T0181667

Lecture Notes in Computer Science

Lecture Notes in Artificial Intelligence   **14171**

Founding Editor

Jörg Siekmann

Series Editors

Randy Goebel, *University of Alberta, Edmonton, Canada*
Wolfgang Wahlster, *DFKI, Berlin, Germany*
Zhi-Hua Zhou, *Nanjing University, Nanjing, China*

The series Lecture Notes in Artificial Intelligence (LNAI) was established in 1988 as a topical subseries of LNCS devoted to artificial intelligence.

The series publishes state-of-the-art research results at a high level. As with the LNCS mother series, the mission of the series is to serve the international R & D community by providing an invaluable service, mainly focused on the publication of conference and workshop proceedings and postproceedings.

Danai Koutra · Claudia Plant ·
Manuel Gomez Rodriguez · Elena Baralis ·
Francesco Bonchi
Editors

Machine Learning and Knowledge Discovery in Databases

Research Track

European Conference, ECML PKDD 2023
Turin, Italy, September 18–22, 2023
Proceedings, Part III

 Springer

Editors
Danai Koutra (iD)
University of Michigan
Ann Arbor, MI, USA

Claudia Plant (iD)
University of Vienna
Vienna, Austria

Manuel Gomez Rodriguez (iD)
Max Planck Institute for Software Systems
Kaiserslautern, Germany

Elena Baralis (iD)
Politecnico di Torino
Turin, Italy

Francesco Bonchi (iD)
CENTAI
Turin, Italy

ISSN 0302-9743   ISSN 1611-3349 (electronic)
Lecture Notes in Artificial Intelligence
ISBN 978-3-031-43417-4   ISBN 978-3-031-43418-1 (eBook)
https://doi.org/10.1007/978-3-031-43418-1

LNCS Sublibrary: SL7 – Artificial Intelligence

Preface

The 2023 edition of the European Conference on Machine Learning and Principles and Practice of Knowledge Discovery in Databases (ECML PKDD 2023) was held in Turin, Italy, from September 18 to 22, 2023.

The ECML PKDD conference, held annually, acts as a worldwide platform showcasing the latest advancements in machine learning and knowledge discovery in databases, encompassing groundbreaking applications. With a history of successful editions, ECML PKDD has established itself as the leading European machine learning and data mining conference, offering researchers and practitioners an unparalleled opportunity to exchange knowledge and ideas.

The main conference program consisted of presentations of 255 accepted papers and three keynote talks (in order of appearance):

- Max Welling (University of Amsterdam): Neural Wave Representations
- Michael Bronstein (University of Oxford): Physics-Inspired Graph Neural Networks
- Kate Crawford (USC Annenberg): Mapping Generative AI

In addition, there were 30 workshops, 9 combined workshop-tutorials, 5 tutorials, 3 discovery challenges, and 16 demonstrations. Moreover, the PhD Forum provided a friendly environment for junior PhD students to exchange ideas and experiences with peers in an interactive atmosphere and to get constructive feedback from senior researchers. The conference included a Special Day on Artificial Intelligence for Financial Crime Fight to discuss, share, and present recent developments in AI-based financial crime detection.

In recognition of the paramount significance of ethics in machine learning and data mining, we invited the authors to include an ethical statement in their submissions. We encouraged the authors to discuss the ethical implications of their submission, such as those related to the collection and processing of personal data, the inference of personal information, or the potential risks. We are pleased to report that our call for ethical statements was met with an overwhelmingly positive response from the authors.

The ECML PKDD 2023 Organizing Committee supported Diversity and Inclusion by awarding some grants that enable early career researchers to attend the conference, present their research activities, and become part of the ECML PKDD community. A total of 8 grants covering all or part of the registration fee (4 free registrations and 4 with 50% discount) were awarded to individuals who belong to underrepresented communities, based on gender and role/position, to attend the conference and present their research activities. The goal of the grants was to provide financial support to early-career (women) scientists and Master and Ph.D. students from developing countries. The Diversity and Inclusion action also includes the SoBigData Award, fully sponsored by the SoBigData++ Horizon2020 project, which aims to encourage more diverse participation in computer science and machine learning events. The award is intended to cover expenses for transportation and accommodation.

The papers presented during the three main conference days were organized in four different tracks:

- Research Track: research or methodology papers from all areas in machine learning, knowledge discovery, and data mining;
- Applied Data Science Track: papers on novel applications of machine learning, data mining, and knowledge discovery to solve real-world use cases, thereby bridging the gap between practice and current theory;
- Journal Track: papers published in special issues of the journals Machine Learning and Data Mining and Knowledge Discovery;
- Demo Track: short papers introducing new prototypes or fully operational systems that exploit data science techniques and are presented via working demonstrations.

We received 829 submissions for the Research track and 239 for the Applied Data Science Track.

We accepted 196 papers (24%) in the Research Track and 58 (24%) in the Applied Data Science Track. In addition, there were 44 papers from the Journal Track and 16 demo papers (out of 28 submissions).

We want to thank all participants, authors, all chairs, all Program Committee members, area chairs, session chairs, volunteers, co-organizers, and organizers of workshops and tutorials for making ECML PKDD 2023 an outstanding success. Thanks to Springer for their continuous support and Microsoft for allowing us to use their CMT software for conference management and providing support throughout. Special thanks to our sponsors and the ECML PKDD Steering Committee for their support. Finally, we thank the organizing institutions: CENTAI (Italy) and Politecnico di Torino (Italy).

September 2023

Elena Baralis
Francesco Bonchi
Manuel Gomez Rodriguez
Danai Koutra
Claudia Plant
Gianmarco De Francisci Morales
Claudia Perlich

Organization

General Chairs

Elena Baralis   Politecnico di Torino, Italy
Francesco Bonchi   CENTAI, Italy and Eurecat, Spain

Research Track Program Chairs

Manuel Gomez Rodriguez   Max Planck Institute for Software Systems, Germany
Danai Koutra   University of Michigan, USA
Claudia Plant   University of Vienna, Austria

Applied Data Science Track Program Chairs

Gianmarco De Francisci Morales   CENTAI, Italy
Claudia Perlich   NYU and TwoSigma, USA

Journal Track Chairs

Tania Cerquitelli   Politecnico di Torino, Italy
Marcello Restelli   Politecnico di Milano, Italy
Charalampos E. Tsourakakis   Boston University, USA and ISI Foundation, Italy
Fabio Vitale   CENTAI, Italy

Workshop and Tutorial Chairs

Rosa Meo   University of Turin, Italy
Fabrizio Silvestri   Sapienza University of Rome, Italy

Demo Chairs

Nicolas Kourtellis   Telefonica, Spain
Natali Ruchansky   Netflix, USA

Local Chairs

Daniele Apiletti   Politecnico di Torino, Italy
Paolo Bajardi   CENTAI, Italy
Eliana Pastor   Politecnico di Torino, Italy

Discovery Challenge Chairs

Danilo Giordano   Politecnico di Torino, Italy
André Panisson   CENTAI, Italy

PhD Forum Chairs

Yllka Velaj   University of Vienna, Austria
Matteo Riondato   Amherst College, USA

Diversity and Inclusion Chair

Tania Cerquitelli   Politecnico di Torino, Italy

Proceedings Chairs

Eliana Pastor   Politecnico di Torino, Italy
Giulia Preti   CENTAI, Italy

Sponsorship Chairs

Daniele Apiletti   Politecnico di Torino, Italy
Paolo Bajardi   CENTAI, Italy

Web Chair

Alessandro Fiori   Flowygo, Italy

Social Media and Publicity Chair

Flavio Giobergia   Politecnico di Torino, Italy

Online Chairs

Alkis Koudounas   Politecnico di Torino, Italy
Simone Monaco   Politecnico di Torino, Italy

Best Paper Awards Chairs

Peter Flach   University of Bristol, UK
Katharina Morik   TU Dortmund, Germany
Arno Siebes   Utrecht University, The Netherlands

ECML PKDD Steering Committee

Massih-Reza Amini   Université Grenoble Alpes, France
Annalisa Appice   University of Bari, Aldo Moro, Italy
Ira Assent   Aarhus University, Denmark
Tania Cerquitelli   Politecnico di Torino, Italy
Albert Bifet   University of Waikato, New Zealand
Francesco Bonchi   CENTAI, Italy and Eurecat, Spain
Peggy Cellier   INSA Rennes, France
Saso Dzeroski   Jožef Stefan Institute, Slovenia
Tias Guns   KU Leuven, Belgium
Alípio M. G. Jorge   University of Porto, Portugal
Kristian Kersting   TU Darmstadt, Germany
Jefrey Lijffijt   Ghent University, Belgium
Luís Moreira-Matias   Sennder GmbH, Germany
Katharina Morik   TU Dortmund, Germany
Siegfried Nijssen   Université catholique de Louvain, Belgium
Andrea Passerini   University of Trento, Italy

Program Committee

Guest Editorial Board, Journal Track

Marco Cotogni	University of Pavia, Italy
Gabriele D'Acunto	Sapienza University of Rome, Italy
Cassio Fraga Dantas	TETIS, Université Montpellier, INRAE, France
Jérôme Darmont	Université Lumière Lyon 2, France
George Dasoulas	Harvard University, USA
Sébastien Destercke	Université de Technologie de Compiègne, France
Shridhar Devamane	Global Academy of Technology, India
Claudia Diamantini	Università Politecnica delle Marche, Italy
Gianluca Drappo	Politecnico di Milano, Italy
Pedro Ferreira	University of Lisbon, Portugal
Cèsar Ferri	Universitat Politècnica de València, Spain
M. Julia Flores	Universidad de Castilla-La Mancha, Spain
Germain Forestier	University of Haute-Alsace, France
Elisa Fromont	Université de Rennes 1, France
Emanuele Frontoni	University of Macerata, Italy
Esther Galbrun	University of Eastern Finland, Finland
Joao Gama	University of Porto, Portugal
Jose A. Gamez	Universidad de Castilla-La Mancha, Spain
David García Soriano	ISI Foundation, Italy
Paolo Garza	Politecnico di Torino, Italy
Salvatore Greco	Politecnico di Torino, Italy
Riccardo Guidotti	University of Pisa, Italy
Francesco Gullo	UniCredit, Italy
Shahrzad Haddadan	Rutgers Business School, USA
Martin Holena	Czech Academy of Sciences, Czech Republic
Jaakko Hollmén	Stockholm University, Sweden
Dino Ienco	INRAE, France
Georgiana Ifrim	University College Dublin, Ireland
Felix Iglesias	TU Vienna, Austria
Angelo Impedovo	Niuma, Italy
Manfred Jaeger	Aalborg University, Denmark
Szymon Jaroszewicz	Warsaw University of Technology, Poland
Panagiotis Karras	Aarhus University, Denmark
George Katsimpras	National Center for Scientific Research Demokritos, Greece
Mehdi Kaytoue	Infologic R&D, France
Dragi Kocev	Jožef Stefan Institute, Slovenia
Yun Sing Koh	University of Auckland, New Zealand
Sotiropoulos Konstantinos	Boston University, USA
Lars Kotthoff	University of Wyoming, USA
Alkis Koudounas	Politecnico di Torino, Italy
Tommaso Lanciano	Sapienza University of Rome, Italy

Helge Langseth	Norwegian University of Science and Technology, Norway
Thien Le	MIT, USA
Hsuan-Tien Lin	National Taiwan University, Taiwan
Marco Lippi	University of Modena and Reggio Emilia, Italy
Corrado Loglisci	University of Bari, Aldo Moro, Italy
Manuel López-ibáñez	University of Manchester, UK
Nuno Lourenço	CISUC, Portugal
Claudio Lucchese	Ca' Foscari University of Venice, Italy
Brian Mac Namee	University College Dublin, Ireland
Gjorgji Madjarov	Ss. Cyril and Methodius University in Skopje, North Macedonia
Luigi Malagò	Transylvanian Institute of Neuroscience, Romania
Sagar Malhotra	Fondazione Bruno Kessler, Italy
Fragkiskos Malliaros	CentraleSupélec, Université Paris-Saclay, France
Giuseppe Manco	ICAR-CNR, Italy
Basarab Matei	Sorbonne Université Paris Nord, France
Michael Mathioudakis	University of Helsinki, Finland
Rosa Meo	University of Turin, Italy
Mohamed-Lamine Messai	Université Lumière Lyon 2, France
Sara Migliorini	University of Verona, Italy
Alex Mircoli	Università Politecnica delle Marche, Italy
Atsushi Miyauchi	University of Tokyo, Japan
Simone Monaco	Politecnico di Torino, Italy
Anna Monreale	University of Pisa, Italy
Corrado Monti	CENTAI, Italy
Katharina Morik	TU Dortmund, Germany
Lia Morra	Politecnico di Torino, Italy
Arsenii Mustafin	Boston University, USA
Mirco Mutti	Politecnico di Milano/University of Bologna, Italy
Amedeo Napoli	University of Lorraine, CNRS, LORIA, France
Kleber Oliveira	CENTAI, Italy
Gabriella Olmo	Politecnico di Torino, Italy
Marios Papachristou	Cornell University, USA
Panagiotis Papapetrou	Stockholm University, Sweden
Matteo Papini	Universitat Pompeu Fabra, Spain
Vincenzo Pasquadibisceglie	University of Bari, Aldo Moro, Italy
Eliana Pastor	Politecnico di Torino, Italy
Andrea Paudice	University of Milan, Italy
Charlotte Pelletier	IRISA - Université Bretagne-Sud, France
Ruggero G. Pensa	University of Turin, Italy
Simone Piaggesi	University of Bologna/ISI Foundation, Italy

Matteo Pirotta	Meta, France
Marc Plantevit	EPITA, France
Konstantinos Pliakos	KU Leuven, Belgium
Kai Puolamäki	University of Helsinki, Finland
Jan Ramon	Inria, France
Rita P. Ribeiro	INESC TEC/University of Porto, Portugal
Matteo Riondato	Amherst College, USA
Antonio Riva	Politecnico di Milano, Italy
Shota Saito	University College London, UK
Flora Salim	University of New South Wales, Australia
Roberto Santana	University of the Basque Country, Spain
Lars Schmidt-Thieme	University of Hildesheim, Germany
Thomas Seidl	LMU Munich, Germany
Kijung Shin	KAIST, South Korea
Shinichi Shirakawa	Yokohama National University, Japan
Konstantinos Sotiropoulos	Boston University, USA
Fabian Spaeh	Boston University, USA
Gerasimos Spanakis	Maastricht University, The Netherlands
Myra Spiliopoulou	Otto-von-Guericke-University Magdeburg, Germany
Jerzy Stefanowski	Poznan University of Technology, Poland
Mahito Sugiyama	National Institute of Informatics, Japan
Nikolaj Tatti	University of Helsinki, Finland
Maximilian Thiessen	TU Vienna, Austria
Josephine Thomas	University of Kassel, Germany
Kiran Tomlinson	Cornell University, USA
Leonardo Trujillo	Tecnológico Nacional de México, Mexico
Grigorios Tsoumakas	Aristotle University of Thessaloniki, Greece
Genoveva Vargas-Solar	CNRS, LIRIS Lab, France
Edoardo Vittori	Politecnico di Milano/Intesa Sanpaolo, Italy
Christel Vrain	University of Orléans, France
Willem Waegeman	Ghent University, Belgium
Yanbang Wang	Cornell University, USA
Pascal Welke	University of Bonn, Germany
Marcel Wever	LMU Munich, Germany
Stefan Wrobel	University of Bonn/Fraunhofer IAIS, Germany
Guoxian Yu	Shandong University, China
Ilias Zavitsanos	National Center for Scientific Research Demokritos, Greece
Ye Zhu	Deakin University, Australia
Albrecht Zimmermann	Université de Caen Normandie, France

Area Chairs, Research Track

Fabrizio Angiulli	University of Calabria, Italy
Annalisa Appice	University of Bari, Aldo Moro, Italy
Antonio Artés	Universidad Carlos III de Madrid, Spain
Martin Atzmueller	Osnabrück University, Germany
Christian Böhm	University of Vienna, Austria
Michael R. Berthold	KNIME, Switzerland
Albert Bifet	Université Paris-Saclay, France
Hendrik Blockeel	KU Leuven, Belgium
Ulf Brefeld	Leuphana University, Germany
Paula Brito	INESC TEC - LIAAD/University of Porto, Portugal
Wolfram Burgard	University of Technology Nuremberg, Germany
Seshadhri C.	UCSC, USA
Michelangelo Ceci	University of Bari, Aldo Moro, Italy
Peggy Cellier	IRISA - INSA Rennes, France
Duen Horng Chau	Georgia Institute of Technology, USA
Nicolas Courty	IRISA - Université Bretagne-Sud, France
Bruno Cremilleux	Université de Caen Normandie, France
Jesse Davis	KU Leuven, Belgium
Abir De	IIT Bombay, India
Tom Diethe	AstraZeneca, UK
Yuxiao Dong	Tsinghua University, China
Kurt Driessens	Maastricht University, The Netherlands
Tapio Elomaa	Tampere University, Finland
Johannes Fürnkranz	JKU Linz, Austria
Sophie Fellenz	RPTU Kaiserslautern-Landau, Germany
Elisa Fromont	IRISA/Inria rba - Université de Rennes 1, France
Thomas Gärtner	TU Vienna, Austria
Patrick Gallinari	Criteo AI Lab - Sorbonne Université, France
Joao Gama	INESC TEC - LIAAD, Portugal
Rayid Ghani	Carnegie Mellon University, USA
Aristides Gionis	KTH Royal Institute of Technology, Sweden
Chen Gong	Nanjing University of Science and Technology, China
Francesco Gullo	UniCredit, Italy
Eyke Hüllermeier	LMU Munich, Germany
Junheng Hao	University of California, Los Angeles, USA
José Hernández-Orallo	Universitat Politècnica de Valencia, Spain
Daniel Hernández-Lobato	Universidad Autonoma de Madrid, Spain
Sibylle Hess	TU Eindhoven, The Netherlands

Jaakko Hollmén	Aalto University, Finland
Andreas Hotho	University of Würzburg, Germany
Georgiana Ifrim	University College Dublin, Ireland
Jayaraman J. Thiagarajan	Lawrence Livermore, USA
Alipio M. G. Jorge	INESC TEC/University of Porto, Portugal
Ross King	Chalmers University of Technology, Sweden
Yun Sing Koh	University of Auckland, New Zealand
Lars Kotthoff	University of Wyoming, USA
Peer Kröger	Christian-Albrecht University of Kiel, Germany
Stefan Kramer	JGU Mainz, Germany
Jörg Lücke	University of Oldenburg, Germany
Niklas Lavesson	Blekinge Institute of Technology, Sweden
Bruno Lepri	Fondazione Bruno Kessler, Italy
Jefrey Lijffijt	Ghent University, Belgium
Marius Lindauer	Leibniz University Hannover, Germany
Patrick Loiseau	Inria, France
Jose A. Lozano	UPV/EHU, Spain
Emmanuel Müller	TU Dortmund, Germany
Donato Malerba	University of Bari, Aldo Moro, Italy
Fragkiskos Malliaros	CentraleSupelec, France
Giuseppe Manco	ICAR-CNR, Italy
Pauli Miettinen	University of Eastern Finland, Finland
Dunja Mladenic	Jožef Stefan Institute, Slovenia
Anna Monreale	University of Pisa, Italy
Luis Moreira-Matias	Sennder GmbH, Germany
Katharina J. Morik	TU Dortmund, Germany
Siegfried Nijssen	Université catholique de Louvain, Belgium
Evangelos Papalexakis	UC, Riverside, USA
Panagiotis Papapetrou	Stockholm University, Sweden
Andrea Passerini	University of Trento, Italy
Mykola Pechenizkiy	TU Eindhoven, The Netherlands
Jaakko Peltonen	Tampere University, Finland
Franz Pernkopf	TU Graz, Austria
Bernhard Pfahringer	University of Waikato, New Zealand
Fabio Pinelli	IMT Lucca, Italy
Goran Radanovic	Max Planck Institute for Software Systems, Germany
Jesse Read	École Polytechnique, France
Matthias Renz	Christian-Albrecht University of Kiel, Germany
Marian-Andrei Rizoiu	University of Technology, Sydney, Australia
Celine Robardet	INSA Lyon, France
Juho Rousu	Aalto University, Finland

Sriparna Saha	IIT Patna, India
Ute Schmid	University of Bamberg, Germany
Lars Schmidt-Thieme	University of Hildesheim, Germany
Michele Sebag	LISN CNRS, France
Thomas Seidl	LMU Munich, Germany
Junming Shao	University of Electronic Science and Technology of China, China
Arno Siebes	Utrecht University, The Netherlands
Fabrizio Silvestri	Sapienza University of Rome, Italy
Carlos Soares	University of Porto, Portugal
Christian Sohler	University of Cologne, Germany
Myra Spiliopoulou	Otto-von-Guericke-University Magdeburg, Germany
Jie Tang	Tsinghua University, China
Nikolaj Tatti	University of Helsinki, Finland
Evimaria Terzi	Boston University, USA
Marc Tommasi	Lille University, France
Heike Trautmann	University of Münster, Germany
Herke van Hoof	University of Amsterdam, The Netherlands
Celine Vens	KU Leuven, Belgium
Christel Vrain	University of Orleans, France
Jilles Vreeken	CISPA Helmholtz Center for Information Security, Germany
Wei Ye	Tongji University, China
Jing Zhang	Renmin University of China, China
Min-Ling Zhang	Southeast University, China

Area Chairs, Applied Data Science Track

Annalisa Appice	University of Bari, Aldo Moro, Italy
Ira Assent	Aarhus University, Denmark
Martin Atzmueller	Osnabrück University, Germany
Michael R. Berthold	KNIME, Switzerland
Hendrik Blockeel	KU Leuven, Belgium
Michelangelo Ceci	University of Bari, Aldo Moro, Italy
Peggy Cellier	IRISA - INSA Rennes, France
Yi Chang	Jilin University, China
Nicolas Courty	IRISA - UBS, France
Bruno Cremilleux	Université de Caen Normandie, France
Peng Cui	Tsinghua University, China
Anirban Dasgupta	IIT Gandhinagar, India

Tom Diethe	AstraZeneca, UK
Carlotta Domeniconi	George Mason University, USA
Dejing Dou	BCG, USA
Kurt Driessens	Maastricht University, The Netherlands
Johannes Fürnkranz	JKU Linz, Austria
Faisal Farooq	Qatar Computing Research Institute, Qatar
Paolo Frasconi	University of Florence, Italy
Elisa Fromont	IRISA/Inria rba - Université de Rennes 1, France
Glenn Fung	Liberty Mutual, USA
Joao Gama	INESC TEC - LIAAD, Portugal
Jose A. Gamez	Universidad de Castilla-La Mancha, Spain
Rayid Ghani	Carnegie Mellon University, USA
Aristides Gionis	KTH Royal Institute of Technology, Sweden
Sreenivas Gollapudi	Google, USA
Francesco Gullo	UniCredit, Italy
Eyke Hüllermeier	LMU Munich, Germany
Jingrui He	University of Illinois at Urbana-Champaign, USA
Jaakko Hollmén	Aalto University, Finland
Andreas Hotho	University of Würzburg, Germany
Daxin Jiang	Microsoft, Beijing, China
Alipio M. G. Jorge	INESC TEC/University of Porto, Portugal
George Karypis	University of Minnesota, USA
Eamonn Keogh	UC, Riverside, USA
Yun Sing Koh	University of Auckland, New Zealand
Parisa Kordjamshidi	Michigan State University, USA
Lars Kotthoff	University of Wyoming, USA
Nicolas Kourtellis	Telefonica Research, Spain
Stefan Kramer	JGU Mainz, Germany
Balaji Krishnapuram	Pinterest, USA
Niklas Lavesson	Blekinge Institute of Technology, Sweden
Chuan Lei	Amazon Web Services, USA
Marius Lindauer	Leibniz University Hannover, Germany
Patrick Loiseau	Inria, France
Giuseppe Manco	ICAR-CNR, Italy
Gabor Melli	PredictionWorks, USA
Anna Monreale	University of Pisa, Italy
Luis Moreira-Matias	Sennder GmbH, Germany
Nuria Oliver	ELLIS Alicante, Spain
Panagiotis Papapetrou	Stockholm University, Sweden
Mykola Pechenizkiy	TU Eindhoven, The Netherlands
Jian Pei	Simon Fraser University, Canada
Julien Perez	Naver Labs Europe, France

Fabio Pinelli   IMT Lucca, Italy
Zhiwei (Tony) Qin   Lyft, USA
Visvanathan Ramesh   Goethe University, Germany
Zhaochun Ren   Shandong University, China
Sriparna Saha   IIT Patna, India
Ute Schmid   University of Bamberg, Germany
Lars Schmidt-Thieme   University of Hildesheim, Germany
Thomas Seidl   LMU Munich, Germany
Fabrizio Silvestri   Sapienza University of Rome, Italy
Myra Spiliopoulou   Otto-von-Guericke-University Magdeburg,
                                   Germany

Karthik Subbian   Amazon, USA
Liang Sun   Alibaba Group, China
Jie Tang   Tsinghua University, China
Jiliang Tang   Michigan State University, USA
Sandeep Tata   Google, USA
Nikolaj Tatti   University of Helsinki, Finland
Marc Tommasi   Lille University, France
Yongxin Tong   Beihang University, China
Vincent S. Tseng   National Yang Ming Chiao Tung University,
                                   Taiwan

Antti Ukkonen   University of Helsinki, Finland
Willem Waegeman   Ghent University, Belgium
Fei Wang   Cornell University, USA
Jie Wang   University of Science and Technology of China,
                                   China

Sinong Wang   Meta AI, USA
Zheng Wang   Alibaba DAMO Academy, China
Lingfei Wu   Pinterest, USA
Yinglong Xia   Meta, USA
Hui Xiong   Rutgers University, USA
Hongxia Yang   Alibaba Group, China
Min-Ling Zhang   Southeast University, China
Jiayu Zhou   Michigan State University, USA
Xingquan Zhu   Florida Atlantic University, USA
Fuzhen Zhuang   Institute of Artificial Intelligence, China
Albrecht Zimmermann   Université de Caen Normandie, France

Program Committee, Research Track

Matthias Aßenmacher	LMU Munich, Germany
Sara Abdali	Microsoft, USA
Evrim Acar	Simula Metropolitan Center for Digital Engineering, Norway
Homayun Afrabandpey	Nokia Technologies, Finland
Reza Akbarinia	Inria, France
Cuneyt G. Akcora	University of Manitoba, Canada
Ranya Almohsen	West Virginia University, USA
Thiago Andrade	INESC TEC/University of Porto, Portugal
Jean-Marc Andreoli	Naverlabs Europe, France
Giuseppina Andresini	University of Bari, Aldo Moro, Italy
Alessandro Antonucci	IDSIA, Switzerland
Xiang Ao	Institute of Computing Technology, CAS, China
Héber H. Arcolezi	Inria/École Polytechnique, France
Jerónimo Arenas-García	Universidad Carlos III de Madrid, Spain
Yusuf Arslan	University of Luxembourg, Luxemburg
Ali Ayadi	University of Strasbourg, France
Steve Azzolin	University of Trento, Italy
Pierre-Luc Bacon	Mila, Canada
Bunil K. Balabantaray	NIT Meghalaya, India
Mitra Baratchi	LIACS/Leiden University, The Netherlands
Christian Bauckhage	Fraunhofer IAIS, Germany
Anna Beer	Aarhus University, Denmark
Michael Beigl	Karlsruhe Institute of Technology, Germany
Khalid Benabdeslem	Université de Lyon, Lyon 1, France
Idir Benouaret	Epita Research Laboratory, France
Paul Berg	IRISA, France
Christoph Bergmeir	Monash University, Australia
Gilberto Bernardes	INESC TEC/University of Porto, Portugal
Eva Besada-Portas	Universidad Complutense de Madrid, Spain
Jalaj Bhandari	Columbia University, USA
Asmita Bhat	TU Kaiserslautern, Germany
Monowar Bhuyan	Umeå University, Sweden
Adrien Bibal	University of Colorado Anschutz Medical Campus, USA
Manuele Bicego	University of Verona, Italy
Przemyslaw Biecek	Warsaw University of Technology, Poland
Alexander Binder	University of Oslo, Norway
Livio Bioglio	University of Turin, Italy
Patrick Blöbaum	Amazon Web Services, USA

Nanqing Dong	University of Oxford, UK
Haizhou Du	Shanghai University of Electric Power, China
Qihan Du	Renmin University of China, China
Songlin Du	Southeast University, China
Xin Du	University of Edinburgh, UK
Wouter Duivesteijn	TU Eindhoven, The Netherlands
Inês Dutra	University of Porto, Portugal
Sourav Dutta	Huawei Research Centre, Ireland
Saso Dzeroski	Jožef Stefan Institute, Slovenia
Nabil El Malki	IRIT, France
Mohab Elkaref	IBM Research Europe, UK
Tapio Elomaa	Tampere University, Finland
Dominik M. Endres	University of Marburg, Germany
Georgios Exarchakis	University of Bath, UK
Lukas Faber	ETH Zurich, Switzerland
Samuel G. Fadel	Leuphana University, Germany
Haoyi Fan	Zhengzhou University, China
Zipei Fan	University of Tokyo, Japan
Hadi Fanaee-T	Halmstad University, Sweden
Elaine Ribeiro Faria	UFU, Brazil
Fabio Fassetti	University of Calabria, Italy
Anthony Faustine	ITI/LARSyS - Técnico Lisboa, Portugal
Sophie Fellenz	RPTU Kaiserslautern-Landau, Germany
Wenjie Feng	National University of Singapore, Singapore
Zunlei Feng	Zhejiang University, China
Daniel Fernández-Sánchez	Universidad Autónoma de Madrid, Spain
Luca Ferragina	University of Calabria, Italy
Emilio Ferrara	USC ISI, USA
Cèsar Ferri	Universitat Politècnica València, Spain
Flavio Figueiredo	Universidade Federal de Minas Gerais, Brazil
Lucie Flek	University of Marburg, Germany
Michele Fontana	University of Pisa, Italy
Germain Forestier	University of Haute-Alsace, France
Raphaël Fournier-S'niehotta	CNAM, France
Benoît Frénay	University of Namur, Belgium
Kary Främling	Umeå University, Sweden
Holger Froening	University of Heidelberg, Germany
Fabio Fumarola	Prometeia, Italy
María José Gómez-Silva	Universidad Complutense de Madrid, Spain
Vanessa Gómez-Verdejo	Universidad Carlos III de Madrid, Spain
Pratik Gajane	TU Eindhoven, The Netherlands
Esther Galbrun	University of Eastern Finland, Finland

Claudio Gallicchio	University of Pisa, Italy
Chen Gao	Tsinghua University, China
Shengxiang Gao	Kunming University of Science and Technology, China
Yifeng Gao	University of Texas Rio Grande Valley, USA
Luis Garcia	University of Brasilia, Brazil
Dominique Gay	Université de La Réunion, France
Suyu Ge	University of Illinois at Urbana-Champaign, USA
Zhaocheng Ge	Huazhong University of Science and Technology, China
Alborz Geramifard	Facebook AI, USA
Ahana Ghosh	Max Planck Institute for Software Systems, Germany
Shreya Ghosh	Penn State University, USA
Flavio Giobergia	Politecnico di Torino, Italy
Sarunas Girdzijauskas	KTH Royal Institute of Technology, Sweden
Heitor Murilo Gomes	University of Waikato, Sweden
Wenwen Gong	Tsinghua University, China
Bedartha Goswami	University of Tübingen, Germany
Anastasios Gounaris	Aristotle University of Thessaloniki, Greece
Michael Granitzer	University of Passau, Germany
Derek Greene	University College Dublin, Ireland
Moritz Grosse-Wentrup	University of Vienna, Austria
Marek Grzes	University of Kent, UK
Xinyu Guan	Xian Jiaotong University, China
Massimo Guarascio	ICAR-CNR, Italy
Riccardo Guidotti	University of Pisa, Italy
Lan-Zhe Guo	Nanjing University, China
Lingbing Guo	Zhejiang University, China
Shanqing Guo	Shandong University, China
Karthik S. Gurumoorthy	Walmart, USA
Thomas Guyet	Inria, France
Huong Ha	RMIT University, Australia
Benjamin Halstead	University of Auckland, New Zealand
Massinissa Hamidi	LIPN-UMR CNRS 7030, France
Donghong Han	Northeastern University, USA
Marwan Hassani	TU Eindhoven, The Netherlands
Rima Hazra	Indian Institute of Technology, Kharagpur, India
Mark Heimann	Lawrence Livermore, USA
Cesar Hidalgo	University of Toulouse, France
Martin Holena	Institute of Computer Science, Czech Republic
Mike Holenderski	TU Eindhoven, The Netherlands

Adrian Horzyk	AGH University of Science and Technology, Poland
Shifu Hou	Case Western Reserve University, USA
Hongsheng Hu	CSIRO, Australia
Yaowei Hu	University of Arkansas, USA
Yang Hua	Queen's University Belfast, UK
Chao Huang	University of Hong Kong, China
Guanjie Huang	Penn State University, USA
Hong Huang	Huazhong University of Science and Technology, China
Nina C. Hubig	Clemson University, USA
Dino Ienco	Irstea Institute, France
Angelo Impedovo	Niuma, Italy
Roberto Interdonato	CIRAD, France
Stratis Ioannidis	Northeastern University, USA
Nevo Itzhak	Ben-Gurion University, Israel
Raghav Jain	IIT Patna, India
Kuk Jin Jang	University of Pennsylvania, USA
Szymon Jaroszewicz	Polish Academy of Sciences, Poland
Shaoxiong Ji	University of Helsinki, Finland
Bin-Bin Jia	Lanzhou University of Technology, China
Caiyan Jia	School of Computer and Information Technology, China
Xiuyi Jia	Nanjing University of Science and Technology, China
Nan Jiang	Purdue University, USA
Renhe Jiang	University of Tokyo, Japan
Song Jiang	University of California, Los Angeles, USA
Pengfei Jiao	Hangzhou Dianzi University, China
Di Jin	Amazon, USA
Guangyin Jin	National University of Defense Technology, China
Jiahui Jin	Southeast University, China
Ruoming Jin	Kent State University, USA
Yilun Jin	The Hong Kong University of Science and Technology, Hong Kong
Hugo Jonker	Open University of the Netherlands, The Netherlands
Adan Jose-Garcia	Lille University, France
Marius Köppel	JGU Mainz, Germany
Vana Kalogeraki	Athens University of Economics and Business, Greece
Konstantinos Kalpakis	University of Maryland Baltimore County, USA

Andreas Kaltenbrunner	ISI Foundation, Italy
Shivaram Kalyanakrishnan	IIT Bombay, India
Toshihiro Kamishima	National Institute of Advanced Industrial Science and Technology, Japan
Bo Kang	Ghent University, Belgium
Murat Kantarcioglu	UT Dallas
Thommen Karimpanal George	Deakin University, Australia
Saurav Karmakar	University of Galway, Ireland
Panagiotis Karras	Aarhus University, Denmark
Dimitrios Katsaros	University of Thessaly, Greece
Eamonn Keogh	UC, Riverside, USA
Jaleed Khan	University of Galway, Ireland
Irwin King	Chinese University of Hong Kong, China
Mauritius Klein	LMU Munich, Germany
Tomas Kliegr	Prague University of Economics and Business, Czech Republic
Dmitry Kobak	University of Tübingen, Germany
Dragi Kocev	Jožef Stefan Institute, Slovenia
Lars Kotthoff	University of Wyoming, USA
Anna Krause	University of Würzburg, Germany
Amer Krivosija	TU Dortmund, Germany
Daniel Kudenko	L3S Research Center, Germany
Meelis Kull	University of Tartu, Estonia
Sergey O. Kuznetsov	HSE, Russia
Beatriz López	University of Girona, Spain
Jörg Lücke	University of Oldenburg, Germany
Firas Laakom	Tampere University, Finland
Mateusz Lango	Poznan University of Technology, Poland
Hady Lauw	Singapore Management University, Singapore
Tuan Le	New Mexico State University, USA
Erwan Le Merrer	Inria, France
Thach Le Nguyen	Insight Centre, Ireland
Tai Le Quy	L3S Research Center, Germany
Mustapha Lebbah	UVSQ - Université Paris-Saclay, France
Dongman Lee	KAIST, South Korea
Yeon-Chang Lee	Georgia Institute of Technology, USA
Zed Lee	Stockholm University, Sweden
Mathieu Lefort	Université de Lyon, France
Yunwen Lei	University of Birmingham, UK
Vincent Lemaire	Orange Innovation, France
Daniel Lemire	TÉLUQ University, Canada
Florian Lemmerich	RWTH Aachen University, Germany

Youfang Leng	Renmin University of China, China
Carson K. Leung	University of Manitoba, Canada
Dan Li	Sun Yat-Sen University, China
Gang Li	Deakin University, Australia
Jiaming Li	Huazhong University of Science and Technology, China
Mark Junjie Li	Shenzhen University, China
Nian Li	Tsinghua University, China
Shuai Li	University of Cambridge, UK
Tong Li	Hong Kong University of Science and Technology, China
Xiang Li	East China Normal University, China
Yang Li	University of North Carolina at Chapel Hill, USA
Yingming Li	Zhejiang University, China
Yinsheng Li	Fudan University, China
Yong Li	Huawei European Research Center, Germany
Zhihui Li	University of New South Wales, Australia
Zhixin Li	Guangxi Normal University, China
Defu Lian	University of Science and Technology of China, China
Yuxuan Liang	National University of Singapore, Singapore
Angelica Liguori	University of Calabria, Italy
Nick Lim	University of Waikato, Sweden
Baijiong Lin	The Hong Kong University of Science and Technology, Hong Kong
Piotr Lipinski	University of Wrocław, Poland
Marco Lippi	University of Modena and Reggio Emilia, Italy
Bowen Liu	Stanford University, USA
Chien-Liang Liu	National Chiao Tung University, Taiwan
Fenglin Liu	University of Oxford, UK
Junze Liu	University of California, Irvine, USA
Li Liu	Chongqing University, China
Ninghao Liu	University of Georgia, USA
Shenghua Liu	Institute of Computing Technology, CAS, China
Xiao Fan Liu	City University of Hong Kong, Hong Kong
Xu Liu	National University of Singapore, Singapore
Yang Liu	Institute of Computing Technology, CAS, China
Zihan Liu	Zhejiang University/Westlake University, China
Robert Loftin	TU Delft, The Netherlands
Corrado Loglisci	University of Bari, Aldo Moro, Italy
Mingsheng Long	Tsinghua University, China
Antonio Longa	Fondazione Bruno Kessler, Italy

Grigorios Loukides	King's College London, UK
Tsai-Ching Lu	HRL Laboratories, USA
Zhiwu Lu	Renmin University of China, China
Pedro Henrique Luz de Araujo	University of Vienna, Austria
Marcos M. Raimundo	University of Campinas, Brazil
Maximilian Münch	University of Applied Sciences Würzburg-Schweinfurt, Germany
Fenglong Ma	Pennsylvania State University, USA
Pingchuan Ma	The Hong Kong University of Science and Technology, Hong Kong
Yao Ma	New Jersey Institute of Technology, USA
Brian Mac Namee	University College Dublin, Ireland
Henryk Maciejewski	Wrocław University of Science and Technology, Poland
Ayush Maheshwari	IIT Bombay, India
Ajay A. Mahimkar	AT&T, USA
Ayan Majumdar	Max Planck Institute for Software Systems, Germany
Donato Malerba	University of Bari, Aldo Moro, Italy
Aakarsh Malhotra	IIIT-Delhi, India
Fragkiskos Malliaros	CentraleSupelec, France
Pekka Malo	Aalto University, Finland
Hiroshi Mamitsuka	Kyoto University, Japan/Aalto University, Finland
Domenico Mandaglio	University of Calabria, Italy
Robin Manhaeve	KU Leuven, Belgium
Silviu Maniu	Université Paris-Saclay, France
Cinmayii G. Manliguez	National Sun Yat-Sen University, Taiwan
Naresh Manwani	IIIT Hyderabad, India
Giovanni Luca Marchetti	KTH Royal Institute of Technology, Sweden
Koji Maruhashi	Fujitsu Research, Fujitsu Limited, Japan
Florent Masseglia	Inria, France
Sarah Masud	IIIT-Delhi, India
Timothée Mathieu	Inria, France
Amir Mehrpanah	KTH Royal Institute of Technology, Sweden
Wagner Meira Jr.	Universidade Federal de Minas Gerais, Brazil
Joao Mendes-Moreira	INESC TEC, Portugal
Rui Meng	BNU-HKBU United International College, China
Fabio Mercorio	University of Milan-Bicocca, Italy
Alberto Maria Metelli	Politecnico di Milano, Italy
Carlo Metta	CNR-ISTI, Italy
Paolo Mignone	University of Bari, Aldo Moro, Italy
Tsunenori Mine	Kyushu University, Japan

Nuno Moniz   INESC TEC, Portugal
Pierre Monnin   Université Côte d'Azur, Inria, CNRS, I3S, France
Carlos Monserrat-Aranda   Universitat Politècnica de València, Spain
Raha Moraffah   Arizona State University, USA
Davide Mottin   Aarhus University, Denmark
Hamid Mousavi   University of Oldenburg, Germany
Abdullah Mueen   University of New Mexico, USA
Shamsuddeen Hassan Muhamamd   University of Porto, Portugal
Koyel Mukherjee   Adobe Research, India
Yusuke Mukuta   University of Tokyo, Japan
Pranava Mummoju   University of Vienna, Austria
Taichi Murayama   NAIST, Japan
Ankur Nahar   IIT Jodhpur, India
Felipe Kenji Nakano   KU Leuven, Belgium
Hideki Nakayama   University of Tokyo, Japan
Géraldin Nanfack   University of Namur, Belgium
Mirco Nanni   CNR-ISTI, Italy
Franco Maria Nardini   CNR-ISTI, Italy
Usman Naseem   University of Sydney, Australia
Reza Nasirigerdeh   TU Munich, Germany
Rajashree Nayak   MIT ADT University, India
Benjamin Negrevergne   Université Paris Dauphine, France
Stefan Neumann   KTH Royal Institute of Technology, Sweden
Anna Nguyen   IBM, USA
Shiwen Ni   SIAT, CAS, China
Siegfried Nijssen   Université catholique de Louvain, Belgium
Iasonas Nikolaou   Boston University, USA
Simona Nisticò   University of Calabria, Italy
Hao Niu   KDDI Research, Japan
Mehdi Nourelahi   University of Wyoming, USA
Slawomir Nowaczyk   Halmstad University, Sweden
Eirini Ntoutsi   Bundeswehr University Munich, Germany
Barry O'Sullivan   University College Cork, Ireland
Nastaran Okati   Max Planck Institute for Software Systems,
                                          Germany
Tsuyoshi Okita   Kyushu Institute of Technology, Japan
Pablo Olmos   Universidad Carlos III de Madrid, Spain
Luis Antonio Ortega Andrés   Autonomous University of Madrid, Spain
Abdelkader Ouali   Université de Caen Normandie, France
Latifa Oukhellou   IFSTTAR, France
Chun Ouyang   Queensland University of Technology, Australia
Andrei Paleyes   University of Cambridge, UK

Jiaming Shen	Google Research, USA
Qiang Sheng	Institute of Computing Technology, CAS, China
Bin Shi	Xi'an Jiaotong University, China
Jimeng Shi	Florida International University, USA
Laixi Shi	Carnegie Mellon University, USA
Rongye Shi	Columbia University, USA
Harsh Shrivastava	Microsoft Research, USA
Jonathan A. Silva	Universidade Federal de Mato Grosso do Sul, Brazil
Esther-Lydia Silva-Ramírez	Universidad de Cádiz, Spain
Kuldeep Singh	Cerence, Germany
Moshe Sipper	Ben-Gurion University of the Negev, Israel
Andrzej Skowron	University of Warsaw, Poland
Krzysztof Slot	Lodz University of Technology, Poland
Marek Smieja	Jagiellonian University, Poland
Gavin Smith	University of Nottingham, UK
Carlos Soares	University of Porto, Portugal
Cláudia Soares	NOVA LINCS, Portugal
Andy Song	RMIT University, Australia
Dongjin Song	University of Connecticut, USA
Hao Song	Seldon, UK
Jie Song	Zhejiang University, China
Linxin Song	Waseda University, Japan
Liyan Song	Southern University of Science and Technology, China
Zixing Song	Chinese University of Hong Kong, China
Arnaud Soulet	University of Tours, France
Sucheta Soundarajan	Syracuse University, USA
Francesca Spezzano	Boise State University, USA
Myra Spiliopoulou	Otto-von-Guericke-University Magdeburg, Germany
Janusz Starzyk	WSIZ, Poland
Jerzy Stefanowski	Poznan University of Technology, Poland
Julian Stier	University of Passau, Germany
Michiel Stock	Ghent University, Belgium
Eleni Straitouri	Max Planck Institute for Software Systems, Germany
Łukasz Struski	Jagiellonian University, Poland
Jinyan Su	University of Electronic Science and Technology of China, China
David Q. Sun	Apple, USA
Guangzhong Sun	University of Science and Technology of China, China

Mingxuan Sun	Louisiana State University, USA
Peijie Sun	Tsinghua University, China
Weiwei Sun	Shandong University, China
Xin Sun	TU Munich, Germany
Maryam Tabar	Pennsylvania State University, USA
Anika Tabassum	Virginia Tech, USA
Shazia Tabassum	INESC TEC, Portugal
Andrea Tagarelli	University of Calabria, Italy
Acar Tamersoy	NortonLifeLock Research Group, USA
Chang Wei Tan	Monash University, Australia
Cheng Tan	Zhejiang University/Westlake University, China
Garth Tarr	University of Sydney, Australia
Romain Tavenard	LETG-Rennes/IRISA, France
Maguelonne Teisseire	INRAE - UMR Tetis, France
Evimaria Terzi	Boston University, USA
Stefano Teso	University of Trento, Italy
Surendrabikram Thapa	Virginia Tech, USA
Maximilian Thiessen	TU Vienna, Austria
Steffen Thoma	FZI Research Center for Information Technology, Germany
Simon Tihon	Euranova, Belgium
Kai Ming Ting	Nanjing University, China
Abhisek Tiwari	IIT Patna, India
Gabriele Tolomei	Sapienza University of Rome, Italy
Guangmo Tong	University of Delaware, USA
Sunna Torge	TU Dresden, Germany
Giovanni Trappolini	Sapienza University of Rome, Italy
Volker Tresp	Siemens AG/LMU Munich, Germany
Sofia Triantafillou	University of Crete, Greece
Sebastian Trimpe	RWTH Aachen University, Germany
Sebastian Tschiatschek	University of Vienna, Austria
Athena Vakal	Aristotle University of Thessaloniki, Greece
Peter van der Putten	Leiden University, The Netherlands
Fabio Vandin	University of Padua, Italy
Aparna S. Varde	Montclair State University, USA
Julien Velcin	Université Lumière Lyon 2, France
Bruno Veloso	INESC TEC/University of Porto, Portugal
Rosana Veroneze	LBiC, Brazil
Gennaro Vessio	University of Bari, Aldo Moro, Italy
Tiphaine Viard	Télécom Paris, France
Herna L. Viktor	University of Ottawa, Canada

Joao Vinagre	Joint Research Centre - European Commission, Belgium
Jordi Vitria	Universitat de Barcelona, Spain
Jean-Noël Vittaut	LIP6 - CNRS - Sorbonne Université, France
Marco Viviani	University of Milan-Bicocca, Italy
Paola Vocca	Tor Vergata University of Rome, Italy
Tomasz Walkowiak	Wrocław University of Science and Technology, Poland
Ziwen Wan	University of California, Irvine, USA
Beilun Wang	Southeast University, China
Chuan-Ju Wang	Academia Sinica, Taiwan
Deng-Bao Wang	Southeast University, China
Di Wang	KAUST, Saudi Arabia
Dianhui Wang	La Trobe University, Australia
Hongwei Wang	University of Illinois at Urbana-Champaign, USA
Huandong Wang	Tsinghua University, China
Hui (Wendy) Wang	Stevens Institute of Technology, USA
Jiaqi Wang	Penn State University, USA
Puyu Wang	City University of Hong Kong, China
Qing Wang	Australian National University, Australia
Ruijie Wang	University of Illinois at Urbana-Champaign, USA
Senzhang Wang	Central South University, China
Shuo Wang	University of Birmingham, UK
Suhang Wang	Pennsylvania State University, USA
Wei Wang	Fudan University, China
Wenjie Wang	Shanghai Tech University, China
Yanhao Wang	East China Normal University, China
Yimu Wang	University of Waterloo, Canada
Yue Wang	Microsoft Research, USA
Yue Wang	Waymo, USA
Zhaonan Wang	University of Tokyo, Japan
Zhi Wang	Southwest University, China
Zijie J. Wang	Georgia Tech, USA
Roger Wattenhofer	ETH Zurich, Switzerland
Pascal Weber	University of Vienna, Austria
Jörg Wicker	University of Auckland, New Zealand
Michael Wilbur	Vanderbilt University, USA
Weng-Fai Wong	National University of Singapore, Singapore
Bin Wu	Zhengzhou University, China
Chenwang Wu	University of Science and Technology of China, China

Di Wu	Chongqing Institute of Green and Intelligent Technology, CAS, China
Guoqiang Wu	Shandong University, China
Peng Wu	Shanghai Jiao Tong University, China
Xiaotong Wu	Nanjing Normal University, China
Yongkai Wu	Clemson University, USA
Danyang Xiao	Sun Yat-Sen University, China
Zhiwen Xiao	Southwest Jiaotong University, China
Cheng Xie	Yunnan University, China
Hong Xie	Chongqing Institute of Green and Intelligent Technology, CAS, China
Yaqi Xie	Carnegie Mellon University, USA
Huanlai Xing	Southwest Jiaotong University, China
Ning Xu	Southeast University, China
Xiaolong Xu	Nanjing University of Information Science and Technology, China
Hao Xue	University of New South Wales, Australia
Yexiang Xue	Purdue University, USA
Sangeeta Yadav	Indian Institute of Science, India
Qiao Yan	Shenzhen University, China
Yan Yan	Carleton University, Canada
Yu Yan	People's Public Security University of China, China
Yujun Yan	Dartmouth College, USA
Jie Yang	University of Wollongong, Australia
Shaofu Yang	Southeast University, China
Yang Yang	Nanjing University of Science and Technology, China
Liang Yao	Tencent, China
Muchao Ye	Pennsylvania State University, USA
Michael Yeh	Visa Research, USA
Kalidas Yeturu	Indian Institute of Technology Tirupati, India
Hang Yin	University of Copenhagen, Denmark
Hongwei Yong	Hong Kong Polytechnic University, China
Jaemin Yoo	KAIST, South Korea
Mengbo You	Iwate University, Japan
Hang Yu	Shanghai University, China
Weiren Yu	University of Warwick, UK
Wenjian Yu	Tsinghua University, China
Jidong Yuan	Beijing Jiaotong University, China
Aras Yurtman	KU Leuven, Belgium
Claudius Zelenka	Christian-Albrechts University of Kiel, Germany

Akka Zemmari	University of Bordeaux, France
Bonan Zhang	Princeton University, USA
Chao Zhang	Zhejiang University, China
Chuang Zhang	Nanjing University of Science and Technology, China
Danqing Zhang	Amazon, USA
Guoqiang Zhang	University of Technology, Sydney, Australia
Guoxi Zhang	Kyoto University, Japan
Hao Zhang	Fudan University, China
Junbo Zhang	JD Intelligent Cities Research, China
Le Zhang	Baidu Research, China
Ming Zhang	National Key Laboratory of Science and Technology on Information System Security, China
Qiannan Zhang	KAUST, Saudi Arabia
Tianlin Zhang	University of Manchester, UK
Wenbin Zhang	Michigan Tech, USA
Xiang Zhang	National University of Defense Technology, China
Xiao Zhang	Shandong University, China
Xiaoming Zhang	Beihang University, China
Xinyang Zhang	University of Illinois at Urbana-Champaign, USA
Yaying Zhang	Tongji University, China
Yin Zhang	University of Electronic Science and Technology of China, China
Yongqi Zhang	4Paradigm, China
Zhiwen Zhang	University of Tokyo, Japan
Mia Zhao	Airbnb, USA
Sichen Zhao	RMIT University, Australia
Xiaoting Zhao	Etsy, USA
Tongya Zheng	Zhejiang University, China
Wenhao Zheng	Shopee, Singapore
Yu Zheng	Tsinghua University, China
Yujia Zheng	Carnegie Mellon University, USA
Jiang Zhong	Chongqing University, China
Wei Zhou	School of Cyber Security, CAS, China
Zhengyang Zhou	University of Science and Technology of China, China
Chuang Zhu	Beijing University of Posts and Telecommunications, China
Jing Zhu	University of Michigan, USA
Jinjing Zhu	Hong Kong University of Science and Technology, China

Junxing Zhu	National University of Defense Technology, China
Yanmin Zhu	Shanghai Jiao Tong University, China
Ye Zhu	Deakin University, Australia
Yichen Zhu	Midea Group, China
Zirui Zhuang	Beijing University of Posts and Telecommunications, China
Tommaso Zoppi	University of Florence, Italy
Meiyun Zuo	Renmin University of China, China

Program Committee, Applied Data Science Track

Jussara Almeida	Universidade Federal de Minas Gerais, Brazil
Mozhdeh Ariannezhad	University of Amsterdam, The Netherlands
Renato M. Assuncao	ESRI, USA
Hajer Ayadi	York University, Canada
Ashraf Bah Rabiou	University of Delaware, USA
Amey Barapatre	Microsoft, USA
Patrice Bellot	Aix-Marseille Université - CNRS LSIS, France
Ludovico Boratto	University of Cagliari, Italy
Claudio Borile	CENTAI, Italy
Yi Cai	South China University of Technology, China
Lei Cao	University of Arizona/MIT, USA
Shilei Cao	Tencent, China
Yang Cao	Hokkaido University, Japan
Aniket Chakrabarti	Amazon, USA
Chaochao Chen	Zhejiang University, China
Chung-Chi Chen	National Taiwan University, Taiwan
Meng Chen	Shandong University, China
Ruey-Cheng Chen	Canva, Australia
Tong Chen	University of Queensland, Australia
Yi Chen	NJIT, USA
Zhiyu Chen	Amazon, USA
Wei Cheng	NEC Laboratories America, USA
Lingyang Chu	McMaster University, Canada
Xiaokai Chu	Tencent, China
Zhendong Chu	University of Virginia, USA
Federico Cinus	Sapienza University of Rome/CENTAI, Italy
Francisco Claude-Faust	LinkedIn, USA
Gabriele D'Acunto	Sapienza University of Rome, Italy
Ariyam Das	Google, USA

Jingtao Ding	Tsinghua University, China
Kaize Ding	Arizona State University, USA
Manqing Dong	eBay, Australia
Yushun Dong	University of Virginia, USA
Yingtong Dou	University of Illinois, Chicago, USA
Yixiang Fang	Chinese University of Hong Kong, China
Kaiyu Feng	Beijing Institute of Technology, China
Dayne Freitag	SRI International, USA
Yanjie Fu	University of Central Florida, USA
Matteo Gabburo	University of Trento, Italy
Sabrina Gaito	University of Milan, Italy
Chen Gao	Tsinghua University, China
Liangcai Gao	Peking University, China
Yunjun Gao	Zhejiang University, China
Lluis Garcia-Pueyo	Meta, USA
Mariana-Iuliana Georgescu	University of Bucharest, Romania
Aakash Goel	Amazon, USA
Marcos Goncalves	Universidade Federal de Minas Gerais, Brazil
Francesco Guerra	University of Modena e Reggio Emilia, Italy
Huifeng Guo	Huawei Noah's Ark Lab, China
Ruocheng Guo	ByteDance, China
Zhen Hai	Alibaba DAMO Academy, China
Eui-Hong (Sam) Han	The Washington Post, USA
Jinyoung Han	Sungkyunkwan University, South Korea
Shuchu Han	Stellar Cyber, USA
Dongxiao He	Tianjin University, China
Junyuan Hong	Michigan State University, USA
Yupeng Hou	UC San Diego, USA
Binbin Hu	Ant Group, China
Jun Hu	National University of Singapore, Singapore
Hong Huang	Huazhong University of Science and Technology, China
Xin Huang	Hong Kong Baptist University, China
Yizheng Huang	York University, Canada
Yu Huang	University of Florida, USA
Stratis Ioannidis	Northeastern University, USA
Radu Tudor Ionescu	University of Bucharest, Romania
Murium Iqbal	Etsy, USA
Shoaib Jameel	University of Southampton, UK
Jian Kang	University of Rochester, USA
Pinar Karagoz	METU, Turkey
Praveen C. Kolli	Carnegie Mellon University, USA

Deguang Kong	Yahoo Research, USA
Adit Krishnan	University of Illinois at Urbana-Champaign, USA
Mayank Kulkarni	Amazon, USA
Susana Ladra	University of A Coruña, Spain
Renaud Lambiotte	University of Oxford, UK
Tommaso Lanciano	KTH Royal Institute of Technology, Sweden
Md Tahmid Rahman Laskar	Dialpad, Canada
Matthieu Latapy	CNRS, France
Noah Lee	Meta, USA
Wang-Chien Lee	Pennsylvania State University, USA
Chang Li	Apple, USA
Chaozhuo Li	Microsoft Research Asia, China
Daifeng Li	Sun Yat-Sen University, China
Lei Li	Hong Kong University of Science and Technology, China
Shuai Li	University of Cambridge, UK
Xiang Lian	Kent State University, USA
Zhaohui Liang	National Library of Medicine, NIH, USA
Bang Liu	University of Montreal, Canada
Ji Liu	Baidu Research, China
Jingjing Liu	MD Anderson Cancer Center, USA
Tingwen Liu	Institute of Information Engineering, CAS, China
Weiwen Liu	Huawei Noah's Ark Lab, China
Andreas Lommatzsch	TU Berlin, Germany
Jiyun Luo	Pinterest, USA
Ping Luo	CAS, China
Xin Luo	Shandong University, China
Jing Ma	University of Virginia, USA
Xian-Ling Mao	Beijing Institute of Technology, China
Mirko Marras	University of Cagliari, Italy
Zoltan Miklos	Université de Rennes 1, France
Ahmed K. Mohamed	Meta, USA
Mukesh Mohania	IIIT Delhi, India
Corrado Monti	CENTAI, Italy
Sushant More	Amazon, USA
Jose G. Moreno	University of Toulouse, France
Aayush Mudgal	Pinterest, USA
Sepideh Nahali	York University, Canada
Wolfgang Nejdl	L3S Research Center, Germany
Yifan Nie	University of Montreal, Canada
Di Niu	University of Alberta, Canada
Symeon Papadopoulos	CERTH/ITI, Greece

Manos Papagelis	York University, Canada
Leonardo Pellegrina	University of Padua, Italy
Claudia Perlich	TwoSigma, USA
Fabio Pinelli	IMT Lucca, Italy
Giulia Preti	CENTAI, Italy
Buyue Qian	Xi'an Jiaotong University, China
Chuan Qin	BOSS Zhipin, China
Xiao Qin	Amazon Web Services AI/ML, USA
Yanghui Rao	Sun Yat-Sen University, China
Yusuf Sale	LMU Munich, Germany
Eric Sanjuan	Avignon University, France
Maria Luisa Sapino	University of Turin, Italy
Emmanouil Schinas	CERTH/ITI, Greece
Nasrullah Sheikh	IBM Research, USA
Yue Shi	Meta, USA
Gianmaria Silvello	University of Padua, Italy
Yang Song	Apple, USA
Francesca Spezzano	Boise State University, USA
Efstathios Stamatatos	University of the Aegean, Greece
Kostas Stefanidis	Tampere University, Finland
Ting Su	Imperial College London, UK
Munira Syed	Procter & Gamble, USA
Liang Tang	Google, USA
Ruiming Tang	Huawei Noah's Ark Lab, China
Junichi Tatemura	Google, USA
Mingfei Teng	Amazon, USA
Sofia Tolmach	Amazon, Israel
Ismail Hakki Toroslu	METU, Turkey
Kazutoshi Umemoto	University of Tokyo, Japan
Yao Wan	Huazhong University of Science and Technology, China
Chang-Dong Wang	Sun Yat-Sen University, China
Chong Wang	Amazon, USA
Chuan-Ju Wang	Academia Sinica, Taiwan
Hongzhi Wang	Harbin Institute of Technology, China
Kai Wang	Shanghai Jiao Tong University, China
Ning Wang	Beijing Jiaotong University, China
Pengyuan Wang	University of Georgia, USA
Senzhang Wang	Central South University, China
Sheng Wang	Wuhan University, China
Shoujin Wang	Macquarie University, Australia
Wentao Wang	Michigan State University, USA

Yang Wang	University of Science and Technology of China, China
Zhihong Wang	Tsinghua University, China
Zihan Wang	Shandong University, China
Shi-ting Wen	Ningbo Tech University, China
Song Wen	Rutgers University, USA
Zeyi Wen	Hong Kong University of Science and Technology, China
Fangzhao Wu	Microsoft Research Asia, China
Jun Wu	University of Illinois at Urbana-Champaign, USA
Wentao Wu	Microsoft Research, USA
Yanghua Xiao	Fudan University, China
Haoyi Xiong	Baidu, China
Dongkuan Xu	North Carolina State University, USA
Guandong Xu	University of Technology, Sydney, Australia
Shan Xue	Macquarie University, Australia
Le Yan	Google, USA
De-Nian Yang	Academia Sinica, Taiwan
Fan Yang	Rice University, USA
Yu Yang	City University of Hong Kong, China
Fanghua Ye	University College London, UK
Jianhua Yin	Shandong University, China
Yifang Yin	A*STAR-I2R, Singapore
Changlong Yu	Hong Kong University of Science and Technology, China
Dongxiao Yu	Shandong University, China
Ye Yuan	Beijing Institute of Technology, China
Daochen Zha	Rice University, USA
Feng Zhang	Renmin University of China, China
Mengxuan Zhang	University of North Texas, USA
Xianli Zhang	Xi'an Jiaotong University, China
Xuyun Zhang	Macquarie University, Australia
Chen Zhao	Baylor University, USA
Di Zhao	University of Auckland, New Zealand
Yanchang Zhao	CSIRO, Australia
Kaiping Zheng	National University of Singapore, Singapore
Yong Zheng	Illinois Institute of Technology, USA
Jingbo Zhou	Baidu, China
Ming Zhou	University of Technology, Sydney, Australia
Qinghai Zhou	University of Illinois at Urbana-Champaign, USA
Tian Zhou	Alibaba DAMO Academy, China
Xinyi Zhou	University of Washington, USA

Yucheng Zhou	University of Macau, China
Jiangang Zhu	ByteDance, China
Yongchun Zhu	CAS, China
Ziwei Zhu	George Mason University, USA
Jia Zou	Arizona State University, USA

Program Committee, Demo Track

Ferran Diego	Telefonica Research, Spain
Jan Florjanczyk	Netflix, USA
Mikko Heikkila	Telefonica Research, Spain
Jesus Omaña Iglesias	Telefonica Research, Spain
Nicolas Kourtellis	Telefonica Research, Spain
Eduard Marin	Telefonica Research, Spain
Souneil Park	Telefonica Research, Spain
Aravindh Raman	Telefonica Research, Spain
Ashish Rastogi	Netflix, USA
Natali Ruchansky	Netflix, USA
David Solans	Telefonica Research, Spain

Sponsors

Platinum

Gold

Silver

Bronze

PhD Forum Sponsor

Publishing Partner

Invited Talks Abstracts

Neural Wave Representations

Max Welling

University of Amsterdam, The Netherlands

Abstract. Good neural architectures are rooted in good inductive biases (a.k.a. priors). Equivariance under symmetries is a prime example of a successful physics-inspired prior which sometimes dramatically reduces the number of examples needed to learn predictive models. In this work, we tried to extend this thinking to more flexible priors in the hidden variables of a neural network. In particular, we imposed wavelike dynamics in hidden variables under transformations of the inputs, which relaxes the stricter notion of equivariance. We find that under certain conditions, wavelike dynamics naturally arises in these hidden representations. We formalize this idea in a VAE-over-time architecture where the hidden dynamics is described by a Fokker-Planck (a.k.a. drift-diffusion) equation. This in turn leads to a new definition of a disentangled hidden representation of input states that can easily be manipulated to undergo transformations. I also discussed very preliminary work on how the Schrödinger equation can also be used to move information in the hidden representations.

Biography. Prof. Dr. Max Welling is a research chair in Machine Learning at the University of Amsterdam and a Distinguished Scientist at MSR. He is a fellow at the Canadian Institute for Advanced Research (CIFAR) and the European Lab for Learning and Intelligent Systems (ELLIS) where he also serves on the founding board. His previous appointments include VP at Qualcomm Technologies, professor at UC Irvine, postdoc at the University of Toronto and UCL under the supervision of Prof. Geoffrey Hinton, and postdoc at Caltech under the supervision of Prof. Pietro Perona. He finished his PhD in theoretical high energy physics under the supervision of Nobel laureate Prof. Gerard 't Hooft. Max Welling served as associate editor-in-chief of IEEE TPAMI from 2011–2015, he has served on the advisory board of the NeurIPS Foundation since 2015 and was program chair and general chair of NeurIPS in 2013 and 2014 respectively. He was also program chair of AISTATS in 2009 and ECCV in 2016 and general chair of MIDL in 2018. Max Welling was a recipient of the ECCV Koenderink Prize in 2010 and the ICML Test of Time Award in 2021. He directs the Amsterdam Machine Learning Lab (AMLAB) and co-directs the Qualcomm-UvA deep learning lab (QUVA) and the Bosch-UvA Deep Learning lab (DELTA).

Physics-Inspired Graph Neural Networks

Michael Bronstein

University of Oxford, UK

Abstract. The message-passing paradigm has been the "battle horse" of deep learning on graphs for several years, making graph neural networks a big success in a wide range of applications, from particle physics to protein design. From a theoretical viewpoint, it established the link to the Weisfeiler-Lehman hierarchy, allowing us to analyse the expressive power of GNNs. We argue that the very "node-and-edge"-centric mindset of current graph deep learning schemes may hinder future progress in the field. As an alternative, we propose physics-inspired "continuous" learning models that open up a new trove of tools from the fields of differential geometry, algebraic topology, and differential equations so far largely unexplored in graph ML.

Biography. Michael Bronstein is the DeepMind Professor of AI at the University of Oxford. He was previously a professor at Imperial College London and held visiting appointments at Stanford, MIT, and Harvard, and has also been affiliated with three Institutes for Advanced Study (at TUM as a Rudolf Diesel Fellow (2017–2019), at Harvard as a Radcliffe fellow (2017–2018), and at Princeton as a short-time scholar (2020)). Michael received his PhD from the Technion in 2007. He is the recipient of the Royal Society Wolfson Research Merit Award, Royal Academy of Engineering Silver Medal, five ERC grants, two Google Faculty Research Awards, and two Amazon AWS ML Research Awards. He is a Member of the Academia Europaea, Fellow of the IEEE, IAPR, BCS, and ELLIS, ACM Distinguished Speaker, and World Economic Forum Young Scientist. In addition to his academic career, Michael is a serial entrepreneur and founder of multiple startup companies, including Novafora, Invision (acquired by Intel in 2012), Videocites, and Fabula AI (acquired by Twitter in 2019).

Mapping Generative AI

Kate Crawford

USC Annenberg, USA

Abstract. Training data is foundational to generative AI systems. From Common Crawl's 3.1 billion web pages to LAION-5B's corpus of almost 6 billion image-text pairs, these vast collections – scraped from the internet and treated as "ground truth" – play a critical role in shaping the epistemic boundaries that govern generative AI models. Yet training data is beset with complex social, political, and epistemological challenges. What happens when data is stripped of context, meaning, and provenance? How does training data limit what and how machine learning systems interpret the world? What are the copyright implications of these datasets? And most importantly, what forms of power do these approaches enhance and enable? This keynote is an invitation to reflect on the epistemic foundations of generative AI, and to consider the wide-ranging impacts of the current generative turn.

Biography. Professor Kate Crawford is a leading international scholar of the social implications of artificial intelligence. She is a Research Professor at USC Annenberg in Los Angeles, a Senior Principal Researcher at MSR in New York, an Honorary Professor at the University of Sydney, and the inaugural Visiting Chair for AI and Justice at the École Normale Supérieure in Paris. Her latest book, *Atlas of AI* (Yale, 2021) won the Sally Hacker Prize from the Society for the History of Technology, the ASIS&T Best Information Science Book Award, and was named one of the best books in 2021 by *New Scientist* and the *Financial Times*. Over her twenty-year research career, she has also produced groundbreaking creative collaborations and visual investigations. Her project *Anatomy of an AI System* with Vladan Joler is in the permanent collection of the Museum of Modern Art in New York and the V&A in London, and was awarded with the Design of the Year Award in 2019 and included in the Design of the Decades by the Design Museum of London. Her collaboration with the artist Trevor Paglen, *Excavating AI*, won the Ayrton Prize from the British Society for the History of Science. She has advised policymakers in the United Nations, the White House, and the European Parliament, and she currently leads the Knowing Machines Project, an international research collaboration that investigates the foundations of machine learning.

Contents – Part III

Graphs

Interpretability

Knowledge Graphs

Large-Scale Learning

Graph Neural Networks

Learning to Augment Graph Structure for both Homophily and Heterophily Graphs

Lirong Wu, Cheng Tan, Zihan Liu, Zhangyang Gao, Haitao Lin, and Stan Z. Li[✉]

AI Lab, Research Center for Industries of the Future, Westlake University, Hangzhou, China
{wulirong,tancheng,liuzihan,gaozhangyang, linhaitao,stan.zq.li}@westlake.edu.cn

Abstract. Recent years have witnessed great successes in performing graph structure learning for Graph Neural Networks (GNNs). However, comparatively little work studies structure augmentation for graphs, where the augmented structures are only used for training and are not available during inference. This is mainly due to that structure augmentation is a discrete combinatorial optimization problem rather than a continuous optimization problem like structure learning. In this paper, we propose *Learning to Augment* (L2A), a novel structure augmentation framework that learns customized augmentation strategies for graphs with different homophily levels. Specifically, L2A simultaneously performs the maximum likelihood estimation of GNN parameters and the learning of optimal structure augmentations in a variational inference framework. Moreover, L2A applies two auxiliary self-supervised tasks to exploit both global position and label distribution information in the graph structure to further reduce the reliance on annotated labels and improve applicability to heterophily graphs. Extensive experiments have shown that L2A can produce truly encouraging results at various homophily levels compared with other leading methods and can learn customized structure augmentation strategies across various GNNs architectures and graph datasets. Codes are available at: https://github.com/LirongWu/L2A.

Keywords: Graph Neural Networks · Graph Structure Augmentation · Variational Inference · Graph Self-supervised Learning

1 Introduction

Recently, the emerging Graph Neural Networks (GNNs) [27,31] have demonstrated their powerful capability to handle a variety of graph-related tasks. However, existing methods are prone to suffer from poor generalization or weak robustness due to their heavy reliance on the quantity of annotated labels and the quality of the graph structure [16,17]. To improve the generalization capability, a natural solution is to augment training data by creating plausible variations

D. Koutra et al. (Eds.): ECML PKDD 2023, LNAI 14171, pp. 3–18, 2023.
https://doi.org/10.1007/978-3-031-43418-1_1

of existing data without additional ground-truth labels, which have been widely adopted in fields such as computer vision [3,8] and natural language processing [5,22]. The data augmentation on graphs mainly includes two branches: node feature augmentation and graph structure augmentation. While the former has been well studied by directly extending existing approaches for image and text data to graph data [9,12,30,33], comparatively little work has been done to study graph structure augmentation [2,19,21,34]. For example, *DropEdge* [21] randomly removes a fraction of edges before each training epoch, somewhat similar to dropout [24]. Different from the ad-hoc, two-stage *DropEdge*, *GAUG* [34] proposes to optimize the structure augmentation and GNN parameters in an end-to-end manner. Despite their great success, the above methods are based on the class-homophily assumption which greatly limits their applicability to heterophily graphs, where connected nodes may have different class labels. Thus, a crucial question here is: *Can we adaptively perform graph structure augmentation in an end-to-end framework for graphs with low-to-high homophily levels?*

In this paper, we explore whether one can adaptively learn customized augmentation strategies for different graphs. There are several tricky challenges on the way: *(1)* The structure augmentation is a discrete combinatorial optimization problem with complexity $\mathcal{O}(2^{N^2})$, which is computationally expensive to solve. *(2)* The graph data is too complex to create hand-crafted or heuristic augmentation rules, especially when we know little about the underlying graph properties, e.g., homophily ratio. *(3)* It is hard to directly obtain the optimal strategies for structure augmentation as supervision signals for model optimization.

To address the above challenges, we propose a simple yet effective *Learning to Augment* (L2A) framework that learns customized augmentation strategies for graphs with different homophily levels. To achieve this, we adopt the probabilistic generative model and take the optimal augmentations as latent variables [14,32], which transforms structure augmentation from a discrete combinatorial optimization problem into a continuous optimization problem. Moreover, to further reduce the reliance on annotated labels and improve the applicability to heterophily graphs, we apply two auxiliary self-supervised tasks to incorporate both global position and label distribution information embedded in the graph.

Our contributions are summarized as: (1) Proposing a general graph structure augmentation framework to learn customized augmentation strategies for both homophily and heterophily graphs. (2) Transforming discrete structure augmentation into a continuous optimization problem and solving it in a variational inference framework. (3) Two important contextual topological information, *global position and label distribution*, are incorporated to improve graph structure augmentation. (4) Extensive experiments show that L2A outperforms other leading methods covering the full spectrum of low-to-high homophily ratios.

2   Related Work

2.1   Graph Neural Networks

Graph Neural Networks (GNNs) can be mainly divided into two categories: spectral-based GNNs and spatial-based GNNs. The spectral-based GNNs, such as GCN-Cheby [4] and GCN [15], define convolution kernels in the spectral domain based on the graph signal processing theory. Instead, the spatial-based GNNs, including GraphSAGE [7] and GAT [15], focus on the design of aggregation functions. However, the above four GNNs are based on the class-homophily assumption, so they cannot be directly generalized to heterophily settings, where the homophily level h is defined as the fraction of edges in a graph that connect nodes that have the same class label, i.e., intra-class edges. To solve this problem, several works have been specifically proposed to deal with heterophily graphs [26]. For example, *Geom-GNN* [20] exploits structural similarity to directly capture long-range dependencies in heterophily graphs. In addition, *H2GNN* [36] separates raw and aggregated features so that both low- and high-frequency information can be preserved. Moreover, *FAGCN* [1] proposes a self-gating mechanism to adaptively weigh between low- and high-frequency signals. For more GNNs for heterophily graphs, please refer to a recent survey [35].

2.2 Graph Structure Augmentation

The mainstream algorithms for graph structure augmentation can be divided into three categories: hand-crafted, heuristic, and end-to-end. As a typical hand-crafted algorithm, *DropEdge* [21] randomly removes a fraction of edges before each training epoch according to the hand-crafted probability. In a heuristic way, *AddEdge* [2] iteratively adds (removes) edges between nodes predicted to have the same (different) labels. Different from the above methods, *GAUG* [34] propose to optimize the structure augmentation and GNN parameters in an end-to-end manner. Instead, *MH-Aug* [19] proposes a sampling-based augmentation, where a sequence of augmented graphs are directly drawn from an explicit target distribution. However, due to the overemphasis on the class-homophily assumption, these methods may not be applicable to graphs with strong heterophily. A recent work, KDGA [28], provides deep insights into the potential distribution shift problem in structure augmentation, extending it to heterophily settings for the first time, but it is essentially a post-processing operation based on knowledge distillation rather than an architectural design for graph structure augmentation.

2.3 Variational Inference for GNNs

Inspired by variational autoencoder [14], there have been a lot of works applying variational inference to GNN learning. Our work is greatly inspired by L2P [32], which studies the problem of learning message propagation strategies in a variational Expectation-Maximization (VEM) framework. However, we differ from it in the following three aspects: *(1) Research Objectives.* L2A and L2P focus on two completely different research areas, L2P for message propagation and L2A for structure augmentation, which are orthogonal and compatible. Besides, L2P considers node-level propagation with the distribution space size of latent variables as $\mathcal{O}(k^N)$ (k is the layer number, N is the node number), but L2A considers edge-level augmentation with the distribution space size of $\mathcal{O}(2^{N^2})$, which is more challenging. *(2) Learning Strategy.* L2P is formulated in a bi-level optimization framework, while L2A can be directly optimized in an end-to-end manner. *(3) Evaluation Protocol.* The augmented graphs learned by L2A are only used during training and are not available during testing. In contrast, the learned propagation strategy of L2P is used during both training and testing.

3   Methodology

3.1   Problem Statement

Given a graph $\mathcal{G} = (\mathcal{V}, \mathcal{E})$, where $\mathcal{V}$ is the set of N nodes with features $\mathbf{X} = [\mathbf{x}_1, \mathbf{x}_2, \cdots, \mathbf{x}_N] \in \mathbb{R}^{N \times d}$ and $\mathcal{E} \subseteq \mathcal{V} \times \mathcal{V}$ is the edge set. Each node $v_i \in \mathcal{V}$ is associated with a d-dimensional features vector $\mathbf{x}_i$. The graph structure can also be denoted by an adjacency matrix $\mathbf{A} \in [0,1]^{N \times N}$ with $A_{i,j} = 1$ if $e_{i,j} \in \mathcal{E}$ and $A_{i,j} = 0$ if $e_{i,j} \notin \mathcal{E}$. For semi-supervised node classification, only a subset of node $\mathcal{V}_L$ with corresponding labels $\mathcal{Y}_L$ are known, and we denote the labeled set as $\mathcal{D}_L = (\mathcal{V}_L, \mathcal{Y}_L)$ and unlabeled set as $\mathcal{D}_U = (\mathcal{V}_U, \mathcal{Y}_U)$, where $\mathcal{V}_U = \mathcal{V} \backslash \mathcal{V}_L$. The task of semi-supervised node classification is to learn a mapping $f_\theta : \mathcal{V} \rightarrow \mathcal{Y}$ on labeled data $\mathcal{D}_L$, so that it is used to infer the labels $\mathcal{Y}_U$ of unlabeled data $\mathcal{D}_U$.

Learning to Augment. In this section, we introduce *Learning to Augment* (L2A) framework, which allows for learning customized structure augmentation as well as GNN parameters. The key here is to transform structure augmentation from a discrete combinatorial optimization problem to a continuous optimization problem. To this end, we introduce a set of discrete latent variables $\{t_{i,j}\}_{i,j=1}^N$, where $t_{i,j} \in \{0,1\}$ denotes the optimal augmentation selection between node v_i and v_j. Furthermore, we follow [32] to propose a generative model for modeling the joint distribution of node labels and structure augmentation conditioned on node features and adjacency matrix, i.e., $p(y_n, \mathbf{T} \mid \mathbf{X}, \mathbf{A})$, where $\mathbf{T} \in \mathbb{R}^{N \times N}$ and $\mathbf{T}_{i,j} = t_{i,j}$. The distribution space size of latent variables $\mathbf{T}$ is 2^{N^2}, and without loss of generality, we can denote all possible permutation schemes in this distribution space by $\{T_1, T_2, \cdots, T_{2^{N^2}}\}$. Finally, we can formulate it in a variational inference framework, that learns optimal GNN parameters and structure augmentation distribution in an end-to-end manner, as shown in Fig. 1.

3.2   Augmentation from a Probabilistic Generation Perspective

In the proposed L2A framework, we treat the optimal augmentation (e.g., adding or removing edge) between node v_i and v_j as a discrete latent variable $t_{i,j}$ and adopt the principle of the probabilistic generative model, which has been shown to be effective in estimating the underlying data distribution [18,32]. In practice, $t_{i,j}$ is edge-wise since the optimal augmentation for node pairs may vary largely from one to another. With a set of latent variables $\{t_{i,j}\}_{i,j=1}^N$, we can model the joint distribution of observed label y_i and latent variables $\mathbf{T}$ as follows

$$p_\theta(y_i, \mathbf{T} \mid \mathbf{X}, \mathbf{A}) = p_\theta(y_i \mid \mathbf{X}, \mathbf{A}, \mathbf{T}) \, p(\mathbf{T}), \tag{1}$$

where $p(\mathbf{T})$ is the prior of latent variables and $p_\theta(y_i \mid \mathbf{X}, \mathbf{A}, \mathbf{T})$ represents the label prediction probability of node v_i based on latent variables $\mathbf{T}$. Given the generative model in Eq. (1), our learning objective is twofold as in [32]:

- Learning GNN parameters by maximizing the marginal likelihood:

$$\log p_\theta(y_i \mid \mathbf{X}, \mathbf{A}) = \log \sum_{n=1}^{2^{N^2}} p_\theta(y_i \mid \mathbf{X}, \mathbf{A}, T_n) \, p(T_n). \tag{2}$$

- Inferring posterior $p(\mathbf{T} \mid \mathbf{X}, \mathbf{A}, y_n)$ of latent variables $\mathbf{T}$:

$$p(\mathbf{T} = T_k \mid \mathbf{X}, \mathbf{A}, y_i) = \frac{p_\theta(y_i \mid \mathbf{X}, \mathbf{A}, T_k) \, p(T_k)}{\sum_{n=1}^{2^{N^2}} p_\theta(y_i \mid \mathbf{X}, \mathbf{A}, T_n) \, p(T_n)}. \tag{3}$$

For learning, since it involves marginalizing 2^{N^2} latent variables, we cannot directly learn GNN parameters θ. For inferring, the non-parametric true posterior in Eq. (3) is not applicable since we don't have access to all the ground-truth labels [32]. Therefore, we adopt the variational inference principle [14] and consider the lower bound $\mathcal{L}(\theta, q)$ of the marginal log-likelihood in Eq. (2) as follows

$$\begin{aligned}
\log p_\theta(y_i \mid \mathbf{X}, \mathbf{A}) &= \mathbb{E}_{q(\mathbf{T})}[\log p_\theta(y_i \mid \mathbf{X}, \mathbf{A}, \mathbf{T})] \\
&\quad - KL(q(\mathbf{T}) \| p(\mathbf{T})) + KL(q(\mathbf{T}) \| p(\mathbf{T} \mid \mathbf{X}, \mathbf{A}, y_i)) \\
&\geq \mathbb{E}_{q(\mathbf{T})}[\log p_\theta(y_i \mid \mathbf{X}, \mathbf{A}, \mathbf{T})] - KL(q(\mathbf{T}) \| p(\mathbf{T})) = \mathcal{L}(\theta, q)
\end{aligned} \tag{4}$$

where the detailed derivation of Eq. (4) can be referred to [14]. Maximizing the ELBO $\mathcal{L}(\theta, q)$ means (i) maximize the posterior defined in Eq. (2) and to (ii) make the introduced variational distributions $q(\mathbf{T})$ be close to its intractable true posteriors $p(\mathbf{T} \mid \mathbf{X}, \mathbf{A}, y_i)$ as derived in [32]. When we do not have any prior about how to augment, $p(\mathbf{T} = T_k) = \frac{1}{2^{N^2}} (k = 1, 2, \cdots, 2^{N^2})$ can be defined as uniform distribution. In practice, overly drastical topological perturbations to the graph structure not only fails to increase generalizability but also hinders performance. Therefore, we can use Dirichlet distribution $p(\mathbf{T} = \mathbf{A}) = 1$ as augmentation prior. In this case, the second KL divergence term in $\mathcal{L}(\theta, q)$ is equivalent to approximate $\mathbf{A}$ by the probability $q(\mathbf{T} = 1)$ directly. Thus, the lower bound $\mathcal{L}(\theta, q)$ of Eq. (4) can be approximated and re-written as follows:

$$\mathcal{L}(\theta, q) \approx \mathbb{E}_{q(\mathbf{T})}[\log p_\theta(y_i \mid \mathbf{X}, \mathbf{A}, \mathbf{T})] - CE(q(\mathbf{T} = 1) \| \mathbf{A}), \tag{5}$$

where $CE(q(\mathbf{T} = 1) \| \mathbf{A})$ denotes the cross entropy between $q(\mathbf{T} = 1)$ and $\mathbf{A}$.

3.3   Iterative Variational Inference

Since directly maximizing the ELBO $\mathcal{L}(\theta, q)$ in Eq. (5) is challenging, we adopt an end-to-end iterative variational inference algorithm to minimize negative ELBO in this paper. Specifically, we introduce the parameterized posterior $q_\phi(\mathbf{T} \mid \mathbf{X}, \mathbf{A})$

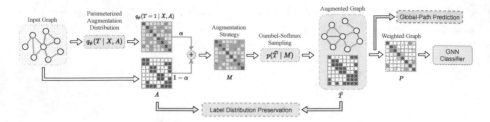

Fig. 1. Illustration of the proposed *Learning to Augment* (L2A) framework, which consists of five major components: (1) Estimating latent variables **T** by parameterized augmentation distribution $q_\phi(\mathbf{T} \mid \mathbf{X}, \mathbf{A})$; (2) Obtaining the optimal augmentation strategy **M** by the weighted fusion; (3) Sampling augmented graph $\widehat{\mathbf{T}}$ from augmentation strategy **M** through differentiable Gumbel-Softmax Sampling; (4) Learning a weighted graph **P** and classifying nodes based on it; (5) Capturing global position information and label distribution information through two auxiliary pretext tasks.

(how to exactly parameterize the variational distribution $q(\mathbf{T})$ is deferred until the next section) into Eq. (5) and then simultaneously learn the optimal augmentation distribution $q_\phi(\mathbf{T} \mid \mathbf{X}, \mathbf{A})$ and GNN parameters in an end-to-end manner. Furthermore, we follow [11,32] to adopt Gumbel-Softmax Sampling, which substitutes non-differentiable sampling from a discrete distribution with a differentiable Gumbel-Softmax distribution. Finally, the learning objective is to minimize the following negative ELBO, as follows

$$\mathcal{L}_{cla}(\theta, \phi) = -\log p_\theta(\mathbf{y} \mid \mathbf{X}, \mathbf{A}, \widehat{\mathbf{T}}) + CE\left(q_\phi(\mathbf{T} = 1 \mid \mathbf{X}, \mathbf{A}) \,\|\, \mathbf{A}\right), \qquad (6)$$

where $\widehat{\mathbf{T}}$ is drawn from a categorical distribution, defined as follows,

$$\widehat{T}_{i,j} = \left\lfloor \frac{1}{1 + \exp^{-\left(\log \mathbf{M}_{i,j} + G\right)/\tau}} + \frac{1}{2} \right\rfloor, 1 \leq i, j \leq N, \qquad (7)$$

where $\mathbf{M}_{i,j} = \alpha q_\phi(\mathbf{T} = 1 \mid \mathbf{X}, \mathbf{A})[i,j] + (1 - \alpha)\mathbf{A}_{i,j}$ is defined as the learned *optimal augmentation strategy*. Besides, $\alpha \in [0,1]$ is the fusion factor, which aims to prevent the sampled augmentation $\widehat{\mathbf{T}}$ from deviating too much from the original graph **A**. τ is the temperature of Gumbel-Softmax distribution, and $G \sim$ Gumbel$(0,1)$ is a Gumbel random variate. Next, we will discuss in detail how to model parameterized posterior $q_\phi(\mathbf{T} \mid \mathbf{X}, \mathbf{A})$ and posterior $p_\theta(\mathbf{y} \mid \mathbf{X}, \mathbf{A}, \widehat{\mathbf{T}})$.

3.4 Parameterized Augmentation Distribution

In the variational inference principle, we adopt the amortization inference [14,32] to fit a shared neural network to model parameterized posterior. Specifically, a two-layer shared GCN encoder and an inner-product decoder are used to parameterize the augmentation distribution $q_\phi(\mathbf{T} \mid \mathbf{X}, \mathbf{A})$ as follows

$$q_\phi(\mathbf{T} = 1 \mid \mathbf{X}, \mathbf{A}) = \sigma\left(\mathbf{Z}\mathbf{Z}^T\right), \text{ where } \mathbf{Z} = f_{GCN}^{(1)}\left(\mathbf{A}, f_{GCN}^{(0)}(\mathbf{A}, \mathbf{X})\right), \qquad (8)$$

where $\mathbf{Z}$ denotes the hidden embeddings learned by the encoder, and $\sigma(\cdot)$ is an element-wise sigmoid function. As many previous works, such as GAUG, have pointed out, overly severe topological perturbation to graph structure not only fails to improve robustness, but also hinders generalizability, especially for heterophily graphs. In practice, augmenting a graph from heterophily to homophily inevitably changes the contextual information of the graph, which may further affect the model performance. Therefore, we **treat the label distribution of nodes as important contextual information and take its preservation as a constraint** to control the perturbation level of graph structure during structure augmentation. Specifically, we propose a self-supervised pretext task *Label Distribution Preservation*, which forces the augmented graph $\widehat{\mathbf{T}}$ to have a consistent label distribution with the original graph $\mathbf{A}$. First, we take the original graph $\mathbf{A}$ as an example to define the local label distribution. Given labeled set $\mathcal{D}_L = (\mathcal{V}_L, \mathcal{Y}_L)$, we first assign labels for those unlabeled nodes through label propagation [37] on graph $\mathbf{A}$ and then defines the local label distribution $\mathbf{y}_i^A$ for each node v_i within its k-hop neighborhood, with the c-th element $\mathbf{y}_{i,c}^A$ is

$$\mathbf{y}_{i,c}^A = \frac{\left|\mathcal{N}_i^L(c)\right| + \left|\mathcal{N}_i^U(c)\right|}{\left|\mathcal{N}_i^L\right| + \left|\mathcal{N}_i^U\right|}, c = 1, 2, \cdots, C \tag{9}$$

where $\mathcal{N}_i^L$ and $\mathcal{N}_i^U$ are labeled and unlabeled nodes within k-hop neighborhood of node v_i, respectively. $\mathcal{N}_i^L(c)$ denotes only those in the neighborhood with the ground-truth label c, and $\mathcal{N}_i^U(c)$ denotes those in the neighborhood that are assigned label c by label propagation. Similarity, we obtain the label distribution $\mathbf{y}_i^{\widehat{T}}$ for the augmented graph $\widehat{\mathbf{T}}$. Finally, the learning objective is defined as

$$\mathcal{L}_{ldp} = \frac{1}{|\mathcal{V}|} \sum_{v_i \in \mathcal{V}} \left\|\mathbf{y}_i^{\widehat{\mathbf{T}}} - \mathbf{y}_i^A\right\|^2. \tag{10}$$

The experimental results in Fig. 2 have demonstrated the effectiveness of the label distribution preservation, especially for heterophily graphs. Due to space limitations, more discussions on the motivations behind the proposed self-supervised pretext tasks and how they differ from existing work [29] can be found in **Appendix A** at https://github.com/LirongWu/L2A/tree/main/appendix.

3.5 GNN Classifier Module for Node Classification

Next, we detail how to model posterior $p_\theta(\mathbf{y} \mid \mathbf{X}, \mathbf{A}, \widehat{\mathbf{T}})$. Specifically, we first transform the input nodes to a low-dimensional space by a parameter matrix $\mathbf{W}_h \in \mathbb{R}^{F \times d}$, that is $\mathbf{h}_i' = \mathbf{W}_h \mathbf{x}_i$. The transformed features are finally used to generate a weighted graph $\mathbf{P}$ based on the augmented graph $\widehat{\mathbf{T}}$, defined as

$$\mathbf{P}_{i,j} = \sigma\left(\Omega_\psi(\mathbf{h}_i', \mathbf{h}_j')\right) \cdot \widehat{\mathbf{T}}_{i,j}, \quad 1 \le i, j \le N, \tag{11}$$

where $\sigma = \tanh(\cdot)$ is an activation function, and $\Omega_\psi(\cdot)$ is a function that takes the contacted features of node v_i and v_j as input and takes the form of a one-layer

MLP in our implementation. To improve the applicability of L2A to graphs with different homophily levels, **the global position information embedded in the graph structure needs to be further exploited**. To this end, we apply a self-supervised auxiliary task *Global-Path Prediction* [12], which takes the shortest path length between nodes as the target, enables the model to consider both label information and global position topological information in the feature extraction process, and thus models the long-distance dependencies between nodes. It pre-obtains a set of clusters from the node set $\mathcal{V}$ and then guides the model to *preserve global topology information* by predicting the shortest path from each node to the anchor nodes associated with cluster centers. Specifically, it firstly partitions the graph into K clusters $\{M_1, M_2, \cdots, M_K\}$ by applying graph partition algorithm [13]. Inside each cluster M_k ($1 \leq k \leq K$), the node with the highest degree is taken as the cluster center, denoted as m_t. Secondly, it calculates the distance $\mathbf{l}_i \in \mathbb{R}^K$ from node v_i to cluster centers $\{m_k\}_{k=1}^K$. Finally, the learning objective of Global-Path Prediction can be defined as follows

$$\mathcal{L}_{global} = \frac{1}{|\mathcal{V}|} \sum_{v_i \in \mathcal{V}} \|f_\omega(\mathbf{h}_i') - \mathbf{l}_i\|^2, \tag{12}$$

where $f_\omega(\cdot)$ linearly maps the input to K-dimension values.

Once the weighted graph $\mathbf{P}$ is obtained, we can aggregate features by taking the weighted sum of its neighbors:

$$\mathbf{h}_i^{(l)} = (1 - \beta) \sum_{j \in \mathcal{N}_i} \mathbf{P}_{i,j} \mathbf{h}_j^{(l-1)} + \beta \mathbf{h}_i^{(0)}, \tag{13}$$

where $1 \leq l \leq L$ and $\mathbf{h}_i^{(0)} = \text{ReLu}(\mathbf{W}_1 \mathbf{x}_i)$. β and L are the teleport probability and aggregation layer, respectively. Finally, we make a prediction on node v_i by

$$\widehat{\mathbf{y}}_i = softmax(\mathbf{W}_2 \cdot \mathbf{h}_i^{(L)}), \tag{14}$$

where $\mathbf{W}_1 \in \mathbb{R}^{F \times F}$ and $\mathbf{W}_2 \in \mathbb{R}^{C \times F}$ are weight matrices.

The total loss to train the whole model is defined as

$$\mathcal{L}_{total} = \mathcal{L}_{cla}(\theta, \phi) + \lambda \mathcal{L}_{ldp} + \kappa \mathcal{L}_{global}. \tag{15}$$

where λ and κ are the weights to balance the influence of the two self-supervised losses $\mathcal{L}_{ldp}$ and $\mathcal{L}_{global}$. The pseudo-code of L2A is summarized in Algorithm 1.

3.6   Complexity Analysis

The time complexity of L2A mainly comes from three parts: (1) augmentator $\mathcal{O}(|\mathcal{V}|dF + |\mathcal{V}|^2F)$ (2) self-supervised tasks $\mathcal{O}(|\mathcal{E}|F)$, and (3) GNN classifier $\mathcal{O}(|\mathcal{V}|dF + |\mathcal{E}|F)$, where d and F are the dimensions of the input and hidden space. The total complexity $\mathcal{O}(|\mathcal{V}|dF + |\mathcal{V}|^2F + |\mathcal{E}|F)$ is squared to the number of nodes $|\mathcal{V}|$ and linear to the number of edges $|\mathcal{E}|$, which is nearly in the same order as the leading method GAUG and other graph generation algorithms. Compared to GAUG, the additional computational burden of L2A comes mainly from the two self-supervised pretext tasks $\mathcal{O}(|\mathcal{E}|F)$, which is negligible as $\mathcal{E} \ll \mathcal{V}^2$.

Algorithm 1 . Algorithm for the proposed L2A framework
Input: Feature Matrix: $\mathbf{X}$; Adjacency Matrix: $\mathbf{A}$.
Output: Predicted Labels $\mathcal{Y}_U$.
1: Randomly initialize Augmentator ϕ and GNN Classifier θ;
2: Pretrain Augmentator until convergence based on $CE\left(q_\phi\left(\mathbf{T} = \mathbf{1} \mid \mathbf{X}, \mathbf{A}\right) \| \mathbf{A}\right)$ and L_{ldp} defined in Eq. (6) and Eq. (10).
3: Pretrain GNN Classifier until convergence based on L_{global} and $-\log p_\theta(\mathbf{y} \mid \mathbf{X}, \mathbf{A}, \widehat{\mathbf{T}})$ defined in Eq. (12) and Eq. (6).
4: **while** Not Converged **do**
5:     *# Graph Augmentation*
6:     Obtain augmentated graph $\widehat{\mathbf{T}}$ by Eq. (8) and Eq. (7);
7:     Make label prediction by Eq. (11), Eq. (13), and Eq. (14);
8:     Compute total loss $\mathcal{L}_{total}$ by Eq. (15);
9:     Update the parameters θ and ϕ by back propagation.
10: **end while**
11: Predict labels $\mathcal{Y}_U$ for unlabeled nodes $\mathcal{V}_U$ with GNN Classifier on the original structure $\mathbf{A}$ (rather than augmentated graph $\widehat{\mathbf{T}}$).
12: **return** Predicted labels $\mathcal{Y}_U$, Augmentor ϕ and Classifier θ.

---

4 Experiments

In this section, we conduct extensive experiments to evaluate the effectiveness of the L2A framework. Specifically, the experiments aim to answer five questions: **Q1.** How effective is L2A for the task of semi-supervision node classification on various real-world graph datasets **Q2.** Is L2A robust to different GNN architectures? Is L2A robust to different homophily and homophily levels? **Q3.** How do the two self-supervised pretext tasks and structure augmentation influence the performance of L2A? **Q4.** Could L2A effectively learn the customized augmentation strategies for graphs with different homophily levels? **Q5.** How do the two key hyperparameters α and L influence the performance of L2A?

4.1 Experimental Setups

Datasets. There are totally *Eight* graph datasets (including ONE synthetic and seven real-world datasets) used to evaluate the proposed L2A framework. An overview summary of the statistic characteristics of datasets is given in Table 1. Three common homophily citation networks, e.g., *Cora* [23], *Citeseer* [6], and *BlogCatalog* [10] are included in the comparison. Besides, we consider four heterophily datasets: *Cornell, Texas, Wisconsin* and *Aactor* [25]. Finally, one synthetic dataset *Syn-Cora* is generated to evaluate the capabilities of the model to handle graphs with different homophily levels. The *Syn-Cora* dataset is generated with various heterophily ratios h by adopting a modified preferential attachment process. Starting from an empty initial graph, new nodes are added into the graph one by one until the number of nodes $|\mathcal{V}|$ reaches 1490. Let $p_{i,j}$ denote the probability that a newly added node u in class i is connected with an existing node v in class j. As a result, heterophily ratio h can be controlled by

$\{p_{i,j}\}_{i,j=1}^{C}$. We first randomly select $C = 5$ classes from the Cora dataset. Then, the node features of *Syn-Cora* dataset in each class are generated by sampling node features from the corresponding class in the real-world Cora dataset.

Table 1. Statistical information of the datasets.

Dataset	Syn-Cora	Cora	Citeseer	BlogCatalog	Texas	Cornell	Wisconsin	Actor
# Nodes	1490	2708	3327	5196	183	183	251	7600
# Edges	2965-2968	5278	4552	171743	279	277	450	26659
# Features	1433	1433	3703	8189	1703	1703	1703	932
# Classes	5	7	3	6	5	5	5	5
Homophily Ratio h	0.00-1.00	0.81	0.74	0.40	0.11	0.30	0.21	0.22

Baselines. To demonstrate the powerful capability of the proposed L2A for structure augmentation, we compare it with five state-of-the-art baselines: And-Edge, DropEdge, MH-Aug, GAUG, and KDGA. Besides, we compare L2A with Geom-GCN, H2GCN, and FAGCN to demonstrate that L2A may work well for graphs with low-to-high homophily levels. In particular, four classical methods, MLP, GCN, GraphSAGE, and GAT, are also included in the comparison as baselines. Note that L2A is a plug-and-play augmentation module that can theoretically be combined with any GNN architecture to further improve performance, such as with FAGCN to create a more powerful variant of *L2A-FAGCN*.

Hyperparameters. The following hyperparameters are set the same for all datasets: Adam optimizer with learning rate $lr = $ 1e-2 and weight decay *decay* $= $ 5e-4; Epoch $E = 500$; teleport probability $\beta = 0.1$. The other hyperparameters are determined by a hyperparameter search tool - NNI for each dataset, including hidden dimension $F = \{16, 32, 64, 128\}$, fusion factor $\alpha = \{0.1, 0.3, 0.8, 1.0\}$, aggregation layer $L = \{1, 2, 3, 4, 5, 6, 7, 8\}$, and loss weights $\lambda, \kappa = \{0.1, 0.5, 1.0\}$. All methods are implemented with PyTorch 1.6.0 library running on NVIDIA v100 GPU, and the model with the highest accuracy on the validation set is selected for testing. Each set of experiments is run five times with different random seeds, and the average performance and standard deviation are reported.

4.2 Classification on Real-World Datasets (Q1)

To answer Q1, we conduct experiments on seven datasets with different homophily levels. The GNN classifier module proposed in this paper is used as a benchmark GNN architecture to compare L2A with four state-of-the-art structure augmentation methods: AndEdge, DropEdge, MH-Aug, GAUG, and KDGA. Besides, the original implementations of MLP, GCN, GraphSAGE, and GAT are also included as baselines. Moreover, we also compare L2A with algorithms specifically designed for heterophily graphs, such as Geom-GCN, H2GCN,

Table 2. Classification accuracy (%) on *seven* real-world datasets. The homophily ratios h is defined as the fraction of intra-class edges among all the edges in a graph: $h = |\{(u,v) \in \mathcal{E} \mid y_u = y_v\}| / |\mathcal{E}|$. In practice, a graph with category number C displays a homophily tendency if $h < \frac{2}{C}$, otherwise it displays a heterophily tendency.

	Heterophily				Homophily		
	Texas	Wisconsin	Actor	Cornell	BlogCatalog	Citeseer	Cora
Homophily Ratio h	0.11	0.21	0.22	0.30	0.40	0.74	0.81
# Nodes $|\mathcal{V}|$	183	251	7,600	183	5,196	3,327	2,708
# Edges $|\mathcal{E}|$	279	450	26,659	277	171,743	4,552	5,278
MLP	81.9±4.8	85.3±3.6	35.8±1.0	81.1±6.4	65.7±2.1	46.5±0.5	55.1±0.5
GCN	59.5±5.3	59.8±7.0	30.3±0.8	57.0±4.7	75.0±0.4	70.3±0.5	81.5±0.8
GraphSAGE	82.4±6.1	81.2±5.6	34.2±1.0	76.0±5.0	73.4±0.4	71.2±0.4	82.2±0.7
GAT	58.4±4.5	55.3±8.7	26.3±1.7	58.9±3.3	63.8±5.2	72.5±0.5	83.1±0.5
DropEdge	82.8±4.7	85.3±5.1	36.5±1.3	79.1±4.1	77.4±0.3	72.4±0.2	82.5±0.8
AddEdge	83.4±5.2	84.9±4.6	35.9±0.9	78.8±4.0	77.3±0.3	72.8±0.7	82.4±0.6
MH-Aug	82.3±3.8	85.4±3.0	35.3±1.1	79.8±3.3	79.1±0.6	72.9±0.5	83.6±0.4
GAUG	80.7±3.5	83.7±3.4	34.5±1.0	78.4±2.9	78.6±0.4	73.1±0.6	83.9±0.5
KDGA	84.0±4.2	86.7±3.8	36.4±1.2	81.8±3.5	78.8±0.3	72.8±0.6	84.4±0.6
L2A (ours)	**85.6±3.4**	**90.2±3.2**	**38.8±0.7**	**84.7±1.3**	**80.2±1.0**	**73.3±0.2**	**84.7±0.6**
GEOM-GCN	67.6	64.1	31.6	60.8	-	-	-
H2GCN	82.2±5.3	85.9±4.2	35.6±1.3	82.2±6.0	77.6±0.8	**72.8±0.4**	83.5±0.5
FAGCN	84.0±4.7	88.4±3.6	35.9±1.1	84.3±4.8	78.5±0.6	72.7±0.8	84.1±0.5
L2A-FAGCN	**86.2±3.9**	**89.1±3.7**	**37.8±0.9**	**85.2±3.3**	**81.9±0.9**	72.4±0.5	**84.5±0.4**

and FAGCN, to demonstrate that L2A may well work for the full spectrum of low-to-high homophily levels. Table 2 summarizes the graph properties and classification performance, from which it can be seen that (1) It can be seen that L2A consistently achieves the best overall performance on all seven datasets, especially in strong heterophily settings. For example, L2A obtains the best performance on the Wisconsin and Cornell datasets, and more notably, our accuracy outperforms GAUG by 6.5% and 6.3%, respectively. (2) Though GAUG and MH-Aug perform well on homophily graphs, it falls behind even DropEdge and AddEdge on heterophily graphs due to the overemphasis on class-homophily. (3) More importantly, L2A shows great advantages even when compared to algorithms specifically designed for heterophily graphs, including Geom-GCN, H2GCN, and FAGCN. More importantly, L2A can be easily combined with existing GNNs to further improve their performance. For example, the variant *L2A-FAGCN*, obtained by combining L2A with FAGCN, significantly improves the performance of the vanilla FAGCN by 2.2% and 3.4% on the Texas and BlogCatalog datasets.

4.3 Homophily Ratios and GNN Architectures (Q2)

The performance on the *Syn-Cora* dataset is reported in Table 2. Experiments are conducted on the *Syn-Cora* dataset by varying homophily ratio h as $\{0.0, 0.1, \cdots, 0.9\}$ with three classical GNN architectures: GCN, GraphSAGE, and GAT. It can be observed from Table 2 that: (1) The proposed L2A framework generalizes well to different homophily levels and achieves the best overall performance across all settings. This suggests that L2A favors learning in homophily settings without sacrificing excellent performance in heterophily data. In contrast, while GAUG can work well in homophily settings, it cannot even match the results of baselines on heterophily data. (2) L2A achieves consistent improvements across all three GNN architectures. For example, L2A improves 3.5% (GCN), 1.8% (GraphSAGE), and 1.8% (GAT) averaged across all 10 homophily ratios compared to baselines, respectively. However, *GAUA* improves only 0.2% (GCN), 0.3% (GraphSAGE), and 0.3% (GAT), respectively (Table 3).

Table 3. Classification accuracy $\pm$ std(%) on the *Syn-Cora* dataset under different homophily ratios h and three GNN architectures (GCN, GraphSAGE, and GAT).

h	0.00	0.10	0.20	0.30	0.40	0.50	0.60	0.70	0.80	0.90
GCN	33.7±1.7	37.1±4.6	42.8±1.9	51.1±0.8	56.9±2.6	66.2±1.0	77.3±1.2	84.5±0.5	91.2±1.3	96.1±0.8
GAUG-GCN	35.2±1.3	37.0±0.8	41.5±1.2	50.1±1.2	57.5±1.6	65.7±0.9	78.4±1.1	**84.9±0.8**	91.4±1.5	**97.3±0.6**
L2A-GCN	**40.2±1.0**	**45.0±1.0**	**47.3±1.8**	**56.0±2.0**	**61.7±1.2**	**68.6±1.4**	**79.9±2.5**	84.7±0.7	**91.9±1.7**	96.9±0.4
GraphSAGE	**76.0±1.9**	72.9±2.4	70.6±1.4	71.8±0.7	72.0±1.7	76.6±0.8	81.3±1.0	85.1±0.5	90.8±1.0	95.1±1.2
GAUG-GraphSAGE	73.8±1.4	71.9±1.0	71.1±0.7	70.9±0.9	72.3±1.5	76.0±0.9	83.0±1.3	87.3±0.6	92.5±1.2	96.5±0.7
L2A-GraphSAGE	74.2±0.6	**73.6±1.1**	**73.1±0.6**	**74.8±0.7**	**74.1±0.7**	**77.5±0.9**	**84.2±0.7**	**88.0±0.7**	**93.6±1.2**	**96.7±0.6**
GAT	30.2±1.3	33.1±1.2	39.1±0.3	48.8±1.6	55.4±2.4	64.5±0.5	76.3±1.8	84.0±1.0	90.9±1.5	95.9±0.2
GAUG-GAT	31.2±1.2	32.9±1.1	38.5±0.9	47.9±1.3	55.2±1.3	64.8±1.4	77.0±1.2	**84.2±0.8**	92.8±1.3	**97.1±0.8**
L2A-GAT	**33.5±1.4**	**35.8±1.4**	**42.6±2.5**	**50.3±1.4**	**55.6±1.5**	**65.5±0.9**	**78.8±0.9**	83.9±0.9	**93.7±1.5**	96.9±0.5

4.4 Ablation Study (Q3)

This evaluates the effectiveness of the structure augmentation and the two auxiliary self-supervised tasks in the L2A framework through four sets of experiments: the model without (A) structure augmentation (*w/o Augmentor*); (B) Global-Path Prediction (*w/o $\mathcal{L}_{global}$*); (C) Label Distribution Preservation (*w/o $\mathcal{L}_{ldp}$*), and (D) the full model. Experiments are conducted on seven datasets, and classification accuracy is reported as the metric. After analyzing the reported results in Fig. 2, we find that both Global-Path Prediction and Label Distribution Preservation contribute to improving performance. More importantly, applying these two tasks together can further improve performance on top of each, which demonstrates the benefit of capturing global position information and preserving label distribution in the graph structure. Moreover, the removal of the structure augmentation will lead to a sharp drop in performance, e.g., 4.7%, 3.2%, 8.9% on the BlogCatalog, Actor, and Texas datasets, which demonstrates the importance of structure augmentation and the effectiveness of the L2A framework.

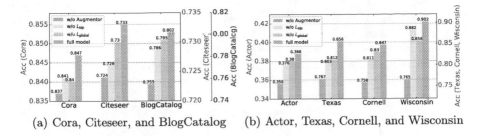

(a) Cora, Citeseer, and BlogCatalog   (b) Actor, Texas, Cornell, and Wisconsin

Fig. 2. Ablation study on the structure augmentation and the two self-supervised tasks.

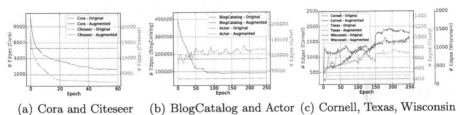

(a) Cora and Citeseer   (b) BlogCatalog and Actor   (c) Cornell, Texas, Wisconsin

Fig. 3. Relationship between augmentation strategy and graph homophily levels.

4.5 Augmentation Strategy Learning (Q4)

To explore the relationship between the structure augmentation strategy and the level of homophily, we visualized the change in the number of edges on the augmented graph $\widehat{\mathbf{T}}$ as training proceeds on all datasets in Fig. 3. Additionally, we provide the number of edges in the original graph $\mathbf{A}$ as baselines, denoted by dotted lines. It can be seen that for three relatively homophily graphs, Cora, Citeseer, and BlogCatalog, the number of edges in the augmented graph decreases consistently with training to produce a *relatively sparse* augmented graph, which helps to alleviate the common over-smoothing problem in homophily data. However, for relatively heterophily graphs, the optimal augmentation strategy is to increase the number of edges to obtain a *densely connected* augmented graph. This is because heterophily data are less affected by the over-smoothing problem, and more dense connectivity helps to establish long-range dependencies between nodes, allowing a larger receptive field to capture contextual information, which is beneficial for node classification on heterophily graphs.

4.6 Parameter Sensitivity Analysis (Q5)

To answer Q5, we evaluate the sensitivity analysis w.r.t two key hyperparameters: fusion factor α in Eq. (7) and aggregation layer L in Eq. (13). The results are

16   L. Wu et al.

reported in Fig. 4 with the best performance circled, from which we can observe:
(1) The performance gain of L2A becomes larger as α increases. However, when
α becomes too large, L2A in turn yields lower performance gains. This is because
a too-small α weakens the contribution of structure augmentation to model performance, while a too-large α can cause the topology of the augmented graph
to deviate too much from the original graph, bringing misleading information
or noise. (2) The model performance can be improved with a larger aggregation
layer L, which enables each node to establish connections with nodes in a larger
multi-hop neighborhood, capturing more contextual information. However, the
performance gain becomes lower when L becomes too large.

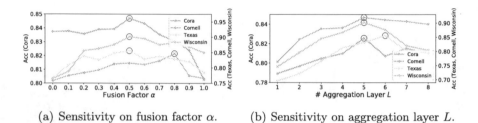

(a) Sensitivity on fusion factor α.   (b) Sensitivity on aggregation layer L.

Fig. 4. Parameter sensitivity analysis on *four* datasets.

5   Conclusion

In this paper, we propose *Learning to Augment* (L2A), a general structure augmentation framework that learns customized augmentation strategies for graphs
with different homophily levels. Specifically, L2A transforms structure augmentation from a discrete combinatorial optimization problem to a continuous optimization problem. This further enables us to simultaneously perform the maximum likelihood estimation of GNN parameters and learning of optimal augmentations in a variational inference framework. Extensive experiments on synthetic
and real-world datasets have shown that L2A outperforms other leading graph
structure augmentation methods. Despite the great progress, limitations still
exist, for example, L2A has only been evaluated on some small-scale datasets.
In our opinion, decoupling edge addition and removal may be helpful to achieve
better scalability for large-scale graphs, which will be left for future work.

Acknowledgement. This work was supported by the National Key R&D Program
of China (No. 2022ZD0115100), the National Natural Science Foundation of China
Project (No. U21A20427), and Project (No. WU2022A009) from the Center of Synthetic Biology and Integrated Bioengineering of Westlake University.

Ethical Statement. Our submission does not involve any ethical issues, including
but not limited to privacy, security, etc.

References

1. Bo, D., Wang, X., Shi, C., Shen, H.: Beyond low-frequency information in graph convolutional networks. arXiv preprint arXiv:2101.00797 (2021)
2. Chen, D., Lin, Y., Li, W., Li, P., Zhou, J., Sun, X.: Measuring and relieving the over-smoothing problem for graph neural networks from the topological view. In: Proceedings of the AAAI Conference on Artificial Intelligence, vol. 34, pp. 3438–3445 (2020)
3. Cubuk, E.D., Zoph, B., Mane, D., Vasudevan, V., Le, Q.V.: Autoaugment: learning augmentation strategies from data. In: Proceedings of the IEEE/CVF Conference on Computer Vision and Pattern Recognition, pp. 113–123 (2019)
4. Defferrard, M., Bresson, X., Vandergheynst, P.: Convolutional neural networks on graphs with fast localized spectral filtering. arXiv preprint arXiv:1606.09375 (2016)
5. Fadaee, M., Bisazza, A., Monz, C.: Data augmentation for low-resource neural machine translation. arXiv preprint arXiv:1705.00440 (2017)
6. Giles, C.L., Bollacker, K.D., Lawrence, S.: Citeseer: an automatic citation indexing system. In: Proceedings of the Third ACM Conference on Digital Libraries, pp. 89–98 (1998)
7. Hamilton, W., Ying, Z., Leskovec, J.: Inductive representation learning on large graphs. In: Advances in Neural Information Processing Systems, pp. 1024–1034 (2017)
8. Ho, D., Liang, E., Chen, X., Stoica, I., Abbeel, P.: Population based augmentation: efficient learning of augmentation policy schedules. In: International Conference on Machine Learning, pp. 2731–2741. PMLR (2019)
9. Hu, W., et al.: Strategies for pre-training graph neural networks. arXiv preprint arXiv:1905.12265 (2019)
10. Huang, X., Li, J., Hu, X.: Label informed attributed network embedding. In: Proceedings of the Tenth ACM International Conference on Web Search and Data Mining, pp. 731–739 (2017)
11. Jang, E., Gu, S., Poole, B.: Categorical reparameterization with gumbel-softmax. arXiv preprint arXiv:1611.01144 (2016)
12. Jin, W., et al.: Self-supervised learning on graphs: deep insights and new direction. arXiv preprint arXiv:2006.10141 (2020)
13. Karypis, G., Kumar, V.: A fast and high quality multilevel scheme for partitioning irregular graphs. SIAM J. Sci. Comput. **20**(1), 359–392 (1998)
14. Kingma, D.P., Welling, M.: Auto-encoding variational bayes. arXiv preprint arXiv:1312.6114 (2013)
15. Kipf, T.N., Welling, M.: Semi-supervised classification with graph convolutional networks. arXiv preprint arXiv:1609.02907 (2016)
16. Liu, Z., Luo, Y., Wu, L., Li, S., Liu, Z., Li, S.Z.: Are gradients on graph structure reliable in gray-box attacks? In: Proceedings of the 31st ACM International Conference on Information & Knowledge Management, pp. 1360–1368 (2022)
17. Liu, Z., Luo, Y., Wu, L., Liu, Z., Li, S.Z.: Towards reasonable budget allocation in untargeted graph structure attacks via gradient debias. In: Advances in Neural Information Processing Systems (2022)
18. Mohamed, S., Rezende, D.J.: Variational information maximisation for intrinsically motivated reinforcement learning. arXiv preprint arXiv:1509.08731 (2015)
19. Park, H., et al.: Metropolis-hastings data augmentation for graph neural networks. In: Advances in Neural Information Processing Systems, vol. 34 (2021)

20. Pei, H., Wei, B., Chang, K.C.C., Lei, Y., Yang, B.: Geom-GCN: geometric graph convolutional networks. arXiv preprint arXiv:2002.05287 (2020)
21. Rong, Y., Huang, W., Xu, T., Huang, J.: Dropedge: towards deep graph convolutional networks on node classification. arXiv preprint arXiv:1907.10903 (2019)
22. Şahin, G.G., Steedman, M.: Data augmentation via dependency tree morphing for low-resource languages. arXiv preprint arXiv:1903.09460 (2019)
23. Sen, P., Namata, G., Bilgic, M., Getoor, L., Galligher, B., Eliassi-Rad, T.: Collective classification in network data. AI Mag. **29**(3), 93 (2008)
24. Srivastava, N., Hinton, G., Krizhevsky, A., Sutskever, I., Salakhutdinov, R.: Dropout: a simple way to prevent neural networks from overfitting. J. Mach. Learn. Res. **15**(1), 1929–1958 (2014)
25. Tang, J., Sun, J., Wang, C., Yang, Z.: Social influence analysis in large-scale networks. In: Proceedings of the 15th ACM SIGKDD International Conference on Knowledge Discovery and Data Mining, pp. 807–816 (2009)
26. Wu, L., et al.: Beyond homophily and homogeneity assumption: relation-based frequency adaptive graph neural networks. IEEE Trans. Neural Netw. Learn. Syst. (2023)
27. Wu, L., Lin, H., Huang, Y., Fan, T., Li, S.Z.: Extracting low-/high-frequency knowledge from graph neural networks and injecting it into MLPs: an effective GNN-to-MLP distillation framework. arXiv preprint arXiv:2305.10758 (2023)
28. Wu, L., Lin, H., Huang, Y., Li, S.Z.: Knowledge distillation improves graph structure augmentation for graph neural networks. In: Advances in Neural Information Processing Systems (2022)
29. Wu, L., Lin, H., Tan, C., Gao, Z., Li, S.Z.: Self-supervised learning on graphs: contrastive, generative, or predictive. IEEE Trans. Knowl. Data Eng. (2021)
30. Wu, L., Xia, J., Gao, Z., Lin, H., Tan, C., Li, S.Z.: Graphmixup: improving class-imbalanced node classification by reinforcement mixup and self-supervised context prediction. In: Amini, M.R., Canu, S., Fischer, A., Guns, T., Kralj Novak, P., Tsoumakas, G. (eds.) PKDD 2022. LNCS, vol. 13716, pp. 519–535. Springer, Cham (2023). https://doi.org/10.1007/978-3-031-26412-2_32
31. Wu, Z., Pan, S., Chen, F., Long, G., Zhang, C., Philip, S.Y.: A comprehensive survey on graph neural networks. IEEE Trans. Neural Netw. Learn. Syst. **32**(1), 4–24 (2020)
32. Xiao, T., Chen, Z., Wang, D., Wang, S.: Learning how to propagate messages in graph neural networks. In: Proceedings of the 27th ACM SIGKDD Conference on Knowledge Discovery & Data Mining, pp. 1894–1903 (2021)
33. You, Y., Chen, T., Sui, Y., Chen, T., Wang, Z., Shen, Y.: Graph contrastive learning with augmentations. In: Advances in Neural Information Processing Systems, vol. 33 (2020)
34. Zhao, T., Liu, Y., Neves, L., Woodford, O., Jiang, M., Shah, N.: Data augmentation for graph neural networks. arXiv preprint arXiv:2006.06830 (2020)
35. Zheng, X., Liu, Y., Pan, S., Zhang, M., Jin, D., Yu, P.S.: Graph neural networks for graphs with heterophily: a survey. arXiv preprint arXiv:2202.07082 (2022)
36. Zhu, J., Yan, Y., Zhao, L., Heimann, M., Akoglu, L., Koutra, D.: Beyond homophily in graph neural networks: current limitations and effective designs. In: Advances in Neural Information Processing Systems, vol. 33 (2020)
37. Zhu, X., Ghahramani, Z., Lafferty, J.D.: Semi-supervised learning using gaussian fields and harmonic functions. In: Proceedings of the 20th International conference on Machine learning (ICML 2003), pp. 912–919 (2003)

Learning Representations for Bipartite Graphs Using Multi-task Self-supervised Learning

Akshay Sethi[✉], Sonia Gupta, Aakarsh Malhotra, and Siddhartha Asthana

AI Garage, Mastercard, Gurugram, India
{akshay.sethi,sonia.gupta,aakarsh.malhotra,
siddhartha.asthana}@mastercard.com

Abstract. Representation learning for bipartite graphs is a challenging problem due to its unique structure and characteristics. The primary challenge is the lack of extensive supervised data and the bipartite graph structure, where two distinct types of nodes exist with no direct connections between the nodes of the same kind. Hence, recent algorithms utilize Self Supervised Learning (SSL) to learn effective node embeddings without needing costly labeled data. However, conventional SSL methods learn through a single pretext task, making the trained model specific to the downstream task. This paper proposes a novel approach for learning generalized representations of bipartite graphs using multi-task SSL. The proposed method utilizes multiple self-supervised tasks to learn improved embeddings that capture different aspects of the bipartite graphs, such as graph structure, node features, and local-global information. We utilize deep multi-task learning (MTL) to further assist in learning generalizable self-supervised solution. To mitigate negative transfer when related and unrelated tasks are trained in MTL, we propose a novel DST++ algorithm. The proposed DST++ optimization algorithm improves existing DST by considering task affinities and groupings for better initialization and training. The end-to-end proposed method with complimentary SSL tasks and DST++ multi-task optimization is evaluated on three tasks: node classification, link prediction, and node regression, using four publicly available benchmark datasets. The results demonstrate that our proposed method outperforms state-of-the-art methods for representation learning in bipartite graphs. Specifically, our method achieves up to 12% improvement in accuracy for node classification and up to 9% improvement in AUC for link prediction tasks compared to the baseline methods.

Keywords: GNNs · Multi Task · Unsupervised · Self-Supervised

1 Introduction

Bipartite graphs are versatile structures representing the relationship between two distinct types of nodes. Its applicability extends to a wide range of real-world

D. Koutra et al. (Eds.): ECML PKDD 2023, LNAI 14171, pp. 19–35, 2023.
https://doi.org/10.1007/978-3-031-43418-1_2

scenarios, such as recommender systems [1], drug discovery [42], and information retrieval [49]. For instance, in recommender systems, users and items can be modeled as two types of nodes within a bipartite graph. The edges in this graph represent interactions between users and items. Additionally, bipartite graphs possess unique structural features that set them apart from heterogeneous graphs. Notably, there are no direct connections between nodes of the same type in a bipartite graph.

In recent years, significant progress has been made in graph embedding generation [3,13]. While these methods have proven effective for homogeneous and heterogeneous graphs, developing meaningful node representations for bipartite graphs remains a persistent challenge. Primarily, such algorithms must be optimized for modeling bipartite graphs, otherwise the resulting node and graph embeddings prove to be suboptimal [9]. To address this, researchers have proposed algorithms specific to bipartite graphs [1,9,41,43,46,47,50].

However, in such a domain, SSL can assist in generating meaningful representation as most problems in bipartite graph domain lack labelled data. SSL based methods can learn effective embeddings without the use of costly labelled data. Motivated by SSL for homogeneous graphs, the current state-of-the-art studies in bipartite graphs utilizing SSL include BiGi [4] and COIN [21]. These approaches build upon a single pretext task with a particular philosophy, such as maximizing mutual information. Such methods have illustrated promising results for bipartite graph representation learning. However, their efficacy is usually limited to only one task and performs lower across other downstream tasks and datasets. For instance, BiGi [4], which is based on mutual information maximization between local and global representations, performs well in link prediction tasks but poorly in node classification tasks. Additionally, COIN [21], deliver excellent results for clustering task as it maximize the mutual information of co-clusters to captures the cluster-level information whereas it doesn't perform well on other tasks like link prediction.

This issue has been studied in other domains, such as Natural Language Processing [33,34] and Computer Vision [6,29]. These research studies have indicated that models enhanced by SSL over multiple pretext tasks have demonstrated strong task generalization and the ability to learn transferable intrinsic patterns. Similarly, there has been some work in the homogeneous graph domain [22] showing that MTL for homogeneous graphs enables better task performance (Fig. 1).

In this work, we propose a multi-task SSL algorithm for bipartite graphs with pretext tasks to impart generalized knowledge to the model. We use different SSL tasks used in homogeneous graph learning literature, which include feature reconstruction, edge reconstruction, contrastive learning, and mutual information maximization. We simultaneously optimize and dynamically coordinate the pretext tasks by proposing a novel MTL optimization algorithm DST++. The proposed DST++ improves upon DST [27] by modeling task affinities and groupings, eventually dropping and scheduling the grouped tasks together. Furthermore, using the task groupings, we better initialize the shared backbone of

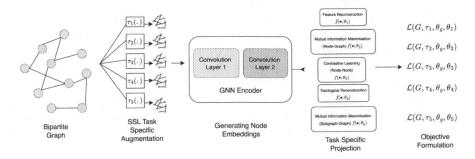

Fig. 1. Multi-Task Network for Self Supervised learning

the multi-task network to promote weaker tasks. The overall contributions of this study are summarised as follows:

– As an initial step towards exploring foundational bipartite graph models [2] and improving overall generalization, we developed five pretext tasks for SSL. We introduce a multi-task SSL algorithm called MultiBipGNN, which is self-supervised by pretext tasks and dynamically reconciles them according to DST++. This ensures the graph encoder learns knowledge from every pretext task while minimizing conflicts.
– We also propose a novel bipartite graph encoder that aggregates information from two hops (same type) nodes and one hop (different type) nodes via multi-head soft attention (MHSA) [38,39].
– We evaluate MultiBipGNN against seven state-of-the-art unsupervised bipartite representation methods on four public benchmark datasets across three downstream tasks (node classification, node regression, and link prediction). Our experiments demonstrate that MultiBipGNN outperforms the state-of-the-art unsupervised methods by +7.1% in overall performance, indicating better task generalization by learning disjoint yet complementary knowledge from different tasks.

2   Background Work

This section describes the background work in SSL for bipartite graphs. We explain SSL in bipartite graphs and then move to SSL in homogeneous graphs via GNNs. Next, we list research studies in multi-task SSL in different domains, such as language, vision, and graphs. Finally, we illustrate how to optimize multiple tasks better while learning to avoid negative transfer.

2.1   Bipartite Graph Representation Learning

Bipartite graphs are commonly modeled using (i) homogeneous or (ii) heterogeneous graph embeddings. Some **homogeneous** random-walk-based methods include Node2vec [10], DeepWalk [32], LINE [37], or, GNN ones like GraphSAGE

[12] and GAT [39]. Random-walk-based methods employ Skip-Gram to acquire node embeddings to maintain the graph structure but seldom employ the node features. Alternatively, GNN-based methods recursively aggregate features of neighboring nodes and learn node representations.

On the other hand, **heterogeneous** graph embedding methods include studies such as Metapath2vec [7] and DMGI [30]. Metapath2vec constructs diverse node neighborhoods using meta path-based random walks. Such heterogeneous methods, however, are not tailored for bipartite graphs and may lose their structural characteristics [9]. To preserve structural detail, several methods are designed for bipartite graphs, including PinSage [43], BiNE [9], C-BGNN [15], BiGI [4], and COIN [21]. BiNE [9] proposes a biased random walk that generates vertex sequences to preserve the long-tail distribution of vertices and trains skip-gram-based embeddings on them. C-BGNN [15], on the other hand, aggregates information across and within the two partitions of a bipartite graph by utilizing a customized Inter-domain Message Passing and Intra-domain Alignment. BiGI [4] focuses on learning better representations by using mutual information maximization between global and local graph embeddings. Recently, COIN [21] also utilized mutual information maximization between co-clusters to capture the cluster-level information.

2.2   Self Supervised Learning (SSL) for GNNs

SSL has attracted a lot of attention in graphs due to its ability to learn effective node embeddings without costly labeled data. Most graph SSL frameworks for node-level tasks rely on a single philosophy and pretext task. Such tasks include mutual information maximization, contrastive learning, or generative reconstruction. Although initially used in computer vision, contrastive learning methods are adapted to graph representation learning. For instance, DGI [39] learns node representations by contrasting local and global embeddings. Due to contrastive learning, DGI achieved impressive results in node classification benchmarks. GIC [28] proposes an unsupervised method that maximizes the mutual information between node-level and cluster-level representations. GMI [31] generalizes conventional mutual information computations from the vector space to the graph domain, measuring mutual information from node features and topological structure. Lastly, by creating two views of the graph to learn node representations GRACE [51] and GCA [52] use contrastive learning. They pull the representation of the same node in two views close while pushing the embedding of every other node apart.

2.3   Multi-task Self Supervised Learning and Optimization

Multi-task SSL is extensively studied in computer vision and natural language processing [6,26,29,33,34]. Within the graph domain, AutoSSL [20] examines a multi-task setting where tasks are reconciled to promote graph homophily. Additionally, Hu et al. [18] focus on graph-level tasks and pre-trained GNNs in separate stages. The tasks were reconciled using either weighted summation or pre-defined heuristics. Recently, Ju et al. [22] proposed a multi-task self-supervised framework for learning in homogeneous graphs. The different tasks are coordinated using multiple gradient descent. Though some of these studies [18,22] work towards unsupervised learning or pretraining in graphs using multiple tasks, they cannot be extended to bipartite graphs directly.

When optimizing an MTL network, the aim is to orchestrate priorities of tasks dynamically during training. Two commonly used approaches in MTL optimization are (i) task grouping and (ii) task prioritization. The former method groups the tasks based on their relatedness and selects a group of tasks or sub-network for efficient MTL. Various methods are used to compute task grouping, such as measuring affinities [48], cross-task consistencies [45], or probability of concurrently simple/difficult tasks [25]. After grouping, different sub-networks may be generated [25], or MTL be orchestrated [45,48].

On the other hand, in weight-based task prioritization, each task is weighed individually and optimized using $\widetilde{L} = \sum_{t=1}^{k} w_t L_t$. Studies use informative task-specific loss value, validation performance, or gradients to balance training dynamically. For instance, GradNorm [5] and LBTW [24] alter the gradients of the network and prioritize tasks. Alternatively, some studies utilize train or validation set performance to determine the difficulty or the incompleteness of the task [11,19]. Task-wise weights can also be added as learnable parameters and constrained using regularization terms to enforce non-trivial solutions as done in [23]. Recently, DST [27] proposed a dropping mechanism to drop tasks during MTL training. The tasks were dropped to prioritize the remaining weaker tasks.

3 Proposed Algorithm

In this section, we first describe the notations, followed by our proposed algorithm MultiBipGNN and its three components: (i) Bipartite Graph Encoder, (ii) Multi Task Self Supervised Learning, and (iii) DST++.

3.1 Notation

Let G be a bipartite graph $= (U, V, E)$, where U and V are two separate sets of nodes, and $E \subseteq U \times V$ represents the edges. G comprises two types of nodes: those that belong to the same set are similar, while those in different sets are dissimilar. Let A be a binary adjacency matrix of size $|U| \times |V|$, where each element A_{ij} indicates whether a node $u_i \in U$ has a connection with a node $v_j \in V$. The aim of bipartite graph embedding is to assign a d-dimensional vector to each node in G, denoted as $\mathbf{u_i}$ and $\mathbf{v_j}$ for u_i and v_j, respectively.

3.2 Bipartite Graph Encoder

We propose a bipartite graph encoder for the shared backbone of the multi-task network. We train two encoders, the first one learning representations of u-type nodes and the other for v-type nodes.

Since the direct neighbors in a bipartite graph are of different types, the message-passing mechanism of homogeneous graphs cannot be applied to bipartite graphs. Hence, we describe the message passing for u_i^k as follows, with v_j^k also following the same process. First, we generate temporary representations $\hat{v}_j^k$ via a mean aggregation as:

$$\hat{v}_j^k = \delta(\hat{W}_v^k.MEAN(u_i^{k-1} : u_i \in N(v_j))), \tag{1}$$

where, k is the layer, δ the non-linear activation, W^k is a weight matrix, and $N(v_j)$ denotes one-hop neighbors of v_j. Due to its construction, $\hat{v}_j^k$ can be considered a u-type embedding. Now at the one hop, we have two types of neighbors: v_j^{k-1}, the natural neighbor, and $\hat{v}_j^k$, the constructed temporary neighbor. We apply a non-linear transform on v_j using an MLP and then aggregate both kinds of neighbors and the self-node using multi-head soft attention (MHSA) (Fig. 2).

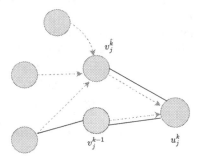

Fig. 2. Message Passing in Proposed Bipartite Graph Encoder

We define an augmented neighborhood for a node u_i, consisting of all the one-hop natural neighbors v_j and temporary neighbors $\hat{v}_j$. We then perform a graph attention-based convolution using MHSA on the augmented neighborhood to learn the feature representations for the node u_i.

$$\alpha_{ij}^k = \frac{exp(\delta(a^T[W_u^k u_i^{k-1} \| W_u^k v_j^{k-1}]))}{\sum_{l \in N_i} exp(\delta(a^T[W_u^k u_i^{k-1} \| W_u^k v_l^{k-1}]))} \tag{2}$$

$$\mathbf{u^i} = \delta \left(\frac{1}{N} \sum_{n=1}^{N} \sum_{j \in N_i} \alpha_{ij}^k W_u^k v_j^{k-1} \right) \tag{3}$$

Here, α_{ij}^k denotes the attention weights that aggregate information over the augmented neighborhood. δ is the non-linear activation, and a is an MLP which adds further expressivity to the attention mechanism. To stabilize attention, we use N heads [38,39] and take an average to obtain the final embedding.

Building the intuition of the algorithm, we require information from the same type of nodes for message passing. However, complementary information from the other node type can also assist. Hence, we aggregate the two kinds of neighbors using MHSA, which can decide how much to weigh each piece of information. We use an MLP for implicit domain alignment between the two feature domains u and v, as followed by C-BGNN [15].

3.3   Multi Task Self Supervised Learning

This work proposes five pretext tasks to cover three high-level philosophies: generative reconstruction, contrastive learning, and maximizing mutual information between local and global representations. The details of these five tasks are:

Generative Reconstruction: This aims to generate the node features (feature reconstruction) and topology (topological reconstruction) from its embedding.

Feature Reconstruction: Using MultiBipGNN, we first encode node features by masking the features of a random batch of nodes. Next, we reconstruct the masked node features after remasking them against the node representations [17]. For the same, we utilize the u encoder, $f_{g,u}$, to reconstruct the representations for u-type nodes and v encoder, $f_{g,v}$ to reconstruct for v-type nodes. The following equations describe the reconstruction loss for u type nodes.

$$\hat{X}_u{}' = A'.f_{g,u}(G'; \theta_{g,u}) \odot M_u.W_u^{Dec} \tag{4}$$

$$\mathcal{L}_{FeatRec,u} = \frac{\|\hat{X}_u' \odot \hat{M}_u - X_u' \odot \hat{M}_u\|_F}{\|X_u' \odot \hat{M}_u\|_F} \tag{5}$$

Here $\odot$ refers to the Hadamard product, X_u' is the feature matrix of the sampled subgraph, A' is the adjacency matrix for the same and M_u and $\hat{M}_u$ are the masked and remasked feature matrices. The final loss to be minimized for feature reconstruction is the sum of u-type and v-type losses.

Topological Reconstruction: We also reconstruct links between connected nodes to retain pair-wise topological knowledge. Given a sampled sub-graph G', we randomly sample B positive node pairs where the links exist and B negative node pairs where no edge exists. The probability of connection between two nodes is calculated as:

$$P_{link}(i,j) = \delta\left((f_u(G'; \theta_{g,u})[u_i] \odot f_v(G'; \theta_{g,v})[v_j]).W^{Topo}\right) \tag{6}$$

Finally, topological reconstruction maximizes the probabilities of positive node pairs and minimizes for negative node pairs as:

$$\mathcal{L}_{TopoRec} = \frac{-1}{2B} \sum_{(u_i,v_j)\in V^+} log(P_{link}(u_i, v_j)) + \sum_{(u_i,v_j)\in V^-} log(1 - (P_{link}(u_i, v_j)))$$
$$\tag{7}$$

Contrastive Learning: Contrastive learning aims to maximize mutual information by contrasting positive pairs with negative-sampled counterparts. Motivated by GraphCL [44], we define a formulation for bipartite graphs. While pre-training the GNN, a random set of N sub-graphs is chosen and used in contrastive learning. This process results in $2N$ augmented graphs, which are used to optimize the contrastive loss. Here, u nodes are contrasted with u-type nodes to obtain positive examples for the u-type anchor. On the contrary, negative pairs are not explicitly sampled but obtained from the other augmented graphs in the same set of N sub-graphs. $u_{n,i}$ and $u_{n,j}$ are the positive samples generated using augmentation from the same node. sim is a similarity measure like cosine similarity. We follow the same process for v type nodes. Lastly, the final contrastive learning loss to be minimised is the sum of u-type and v-type losses.

$$\mathcal{L}_{Contrastive,u} = -log\frac{exp(sim(u_{n,i}, u_{n,j})/\tau)}{\sum_{n'=1, n' \neq n}^{N} exp(sim(u_{n,i}, u_{n',j})/\tau)} \tag{8}$$

Mutual Information Maximization: This involves maximizing the mutual information between two views of the same target, which assists in learning intrinsic patterns [16]. To maximize local-global mutual information, we minimize the distance between the intact graph-level representation and its edge representations while simultaneously maximizing the distance between the former and the corrupted edge representations. We extend the DGI [39] method for a bipartite graph by maximizing the mutual information between the edge embeddings and the global representation of the graph.

$$\mathcal{L}_{MI}^{1} = \frac{1}{N+M} \left(\sum_{i=1}^{N} E_{(\mathbf{X},\mathbf{A})} \left[logD(\mathbf{h_i}, g) \right] + \sum_{j=1}^{M} E_{(\widetilde{\mathbf{X}}, \widetilde{\mathbf{A}})} \left[log(1 - D(\widetilde{\mathbf{h}}_j, g)) \right] \right) \tag{9}$$

Here, g is the graph representation, defined using mean over node representations for both u-type and v-type and then concatenated. Similarly, we compute local edge representation $\mathbf{h}$ by concatenating node representations of u and v. As a proxy for maximizing the mutual information, we employ a discriminator $D(\mathbf{h_i}, g)$ [4,39]. It represents the probability scores assigned to the patch-summary pair (higher score for patches contained within the summary).

Motivated from BiGI [4], we also maximize the mutual information between sub-graph and global graph representations. Here, we maximize the mutual information between the embeddings of a subgraph defined around an edge and the global representation.

$$\mathbf{p}_u = MEAN(\mathbf{u_i}; u_i \in U), \mathbf{p}_v = MEAN(\mathbf{v_i}; v_i \in V),$$
$$g = COM(p_u, p_v) = [\sigma(p_u)|\sigma(p_v)] \tag{10}$$

$$\mathbf{g}_{(u,v)}^{h} = \left[\sigma\left(\sum_{v_i \in G^h(u)} \alpha_{u,i} v_i + u \right) | \sigma\left(\sum_{u_i \in G^h(u)} \alpha_{v,i} u_i + v \right) \right] \tag{11}$$

Here g is the global graph representation and $\mathbf{g}^h_{(u,v)}$ is the sub-graph representation. $\mathbf{g}^h_{(u,v)}$ is computed around edge u,v and is defined by taking a h-hop neighbourhood and learning attention weights for both u and v. Finally, as described below, we maximize the mutual information between the subgraph and global graph representation using the actual graph and its corrupted version.

$$\mathcal{L}^2_{MI} = \frac{1}{N+M} \left(\sum_{i=1}^{N} E_{(\mathbf{X},\mathbf{A})} \left[log D(\mathbf{g}^h_{(u,v)}, g) \right] + \sum_{j=1}^{M} E_{(\widetilde{\mathbf{X}},\widetilde{\mathbf{A}})} \left[log(1 - D(\widetilde{\mathbf{g}^h_{(u,v)}}, g)) \right] \right)$$

(12)

3.4 DST++: Dropped Schedule Task MTL with Task Affinity

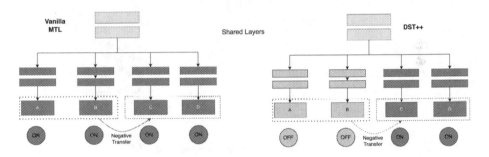

Fig. 3. DST++ Task Dropping Mechanism

Empirical observations show that combining pre-text SSL tasks with weighted summation can improve task generalization, but a multi-task self-supervised GNN may not always perform as well as expert models on some downstream tasks due to potential conflicts between SSL tasks (Fig. 3).

Malhotra et al. [27] recently proposed the DST algorithm for optimized training of weaker tasks and avoiding negative transfer in MTL. They encoded a cumulative activation probability $P_{k,t}$ with five different metrics. This activation probability $P_{k,t}$ denoted the probability with which the tth task will remain active in the kth epoch. Stochastically, the dropped task was removed from joint optimization in the epoch, and the remaining tasks jointly optimized the network. However, the DST algorithm fails to consider task relatedness and affinities. Independent task-level activation can result in dissimilar tasks being "switched ON" together. Hence, in this research, we proposed DST++. The enhanced DST++ includes task affinity alongside three original key metrics of task completion, task stagnancy, and regularization to avoid catastrophic forgetting.

Task Affinity Metric: First, we require a task affinity matrix based on which task affinity metric $\mathcal{P}^a_{k,t}$ can be defined. This task affinity metric $\mathcal{P}^a_{k,t}$ will then be used to obtain the task activation probability $P_{k,t}$. Inspired by Fifty et al. [8], the idea is to compute how gradient update due to a task T_i affects another task T_j at the shared layers. If the *forward looking* weight update due to T_i positively impacts T_j (loss L_j decreases), the task can be said to be related. Hence, the affinity at iteration k can be defined as:

$$Z^k_{j \to i} = 1 - \frac{L_j^{(k+1)|\theta_i^{k+1}}}{L_j^k} \tag{13}$$

On a positive impact, $L_j^{(k+1)|\theta_i^{k+1}} < L_j^k$ and hence, $Z^k_{j \to i}$ indicates a positive affinity. On the contrary, if $L_j^{(k+1)|\theta_i^{k+1}} > L_j^k$, the weight update on shared layers due to T_i harmed the learning of T_j, and hence a negative affinity. A generalized score at training or epoch level can then be computed as $\hat{Z}^k_{j \to i} = \frac{1}{K} \sum_{k=1}^K Z^k_{j \to i}$. Lastly, using $\hat{Z}^k_{j \to i}$, the task groupings are computed using a branch and bound algorithm [8]. Once the groups are created based on task affinity, the next step is to create the task affinity metric $\mathcal{P}^a_{k,t}$. For all tasks $T_i \subseteq T$, where T_i are number of task in the ith group, the task affinity metric $\mathcal{P}^a_{k,t}$ can be defined as:

$$\mathcal{P}^a_{(k,t)} = \begin{cases} \frac{1}{2} * (1 + sin\frac{2\pi k}{M}) & \text{if } k \in (n * (i-1), n * i]; \\ \frac{1}{2} * sin\frac{2\pi k}{M} \end{cases} \tag{14}$$

Here k is the training epoch, M is the total number of groups and it operates same for all tasks in the ith group. n represents a natural number, which takes on values 1,2,3 .... depending on values of k to make the entire metric periodic.

As a last step, we also utilize $\mathcal{P}^b_{k,t}$, $\mathcal{P}^c_{k,t}$, and $\mathcal{P}^d_{k,t}$ for task completion, task stagnancy, and regularization from DST [27], respectively. Task completion metric is $\mathcal{P}^b_{(k,t)} = \min\left(1, \frac{I_{(k,t)}}{E(I_{(k)})}\right)$, where $I_{(k,t)}$ is the ratio of current loss value over initial loss value for t^{th} task and $E(I_{(k)})$ is expected value across all task. Similarly, $\mathcal{P}^c_{k,t}$ computes the duration for which the loss value for each task has been stagnant and prefers activation of longer stagnant tasks. Lastly, $\mathcal{P}^d_{k,t}=1$ is a regularization to prevent tasks from remaining OFF forever and limits catastrophic forgetting.

With all four metrics computed, the overall task activation probability $P_{k,t}$ can be defined as:

$$P_{(k,t)} = \lambda_1 \mathcal{P}^a_{(k,t)} + \lambda_2 \mathcal{P}^b_{(k,t)} + \lambda_3 \mathcal{P}^c_{(k,t)} + \lambda_4 \mathcal{P}^d_{(k,t)} \tag{15}$$

where $\sum \lambda_i = 1$. For each task, its activation is decided by sampling 1 or 0 gate using the $P_{(k,t)}$, sampled from an independent Bernoulli distribution, hence scheduling tasks at each epoch.

DST++ Multi-task Network Initialization: Another extension we propose to DST in DST++ is in the area of better network initialization. DST uses random init, with no emphasis on initialization based on tasks. Once we obtain the task affinities and groupings, we then compute inter-group affinities. Using these inter-group affinities, we initialize the multi-task network by network weights of tasks belonging to the group with minimum inter-group affinity. This takes the network weights in a space where the remaining tasks don't dominate the less related task group. The formulation for inter-group affinity is given as follows:

$$A_i = \frac{\sum_{t=1}^{T} \sum_{j=1}^{J} \tau_{t,j}}{N_t * N_j} \tag{16}$$

Here A_i is the affinity of task group i and $\tau_{t,j}$ is the task affinity of the tasks t and j. Here, task t belongs to group i while task j is outside group i. Finally, N_t is the number of tasks in group i and N_j is the remaining number of tasks.

4   Experiments

In this section, we go into detail about the datasets, tasks, and experimental setup that MultiBipGNN was trained and tested on. Furthermore, we will also describe the baselines it has been compared with.

4.1   Datasets

We conduct extensive experimentation with different tasks using four open benchmark datasets. These include MovieLens-100k (ML) [14], Amazon CD (AC) [36], Amazon Movie (AM) [35] and Aminer Paper-Author (PA) [40] datasets. Table 1 lists the statistics for different datasets, comprising the number of nodes, types of nodes, and number of edges in the graph. The aim of using such a wide range of datasets and tasks is to thoroughly evaluate how generalizable the proposed approach is.

Table 1. Dataset Statistics

Dataset	Node Types	$|U|$	$|V|$	$|E|$
MovieLens-100k [14]	User, Movie	943	1,682	100,000
Amazon Music [35]	User, Movie	53,986	54,523	453,228
Amazon CD [36]	User, CD	44,025	48,856	946,138
Paper-Author [40]	Author, Paper	79,250	47,385	260,897

4.2   Downstream Tasks and Evaluation Metrics

We assess the performance of our proposed method using the node classification, node regression, and link prediction tasks as three common downstream tasks. The metrics used to evaluate each task's performance are Accuracy (Acc), Mean Squared Error (MSE), and Area under the Curve (AUC).

To carry out node regression, we rely on three datasets, Amazon CD, Amazon Music and MovieLens-100k. For the link prediction we again rely on three datasets, Amazon CD, Amazon Music and MovieLens-100k. To perform node classification, we make use of the Paper-Author dataset, which involves a subset of Aminer papers published in the top 10 venues.

4.3   Evaluation Protocol

To conduct various downstream tasks, we utilize the standard linear-evaluation protocol on graphs, as proposed by [22,39]. For all three tasks, this entails freezing the parameters of the GNN encoder, retrieving the embeddings of the corresponding nodes during inference, and training only linear models. For datasets whose splits are available we utilize the public splits provided for evaluation. However, for other datasets, we adopt a 80%/10%/10% split for train/validation /test, which is consistent with the methodology used in other works [4,22,39].

4.4   Baselines

We compared the state of the art (SoTA) unsupervised graph representation learning methods from the homogeneous, heterogeneous, and bipartite graph literature with our proposed algorithm.

- **Homogeneous and Heterogeneous Graph Embeddings:** We compare our algorithm with strong homogeneous methods like Node2Vec, GraphSAGE and GAT. Node2Vec employs Skip-Gram to acquire node embeddings that maintain the graph's structure, but it never employs the features of the nodes. GraphSAGE and GAT aim to preserve the local graph structure by aggregating neighbouring features. On the Heterogeneous side, we compare with Metapath2Vec.
- **Bipartite Graph Embeddings:** As mentioned in the related work section, there are several works which learn representations for bipartite graphs as homogeneous and heterogeneous methods prove to be suboptimal. We do a comparison with algorithms like BiNE, C-BGNN and BiGI.

5   Results and Analysis

Results of the proposed algorithm, MultiBipGNN are discussed in this section. We extensively experiment on different datasets and tasks, and compare with various strong baselines.

5.1   Comparison with Unsupervised Baselines

We evaluate MultiBipGNN by comparing it with seven other unsupervised learning methods, which are considered as strong baselines. Table 2 shows that none of the baseline algorithms can perform favorably on all downstream tasks across all datasets. When it comes to specific tasks, BiGI excels at link prediction but struggles with node classification and node regression. However, C-BGNN is less effective for other tasks than node regression and classification.

As detailed in above sections, we carry out node regression using three datasets AC, AM and ML. In AC and AM the task is the predict the mean rating of a CD and Movie respectively, whereas in ML we predict the user's age. We use Mean Squared Error (MSE) to compare the performance of all methods on this task. We see a relative improvement of about 10% using our algorithm across all three datasets relative to the corresponding best performing baseline. For the link prediction we again rely on three datasets, Amazon CD, Amazon Music and MovieLens-100k. In the AC dataset, a connection between a user and a CD signifies that the user has given a rating to that particular CD. Likewise, in the AM and ML datasets, a link exists if a user has rated a movie. Our algorithm has shown a comparative improvement of approximately 7% in all three datasets. We use the PA dataset for the node classification task where the aim is to predict the venue of a paper. Here also we beat the baselines with an improvement of 5%.

The results reveal that our technique can generalize across tasks and datasets due to the usage of multiple SSL tasks and DST++ to coordinate them. Multi-BipGNN outperforms baselines on all tasks, in contrast to competing baselines, which excel on a single task.

Table 2. Performance Comparison with existing Literature

Method	Regression(MSE)			Link Prediction(AUC)			Classification (Acc)
	AC	AM	ML	AC	AM	ML	PA
Node2Vec	0.50	0.52	0.71	0.80	0.82	0.62	0.50
GraphSage	0.32	0.41	0.67	0.76	0.80	0.64	0.55
GAT	0.32	0.38	0.79	0.72	0.75	0.70	0.56
Metapath2vec	0.36	0.42	0.70	0.85	0.86	0.62	0.55
BINE	0.34	0.50	0.71	0.86	0.86	0.75	0.54
BiGi	0.36	0.4	0.81	0.91	0.92	0.82	0.54
C-BGNN	0.31	0.37	0.65	0.85	0.88	0.75	0.58
MultiBipGNN	**0.27**	**0.34**	**0.58**	**0.95**	**0.96**	**0.90**	**0.62**

5.2   Ablation Study

We perform experiments on our pretext tasks and evaluate their performance individually as shown in Table 3. Our observations shows that a model designed for single-task is not efficient to give competitive results on different downstream task for all datasets. This reveals that knowledge learned through a single methodology is not enough for consistent task generalization. Models trained on a single pretext task alone can only provide satisfactory results on a few tasks or datasets, making them narrow experts.

For example, Feature Reconstruction performs well on node classification and regression but performs poorly on all other tasks. Similarly, MI-Subgraph-Graph (BiGI) performs well on link prediction but underperforms on other tasks. However, when we compared these models with the model which is trained on combination of all pretext tasks through weighted summation (i.e., w/o DST++), we discover that the latter achieved both robust task generalization and stronger single-task performance. Multiple objectives help regularize the learning model against extracting unessential information, enabling the model to learn multiple complementary views of the given bipartite graphs.

Table 3. Ablation Results

Method	Regression (MSE)			Link Prediction (AUC)			Classification (Acc)
	AC	AM	ML	AC	AM	ML	PA
MI-Edge-Graph	0.35	0.38	0.78	0.88	0.90	0.80	0.55
MI-Subgraph-Graph	0.36	0.40	0.81	0.91	0.92	0.82	0.54
Topological Reconstruction	0.34	0.40	0.76	0.86	0.89	0.80	0.52
Feature Reconstruction	0.31	0.38	0.65	0.80	0.80	0.73	0.58
Contrastive Learning	0.32	0.37	0.70	0.84	0.80	0.76	0.56
MultiBipGNN (w/o DST++)	0.29	0.39	0.62	0.90	0.92	0.84	0.58
MultiBipGNN	**0.27**	**0.34**	**0.58**	**0.95**	**0.96**	**0.90**	**0.62**

In some cases, we notice significant performance differences between the best-performing single-task models and the vanilla multi-task model w/o DST++. MultiBipGNN addresses this issue by dropping and scheduling tasks. Table 3 shows that MultiBipGNN is the highest-performing model in terms of both average metric and individual downstream tasks, indicating strong task generalization and promising single-task performance.

6   Conclusion

We present MultiBipGNN, a multi-task self supervised approach for learning representations in bipartite graphs. We furthermore propose DST++ to minimize conflicts and negative transfer among the SSL pretext tasks. Through extensive experimentation across four public graph datasets and three tasks, node classification, node regression and link prediction we show that our algorithm is able to capture complementary knowledge from diverse SSL philosophies and is able to comprehensively beat strong baselines and individual SSL tasks it is trained on. We believe our work is a first step towards training a generalist model (foundation model) for bipartite graphs.

Ethics Statement. Our proposed algorithm does not raise any ethical concerns, however, it is important to note that ethical applications of graphs can potentially benefit from the improved task generalization and performance provided by our work. To ensure positive and socially beneficial outcomes of machine learning algorithms, it is crucial to exercise caution and responsibility.

References

1. Berg, R.V.D., Kipf, T.N., Welling, M.: Graph convolutional matrix completion. arXiv preprint arXiv:1706.02263 (2017)
2. Bommasani, R., et al.: On the opportunities and risks of foundation models. arXiv preprint arXiv:2108.07258 (2021)
3. Cai, H., Zheng, V.W., Chang, K.C.C.: A comprehensive survey of graph embedding: problems, techniques, and applications. IEEE Trans. Knowl. Data Eng. **30**(9), 1616–1637 (2018)
4. Cao, J., Lin, X., Guo, S., Liu, L., Liu, T., Wang, B.: Bipartite graph embedding via mutual information maximization. In: ACM International Conference on Web Search and Data Mining, pp. 635–643 (2021)
5. Chen, Z., Badrinarayanan, V., Lee, C.Y., Rabinovich, A.: Gradnorm: gradient normalization for adaptive loss balancing in deep multitask networks. In: International Conference on Machine Learning, pp. 794–803 (2018)
6. Doersch, C., Zisserman, A.: Multi-task self-supervised visual learning. In: IEEE International Conference on Computer Vision, pp. 2051–2060 (2017)
7. Dong, Y., Chawla, N.V., Swami, A.: metapath2vec: scalable representation learning for heterogeneous networks. In: ACM International Conference on Knowledge Discovery and Data Mining, pp. 135–144 (2017)
8. Fifty, C., Amid, E., Zhao, Z., Yu, T., Anil, R., Finn, C.: Efficiently identifying task groupings for multi-task learning. Adv. Neural. Inf. Process. Syst. **34**, 27503–27516 (2021)
9. Gao, M., Chen, L., He, X., Zhou, A.: Bine: bipartite network embedding. In: ACM Conference on Research & Development in Information Retrieval, pp. 715–724 (2018)
10. Grover, A., Leskovec, J.: node2vec: scalable feature learning for networks. In: ACM International Conference on Knowledge Discovery and Data Mining, pp. 855–864 (2016)
11. Guo, M., Haque, A., Huang, D.A., Yeung, S., Fei-Fei, L.: Dynamic task prioritization for multitask learning. In: European Conference on Computer Vision, pp. 270–287 (2018)
12. Hamilton, W., Ying, Z., Leskovec, J.: Inductive representation learning on large graphs. In: Advances in Neural Information Processing Systems, vol. 30 (2017)
13. Hamilton, W.L., Ying, R., Leskovec, J.: Representation learning on graphs: methods and applications. arXiv preprint arXiv:1709.05584 (2017)

14. Harper, F.M., Konstan, J.A.: The movielens datasets: history and context. ACM Trans. Interact. Intell. Syst. **5**(4), 1–19 (2015)
15. He, C., et al.: Cascade-BGNN: toward efficient self-supervised representation learning on large-scale bipartite graphs. arXiv preprint arXiv:1906.11994 (2019)
16. Hjelm, R.D., et al.: Learning deep representations by mutual information estimation and maximization. arXiv preprint arXiv:1808.06670 (2018)
17. Hou, Z., Liu, X., Dong, Y., Wang, C., Tang, J., et al.: Graphmae: self-supervised masked graph autoencoders. arXiv preprint arXiv:2205.10803 (2022)
18. Hu, W., et al.: Strategies for pre-training graph neural networks. arXiv preprint arXiv:1905.12265 (2019)
19. Jean, S., Firat, O., Johnson, M.: Adaptive scheduling for multi-task learning. arXiv preprint arXiv:1909.06434 (2019)
20. Jin, W., Liu, X., Zhao, X., Ma, Y., Shah, N., Tang, J.: Automated self-supervised learning for graphs. arXiv preprint arXiv:2106.05470 (2021)
21. Jing, B., Yan, Y., Zhu, Y., Tong, H.: Coin: co-cluster infomax for bipartite graphs. arXiv preprint arXiv:2206.00006 (2022)
22. Ju, M., et al.: Multi-task self-supervised graph neural networks enable stronger task generalization. arXiv preprint arXiv:2210.02016 (2022)
23. Liebel, L., Körner, M.: Auxiliary tasks in multi-task learning. arXiv preprint arXiv:1805.06334 (2018)
24. Liu, S., Liang, Y., Gitter, A.: Loss-balanced task weighting to reduce negative transfer in multi-task learning. In: AAAI Conference on Artificial Intelligence, vol. 33, no. 01, pp. 9977–9978 (2019)
25. Lu, Y., Kumar, A., Zhai, S., Cheng, Y., Javidi, T., Feris, R.: Fully-adaptive feature sharing in multi-task networks with applications in person attribute classification. In: IEEE Conference on Computer Vision and Pattern Recognition, pp. 5334–5343 (2017)
26. Malhotra, A., et al.: Multi-task driven explainable diagnosis of COVID-19 using chest X-ray images. Pattern Recogn. **122**, 108243 (2022)
27. Malhotra, A., Vatsa, M., Singh, R.: Dropped scheduled task: mitigating negative transfer in multi-task learning using dynamic task dropping. Trans. Mach. Learn. Res. (2022)
28. Mavromatis, C., Karypis, G.: Graph infoclust: maximizing coarse-grain mutual information in graphs. In: Advances in Knowledge Discovery and Data Mining, pp. 541–553 (2021)
29. Ni, M., et al.: M3P: learning universal representations via multitask multilingual multimodal pre-training. In: IEEE Conference on Computer Vision and Pattern Recognition, pp. 3977–3986 (2021)
30. Park, C., Kim, D., Han, J., Yu, H.: Unsupervised attributed multiplex network embedding. In: AAAI Conference on Artificial Intelligence, vol. 34, no. 04, pp. 5371–5378 (2020)
31. Peng, Z., et al.: Graph representation learning via graphical mutual information maximization. In: The Web Conference, pp. 259–270 (2020)
32. Perozzi, B., Al-Rfou, R., Skiena, S.: Deepwalk: online learning of social representations. In: ACM International Conference on Knowledge Discovery and Data Mining, pp. 701–710 (2014)
33. Radford, A., Wu, J., Child, R., Luan, D., Amodei, D., Sutskever, I., et al.: Language models are unsupervised multitask learners. OpenAI Blog **1**(8), 9 (2019)
34. Sanh, V., et al.: Multitask prompted training enables zero-shot task generalization. arXiv preprint arXiv:2110.08207 (2021)

35. Stratigi, M., Li, X., Stefanidis, K., Zhang, Z.: Ratings vs. reviews in recommender systems: a case study on the amazon movies dataset. In: New Trends in Databases and Information Systems, pp. 68–76 (2019)
36. Sun, J., Cheng, Z., Zuberi, S., Pérez, F., Volkovs, M.: HGCF: hyperbolic graph convolution networks for collaborative filtering. In: The Web Conference, pp. 593–601 (2021)
37. Tang, J., Qu, M., Wang, M., Zhang, M., Yan, J., Mei, Q.: Line: large-scale information network embedding. In: International Conference on World Wide Web, pp. 1067–1077 (2015)
38. Vaswani, A., et al.: Attention is all you need. In: Advances in Neural Information Processing Systems, vol. 30 (2017)
39. Veličković, P., Cucurull, G., Casanova, A., Romero, A., Lio, P., Bengio, Y.: Graph attention networks. arXiv preprint arXiv:1710.10903 (2017)
40. Wan, H., Zhang, Y., Zhang, J., Tang, J.: Aminer: search and mining of academic social networks. Data Intell. 1(1), 58–76 (2019)
41. Wang, X., He, X., Wang, M., Feng, F., Chua, T.S.: Neural graph collaborative filtering. In: ACM International Conference on Research and Development in Information Retrieval, pp. 165–174 (2019)
42. Yamanishi, Y., Kotera, M., Kanehisa, M., Goto, S.: Drug-target interaction prediction from chemical, genomic and pharmacological data in an integrated framework. Bioinformatics 26(12), i246–i254 (2010)
43. Ying, R., He, R., Chen, K., Eksombatchai, P., Hamilton, W.L., Leskovec, J.: Graph convolutional neural networks for web-scale recommender systems. In: ACM International Conference on Knowledge Discovery & Data Mining, pp. 974–983 (2018)
44. You, Y., Chen, T., Sui, Y., Chen, T., Wang, Z., Shen, Y.: Graph contrastive learning with augmentations. Adv. Neural. Inf. Process. Syst. 33, 5812–5823 (2020)
45. Zamir, A.R., et al.: Robust learning through cross-task consistency. In: IEEE Conference on Computer Vision and Pattern Recognition, pp. 11197–11206 (2020)
46. Zhang, M., Chen, Y.: Inductive matrix completion based on graph neural networks. arXiv preprint arXiv:1904.12058 (2019)
47. Zhang, Y., Xiong, Y., Kong, X., Zhu, Y.: Learning node embeddings in interaction graphs. In: ACM Conference on Information and Knowledge Management, pp. 397–406 (2017)
48. Zhang, Y., Yeung, D.Y.: A regularization approach to learning task relationships in multitask learning. ACM Trans. Knowl. Discov. Data (TKDD) 8(3), 1–31 (2014)
49. Zhang, Y., Wang, D., Zhang, Y.: Neural IR meets graph embedding: a ranking model for product search. In: The World Wide Web Conference, pp. 2390–2400 (2019)
50. Zhang, Z., Cui, P., Wang, X., Pei, J., Yao, X., Zhu, W.: Arbitrary-order proximity preserved network embedding. In: ACM International Conference on Knowledge Discovery & Data Mining, pp. 2778–2786 (2018)
51. Zhu, Y., Xu, Y., Yu, F., Liu, Q., Wu, S., Wang, L.: Deep graph contrastive representation learning. arXiv preprint arXiv:2006.04131 (2020)
52. Zhu, Y., Xu, Y., Yu, F., Liu, Q., Wu, S., Wang, L.: Graph contrastive learning with adaptive augmentation. In: The Web Conference, pp. 2069–2080 (2021)

ChiENN: Embracing Molecular Chirality with Graph Neural Networks

Piotr Gaiński[1(✉)], Michał Koziarski[2,3], Jacek Tabor[1], and Marek Śmieja[1]

[1] Faculty of Mathematics and Computer Science, Jagiellonian University, Kraków,
Poland
piotr.gainski@doctoral.uj.edu.pl
[2] Mila - Quebec AI Institute, Montreal, QC, Canada
[3] Université de Montréal, Montreal, QC, Canada

Abstract. Graph Neural Networks (GNNs) play a fundamental role in many deep learning problems, in particular in cheminformatics. However, typical GNNs cannot capture the concept of chirality, which means they do not distinguish between the 3D graph of a chemical compound and its mirror image (enantiomer). The ability to distinguish between enantiomers is important especially in drug discovery because enantiomers can have very distinct biochemical properties. In this paper, we propose a theoretically justified message-passing scheme, which makes GNNs sensitive to the order of node neighbors. We apply that general concept in the context of molecular chirality to construct Chiral Edge Neural Network (ChiENN) layer which can be appended to any GNN model to enable chirality-awareness. Our experiments show that adding ChiENN layers to a GNN outperforms current state-of-the-art methods in chiral-sensitive molecular property prediction tasks.

Keywords: Graph Neural Networks · GNN · Message-passing · Chirality · Molecular Property Prediction

1 Introduction

Recent advances in Graph Neural Networks (GNNs) have revolutionized cheminformatics and enabled learning the molecular representation directly from chemical structures [9,30]. GNNs are widely used in molecular property prediction [20,31,34,36], synthesis prediction [3,17], molecule generation [2,21,22], or conformer generation [6,11,19,33]. Surprisingly, typical GNNs cannot capture the concept of chirality, roughly meaning they do not distinguish between a molecule and its mirror image, called enantiomer (see Fig. 1). Although enantiomers share many physical, chemical, and biological properties, they may behave remarkably differently when interacting with other chiral molecules, e.g. chiral proteins. For this reason, capturing chirality is critical in the context of drug design [10,12,16,23,25] and should not be ignored by the design of GNN architecture.

A chiral molecule is a molecule with at least one chiral center which is usually a carbon atom with four non-equivalent constituents. The mirror image

© The Author(s), under exclusive license to Springer Nature Switzerland AG 2023
D. Koutra et al. (Eds.): ECML PKDD 2023, LNAI 14171, pp. 36–52, 2023.
https://doi.org/10.1007/978-3-031-43418-1_3

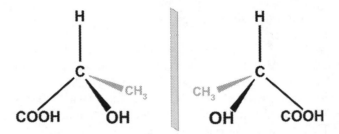

Fig. 1. An example of a chiral molecule (left) and its mirror image (right).

of a chiral molecule, called an enantiomer, cannot be superposed back to the original molecule by any combination of rotations, translations, and conformational changes (see Fig. 1). Therefore, enantiomers are molecules with different bond arrangements and the same graph connectivity. There are many examples of chiral drugs used in pharmacy whose enantiomers cause substantially different effects [23]. For instance (S)-penicillamine is an antiarthritic drug while its enantiomer (R)-penicillamine is extremely toxic [15].

Actually, chirality can be a characteristic of any class of graphs embedded in euclidean space (where we have an intuitive notion of reflection). For instance, Fig. 2 shows two 2D road maps that are mirror images of each other and possess different properties. For this reason, modeling chirality in GNNs is not restricted to the chemical domain.

In this paper, we propose and theoretically justify a novel order-sensitive message-passing scheme, which makes GNNs sensitive to chirality. In contrast to existing methods of embracing chirality, our framework is not domain specific and does not rely on arbitrary chiral tagging or torsion angles (see Sect. 2). The only inductive bias our method introduces to a GNN is the dependency on the orientation of the neighbors around a node, which lies at the core of chirality.

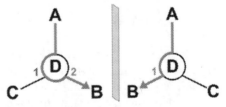

Fig. 2. An illustration of a road map (left) and its mirror image (right). We see that the maps share the same connectivity between cities, however, to get from city A to city B one has to take the second exit on a roundabout D for the left map, and the first exit for the right map.

The key component of the proposed framework is the message aggregation function. In a typical GNN, the messages incoming to a node from its neighbors are treated as a set and aggregated with a permutation-invariant function (sum, max, etc.). It makes the model unable to distinguish between chiral graphs with the same connectivity, but with different spatial arrangements. We re-invent this approach and introduce a message aggregation function that is sensitive to the spatial arrangement (order) of the neighbors. Our approach can be used in any chiral-sensitive graph domain where chirality can be expressed by an order of the neighboring nodes.

We apply that general order-sensitive message-passing framework in the context of molecular chirality to construct Chiral Edge Neural Network (ChiENN) layer. The ChiENN layer can be appended to most molecular GNN models to enable chirality sensitiveness. Our experiments show that ChiENN can be successfully used within existing GNN models and as a standalone model consisting of stacked ChiENN layers. In both cases, ChiENN outperforms current state-of-the-art methods in chiral-sensitive molecular property prediction tasks by a large margin. We make our code publicly available[1].

Our contributions are as follows:

1. We propose and theoretically justify a general order-sensitive message-passing scheme. Our method can be adapted to any chiral-sensitive graph domain where chirality can be expressed by an order of the neighboring nodes (Sect. 3).
2. We use the proposed framework to construct a novel ChiENN layer that enables chirality awareness in any GNN model in the domain of molecular graphs (Sect. 4). The proposed ChiENN can be applied to any 3D graph task with the notion of chirality.
3. We evaluate and analyze the ChiENN layer and show that it outperforms current state-of-the-art methods in chiral-sensitive molecular property prediction tasks (Sect. 5).

2   Related Work

Explicit Tagging of Chiral Center. The most common approach for incorporating chirality into GNN is to use local or global chiral tags [13,18,27]. Both local and global tagging can be seen in the following way. Every carbon atom with four non-equivalent constituents, called a chiral center, is given a tag (CCW or CW) describing the orientation of its constituents. The orientation is defined using the enumeration of constituents computed by an arbitrary algorithm. The constituent with the highest number (4) is positioned so that it points away from the observer. The curve passing through the constituents with numbers 1, 2, and 3 respectively determines a clockwise (CW) or counterclockwise (CCW) orientation of the chiral center. Although enumeration algorithms for global and local tagging differ (the latter is not explicitly used in practice), the expressivity of both methods is limited, as we show in Sect. 5.

3D GNNs with Torsion Angles. Some recent GNN models enrich graphs with 3D information, like distances between atoms [4,20], angles between bonds [8,28], and torsion angles between two bonds joined by another bond [5,7]. As distances and angles are invariant to chirality, the torsion angles (that are negated

---

[1] https://github.com/gmum/ChiENN.

upon reflection) are required for 3D GNN to express the chirality. However, even access to a complete set of torsion angles does not guarantee expressivity in chiral-sensitive tasks as shown in [1]. Torsion angles are sensitive to bond rotations and can also be negated by the reflection of a non-chiral molecule. In [1], the authors proposed the ChIRo model that instead of embedding single torsion angles, embeds sets of torsion angles with a common bond. ChIRo is the current state-of-the-art method for chiral-sensitive tasks. In contrast to ChIRo, our proposed method does not incorporate distances, angles, or torsion angles. It only relies on the orientation of neighbors around a node, making it more general and easily adaptable to other chiral graph domains. Moreover, our experiments show that the ChiENN layer outperforms ChIRo by a large margin on chiral-sensitive molecular tasks (see Sect. 5).

Changing Aggregation Scheme. The method most related to our approach is the Tetra-DMPNN model from [24] which replaces a classic message-passing scheme with a chiral-sensitive one. The proposed aggregation scheme is guided by local chiral tags, meaning that it relies on some arbitrary rules for enumerating neighbors and cannot be applied to nodes other than chiral centers. Moreover, the Tetra-DMPNN method is computationally expensive and does not scale with the number of possible neighbors of a chiral center, making the model useful only in the context of chemistry. Our approach provides a general, efficient, and scalable chiral-sensitive message passing and outperforms the Tetra-DMPNN on chiral-sensitive molecular tasks by a large margin (see Sect. 5).

3   Order-Sensitive Message-Passing Scheme

Setting. Let us consider a directed graph $G = (X, E)$ in which every node $x_i \in X$ is represented by a N-dimensional encoding ($x_i \in \mathbb{R}^N$). Edge e_{ij} connects nodes x_i and x_j and is represented by M-dimensional encoding ($e_{ij} \in \mathbb{R}^M$).

In addition, we assume that for every node $x \in X$, we are given an order o of all its neighbors $o = (x_0, x_1, \ldots, x_{d-1})$. The order of neighbors forms a sequence, which stands in contrast to typical graphs, where neighbors are treated as an unordered set. Given a permutation π on $\{0, 1, \ldots, d-1\}$, we assume that two orders $o_1 = (x_0, \ldots, x_{d-1})$ and $o_2 = (x_{\pi(0)}, \ldots, x_{\pi(d-1)})$ are equivalent if and only if π is a shift i.e. $\pi(i) = (i + k) \bmod d$, for a fixed $k \in \mathbb{Z}$. In other words, the neighbors form the sequence on a ring.

One of the most common mechanisms in GNN is message-passing, which updates the representation of a node x by the information coming from its neighbors $(x_0, \ldots, x_{d-1})$, which can be written as:

$$x' = f(x; x_0, \ldots, x_{d-1}).$$

In this paper, we are going to describe the general message-passing scheme, which is aware of the neighbors' order. Before that, we discuss possible choices of the aggregation function f.

Vanilla Message-Passing as a Permutation-Invariant Transformation.
Let us first discuss a basic case, where f is a permutation-invariant function, i.e.

$$f(x; x_0, \ldots, x_{d-1}) = f(x; x_{\pi(0)}, \ldots, x_{\pi(d-1)}),$$

for every permutation π of $\{0, 1, \ldots, d-1\}$. This aggregation ignores the order
of neighbors and lies in a heart of typical GNNs.

Let us recall that f is permutation-invariant with respect to $\{x_0, x_1, \ldots, x_{d-1}\}$
if and only if it can be decomposed in the form [35]:

$$f(x_0, x_1, \ldots, x_{d-1}) = \rho(\sum_{i=0}^{d-1} \phi(x_i)),$$

for suitable transformations ϕ and ρ. In the context of graphs, a general form of
a permutation-invariant aggregation of neighbors $\{x_0, x_1, \ldots, x_{d-1}\}$ of x is:

$$x' = f(x; x_0, \ldots, x_{d-1}) = \rho(x; \sum_{i=0}^{d-1} \phi(x; x_i)), \tag{1}$$

for suitable transformations ϕ and ρ. By specifying ρ, ϕ as neural networks, we
get the basic formula of vanilla message-passing.

Shift-Invariant Aggregation. Vanilla message-passing relies on permutation-
invariant aggregation and it does not take into account the neighbor's order.
Thus we are going to discuss the weaker case of aggregation function f and
assume that f is shift-invariant, i.e.

$$f(x; x_0, \ldots, x_{d-1}) = f(x; x_{0+p}, \ldots, x_{d-1+p}),$$

for any shift by a number $p \in 0, \ldots, d-1$, where the additions on indices are
performed modulo d. This assumption is consistent with our initial requirement
that shifted orders are equivalent.

The following theorem gives a general formula for shift-invariant mappings.

Theorem 1. *The function f is shift-invariant if and only if f can be written
as:*

$$f(x_0, \ldots, x_{d-1}) = \sum_{p=0}^{d-1} g(x_{0+p}, \ldots, x_{d-1+p})$$

for an arbitrary function g.

Proof. If f is shift invariant, then $f(x_0, \ldots, x_{d-1}) = f(x_{0+p}, \ldots, x_{d-1+p})$ for
every p, and consequently

$$f(x_0, \ldots, x_{d-1}) = \sum_{p=0}^{d-1} \frac{1}{d} f(x_{0+p}, \ldots, x_{d-1+p}).$$

On the other hand, if the function f can be written as $\sum_{p=0}^{d-1} g(x_{0+p}, \ldots, x_{d-1+p})$,
then it is shift-invariant for arbitrary function g.

Following the above theorem, we get a general formula for shift-invariant aggregation applicable to graphs:

$$x' = \rho(x; \sum_{p=0}^{d-1} \psi(x; x_{0+p}, \dots, x_{d-1+p})), \qquad (2)$$

for suitable ρ and ψ, where all additions are performed modulo d.

Now, we want to ensure that our function f is not only shift-invariant but also order-sensitive

Order-Sensitive Message-Passing. Let us assume that we are in the class of shift-invariant transformations. We are going to specify the formula (2) to obtain ab aggregation, which is sensitive to any permutation other than shift. More precisely, we say that f is order-sensitive if and only if for every permutation π, we have:

$$f(x; x_0, \dots, x_{d-1}) = f(x; x_{\pi(0)}, \dots, x_{\pi(d-1)}) \iff \pi(i) = (i + k) \bmod d.$$

Let us investigate typical functions ψ in formula (2), which can be implemented using neural networks. We start with the simplest case, where ψ is linear. Then

$$\sum_{p=0}^{d-1} \psi(x_{0+p}, \dots, x_{d-1+p}) = \sum_{p=0}^{d-1}\sum_{i=0}^{d-1} w_i x_{i+p} = \sum_{i=0}^{d-1} w_i \sum_{p=0}^{d-1} x_{i+p} = \sum_{i=0}^{d-1} w_i \sum_{j=0}^{d-1} x_j,$$

does not depend on the order of the neighbors $(x_0, \dots, x_{d-1})$. To construct more complex functions, we use an arbitrary Multi-Layer Perceptron (MLP) as ψ. Since MLPs are universal approximators (for a sufficiently large number of hidden units), we can find such parameters θ that $\sum_{p=0}^{d-1} \psi_\theta(x_{\pi(0)+p}, \dots, x_{\pi(d-1)+p})$ returns a different value for every permutation π that is not a shift. Therefore our aggregation scheme with ψ given by MLP can learn order-sensitive mapping.

Following the above observations, we implement our order-sensitive message-passing using MLP as ψ. To match our construction to various numbers of neighbors in a graph, we restrict ψ to be k-ary (denoted as ψ^k) for some fixed $k > 1$ and overload it so that:

$$\psi^k(x_0, \dots, x_{d-1}) = \psi^k(x_0, \dots, x_{d-1}, \underbrace{0, \dots, 0}_{k-d}) \text{ for } d < k.$$

Given that, we implement the Eq. (2) with the following neural network layer:

$$x' = Wx + \sum_{p=0}^{d-1} \psi^k(x_{0+p}, \dots, x_{k-1+p}), \qquad (3)$$

$$\psi^k(x_{0+p}, \dots, x_{k-1+p}) = W_1\sigma(W_2(x_{0+p}|\dots|x_{k-1+p})).$$

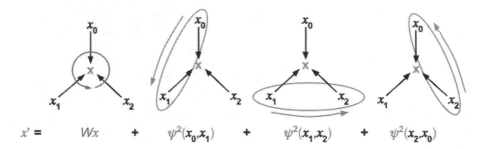

$$x' = \quad Wx \quad + \quad \psi^2(x_0, x_1) \quad + \quad \psi^2(x_1, x_2) \quad + \quad \psi^2(x_2, x_0)$$

Fig. 3. An illustration of our update rule for node x with 3 ordered neighbors (x_0, x_1, x_2) and for $k = 2$. We see that ψ^k is used to embed pairs of consecutive nodes.

Our k-ary message function ψ^k is composed of concatenation operator | and two-layer MLP with ELU as σ. Intuitively, the output of $\psi^k(x_{0+p}, ..., x_{k-1+p})$ can be seen as a message obtained jointly from k consecutive neighbors starting from a neighbor p in order $(x_0, ..., x_{d-1})$ which is illustrated in Fig. 3.

4 ChiENN: Chiral-Aware Neural Network

In this section, we apply the order-sensitive message-passing framework to molecular graphs. We show that order-sensitive aggregation is a key factor for embracing molecular chirality. Roughly speaking, in contrast to vanilla message-passing, the proposed ChiENN (Chiral-aware Edge Neural Network) is able to distinguish enantiomers, where one molecule is a mirror image of the second. Although we evaluate the ChiENN model in the context of molecular property prediction, the proposed model can be applied to any 3D graph task with the notion of chirality.

To construct ChiENN based on our order-sensitive message-passing scheme from Eq. (3), we need to define a notion of neighbors' order in molecular graphs that grasps the concept of chirality (see Fig. 4). We introduce this notion of order for edge (dual) molecular graphs and provide a simple transformation from standard molecular graphs to edge molecular graphs. Therefore the rest of the section is organized into three subsections:

1. **Edge Graph** describing the transformation from a molecular graph to its edge (dual) form used in our ChiENN model,
2. **Neighbors Order** defining the order of the neighbors in an edge graph,
3. **Chiral-Aware Update** constructing order-sensitive update rule using our order-sensitive framework from the Sect. 3.

4.1 Edge Graph

Let us suppose, we have a directed graph $G = (X, C, E)$ that represents a concrete conformation (3D embedding) of a molecule. The node encoding $x_i \in X$

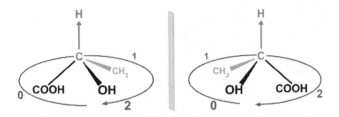

Fig. 4. An intuitive illustration of the neighbor ordering in a molecule. First, we pick a directed bond from atom C to H and then order the rest of the neighbors around that bond. We observe that for a chiral molecule (left) and its mirror image (right), we obtain different orders of the $COOH$, CH_3, and OH constituents.

corresponds to an i-th atom from a molecule, $c_i \in C \subseteq \mathbb{R}^3$ are its coordinates in 3D space, and the edge encoding $e_{ij} \in E$ represents a bond between i-th and j-th atoms.

To make the definition of neighbor order straightforward, our ChiENN model operates on an edge (dual) graph $G' = (X', C', E')$ which swaps nodes with edges from the original graph G. It means that the node $x_{ij} \in X'$ represents the edge $e_{ij} \in E$, while the edge $e_{ij,jk} \in E'$ represents the node x_j that connects edge $e_{ij} \in E$ with $e_{jk} \in E$. Similarly, $c'_{ij} \in \mathbb{R}^3 \times \mathbb{R}^3$ is now a 3D coordinate vector that links positions c_i and c_j. Formally, we have:

$$X' = \{x_{ij} = e_{ij} : e_{ij} \in E\},$$
$$C' = \{c_{ij} = c_i | c_j : c_i, c_j \in C, e_{ij} \in E\},$$
$$E' = \{e_{ij,jk} = e_{ij} | x_j | e_{jk} : e_{ij}, e_{jk} \in E, x_j \in X\},$$

where | stands for a concatenation operator. Clearly, the constructed edge graph $G' = (X', C', E')$ can be fed to any GNN that can take as an input the original graph $G = (X, C, E)$.

4.2   Neighbors Order

In an edge molecular graph $G = (X, C, E)$, a node $x_{jk} \in E$ represents a directed bond from atom j to atom k in the original molecule. It is assigned with a 3D vector $c_{jk} \in C \subseteq \mathbb{R}^3 \times \mathbb{R}^3$ spanned from atom j to atom k. Therefore, we will sometimes refer to nodes as if they were 3D vectors.

Let us consider the node x_{jk} and the set of its incoming neighbors: $N(x_{jk}) = \{x_{i_1j}, x_{i_2j}, ..., x_{i_dj}\}$. By construction of G, every node x_{jk} has a corresponding parallel node x_{kj}. For simplicity, we will treat this parallel node separately and exclude it from the set of neighbors, i.e. $x_{kj} \notin N(x_{jk})$.

The construction of the neighbors $N(x_{jk})$ order is illustrated in Fig. 5 and consists of two steps:

1. Transformation: first, we perform a sequence of 3D transformations on x_{jk} and $N(x_{jk})$ to make x_{jk} anchored to coordinate origin, perpendicular to yz plane and pointed away from the observer (see Fig. 5b)).

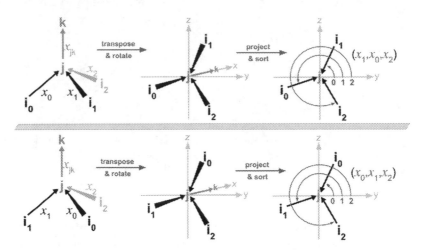

Fig. 5. An illustration of ordering the neighbors $\{x_0, x_1, x_2\}$ of x_{jk} for a chiral molecule (top) and its mirror image (bottom) around the chiral center j. First, we perform a sequence of 3D transformations on x_{jk} and its neighbors to make x_{jk} anchored to coordinate origin, perpendicular to yz plane and pointed away from the observer. Next, we project the transformed neighbors to the yz plane and sort the projections by the angle to the y axis. We see that for the chiral molecule (top) and its mirror image (bottom), we obtained non-equivalent orders (x_1, x_0, x_2) and (x_0, x_1, x_2).

2. Sorting: second, we project the transformed neighbors $N(x_{jk})$ to the yz plane and sort the projections by the angle to the y axis.

Details of the above construction are presented in the supplementary materials.
Two observations can be made regarding the above construction:

Observation 1. *The above construction returns non-equivalent orders for a chiral center and its mirror image.*

Observation 2. *Any $SE(3)$ transformation of a molecule coordinates C and any internal rotation of its bonds (conformation) can only change the shift of the order o, resulting in equivalent order o'.*

Therefore, the above construction grasps the notion of chirality in a molecule and is additionally $SE(3)$- and conformation-invariant.

We artificially excluded x_{kj} from a set of x_{jk} neighbors, because its parallel to x_{jk} and therefore its angle to y axis after the sequence of transformations is undefined. In theory, another neighbor x_{ij} can also be parallel to x_{jk} and should also be excluded from the neighbor set, but we have not observed such a case in our experiments and decided not to take it into account.

4.3   Chiral-Aware Update

Once we transformed a molecular graph to edge (dual) molecular graph $G = (X, E, C)$ using transformation from Sect. 4.1 and assigned every node x_{jk} with an order of its neighbors $(x_1, ..., x_d)$ using construction from Sect. 4.2, we can define the order-sensitive update rule of our ChiENN model:

$$x'_{jk} = W_1 x_{jk} + W_2 x_{kj} + \sum_{p=0}^{d-1} \psi^k(x_{0+p}, ..., x_{k-1+p}),$$

$$\psi^k(x_{0+p}, ..., x_{k-1+p}) = W_3 \sigma(W_4(x_{0+p}|...|x_{k-1+p})),$$

$$(4)$$

where ψ^k is k-ary message function and σ is ELU non-linear activation. The update rule is almost the same as that from Eq. (3), but here we add a term that explicitly embeds x_{kj} node, which was artificially excluded from the order of the x_{jk} neighbors.

5   Experiments

We compare ChiENN with several state-of-the-art models on a variety of chiral-sensitive tasks. Details of experiments are described in Sect. 5.1, while the results can be found in Sect. 5.2. Furthermore, to validate design choices behind ChiENN we also conducted an ablation study, presented in Sect. 5.3.

5.1   Set-Up

Datasets. We conduct our experiments on five different datasets affected by molecule chirality. First, two datasets proposed in [1] which are designed specifically to evaluate the capability of a model to express chirality: classification of tetrahedral chiral centers as R/S (which should be a necessary, but not sufficient, condition to learn meaningful representations of chiral molecules); and enantiomer ranking, in which pairs of enantiomers with enantioselective docking scores were selected, and the task was to predict which molecule of the pair had a lower binding affinity in a chiral protein pocket.

Second, the binding affinity dataset, which is an extension of the previously described enantiomer ranking, with the same underlying molecules, but the task being regression of the binding affinity.

Additionally, we take two datasets from the MoleculeNet benchmark [32] that do not explicitly require prediction of molecule chirality, but contain some percentage of molecules with chiral centers, and the underlying biological task in principle might be chirality-dependant: BACE, a binary classification dataset for prediction of binding results for a set of inhibitors of human β-secretase 1 (BACE-1) [29]; and Tox21, a multilabel classification dataset containing qualitative toxicity measurements on 12 different targets, including nuclear receptors and stress response pathways.

Reference Methods. As reference models we consider several state-of-the-art neural network architectures for processing graphs, both chirality-aware and general: GPS [26], SAN [14], DMPNN [34], ChIRo [1], and Tetra-DMPNN [24].

Table 1. Comparison of ChiENN-based approaches with the reference methods on chiral-sensitive tasks. Methods are split into groups by the underlying base model, except for the bottom group which includes models specifically designed to be chiral-sensitive. We **bold** the best results in every group and underline the best results across all groups. All variations of our method (ChiENN, SAN+ChiENN, and GPS+ChiENN) significantly outperform current state-of-the-art chiral-sensitive models. Note that for the R/S task, we omitted the results for models with chiral tags encoded in node features, for which the task is trivial.

Model	R/S	Enantiomer ranking	Binding affinity
	Accuracy ↑	R. Accuracy ↑	MAE ↓
DMPNN	0.500 ± 0.000	0.000 ± 0.000	0.310 ± 0.001
DMPNN+tags	-	$\mathbf{0.701 \pm 0.003}$	$\mathbf{0.285 \pm 0.001}$
GPS	0.500 ± 0.000	0.000 ± 0.000	0.330 ± 0.003
GPS+tags	-	0.669 ± 0.037	0.318 ± 0.004
GPS+ChiENN	$\underline{\mathbf{0.989 \pm 0.000}}$	$\mathbf{0.753 \pm 0.004}$	$\mathbf{0.258 \pm 0.001}$
SAN	0.500 ± 0.000	0.000 ± 0.000	0.317 ± 0.004
SAN+tags	-	0.722 ± 0.004	0.278 ± 0.003
SAN+ChiENN	$\mathbf{0.987 \pm 0.001}$	$\underline{\mathbf{0.764 \pm 0.005}}$	$\underline{\mathbf{0.257 \pm 0.002}}$
ChIRo	0.968 ± 0.019	0.691 ± 0.006	0.359 ± 0.009
Tetra-DMPNN	0.935 ± 0.001	0.690 ± 0.006	0.324 ± 0.026
ChiENN	$\underline{\mathbf{0.989 \pm 0.000}}$	$\mathbf{0.760 \pm 0.002}$	$\mathbf{0.275 \pm 0.003}$

For models not designed to process chirality, that is DMPNN, GPS, and SAN, we additionally considered their variants with chiral atom tags included in the node features, similar to [1]. For the proposed approach we consider both a pure model obtained by stacking several ChiENN layers, as well as combining ChiENN layers with other architectures (ChiENN+GPS and ChiENN+SAN).

Training Details. All models were trained using Adam optimizer for up to 100 epochs, with a cosine learning rate scheduler with 10 warm-up epochs and gradient norm clipping, following the set-up of [26]. Cross-entropy and L1 loss functions were used for classification and regression, respectively. Note that in contrast to [1], to keep the set-up consistent across models we did not use triplet margin loss for ChIRo, and observed worse results than reported in [1].

We also performed a grid search of parameters with the identical budget. For all datasets and models, we reported results averaged from three runs.

For enantiomer ranking, binding affinity, and R/S, we used data splits provided by [1] and for BACE and Tox21, we used random splits with a train-valid-test ratio of 7:1:2. For each model and dataset, we report mean results from 3 independent runs with the best parameters picked by grid search.

Evaluation. Note that for the binding rank task we used accuracy modified with respect to [1]. We required the difference between the predicted affinity of two enantiomers to be higher than the threshold of 0.001. This led to ranking accuracy being equal to 0 for models unable to distinguish chiral molecules.

5.2 Comparison with Reference Methods

In this section, we compare ChiENN-based networks with state-of-the-art reference architectures using the experimental setting described in Sect. 5.1.

Chiral-Sensitive Tasks. The results on chiral-sensitive tasks are presented in Table 1. For both the enantiomer ranking and binding affinity, ChiENN-based approaches achieved the best results, producing a significant improvement in performance over the state-of-the-art chiral-aware architectures, that is ChIRo and Tetra-DMPNN. For both GPS and SAN, there was a significant improvement in performance due to the addition of ChiENN layers when compared to chiral tag inclusion. It demonstates that ChiENN model can enable chiral-awareness demonstrating the general usefulness of the proposed layer, and the fact that it can be combined with a model preferred in a given task.

Finally, as expected, all of the chirality-aware methods can properly distinguish chiral centers in the R/S task, while the baselines that do not capture the concept of chirality (DMPNN, GPS and SAN) cannot. Note that for this task, we omitted the results for models with chiral tags encoded in node features, for which the task is trivial.

Remaining Tasks. The results on BACE and Tox21 tasks are in Table 2. We see that the ChiENN model achieves results comparable to state-of-the-art models, however the influence of chirality-sensitiveness on these tasks is not clear. For SAN we actually observed a slight drop in performance when using Chi-ENN layers, and for GPS the results remained roughly the same. The possible explanations for that might be either 1) lack of importance of chirality on predicted tasks, or 2) small dataset size, leading to overfitting in presence of chiral information. Our conclusion is that ChiENN layers significantly improve the performance in chiral-sensitive tasks, and produce comparable results in the other tasks, where the influence of chirality is not clear. We believe that further investigation on the influence of chirality on the tasks commonly used in the molecular property prediction domain would be beneficial and we leave it for future work.

5.3 Ablation Studies

Comparison of k-Ariness of the Message Function. We began with an analysis of the impact of k-ariness (Eq. 3) of the message function used by Chi-ENN. Specifically, in this experiment, we used the pure variant of ChiENN, which is a graph neural network using ChiENN layers as message-passing layers.

Table 2. Comparison of ChiENN-based approaches with the reference methods on tasks **not** explicitly requiring chirality. We see that the ChiENN model achieves results comparable to state-of-the-art models.

Model	BACE	Tox21
	AUC ↑	AUC ↑
DMPNN	**0.847 ± 0.015**	0.813 ± 0.008
DMPNN+tags	0.840 ± 0.004	**0.824 ± 0.006**
GPS	**0.841 ± 0.004**	0.821 ± 0.000
GPS+tags	0.812 ± 0.017	**0.825 ± 0.002**
GPS+ChiENN	0.839 ± 0.008	0.821 ± 0.007
SAN	**0.846 ± 0.012**	0.842 ± 0.007
SAN+tags	0.829 ± 0.009	0.841 ± 0.004
SAN+ChiENN	0.826 ± 0.014	0.834 ± 0.005
ChIRo	0.815 ± 0.010	**0.847 ± 0.005**
Tetra-DMPNN	0.824 ± 0.017	0.807 ± 0.003
ChiENN	**0.838 ± 0.003**	0.838 ± 0.003

Table 3. Comparison of k-ariness of the message function.

k-ary	R/S	Enantiomer ranking	Binding affinity	BACE	Tox21
	Accuracy ↑	R. Accuracy ↑	MAE ↓	AUC ↑	AUC ↑
$k = 1$	0.500 ± 0.000	0.000 ± 0.000	0.328 ± 0.000	0.831 ± 0.028	0.833 ± 0.005
$k = 2$	**0.989 ± 0.001**	0.759 ± 0.003	**0.267 ± 0.001**	0.788 ± 0.014	0.836 ± 0.004
$k = 3$	**0.989 ± 0.000**	**0.760 ± 0.002**	0.275 ± 0.003	**0.838 ± 0.003**	**0.838 ± 0.003**

We varied $k \in \{1, 2, 3\}$, where $k = 1$ disables the ability of the network to distinguish enantiomers as it collapses our order-sensitive message passing scheme from Eq. (3) to vanilla message-passing from Eq. (1). We considered values of k up to 3 since it corresponds to the airiness of standard chiral centers observed in the edge graphs (see Sect. 4.1) of molecules.

The results are presented in Table 3. As expected, choosing $k = 1$ leads to a failure in distinguishing enantiomers (makes message passing permutation invariant), as demonstrated by minimum performance in R/S and enantiomer ranking tasks. Interestingly, for most datasets choosing $k = 2$ was sufficient, leading to a comparable performance to $k = 3$. The only exception to that was BACE dataset, for which a noticeable drop in performance was observed when using $k = 2$. We used $k = 3$ in the remainder of this paper.

Using ChiENN Layer with Existing Models. Secondly, we conducted an ablation of different design choices that can be made to enable enantiomer recognition within the existing architectures. Specifically, we focused on the GPS model and considered using three different strategies: conversion to edge graph

Table 4. Ablation study of different design choices for GPS+ChiENN model. The "Graph" column indicates conversion to the edge graph; the "Tags" column indicates the inclusion of the chiral tags as node features; the "ChiENN" column indicates the usage of ChiENN as a message-passing layer.

Graph	Tags	ChiENN	R/S	Enantiomer ranking	Binding affinity	BACE	Tox21
			Accuracy ↑	R. Accuracy ↑	MAE ↓	AUC ↑	AUC ↑
No	No	No	0.500 ± 0.000	0.000 ± 0.000	0.330 ± 0.003	0.841 ± 0.004	0.821 ± 0.000
Yes	No	No	0.500 ± 0.000	0.000 ± 0.000	0.306 ± 0.001	$\mathbf{0.851 \pm 0.007}$	0.821 ± 0.007
No	Yes	No	$\mathbf{1.000 \pm 0.000}$	0.669 ± 0.037	0.318 ± 0.004	0.812 ± 0.017	0.825 ± 0.002
Yes	Yes	No	$\mathbf{1.000 \pm 0.000}$	0.720 ± 0.002	0.283 ± 0.008	0.802 ± 0.019	$\mathbf{0.838 \pm 0.003}$
Yes	No	Yes	0.989 ± 0.000	$\mathbf{0.753 \pm 0.004}$	$\mathbf{0.258 \pm 0.001}$	0.839 ± 0.008	0.821 ± 0.007

proposed in this paper, the inclusion of chiral tags in the node features of the graph, and finally, replacement of message passing layers with ChiENN layers.

The results are presented in Table 4. Several observations can be made: first of all, in the case of R/S task, we can see that both using chiral tags and the ChiENN layers allows us to properly recognize chiral centers (and as stated before, due to the simplicity of the task, good performance here is a necessary, but not sufficient, requirement for learning meaningful chiral representations).

Secondly, using ChiENN layers significantly improves the performance in the enantiomer ranking (explicitly requiring chirality) and binding affinity (implicitly requiring it) tasks, more than simply including chiral tags. Interestingly, combining chiral tags with edge graph transformation improves the performance compared to using the tags alone (though not as much as using ChiENN layers), suggesting that it might be a feasible general strategy.

Finally, the results on two remaining tasks, that is BACE and Tox21, for which the impact of chirality is unclear, are less straightforward: in the case of BACE, GPS with edge graph transformation achieves the best performance, and in the case of Tox21, using both the edge graph transformation and including the chiral tags. However, we can conclude that using ChiENN layers outperforms simply including chiral tags in tasks requiring chirality, and have comparable performance to the baseline GPS in other tasks.

6   Conclusions

In this paper, we proposed and theoretically justify a general order-sensitive message-passing scheme that can be applied to any chiral-sensitive graph domain where chirality can be expressed by an order of the neighboring nodes. We used the proposed framework to construct a novel ChiENN layer that enables chirality awareness in any GNN model in the domain of molecular graphs, where chirality plays an important role as it can strongly alter the biochemical properties of molecules. Our experiments showed that the ChiENN layer allows to outperform the current state-of-the-art methods in chiral-sensitive molecular property prediction tasks.

Acknowledgements. The research of J. Tabor was supported by the Foundation for Polish Science co-financed by the European Union under the European Regional Development Fund in the POIR.04.04.00-00-14DE/18-00 project carried out within the Team-Net program. The research of P. Gaiński and M. Śmieja was supported by the National Science Centre (Poland), grant no. 2022/45/B/ST6/01117.

Ethical Statement. As we consider our work to be fundamental research, there are no direct ethical risks or societal consequences; these have to be analyzed per concrete applications.

References

1. Adams, K., Pattanaik, L., Coley, C.W.: Learning 3D representations of molecular chirality with invariance to bond rotations. In: The Tenth International Conference on Learning Representations, ICLR 2022, Virtual Event, 25–29 April 2022. OpenReview.net (2022)
2. Brown, N., Fiscato, M., Segler, M.H.S., Vaucher, A.C.: GuacaMol: benchmarking models for de novo molecular design. J. Chem. Inf. Model. **59**(3), 1096–1108 (2019)
3. Chen, S., Jung, Y.: Deep retrosynthetic reaction prediction using local reactivity and global attention. JACS Au **1**(10), 1612–1620 (2021)
4. Choukroun, Y., Wolf, L.: Geometric transformer for end-to-end molecule properties prediction. arXiv preprint arXiv:2110.13721 (2021)
5. Coors, B., Condurache, A.P., Geiger, A.: Spherenet: learning spherical representations for detection and classification in omnidirectional images. In: Proceedings of the European Conference on Computer Vision (ECCV), pp. 518–533 (2018)
6. Ganea, O., et al.: Geomol: torsional geometric generation of molecular 3D conformer ensembles. Adv. Neural. Inf. Process. Syst. **34**, 13757–13769 (2021)
7. Gasteiger, J., Becker, F., Günnemann, S.: Gemnet: universal directional graph neural networks for molecules. Adv. Neural. Inf. Process. Syst. **34**, 6790–6802 (2021)
8. Gasteiger, J., Groß, J., Günnemann, S.: Directional message passing for molecular graphs. arXiv preprint arXiv:2003.03123 (2020)
9. Gilmer, J., Schoenholz, S.S., Riley, P.F., Vinyals, O., Dahl, G.E.: Neural message passing for quantum chemistry. In: International Conference on Machine Learning, pp. 1263–1272. PMLR (2017)
10. Gómez-Hortigüela, L., Bernardo-Maestro, B.: Chiral organic structure-directing agents. In: Gómez-Hortigüela, L. (ed.) Insights into the Chemistry of Organic Structure-Directing Agents in the Synthesis of Zeolitic Materials. SB, vol. 175, pp. 201–244. Springer, Cham (2017). https://doi.org/10.1007/430_2017_9
11. Hawkins, P.C., Skillman, A.G., Warren, G.L., Ellingson, B.A., Stahl, M.T.: Conformer generation with omega: algorithm and validation using high quality structures from the protein databank and Cambridge structural database. J. Chem. Inf. Model. **50**(4), 572–584 (2010)
12. Jamali, F., Mehvar, R., Pasutto, F.: Enantioselective aspects of drug action and disposition: therapeutic pitfalls. J. Pharm. Sci. **78**, 695–715 (1989)
13. Kovatcheva, A., Golbraikh, A., Oloff, S., Feng, J., Zheng, W., Tropsha, A.: QSAR modeling of datasets with enantioselective compounds using chirality sensitive molecular descriptors. SAR QSAR Environ. Res. **16**(1–2), 93–102 (2005)
14. Kreuzer, D., Beaini, D., Hamilton, W., Létourneau, V., Tossou, P.: Rethinking graph transformers with spectral attention. Adv. Neural. Inf. Process. Syst. **34**, 21618–21629 (2021)

15. Krstulović, A.M.: Chiral Separations by HPLC. Ellis Horwood, Chichester (1989)
16. Liao, K., et al.: Design of catalysts for site-selective and enantioselective functionalization of non-activated primary C-H bonds. Nat. Chem. **10**, 1048–1055 (2018)
17. Liu, C., Korablyov, M., Jastrzebski, S., Wlodarczyk-Pruszynski, P., Bengio, Y., Segler, M.H.S.: RetroGNN: fast estimation of synthesizability for virtual screening and de novo design by learning from slow retrosynthesis software. J. Chem. Inf. Model. **62**(10), 2293–2300 (2022)
18. Mamede, R., de Almeida, B.S., Chen, M., Zhang, Q., Aires-de Sousa, J.: Machine learning classification of one-chiral-center organic molecules according to optical rotation. J. Chem. Inf. Model. **61**(1), 67–75 (2020)
19. Mansimov, E., Mahmood, O., Kang, S., Cho, K.: Molecular geometry prediction using a deep generative graph neural network. Sci. Rep. **9**(1), 20381 (2019)
20. Maziarka, L., Danel, T., Mucha, S., Rataj, K., Tabor, J., Jastrzebski, S.: Molecule attention transformer. CoRR abs/2002.08264 (2020)
21. Maziarka, Ł, Pocha, A., Kaczmarczyk, J., Rataj, K., Danel, T., Warchoł, M.: Mol-CycleGAN: a generative model for molecular optimization. J. Cheminform. **12**(1), 2 (2020)
22. Maziarz, K., et al.: Learning to extend molecular scaffolds with structural motifs. In: The Tenth International Conference on Learning Representations, ICLR 2022, Virtual Event, 25–29 April 2022. OpenReview.net (2022). https://openreview.net/forum?id=ZTsoE8G3GG
23. Nguyen, L., He, H., Pham-Huy, C.: Chiral drugs: an overview. Int. J. Biomed. Sci. IJBS **2**, 85–100 (2006)
24. Pattanaik, L., Ganea, O.E., Coley, I., Jensen, K.F., Green, W.H., Coley, C.W.: Message passing networks for molecules with tetrahedral chirality. arXiv preprint arXiv:2012.00094 (2020)
25. Pfaltz, A., Drury, W.: Design of chiral ligands for asymmetric catalysis: from C2-symmetric P, P- and N, N-ligands to sterically and electronically nonsymmetrical P, N-ligands. Proc. Natl. Acad. Sci. USA **101**, 5723–5726 (2004)
26. Rampášek, L., Galkin, M., Dwivedi, V.P., Luu, A.T., Wolf, G., Beaini, D.: Recipe for a general, powerful, scalable graph transformer. Adv. Neural. Inf. Process. Syst. **35**, 14501–14515 (2022)
27. Schneider, N., Lewis, R.A., Fechner, N., Ertl, P.: Chiral cliffs: investigating the influence of chirality on binding affinity. ChemMedChem **13**(13), 1315–1324 (2018)
28. Schütt, K.T., Sauceda, H.E., Kindermans, P.J., Tkatchenko, A., Müller, K.R.: SchNet-a deep learning architecture for molecules and materials. J. Chem. Phys. **148**(24), 241722 (2018)
29. Subramanian, G., Ramsundar, B., Pande, V., Denny, R.A.: Computational modeling of β-secretase 1 (BACE-1) inhibitors using ligand based approaches. J. Chem. Inf. Model. **56**(10), 1936–1949 (2016)
30. Veličković, P., Cucurull, G., Casanova, A., Romero, A., Lio, P., Bengio, Y.: Graph attention networks. arXiv preprint arXiv:1710.10903 (2017)
31. Wang, Y., Wang, J., Cao, Z., Barati Farimani, A.: Molecular contrastive learning of representations via graph neural networks. Nat. Mach. Intell. **4**(3), 279–287 (2022)
32. Wu, Z., et al.: MoleculeNet: a benchmark for molecular machine learning. Chem. Sci. **9**(2), 513–530 (2018)
33. Xu, M., Luo, S., Bengio, Y., Peng, J., Tang, J.: Learning neural generative dynamics for molecular conformation generation. In: 9th International Conference on Learning Representations, ICLR 2021, Virtual Event, Austria, 3–7 May 2021. OpenReview.net (2021)

34. Yang, K., et al.: Analyzing learned molecular representations for property prediction. J. Chem. Inf. Model. **59**(8), 3370–3388 (2019)
35. Zaheer, M., Kottur, S., Ravanbakhsh, S., Poczos, B., Salakhutdinov, R.R., Smola, A.J.: Deep sets. In: Advances in Neural Information Processing Systems, vol. 30 (2017)
36. Zhu, J., et al.: Unified 2D and 3D pre-training of molecular representations. In: Zhang, A., Rangwala, H. (eds.) KDD 2022: The 28th ACM SIGKDD Conference on Knowledge Discovery and Data Mining, Washington, DC, USA, 14–18 August 2022, pp. 2626–2636. ACM (2022)

Multi-label Image Classification with Multi-scale Global-Local Semantic Graph Network

Wenlan Kuang[1,2], Qiangxi Zhu[1,2], and Zhixin Li[1,2(✉)]

[1] Key Lab of Education Blockchain and Intelligent Technology, Ministry of Education, Guangxi Normal University, Guilin 541004, China
[2] Guangxi Key Lab of Multi-source Information Mining and Security, Guangxi Normal University, Guilin 541004, China
`lizx@gxnu.edu.cn`

Abstract. With the development of deep learning techniques, multi-label image classification tasks have achieved good performance. Recently, graph convolutional network has been proved to be an effective way to explore the labels dependencies. However, due to the complexity of label semantic relations, the static dependencies obtained by existing methods cannot consider the overall characteristics of an image and accurately locate the target region. Therefore, we propose the Multi-scale Global-local Semantic Graph Network (MGSGN) for multi-label image classification, which mainly includes three important parts. First, the multi-scale feature reconstruction aggregates complementary information at different levels in CNN through cross-layer attention, which can effectively identify target categories of different sizes. We then design a channel dual-branch cross-attention module to explore the correlation between global information and local features in multi-scale features, which using the way of adaptive cross-fusion to locate the target area more accurately. Moreover, we propose the multi-perspective weighted cosine measure in multi-perspective dynamic semantic representation module to construct content-based label dependencies for each image to dynamically construct a semantic relationship graph. Extensive experiments on the two public datasets have verified that the classification performance of our model is better than many state-of-the-art methods.

Keywords: Multi-label image classification · Multi-scale feature · Attention mechanisms · Semantic relationship graph

1 Introduction

Multi-label image classification (MLIC) is a challenging fundamental task in the field of computer vision, which aims to assign multiple labels to an image. At present, MLIC has been widely used in various application scenarios such as image annotation [24], image retrieval [35], human attribute recognition [23], medical image recognition [14], etc. Unlike single-label classification tasks, MLIC

D. Koutra et al. (Eds.): ECML PKDD 2023, LNAI 14171, pp. 53–69, 2023.
https://doi.org/10.1007/978-3-031-43418-1_4

is more challenging because each image in the real world usually contains not just a single object, but multiple foreground objects. More importantly, objects in multi-label images usually have different sizes and location distributions, with foreground objects often occluding other objects. Therefore, it is necessary to simultaneously explore image features and consider the relationship between labels to the performance of the MLIC.

The simplest approach to MLIC is to convert it to multiple binary classification problems or single-label classification [1]. However, the problem with this approach is that the underlying relationship between labels is not completely explored resulting the not good classification effect. Many works have been proposed to effectively capture the dependencies between labels, including probabilistic graphical models [22] and structured inference networks [18]. The appearance of recurrent neural networks (RNN) has nicely alleviated the scalability challenges of probabilistic graphical model-based methods. For example, Wang et al. [28] combined RNN with convolutional neural network (CNN) for the first time in an MLIC task to capture semantic label dependencies. They unify CNN and RNN into a framework (CNN-RNN) that mines label dependencies on a global level and predicts labels in a predefined order. However, the pre-defined label prediction order of the RNN will affect the performance of the model. Therefore, Chen et al. [2] proposed using a long short-term memory model to learn label dependencies without pre-defining the order of prediction, thereby reducing the constraint of label order. These RNN-based methods explore the limited relationships between labels in a sequential manner.

In addition, some researchers have also introduced the attention mechanism [43] into MLIC to implicitly model the spatial relationship between different labels. For example, Chen et al. [5] first introduced reinforcement learning to learn a local region of the attention area. Zhu et al. [41] proposed a spatial regularization network (ResNet-SRN) to learn the semantic and spatial correlation between image labels by employing an attention mechanism. However, SRN relies on image-level supervision to obtain attention regions, without considering the correlation between attention regions and each label. Recently, some studies have introduced graph convolutional networks (GCN) to take full advantage of the image-label pairwise relationship. Chen et al. [8] proposed a multi-label image recognition with graph convolutional networks (ML-GCN), which utilizes a directed graph of label embeddings to model label correlations. Li et al. [21] proposes a label graph module to learn label information for word embeddings, and augments the tag graph module with sparse correlation constraints. Wang et al. [29] proposes an operation of superimposing statistical label maps and knowledge prior label maps (KSSNet), and fuses the label structure information generated by GCN at different stages of CNN. However, these above methods builds a global graph for the entire dataset, which leads to each image sharing a static graph, and the co-occurrence probability will cause the frequency deviation problem of the dataset under different scenarios. In particular, these ML-GCN based extension methods [3,7] may learn spurious correlations when label statistics are insufficient. To alleviate the limitations caused by static graphs, these methods [6,33,34] explore high-level semantic feature descriptors based on specific images, which can dynamically generate individual graphs for each image and mine the correlation between them through the graph propagation mechanism. These MLIC methods consider the features of each image in constructing the relational graph, which solves the negative impact brought about by the co-occurrence probability. However, the high-level semantic features at a single scale may lack sufficient supervision information, this modeling approach does not fully exploit the deeper semantic information in multi-scale feature descriptors. Therefore, it is still necessary to further improve the semantic representation abilities of dynamic graphs.

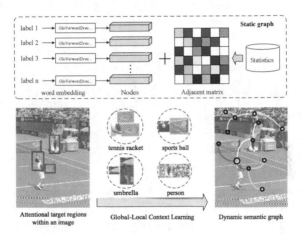

Fig. 1. Motivation of the proposed dynamic semantic graph. Different images have their own graphs that provide global and local information to dynamically learn category dependencies related to the content of each image, instead of all images sharing a fixed adjacency matrix.

To solve the aforementioned problems, we propose the Multi-scale Global-local Semantic Graph Network (MGSGN) for MLIC. As shown in Fig. 1, the key of our model is to dynamically learn the category dependencies related to the content of each image, through the extracted multi-scale global-local information in the image target region features. Our model consists of three important parts: multi-scale feature reconstruction, channel dual-branch cross-attention module, and multi-perspective dynamic semantic representation module. The multi-scale features involved in this paper refer to the shallow, middle and deep features of CNN. And, the channel dual-branch cross-attention module is divided into upper and lower branches according to the channel dimension. We design the gated adaptive convolution for the first branch to capture fine-grained local features. In the second branch, we employ self-attention to learn the global contextual information. Finally, we employ a semantic attention module on the global-local information to obtain class-specific semantic representations as nodes of the semantic relation graph. Different from the co-occurrence matrix based on label statistics, we construct a multi-perspective weighted cosine similarity metric to calculate the semantic correlation between node vectors, and average the similarity matrices of all perspectives as a new adjacency matrix. The main contributions of this paper can be summarized as:

- To increase the diversity and complementarity of image features, we fuse the cross-layer attention features into the feature maps of different levels in the CNN during the multi-scale feature reconstruction module.
- We design the channel dual-branch cross-attention module that extracts the global-local information from the reconstructed multi-scale features. Then, the local and global feature representations are regarded as queries, the correlation between each local-global token pair is adaptively explored through the cross-attention mechanisms in order to enhance the objects perception of different sizes for our model.
- We construct a multi-perspective dynamic semantic representation module to mine class-specific semantic representations for multi-scale global-local features. The key to this module is to use the weighted cosine measure to jointly construct the semantic graph structure related to specific content of each image from multiple perspectives.

2   Proposed Method

The overall framework is shown in Fig. 2. The proposed MGSGN primarily includes: (1) multi-scale feature reconstruction, (2) channel dual-branch cross-attention module, and (3) multi-perspective dynamic semantic representation.

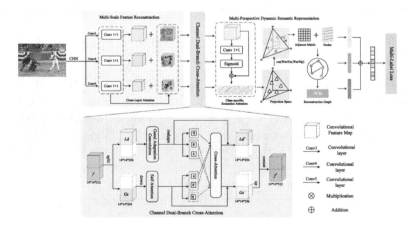

Fig. 2. Overview of our proposed MGSGN. The key of the proposed model is to dynamically learn the category dependencies related to the content of each image through the extracted multi-scale global-local information.

2.1   Multi-scale Feature Reconstruction

We use the ResNet-101 [17] pre-trained on the ImageNet [10] dataset to extract image features, we employ the outputs of three convolutional layers (i.e.

"conv3_x", "conv4_x" and "conv5_x") of ResNet-101 serve as the multi-scale feature representation in our model, from which three different sizes of features $f_l \in \Re^{C_l \times H_l \times W_l}$, $f_m \in \Re^{C_m \times H_m \times W_m}$, and $f_h \in \Re^{C_h \times H_h \times W_h}$ are extracted, where C, H, and W are the channel number, height, and width of the feature map, respectively. $C_l \times H_l \times W_l = 512 \times 56 \times 56$, $C_m \times H_m \times W_m = 1024 \times 28 \times 28$ and $C_h \times H_h \times W_h = 2048 \times 14 \times 14$. Specifically, given an input image I, the multi-layer feature extraction process can be described as:

$$f_l, f_m, f_h = F_{cnn}(I, \theta) \tag{1}$$

where F_{cnn} is the feature extractor, and θ is the network weight parameter.

However, while increasing information diversity and complementarity, different levels of features also increase the computational burden and redundant information. To suppress the noise at different levels of features, we use the cross-layer attention module [34] to effectively integrate the feature maps from different layers to enhance the location information of objects. We first utilize 1×1 convolutional layers to compress their channel numbers respectively to reduce the computational cost. Secondly, the feature map f'_l, f'_m, and f'_h is up-sampled, and the common location information of the target in different levels of feature maps is extracted by performing position multiplication on the three up-sampled feature maps. Subsequently, the three extracted feature maps are down-sampled and location information enhanced to obtain new feature maps $f^p_l \in \Re^{C \times H_l \times W_l}$, $f^p_m \in \Re^{C \times H_m \times W_m}$, and $f^p_h \subset \Re^{C \times H_h \times W_h}$, which is expressed as

$$f'_l = F^{1 \times 1}(f_l), f'_m = F^{1 \times 1}(f_m), f'_h = F^{1 \times 1}(f_h)$$
$$f^p_i = F^{down}\left(\prod_i^j F^{up}(f'_i) + f'_i\right) \tag{2}$$

where $F^{1 \times 1}$ represent convolutional layers, F^{up} and F^{down} are upsampling and downsampling operations.

2.2 Channel Dual-Branch Cross Attention

The CNN and attention mechanisms are both considered as the powerful representation learning technologies, which have achieved excellent performance in image recognition, semantic segmentation and so on. Different from previous attention mechanism and CNN-related researches [37,44], we develop a dual-branch cross-attention module (DBCAM) in this paper, which effectively explores the interaction of attention aggregation and gated convolutional features in the multi-scale reconstruction module. We first add position embedding (generated by convolution operation) to f^p_l, f^p_m, f^p_h, and divide the channel dimension into upper and lower parts (taking the reconstructed shallow feature f^p_l as an example, we divide it into $f^L_l \in \Re^{C_{1/2} \times H_{l/2} \times W_{l/2}}$ and $f^G_l \in \Re^{C_{1/2} \times H_{l/2} \times W_{l/2}}$). Subsequently, the self-attention and gated adaptive convolution are integrated into two paths, and feature maps of different resolutions are processed respectively to obtain global context and local details. Finally, the information interactions are performed through the process of cross fusion.

As shown in Fig. 2, the DBCAM module includes: 1) local feature extraction, through a gated adaptive convolution layer to effectively capture the fine-grained local features in f_l^G; 2) global feature extraction, here, we downsample f_l^G and use self-attention to learn the global context information in feature map f_l^G; 3) cross fusion, two different types of local-global features are dynamically integrated via cross attention. Thus, DBCAM can enjoy the benefits of both self-attention and CNN while having minimal computational overhead compared to pure convolution operations or self-attention.

(1) Local feature extraction: To realize the consistency of the channel dimensions of the two branches in DBCAM, we extract local features using depthwise separable convolutions [9] in the first branch. However, a convolution kernel is responsible for the feature extraction of one channel for depthwise separable convolution, and the communication between channels (i.e., depth) is missing. Therefore, the gated adaptive convolution module is proposed, we introduce a gated conversion unit before the depth separable convolution layer to promote "competition" and "cooperation" between channel features (here, "competition" means increasing the variance of channel activation, and "cooperation" means decreasing the variance of channel activation), so that the model learns better channel feature correlation. Considering the reconstructed shallow feature input $f_l^L \in \Re^{C_{1/2} \times H_{l/2} \times W_{l/2}}$, the gated adaptive convolution is expressed as

$$f_l^{L_d} = F^{depth} \left(f_l^L * \left[1 + \delta \left(\gamma \left(\alpha \| f_l^L \|_2 \right) + \beta \right) \right] \right) \qquad (3)$$

where $\|\cdot\|_2$ is l_2-norm, $\delta(\cdot)$ represents the activation function, here we use the tanh function. We use 3×3 depthwise separable convolution layer $F^{depth}(\cdot)$ to extract features. Three trainable parameters $\alpha \in \Re^{C_{1/2} \times 1 \times 1}$, $\beta \in \Re^{C_{1/2} \times 1 \times 1}$, and $\gamma \in \Re^{C_{1/2} \times 1 \times 1}$ are introduced into the gating conversion unit to evaluate channel features, and these three parameters can be optimized for training together with network weights. α is a learnable parameter that facilitates the adaptability of feature embeddings. The weights γ and biases β are used to control the activation of the channel features, i.e. they determine the behavior of the gated conversion unit on each channel. During training, we initialize α to 1, γ and β are initialized to 0. After enhancing the channel correlation through the gating conversion unit, the final features $f_l^{L_d}$ containing local details are obtained. Similarly, the local detail features $f_m^{L_d}$ and $f_h^{L_d}$ in the middle and deep features are obtained.

(2) Global feature extraction: The convolution operation is a local operation, the receptive field of the CNN is limited, so the global dependency between features cannot be effectively explored. Here, we introduce the self-attention to strengthen the global correlation among target attributes. Considering the feature input $f_l^G \in \Re^{C_{l/2} \times H_{l/2} \times W_{l/2}}$, we first downsample the feature input f_l^G to reduce the computational complexity of self-attention while retaining important information. Then, the processed features are flattened into $\hat{f}_l^G \in \Re^{C_{l/2} \times L}$, $L = H_{l/2} \times W_{l/2}$, and input into self-attention, so the captured global context information $f_l^{G_s}$ is defined as:

$$f_l^{G_s} = F^{self} \left(F^{down} \left(f_l^G \right) \right) \qquad (4)$$

where $F^{self}(\cdot)$ represents the self-attention layer. Similarly, the global context information of mid-level and deep features are denoted as $f_m^{G_s}$ and $f_h^{G_s}$.

(3) Cross Attention Fusion (CAF): Inspired by works [13,32], we employ cross-attention to align two types of features obtained from CNN and self-attention. Specifically, given the local features $f_l^{L_d}$ and global features $f_l^{G_s}$ extracted from shallow features f_l^p, they are transformed as follows:

$$Q_L = f_l^{L_d} W_q^L, K_L = f_l^{L_d} W_k^L, V_L = f_l^{L_d} W_v^L$$
$$Q_G = f_l^{G_s} W_q^G, K_L = f_l^{G_s} W_k^G, V_L = f_l^{G_s} W_v^G \tag{5}$$

where $W_q^L, W_k^L, W_v^L, W_q^G, W_k^G, W_v^G$ are the learnable hyperparameters. After obtaining the transformed local and global representations, we compute the cross-attention fusion between each pair of $f_l^{L_d}$ and $f_l^{G_s}$:

$$\text{CAF}_{G \to L}(Q_L, K_G, V_G) = \text{softmax}\left(\frac{Q_L K_G^T}{\sqrt{d}}\right) V_G$$
$$\text{CAF}_{L \to G}(Q_G, K_L, V_L) = \text{softmax}\left(\frac{Q_G K_L^T}{\sqrt{d}}\right) V_L \tag{6}$$

where d is the dimension of Q_L and Q_G. By taking local features and global information as queries at the same time, the correlation and importance between each local-global token pair can be adaptively explored in three different levels feature maps, so that the fused multi-scale features are more representative and informative. After cross-attention fusion, local and global features are concatenated to complete the final information fusion. Finally, the reconstructed feature maps of the three levels pass through the channel dual-branch cross-attention module to obtain new feature maps f_l^{CA}, f_m^{CA} and f_h^{CA}.

2.3   Multi-perspective Dynamic Semantic Representation

To fully mine the semantic relationships of labels, we propose a multi-view dynamic semantic representation module in Fig. 2, which takes multi-level global-local feature maps as input to generate class-specific semantic representations for explicit embedding. Then, a learnable weighted similarity metric mechanism is used to explore the semantic correlation between class-specific vectors from multiple perspectives, thus dynamically building a semantic relationship graph for each input image.

(1) Semantic attention module (SAM) [33]: Given the new feature maps f_l^{CA}, f_m^{CA} and f_h^{CA}, obtained in Sect. 2.2, taking f_l^{CA} as an example, first we utilize the SAM to compute category-specific activation maps $M_l \in \Re^{C \times H_l \times W_l}$. Through M_l, the transformed feature map is mapped to a class-specific semantic representation $\mathbf{H}_l \in \Re^{C \times D}$, D represents the number of categories, and the specific process of generating a class-specific semantic representation can be expressed as

$$\mathbf{H}_l = \varsigma\left(f_l^{CA}\right) M_l^T, \quad M_l = \text{softmax}\left(\varsigma\left(F^{1 \times 1}\left(f_l^{CA}\right)\right)\right) \tag{7}$$

where $\varsigma(\cdot)$ represents the feature dimension conversion operation, $F^{1 \times 1}(\cdot)$ and is a 1×1 convolutional layer. The SAM is able to expose the hidden attention

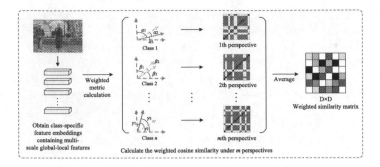

Fig. 3. Illustration of the multi-perspective dynamic semantic representation module.

on the feature map without bounding box and segmentation, and the resulting class-specific semantic representation $\mathbf{H}_l$ can selectively describe the features related to a specific class.

(2) Multi-perspective dynamic semantic representation module (MDSR): Given a feature matrix $\mathbf{H}_l \in \Re^{C \times D}$ containing D node (category) objects $k \in \Re^C$. Inspired by the multi-head attention mechanism, we propose a multi-perspective weighted cosine measure to calculate the similarity between each node, to construct a new adjacency matrix and enhance the expressive ability of similarity, shown in Fig. 3. In particular, the multi-perspective weighted cosine similarity is expressed as

$$\mathbf{u}_{ij} = \frac{1}{n} \sum_{m=1}^{n} \mathbf{u}_{ij}^m, \ \mathbf{u}_{ij}^m = \cos\left(W_m \odot k_i, W_m \odot k_j\right) \tag{8}$$

where $\odot$ represents the Hadamard product, and W represents the learnable weight vector. $\mathbf{u}_{ij}^m$ represents the similarity matrix of two input node vectors k_i and k_j from the mth perspective, and $\mathbf{u}_{ij}$ represents the average value of the similarity matrix calculated using n independent weight vectors W_m (similar to the multi-head attention mechanism, each weight vector represents a perspective), which is used as the final similarity matrix.

However, the usual adjacency matrix is a non-negative matrix, so we extract a new adjacency matrix $\mathbf{A}_{ij} \in \Re^{D \times D}$ from the final similarity matrix through a non-negative threshold τ, which is represented as follows:

$$A_{ij} = \begin{cases} 0, & \text{otherwise,} \\ \mathbf{u}_{ij}, & \mathbf{u}_{ij} > \tau. \end{cases} \tag{9}$$

We dynamically construct new adjacency matrices $\mathbf{A}_l$, $\mathbf{A}_m$, and $\mathbf{A}_h$ for the feature maps of the shallow, middle and deep branches of the network according to Eqs. 8 and 9. Subsequently, this paper adopts the GCN [19] to model the content-related category dependencies, and the result of dynamic semantic graph of the shallow feature map branch can be expressed as

$$\mathbf{Z}_l = \delta\left(\mathbf{A}_l \mathbf{H}_l \mathbf{W}_l\right) \tag{10}$$

where $\mathbf{W}_l$ denotes the state update weight, $\delta\left(\cdot\right)$ and denotes the LeakyReLU activation function [26]. $\mathbf{Z}_l$ represents the updated multi-perspective semantic relation graph. Notably, the dynamic adjacency matrix $\mathbf{A}$ is constructed by learning weighted correlations between class-specific semantic representations for each specific image from multiple perspectives. It captures the content-related category dependencies of each image from different semantic aspects, and also solves the problem of semantic deviation caused by rough label dependencies in static statistical graphs.

2.4 Classification and Loss

In order to speed up the convergence process, after obtaining three levels of local-global visual features and multi-perspective semantic relationship graphs, we further jointly train the prediction results $\mathbf{F}_{fusion}$ of visual features and $\mathbf{F}_{sac}$ of semantic features.

$$
\begin{aligned}
\mathbf{F}_{fusion} &= \psi\left(F_{cat}\left(\mathrm{GMP}\left(f_l^{CA}, f_m^{CA}, f_h^{CA}\right)\right)\right) \\
\mathbf{F}_{sac} &= \varphi\left(\nabla\left(Z_l, Z_m, Z_h\right)\right)
\end{aligned}
\tag{11}
$$

where $\psi\left(\cdot\right)$ represents the category classifier of visual features, $\mathrm{GMP}\left(\cdot\right)$ is the global average pooling operation, $\nabla\left(\cdot\right)$ denotes the fusion of three levels semantic features. $\varphi\left(\cdot\right)$ represents the category classifier of semantic features. We train the entire MGSGN with the traditional multi-label cross-entropy loss function, and train the loss function of visual features ℓ_{fusion} and the loss function of semantic features ℓ_{sac} in a collaborative learning manner. Therefore, the final loss function is expressed as

$$
\ell_{total} = \ell_{fusion} + \ell_{sac}
\tag{12}
$$

Through the above collaborative training approach, our model can jointly perceive different levels of global-local visual features and multi-perspective dynamic semantic features, thereby achieving better MLIC results.

3 Experiments

Datasets and Evaluation Metrics. We use two public image datasets, MS-COCO [25] and Pascal VOC 2007 [11], to verify our proposed method. The statistics of the experimental dataset are shown in Table 1. In order to achieve a fair comparison, we discuss the effectiveness of the proposed method using the following evaluation metrics in the MS-COCO dataset, namely mean average precision(mAP), the average per-class precision(CP), recall(CR), F1(CF1) and the overall precision(OP), recall(OR), F1(OF1). We will also list the classification scores for the top-3 labels in the experimental results. Furthermore, an average precision for each class is reported in the Pascal VOC 2007 dataset.

Implementation Details. We employ ResNet-101 pretrained on ImageNet as our image feature extractor. During the training phase, all input images are rescaled to 512×512, augmented by random cropping and resizing to 448×448, and then randomly horizontally flipped. In the testing stage, we simply resize the input image to 448×448. The optimizer uses stochastic gradient descent (SGD)

Table 1. Statistics of the experimental datasets.

Datasets	Class	Training	Testing	Total	Class per image
MS-COCO 2014	80	82,081	40,137	122218	2.9
Pascal VOC 2007	20	5011	4952	9963	1.5

with a momentum of 0.9 and weight decay set to 0.0001. In particular, for the basic convolutional neural network and other parts, the initial learning rate of MS-COCO is 0.03, and the initial learning rate of VOC 2007 is 0.01, which is decayed by a factor of 10 every 30 epochs. Our model MGSGN is trained in 50 epochs with a batch size of 64. Our method is implemented based on PyTorch [27] and all experiments are carried out on NVIDIA GeForce RTX 3090.

3.1   Comparison with State of the Arts

Results on MS-COCO. In Table 2, when the resolution of the input image is 448×448 and the image feature extractor is ResNet101, our model MGSGN can reach 85.1% on mAP and is superior to the above comparison methods in most indicators. Specifically, the mAP of MGSGN is significantly improved by 7.8% over the ResNet101 baseline, which illustrates the superiority of our method. The MGSGN model is better than ML-GCN 2.1%, CPCL 2.3%, KSSNet 1.4% and TDRG 0.5% in the mAP, which also uses the GCN method. In addition, the performance of the MGSGN model on mAP is 1.2%, 1.1% and 0.9% higher than the SOTA methods LGR, FL-Tran and AAMN, respectively. Meanwhile, after we resize the input image to 576×576, the performance of the MGSGN model can be further improved to 86.6%. The MGSGN model outperforms the SSGRL model with mAP increased by 2.8%, CF1(ALL) increased by 4.5%, OF1(ALL) increased by 3.2%, CF1(top-3) increased by 3.9%, and OF1(top-3) increased by 2.3%. Compared with the recently released C-Tran and DA-GAT, the MGSGN model greatly outperforms these methods on most metrics.

Results on Pascal VOC 2007. In Table 3, compared with other state-of-the-art methods, our proposed model MGSGN achieves the best performance. Specifically, when the input image resolution is 448×448, compared to the baseline method ResNet-101, which obtains 89.9% mAP, the MGSGN model significantly improves to 95.7%, an increase of 5.8%. Even when MCAR uses larger image sizes, the MGSGN model outperforms the method by 0.9%. Although the TDRG and FL-Tran models also utilize the multi-scale feature mechanism of the CNN to learn object features at different scales of the image, the mAP of MGSGN model is 0.7% and 1.8% higher than these two advanced methods, respectively, MGSGN also outperforms the two methods in AP values for most categories. It is worth noting that when the input image resolution is 576×576, it can be found that the mAP of the MGSGN model is further improved to 96.4%. Compared with the state-of-the-art methods such as ADD-GCN, AAMN, and MCAR, our MGSGN model also achieves the best performance.

Table 2. Comparisons with state-of-the-art methods on the MS-COCO dataset. S_{tr} and S_{te} denote image resolution used in the training and testing stage.

Methods	(S_{tr}, S_{te})	Backbone	mAP	ALL						top-3					
				C-P	C-R	C-F1	O-P	O-R	O-F1	C-P	C-R	C-F1	O-P	O-R	O-F1
CNN-RNN [28]	(-, -)	vgg-16	61.2	-	-	-	-	-	-	66.0	55.6	60.4	69.2	66.4	67.8
RNN-Attention [31]	(-, -)	vgg-16	-	-	-	-	-	-	-	79.1	58.7	67.4	84.0	63.0	72.0
ResNet-SRN [41]	(224, 224)	ResNet-101	77.1	81.6	65.4	71.2	82.7	69.9	75.8	85.2	58.8	67.4	87.4	62.5	72.9
ResNet101 [17]	(224, 224)	ResÑet-101	77.3	80.2	66.7	72.8	83.9	70.8	76.8	84.1	59.4	69.7	89.1	62.8	73.6
ResNet101-ACfs [15]	(224, 224)	ResNet-101	77.5	77.4	68.3	72.2	79.8	73.1	76.3	85.2	59.4	68.0	86.6	63.3	73.1
CPCL [36]	(448, 448)	ResNet-101	82.8	85.6	71.1	77.6	86.1	74.5	79.9	89.0	63.5	74.1	90.5	65.9	76.3
ML-GCN [8]	(448, 448)	ResNet-101	83.0	85.1	72.0	78.0	85.8	75.4	80.3	89.2	64.1	74.6	90.5	66.5	76.7
KSSNet [29]	(448, 448)	ResNet-101	83.7	84.6	73.2	77.2	**87.8**	76.2	**81.5**	-	-	-	-	-	-
LGR [7]	(448, 448)	ResNet-101	83.9	85.0	73.3	78.4	86.2	76.4	81.0	89.0	**64.8**	75.0	90.7	67.0	77.1
FL-Tran [38]	(448, 448)	ResNet-101	84.0	84.9	73.5	78.8	86.0	76.3	80.9	88.7	65.2	75.1	90.6	67.0	77.0
AAMN [39]	(448, 448)	ResNet-101	84.2	86.2	72.7	78.9	87.0	76.0	81.1	89.7	64.8	75.2	**91.2**	66.9	77.2
TDRG [34]	(448, 448)	ResNet-101	84.6	86.0	73.1	79.0	86.6	76.4	81.2	**89.9**	64.4	75.0	**91.2**	67.0	77.2
SSGRL [6]	(576, 576)	ResNet-101	83.8	**89.9**	68.5	76.8	**91.3**	70.8	79.7	91.9	62.5	72.7	**93.8**	64.1	76.2
KGGR [4]	(576, 576)	ResNet-101	84.3	85.6	72.7	78.6	87.1	75.6	80.9	89.4	64.6	75.0	91.3	66.6	77.0
DA-GAT [40]	(576, 576)	ResNet-101	84.8	87.0	74.2	80.1	87.3	77.5	82.1	89.2	65.6	75.6	91.6	67.7	77.9
C-Tran [20]	(576, 576)	ResNet-101	85.1	86.3	74.3	79.9	87.7	76.5	81.7	90.1	65.7	76.0	92.1	**71.4**	77.6
TDRG [34]	(576, 576)	ResNet-101	86.0	87.0	74.7	80.4	87.5	**77.9**	82.4	90.7	65.6	76.2	91.9	68.0	78.1
MGSGN(ours)	(448, 448)	ResNet-101	85.1	86.3	73.9	79.6	86.1	77.1	81.4	89.9	64.8	75.3	90.9	67.2	77.3
MGSGN(ours)	(576, 576)	ResNet-101	86.6	87.4	76.9	81.3	88.1	77.1	82.9	92.1	67.1	76.6	92.7	67.1	78.5

Table 3. Comparisons with state-of-the-art methods on the VOC 2007 dataset. The performance based on two resolution settings are reported.

Methods	aero	bike	bird	boat	bottle	bus	car	cat	chair	cow	table	dog	horse	mbike	person	plant	sheep	sofa	trian	tv	mAP
CNN-RNN [28]	96.7	83.1	94.2	92.8	61.2	82.1	89.1	94.2	64.2	83.6	70.0	92.4	91.7	84.2	93.7	59.8	93.2	75.3	99.7	78.6	84.0
ResNet-101 [17]	99.5	97.7	97.8	96.4	65.7	91.8	96.1	97.6	74.2	80.9	85.0	98.4	96.5	95.9	98.4	70.1	88.3	80.2	98.9	89.2	89.9
RARL [5]	98.6	97.1	97.1	95.5	75.6	92.8	96.8	97.3	78.3	92.2	87.6	96.9	96.5	93.6	98.5	81.6	93.1	83.2	98.5	89.3	92.0
SSNP [30]	97.1	94.0	95.4	93.7	59.6	88.2	94.4	94.9	71.7	85.3	81.9	94.1	95.4	91.7	97.4	74.8	87.1	78.7	96.9	84.0	87.8
LDR [16]	99.6	98.3	98.0	98.2	78.2	94.2	97.0	97.8	80.8	94.9	84.9	97.7	97.5	96.6	98.7	85.0	96.2	83.2	98.5	92.6	93.4
FL-Tran [38]	99.7	97.7	98.2	98.4	81.5	95.4	97.3	97.0	82.1	95.5	85.5	97.9	96.9	95.7	98.7	86.1	96.7	83.9	98.9	93.9	93.9
ML-GCN [8]	99.5	98.5	**98.6**	98.1	80.8	94.6	97.2	98.2	82.3	95.7	86.4	98.2	98.4	96.7	99.0	84.7	96.7	84.3	98.9	93.7	94.0
LGR [7]	99.6	95.6	97.3	96.4	**84.0**	95.8	94.1	**98.9**	**86.9**	**96.8**	86.8	98.7	98.6	96.9	98.8	84.8	97.2	83.7	98.8	93.6	94.2
CSRA [42]	**99.9**	98.4	98.1	98.9	82.2	95.3	97.8	97.9	84.6	94.8	90.8	98.1	97.6	96.2	99.1	86.4	95.9	88.3	98.9	94.4	94.7
TDRG [34]	**99.9**	98.9	98.4	**98.7**	81.9	95.8	97.8	98.0	85.2	95.6	89.5	98.8	98.6	97.1	99.1	86.2	97.7	87.2	99.1	95.3	95.0
KGGR [4]	99.8	97.1	98.4	98.0	84.2	95.1	96.9	98.4	78.6	94.9	87.0	98.1	97.7	97.4	98.7	82.4	97.1	82.5	98.7	92.0	93.6
AAMN [39]	99.8	97.0	98.2	97.9	83.6	95.5	97.7	98.2	82.4	96.6	85.6	98.3	98.6	96.2	99.0	87.9	97.6	86.4	98.7	93.8	94.4
FL-Tran [38]	99.8	98.6	98.7	98.4	83.2	95.9	97.4	98.4	81.5	96.2	86.1	98.9	98.7	97.1	99.0	84.9	96.9	83.1	99.2	95.4	94.4
MCAR [12]	99.7	99.0	98.5	98.2	85.4	96.9	97.4	98.9	83.7	95.5	88.8	**99.1**	98.2	95.1	99.1	84.8	97.1	87.8	98.3	94.8	94.8
ADD-GCN [33]	99.8	99.0	98.4	99.0	86.7	**98.1**	98.5	98.3	85.8	98.3	88.9	98.8	99.0	97.4	99.2	88.3	98.7	90.7	**99.5**	97.0	96.0
MGSGN(ours)	99.8	99.0	98.5	**98.7**	83.8	96.0	98.1	98.9	86.4	96.4	91.3	98.9	99.3	97.1	99.2	86.5	98.6	90.1	99.6	96.4	95.7
MGSGN(ours)	99.8	99.3	98.9	99.1	87.5	97.6	98.7	99.2	86.7	98.6	90.8	99.0	99.2	97.9	99.5	88.9	99.0	91.2	99.3	97.3	96.4

In summary, the significant accuracy improvement is attributed to our proposed MLIC framework with the multi-scale global-local semantic graph network. Compared with static graph-based models, our multi-perspective dynamic semantic graph constructed from multi-scale global-local information in image target region features has better performance, especially in predicting some semantically dependent labels.

3.2 Ablation Studies

Effect of Multi-scale Mechanisms in MGSGN. To verify the effectiveness of our proposed MGSGN, we analyzed the impact analysis of the combination of different levels of the CNN features on our model, and the experiment was

Table 4. Analysis of the impact of CNN different level feature combinations on the proposed model MGSGN. The dataset used for this experiment is MS-COCO.

Methods	mAP	ALL		Top-3	
		C-F1	O-F1	C-F1	O-F1
Conv3+DBCA+MDSR	83.9	78.5	80.5	74.6	76.6
Conv4+DBCA+MDSR	84.1	78.7	80.7	74.7	76.8
Conv5+DBCA+MDSR	84.4	79.0	80.9	74.9	77.2
(Conv3, Conv5)+DBCA+MDSR	84.6	79.1	81.2	75.0	77.2
(Conv4, Conv5)+DBCA+MDSR	84.7	79.5	81.2	75.1	77.9
(Conv3, Conv4)+DBCA+MDSR	84.5	79.2	81.1	74.9	77.1
MGSGN (ours)	**85.1**	**79.6**	**81.4**	**75.3**	**77.3**

implemented on the MS-COCO dataset. The input image resolution is 448 × 448. In Table 4, the model that fuses shallow, middle and deep features works best. Specifically, the mAPs of MGSGN are 0.7%, 1.0% and 1.2% higher than the three methods using only single-level features, respectively. When equipped with two-level features, the performance of the model is also improved on the basis of single-level features. Finally, our model achieves the highest mAP of 85.1% when combining three-scale features. This shows that a single-level feature representation is not enough for object recognition of multiple different sizes, and our model incorporates the complementarity and diversity of features at different levels, which contains richer semantic correlation and feature-aware capabilities.

Table 5. Performance comparisons of different components in the MGSGN.

Architecture				mAP	ALL		Top-3	
ResNet-101	CLA	DBCA	MDSR		C-F1	O-F1	C-F1	O-F1
✓				77.3	72.8	76.8	69.7	73.6
✓	✓			82.8	77.3	79.4	73.8	75.9
✓		✓		83.2	77.9	80.0	74.2	76.3
✓			✓	83.3	78.0	80.0	74.4	76.4
✓	✓	✓		84.0	78.5	80.5	74.5	76.6
✓	✓		✓	84.1	78.7	80.7	74.7	76.8
✓		✓	✓	84.6	79.0	81.1	75.0	77.1
✓	✓	✓	✓	**85.1**	**79.6**	**81.4**	**75.3**	**77.3**

Comparison of Different Module Structures in MGSGN. To analyze the contribution of individual components in MGSGN, we conduct ablation experiments on MS-COCO. In Table 5, we first apply cross-layer attention (CLA)

Table 6. Performance comparison of the label dependency modeling method in MGSGN on the MS-COCO dataset.

Methods	mAP	ALL		Top-3	
		C-F1	O-F1	C-F1	O-F1
MGSGN(*)	84.2	78.7	80.7	74.7	**78.7**
MGSGN(†)	**85.1**	**79.6**	**81.4**	**75.3**	77.3

to the baseline, and the model performance is significantly improved by more than 5.5%. This shows that CLA is able to allow the model to learn multi-scale features from images, thus improving the model's performance. Next, we equip the baseline with a dual-branch cross-attention module (DBCA) and observe a model performance improvement of 5.9% relative to the baseline, which demonstrates that our DBCA can effectively capture local-global features in images. Subsequently, we add multi-perspective dynamic semantic representation module (MDSR) to the baseline, which improves the baseline's performance by 6%, illustrating that a multi-perspective dynamic semantic representation module can effectively model content-related category dependencies. Finally, under the full architecture, our model MGSGN achieves the best performance of 85.1%, which greatly exceeds the baseline. This shows that the three modules we propose can mutually promote each other in improving the performance of the model.

Performance Comparison of Different Label Graphs in MGSGN. In Table 6, * means that the static graph shared by the entire dataset obtained according to statistical probability is added to the semantic graph learning module [8]. † represents the proposed dynamic semantic relationship. We can see that the overall classification performance of the dynamic semantic map we constructed is better than that of the static graph, increasing mAP by 0.9%, and it is better than the MGSGN method under the static graph in most indicators. This is because the semantic information of the target object contained in the image is not only determined by its intrinsic attributes, but also needs to consider the context information of the target object. More importantly, our multi-view dynamic semantic graph module establishes the dependencies between different semantics from a global perspective, which can better explore label correlation.

3.3   Visual Analysis

In this section, we visualize the learned attention maps to illustrate the ability of the proposed model to exploit meaningful regions and capture spatially global-local semantic dependencies. In Fig. 4, the three columns of example images from left to right are the original image, the classification attention map generated by ResNet101 and MGSGN. The results show that the MGSGN model can focus on more semantic regions and has stronger modeling ability than

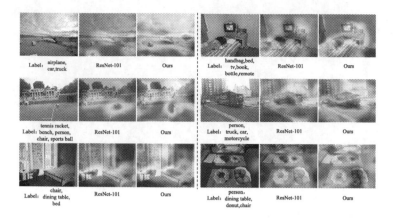

Fig. 4. Visualization results of salient features on MS-COCO.

ResNet101 to mine more discriminative and meaningful information. Furthermore, our MGSGN model has the ability to capture spatial global-local semantic dependencies, especially for invisible or small objects appearing in images. For example, when recognizing tennis racket and sports ball, due to their similar semantics, people pay attention to sports ball and also pay attention to tennis racket, thus recognizing these objects requires richer contextual information. Thanks to the multi-scale feature reconstruction module and the channel dual-branch cross-attention module, our method captures the global-local information in multi-scale features and adaptively explores the correlation between global-local feature pairs through cross-attention, so that the model can more accurately locate and perceive objects of different sizes.

4   Conclusion

We propose the Multi-scale Global-local Semantic Graph Network for MLIC. First, we exploit the multi-scale feature reconstruction module to extract complementary information from shallow, middle and deep features in CNN. In addition, the channel dual-branch cross-attention module is designed to further process the complementary information of the CNN to fuse the global-local features extracted from multiple scale mechanisms in an adaptive cross-fusion manner. Finally, we propose a multi-perspective dynamic semantic representation module that explores complex semantic correlations from multiple perspectives. Extensive experiments on benchmark datasets demonstrate that our proposed MGSGN significantly improves the performance of MLIC models.

Acknowledgments. This work is supported by National Natural Science Foundation of China (Nos. 62276073, 61966004), Guangxi Natural Science Foundation (No. 2019GXNSFDA245018), Innovation Project of Guangxi Graduate Education (No. YCBZ2022060), Guangxi "Bagui Scholar" Teams for Innovation and Research Project, and Guangxi Collaborative Innovation Center of Multi-source Information Integration and Intelligent Processing.

Ethical Statement. We affirm that the ideas, concepts, and findings presented in this paper are the result of our own original work, conducted with honesty, rigor, and transparency. We have provided proper citations and references for all sources used, and have clearly acknowledged the contributions of others where applicable.

References

1. Boutell, M.R., Luo, J., Shen, X., Brown, C.M.: Learning multi-label scene classification. Pattern Recogn. **37**(9), 1757–1771 (2004)
2. Chen, S.F., Chen, Y.C., Yeh, C.K., Wang, Y.C.: Order-free RNN with visual attention for multi-label classification. In: Proceedings of the 32th AAAI Conference on Artificial Intelligence, vol. 32 (2018)
3. Chen, S., Li, Z., Tang, Z.: Relation R-CNN: a graph based relation-aware network for object detection. IEEE Signal Process. Lett. **27**, 1680–1684 (2020)
4. Chen, T., Lin, L., Chen, R., Hui, X., Wu, H.: Knowledge-guided multi-label few-shot learning for general image recognition. IEEE Trans. Pattern Anal. Mach. Intell. **44**(3), 1371–1384 (2020)
5. Chen, T., Wang, Z., Li, G., Lin, L.: Recurrent attentional reinforcement learning for multi-label image recognition. In: Proceedings of the 32th AAAI Conference on Artificial Intelligence, vol. 32 (2018)
6. Chen, T., Xu, M., Hui, X., Wu, H., Lin, L.: Learning semantic-specific graph representation for multi-label image recognition. In: Proceedings of the IEEE/CVF International Conference on Computer Vision, pp. 522–531 (2019)
7. Chen, Y., Zou, C., Chen, J.: Label-aware graph representation learning for multi-label image classification. Neurocomputing **492**, 50–61 (2022)
8. Chen, Z.M., Wei, X.S., Wang, P., Guo, Y.: Multi-label image recognition with graph convolutional networks. In: Proceedings of the IEEE/CVF Conference on Computer Vision and Pattern Recognition, pp. 5177–5186 (2019)
9. Chollet, F.: Xception: deep learning with depthwise separable convolutions. In: Proceedings of the IEEE Conference on Computer Vision and Pattern Recognition, pp. 1251–1258 (2017)
10. Deng, J., Dong, W., Socher, R., Li, L.J., Li, K., Fei-Fei, L.: Imagenet: a large-scale hierarchical image database. In: Proceedings of the IEEE Conference on Computer Vision and Pattern Recognition, pp. 248–255. IEEE (2009)
11. Everingham, M., Eslami, S.A., Van Gool, L., Williams, C.K., Winn, J., Zisserman, A.: The pascal visual object classes challenge: a retrospective. Int. J. Comput. Vision **111**, 98–136 (2015)
12. Gao, B.B., Zhou, H.Y.: Learning to discover multi-class attentional regions for multi-label image recognition. IEEE Trans. Image Process. **30**, 5920–5932 (2021)
13. Gao, P., et al.: Dynamic fusion with intra-and inter-modality attention flow for visual question answering. In: Proceedings of the IEEE/CVF Conference on Computer Vision and Pattern Recognition, pp. 6639–6648 (2019)
14. Ge, Z., Mahapatra, D., Sedai, S., Garnavi, R., Chakravorty, R.: Chest X-rays classification: a multi-label and fine-grained problem. arXiv preprint arXiv:1807.07247 (2018)

15. Guo, H., Zheng, K., Fan, X., Yu, H., Wang, S.: Visual attention consistency under image transforms for multi-label image classification. In: Proceedings of the IEEE/CVF Conference on Computer Vision and Pattern Recognition, pp. 729–739 (2019)
16. Hassanin, M., Radwan, I., Khan, S., Tahtali, M.: Learning discriminative representations for multi-label image recognition. J. Vis. Commun. Image Represent. **83**, 103448 (2022)
17. He, K., Zhang, X., Ren, S., Sun, J.: Deep residual learning for image recognition. In: Proceedings of the IEEE Conference on Computer Vision and Pattern Recognition, pp. 770–778 (2016)
18. Hu, H., Zhou, G.T., Deng, Z., Liao, Z., Mori, G.: Learning structured inference neural networks with label relations. In: Proceedings of the IEEE Conference on Computer Vision and Pattern Recognition, pp. 2960–2968 (2016)
19. Kipf, T.N., Welling, M.: Semi-supervised classification with graph convolutional networks. arXiv preprint arXiv:1609.02907 (2016)
20. Lanchantin, J., Wang, T., Ordonez, V., Qi, Y.: General multi-label image classification with transformers. In: Proceedings of the IEEE/CVF Conference on Computer Vision and Pattern Recognition, pp. 16478–16488 (2021)
21. Li, Q., Peng, X., Qiao, Y., Peng, Q.: Learning category correlations for multi-label image recognition with graph networks. arXiv preprint arXiv:1909.13005 (2019)
22. Li, X., Zhao, F., Guo, Y.: Multi-label image classification with a probabilistic label enhancement model. In: Proceedings of the 30th Conference on Uncertainty in Artificial Intelligence, vol. 1, pp. 1–10 (2014)
23. Li, Y., Huang, C., Loy, C.C., Tang, X.: Human attribute recognition by deep hierarchical contexts. In: Leibe, B., Matas, J., Sebe, N., Welling, M. (eds.) ECCV 2016. LNCS, vol. 9910, pp. 684–700. Springer, Cham (2016). https://doi.org/10. 1007/978-3-319-46466-4_41
24. Li, Z., Lin, L., Zhang, C., Ma, H., Zhao, W., Shi, Z.: A semi-supervised learning approach based on adaptive weighted fusion for automatic image annotation. ACM Trans. Multimedia Comput. Commun. Appl. (TOMM) **17**(1), 1–23 (2021)
25. Lin; T.-Y., et al.: Microsoft COCO: common objects in context. In: Fleet, D., Pajdla, T., Schiele, B., Tuytelaars, T. (eds.) ECCV 2014. LNCS, vol. 8693, pp. 740–755. Springer, Cham (2014). https://doi.org/10.1007/978-3-319-10602-1_48
26. Maas, A.L., Hannun, A.Y., Ng, A.Y., et al.: Rectifier nonlinearities improve neural network acoustic models. In: Proceedings of the 30th International Conference on Machine Learning, Atlanta, Georgia, USA, vol. 30, p. 3 (2013)
27. Paszke, A., et al.: Automatic differentiation in pytorch (2017)
28. Wang, J., Yang, Y., Mao, J., Huang, Z., Huang, C., Xu, W.: CNN-RNN: a unified framework for multi-label image classification. In: Proceedings of the IEEE Conference on Computer Vision and Pattern Recognition, pp. 2285–2294 (2016)
29. Wang, Y., et al.: Multi-label classification with label graph superimposing. In: Proceedings of the 34th AAAI Conference on Artificial Intelligence, vol. 34, pp. 12265–12272 (2020)
30. Wang, Z., Fang, Z., Li, D., Yang, H., Du, W.: Semantic supplementary network with prior information for multi-label image classification. IEEE Trans. Circuits Syst. Video Technol. **32**(4), 1848–1859 (2021)
31. Wang, Z., Chen, T., Li, G., Xu, R., Lin, L.: Multi-label image recognition by recurrently discovering attentional regions. In: Proceedings of the IEEE International Conference on Computer Vision, pp. 464–472 (2017)
32. Xian, T., Li, Z., Tang, Z., Ma, H.: Adaptive path selection for dynamic image captioning. IEEE Trans. Circuits Syst. Video Technol. **32**(9), 5762–5775 (2022)

33. Ye, J., He, J., Peng, X., Wu, W., Qiao, Yu.: Attention-driven dynamic graph convolutional network for multi-label image recognition. In: Vedaldi, A., Bischof, H., Brox, T., Frahm, J.-M. (eds.) ECCV 2020. LNCS, vol. 12366, pp. 649–665. Springer, Cham (2020). https://doi.org/10.1007/978-3-030-58589-1_39
34. Zhao, J., Yan, K., Zhao, Y., Guo, X., Huang, F., Li, J.: Transformer-based dual relation graph for multi-label image recognition. In: Proceedings of the IEEE/CVF International Conference on Computer Vision, pp. 163–172 (2021)
35. Zhao, Q., Wang, X., Lyu, S., Liu, B., Yang, Y.: A feature consistency driven attention erasing network for fine-grained image retrieval. Pattern Recogn. **128**, 108618 (2022)
36. Zhou, F., Huang, S., Liu, B., Yang, D.: Multi-label image classification via category prototype compositional learning. IEEE Trans. Circuits Syst. Video Technol. **32**(7), 4513–4525 (2021)
37. Zhou, T., Li, Z., Zhang, C., Ma, H.: Classify multi-label images via improved CNN model with adversarial network. Multimedia Tools Appl. **79**, 6871–6890 (2020)
38. Zhou, W., Dou, P., Su, T., Hu, H., Zheng, Z.: Feature learning network with transformer for multi-label image classification. Pattern Recogn. **136**, 109203 (2023)
39. Zhou, W., Hou, Y., Chen, D., Hu, H., Su, T.: Attention-augmented memory network for image multi-label classification. ACM Trans. Multimedia Comput. Commun. Appl. **19**(3), 1–24 (2022)
40. Zhou, W., Xia, Z., Dou, P., Su, T., Hu, H.: Double attention based on graph attention network for image multi-label classification. ACM Trans. Multimed. Comput. Commun. Appl. **19**(1), 1–23 (2023)
41. Zhu, F., Li, H., Ouyang, W., Yu, N., Wang, X.: Learning spatial regularization with image-level supervisions for multi-label image classification. In: Proceedings of the IEEE Conference on Computer Vision and Pattern Recognition, pp. 5513–5522 (2017)
42. Zhu, K., Wu, J.: Residual attention: a simple but effective method for multi-label recognition. In: Proceedings of the IEEE/CVF International Conference on Computer Vision, pp. 184–193 (2021)
43. Zhu, Q., Kuang, W., Li, Z.: Dual attention interactive fine-grained classification network based on data augmentation. J. Vis. Commun. Image Represent. **88**, 103632 (2022)
44. Zhu, Q., Kuang, W., Zhixin, L.: Fusing bilinear multi-channel gated vector for fine-grained classification. Mach. Vis. Appl. **34**(2), 26 (2023)

CasSampling: Exploring Efficient Cascade Graph Learning for Popularity Prediction

Guixiang Cheng[1,2], Xin Yan[1,2(✉)], Shengxiang Gao[1,2], Guangyi Xu[3], and Xianghua Miao[1,2]

[1] Faculty of Information Engineering and Automation, Kunming University of Science and Technology, Kunming, China
kg_yanxin@sina.com
[2] Yunnan Key Laboratory of Artificial Intelligence, Kunming University of Science and Technology, Kunming, China
[3] Yunnan Nantian Electronics Information Co., Ltd., Kunming, China

Abstract. Predicting the growth size of an information cascade is one of the primary challenges in understanding the diffusion of information. Recent efforts focus on utilizing graph neural networks to capture graph structure. However, there is considerable variance in the information cascade size (from few to million). From the perspective of efficiency and performance, the method of modeling each node is inappropriate for graph neural networks. In this paper, we propose a novel deep learning framework for popularity prediction called CasSampling. Firstly, we exploit a heuristic algorithm to sample the critical part of cascade graph. For the loss of structure information due to sampling, we keep outdegree of sampled node in the global graph as part of the node feature into the graph attention networks. For the loss of temporal information due to sampling, we utilize the time series to learn the global propagation time flow. Then, we design an attention aggregator for node-level representation to better integrate local-level propagation into the global-level time flow. Experiments conducted on two benchmark datasets demonstrate that our method significantly outperforms the state-of-the-art methods for popularity prediction. Additionally, the computation cost is much less than the baselines. Code and (public) datasets are available at https://github.com/Gration-Cheng/CasSampling.

Keywords: Popularity prediction · Cascade graph sampling · Graph neural network

1 Introduction

With the improvement of communication technology, the rapid development of online social media has promoted the propagation and interaction of massive information. Through social media, people spread news, politics, and life hot spots in a cascading way. Therefore, the prediction of the information propagation cascade is significant, and the effective prediction of the number of retweets

D. Koutra et al. (Eds.): ECML PKDD 2023, LNAI 14171, pp. 70–86, 2023.
https://doi.org/10.1007/978-3-031-43418-1_5

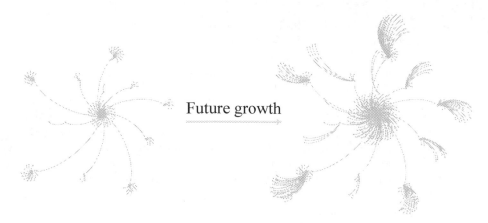

Future growth

Fig. 1. A real-world example of a propagation graph in the Weibo dataset. The left figure shows the propagation graph during the observation time 1 h, while the right figure shows the propagation graph after 23 h. The blue nodes denote the observed nodes, while the orange nodes represent the nodes that will propagate in the future.

in a period is beneficial for understanding the cascade, which has attracted considerable attention in academia and industry. Cascading propagation plays a crucial role in many downstream tasks, such as accelerating or suppressing the spread of information [1,2], rumor detection, and even epidemic prediction. However, social media are large open platforms, and the uncertainty about cascading effects makes popularity prediction an extremely challenging problem.

In recent years, Most of the research uses deep learning-based approaches to learn the representation of cascades. Most of them [3–6], view an information propagation as a sequence of events and use subgraphs or subsequences to represent the cascade. However, modeling subgraph or subsequence is difficult to learn the cascade effect of information propagation.

Recent research has focused on using graph neural networks to capture the cascade effect [4,6–8]. Graph Neural Networks (GNN) are able to effectively model graph-structured data by integrating node attributes and topology. However, when facing a large number of nodes, GNNs can be computationally expensive and inefficient. As shown in Fig. 1, many of the nodes within the observation time do not bring new forwarding propagation. These nodes have little effect on propagation. It is obvious that nodes with more propagation during the observation time will have a larger cascading effect.

Note that with these problems, existing methods confront several challenges: (1) Some methods model each node to learn node-level representation, but it is not efficient because of the cascade size (from few to million). (2) The method of modeling subgraphs or subsequences is difficult to learn the cascade effect of information propagation. (3) Time is crucial information. Existing methods lack the extensive use of time information both at the local-level and the global-level.

To address these challenges, we proposed a novel neural network model named CasSampling. The model focuses on sampling the cascade graph and compensates for the loss of time and structure information due to sampling, making the model more efficient and performing better. Our main contributions can be summarized as follows:

- **Efficiency graph representation**. We implemented a heuristic algorithm to sample the key part of cascade graph, which address the problem of the large variable size of graphs that make it difficult to model with GNNs. To compensate for the loss of graph structure due to sampling, we retain the outdegree of sampled nodes as part of the sampled nodes feature. It efficiently models cascade graphs with the large variable sizes and is effective for explicitly capturing cascading effects.
- **Multi-scale time information**. We design an attention aggregator that combines the node's propagation embedding with the time stamp of nodes. To compensate for the loss of time information caused by graph sampling, we use time series to learn the global propagation time flow. We have successfully integrated two types of temporal information for the first time, which enables us capture the potential information between the retweet time of the active node and the global propagation time flow, and it can more fully model the information diffusion process.
- **Evaluation on benchmark datasets.** We conduct extensive evaluations on two publicly available benchmark datasets, demonstrating that CasSampling significantly outperforms the state-of-the-art (SOTA) baselines and reduces the computational cost.

2   Related Work

We review the related work grouped into three main categories: featured-based, generative process and deep learning-based approaches.

Featured-Based Approaches. It usually extracts features from specific platforms, such as Arxiv; Weibo [3]; Twitter [9]; These features include user-related features [10,11], content-related features [12], cascades structural [13,14] and temporal features [15]. However, feature-based approaches extract features from different platforms, making the learned features difficult to generalize into different scenarios, and the prediction performance heavily relies on the quality of the hand-crafted feature.

Generative Process Approaches. It mainly regards the process of message diffusion as an arrival time sequence [16–19]. These methods focus on modeling the intensity function for the arrival process. The popularity prediction can be obtained by event simulation of the intensity function. These methods demonstrate enhanced comprehensibility, but they rely on certain assumptions, and we do not know whether these assumptions are valid in real situations, limiting model performance.

Deep Learning-Based Approaches. Generally, existing methods for popularity prediction mainly focus on four types of information, i.e., temporal information, node representation, structure representation, and content.

For node and structure representation. DeepHawkes [3] integrates an interpretable Hawkes process for information cascade prediction. With the booming development of graph neural networks (GNN), CasCN [4] uses it to model the structural information of cascade subgraphs (via cascade Laplacian). CasFlow [20] uses a variational autoencoder to learn the uncertainty of the cascade. TempCas [5] exploits a heuristic algorithm to sample critical paths and utilizes some handcraft features as compensation for the sampled graph. All the work above depicts the subgraph of participating users. However, modeling subgraphs or subsequences is difficult to learn the cascade effect of information propagation. CouledGNN [7] uses the global propagation graph to capture the interaction between node activation states and diffusion; CasGCN [21] considers that the cascade effect is bidirectional, uses in-coming and out-going adjacency matrices as the representation of graph structure, and combines the time information with the graph structure by attention mechanism. These GNN-based methods model each node for graph embedding. However, from the perspective of efficiency and performance, the method of modeling each node is inappropriate for GNN.

For temporal information modeling, DeepHawkes [3] introduced a nonparametric time decay function into the path modeling of recurrent neural networks. DFTC [22] represents temporal information by time series, which used a Convolution-1d neural network for capturing short-term outbreaks and LSTM for long-term fluctuations. TempCas [5] improves the DFTC [22] by combining the short-term and long-term rather than capturing them separately. However, these methods do not fully utilize global-level and local-level time information.

Note these problems. We propose a novel model, called CasSampling, which implements a heuristic algorithm to sample the cascade graph and compensate for the loss of time and structure information caused by sampling. Compared with the same model, we sample cascade at the graph-level for the first time and fully utilize multi-scale time information. It achieved better performance and less computation cost.

3   Preliminaries

We now present the essential background and formally define the popularity prediction problem.

Definition 1 (Cascade Graph). *Suppose that we have n posts, $P = \{p_c, c \in [1, n]\}$. For each post p_c, there is a cascade graph denoted by $\mathcal{G}_c = (\mathcal{V}_c, \mathcal{E}_c, \mathcal{T}_c)$, where $\mathcal{V}_c$ is a set of nodes that have been involved in the cascade during the observation time T, a directed edge $(v_i, v_j) \in \mathcal{E}_c$ represents that node v_j retweet from node v_i, and a tuple of node time label $(v_i : t_i) \in \mathcal{T}_c$ denotes the time elapsed between the original post and node v's retweet.*

Definition 2 (Growth size). *It is defined as the amount of cascade growth number over observation time window T after it has spread for Δt. According to* **Definition 1**, *we obtain $\mathcal{G}_c = (\mathcal{V}_c, \mathcal{E}_c, \mathcal{T}_c), \mathcal{T}_c < T$. Our task is to predict the growth size ΔS_i of a cascade after a given time interval Δt. The growth size can be defined as $\Delta S_i = |\mathcal{V}_i^{T+\Delta t}| - |\mathcal{V}_i^T|$.*

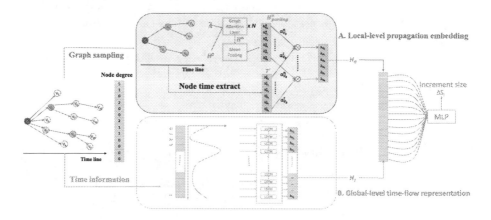

Fig. 2. The framework of CasSampling for popularity prediction.

4   Method

Before introducing the details of the CasSampling model, we present the overall framework of CasSampling in Fig. 2. It contains four major parts:(1)A heuristic algorithm to sample the critical parts of a graph. (2) Local-level propagation embedding model graph structure with GAT and uses the attention aggregator to combine it with node time information. (3) Global-level time flow representation adopts LSTM on time series to capture the propagation trend. (4) Prediction layer concatenates local-level propagation and global-level time flow into the self-attention layer to fuse each other and feed into Multilayer-Perception(MLP) to predict the increment size.

4.1   Graph Sampling

Efficient node representation is challenging due to the variable size of cascades(from few to million). Specifically, the millions of nodes for the GNN are computation expensive. To achieve an efficient graph representation, we used rule-based graph sampling to reduce the number of nodes while preserving the original graph information as much as possible.

Algorithm 1 Graph sampling

Input: A cascade graph $\mathcal{G}_c$, degree vector D of $\mathcal{G}_c$; the maximum number of nodes K.
Output: Sampled graph$\mathcal{G}_c^{sampled}$ and out-degree vector $D_{sampled}$ of $\mathcal{G}_c^{sampled}$
1: $\mathcal{V}_c, \mathcal{E}_c, \mathcal{T}_c \leftarrow \mathcal{G}_c$
2: **if** $|\mathcal{V}_c| < K$ **then**
3:      **return** $\mathcal{G}_c, D$
4: **end if**
5: $D_{sorted}, \mathcal{V}_{sorted} = \text{sort}(D, \mathcal{V}_c, \mathcal{T}_c) \# $ Sort by Rule 1 and Rule 2
6: $D_{sampled}, \mathcal{V}_{sampled} = \text{selectTop}(D_{sorted}, \mathcal{V}_{sorted}, K)$
7: $\mathcal{E}_{sampled} \leftarrow \varnothing, \mathcal{T}_{sampled} \leftarrow \varnothing$
8: **for** each $\{v_i, v_j\}$ in $\mathcal{E}_c$ **do**
9:      **if** $v_j \notin \mathcal{V}_{sampled}$ **then**
10:          continue
11:      **else if** $v_i \in \mathcal{V}_{sampled}$ **then**
12:          $\mathcal{E}_{sampled} \leftarrow \mathcal{E}_{sampled} \cup \{v_i, v_j\}$
13:      **else**
14:          $v_k = \text{findAncestor}(v_i, \mathcal{E}_c, \mathcal{V}_{sampled}) \#$ Find the nearest ancestor of node v_i in the $\mathcal{V}_{sampled}$.
15:          $\mathcal{E}_{sampled} \leftarrow \mathcal{E}_{sampled} \cup \{v_k, v_j\}$
16:      **end if**
17: **end for**
18: **for** each v in $\mathcal{V}_{sampled}$ **do**
19:      $\mathcal{T}_{sampled} \leftarrow \mathcal{T}_{sampled} \cup (v : T(v))$
20: **end for**
21: $\mathcal{G}_c^{sampled} = \{\mathcal{V}_{sampled}, \mathcal{E}_{sampled}, \mathcal{T}_{sampled}\}$
22: **return** $\mathcal{G}_c^{sampled}, D_{sampled}$

Given a cascade graph $\mathcal{G}_c$ and the adjacency matrix $\mathbf{A_c}$. The outdegree vector $D = \{d_i, i \in [1, n]\}$ can be computed with:

$$d_i = log_2(\sum_{j=1}^{N} a_{ij}), \tag{1}$$

where N is the number of nodes and a_{ij} is one element of $\mathbf{A_c}$. The d_i denotes the outdegree of node i after logarithmic scaling.

Since the node with a larger out-degree is more critical, and according to the Hawkes process [3], the point closer to the occurrence of time has the more significant influence, there are two rules for sorting:

Rule 1: Sort the $\mathcal{V}_c$ by the outdegree D of nodes.(from large to small).
Rule 2: For nodes with the same outdegree, make a second sort according to their time(from late to early).

To reduce computation costs and improve performance, we sampled nodes based on their sorted out-degree vector and selected the top K nodes. However, this process may result in some nodes missing parent nodes. To address this issue, we identified the nearest ancestor node that was not filtered out and used it as the parent node. To preserve the original graph information, we used the out-degree of the original graph node as the feature for the sampled node.

The process of graph sampling is shown in Algorithm 1.

4.2 Local-Level Propagation Embedding

Graph Attention Layer. Recently, Graph neural networks have been advanced in graph learning. To capture the local information and achieve node-level representation, we utilize graph neural networks to learn hidden information among cascade nodes. Each tweet has a different cascade graph which is an inductive task, so we choose Graph Attention networks [23] (GAT) to learn the graph structure.

The input of GAT consists of two parts, adjacency of the graph and the node's feature matrix. After graph sampling, we obtain the $\mathcal{G}_c^{sampled}$ and $D^{sampled}$ of a cascade. To retain the original graph information, we reserve the outdegrees of nodes as part of nodes feature to learn the node influence and the size of the original cascade. The node input feature H^0 can be defined as:

$$H^0 = \mathbf{A} + \mathrm{diag}(D_{sampled}) = \begin{bmatrix} - \ h_1^0 \ - \\ - \ h_2^0 \ - \\ \vdots \\ - \ h_N^0 \ - \end{bmatrix}, \tag{2}$$

where $\mathbf{A}$ is the adjacency matrix of $\mathcal{G}_c^{sampled}$. $\mathrm{diag}(D_{sampled})$ indicates diagonalizing the $D_{sampled}$ vector. $h_i^0 \in \mathbb{R}^F$ is the input feature of node i, $F = N$, and N is the number of nodes.

For the adjacency matrix, we add self-connection to prevent loss of self-information during aggregation. The Adjacency $\tilde{\mathbf{A}}$ is formulated as:

$$\tilde{\mathbf{A}} = \mathbf{A} + \mathbf{I_n}, \tag{3}$$

where $\mathbf{I_n} \in \mathbb{R}^{N \times N}$ is an identity matrix.

The main idea of GAT is to aggregate node features by calculating the attention weight between connected nodes. After n layers of GAT, the node receives messages from other nodes within n-hops. The aggregate function is as follows:

$$h_i^n = \sigma(\sum_{j \in \mathcal{N}_i} \alpha_{ij} \mathbf{W} h_j^{n-1}), \tag{4}$$

where $\mathcal{N}_i$ is the neighborhood of node v_i in the graph, which can be obtained from $\tilde{\mathbf{A}}$. The h_j^{n-1} represents embedding of node j after n-1 layers of GAT. The α_{ij} is the attention score between node i and node j. It can be calculated by:

$$\alpha_{ij} = \frac{\exp(\mathrm{LeakyReLU}(\mathbf{a}^T[\mathbf{W}h_i\|\mathbf{W}h_j]))}{\sum_{k \in \mathcal{N}_i} \exp(\mathrm{LeakyReLU}(\mathbf{a}^T[\mathbf{W}h_i\|\mathbf{W}h_k]))}, \tag{5}$$

where $\mathbf{a} \in \mathbb{R}^{2F'}$ denote the learnable parameters. LeakyReLU is an activation function. $\|$ is the concatenation operation. A weight matrix $\mathbf{W} \in \mathbb{R}^{F' \times F}$ is shared to every node.

We do mean pooling with the output H^n of the n layers of GAT, and pooling the feature of each node.

$$H^n_{pooling} = \mathbf{MeanPooling}(H^n). \tag{6}$$

The final graph embedding can be expressed as: $H^n_{pooling} = [h^n_1, h^n_2, \ldots, h^n_N]^T$, $H^n \in \mathbb{R}^N$, where $h^n_i \in \mathbb{R}$ is the embedding of node i.

Node Time Information. To integrate graph structure and global temporal flow, we preserve the original time information of nodes instead of incorporating it into GAT input features. We utilize the attention aggregator to merge node structure and time information as the graph represents. Let $T' = [h^t_1, h^t_2, \ldots, h^t_N]^T$, $T' \in \mathbb{R}^N$ denote the time stamp of the node, which is obtained from $\mathcal{T}_{sampled}$. $h'_i = [h^n_i \| h^t_i]$ represents node i concatenating GAT output and time information.

$$e^j_i = \mathbf{v}^T tanh(\mathbf{W_a}[h^j_i \| h'_i]), \tag{7}$$

where h^j_i denotes one of the node feature of h'_i. $\mathbf{W_a}$ and $\mathbf{v}$ denote the learnable parameter.

$$\alpha^j_i = \frac{\exp(e^j_i)}{\sum_{k \in \{t,n\}} \exp(e^k_i)}, \tag{8}$$

where α^j_i represents the attention score of h_{ij}.

Aggregate the features of node i, and the aggregate function is as follows:

$$h_i = \sum_{j \in \{t,n\}} \alpha^j_i h^j_i. \tag{9}$$

$H_G = [h_1, h_2, \ldots, h_N], H_G \in \mathbb{R}^N$ contains nodes structure embedding and nodes time information.

4.3 Global-Level Time Flow Representation

Given a fixed interval of time t_s, We have T/t_s time slots. From $\mathcal{G}_c$, we can get the global graph node's time information, then calculate the time slot of each node. Let $R_T = \{r_1, r_2, \ldots, r_{T/t_s}\}$, $R_T \in \mathbb{R}^{T/t_s}$ denote the temporal flow sequence. We utilize LSTM to capture the time flow information.

$$H_T = \mathbf{LSTM}(R_T), \tag{10}$$

where $H_T \in \mathbb{R}^{T/t_s}$ is the global propagation time flow representation.

4.4 Prediction Layer

Each node in H_G represents graph structure information. H_T contains global temporal information. We concatenate the two parts into Self-Attention [24] layer to fuse each other and feed into MLP to predict the increment size.

$$H = H_G \oplus H_T, \tag{11}$$

$$H' = \textbf{Self Attention}(H) + H, \tag{12}$$

$$\Delta S_i = \textbf{MLP}(H'), \tag{13}$$

Our ultimate task is to predict the increment size for a fixed time interval, which can be done by minimizing the following loss function:

$$\mathcal{L}(\Delta S_i, \Delta \hat{S}_i) = \frac{1}{P} \sum_{i=1}^{P} (\log_2 \Delta S_i - \log_2 \Delta \hat{S}_i)^2, \tag{14}$$

where P is the number of posts, ΔS_i is the predicted amount of growth, $\Delta \hat{S}_i$ is the ground truth.

4.5 Complexity Analysis

The complexity based on the sparse matrix operation of GAT is $\mathcal{O}(|\mathcal{V}_c|F'F + |\mathcal{E}_c|F)$, where F is the number of input features and F' is the number of output features. The complexity of the node-level time attention mechanism is $\mathcal{O}(|\mathcal{V}_c|)$. Compare with the subsequence-based method, our method can be parallelized. The complexity of global time flow representation is $\mathcal{O}(T/t_s)$. The complexity of Self-Attention layer is $\mathcal{O}((|\mathcal{V}_c| + T/t_s)^2)$. Sum up, the complexity approximates to $\mathcal{O}(|\mathcal{V}_c|F'F + |\mathcal{E}_c|F + (|\mathcal{V}_c| + T/t_s)^2)$.

5 Experiments

To evaluate the performance of our model, we compare CasSampling with several SOTA methods on two benchmark datasets under various evaluation metrics.

5.1 Datasets

Sina Weibo. The dataset [3] comes from Sina Weibo, a major microblogging site that is similar to Twitter. It contains posts that were published between 0:00 to 24:00 on June 1, 2016.

Twitter. The dataset is collected by [9] and contains public English written tweets published between Mar 24 and Apr 25, 2012.

The observation time T for Weibo is set to 0.5 h, 1 h and 2 h, and 1 days,2 days and 3 days for Twitter. We select 24 h as the prediction time for the Weibo dataset and 32 days for the Twitter dataset. Following earlier methods [3,20], we filter out cascades whose $|\mathcal{V}_c| < 10$, and due to the effect of diurnal rhythm in Weibo, we focused on tweets published between 8 a.m. and 6 p.m. to give each tweet at least 6 h to gain retweets. For Twitter, we only tracked tweets published before Apr 10, ensuring at least 15 days for each tweet to grow adopters. For each of two datasets, we randomly split it into training set (70%), validation set (15%), and test set (15%). The statistics and visualization of these two datasets are shown in Table 1 and Fig. 3.

5.2   Baseline

To validate CasSampling's performance in popularity prediction, we chose the following SOTA baselines for comparison:

Table 1. Descriptive statistics of two datasets.

Dataset	Ori. Cascade	Avg. path length	Avg. popularity	0.5 h/1 day			1 h/2 days			2h/3days		
				Train	Val	Test	Train	Val	Test	Train	Val	Test
Weibo	119313	1.217	171.098	21461	4598	4598	27353	5860	5860	32943	7059	7059
Twitter	88440	1.201	142.672	9640	2065	2065	12740	2729	2729	15777	3380	3380

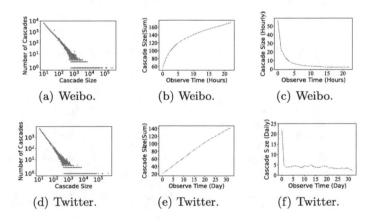

(a) Weibo.   (b) Weibo.   (c) Weibo.

(d) Twitter.   (e) Twitter.   (f) Twitter.

Fig. 3. Cascade size distribution of each dataset. In the 1st column, each figure shows the distribution of cascade sizes. The 2nd column denotes the mean sum cascade size changing over observation time. The 3rd column describes the mean hourly cascade size change over the observation time.

Feature-Linear and Feature-Deep. We have extracted all the predictable features from recent research [10,12,13,15]. Then, we feed it into a linear regression model and a fully-connected layer to predict the increment size.

DeepHawkes [3]. DeepHawkes considers three important aspects of the Hawkes process: user influence, time decay effect, and self-exciting mechanism.

CasCN [4]. CasCN is the first GNN-based framework exploiting both structural and employs a sequence of sub-cascade graphs with cascade Laplacian.

CasFlow [20]. CasFlow combines the local structure of cascade graph with global social collaboration network.

TempCas [5]. TempCas sample the critical path of cascade and utilizes hand-crafted features to compensate for structural loss. It uses LSTM and attention CNN to model long-short term time information.

5.3   Evaluation Metrics

Following existing works [3,4,25], we use Mean Square Logarithmic Error (MSLE) and Symmetric Mean Absolute Percentage Error (SMAPE) for prediction performance evaluation, which are defined as:

$$\text{MSLE} = \frac{1}{P} \sum_{i=1}^{P} (\log_2 \Delta S_i - \log_2 \Delta \hat{S}_i)^2, \tag{15}$$

$$\text{SMAPE} = \frac{1}{P} \sum_{i=1}^{P} \frac{|\log_2 \Delta S_i - \log_2 \Delta \hat{S}_i|}{(\log_2 \Delta S_i + \log_2 \Delta \hat{S}_i)/2}, \tag{16}$$

where P is the number of posts, ΔS_i is the predicted amount of growth, $\Delta \hat{S}_i$ is the ground truth.

Table 2. Results on Weibo and Twitter dataset.

Model	Weibo						Twitter					
	0.5 h		1 h		2 h		1 Day		2 Days		3 Days	
	MSLE	SMAPE	MSLE	SMAPE	MSLE	SMAPE	MSLE	SMAPE	MSLE	SMAPE	MSLE	SMAPE
Feature-Linear	3.025	0.305	2.653	0.323	2.451	0.332	9.123	0.698	6.729	0.632	5.833	0.602
Feature-Deep	2.891	0.281	2.612	0.319	2.332	0.311	7.801	0.669	6.330	0.599	5.439	0.574
DeepHawkes	2.674	0.277	2.538	0.303	2.312	0.302	6.874	0.635	5.085	0.545	4.281	0.463
CasCN	2.660	0.275	2.613	0.323	2.452	0.310	7.121	0.638	5.438	0.560	4.482	0.463
CasFlow	2.418	0.247	2.298	0.257	2.003	0.281	6.989	0.625	5.143	0.552	4.102	0.449
TempCas	2.332	0.243	2.219	0.248	2.001	0.278	6.232	0.611	4.332	0.525	3.680	0.455
CasSampling-Struct	2.553	0.246	2.483	0.283	2.339	0.307	7.329	0.667	5.773	0.591	4.681	0.483
CasSampling-St.ND	2.793	0.287	2.681	0.312	2.539	0.352	7.811	0.687	5.983	0.610	4.997	0.498
CasSampling-TimeFlow	2.388	0.244	2.241	0.248	2.021	0.281	6.322	0.602	4.349	0.521	3.757	0.457
CasSampling-NNT	2.311	0.244	2.178	0.247	1.988	**0.273**	6.198	0.599	4.298	0.516	3.658	0.451
CasSampling	**2.194**	**0.227**	**2.113**	**0.243**	**1.883**	0.276	**5.908**	**0.594**	**4.125**	**0.512**	**3.433**	**0.447**

Table 3. Computation cost on Weibo dataset with 1h observation time.

Models	Time cost			Parameter
	Preprocessing	Trainning	Inference	
DeepHawkes	~1 min	~40 min	323 samples/s	~103M
CasCN	~3 h	~2 h	158 samples/s	~210M
CasFlow	~28 min	~15 min	1432 samples/s	~11M
TempCas	~6 min	~13 min	1591 samples/s	~12M
CasSampling	~2 min	~5 min	6328 samples/s	~720K

5.4   Experiment Settings

Parameter Settings. For baselines, we follow the settings of their works. In our experiment, the maximum number of nodes in cascade graph K is set to 128. For local propagation embedding, CasSampling contains 2 layers of GAT, the hidden dimension feature is set to 512 and the output dimension of the node feature is set to 8. For the global propagation time flow, the number of time slots is set to 64. For the prediction layer, the number of neurons in each layer of the MLP is {64,32}. The optimizer is Adam with learning rate = 0.0001. We set the batch size as 64 and the training epochs as 50.

Experimental Environment. We ran the experiment on a PC with an AMD 5600X 3.70 Ghz, an NVIDIA GTX 3090 24 GB, and 64 GB memory. CasSampling was trained by using PyTorch 1.11.0.

6   Results and Analysis

In this section, we report experimental results and conduct further analysis.

6.1   Experiment Results

The experimental results are shown in Table 2. Our approach outperforms the baseline methods for all metrics. CasCN and DeepHawkes only focus on node-level modeling, which is inadequate for large graphs. CasFlow combines cascade graphs with a global social network for structure learning. However, the method above does not take into account the importance of time information, which may be the reason to limit their performance. TempCas implements a heuristic algorithm to sample critical paths, but compensates for structural losses using hand-crafted features without alignment with structural representation. Although it uses LSTM and attention CNN to model long-short term global propagation time information, the node-level time information is not integrated into the structure representation, which may result in poor integration between the structure embedding and the time-flow representation.

Our proposed CasSampling model beats all counterparts on all datasets. Compared with the classic models DeepHawkes and CasCN, our method has

Table 4. Effect of varying maximum number of node K on the performance of the model.

Model	Weibo Dataset								
	MSLE								
	0.5 h			1 h			2 h		
	K = 64	K = 128	K = 256	K = 64	K = 128	K = 256	K = 64	K = 128	K = 256
CasSampling-Struct	2.612	2.553	2.501	2.551	2.483	2.432	2.389	2.339	2.302
CasSampling	2.282	2.231	**2.228**	2.158	**2.113**	2.128	1.924	**1.883**	1.891

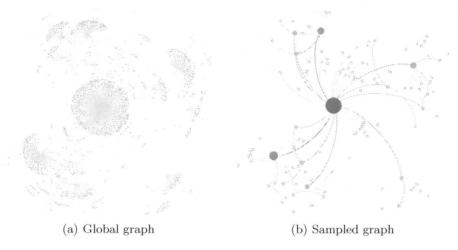

(a) Global graph   (b) Sampled graph

Fig. 4. An example of graph sampling. The left is the original global graph, which has over 3000 nodes. The right is the sampled graph, with colored edges and points being selected (The max number of node K is 128). The depth of color and the size of nodes indicate the activity of nodes, which is derived from the degree of sampling nodes in the global graph.

improved by 10%–25% on each evaluation metrics. Compared with the recent SOTA models (CasFlow, TempCas), our method also has improved by 5%–15% on MSLE. This shows that our method is significantly better than the baseline in information popularity prediction.

We compute the time cost and parameter for baselines and CasSampling, as shown in Table 3. It demonstrates that CasSampling is more efficient compared with all the SOTA baselines.

Table 4 illustrates the impact of different maximum node number of K on the model's performance. As K increases, we observe a consistent improvement in the performance of CasSampling-Struct, since a larger number of nodes leads to more temporal information being captured. However, the overall performance of the model is best at $K = 128$, indicating that an appropriate value of K can facilitate better capturing of cascading effects.

6.2   Ablation Study

To study the relative importance of each module in the CasSampling, we conduct ablation studies over the different parts of the model as follows:

– **CasSampling-Struct**. It only uses the local-level propagation embedding part to predict increment size.
– **CasSampling-St.ND**. It only uses the local-level propagation embedding part and removes the outdegree feature of node.
– **CasSampling-TimeFlow**. It only uses global-level time flow representation to predict increment size.

– **CasSampling-NNT**. It removed the attention aggregator module of node time information.

The results are shown in Table 2. **CasSampling-Struct** demonstrates that the sampled graph can still represent global propagation. Figure 4 is an example of graph sampling. The performance of **CasSampling-St.ND** decreases considerably, which shows that the importance of maintaining the outdegree of the node plays a great role in compensating for the graph structure. The performance of **CasSampling-NNT** is not as good as **CasSampling**, which proves that adding time information to nodes can make local-level propagation embedding better integrated with global-level time flow representation. **CasSampling-TimeFlow** shows an interesting result that only time information is better than most models, so we did a further analysis to explore the underlying reason.

6.3 Further Analysis

We select samples based on the average path length of the graph to further analysis the time-flow based method and graph-embedding based method.

We link the performance with the graph structure. Figure 5 indicates that CasSampling-TimeFlow's performance slightly decreases with longer average path lengths in the cascade graph, while CasSampling-Struct performs better under these conditions. This suggests that CasSampling-Struct can learn the intrinsic information of complex cascades, while CasSampling-TimeFlow cannot.

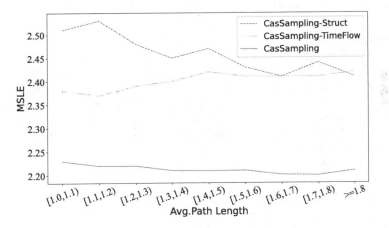

Fig. 5. The Relationship between performance and average path length of cascade graph.

7 Conclusion

We present CasSampling, a new deep learning framework for efficient popularity prediction. It captures cascade graph structure and leverages multi-scale time information. CasSampling consists of four main components: (1) a heuristic algorithm for sampling critical parts of a graph, (2) a local-level propagation embedding model that uses GAT and an attention aggregator to combine graph structure with node time information, (3) A global-level time flow representation using LSTM to capture propagation trends, and (4) a prediction layer that fusing local-level propagation and global-level time flow and feeds it into an MLP to predict the increment size. We conducted extensive experiments on Weibo and Twitter datasets, and achieved SOTA performance on information cascade size prediction with much less computation cost than the baselines.

Our future work mainly focuses on the following aspects: (1) Exploit a better strategy to sample graph. (2) Explore the relationship between structural information and temporal information, and better integrate each other.

Acknowledgments. The work was supported by National Natural Science Foundation of China (Grant Nos. 61966020, 61972186, U21B2027), Yunnan high-tech industry development project (Grant No. 201606), Yunnan provincial major science and technology special plan projects (Grant No. 202103AA080015, 202002AD080001-5), Yunnan Basic Research Project (Grant No. 202001AS070014), and Talents and Platform Program of Science and Technology of Yunnan (Grant No. 202105AC160018).

Ethical Statement. The purpose of this paper is to explore efficient and effective methods for learning cascade graphs for popularity prediction while adhering to academic integrity and research ethics requirements. We used publicly available data from social media datasets that have been authorized by Twitter and Weibo officials. To ensure the confidentiality of personal information, all data is anonymized and stored securely. We obtained approval and permission from the ethics committee of our institution to conduct this research.

The models and algorithms used in this study are based on publicly available data and previous research results, and we have thoroughly tested and verified them. We commit to conducting a transparent and fair evaluation of the algorithms and models used in this research, and we will present them fully in the paper.

Throughout this study, we will adhere to academic standards and ethical requirements, striving to avoid any behavior that may violate these requirements. We hope that this research will contribute to the development of cascade graph learning and popularity prediction, promoting further research in this area.

References

1. Mishra, S., Rizoiu, M.A., Xie, L.: Modeling popularity in asynchronous social media streams with recurrent neural networks. In: Twelfth International AAAI Conference on Web and Social Media (2018)

2. Li, G., Chen, S., Feng, J., Tan, K.l., Li, W.S.: Efficient location-aware influence maximization. In: Proceedings of the 2014 ACM SIGMOD International Conference on Management of Data, pp. 87–98 (2014)
3. Cao, Q., Shen, H., Cen, K., Ouyang, W., Cheng, X.: Deephawkes: bridging the gap between prediction and understanding of information cascades. In: Proceedings of the 2017 ACM on Conference on Information and Knowledge Management, pp. 1149–1158 (2017)
4. Chen, X., Zhou, F., Zhang, K., Trajcevski, G., Zhong, T., Zhang, F.: Information diffusion prediction via recurrent cascades convolution. In: 2019 IEEE 35th International Conference on Data Engineering (ICDE), pp. 770–781. IEEE (2019)
5. Tang, X., Liao, D., Huang, W., Xu, J., Zhu, L., Shen, M.: Fully exploiting cascade graphs for real-time forwarding prediction. In: Proceedings of the AAAI Conference on Artificial Intelligence, vol. 35, pp. 582–590 (2021)
6. Yuan, C., Li, J., Zhou, W., Lu, Y., Zhang, X., Hu, S.: DyHGCN: a dynamic heterogeneous graph convolutional network to learn users' dynamic preferences for information diffusion prediction. In: Hutter, F., Kersting, K., Lijffijt, J., Valera, I. (eds.) ECML PKDD 2020. LNCS (LNAI), vol. 12459, pp. 347–363. Springer, Cham (2021). https://doi.org/10.1007/978-3-030-67664-3_21
7. Cao, Q., Shen, H., Gao, J., Wei, B., Cheng, X.: Popularity prediction on social platforms with coupled graph neural networks. In: Proceedings of the 13th International Conference on Web Search and Data Mining, pp. 70–78 (2020)
8. Wu, Z., Zhou, J., Liu, L., Li, C., Gu, F.: Deep popularity prediction in multi-source cascade with HERI-GCN. In: 2022 IEEE 38th International Conference on Data Engineering (ICDE) (2022)
9. Weng, L., Menczer, F., Ahn, Y.Y.: Virality prediction and community structure in social networks. Sci. Rep. **3**(1), 1–6 (2013)
10. Cui, P., Jin, S., Yu, L., Wang, F., Zhu, W., Yang, S.: Cascading outbreak prediction in networks: a data-driven approach. In: Proceedings of the 19th ACM SIGKDD International Conference on Knowledge Discovery and Data Mining, pp. 901–909 (2013)
11. Ma, Z., Sun, A., Cong, G.: On predicting the popularity of newly emerging hashtags in twitter. J. Am. Soc. Inform. Sci. Technol. **64**(7), 1399–1410 (2013)
12. Petrovic, S., Osborne, M., Lavrenko, V.: Rt to win! predicting message propagation in twitter. In: Proceedings of the International AAAI Conference on Web and Social Media, vol. 5, pp. 586–589 (2011)
13. Shulman, B., Sharma, A., Cosley, D.: Predictability of popularity: gaps between prediction and understanding. In: Tenth International Conference on Web and Social Media (2016)
14. Bao, P., Shen, H.W., Huang, J., Cheng, X.Q.: Popularity prediction in microblogging network: a case study on Sina Weibo. In: Proceedings of the 22nd International Conference on World Wide Web, pp. 177–178 (2013)
15. Cheng, J., Adamic, L., Dow, P.A., Kleinberg, J.M., Leskovec, J.: Can cascades be predicted? In: Proceedings of the 23rd International Conference on World Wide Web, pp. 925–936 (2014)
16. Rizoiu, M.A., Xie, L., Sanner, S., Cebrian, M., Yu, H., Van Hentenryck, P.: Expecting to be hip: hawkes intensity processes for social media popularity. In: Proceedings of the 26th International Conference on World Wide Web, pp. 735–744 (2017)
17. Mishra, S., Rizoiu, M.A., Xie, L.: Feature driven and point process approaches for popularity prediction. In: Proceedings of the 25th ACM International on Conference on Information and Knowledge Management, pp. 1069–1078 (2016)

18. Shen, H., Wang, D., Song, C., Barabási, A.L.: Modeling and predicting popularity dynamics via reinforced poisson processes. In: Proceedings of the AAAI Conference on Artificial Intelligence, vol. 28 (2014)
19. Yang, S.H., Zha, H.: Mixture of mutually exciting processes for viral diffusion. In: International Conference on Machine Learning, pp. 1–9. PMLR (2013)
20. Xu, X., Zhou, F., Zhang, K., Liu, S., Trajcevski, G.: Casflow: exploring hierarchical structures and propagation uncertainty for cascade prediction. IEEE Trans. Knowl. Data Eng. (2021)
21. Xu, Z., Qian, M., Huang, X., Meng, J.: CasGCN: predicting future cascade growth based on information diffusion graph. arXiv preprint arXiv:2009.05152 (2020)
22. Liao, D., Xu, J., Li, G., Huang, W., Liu, W., Li, J.: Popularity prediction on online articles with deep fusion of temporal process and content features. In: Proceedings of the AAAI Conference on Artificial Intelligence, vol. 33, pp. 200–207 (2019)
23. Veličković, P., Cucurull, G., Casanova, A., Romero, A., Liò, P., Bengio, Y.: Graph attention networks. In: International Conference on Learning Representations (2018, accepted as poster). https://openreview.net/forum?id=rJXMpikCZ
24. Vaswani, A., et al.: Attention is all you need. In: Advances in Neural Information Processing Systems, vol. 30 (2017)
25. Chen, X., Zhang, F., Zhou, F., Bonsangue, M.: Multi-scale graph capsule with influence attention for information cascades prediction. Int. J. Intell. Syst. **37**(3), 2584–2611 (2022)

Boosting Adaptive Graph Augmented MLPs via Customized Knowledge Distillation

Shaowei Wei, Zhengwei Wu, Zhiqiang Zhang, and Jun Zhou[✉]

Ant Group, Hangzhou, China
{weishaowei.wsw,zejun.wzw,lingyao.zzq,jun.zhoujun}@antgroup.com

Abstract. While Graph Neural Networks (GNNs) have shown convinced performance on handling non-Euclidean network data, the high inference latency caused by message-passing mechanism hinders their deployment on real-time scenarios. One emerging inference acceleration approach is to distill knowledge derived from teacher GNNs into message-passing-free student multi-layer perceptrons (MLPs). Nevertheless, due to the graph heterophily causing performance degradation of teacher GNNs, as well as the unsatisfactory generalization ability of student MLPs on graph data, GNN-MLP like designs often achieve inferior performance. To tackle this challenge, we propose boosting adaptive **GR**aph **A**ugmented MLPs via **C**ustomized knowl**E**dge **D**istillation (GRACED), a novel approach to learn graph knowledge effectively and efficiently. Specifically, we first design a novel customized knowledge distillation strategy to modify the guided knowledge to mitigate the adverse influence of heterophily to student MLPs. Then, we introduce an adaptive graph propagation approach to precompute aggregation feature for node considering both of homophily and heterophily to boost the student MLPs for learning graph information. Furthermore, we design an aggregation feature approximation technique for inductive scenarios. Extensive experiments on node classification task and theoretical analyses demonstrate the superiority of GRACED by comparing with the state-of-the-art methods under both transductive and inductive settings across homophilic and heterophilic datasets.

Keywords: Graph learning · Inference acceleration · Knowledge distillation · Inductive learning

1 Introduction

Graph Neural Networks (GNNs) have shown remarkable effectiveness in processing non-Euclidean structural data and achieved enormous success in diverse

Supplementary Information The online version contains supplementary material available at https://doi.org/10.1007/978-3-031-43418-1_6.

graph mining tasks [5,22]. The achievement of current GNNs relies on the employment of message passing paradigm, which extracts graph information by propagating node feature on graph iteratively to learn node representation. However, the number of neighbor for each node would exponentially explodes as the time of feature propagation increases. Therefore, the time-consuming and computation-intensive problem caused by neighbor explosion severely hinders the deployment of GNNs for practical scenarios that have strict constraint on inference latency, especially for large-scale graphs.

Common inference acceleration techniques like hardware improvement [4, 10], pruning [31], quantization [29] and distillation [23] can accelerate GNNs to some extent by reducing Multiplication-and-ACcumulation (MAC) operations. Nevertheless, their improvements are limited, since they cannot completely get rid of time-consuming neighborhood fetching imposed by message passing.

Inspired by the promising effectiveness of MLP-like models in computer vision [12], graph-less neural networks (GLNN) [28] transfers the graph knowledge from GNNs to MLPs using knowledge distillation (KD) [7]. This idea combines the performance advantage of GNNs and the latency advantage of MLPs. Hence, the performance of deployed MLPs is improved while the fast inference speed of MLPs is retained without requiring explicit message passing.

GLNN has proved that KD can help MLP to find fitted parameters to bridge the gaps in model structure through transferring inductive bias of GNNs when node feature and topology are strongly correlated. However, common GNNs are built on the homophily assumption [14] that the edges with a higher tendency to connect nodes of same types. This assumption fails when meeting heterophilous graph data which results in GNNs underperforming corresponding graph-agnostic models [3,13,32]. Under the circumstances, simply transferring knowledge of teacher GNN that ignores this harmful heterophily would degrade distillation effectiveness.

On the other hand, we observe the performance of GLNN under inductive setting is closer to MLP that lack of utilization of graph structure information as present in Fig. 1. This can be explained by PMLP [24], which pinpoints the message passing mechanism inherently improves model's generalization capability for dealing with unobserved samples. Specifically, in transductive settings, since all node features and graph structures are available in training phase, student MLPs can memorize teachers' outputs on all nodes, which may lead to proper performance. However, in inductive setting, since test information is unseen in training phase, the lack of structure information limits the generalization of MLPs. Thus the structure information plays an important role to generalize knowledge learned from training set to test set. In summary, due to the neglect of harmful heterophily and lack of structure information, GLNN-like approaches are difficult to achieve satisfactory results, especially under the inductive setting.

To address above mentioned issues, we propose boosting adaptive **GR**aph **A**ugmented MLPs via **C**ustomized knowl**E**dge **D**istillation (GRACED), a novel approach to learn graph knowledge with effectiveness and efficiency. Specifically, to mitigate the heterophily problem, we first design a novel customized knowledge distillation approach that adaptively utilizes label information to modify

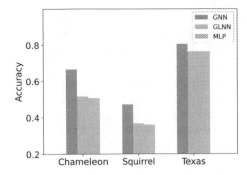

Fig. 1. Performance of GNN, GLNN and MLP on three webpage datasets under inductive setting.

the guided knowledge from teacher GNNs, and thereby mitigates the harmful influence of heterophily to student MLPs. To further improve the generalization capability of student MLPs, we introduce adaptive graph propagation (AGP) approach to precompute aggregation node feature considering both of homophily and heterophily in weighted manner. Hence student MLPs can fully capture graph structure information as well as node content information of different types of graphs. Finally, we introduce a method to approximate the aggregated node features to alleviate performance degradation caused by neighbor missing in inductive setting. In addition, we provide theoretical analyses on gradient perspective to facilitate a better understanding of the model. The core contributions of this work are summarized as follows:

(i) We design a customized knowledge distillation strategy that modifies the teacher's knowledge to mitigate the heterophily problem.
(ii) We introduce adaptive graph propagation which make MLPs capture structure information of homophilic graphs and heterophilic graphs to improve the model's generalization capability, especially under the inductive setting.
(iii) We propose a method to approximate the aggregated node features to alleviate performance degradation caused by neighbor missing in inductive setting.
(iv) Comprehensive experiments, including performance comparisons, sensitivity analyses, efficiency comparisons, ablation studies and online deployment demonstrate the superiority of GRACED.

2   Related Work

2.1   Inference Acceleration

Existing technical approaches for speeding up GNNs inference can be broadly divided into two categories: data reduction and model compression. Data reduction is to reduce the data scale. GraphSAINT [27] proposes an sampling algorithms for variance reduction. Further, it can decouple the sampling from the forward and backward propagation. Zhou *et al.* propose a pruning framework [31] via a novel LASSO regression formulation. LPGNAS is [29] a novel network architecture search (NAS) mechanism, constrains both architecture and quantisation choices to be differentiable. Both data reduction and model compression can not eliminate the latency to fetch neighbor. Concurrently, Graph-Augmented Multi-Layer Perceptrons (GA-MLPs) attempts to bypass GNN neighbor fetching [17] by decoupling the feature transformation and message propagation.

2.2 GNN Distillation

Most GNN knowledge distillation works attempt to distill large GNNs to smaller GNNs. LSP [26] conducts Knowledge distillation while preserving local information. GraphAKD [6] adversarially trains a discriminator and a generator to adaptively detect and decrease the discrepancy between teacher and student networks. GKD [25] proposes geometric knowledge distillation to transfer geometric knowledge from a teacher GNN to a student GNN. These GNN-GNN distillation designs still suffer from latency-inducing neighbor fetching. GLNN [28] distills GNN to MLP, which solves the neighbor fetching problem. Cold Brew [30] attempts to solve the cold start problem and noisy-neighbor challenges for GNNs. NOSMOG [20] learn Noise-robust and Structure-aware MLPs on graphs that considers position encoding, similarity distillation, and attribute augmentation.

2.3 GNN on Addressing Heterophily

Geom-GCN [15] precomputes unsupervised node embedding and utilizes graph structure defined by geometric relationships in the embedding space to execute the bi-level aggregation. FAGCN [1] learns edge-level attention scores as GAT [21] but allows the scores to be negative which enables the network to capture the high-frequency graph signals. GPRGNN [3]uses learnable weights that can be both positive and negative for message passing. Thus it is able to handle both homophily and heterophily of the graph. ACM-GNN [13] proposes an adaptive channel mixing framework to adaptively exploit aggregation, diversification and identity channels in each GNN layer to address heterophily. The inference speed of these models is normally slower than that of general GNNs due to the special design for heterophily.

3 Preliminaries

Notations. Consider an undirected graph $\mathcal{G} = (\mathcal{V}, \mathcal{E})$ with node set $\mathcal{V}$ and edge set $\mathcal{E} \subseteq \mathcal{V} \times \mathcal{V}$. $N = |\mathcal{V}|$ denotes the total number of nodes, assumed to be assigned to one of $C \geq 2$ classes. The initial nodes feature is represent by matrix $\mathbf{X} \in \mathbb{R}^{N \times d}$, where d stands for the number of features per node. The topological structure of $\mathcal{G}$ is described by the adjacency matrix $\mathbf{A} \in \mathbb{R}^{N \times N}$, in which $A_{u,v} = 1$ if edge$(u, v) \in \mathcal{E}$, otherwise $A_{u,v} = 0$. The diagonal degree matrix is denoted as $\mathbf{D}$. Let $\tilde{\mathbf{A}} = \mathbf{A} + \mathbf{I}$ and $\tilde{\mathbf{D}} = \mathbf{D} + \mathbf{I}$ denote the adjacency matrix and the degree matrix for a graph with added self-loops, respectively. Then

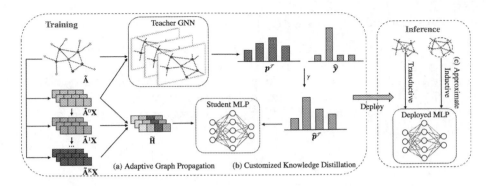

Fig. 2. The overall framework of GRACED: In training phase, a teacher GNN is trained on graph data for soft labels. Furthermore, GRACED modifies the obtained soft labels by customized knowledge distillation method. Then the aggregated node feature precomputed through adaptive graph propagation is used to train a student MLP, which is guided by the modified soft labels of teacher GNN. In inference phase, GRACED merely relies on the precomputed aggregated feature of node itself or its one-hop neighbors, and hence GRACED infers much faster than GNNs.

the symmetric normalized adjacency matrix with self-loops can be represent by $\tilde{\mathbf{A}}_{sym} = \tilde{\mathbf{D}}^{-1/2}\tilde{\mathbf{A}}\tilde{\mathbf{D}}^{-1/2}$.

Metric of Homophily. The metric of homophily is defined by considering the different correlation between node labels and graph structure described by adjacency matrix. Following work in [11], we calculate the homophily of graphs as:

$$Q(\mathcal{G}) = \frac{1}{C-1}\sum_{c=1}^{C}\max(Q_c - \frac{|\{v|\mathbf{Y}_{v,c}=1\}|}{N}, 0), \tag{1}$$

$$Q_c = \frac{\sum_{v\in\mathcal{V}}|\{u|\mathbf{Y}_{v,c}=1, u\in\mathcal{N}_v, \mathbf{Y}_{u,:}=\mathbf{Y}_{v,:}\}|}{\sum_{v\in\{v|\mathbf{Y}_{v,c}=1\}}|\mathcal{N}(v)|}, \tag{2}$$

where $Q(\mathcal{G}) \in [0, 1]$, which closes to 1 corresponds to strong homophily, while closes to 0 indicates strong heterophily. Q_c is the class-wise homophily metric. $\mathbf{Y} \in \mathbb{R}^{N\times C}$ denotes the label encoding matrix, whose v-th row $\mathbf{Y}_{v,:}$ is the one-hot encoding of the label of node v. $|\mathcal{N}(v)|$ is the degree of node v.

4 Methodology

The key idea of our approach is to solve the heterophily problem of teacher GNN and the generalization problem of student MLP on graph data. We explicitly boost the low-latency student MLP with a carefully designed distillation strategy and an innovative adaptive graph propagation method.

In this section, we introduce the proposed methodology in detail, along with its implementation. An overview of the proposal is depicted in Fig. 2.

4.1   Customized Knowledge Distillation

Training MLPs with the knowledge derived from fixed GNNs is a forthright idea as in GLNN [28]. Given the output generated by a cumbersome teacher GNN and the ground truth labels, the target is to learn a "boosted" student MLP. For a single sample, the objective function of the distillation process is weighted by distillation loss (corresponding to teacher output) and label supervised loss (corresponding to ground truth labels):

$$\mathcal{L} = (1 - \lambda)\mathcal{L}_{kd} + \lambda\mathcal{L}_{label}, \tag{3}$$

where λ is a trade-off hyper-parameter for balancing two loss terms.

Specifically, $\mathcal{L}_{kd}$ is the knowledge distillation loss between the classification probabilities $\mathbf{p}^{\mathcal{T},t}$ of teacher GNN $\mathcal{T}$ and that of student MLP $\mathcal{S}$ in temperature t. It is calculated by KL-divergence:

$$\mathcal{L}_{kd} = KL(\mathbf{p}^{\mathcal{T},t}||\mathbf{p}^{\mathcal{S},t}) = \sum_{i=1}^{C} p_i^{\mathcal{T},t} \log(\frac{p_i^{\mathcal{T},t}}{p_i^{\mathcal{S},t}}), \tag{4}$$

where

$$p_i^{\mathcal{S},t} = \frac{e^{z_i^{\mathcal{S}}/t}}{\sum_{c=1}^{C} e^{z_c^{\mathcal{S}}/t}}, \\ p_i^{\mathcal{T},t} = \frac{e^{z_i^{\mathcal{T}}/t}}{\sum_{c=1}^{C} e^{z_c^{\mathcal{T}}/t}}. \tag{5}$$

$\mathbf{z}^{\mathcal{T}}$ and $\mathbf{z}^{\mathcal{S}}$ are the output logits of teacher GNN and that of student MLP respectively.

The cross-entropy loss between the ground truth labels $\mathbf{y}$ and classification probabilities $\mathbf{p}^{\mathcal{S},1}$ of the student MLP is as following:

$$\mathcal{L}_{label} = CE(\mathbf{y}, \mathbf{p}^{\mathcal{S},1}) = - \sum_{i=1}^{C} y_i \log p_i^{\mathcal{S},1}. \tag{6}$$

However, this simple design does not consider that GNN can be affected by graph heterophily, resulting in unreasonable probabilities output, which is then transferred as injurious distillation knowledge, causing degradation of the student model performance. Therefore, how to avoid the adverse influence of heterophily while retaining the distillation effectiveness of teachers' knowledge is a significant challenge. Distinguishing from specific design on addressing heterophily, we start from the distillation task and propose customized knowledge distillation (CKD) to jointly utilize the ground truth labels and cross-entropy to modify the teacher's output, thereby improving the distillation effect.

Original ground truth labels are one-hot vectors, which take a value of 1 in the target dimension and 0 in other dimensions. This characteristic allows labels to only change the value of teacher's output on target dimension. To make modification effective for all dimensions, a simple idea is to assign a non-zero value to the dimension with value 0 in advance. Therefore, we introduce label smooth regularization (LSR) [19], a method proposed at first to encourage deep models to generalize and exploit inter-class information, to soften the ground truth one-hot labels. Considering a sample of class m with ground truth label distribution $\mathbf{y} = \delta(m)$, where $\delta(\cdot)$ is impulse signal, the LSR label is given as:

$$\hat{\mathbf{y}} = (1 - \epsilon)\delta(m) + \epsilon/C, \tag{7}$$

where ϵ is a hyper-parameter. Comparing with one-hot labels distribution, it gives a less confident probability (but still the most confident among all the classes) to the ground truth labels, and allocates the remainder of the probability equally to other classes. The obtained LSR labels is subsequently used to modify the output logits of teacher GNN.

Furthermore, we define a weight according to the teacher's cross entropy $CE^{\mathcal{T}}$ and the student's cross entropy $CE^{\mathcal{S}}$. The weight can be formulated as:

$$\gamma = 1 - \exp(-\frac{CE^{\mathcal{S}}}{CE^{\mathcal{T}}}),$$

$$CE^{\mathcal{S}} = -\sum_{i=1}^{C} y_i \log p_i^{\mathcal{S},1}, \tag{8}$$

$$CE^{\mathcal{T}} = -\sum_{i=1}^{C} y_i \log p_i^{\mathcal{T},1},$$

where $\gamma \in (0,1)$. Intuitively, the greater the cross entropy, the worse model is trained on the sample. Thus, when student MLP learns worse than teacher GNN, γ will become greater.

Then we use γ to weight the teacher's original classification probabilities and the LSR labels, and the modified probabilities is rewritten as:

$$\hat{p}_i^{\mathcal{T},l} = \gamma p_i^{\mathcal{T},t} + (1 - \gamma)\hat{y}_i. \tag{9}$$

The above equation means that a weighting factor is assigned to teacher's probabilities and LSR labels according to the discrepancy extent of the teacher and the student on sample i. When $\gamma = 1$, $\hat{\mathbf{p}}^{\mathcal{T}}$ degenerates into teacher's probabilities; when $\gamma = 0$ and $\epsilon = 0$, $\hat{\mathbf{p}}^{\mathcal{T}}$ degenerates into ground truth labels. In this way, if compared to the student, a teacher network is relatively worse trained on a sample, a smaller weight is assigned to teacher's probabilities.

We then substitute Eq. (9) into Eq. (4) to calculate the distillation loss. Hereto, we obtain a more powerful KD to transfer knowledge with less heterophily from the teacher GNN into the student MLP to achieve better performance.

Analysis of effectiveness of CKD. We attempt to analyze the gradient of KD loss $\mathcal{L}_{kd}$ to explain the effectiveness of CKD. Specifically, for any single sample, we compute the gradient of $\mathcal{L}_{kd}$ for its i-th output:

$$\frac{\partial \mathcal{L}_{kd}}{\partial z_i^S} = -\frac{\partial}{\partial z_i^S} \sum_{c=1}^{C} \hat{p}_c^{T,t} \log p_c^{S,t} = \frac{1}{t}(p_i^{S,t} - \hat{p}_i^{T,t})$$

$$= \frac{1}{t}(\frac{e^{z_i^S/t}}{\sum_{c=1}^{C} e^{z_c^S/t}} - \frac{e^{\hat{z}_i^T/t}}{\sum_{c=1}^{C} e^{\hat{z}_c^T/t}}). \tag{10}$$

Then the gradient of KD loss function for this sample should be:

$$\frac{\partial \mathcal{L}_{kd}}{\partial \mathbf{z}^S} = \frac{1}{t} \sum_{i=1}^{C} (p_i^{S,t} - \hat{p}_i^{T,t}) = \frac{1}{t} \sum_{i=1}^{C} (p_i^{S,t} - \gamma p_i^{T,t}) + (\gamma - 1). \tag{11}$$

As reflected in Eq. (11), when the teacher GNN predicts a sample with high heterophily, the cross entropy of the sample is greater than that with low heterophily. The weight γ decreases thereby, and then the teacher's output related information will play less important role in gradient computation.

4.2   Adaptive Graph Propagation

Though KD helps MLP to explore suitable parameters which can well approximate the prediction function from transferring inductive bias of GNNs [28] on training set, the generalization capability of student MLP on unseen samples is poor stemming from lack of graph information. Specifically, the input of MLP only contains node content features, while the input of GNN also contains both of node content features and topology information. This difference in input limits the expression and generalization ability of MLP on graph data [2,24]. In order for MLP to make full use of graph structure information without losing the advantage of inference efficiency, we attempt to augment node feature via computing propagation during preprocessing.

Generalized PageRank (GPR) [9] methods were first used in the context of unsupervised graph clustering, which is defined as follows:

$$\tilde{\mathbf{H}} = \sum_{k=0}^{\infty} \alpha_k \mathbf{H}^k,$$

$$\mathbf{H}^k = \tilde{\mathbf{A}}_{sym}^k \mathbf{X}, \tag{12}$$

where α_k is the weights of the k-th order convolution matrix. If we truncate the infinite sum in the definition of GPR at some natural number K, $\sum_{k=0}^{K} \alpha_k \tilde{\mathbf{A}}_{sym}^k$ corresponds to a polynomial graph filter of order K. Thus, learning the optimal GPR weights is equivalent to learning the optimal polynomial graph filter. Note that one can approximate any graph filter using a polynomial graph filter [18] and hence the GPR method is able to deal with different category of graph, including heterophilic graphs. However, Eq. (12) only considers the weights from the perspective of the base filter with different hops, which is too coarse for sundry and heterophilic node feature. Therefore, we explicitly model the weights for node features by introducing diagonal parameter matrices $\mathbf{B}_k$. Then we rewrite Eq. (12) as follows:

$$\tilde{\mathbf{H}} = \sum_{k=0}^{K} \alpha_k \mathbf{H}^k \mathbf{B}_k,$$

$$\mathbf{B}_k = diag(\beta_k^1, \beta_k^2, ..., \beta_k^d),$$

(13)

where $\mathbf{B}_k$ represents the weight of the features in the k-th basic propogation. It performs as a $1D$ convolution to reduce the number of input parameters to the subsequent student MLP, avoiding a multiplicative increase in the number of model parameters by a factor of N.

Before training the student MLP, we precompute the message propogation as:

$$\mathcal{X} = \{\mathbf{X}, \mathbf{H}^1, \mathbf{H}^2, ..., \mathbf{H}^K\}.$$

(14)

In this way, we can greatly reduce the time overhead caused by message propagation during training and inference phase. Subsequently, the graph augmented feature is decoded by MLP to obtain the output predictions. The parameters of MLP are trained together with α_k and $\mathbf{B}_k$ in an end-to-end fashion.

$$\mathbf{Z} = MLP(\tilde{\mathbf{H}}).$$

(15)

4.3 Approximate Aggregation Feature

In practical deployment, the model often conducts inference in inductive setting. For example, in recommendation scenario, one user is newly added who is unseen in train set and test set, and thereby has not precomputed aggregation feature. We should compute the aggregation feature for this user on existing user-item bipartite graph. However, the time cost grows exponentially with the number of hops is unacceptable under strict latency limitation in inference phase. As a result, we propose an approach to approximate K-hop node aggregation feature merely with linear time complexity.

Specifically, for a target node v to be predicted, we attempt to utilize precomputed feature in $\mathcal{X}$ of its neighbor $u \in \mathcal{N}(v)$ to represent approximate aggregation feature.

Firstly, we initialize $\overline{\mathbf{h}}_v^0$ and $\overline{\mathbf{h}}_u^0$ as node content feature:

$$\overline{\mathbf{h}}_v^0 = \mathbf{x}_v, \overline{\mathbf{h}}_u^0 = \mathbf{x}_u.$$

(16)

Then, the k-hop feature $\overline{\mathbf{h}}_v^k$ of v is aggregated in mean pooling manner:

$$\overline{\mathbf{h}}_v^k = \sum_{u \in \mathcal{N}(v)} \frac{1}{|\mathcal{N}(v)|} \overline{\mathbf{h}}_u^{k-1}.$$

(17)

The k-hop representation $\overline{\mathbf{h}}_u^k$ of u is approximate by $\overline{\mathbf{h}}'^k_u$:

$$\overline{\mathbf{h}}_u^k \approx \overline{\mathbf{h}}'^k_u = \frac{|\mathcal{N}(u)|}{|\mathcal{N}(u)| + 1}(\frac{l}{l+1})^{k-1}\mathbf{h}_u^k + \frac{1}{|\mathcal{N}(u)| + 1}\overline{\mathbf{h}}_v^{k-1}$$
$$+ \sum_{i=0}^{k-2}\frac{|\mathcal{N}(u)|}{|\mathcal{N}(u)| + 1}(\frac{l}{l+1})^i\frac{1}{l+1}\overline{\mathbf{h}}_v^{k-2-i}, \tag{18}$$

where l is a constant set manually. After replacing $\overline{\mathbf{h}}_u^k$ with $\overline{\mathbf{h}}'^k_u$, we can obtain the approximate aggregation feature $\{\overline{\mathbf{h}}_v^k\}_{k=0}^K$ of node v in time complexity $\mathcal{O}(|\mathcal{N}(v)|Kd)$ through alternately calculating Eq. (17) and Eq. (18).

Table 1. Statistics of used datasets.

Datasets	Homophily	#Nodes	#Edges	#Features	#Classes
Cora	0.766	2708	5429	1433	7
Citeseer	0.627	3327	4732	3703	6
Pubmed	0.664	19717	44338	500	3
Texas	0.001	183	309	1703	5
Chameleon	0.062	2277	36101	2325	5
Squirrel	0.025	5201	217073	2089	5

The error caused by approximation is bounded by:

$$||\overline{\mathbf{h}}_u^k - \overline{\mathbf{h}}'^k_u|| \leq \frac{|\mathcal{N}(u)|}{|\mathcal{N}(u)| + 1}$$
$$+ \frac{|\mathcal{N}(u)|}{|\mathcal{N}(u)| + 1}\sum_{i=0}^{k-2}[\frac{f^i}{2^i} + (\frac{l}{l+1})^i\frac{1}{l+1}], \tag{19}$$

where f is the max degree of neighbors of node v within K hop.

5   Experiments

5.1   Datasets

we evaluate the performance of our proposed GRACED on three benchmark homophilous graphs and three benchmark heterophilous graphs respectively. The statistics is as described in Table 1.

Homophilous Graphs. We choose the commonly used citation datasets, e.g., Cora, Citeseer and Pubmed as homophilous graphs. Edges in these networks represent the citation relationship between two papers, node features are the bag-of-words embedding of the papers and labels are the fields of papers. In each network, we use 20 labeled nodes per class for training, 500 nodes for validation and 1000 nodes for testing. More details can be found in [22].

Heterophilous Graphs. Texas is webpage graph from WebKB[1]. Chameleon and Squirrel are two Wikipedia networks[2]. Edges represent the hyperlinks between two pages, node features are some informative nouns in the pages and labels correspond to the traffic of the pages. We split labeled nodes into train/validation/test set according to ratio of 60%, 20% and 20% as Geom-GCN [15].

5.2   Experimental Setup

Baseline Methods. We choose three types of methods that are most relevant to our proposal as competitive baselines: neighbor-fetching free methods, i.e., MLP and GLNN [28]; Methods designed for heterophily, i.e., FAGCN [1], GPRGNN [3], Geom-GCN [15] and ACM-GCN [13]; distillation methods, i.e., the traditional logit-based knowledge distillation (KD) [7], the feature mimicking algorithm FitNet [16], the recent local structure preserving (LSP) method [26] and the adversarial knowledge distillation methods (GraphAKD) [6]. We also compare GRACED with classical GCN [22].

Parameter Settings. For all GNN-based methods, we set the number of layers as 2 or 3. The embedding size is fixed to 64 for all methods. For GLNN and GRACED, We choose classical GCN and ACM-GCN as teacher models for homophilic datasets and heterophilic datasets respectively. We optimize all methods using Adam [8] optimizer. The hyper-parameter search space is: learning rate $lr \in [0.005, 0.05]$, droupout rate $dp \in [0.5, 0.7]$, $\epsilon \in [0.1, 0.6]$, $\lambda \in [0.2, 0.8]$, and distillation temperature $t \in [10^{-2}, 10^{2}]$.

5.3   Node Classification on Different Types of Graph

To fully evaluate the model, we conduct node classification in two settings: transductive and inductive as in GLNN [28]. Table 2 and Table 3 show the transductive/inductive performance comparison between proposal and state-of-the-art competitors on node classification task. We run 10 times and report the mean accuracy with standard deviation.

From the transductive results, we observe that GRACED outperforms all comparing methods on 5/6 datasets. Specifically, MLP performs worst, because it merely encodes node context feature. Furthermore, GRACED outperforms GLNN due to additionally encode the structure information in an adaptive way. By combining customized knowledge distillation and adaptive graph propagation, our proposal can achieve outstanding performance on graph data.

---

[1]   http://www.cs.cmu.edu/afs/cs.cmu.edu/project/theo-11/www/wwkb.

[2]   https://github.com/benedekrozemberczki/datasets.

The results demonstrate the effectiveness of GRACED learning on both of homophilous graphs and heterophilous graphs.

Moreover, we also conduct comparison experiment under inductive setting as shown in Table 3. The performance of GLNN drops significantly, since the graph information learned in training set cannot be generalized to the test set. In contrast, GRACED still maintains competitive performance on most datasets, which proves the effectiveness of the approximate aggregation feature module.

5.4   Comparing with GNN Distillation Methods

To further demonstrate the effectiveness of GRACED, we compare the proposed framework with several GNN distillation methods and present comparisons in Table 4. Although the student model of these four compared distillation methods is GCN, which can better capture the graph structure information than MLP, our method still achieves competitive performance. That's because the precomputed adaptive graph propagation serves as message passing in GCN to boost generalization ability of MLP on graph data. As for distillation, these four comparison methods directly feed the teacher's output to the student, ignoring the heterophily problem, as we specially design a specialized strategy to elude heterophily. Therefore, GRACED is comparable to GNN distillation methods.

Table 2. Mean accuracy (%) with standard deviation on real world benchmark datasets under the transductive setting. Bold letters are used to mark the best results while underlined letters represent suboptimal results.

	Cora	Citeseer	Pubmed	Chameleon	Squirrel	Texas
MLP	58.89±1.32	60.58±0.60	70.07±0.63	50.81±1.91	35.98±1.60	76.49±4.37
GCN	81.25±0.63	72.06±0.61	78.88±0.31	63.46±2.06	46.39±2.25	59.19±4.65
GLNN	81.07±0.50	71.46±0.93	79.95 ± 0.42	57.04±2.26	43.37±1.68	81.62 ± 6.92
FAGCN	83.83 ± 0.59	72.37 ± 0.68	79.42±0.35	59.47±2.83	43.45±1.97	74.59±3.46
GPRGNN	81.33±0.52	71.77±0.82	79.83±0.38	62.59±2.04	46.31±2.46	81.35±5.32
Geom-GCN	73.22±0.34	58.45±1.01	71.86±0.66	60.00±2.81	38.15±0.92	66.76±2.72
ACM-GCN	79.75±1.13	69.04±1.21	77.01±0.49	68.15 ± 1.05	51.66± 1.29	81.35±5.60
OURS	83.99±0.45	72.56±0.69	81.07±0.47	68.44±1.56	49.88 ± 1.81	83.51±4.90

Table 3. Mean accuracy (%) with standard deviation on real world benchmark datasets under the inductive setting. Bold letters are used to mark the best results while underlined letters represent suboptimal results.

	Cora	Citeseer	Pubmed	Chameleon	Squirrel	Texas
MLP	58.89±1.32	60.58±0.60	70.07±0.63	50.81±1.91	35.98±1.60	76.49±4.37
GCN	77.72±1.36	68.17 ± 1.52	76.72 ± 0.79	62.46±1.86	44.87±2.13	60.00±7.03
GLNN	63.37±0.94	61.46±0.53	74.17±0.56	51.73±2.01	36.76±1.19	76.49±6.05
FAGCN	78.61 ± 2.41	66.27±2.23	76.49±0.65	59.14±2.53	41.37±1.87	77.54±3.02
GPRGNN	78.54±1.01	67.98±1.33	75.41±0.98	64.12±2.52	46.39±2.22	81.00 ± 4.75
Geom-GCN	24.60±3.49	42.44±1.40	59.26±3.24	61.04±1.99	46.36±1.49	66.22±8.04
ACM-GCN	74.28±0.97	65.06±1.42	74.38±0.70	66.51±1.92	47.18±2.08	80.54±3.15
OURS	78.77±1.02	68.18±2.09	77.70±0.53	65.99 ± 1.83	46.74 ± 2.17	81.89±3.91

5.5 Ablation Study

To evaluate the capability of designed modules, we conduct ablation experiment on the same six graph datasets. Specifically, we separately test each component to clarify the essential improvement. As present in Fig. 3, only employing KD or AGP is always inferior to teacher GNN. Through combining KD and AGP, we can obtain compared results. While we use CKD to further modify the output of teacher GNN that even is specifically designed to address heterophily, the performance can still be improved.

The fact that GRACED outperforms the variants demonstrates that each component can capture orthogonal and useful knowledge.

Table 4. Comparison results of GRACED and other GNN distillation methods.

	Cora	Citeseer	Pubmed
KD	83.2	71.4	80.3
FitNet	82.4	71.6	**81.3**
LSP	81.7	68.8	80.8
GraphAKD	83.6	**72.9**	**81.3**
GRACED	**84.0**	72.6	81.1

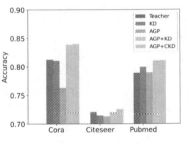
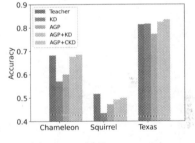

(a) Homophilous graphs.   (b) Heterophilous graphs.

Fig. 3. Performance of GRACED and its variants

5.6 Parameter Sensitivity Analysis

We further examine the effects of important hyper-parameters λ, ϵ and distillation temperature t on Citeseer and Squirrel.

As reflected in Fig. 4, for each parameter, increasing the value promotes the performance, but further increasing will degrade the performance. This indicates that selecting the suitable parameter will result in the optimal model performance.

5.7   Inference Acceleration and Practical Deployment

We finally verify the efficiency and effectiveness of GRACED on Pumbed and a real-world recommendation system. As shown in Table 5, GLNN infers as MLP and so is the fast method on Pumbed. The inference efficiency of GRACED is close to GLNN. Other GCN-like methods suffer from message passing and heterophily design, and thus are obviously slower than GLNN and GRACED.

We further train and deploy GCN, GLNN and GRACED on a real-world recommendation system from 2022-12 to 2023-01. Comparing with GCN, GLNN and GRACED still have obvious efficiency advantages in offline and online scenarios. Besides, the Click-Through-Rate(CTR) of GRACED has no statistical difference w.r.t GCN in online inference. Once we attempt to expand the traffic, GCN will encounter out of time(OOT) problem due to the limited online

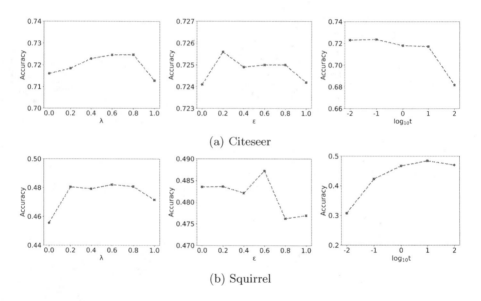

(a) Citeseer

(b) Squirrel

Fig. 4. Parameter analysis of λ, ϵ and t.

Table 5. Inference time of compared methods.

	Pubmed	Offline	Online
GCN	62.3 s	2025.7 s	40.2 ms
GLNN	**19.6 s**	**810.1 s**	**15.1 ms**
FAGCN	93.7 s	–	–
GPRGNN	54.5 s	–	–
Geom-GCN	>10 h	–	–
ACM-GCN	2366.1 s	–	–
GRACED	22.8 s	860.4 s	15.9 ms

resources of the inference service. Thus we merely observe the model performance at 5% traffic for the sake of fair comparison. In other word, GRACED still has advantages in large-scale inference scenarios.

6   Conclusion

In this paper, we present GRACED, a practical solution to address the deployment of GNNs via knowledge distillation and graph propagation. This is achieved by designing an customized knowledge distillation strategy and combining it with a novel adaptive graph propagation approach. We also design an approximation technique to deal with new nodes without precomputed aggregation feature in inductive setting. Experimental results on benchmark datasets confirm the effectiveness, efficiency and versatility of proposed GRACED. We will make further attempts to explore how to learn MLPs on graphs for link prediction task.

Ethical Statement. As machine learning and data mining researchers, we recognize the importance of ethical considerations in our work. The ethical implications of our research can have a significant impact on individuals, communities, and society as a whole. Therefore, we believe that it is our responsibility to carefully consider and address any ethical concerns that may arise from our work. We acknowledge that the collection and processing of personal data can have significant ethical implications. As such, we have taken steps to ensure that our research adheres to ethical guidelines and regulations. We have obtained all necessary permissions and have taken encryption measures to protect the privacy and confidentiality of any personal data used in our research. Additionally, we have implemented measures to ensure that any inferences made from data are transparent and are not used to perpetuate any forms of bias or discrimination. Our research aims to provide insights that are beneficial to society, while avoiding any potential negative impacts on individuals or communities. Our research does not relate to, nor collaborate with, the police or military. We believe that by addressing ethical concerns in our work, we can promote the responsible and beneficial use of machine learning and data mining technologies.

References

1. Bo, D., Wang, X., Shi, C., Shen, H.: Beyond low-frequency information in graph convolutional networks. In: AAAI (2021)
2. Chen, L., Chen, Z., Bruna, J.: On graph neural networks versus graph-augmented MLPs. In: ICLR (2021)
3. Chien, E., Peng, J., Li, P., Milenkovic, O.: Adaptive universal generalized pagerank graph neural network. In: ICLR (2021)
4. Geng, T., et al.: AWB-GCN: a graph convolutional network accelerator with runtime workload rebalancing. In: MICRO (2020)
5. Hamilton, W.L., Ying, Z., Leskovec, J.: Inductive representation learning on large graphs. In: NeurIPS (2017)
6. He, H., Wang, J., Zhang, Z., Wu, F.: Compressing deep graph neural networks via adversarial knowledge distillation. arXiv preprint: arXiv:2205.11678 (2022)

7. Hinton, G., Vinyals, O., Dean, J., et al.: Distilling the knowledge in a neural network. arXiv preprint: arXiv:1503.02531 (2015)
8. Kingma, D.P., Ba, J.: Adam: a method for stochastic optimization. arXiv preprint: arXiv:1412.6980 (2014)
9. Li, P., Chien, I., Milenkovic, O.: Optimizing generalized pagerank methods for seed-expansion community detection. In: NeurIPS (2019)
10. Liang, S., et al.: EnGN: a high-throughput and energy-efficient accelerator for large graph neural networks. IEEE Trans. Comput. **70**, 1511–1525 (2021)
11. Lim, D., Li, X., Hohne, F., Lim, S.: New benchmarks for learning on non-homophilous graphs (2021). https://arxiv.org/abs/2104.01404
12. Liu, H., Dai, Z., So, D.R., Le, Q.V.: Pay attention to MLPs. In: NeurIPS (2021)
13. Luan, S., Hua, C., Lu, Q., Zhu, J., Zhao, M., Zhang, S., Chang, X.W., Precup, D.: Is heterophily a real nightmare for graph neural networks to do node classification? arXiv preprint: arXiv:2109.05641 (2021)
14. McPherson, M., Smith-Lovin, L., Cook, J.M.: Birds of a feather: homophily in social networks. Ann. Rev. Sociol. **27**(1), 415–444 (2001)
15. Pei, H., Wei, B., Chang, K.C.C., Lei, Y., Yang, B.: Geom-GCN: geometric graph convolutional networks. In: ICLR (2019)
16. Romero, A., Ballas, N., Kahou, S.E., Chassang, A., Gatta, C., Bengio, Y.: FitNets: hints for thin deep nets. In: ICLR (2015)
17. Rossi, E., Frasca, F., Chamberlain, B., Eynard, D., Bronstein, M.M., Monti, F.: SIGN: scalable inception graph neural networks (2020). https://arxiv.org/abs/2004.11198
18. Shuman, D.I., Narang, S.K., Frossard, P., Ortega, A., Vandergheynst, P.: The emerging field of signal processing on graphs: extending high-dimensional data analysis to networks and other irregular domains. IEEE Sig. Process, Mag. **30**, 83–98 (2013)
19. Szegedy, C., Vanhoucke, V., Ioffe, S., Shlens, J., Wojna, Z.: Rethinking the inception architecture for computer vision. In: CVPR (2016)
20. Tian, Y., Zhang, C., Guo, Z., Zhang, X., Chawla, N.: Learning MLPs on graphs: a unified view of effectiveness, robustness, and efficiency. In: ICLR (2023)
21. Veličković, P., Cucurull, G., Casanova, A., Romero, A., Lio, P., Bengio, Y.: Graph attention networks. arXiv preprint: arXiv:1710.10903 (2017)
22. Welling, M., Kipf, T.N.: Semi-supervised classification with graph convolutional networks. In: ICLR (2016)
23. Yan, B., Wang, C., Guo, G., Lou, Y.: TinyGNN: learning efficient graph neural networks. In: KDD (2020)
24. Yang, C., Wu, Q., Wang, J., Yan, J.: Graph neural networks are inherently good generalizers: isights by bridging GNNs and MLPs. In: ICLR (2023)
25. Yang, C., Wu, Q., Yan, J.: Geometric knowledge distillation: topology compression for graph neural networks. In: NeurIPS (2023)
26. Yang, Y., Qiu, J., Song, M., Tao, D., Wang, X.: Distilling knowledge from graph convolutional networks. In: CVPR (2020)
27. Zeng, H., Zhou, H., Srivastava, A., Kannan, R., Prasanna, V.K.: Graphsaint: Graph sampling based inductive learning method. In: ICLR (2020)
28. Zhang, S., Liu, Y., Sun, Y., Shah, N.: Graph-less neural networks: teaching old MLPs new tricks via distillation. In: ICLR (2022)
29. Zhao, Y., Wang, D., Bates, D., Mullins, R.D., Jamnik, M., Liò, P.: Learned low precision graph neural networks (2020). https://arxiv.org/abs/2009.09232

30. Zheng, W., Huang, E.W., Rao, N., Katariya, S., Wang, Z., Subbian, K.: Cold brew: distilling graph node representations with incomplete or missing neighborhoods. In: ICLR (2022)

31. Zhou, H., Srivastava, A., Zeng, H., Kannan, R., Prasanna, V.: Accelerating large scale real-time GNN inference using channel pruning. VLDB (2021)

32. Zhu, J., Yan, Y., Zhao, L., Heimann, M., Akoglu, L., Koutra, D.: Beyond homophily in graph neural networks: current limitations and effective designs. In: NeurIPS (2020)

ENGAGE: Explanation Guided Data Augmentation for Graph Representation Learning

Yucheng Shi[1], Kaixiong Zhou[2], and Ninghao Liu[1(✉)]

[1] University of Georgia, Athens, GA 30602, USA
{yucheng.shi,ninghao.liu}@uga.edu
[2] Rice University, Houston, TX 77005, USA
kaixiong.zhou@rice.edu

Abstract. The recent contrastive learning methods, due to their effectiveness in representation learning, have been widely applied to modeling graph data. Random perturbation is widely used to build contrastive views for graph data, which however, could accidentally break graph structures and lead to suboptimal performance. In addition, graph data is usually highly abstract, so it is hard to extract intuitive meanings and design more informed augmentation schemes. Effective representations should preserve key characteristics in data and abandon superfluous information. In this paper, we propose ENGAGE (ExplaNation Guided data AuGmEntation), where explanation guides the contrastive augmentation process to preserve the key parts in graphs and explore removing superfluous information. Specifically, we design an efficient unsupervised explanation method called smoothed activation map as the indicator of node importance in representation learning. Then, we design two data augmentation schemes on graphs for perturbing structural and feature information, respectively. We also provide justification for the proposed method in the framework of information theories. Experiments of both graph-level and node-level tasks, on various model architectures and on different real-world graphs, are conducted to demonstrate the effectiveness and flexibility of ENGAGE. The code of ENGAGE can be found here (https://github.com/sycny/ENGAGE).

Keywords: Graph learning · Contrastive learning · Explainability

1 Introduction

Graph representation learning has been shown to be powerful in many graph analysis tasks [10,30,51,52,57]. In particular, unsupervised graph representation learning methods [16,21,23] have attracted substantial attention, as they are adaptive to various applications especially when labels are scarce. Among them, recently contrastive learning [35,57] has achieved superior performance by learning representations from contrastive views to reduce superfluous information. However, most existing works [2,3,52,57] simply apply random sampling for

© The Author(s), under exclusive license to Springer Nature Switzerland AG 2023
D. Koutra et al. (Eds.): ECML PKDD 2023, LNAI 14171, pp. 104–121, 2023.
https://doi.org/10.1007/978-3-031-43418-1_7

data augmentation, which could accidentally break the graph structures, thus reducing the effectiveness of representations. In other domains such as computer vision and natural language processing, more intelligent data augmentation methods have been proposed by leveraging the semantic information [22,35] or domain knowledge [4]. However, it is obscure to define and extract meaningful elements from abstract data types such as graphs. Also, the non-Euclidean property of graph increases the augmentation difficulty.

Some preliminary efforts have been made to tackle the problem. For example, Fang et al. [5] propose using knowledge graphs to augment the original input graph and help construct contrastive pairs, which is applicable to computational chemistry. However, a more common and intriguing problem is how to design intelligent augmentation without external information sources. In addition, Zhu et al. [58] apply centrality as the node importance indicator and encourage perturbing nodes of lower centrality. However, node centrality is a static metric and is not necessarily relevant to downstream tasks in all scenarios. Some work [11,51] design end-to-end frameworks to automatically formulate data augmentation policies, but they could induce high computational costs. Also, their black-box nature would fail to explicitly locate task-relevant information in graph data.

To solve the problem, this work proposes ENGAGE (ExplaNation Guided data AuGmEntation), where we use explanation to guide the generation of contrastive views for learning effective unsupervised representations on graph data. Specifically, we first propose a new explanation method called Smoothed Activation Map (SAM). Different from existing explanation methods that focus on understanding model predictions, SAM measures node importance based on the distribution of representations in the latent space. Then, with the node importance scores, we design an explanation guided graph augmentation method by perturbing edges and node features, which is used to construct paired graph views for contrastive learning. By leveraging explanations, significant graph structures are less likely to be damaged by accidents. Meanwhile, our SAM method is efficient by using the quantization technique [14], so that it can be applied into the training process. Finally, we conduct experiments on multiple datasets and tasks to demonstrate the effectiveness and flexibility of our proposed method. The contributions can be summarized as below:

- We propose the ENGAGE framework which leverages explanation to inform graph augmentation, and uses contrastive learning for training representations to preserve the key parts in graphs while removing uninformative artifacts.
- We propose a new efficient explanation method called SAM for unsupervised representation learning on graph data.
- We conduct comprehensive experiments on both node-level and graph-level classification tasks, with two representative contrastive learning models and different encoders, demonstrating the effectiveness and flexibility of ENGAGE.

2   Related Work

2.1   Representation Learning for Graph Data

Learning effective node or graph representations benefits various graph mining tasks. There are several major types of representation learning methods for graph data, including random-walk based methods [8,23,25,33], graph neural networks (GNNs) [7,9,37,38,43,44], and graph contrastive learning [2,32,46,57]. As the pioneering methodology of representation learning on graphs, random-walk based methods optimize node representations so that nodes within similar contexts tend to have similar representations. Then, graph neural networks become the new state-of-the-art architecture to process graph data. Finally, graph contrastive learning could be used to further refine the representation learning process with GNNs as the encoder.

2.2   Graph Contrastive Learning

Contrastive learning trains representations by maximizing the mutual information between different augmented views [2,3,12,34,38]. For example, GRACE [57] constructs the negative node examples by dropping edges and masking features, and employs a contrastive model similar to SimCLR [2]. GraphCL [52] perturbs graphs with four kinds of data augmentations on the graph level, and employs NT-Xent loss [2] for training. SimGRACE [46] gets rid of input data augmentation, and chooses to perturb model parameters. Data augmentation is vital for contrastive learning to achieve good performance on downstream tasks [22,35]. However, existing methods mainly rely on random perturbation, which could hurt graph information in the augmented views. To tackle the issue, Zhu et al. [58] propose to use node centrality as an importance indicator and perturb nodes with lower node centrality. Xu et al. [47] propose an information-aware representation learning model [36] to keep task-relevant information both in local and global views. Li et al. [17] propose a graph rationale guided data augmentation to better preserve semantic information. You et al. [51] design an end-to-end framework to automatically optimize data augmentation. However, it remains a challenge how to design data augmentation that is adaptive to different graph/node samples while keeping relatively low computing costs.

2.3   Explanation for Graph Neural Networks

Existing approaches for explaining GNN models can be divided into several categories [54], such as substitute-based, relevance-based, perturbation-based, generation-based, and rationale-based methods. Substitute-based methods approximate the original model with simplified but explainable substitutes, which either leverage GNN mechanisms [1,24,42] or bypass the model information [13,39,55]. Relevance-based methods compute input contributions by redistributing activations between neurons from the output layer to the input layer [24,27,28]. Perturbation-based methods [19,20,26,41,50] estimate input scores with the assumption that removing important features will have a large impact on the prediction. Generation-based methods produce synthetic graphs that maximally activate the target neuron [53]. Rationale-based methods find a small subgraph which best guides the model prediction as explanation [17,18,45]. Existing methods mainly focus on supervised graph learning models, while we attempt to obtain explanation for unsupervised graph learning. Meanwhile, we propose to leverage explanation for improving models, which further requires the explanation algorithm to be efficient.

3 Preliminaries

3.1 Notations

Let $G = \{\mathcal{V}, \mathcal{E}, \boldsymbol{A}, \boldsymbol{X}\}$ be a graph, where $\mathcal{V}$ and $\mathcal{E}$ denote the set of nodes and edges, respectively. $\boldsymbol{A} \in \{0,1\}^{|\mathcal{V}| \times |\mathcal{V}|}$ is the adjacency matrix. If node v_i and node v_j are connected, then $A_{ij} = 1$, where we use $e_{i,j}$ to denote that edge. $\boldsymbol{X} \in \mathbb{R}^{|\mathcal{V}| \times D}$ is the feature matrix and $\boldsymbol{x}_i = \boldsymbol{X}_{i,:}$ is the feature vector of node v_i. The GNN encoder is denoted as $f(\cdot)$, which transforms the nodes to representations $\boldsymbol{Z} = f(\boldsymbol{X}, \boldsymbol{A})$, $\boldsymbol{Z} \in \mathbb{R}^{|\mathcal{V}| \times K}$, where K is the latent dimension and $\boldsymbol{z}_i = \boldsymbol{Z}_{i,:}$ denotes the representation of node v_i. Meanwhile, we also consider graph-level tasks in this work. Let $\mathcal{G} = \{G_1, G_2, ..., G_N\}$ denote a set of graphs. In this case, the representation of a graph G_n is obtained as $\boldsymbol{z}_n = f(G_n)$, where $\boldsymbol{z}_n \in \mathbb{R}^K$. Our proposed method is applicable to both types of tasks. Unless otherwise stated, the methodology part in this paper assumes using graph-level tasks for illustration.

3.2 Contrastive Learning Frameworks

In this work, we adopt contrastive learning for learning node/graph representations. We consider two types of contrastive learning frameworks. The first type includes GraphCL [52] and GRACE [57] that are motivated by SimCLR [2] and learn to maximize the consistency between positive views compared with negative views. The second type is based on Simsiam [3] and could get rid of negative samples by using the stop gradient to prevent model collapse. We modify SimCLR and Simsiam frameworks to adapt to graph representation learning, and apply ENGAGE on both frameworks.

Learning Objectives. In contrastive learning, each instance is augmented into two *positive views* whose representations are $\boldsymbol{z}^1$ and $\boldsymbol{z}^2$, respectively. In SimCLR [2], the loss for learning the representation of i-th instance is:

$$\ell_i = -\log \frac{\exp\left(\text{sim}\left(\boldsymbol{z}_i^1, \boldsymbol{z}_i^2\right)/\tau\right)}{\sum_j \mathbb{1}_{[j \neq i]} \exp\left(\text{sim}\left(\boldsymbol{z}_i^+, \boldsymbol{z}_j\right)/\tau\right)}, \tag{1}$$

where z_i^+ refers to z_i^1 or z_i^2, and z_j denotes the embeddings of other instances as negative views. Positive views are expected to preserve the core information of the original instance, while negative views are expected to be irrelevant to the original instance. $\operatorname{sim}\left(z^1, z^2\right) = z^{1^T} z^2 / \|z^1\| \|z^2\|$. The Simsiam [3] model gets rid of the negative views, and its loss function is defined as below:

$$\ell_i = -(z_i^1 / \|z_i^1\|_2) \cdot (z_i^2 / \|z_i^2\|_2). \tag{2}$$

Encoder and MLP Heads. We use graph neural networks as the encoder $f(\cdot)$ to learn graph/node representations z. To comprehensively test our proposed framework, we apply several architectures, including graph convolutional networks (GCN) [15] and graph attention networks (GAT) [37] for node-level tasks. Also, we employ graph isomorphism networks (GIN) [48] for graph-level tasks. Then, the representations are fed into different MLP heads depending on the CL framework. In SimCLR, there is only one MLP head called $p_o(\cdot)$. In Simsiam, there are two MLP heads, namely $p_o(\cdot)$ and $p_e(\cdot)$.

4   The ENGAGE Framework

4.1   Mitigating Superfluous Information in Representations

We begin by introducing the guideline of minimizing superfluous information, which we will follow throughout this work, for learning effective and robust representations. Without loss of generality, we denote the original input and downstream task label as X and y, respectively.

Definition 1. *(Sufficiency) A representation z is defined as sufficient for label y iff $I(X; y) = I(z; y)$.*

An illustration of sufficient representation is shown in Fig. 3(a). To achieve good downstream task performance, it is encouraged to learn z from X without losing task-relevant information. Meanwhile, according to the information bottleneck principle [36], by reducing superfluous information from X, the sufficient representation z becomes more robust and gives better performance. This can be better understood by splitting the mutual information between X and z into two parts as below:

$$I(X; z) = \underbrace{I(X; z \mid y)}_{\text{superfluous information}} + \underbrace{I(z; y)}_{\text{task-relevant information}} . \tag{3}$$

The first term is the information in z that is not useful for predicting y, which should be minimized. The second term denotes the predictive information, which is not affected by the representation as long as z is sufficient for y.

Recent research shows contrastive learning (CL) can control the amount of information preserved in representations [35,40]. However, without label information, it is difficult to specify which part of input information to be preserved in CL. In this work, we utilize explanation to identify non-trivial structural information in graphs. Then, the information recommended by explanation is given higher priority to be preserved in representations, while other information is more likely to be discarded. This is done by using explanation, instead of random perturbation, to guide data augmentation in contrastive learning.

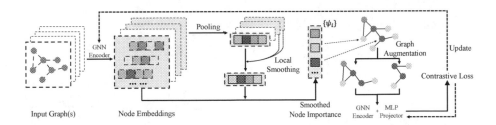

Fig. 1. Graph augmentation guided by Smoothed Activation Map (SAM) for contrastive learning.

4.2 Efficient Explanations for Unsupervised Representations

Class Activation Map. The goal of explanation is to identify the key components in input. We use GCN to illustrate the idea of explaining graph neural networks. A graph convolutional layer is defined as $F^l = \sigma(\tilde{D}^{-\frac{1}{2}}\tilde{A}\tilde{D}^{-\frac{1}{2}}F^{(l-1)}W^l)$, where F^l is output of l-th layer, $F^0 = X$, $\tilde{A} = A + I_N$ is the adjacency matrix with self-connections, and $\tilde{D}$ is the degree matrix of $\tilde{A}$. W^l denotes trainable weights, and $\sigma(\cdot)$ is the activation function. In supervised learning, the Class Activation Map (CAM) [24,56] can be used to compute the importance of node v_i as: $\psi_i^c = \text{ReLU}(\sum_k w_k^c F_{k,i}^L)$, where L is the final convolutional layer, and $F_{k,i}^l$ is the k-th latent dimension (i.e., channel) of node v_i at the l-th layer. w_k^c is the weight of channel k at the output layer towards predicting class c.

However, there are two challenges that impede us from directly applying CAM to our problem. First, CAM is designed for specific model architectures with a GCN and a fully-connected output layer (consisting of the w_k^c weights), where its applicability is limited. Second, CAM works for supervised models, while we focus on unsupervised learning.

Smoothed Activation Map. To tackle the challenges, we propose Smoothed Activation Map (SAM) to explain representations without class labels. The key idea is to leverage the distribution of graph/node representations to identify the locally important and reliable graph components, as shown in Fig. 2. Unlike CAM, our method works for different types of

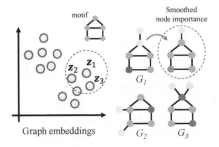

Fig. 2. Extracting reliable explanations via local smoothing.

Algorithm 1 SAM-based node importance estimation for graph-level tasks.

Input: Encoder $f(\cdot)$, the target graph $G_n = \{\mathcal{V}, \mathcal{E}, \boldsymbol{A}, \boldsymbol{X}\} \in \mathcal{G}$.

1: $\boldsymbol{Z} \leftarrow f(\boldsymbol{X}, \boldsymbol{A}); z \leftarrow \text{Pool}(\boldsymbol{Z});$ // $z \in \mathbb{R}^K$, the graph-level embedding of G_n
2: For G_n, find its m nearest-neighbor graphs $\tilde{\mathcal{N}}_n$ in the latent space;
3: $\tilde{w}_k^{graph} \leftarrow \text{Norm}(z + \sum_{n' \in \tilde{\mathcal{N}}_n} z_{n'})[k];$ // smoothed importance score
4: **for** $v_i \in G_n$ **do**
5:      $F_{k,i}^L \leftarrow \boldsymbol{Z}[i, k];$
6:      $\psi_i \leftarrow \text{ReLU}(\sum_k \tilde{w}_k^{graph(n)} F_{k,i}^L);$ // node importance score
7: **end for**

Output: Node importance scores $\{\psi_i\}$.

GNN models and does not require supervised signals. Without loss of generality, we write the feedforward process of GNNs as follows:

$$\boldsymbol{a}_i^l = \text{AGGREGATION}^l(\{F_{i'}^{(l-1)} : n' \in \mathcal{N}_i\}), \quad F_i^l = \text{COMBINE}^l(F_i^{(l-1)}, \boldsymbol{a}_i^l), \tag{4}$$

where F_i^l is the embedding of v_i at l-th layer. $\mathcal{N}_i$ denotes the neighbors of v_i. Then, the SAM heat-map is calculated as:

$$\psi_i = \text{ReLU}(\sum_k \tilde{w}_k F_{k,i}^L), \tag{5}$$

where ψ_i explains the importance score of v_i, $\tilde{w}_k$ is the smoothed importance of channel k, and L is the final layer. For graph-level tasks, the channel importance of graph G_n is estimated based on its local context, so $\tilde{w}_k^{graph(n)} = \text{Norm}(\sum_{n' \in \tilde{\mathcal{N}}_n} \text{Pool}\{F_{i'}^L : i' \in G_{n'}\})[k]$, where $\tilde{\mathcal{N}}_n$ denotes the set of neighbors graphs around G_n in the embedding space. The Pool() operation produces the heat-map of $G_{n'}$ from its nodes embeddings, where we use Average Pooling in experiments. The Norm() operation means performing L_2 normalization for heat-maps. The set $\tilde{\mathcal{N}}_n$ of neighbors can be retrieved efficiently by using quantization techniques [14]. For node-level tasks, the channel importance is estimated by averaging the heat-maps of nearby node embeddings, i.e., $\tilde{w}_k^{node(i)} = \text{Norm}(\sum_{i' \in \tilde{\mathcal{N}}_i} F_{i'}^L)[k]$, where $\tilde{\mathcal{N}}_i$ is the set of neighbors that are close to v_i in the embedding space. The explanation process is shown in Fig. 1.

Both $\tilde{w}_k^N$ and $\tilde{w}_k^G$ are estimated in unsupervised learning, and they play a similar role as w_k^c in CAM. By considering nearby nodes and graphs, explanation information of the target node/graph is smoothed. Another perspective to understand SAM is that it provides explanation not only for a single node or graph, but for a group of nodes or graphs in the local manifold region.

Finally, many explanation methods have been proposed for graph neural networks (e.g., perturbation-based, substitute-based, and generation-base methods), so we want to justify our selection of CAM-style explanation in this work. The main consideration is computational efficiency. The heat-maps in CAM-style methods are directly obtainable in the feedforward process of GNNs, requiring minimal additional computation. In contrast, both perturbation-based and substitute-based methods require sending a number of perturbed inputs to estimate the effect of different graph features, which leads to significantly greater time costs. Generation-based methods face the similar issue, as they require training a global explainer on a large number of graph samples.

4.3   Explanation-Guided Contrastive Views Generation

We design two data augmentation operations utilizing explanation results, where graph components highlighted by explanation are considered as important [22, 24]. The general idea is to keep important information intact, while maximally perturbing unimportant information.

Edge Perturbation. We define two masks $M^{\text{edge},1}, M^{\text{edge},2} \in \{0,1\}^{|\mathcal{V}| \times |\mathcal{V}|}$ to perturb edges and obtain different data views from the original graph. The adjacency matrix of the two new views are

$$A_1 = A \odot M^{\text{edge},1}, \ \ A_2 = A \odot M^{\text{edge},2}, \tag{6}$$

where $\odot$ denotes the Hadamard product. The masks are obtained based on the explanation results:

$$M_{i,j}^{\text{edge},1} = \begin{cases} 1, & \text{if } \phi_{i,j} > \theta_e \\ \text{Bernoulli}(\phi_{i,j}) & \text{if } \phi_{i,j} \le \theta_e \end{cases}, M_{i,j}^{\text{edge},2} = \begin{cases} 1, & \text{if } \phi_{i,j} > \theta_e \\ 1 - M_{i,j}^{\text{edge},1} & \text{if } \phi_{i,j} \le \theta_e \end{cases}, \tag{7}$$

where θ_e is a threshold, and $\phi_{i,j} = (\psi_i + \psi_j)/2$ is the edge importance between v_i and v_j. The edge importance averages the explanation scores of end nodes. The intuition of edge masking is that, with explanations, we want to maintain the important connections intact while perturbing the relatively unimportant part as much as possible. Based on the above definition, the two views are set to keep minimal mutual information while both contain task-relevant information. Here θ_e is a threshold that controls the degree of distinction between the two graph views. Empirically, we set $\theta_e = \mu_\phi + \lambda_e * \sigma_\phi$, where μ_ϕ and σ_ϕ are the mean value and standard deviation of all the edge interpretability from a graph or a batch of graphs. λ_e is the hyperparameter used to control the size of important part, because the range of importance scores can be different for different datasets.

Feature Perturbation. We also define two masks $M^{\text{feat},1}, M^{\text{feat},2} \in \{0,1\}^{|\mathcal{V}| \times D}$ to perturb node features. The feature matrix of the two views are

$$X_1 = X \odot M^{\text{feat},1}, \ \ X_2 = X \odot M^{\text{feat},2}. \tag{8}$$

The masks are obtained based on explanation results:

$$M_{i,d}^{\text{feat},1} = \begin{cases} 1, & \text{if } \psi_i > \theta_f \\ \text{Bernoulli}(\psi_i) & \text{if } \psi_i \le \theta_f, \end{cases}, M_{i,d}^{\text{feat},2} = \begin{cases} 1, & \text{if } \psi_i > \theta_f \\ 1 - M_i^{\text{feat},1} & \text{if } \psi_i \le \theta_f, \end{cases} \tag{9}$$

where θ_f is a threshold, and ψ_i is the explanation of node v_i. Similar to edge perturbation, we set the threshold as $\theta_f = \mu_\psi + \lambda_f * \sigma_\psi$, where μ_ψ and σ_ψ are the mean and standard deviation of node explanations from a graph or a batch of graphs. By this design, we can keep important information intact, while the features of unimportant nodes are more likely to be perturbed. Also, the two views are constructed in a way to reduce their mutual information $I(\boldsymbol{X}_1, \boldsymbol{X}_2)$.

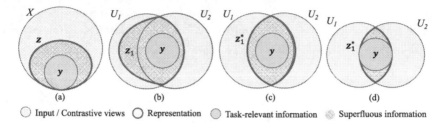

Fig. 3. Illustration of theoretical justification (best viewed in color): (a) z contains all task-relevant information and is a sufficient representation of X; (b) z_1 is a sufficient representation of U_1 containing task-relevant and non-shared information; (c)(d) z_1^* is the approximate minimal sufficient representation of U_1 that only includes shared information between U_1 and U_2.

4.4   Theoretical Justification

In this part, we theoretically justify the design of our explanation guided method for building the contrastive views. The original input is denoted as X, the positive pair containing two data views obtained through augmentation is $\{U_1, U_2\}$, and $\boldsymbol{y}$ is the downstream task label.

Definition 2. *(Redundancy) The view U_1 is redundant with respect to view U_2 for $\boldsymbol{y}$ iff $I(U_1; \boldsymbol{y}|U_2) = 0$.*

The intuition behind is that a view U_1 is redundant for the task if the information in $\boldsymbol{y}$ is already observed in U_2. Let z_1 and z_2 denote the representation of U_1 and U_2, respectively. When U_1 and U_2 are mutually redundant, if z_1 is sufficient for U_2 (refer to Definition 1 for "sufficiency"), then z_1 retains task-relevant information about $\boldsymbol{y}$, as shown in Fig. 3(b). The proofs for the above statements are provided in Appendix A[2].

The statements above suggest that, in contrastive learning, the task-relevance of the representations z_1 and z_2 depends on the quality of the constructed contrastive views U_1 and U_2, where it is crucial to keep important task-relevant information intact when building U_1 and U_2. However, in unsupervised learning, the task label is not accessible. Thus, our assumption in this work is that, the graph information important for z in unsupervised representation distribution

---

[2] The appendix file is provided here: https://github.com/sycny/ENGAGE.

could also be important for downstream tasks, and should be preserved in U_1 and U_2 with higher priority. This motivates the design of explanation guided contrastive views construction from Eq. 6–9, since graph components with high importance scores could be regarded as approximately preserving the key information of graphs. In addition, to mitigate noises in a single node/graph instance, our proposed SAM method gathers the explanatory information from the local context.

Definition 3. *(Sufficient Contrastive Representation) A representation z_1 of U_1 is sufficient for U_2 iff $I(z_1; U_2) = I(U_1; U_2)$.*

Definition 4. *(Minimal Sufficient Contrastive Representation) The sufficient contrastive representation z_1 of U_1 is defined as minimal iff $I(z_1; U_1) \leq I(z_1'; U_1)$, $\forall z_1'$ that is a sufficient contrastive representation.*

Let z_1^* denote the minimal sufficient contrastive representation learned from U_1. We can have $I(z_1^*; U_2) = I(U_1; U_2)$, which implies that the shared information $I(U_1; U_2)$ is retained in the contrastive representation while the non-shared information is ignored [6]. To obtain such representations, the encoder in contrastive learning is trained so that $z_1 \approx z_1^*$ and $z_2 \approx z_2^*$ (it also implies $I(z_1, z_2) \approx I(U_1, U_2)$) [40]. After encoding, the minimal sufficient representation z_1 (or z_2) is obtained from U_1 (or U_2), and is used for prediction in downstream tasks. An illustration of z_1^* is presented in Fig. 3(c). However, the representation may still contain a significant amount of superfluous information, which could degrade the downstream task performance.

Our design in Eq. 6–9 aims to address the above problem. In our ENGAGE method, when thresholds θ_e and θ_f are set higher in Eq. 6 and 8, more information in U_1 and U_2 is deleted, making $I(U_1, z_1 | y)$ further reduced after training for z_1. Thus, assuming $I(z; y)$ is untouched (i.e., U_1 and U_2 remain mutually redundant) by setting appropriate thresholds, our proposed method reduces $I(X; z)$ by suppressing the superfluous information contained in z, as depicted in Fig. 3(d). On the other hand, when θ_e and θ_f values are set smaller, we keep more information in z after contrastive learning.

5   Experiments

We answer the following research questions in experiments. **RQ1**: How effective is the proposed ENGAGE method in building contrastive views and learning graph representations? **RQ2**: How does the proposed method influence representation learning as indicated by explanations? **RQ3**: What is the effect of hyperparameters (e.g., λ_e and λ_f) on the proposed method?

5.1   Experimental Setup

We apply ENGAGE to contrastive learning models for both unsupervised graph-level and node-level classification tasks. For graph classification, we follow the

Table 1. Graph classification performance comparison.

Method	NCI1	PROTEINS	DD	PTC-MR	COLLAB	RDT-B	RDT-M5K	IMDB-B	A.R.
WL	80.01 ± 0.50	72.92 ± 0.56	74.02 ± 2.28	58.00 ± 0.50	69.30 ± 3.44	68.82 ± 0.41	46.06 ± 0.21	**72.30 ± 3.44**	9.62
DGK	**80.31 ± 0.46**	73.30 ± 0.82	74.85 ± 0.74	60.10 ± 2.60	64.66 ± 0.50	78.04 ± 0.39	41.27 ± 0.18	66.96 ± 0.56	9.88
node2vec	54.89 ± 1.61	57.49 ± 3.57	—	58.60 ± 8.00	56.10 ± 0.20	—	—	—	6.25
sub2vec	52.84 ± 1.47	53.03 ± 5.55	54.33 ± 2.44	60.00 ± 6.40	55.26 ± 1.54	71.48 ± 0.41	36.68 ± 0.42	55.26 ± 1.54	13.12
graph2vec	73.22 ± 1.81	73.30 ± 2.05	70.32 ± 2.32	60.20 ± 6.90	71.10 ± 0.54	75.78 ± 1.03	47.86 ± 0.26	71.10 ± 0.54	9.62
MVGRL	77.00 ± 0.80	—	—	62.50 ± 1.70	**76.00 ± 1.20**	84.50 ± 0.60	—	**74.20 ± 0.70**	3.12
InfoGraph	76.20 ± 1.06	74.44 ± 0.31	72.85 ± 1.78	**61.70 ± 1.40**	70.65 ± 1.13	82.50 ± 1.42	53.46 ± 1.03	**73.03 ± 0.87**	7.62
GraphCL	77.87 ± 0.41	74.39 ± 0.45	**78.62 ± 0.40**	61.30 ± 2.10	71.36 ± 1.15	**89.53 ± 0.84**	55.99 ± 0.28	71.14 ± 0.44	5.38
JOAO	78.07 ± 0.47	74.55 ± 0.41	77.32 ± 0.54	—	69.50 ± 0.36	85.29 ± 1.35	55.74 ± 0.63	70.21 ± 3.08	6.75
JOAOv2	78.36 ± 0.53	74.07 ± 1.10	77.40 ± 1.15	—	69.33 ± 0.34	86.42 ± 1.45	**56.03 ± 0.27**	70.83 ± 0.25	6.12
SimGRACE	79.12 ± 0.44	75.35 ± 0.09	77.44 ± 1.11	—	71.72 ± 0.82	**89.51 ± 0.89**	55.91 ± 0.34	71.30 ± 0.77	4.00
RD-SimCLR	79.02 ± 0.52	74.61 ± 0.56	77.40 ± 0.81	58.55 ± 2.01	69.32 ± 1.54	85.67 ± 5.40	55.52 ± 0.74	69.08 ± 2.47	8.00
EG-SimCLR	**82.97 ± 0.20**	75.44 ± 0.65	**78.86 ± 0.51**	61.51 ± 2.41	**76.60 ± 1.26**	**90.70 ± 0.46**	**56.22 ± 0.56**	71.78 ± 0.34	**2.12**
RD-Simsiam	79.62 ± 0.59	**75.42 ± 0.50**	77.20 ± 1.33	58.55 ± 1.85	66.50 ± 2.31	86.12 ± 1.80	54.30 ± 0.64	69.86 ± 0.86	7.88
EG-Simsiam	**81.49 ± 0.19**	76.06 ± 0.51	**78.35 ± 0.83**	**62.67 ± 1.50**	74.73 ± 0.79	89.17 ± 0.43	**56.37 ± 0.17**	71.93 ± 0.40	2.38

evaluation pipeline in [31] by training an SVM as the classifier. The whole dataset is used to learn graph-level representations, which are evaluated under the SVM classifier with cross-validation. Eight benchmark datasets are all selected from the TUDataset. We modify SimCLR and Simsiam to adapt to graph representation learning and select GIN [48] as the encoder network. Besides using contrastive learning models with random perturbation as baselines, we compare our proposed model with graph kernel methods like WL [29] and DGK [49]. We also choose state-of-the-art graph self-supervised learning methods including GraphCL [52], JOAO [51], JOAO(v2) [51], SimGRACE [46] and MVGRL [10].

For node classification, we follow [57] where the whole dataset is used to learn node representations, which are evaluated under a logistic regression classifier with cross-validation. Popular datasets like Cora and CiteSeer are selected, and other real-world datasets, including Wiki-CS, Amazon-Computers, and Amazon-Photo are also used. Similar to graph-level tasks, we modify SimCLR and Simsiam frameworks to adapt to node representation learning. Both GCN [15] and GAT [37] models are used as encoders. We also compare with other self-supervised learning models including GCA [58], MVGRL [10], DGI [38]. We evaluate model performance using the *accuracy* metric. For each model, we report mean accuracy and standard deviation of five runs. The '—' in Table 1 and Table 2 means that these results are not available in currently published papers. The implementation details of our experiments can be found in Appendix G.

5.2 Experiment Results and Comparisons

Table 1 lists the result for graph classification, where the top three results are highlighted in bold. The proposed ENGAGE models are abbreviated as EG-SimCLR and EG-Simsiam, corresponding to their vanilla versions RD-SimCLR and RD-Simsiam, respectively. The results show that the average ranks (A.R.) of EG-SimCLR and EG-Simsiam are highest as 2.12 and 2.38, respectively, compared with other state-of-the-art methods. Among them, NCI1 has the biggest improvement of 2.66% over the most competitive baselines. Most importantly,

Table 2. Node classification performance comparison.

Method	Cora	Citeseer	Wiki-CS	Amazon-Computers	Amazon-Photo	A.R
GCN	81.50 ± 0.00	70.30 ± 0.00	77.19 ± 0.12	86.51 ± 0.54	92.42 ± 0.22	11.6
GAT	83.00 ± 0.70	$\mathbf{72.50 \pm 0.70}$	77.65 ± 0.11	86.93 ± 0.29	92.56 ± 0.35	7.2
DeepWalk	70.70 ± 0.60	51.40 ± 0.50	77.21 ± 0.03	86.28 ± 0.07	90.05 ± 0.08	13.6
GAE	71.50 ± 0.40	65.80 ± 0.40	70.15 ± 0.01	85.27 ± 0.19	91.62 ± 0.13	13.6
DGI	82.30 ± 0.60	71.80 ± 0.70	75.35 ± 0.14	83.95 ± 0.47	91.61 ± 0.22	11.4
MVGRL	$\mathbf{86.80 \pm 0.50}$	$\mathbf{73.30 \pm 0.50}$	77.52 ± 0.08	87.52 ± 0.11	91.74 ± 0.07	6.8
GCA	—	—	78.35 ± 0.05	87.85 ± 0.31	92.53 ± 0.16	8.3
GRACE	82.01 ± 0.56	71.51 ± 0.33	$\mathbf{79.12 \pm 0.15}$	88.36 ± 0.18	92.52 ± 0.26	6.8
EG-SimCLR(GCN)	$\mathbf{84.07 \pm 0.18}$	72.40 ± 0.46	$\mathbf{79.21 \pm 0.12}$	$\mathbf{88.53 \pm 0.13}$	92.65 ± 0.19	**3.0**
GRACE(GAT)	83.57 ± 0.55	71.70 ± 0.55	78.48 ± 0.18	88.09 ± 0.15	$\mathbf{92.74 \pm 0.20}$	5.4
EG-SimCLR(GAT)	$\mathbf{83.78 \pm 0.53}$	72.28 ± 0.40	78.76 ± 0.07	$\mathbf{88.56 \pm 0.17}$	$\mathbf{92.97 \pm 0.07}$	3.2
RD-Simsiam(GCN)	82.65 ± 0.62	70.72 ± 0.64	78.79 ± 0.10	87.40 ± 0.31	92.53 ± 0.17	8.2
EG-Simsiam(GCN)	83.46 ± 0.56	71.49 ± 0.31	$\mathbf{79.27 \pm 0.34}$	$\mathbf{88.66 \pm 0.19}$	$\mathbf{92.77 \pm 0.14}$	3.4
RD-Simsiam(GAT)	80.31 ± 0.34	70.18 ± 0.54	78.61 ± 0.27	87.96 ± 0.27	92.63 ± 0.12	8.8
EG-Simsiam(GAT)	82.31 ± 0.43	70.73 ± 0.17	78.93 ± 0.20	88.28 ± 0.18	92.73 ± 0.28	6.0

ENGAGE methods consistently outperform random perturbation based models (e.g., RD-SimCLR and RD-Simsiam) on the eight datasets, with an average improvement of 2.90%. In addition, ENGAGE reduces performance variance compared with random perturbation, indicating that representation learning becomes more stable. These observations validate the effectiveness of using explanation toward a more adaptive and intelligent data augmentation scheme.

The result for the node classification is presented in Table 2 with the top three results highlighted. Our ENGAGE models are named as EG-SimCLR and EG-Simsiam, while their vanilla counterparts are GRACE [57] and RD-Simsiam, respectively. Many observations are similar to graph classification, such as improved performance and representation learning stability. In addition, we observe that ENGAGE works better for the GCN architecture than GAT. The reason could be that the attention mechanism in GAT already equips it with some abilities to select graph components during training. The proposed ENGAGE is compatible with various GNN backbones and contrastive learning models.

5.3   Ablation Study

We conduct ablation studies to further verify the effect of using SAM explanations for guiding graph representation learning, and the influence of hyperparameters.

Does ENGAGE Remove Redundant Information?   The explanation extracted from the model should become sparser as training goes on, since ENGAGE gradually removes superfluous information from representations. Thus, we define explanation *sparsity* [24,54] for graph G_n as $\mathcal{S}_n = 1 -$

$(\sum_{i=1}^{|\mathcal{V}_n|} \mathbb{1}[\psi_i > \mu_\psi])/|\mathcal{V}_n|$, where $|\mathcal{V}_n|$ is the number of nodes in G_n. ψ_i is the importance score of node v_i. μ_ψ is the mean importance score of all nodes in graphs $\mathcal{G}$. The changes of explanation sparsity on DD, PROTEINS, and RDT-B at different training iterations are shown in Fig. 4. We can observe that if we choose to perturb the original view radically ($\lambda_e = 2$, $\lambda_f = 2$), then sparsity tends to increase during the training process. In this mode, only the most crucial graph components will be kept, while other information will be discarded. If we perturb graphs softly ($\lambda_e = -2$, $\lambda_f = -2$), then the sparsity will remain stable or even decrease slightly, which means most of graph information is kept intact during training. We also provide visualization and quantitative analysis for explanation results of SAM in Appendix H and I, respectively.

Table 3. Effect of proposed SAM guided data augmentation.

Method	NCI1	PROTEINS	DD	PTC-MR	COLLAB	RDT-B	RDT-M5K	IMDB-B
RD-SimCLR	79.02 ± 0.52	74.61 ± 0.56	77.40 ± 0.81	58.55 ± 2.01	69.32 ± 1.54	85.67 ± 5.40	55.52 ± 0.74	69.08 ± 2.47
RD-Simsiam	79.62 ± 0.59	75.42 ± 0.50	77.20 ± 1.33	58.55 ± 1.85	66.50 ± 2.31	86.12 ± 1.80	54.30 ± 0.64	69.86 ± 0.86
HG-SimCLR	80.48 ± 0.44	74.93 ± 0.62	78.40 ± 0.69	56.62 ± 3.16	72.53 ± 0.97	89.92 ± 0.53	56.01 ± 0.25	69.88 ± 2.29
HG-Simsiam	80.70 ± 0.64	75.45 ± 0.72	77.87 ± 1.10	58.61 ± 1.99	72.84 ± 0.91	89.63 ± 0.55	55.92 ± 0.60	71.28 ± 0.82
EG-SimCLR	**82.97 ± 0.20**	75.44 ± 0.65	**78.86 ± 0.51**	61.51 ± 2.41	**76.60 ± 1.26**	**90.70 ± 0.46**	56.22 ± 0.56	71.78 ± 0.34
EG-Simsiam	81.49 ± 0.19	**76.06 ± 0.51**	78.35 ± 0.83	**62.67 ± 1.50**	74.73 ± 0.79	89.17 ± 0.43	**56.37 ± 0.17**	**71.93 ± 0.40**

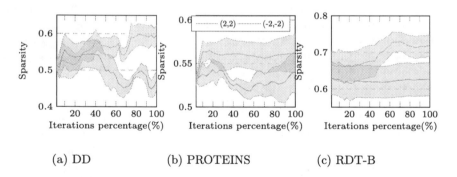

(a) DD   (b) PROTEINS   (c) RDT-B

Fig. 4. Evolution of explanation sparsity of three datasets during training.

SAM Guided Data Augmentation. We first compare our proposed EG-SimCLR, EG-Simsiam models with RD-SimCLR and RD-Simsiam using random perturbation. Besides that, we formulate two variants of our method, called HG-SimCLR and HG-Simsiam ("HG" refers to "heatmap guided"), which do not employ local smoothing to obtain explanations. The comparison is in Table 3. The result shows that the explanation guided models (HG and EG models) generally perform better than models with random data augmentation, which means the explanations can be successfully leveraged to improve representation learning with contrastive views. In addition, it can be observed that our proposed SAM-based methods consistently outperform other baselines, showing that local smoothing helps capture the important information more accurately.

Hyperparameter Analysis. We now explore the effect of different (λ_e, λ_f) combinations on model performance. We conduct a detailed study on 13 datasets, where λ_e and λ_f are changed, and all the other settings are the same. Larger λ means a greater portion of data is perturbed. The results of DD, PROTEINS, and RDT-B datasets are shown in Fig. 5. The results on other datasets are provided in Appendix C.

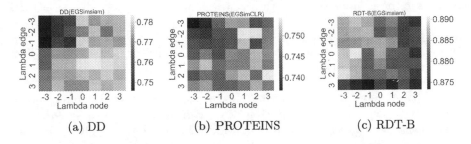

| (a) DD | (b) PROTEINS | (c) RDT-B |

Fig. 5. Model performances with different combinations of λ_e and λ_f.

Some observations are made as follows. First, the optimal data augmentation threshold varies for different datasets. For example, Fig. 5(a) and (c) show that DD benefits from more perturbation, but RDT-B does not. The reason could be that, without data augmentation and contrastive learning, the vanilla representations in different datasets contain different levels of superfluous information. Second, the sensitivity to λ_e and λ_f varies across different datasets. Here we define performance gap as the difference between the best accuracy and the worst one. For graph-level and node-level tasks, COLLAB and CiteSeer have a maximum performance gap of 9.55% and 2.45%, respectively, while the RDT-M5K and Amazon-Photo have a minimum performance gap of 0.97% and 0.23%. The possible reason could be that in some datasets, the task-relevant information is redundant, so it does not hurt performance when more graph components are removed. We thus benefit more from searching for the optimal hyperparameters for datasets like COLLAB and CiteSeer. Third, Simsiam-based models generally show better stability than SimCLR-based models. The average performance gap of Simsiam-based models is 3.39% and 0.75% in graph-level and node-level tasks, respectively. By comparison, the corresponding numbers are 3.96% and 1.08% for SimCLR ones.

6   Conclusion and Future Work

In this paper, we propose an explanation guided data augmentation methods for graph representation learning. First, we design a new explanation method for interpreting unsupervised graph learning models by leveraging the information shared by local embeddings. Then we propose guided data augmentation using explanation results. We will preserve the graph structure and features whose importance exceeds the importance threshold. For the other part, we try to keep the mutual information between two views as low as possible. The final results show that our proposed methods achieve superior performance on multiple datasets. The ablation study also shows that the optimal thresholds vary across different datasets, while a general random perturbing may hurt task performance. For future work, we will (1) design more faithful unsupervised GNN explanation methods; (2) design intelligent explanation guided augmentation methods for other applications with domain knowledge.

Acknowledgements. The work is in part supported by NSF grant IIS-2223768. The views and conclusions contained in this paper are those of the authors and should not be interpreted as representing any funding agencies.

Ethical Statement. Our team acknowledges the importance of ethical considerations in the development and deployment of our ENGAGE framework. We ensure that our work does not lead to any potential negative societal impacts. We only use existing datasets and cite the creators of those datasets to ensure they receive proper credit. Additionally, we do not allow our work to be used for policing or military purposes. We believe it is essential to prioritize ethical considerations in all aspects of machine learning and data mining to ensure that these technologies are used for the benefit of society as a whole.

References

1. Baldassarre, F., Azizpour, H.: Explainability techniques for graph convolutional networks. arXiv preprint: arXiv:1905.13686 (2019)
2. Chen, T., Kornblith, S., Norouzi, M., Hinton, G.: A simple framework for contrastive learning of visual representations. In: International Conference on Machine Learning, pp. 1597–1607. PMLR (2020)
3. Chen, X., He, K.: Exploring simple Siamese representation learning. In: Proceedings of the IEEE/CVF Conference on Computer Vision and Pattern Recognition, pp. 15750–15758 (2021)
4. Cheng, P., Hao, W., Yuan, S., Si, S., Carin, L.: FAIRFIL: contrastive neural debiasing method for pretrained text encoders. arXiv preprint: arXiv:2103.06413 (2021)
5. Fang, Y., et al.: Molecular contrastive learning with chemical element knowledge graph. arXiv preprint: arXiv:2112.00544 (2021)
6. Federici, M., Dutta, A., Forré, P., Kushman, N., Akata, Z.: Learning robust representations via multi-view information bottleneck. arXiv preprint: arXiv:2002.07017 (2020)
7. Gao, H., Ji, S.: Graph U-Nets. In: ICML, pp. 2083–2092. PMLR (2019)
8. Grover, A., Leskovec, J.: node2vec: scalable feature learning for networks. In: Proceedings of the 22nd ACM SIGKDD International Conference on Knowledge Discovery and Data Mining, pp. 855–864 (2016)
9. Hamilton, W., Ying, Z., Leskovec, J.: Inductive representation learning on large graphs. In: NeurIPS, pp. 1024–1034 (2017)
10. Hassani, K., Khasahmadi, A.H.: Contrastive multi-view representation learning on graphs. In: International Conference on Machine Learning, pp. 4116–4126. PMLR (2020)

11. Hassani, K., Khasahmadi, A.H.: Learning graph augmentations to learn graph representations. arXiv preprint: arXiv:2201.09830 (2022)
12. He, K., Fan, H., Wu, Y., Xie, S., Girshick, R.: Momentum contrast for unsupervised visual representation learning. In: Proceedings of the IEEE/CVF Conference on Computer Vision and Pattern Recognition, pp. 9729–9738 (2020)
13. Huang, Q., Yamada, M., Tian, Y., Singh, D., Yin, D., Chang, Y.: GraphLIME: local interpretable model explanations for graph neural networks. arXiv preprint: arXiv:2001.06216 (2020)
14. Johnson, J., Douze, M., Jégou, H.: Billion-scale similarity search with GPUs. IEEE Trans. Big Data **7**(3), 535–547 (2019)
15. Kipf, T.N., Welling, M.: Semi-supervised classification with graph convolutional networks. arXiv preprint: arXiv:1609.02907 (2016)
16. Kipf, T.N., Welling, M.: Variational graph auto-encoders. arXiv preprint: arXiv:1611.07308 (2016)
17. Li, S., Wang, X., Zhang, A., Wu, Y.X., He, X., Chua, T.S.: Let invariant rationale discovery inspire graph contrastive learning. In: ICML (2022)
18. Liu, G., Zhao, T., Xu, J., Luo, T., Jiang, M.: Graph rationalization with environment-based augmentations. arXiv:abs/2206.02886 (2022)
19. Lucic, A., Ter Hoeve, M., Tolomei, G., de Rijke, M., Silvestri, F.: CF-GNNExplainer: counterfactual explanations for graph neural networks. arXiv preprint: arXiv:2102.03322 (2021)
20. Luo, D., et al.: Parameterized explainer for graph neural network. In: Advances in neural information processing systems, vol. 33, pp. 19620–19631 (2020)
21. Pan, S., Hu, R., Long, G., Jiang, J., Yao, L., Zhang, C.: Adversarially regularized graph autoencoder for graph embedding. arXiv preprint: arXiv:1802.04407 (2018)
22. Peng, X., Wang, K., Zhu, Z., You, Y.: Crafting better contrastive views for Siamese representation learning. arXiv preprint: arXiv:2202.03278 (2022)
23. Perozzi, B., Al-Rfou, R., Skiena, S.: DeepWalk: online learning of social representations. In: Proceedings of the 20th ACM SIGKDD International Conference on Knowledge Discovery and Data Mining, pp. 701–710 (2014)
24. Pope, P.E., Kolouri, S., Rostami, M., Martin, C.E., Hoffmann, H.: Explainability methods for graph convolutional neural networks. In: Proceedings of the IEEE/CVF Conference on Computer Vision and Pattern Recognition, pp. 10772–10781 (2019)
25. Qiu, J., Dong, Y., Ma, H., Li, J., Wang, K., Tang, J.: Network embedding as matrix factorization: unifying DeepWalk, LINE, PTE, and node2vec. In: Proceedings of the Eleventh ACM International Conference on Web Search and Data Mining, pp. 459–467 (2018)
26. Schlichtkrull, M.S., De Cao, N., Titov, I.: Interpreting graph neural networks for nlp with differentiable edge masking. arXiv preprint: arXiv:2010.00577 (2020)
27. Schnake, T., et al.: XAI for graphs: explaining graph neural network predictions by identifying relevant walks. arXiv preprint: arXiv:2006.03589 (2020)
28. Schwarzenberg, R., Hübner, M., Harbecke, D., Alt, C., Hennig, L.: Layerwise relevance visualization in convolutional text graph classifiers. arXiv preprint: arXiv:1909.10911 (2019)
29. Shervashidze, N., Schweitzer, P., Van Leeuwen, E.J., Mehlhorn, K., Borgwardt, K.M.: Weisfeiler-lehman graph kernels. J. Mach. Learn. Res. **12**(9) (2011)
30. Shi, Y., et al.: Chatgraph: interpretable text classification by converting ChatGPT knowledge to graphs. arXiv preprint: arXiv:2305.03513 (2023)

31. Sun, F.Y., Hoffmann, J., Verma, V., Tang, J.: InfoGraph: unsupervised and semi-supervised graph-level representation learning via mutual information maximization. arXiv preprint: arXiv:1908.01000 (2019)

32. Tan, Q., et al.: S2GAE: self-supervised graph autoencoders are generalizable learners with graph masking. In: Proceedings of the Sixteenth ACM International Conference on Web Search and Data Mining, pp. 787–795 (2023)

33. Tang, J., Qu, M., Wang, M., Zhang, M., Yan, J., Mei, Q.: Line: large-scale information network embedding. In: Proceedings of the 24th International Conference on World Wide Web, pp. 1067–1077 (2015)

34. Tian, Y., Krishnan, D., Isola, P.: Contrastive multiview coding. In: Vedaldi, A., Bischof, H., Brox, T., Frahm, J.-M. (eds.) ECCV 2020. LNCS, vol. 12356, pp. 776–794. Springer, Cham (2020). https://doi.org/10.1007/978-3-030-58621-8_45

35. Tian, Y., Sun, C., Poole, B., Krishnan, D., Schmid, C., Isola, P.: What makes for good views for contrastive learning? In: Advances in Neural Information Processing Systems, vol. 33, pp. 6827–6839 (2020)

36. Tishby, N., Pereira, F.C., Bialek, W.: The information bottleneck method. arXiv preprint: arXiv:physics/0004057 (2000)

37. Veličković, P., Cucurull, G., Casanova, A., Romero, A., Liò, P., Bengio, Y.: Graph attention networks. In: ICLR (2018)

38. Veličković, P., Fedus, W., Hamilton, W.L., Liò, P., Bengio, Y., Hjelm, R.D.: Deep graph infomax. arXiv preprint: arXiv:1809.10341 (2018)

39. Vu, M.N., Thai, M.T.: PGM-explainer: probabilistic graphical model explanations for graph neural networks. arXiv preprint: arXiv:2010.05788 (2020)

40. Wang, H., Guo, X., Deng, Z.H., Lu, Y.: Rethinking minimal sufficient representation in contrastive learning. arXiv preprint: arXiv:2203.07004 (2022)

41. Wang, X., Wu, Y., Zhang, A., He, X., Seng Chua, T.: Causal screening to interpret graph neural networks (2021)

42. Wiltschko, A.B., et al.: Evaluating attribution for graph neural networks (2020)

43. Wu, F., Souza, A., Zhang, T., Fifty, C., Yu, T., Weinberger, K.: Simplifying graph convolutional networks. In: ICML, pp. 6861–6871. PMLR (2019)

44. Wu, X., Zhou, K., Sun, M., Wang, X., Liu, N.: A survey of graph prompting methods: techniques, applications, and challenges. arXiv preprint: arXiv:2303.07275 (2023)

45. Wu, Y., Wang, X., Zhang, A., He, X., Chua, T.S.: Discovering invariant rationales for graph neural networks. In: International Conference on Learning Representations (2022)

46. Xia, J., Wu, L., Chen, J., Hu, B., Li, S.Z.: SimGRACE: a simple framework for graph contrastive learning without data augmentation. arXiv preprint: arXiv:2202.03104 (2022)

47. Xu, D., Cheng, W., Luo, D., Chen, H., Zhang, X.: InfoGCL: information-aware graph contrastive learning. In: Advances in Neural Information Processing Systems, vol. 34 (2021)

48. Xu, K., Hu, W., Leskovec, J., Jegelka, S.: How powerful are graph neural networks? arXiv preprint: arXiv:1810.00826 (2018)

49. Yanardag, P., Vishwanathan, S.: Deep graph kernels. In: Proceedings of the 21th ACM SIGKDD International Conference on Knowledge Discovery and Data Mining, pp. 1365–1374 (2015)

50. Ying, Z., Bourgeois, D., You, J., Zitnik, M., Leskovec, J.: GNNExplainer: generating explanations for graph neural networks. In: Advances in Neural Information Processing Systems, vol. 32 (2019)

51. You, Y., Chen, T., Shen, Y., Wang, Z.: Graph contrastive learning automated. In: International Conference on Machine Learning, pp. 12121–12132. PMLR (2021)
52. You, Y., Chen, T., Sui, Y., Chen, T., Wang, Z., Shen, Y.: Graph contrastive learning with augmentations. In: Advances in Neural Information Processing Systems, vol. 33, pp. 5812–5823 (2020)
53. Yuan, H., Tang, J., Hu, X., Ji, S.: XGNN: towards model-level explanations of graph neural networks. In: Proceedings of the 26th ACM SIGKDD International Conference on Knowledge Discovery & Data Mining, pp. 430–438 (2020)
54. Yuan, H., Yu, H., Gui, S., Ji, S.: Explainability in graph neural networks: a taxonomic survey. arXiv preprint: arXiv:2012.15445 (2020)
55. Zhang, Y., Defazio, D., Ramesh, A.: Relex: a model-agnostic relational model explainer. arXiv preprint: arXiv:2006.00305 (2020)
56. Zhou, B., Khosla, A., Lapedriza, A., Oliva, A., Torralba, A.: Learning deep features for discriminative localization. In: Proceedings of the IEEE Conference on Computer Vision and Pattern Recognition, pp. 2921–2929 (2016)
57. Zhu, Y., Xu, Y., Yu, F., Liu, Q., Wu, S., Wang, L.: Deep graph contrastive representation learning. arXiv preprint: arXiv:2006.04131 (2020)
58. Zhu, Y., Xu, Y., Yu, F., Liu, Q., Wu, S., Wang, L.: Graph contrastive learning with adaptive augmentation. In: Proceedings of the Web Conference 2021, pp. 2069–2080 (2021)

Modeling Graphs Beyond Hyperbolic: Graph Neural Networks in Symmetric Positive Definite Matrices

Wei Zhao[1,2(✉)], Federico Lopez[1], J. Maxwell Riestenberg[2], Michael Strube[1], Diaaeldin Taha[2], and Steve Trettel[3]

[1] Heidelberg Institute for Theoretical Studies, Heidelberg, Germany
{Wei.Zhao,Federico.Lopez,Michael.Strube}@h-its.org
[2] Heidelberg University, Heidelberg, Germany
{mriestenberg,dtaha}@mathi.uni-heidelberg.de
[3] University of San Francisco, San Francisco, USA
strettel@usfca.edu

Abstract. Recent research has shown that alignment between the structure of graph data and the geometry of an embedding space is crucial for learning high-quality representations of the data. The uniform geometry of Euclidean and hyperbolic spaces allows for representing graphs with uniform geometric and topological features, such as grids and hierarchies, with minimal distortion. However, real-world graph data is characterized by multiple types of geometric and topological features, necessitating more sophisticated geometric embedding spaces. In this work, we utilize the Riemannian symmetric space of symmetric positive definite matrices (SPD) to construct graph neural networks that can robustly handle complex graphs. To do this, we develop an innovative library that leverages the SPD gyrocalculus tools [26] to implement the building blocks of five popular graph neural networks in SPD. Experimental results demonstrate that our graph neural networks in SPD substantially outperform their counterparts in Euclidean and hyperbolic spaces, as well as the Cartesian product thereof, on complex graphs for node and graph classification tasks. We release the library and datasets at https://github.com/andyweizhao/SPD4GNNs.

Keywords: Graph Neural Networks · Riemannian Geometry · Symmetric Space · Space of Symmetric Positive Definite Matrices

1 Introduction

Complex structures are a common feature in real-world graph data, where the graphs often contain a large number of connected subgraphs of varying topologies (including grids, trees, and combinations thereof). While accommodating the

---

F. Lopez and D. Taha—These authors contributed equally to this work.

© The Author(s), under exclusive license to Springer Nature Switzerland AG 2023
D. Koutra et al. (Eds.): ECML PKDD 2023, LNAI 14171, pp. 122–139, 2023.
https://doi.org/10.1007/978-3-031-43418-1_8

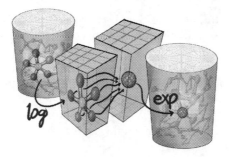

Fig. 1. Propagation schema for utilizing SPD geometry while performing calculations in the tangent (Euclidean) space: starting from an SPD embedding, map a node and its neighbors to the tangent space via the logarithm, and perform a modified Euclidean aggregation (Table 1) before returning to SPD via the Riemannian exponential map.

diversity of such graphs is necessary for robust representation learning, neither Euclidean nor hyperbolic geometry alone has been sufficient [23].

This inefficiency stems from geometric reasons. Properties of the embedding space strongly control which graph topologies embed with low distortion, with simple geometries selecting only narrow classes of graphs. Euclidean geometry provides the foundational example, where its abundant families of equidistant lines allow for efficient representation of grid-like structures, but its polynomial volume growth is too slow to accommodate tree-like data. This is somewhat ameliorated by moving to higher dimensions (with faster polynomial volume growth), though with a serious trade-off in efficiency [4]. An alternative is to move to hyperbolic geometry, where volume growth is exponential, providing plenty of room for branches to spread out for the isometric embedding of trees [7,35]. However, hyperbolic geometry has a complementary trade-off: it does not contain equidistant lines, which makes it unfit for embedding the grid-like structures Euclidean space excelled at [8].

Many proposed graph neural networks utilize representations of graph data to perform machine learning tasks in various graph domains, such as social networks, biology and molecules [2,11,13,14,22,31,32,37]. A subset of these networks take seriously the constraints of geometry on representation capability, and work to match various non-Euclidean geometries to common structures seen in graph data. For instance, Chami et al. [11] and Defferrard et al. [13] show that constructing graph neural networks in hyperbolic and spherical spaces have been successful in embedding graphs with hierarchical and cyclical structures, respectively. However, the relative geometric simplicity of these spaces poses serious limitations including (a) the need to know the graph structure prior to choosing the embedding space, and (b) the inability to perform effectively with graphs built of geometrically distinct sub-structures, a common feature of real-world data.

Avoiding these limitations may necessitate resorting to more complex geometric spaces. For example, Gu et al. [18] employed Cartesian products of various geometric spaces to represent graphs with mixed geometric structures. But any such choice must be carefully considered: isometries play an essential role in the construction of the above architectures, and any increase in complexity accompanied by too great a decrease in symmetry may render a space computationally intractable.

Riemannian symmetric spaces, which have a rich geometry encompassing all the aforementioned spaces, strike an effective balance between geometric generality and ample symmetry. Lopez et al. [25] proposed particular symmetric spaces, namely Siegel spaces, for graph embedding tasks, and demonstrated that many different classes of graphs embed in these spaces with low distortion. Lopez et al. [26] suggested utilizing the symmetric space SPD of symmetric positive definite matrices that is less computationally expensive than Siegel spaces. Furthermore, they developed gyrocalculus tools that enable "vector space operations" on SPD.

Here we extend the idea of Lopez et al. [26] to construct graph neural networks in SPD, particularly by utilizing their gyrocalculus tools to implement the building blocks of graph neural networks in SPD (Fig. 1). The building blocks include (a) feature transformation via isometry maps, (b) propagation via graph convolution in the tangent space of SPD (the space of symmetric matrices S_n), (c) bias addition via gyrocalculus, (d) non-linearity acting on eigenspace, and (e) three classification layers. We develop *SPD4GNNs*, an innovative library that showcases training five popular graph neural networks in SPD_n, alongside the functionality for training them in Euclidean and hyperbolic spaces.

We perform experiments to compare four ambient geometries (Euclidean, hyperbolic, products thereof, and SPD) across popular graph neural networks, evaluated on the node and graph classification tasks on nine datasets with varying complexities. Results show that constructing graph neural networks in SPD space leads to big improvements in accuracy over Euclidean and hyperbolic spaces on complex graphs, at the cost of doubling (resp. quadrupling) the training time of graph neural networks compared to hyperbolic space (resp. Euclidean space).

Finally, we provide a summary of the numerical issues we encountered and the solutions to addressing them (see Appendix F).

2   Related Work

Graph Neural Networks. Graph neural networks (GNNs) have been profiled as the de facto solutions for learning graph embeddings [2,14,22,31,37,38]. These networks can be differentiated into two dimensions: (a) how they propagate information over graph nodes and (b) which geometric space they use to embed the nodes. In **Euclidean space**, a class of GNNs has been proposed that represents graph nodes in a flat space and propagates information via graph convolution in various forms, such as using Chebyshev polynomial filters [12,22], high-order filters [38], importance sampling [19], attention mechanisms [37], graph-isomorphism designs [2,32,39], and differential equations [14,16,31]. In contrast, **non-Euclidean spaces** have a richer structure for representing geometric graph structures in curved spaces. Recently, there has been a line of GNNs developed in these spaces that performs graph convolution on different Riemannian manifolds in order to accommodate various graph structures, such as hyperbolic space on tree-like graphs [11,24,40], spherical space on spherical graphs [13], and Cartesian products of thereof [18].

SPD *Space.* Representing data with SPD matrices has been researched for many years, with the representations being primarily in the form of covariance matrices [9,15,17,21,42]. These matrices capture the statistical dependencies between Euclidean features. Recent research focused on designing the building blocks of neural networks in the space of covariance matrices. This includes feature transformation that maps Euclidean features to covariance matrices via geodesic Gaussian kernels [6,15], nonlinearity on the eigenvalues of covariance matrices [21], convolution through SPD filters [42] and Fréchet mean [9], Riemannian recurrent networks [10], and Riemannian batch normalization [5].

Nguyen et al. [29] recently approached hand gesture classification by embedding graphs into SPD via a neural network. The architectures we consider here are different. While we alternate between SPD and its tangent space using the exponential and logarithm maps, Nguyen et al. [29] do so via an aggregation operation and the log map. Further, we couple this alternation with our building blocks to operate graph neural networks in SPD.

3   Background

3.1   The Space SPD

We let SPD_n denote the space of positive definite real symmetric $n \times n$ matrices. This space has the structure of a Riemannian manifold of non-positive curvature of $n(n+1)/2$ dimensions. The tangent space to any point of SPD_n can be identified with the vector space S_n of all real symmetric $n \times n$ matrices. SPD_n is more flexible than Euclidean or hyperbolic geometries, or products thereof. In particular, it contains n-dimensional Euclidean subspaces, $(n-1)$-dimensional hyperbolic subspaces, products of $\lfloor \frac{n}{2} \rfloor$ hyperbolic planes, and many other interesting spaces as totally geodesic submanifolds; see the reference [20] for an in-depth introduction to these well-known facts. While it is not yet fully understood how our proposed models leverage the Euclidean and hyperbolic subspaces in SPD_n, we hypothesize that the presence of these subspaces is an important factor in the superior performance of SPD_n graph neural networks. Refer to Fig. 2 for a demonstration of how this hypothesis may manifest.

Riemannian Exponential and Logarithmic Maps. For SPD_n, the Riemannian exponential map at the basepoint I_n agrees with the standard matrix exponential $\exp \colon S_n \to \mathrm{SPD}_n$. This map is a diffeomorphism with inverse the matrix logarithm $\log \colon \mathrm{SPD}_n \to S_n$. These maps allow us to pass from SPD_n to S_n and back again. Given any two points $X, Y \in \mathrm{SPD}_n$, there exists an isometry (i.e., a distance-preserving transformation) that maps X to Y. As such, the choice of a basepoint for the exponential and logarithm maps is arbitrary since any other point can be mapped to the basepoint by an isometry. In particular, there is no loss of generality with fixing the basepoint I_n as we do.

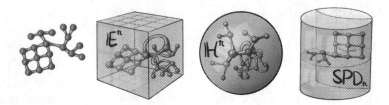

Fig. 2. Graphs exhibiting both euclidean/grid-like and hyperbolic/tree-like features (left) cannot embed well in either euclidean or hyperbolic spaces due to the impossibility of isometrically embedding trees in Euclidean spaces and grids in hyperbolic spaces (center). However, SPD_n (right) contains both euclidean and hyperbolic subspaces, which allows embedding a broad class of graphs, including the example in the figure.

Non-linear Activation Functions in SPD_n. We use two non-linear functions on SPD matrices, namely (i) ReEig [21]: factorizing a point $P \in \mathrm{SPD}_n$ and then employing the ReLU-like non-linear activation function φ_a to suppress the positive eigenvalues that are bigger than 0.5 [1]:

$$\varphi^{\mathrm{SPD}}(P) = U\varphi_a(\Sigma)U^T \qquad P = U\Sigma U^T \qquad (1)$$

(ii) TgReEig: projecting $P \in \mathrm{SPD}_n$ into the tangent space and then suppressing the negative eigenvalues of the projected point $\in S_n$ with the ReLU non-linear activation function φ_b, i.e. $\varphi^{\mathrm{SPD}}(P) = U\exp(\varphi_b(\log(\Sigma)))U^T$.

3.2 Gyrocalculus on SPD

Addition and Subtraction. Gyro-calculus is a way of expressing natural analogues of vector space operations in Riemannian manifolds. Following Lopez et al. [26], given two points $P, Q \in \mathrm{SPD}_n$, we denote gyro-addition and gyro-inversion by:

$$P \oplus Q = \sqrt{P}Q\sqrt{P} \qquad \ominus P = P^{-1} \qquad (2)$$

For $P, Q \in \mathrm{SPD}_n$, the value $P \oplus Q \in \mathrm{SPD}_n$ is the result of applying the SPD_n-translation moving the basepoint I_n to P, evaluated on Q.

Isometry Maps. Any invertible $n \times n$ real matrix $M \in \mathrm{GL}(n, \mathbb{R})$ defines an isometry of SPD_n by

$$M \odot P = MPM^T \qquad (3)$$

where $P \in \mathrm{SPD}_n$.

Lopez et al. [26] proposed defining M in two forms, namely a rotation element in $SO(n)$ and a reflection element in $O(n)$. In this case, the choice of rotation and reflection becomes a hyperparameter for M, and that needs to be selected before training. In contrast, the form of M we considered is more flexible and can be automatically adjusted by training data. To do so, we first let M denote the

---

[1] TgReEig equals ReEig in the case of $\varphi_a(x) = \max(x, 1)$.

orthogonal basis of a learnable square matrix, and then tune the square matrix from training data. Thus, M, as an orthogonal matrix that extends rotations and reflections, is better suited to fit the complexity of graph data.

Table 1. Comparison of operations in different spaces across three graph neural networks, i.e., GCN [22], GAT [37] and 1-order Cheb [12]. SGC [38] and GIN [39] are presented in Appendix B, which indeed apply propagation before feature transformation.

Operations	GNNs	Euclidean Space	Hyperbolic and SPD Space
Feature Trans	All	$h_i^l = W^l x_i^{l-1}$	$Q_i^l = M^l \odot Z_i^{l-1}$
Propagation	GCN	$p_i^l = \sum_{j \in \mathcal{N}(i)} k_{i,j} h_j^l$	$P_i^l = \exp(\sum_{j \in \mathcal{N}(i)} k_{i,j} \log(Q_j^l))$
	GAT	$p_i^l = \alpha_{i,i} h_i^l + \sum_{j \in \mathcal{N}(i)} \alpha_{i,j} h_j^l$	$P_i^l = \exp(\alpha_{i,i} \log(Q_i) + \sum_{j \in \mathcal{N}(i)} \alpha_{i,j} \log(Q_j^l))$
	Cheb	$p_i^l = h_i^l + W^l \sum_{j \in \mathcal{N}(i)} k_{i,j} h_j^l$	$P_i^l = Q_i^l \oplus (M^l \odot \exp(\sum_{j \in \mathcal{N}(i)} k_{i,j} \log Z_j^{l-1}))$
Bias&Nonlin	All	$x_i^l = \varphi(p_i^l + b^l)$	$Z_i^l = \varphi(P_i^l \oplus B^l)$

4 Graph Neural Networks

In this section, we introduce the notation and building blocks of graph neural networks using graph convolutional network (GCN) [22] as an example, and present modifications for operating these building blocks in SPD. Table 1 establishes parallels between five popular graph neural networks in Euclidean, hyperbolic and SPD spaces.

4.1 GCN in Euclidean Space

Given a graph $\mathcal{G} = (\mathcal{V}, \mathcal{E})$ with a vertex set $\mathcal{V}$ and an edge set $\mathcal{E}$, we define d-dimensional input node features $(x_i^0)_{i \in \mathcal{V}}$, where the superscript 0 indicates the first layer. The goal of a graph neural network is to learn a mapping denoted by:

$$f : (\mathcal{V}, \mathcal{E}, (x_i^0)_{i \in \mathcal{V}}) \to \mathcal{Z} \in \mathbb{R}^{|\mathcal{V}| \times d}$$

where $\mathcal{Z}$ is the space of node embeddings obtained from the final layer of GCN, which we take as the input of classification layer to perform downstream tasks.

Let $\mathcal{N}(i) = \{j : (i,j) \in \mathcal{E}\} \cup \{i\}$ be the set of neighbors of $i \in \mathcal{V}$ with self-loops, and (W^l, b^l) be a matrix of weights and a vector of bias parameters at layer l, and $\varphi(\cdot)$ be a non-linear activation function. We now introduce **message passing**, which consists of the following three components for exchanging information between the node i and its neighbors at layer l:

$$h_i^l = W^l x_i^{l-1} \qquad \text{Feature transform} \qquad (4)$$

$$p_i^l = \sum_{j \in \mathcal{N}(i)} k_{i,j} h_j^l \qquad \text{Propagation} \qquad (5)$$

$$x_i^l = \varphi(p_i^l + b^l) \qquad \text{Bias \&Nonlinearity} \qquad (6)$$

where $k_{i,j} = c_i^{-\frac{1}{2}} c_j^{-\frac{1}{2}}$ with c_i as the cardinality of $\mathcal{N}(i)$. $k_{i,j}$ represents the relative importance of the node j to the node i.

4.2   GCN in SPD

Mapping from Euclidean to SPD space. Oftentimes, input node features are not given in SPD, but in Euclidean space $(x_i^0)_{i \in \mathcal{V}} \in \mathbb{R}^d$. Therefore, we design a transformation that maps Euclidean features to a point in SPD. To do so, we first learn a linear map that transforms the d-dimensional input features into a vector of dimension $n(n+1)/2$, that we arrange as the upper triangle of an initially zero matrix $A \in \mathbb{R}^{n \times n}$. We then define a symmetric matrix $U \in S_n$ such that $U = A + A^T$. We now apply the exponential map such that $Z = \exp(U)$, which moves the coordinates from the tangent space S_n to the original manifold SPD_n. Thus, the resulting node embeddings $(Z_i^0)_{i \in \mathcal{V}}$ are in SPD_n. By performing this mapping only once, we enable GNNs to operate in SPD_n.

Feature Transform. We apply isometry maps to transform points in SPD at different layers, denoted by: $Q_i^l = M^l \odot Z_i^{l-1}$, where $Q_i^l, Z_i^{l-1} \in \mathrm{SPD}_n$ and M^l is a isometry map (see §3.2) at layer l of the GNN.

Propagation. This step aggregates information from all the neighbors $\mathcal{N}(i)$ of a given node i, with the information weighted by the importance of a neighbor to the node i (see Eq. 5). We note that propagation involves addition and scaling operators. This results in two alternative approaches for computing propagation: (a) employing gyro-addition to aggregate information over the neighbors for each node; (b) computing the Riemannian Fréchet mean in SPD_n—which requires hundreds of iterations to find a geometric center. Therefore, these approaches are costly to compute and also involve the use of cumbersome Riemannian optimization algorithms (see Appendix A for optimization). Here we perform aggregation via graph convolution in the space of symmetric matrices S_n denoted by: $P_i^l = \exp(\sum_{j \in \mathcal{N}(i)} k_{i,j} \log(Q_j^l))$, where $P_i^l \in \mathrm{SPD}_n$ and $k_{i,j} = c_i^{-\frac{1}{2}} c_j^{-\frac{1}{2}}$ (as in the Euclidean case). This is similar to the approach of Chami et al. [11] by performing propagation in the tangent pace and the posterior projection through the exponential map.

Bias Addition and Non-linearity. Finally, we add the bias B^l at layer l to the result of propagation through gyro-addition followed by applying a non-linear function, denoted by: $Z_i^l = \varphi^{\mathrm{SPD}}(P_i^l \oplus B^l)$, with $Z_i^l \in \mathrm{SPD}_n$ as the new embedding for the node i at layer l and $B^l \in \mathrm{SPD}_n$.

Message Passing in SPD. We establish a one-to-one correspondence between the Euclidean and SPD versions of GCN at layer l for node i:

$$Q_i^l = M^l \odot Z_i^{l-1} \qquad\qquad \text{Feature transform} \qquad (7)$$

$$P_i^l = \exp\left(\sum_{j \in \mathcal{N}(i)} k_{i,j} \log(Q_j^l) \right) \qquad \text{Propagation} \qquad (8)$$

$$Z_i^l = \varphi^{\mathrm{SPD}}(P_i^l \oplus B^l) \qquad\qquad \text{Bias \& non-lin} \qquad (9)$$

Classification. In node classification setups[2], we are given $\{Z_i, y_i\}_{i=1}^N$ on a dataset, with N as the number of instances, $Z_i \in \text{SPD}_n$ as the i-th node embedding obtained from the final layer of a graph neural network, and $y_i \in \{1, \ldots, K\}$ as the true class of i-th node. Let $h : \text{SPD} \mapsto \{1, \ldots, K\}$ be a classifier that best predicts the label y_i of a given input Z_i. Indeed, the input space of h can be in various forms, not limited to SPD_n. Here we introduce three classifiers in two alternative input spaces: (a) $\mathbb{R}^{d(d+1)/2}$ and (b) S_n[3]. To do so, we first take Riemannian logarithm $\log: \text{SPD}_n \rightarrow S_n$ of each Z_i at the identity. For (a), we vectorize the upper triangle elements of X as $\mathbf{x} = (X_{1,1} \cdots X_{1,d}, X_{2,2}, \cdots, X_{d,d}) \in \mathbb{R}^{d(d+1)/2}$, and then design two classifiers, i.e., LINEAR-XE (Linear Classifier coupled with Cross-Entropy loss) and NC-MM (Nearest Centroid Classifier with Multi-Margin loss). For (b), we design a SVM-like classifier SVM-MM acting in S_n, a similar approach to the proposal of Nguyen et al. [29]. We present the details of these classifiers in Appendix G.

5   Experiments

In this section, we first perform experiments for node and graph classification, and then analyze the ability of three geometric spaces in arranging and separating nodes with different classes. Further, we compare the training efficiency of different spaces and the usefulness of three classifiers. Lastly, we discuss **product space** (the Cartesian product of Euclidean and hyperbolic spaces) and compare it with SPD in Appendix H.

Baselines. To investigate the usefulness of different geometric spaces on graph neural networks, we choose five well-known graph architectures as representatives: GCN [22], GAT [37], Cheb [12], SGC [38] and GIN [39], and evaluate these architectures in Euclidean, hyperbolic and SPD spaces. For the hyperbolic versions of these architectures, we use Poincaré models and extend the implementation of Poincaré GCN [11] to other four architectures.

5.1   Node Classification

Datasets. We evaluate graph neural networks in the three spaces on 5 popular datasets for node classification: Disease [1], Airport [41], Pubmed [28], Citeseer and Cora [34]. Overall, each dataset has a single graph that contains up to thousands of labeled nodes. We use the public train, validation and test splits of each dataset, and provide dataset statistics in Appendix C. Unlike previous works [11,40], we only use original node features to ensure a fair and transparent comparison.

---

[2] For graph classification, Z_i and y_i denote the 'center' of the graph i and its true class. We take the arithmetic mean of node embeddings in SPD_n to produce $Z_i \in \text{SPD}_n$.

[3] We also design several classifiers with the input space in SPD_n, but these do not yield better results than those in S_n.

Setup. We compare three geometries, namely Euclidean, hyperbolic and SPD, in two low-dimensional spaces: (i) 6 dimensions: $\mathbb{R}^6$, $\mathbb{H}^6$ and SPD$_3$, and (ii) 15 dimensions: $\mathbb{R}^{15}$, $\mathbb{H}^{15}$ and SPD$_5$, a common choice of dimensions in previous work [11,40]. The reason we considered for low-dimensional space is the following: If the structure of data matches the geometry of embedding space, a low-dimensional space can be leveraged efficiently for producing high-quality embeddings. If they do not match, a large dimension is needed to compensate for the wrong use of unsuitable geometric spaces. Here we investigate the efficiencies of different geometries in space use when given a small dimension. We report mean accuracy and standard deviation of binary/multi-label classification results under 10 runs, and provide training details in Appendix A.

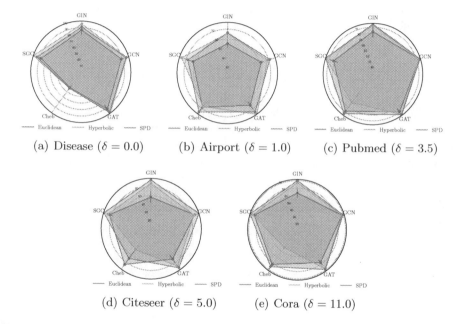

(a) Disease ($\delta = 0.0$)   (b) Airport ($\delta = 1.0$)   (c) Pubmed ($\delta = 3.5$)

(d) Citeseer ($\delta = 5.0$)   (e) Cora ($\delta = 11.0$)

Fig. 3. Evaluation of five graph neural networks coupled with LINEAR-XE on five node classification datasets in the three 6-dimensional spaces: $\mathbb{R}^6$, $\mathbb{H}^6$ and SPD$_3$. Each radar chart shows classification accuracy (on a varying scale, as noted by the gridlines with circular shapes) from the five GNN architectures on a dataset. Each dataset has only one graph. δ-hyperbolicity shows the degree to which the dataset graph is a hyperbolic tree. A smaller δ indicates a more tree-like dataset.

Results. Figure 3 shows the accuracy results of a node classification task in the three 6-dimensional geometries across five datasets on five GNNs, see also Table 6 (appendix). For graphs with δ-hyperbolicity > 1, SPD$_3$ achieves the best accuracy in all cases except the Cheb architecture on the Citeseer dataset. We also observe that the accuracy of SPD is similar to hyperbolic space on the Airport dataset $\delta = 1$. The Disease graph is a tree ($\delta = 0$) and has optimal

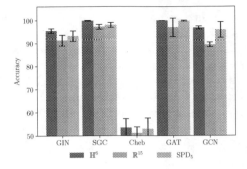

Fig. 4. Comparison of 6d and 15d spaces on Disease. SPD_5 has 15 dimensions.

performance in hyperbolic space. The accuracy is much lower for these two tree-like datasets in Euclidean geometry for all GNNs except Cheb.

In the case of tree-like datasets, hyperbolic space provides not only accuracy for these tasks but also efficiency. Figure 4 compares 6-dimensional hyperbolic space to $\mathbb{R}^{15}$ and SPD_5 (also 15-dimensional), showing that even a much smaller dimensional hyperbolic space achieves the best performance on Disease. Notably, the poor performance of Cheb across all spaces might be attributed to the low representational capacity of the first-order Chebyshev polynomial used in the graph neural network for embedding the tree structure of Disease. Results comparing the 6d and 15d geometries are reported in Table 7 (appendix).

5.2   Graph Classification

Datasets. We evaluate graph neural networks in three spaces on the popular TUDataset benchmark [27]. Here we focus on datasets with node features, and choose a sample of 4 popular datasets in two domains, namely (a) Biology: ENZYMES [33] and PROTEINS [3]; (b) Molecules: COX2 [36] and AIDS [30]. Overall, each dataset instance has one labeled graph with dozens of nodes. We use the first split of train and test sets in the 10-fold cross-validation setup, and select 10% of the training set uniformly at random as the development set. We provide data statistics in Appendix C.

Setup. Following Morris et al. [27], we predict the class of an unlabeled graph by classifying its center. In particular, we produce the graph center by using mean pooling to take the arithmetic mean of node embeddings in a graph. To compare efficiency in space use, we conduct experiments in three spaces with the same dimension size of 36, namely $\mathbb{R}^{36}$, $\mathbb{H}^{36}$ and SPD_8, the smallest dimension size in the grid search from Morris et al. [27]. We report the mean accuracy and standard deviation of graph classification results under 10 runs, and provide training details in Appendix A.

Results. Figure 5 shows the accuracy results of a graph classification task in three geometries across five datasets on five GNNs, see also Table 8 (appendix). Figure 6 shows the distribution of δ-hyperbolicity over instances. We see that SPD$_8$ achieves better or similar accuracy than its counterparts of the same dimension in all cases except Cheb on COX2 and GIN on ENZYMES. On the AIDS dataset, SPD achieves much better accuracy across all GNNs, and on ENZYMES SPD achieves much better accuracy on SGC.

We also observe that hyperbolic space does not yield much increased accuracy over Euclidean space in most cases, except the AIDS data set. Furthermore, SPD significantly outperforms hyperbolic space on the AIDS dataset but not the COX2 data set. Both of these datasets have the property that almost all instances are tree-like ($\delta \leq 1$) (see Fig. 6), but the hyperbolicity constants are less concentrated in the AIDS dataset than in the COX2 dataset. It is possible that the flexibility of SPD explains the increased performance over hyperbolic space in this case. For example, SPD admits totally geodesic submanifolds isometric to hyperbolic spaces of varying constant curvatures. It would be interesting to find out, for example, if these graphs of different hyperbolicity constants stay near copies of hyperbolic space of different curvatures.

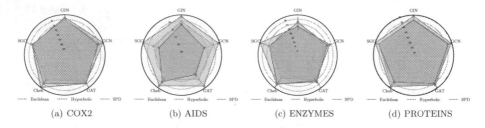

(a) COX2   (b) AIDS   (c) ENZYMES   (d) PROTEINS

Fig. 5. Evaluation of five graph neural networks with LINEAR-XE on four graph classification datasets in the three 36-dimensional spaces: $\mathbb{R}^{36}$, $\mathbb{H}^{36}$ and SPD$_8$.

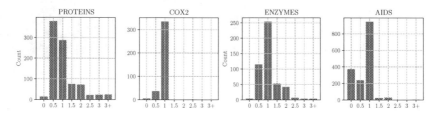

Fig. 6. Distributions of δ-hyperbolicity on four graph classification datasets, where each instance consists of one graph. Y-axis shows the number of graphs for a given δ-hyperbolicity on X-axis.

5.3   Analysis

Class Separation. Figure 7 shows a visualization of node embeddings obtained from the final layer of SGConv on Cora. In each space, we vectorize node embeddings, and then use PCA to extract the top 3 dimensions. We then look at the projections to that 3-dimensional space by further projecting to the x-y, y-z, and x-z planes. For instance, the x-y plane is the projection to the top 2 dimensions of PCA. The x-x, y-y and z-z planes show the informativeness of each dimension in terms of class separation.

Figure 7 (a) depicts the case when the ambient geometry is Euclidean. In this example, nodes from the pink, blue and green classes are well-separated but the nodes in red and orange cannot be easily distinguished. Figure 7 (b) depicts the case when the nodes are embedded in the Poincaré ball model of hyperbolic space. In the x-z plane five classes are well-separated, including the red and orange classes. Figure 7 (c) depicts the case when the nodes are embedded into SPD where the best class separation is achieved. Indeed, the Cora graph has hyperbolicity constant $\delta = 11$, so one cannot expect it to embed well into hyperbolic space.

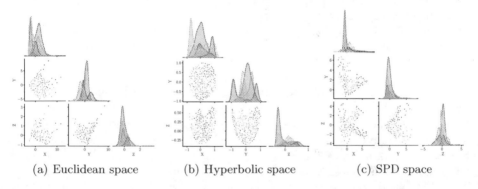

(a) Euclidean space   (b) Hyperbolic space   (c) SPD space

Fig. 7. Vizualizations of the node embeddings into three 6-dimensional geometries for SGC on the Cora dataset. In each space, the nodes are vectorized and then projected linearly to $\mathbb{R}^3$ via PCA.

Training Time. As a case study on the impact of the choice of the latent space geometry on the training time of GNN models, Fig. 8 compares the training efficiency of three graph neural networks on Citeseer across three 6-dimensional manifolds: $\mathbb{R}^6$, $\mathbb{H}^6$, and SPD_3. Overall, we see that models with Euclidean latent spaces needed the least amount of training time, but produced the lowest accuracy. Moreover, hyperbolic space slows down the training in Euclidean space by up to four times, and the effect on accuracy is either slightly positive or negative. For instance, using hyperbolic space with the SGC architecture only brought small accuracy improvements, while applying it to GCN resulted in a drop in accuracy. On the other hand, even though SPD models require nearly double the training time of hyperbolic models, the SPD models bring big improvements in accuracy, not only on Citeseer in the current study case, but also on many datasets such as AIDS and PROTEINS (see Fig. 5). We note that the longer training times for SPD models can be attributed to the involvement of eigende-compositions. However, the benefits of using SPD space in graph neural networks appear to outweigh this drawback.

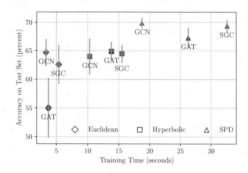

Fig. 8. Evaluation of three 6-dimensional spaces across graph neural networks in terms of training time and accuracy on Citeseer ($\delta = 5.0$). Each point has a unique pattern that combines color and shape. For instance, a red triangular means GCN in SPD. (Color figure online)

Classifiers. Our three classification layers are built upon traditional classification methods. LINEAR-XE and SVM-MM are both linear classifiers that separate classes with hyperplanes, differing in the choice of loss functions: cross-entropy and multi-margin loss. In contrast, NC-MM layer learns class-specific centroids and then determining the class of an unlabeled node (or graph) by examining which centroid it is closest to according to a similarity function.

Table 2 shows the usefulness of our classifiers in SPD on Citesser and Cora. Overall, we see that the MM-based classifiers (SVM-MM and NC-MM) are often helpful, outperforming LINEAR-XE in SPD, and when they succeed, their improvements are substantial. This means the benefits of using SPD and these advanced classifiers are complementary, resulting in stacked performance gains. This is an important finding as it hints at the possibility of accommodating more advanced classification methods recently developed in Euclidean space, when constructing graph neural networks in SPD. Note that the results on other datasets are similar, which we present in Appendix D and E.

Table 2. Comparison of different classifiers on Citeseer (top) and Cora (bottom). We bold the best accuracy in each row.

| | $\mathbb{R}^6$ | SPD_3 | | |
	Lin-XE	Lin-XE	SVM-MM	NC-MM
GIN	48.2 ± 6.3	$\mathbf{68.0 \pm 1.3}$	67.3 ± 1.2	67.0 ± 0.8
SGC	62.6 ± 3.4	69.4 ± 1.0	$\mathbf{69.7 \pm 0.8}$	67.9 ± 1.5
Cheb	63.2 ± 2.1	54.6 ± 10.4	61.4 ± 4.4	$\mathbf{64.0 \pm 2.3}$
GAT	55.0 ± 5.2	67.3 ± 1.7	$\mathbf{69.2 \pm 0.7}$	68.1 ± 1.1
GCN	64.7 ± 2.3	$\mathbf{69.9 \pm 0.8}$	69.2 ± 0.8	68.2 ± 1.0
GIN	77.1 ± 1.0	$\mathbf{79.9 \pm 0.6}$	79.5 ± 0.6	78.8 ± 1.0
SGC	75.7 ± 3.6	81.5 ± 0.9	$\mathbf{81.8 \pm 0.3}$	81.1 ± 0.6
Cheb	71.9 ± 2.8	75.5 ± 3.9	77.9 ± 2.4	$\mathbf{79.2 \pm 1.3}$
GAT	67.9 ± 4.2	79.4 ± 0.9	$\mathbf{81.2 \pm 1.4}$	$\mathbf{81.2 \pm 1.1}$
GCN	78.1 ± 1.7	79.7 ± 0.9	$\mathbf{80.7 \pm 0.5}$	80.2 ± 1.3

6   Conclusions

This work brings sophisticated geometric tools to graph neural networks (GNNs). Following the maxim 'complex data requires complex geometry', we leverage the flexibility of the space of symmetric positve definite (SPD) matrices to construct GNNs which do not require careful prior knowledge of graph topologies. This is a distinct advantage over familiar spaces such as Euclidean, spherical or hyperbolic geometries, where only narrow classes of graphs embed with low distortion.

To operate GNNs in SPD, we designed several building blocks, and developed a library (SPD4GNN) that enables training five popular GNNs in SPD, Euclidean and hyperbolic spaces. Our results confirm the strong connection between graph topology and embedding geometry: GNNs in SPD provide big improvements on graph datasets with multi-modal structures, with their counterparts in hyperbolic space performing better on strictly tree-like graphs.

Determining the optimal classifier for training GNNs in the complex geometry of SPD is challenging, and presents an avenue for continued improvement. This work only begins the process of designing geometrically meaningful classifiers and identifying the conditions which guarantee good performance. Additional performance gains may come through careful implementation of the computationally demanding functions in SPD. While this work contains techniques for accelerating computations in SPD, further optimization is likely possible.

Constructing tools to aid the interpretability of SPD embeddings is an important direction of future work, including quantitative measures for (a) comparing the geometry of the learned embeddings to the real-world graphs' topology and (b) understanding how the geometric features of SPD are leveraged in for graph tasks. While the results of this current work suggest some of SPD's superior performance may be due to graphs of varying hyperbolicity finding geometric subspaces optimally adapted to their curvature, such measures would enable the precise quantitative analysis required for verification.

Acknowledgements. We thank Anna Wienhard and Maria Beatrice Pozetti for insightful discussions, as well as the anonymous reviewers for their thoughtful feedback that greatly improved the texts. This work has been supported by the Klaus Tschira Foundation, Heidelberg, Germany, as well as under Germany's Excellence Strategy EXC-2181/1 - 390900948 (the Heidelberg STRUCTURES Cluster of Excellence).

Ethical Considerations. We have not identified any immediate ethical concerns such as bias and discrimination, misinformation dissemination, privacy issues, originating from the contributions presented in this work. However, it is important to note that our SPD models use computationally demanding functions, such as determining eigenvalues and eigenvectors, which may incur a negative environmental impact due to increased energy consumption. Nevertheless, SPD models do not outsuffer Euclidean and hyperbolic counterparts in terms of computational overhead. This is because Euclidean and hyperbolic models would require substantial computing resources when dealing with larger dimensions, a necessity for compensating for the challenges of embedding complex graphs into these ill-suited spaces.

References

1. Anderson, R.M., May, R.M.: Infectious Diseases of Humans: Dynamics and Control. Oxford University Press, Oxford (1992)
2. Barcelo, P., Galkin, M., Morris, C., Orth, M.R.: Weisfeiler and leman go relational. In: The First Learning on Graphs Conference (2022). https://openreview.net/forum?id=wY_IYhh6pqj
3. Borgwardt, K.M., Ong, C.S., Schönauer, S., Vishwanathan, S., Smola, A.J., Kriegel, H.P.: Protein function prediction via graph kernels. Bioinformatics **21**(suppl_1), i47–i56 (2005)
4. Bronstein, M.M., Bruna, J., LeCun, Y., Szlam, A., Vandergheynst, P.: Geometric deep learning: going beyond euclidean data. IEEE Signal Process. Mag. **34**(4), 18–42 (2017)
5. Brooks, D., Schwander, O., Barbaresco, F., Schneider, J.Y., Cord, M.: Riemannian batch normalization for SPD neural networks. In: Wallach, H., Larochelle, H., Beygelzimer, A., d'Alché-Buc, F., Fox, E., Garnett, R. (eds.) Advances in Neural Information Processing Systems, vol. 32, pp. 15489–15500. Curran Associates, Inc. (2019). https://proceedings.neurips.cc/paper/2019/file/6e69ebbfad976d4637bb4b39de261bf7-Paper.pdf
6. Brooks, D.A., Schwander, O., Barbaresco, F., Schneider, J.Y., Cord, M.: Exploring complex time-series representations for Riemannian machine learning of radar data. In: ICASSP 2019–2019 IEEE International Conference on Acoustics, Speech and Signal Processing (ICASSP), pp. 3672–3676 (2019). https://doi.org/10.1109/ICASSP.2019.8683056
7. Buyalo, S., Schroeder, V.: Embedding of hyperbolic spaces in the product of trees. Geom. Dedicata. **113**(1), 75–93 (2005)
8. Cannon, J.W., Floyd, W.J., Kenyon, R., Parry, W.R., et al.: Hyperbolic geometry. Flavors Geom. **31**(59–115), 2 (1997)

9. Chakraborty, R., Bouza, J., Manton, J., Vemuri, B.C.: ManifoldNet: A deep neural network for manifold-valued data with applications. IEEE Trans. Pattern Anal. Mach. Intell., 1 (2020). https://doi.org/10.1109/TPAMI.2020.3003846

10. Chakraborty, R., et al.: A statistical recurrent model on the manifold of symmetric positive definite matrices. In: Bengio, S., Wallach, H., Larochelle, H., Grauman, K., Cesa-Bianchi, N., Garnett, R. (eds.) Advances in Neural Information Processing Systems, vol. 31. Curran Associates, Inc. (2018). https://proceedings.neurips.cc/paper/2018/file/7070f9088e456682f0f84f815ebda761-Paper.pdf

11. Chami, I., Ying, Z., Ré, C., Leskovec, J.: Hyperbolic graph convolutional neural networks. In: Advances in Neural Information Processing Systems, vol. 32, pp. 4869–4880. Curran Associates, Inc. (2019). https://proceedings.neurips.cc/paper/2019/file/0415740eaa4d9decbc8da001d3fd805f-Paper.pdf

12. Defferrard, M., Bresson, X., Vandergheynst, P.: Convolutional neural networks on graphs with fast localized spectral filtering. In: Advances in Neural Information Processing Systems, vol. 29 (2016)

13. Defferrard, M., Milani, M., Gusset, F., Perraudin, N.: DeepSphere: a graph-based spherical CNN. In: International Conference on Learning Representations (2020). https://openreview.net/forum?id=B1e3OlStPB

14. Di Giovanni, F., Rowbottom, J., Chamberlain, B.P., Markovich, T., Bronstein, M.M.: Graph neural networks as gradient flows. arXiv preprint: arXiv:2206.10991 (2022)

15. Dong, Z., Jia, S., Zhang, C., Pei, M., Wu, Y.: Deep manifold learning of symmetric positive definite matrices with application to face recognition. In: Proceedings of the Thirty-First AAAI Conference on Artificial Intelligence, AAAI'17, pp. 4009–4015. AAAI Press (2017)

16. Eliasof, M., Haber, E., Treister, E.: PDE-GCN: novel architectures for graph neural networks motivated by partial differential equations. In: Advances in Neural Information Processing Systems, vol. 34, pp. 3836–3849 (2021)

17. Gao, Z., Wu, Y., Bu, X., Yu, T., Yuan, J., Jia, Y.: Learning a robust representation via a deep network on symmetric positive definite manifolds. Pattern Recogn. **92**, 1–12 (2019). https://doi.org/10.1016/j.patcog.2019.03.007, https://www.sciencedirect.com/science/article/pii/S0031320319301062

18. Gu, A., Sala, F., Gunel, B., Ré, C.: Learning mixed-curvature representations in product spaces. In: International Conference on Learning Representations (2019). https://openreview.net/forum?id=HJxeWnCcF7

19. Hamilton, W., Ying, Z., Leskovec, J.: Inductive representation learning on large graphs. In: Guyon, I., et al. (eds.) Advances in Neural Information Processing Systems, vol. 30. Curran Associates, Inc. (2017). https://proceedings.neurips.cc/paper/2017/file/5dd9db5e033da9c6fb5ba83c7a7ebea9-Paper.pdf

20. Helgason, S.: Differential Geometry, Lie Groups, and Symmetric Spaces. Academic Press, New York (1978)

21. Huang, Z., Van Gool, L.: A Riemannian network for SPD matrix learning. In: Proceedings of the Thirty-First AAAI Conference on Artificial Intelligence, AAAI'17, pp. 2036–2042. AAAI Press (2017)

22. Kipf, T.N., Welling, M.: Semi-supervised classification with graph convolutional networks. In: 5th International Conference on Learning Representations, ICLR 2017, Toulon, France, 24–26 April 2017. Conference Track Proceedings (2017). https://openreview.net/forum?id=SJU4ayYgl

23. Krioukov, D., Papadopoulos, F., Kitsak, M., Vahdat, A., Boguná, M.: Hyperbolic geometry of complex networks. Phys. Rev. E **82**(3), 036106 (2010)

24. Liu, Q., Nickel, M., Kiela, D.: Hyperbolic graph neural networks. In: Wallach, H., Larochelle, H., Beygelzimer, A., d'Alché-Buc, F., Fox, E., Garnett, R. (eds.) Advances in Neural Information Processing Systems, vol. 32. Curran Associates, Inc. (2019)

25. López, F., Pozzetti, B., Trettel, S., Strube, M., Wienhard, A.: Symmetric spaces for graph embeddings: a finsler-riemannian approach. In: Meila, M., Zhang, T. (eds.) Proceedings of the 38th International Conference on Machine Learning. Proceedings of Machine Learning Research, vol. 139, pp. 7090–7101. PMLR (2021). https://proceedings.mlr.press/v139/lopez21a.html

26. López, F., Pozzetti, B., Trettel, S., Strube, M., Wienhard, A.: Vector-valued distance and gyrocalculus on the space of symmetric positive definite matrices. In: Larochelle, H., Ranzato, M., Hadsell, R., Balcan, M.F., Lin, H. (eds.) Advances in Neural Information Processing Systems, vol. 34. Curran Associates, Inc. (2021)

27. Morris, C., Kriege, N.M., Bause, F., Kersting, K., Mutzel, P., Neumann, M.: TUDataset: a collection of benchmark datasets for learning with graphs. In: ICML 2020 Workshop on Graph Representation Learning and Beyond (GRL+ 2020) (2020). https://www.graphlearning.io

28. Namata, G., London, B., Getoor, L., Huang, B., Edu, U.: Query-driven active surveying for collective classification. In: 10th International Workshop on Mining and Learning with Graphs, vol. 8, p. 1 (2012)

29. Nguyen, X.S., Brun, L., Lezoray, O., Bougleux, S.: A neural network based on SPD manifold learning for skeleton-based hand gesture recognition. In: Proceedings of the IEEE/CVF Conference on Computer Vision and Pattern Recognition (CVPR) (2019)

30. Riesen, K., Bunke, H.: IAM graph database repository for graph based pattern recognition and machine learning. In: da Vitoria Lobo, N., et al. (eds.) SSPR /SPR 2008. LNCS, vol. 5342, pp. 287–297. Springer, Heidelberg (2008). https://doi.org/10.1007/978-3-540-89689-0_33

31. Rusch, T.K., Chamberlain, B., Rowbottom, J., Mishra, S., Bronstein, M.: Graph-coupled oscillator networks. In: International Conference on Machine Learning, pp. 18888–18909. PMLR (2022)

32. Satorras, V.G., Hoogeboom, E., Welling, M.: E (n) equivariant graph neural networks. In: International Conference on Machine Learning, pp. 9323–9332. PMLR (2021)

33. Schomburg, I., et al.: BRENDA, the enzyme database: updates and major new developments. Nucleic Acids Res. **32**(suppl_1), D431–D433 (2004)

34. Sen, P., Namata, G., Bilgic, M., Getoor, L., Galligher, B., Eliassi-Rad, T.: Collective classification in network data. AI Mag. **29**(3), 93 (2008)

35. Sonthalia, R., Gilbert, A.: Tree! i am no tree! i am a low dimensional hyperbolic embedding. In: Advances in Neural Information Processing Systems, vol. 33, pp. 845–856 (2020)

36. Sutherland, J.J., O'brien, L.A., Weaver, D.F.: Spline-fitting with a genetic algorithm: a method for developing classification structure- activity relationships. J. Chem. Inf. Comput. Sci. **43**(6), 1906–1915 (2003)

37. Veličković, P., Cucurull, G., Casanova, A., Romero, A., Lió, P., Bengio, Y.: Graph attention networks. In: International Conference on Learning Representations (2018). https://openreview.net/forum?id=rJXMpikCZ
38. Wu, F., Souza, A., Zhang, T., Fifty, C., Yu, T., Weinberger, K.: Simplifying graph convolutional networks. In: International Conference on Machine Learning, pp. 6861–6871. PMLR (2019)
39. Xu, K., Hu, W., Leskovec, J., Jegelka, S.: How powerful are graph neural networks? In: 7th International Conference on Learning Representations, ICLR 2019, New Orleans, LA, USA, 6–9 May 2019. OpenReview.net (2019). https://openreview.net/forum?id=ryGs6iA5Km
40. Yu, T., De Sa, C.: HyLa: hyperbolic Laplacian features for graph learning. arXiv preprint: arXiv:2202.06854 (2022)
41. Zhang, M., Chen, Y.: Link prediction based on graph neural networks. In: Advances in Neural Information Processing Systems, vol. 31 (2018)
42. Zhang, T., Zheng, W., Cui, Z., Li, C.: Deep manifold-to-manifold transforming network. In: 2018 25th IEEE International Conference on Image Processing (ICIP), pp. 4098–4102 (2018). DOI: https://doi.org/10.1109/ICIP.2018.8451626

Leveraging Free Labels to Power up Heterophilic Graph Learning in Weakly-Supervised Settings: An Empirical Study

Xugang Wu, Huijun Wu, Ruibo Wang$^{(\boxtimes)}$, Duanyu Li, Xu Zhou, and Kai Lu$^{(\boxtimes)}$

College of Computer, National University of Defense Technology, Changsha, China
{wuxugang13,wuhuijun,wangruibo,liduanyu,zhouxu,kailu}@nudt.edu.cn

Abstract. Graph learning on heterophilic graphs is challenging for classic graph neural network models. Recent research addresses this issue by using adaptive graph filters that consider signals with different frequencies. Although such models provide insightful design patterns for heterophilic graph analysis, their practical effect has been overlooked. Previous studies have evaluated adaptive graph filters with a large proportion of training data to demonstrate their effectiveness. However, such dense labeling is often impractical. Empirically, we observed that typical adaptive filters perform badly in weakly-supervised settings, making them easily outperformed by fixed filters. With empirical evidence, we demonstrate that the key reason is that sparse node labels make it difficult to learn effective filters. Fortunately, although labeled nodes are sparse in weakly-supervised settings, graph structures provide substantial supervision by indicating whether an edge is present. Through theoretical analysis on contextual Stochastic Block Models, we show that a good link predictor can imply the knowledge needed by a good node classifier. Therefore, we propose to use the "free labels" from the graph structure to form link prediction tasks and obtain an effective graph filter, which can be used to initialize the node classification model. Experimental results on both synthetic and real-world heterophilic graphs demonstrate the effectiveness of our approach. We also provide an in-depth analysis of the learned filters, which sheds light on the underlying mechanisms of our proposed approach. Codes are available at https://github.com/lucio-win/PKDD2023.

Keywords: Heterophilic Graph Learning · Adaptive Filter · Weakly-Supervised Learning

1 Introduction

In recent years, graph neural networks (GNNs) have gained considerable attention as a powerful method for analyzing graph-structured data across various domains [2,30,32,33]. Most classic GNNs are designed with explicit or implicit assumptions of homophily [7,22]. However, homophily does not hold for heterophilic graphs, thus making existing GNNs inefficient on heterophilic graphs.

© The Author(s), under exclusive license to Springer Nature Switzerland AG 2023
D. Koutra et al. (Eds.): ECML PKDD 2023, LNAI 14171, pp. 140–156, 2023.
https://doi.org/10.1007/978-3-031-43418-1_9

To address this issue, recent work introduces adaptive filters, which learn adaptive graph filters based on the graph data [3,4,6,11,23,28,34–36]. Such models have shown great potential in enhancing the performance of learning tasks on heterophilic graphs.

It should be noted, however, that a large proportion of training data is typically used to evaluate adaptive spectral GNNs on heterophilic graphs [19,23,24]. A common practice is to divide data into train, validation, and test sets with a ratio of 60%, 20% and 20%, respectively. Although a large amount of training nodes enables the adaptive models to learn better graph filters, such a partition is less practical in real-world scenarios where we normally know less but predict more. Moreover, a high training ratio means that a substantial number of labeled nodes is required to predict an unknown node, making the learning process cost-ineffective. It remains unclear how adaptive filter-based GNNs perform in weakly-supervised settings.

To figure this out, we investigate the performance of the adaptive spectral GNNs under different data splits. Surprisingly, as the amount of training data decreases, the performance of the adaptive spectral GNNs deteriorates rapidly. In some cases, they can even be easily outperformed by GNNs with fixed filters. For example, when the proportion of the training set is less than 15%, typical adaptive filter-based GNNs like GPR-GNN can be outperformed by GCN. To understand why adaptive filter-based GNNs are sensitive to the amount of training data, we further analyzed the graph filters learned by the model under different data splits. The results indicate that when the training sample ratio is low, the model is unable to learn an effective filter, resulting in poor performance. By using an effective initial filter, which accounts for less than **0.2%**[1] of all trainable parameters, the performance of the model can be significantly improved in weakly-supervised settings.

Motivated by the above observations, we propose a novel approach to learn an effective graph filter in a weakly-supervised setting. According to the above analysis, the lack of supervision and the resulting ineffective filters should be blamed for the poor performance. The key to the solution is therefore obtaining a good filter without heavy labeling. To achieve this, we utilize the *free link labels* in the graphs. To be specific, although getting labeled nodes requires a non-trivial amount of annotations, labeled edges are free to get in a graph. The graph structure already tells whether an edge exists, which provides N^2 edge labels where N is the number of nodes. Through theoretical analysis, we found that a good link predictor also implied the knowledge needed by a good node classifier. Hence, we leverage the edge information to form a problem of link prediction. The graph filter learned for the link prediction problem is used to initialize the filter of the node classifier. Such prior powers the node classifier with the ability to keep informative signals in the graph, thus improving the classification accuracy.

---

[1] This value depends on the number of node features, classes, hidden units, hidden layers and propagation layers. The calculation is provided in the supplementary material.

Our experiments on synthetic and real-world datasets demonstrate the effectiveness of our approach in node classification tasks. We also provide an in-depth analysis of the learned filters, which sheds light on the underlying mechanisms of our proposed approach.

2   Related Work

2.1   Adaptive Filters for Heterophilic Graph Learning

Graph neural networks (GNNs) have achieved remarkable success in learning representation for graph data. From the perspective of graph signal processing, most GNNs can be viewed as fixed low-pass graph filters that smooth features over graph topology [5,10,12,14–16,27,29,31]. These models are designed with the assumption of homophily which assumes similar nodes tend to connect in a graph. In homophilic graphs, low-frequency signals dominate so that low-pass filters work well. For heterophilic graphs, however, the information lies at different frequencies due to complex edge patterns. Therefore, existing low-pass filters are not applicable in such graphs. In response to this challenge, a recent line of research focuses on designing adaptive filters which adapt their frequency response according to the graph patterns in both homophilic and heterophilic settings. GPR-GNN [6] uses a polynomial function to represent the graph filter and learn the optimal polynomial coefficients that can automatically adjust to the node label pattern. BernNet [11] approximates the optimal filter using a Bernstein polynomial of order-k and utilizes the coefficients of the Bernstein basis to design its spectral property. JacobiConv [28] employs the Jacobi basis which is orthogonal and adaptable to a diverse array of weight functions. AdaGNN [9] utilizes a trainable filter that spans over several layers. ARMA [3] introduces a new graph convolutional layer inspired by the auto-regressive moving average (ARMA) filter, which could offer a more adaptable frequency response. ARMA is more resilient to noise and is better equipped to capture the overall structure of the graph. PP-GNN [21] proposes a piece-wise polynomial filter to model more complex frequency responses. Compared with GNNs that employ fixed filters, the above methods with adaptive filters can better adjust their frequency response based on data characteristics, thus achieving good performance on heterophilic graphs. However, it is worth noting that the current evaluation of these methods often uses a large proportion of nodes for training. Their performance in weakly supervised scenarios remains to be explored.

2.2   Evaluation on Heterophilic Graph Learning

There are three primary benchmarks in evaluating graph neural network models for heterophilic graphs. The most widely used benchmarks are the six datasets proposed by Pei et al [23], which include Wikipedia graphs, *chameleon* and *squirrel*, the Actor co-occurrence graph, and the webpage graph *Texas* and

Cornell from WebKB3. The majority of works on heterophilic graph learning adopt these datasets as standard benchmarks for performance evaluation [6,11,20,23,28,35,36]. Lim et al. [19] address the large-scale heterophilic graph learning and present larger heterophilic datasets with a wider range of applications. Platonov et al. [24] point out that the prior datasets used for evaluating heterophily-specific models suffer from serious drawbacks, including duplicate nodes and unstable performance due to their small scale. To address these issues, they propose a new benchmark dataset with graphs of varying properties. Evaluation of spectral GNNs with adaptive filters on these heterophilic graphs verifies that they can learn adaptive frequency responses from the data, thereby achieving better performance than the GNNs with fixed filters.

However, we notice that current evaluations for these models often use a large proportion of graph nodes for training. For example, the dataset proposed by Pei et al. [23] adopts a 60%, 20%, and 20% split for training, validation, and testing, respectively. In addition, the datasets proposed by Lim et al. [19] and Platonov et al. [24] adopt a 50%, 25%, and 25% split for training, validation, and testing, respectively. Such dense training splits indeed help with filter training but are not practical for real applications. In real-world scenarios, we normally only know the true labels of a small portion of nodes and expect to predict the labels of more. Therefore, it is crucial to understand the effectiveness of these adaptive methods in weakly supervised scenarios, motivating us to conduct the empirical studies in this paper.

3   Motivation

In this section, we start with an empirical investigation into the performance of GPR-GNN [6], a pervasive model utilizing an adaptive filter, across diverse partitions of heterophilic graph data. We observe a notable performance degradation of GPR-GNN under weakly supervised settings. Intriguingly, with inadequate training data, GPR-GNN may even exhibit inferior performance compared to GNNs with fixed graph filters, such as GCN.

3.1   Experimental Setups

Problem Setup. The empirical study focuses on the semi-supervised node classification task on heterophilic graphs. Given a graph $\mathcal{G} = (\mathcal{V}, \mathcal{E}, \mathbf{X})$ with n nodes, where $\mathcal{V}$ is the set of nodes $\{v_1, \cdots, v_n\}$ with $|\mathcal{V}| = n$, $\mathcal{E}$ is the set of edges, and $\mathbf{X} = (\boldsymbol{x}_1, \boldsymbol{x}_2, \cdots, \boldsymbol{x}_n)^{\mathrm{T}} \in \mathbb{R}^{n \times m}$ is the corresponding feature matrix. The feature of each node $v \in \mathcal{V}$ can be denoted as an m-dimensional row vector $\boldsymbol{x}_v \in \mathbb{R}^m$. The adjacency matrix $\mathbf{A} \in \mathbb{R}^{n \times n}$ can be constructed by setting $\mathbf{A}_{ij} = 1$ if $(v_i, v_j) \in \mathcal{E}$ and $\mathbf{A}_{ij} = 0$, otherwise. $\tilde{\mathbf{A}}$ stands for the adjacency matrix with self-loops. Let $\tilde{\mathbf{D}}$ be the diagonal degree matrix of $\tilde{\mathbf{A}}$ and the symmetric normalized adjacency matrix with self-loops can be expressed as $\tilde{\mathbf{A}}_{\mathrm{sym}} = \tilde{\mathbf{D}}^{-1/2} \tilde{\mathbf{A}} \tilde{\mathbf{D}}^{-1/2}$. $\mathbf{y} \in \mathcal{Y}^{|\mathcal{V}|}$ denotes the ground truth label for each node. Our goal is to predict the classes of unlabeled nodes.

Table 1. Real-world Dataset Statistics.

Dataset	Chameleon	Squirrel	Actor	Genius	Tolokers	Questions
# Nodes	2,277	5,201	7,600	421,961	11,758	48,921
# Edges	36,101	216,933	29,926	984,979	519,000	153,540
# Features	2,325	2,089	931	12	10	301
# Classes	5	5	5	2	2	2

Datasets and Splits. For the experiments, we adopt one synthetic dataset: the cSBM dataset from [8], as well as six real-world datasets: *chameleon, squirrel* and *actor* from [23], *tolokers* and *question* from [24] and *genius* from [19].

The cSBM dataset is a synthetic dataset generated from a stochastic block model (SBM) [8]. Within the framework of cSBM, the node features are modeled as Gaussian random vectors, with their means conditioned on the corresponding community assignments. The difference in means is modulated by a parameter μ, whereas the difference in edge densities between and within communities is governed by a parameter λ. In our experiments, we consider the same setting of the cSBM dataset as in [6]. Specifically, we generate two communities with equal sizes. The parameter $\phi = \arctan\left(\frac{\lambda\sqrt{\xi}}{\mu}\right) \times \frac{2}{\pi}$ is used to control the relative information of node features and graph structures. A value of $\phi = 0$ implies that only node features contain pertinent information, whereas a value of $|\phi| = 1$ implies that solely the graph topology contains informative signals. Since we focus on heterophilic graph learning, we generate the cSBM dataset with a list of ϕ as $[-1, -0.75, -0.5]$. We refer readers to [1,6,8] for more detailed settings and the generating process of the cSBM dataset.

Chameleon and *squirrel* are two of the most widely utilized heterophilic datasets for node classification tasks. The two datasets were originally collected by Rozemberczki et al. [25]. Nodes in these graphs correspond to articles from the English Wikipedia and the edges represent mutual hyperlinks between them. Node features denote the occurrence of specific nouns within the articles. *Actor* is an actor-only induced subgraph derived from the film-director-actor-writer network proposed by Tang et al. [26]. Each node in the graph represents an actor, while edges denote their co-occurrence on the same Wikipedia page. Node features correspond to certain keywords extracted from the corresponding Wikipedia page. The task is to classify the actors into five categories. *Tolokers* is derived from the data collected from the Toloka crowdsourcing platform [17]. Each node in the graph corresponds to a toloker who has taken part in at least one of the 13 chosen projects. An edge connects two tolokers if they have collaborated on the same task. The objective is to predict which tolokers have been banned in any of the projects. Node features are derived from the profile information and task performance of the workers. *Questions* dataset is derived from data collected from the Yandex Q question-answering website. Nodes in the graph correspond to users, with an edge connecting two nodes if one user answered the other user's question within one year. The classification task aims to predict which users were active on the website at the end of the period. *Genius* is a social network introduced in [18], the task is to predict the reported gender of the users. Node features are the bag-of-words representation of the bios of the users. Key statistics of these datasets are shown in Table 1.

In terms of data splits, we are interested in the performance of GPR-GNN under different data partitions. Since node classification tasks on synthetic data are relatively easy, we evaluate with lower training sample ratios, namely [0.005, 0.01, 0.025, 0.05]. For real-world datasets, the training sample ratios include [0.025, 0.05, 0.1, 0.15, 0.2, 0.25, 0.3, 0.35, 0.4, 0.45, 0.5, 0.55, 0.6]. We fix the validation set ratio as 0.1, and the remaining nodes are used as the test data. We repeat the random sampling process 10 times and report the average performance.

Model. In our evaluation, We employ the GPR-GNN as the representative GNN model which adopts the idea of adaptive filters. Taking a graph with feature $\mathbf{X}$ and normalized adjacency matrix $\tilde{\mathbf{A}}_{\text{sym}}$ as the input, GPR-GNN first extracts the embeddings of each node by a 2-layer MLP, $\mathbf{H}^{(0)} = f_\theta(\mathbf{X})$ and then applies a K-layer Generalized PageRank propagation to obtain the final representations of each node $\mathbf{Z} = \sum_{k=0}^{K} \gamma_k \tilde{\mathbf{A}}_{\text{sym}}^k \mathbf{H}^{(0)}$, where γ_k is the weight of the k-th layer and θ correspond to the MLP parameter. From the spectral perspective, it parameterizes the graph filter as a polynomial of degree K: $g(\lambda) := \sum_{k=0}^{K} \gamma_k \lambda^k$, where λ is the eigenvalue of the normalized adjacency matrix. Given the fact that GPR-GNN is one of the most representative prototypes of adaptive filter-based models, results obtained from it can be potentially generalized to other similar models. Meanwhile, we adopt the GCN model as the representative of fixed filter-based GNN for comparison.

Implementation Details. For all datasets, we set the number of training epochs as 1000 and the early stopping patience as 200, using the validation accuracy as the supervision. We use Adam optimizer [13] with the learning rate tuned in [0.005, 0.01, 0.05] and the weight decay tuned in [0, 0.0005] for all trainable parameters. For GPR-GNN, we set the number of MLP layers as 2, the number of hidden units as 64 and the number of propagating layers as 10. For GCN, we utilize a 2-layer convolution structure with 64 hidden units.

3.2   Results and Observations

Figure 1 show the mean accuracy of GPR-GNN and GCN on the synthetic and real-world datasets, respectively. From the results, we make the following observation. GPR-GNN outperforms GCN in most cases when the training ratio is high. However, as the volume of training data decreases, the performance of GPR-GNN deteriorates much more severely than that of GCN. For example, on the *chameleon* dataset, GPR-GNN exhibits up to 5% improvements in performance over GCN when the training sample ratio exceeds 0.25. However, with lower training sample ratios, GPR-GNN is inferior to GCN. Intriguingly, we

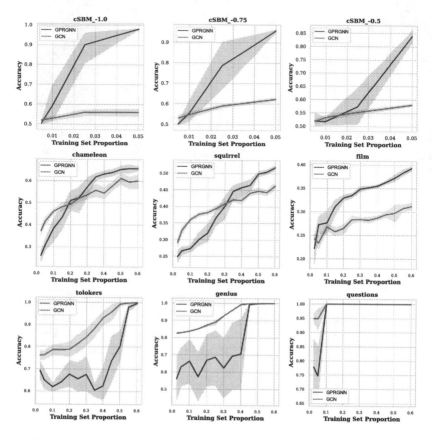

Fig. 1. The performance of GPR-GNN and GCN on synthetic and real-world datasets under different data splits

observed that when the training ratio is as low as 0.025, the performance of GPR-GNN is over 10% lower than that of GCN, highlighting the significant impact of the training sample ratio on model performance in heterophilic graph analysis.

3.3   Analysis

Based on the experimental results, it appears that the adaptive filter-based GNN is particularly sensitive to the density of the training data. To gain a deeper understanding of the underlying reasons for this phenomenon, we make a detailed analysis of the frequency response of the learned filters of GPR-GNN under different splits. Figure 2 displays the frequency response of the learned filters and the mean accuracy of GPR-GNN on the *chameleon* dataset. Each curve with different colors corresponds to a different initialization. The results demonstrate that, in scenarios where the training data is insufficient, the model is unable to learn an effective filter from the data, and the frequency response is primarily a

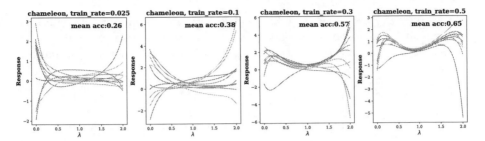

Fig. 2. The learned response filter and mean accuracy of GPR-GNN for *chameleon* dataset under different data splits

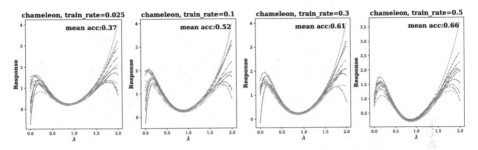

Fig. 3. The learned response filter and mean accuracy of GPR-GNN for *chameleon* dataset under different data splits, using the learned filters of GPR-GNN at a training ratio of 0.6 as the initialization for γ

result of random initialization. This is further reflected by the decreasing speed of accuracy as the training ratio drops. Specifically, when the training ratio decreases from 0.5 to 0.3, the model is still able to learn a decent filter, resulting in only an 8% decrease in accuracy. However, when it further drops from 0.3 to 0.1, the accuracy significantly decreases by 19%. The results suggest that a critical factor leading to the performance degradation of GPR-GNN under conditions of insufficient training data is its inability to learn an effective filter. As a consequence, the filter's performance is primarily determined by random initialization, eliminating its ability to capture graph features.

To verify this hypothesis, we design another set of experiments. We adopt the filters learned by GPR-GNN at a training ratio of 0.6 as initialization for γ (where γ represents the coefficients of the polynomial filter) and evaluated the performance of GPR-GNN under different training ratios. Notably, the γ parameters only account for less than **0.2%** of all trainable parameters in GPR-GNN. The results, as depicted in Fig. 3, demonstrate a significant improvement in GPR-GNN's performance when the training ratio is low, suggesting that the model's performance is closely correlated to the quality of the learned filter. Surprisingly, providing a good initialization for only a tiny subset of the parameters can lead to such significant improvement. For instance, when the training ratio is as low as 0.1, adopting the well-pre-trained filter can improve the performance by

14%. Confirming the impact of filters on the performance in cases of insufficient training data, the challenge now becomes how to obtain an efficient filter that is well-suited to the characteristics of graph data in weakly supervised scenarios.

4   Proposed Approach

The empirical results clearly illustrate the critical role of an effective filter in improving the performance of the adaptive filter-based GNNs in weakly supervised scenarios. However, it is also indicated that, when the training data is insufficient, the model is unable to learn an effective filter solely based on the available node labels. Motivated by the recent work [2] that presents the connection between node classification (NC) and link prediction (LP) on knowledge graphs, we propose to leverage the edge information, which comes "free" with the graph data, to learn an effective filter for the initialization of the adaptive filter-based GNNs in node classification tasks. Specifically, we first train a link prediction model on the graph data, and then use the learned filter as an initialization for the adaptive filter-based GNNs to conduct node classification on the same graph. The intuition behind this approach is that, in the process of learning the link prediction model, the model should capture the intrinsic properties of the graph data, such as the node relationships, and therefore encourage its adaptive filter to respond to the "informative frequency". In this way, the model can learn an effective initial filter from the data, and the performance of the adaptive filter-based GNNs in weakly-supervised settings can be significantly improved.

To further illustrate the connection between node classification and link prediction on the same graph, we provide a theoretical analysis of the relationship between the two tasks on a generative graph model presented in Sect. 3.1, the cSBM [8]. In essence, our theoretical analysis demonstrates how, on the cSBM, an optimal model learned from one task can be transformed into an optimal model for another task.

Problem Setup. Let $G = (V, E)$ be an undirected graph, where $V = 1, 2, ..., N$ is the set of nodes and A is the adjacency matrix. We assume that the graph is generated by the contextual stochastic block model (cSBM) with 2 clusters. Let $C = C_1, C_2$ be the partition of the nodes. The cSBM model assumes that the probability of an edge between two nodes depends only on their clusters. Let p_{ij} be the probability of an edge between node i and node j, where $i, j \in V$. Then, the SBM model is defined as follows:

$$p_{ij} = \begin{cases} p_{in}, & \text{if } i, j \in C_l \text{ for } l \in 1, 2 \\ p_{out}, & \text{if } i \in C_l \text{ and } j \in C_m \text{ for } l \neq m \end{cases}$$

where p_{in} is the in-cluster probability and p_{out} is the inter-cluster probability.

From NC to LP. Assuming we have an optimal node classifier $NC^*(i)$, we can construct an optimal link predictor $LP^*(i, j)$ that outputs the probability of there being an edge between nodes i and j as:

$$LP^*(i, j) = \begin{cases} \hat{p}_{in}, & \text{if } NC^*(i) = NC^*(j), \\ \hat{p}_{out}, & \text{if } NC^*(i) \neq NC^*(j) \end{cases}$$

where $\hat{p}_{in}$ and $\hat{p}_{out}$ can be estimated by Maximum Likelihood Estimation (MLE) as follows:

$$\hat{p}_{in} = \frac{\sum_{i \in V} \sum_{j \in V} A_{ij}[i \in C_l \text{ and } j \in C_l, l \in 1, 2]}{\sum_{i \in V} \sum_{j \in V}[i \in C_l \text{ and } j \in C_l]},$$

$$\hat{p}_{out} = \frac{\sum_{i \in V} \sum_{j \in V} A_{ij}[i \in C_l \text{ and } j \in C_m, l \neq m]}{\sum_{i \in V} \sum_{j \in V}[i \in C_l \text{ and } j \in C_m]},$$

where the [] denotes the Iverson bracket, which converts a boolean expression to 0 if the boolean expression in the bracket is false, and 1 otherwise. The complete MLE procedure can be found in the supplementary material.

From LP to NC. Assuming we have an optimal link predictor $LP^*(i, j)$ and a subset of the node labels y_{sub}, the procedure of constructing an optimal node classifier $NC^*(i)$ is derived as follows:

1. Randomly select an anchor node a.
2. Compute the link probabilities of all other nodes with the anchor node: $p_i = LP^*(a, i)$ for all $i \neq a$.
3. Sort the nodes in descending order of their link probabilities.
4. Assign the first $N/2$ nodes to the same community and the remaining nodes to another community.
5. Repeat steps 1–4 with different anchor nodes and take the partition that yields the highest modularity score as the optimal partition.
6. Based on the optimal partition and the y_{sub}, construct the node classifier $NC^*(i)$ by assigning node i to the label of the community that it belongs to in the optimal partition.

The modularity score is a measure of the quality of the partition and is defined as:

$$Q = \left| \frac{1}{2m} \sum_{i,j} (A_{ij} - \frac{k_i k_j}{2m}) \delta(c_i, c_j) \right|$$

where A_{ij} is the observed edge between nodes i and j, k_i and k_j are the degrees of nodes i and j, respectively, m is the total number of edges in the network, and $\delta(c_i, c_j)$ is an indicator function that equals 1 if nodes i and j belong to the same community and 0 otherwise.

We take the absolute value of Q here because we cannot determine the relative magnitudes of p_{in} and p_{out}. Furthermore, when p_{in} and p_{out} are close, LP may have difficulties in distinguishing intra-class edges from inter-class edges, resulting in non-trivial noise in the partition. Therefore, we use multiple anchors and repetitions to improve the robustness of the partition. Once the optimal partition is obtained, we only need a small number of node labels as the partition labels to complete the classification.

The above analysis indicates how the node classification tasks relate to the link prediction tasks on the cSBM, which motivates us to solve the challenge of node classification on the heterophilic graph under weakly-supervised settings via utilizing the "free label". That is, using the link prediction tasks to obtain a filter that well captures the informative graph signals and initializes the node classification model with such a filter.

4.1   Implementation

Our proposed approach is implemented as follows. For each node classification task on the heterophilic graph, we first formulate a link prediction task on the same graph. To prepare the edge data for the link prediction, we randomly split all edges into training, validation, and testing edges with a split of 0.85:0.1:0.05. Note that the testing split is only reserved to check the performance of the link predictor. During each training epoch, we sample pairs of unconnected nodes in the graph as negative edges, which have the same number as the training edges. The model is trained to predict the link probability of each edge, where 1 indicates a positive edge and 0 refers to a negative edge.

The link predictor uses the same backbone as the model used for the node classification task, with only one exception: we remove the softmax layer and replace it with a linear layer combined with a sigmoid layer, which takes the concatenation of the node embeddings of a pair of nodes as input and outputs the link probability. The link predictor is trained with the same hyperparameters as the node classification task, using binary cross-entropy loss as the training loss. After the link predictor is fully trained, we obtain the learned filter, denoted by the parameter γ_L.

To conduct the node classification task, we initialize the filter as γ_L and randomly initialize the other parameters. We keep the rest of the training details, including hyperparameters and training procedure, the same as described in Sect. 3.1.

5   Experiments

To evaluate the effectiveness of our proposed methods, we conduct the following experiments on both synthetic and real-world heterophilic graphs. Specifically, we are examining the following aspects: (1) whether the proposed approach can effectively utilize the "free label" to improve the performance of node classification on heterophilic graphs. (2) whether the proposed approach can be applied to other adaptive filter-based GNNs. (3) the visualization of the learned filters. The experiment setups we used in this section keep the same as presented in Sect. 3.1.

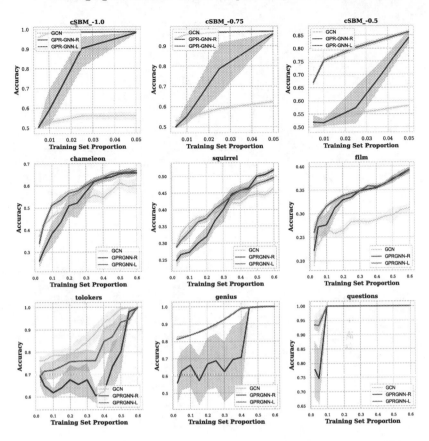

Fig. 4. The performance of GCN, GPRGNN-R and GPRGNN-L on both synthetic and real-world heterophilic graphs under different data splits

5.1 Performance Improvements on GPR-GNN

We first evaluate our proposed method on GPR-GNN. The main results are shown in Fig. 4, we also provide a detailed accuracy table in the supplementary material. GPRGNN-R denotes the original GPR-GNN that uses random initialization of the filter. GPRGNN-L denotes our approach that first trains a link predictor to obtain a learned filter and then uses the filter to initialize the filter of the node classifier. The results show that our approach can significantly improve the performance of GPR-GNN on heterophilic graphs, especially when the training sample ratio is low. For example, when the training set proportion is 0.1, GPRGNN-L achieves 14% and 8% improvements over GPRGNN-R on the *chameleon* and *squirrel* datasets, respectively. This indicates that our approach can effectively utilize the "free label" to improve the performance of node classification under weakly-supervised settings. Furthermore, we also observe a smaller variance in the performance of GPRGNN-L than that of GPRGNN-R, meaning that our approach also enhances the stability of GPR-GNN.

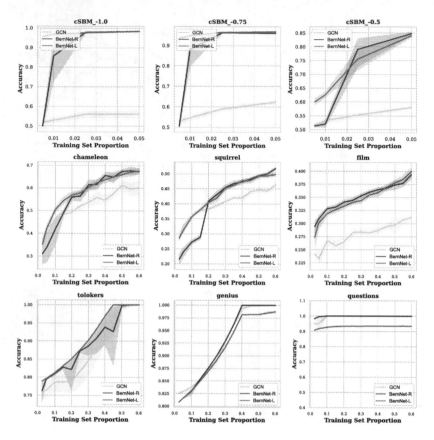

Fig. 5. The performance of GCN, BernNet-R and BernNet-L on both synthetic and real-world heterophilic graphs under different data splits.

5.2   Performance Improvements on BernNet

To verify that the proposed approach can be applied to other adaptive filter-based GNNs, we also evaluate our approach on BernNet [11], a GNN model that learns a filter with Bernstein basis. The results are shown in Fig. 5, which demonstrates that our approach can also improve the performance of BernNet under weakly-supervised settings. In addition, we find that the amount of data that BernNet requires to learn an effective filter is smaller than GPR-GNN. For example, on the *squirrel* dataset, BernNet-R achieves comparable performance to BernNet-L with a training set proportion of 0.2 for *chameleon* and *squirrel* datasets, whereas GPRGNN-R requires a proportion of 0.35. We also notice that on specific datasets like *questions*, the adaptive filter is insensitive to the training set proportion.

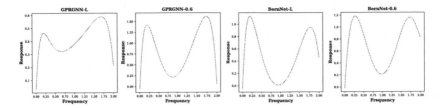

Fig. 6. The learned initial filter of GPRGNN-L and BernNet-L on squirrel, compared with the optimal filter learned with a training ratio of 0.6, denoted as GPRGNN-0.6 and BernNet-0.6. (More learned filters on other datasets are provided in the supplementary material.)

5.3   Visualization of the Learned Filters

To verify that the learned filters are effective, in this section we visualize the learned filters and compare them with the optimal filters. The visualization results are shown in Fig. 6. We can see that the learned filters are consistent with the well-optimized filters learned with sufficient training data, which verifies the effectiveness of using the link predictor to initialize the adaptive filter.

6   Conclusion

This paper addresses a pitfall inherent in the evaluation of adaptive filter-based GNNs in heterophilic graph learning: the common practice of data splitting is to allocate a high proportion of data for training, making the evaluation impractical. To fill this gap, we conducted a series of empirical experiments and verified that in weakly supervised scenarios, the performance of adaptive filter-based GNNs rapidly deteriorates, and they may even be outperformed by fixed filter-based GNNs. Through additional experiments, we highlighted that the ineffectiveness of the learned filters is a key factor leading to the performance degradation. To address this issue, we proposed an edge information-based approach to learn an effective initial filter. We conducted experiments on two adaptive filter-based GNNs, GPR-GNN and BernNet, and verified that the proposed approach can effectively learn a good initialization and therefore improve the performance of adaptive filter-based GNNs under weakly-supervised settings.

Acknowledgements. This work is supported by the National University of Defense Technology Foundation under Grant Nos. ZK20-09 and ZK21-17, the Natural Science Foundation of Hunan Province of China under Grant No. 2021JJ40692 and the National Key Research and Development Program of China under Grant 2021YFB0300101.

Ethical Statement. The purpose of this research is to study the performance of adaptive filters on heterophilic graphs in weakly-supervised settings. The research involves the usage of several open-sourced real-world datasets proposed and used by the heterophilic graph learning community. The potential risks associated with the research include the potential privacy issues on these datasets. We take the following measures to minimize these risks: when conducting the experiments, we will not track the original source of the dataset, but use the data anonymized by the dataset builders. The results of the research will be presented in an unbiased and objective manner.

References

1. Abbe, E.: Community detection and stochastic block models: recent developments. J. Mach. Learn. Res. **18**(1), 6446–6531 (2017)
2. Abboud, R., Ceylan, İ.İ.: Node classification meets link prediction on knowledge graphs. arXiv preprint arXiv:2106.07297 (2021)
3. Bianchi, F.M., Grattarola, D., Livi, L., Alippi, C.: Graph neural networks with convolutional ARMA filters. IEEE Trans. Pattern Anal. Mach. Intell. **44**(7), 3496–3507 (2021)
4. Bo, D., Wang, X., Shi, C., Shen, H.: Beyond low-frequency information in graph convolutional networks. In: Proceedings of the AAAI Conference on Artificial Intelligence, vol. 35, pp. 3950–3957 (2021)
5. Bojchevski, A., et al.: Scaling graph neural networks with approximate pagerank. In: Proceedings of the 26th ACM SIGKDD International Conference on Knowledge Discovery & Data Mining, pp. 2464–2473 (2020)
6. Chien, E., Peng, J., Li, P., Milenkovic, O.: Adaptive universal generalized pagerank graph neural network. In: 9th International Conference on Learning Representations, ICLR 2021, Virtual Event, Austria, 3–7 May 2021 (2021)
7. Ciotti, V., Bonaventura, M., Nicosia, V., Panzarasa, P., Latora, V.: Homophily and missing links in citation networks. EPJ Data Sci. **5**(1), 7 (2016)
8. Deshpande, Y., Sen, S., Montanari, A., Mossel, E.: Contextual stochastic block models. In: Bengio, S., Wallach, H.M., Larochelle, H., Grauman, K., Cesa-Bianchi, N., Garnett, R. (eds.) Advances in Neural Information Processing Systems 31: Annual Conference on Neural Information Processing Systems 2018, NeurIPS 2018, Montréal, Canada, 3–8 December 2018, pp. 8590–8602 (2018)
9. Dong, Y., Ding, K., Jalaian, B., Ji, S., Li, J.: AdaGNN: graph neural networks with adaptive frequency response filter. In: Proceedings of the 30th ACM International Conference on Information & Knowledge Management, pp. 392–401 (2021)
10. Hamilton, W.L., Ying, Z., Leskovec, J.: Inductive representation learning on large graphs. In: Advances in Neural Information Processing Systems 30: Annual Conference on Neural Information Processing Systems, Long Beach, CA, USA, pp. 1024–1034 (2017)
11. He, M., Wei, Z., Xu, H., et al.: BernNet: learning arbitrary graph spectral filters via Bernstein approximation. Adv. Neural. Inf. Process. Syst. **34**, 14239–14251 (2021)
12. Kenlay, H., Thanou, D., Dong, X.: Interpretable stability bounds for spectral graph filters. In: International Conference on Machine Learning, pp. 5388–5397. PMLR (2021)
13. Kingma, D.P., Ba, J.: Adam: A method for stochastic optimization. arXiv preprint arXiv:1412.6980 (2014)
14. Kipf, T.N., Welling, M.: Semi-supervised classification with graph convolutional networks. In: 5th International Conference on Learning Representations, ICLR 2017, Toulon, France, 24–26 April 2017, Conference Track Proceedings. OpenReview.net (2017)

15. Klicpera, J., Bojchevski, A., Günnemann, S.: Predict then propagate: graph neural networks meet personalized pagerank. In: 7th International Conference on Learning Representations, ICLR 2019, New Orleans, LA, USA, 6–9 May 2019. OpenReview.net (2019)
16. Levie, R., Isufi, E., Kutyniok, G.: On the transferability of spectral graph filters. In: 2019 13th International conference on Sampling Theory and Applications (SampTA), pp. 1–5. IEEE (2019)
17. Likhobaba, D., Pavlichenko, N., Ustalov, D.: Toloker Graph: Interaction of Crowd Annotators (2023)
18. Lim, D., Benson, A.R.: Expertise and dynamics within crowdsourced musical knowledge curation: a case study of the genius platform. In: Proceedings of the International AAAI Conference on Web and Social Media, vol. 15, pp. 373–384 (2021)
19. Lim, D., et al.: Large scale learning on non-homophilous graphs: new benchmarks and strong simple methods. Adv. Neural. Inf. Process. Syst. **34**, 20887–20902 (2021)
20. Lim, D., et al.: Large scale learning on non-homophilous graphs: new benchmarks and strong simple methods, pp. 20887–20902 (2021)
21. Lingam, V., Sharma, M., Ekbote, C., Ragesh, R., Iyer, A., Sellamanickam, S.: A piece-wise polynomial filtering approach for graph neural networks. In: Amini, M.R., Canu, S., Fischer, A., Guns, T., Kralj Novak, P., Tsoumakas, G. (eds.) ECML PKDD 2022, Part II. LNCS, vol. 13714, pp. 412–452. Springer, Cham (2023). https://doi.org/10.1007/978-3-031-26390-3_25
22. McPherson, M., Smith-Lovin, L., Cook, J.M.: Birds of a feather: homophily in social networks. Ann. Rev. Sociol. **27**(1), 415–444 (2001)
23. Pei, H., Wei, B., Chang, K.C., Lei, Y., Yang, B.: Geom-GCN: geometric graph convolutional networks. In: 8th International Conference on Learning Representations, ICLR 2020, Addis Ababa, Ethiopia, 26–30 April 2020 (2020)
24. Platonov, O., Kuznedelev, D., Diskin, M., Babenko, A., Prokhorenkova, L.: A critical look at evaluation of GNNs under heterophily: are we really making progress? In: International Conference on Learning Representations
25. Rozemberczki, B., Allen, C., Sarkar, R.: Multi-scale attributed node embedding. J. Complex Netw. **9**(2), cnab014 (2021)
26. Tang, J., Sun, J, Wang, C., Yang, Z.: Social influence analysis in large-scale networks. In: Proceedings of the 15th ACM SIGKDD International Conference on Knowledge Discovery and Data Mining, pp. 807–816 (2009)
27. Velickovic, P., Cucurull, G., Casanova, A., Romero, A., Liò, P., Bengio, Y.: Graph attention networks. In: 6th International Conference on Learning Representations, ICLR 2018, Vancouver, BC, Canada, April 30 - May 3, 2018, Conference Track Proceedings. OpenReview.net (2018)
28. Wang, X., Zhang, M.: How powerful are spectral graph neural networks. In: International Conference on Machine Learning, pp. 23341–23362. PMLR (2022)
29. Wu, F., Jr., A.H.S., Zhang, T., Fifty, C., Yu, T., Weinberger, K.Q.: Simplifying graph convolutional networks. In: Proceedings of the 36th International Conference on Machine Learning, ICML 2019, Long Beach, California, USA, 9–15 June 2019, pp. 6861–6871 (2019)
30. Wu, Z., Pan, S., Long, G., Jiang, J., Chang, X., Zhang, C.: Connecting the dots: multivariate time series forecasting with graph neural networks. In: Gupta, R., Liu, Y., Tang, J., Prakash, B.A. (eds.) KDD 2020: The 26th ACM SIGKDD Conference on Knowledge Discovery and Data Mining, Virtual Event, CA, USA, 23–27 August 2020, pp. 753–763. ACM (2020)

31. Xu, K., Li, C., Tian, Y., Sonobe, T., Kawarabayashi, K., Jegelka, S.: Representation learning on graphs with jumping knowledge networks. In: Proceedings of the 35th International Conference on Machine Learning, ICML 2018, Stockholmsmässan, Stockholm, Sweden, 10–15 July 2018. Proceedings of Machine Learning Research, vol. 80, pp. 5449–5458. PMLR (2018)
32. Ying, R., He, R., Chen, K., Eksombatchai, P., Hamilton, W.L., Leskovec, J.: Graph convolutional neural networks for web-scale recommender systems. In: Guo, Y., Farooq, F. (eds.) Proceedings of the 24th ACM SIGKDD International Conference on Knowledge Discovery & Data Mining, KDD 2018, London, UK, 19–23 August 2018, pp. 974–983. ACM (2018)
33. Zhang, Z., Cui, P., Zhu, W.: Deep learning on graphs: a survey. IEEE Trans. Knowl. Data Eng. **34**(1), 249–270 (2022)
34. Zheng, X., Liu, Y., Pan, S., Zhang, M., Jin, D., Yu, P.S.: Graph neural networks for graphs with heterophily: A survey. arXiv preprint arXiv:2202.07082 (2022)
35. Zhu, J., et al.: Graph neural networks with heterophily. In: Thirty-Fifth AAAI Conference on Artificial Intelligence, Virtual Event, 2–9 February 2021, pp. 11168–11176 (2021)
36. Zhu, J., Yan, Y., Zhao, L., Heimann, M., Akoglu, L., Koutra, D.: Beyond homophily in graph neural networks: current limitations and effective designs. In: Annual Conference on Neural Information Processing Systems 2020, NeurIPS 2020, 6–12 December 2020, virtual (2020)

Train Your Own GNN Teacher: Graph-Aware Distillation on Textual Graphs

Costas Mavromatis[1]($\boxtimes$), Vassilis N. Ioannidis[2], Shen Wang[2], Da Zheng[2],
Soji Adeshina[2], Jun Ma[3], Han Zhao[2,4], Christos Faloutsos[2,5],
and George Karypis[1,2]

[1] University of Minnesota, Minneapolis, USA
mavro016@umn.edu
[2] Amazon Web Services, Seattle, USA
[3] Walgreens AI Labs, Seattle, USA
[4] University of Illinois at Urbana-Champaign, Champaign, USA
[5] Carnegie Mellon University, Pittsburgh, USA

Abstract. How can we learn effective node representations on textual graphs? Graph Neural Networks (GNNs) that use Language Models (LMs) to encode textual information of graphs achieve state-of-the-art performance in many node classification tasks. Yet, combining GNNs with LMs has not been widely explored for practical deployments due to its scalability issues. In this work, we tackle this challenge by developing a Graph-Aware Distillation framework (GRAD) to encode graph structures into an LM for graph-free, fast inference. Different from conventional knowledge distillation, GRAD jointly optimizes a GNN teacher and a graph-free student over the graph's nodes via a shared LM. This encourages the graph-free student to exploit graph information encoded by the GNN teacher while at the same time, enables the GNN teacher to better leverage textual information from unlabeled nodes. As a result, the teacher and the student models learn from each other to improve their overall performance. Experiments in eight node classification benchmarks in both transductive and inductive settings showcase GRAD's superiority over existing distillation approaches for textual graphs. Our code and supplementary material are available at: https://github.com/cmavro/GRAD.

Keywords: Graph Neural Networks · Language Models · Knowledge Distillation

1 Introduction

Graph Neural Networks (GNNs) offer state-of-the-art performance on graph learning tasks in real world applications, including social networks, recommendation systems, biological networks and drug interactions. GNNs [10,17,26] learn

---

C. Mavromatis—Work done while interning at Amazon Web Services, Santa Clara.

© The Author(s), under exclusive license to Springer Nature Switzerland AG 2023
D. Koutra et al. (Eds.): ECML PKDD 2023, LNAI 14171, pp. 157–173, 2023.
https://doi.org/10.1007/978-3-031-43418-1_10

node representations via a recursive neighborhood aggregation scheme [8], which takes as input the node features and the graph structure. In textual graphs, text-based information is associated with the graph's nodes. Methods such as bag-of-words, word2vec [21] or pre-trained Language Models (LMs), e.g., BERT [5], are used to transform raw texts of nodes into features. Transforming raw text to numerical features is usually associated with a non-negligible cost. For example, LMs that rely on transformers [25] have a very large number of parameters and their cost depends on the LM's architecture[1]. This high computational cost results in expensive and/or slow inference during deployment.

Recent works show that combining GNNs with LMs in an end-to-end manner [15,31] leads to state-of-the-art performance for node classification and link prediction tasks. Although powerful, these models are associated with expensive inference costs. During mini-batch inference, a K-layer GNN fetches an exponential number of nodes w.r.t. K, where raw texts of the fetched nodes need to be transformed to numerical features on the fly. As a result, combining LMs with GNNs in a cascaded manner exponentially grows the LM inference cost for each target node. This cost is prohibitive for applications where fast inference is vital, such as providing instant query-product matching in e-commence.

Aiming at a balance between effectiveness and efficiency, we seek to transfer useful knowledge from a GNN teacher to a graph-free student via distillation. As the graph-free student does not use the graph structure during inference, the inference cost depends only on the LM employed. However, existing knowledge distillation (KD) approaches for graphs either do not take full advantage of the graph structure [39] or they require powerful student models (e.g., large LMs) to achieve good performance [42].

To address these limitations, we developed a Graph-Aware Distillation approach (GRAD) that *jointly* optimizes the GNN teacher with its graph-free student via a shared LM. The shared LM serves as an interaction module that allows the two models to learn from each other. On the one hand, the GNN teacher updates the LM's parameters with graph-aware information and distills graph knowledge as soft-labels, which are provided to the student. On the other hand, the graph-free student imitates the GNN's predictions and leverages textual information from unlabeled nodes to improve the fine-tuning of the shared LM. This dynamic interplay between

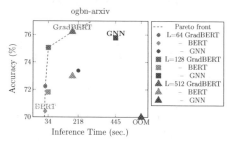

Fig. 1. **GraDBERT** is on the Pareto front: Accuracy performance w.r.t. inference time for ogbn-arxiv. L is the input sequence length and OOM (out of memory) means that the model encountered GPU failure.

---

[1] For example, the inference cost of a single transformer layer is $\mathcal{O}(L^2 d + L d^2)$, where L is the sequence length and d is the number of hidden dimensions.

the two models stimulates the student to not only mimic the GNN predictions but to learn node features that improve its teacher's performance.

GRAD is formulated as a multi-task learning for the shared LM, whose goal is to achieve good performance for both the GNN teacher and the graph-free student models. We designed three different strategies for optimizing the GRAD framework. Their key differences is on how tight the teacher and student models are coupled and on how much flexibility the student model has to fit to its teacher's predictions. As a result, GRAD can be applied in both large-scale graphs, where the student model is a powerful LM, and in small-scale graphs, where the LM is substituted by simple MLPs.

Figure 1 illustrates the superiority of GRAD when the graph-free student model is a BERT model (GRADBERT). It outperforms a fine-tuned BERT model for node classification by 3.24%, and it is as effective as combining BERT with a GNN with 2.4x–13x smaller inference time. Our contributions are summarized below:

- We analyze and identify the limitations of conventional knowledge distillation for textual graphs, which have been previously under-studied (Sect. 3.2).
- We present a graph-aware distillation (GRAD) framework that couples a GNN teacher and a graph-free student together to fully exploit the underlying graph structure. GRAD improves classification for both seen and unseen nodes, that are present in either large or small-scale graphs (Sect. 6.1 and Sect. 6.2).
- We developed three different strategies (Sect. 4) to effectively optimize GRAD framework, which we comprehensively study. This enables GRAD to scale to large graphs and achieve state-of-the-art performance in node classification tasks.

2   Background

2.1   Problem Formulation

In an input *textual graph* $\mathcal{G} = \{\mathcal{V}, \mathcal{E}\}$, each node $v \in \mathcal{V}$ is associated with raw text, which we denote as X_v. $\mathcal{V}$ is the node set and $\mathcal{E}$ is the edge set. Let N denote the total number of nodes. For node classification, the prediction targets are $\boldsymbol{Y} \in \mathbb{R}^{N \times m}$, where row $\boldsymbol{y}_v$ is a m-dim one-hot vector for node v. The node set is divided into labeled nodes $\mathcal{V}^L$ and unlabeled nodes $\mathcal{V}^U$, i.e., $\mathcal{V} = \mathcal{V}^L \cup \mathcal{V}^U$. In inductive scenarios, the input graph $\mathcal{G}$ is divided into two subgraphs $\mathcal{G} = \mathcal{G}^{\text{tran}} \cup \mathcal{G}^{\text{ind}}$, where $\mathcal{G}^{\text{tran}}$ is used for learning (transductive part) and $\mathcal{G}^{\text{ind}}$ is used only during inference ($\mathcal{G}^{\text{ind}}$ is the inductive part that is not observed during learning). In transductive scenarios, we have $\mathcal{G} = \mathcal{G}^{\text{tran}}$ and $\mathcal{G}^{\text{ind}} = \emptyset$.

As introduced Sect. 1, utilizing the textual graph $\mathcal{G}$ for making predictions at test time results in slow inference. Thus, we seek to learn a graph-free model τ', e.g., a LM, that only takes node text X_v during inference. It is desired that $\tau'(X_v) \approx f(\mathcal{G}, X_v)$, where f is a model that uses the graph, e.g., a GNN, so that the graph-free model achieves as effective node classification as a graph-based model.

2.2   GNNs on Textual Graphs

To handle raw texts in textual graphs, X_v is transformed to numerical features $\boldsymbol{x}_v \in \mathbb{R}^d$ via a function $\tau(\cdot)$,

$$\boldsymbol{x}_v = \tau(X_v). \tag{1}$$

For example, LMs, such as BERT [5] for modelling $\tau(\cdot)$, transform each token of the input sequence X_v to a representation. The final $\boldsymbol{x}_v$ can be obtained as the representation of a specific token, which is usually the [CLS] token.

GNNs [17,26] transform a computation graph $\mathcal{G}_v$ that is centered around node v to a d-dimensional node representation $\boldsymbol{h}_v$. We write the GNN transformation as

$$\boldsymbol{h}_v = \text{GNN}\big(\{\tau(X_u) : u \in \mathcal{G}_v\}\big), \tag{2}$$

where $\tau(X_u)$ generates the input features $\boldsymbol{x}_u$ of node u. For a GNN with K layers, $\mathcal{G}_v$ includes nodes and edges (with self-loops) up to K hops away from v.

The $(k+1)$-th GNN layer takes as input a node's representation $\boldsymbol{h}_v^{(k)}$ of the previous layer k as well as the representations of its 1-hop neighbors. It aggregates them to a new representation $\boldsymbol{h}_v^{(k+1)}$ as follows,

$$\boldsymbol{h}_v^{(k+1)} = \phi\big(\{\boldsymbol{h}_u^{(k)} : u \in \mathcal{N}_v\}\big), \tag{3}$$

where $\mathcal{N}_v$ is the set of direct neighbors of v and $\phi(\cdot)$ is an aggregation function. For example, a common GNN update $\phi(\cdot)$, which is employed in GraphSAGE [10] and RGCN [24], can be described as follows,

$$\boldsymbol{h}_v^{(k+1)} = \sigma\Big(\boldsymbol{W}_{\text{self}}^{(k)}\boldsymbol{h}_v^{(k)} + \sum_{u \in \mathcal{N}_v} \boldsymbol{W}^{(k)}\boldsymbol{h}_u^{(k)}\Big), \tag{4}$$

where $\boldsymbol{W}_{\text{self}}^{(k)}, \boldsymbol{W}^{(k)}$ are learnable parameters and $\sigma(\cdot)$ is a nonlinearity mapping. At the first layer, we usually have $\boldsymbol{h}_v^{(0)} = \boldsymbol{x}_v$, that are text features extracted from the node. Computing $\boldsymbol{h}_v$ can be as expensive as $\mathcal{O}(S^K C)$, where $\tau(\cdot)$ is a LM with inference cost C, S is the neighborhood size, and K is the number of GNN layers.

3   Towards Graph-Aware Knowledge Distillation

As discussed in Sect. 2.1, we seek to learn a graph-free model τ' for fast inference, that also achieves as effective node classification as a GNN model f.

3.1   Knowledge Distillation

A straightforward solution is to use the Knowledge Distillation (KD) technique [11], where a powerful teacher model transfers knowledge to a simpler student model. In our case, the teacher model corresponds to a graph-based model (GNN), while the student model is a graph-free model, such as an LM.

We follow the standard KD paradigm, in which the teacher distills knowledge via soft-labels. At a high level, the algorithmic procedure is

- **First Stage.** The GNN teacher is trained for node classification. The objective is given by

$$\mathcal{L}_{\mathrm{nc}} = \sum_{v \in \mathcal{V}^L} l_{\mathrm{CE}}(\hat{\boldsymbol{t}}_v, \boldsymbol{y}_v), \tag{5}$$

where l_{CE} is the standard cross-entropy and

$$\hat{\boldsymbol{t}}_v = \mathrm{MLP}\Big(\mathrm{GNN}\big(\{\boldsymbol{x}_u : u \in \mathcal{G}_v\}\big)\Big) \tag{6}$$

are teacher's label predictions (logits). Numerical features $\boldsymbol{x}_u$ are learned by fine-tuning an LM $\tau(\cdot)$ in an end-to-end manner; see Eq. (1). The trained GNN teacher generates soft-labels $\hat{\boldsymbol{t}}_v$ for all nodes $v \in \mathcal{G}$.
- **Second Stage.** Another LM $\tau'(\cdot)$ is trained to mimic GNN's predictions $\hat{\boldsymbol{t}}_v$. The LM is optimized via

$$\mathcal{L}_{\mathrm{KD}} = \sum_{v \in \mathcal{V}^L} l_{\mathrm{CE}}(\hat{\boldsymbol{s}}_v, \boldsymbol{y}_v) + \lambda \sum_{v \in \mathcal{V}} l_{\mathrm{KL}}(\hat{\boldsymbol{s}}_v, \hat{\boldsymbol{t}}_v), \tag{7}$$

where

$$\hat{\boldsymbol{s}}_v = \mathrm{MLP}\big(\tau'(X_v)\big) \tag{8}$$

are the student's predictions and l_{KL} is the KL-divergence between the student's and teacher's logits. Hyper-parameter $\lambda \in \mathbb{R}$ controls the relative importance of the knowledge distillation term.

3.2   What Does Knowledge Distillation Learn? An Analysis

In many cases, only a subset of the nodes in a graph is labeled; it is denoted as $\mathcal{V}^L$. Since the GNN's predictions $\hat{\boldsymbol{t}}_v$ are treated as soft-labels, the second term in Eq. (7) allows KD to fine-tune its LM τ' over both labeled and unlabeled nodes. However, as $\hat{\boldsymbol{t}}_v$ are pre-computed after the first stage of GNN training, the graph-free student does not use the actual graph structure during learning (second stage). In other words, nodes are treated independently from the underlying graph and the graph-free model can only infer how nodes interact via the provided soft-labels by the GNN.

Next, we quantify the importance of capturing node interactions, which benefits many applications such as community detection and label propagation in graphs [16]. As discussed in Sect. 2.2, the node classification objective aims at transforming a subgraph $\mathcal{G}_v$ centered around node v to its label $\boldsymbol{y}_v$. In information theory, this is equivalent to maximizing the mutual information $I(\cdot)$,

$$\max_f \sum_{v \in \mathcal{V}^L} I_f(\boldsymbol{y}_v; \mathcal{G}_v), \tag{9}$$

between $\mathcal{G}_v$ and label distribution $\boldsymbol{y}_v$, where I_f is parametrized by the GNN function f. It is always true that $I(\cdot) \geq 0$.

If we consider $\mathcal{G}_v$ as a joint distribution of the feature set $\mathcal{X}_v = \{X_u : u \in \mathcal{G}_v\}$ and edge set $\mathcal{E}_v$, we have

$$I(\boldsymbol{y}_v; \mathcal{G}_v) = I(\boldsymbol{y}_v; (\mathcal{X}_v, \mathcal{E}_v)) = I(\boldsymbol{y}_v; \mathcal{X}_v) + I(\boldsymbol{y}_v; \mathcal{E}_v | \mathcal{X}_v), \tag{10}$$

which is obtained via the chain rule of mutual information. Now by setting $\tilde{\mathcal{X}}_v = \mathcal{X}_v \setminus \{X_v\}$, we can further obtain

$$I(\boldsymbol{y}_v; \mathcal{G}_v) = I(\boldsymbol{y}_v; X_v) + I(\boldsymbol{y}_v; \tilde{\mathcal{X}}_v | X_v) + I(\boldsymbol{y}_v; \mathcal{E}_v | \mathcal{X}_v). \tag{11}$$

The joint mutual information is decomposed into three terms, (i) the information that comes from the node itself, (ii) the information that comes from other nodes in $\mathcal{G}_v$, and (iii) the additional information that comes from the actual links between nodes.

Remark 1. If the neighbor set or the graph structure is not utilized during learning, only $I(\boldsymbol{y}_v; X_v)$ of Eq. (11) can be maximized.

Corollary 1. *Assume that predictions $\hat{\boldsymbol{t}}_u$ for unlabeled nodes $u \in \mathcal{V}^U$ are obtained via Eq. (6) with a GNN f and an LM τ. The graph-free student of KD, that employs an LM τ', solves*

$$\max_{\tau'} \sum_{u \in \mathcal{V}^U} I_{\tau'}(\hat{\boldsymbol{t}}_u; X_u), \tag{12}$$

where

$$\hat{\boldsymbol{t}}_u = f(\tau(X_{u'}) : u' \in \mathcal{G}_u),$$
$$s.t. \quad f, \tau = \arg\max_{\tilde{f}, \tilde{\tau}} \sum_{v \in \mathcal{V}^L} I_{\tilde{f}, \tilde{\tau}}(\boldsymbol{y}_v; \mathcal{G}_v). \tag{13}$$

The student models solves Eq. (12) without directly accessing the graph structure $\mathcal{G}$. Since $\hat{\boldsymbol{t}}_u$ are obtained through a teacher GNN in Eq. (13), which maximizes all three parts of Eq. (11), it is possible that $\hat{\boldsymbol{t}}_u$ can still implicitly contain graph information from $\mathcal{G}_u$. However, due to the data-processing inequality of mutual information, it holds that

$$I_{f, \tau}(\boldsymbol{y}_u; \mathcal{G}_u) \geq I(\boldsymbol{y}_u; \hat{\boldsymbol{t}}_u). \tag{14}$$

This means that, despite being a function of $\mathcal{G}_u$, the information contained in $\hat{\boldsymbol{t}}_u$ w.r.t. $\boldsymbol{y}_u$ is less than that of the original $\mathcal{G}_u$. Thus, student's performance depends on *how informative $\hat{\boldsymbol{t}}_u$ are*, compared to $\mathcal{G}_u$.

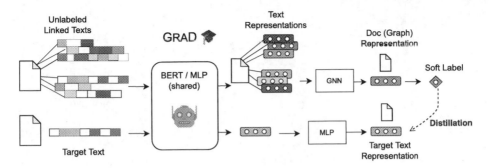

Fig. 2. GRAD framework. GRAD captures textual information among unlabeled linked texts by allowing the teacher GNN and the graph-free student to jointly update the shared text encoding function.

Note that the objectives of Eq. (12) and Eq. (13) are applied over different sets of nodes $\mathcal{V}^U$ and $\mathcal{V}^L$, which does not ensure that GNN f is the optimal function to encode graph information for nodes $u \in \mathcal{V}^U$. For example, a GNN might overfit to nodes that appear frequently in the training subgraphs, and ignore nodes that appear infrequently. In Sect. 4, we present a framework that aims at better capturing the existing graph and textual information during distillation.

4   GRAD 🎓 Framework

In this work, we take a different approach from the traditional KD, as implemented in Eq. (12). As we cannot use the graph structure during inference, our GRaph-Aware Distillation (GRAD) improves structure utilization during training. The motivation is to use the original graph $\mathcal{G}$ while training the graph-free student, even if GNN predictions $\hat{t}_u$ may (or may not) implicitly contain such graph information.

Our GRAD framework does this by coupling the teacher GNN with its graph-free student with a shared function $\tau(\cdot)$. This allows the GNN to directly encode structural information into τ, that is then used by the graph-free model during inference. The overall framework is illustrated in Fig. 2. GRAD is posed as a multi-task learning for the shared LM, whose goal is to collectively optimize the GNN teacher and the graph-free student models. The learning problem is given by

$$\max_{f,\tau} \sum_{v \in \mathcal{V}^L} I_{f,\tau}(\boldsymbol{y}_v; \mathcal{G}_v) + \sum_{v \in \mathcal{V}^U} I_\tau(\hat{\boldsymbol{t}}_u; X_u),$$

$$\text{where} \quad \hat{\boldsymbol{t}}_u = f\big(\tau(X_{u'}) : u' \in \mathcal{G}_u\big), \tag{15}$$

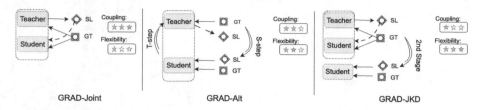

Fig. 3. GRAD strategies for coupling the GNN teacher and the graph-free student. *SL* denotes soft-label and *GT* denotes ground-truth label. GRAD-Joint couples the two models in a single step, GRAD-Alt couples them in an alternate fashion, while GRAD-JKD couples them in the first stage and decouples them in the second stage. For illustration purposes only, the star metric ($\star$) quantifies the teacher-student coupling tightness and the flexibility of the student model.

and function τ contributes in both objectives that GRAD maximizes. This results in a *coupled* multi-objective optimization, since predictions $\hat{t}_u$ depend on function τ and thus, tie the GNN f with the graph-free model together.

Notably, the graph-free student uses soft-labels provided by the GNN to fine-tune the LM over textual information from unlabeled nodes; see second term of Eq. (15). This, consequently, ensures that the GNN leverages all the graph's textual information (in an implicit manner) to compute $\hat{t}_u$, which might have been neglected in Eq. (13). As the GNN teacher better encodes graph-aware textual information from the input (transdutive) nodes, the graph-free student manages to *train its own GNN teacher* via the shared LM.

In what follows, we present three different optimization strategies (GRAD-Joint, GRAD-Alt, and GRAD-JKD) for solving Eq. (15). Figure 3 presents them at a high-level, and their key difference is on how tight they couple the teacher and the student model.

4.1 GRAD-Joint

The first strategy (GRAD-Joint) optimizes GRAD framework in a single-stage, where the teacher and the student are jointly updating τ. GRAD-Joint objective is given by

$$\mathcal{L}_{\text{Joint}} = \lambda \sum_{v \in \mathcal{V}} l_{\text{KL}}(\hat{s}_v, \hat{t}_v) + \sum_{v \in \mathcal{V}^L} \left[\alpha l_{\text{CE}}(\hat{t}_v, \boldsymbol{y}_v) + (1 - \alpha) l_{\text{CE}}(\hat{s}_v, \boldsymbol{y}_v) \right], \quad (16)$$

where $\lambda \in \mathbb{R}$ and $\alpha \in [0, 1]$ are hyperparameters that control the importance of each term and ensure that the GNN models does not learn to ignore the structure. The first term is the KD loss between GNN teacher's predictions $\hat{t}_v$ and graph-free student's predictions $\hat{s}_v$, and the other two terms are for ground-truth labels $\boldsymbol{y}_v$. Predictions $\hat{s}_v$ and $\hat{t}_v$ are optimized via a shared encoding function $\tau(\cdot)$ (multi-task learning).

We highlight the dynamic interplay between the GNN teacher and the graph-free student in Eq. (16). The GNN teacher provides a soft-label $\hat{t}_v$, which the graph-free student tries to mimic via $l_{\mathrm{KL}}(\hat{\boldsymbol{s}}_v, \hat{\boldsymbol{t}}_v)$. However, instead of training $\tau(\cdot)$ to simply mimic the GNN predictions, term $l_{\mathrm{CE}}(\hat{\boldsymbol{t}}_v, \boldsymbol{y}_v)$ encourages $\tau(\cdot)$ to generate text representations that are beneficial for the GNN teacher. This co-learning between the GNN teacher and the graph-free student leads to graph-aware text representations, as the two models learn from each other.

4.2 GRaD-Alt

A common challenge in multi-task learning is negative transfer [40], in which the performance improvement of a specific task leads to performance degradation of other tasks. Our second strategy (GRaD-Alt) alleviates this issue, which might be present in GRaD-Joint, by optimizing the teacher and the student model in an alternate fashion. GRaD-Alt objective is given by

$$\mathcal{L}_{\text{T-step}} = \sum_{v \in \mathcal{V}^L} l_{\mathrm{CE}}(\hat{\boldsymbol{t}}_v, \boldsymbol{y}_v), \tag{17}$$

$$\mathcal{L}_{\text{S-step}} = \lambda \sum_{v \in \mathcal{V}} l_{\mathrm{KL}}(\hat{\boldsymbol{s}}_v, \hat{\boldsymbol{t}}_v) + \sum_{v \in \mathcal{V}^L} l_{\mathrm{CE}}(\hat{\boldsymbol{s}}_v, \boldsymbol{y}_v), \tag{18}$$

where the teacher objective $\mathcal{L}_{\text{T-step}}$ and the student objective $\mathcal{L}_{\text{S-step}}$ alternately update function τ. Different from GRaD-Joint, decoupling S-step from the teacher gives more flexibility to the student to fit to its teacher's predictions.

4.3 GRaD-JKD

Solving Eq. (17) and Eq. (18) consists of many alternate optimization steps that update τ. This is associated with significant computational costs when τ is a large LM and when the input graph consists of a large number of nodes.

Our third strategy (GRaD-JKD) is motivated by the benefits discussed in Sect. 4.1 that lead to improving the GNN teacher as well as the benefits discussed in Sect. 4.2 that lead to improving the flexibility of the graph-free student. GRaD-JKD consists of two distinct stages, as summarized below

- **First Stage.** The GNN teacher is jointly trained with its graph-free student via objective $\mathcal{L}_{\text{Joint}}$; see Eq. (16).
- **Second Stage.** The GNN teacher is decoupled by its student, and the student is retrained alone to mimic the teacher's predictions via

$$\mathcal{L}_{\mathrm{KD}} = \lambda \sum_{v \in \mathcal{V}} l_{\mathrm{KL}}(\hat{\boldsymbol{s}}_v, \hat{\boldsymbol{t}}_v) + \sum_{v \in \mathcal{V}^L} l_{\mathrm{CE}}(\hat{\boldsymbol{s}}_v, \boldsymbol{y}_v). \tag{19}$$

The second stage is similar to conventional KD, which is why we term this strategy GRaD-JKD (Joint +KD). In our case, however, the GNN teacher has been trained with a graph-free student, which allows it to better leverage textual information from unlabeled nodes.

4.4   Student Models

A powerful function $\tau(\cdot)$, that can encode information from both the GNN and the graph-free model, is a key factor in the co-optimization of the teacher and student model. We use LMs, such as BERT [5], to instantiate $\tau(\cdot)$, and name our method GRADBERT. GRADBERT is fine-tuned end-to-end, which is shown to benefit node classification tasks [15].

GRADBERT requires raw texts on nodes and assumes the graphs have adequate data for training. Although not common in practical scenarios, some graphs might be of small scale and not associated with raw texts. In such cases, we model $\tau(\cdot)$ by bag-of-words or TF-IDF text vectors (if provided), followed by trainable MLPs, which we name GRADMLP.

5   Experimental Setup

5.1   Datasets

For GRADBERT, we use three widely used node classification benchmarks that provide raw text on nodes, ogbn-arxiv (Arxiv), ogbn-products (Products), and a smaller version of ogbn-papers100M (Papers1.5M) [3,12]. For GRADMLP, we use Cora, Citeseer, Pubmed, A-Computer, and A-Photo [29], where input features are bag-of-words or TF-IDF word encodings.

5.2   Implementation Details

For our GNN teacher, we use GraphSAGE [10] for both the GRADBERT and the GRADMLP students. To further reduce the training computation cost for GRADBERT, we use an 1-layer GraphSAGE and sample $S \in \{8, 12\}$ neighbors for Eq. (4), which has a training cost of $\mathcal{O}(SC)$ per node. We initialize GRADBERT parameters with SciBERT [2] for Arxiv and Papers1.5M that provides better tokenization for scientific texts. Due to computational constraints, we use a smaller LM for Products, i.e., DistilBERT [23], and we only use GRAD-Alt for small-scale graphs. Further implementation details and ablation studies on GRAD's framework can be found in the Appendix.

5.3   Compared Methods

We develop the BERT+KD baseline, which employs conventional GNN-to-BERT KD via Eq. (7). GLNN [39] is a GNN-to-MLP distillation approach that does not leverage LMs, to which we refer as MLP+KD baseline. We also compare GRADBERT with methods that fine-tune LMs on graphs. Graph-Aware BERT (GA-BERT) [15] and BERT-LP [3] fine-tune BERT models to solve the link prediction task. GIANT [3] fine-tunes BERT to solve neighborhood prediction, which is a task similar to link prediction. E2EG [6] trains GIANT for neighborhood prediction and node classification end-to-end. GLEM [42] utilizes

Table 1. Performance comparison of graph-free methods. Bold font denotes the overall best results. We also report the number of trainable parameters of each LM model in millions (#Params).

	Arxiv		Products		Papers1.5M	
	Acc. (%)	#Params	Acc. (%)	#Params	Acc. (%)	#Params
MLP	$62.91_{\pm 0.60}$	No LM	$61.06_{\pm 0.08}$	No LM	$47.24_{\pm 0.39}$	No LM
GLNN	$72.15_{\pm 0.27}$	No LM	$77.65_{\pm 0.48}$	No LM	-	
BERT	$72.81_{\pm 0.12}$	110M	$77.64_{\pm 0.08}$	110M	$61.45_{\pm 0.07}$	110M
BERT-LP	$67.33_{\pm 0.54}$	110M	$73.83_{\pm 0.06}$	110M	-	
GIANT	$73.06_{\pm 0.11}$	110M	$80.49_{\pm 0.28}$	110M	$61.10_{\pm 0.19}$	110M
E2EG	$73.62_{\pm 0.14}$	110M	$81.11_{\pm 0.37}$	110M	-	
GLEM	$74.53_{\pm 0.12}$	138M	$81.25_{\pm 0.15}$	138M	-	
BERT+KD	$74.39_{\pm 0.32}$	110M	$\underline{81.91}_{\pm 0.64}$	66M	$61.85_{\pm 0.04}$	110M
GRaDBERT						
Joint	$\underline{74.92}_{\pm 0.16}$	110M	$81.42_{\pm 0.40}$	66M	$\underline{63.44}_{\pm 0.05}$	110M
JKD	$\mathbf{75.05}_{\pm 0.11}$	110M	$\mathbf{82.89}_{\pm 0.07}$	66M	$\mathbf{63.60}_{\pm 0.05}$	110M

variational inference to jointly optimize the LM and the GNN for node classification. For a fair comparison, we have the same GNN architecture (GraphSAGE) among methods that use GNNs (GRaD, KD, GA-BERT, and GLEM) during training.

6 Experimental Results

In the following experiments, we assess GRaD's performance for node classification over textual graphs. In Sect. 6.1, we compare GRaDBERT with other methods that do not use graph structure during inference, as well as we assess the performance of GRaD's GNN teacher. In Sect. 6.2, we evaluate how well different GRaD strategies generalize to inductive (unseen) nodes. Furthermore, we conduct inference time analysis to demonstrate the efficiency advantage of GRaD and provide qualitative examples in the Appendix.

6.1 GRaDBERT Results

Table 1 shows performance results for methods that do not use graph structure during inference. Clearly, GRaDBERT is the method that performs the best. MLP and GLNN are methods that do not fine-tune LMs, and thus, perform poorly. GIANT and BERT-LP pretrain BERT to encode structural information, but BERT is fixed for node classification, which may be suboptimal. For example, E2EG, that adapts GIANT for node classification, improves GIANT by 0.61% points on average. GLEM relies on powerful LMs to alternately fine-tune the teacher and the student models, and thus outperforms previous methods. However, GLEM does not show a clear advantage over our baseline BERT+KD

Table 2. GNN performance comparison for different methods that jointly fine-tune LMs for node classification. The underlying GNN model is GraphSAGE. We also report the number of trainable parameters of each backbone LM model in millions (#Params).

	Arxiv		Products		Papers1.5M	
	Acc. (%)	#Params	Acc. (%)	#Params	Acc. (%)	#Params
BERT-GNN	$74.78_{\pm 0.52}$	110M	$82.01_{\pm 0.43}$	110M	$65.80_{\pm 0.23}$	110M
GA-BERT-GNN	74.97	110M	82.35	110M	-	
GLEM-GNN	$75.50_{\pm 0.24}$	138M	$83.16_{\pm 0.19}$	138M	-	
GRAD-GNN	$\mathbf{76.42}_{\pm 0.21}$	110M	$\mathbf{83.34}_{\pm 0.24}$	66M	$\mathbf{66.61}_{\pm 0.22}$	110M

Table 3. Performance comparison of different distillation strategies in the inductive setting, in which we hold 50% of validation and test nodes out of the full graph. *Full* means that methods are trained and evaluated on the full graph, while *ind* shows performance on inductive nodes. Δ_{acc} reports the relative performance degradation between the two settings.

Dataset		MLP+KD	BERT+KD	GRADBERT	
				Joint	JKD
Arxiv	full	68.26	74.43	74.45	75.15
	ind	59.34	73.45	**74.22**	73.81
	Δ_{acc}	-13.06%	-1.32%	-0.31%	-1.78%
Products	full	77.20	82.31	81.47	82.82
	ind	72.93	80.94	81.24	**81.69**
	Δ_{acc}	-5.53%	-1.66%	-0.28%	-1.36%

method, while it utilizes 28M or 77M more parameters. GRADBERT outperforms BERT+KD by 0.66%, 0.98%, and 1.75% points for Arxiv, Products, and Papers, respectively, which is a considerable improvement for these large-scale graphs. In Products, GRAD-JKD improves over GRAD-Joint by 1.45% points, and shows that JKD allows the student model to better fit to its teacher's predictions.

Table 2 evaluates the performance of GNNs combined with LMs (LM-GNN methods). GRAD's GNN teacher performs the best, which verifies that GRAD's student improves its teacher's effectiveness. BERT-GNN is the baseline LM-GNN with end-to-end training, which performs the worst. GA-BERT enhances BERT with a link prediction task and leads to better results than BERT-GNN. GLEM that leverages unlabeled nodes, as GRAD does, performs better than BERT and GA-BERT. However, it does not train the LM-GNN model end-to-end, which limits its performance compared to GRAD, while it requires larger LM models.

In transductive settings, graph-free students could perform well by imitating their GNN teachers' predictions without learning effective features (Sect. 3.2). Thus, we evaluate our GRAD approach in the inductive setting, where

Table 4. Performance comparison of different GRAD strategies on transductive (tran) and inductive (ind) nodes. We sample 50% nodes from the test set as the inductive nodes to evaluate every method. We report mean accuracy over 10 runs.

Dataset		GLNN (MLP+KD)	GLEM (MLP)	GRADMLP (ours)		
				Joint	Alt	JKD
Cora	tran	76.72	76.78	79.39	79.20	79.04
	ind	70.74	70.44	**73.00**	72.86	72.51
Citeseer	tran	69.55	69.06	70.33	70.96	68.69
	ind	69.72	69.33	70.38	**70.80**	69.28
Pubmed	tran	74.00	76.38	78.13	77.71	77.72
	ind	73.61	75.53	**77.54**	76.96	76.89
A-Comp	tran	82.12	81.15	81.20	82.60	82.28
	ind	79.11	78.07	78.79	**80.09**	79.41
A-Photo	tran	92.21	89.83	91.68	91.70	92.36
	ind	89.96	86.49	88.83	89.03	**90.09**

well-trained students are essential to generalize to features of unseen nodes, which are not connected to the existing graph during training. Table 3 shows GRADBERT's performance in inductive settings. GRADBERT outperforms the baseline BERT+KD by more than 0.7% points, on average. Note that MLP+KD uses a static BERT model and cannot generalize well to unseen nodes. As Table 3 shows, methods that use conventional KD (BERT+KD and GRAD-JKD) have a higher performance drop for inductive nodes. This suggests that conventional KD favors transductive settings while it might be limited for inductive nodes.

6.2   GRADMLP Results

Table 4 shows the performance of different GRAD strategies for small-scale graphs, where MLPs uses as the backbone share function τ. Methods that employ KD do not couple the teacher and student models sufficiently, and thus do not learn as effective node features in these small-scale graphs. GLEM performs the worst as it requires a powerful student model that generates high-quality soft-labels, which is not the case for simple MLPs. GRAD-Alt performs the best on Citeseer and A-Comp, while GRAD-Joint performs the best on Cora and Pubmed. We suspect that, in the second case, node texts are more informative (paper keywords) and thus, coupling the teacher and student models tightly improves the performance.

Moreover, Fig. 4 shows that GRADMLP consistently outperforms MLP+KD with different inductive rates, ranging from 10% to 75%. In these small graphs, having an inductive ration close to 90% results in training graphs with few connections among nodes. Thus, in this case, GRADMLP does not have useful graph information to leverage.

7   Related Work

Learning on Textual Graphs. A common approach for effective learning on textual graphs is to combine LMs [5,19,22] with GNNs [10,17,26]. Methods such as [3,15,34] focus on pre-training LMs over graph data to preserve node-level structure, while [35] focuses on token-level information. Methods such as [6,31,37,42] focus on fine-tuning LMs for solving node classification directly, which is more related to our work. Experiments showed that GRAD outperforms these competing approaches. Apart from node classification, leveraging GNNs for learning on textual graphs has been applied to question answering [20,41], sponsored search [18,45], and document classification [14,33].

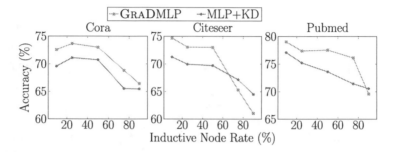

Fig. 4. Performance on inductive nodes w.r.t. inductive node rate (inductive node rate equals to #ind test nodes/#total test nodes). GRADMLP consistently outperforms MLP+KD for reasonable inductive rates.

Distillation Approaches. Distillation approaches mainly focus on model compression (see a survey in [9]). It is worth to mention that [38] proposed a self-distillation technique that distills knowledge from deeper layers to shallow ones of the same architecture. Inspired by self-distillation, GRAD-Joint self-distills knowledge from deeper layers (GNN) to shallow layers (LM or MLP). However, our work is motivated by capturing node interactions, and not by model compression. Moreover, [36] shows a connection between self-distillation and label smoothing, which may be interpreted as a graph-aware label smoothing in our case. Closely related to our work, GLNN [39] and ColdBrew [43] propose to distill knowledge from a graph modality to a graph-less modality. However, experiments showed that GRAD learns better graph information than GLNN for both inductive and transductive settings, while ColdBrew can only be applied to transductive settings. Graph-regularized MLPs [1,7,13,30,44] are also methods that improve MLP performance for node classification. However, their performance is inferior to the one achieved by KD approaches. Other graph-based distillation approaches focus on distilling large GNNs to smaller GNNs [28,32] or to simpler graph models [29]. Finally, the work in [4] distills knowledge from pretrained GNNs and the work in [27] applies graph-based distillation for incremental learning in recommender systems.

8   Conclusion

In this paper, we developed a graph-aware distillation approach (GRAD) that jointly trains a teacher GNN and a graph-free student via a shared LM. This allows the two models to learn from each other and improve their overall performance. We have evaluated GRAD in eight node classification benchmarks in both transductive and inductive settings, in all of which GRAD outperforms conventional knowledge distillation. GRAD is a method that achieves a balance among efficiency and effectiveness in textual graphs.

Acknowledgment. Part of this work was supported by NSF (1704074, 1757916, 1834251, 1834332). Access to research and computing facilities was provided by the College of Science & Engineering and the Minnesota Supercomputing Institute.

Limitations and Ethical Statement. GRAD relies on informative input node features to learn effective shared LMs (or MLPs) that can generalize to unseen nodes, which is the case in textual graphs. Thus, one limitation is that it is not certain how GRAD generalizes to other graphs, e.g., to featureless graphs. Moreover as a knowledge distillation approach, GRAD trades accuracy for computation efficiency and it cannot adapt to dynamic graphs with edge changes the same way as GNN could. To overcome biases encoded in the training graph, e.g., standard stereotypes in recommender graphs, GRAD needs to be retrained over the new unbiased graph.

References

1. Ando, R., Zhang, T.: Learning on graph with laplacian regularization. In: NIPS (2006)
2. Beltagy, I., Lo, K., Cohan, A.: SciBERT: a pretrained language model for scientific text. In: EMNLP-IJCNLP (2019)
3. Chien, E., et al.: Node feature extraction by self-supervised multi-scale neighborhood prediction. In: ICLR (2022)
4. Deng, X., Zhang, Z.: Graph-free knowledge distillation for graph neural networks. arXiv (2021)
5. Devlin, J., Chang, M.W., Lee, K., Toutanova, K.: BERT: pre-training of deep bidirectional transformers for language understanding. In: ACL (2019)
6. Dinh, T.A., Boef, J.D., Cornelisse, J., Groth, P.: E2EG: end-to-end node classification using graph topology and text-based node attributes. arXiv (2022)
7. Dong, W., Wu, J., Luo, Y., Ge, Z., Wang, P.: Node representation learning in graph via node-to-neighbourhood mutual information maximization. In: IEEE/CVF CVPR (2022)
8. Gilmer, J., Schoenholz, S.S., Riley, P.F., Vinyals, O., Dahl, G.E.: Neural message passing for quantum chemistry. In: ICML (2017)
9. Gou, J., Yu, B., Maybank, S.J., Tao, D.: Knowledge distillation: a survey. In: IJCV (2021)
10. Hamilton, W., Ying, Z., Leskovec, J.: Inductive representation learning on large graphs. In: NeurIPS (2017)
11. Hinton, G., Vinyals, O., Dean, J., et al.: Distilling the knowledge in a neural network. arXiv (2015)

12. Hu, W., et al.: Open graph benchmark: datasets for machine learning on graphs. In: NeurIPS (2020)
13. Hu, Y., You, H., Wang, Z., Wang, Z., Zhou, E., Gao, Y.: Graph-MLP: node classification without message passing in graph (2021)
14. Huang, L., Ma, D., Li, S., Zhang, X., Wang, H.: Text level graph neural network for text classification. In: EMNLP (2019)
15. Ioannidis, V.N., et al.: Efficient and effective training of language and graph neural network models. arXiv (2022)
16. Jia, J., Benson, A.R.: Residual correlation in graph neural network regression. In: KDD (2020)
17. Kipf, T.N., Welling, M.: Semi-supervised classification with graph convolutional networks. In: ICLR (2017)
18. Li, C., et al.: AdsGNN: behavior-graph augmented relevance modeling in sponsored search. In: ACM SIGIR (2021)
19. Liu, Y., et al.: Roberta: a robustly optimized bert pretraining approach. arXiv (2019)
20. Mavromatis, C., Karypis, G.: ReaRev: adaptive reasoning for question answering over knowledge graphs. arXiv (2022)
21. Mikolov, T., Sutskever, I., Chen, K., Corrado, G.S., Dean, J.: Distributed representations of words and phrases and their compositionality. In: NIPS (2013)
22. Raffel, C., et al.: Exploring the limits of transfer learning with a unified text-to-text transformer. JMLR **21**(1), 5485–5551 (2020)
23. Sanh, V., Debut, L., Chaumond, J., Wolf, T.: Distilbert, a distilled version of bert: smaller, faster, cheaper and lighter. arXiv (2019)
24. Schlichtkrull, M., Kipf, T.N., Bloem, P., Berg, R.V.D., Titov, I., Welling, M.: Modeling relational data with graph convolutional networks. In: ESWC (2018)
25. Vaswani, A., et al.: Attention is all you need. In: NIPS (2017)
26. Veličković, P., Cucurull, G., Casanova, A., Romero, A., Lio, P., Bengio, Y.: Graph attention networks. In: ICLR (2018)
27. Xu, Y., Zhang, Y., Guo, W., Guo, H., Tang, R., Coates, M.: Graphsail: graph structure aware incremental learning for recommender systems. In: CIKM (2020)
28. Yan, B., Wang, C., Guo, G., Lou, Y.: Tinygnn: learning efficient graph neural networks. In: KDD (2020)
29. Yang, C., Liu, J., Shi, C.: Extract the knowledge of graph neural networks and go beyond it: an effective knowledge distillation framework. In: WWW (2021)
30. Yang, H., Ma, K., Cheng, J.: Rethinking graph regularization for graph neural networks. In: AAAI (2021)
31. Yang, J., et al.: Graphformers: GNN-nested transformers for representation learning on textual graph. In: NeurIPS (2021)
32. Yang, Y., Qiu, J., Song, M., Tao, D., Wang, X.: Distilling knowledge from graph convolutional networks. In: IEEE/CVF CVPR (2020)
33. Yao, L., Mao, C., Luo, Y.: Graph convolutional networks for text classification. In: AAAI (2019)
34. Yasunaga, M., et al.: Deep bidirectional language-knowledge graph pretraining. In: NeurIPS (2022)
35. Yasunaga, M., Leskovec, J., Liang, P.: Linkbert: pretraining language models with document links. In: ACL (2022)
36. Yuan, L., Tay, F.E., Li, G., Wang, T., Feng, J.: Revisiting knowledge distillation via label smoothing regularization. In: IEEE/CVF CVPR (2020)
37. Zhang, J., Zhang, H., Xia, C., Sun, L.: Graph-bert: only attention is needed for learning graph representations. arXiv (2020)

38. Zhang, L., Song, J., Gao, A., Chen, J., Bao, C., Ma, K.: Be your own teacher: improve the performance of convolutional neural networks via self distillation. In: IEEE/CVF ICCV (2019)
39. Zhang, S., Liu, Y., Sun, Y., Shah, N.: Graph-less neural networks: teaching old MLPs new tricks via distillation. In: ICLR (2022)
40. Zhang, W., Deng, L., Zhang, L., Wu, D.: A survey on negative transfer. arXiv (2020)
41. Zhang, X., et al.: GreaseLM: graph REASoning enhanced language models. In: ICLR (2022)
42. Zhao, J., et al.: Learning on large-scale text-attributed graphs via variational inference. arXiv (2022)
43. Zheng, W., Huang, E.W., Rao, N., Katariya, S., Wang, Z., Subbian, K.: Cold brew: distilling graph node representations with incomplete or missing neighborhoods. In: ICLR (2022)
44. Zhou, D., Bousquet, O., Lal, T., Weston, J., Schölkopf, B.: Learning with local and global consistency. In: NIPS (2003)
45. Zhu, J., et al.: Textgnn: improving text encoder via graph neural network in sponsored search. In: WWW (2021)

Graphs

The Mont Blanc of Twitter: Identifying Hierarchies of Outstanding Peaks in Social Networks

Maximilian Stubbemann$^{(\boxtimes)}$ and Gerd Stumme

Knowledge and Data Engineering Group, University of Kassel, Kassel, Germany
{stubbemann,stumme}@cs.uni-kassel.de

Abstract. The investigation of social networks is often hindered by their size as such networks often consist of at least thousands of vertices and edges. Hence, it is of major interest to derive compact structures that represent important connections of the original network. In this work, we derive such structures with orometric methods that are originally designed to identify outstanding mountain peaks and relationships between them. By adapting these methods to social networks, it is possible to derive family trees of important vertices. Our approach consists of two steps. We first apply a novel method for discarding edges that stand for weak connections. This is done such that the connectivity of the network is preserved. Then, we identify the important "peaks" in the network and the "key cols", i.e., the lower points that connect them. This gives us a compact network that displays which peaks are connected through which cols. Thus, a natural hierarchy on the peaks arises by the question which higher peak comes behind the col, yielding to chains of peaks with increasing heights. The resulting "line parent hierarchy" displays dominance relations between important vertices. We show that networks with hundreds or thousands of edges can be condensed to a small set of vertices and key connections between them.

Keywords: Social Networks · Orometry · Hierarchies

1 Introduction

Relationships in social networks are usually modelled as graphs. Examples of this are follower relations on Twitter or friendships on Facebook. However, even for medium-sized graphs with thousands of nodes to display and comprehend the full structure is often not possible. Another problem is that the importance of different edges often varies. This is especially possible in networks that arise as projections from other graphs. Examples for this are networks of co-group memberships of Youtube users or co-Follower networks on Twitter. Here, there will be a large amount of "weak" edges where the set of shared neighbors in the original graph was small. In such cases, it is crucial to derive compact representations of structurally important relationships.

© The Author(s), under exclusive license to Springer Nature Switzerland AG 2023
D. Koutra et al. (Eds.): ECML PKDD 2023, LNAI 14171, pp. 177–192, 2023.
https://doi.org/10.1007/978-3-031-43418-1_11

Often, the importance of individual vertices can be measured by a given "height" function. For example, Twitter users can be evaluated by the amount of followers and academic authors by their h-index. While it is intuitive to sample the "top k" users as a subset, this may not lead to a reasonable representation of the important nodes. This is for example the case if Twitter users with high follower counts are surrounded by users with even higher counts. Hence, they may have a overall large height which is however not outstanding for the specific community they belong to. In contrast to just assume the "highest" vertices as important, we propose a way to identify *locally outstanding* nodes in networks, i.e., nodes with a large height with respect to their surrounding community. Additionally, we derive hierarchical relations between these outstanding nodes.

Our approach adopts notions from the realm of orometry which are originally designed to evaluate the outstandingness of mountains. The *(topographic) prominence* of a mountain quantifies its local outstandingness by computing the minimal vertical descent that is needed to reach a higher peak. Paths with minimal descent to a higher peak deliver two important reference points for each mountain. First, the lowest point of this path determines the prominence value. This point is called the *key col*. Secondly, the first higher peak reached after the key col is called the *line parent*. Adopting these notions to networks allows to find locally outstanding nodes and to derive a compact tree structure which displays how these outstanding nodes are dominated by each other.

When deriving such structures, the question arises on how to traverse the network to find key cols and line parents. Here, it is natural to use the edges of the graph. However, as mentioned above, some edges in the graph may represent weak connections and should not contribute to the derived landscape. Hence, it can be beneficial to remove edges as a preprocessing step. To this point, we propose a method for parameter-free edge-reducing based on the *relative neighborhood graph* (RNG) [26]. We will show that our edge-reduction technique preserves connectivity. This is not guaranteed by other approaches which discard edges via a weight threshold or only keep the k most important edges. Note, that the key contribution of our approach are mountain graphs and line parent trees. Discarding unimportant edges is an optional preprocessing step.

To sum up, our approach derives line-parent trees between locally outstanding nodes. This significantly simplifies the study of networks because trees can be satisfactory visualized and navigating through them is possible for larger node sets. Furthermore, the derived hierarchy is not a subset of the original edge relation. Thus, we create a novel view on social networks which is not captured by existing approaches. We provide our experimental code for the sake of reproducibility[1].

2   Related Work

Deriving compact structures that display important relations in the original network is often done via sampling vertices or edges [10, 12, 15, 16, 21]. In contrast,

---

[1] https://github.com/mstubbemann/mont-blanc-of-twitter.

Table 1. Important Notations

Name	Notation	Description
Landscape	$L = (G, d, h)$	Triple of a graph, a metric and a height function
Mountain Graph	$MG = (V_{MG(L)}, E_{MG(L)})$	Graph that reflects connections between peaks and key cols
Line Parent Tree	$LP(L) = (P(L), E_{LP(L)})$	The line parent hierarchy of the peaks
Relative Neighborhood Graph (RNG)	$RNG(d) = (M, E_{RNG(d)})$	The relative neighborhood graph of a metric space
Essential Landscape	$L(G, h) = (RNG(G), d_{SP}, h)$	The landscape of a graph that uses the shortest path distance as metric and the RNG of the shortest path metric

other works focus on the aggregation of vertices and edges such that the original network can be reconstructed [14, 22, 25]. All these methods have in common that they return a proxy of the original network. Thus, they are not able to identify hierarchies and connections of outstanding vertices that are not approximations or explicit subgraphs of the original graph.

The study of hierarchic structures has gained recent interest. Lu et al. [17] derives acyclic graphs by removing cycles. Other works use likelihoods to derive suitable hierarchies [5, 18] or provide a quantification on how "hierarchical" a graph is [6]. In contrast to our approach, these methods are solely based on the graph structure and are not able to incorporate the "height" of nodes. The usage of the height function is a unique feature of our line-parent hierarchy, resulting in a tree structure that capture different connections than existing approaches.

The idea of adapting methods from orometry to different areas has been followed in recent works [9, 19]. On the other hand, there is a variety of works which study prominence in different abstract settings [20, 23, 24]. All these works have in common, that they focus on the computation of prominence and not on the underlying structure, i.e., the connections to key cols and line parents which determine prominence values.

3   Mountain Graphs and Line Parent Trees

In this section we present our approach to derive small hierarchies between peaks from larger networks. We first explain how one can derive mountain graphs and line parents from networks that provide distance and height information. Afterwards, we propose an optional preprocessing step that uses the notion of relative neighborhood graphs (RNGs) [26] to remove a significant amount of edges while preserving the connectivity of the original network. This will provide us with an end-to-end pipeline for extracting line parent hierarchies from networks by first discarding unimportant edges, which is described in Sect. 3.3 and by

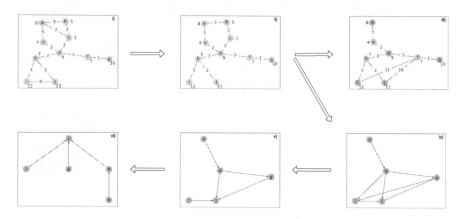

Fig. 1. Generating the mountain graph and the line parent tree. In i), a graph is displayed with the heights next to the nodes and with the edge weight put in the middle of each edge. The RNG in ii) is derived by discarding the edge between i and j, because h is closer to both i and j than they are to each other and by discarding the edge between a and c because node b is closer to both of them than they are to each other. From this, the Mountain Graph is derived in iii), where we display the shortest path distances between the cols and peaks. Additionally, we derive from ii) the Peak Graph which is displayed in iv). According to Definition 8, we then discard the edge from g to i because j is closer to the key col f than i and we discard the edge between d and i because j is closer to the key col h to arrive at v). From this, the line parent tree vi) is derived by discarding the edge between d and g because the key col h over which j is reached is closer to g than the key col f over which g is reached.

secondly computing the mountain graph and line parent tree from the resulting network as described in Sect. 3.1 and Sect. 3.2. We rely on the prominence term from Schmidt and Stumme [23]. A complete example of the procedure which we develop in the following is given by Fig. 1. Table 1 contains the most important notations. The proofs of all theorems presented in the following can be found in the supplementary material which is available at https://github.com/mstubbemann/mont-blanc-of-twitter.

3.1 Landscapes and Mountain Graphs

In the following, we will work with undirected graphs $G = (V, E)$, where $E \subseteq \binom{V}{2}$. We call a function $w : E \to \mathbb{R}_{>0}$ a *weighting function* of (V, E). If we have a triple $G = (V, e, w)$ where (V, E) is an undirected graph and w a weighting function on (V, E), we call G a *weighted* graph. If we simply speak of graphs, we refer to undirected and unweighted graphs.

A *walk* p of a graph G is a finite sequence $p = (v_i)_{i=0}^n$ with $v_i \in V$ for all $i \in \{0, \dots n\}$ and $\{v_{j-1}, v_j\} \in E$ for all $j \in \{1, \dots, n\}$. We call a walk p a *path*, if for all $i \neq j$ it holds that $v_i \neq v_j$ or $\{i, j\} = \{1, n\}$. For each walk $p = (v)_{i=0}^n$, we call $\text{start}(p) := v_0$ the *starting point* and $\text{end}(p) := v_n$ the *end point* of p. We follow the usual convention to not distinguish between walks $p = (v_i)_{i=0}^n$

and the corresponding set $\{v_i \mid i \in \{0, \ldots n\}\}$, meaning that we say that v is element of p and write $v \in p$. A graph is *connected*, if for all pairs $u, v \in V$ there is a walk from u to v. Additionally, let $N_G(v) := \{u \in V \mid \{u, v\} \in E\}$ be the neighborhood of v in G. If clear from the context, we omit G and write $N(v)$.

We consider graphs with a *height function* $h \colon V \to \mathbb{R}_{\geq 0}$ and a *metric*, i.e., $d \colon V \times V \to \mathbb{R}_{\geq 0}$ with • $\forall x, y \in V : d(x, y) = 0 \iff x = y$ (reflexivity), • $\forall x, y \in V : d(x, y) = d(y, x)$ (symmetry) and • $\forall x, y, z \in V : d(x, z) \leq d(x, y) + d(y, z)$ (triangle inequality).

Definition 1 (Landscape). *We call $L = (G, d, h)$ a landscape if $G = (V, E)$ is a connected[2] and finite graph, d is a metric on V and h is a height function on V such that h has a unique maximum. We denote the highest point by $\max(L)$.*

To sum up, a landscape is given by a set of points, where we can traverse the points (via the given graph structure), where we know, how "high" each point is and where we can measure distances. If G has a weighting function w on it, a metric on the nodes of G is provided by the weighted shortest path distance.

As mentioned earlier, our aim is to display hierarchies of peaks and connections between peaks and cols. For this, we first have to define peaks and cols. In the following, we will always assume to have given a landscape $L = (G, d, h)$.

Definition 2 (Peaks, Mountain paths and Cols[3]). *We call a node $v \in V$ a peak of L if $h(v) > h(u)$ for all $u \in N(v)$ and denote by $P(L)$ the set of peaks of L. A path p of G is a mountain path if $\mathrm{start}(p), \mathrm{end}(p) \in P(L)$. We denote by $M(L)$ the set of all mountain paths. For each $p \in M(L)$ we call $c(p) := \mathrm{argmin}_{v \in p} h(p)$ the col of p. If this argmin is not unique, we choose the point in the path which is visited first.*

To compute the prominence of a peak, we have to identify the cols which connect it with higher peaks.

Definition 3 (Cols of Peaks). *For each peak $v \in P(L) \setminus \{\max(L)\}$ we call the set $\uparrow_L (v) := \{p \in M(L) \mid \mathrm{start}(p) = v, h(\mathrm{end}(p)) > h(v), \nexists u \in p \setminus \{\mathrm{end}(p), v\} : u \in P(L) \wedge h(u) > h(v)\}$ the ascending paths of v and denote by $C_L(v) := \{c(p) \mid p \in \uparrow_L (v)\}$ the set of all cols of v.*

To sum up, the ascending paths $p \in \uparrow_L (v)$ are the paths from v to higher peaks such that there is no higher peak $w \in p$ and the cols of v are the lowest points of the ascending paths. We omit the L in the index if clear from the context. As prominence for mountain peaks is the *minimal* descent needed to go to higher points, we are just interested in the *highest* cols.

---

[2] This is assumed for simplicity. The following foundations can be applied to unconnected graphs by studying every connected component for itself.

[3] To simplify notations, our definition of cols allow only one col per path which differs from the definition in geography,.

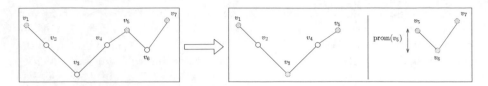

Fig. 2. Prominence: Here, the vertical positioning displays the height of the different points. To compute the prominence of v_5, we first identify the paths that lead to higher peaks. Then, we determine the cols of these paths and compute the height difference of v_5 to these cols. The lower difference yield the prominence of v_5.

Definition 4 (Key Cols and Prominence). *Let* $\mathrm{prom}_L(\max(L)) := h(\max(L))$. *For each peak* $v \in P(L) \setminus \{\max(L)\}$ *we call the elements of* $K_L(v) := \{u \in C_L(v) \mid h(u) = \max_{\tilde{u} \in C_L(v)} h(\tilde{u})\}$ *the key cols of* v. *For* $u \in K_L(v)$ *the prominence of* v *is given via*

$$\mathrm{prom}_L(v) := h(v) - h(u).$$

Thus, the prominence of a peak v displays the vertical distance to the key cols. For $v \in P(L) \setminus \{\max(L)\}$ the prominence is the minimal height difference to a col, i.e., $\mathrm{prom}_L(v) = \min_{u \in C(v)} h(v) - h(u)$. Again, we write $\mathrm{prom}(v)$ and $K(v)$ if the choice of the landscape is clear. An illustration of the definition of prominence is given by Fig. 2.

We are interested in the structure which determines the prominence of peaks, i.e., in the higher peaks to reach from a specific peak and in the cols which connects the peaks of the mountain landscape. Hence, we do not only study the key cols of peaks but also the higher peaks that can be reached from their cols.

Definition 5 (Dominators). *Let* v *be a peak of the landscape* L. *We then call the set* $D_L(v) := \{\mathrm{end}(p) \mid p \in \uparrow_L(v) \wedge c(p) \in K(v)\}$ *the dominators of* v.

Definition 6 (Mountain Graph). *For a given landscape* $L = ((V, E), d, h)$, *let* $K(L) := \cup_{v \in P(L)} K_L(v)$ *be the set of* key cols *of L and let* $V_{\mathrm{MG}}(L) := P(L) \cup K(L)$ *be the* critical points *of L. Let for* $v \in P(L)$ *be* $\uparrow_L^K(v) := \{p \in \uparrow_L(v) \mid c(p) \in K_L(v)\}$ *the* ascending paths *of* v *with key cols as cols. Let then*

$$E_{\mathrm{MG}}(L) := \bigcup_{v \in P(L)} \left(\bigcup_{p \in \uparrow_L^K(v)} \{\{v, c(p)\}, \{c(p), \mathrm{end}(p)\}\} \right).$$

The graph $\mathrm{MG} = (V_{\mathrm{MG}}(L), E_{\mathrm{MG}}(L))$ *is called the* mountain graph *of L and the landscape* $L_{\mathrm{MG}} := (\mathrm{MG}_L, d|_{\mathrm{MG}}, h|_{\mathrm{MG}})$ *the* mountain landscape *of L.*

To sum up, if a peak v_1 is connected via a key col u to a higher peak v_2, we add edges between v_1 and u and between u and v_2 to the mountain graph. Thus, the mountain graph displays which peaks are connected through which key cols. If clear from the context, we omit L and simply write $\mathrm{MG} = (V_{\mathrm{MG}}, E_{\mathrm{MG}})$. The mountain graph contains all relevant information for the computation of prominence values as the following theorem shows.

Theorem 1. *The following statements hold:*

1. MG *is connected.*
2. $P(L) = P(L_{\mathrm{MG}})$
3. *Consider for each peak* $v \in P(L) \setminus \{\max(L)\}$ *of* L *the set* $N'_{\mathrm{MG}}(v) := \{u \in N_{\mathrm{MG}}(v) \mid \exists v' \in N_{\mathrm{MG}}(u) : h(v') > h(v)\}$. *Then:*

$$u \in N'_{\mathrm{MG}}(v) \Rightarrow \exists u' \in C_L(v) : h(u') \geq h(u).$$

4. *It holds for* $v \in P(L) \setminus \{\max(L)\}$ *that:*

$$\mathrm{prom}_L(v) = \min_{u \in N'_{\mathrm{MG}}(v)} (h(v) - h(u)).$$

Theorem 1 shows that to study relations between cols and peaks that determine prominence values, it is sufficient to check the cols to which a peak is connected in the mountain graph. Note, that the key cols and the paths between peaks passing through them have to be determined to derive the mountain graph. Hence, Theorem 1 does not allow for a faster computation of prominence values. Instead, it provides a representation that can be used to observe important connections between peaks and cols.

3.2 Line Parent Trees

As the prominence of mountain peaks is computed by descending to key cols and then ascending to higher peaks, a hierarchy between peaks arises by the question to which higher peak one can traverse from a key col of a given peak.

Definition 7 (Peak Graph). *Let*

$$E_P(L) := \bigcup_{v \in P(L)} \{\{\mathrm{start}(p), \mathrm{end}(p)\} \mid p \in \uparrow_L^K(v)\}.$$

We call $\mathrm{PG}(L) := (P(L), E_P(L))$ *the* peak graph *of* L *and we call*

$$T_{\mathrm{PG}(L)} := \{(\mathrm{start}(p), c(p), \mathrm{end}(p)) \mid p \in \uparrow_L^K(v)\}$$

the defining triples *of* $\mathrm{PG}(L)$.

Peaks may be connected to different key cols and different higher peaks. To define a meaningful hierarchy on the peaks, we use the metric d to determine a unique line parent for all peaks.

Definition 8 (Line Parents). *Let* $T'_{\mathrm{PG}}(L) := \{(v, u, \tilde{v}) \in T_{\mathrm{PG}} \mid \nexists v' : (v, u, v') \in T_{\mathrm{PG}} \wedge (d(u, v') < d(u, \tilde{v}) \vee (d(u, v') = d(u, \tilde{v}) \wedge h(v') > h(\tilde{v})))\}$. *Let* $E_{\mathrm{LP}}(L) := \{\{v, \tilde{v}\} \mid \exists u : (v, u, \tilde{v}) \in T'_{\mathrm{PG}}(L) \wedge \nexists u', v' : (v, u', v') \in T'_{\mathrm{PG}}(L) \wedge d(v, u') < d(v, u)\}$. *We call* $\mathrm{LP}(L) := (P(L), E_{\mathrm{LP}}(L))$ *the* line parent graph *of* L. *If* $\{u, v\} \in E_{\mathrm{LP}}(L)$ *with* $h(v) > h(u)$, v *is a* line parent *of* u.

Again, we omit L when possible without confusion. In Definition 8, we first remove edges to higher peaks that are further away from the corresponding key col. If there are multiple higher peaks with the exact same distance to the key col, we keep the highest peak. Then we remove edges where the key col is further away. If for all $v \in P(L) \setminus \max(L)$ the line parent is unique, $\mathrm{LP}(L)$ is a tree.

Theorem 2. *If for each peak $v \in P(L) \setminus \{\max(L)\}$ the line parent is unique, then $\mathrm{LP}(L)$ is a tree.*

The uniqueness of the line parent is only violated in two cases. First, if there are multiple peaks being reached after the same key col with the exactly same distance to the key col and the same height. In such a case, we can enforce the uniqueness by sampling one of the peaks. Secondly, if there are key cols $c_1, \ldots, c_n$ with corresponding higher peaks $p_1 \ldots p_n$ with the exact same distance to the point. In such a case, we choose p_i such that $d(c_i, p_i)$ is minimal. If these minimum is reached multiple times, we enforce uniqueness by sampling one of the higher peaks with minimal distance to the corresponding key col.

To sum up, we enforce the uniqueness of the line parent. The simple edge structure of trees enables a satisfactory visualization even for medium sized node sets. The line parent tree can also be used to study dominance relationships with a non peak as a starting point. In this case, we suggest to navigate through the line parent tree starting with the closest peak with respect to the given metric.

3.3 Discarding Edges via Relative Neighborhood Graphs

Let $G = (V, E, w)$ be a weighted graph and let $h: V \to \mathbb{R}_{\geq 0}$ be a height function on G. In the following, we extend this structure to a landscape by using the shortest path metric on G. In practical applications, the amount of peaks will often be very low. One reason for this is the huge amount of connections one may have in social networks. Let us for example assume to have a weighted co-follower graph (for example weighted with Jaccard-distance) where the height function is given by the amount of followers. Here, all pairs of users with just one common follower would be connected and thus nearly all users would have a "higher" neighbor and thus will not be peaks. Hence, it is of major interest to only keep edges which stand for a strong connection, i.e., edges between users with a large amount of common followers.

A straight-forward way to remove edges would be by choosing a $k \in \mathbb{N}$ and keep for all vertices only the k edges with the smallest weights or to choose a $t \in (0,1)$ and remove all edges with weights higher than t. However, besides the disadvantage that in both cases a parameter has to be chosen, this procedure can lead to disconnected graphs. Restricting to the biggest connected component of the resulting graph would then lead to the discarding of whole regions of the graph. To this end, we develop in the following a parameter free, deterministic edge sampling approach which always preserves connectivity. This approach is based on the relative neighborhood graph (RNG) [26]. The RNG derives a graph structure from a metric space by connecting points nearby. More specifically, two points are connected if there is no third point which is closer to both of them.

Definition 9 (Relative Neighborhood Graph). *The* relative neighborhood graph *of a metric space* (M, d) *is given by the undirected graph* $\mathrm{RNG}(d) :=$ $(M, E_{\mathrm{RNG}(d)})$ *with* $E_{\mathrm{RNG}(d)} \subseteq \binom{M}{2}$ *such that* $\{m_1, m_2\} \in E_{\mathrm{RNG}(d)}$ *if and only if there does not exist* $m_3 \in M$ *with* $\max(\{d(m_1, m_3), d(m_2, m_3)\}) < d(m1, m2)$.

Our goal is to thin out graphs by computing the RNGs. Hence, it is of fundamental interest that RNGs are connected. For points in $\mathbb{R}^2$, it has been shown that the RNG is a supergraph of the minimum-spanning-tree [26] which implies connectivity [8]. Because RNGs are commonly only studied in $\mathbb{R}^d$ with L^p metrics we could not find a proof for the connectivity in arbitrary finite metric spaces. Hence, we prove it in the supplementary material.

Theorem 3 (Connectivity of relative neighborhood graph). *Let* (M, d) *be a finite metric space. Then* $\mathrm{RNG}(d)$ *is connected.*

What still needs to be shown is that deriving RNGs from the shortest-path metric is indeed an edge-reduction technique, i.e., that edges are just removed and that is not possible that new edges are added.

Theorem 4 (RNG as Edge-Reduction). *Let* $G = (V, E, w)$ *be a connected, undirected and weighted graph and* $d_{\mathrm{SP}} : V \times V \to \mathbb{R}_{\geq 0}$ *be the shortest path metric on* G. *Then it holds that* $E_{\mathrm{RNG}(d_{\mathrm{SP}})} \subseteq E$.

In the following, we use the term *relative neighborhood graph of* G, denoted by $\mathrm{RNG}(G)$, which will always refer to the RNG with respect to the shortest-path-metric. A sketch of an edge-reduction on a graph is given as part of Fig. 1.

For a weighted graph $G = (V, E, w)$ with a height function h, our standard procedure is to 1. compute the weighted shortest path metric d_{SP}, 2. compute $\mathrm{RNG}(G)$, 3. derive from this the following landscape.

Definition 10 (Essential Landscape). *Let* $h : V \to R_{\geq 0}$ *be a height function on a graph* $G = (V, E, w)$. *Let* d_{SP} *be the weighted shortest path metric on* G. *We call*

$$L(G, h) := (\mathrm{RNG}(G), d_{\mathrm{SP}}, h)$$

the (essential) landscape of G *and* $\mathrm{MG}(G, h) := \mathrm{MG}(L(G, h))$ *the essential mountain graph of* G. *We call* $\mathrm{LP}(G, h) := \mathrm{LP}(L(G, h))$ *the (essential) line parent tree of* G. *If clear from the context, we simply write* $\mathrm{MG}(G)$ *and* $\mathrm{LP}(G)$.

Complexity. The naive approach to compute the RNG for a finite metric space (M, d) would be to check for all pairs $m_1 \neq m_2 \in M$ whether there exists m_3 which is closer to both of them. This results in an algorithm with runtime $\mathcal{O}(|M|^3)$ [26]. For $\mathbb{R}^d$ with a l_p metric, there are algorithms with better runtime [1,7,26]. However, these results can not be applied to shortest path metrics. To compute $\mathrm{RNG}(G)$ for a graph $G = (V, E)$, we can use Theorem 4 to speed up the computation as we only have to check the elements of E and not all node pairs. Hence, computing the RNG has complexity $\mathcal{O}(|E||V|)$.

Table 2. Network statistics. In the first table, we display from left to right: 1.) the number of vertices of the network, 2.) its density 3.) the density of the RNG 4.) the number of vertices of the mountain graph, 5.) the density of the mountain graph, 6.) the number of vertices in the line parent tree, 7.) its maximum width and 8.) its depth. In the second table, we show the node sizes and degrees of the sampled graphs serving a) as a comparison for discarding edges via the RNG procedure and b) for serving as a comparison for the mountain graph which is computed from the RNG. For the latter, we apply the sampling baselines on the RNG, not on the original network itself.

	$|V|$	D_G	$D_{RNG(G)}$	$|V_{MG}|$	D_{MG}	$|V_{LP}|$	W_{LP}	DP_{LP}
Twitter>10K	6635	.9958	.0005	1171	.1089	652	88	20
Twitter>100K	430	1.0000	.0064	146	.1084	84	14	13
ECML/PKDD	742	.0123	.0052	190	.1957	98	21	10
KDD	1674	.0100	.0036	219	.2236	115	30	8
PAKDD	889	.0124	.0054	132	.2155	67	27	5

	RNG Baselines				MG Baselines			
	ES		CNARW [16]		RPN [12]		RCMH [15]	
	$|V|$	D_G	$|V|$	D_G	$|V|$	D_G	$|V|$	D_G
Twitter>10K	5192.8	.0008	5174	.0007	271.1	.0079	1171	.0021
Twitter>100K	374.8	.0084	325.5	.0112	35.9	.0652	146	.0168
ECML/PKDD	650.7	.0067	560	.0092	77.1	.0304	190	.0153
KDD	1575.5	.0041	1407.5	.0041	67.2	.0390	219	.0138
PAKDD	814.7	.0064	704.1	.0087	34.3	.0812	132	.0222

4 Line Parent Trees of Real-World Networks

We experiment with networks built from a Twitter follower network [3,4,11] which we found at SNAP [13] and with networks that display co-author relations. These networks are derived from the *Semantic Scholar Open Research Corpus* [2]. From the Twitter dataset, we derive two weighted co-follower networks. In these networks two users have an edge if they have a common follower. The edges are weighted via Jaccard distance. We derive a version containing users with at least 10,000 followers (**Twitter>10K**) and a network containing users with at least 100,000 followers (**Twitter>100K**). Here, the height of a user is given via the amount of followers.

The co-author networks are derived by considering communities of authors that regularly publish at a specific conference. We derive datasets for the *European Conference on Machine Learning and Principles and Practice of Knowledge Discovery in Databases* (**ECML/PKDD**), the *SIGKDD Conference on Knowledge Discovery and Data Mining* (**KDD**) and the *Pacific-Asia Conference on Knowledge Discovery and Data Mining* (**PAKDD**). The heights of the authors are given via h-indices.

For all graphs, we use well-established measures to get further insights. To be more detailed, we display node sizes and densities of the networks themselves, the RNGs and the mountain graphs derived from the RNGs. Additionally, we display node sizes, maximum widths and depths of the line-parent trees derived from the RNGs. The results can be found in Table 2. Plots of labeled trees and details on dataset creation are part of the supplementary material.[4]

4.1 Comparison with Sampling Approaches

To further understand the steps of our approach, we compare them with commonly used sampling approaches [12, 15, 16]. To be more specific, we sample edges from the original network to get graphs which have an equal amount of edges as the RNG. Then we take the biggest connected component of these graphs. We call these methods the **RNG Baselines**. We use two sampling approaches: First, we sample edges with the probability of an edge e to be chosen being proportional to $1 - w(e)$, where $w(e)$ is the weight of the edge[5]. We call the resulting baseline the *Edge Sampling* (ES) approach. As a second comparison, we use a weighted version of *CNARW* [16], a modern random walk approach.

Additionally, we use sampling approaches to sample from the RNG in such a way, that we have an equal amount of nodes as in the mountain graph and take the biggest component of the resulting network. We call these methods the **MG Baseline**. First, we sample nodes by their PageRank value via*RPN* [12]. Again, we also use a modern random walk based approach, namely *RCMH* [15]. The CNARW method used above relies on common neighbors. Since triangles in the RNG are very uncommon (for these, 2 of the 3 corresponding edges in the original graph need to have the same distance weight), we use RCMH instead.

Note, that we use the comparison with other methods to contextualize our novel structures. As our structures have a different purpose, namely displaying important connections that are derived from the original network, they are not directly comparable to regular sampling approaches. These approaches derive small graphs that behave similar to the original graph with respect to specific measures. This makes it unreasonable to interpret the comparison to our baselines as a competition where higher/lower node sizes or densities are, in some way, better. As our comparison methods include random sources, we repeat them 10 times and report means. Statistics, including sizes of the derived RNGs, mountain graphs and line parent trees, can be found in Table 2. Additionally, we include node sizes and densities for all comparison approaches.

We observe that computing the RNG reduces the density by a large margin. It stands out, that this effect is stronger for the dense Twitter networks. When sampling an equal amount of edges, there are nodes which do not belong to the biggest connected component anymore. This results in a higher density of the (biggest component) of the networks created by sampling compared to the RNG.

---

[4] https://github.com/mstubbemann/mont-blanc-of-twitter.
[5] We use $1 - w(e)$ instead of $w(e)$ because we assume edge weights to be distances, not similarities.

Table 3. Mean, median and maximum of the minimal shortest path distance (MSPD) from all non-peaks v to the set P of all peaks (left) to the set H which contains the $|P|$ highest nodes of the network (right).

	$d(P)_{\text{Mean}}$	$d(P)_{\text{Median}}$	$d(P)_{\text{Max}}$	$d(H)_{\text{Mean}}$	$d(H)_{\text{Median}}$	$d(H)_{\text{Max}}$
Twitter>10K	0.87	0.88	1.00	0.90	0.91	1.00
Twitter>100k	0.86	0.87	0.97	0.92	0.95	0.99
ECML	1.28	1.00	2.98	1.74	1.91	4.91
KDD	1.30	1.00	2.95	1.83	1.95	3.90
PAKDD	1.46	1.00	3.78	1.94	1.96	4.90

The resulting line parent trees are much smaller than the original network, reducing the node set by a factor of about 5 to 10 times. Another remarkable point is that the mountain graph is always denser than the RNG from which it is computed and than the graphs which are sampled via the comparison methods. An explanation is that edges from a peak v to a col u in the mountain graph correspond to paths (not edges!) in the RNG. As the amount of paths in a graph is commonly remarkably higher than the amount of edges, this could be one reason for the higher density of the mountain graph.

4.2 Distances to Line-Parent Trees

To investigate to which extent line parent trees are representative for the structure of the whole network, we compute how "dense" the line parent trees lay in the networks, i.e. the shortest path lengths from all non-peaks to the peaks. To evaluate whether choosing locally outstanding nodes lead to a better representation than choosing nodes solely based on their height, we compare our approach with a "naive" approach of assuming the n highest points to be relevant, where n is the amount of peaks. To be more detailed, we compute for each non-peak v the minimal shortest path distances (MSPD) to all peaks in the original graph G. We do the same using the n highest points instead of the set of peaks. We report means, medians and maximum values over the MSPDs of all non-peaks, the results can be found in Table 3.

Our results show that locally outstanding nodes better reflect the overall network then just choosing the highest nodes, with median and mean values of the MSPDs being fundamentally lower. Furthermore, median MSPDs to peaks are always not higher then 1. In contrast, MSPDs to the "highest" nodes have median values of nearly 2 for the sparse co-author networks. This indicates that selecting locally outstanding points indeed lead to a more reasonable representation instead of selecting nodes solely by their height, ignoring spatial information. Note, that we compute distances in a weighted graph. Hence, shortest path distances (and thus medians and maxima over them) do not have to be integers.

5   Experiments on Random Data

To investigate sizes and densities of the RNG, the mountain graph and the line parent tree, we additionally experiment with randomly generated data. Here,

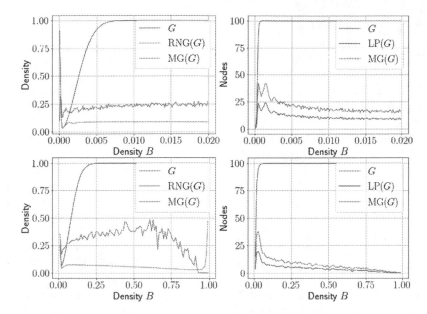

Fig. 3. Experiments on random data. In both rows, the set A on which is projected has size 100. The other set has size $100,000$ on the first row and size 100 in the second row. The x-axes display the densities of the original bipartite graph B. The left plots display the densities for the resulting network G, which is the biggest connected component of the weighted projection, the line parent tree RNG(G) and the mountain graph MG(G). The right pictures plot the node size of G, MG(G) and LP(G).

we start with a randomly generated bipartite graph with vertex sets M_1, M_2 with $|M_1| = 100$ and $|M_2| \in \{100000, 100\}$. We then project on the vertex set A and set for two vertices with an edge in the resulting graph the edge weight to the Jaccard distance. The graph G is then given via the biggest connected component of this graph. As height function, we map each vertex to the amount of neighbors in the original bipartite network. This procedure is motivated by the background of often investigated real-world networks. Co-author networks are for example projection from the bipartite author-publication graph. Here, the corresponding height function then would be the amount of papers of an author, where each author is connected to multiple publications but only a small amount of the overall publications. This leads to a small density of the bipartite network.

We generate networks for different densities d. Namely, we iterate d through $\{0.0001, 0.0002, \ldots, 0.01999\}$ for $|M_2| = 100,000$ and through $\{0.01, 0.02, \ldots 0.99\}$ for $|M_2| = 100$. The experiments with different sizes of $|M_2|$ allow us to investigate if our methods behave fundamentally different for networks of different kinds. From G we compute the RNG(G), the mountain graph MG(G) and the line parent hierarchy LP(G)) of the essential landscape. For each d and $|M_2|$, we repeat this procedure 20 times and display means. The results can be found in Fig. 3. The following facts stand out.

- The density of both the RNG and the mountain graph of the RNG are growing in a significant smaller pace than the density of G. Considering the case $|M_2| = 100,000$ it is remarkable, that, when G has a density of nearly 1, the density of both other graphs are still under 0.3.
- The characteristic points for describing the resulting mountain landscape build indeed a subset that is remarkably smaller than the vertex size of the biggest component of G.
- Considering the second row, it stands out that for very high densities of nearly 1 of the original bipartite network, the density and thus the amount of edges of the RNG start to rise rapidly. We assume that this is driven by the case, that, if the bipartite graph is nearly complete, there will be a large amount of vertex pairs with the same neighbor set in the bipartite graph. Thus, nearly all shortest path distances are equal and just very few edges will be discarded. In consequence, the mountain graph is built from a nearly complete graph where nearly all edges have similar weights. Thus, there will be only a small amount of peaks and the mountain graph is nearly vanishing.

Note, that we use a height that is directly derived from the graph. Such height functions are indeed reasonable. For example, the amount of followers of Twitter users in co-follower graphs is indeed a useful indicator of importance.

6   Conclusion and Future Work

In this work, we showed how the notions of peaks, cols and line parents, which are originally designed to characterize connections and hierarchies between mountains, can be adapted to networks. We discussed how these notions can be used to identify important vertices and meaningful connections and hierarchies between them. Our method further benefits from a novel preprocessing procedure that removes unimportant edges without hurting the connectivity of the network. This preprocessing step is based on relative neighborhood graphs which were originally invented to connect data points in two-dimensional euclidean spaces.

Our experiments indicate that our method finds dependencies and hierarchies from the original network that are remarkably smaller than the original graph and therefore can enhance the comprehension of real-world social networks.

Future work will investigate the application to further kinds of networks such as friendship networks on Facebook. As some of these networks may be unweighted, the question arises on how to use our RNG procedure in this case. On the other hand, it would be interesting to involve temporal aspects in networks. How does the line parent hierarchy of social networks change over time?

Acknowledgment. This work is partially funded by the German Federal Ministry of Education and Research (BMBF) under grant 01PU17012A.

References

1. Agarwal, P.K., Matousek, J.: Relative neighborhood graphs in three dimensions. In: Annual Symposium on Discrete Algorithms (1992)
2. Ammar, W., et al.: Construction of the literature graph in semantic scholar. In: NAACL (2018)
3. Boldi, P., Rosa, M., Santini, M., Vigna, S.: Layered label propagation: a multiresolution coordinate-free ordering for compressing social networks. In: WWW (2011)
4. Boldi, P., Vigna, S.: The webgraph framework I: compression techniques. In: WWW (2004)
5. Clauset, A., Moore, C., Newman, M.E.: Hierarchical structure and the prediction of missing links in networks. Nature **453**, 98–101 (2008)
6. Gupte, M., Shankar, P., Li, J., Muthukrishnan, S., Iftode, L.: Finding hierarchy in directed online social networks. In: WWW (2011)
7. Jaromczyk, J.W., Kowaluk, M.: A note on relative neighborhood graphs. In: Annual Symposium on Computational Geometry, Waterloo (1987)
8. Jaromczyk, J.W., Toussaint, G.T.: Relative neighborhood graphs and their relatives. Proc. IEEE **80**, 1502–1517 (1992)
9. Karatzoglou, A.: Applying topographic features for identifying speed patterns using the example of critical driving. In: ACM SIGSPATIAL International Workshop on Computational Transportation Science (2020)
10. Krishnamurthy, V., Sun, J., Faloutsos, M., Tauro, S.L.: Sampling internet topologies: how small can we go? In: International Conference on Internet Computing (2003)
11. Kwak, H., Lee, C., Park, H., Moon, S.B.: What is twitter, a social network or a news media? In: WWW (2010)
12. Leskovec, J., Faloutsos, C.: Sampling from large graphs. In: KDD (2006)
13. Leskovec, J., Krevl, A.: SNAP Datasets: Stanford large network dataset collection (2014). http://snap.stanford.edu/data
14. Li, F., Zou, Z., Li, J., Li, Y.: Graph compression with stars. In: Yang, Q., Zhou, Z.-H., Gong, Z., Zhang, M.-L., Huang, S.-J. (eds.) PAKDD 2019. LNCS (LNAI), vol. 11440, pp. 449–461. Springer, Cham (2019). https://doi.org/10.1007/978-3-030-16145-3_35
15. Li, R., Yu, J.X., Qin, L., Mao, R., Jin, T.: On random walk based graph sampling. In: IEEE International Conference on Data Engineering (2015)
16. Li, Y., et al.: Walking with perception: efficient random walk sampling via common neighbor awareness. In: IEEE International Conference on Data Engineering (2019)
17. Lu, C., Yu, J.X., Li, R., Wei, H.: Exploring hierarchies in online social networks. IEEE Trans. Knowl. Data Eng. **28**, 2086–2100 (2016)
18. Maiya, A.S., Berger-Wolf, T.Y.: Inferring the maximum likelihood hierarchy in social networks. In: IEEE International Conference on Computational Science and Engineering (2009)
19. Nelson, G.D., McKeon, R.: Peaks of people: using topographic prominence as a method for determining the ranked significance of population centers. Prof. Geogr. **71**, 342–354 (2019)
20. Pavlík, J.: Topographic spaces over ordered monoids. Math. Appl. **4**, 31–59 (2015)
21. Rafiei, D., Curial, S.: Effectively visualizing large networks through sampling. In: IEEE Visualization Conference (2005)
22. Royer, L., Reimann, M., Andreopoulos, B., Schroeder, M.: Unraveling protein networks with power graph analysis. PLoS Comput. Biol. **4**, e1000108 (2008)

23. Schmidt, A., Stumme, G.: Prominence and dominance in networks. In: Faron Zucker, C., Ghidini, C., Napoli, A., Toussaint, Y. (eds.) EKAW 2018. LNCS (LNAI), vol. 11313, pp. 370–385. Springer, Cham (2018). https://doi.org/10.1007/978-3-030-03667-6_24
24. Stubbemann, M., Hanika, T., Stumme, G.: Orometric methods in bounded metric data. In: IDA (2020)
25. Toivonen, H., Zhou, F., Hartikainen, A., Hinkka, A.: Compression of weighted graphs. In: KDD (2011)
26. Toussaint, G.T.: The relative neighbourhood graph of a finite planar set. Pattern Recognit. **12**, 261–268 (1980)

RBNets: A Reinforcement Learning Approach for Learning Bayesian Network Structure

Zuowu Zheng, Chao Wang, Xiaofeng Gao$^{(\boxtimes)}$, and Guihai Chen

MoE Key Lab of Artificial Intelligence, Department of Computer Science and
Engineering, Shanghai Jiao Tong University, Shanghai, China
{waydrow,wangchao.2014}@sjtu.edu.cn, {gao-xf,gchen}@cs.sjtu.edu.cn

Abstract. Bayesian networks are graphical models that are capable
of encoding complex statistical and causal dependencies, thereby facilitating powerful probabilistic inferences. To apply these models to real-
world problems, it is first necessary to determine the Bayesian network
structure, which represents the dependencies. Classic methods for this
problem typically employ score-based search techniques, which are often
heuristic in nature and have limited running times and performances that
do not scale well for larger problems. In this paper, we propose a novel
technique called RBNets, which uses deep reinforcement learning along
with an exploration strategy guided by Upper Confidence Bound for
learning Bayesian Network structures. RBNets solves the highest-value
path problem and progressively finds better solutions. We demonstrate
the efficiency and effectiveness of our approach against several state-
of-the-art methods in extensive experiments using both real-world and
synthetic datasets.

Keywords: Bayesian network · Structure learning · Reinforcement
learning

1 Introduction

A Bayesian network is a probabilistic graphical model that represents probabilistic dependencies between random variables in a domain compactly and
intuitively. It has a wide range of applications in data mining, classification problems, medical diagnosis and engineering decisions, etc. Learning the structure of
Bayesian networks involves finding the acyclic graph that fits a discrete dataset
best over the random variables. It is the basis for solving practical problems, but
is a very challenging task in machine learning.

This work was supported by the National Key R&D Program of China
[2020YFB1707900], the National Natural Science Foundation of China [62272302,
62202055, 62172276], Shanghai Municipal Science and Technology Major Project
[2021SHZDZX0102], and CCF-Ant Research Fund [CCF-AFSG RF20220218].

D. Koutra et al. (Eds.): ECML PKDD 2023, LNAI 14171, pp. 193–208, 2023.
https://doi.org/10.1007/978-3-031-43418-1_12

In this work, we consider the problem of learning an appropriate Bayesian network structure for a given dataset and scoring function. Such score-based learning has been shown to be NP-hard [6], so much early research focused on local search strategies, searching for a structure that optimizes a particular scoring function, such as greedy hill climbing approaches [9,10,12], ordering-based search [14,19,25], and ant colony optimization [4]. They all take as input scores of candidate parent sets of all variables, and use various optimization techniques to find a structure that is a good predictor of the data. Unfortunately, these algorithms are unable to guarantee the quality of the learned networks. Thus, it motivates the research of more principled search algorithms.

Over the past several decades, exact algorithms have been studied extensively and there have been proposals based on A* search [5,28], dynamic programming [21,23], branch and bound [3,16], model averaging [15], and integer linear programming [7,8,13]. Besides, some reinforcement learning based methods are proposed, such as RL-BIC [29] and CORL [26]. These methods achieve good performance on smaller networks but fail in domains with a large number of variables unless the cardinality of parent sets is severely restricted.

In this paper, we view the problem of learning a Bayesian network structure via the optimization of a scoring function as a path-finding problem in an order graph [28]. A straightforward approach to solve this path-finding problem is to resort to A* [28]. However, because the number of nodes in this order graph is exponential in the number of variables, even A* struggles to solve this problem as the number of variables increases. The goal of this paper is to propose a novel method based on reinforcement learning (RL) to improve the learning performance.

RL is a machine learning method [24] concerned with how agents ought to take actions in an environment so as to maximize some notion of expected cumulative reward. Recently, it has been shown [17,22] that it can scale to decision-making problems that were previously intractable, such as high-dimensional state and action spaces. It is therefore natural to use RL to tackle this path-finding problem. To demonstrate this idea, we apply Deep Q-network (DQN) to find a highest-value path in the order graph, which achieves good performance in many fields. The proposed approach RBNets amounts to doing a stochastic search guided by the costs of the edges of the graph while A* searches for a shortest path guided by a heuristic function. Upper Confidence Bound (UCB) based strategy is utilized for better exploration rather than simple ϵ-greedy strategy.

The contributions of this paper are as follows: (1) we propose a novel method RBNets based on deep reinforcement learning for Bayesian network structure learning; (2) we integrate it with a UCB-based exploration strategy to tackle the dilemma of exploration and exploitation; (3) we thoroughly validate our propositions on diverse sets of experiments using several real-world and synthetic datasets, which shows the efficiency and effectiveness of our proposition.

2   Preliminaries

In this section, we first review the problem of Bayesian Network Structure Learning (BNSL). Then we introduce the local score and pruning rules for calculating the candidate parent sets. We formulate the BNSL as a shortest-path problem [28] using order graph. It is the basis of our proposed method.

2.1   Bayesian Network Structure Learning

A Bayesian network is a directed acyclic graph (DAG) defined as $G = (\mathcal{V}, \mathcal{E})$, where $\mathcal{V} = \{X_1, X_2, ..., X_n\}$ is a set of random variables and $\mathcal{E} \subseteq \mathcal{V} \times \mathcal{V}$ is a collection of arcs. A directed arc from X_i to X_j denotes a probabilistic dependence between the two variables, which also means X_i is a parent of X_j. The parent set of X_j is denoted by Π_j. Numerically, a conditional probability distribution $P(X_j \mid \Pi_j)$ describes the dependence between X_j and the variables in Π_j. The joint probability over all variables factorizes as the product of all the conditional probability distributions in the Bayesian network, $P(X_1, X_2, ..., X_n) = \prod_{i=1}^{n} P(X_i \mid \Pi_i)$.

Given a dataset $\mathcal{D} = \{D_1, D_2, ..., D_m\}$, where D_i is a set of values over variables in $\mathcal{V}$. The goal of structure learning is to find a DAG G that optimizes a given scoring function, which measures the goodness of fit of a network structure to $\mathcal{D}$. In this work, as customary, we assume that each variable is discrete with a finite number of possible values, and no data point has missing values in $\mathcal{D}$. Thus we can define the BNSL as follows.

Definition 1 (BNSL). *The optimal Bayesian network structure*

$$G^* = \arg \max_{G \in \mathcal{G}} \hat{s}(G, \mathcal{D}), \tag{1}$$

where $\mathcal{G}$ is the set of all possible DAGs and $\hat{s}$ is the scoring function.

To make the problem tractable, the standard approach is to use a scoring function that is decomposable over the Bayesian network's structure, i.e., the score of a network can be decomposed into a sum of node scores $\hat{s}(G) = \sum_i^n \hat{s}_i(\Pi_i)$ [12]. The values of $\hat{s}_i(\Pi_i)$ are often called *local* scores.

2.2   Local Scores

Many decomposable scoring functions can be used to measure the quality of a network structure, such as the K2, BDeu, BDe, MDL or BIC scores [15]. For concreteness, we present our work with the Bayesian Information Criterion (BIC), i.e., $\hat{s}_i = BIC$. However, our method could be extended to other decomposable scoring functions. BIC is defined as follows.

$$BIC(G) = \sum_{i=1}^{n} BIC(X_i, \Pi_i) \qquad \text{where}$$

$$BIC(X, \Pi) = \sum_{\pi \in \Pi} \sum_{x \in X} \left(m_{x,\pi} \log \hat{\theta}_{x|\pi} \right) - \frac{\log m}{2}(|X| - 1)|\Pi|,$$

where $\pi \in \Pi$ (resp. $x \in X$) denotes an assignment of all variables in Π (resp. of variable X), $\hat{\theta}_{x|\pi}$ is the maximum likelihood estimate of the conditional probability $P(X = x \mid \Pi = \pi)$, $m_{x,\pi}$ denotes the number of data points consistent with $(X = x \wedge \Pi = \pi)$, and $|\Pi|$ (resp. $|X|$) represents the number of possible instantiations of variables in Π (resp. of variable X) with the convention that $|\varnothing| = 1$.

Given n variables, there are 2^{n-1} possible parent sets for each variable. Thus, the size of the solution space grows exponentially in the number of variables. It is therefore impractical to calculate local scores for all parent sets. The computation of this process can be sped up by adopting exact pruning approaches, which guarantees not to remove the optimal network from consideration. There are also other pruning strategies, e.g., restricting the cardinality of parent sets. However, they could eliminate parent sets that are in a globally optimal network. We utilize the following theorems that hold in particular for the BIC scoring function. The first theorem [3] is useful and can handle the issue of having to compute scores for all possible parent sets.

Theorem 1. *The optimal graph G has at most $O(\log m)$ parents per node.*

Therefore, there is no need to compute scores for any parent set with a size larger than $O(\log m)$, because these parent sets are guaranteed to be suboptimal.

This second theorem [3] provides a bound to discard parent sets without even inspecting them.

Theorem 2. *Let X_i be a variable with $\Pi_i \subset \Pi_i'$ two possible parent sets such that $t_i(\Pi_i') + \hat{s}_i(\Pi_i) > 0$, where $t_i(\Pi_i') = |\Pi_i'| \, (|X_i| - 1)$. Then Π_i' and all supersets $\Pi_i'' \supset \Pi_i'$ are not optimal parent set of X_i.*

The entropy of a parent set is also a useful measure for pruning. [2] gave a pruning rule that provides an upper bound on conditional entropy of candidate parent sets and their subsets. The entropy for a variable X_i and parent set Π_i are defined as follows, respectively.

$$H(X_i) = -\sum_{k=1}^{|X_i|} \frac{m_{ik}}{m} \log \frac{m_{ik}}{m} \tag{2}$$

$$H(\Pi_i) = -\sum_{j=1}^{|\Pi_i|} \frac{m_{ij}}{m} \log \frac{m_{ij}}{m}, \tag{3}$$

where m_{ik} and m_{ij} represent, respectively, the number of times $(X_i = x_{ik})$ and $(\Pi_i = \pi_{ij})$ appear in the dataset. The conditional information is defined as usual,

$$H(X \mid Y) = H(X \cup Y) - H(Y). \tag{4}$$

Theorem 3. *Let X_i be a variable, and Π_i be a parent set for X_i. Let $X_j \notin \Pi_i$ such that $m \cdot \min\{H(X_i \mid \Pi_i), H(X_j \mid \Pi_i)\} \geq (1 - |X_j|) \cdot t_i(\Pi_i)$. Then the parent set $\Pi_i' = \Pi_i \cup \{X_j\}$ and all its supersets can be safely ignored when building the list of parent sets for X_i.*

It can be used for pruning the search space of parent sets without having to compute their BIC scores.

After pruning, the remaining parent sets are defined as *potentially optimal parent sets* (POPS). We denote the set of POPS as $\mathcal{P}_i$ for variable X_i. Given POPS as the input, the BNSL problem can be converted into the following form.

$$G^* = \arg\max_{G \in \mathcal{G}} \sum_{i=1}^{n} \hat{s}_i(X_i, \Pi_i), \tag{5}$$

where Π_i is the parent set of X_i in G and $\Pi_i \in \mathcal{P}_i$. In practice, POPS are of course not computed, but the two previous theorems are used to stop the search for known suboptimal subsets.

2.3 Order Graph

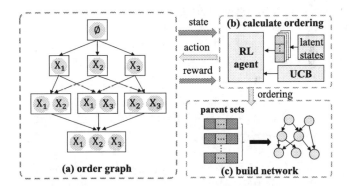

Fig. 1. RBNets framework. We have three components in our method. (a) Order graph is the environment of the agent, from which it can extract states and return rewards. This figure is an example order graph with three variables. (b) We use random walk to learn latent representations of states in the order graph. The agent explores order graph based on UCB search strategy and takes action in the environment. Finally it finds the ordering of variables. (c) From the ordering and POPS, we can calculate the parent sets and rebuild the Bayesian network structure.

Learning the structure of a Bayesian network can be seen as a search in a state-space graph (see Fig. 1(a) for an example with three variables). For a problem with n variables, this graph contains 2^n nodes. Each node represents a subset of variables. For ease of presentation, we identify nodes and subsets. They can be organized into $n + 1$ layers. The top node corresponding to the empty set is the start node at layer 0, while the bottom node, which includes all variables, is the goal node at layer n. For any subset U and any variable $X_i \notin U$, an arc connects U to $U \cup \{X_i\}$. In our context, an arc corresponds to adding a new variable X_i

to a subnetwork whose variables are in U. The value of an arc is defined as

$$cost(U \to U \cup \{X_i\}) = BestCost(U, X_i)$$
$$= \max_{\Pi_i \subseteq U, \Pi_i \in \mathcal{P}_i} \hat{s}_i(X_i, \Pi_i), \qquad (6)$$

where $BestCost(U, X_i)$ is the score of an optimal parent set for X_i in predecessor set U with the POPS constraint. For example, the edge from $\{X_1, X_3\}$ to $\{X_1, X_2, X_3\}$ has a cost equal to $BestCost(\{X_1, X_3\}, X_2)$, which is the score of the parent set of X_2 optimal in $\{X_1, X_3\}$.

With this definition of search graph, each path from the start node to the goal node represents an order of the variables; that is, each node can only find their parents in its predecessor. For example, the path $\varnothing, \{X_2\}, \{X_1, X_2\}, \{X_1, X_2, X_3\}$ denotes the variable ordering X_2, X_1, X_3, so this graph is called *order graph*. The value of a path is equal to the sum of the value of all the edges over the path. The longest path is then the path with the maximum total value in the order graph.

From a longest path from the start node to the goal node, we can reconstruct a Bayesian network structure by noting that each edge on the path encodes the choice of good parents for one of the variables out of the preceding variables. Therefore, we can generate a valid Bayesian network by putting together all the good parent choices.

3   Deep Reinforcement Learning-Based Bayesian Network Structure Learning

In this section, we present our proposed approach for solving BNSL problem. First, we formulate the BNSL problem by Reinforcement learning. Then we introduce Upper-Confidence Bound based exploration strategy for the agent. Finally, we present Deep Q-learning algorithm for our method. The framework is depicted in Fig. 1.

3.1   Reinforcement Learning Formulation

We propose to solve the previously-described highest-value path problem with a reinforcement learning (RL) approach. In RL, an agent interacts with its environment in order to learn a *policy* (i.e., which determines how to select actions in each state) in order to maximize an expected sum of rewards. As shown in Fig. 1(a), we use the order graph as the environment of the RL agent. Formally, the problem is defined as an episodic RL problem with a deterministic transition function, i.e.,

(a) state. Each node represents a state s of the agent. The initial state corresponds to the start node and the final state is the goal node.

(b) action. In time step t, the agent arrives at a state s_t from s_{t-1} and then selects an action a_t from a discrete action set A_t according to a policy π. In our formulation, A_t is the set of the neighbor states of s_t. Since each state has a varying number of actions, $|A_t|$ is set to the maximum number of actions of states. The illegal actions (i.e., there exists no corresponding arc in the order graph) are not considered.

(c) transition function. Following an action a_t in state s_t, a transition to s_{t+1} occurs with probability one if there exists an arc between the corresponding nodes in the order graph.

(d) reward. We use the value of each arc as the reward signal r_t at each time step t, that is, if the agent arrives at s_t from U to $U \cup \{X_i\}$, the reward is

$$r_t = \max_{\Pi_i \subseteq U, \Pi_i \in \mathcal{P}_i} \hat{s}_i(\Pi_i) \tag{7}$$

The RL agent interacts with the environment as follows: The agent starts in the initial state (i.e., start state). The agent repeatedly chooses an action in its current state, observes a reward and moves to a new state (i.e., adjacent node in the order graph). When the agent reaches the goal node, it returns automatically to the initial state.

Q-learning [24] is a standard algorithm for solving an RL problem. While interacting with the environment, it consists in learning the value $Q(s,a)$ of actions a in states s. It is updated as follows after an action a is performed in state s, observing reward r and moving to s':

$$Q(s,a) \leftarrow Q(s,a) + \alpha[r + \gamma \max_{a'} Q(s',a') - Q(s,a)],$$

where α is the learning rate ($0 < \alpha \leq 1$) determining to what extent newly acquired information overrides old information and $\gamma \in [0,1]$ is a discount factor determining the importance of future rewards. In our episodic problem, γ is set to one so that sum of rewards corresponds to the value of a path.

When Q-learning is used to solve a path problem, $Q(s,a)$ has a simple interpretation: it is the estimated score of the best path found so far from s to the final state starting from the arc corresponding to a. When learning stops, the best found path can be recovered by choosing the actions that maximizes $Q(s,a)$ starting from the initial state. Using Q-learning makes the algorithm progressively find better and better solution. However, its efficiency depends on the exploration strategy used in the algorithm, which decides which action to try during learning.

3.2   Upper Confidence Bounds Based Strategy

The exploration strategy makes a trade-off between exploration (i.e., try actions that are currently considered sub-optimal but that may reveal to be good later on) and exploitation (i.e., select the best action found so far, which may in fact not be optimal).

Classically, Q-learning is run with an ϵ-greedy action selection: in current state s, select $\arg\max_a Q(s, a)$ with probability $1 - \epsilon$ or choose a uniform random action otherwise. Running Q-learning amounts then to perform a local random search in each encountered state in order to find the best subpath to the final state. Although such strategy guarantees the convergence to an optimal solution (under some technical conditions) [24], it is clearly inefficient as actions will continue to be chosen with some non-negligible probability even if they revealed to be very bad. A better approach is to use an exploration based on an Upper-Confidence Bound (UCB), which is optimal (in terms of regret) in multi-armed bandits [1].

In every state and for each action, we define the following bonus $b(s, a)$ as

$$b(s, a) = \sqrt{\frac{2 \ln \tau(s)}{\tau(s, a)}},$$

where $\tau(s)$ is the number of times s has been visited so far and $\tau(s, a)$ is the number of times action a has been tried in state s. Note that the bonus is higher for less-tried actions. A UCB-based exploration strategy chooses actions in a state s with $\arg\max_a [Q(s, a) + b(s, a)]$. This strategy automatically finds a good balance between exploration (i.e., high bonus) and exploitation (i.e., high Q value).

3.3   Deep Q-Learning Algorithm

When the number of Bayesian network variables becomes large, the number of states grows exponentially, which prevents the direct application of Q-learning. For large or continuous state-space, a function approximation scheme is needed to approximate the Q function. In this paper, we use the deep Q-network (DQN) algorithm [17] for its proven efficiency and performance. DQN learns $Q(s, a; \theta)$, an approximation of the Q values, with θ representing the parameter of the neural network, by minimizing the following loss function:

$$L(\theta) = E_{s,a,r,s'}[(\hat{y} - Q(s, a; \theta))^2], \tag{8}$$

where $\hat{y} = r + \gamma \max_{a'} Q(s', a'; \theta^-)$, and θ^- represents the independent target network's parameters that is a copy of θ, which is updated at a lower frequency.

In addition, experience replay is adopted to improve the stability of the DQN training. It consists in (1) storing in a replay buffer the transitions (s, a, r, s') experienced by the agent during its interactions with the environment, then (2) minimizing the previous loss function on mini-batches uniformly sampled from the buffer.

Besides, both DQN and Q-learning are known to overestimate the Q values, as the max operator uses the same values to both select and evaluate an action. Correspondingly, the Deep Double Q-network (DDQN) [11] is proposed to solve this problem by redefining the target $\hat{y}$ with:

$$\hat{y} = r + \gamma Q(s', \arg\max_{a'} Q(s', a'; \theta); \theta^-), \tag{9}$$

Algorithm 1: DDQN Algorithm with UCB

Input: empty replay buffer B, initial network parameters θ, θ^--copy of θ, replay buffer maximum size N_r, training batch size N_b, target network replacement frequency N^-

Output: the parameters of Q-network

1   **for** *episode* $e \in 1, 2, ..., M$ **do**
2   Initialize node sequence $\mathbf{x} \leftarrow ()$;
3   **for** $t \in 0, 1, ...$ **do**
4   Set state $s \leftarrow \mathbf{x}$, take action a with $\arg\max_a [Q(s,a) + b(s,a)]$;
5   Sample next node x^t from environment given (s,a) and receive reward r, and append x^t to $\mathbf{x}$;
6   **if** $|\mathbf{x}| > N_r$ **then**
7   delete oldest node $x_{t_{min}}$ from $\mathbf{x}$;
8   Set $s' \leftarrow \mathbf{x}$, and add transition tuple (s,a,r,s') to B, replacing the oldest tuple if $|B| \geq N_r$;
9   Sample a minibatch of N_b tuples $(s,a,r,s') \sim Uniform(B)$;
10   Construct target values, one for each of the N_b tuples;
11   **if** s' *is terminal* **then**
12        $y_i = r$; break;
13   **else**
14        $y_i = r + \gamma Q(s', \arg\max_{a'} Q(s', a'; \theta_i); \theta^-)$;
15   Do a gradient descent step with loss $\|y_i - Q(s,a;\theta)\|^2$;
16   Replace target parameters $\theta^- \leftarrow \theta$ every N^- steps;

---

while the other parts are identical to DQN. For simplicity, we base our work on DDQN. It would be straightforward to use instead other variants of DQN, such as prioritized experience replay [20], dueling network [27], or bootstrapped DQN [18].

We illustrate the DDQN algorithm with UCB in Algorithm 1. The whole process of BNSL in our framework RBNets is summarized in Algorithm 2.

4 Experimental Validation

In this section, we present extensive experiment results over the performance of our method, against state-of-the-art methods.

4.1 Experiment Setup

The experiments were performed on a PC with 2.10 GHz Intel Xeon E5-2620 processor, 64 GB of RAM, 1024 GB of hard disk space, and running Ubuntu 16.04. About parameter setting, the reward discount factor $\gamma = 1$ and the maximum episodes $M = 300$. We used RMSProp for learning parameters with the learning rate α of 0.001. We used a replay buffer size N_r of 2000, batch size N_b of 200, and target network replacement frequency N^- of 300.

Algorithm 2: RBNets Algorithm

Input: Dataset $\mathcal{D} = \{D_1, D_2, ..., D_m\}$ and variables $\mathcal{V} = \{X_1, X_2, ..., X_n\}$
Output: The Bayesian network structure G^*

1 Extract POPS $\mathcal{P}_i$ for each variable X_i based on Theorem 1, Theorem 2 and Theorem 3;
2 Build a search graph and calculate the value of each edge using Equation (6);
3 Find a good ordering of variables using Algorithm 1;
4 Obtain the parent sets Π_i of each variable X_i according to POPS given the ordering of variables;
5 Rebuild the network structure by the parent sets.

Table 1. The description of datasets sorted according to the number n of variables and the number m of instances. An asterisk indicates that the dataset is from BNR and we generate instances from it, otherwise it is from UCI.

Small			Medium			Large			Very large			Very Large and Massive		
Dataset	n	m	Dataset	n	m	Dataset	n	m	Dataset	n	m	Dataset	n	m
shuttle	9	58000	horse colic	27	368	hailfinder*	56	500	pathfinder*	109	1000	isolet	617	7797
adult	14	48842	water*	32	500	hepar*	72	1000	gas sensor	128	13910	parkinson	754	756
voting	16	435	alarm*	37	1000	ozone	73	2536	semeion	256	1593	androgen	1024	1687
segment	19	2310	sponge	45	76	insurance	86	9000	madelon	500	4400	wikipedia	1068	731

4.2 Datasets

The datasets are from UCI repository[1] and Bayesian Network Repository (BNR)[2]. We removed the lines with missing data and discretized continuous variables into two states using the mean values. The BNR classifies networks as small (less than 20 variables), medium (20–50 variables), large (50–100 variables), very large (100–1000 variables), and massive (more than 1000 variables). The description is depicted in Table 1.

4.3 Baseline Methods

Many existing techniques in heuristic search and exact solver can be used to handle the problem of Bayesian network structure learning. We compare our method with the following two exact methods (A* and GOBNILP), three heuristic methods (GHC, OBS, and ASOBS), and one reinforcement learning based method (RL-BIC).

- **A*** [28] is developed based on the dynamic programming recurrences to learn optimal network structures. It formulates learning optimal Bayesian network as a shortest path finding problem. With the guidance of a consistent heuristic, the algorithm learns an optimal Bayesian network. We use the version 2017 from URLearning[3].

---

[1] http://archive.ics.uci.edu/ml/.
[2] https://www.bnlearn.com/bnrepository/.
[3] http://www.urlearning.org/.

Table 2. The running time (in seconds) of different methods. Note that the extraction of POPS was computed in a preprocessing step and the running time does not include it. We use the same extracted POPS in different methods. Running time of RBNets includes model training time. Resource limits of 12 h of CPU time and 64 GB of memory were imposed: OT = out of time; OM = out of memory. Bold indicates that the time is the best result among all tested methods. An asterisk indicates that the dataset is generated from BNR.

Dataset	Time (s)						
	A*	GOBNILP	GHC	OBS	ASOBS	RL-BIC	RBNets
shuttle	**0.8**	3.6	5.6	3.2	3.0	2.8	1.2
adult	9.6	**0.9**	28.4	12.8	6.4	3.6	2.3
voting	4.4	3.1	19.2	18.6	12.5	8.3	**2.6**
segment	**2.8**	4.0	26.7	10.2	5.8	6.1	3.5
horse colic	**8.5**	11.8	121.6	64.0	42.3	29.6	12.4
water*	6.2	**4.7**	239.4	43.9	26.6	25.7	15.8
alarm*	70.1	**6.9**	1385.1	482.3	320.7	105.4	80.5
sponge	138.4	20.6	OT	215.6	68.5	29.8	**19.7**
hailfinder*	OM	129.3	OT	673.3	104.3	105.6	**71.1**
hepar*	OM	OT	OT	1204.7	382.4	309.1	**209.2**
ozone	OM	OT	OT	3420.0	715.7	769.2	**526.4**
insurance	OM	OT	OT	3257.8	2802.5	2035.7	**1953.0**
pathfinder*	OM	OM	OT	3070.6	1961.0	1544.9	**1194.1**
gas sensor	OM	OM	OT	3641.2	3409.4	3284.8	**3026.5**
semeion	OM	OM	OT	18530.6	13298.5	12037.0	**10573.2**
madelon	OM	OM	OT	30268.9	22746.6	22453.7	**19281.7**
isolet	OM	OM	OT	38211.4	29682.3	28444.8	**26318.6**
parkinson	OM	OM	OT	OT	31842.1	28373.5	**27805.9**
androgen	OM	OM	OT	OT	39467.4	37009.2	**36256.0**
wikipedia	OM	OM	OT	OT	40369.2	38675.1	**38096.8**

- **GOBNILP** [7] is based on the integer programming (IP) for exact BN learning, which learns Bayesian networks from complete discrete data or from local scores. It adds acyclicity constraints to the ILP during solving in the form of cutting planes. We use the version 1.6.1 with SCIP 3.2.1 of GOBNILP[4].
- **Greedy Hill Climbing (GHC)** [9] examines all possible local changes (edge addition, edge deletion, and edge reversal) in each step and apply the one that leads to the biggest improvement in score and optimizes the network structure. We use the implementation of bnlearn[5] package with version 4.5.
- **OBS** [25] makes use of the topological orderings of variables as a search space, selecting for each ordering the best network consistent with it. This search space is much smaller, makes more global search steps, has a lower branching factor, and avoids costly acyclicity checks.

---

[4] https://www.cs.york.ac.uk/aig/sw/gobnilp/.
[5] https://www.bnlearn.com/.

- **ASOBS** [19] performs approximated structure learning without constraints on the in-degree. It is made of two parts: parent set identification for exploring the space of possible parent sets of a node; structure optimization for maximizing the score of the resulting structure.
- **RL-BIC** [29] proposes an encoder-decoder model, which takes observable data as input and generates graph adjacency matrices that are used to compute rewards. The reward incorporates both the predefined score function and two penalty terms for enforcing acyclicity.

4.4   Evaluation Metrics

The explicit goal of Bayesian network structure learning is to maximize the BIC score. Therefore, in addition to the running time, we evaluate the performance of methods by the BIC score. The difference in BIC scores between the two alternative networks is an asymptotic approximation of the logarithm of the Bayesian factor, which is the ratio of two posterior probabilities [19]. $\Delta BIC_{1,2} = BIC_1 - BIC_2$ represents the difference between the BIC scores of network net_1 and network net_2. If $\Delta BIC_{1,2} > 0$, it means that net_1 is better than net_2. In order to quantify this metric, the evidence in favor of net_1 is respectively {neutral, positive, strongly positive, very strong} if $\Delta BIC_{1,2}$ is between {0 and 2; 2 and 6; 6 and 10; beyond 10} [19]. In the same way, the evidence in favor of net_2 is respectively {neutral, negative, strongly negative, very negative} if $\Delta BIC_{1,2}$ is between {−2 and 0; −6 and −2; −10 and −6; smaller than −10}.

Table 3. The comparison of RBNets with four heuristic baselines in unknown network structures.

RBNets vs	GHC	OBS	ASOBS	RL-BIC
$\Delta BIC(K)$				
Very positive ($K > 10$)	24	21	15	12
Strongly positive ($6 < K < 10$)	3	4	3	6
Positive ($2 < K < 6$)	2	2	6	5
Neutral ($-2 < K < 2$)	1	3	5	6
Negative ($-6 < K < -2$)	0	0	1	1
Strongly negative ($-10 < K < -6$)	0	0	0	0
Very negative ($K < -10$)	0	0	0	0

4.5   Performance Evaluation of Time

We first tested the running time of different methods in solving the benchmark datasets. We terminate a method early if it runs for more than 12 h on a dataset, which means out of time in our scenario. The result is presented in Table 2, from

Table 4. The comparison of RBNets with four heuristic baselines in known network structures.

RBNets vs	GHC	OBS	ASOBS	RL-BIC
$\Delta BIC(K)$				
Very positive $(K > 10)$	29	23	19	14
Strongly positive $(6 < K < 10)$	0	1	0	5
Positive $(2 < K < 6)$	1	3	2	3
Neutral $(-2 < K < 2)$	0	3	5	4
Negative $(-6 < K < -2)$	0	0	2	2
Strongly negative $(-10 < K < -6)$	0	0	1	2
Very negative $(K < -10)$	0	0	1	0

which we can draw that the running time mainly depends on the scale of the datasets, including the number of variables and instances. The conclusions are as follows.

- Small networks and medium networks datasets are easy for exact algorithms, A* and GOBNILP, while heuristic methods including GHC, OBS, ASOBS, and RL-BIC need more time to find a solution. However, our proposed RBNets achieves satisfactory results and are even better than exact methods in voting and sponge datasets.
- In large networks, it can be challenging for both A* and GOBNILP, either out of memory or out of time. As for the heuristic methods, GHC does not work when number of variables is larger than 40, which is understandable because it examines all possible local changes in each step. ASOBS performs better than OBS because it extends the ordering-based algorithm and provides an effective approach for model selection with reduced computational cost. RL-BIC achieves good performance among baseline methods. Our RBNets has the best performance compared with all baselines.
- In very large and massive networks, A*, GOBNILP, and GHC fail to complete the finding process due to out of memory or out of time. OBS, ASOBS, and RL-BIC can be applied to very large networks, but is still slower than RBNets.
- A* method can easily exceed the memory limit in large datasets, the reason is that it requires all the search information, such as parent and order graphs, to be stored in memory during the search process.

To sum up, the improvement of RBNets is significant in running time when compared with baselines, especially in large, very large, and massive networks.

4.6   Learning Performance from Datasets

In addition to running time, we measure the quality of networks that are learned from datasets of different methods. Based on the datasets mentioned in Table 1, there are 15 datasets from UCI with unknown network structures and 5 datasets from BNR with known network structures. For the former, we randomly divide each dataset into two subsets of instances, which forms 30 datasets with unknown network structures. For the latter, we generated instances from these networks using logic sampling. Each instance corresponds to a value assignment for all nodes. Then we run each method when given the first 200, 500, 1000, 2000, 3000, and 5000 instances from each dataset, i.e., overall we consider 30 datasets (5 original datasets multiplied by 6 different number of instances) with known network structures.

Then we compare our RBNets with four heuristic methods GHC, OBS, ASOBS, and RL-BIC respectively. It should be noted that exact methods A* and GOBNILP are not appropriate here since they aim to learn the optimal Bayesian networks. Besides, A* and GOBNILP can not work in very large networks unless the in-degree is restricted. A positive ΔBIC means that RBNets yields a network with higher BIC score than the network obtained using other approaches; vice versa for negative values of ΔBIC. The comparison results are shown in Table 3 and Table 4, from which we draw following conclusions.

– The ΔBIC of the learned network is larger than 10 in most cases, implying very effective calculation for the networks learned by RBNets.
– Especially comparing with GHC and OBS, RBNets acts much better than them whether the network structure is known or not. $\Delta BIC > 10$ is obtained in 24/30 cases and 29/30 cases in unknown and known structures, respectively.
– ASOBS and RL-BIC have good performance in a few datasets, e.g., ASOBS leads to $\Delta BIC < -2$ in 1/30 cases in unknown structures and 4/30 cases in known structures. However, they still perform worse than RBNets in most cases.
– RL-BIC yields $\Delta BIC < -2$ in 1/30 cases and 4/30 cases in different data scenarios. However, RBNets performs better than R-RBNets in most cases.

5   Conclusion

In this paper, we discuss the problem of learning Bayesian network structures from a given dataset and scoring function, which has been shown to be NP-hard. The running time and learning performance of traditional methods are not satisfactory, which calls for further research. In this paper, we propose a novel deep Reinforcement learning based Bayesian Network structure learning approach (RBNets). We formulate this problem as a highest-value path problem and calculate the ordering of variables using the Deep Double Q-network algorithm with Upper Confidence Bound based exploration strategy. Then we can reconstruct the structure of Bayesian networks from the potential optimal parent sets and the ordering of variables. Substantial experiments on real and synthetic datasets show the efficiency and effectiveness of our method against baseline methods. RBNets has better performance over running time and BIC score when compared with state-of-the-art methods, especially in large networks.

References

1. Auer, P., Cesa-Bianchi, N., Fischer, P.: Finite-time analysis of the multiarmed bandit problem. Mach. Learn. (ML) **47**(2–3), 235–256 (2002)
2. de Campos, C.P., Scanagatta, M., Corani, G., Zaffalon, M.: Entropy-based pruning for learning Bayesian networks using BIC. Artif. Intell. (AI) **260**, 42–50 (2018)
3. Campos, C.P.D., Ji, Q.: Efficient structure learning of Bayesian networks using constraints. J. Mach. Learn. Res. (JMLR) **12**, 663–689 (2011)
4. de Campos, L.M., Fernández-Luna, J.M., Gámez, J.A., Puerta, J.M.: Ant colony optimization for learning Bayesian networks. Int. J. Approx. Reason. **31**(3), 291–311 (2002)
5. Chen, C., Yuan, C.: Learning diverse Bayesian networks. In: AAAI Conference on Artificial Intelligence (AAAI), pp. 7793–7800 (2019)
6. Chickering, D.M.: Learning Bayesian networks is NP-complete. Networks **112**(2), 121–130 (1996)
7. Cussens, J.: Bayesian network learning with cutting planes. In: Conference on Uncertainty in Artificial Intelligence (UAI), pp. 153–160 (2011)
8. Cussens, J., Bartlett, M.: Advances in Bayesian network learning using integer programming. In: Conference on Uncertainty in Artificial Intelligence (UAI), pp. 182–191 (2013)
9. Friedman, N., Nachman, I., Peér, D.: Learning Bayesian network structure from massive datasets: the "sparse candidate" algorithm. In: Conference on Uncertainty in Artificial Intelligence (UAI), pp. 206–215 (1999)
10. Gasse, M., Aussem, A., Elghazel, H.: An experimental comparison of hybrid algorithms for Bayesian network structure learning. In: Flach, P.A., De Bie, T., Cristianini, N. (eds.) ECML PKDD 2012. LNCS (LNAI), vol. 7523, pp. 58–73. Springer, Heidelberg (2012). https://doi.org/10.1007/978-3-642-33460-3_9
11. van Hasselt, H., Guez, A., Silver, D.: Deep reinforcement learning with double q-learning. In: AAAI Conference on Artificial Intelligence (AAAI), pp. 2094–2100 (2016)
12. Heckerman, D.: A tutorial on learning with Bayesian networks. In: NATO Advanced Study Institute on Learning in Graphical Models, pp. 301–354 (1998)
13. Jaakkola, T., Sontag, D., Globerson, A., Meila, M.: Learning Bayesian network structure using LP relaxations. J. Mach. Learn. Res. (JMLR) **9**, 358–365 (2010)
14. Lee, C., van Beek, P.: Metaheuristics for score-and-search Bayesian network structure learning. In: Canadian Conference on Artificial Intelligence (Canadian AI), pp. 129–141 (2017)
15. Liao, Z.A., Sharma, C., Cussens, J., van Beek, P.: Finding all Bayesian network structures within a factor of optimal. In: AAAI Conference on Artificial Intelligence (AAAI), pp. 7892–7899 (2019)
16. Malone, B., Yuan, C., Hansen, E.A., Bridges, S.: Improving the scalability of optimal Bayesian network learning with external-memory frontier breadth-first branch and bound search. In: Conference on Uncertainty in Artificial Intelligence (UAI), pp. 479–488 (2011)
17. Mnih, V., et al.: Human-level control through deep reinforcement learning. Nature **518**, 529–533 (2015)
18. Osband, I., Blundell, C., Pritzel, A., Roy, B.V.: Deep exploration via bootstrapped DQN. In: Neural Information Processing Systems (NeurIPS), pp. 4026–4034 (2016)
19. Scanagatta, M., de Campos, C.P., Corani, G., Zaffalon, M.: Learning Bayesian networks with thousands of variables. In: Neural Information Processing Systems (NeurIPS), pp. 1864–1872 (2015)

20. Schaul, T., Quan, J., Antonoglou, I., Silver, D.: Prioritized experience replay. In: International Conference on Learning Representations (ICLR) (2016)
21. Silander, T., Myllymaki, P.: A simple approach for finding the globally optimal Bayesian network structure. In: Conference on Uncertainty in Artificial Intelligence (UAI) (2006)
22. Silver, D., et al.: A general reinforcement learning algorithm that masters chess, shogi, and go through self-play. Science **362**(6419), 1140–1144 (2018)
23. Singh, A.P., Moore, A.W.: Finding optimal Bayesian networks by dynamic programming. In: USENIX Annual Technical Conference (USENIX ATC) (2005)
24. Sutton, R., Barto, A.: Reinforcement Learning: An Introduction. MIT Press, Cambridge (1998)
25. Teyssier, M., Koller, D.: Ordering-based search: a simple and effective algorithm for learning Bayesian networks. In: Conference on Uncertainty in Artificial Intelligence (UAI), pp. 548–549 (2005)
26. Wang, X., et al.: Ordering-based causal discovery with reinforcement learning. In: International Joint Conference on Artificial Intelligence (IJCAI), pp. 3566–3573 (2021)
27. Wang, Z., Schaul, T., Hessel, M., van Hasselt, H., Lanctot, M., de Freitas, N.: Dueling network architectures for deep reinforcement learning. In: International Conference on Machine Learning (ICML), pp. 1995–2003 (2016)
28. Yuan, C., Malone, B.M., Wu, X.: Learning optimal Bayesian networks using A* search. In: International Joint Conference on Artificial Intelligence (IJCAI), pp. 2186–2191 (2011)
29. Zhu, S., Ng, I., Chen, Z.: Causal discovery with reinforcement learning. In: International Conference on Learning Representations (ICLR) (2020)

A Unified Spectral Rotation Framework Using a Fused Similarity Graph

Yuting Liang[1], Wen Bai[2], and Yuncheng Jiang[1,2]($\boxtimes$)

[1] School of Artificial Intelligence, South China Normal University,
Foshan 528225, China
ytliang@m.scnu.edu.cn
[2] School of Computer Science, South China Normal University,
Guangzhou 510631, China
{wbai,ycjiang}@scnu.edu.cn

Abstract. Multi-view spectral clustering has recently received a lot of attention. Existing methods, however, have two problems to be addressed: 1) similarity matrices used in clustering omit the high-order neighbor information, reducing embedding accuracy; 2) two independent procedures of embedding and discretization may result in a suboptimal result, lowering the final performance. To address the abovementioned issues, we propose a unified spectral rotation framework for multi-view clustering using a fused similarity graph. The method begins with establishing similarity graphs for each view and constructing first-order and high-order Laplacian matrices for capturing the hidden similarity among different nodes. Then embedding and discretization procedures are integrated into a new framework for performing a spectral rotation to obtain a global clustering result. Finally, a three-step optimization method for obtaining the final clustering labels is proposed. We conduct extensive experiments on a variety of real-world and synthetic datasets to validate the effectiveness of the proposed algorithm. Our method outperforms state-of-the-art methods by 8.0% on average, according to experimental results. The code of the proposed method is available at https://github.com/lting0120/USRF_FSG.git.

Keywords: Multi-view clustering · Spectral clustering · High-order Laplacian

1 Introduction

Multi-view clustering is a hot topic in unsupervised learning, widely applied in data mining, machine learning, image processing, and so on [7,9]. A large number of multi-view clustering methods are proposed, including multi-kernel learning [5], multi-view spectral clustering [13], multi-view subspace clustering [31], etc. Among them, multi-view spectral clustering becomes more popular [29,30] because of its good performance and simple implementation, which is successfully applied to many applications, such as image segmentation [1], social multimedia [21], and cancer biology [12]. The classical multi-view spectral clustering

© The Author(s), under exclusive license to Springer Nature Switzerland AG 2023
D. Koutra et al. (Eds.): ECML PKDD 2023, LNAI 14171, pp. 209–225, 2023.
https://doi.org/10.1007/978-3-031-43418-1_13

algorithm can be summarized in three steps: 1) constructing a similarity graph for every view; 2) finding a fusion graph between all similarity graphs and perform spectral embedding; 3) performing spectral discretization by k-means after spectral embedding to obtain the final clustering results.

One of the important tasks of classical multi-view clustering methods that has received much attention is how to improve accuracy. According to the task, the existing algorithms can be divided into two categories. The **first** category pays attention to constructing similarity graphs effectively, aiming to mine hidden neighbor information from multiple views. To be specific, the category mainly includes anchor approximation [22,26], high-order information acquisition [20,33], and graph information fusion [8,25]. These methods often calculate the distance among local neighbors to establish contact and construct similarity graphs. The **second** category commits to fusing the second and third steps thus avoiding the extra k-means step. These methods make the obtained discrete clustering results closer to the real clustering labels by imposing the rank constraint on the fusion matrix to avoid the suboptimal result [14,32]. Besides, some studies [19,24] may obtain the discrete clustering allocation matrix by rotating the continuous allocation matrix.

Although the first category of studies obtained a representative embedding matrix, the two individual steps of spectral embedding and spectral discretization resulted in a suboptimal clustering result. The algorithms in the second category, on the other hand, obtained the best discrete clustering allocation matrix. Still, the embedding matrix lacked sufficient information to capture node features, lowering the final performance. Overall, the current multi-view spectral clustering still has two flaws: 1) lack of a suitable matrix to distinguish similarity among different nodes; 2) individual embedding and discretization processes lead to a suboptimal clustering result.

To solve the above problems, we propose a unified spectral rotation framework using a fused similarity graph. First, instead of conventional similarity graphs, anchor graphs are produced, which selects more representative anchors. Then, we construct the first-order and high-order Laplacian matrices for capturing the hidden similarities among different nodes, where the first-order and high-order Laplacian matrices complement the information held by each other and the optimal Laplacian matrix can be learned for clustering. Finally, embedding and discretization procedures are integrated into a unified framework for performing a spectral rotation to obtain a global clustering result. Furthermore, we design a three-step optimization method for obtaining the final clustering labels. Extensive experiments are conducted on eight benchmark datasets to validate the effectiveness of the proposed algorithm. Experimental results show that our method outperforms the state-of-the-art techniques by 8.0% on average.

The main contributions of our work are summarized below:

- We fuse the information of first-order and high-order Laplacian matrices to capture the hidden similarity among different nodes. In this way, sample-to-sample information can be fully exploited, leading to better clustering performance.

– We propose a new unified framework for integrating the spectral embedding and discretization procedures and performing a spectral rotation to obtain a global clustering result. Also, a three-step optimization method is designed for obtaining the final clustering labels.
– Comprehensive experiments are conducted on a variety of real-world and synthetic datasets to evaluate the effectiveness of our proposed algorithm. As demonstrated, when compared to other state-of-the-art baselines, the proposed algorithm can show its superiority, validating its effectiveness.

The rest of this paper is organized as follows. Related works are introduced in Sect. 2. We propose our method and its optimization in Sect. 3. The experimental results are given in Sect. 4. Finally, we conclude our work in Sect. 5.

2   Related Work

This section introduces the previous studies close to our work. Multi-view clustering aims to exploit the mutual agreement of diverse views information to obtain better clustering performance. Hence, most multi-view clustering methods are similarity-based.

To exploit the similarity between each sample, many researchers constructed affinity matrices by proximity functions, such as local proximity function [15], Gaussian proximity [25], and k-nearest proximity [33]. Considering the noise damage caused by clustering measurement, some studies adopted anchor-based methods such as k-means policy [11] and directly alternate sampling method [14]. Moreover, Sun et al. [22] and Wang et al. [26] performed subspace clustering by integrating the two processes of anchor learning and graph construction. However, the first-order proximity information is insufficient to handle the similarity between nodes. Therefore, another research of multi-view spectral clustering [33] was put forward that searches for the information in the linear combination of the first-order and high-order Laplacian matrices simultaneously. However, there is no effective method to explore hidden information between neighbors.

After the graph construction stage, the clustering process needs an extra step to generate clustering labels. Zong et al. [34] used an extra k-means stage to generate final clustering labels. However, the continuous solution obtained from the graph cutting may deviate far from the discrete solution. Therefore, Huang et al. [10] applied spectral rotation to get the continuous spectral vector closer to the discrete cluster indicator. Because the solution of traditional spectral rotation is approximate, Chen et al. [3] proposed an improved spectral rotation directly obtaining the discrete solution. However, the two-stage method may not lead to a globally optimal solution. Therefore, Nie et al. [19] performed the fusion spectral rotation on all graph matrices to obtain the discrete solution directly. Besides, some works [2, 27] performed spectral embedding and spectral rotation on a single view simultaneously. But there is a lack of combination with neighbor information in terms of multiple views.

3   Methodology

This section proposes a unified spectral rotation framework using a fused similarity graph. This framework makes the first-order and high-order information of the matrix complementary to each other for mining the hidden neighbor information. More importantly, we can search for the optimal Laplacian matrix and the global optimal clustering result simultaneously.

3.1   Similarity Matrix Construction

We first introduce how to construct first-order similarity matrices by the anchor-based method. As we know, random sampling is less representative than k-means based strategy. In this work, we utilize k-means to produce anchors. When choosing anchors, there are numerous ways adopting the clustering centers of k-means. Although these methods can improve the clustering performance, it is unstable due to the random initialization of k-means. In this work, we take the nearest nodes of the centroids generated by k-means as anchors, which is named k-nearest point (KNP) method.

Given a dataset $\mathbf{X} = \{\mathbf{X}_1, \mathbf{X}_2, ..., \mathbf{X}_v\}$, where $\mathbf{X}_v \in \mathbb{R}^{n \times d}$, consisting of n samples from v views and d is the feature number. The KNP method firstly selects m anchors $\mathbf{A} \in \mathbb{R}^{m \times d}$, where $m = \gamma \times n \ll n$ and γ is the anchor rate of samples n. To be specific, we first concatenate all feature as $\mathbf{X}' = [\mathbf{X}_1, \mathbf{X}_2, ..., \mathbf{X}_v]$. Second, we adopt k-means method to generate the nearest nodes of the m clustering centers as anchors. Then by calculating the euclidean distance between anchors and all samples to build the representation matrix $\mathbf{C} \in \mathbb{R}^{n \times m}$ for each view, which is calculated by

$$\min_{\boldsymbol{c}_{i(v)}\mathbf{1}=\mathbf{1},\left(\boldsymbol{c}_{i(v)}\right)^T \succeq \mathbf{0}} \sum_{j=1}^{m} \|\mathbf{x}_i - \mathbf{a}_j\|_2^2 \, c_{ij(v)} + \tau \sum_{j=1}^{m} \left(c_{ij(v)}\right)^2 \tag{1}$$

where $\boldsymbol{c}_{i(v)}$ denotes the ith row of $\mathbf{C}$ and the first term measures the distances between the ith sample and jth anchor. According to [3], the optimal solution $c_{ij(v)}$ to problem (1) is

$$c_{ij(v)} = \begin{cases} \dfrac{E_{i,g+1} - \|\mathbf{x}_i - \mathbf{a}_j\|_2^2}{g E_{i,g+1} - \sum_{\varepsilon=1}^{g} E_{i,\varepsilon}} & \mathbf{x}_j \in \mathcal{N}_g(\mathbf{x}_i) \\ 0 & \text{otherwise} \end{cases} \tag{2}$$

where $E_{i,\varepsilon}$ is the square of Euclidean distance between $\mathbf{x}_i$ and its εth neighbor, and $\mathcal{N}_g$ contains the g nearest neighbors of $\mathbf{x}_i$. After this, the adjacency matrix is calculated by

$$\mathbf{W} = \mathbf{C}\mathbf{\Lambda}^{-1}\mathbf{C}^T \tag{3}$$

where $\mathbf{\Lambda} \in \mathbb{R}^{m \times m}$ is a diagonal matrix which the jth entry is $\Lambda_{jj} = \sum_{i=1}^{n} c_{ij}$.

3.2 High-Order Laplacian Construction

Given a similarity matrix $\mathbf{W}$, each item w_{ij} is the first-order similarity, which indicates the relationship between node i and node j. In addition to the similarity between nodes, we also consider the similarity between the neighbors of nodes [23]. Suppose $\mathbf{\Phi}_i = \{\mathbf{x}_1, \mathbf{x}_2, \cdots, \mathbf{x}_n\}$ is the neighbor set of node i, then its corresponding weight set is $\mathbf{\Omega}_i^{(1)} = \{w_{i1}^{(1)}, w_{i2}^{(1)}, \ldots, w_{in}^{(1)}\}$. If there exist common neighbors between node i and node j, i.e. $\mathbf{\Phi}_i \cap \mathbf{\Phi}_j \neq \varnothing$, then there exists a second-order similarity $w_{ij}^{(2)} = \sum_{t=1}^{n} w_{it}^{(1)} w_{jt}^{(1)} = \mathbf{w}_i^{(1)\mathrm{T}} \mathbf{w}_j^{(1)}, \forall i, j \in [n]$.

Expanding from the second-order similarity, we can deduce the formula for the high-order similarity as $\mathbf{W}^{(o)} = \mathbf{W}^{(o-1)} \mathbf{W}$ [33]. Then the corresponding Laplacian matrix is calculated by: $\mathbf{L}^{(o)} = \mathbf{D}^{(o)} - \mathbf{W}^{(o)} \in \mathbb{R}^{n \times n}$, where $\mathbf{D}$ is degree matrix and the ith element $D_{ii} = \sum_{j=1}^{n} w_{ij}$. To obtain more comprehensive information, we fuse the first-order and high-order Laplacian matrices of multiple views to obtain an optimal synthetic Laplacian matrix [12] $\mathbf{L}^* = \sum_{o=1}^{O} \sum_{p=1}^{v} \alpha_p \mathbf{L}_p^{(o)}$, where α_p is to assign a weight for each Laplacian matrix. Next, we establish the multi-view clustering based on an synthetic Laplacian matrix as follows:

$$\min_{\mathbf{H}^\mathrm{T} \mathbf{D} \mathbf{H} = \mathbf{I}, \alpha} \mathrm{Tr}(\mathbf{H}^\mathrm{T} \mathbf{L}^* \mathbf{H})$$

$$\text{s.t. } \mathbf{L}^* = \sum_{o=1}^{O} \sum_{p=1}^{v} \alpha_p \mathbf{L}_p^{(o)}, \|\alpha\|_1 = 1, \alpha \geq 0, \mathbf{H} = \mathbf{Y}(\mathbf{Y}^\mathrm{T} \mathbf{D} \mathbf{Y})^{-\frac{1}{2}} \tag{4}$$

where $\mathbf{Y} \in \mathbb{B}^{n \times k}$ represents the discrete cluster allocation matrix and k represents the cluster number. The process is designed to optimize the continuous cluster allocation matrix $\mathbf{H} \in \mathbb{R}^{n \times k}$ which also known as spectral embedding.

3.3 Unified Framework

To get the globally optimal result, the spectral rotation is used to perform spectral discretization [10]:

$$\min_{\mathbf{R}^\mathrm{T} \mathbf{R} = \mathbf{I}, \mathbf{Y} \in \mathbb{B}^{n \times k}} \|\mathbf{H}^* \mathbf{R} - \mathbf{Y}\|_F^2 \tag{5}$$

where $\mathbf{H}^*$ is the optimal solution and $\mathbf{R}$ is an orthonormal matrix. Since $\mathbf{HR}$ also a solution of Eq. (4) with the constraint $(\mathbf{HR})^\mathrm{T} \mathbf{D} (\mathbf{HR}) = \mathbf{I}$, the goal of Eq. (5) is to find a suitable $\mathbf{R}$ making the $\mathbf{H}^* \mathbf{R}$ closer to the discrete indicator matrix $\mathbf{Y}$ by minimizing the distance between them [10].

In order to obtain optimal $\mathbf{Y}^*$, there exists a method that transform $\mathbf{H}$ back to the $\mathbf{Y}$ by

$$\mathbf{Y}^* = \mathrm{Diag}\left(\mathrm{diag}^{-\frac{1}{2}}\left(\mathbf{H}^* (\mathbf{H}^*)^\mathrm{T}\right)\right) \mathbf{H}^* \tag{6}$$

Since $\mathbf{Y}^*$ is an approximate solution, the final clustering result may deviate from the proper discrete solution if $\mathbf{Y}$ is solved by Eqs. (5) and (6) only. So we use the original form $\mathbf{Y}(\mathbf{Y}^{\mathrm{T}}\mathbf{D}\mathbf{Y})^{-\frac{1}{2}}$ of $\mathbf{Y}$ such that $\mathbf{Y}$ approximates the correct solution, the improved spectral rotation formula is:

$$\min_{\mathbf{R}^{\mathrm{T}}\mathbf{R}=\mathbf{I},\mathbf{Y}\in\mathbb{B}^{n\times k}} \|\mathbf{H}^*\mathbf{R} - \mathbf{Y}(\mathbf{Y}^{\mathrm{T}}\mathbf{D}\mathbf{Y})^{-\frac{1}{2}}\|_F^2 \tag{7}$$

Finally, we integrate the spectral embedding and spectral rotation in a single framework with a trade-off parameter β for measurement. We also add a diversity inducement term to balance the contribution of different orders with different views:

$$\min_{\mathbf{H}^{\mathrm{T}}\mathbf{D}\mathbf{H}=\mathbf{I},\mathbf{R}^{\mathrm{T}}\mathbf{R}=\mathbf{I},\mathbf{Y}\in\mathbb{B}^{n\times k},\boldsymbol{\alpha}} \left[\mathrm{Tr}(\mathbf{H}^{\mathrm{T}}\mathbf{L}^*\mathbf{H}) + \beta\|\mathbf{H}\mathbf{R} - \mathbf{Y}(\mathbf{Y}^{\mathrm{T}}\mathbf{D}\mathbf{Y})^{-\frac{1}{2}}\|_F^2 + \theta\boldsymbol{\alpha}^{\mathrm{T}}\mathbf{N}\boldsymbol{\alpha} \right]$$

$$\text{s.t. } \mathbf{L}^* = \sum_{o=1}^{O}\sum_{p=1}^{v} \alpha_p \mathbf{L}_p^{(o)}, \|\boldsymbol{\alpha}\|_1 = 1, \boldsymbol{\alpha} > 0$$

$$\mathbf{N}_{pq} = \sum_{o=1}^{O} \frac{\mathrm{Tr}(\mathbf{W}_p^{(o)}\mathbf{W}_q^{(o)})}{\|\mathbf{W}_p^{(o)}\|_F\|\mathbf{W}_q^{(o)}\|_F} (\forall p,q \in [v] \text{ and } o \in [O])$$

$$\tag{8}$$

The first term tries to find a consensus matrix $\mathbf{H}$ among multiple views. The second tends to find a global optimal discrete indication solution $\mathbf{Y}$. The third of the proposed formula is the diversity inducement term, which is introduced to consider the effects between different views of different orders fully. The weight parameter α_p tends to depend only on the adjacency matrix $\mathbf{W}_p^{(o)}$ and a given $\mathbf{H}$, while independent of the other adjacency matrices [16]. So a regularization term is introduced here to characterize the correlation among all adjacency matrices. And the optimal Laplacian matrix is constructed by minimizing this regularization term to update $\boldsymbol{\alpha}$ [33]. θ is the equilibrium coefficient, and $\mathbf{N}$ is the correlation measurement matrix that records the central kernel alignment values among the matrices.

Given the constraint $\mathbf{R}^{\mathrm{T}}\mathbf{R} = \mathbf{I}$, $\mathbf{H}\mathbf{R}$ can be fused into a variable so that $\mathbf{H}$ directly replaces $\mathbf{H}\mathbf{R}$, and then we extend the second term by $\mathbf{D}^{\frac{1}{2}}$. By transforming the above, we obtain the optimization problem of the proposed algorithm as follows:

$$\min_{\mathbf{H}^{\mathrm{T}}\mathbf{D}\mathbf{H}=\mathbf{I},\mathbf{Y}\in\mathbb{B}^{n\times k},\boldsymbol{\alpha}} \left[\mathrm{Tr}(\mathbf{H}^{\mathrm{T}}\mathbf{L}^*\mathbf{H}) + \beta\|\mathbf{D}^{\frac{1}{2}}\mathbf{H} - \mathbf{D}^{\frac{1}{2}}\mathbf{Y}(\mathbf{Y}^{\mathrm{T}}\mathbf{D}\mathbf{Y})^{-\frac{1}{2}}\|_F^2 + \theta\boldsymbol{\alpha}^{\mathrm{T}}\mathbf{N}\boldsymbol{\alpha} \right]$$

$$\text{s.t. } \mathbf{L}^* = \sum_{o=1}^{O}\sum_{p=1}^{v} \alpha_p \mathbf{L}_p^{(o)}, \|\boldsymbol{\alpha}\|_1 = 1, \boldsymbol{\alpha} > 0,$$

$$\mathbf{N}_{pq} = \sum_{o=1}^{O} \frac{\mathrm{Tr}\left(\mathbf{W}_p^{(o)}\mathbf{W}_q^{(o)}\right)}{\left\|\mathbf{W}_p^{(o)}\right\|_F \left\|\mathbf{W}_q^{(o)}\right\|_F} (\forall p,q \in [v] \text{ and } o \in [O])$$

$$\tag{9}$$

The three terms are spectral clustering, spectral rotation, and diversity inducement.

3.4 Optimization

A newly proposed optimization process for Eq. (9) is presented. We decompose it into three optimization sub-problems, namely $\mathbf{H}$-step, $\mathbf{Y}$-step, and $\boldsymbol{\alpha}$-step. In addition, the computational complexity of the optimization algorithm is also discussed.

1) $\boldsymbol{\alpha}$-step. This step aims to update $\boldsymbol{\alpha}$ with the given $\mathbf{H}$ and $\mathbf{Y}$. Then the objective function w.r.t. $\boldsymbol{\alpha}$ can be formulated as

$$\min_{\boldsymbol{\alpha}} \boldsymbol{\alpha}^{\mathrm{T}}\mathbf{N}\boldsymbol{\alpha} + \boldsymbol{b}^{\mathrm{T}}\boldsymbol{\alpha} \qquad \text{s.t. } \|\boldsymbol{\alpha}\|_1 = 1, 0 \leq \alpha_p \leq 1 (p \in [v]) \tag{10}$$

where $b_p = \frac{\beta}{\theta} \mathrm{Tr}\left(\mathbf{H}^{\mathrm{T}} \sum_{o=1}^{O} \mathbf{L}_p^{(o)}\mathbf{H}\right) (p \in [v])$. Because $\mathbf{N}$ is semi-positive definite and the constraint of Eq. (10) is convex, the corresponding QP problem is convex. We can solve it with a standard convex quadratic programming problem. So, the optimal solution can be obtained.

2) $\mathbf{H}$-step. This step aims to update $\mathbf{H}$ with given $\boldsymbol{\alpha}$ and $\mathbf{Y}$. Let $\mathbf{G} = \mathbf{D}^{\frac{1}{2}}\mathbf{H}$, because $\mathbf{G}^{\mathrm{T}}\mathbf{G} = \mathbf{I}$, the objective function can be transformed as:

$$\min_{\mathbf{G}^{\mathrm{T}}\mathbf{G}=\mathbf{I}} \left[\mathrm{Tr}\left(\mathbf{G}^{\mathrm{T}}\mathbf{D}^{-\frac{1}{2}}\mathbf{L}^*\mathbf{D}^{-\frac{1}{2}}\mathbf{G}\right) + \beta \left\|\mathbf{G} - \mathbf{D}^{\frac{1}{2}}\mathbf{Y}\left(\mathbf{Y}^{\mathrm{T}}\mathbf{D}\mathbf{Y}\right)^{-\frac{1}{2}}\right\|_F^2\right] \tag{11}$$

According to $\mathbf{L}^* = \mathbf{D} - \mathbf{W}^*$, we can simplify it as:

$$\max_{\mathbf{G}^{\mathrm{T}}\mathbf{G}=\mathbf{I}} \left[\mathrm{Tr}\left(\mathbf{G}^{\mathrm{T}}\mathbf{D}^{-\frac{1}{2}}\mathbf{W}^*\mathbf{D}^{-\frac{1}{2}}\mathbf{G}\right) + 2\beta\,\mathrm{Tr}\left(\mathbf{G}^{\mathrm{T}}\mathbf{D}^{\frac{1}{2}}\mathbf{Y}\left(\mathbf{Y}^{\mathrm{T}}\mathbf{D}\mathbf{Y}\right)^{-\frac{1}{2}}\right)\right] \tag{12}$$

where $\mathbf{M} = \mathbf{D}^{-\frac{1}{2}}\mathbf{W}^*\mathbf{D}^{-\frac{1}{2}}$. Because of view diversity, we calculate matrix $\mathbf{M}$ by

$$\mathbf{M} = \sum_{o=1}^{O}\sum_{p=1}^{v} \alpha_p \left(\mathbf{D}_p^{(o)}\right)^{-\frac{1}{2}} \mathbf{W}_p^{(o)} \left(\mathbf{D}_p^{(o)}\right)^{-\frac{1}{2}} \tag{13}$$

Then, the $\mathbf{H}$-step can be further expressed as:

$$\max_{\mathbf{G}^{\mathrm{T}}\mathbf{G}=\mathbf{I}} \mathrm{Tr}(\mathbf{G}^{\mathrm{T}}\mathbf{M}\mathbf{G} + 2\beta\mathbf{G}^{\mathrm{T}}\mathbf{K}) \tag{14}$$

where $\mathbf{K} = \mathbf{D}^{\frac{1}{2}}\mathbf{Y}(\mathbf{Y}^{\mathrm{T}}\mathbf{D}\mathbf{Y})^{-\frac{1}{2}} \in \mathbb{R}^{n \times k}$. We consider taking the Lagrangian multipliers to tackle the problem because there is a constraint $\mathbf{G}^{\mathrm{T}}\mathbf{G} = \mathbf{I}$. The Lagrangian function can be written as:

$$\mathcal{L}(\mathbf{G}, \lambda) = \mathrm{Tr}(\mathbf{G}^{\mathrm{T}}\mathbf{M}\mathbf{G} + 2\beta\mathbf{G}^{\mathrm{T}}\mathbf{K}) - \mathrm{Tr}(\lambda(\mathbf{G}^{\mathrm{T}}\mathbf{G} - \mathbf{I})) \tag{15}$$

The λ is the Lagrangian multiplier, and now we need to solve the following:

$$\frac{\partial \mathcal{L}}{\partial \mathbf{G}} = 2\mathbf{M}\mathbf{G} + 2\beta\mathbf{K} - 2\mathbf{G}\lambda = 0 \tag{16}$$

Let $\mathbf{Z} = 2\mathbf{M}\mathbf{G} + 2\beta\mathbf{K}$, the optimal $\mathbf{G}^*$ can be obtained by solving the below question:

$$\max_{\mathbf{G}^{\mathrm{T}}\mathbf{G}=\mathbf{I}} \mathrm{Tr}(\mathbf{G}^{\mathrm{T}}\mathbf{Z}) \tag{17}$$

Because Eqs. (14) and (17) satisfy the KKT condition, we can decompose $\mathbf{Z}$ by single value decomposition (SVD), w.r.t. $\mathbf{Z} = \mathbf{U}\mathbf{\Sigma}\mathbf{V}^{\mathrm{T}}$, then the optimal $\mathbf{G}^*$ is obtained by $\mathbf{G}^{\mathrm{T}*} = \mathbf{V}\mathbf{U}^{\mathrm{T}}$. So the optimal $\mathbf{H}^*$ can be calculated by:

$$\mathbf{H}^* = \mathbf{D}^{-\frac{1}{2}}\mathbf{U}\mathbf{V}^{\mathrm{T}} \tag{18}$$

where $\mathbf{U}, \mathbf{V}^{\mathrm{T}}$ come from the SVD of $\mathbf{Z}$.

3) Y-step. This step aims to update $\mathbf{Y}$ with the given $\boldsymbol{\alpha}$ and $\mathbf{H}$. The objective function of $\mathbf{Y}$ is:

$$\min_{\mathbf{Y}\in\mathbb{B}^{n\times k}} \|\mathbf{D}^{\frac{1}{2}}\mathbf{H} - \mathbf{D}^{\frac{1}{2}}\mathbf{Y}\left(\mathbf{Y}^{\mathrm{T}}\mathbf{D}\mathbf{Y}\right)^{-\frac{1}{2}}\|_F^2 \tag{19}$$

It can be simplified as follows:

$$\max_{\mathbf{Y}\in\mathbb{B}^{n\times k}} \mathrm{Tr}\left(\mathbf{H}^{\mathrm{T}}\mathbf{D}\mathbf{Y}\left(\mathbf{Y}^{\mathrm{T}}\mathbf{D}\mathbf{Y}\right)^{-\frac{1}{2}}\right)$$

Then we can solve the problem above by

$$\max_{\mathbf{Y}\in\mathbb{B}^{n\times k}} \sum_{j=1}^{k} \frac{\sum_{i=1}^{n} h_{ij}D_{ii}y_{ij}}{\sqrt{\mathbf{y}_j^{\mathrm{T}}\mathbf{D}\mathbf{y}_j}} \tag{20}$$

where h_{ij} and y_{ij} denote the i,jth entries of matrix $\mathbf{H}$ and $\mathbf{Y}$ respectively, D_{ii} denotes the ith entry of $\mathbf{D}$, $\mathbf{y}_j$ is the jth column of matrix $\mathbf{Y}$. We are going to fix the other rows and calculate $\mathbf{Y}$ row by row for the reason of $\sqrt{\mathbf{y}_j^{\mathrm{T}}\mathbf{D}\mathbf{y}_j}$ containing all rows of $\mathbf{Y}$. To calculate the ith row of $\mathbf{Y}$, we need to consider the increment in the value of the target function from $y_{ij} = 0$ to $y_{ij} = 1$. The formula for calculating the increment is:

$$s_{ij} = \frac{\sum_{t=1}^{n} h_{tj}D_{tt}y_{tj} + D_{ii}h_{ij}\left(1 - y_{ij}\right)}{\sqrt{\mathbf{y}_j^{\mathrm{T}}\mathbf{D}\mathbf{y}_j + D_{ii}\left(1 - y_{ij}\right)}} - \frac{\sum_{t=1}^{n} h_{tj}D_{tt}y_{tj} - D_{ii}h_{ij}y_{ij}}{\sqrt{\mathbf{y}_j^{\mathrm{T}}\mathbf{D}\mathbf{y}_j - D_{ii}y_{ij}}} \tag{21}$$

Then the optimal value of Y can be obtained by the following equation:

$$y_{ij} = \begin{cases} 1, \ j = \underset{j\in[1,k]}{\arg\max} \ \mathbf{s}_j \\ 0, \qquad \text{else} \end{cases} \tag{22}$$

Iterate $\mathbf{y}_j$ row by row according to the formula above until the process converges and no labels change.

3.5   Complexity Analysis

Finally, we summarize the pseudo code about the optimization process in Algorithm 1, where l_1, l_2 and l_3 indicate the iteration numbers of Algorithm 1, $\mathbf{H}$-step and $\mathbf{Y}$-step respectively. We discuss the time complexity of the proposed algorithm mainly in two parts:

Algorithm 1. A Unified Spectral Rotation Framework Using a Fused Similarity Graph

---

Input: Data from v views $\mathbf{X}_{(1)}, ..., \mathbf{X}_{(v)} \in \mathbb{R}^{n \times d}$, number of clusters k, parameter β and θ, the anchor rate γ.

Output: The indicator matrix $\mathbf{Y} \in \mathbb{B}^{n \times k}$.

1: Construct first-order and high-order similarity matrices for every view according to $\mathbf{W} = \mathbf{C}\Lambda^{-1}\mathbf{C}^{\mathrm{T}}$ and $\mathbf{W}^{(o)} = \mathbf{W}^{(o-1)}\mathbf{W}$ respectively.

2: Construct first-order and high-order Laplacian matrices by $\mathbf{L}^{(o)} = \mathbf{D}^{(o)} - \mathbf{W}^{(o)}$.

3: Initialize $\mathbf{H} \in \mathbb{R}^{n \times k}$, randomly initialize $\mathbf{Y}$, $\boldsymbol{\alpha}$ as $\frac{1_v}{v}$.

4: Calculate: $\mathbf{K} = \mathbf{D}^{\frac{1}{2}}\mathbf{Y}\left(\mathbf{Y}^{\mathrm{T}}\mathbf{D}\mathbf{Y}\right)^{-\frac{1}{2}}$, $\mathbf{G} = \mathbf{D}^{\frac{1}{2}}\mathbf{H}$, and matrix $\mathbf{M}$ by Eq. (13).

5: **while** convergence criterion is not satisfied **do**

6:     Calculate $\mathbf{L}_{(l_1+1)}^{(o)} = \sum_{p=1}^{v} \alpha_{p_{(l_1)}} \mathbf{L}_p^{(o)}$.

7:     Update $\boldsymbol{\alpha}_{(l_1+1)}$ by calculating Eq. (10).

8:     **while** convergence criterion is not satisfied **do**

9:         Calculate $\mathbf{Z}_{(l_2+1)} = 2\mathbf{M}\mathbf{G} + 2\beta\mathbf{K}$.

10:        Calculate the SVD of $\mathbf{Z}_{(l_2+1)}$ that $\mathbf{Z}_{(l_2+1)} = \mathbf{U}\mathbf{\Sigma}\mathbf{V}^{\mathrm{T}}$.

11:        Calculate $\mathbf{H}$ by Eq. (18).

12:    **repeat**

13:        **for** i = 1 to n **do**

14:            **for** j = 1 to k **do**

15:                Calculate s_{ij} according to Eq. (21).

16:            Update $\mathbf{Y}_{(l_3+1)}$ by calculating Eq. (22).

17:    **until** $\mathbf{Y}$ does not change

---

(1) The first part is similarity graphs construction. This part selects m anchors and constructs representation matrices $\mathbf{C}$ which time complexity is $\mathcal{O}\left(vnmd + vnm\log(m)\right)$ where $d = \sum_{p=1}^{v} d_v$. Because $m \ll n, m \ll d$, the complexity of the first part is $\mathcal{O}\left(vnmd\right)$.

(2) The second part is optimization. Specifically, the optimization of $\boldsymbol{\alpha}$-step requires solving a standard convex quadratic programming problem whose complexity is $\mathcal{O}\left(\delta^{-1}v\right)$. δ is the precision of the result. The optimization of $\mathbf{H}$-step includes the calculation of $\mathbf{MG}$, which takes $\mathcal{O}\left(n^2 k\right)$ time. So the $\mathbf{H}$-step needs the complexity of $\mathcal{O}\left(l_2 n^2 k\right)$, where k is the cluster number. The optimization of $\mathbf{Y}$-step needs $\mathcal{O}\left(l_3 nk\right)$ time. In short, the complexity of optimization process is $\mathcal{O}\left(l_1\left(\delta^{-1}v + l_2 n^2 k + l_3 nk\right)\right)$.

In conclusion, the proposed method takes $\mathcal{O}\left(vnmd + l_1\left(\delta^{-1}v + l_2 n^2 k + l_3 nk\right)\right)$ time. Considering $\delta^{-1} \ll n$, $k \ll n$ and l_1, l_2, l_3 are independent with n, the overall complexity of our method is $\mathcal{O}\left(vnmd + n^2 k\right)$, which is reasonable.

4   Experiments

In this section, we evaluate the effectiveness of the proposed algorithm on seven widely used real-world datasets and a synthetic dataset. Yale [24] contains images of 165 different subjects under different conditions. MSRC [28] contains several features of images such as trees, buildings, airplanes, cows, faces, cars, and bicycles. ORL [17] contains detailed pictures of different faces at different times. WikiArticles[1] are selected sections from the Wikipedia's featured articles collection. 100Leaves[2] consists of 100 plant species leaves. NUS [4] contains animal object images. Mnist4 is a subset of MNIST [6], composed of the numbers 0–3. Synthetic3D[3] is a synthetic dataset about 3D objects. The detailed information about the datasets is listed in Table 1.

Table 1. Information of Benchmark Datasets

Dataset	#Sample	#Cluster	#View	#Feature
Yale	165	15	3	4096, 3304, 6750
MSRC	210	7	5	24, 576, 512,256, 254
ORL	400	40	4	512, 59, 864, 254
WikiArticles	693	10	2	10, 128
100Leaves	1600	100	3	64, 64, 64
NUS	2400	12	6	64, 144, 73,128, 225, 500
Mnist4	4000	4	3	30, 9, 30
Synthetic3D	600	3	3	3, 3, 3

4.1   Experimental Setup

In our experiment setup, we mainly set three parameters: trade-off coefficient β, regularization parameter θ, and anchor rate γ, respectively. The trade-off coefficient β is searched in $[10^{-4}, 10^{-3}, \cdots, 10^0]$. The regularization parameter θ is selected from the range $[2^{-15}, 2^{-12}, \cdots, 2^{15}]$. Our proposed method explores the optimal anchor numbers in $[0.1n, 0.2n, ..., 0.9n]$, where n is the sample number. According to the relevant literature [33], the optimal order O of the high-order Laplacian matrix is 2. To eliminate the instability of experimental performance caused by the randomness of anchor selection based on k-means, we ran the experiment 10 times. In addition, we implement the baselines using the author's source codes and set the parameters according to their study. A similarity matrix is pre-calculated with the cosine similarity for the algorithm. The clustering representation uses three widely used metrics: ACC, NMI, and Purity. All our experiments were carried out on Matlab R2021B (64bit) on the same desktop computer.

4.2   Comparison with State-of-the-Art Algorithms

To verify the effectiveness of this algorithm, we compare it with nine multi-view clustering algorithms. The details of the baselines are summarized below:

---

[1] http://www.svcl.ucsd.edu/projects/crossmodal/.

[2] https://archive.ics.uci.edu/dataset/241/one+hundred+plant+species+leaves+data+set.

[3] https://github.com/lting0120/USRF_FSG/tree/main/Datasets.

Table 2. The clustering results in comparing with the state-of-the-art method, where the bolded value is the best.

Dataset	MLAN [18]	WMSC [34]	AWP [19]	MCGC [32]	LMVSC [11]	GMC [25]	SMVSC [22]	SFMC [14]	FPMVS [26]	Proposed
ACC (%)										
Yale	49.8±1.4	61.8±0.0	57.6±0.0	62.4±0.0	54.6±0.0	65.5±0.0	59.4±0.0	52.7±3.3	44.2±0.0	**70.3±0.0**
MSRC	74.3±1.3	83.8±0.0	82.4±0.0	89.1±0.0	34.3±0.0	74.8±0.0	81.4±0.0	81.0±5.1	78.6±0.0	**89.1±0.8**
ORL	55.9±1.5	84.6±1.3	83.8±0.0	81.8±0.0	72.3±0.0	83.8±0.0	57.5±0.0	75.0±3.6	56.5±0.0	**89.3±0.0**
WikiArticles	–	52.5±1.2	45.7±0.0	52.7±0.0	55.1±0.0	44.9±0.0	32.6±0.0	50.0±4.7	32.6±0.0	**62.3±0.0**
100Leaves	58.7±0.3	87.2±1.2	75.7±0.0	31.4±0.0	55.9±0.0	82.4±0.0	38.7±0.0	70.2±1.3	35.4±0.0	**94.6±0.0**
NUS	24.5±0.5	26.2±0.1	24.6±0.0	20.3±0.0	18.5±0.0	16.5±0.0	27.4±0.0	11.4±1.3	25.9±0.0	**28.0±0.6**
Mnist4	69.6±3.7	91.95±0.0	65.6±0.0	88.5±0.0	72.7±0.0	92.0±0.0	88.4±0.0	91.7±0.2	88.5±0.0	**92.0±0.0**
Synthetic3D	46.4±2.8	69.7±0.0	34.7±0.0	33.5±0.0	95.7±0.0	34.8±0.0	96.8±0.0	95.1±1.3	91.5±0.0	**98.3±0.0**
Average	54.2	69.7	58.8	57.5	57.4	61.8	60.3	65.9	56.7	**78.0**
NMI (%)										
Yale	54.1±2.1	65.2±0.2	60.5±0.0	65.9±0.0	59.7±0.0	68.9±0.0	62.2±0.0	58.6±2.7	51.1±0.0	**71.6±0.1**
MSRC	74.6±1.9	75.3±0.0	73.0±0.0	**81.1±0.0**	24.6±0.0	77.1±0.0	70.8±0.0	72.1±3.8	68.6±0.0	79.5±0.2
ORL	73.3±0.1	93.3±0.6	91.0±0.0	93.3±0.0	86.9±0.0	93.9±0.0	79.2±0.0	91.8±1.7	78.9±0.0	**95.5±0.0**
WikiArticles	–	45.1±0.7	32.0±0.0	49.7±0.0	52.4±0.0	41.7±0.0	17.9±0.0	49.1±3.8	17.2±0.0	**56.2±0.0**
100Leaves	80.8±0.2	94.5±0.4	87.9±0.0	41.8±0.0	77.6±0.0	92.9±0.0	71.7±0.0	86.1±0.6	69.8±0.0	**97.1±0.0**
NUS	15.1±0.4	13.7±0.0	13.3±0.0	11.8±0.0	7.8±0.0	12.2±0.0	15.4±0.0	5.3±2.2	14.7±0.0	**16.4±0.5**
Mnist4	65.2±2.0	80.2±0.0	65.1±0.0	72.1±0.0	50.5±0.0	**80.9±0.0**	71.2±0.0	80.1±0.5	71.5±0.0	80.5±0.0
Synthetic3D	46.4±2.0	30.4±0.0	2.4±0.0	0.3±0.0	83.1±0.0	2.1±0.0	86.7±0.0	81.7±4.0	74.2±0.0	**92.1±0.0**
Average	58.5	62.2	53.2	52.0	55.3	58.7	59.4	65.6	55.8	**73.6**
Purity (%)										
Yale	52.1±1.8	61.8±0.0	58.2±0.0	62.4±0.0	66.1±0.0	66.1±0.0	60.0±0.0	52.7±3.1	47.3±0.0	**70.3±0.0**
MSRC	80.5±1.2	83.8±0.0	82.4±0.0	89.1±0.0	38.0±0.0	79.1±0.0	81.4±0.0	81.0±4.1	78.6±0.0	**89.1±0.8**
ORL	64.7±1.4	87.4±1.0	83.8±0.0	86.8±0.0	84.8±0.0	86.8±0.0	60.5±0.0	79.3±2.8	61.5±0.0	**91.5±0.0**
WikiArticles	–	57.0±1.1	49.8±0.0	57.1±0.0	62.3±0.0	48.2±0.0	35.9±0.0	53.2±4.4	37.1±0.0	**64.7±0.0**
100Leaves	63.1±0.3	89.4±0.8	77.1±0.0	36.3±0.0	65.1±0.0	85.1±0.0	40.3±0.0	72.1±1.2	37.1±0.0	**95.6±0.0**
NUS	26.0±0.5	28.3±0.1	27.1±0.0	22.7±0.0	29.9±0.0	17.9±0.0	28.9±0.0	11.8±1.4	27.4±0.0	**30.7±0.6**
Mnist4	74.4±2.2	91.95±0.0	74.3±0.0	88.5±0.0	72.7±0.0	92.0±0.0	88.4±0.0	91.7±0.2	88.5±0.0	**92.0±0.0**
Synthetic3D	46.4±2.5	69.7±0.0	35.7±0.0	33.7±0.0	95.7±0.0	35.5±0.0	96.8±0.0	95.1±1.3	91.5±0.0	**98.3±0.0**
Average	58.2	71.2	61.0	59.6	64.3	63.8	61.5	67.1	58.5	**79.0**

- MLAN [18] performed semi-supervised classification and local structure learning simultaneously to obtain the cluster.
- WMSC [34] used spectral perturbation to model the weight of views and then performed multi-view spectral clustering.
- AWP [19] weighted each view according to their clustering ability and formed a weighted Procrustes Average problem accordingly.
- MCGC [32] extracted consensus information from different views and learned a uniform affinity graph, finally imposing rank constraints to obtain clusters directly without additional operations.
- LMVSC [11] proposed using anchor points on large-scale graphs to learn a smaller one for each view and implement spectral clustering on small graphs.
- GMC [25] proposed a general graph-based multi-view clustering which lets each view graph matrix and the unified graph matrix mutual reinforcement.
- SMVSC [22] proposed to fuse the anchor selection strategy in graph construction to build a unified optimization framework.
- SFMC [14] proposed a parameterless graph fusion framework for multi-view spectral clustering, which looks for a self-supervised weighted joint graph compatible across multi-view.
- FPMVS [26] let anchor selection and subspace graph construction negotiate with each other in a process to improve cluster quality.

Table 2 shows the experimental results running on all baselines and the proposed method. We also report the average of each metric across all datasets and the standard deviation of each method in each dataset. The sign "-" in the table represents the unsuitable dataset for the algorithm. Compared with the baselines, the performance of our proposed algorithm can far exceed the baselines with 8% on average. Regarding ACC and Purity, the proposed algorithm achieves greater than or equal to all baselines. Taking *100Leaves* as an example, it is 7.4%, 6.2% higher than the second-best algorithm in the two criteria, respectively. Meanwhile, under the two criteria, our algorithm has the same effect as MCGC in *MSRC* and GMC in *Mnist4*. In addition, the NMI of *MSRC* and *Mnist4* is slightly worse than that of MCGC and GMC, respectively, due to the robustness of the fusion graph generated by GMC and MCGC. The experiment results demonstrate the effectiveness of fusing the first-order and high-order information in the unified spectral rotation framework.

4.3   Ablation Study

As shown in Table 3, we fix other parameters to explore the effectiveness of fusing similarity matrices which combining first-order and high-order Laplacian matrices. The column L only uses the first-order Laplacian matrices to participate in the clustering process while HL+L combining the first-order and high-order Laplacian matrices for clustering. Table 3 shows the performance of HL+L is superior to that of L. Taking ACC as an example, HL+L is 1.8%, 5.2% and 4.0% higher than L in Yale, MSRC and ORL respectively, which demonstrates the fusing similarity matrices takes full use of neighbor information.

Table 3. Ablation study. Comparing the clustering results of first-order Laplacian matrix and fuse high-order Laplacian matrix on eight benchmark datasets.

Datasets	ACC (%)		NMI (%)		Purity (%)	
	L	HL+L	L	HL+L	L	HL+L
Yale	68.5	**70.3**	70.9	**71.6**	69.1	**70.3**
MSRC	83.8	**89.1**	72.5	**79.5**	83.8	**89.1**
ORL	85.3	**89.3**	93.6	**95.5**	88.8	**91.5**
WikiArticles	58.3	**62.3**	53.2	**56.2**	61.0	**64.7**
100Leaves	89.2	**94.6**	94.7	**97.1**	90.8	**95.6**
NUS	24.5	**28.0**	15.8	**16.4**	27.7	**30.7**
Mnist4	91.8	**92.0**	80.2	**80.5**	91.8	**92.0**
Synthetic3D	98.0	**98.3**	90.7	**92.1**	98.0	**98.3**

4.4   Parameter Sensitivity

This section explores the influence of different parameters within a specific range. Parameter changes on ACC, NMI, and Purity with various datasets are shown in Fig. 1 and Fig. 2.

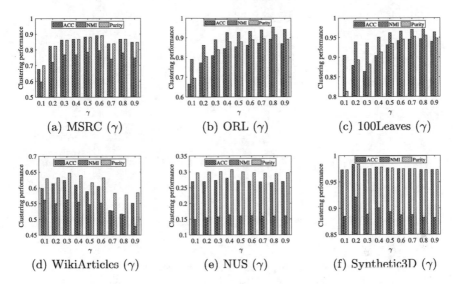

Fig. 1. The clustering results of the proposed method with different γ on six real-world datasets.

To explore the influence of different γ on the clustering result, we fix other coefficients and explore the γ in the range of $[0.1, 0.2, \cdots, 0.9]$. ACC, NMI, and Purity of six real-world datasets are shown in Fig. 1. First, in the four datasets of MSRC, ORL, 100Leaves, and WikiArticles, the practical effects show an upward trend with the increase of anchors. They do not rise with the continuous growth of anchors but fluctuate within a specific range. Second, the experimental effects of NUS and Synthetic3D datasets do not fluctuate significantly with the anchors increase but remain in a small range. So, we can choose the appropriate anchor rate for the similarity matrix construction.

Figure 2a shows the influence of θ with fixed γ and β in six datasets. It can be seen that the ACC has improved as θ changes but it is not promoted so much. Although they fluctuate within a specific range, we can find the suitable θ that balances the spectral clustering and diversity-inducing terms. Specifically, the optimal value of θ in Yale, MSRC, and ORL are $2^{10}, 2^{-12}$ and 2^0 respectively. Figure 2b shows the ACC of β with fixed γ and θ. It can be seen that the ACC increases with the variation of β and reaches its maximum when β is around 0.1.

In short, it can be seen from the above three experiments that all parameters adopted can effectively improve the algorithm's efficiency, both γ and β can enhance the clustering performance more apparently than θ.

4.5   Convergence Analysis

The objective function values of Yale, 100Leaves, and Mnist4 in our algorithm and their convergence are shown in Fig. 3. The values of the objective function decrease monotonically and converge rapidly within thirty iterations. In particular, the Yale monotonically falls the function object value within five iterations and then fluctuates within a small range.

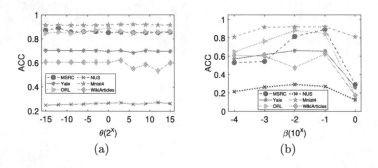

(a)   (b)

Fig. 2. The algorithm sensitivity against the variation of two parameters θ and β.

Thus, the efficiency of our proposed algorithm is verified. The time complexity of our algorithm is reasonable, as displayed in the complexity analysis.

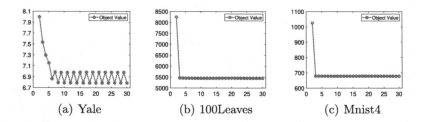

(a) Yale   (b) 100Leaves   (c) Mnist4

Fig. 3. The convergence of the overall objective function on three datasets.

5   Conclusion

This paper proposes a unified spectral rotation framework with a fused similarity graph for multi-view spectral clustering. It combines the first-order Laplacian matrices and high-order Laplacian matrices to find an optimal synthetic Laplacian matrix. Then it embeds the optimal synthetic Laplacian matrix in a new spectral rotation framework that integrates spectral embedding and discretization. Compared with the existing approaches, our method captures the hidden similarity among different nodes and obtains a global clustering result with a three-step optimization. Experiments on eight benchmark datasets validate the effectiveness of the proposed algorithm.

Acknowledgements. The works described in this paper are supported by The National Natural Science Foundation of China under Grant Nos. 61772210 and U1911201; The Project of Science and Technology in Guangzhou in China under Grant No. 202007040006.

Ethical Statement. The authors declare that they have no conflict of interest and this study does not contain any research with human participants and/or animals.

References

1. Cai, X., Nie, F., Huang, H., Kamangar, F.: Heterogeneous image feature integration via multi-modal spectral clustering. In: CVPR 2011, pp. 1977–1984. IEEE (2011)
2. Chen, J., Zhu, J., Xie, S., Yang, H., Nie, F.: FGC_SS: fast graph clustering method by joint spectral embedding and improved spectral rotation. Inf. Sci. **613**, 853–870 (2022)
3. Chen, X., Nie, F., Huang, J.Z., Yang, M.: Scalable normalized cut with improved spectral rotation. In: Proceedings of the Twenty-Sixth International Joint Conference on Artificial Intelligence, pp. 1518–1524 (2017)
4. Chua, T.S., Tang, J., Hong, R., Li, H., Luo, Z., Zheng, Y.: NUS-WIDE: a real-world web image database from national university of Singapore. In: Proceedings of the ACM International Conference on Image and Video Retrieval, pp. 1–9 (2009)
5. De Sa, V.R., Gallagher, P.W., Lewis, J.M., Malave, V.L.: Multi-view kernel construction. Mach. Learn. **79**(1), 47–71 (2010)
6. Deng, L.: The MNIST database of handwritten digit images for machine learning research [best of the web]. IEEE Signal Process. Mag. **29**(6), 141–142 (2012)
7. Djelouah, A., Franco, J.S., Boyer, E., Le Clerc, F., Pérez, P.: Sparse multi-view consistency for object segmentation. IEEE Trans. Pattern Anal. Mach. Intell. **37**(9), 1890–1903 (2015)
8. Greene, D., Cunningham, P.: Producing a unified graph representation from multiple social network views. In: Proceedings of the 5th Annual ACM Web Science Conference, pp. 118–121 (2013)
9. Hong, W., Wright, J., Huang, K., Ma, Y.: Multiscale hybrid linear models for lossy image representation. IEEE Trans. Image Process. **15**(12), 3655–3671 (2006)
10. Huang, J., Nie, F., Huang, H.: Spectral rotation versus k-means in spectral clustering. In: Proceedings of the Twenty-Seventh AAAI Conference on Artificial Intelligence, pp. 431–437 (2013)
11. Kang, Z., Zhou, W., Zhao, Z., Shao, J., Han, M., Xu, Z.: Large-scale multi-view subspace clustering in linear time. In: Proceedings of the Thirty-Fourth AAAI Conference on Artificial Intelligence, pp. 4412–4419 (2020)
12. Khan, A., Maji, P.: Approximate graph Laplacians for multimodal data clustering. IEEE Trans. Pattern Anal. Mach. Intell. **43**(3), 798–813 (2021)
13. Kumar, A., Rai, P., Daume, H.: Co-regularized multi-view spectral clustering. In: Advances in Neural Information Processing Systems, pp. 1413–1421 (2011)

14. Li, X., Zhang, H., Wang, R., Nie, F.: Multiview Clustering: a scalable and parameter-free bipartite graph fusion method. IEEE Trans. Pattern Anal. Mach. Intell. **44**(1), 330–344 (2022)
15. Liu, B.Y., Huang, L., Wang, C.D., Lai, J.H., Yu, P.S.: Multi-view consensus proximity learning for clustering. IEEE Trans. Knowl. Data Eng. **34**(7), 3405–3417 (2022)
16. Liu, X., Dou, Y., Yin, J., Wang, L., Zhu, E.: Multiple kernel k-means clustering with matrix-induced regularization. In: Proceedings of the Thirtieth AAAI Conference on Artificial Intelligence, pp. 1888–1894 (2016)
17. Lu, H., Gao, Q., Zhang, X., Xia, W.: A multi-view clustering framework via integrating k-means and graph-cut. Neurocomputing **501**, 609–617 (2022)
18. Nie, F., Cai, G., Li, X.: Multi-view clustering and semi-supervised classification with adaptive neighbours. In: Proceedings of the Thirty-First AAAI Conference on Artificial Intelligence, pp. 2408–2414 (2017)
19. Nie, F., Tian, L., Li, X.: Multiview clustering via adaptively weighted procrustes. In: Proceedings of the 24th ACM SIGKDD International Conference on Knowledge Discovery & Data Mining, pp. 2022–2030 (2018)
20. Peng, H., Hu, Y., Chen, J., Wang, H., Li, Y., Cai, H.: Integrating tensor similarity to enhance clustering performance. IEEE Trans. Pattern Anal. Mach. Intell. **44**(5), 2582–2593 (2022)
21. Petkos, G., Papadopoulos, S., Kompatsiaris, Y.: Social event detection using multimodal clustering and integrating supervisory signals. In: Proceedings of the 2nd ACM International Conference on Multimedia Retrieval, pp. 1–8 (2012)
22. Sun, M., et al.: Scalable multi-view subspace clustering with unified anchors. In: Proceedings of the 29th ACM International Conference on Multimedia, pp. 3528–3536 (2021)
23. Tang, J., Qu, M., Wang, M., Zhang, M., Yan, J., Mei, Q.: LINE: large-scale information network embedding. In: Proceedings of the 24th International Conference on World Wide Web, pp. 1067–1077 (2015)
24. Wan, Z., Xu, H., Gao, Q.: Multi-view clustering by joint spectral embedding and spectral rotation. Neurocomputing **462**, 123–131 (2021)
25. Wang, H., Yang, Y., Liu, B.: GMC: graph-based multi-view clustering. IEEE Trans. Knowl. Data Eng. **32**(6), 1116–1129 (2020)
26. Wang, S., et al.: Fast parameter-free multi-view subspace clustering with consensus anchor guidance. IEEE Trans. Image Process. **31**, 556–568 (2022)
27. Wang, Z., Li, Z., Wang, R., Nie, F., Li, X.: Large graph clustering with simultaneous spectral embedding and discretization. IEEE Trans. Pattern Anal. Mach. Intell. **43**(12), 4426–4440 (2021)
28. Winn, J., Jojic, N.: LOCUS: learning object classes with unsupervised segmentation. In: Proceedings of the Tenth IEEE International Conference on Computer Vision, pp. 756–763 (2005)
29. Xia, R., Pan, Y., Du, L., Yin, J.: Robust multi-view spectral clustering via low-rank and sparse decomposition. In: Proceedings of the Twenty-Eighth AAAI Conference on Artificial Intelligence, pp. 2149–2155 (2014)
30. Xu, H., Zhang, X., Xia, W., Gao, Q., Gao, X.: Low-rank tensor constrained coregularized multi-view spectral clustering. Neural Netw. **132**, 245–252 (2020)
31. Yin, Q., Wu, S., He, R., Wang, L.: Multi-view clustering via pairwise sparse subspace representation. Neurocomputing **156**, 12–21 (2015)
32. Zhan, K., Nie, F., Wang, J., Yang, Y.: Multiview consensus graph clustering. IEEE Trans. Image Process. **28**(3), 1261–1270 (2019)

33. Zhou, S., et al.: Multi-view spectral clustering with optimal neighborhood Laplacian matrix. In: Proceedings of the Thirty-Fourth AAAI Conference on Artificial Intelligence, pp. 6965–6972 (2020)
34. Zong, L., Zhang, X., Liu, X., Yu, H.: Weighted multi-view spectral clustering based on spectral perturbation. In: Proceedings of the Thirty-Second AAAI Conference on Artificial Intelligence, pp. 4621–4629 (2018)

SimSky: An Accuracy-Aware Algorithm for Single-Source SimRank Search

Liping Yan[1] and Weiren Yu[2(✉)]

[1] Nanjing University of Science and Technology, Jiangsu, China
lipingyan@njust.edu.cn
[2] The University of Warwick, Coventry CV4 7AL, UK
Weiren.Yu@warwick.ac.uk

Abstract. SimRank is a popular node-pair similarity search model based on graph topology. It has received sustained attention due to its wide range of applications in real-world scenarios. Considerable effort has been devoted to devising fast algorithms for SimRank computation through either iterative approaches or random walk based methods. In this paper, we propose an efficient accuracy-aware algorithm for computing single-source SimRank similarity. First, we devise an algorithm, ApproxDiag, to approximate the diagonal correction matrix. Next, we propose an efficient algorithm, named SimSky, which utilizes two Krylov subspaces for transforming high-dimensional single-source SimRank search into low-dimensional matrix-vector multiplications. Extensive experiments on various real datasets demonstrate the superior search quality of SimSky compared to other competitors.

Keywords: SimRank · Single-Source Similarity Search · Low-order Approximation

1 Introduction

A graph is a key structure for modeling complexity networks, in which nodes represent objects and edges represent relationships. Measuring similarity between objects is an important task in graph mining, with many real applications, e.g. link prediction [8], recommendation systems [3], web page ranking [17], and so forth. A variety of similarity measures have been proposed over the past decades, including Personalized PageRank [6], SimRank [5], RoleSim* [14], CoSimRank [10,19], CoSimHeat [20]. Among them, SimRank is considered an influential one. SimRank is based on the simple recursive concept [5] that *"two nodes are similar if their in-neighbors are similar; every node is most similar to itself"*. Let $G = (V, E)$ be a digraph with $|V|$ nodes and $|E|$ edges. We denote by $I(i) = \{j \in V | \exists (j, i) \in E\}$ the in-neighbor set of i, and $|I(i)|$ the in-degree of i. The SimRank score $s(i, j)$ between nodes i and j is defined as

D. Koutra et al. (Eds.): ECML PKDD 2023, LNAI 14171, pp. 226–241, 2023.
https://doi.org/10.1007/978-3-031-43418-1_14

$$s(i,j) - \begin{cases} 1, & i = j; \\ \frac{c}{|I(i)||I(j)|} \sum_{u \in I(i)} \sum_{v \in I(j)} s(u,v), & i \neq j; \\ 0, & |I(i)| \text{ or } |I(j)| = 0, \end{cases} \tag{1}$$

where $c \in (0,1)$ is a decay factor, typically assigned a value of 0.6 or 0.8.

SimRank Matrix Notations. Let $S^{(k)}$ be the k-th iterative SimRank matrix, where each element $[S^{(k)}]_{i,j}$ is the similarity score $s(i,j)$ at iteration k. Let A be the column-normalized adjacency matrix of a graph, and I be the identity matrix. In matrix notations, the SimRank matrix $S^{(k)}$ can be expressed as

$$S^{(k)} = cA^T S^{(k-1)} A + D_k$$
$$= \sum_{i=0}^{k} c^i (A^T)^i D_{k-i} A^i, \tag{2}$$

where $S^{(0)} = D_0 = I$, and $D_k = I - (cA^T S^{(k-1)} A) \circ I$ is called the *diagonal correction matrix*. The symbol $(*)^T$ stands for matrix transpose, and $\circ$ denotes entry-wise multiplication.

Single-Source SimRank. Given a query j, single-source SimRank search returns the similarity scores between node j and each node in the graph. Mathematically, given the query vector e_j (a unit vector with only a 1 in the j-th entry, and 0 s elsewhere), the single-source SimRank vector $[S^{(k)}]_{*,j}$ at the k-th iteration can be represented as

$$[S^{(k)}]_{*,j} = S^{(k)} e_j. \tag{3}$$

Recently, many endeavors [7,9,12,13,15,18] have been invested in designing faster and more efficient algorithms for accelerating single-source SimRank computation at the expense of accuracy. The low accuracy of SimRank arises from two main barriers: (1) the challenge of dealing with the intractable diagonal correction matrix; (2) the problem of high-dimensionality in SimRank iterations.

- *Intractable Diagonal Correction Matrix.* The challenge in retrieving single-source SimRank via Eq. 2 lies in the computation of diagonal correction matrix D_k. There are studies [4,7,16] that attempt to mitigate this issue using the following equation:

$$S^{(k)} = cA^T S^{(k-1)} A + (1-c)I. \tag{4}$$

However, the similarity models represented by Eqs. 2 and 4 are different.

- *High Dimensionality.* In reality, most graphs are large and sparse, leading to the high dimensionality of the adjacency matrix. Most existing work [12,13] employs random walk-based methods through Monte Carlo sampling. While these methods excel in superior scalability on large graphs, they typically exhibit low accuracy with a certain probability. For instance, the state-of-the-art single-source SimRank algorithms (e.g. ExactSim [13] and SLING [12]) using Monte Carlo approaches can only achieve a precision level of up to 10^{-7} on diverse real datasets.

Contributions. Our main contributions to this work are summarized as follows:

- We first design an algorithm, ApproxDiag, to approximate the diagonal correction matrix D with guaranteed accuracy. To make approximation more stable, we resort to a row orthogonal matrix to characterize D (Sect. 2).
- We next propose an efficient algorithm, SimSky, which transforms high-dimensional single-source SimRank search into matrix-vector multiplications over two small Krylov subspaces, eliminating much redundancy (Sect. 3).
- We conduct extensive experiments to demonstrate the superiority of SimSky over other rivals on real datasets (Sect. 4).

2   ApproxDiag: Approximate Diagonal Correction Matrix

For any matrix $X \in \mathbb{R}^{n \times n}$, we denote by the column vectors $\overrightarrow{diag}(X)$ and $\widetilde{diag}(X)$ the exact and approximate solution of the main diagonal elements of X, respectively. Bekas et al. [1] showed that $\widetilde{diag}(X)$ can be obtained by arbitrary column vectors $w_1, w_2, \cdots, w_s \in \mathbb{R}^n$ as follows:

$$\widetilde{diag}(X) = [\sum_{l=1}^{s} w_l \circ (Xw_l)] \oslash [\sum_{l=1}^{s} w_l \circ w_l], \tag{5}$$

where $\oslash$ represents entry-wise division. Let $W = [w_1|w_2|\cdots|w_s]$. If WW^T is a diagonal matrix with all diagonals being nonzeros, then $\widetilde{diag}(X) = \overrightarrow{diag}(X)$.

Construct Matrix W. Bekas et al. [1] chose the matrix W as a Hadamard matrix, which takes only the entries ± 1 so that $WW^T = nI$. This type of matrix W is suitable for approximating the main diagonal elements of a band matrix. However, in practice, the graph adjacency matrix is rarely a band matrix. Therefore, we design a novel method to construct matrix $W \in \mathbb{R}^{n \times s}$ as follows:

1) $W(1 : s, 1 : s)$ is an identity matrix;
2) the element of $W(1+s : n, s)$ is -1 at odd positions and 1 at even positions;
3) the remaining entries in W are all 0s.

As a special case, when $s = n$, W reduces to I and $\widetilde{diag}(X) = \overrightarrow{diag}(X)$.

Subtracting the item $\sum_{i=1}^{k} c^i (A^T)^i D_{k-i} A^i$ from both sides of Eq. 2 and applying Eq. 5 yield the following equation:

$$\widetilde{diag}(D_k) = \overrightarrow{1}_n - (\sum_{l=1}^{s} w_l \circ f(A, w_l, k)) \oslash (\sum_{l=1}^{s} w_l \circ w_l), \tag{6}$$

where $f(A, w_l, k) = \sum_{i=1}^{k} c^i (A^T)^i D_{k-i} A^i w_l$.

By virtue of the idea in [18], for $k \geq 2$, we can express the vector $f(A, w_l, k)$ as follows: $\forall i = 1, 2, \cdots, k$, initialize $x_0 = w_l$,

$$x_i = Ax_{i-1}; \tag{7}$$

Algorithm 1: ApproxDiag(A, c, k)

Input: A - column-normalised adjacency matrix, c - decay factor, k - number of iterations

Output: $\widehat{D}$ - contains $(k+1)$ approximate diagonal correction vectors

1 Custom matrix W and set denom $= (W \circ W) \cdot \vec{1}_s$;
2 Initialise $\widehat{D} = \text{zeros}(n, k+1)$ and set $\widehat{D}(:,1) = \vec{1}_n$;
3 **for** $j = 1$ *to* k **do**
4   Initialise nume $= \text{zeros}(n,1)$, $X = \text{zeros}(n, j+1)$;
5   **for** $i = 1$ *to* s **do**
6        $X(:,1) = W(:,i)$;
7   **for** $a = 1$ *to* j **do**
8           $X(:,a+1) \leftarrow A \cdot X(:,a)$;
9   **end**
10   Initialise $Y = \text{zeros}(n, j+1)$, set $Y(:,1) = \widehat{D}(:,1) \circ X(:, j+1)$;
11   **if** $j = 1$ **then**
12          $Y(:, j+1) \leftarrow cA^T \cdot Y(:, j)$;
13   **else**
14   **for** $b = 2$ *to* j **do**
15             $Y(:,b) \leftarrow cA^T \cdot Y(:, b-1) + \widehat{D}(:,b) \circ X(:, j+2-b)$
16   **end**
17          $Y(:, j+1) \leftarrow cA^T \cdot Y(:, j)$;
18   **end**
19   nume $\leftarrow$ nume $+ W(:,i) \circ Y(:, j+1)$;
20   **end**
21    $\widehat{D}(:, j+1) \leftarrow \vec{1}_n - \text{nume} \oslash \text{denom}$;
22 **end**
23 **return** $\widehat{D}$;

$\forall j = 1, 2, \cdots, k-1$, initialize $y_0 = \overrightarrow{diag}(D_0) \circ x_k$,

$$y_j = cA^T y_{j-1} + \overrightarrow{diag}(D_j) \circ x_{k-j}, \tag{8}$$

thus we can get $f(A, w_l, k) = cA^T y_{k-1}$ easily. Substituting $f(A, w_l, k)$ into Eq. 6, we can get our ApproxDiag algorithm.

Example 1. Given a graph and its column-normalised adjacency matrix A as shown in Fig. 1, decay factor $c = 0.8$, number of iterations $k = 2$. Take 6×2 matrix W_2, 6×3 matrix W_3, 6×4 matrix W_4, 6×5 matrix W_5 and 6×6 identity matrix W_6, where

$$W_2 = \begin{bmatrix} 1 & 0 \\ 0 & 1 \\ 0 & -1 \\ 0 & 1 \\ 0 & -1 \\ 0 & 1 \end{bmatrix}, \quad W_3 = \begin{bmatrix} 1 & 0 & 0 \\ 0 & 1 & 0 \\ 0 & 0 & 1 \\ 0 & 0 & -1 \\ 0 & 0 & 1 \\ 0 & 0 & -1 \end{bmatrix}, \quad W_4 = \begin{bmatrix} 1 & 0 & 0 & 0 \\ 0 & 1 & 0 & 0 \\ 0 & 0 & 1 & 0 \\ 0 & 0 & 0 & 1 \\ 0 & 0 & 0 & -1 \\ 0 & 0 & 0 & 1 \end{bmatrix}, \quad W_5 = \begin{bmatrix} 1 & 0 & 0 & 0 & 0 \\ 0 & 1 & 0 & 0 & 0 \\ 0 & 0 & 1 & 0 & 0 \\ 0 & 0 & 0 & 1 & 0 \\ 0 & 0 & 0 & 0 & 1 \\ 0 & 0 & 0 & 0 & -1 \end{bmatrix}.$$

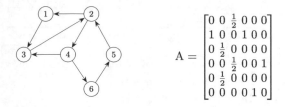

Fig. 1. A digraph with six nodes and its column-normalised adjacency matrix

According to our ApproxDiag algorithm, when W takes W_2, W_3, W_4, W_5, W_6 respectively, the corresponding matrix contains approximate diagonal correction vectors are

$$
\widehat{D}_2 = \begin{bmatrix} 1 & 0.2 & 0.2 \\ 1 & 0.6 & 0.68 \\ 1 & 1 & 1 \\ 1 & 0.2 & 0.2 \\ 1 & 0.2 & 0.04 \\ 1 & 0.6 & 0.92 \end{bmatrix}, \quad
\widehat{D}_3 = \begin{bmatrix} 1 & 0.2 & 0.2 \\ 1 & 0.6 & 0.52 \\ 1 & 1 & 1 \\ 1 & 0.2 & 0.2 \\ 1 & 0.2 & -0.12 \\ 1 & 0.6 & 0.92 \end{bmatrix}, \quad
\widehat{D}_4 = \widehat{D}_5 = \widehat{D}_6 = \begin{bmatrix} 1 & 0.2 & 0.2 \\ 1 & 0.6 & 0.6 \\ 1 & 0.6 & 0.28 \\ 1 & 0.2 & 0.2 \\ 1 & 0.2 & 0.2 \\ 1 & 0.2 & 0.2 \end{bmatrix}.
$$

$\square$

Error Analysis. We analyze the error of $\overrightarrow{diag}(D_k)$ and $\widetilde{diag}(D_k)$. $\|\cdot\|$ represents the L_2 norm for a vector or the spectral norm for a matrix. First of all, suppose that $Z = \sum_{i=1}^{k} c^i (A^T)^i D_{k-i} A^i$, subtract Z from both sides of Eq. 2 and vectorize the main diagonal elements, $\overrightarrow{diag}(D_k) = \overrightarrow{1}_n - \overrightarrow{diag}(Z)$ can be obtained. Similarly, combine with Eq. 5, we can get that $\widetilde{diag}(D_k) = \overrightarrow{1}_n - \widetilde{diag}(WW^T Z)$. According to the definition of W, we know that $(WW^T - I)(1:s-1, 1:s-1) = 0$, and $(WW^T - I)_{ii} = 0$, except that all the other elements either 1 or -1. Given column-normalised adjacency matrix A, due to $c \in (0,1)$, we have spectral radius $\rho(\sqrt{c}A) < 1$. As per Theorem 5 in [2], exists a constant θ depends only on $\sqrt{c}A$ and σ, where $\rho(\sqrt{c}A) < \sigma < 1$, $\theta = \max(1, \frac{\sigma^k}{\|(\sqrt{c}A)^k\|})$, such that $\|(\sqrt{c}A)^{i-1}\| \leq \theta \sigma^{i-1}$. At the same time, it's obvious $\|\sqrt{D_{k-i}}\| \leq 1$. Finally, combine the above equalities and inequalities, the gap between $\overrightarrow{diag}(D_k)$ and $\widetilde{diag}(D_k)$ is bounded by

$$
\|\overrightarrow{diag}(D_k) - \widetilde{diag}(D_k)\|_\infty \leq \theta^2 \frac{c(1-\sigma^{2k})}{1-\sigma^2} \max_{s \leq l \leq n} \sum_{j=s, j \neq l}^{n} \|Ae_l\| \|Ae_j\|, \quad (9)
$$

where e_l (resp. e_j) is a n-dimensional unit vector with only a 1 in the l-th (resp. j-th) entry. The equal sign "=" holds when $s = n$.

Cost Overheads. We analyze the computational cost of ApproxDiag as follows. First, initializing A, W, D requires $\mathcal{O}(nd), \mathcal{O}(ns), \mathcal{O}(nk)$ memory, respectively[1]. Second, computing D (lines 3–22) take $\mathcal{O}(\sum_{j=1}^{k} s(jnd + (j-1)(n + nd)))$ time. Therefore, it requires $\mathcal{O}(n \cdot max(d, s, k))$ memory and takes $\mathcal{O}(k^2 snd)$ time.

---

[1] d denotes the average node degree.

3   SimSky

Yu et al. [18] demonstrated that single-source SimRank search $[S^{(k)}]_{*,j}$ can be expressed as a double loop function, we notice that it can be further rewritten as a piecewise function

$$[S^{(k)}]_{*,j} = r_{2k}, \tag{10}$$

where

$$r_l = \begin{cases} \widetilde{diag}(D_{l+1}) \circ (A^{k-1-l}e_j), & 0 \leq l \leq k-1; \\ \overrightarrow{diag}(D_0) \circ (A^k e_j), & l = k; \\ cA^T r_{l-1} + r_{l-1-k}, & k+1 \leq l \leq 2k. \end{cases} \tag{11}$$

The calculation of the last item r_{2k} can be divided into three parts to complete: (1) approximating $\widetilde{diag}(D_{l+1})$ using our ApproxDiag algorithm, (2) computing $A^{k-1-l}e_j$, $A^k e_j$ via the Arnoldi algorithm [11], (3) computing r_l by means of our SimSky algorithm for $k+1 \leq l \leq 2k$.

For $k+1 \leq l \leq 2k$, r_l can be expressed as

$$r_l = BR_{l-1}, \tag{12}$$

where $B = \begin{bmatrix} cA^T & 0 & \cdots & 0 & I \end{bmatrix}$, $R_{l-1} = \begin{bmatrix} r_{l-1}^T & r_{l-2}^T & \cdots & r_{l-k}^T & r_{l-1-k}^T \end{bmatrix}^T$. Meanwhile, we use the auxiliary equation $\begin{bmatrix} r_{l-1}^T & r_{l-2}^T & \cdots & r_{l-k}^T \end{bmatrix}^T = I_{kn} \cdot \begin{bmatrix} r_{l-1}^T & r_{l-2}^T & \cdots & r_{l-k}^T \end{bmatrix}^T$, I_{kn} is a kn-dimensional identity matrix. Concatenate the Eq. 12 and the auxiliary equation along the vertical direction, we can get the following expression

$$R_l = \begin{bmatrix} B \\ I_{kn} & 0 \end{bmatrix} R_{l-1} = CR_{l-1}, \tag{13}$$

where $R_l = \begin{bmatrix} r_l^T & r_{l-1}^T & \cdots & r_{l-k+1}^T & r_{l-k}^T \end{bmatrix}^T$, 0 is a $kn \times n$ null matrix, C is a sparse block matrix. Set $R_k = \begin{bmatrix} r_k^T & r_{k-1}^T & \cdots & r_1^T & r_0^T \end{bmatrix}^T$, we can get that $R_{2k} = C^k R_k$, and r_{2k} is the first component of R_{2k}.

Therefore, R_k as the initial vector, C as the initial matrix, we can construct the Krylov subspace

$$\mathcal{K}_{m_2} = span\{R_k, CR_k, C^2 R_k, \cdots, C^{m_2-1} R_k\},$$

then we can again use the Arnoldi algorithm [11] to compute its basis matrix and projection matrix, and calculate vector r_{2k} according to Lemma 3.1 in [11].

Example 2. Given the graph and its column-normalised adjacency matrix as shown in Fig. 1. Given the query vector e_1 is a unit vector with only a 1 in the first entry, decay factor $c = 0.8$, low-order parameters $m_1 = m_2 = 3$, number of iterations $k = 2$. For brevity, we assume that diagonal correction matrix D_{k-i} is an identity matrix. Then the process to calculate single-source SimRank search

$$[S^{(2)}]_{*,1} = c^2 (A^T)^2 A^2 e_1 + cA^T A e_1 + e_1 \tag{14}$$

using our SimSky algorithm is as follows.

First, we convert Eq. 14 into a piecewise function

$$r_0 = Ae_1, \quad r_1 = e_1, \quad r_2 = A^2 e_1, \quad r_3 = cA^T r_2 + r_0, \quad r_4 = cA^T r_3 + r_1,$$

it's obvious that $[S^{(2)}]_{*,1} = r_4$.

Second, we construct the first Krylov subspace

$$\mathcal{K}_{m_1} = span\{r_1, r_0, r_2\} = span\{e_1, Ae_1, A^2 e_1\},$$

its column orthonormal matrix U and projection matrix Y can be generated by Arnoldi method [11], and a relationship is established

$$AU(:, 1:3) = UY.$$

As a result, according to Lemma 3.1 in [11], r_0, r_1, r_2 can be rewritten as

$$r_0 = UY e_1', \quad r_1 = U_3 e_1', \quad r_2 = UY Y_3 e_1', \tag{15}$$

where e_1' is a 3-dimensional unit vector with only a 1 in the first component, matrix U_3 consists of the first three columns of matrix U, Y_3 includes the first three rows and first three columns of matrix Y.

Finally, we construct the second Krylov subspace

$$\mathcal{K}_{m_2} = span\{v, Cv, C^2 v\},$$

where block vector $v = [r_2 \ r_1 \ r_0]$, block matrix $C = \begin{bmatrix} B \\ I_{12} \ 0 \end{bmatrix}$ and $B = [cA^T \ 0 \ I]$, I_{12} is a 12-dimensional identity matrix.

Its column orthonormal matrix Q, non-orthonormal matrix P and projection matrix H can be generated through the Arnoldi method [11] and the equality holds as follows

$$cA^T Q(:, 1:m_2) + P(:, 1:m_2) = QH.$$

Thus, r_3, r_4 can be rewritten as

$$r_3 = \|r_2\| QH e_1', \quad r_4 = \|r_2\| QHH_3 e_1',$$

where matrix H_3 includes the first three rows and first three columns of matrix H. In other words, we can transform high-dimensional single-source SimRank search r_4 into low-dimensional matrix vector multiplication $\|r_2\| QHH_3 e_1'$ to eliminate the barrier of redundant dimensionality.   □

Cost Overheads. We analyze SimSky's cost overheads step-by-step. At the beginning, invoking the Arnoldi algorithm takes $\mathcal{O}(m_1 nd)$ time and requires $\mathcal{O}(m_1 n)$ memory. Meanwhile, computing the scalar β takes $\mathcal{O}((k-1)m_1^2)$ time. Second, invoking the ApproxDiag algorithm takes $\mathcal{O}(k^2 snd)$ time and requires $\mathcal{O}(n \cdot max(d, s, k))$ memory. Then, initialising V, H require $\mathcal{O}(km_2 n), \mathcal{O}(m_2^2)$ memory respectively. And, setting the first column $V(:, 1)$ needs $\mathcal{O}(m_1^2 n)$ time. Finally, computing matrices V, H (lines 7–20) take $\mathcal{O}(m_2^2 kn + m_2 nd)$ time, and computing $[S_{m_1, m_2}]_{*,j}$ (line 22) takes $\mathcal{O}(m_2^2 n)$ time. Add them up, in the aggregate, it takes $\mathcal{O}((m_1 + m_2 + k^2 s)nd + (m_1^2 + km_2^2)n)$ time, requires $\mathcal{O}(n \cdot max(km_2, d, s, m_1))$ memory.

Algorithm 2: SimSky(A, m_1, m_2, k, c, e_j)

Input: A - column-normalised adjacency matrix, m_1, m_2 - low-order
      parameters, k - number of iterations, c - decay factor, e_j - query vector

Output: $[S_{m_1,m_2}]_{*,j}$ - single-source SimRank score

1   $[U, Y, m_1] \leftarrow \text{Arnoldi}(A, m_1, e_j)$;

2   Set $Y_m = Y(1 : m_1, 1 : m_1), \beta = \|YY_m^{k-1}e_1\| \neq 0$;

3   $D \leftarrow \text{ApproxDiag}(A, c, k)$;

4   Initialise matrices $V = \text{zeros}((k+1)n, m_2+1), H = \text{zeros}(m_2+1, m_2)$;

5   $e_1(e_2)$ is an $m_1(m_2)$-dimensional unit vector with only a 1 in the first entry;

6   Set $V(:, 1) = \frac{1}{\beta} \begin{bmatrix} D(:, 1) \circ (UYY_m^{k-1}e_1) \\ D(:, k+1) \circ e_j \\ \vdots \\ D(:, 3) \circ (UYY_m^{k-3}e_1) \\ D(:, 2) \circ (UYY_m^{k-2}e_1) \end{bmatrix}$;

7   **for** $i = 1$ *to* m_2 **do**

8      $r \leftarrow cA^T V(1 : n, i) + V(kn+1 : (k+1)n, i)$;

9      $t \leftarrow V(1 : kn, i)$;

10     $s \leftarrow$ concatenate r and t along the vertical direction;

11   **for** $j = 1$ *to* i **do**

12        $temp \leftarrow$ inner product of r and $V(1 : n, j)$;

13        $s \leftarrow s - temp \cdot V(:, j)$;

14        $H(j, i) \leftarrow temp$;

15   **end**

16   **if** $H(i+1, i)$ *satisfies stop criterion* **then**

17        $m_2 = i, V = V(:, 1 : m_2+1), H = H(1 : m_2+1, 1 : m_2)$;

18   **end**

19     $V(:, i+1) \leftarrow \frac{s}{H(i+1,i)}$;

20 **end**

21 $Q = V(1 : n, :), H_m = H(1 : m_2, 1 : m_2), P = V(kn+1 : (k+1)n, :)$;

22 **return** $[S_{m_1,m_2}]_{*,j} = \beta QHH_m^{k-1}e_2$;

Error Analysis. Finally, according to different value ranges of m_1, m_2, k, we analyze the error generated by our SimSky algorithm at length. Taking into account the effects of k, m_1, m_2 on the error, we exclude the interference of diagonal correction matrix D_k on the error, that is, we suppose that W is an identity matrix. The error of single-source SimRank search caused by two aspects. On the one hand, the iterative solution $[S^{(k)}]_{*,j}$ is used to approximate the accurate solution $[S]_{*,j}$, which leads to the iterative error. On the other hand, the dimension-reduced solution $[S_{m_1,m_2}]_{*,j}$ generated by our SimSky algorithm is used to approximate the iterative solution $[S^{(k)}]_{*,j}$, which leads in the dimension-reduced error.

Iterative Error. We analyze the iterative error. First, the same rationale as in the error analysis in Sect. 2, we can obtain that $\|(\sqrt{c}A)^l\| \leq \theta\sigma^l$. Second, Lu et al. [9] proved that $\|D_k - D\| \leq c^{k+2}$. And it's obvious that $\|D\| \leq 1$. Combine the three aforementioned inequalities, we assume that $\theta = \max(1, \frac{\sigma^k}{\|(\sqrt{c}A)^k\|})$, the gap between $[S]_{*,j}$ and $[S^{(k)}]_{*,j}$ is bounded by

$$\|[S]_{*,j} - [S^{(k)}]_{*,j}\| < \theta^2 \|\sqrt{c}Ae_j\| (\frac{\sigma^{2k+1}}{1-\sigma^2} + \frac{c^{k+2}(1-\sigma^{2k+2})}{\sigma - \sigma^3}). \qquad (16)$$

Example 3. Taking the column-normalised adjacency matrix A in Fig. 1 as an example, we set decay factor $c = 0.8$, scalars $\theta = 1$ and $\sigma = \rho(\sqrt{c}A) + 10^{-16}$, query node $j = 3$, number of iterations $k = 5$, the result obtained after 30 iterations is taken as the accurate solution S. By substituting these values for Eq. 16, the values on the left and right sides are 0.0996 and 1.4739. Numerical example shows that our error upper bound is feasible.   □

Dimension-Reduced Error. Dimension-reduced error should be discussed separately according to the value ranges of m_1, m_2, k.

As per Lemma 3.1 in [11], for line 6 of the SimSky algorithm, we know that if $k \geq m_1 + 1$, only those terms $UYY_m^{i-1}e_1$ are accurate solutions to $A^i e_j$ for $1 \leq i \leq m_1$, the rest terms are approximate solutions to $A^i e_j$ for $m_1 + 1 \leq i \leq k$. Through the initial vector $V(:, 1)$, which leads to the gap between the approximate solution and the accurate solution of the last k's terms in Eq. 11. Therefore, if there is the dimension-reduced error on the former m_1-dimensional Krylov subspace, which is transmitted to the latter m_2-dimensional Krylov subspace through the initial vector. It's difficult to give an explicit expression of the nested dimension-reduced error, so our error analysis in theory only considers $1 \leq k \leq m_1$. In the experiments, we cover all value ranges for m_1, m_2, k.

For $1 \leq k \leq m_1$ and $1 \leq k \leq m_2$, in accordance with Lemma 3.1 in [11], we know that $V(:, 1)$ in line 6 and $[S_{m_1, m_2}]_{*,j}$ in line 22 are accurate solutions. Therefore, the gap between the dimension-reduced solution $[S_{m_1, m_2}]_{*,j}$ and the iterative solution $[S^{(k)}]_{*,j}$ is bounded by 0.

For $1 \leq k \leq m_1$ and $k \geq m_2 + 1$, according to Lemma 3.1 in [11], there is no dimension-reduced error on the former m_1-dimensional Krylov subspace, and only exists on the latter m_2-dimensional Krylov subspace. We have to establish a few auxiliary equalities to complete the analysis according to the SimSky algorithm. Due to the limited space, we ignore the specific calculation process and give a direct result. Let $k - m_2 = g$, the gap between the dimension-reduced solution $[S_{m_1, m_2}]_{*,j}$ and the iterative solution $[S^{(k)}]_{*,j}$ is bounded by

$$\|[S_{m_1, m_2}]_{*,j} - [S^{(k)}]_{*,j}\| \leq \beta h_{m_2+1, m_2}(P_1 + P_2), \qquad (17)$$

where h_{m_2+1, m_2} is $(m_2 + 1, m_2)$-th entry of H, $P_1 = \sum\limits_{i=1}^{g} \|c^i A^i\| \|e_{m_2}^T H_m^{m_2+g-1-i} e_2\|$, $P_2 = \sum\limits_{i=0}^{g-1} \|c^i A^i\| \sum\limits_{l=0}^{m_2+g-2-i} e_{m_2}^T H_m^{m_2+g-2-i-l} e_2 Q_l(:, 1+m_2)\|$. When $g = 0$, the equal sign "=" is established.

4   Experiments

Our experiments[2] on real datasets will evaluate the search quality of the SimSky algorithm, and verify our superiority over other competitors. We choose the optimized single-source SimRank [18] as our baseline.

4.1   Experimental Setting

Datasets. We adopt the six real datasets from the Stanford Large Network Dataset Collection[3]. They are email-Eu-core(euc), ca-GrQc(cag), Wiki-Vote(wiv), p2p-Gnutella09(p2p09), ca-AstroPh(caa) and p2p-Gnutella25(p2p25).

Metrics. To evaluate search quality, we use two metrics:

(1) *MaxError.* Given the query node j, the approximate solution $[\widetilde{S}]_{*,j}$ and the accurate solution $[S]_{*,j}$, $MaxError = \|[S]_{*,j} - [\widetilde{S}]_{*,j}\|_\infty = \max\{|[S]_{i,j} - [\widetilde{S}]_{i,j}|\}$ for $1 \leq i \leq n$.
(2) *Precision@k.* Given the query node j, the approximate top-k result $\widehat{V}_k = \{\widehat{v}_1, \widehat{v}_2, \cdots, \widehat{v}_k\}$, the accurate result $V_k = \{v_1, v_2, \cdots, v_k\}$, $Precision@k = \frac{\sum_{i=1}^{k} \delta_{\widehat{v}_i v_i}}{|V_k|}$, where δ is Kronecker delta function. In our experiment, we use *Precision@500*.

Parameters. We set the decay factor $c = 0.8$. In experiments verifying Eqs. 9 and 17, we set $\theta = 1$ and $\sigma = \rho(\sqrt{c}A) + 10^{-16}$, where $\rho(\sqrt{c}A)$ represents the spectral radius of the matrix $\sqrt{c}A$.

We evaluate the search quality of our SimSky algorithm and the other two competitors, including SLING [12] and ExactSim [13]. For each dataset, we generate 50 query nodes randomly and calculate their average value of *MaxError* and *Precision@500*. All experiments are run with an Intel(R) Core(TM) i7-8750H CPU @ 2.20 GHz CPU and 32 GB RAM, on windows 10.

4.2   Comparative Experiments

Our SimSky is a dimensionality reduction algorithm, SLING [12] and ExactSim [13] are random walk algorithms. To be fair, we compare their search precision and the time required under the same value of *MaxError*.

Precision. Fix $k = m_1 = m_2 = 10$, adjust the value of s, resulting in the different values of *MaxError*. We compare the precision of our SimSky with other competitors including ExactSim and SLING under the same value of *MaxError* on real datasets, as shown in Fig. 2. We notice that the ExactSim has only the ability to calculate the value of *MaxError* no less than 10^{-7} on all datasets. When the value of *MaxError* is a double-precision floating-point number, such

---

[2] https://github.com/AnonSimRank/SimSky.
[3] http://snap.stanford.edu/data/index.html.

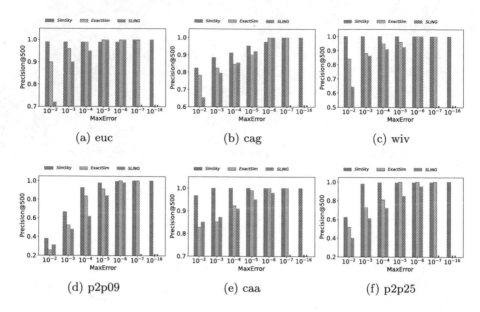

Fig. 2. Precision comparisons on all datasets

as 10^{-16}, none of our competitors are capable of doing so. However, our SimSky is able to do it within a reasonable time. Even the value of *MaxError* exceeds 10^{-6}, our SimSky attains competitive precision compared to our competitors. Especially on dataset wiv, a precision of 100% can be achieved even with the value of *MaxError* takes 10^{-2}.

Time. Parameters are identical to the precision comparison experiments. Figure 3 depicts the cost comparisons of our SimSky with other competitors. The time required for our SimSky remains almost constant as the value of *MaxError* varies. This is consistent with our analysis, the reason lies in whatever the value of *MaxError* is, the deviation between s and n is not too big. Taking the dataset p2p09 as an example, when the values of *MaxError* are $1.0e - 2$, $1.0e - 3$, $1.0e - 4$, $1.0e - 5$, $1.0e - 6$, $1.0e - 7$ and $1.0e - 16$, the corresponding values of s are 7600, 8000, 8085, 8094, 8101, 8102 and 8108, and $n = 8114$, so the time overhead for our SimSky doesn't vary much as the value of *MaxError* varies. For our competitors, although they require less time than our SimSky when the values of *MaxError* are $1.0e - 2$ and $1.0e - 3$, there is no advantage in their search precision.

4.3   Ablation Experiments

We will verify the influences of s, m_1, m_2, k on search quality and error through a series of experiments.

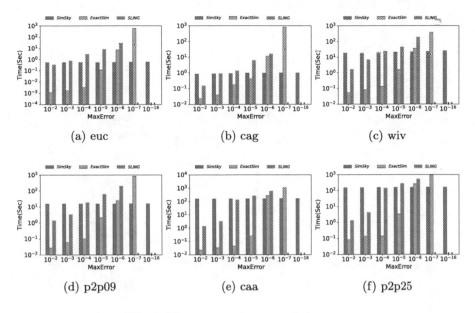

Fig. 3. Time comparisons on all datasets

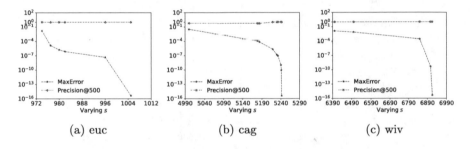

Fig. 4. Effects of s on *Precision@500* and *MaxError*

Effect of s. Fix $k = m_1 = m_2 = 10$, Fig. 4 depicts the effects of s on *Max-Error* and *Precision@500* on the datasets euc, cag and wiv. The gap between the dimension-reduced solution $[S_{m_1,m_2}]_{*,j}$ and the iterative solution $[S^{(k)}]_{*,j}$ narrows, as the value of s approaches the value of n. As a result, the value of error metric *MaxError* gets smaller. Instead, the value of search quality metric *Precision@500* gradually increases. And it demonstrates that our modified row orthogonal matrix W is feasible.

Effects of m_1, m_2, k. Fix $m_2 = k = 10$, $s = n$, Figs. 5a and 5b describe the influences of m_1 on *MaxError* and *Precision@500* respectively. It can be seen that the scale of the y-axis in the Fig. 5a is *logarithmic*. The value of *MaxError* shrinks as the value of m_1 approaches the value of k, which indicates that the gap between our dimension-reduced solution $[S_{m_1,m_2}]_{*,j}$ and the iterative solution $[S^{(k)}]_{*,j}$ is shrinking. It also shows that the search quality of our SimSky is

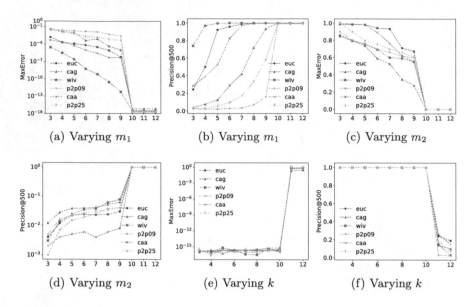

(a) Varying m_1 (b) Varying m_1 (c) Varying m_2

(d) Varying m_2 (e) Varying k (f) Varying k

Fig. 5. Effects of m_1, m_2, k on *Precision@500* and *MaxError*

increasing. Our dimension-reduced solution is equal to the iterative solution if the value of m_1 exceeds the value of k, so that the gap between them can be regarded as infinitesimal, and the value of precision is 1. Theoretical analysis is consistent with Fig. 5b.

Fix $m_1 = k = 10$ and $s = n$, Figs. 5c and 5d describe the influences of m_2 on *MaxError* and *Precision@500* on all datasets respectively. It is noteworthy that the scale of the y-axis in the Fig. 5c is not *logarithmic*. Although the value of *MaxError* decreases as the value of m_2 approaches the value of k, the value of *MaxError* cannot be ignored. In other words, our SimSky is more sensitive to m_2 in comparison to m_1. This is consistent with the idea of our algorithm. Because the dimensionality of the basis matrix is n by m_1+1 on the previous m_1-dimensional Krylov subspace, but the dimensionality of the basis matrix is $(k + 1)n$ by m_2+1 on the subsequent m_2-dimensional Krylov subspace. Experimental results show that the value of m_2 is not expected to be less than the value of k. When the value of m_2 exceeds the value of k, the theoretical analysis and experimental results be similar with m_1.

Fix $m_1 = m_2 = 10$ and $s = n$, Figs. 5e and 5f depict the effects of k on *MaxError* and *Precision@500* on all datasets respectively. When $k \leq 10$, Sim-Sky returns almost the same results as the conventional iterative method. When $k > 10$, only the top-10 solutions are accurate, and the last 2 solutions are approximate in the m_1-dimensional Krylov subspace, leading to the dimension-reduced error. These results will be passed to the m_2-dimensional Krylov subspace by means of the initial vector $V(:,1)$ in the line 6. As such, the nested dimension-reduced error cannot be ignored. This also shows that the precision of our model has been significantly affected, as shown in Fig. 5f.

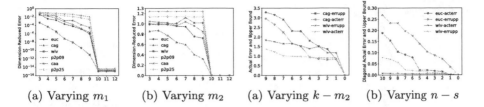

(a) Varying m_1 (b) Varying m_2 (a) Varying $k - m_2$ (b) Varying $n - s$

Fig. 6. Effects of m_1, m_2 on error   **Fig. 7.** Actual error and upper bound

Effects of m_1, m_2 on Dimension-Reduced Error. In the experiments to verify the influences of m_1, m_2 on the dimension-reduced error, we set $s = n$ and $k = 10$, keep the remaining parameter at 10, as shown in Figs. 6a and 6b respectively. Because we use the L_2 norm of the vector to describe the dimension-reduced error, the L_∞ norm of the vector to quantify error metric *MaxError*, therefore the tendency of influence of the single variable on them should be close to consistent, as shown in Figs. 5a and 6a, 5c and 6b respectively.

Actual Error and Upper Bound. Figs. 7a and 7b depict the tendency of the actual error and its upper bound in Eqs. 17 and 9 respectively. Fix $s = n$, $m_1 = m_2 = 10$, the number of iterations k gradually decreases from 19 to 10, Fig. 7a shows that our theoretical upper bound is tight. Figure 7b depicts the tendency of actual error of the diagonal correction vector and its upper bound as the value of $n - s$ varies. When $n = s$, the values of the actual error and upper bound are 0. The theoretical analysis is consistent with the experimental result.

5   Conclusions

In this paper, we propose an accuracy-aware algorithm for efficiently computing single-source SimRank similarity. Firstly, we design an algorithm, ApproxDiag, to approximate the diagonal correction matrix with guaranteed accuracy. Secondly, we present SimSky, an algorithm that leverages two Krylov subspaces to transform high-dimensional single-source SimRank search into low-dimensional matrix-vector multiplications. To evaluate the effectiveness of SimSky, we conducted extensive experiments on various real datasets. Our results demonstrate that SimSky outperforms competing algorithms in terms of search quality.

Acknowledgments. This work has been supported by the National Natural Science Foundation of China under Grant No. 61972203.

Ethical Statement. We acknowledge the importance of ethical considerations in the design of our ApproxDiag and SimSky algorithms. All the datasets used in this paper are publicly-available online, and do not have any privacy issues. We ensure that our algorithms do not lead to any potential negative influences. We declare that we allow our algorithms to be used for the benefit of society.

References

1. Bekas, C., Kokiopoulou, E., Saad, Y.: An estimator for the diagonal of a matrix. Appl. Numer. Math. **57**(11–12), 1214–1229 (2007)
2. Boley, D.L.: Krylov space methods on state-space control models. Circuits Syst. Signal Process. **13**, 733–758 (1994)
3. Fouss, F., Pirotte, A., Renders, J.M., Saerens, M.: Random-walk computation of similarities between nodes of a graph with application to collaborative recommendation. IEEE Trans. Knowl. Data Eng. **19**(3), 355–369 (2007)
4. Fujiwara, Y., Nakatsuji, M., Shiokawa, H., Onizuka, M.: Efficient search algorithm for SimRank. In: 2013 IEEE 29th International Conference on Data Engineering (ICDE), pp. 589–600. IEEE (2013)
5. Jeh, G., Widom, J.: SimRank: a measure of structural-context similarity. In: Proceedings of the Eighth ACM SIGKDD International Conference on Knowledge Discovery and Data Mining, pp. 538–543 (2002)
6. Jeh, G., Widom, J.: Scaling personalized web search. In: Proceedings of the 12th International Conference on World Wide Web, pp. 271–279 (2003)
7. Kusumoto, M., Maehara, T., Kawarabayashi, K.i.: Scalable similarity search for SimRank. In: Proceedings of the 2014 ACM SIGMOD International Conference on Management of Data, pp. 325–336 (2014)
8. Liben-Nowell, D., Kleinberg, J.: The link prediction problem for social networks. J. Am. Soc. Inform. Sci. Technol. **58**(7), 1019–1031 (2007)
9. Lu, J., Gong, Z., Yang, Y.: A matrix sampling approach for efficient SimRank computation. Inf. Sci. **556**, 1–26 (2021)
10. Rothe, S., Schütze, H.: CoSimRank: a flexible & efficient graph-theoretic similarity measure. In: Proceedings of the 52nd Annual Meeting of the Association for Computational Linguistics, pp. 1392–1402 (2014)
11. Saad, Y.: Analysis of some Krylov subspace approximations to the matrix exponential operator. SIAM J. Numer. Anal. **29**(1), 209–228 (1992)
12. Tian, B., Xiao, X.: SLING: a near-optimal index structure for SimRank. In: Proceedings of the 2016 International Conference on Management of Data, pp. 1859–1874 (2016)
13. Wang, H., Wei, Z., Yuan, Y., Du, X., Wen, J.R.: Exact single-source SimRank computation on large graphs. In: Proceedings of the 2020 ACM SIGMOD International Conference on Management of Data, pp. 653–663 (2020)
14. Yu, W., Iranmanesh, S., Haldar, A., Zhang, M., Ferhatosmanoglu, H.: Rolesim*: scaling axiomatic role-based similarity ranking on large graphs. World Wide Web **25**(2), 785–829 (2022). https://doi.org/10.1007/s11280-021-00925-z
15. Yu, W., Lin, X., Zhang, W., Pei, J., McCann, J.A.: Simrank*: effective and scalable pairwise similarity search based on graph topology. VLDB J. **28**(3), 401–426 (2019)
16. Yu, W., McCann, J.A.: Efficient partial-pairs SimRank search on large networks. Proc. VLDB Endow. **8**(5), 569–580 (2015)
17. Yu, W., McCann, J.A., Zhang, C., Ferhatosmanoglu, H.: Scaling high-quality pairwise link-based similarity retrieval on billion-edge graphs. ACM Trans. Inf. Syst. **40**(4), 78:1–78:45 (2022). https://doi.org/10.1145/3495209
18. Yu, W., McCann, J.A.: High quality graph-based similarity search. In: Proceedings of the 38th International ACM SIGIR Conference on Research and Development in Information Retrieval, pp. 83–92 (2015)

19. Yu, W., Wang, F.: Fast exact CoSimRank search on evolving and static graphs. In: Proceedings of the 2018 World Wide Web Conference on World Wide Web, WWW 2018, Lyon, France, 23–27 April 2018, pp. 599–608. ACM (2018). https://doi.org/10.1145/3178876.3186126

20. Yu, W., Yang, J., Zhang, M., Wu, D.: CoSimHeat: an effective heat kernel similarity measure based on billion-scale network topology. In: WWW 2022: The ACM Web Conference 2022, Virtual Event, Lyon, France, 25–29 April 2022, pp. 234–245. ACM (2022). https://doi.org/10.1145/3485447.3511952

Online Network Source Optimization with Graph-Kernel MAB

Laura Toni[1]([⊠]) and Pascal Frossard[2]

[1] EEE Department, University College London, London, UK
l.toni@ucl.ac.uk
[2] LTS4, EPFL, Lausanne, Switzerland

Abstract. We propose `Grab-UCB`, a graph-kernel multi-arms bandit algorithm to learn online the optimal source placement in large scale networks, such that the reward obtained from a priori unknown network processes is maximized. The uncertainty calls for online learning, which suffers however from the curse of dimensionality. To achieve sample efficiency, we describe the network processes with an adaptive graph dictionary model, which typically leads to sparse spectral representations. This enables a data-efficient learning framework, whose learning rate scales with the dimension of the spectral representation model instead of the one of the network. We then propose `Grab-UCB`, an online sequential decision strategy that learns the parameters of the spectral representation while optimizing the action strategy. We derive the performance guarantees that depend on network parameters, which further influence the learning curve of the sequential decision strategy We introduce a computationally simplified solving method, `Grab-arm-Light`, an algorithm that walks along the edges of the polytope representing the objective function. Simulations results show that the proposed online learning algorithm outperforms baseline offline methods that typically separate the learning phase from the testing one. The results confirm the theoretical findings, and further highlight the gain of the proposed online learning strategy in terms of cumulative regret, sample efficiency and computational complexity.

Keywords: multi-arms bandit · graph dictionary · graph-kernel

1 Introduction

Large-scale interconnected systems (transportation networks, social networks, etc.), which create services and produce massive amounts of data, are becoming predominant in many application domains. The management of such networked systems is exceedingly hard because of their intrinsic and constantly growing complexity. Many works have been proposed to tackle this problem (e.g., model based optimal control, consensus works [29,30,34,50,51], Bayesian approaches [1], etc.) but with a limited focus on online learning and control of large-scale networks. The latter becomes extremely challenging with dynamic and high dimensional network processes that controls the evolution of states of network nodes.

ⓒ The Author(s), under exclusive license to Springer Nature Switzerland AG 2023
D. Koutra et al. (Eds.): ECML PKDD 2023, LNAI 14171, pp. 242–258, 2023.
https://doi.org/10.1007/978-3-031-43418-1_15

The dynamics introduce uncertainty about the system environment, which can be addressed by online learning strategies that infer the system behaviour before taking the appropriate adaptation actions or decisions. The high dimensionality of the problem calls for proper information representation methods.

We consider the particular problem of optimal source placement in order to maximize a reward function on a network, which depends on network processes that are a priori unknown and must be learned online. We address this challenge by blending together online learning theory [22] and Graph Signal Processing (GSP) [31,35] with the key intuition that the latter permits to appropriately model the large-scale network processes via sparse graph spectral representations. This generates a data-efficient learning framework, whose learning rate does not scale with the dimension of the network as in most methods of the literature, but rather with the dimension of the spectral representation. Indeed, in classical online learning solutions such as those casted as Multi-arm bandit (MAB) problems, the main learning steps happen in the action (or node) domain and do not scale properly with the search space. The key intuition underpinning our new framework is to consider these learning steps at the crossroad of the search space (or node) domain and the latent space (or spectral) domain. An agent takes sequential decision strategies in the high-dimensional vertex domain based on the uncertainty of the model estimated in the low-dimensional spectral domain. Similar intuition is shared in literature on bandit for spectral graph domains (see Sect. 6), which aims at applying linUCB algorithms while preserving the low-dimensionality assumption of the reward. However, we do not limit ourselves to smoothness assumption in inductive bias and rather model the entire network process as a graph filter that is excited by a set of unknown low-rank inputs (action). As a result, the learning process boils down to inferring spectral graph representations with a learning rate that scales with the dimension of their generating kernels, which is substantially lower than the one of the search space. With our framework, this online learning problem can be reformulated and reduced to a linearUCB problem [9] that is a well-known algorithm achieving good sample efficiency in the literature for linear stochastic bandit problems. We then derive the theoretical bound of the estimation of the graph spectral model and translate it to the MAB upper confidence bound. Finally, we observe that the optimization method leads to an arm selection problem that is NP-hard, and we provide a low-complexity algorithm, Grab-arm-Light, by exploiting the structure of the optimization function (maximization of a convex function over a polytope). Simulations validate the accuracy of the proposed low-complexity algorithm as well as the gains of the proposed graph-kernel MAB strategy, in terms of cumulative regret, sample efficiency and computational complexity, when compared to baseline offline methods.

The reminder of this paper is as follows. The online source optimization problem is formulated in Sect. 2. The proposed Grab-UCB is detailed in Sect. 3, and the low complexity solution Grab-arm-Light is introduced in Sect. 4. Simulation results are discussed in Sect. 5. Related works are presented in Sect. 6, and conclusions in Sect. 7.

2   Online Source Optimization Problem

2.1   Problem Formulation

Let consider a learner (or agent) controlling processes on large scale networks with no *a priori* information on their dynamics. Examples can be network cooling systems [18], opinions spreading across social networks [32], or energy distribution networks [33] that need to be managed online with no a priori information about the underlying processes. In this paper, we model these processes as signals on graphs, as depicted in Fig. 1, with actions and resultant signal defined on the weighted and undirected graph $\mathcal{G} = (\mathcal{V}, \mathcal{E}, \boldsymbol{W})$ with $\mathcal{V}$ being the vertex set ($|\mathcal{V}| = N$), $\mathcal{E}$ the edge sets, and $\boldsymbol{W}$ the $N \times N$ graph adjacency matrix. Namely, we assume that the action taken by the learner at time t, $\boldsymbol{a}_t \in \mathbb{R}^N$, is modelled as an *excitation signal* on the graph and produces a *resultant graph signal* $\boldsymbol{y}_t \in \mathbb{R}^N$. The instantaneous reward $\boldsymbol{w}_t = \mathcal{V} \to \mathbb{R}^N$ can be modelled as a function of the resultant graph signal, and reads $\boldsymbol{w}_t = f(\boldsymbol{y}_t) + \boldsymbol{n}_t$, with $f(\cdot)$ being an affine function[1] and $\boldsymbol{n}_t$ an additive noise. The overall goal of the agent is to learn which actions need to be selected to achieve the maximum reward, with no prior information on the network process (i.e., the mapping from $\boldsymbol{a}_t$ to $\boldsymbol{w}_t$). The problem can be casted as a stochastic MAB problem, aimed minimizing the cumulative loss (or equivalently maximize the cumulative reward) over a time horizon T, which is seen as the minimization of the pseudo regret $R_T = Tr(\boldsymbol{a}^\star) - \sum_{t=1}^{T} r(\boldsymbol{a}_t)$, with $r(\boldsymbol{a})$ being the mean reward for action $\boldsymbol{a}$.

In this following, we consider the online source optimization problem[2], where a decision maker needs to select T_0 sparse actions out of N, i.e., $\mathcal{A} = \{\boldsymbol{h} \mid ||\boldsymbol{h}||_0 \leq T_0 \ \wedge \ h_n \in [0,1], \ n = 1, ..., N\}$, where T_0 is the maximum sparsity level of the actions. We assume that the rewards associated to consecutive actions are independent and model the affine function $f(\cdot)$ as the mapping function $\boldsymbol{M} \in \mathbb{R}^{N \times N}$, a diagonal binary matrix, with the n-th diagonal element being 1 if the signal at the node n is consdiered in computing the reward, or 0 if that signal is masked. Real-world examples are influence maximization problems, such as targeted advertisement online [17,37] or optimization of cooling systems and/or power networks [16]. This online learning problem can be solved by classical MAB problems, with a sublinear regret $R_T = \mathcal{O}(|\mathcal{A}| \log T)$ [22], with $|\mathcal{A}| = \binom{N}{T_o}$, if T_0 is the imposed sparsity of $\boldsymbol{h}$. This regret is not sustainable in large-scale networks with large action space $|\mathcal{A}|$.

2.2   Graph-Kernel MAB Framework

We now propose a graph-kernel MAB problem that exploits the geometry of the network processes to achieve a better regret scaling. Specifically, we model the

---

[1] This includes many reward shapes such as subsampled or filtered signal as well as mean value.

[2] It is worth noting that the formalism introduced in this Section extends to most problem on learning on network process, but for the sake of brevity and clarity we discuss only the source optimization problem.

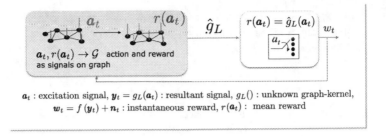

a_t : excitation signal, $y_t = g_L(a_t)$: resultant signal, $g_L()$: unknown graph-kernel, $w_t = f(y_t) + n_t$: instantaneous reward, $r(a_t)$: mean reward

Fig. 1. Graphical visualisation of the proposed framework.

mapping $a_t \to w_t$ as an *unknown* structured function of the graph Laplacian L (defined to be $L = D - W$, with D being the degree matrix), i.e.,

$$w_t = f(y_t) + n_t = f(g_L(a_t)) + n_t \tag{1}$$

with $g_L(\cdot)$ being an *unknown* generating kernel[3] of the graph Laplacian L. The generating kernel models the process on graphs and characterizes the effect of an action in a resulting graph signal, which will impact the mean reward. Hence, the agent infers the mapping $a_t \to r(a_t)$ by learning the graph generating kernel $g_L(\cdot)$ in the spectral domain, which is much more sample-efficient than learning the mapping $a_t \to r(a_t)$ directly in the high-dimensional vertex (action) space.

We formulate the online learning problem via GSP tools, and we cast the problem into a linear MAB problem, in which the confidence bound is defined on the graph spectral parameters of the generating kernel. We model the network process via the graph-based parametric dictionary learning algorithm in [40], with a signal on graph defined as $y = Dh + \epsilon$, with $h = [h_1, h_2, \ldots, h_N]^T$ being the latent variables (localized events) defined on the graph, i.e., the excitation signal defined as actions in our model, and $\epsilon = [\epsilon_1, \epsilon_2, \ldots, \epsilon_N]^T$ is a Gaussian and N-dimensional random variable with $\epsilon_n \sim \mathcal{N}(0, \sigma_e^2)$ [9].

The graph dictionary D is defined as $D = g_L(\cdot) = \sum_{k=0}^{K-1} \alpha_k L^k$ [40] and represents the graph-kernel, which incorporates the intrinsic geometric structure of data domain into the atoms of the dictionary through L. Assuming that signals have a support contained within K hops from vertex n, the resulting signal in n can be represented as combinations of localized events (e.g., local signals) on the graph, which can appear in different vertices and diffuse along the graph. Namely,

$$y_n = \sum_{m=1}^{N} h_m \sum_{k=0}^{K-1} \alpha_k (L^k)_{n,m} + \epsilon_n \tag{2}$$

where $(L^k)_{n,m}$ is the (m, n) entry of L^k and we recall that $(L^k)_{n,m} = 0$ if the shortest path between n and m has a number of hops that is greater than k.

---

[3] Graph filter defined in the spectral domain of the graph, typically in the form of the power series of the graph Laplacian [40].

With the following matrix notations where $P = [L^0, L^1, L^2, \ldots, L^{K-1}]$, with $P \in \mathbb{R}^{N \times NK}$, captures the powers of the Laplacian, and with $\alpha = [\alpha_0, \alpha_1, \ldots, \alpha_{K-1}]^T$ representing the polynomials coefficients in the dictionary, we can rewrite the resulting signal as

$$y = g_L(h; \alpha) = PI_K \otimes h\alpha + \epsilon = PH\alpha + \epsilon \tag{3}$$

with I_K being the $K \times K$ identity matrix, $\otimes$ the Kronecker product, and $H = I_K \otimes h$, with $H \in \mathbb{R}^{NK \times K}$. In our framework, at the decision opportunity t, the agent controls the latent variables h_t while learning the polynomial coefficients α. Given that the instantaneous reward is an affine function of the resultant signal y_t, substituting (3) in the reward expression (4), we achieve the following

$$w_t = My_t = MPH_t\alpha + M\epsilon_t = X\alpha + n_t \tag{4}$$

where and $X = MPH_t$, with $X_t \in \mathbb{R}^{N \times K}$.

In short, the reward can be expressed as a linear combination of the K-degree polynomial α and the matrix X_t, which includes both the graph structure information (via the Laplacian L) and the action h_t. This is important because:

– the reward is a linear mapping between the unknown parameters α and the actions h_t (hence X_t), implying that we can solve the online learning problem with the linUCB [9] theory.
– the reward is given by the generating kernel $g_L(\cdot)$, which is parametrized by the vector α with dimensionality K. Therefore the uncertainty bound in the linUCB is evaluated in the spectral (low-dimensional) domain. This presents an important advantage, as the regret scales as $\mathcal{O}(d\sqrt{T} \log T)$ in LinUCB, where d is the dimension of the unknown (low-dimension) parameter α.

3   Grab-UCB: Proposed Algorithm

We now propose a theoretical bound and algorithmic solution to the online source optimisation problem using the new framework described in Sect. 2, which permits to learn in the spectral domain and to act in the vertex domain, see Fig. 2. There are two interacting subtasks in the algoirthm: 1) refinement of the coefficients estimate, 2) selection of the arm given the updated knowledge of the system.

Step 1: Coefficients Estimation. Let consider the t-th decision opportunity, when $t - 1$ decisions have already been taken and the corresponding signals and rewards have been observed. The training set is built over time thus it corresponds to sequence of pairs $\{(h_\tau, w_\tau)\}_{\tau=1}^{t-1}$, where we recall that $p(y|h, \alpha) \sim \mathcal{N}(g_L(h; \alpha), \sigma_e^2 I_N)$, and that the randomness is due to the random noise ϵ_τ. For large t, maximizing the MAP probability $p(\alpha|y, h)$ corresponds to minimizing the l^2-regularized least-square estimate of α, leading to the following problem: $\hat{\alpha}_t : \arg\min_\alpha \sum_{\tau=1}^{t-1} ||MPH_\tau\alpha - w_\tau||_2^2 + \mu||\alpha||_2^2$. It follows that

$$\hat{\alpha}_t = \left[\sum_{\tau=1}^{t-1} Z_\tau^T Z_\tau + \mu I_K \right]^{-1} \sum_{\tau=1}^{t-1} Z_\tau^T w_\tau = \left[Z_{1:t}^T Z_{1:t} + \mu I_K \right]^{-1} Z_{1:t}^T W_t = V_t^{-1} Z_{1:t}^T W_t \tag{5}$$

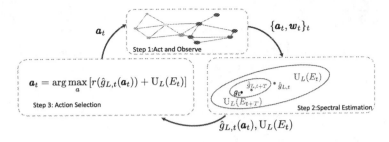

Fig. 2. Figurative example of the online graph-strcutured processing. Green (red) dashed boxes are defined in the vertex (spectral) domain. (Color figure online)

with $\boldsymbol{Z}_{1:t} = [\boldsymbol{Z}_1, \boldsymbol{Z}_2, \ldots, \boldsymbol{Z}_{t-1}]^T$, $\boldsymbol{Z}_\tau = \boldsymbol{MPH}_\tau$, $\boldsymbol{W}_t = [\boldsymbol{w}_1, \boldsymbol{w}_2, \ldots, \boldsymbol{w}_{t-1}]^T$, and $\boldsymbol{V}_t = \boldsymbol{Z}_{1:t}^T \boldsymbol{Z}_{1:t} + \mu \boldsymbol{I}_K$. The l^2-regularized least-square estimate leads to an approximation of the actual polynomial $\boldsymbol{\alpha}$, and this approximated estimate $\hat{\boldsymbol{\alpha}}_t$ is refined at each decision opportunity.

Step 2: Action Selection. Once the estimation of the $\boldsymbol{\alpha}$ coefficients is refined, the decision maker needs to select the best action to take for the t-th decision opportunity. Following the theory of linear UCB [9], the decision maker evaluates the confidence bound E_t as an ellipsoid centered in $\hat{\boldsymbol{\alpha}}_t$ defined such that $\boldsymbol{\alpha} \in E_t$ with probability $1 - \delta$ for all $t \geq 1$, see Fig. 2. Then, the decision maker selects the best action that maximizes the estimated mean reward, for each possible generating kernel in the ellipsoid (optimism in face of uncertainty [22]). Formally, the decision maker selects the action $\boldsymbol{h}$ (and therefore $\boldsymbol{X} = \boldsymbol{MPI}_K \otimes \boldsymbol{h}$) such that

$$\boldsymbol{h}_t : \arg\max_{\boldsymbol{h} \in \mathcal{A}} \max_{\boldsymbol{\alpha} \in E_t} \boldsymbol{X}\boldsymbol{\alpha}. \tag{6}$$

To apply (6), we need to formally derive the confidence bound E_t. This can be derived by the following two Lemmas (proofs in Appendix A in [41]). Lemma 1 bounds the matrix $\boldsymbol{V}_t$, which defines the regularized least-square solution as shown in (5). Lemma 1 is key to evaluate the upper confidence bound in Lemma 2. Specifically, Lemma 2 provides the confidence bound E_t such that $E_t : \{\|\hat{\boldsymbol{\alpha}}_t - \boldsymbol{\alpha}_*\| \leq c_t\}$. It is worth noting that both bounds have explicit dependency on topological features of the graph, such as the sum of eigenvalues power, as we comment later.

Lemma 1: *Suppose $\boldsymbol{Z}_1, \boldsymbol{Z}_2, \ldots, \boldsymbol{Z}_t \in \mathbb{R}^{1 \times K}$, with $\boldsymbol{Z}_\tau = \boldsymbol{MPI}_K \otimes \boldsymbol{h}_\tau$ and for any $1 \leq \tau \leq t - 1$, $\|h_\tau\|_F^2 \leq T_0$, and $\|\boldsymbol{M}\|_F^2 \leq Q$. Let $\boldsymbol{V}_t = \sum_\tau \boldsymbol{Z}_\tau^T \boldsymbol{Z}_\tau + \mu \boldsymbol{I}_K$ with $\mu > 0$, then $|\boldsymbol{V}_t| \leq [\mu + dQT_0]^K$, with $d = \sum_k \sum_l \lambda_l^k$, with λ_l being the l-th eigenvalue of the graph Laplacian.*

Lemma 2: *Assume that $\boldsymbol{V}_t = \sum_\tau \boldsymbol{Z}_\tau^T \boldsymbol{Z}_\tau + \mu \boldsymbol{I}_K$, define $\boldsymbol{w}_\tau = \boldsymbol{Z}_\tau \boldsymbol{\alpha}_* + \boldsymbol{\eta}_\tau$, with $\boldsymbol{Z}_\tau = \boldsymbol{MPI}_K \otimes \boldsymbol{h}_\tau$ and with $\boldsymbol{\eta}_t$ being conditionally R-sub-Gaussian, and assume*

Algorithm 1. Grab–UCB

Input:
N: nr of nodes, T_0: sparsity level of action signal $\boldsymbol{h}$, K: sparsity of the basis coefficients
μ, δ: regularization and confidence parameters
R, S: upper bounds on the noise and $\boldsymbol{\alpha}_*$
$t = 1$
while $t \leq T$ **do**
  Refine estimate of the coefficients
  $\boldsymbol{X}_{1:t} = [\boldsymbol{X}_1, \boldsymbol{X}_2, \ldots, \boldsymbol{X}_{t-1}]^T$
  $\boldsymbol{Y}_{1:t} = [\boldsymbol{y}_1, \boldsymbol{y}_2, \ldots, \boldsymbol{y}_{t-1}]^T$
  $\boldsymbol{V}_t = \boldsymbol{X}_{1:t}^T \boldsymbol{X}_{1:t} + \mu \boldsymbol{I}_{K+1}$
  Step 1: Coefficients estimation:
    $\hat{\boldsymbol{\alpha}}_t = \boldsymbol{V}_t^{-1} \boldsymbol{X}_{1:t}^T \boldsymbol{Y}_{1:t}$
  Step 2: Action Selection
    Evaluate the confidence bound and select the best action
    Select action by solving (7) numerically or via Grab-arm-Light
  Observe the resulting signal $\boldsymbol{y}_t$ and the instantaneous reward
  $t = t + 1$
end while

---

that $||\boldsymbol{\alpha}_*||_2 \leq S$, and $||\boldsymbol{h}_\tau||_F^2 \leq T_0$. Then, for any $\delta > 0$, with probability at least $1 - \delta$, for all $t \leq 0$, $\boldsymbol{\alpha}_*$ lies in the set

$$E_t : \left\{ \boldsymbol{\alpha} \in \mathbb{R}^{1 \times K} : ||\hat{\boldsymbol{\alpha}}_t - \boldsymbol{\alpha}||_{\boldsymbol{V}_t} \leq R \left[\sqrt{K \log(\mu + tdQT_0) + 2\log(\mu^{-1/2}\delta)} \right] + \mu^{1/2} S \right\}$$

with $d = \sum_k \sum_l \lambda_l^k$, with λ_l being the l-th eigenvalue of the graph Laplacian and $\hat{\boldsymbol{\alpha}}_t$ is the l^2-regularized least-square estimate of $\boldsymbol{\alpha}$ with t training samples.

From Lemma 2, the maximization in (6) becomes (see Appendix A in [41] for details)

$$\boldsymbol{h}_t = \arg\max_{\boldsymbol{h} \in \mathcal{A}} \max_{\boldsymbol{\alpha} \in E_t} \boldsymbol{X}\boldsymbol{\alpha} = \arg\max_{\boldsymbol{h} \in \mathcal{A}} \boldsymbol{X}\boldsymbol{\alpha} + c_t \sqrt{\boldsymbol{X} \boldsymbol{V}_t^{-1} \boldsymbol{X}^T}$$

$$= \arg\max_{\boldsymbol{h} \in \mathcal{A}} \boldsymbol{X}\boldsymbol{\alpha} + c_t ||\boldsymbol{X}||_{\boldsymbol{V}_t^{-1}} = \arg\max_{\boldsymbol{h} \in \mathcal{A}} \left[\boldsymbol{MPH}\hat{\boldsymbol{\alpha}}_t + c_t ||\boldsymbol{MPH}||_{\boldsymbol{V}_t^{-1}} \right] \quad (7)$$

with $c_t = R \left[\sqrt{K \log(\mu + tdQT_0) + 2\log(\mu^{-1/2}\delta)} \right] + \mu^{1/2} S$ following Lemma 2. This optimization characterizes the Step 2, *i.e.*, the action selection. However, this cannot be solved efficiently in large scale networks, see Appendix A in [41] for description of the solving method and scalability issues. In the following Section, we propose a computationally effective optimization algorithm.

In Algorithm 1, we summarize the main steps of the proposed Grab–UCB strategy. This algorithm achieves the following regret bound (derived in Appendix B in [41]) of $R_T \leq 2(c_T + 1)\sqrt{2KT \log\left(1 + \frac{QT_0 d}{\mu}\right)}$. It is worth noting the dependency on the topological structure via d, sum of eigenvalues power. Finally, the regret does not depend on the network size N but rather on the sparsity level T_0, hence the strong gain with respect to linUCB like algorithms.

4   Grab-arm-Light: Efficient Action Selection

The methodology proposed in the previous Section entails two main optimization/learning steps that need to be solved. While the solution to the optimization in Step 1 has a closed form, i.e., Eq. (5), in Step 2 the optimization problem in (7) needs to be solved efficiently. This optimization becomes computationally expensive in large-scale graphs, see Appendix C in [41]. Therefore, in the following we propose a computationally effective optimization algorithm to address the scalability issue that we call Grab-arm-Light. It is a computationally light solving method aimed at selecting the action/arm in Step 2 of Grab-UCB. We first rewrite the problem (7) (see Appendix A in [41]) as follows

$$\max_{\boldsymbol{h}} \boldsymbol{Dh} + c_t ||\boldsymbol{L} * \boldsymbol{b}^T \otimes \boldsymbol{h}^T||_2 \qquad \text{s.t. } h(n) \in [0,1], \; \forall n ||\boldsymbol{h}||_0 \leq T_0 \qquad (8)$$

where we have used $\boldsymbol{X} = \boldsymbol{MPI}_{K+1} \otimes \boldsymbol{h} = \boldsymbol{b} \otimes \boldsymbol{h}$. The above problem maximizes a convex objective function over a polytope, defined by both constraints. If the objective function has a maximum value on the feasible region, then it is at the edges of the polytope. Therefore, the problem reduces to a finite computation of the objective function over the finite number of extreme points.

However, in the case of large networks, this computation could be too expensive. Therefore, we propose an algorithm that walks along the edges of the polytope. The intuition is similar to the one of the simplex algorithm or any hill climbing algorithm. Let consider an iterative algorithm, where at each iteration the N variables h_n, with $n = 1, \ldots, N$, are subdivided into basic variables and non-basic variables. The former are the ones such that $h_n = 1$, while the non basic variables are the remaining zero sources. At each iteration, we perform the operation of moving from a feasible solution to an adjacent feasible solution by swapping a basic variable with a non basic one (similar to the pivoting operation in the simplex algorithm). We move in such a way that the objective function always increases. We then stop the algorithm either after a maximum number of iteration steps or when convergence is reached. This is the Grab-arm-Light, presented in Algorithm 2 and further described in the following.

Let $\boldsymbol{h}^{(t-1)} = [h_1^{(t-1)}, h_2^{(t-1)}, \ldots, h_N^{(t-1)}]$ be the optimal variable at the iteration step $i - 1$. Let $\mathcal{B}_t = \{n|h_n^{(t-1)} = 1\}$ be the set of the indices of basic variables at t. Let then denote by J the objective function $J(\boldsymbol{h}) = \boldsymbol{MPI}_{K+1} \otimes \boldsymbol{h}\hat{\boldsymbol{\alpha}}_t + c_t ||\boldsymbol{L} * \boldsymbol{b}^T \otimes \boldsymbol{h}^T||_2$ and by $\partial J/\partial h_n$ be the partial derivative of J with respect the nth variable. Finally, note that vertices are adjacent if they share all but one non-basic variable. Equipped with the above notations and definitions, we now state the following Lemmas (proofs in Appendix A in [41]):

Lemma 3: *One vertex is optimal if there is no better neighboring vertex.*

Algorithm 2. Grab-arm-Light

Input:
number of iterations $MaxIter$, action sparsity level T_0, graph topology (and therefore L and P), reward mask M, estimated polynomial $\hat{\alpha}$, confidence bound c.
Output:
optimal source signal $h^\star$
Initialization:
Definition of the objective function $J(h) = MPI_{K+1} \otimes h\hat{\alpha} + c\|L * b^T \otimes h^T\|_2$
Evaluation of the partial derivatives $a_n = \frac{\partial J}{\partial h_n}\big|_{u_n}, \forall n$
Selection of $h^{(0)}$: $h_n^{(0)} = 1$ if a_n belongs to the T_0 largest partial derivatives.
$t = 1$
for $t \leq MaxIter$ **do**
　　Set $\mathcal{B}_t = \{n | h_n^{(t-1)} = 1\}$
　　Evaluate the IN and OUT variables:

$$in = \arg \max_{n | h_n \notin \mathcal{B}_t} \left\{ \frac{\partial J}{\partial h_n}\Big|_{h^{(t-1)}} \right\}, \qquad out = \arg \min_{n | h_n \in \mathcal{B}_t} \left\{ \frac{\partial J}{\partial h_n}\Big|_{h^{(t-1)}} \right\}$$

　　Set $h^{(t)} = h^{(t-1)}$
　　Set $h_{in}^{(t)} = 1, h_{out}^{(t)} = 0$
　　if $J(h^{(t)}) \leq J(h^{(t-1)})$ **then**
　　　　$h^\star = h^{(t)}$
　　　　break
　　end if
　　$t \leftarrow t + 1$
end for

Lemma 4: *From a vertex, moving to one of the neighboring nodes in the direction of the greatest gradient leads to a no-worse objective function. Let $h_{in}^{(t)}$ and $h_{out}^{(t)}$ be the variable that enters and leaves the set of basic variables, respectively, at the t-th iteration. These variables are evaluated as follows*

$$in = \arg \max_{n | h_n \notin \mathcal{B}_t} \left\{ \frac{\partial J}{\partial h_n}\Big|_{h^{(t-1)}} \right\}, \qquad out = \arg \min_{n | h_n \in \mathcal{B}_t} \left\{ \frac{\partial J}{\partial h_n}\Big|_{h^{(t-1)}} \right\}$$

From Lemma 4, given a vertex $h^{(t-1)}$, at the t-th iteration the algorithm will move to the neighboring vertex $h^{(t)}$ defined as follows:

$$h_{in}^{(t)} = 1, \quad h_{out}^{(t)} = 0, \quad \text{and} \quad h_n^{(t)} = h_n^{(t-1)}, \forall n \neq in, out.$$

As shown in Algorithm 2, if the swap variable leads to an improvement of the objective function, *i.e.*, if $J(h^{(t)}) > J(h^{(t-1)})$, then we proceed to the next step. Otherwise, we set the optimal source signal $h^\star = h^{(t-1)}$ and we break the iterative loop. Further details are provided in Algorithm 2, together with the initialization step. Rather than a randomly generating starting point, we consider the one with the T_0 variables having the maximum partial derivative $a_n = \frac{\partial J}{\partial h_n}\big|_{u_n}, \forall n$, with u_n being a N-dimensional vector all elements null but the

n-th, which is set to 1. Note also that in the algorithm the partial derivative of the objective function can be derived as (see Appendix D.2 in [41] for details)

$$\frac{\partial J(\boldsymbol{h})}{\partial h_n} = \boldsymbol{MPI}_{K+1} \otimes \boldsymbol{1}_n \hat{\boldsymbol{\alpha}} + \frac{(\boldsymbol{L} * \boldsymbol{b}^T \otimes \boldsymbol{h}^T)}{||\boldsymbol{L} * \boldsymbol{b}^T \otimes \boldsymbol{h}^T||_2} \left(\boldsymbol{L} * \boldsymbol{b}^T \otimes \boldsymbol{1}_n^T \right)^T \qquad (9)$$

In summary, the proposed algorithm requires the evaluation of the partial derivative (N operations) instead of exhaustively evaluating the objective function in (8) at all $\binom{N}{T_0}$ possible edges. In the following Section, we show emporically that this complexity reduction does not come at the price of reduced optimality.

5   Simulation Results

5.1   Settings

As benchmark solution, we propose an algorithm denoted as Act After Learning (AAL), in which the exploration and the exploitation phases are separated, while our proposed method finds the best tradeoff between exploitation and exploration automatically. The key intuition is that it first gathers a training set (in the first T_L decision strategies) and therefore experience a reward as a function of random actions. Then, after a training phase of T_L decision opportunities, the generating kernel is estimated and the best arm is selected. In the remaining decision opportunities the best action is taken. Note that we do not compare with the linUCB algorithms since its regret would scale with the cardinality of the decision space $|\mathcal{A}| = \binom{N}{T_o}$, if T_0 is the imposed sparsity of $\boldsymbol{h}$, which is prohibitive in the case of large-scale network. .

We carry out experiments on Barabási-Albert model (BA) graphs [3], on radial basis function (RBF) random graphs, and on non-synthetic graphs (*e.g.*, Minnesota graph[4]). For BA graphs, the network begins with an initial connected network of $m_0 = 10$ nodes. At each iteration, one node is added to the network and it is connected to $m \le m_0$ existing nodes. Connections to existing nodes are built following a preferential attachment mechanism, which eventually builds a scale-free network. For the RBF model, we generate the coordinates of the vertices uniformly at random in the unit square, and we set the edge weights based on a thresholded Gaussian kernel function so that $W(i,j) = \exp(-[dist(i,j)^2]/2\sigma)$ if the distance between vertices i and j is smaller than or equal to T, and zero otherwise. We further set $\sigma = 0.5$ and we vary T to change the edge density of the generated graphs.

We model the network processes as a diffusion processes with generating kernel $g_L = e^{-\tau L}$ [39]. We then consider that each signal on the graph is characterized by the source signal, the generating kernel and an additive random noise ϵ_t with zero mean and variance σ_e^2 (i.e., $R = \sigma_e$ in the spectral UCB). The remaining parameters of the sequential decision strategy are set as $\mu = 0.01$, $\delta = 0.01$. The mask M is randomly generated and it covers 20% of the nodes.

---

[4] Available at https://lts2.epfl.ch/gsp/.

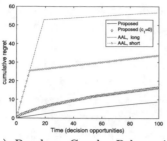
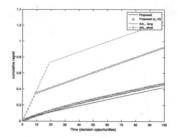

(a) Random Graph, Polynomial Dictionary ($K = 20$)

(b) Community Graph, Diffusion dictionary, $\tau = 5$.

Fig. 3. Cumulative regret vs. time for randomly generated graphs with $N = 100$, diffusion process (with $\tau = 5$) and sparsity level $T_0 = 5$ for Grab-UCB.

5.2   Performance of Grab-UCB

We now study the performance of the proposed Grab-UCB with Grab-arm-Light used in Step 2. First, a randomly generated graph (RBF model) with $N = 100$ nodes is considered, in the case of diffusion process acting on the graph with $\tau = 10$ and with $\sigma_e^2 = 10^{-2}$. Figure 3 depicts the cumulative regret over time (in terms of decision opportunities) for the considered graph. Each point is averaged over 100 realizations (when at each realization both the graph and the noise of the signal on graph are generated). The Grab-UCB is compared to AAL with $T_L = 10$ (AAL short) and $T_L = 20$ (AAL long). Note that a longer exploration leads to a better estimate but for a longer (suboptimal) exploration phse. From Fig. 3, we observe that Grab-UCB outperforms the baseline algorithms in both networks. The proposed algorithm is tested also in the case of $c_t = 0$, which means that the confidence bound is ignored when acting – leading to less exploration. The comparison shows the gain in striking the optimal tradeoff between exploitation and eploraztion ($c_t > 0$). Further results are provided in Appendix E.1 in [41].

We further illustrate in Fig. 4 that optimal placement of sparse resources in high dimensional networks is not necessarily an intuitive step. It depicts the optimal source signal computed by Grab-UCB with optimal solver introduced in Appendix A in [41] and the resulting signal for a randomly generated graph (RBF model) with $N = 100$, and sparsity level $T_0 = 4$. In Fig. 4a, the optimal signal is depicted in red, while the mask signal used to evaluate the reward is depicted in blue. Interestingly, the optimal signal is placed on nodes that do not necessarily belong to the mask and do not necessarily appear to be central in the graph. Yet, this results in the optimal reward signal depicted in Fig. 4b.

We validate now the proposed algorithm for solving the action selection step, which is a priori NP-hard. We empirically compare the numerical solver (FMICON) adopted to optimally solve Step 2 (labelled in the following figure as "Exact") and the Grab-arm-Light (labelled as "Algorithm 2"). Figure 5a depicts the CPU time required by both solvers as a function of the number of nodes N for a randomly generated graph (RBF model), with sparsity level

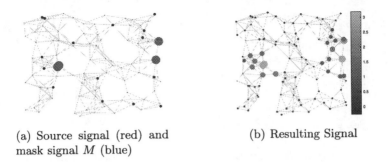

(a) Source signal (red) and
mask signal M (blue)

(b) Resulting Signal

Fig. 4. Optimal source signal and resulting signal for a randomly generated graph (RBF model) with $N = 100$, and sparsity level $T_0 = 4$.

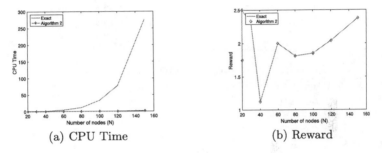

(a) CPU Time

(b) Reward

Fig. 5. Comparison of the optimal solver and Grab-arm-Light (Algorithm 2) for random graphs (RBF model) with different number of nodes, and $T_0 = 5$.

$T_0 = 5$. The achieved reward after 100 decision steps is also depicted in Fig. 5b. Results are averaged over 50 generated graphs. As expected, the problem in (8) is NP-hard (maximization of a convex function under convex -or affine- constraints) and the solver's complexity grows exponentially with N. Conversely, the complexity of Grab-UCB grows linearly with N, as shown by Fig. 5a. From Fig. 5b, it can be observed that the proposed solution still achieves the optimal solution in terms of reward. Note that the reward is not monotonic with N because the density of the graph is not necessarily kept constant for different N values.

Finally, we evaluate the effect of network topology on the estimation error (From Lemma 2, we see that the confidence bound increases with the sparsity level T_0 and $d = \sum_{k=0}^{K} \sum_{l=1}^{N} \lambda_l^k$). We consider a randomly generated training set of 300 signals, and we then estimate the accuracy of the learned polynomial α. To measure the accuracy of the estimate, we evaluate the error on the resulting signal given the action h of test signals. We consider graphs generated with the BA model; by changing the parameter m, we generate more or less connected graphs (the larger the m the more connected is the graph). This is reflected in the power sum d and in a more narrow profile of the eigenvalues of the Laplacian λ_l, as observed from Fig. 6a, where the values of λ_l are provided for different graph

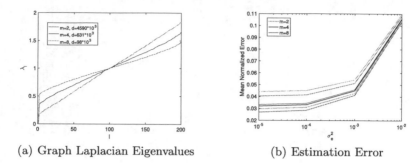

(a) Graph Laplacian Eigenvalues   (b) Estimation Error

Fig. 6. Graph Laplacian distribution and signal estimation error for graphs generated with the BA model with different levels of connectivity, $N = 200$ nodes, and sparsity value $T_0 = 25$. The estimation error is evaluated both in the case of full observability (solid line) or in the case of partial observability (dotted line).

topologies. As a consequence, more connected graphs lead to a more accurate estimate of the generating kernels, see Fig. 6b. This validates the understanding we had from the theoretical bounds, which depend on d.

6   Related Work

Multiple works have looked at graph-based bandit problems with the ultimate goal of addressing sample-efficiency [4,17,28,36,43,46], identifying and leveraging the structure underneath data in optimisation problems where the outputs have semantically rich structure. In this direction, graph knowledge has been used for 1) sharing the payoff throughout the graph Laplacian [10,12,23,27] or reducing the dimensionality of the search space by clustering arms [6,7,11,21,24–26] – those usually perform poorly in irregular datasets [48], typical of most of the real-world problems; 2) modelling each arm as graph [19] – the main goal is optimization over graph domains (set of graphs) while our focus is optimizing over geometrical signal domains (set of signals on a given graph); 3) modelling the reward signal, seen as smooth signal on the graph [44]– this shares most similarities with our work hence they are further describe in the following paragraph where differences with respect to our works are also highligthed.

Looking at the arms as nodes on a graph and the reward as a smooth signal on this graph [13,20,43,44] permits to i) define the reward as a linear combination of the eigenvectors of the graph Laplacian matrix, where the linear coefficients are unknown, ii) apply LinUCB [9] in the spectral domain. These algorithms achieve a regret bound of the order $\sqrt{dT}$, with d being the effective dimension (linked to the dimensionality of the characteristic eigenvalues) and T being the number of rounds. Similar intuitions have been introduced in [42], which performs maximization over the smooth functions that have a small Reproducing kernel Hilbert space (RKHS) norm, or in [38,47] that exploit graph homophily to denoise/generalize the reward. Similarly, our work exploits spectral graph prior to solve a linUCB algorithm with the assumption of low dimensional reward behavior. Yet, we expand the literature on spectral MABs by modelling processing evolving on graphs. Namely, each action represents possibly a set on a graph (not limited to a node only) and the reward is not necessarily smooth on the graph and it is a resultant signal on the entire graph instead of on one node only.

Our work, as well as spectral MAB ones, can be seen as extensions of the rich field of methods for kernelized bandits working under the norm bounded RKHS assumption [5,8,42,49] but they are not limited to Euclidean domains. Another line of works consider bandits theory for decision-making strategy [15,49] (and many references therein), which however differ from our model in which we limit decisions to bandit problems and we exploit GSP tools to learn the dynamic process of the network flow. Our paper share the ultimate goal of [17], focused on online targeted advertising on social networks, where the multi-mode tensor tool can nicely complement our work to extend our signal processing analysis to heterogeneous feature vectors. Complementary to this work, there is also the vast literature on Thompson sampling for the multi-arms bandit problem that could be an interesting alternative to our Grab-arm-Light [2].

Finally, there is a vast literature from the GSP community [31] aimed at capturing structural properties of network processes (i.e., node centrality [14], community detection [45]) for network problems such as diffusion dynamics, pricing experiments, and opinion dynamics: the work in [45] models an unknown network process as a graph filter that is excited by a set of unknown low-rank inputs, the study in [33] models power systems as generative low-pass graph filters. However, no work so far has focused on learning while acting, i.e., inferring network process models while taking sequential actions on those networks.

7   Conclusions

In this work, we study network optimization problems under uncertainty in the case of optimal source placement. As main contributions, we cast the network optimization problem under uncertainty as a linear MAB problem, which infers a K-dimensional polynomial that defines the graph generating-kernel while taking actions over time on the network-graph. We then derive the theoretical bound of the estimation of the graph spectral model and translate it to the MAB upper confidence bound. We show both mathematically and empirically that more connected graphs and sparser signals lead to a more accurate estimation of the network processes. Finally, we observe that the optimization method leads to an arm selection problem that is NP-hard, and we provide a low-complexity algorithm by exploiting the structure of the optimization function. Beyond proposing a data-efficient solution to problems of network optimization, this work aims at opening the gate to new research directions in which graph signal processing tools are blended to online learning frameworks to exploit structural knowledge of network optimization problems.

Ethical Statement. Our work is mostly of theoretical nature, and we do not foresee any direct ethical implications. There is always a risk, as for most works of theoretical and algorithmic nature in machine learning, that the work would be diverted from its original objective, and largely modified to design extensions in non-ethical applications. However, this is not obviously envisaged by the authors at the time of the writing.

References

1. Acemoglu, D., Ozdaglar, A.: Opinion dynamics and learning in social networks. Dyn. Games Appl. **1**(1), 3–49 (2011)
2. Agrawal, S., Goyal, N.: Analysis of Thompson sampling for the multi-armed bandit problem. In: Conference on Learning Theory. JMLR Workshop and Conference Proceedings, pp. 1–26 (2012)
3. Barabási, A.L., Albert, R.: Emergence of scaling in random networks. Science **286**(5439), 509–512 (1999)
4. Bellemare, M.G., et al.: A geometric perspective on optimal representations for reinforcement learning. CoRR abs/1901.11530 (2019)
5. Camilleri, R., Jamieson, K., Katz-Samuels, J.: High-dimensional experimental design and kernel bandits. In: Meila, M., Zhang, T. (eds.) Proceedings of International Conference on Machine Learning (ICML) (2021)
6. Caron, S., Kveton, B., Lelarge, M., Bhagat, S.: Leveraging side observations in stochastic bandits. ArXiv abs/1210.4839 (2012)
7. Cesa-Bianchi, N., Gentile, C., Zappella, G.: A gang of bandits. In: Proceedings of Advances in Neural Information Processing Systems (NIPS), pp. 737–745 (2013)
8. Chowdhury, S.R., Gopalan, A.: On kernelized multi-armed bandits. In: Precup, D., Teh, Y.W. (eds.) Proceedings of International Conference on Machine Learning (ICML) (2017)
9. Chu, W., Li, L., Reyzin, L., Schapire, R.E.: Contextual bandits with linear payoff functions. In: Proceedings of Artificial Intelligence and Statistics Conference (AISTATS), vol. 15, pp. 208–214 (2011)
10. Esposito, E., Fusco, F., van der Hoeven, D., Cesa-Bianchi, N.: Learning on the edge: online learning with stochastic feedback graphs. arXiv:2210.04229 (2022)
11. Gentile, C., Li, S., Zappella, G.: Online clustering of bandits. In: Proceedings of International Conference on Machine Learning (ICML) (2014)
12. Ghari, P.M., Shen, Y.: Online learning with probabilistic feedback. In: Proceedings of IEEE International Conference on Acoustics, Speech and Signal Processing (ICASSP) (2022)
13. Hanawal, M.K., Saligrama, V.: Cost effective algorithms for spectral bandits. In: Proceedings of IEEE Conference on Communication, Control, and Computing (2015)
14. He, Y., Wai, H.T.: Detecting central nodes from low-rank excited graph signals via structured factor analysis. arXiv preprint arXiv:2109.13573 (2021)
15. Hsieh, Y.G., Kasiviswanathan, S.P., Kveton, B., Blöbaum, P.: Thompson sampling with diffusion generative prior (2023)
16. Hölzle, U.: Our commitment to climate-conscious data center cooling. https://blog.google/outreach-initiatives/sustainability/our-commitment-to-climate-conscious-data-center-cooling/ (2022)
17. Idé, T., Murugesan, K., Bouneffouf, D., Abe, N.: Targeted advertising on social networks using online variational tensor regression. arXiv:2208.10627 (2022)
18. Jones, N.: How to stop data centres from gobbling up the world's electricity. Nature **561**(7722), 163–167 (2018)

19. Kassraie, P., Krause, A., Bogunovic, I.: Graph neural network bandits. In: Conference on Neural Information Processing Systems (NeurIPS) (2022)
20. Kocák, T., Valko, M., Munos, R., Agrawal, S.: Spectral thompson sampling. In: Proceedings of AAAI Conference on Artificial Intelligence (2014)
21. Korda, N., Szorenyi, B., Li, S.: Distributed clustering of linear bandits in peer to peer networks. In: Proceedings of International Conference on Machine Learning (ICML) (2016)
22. Lattimore, T., Szepesvári, C.: Bandit algorithms. arXiv (2018)
23. Lee, C.W., Luo, H., Zhang, M.: A closer look at small-loss bounds for bandits with graph feedback. In: Proceedings of International Conference on Algorithmic Learning Theory (ALT) (2020)
24. Li, S., Gentile, C., Karatzoglou, A., Zappella, G.: Data-dependent clustering in exploration-exploitation algorithms. arXiv preprint arXiv:1502.03473 (2015)
25. Li, S., Gentile, C., Karatzoglou, A., Zappella, G.: Online context-dependent clustering in recommendations based on exploration-exploitation algorithms. ArXiv abs/1608.03544 (2016)
26. Li, S., Karatzoglou, A., Gentile, C.: Collaborative filtering bandits. In: Proceedings of International ACM Conference on Research and Development in Information Retrieval (2016)
27. Lykouris, T., Tardos, E., Wali, D.: Feedback graph regret bounds for thompson sampling and ucb. In: Proceedings of International Conference on Algorithmic Learning Theory (ALT) (2020)
28. Mohaghegh Neyshabouri, M., Gokcesu, K., Gokcesu, H., Ozkan, H., Kozat, S.S.: Asymptotically optimal contextual bandit algorithm using hierarchical structures. IEEE Trans. Neural Netw. Learn. Syst. **30**(3), 923–937 (2019)
29. Movric, K.H., Lewis, F.L.: Cooperative optimal control for multi-agent systems on directed graph topologies. IEEE Trans. Autom. Control **59**(3), 769–774 (2014)
30. Nassif, R., Vlaski, S., Sayed, A.H.: Adaptation and learning over networks under subspace constraints. ArXiv 1905.08750 (2019)
31. Ortega, A., Frossard, P., Kovačević, J., Moura, J.M.F., Vandergheynst, P.: Graph signal processing: overview, challenges, and applications. Proc. IEEE **106**(5), 808–828 (2018)
32. Perra, N., Rocha, L.E.: Modelling opinion dynamics in the age of algorithmic personalisation. Sci. Rep. **9**(1), 1–11 (2019)
33. Ramakrishna, R., Scaglione, A.: Grid-graph signal processing (grid-gsp): a graph signal processing framework for the power grid. IEEE Trans. Signal Process. **69**, 2725–2739 (2021)
34. Salami, H., Ying, B., Sayed, A.H.: Social learning over weakly connected graphs. IEEE Trans. Signal Inf. Process. Netw. **3**(2), 222–238 (2017)
35. Shuman, D.I., Narang, S.K., Frossard, P., Ortega, A., Vandergheynst, P.: The emerging field of signal processing on graphs: extending high-dimensional data analysis to networks and other irregular domains. IEEE Signal Process. Maga. **30**(3), 83–98 (2013)
36. Slivkins, A.: Contextual bandits with similarity information. J. Mach. Learn. Res. **15**(1), 2533–2568 (2014)
37. Tang, S.: When social advertising meets viral marketing: sequencing social advertisements for influence maximization. In: AAAI (2018)
38. Thaker, P.K., Malu, M., Rao, N., Dasarathy, G.: Maximizing and satisficing in multi-armed bandits with graph information (2022)
39. Thanou, D., Dong, X., Kressner, D., Frossard, P.: Learning heat diffusion graphs. IEEE Trans. Signal Inf. Process. Netw. **3**(3), 484–499 (2017)

40. Thanou, D., Shuman, D.I., Frossard, P.: Learning parametric dictionaries for signals on graphs. IEEE Trans. Signal Process. **62**(15), 3849–3862 (2014)
41. Toni, L., Frossard, P.: Online network source optimization with graph-kernel MAB. https://arxiv.org/abs/2307.03641 (2023)
42. Valko, M., Korda, N., Munos, R., Flaounas, I., Cristianini, N.: Finite-time analysis of kernelised contextual bandits (2013)
43. Valko, M., Munos, R.: Cheap bandits. In: Proceedings of International Conference on Machine Learning (ICML) (2015)
44. Valko, M., Munos, R., Kveton, B., Kocak, T.: Spectral bandits for smooth graph functions. In: Proceedings of International Conference on Machine Learning (ICML) (2014)
45. Wai, H.T., Segarra, S., Ozdaglar, A.E., Scaglione, A., Jadbabaie, A.: Blind community detection from low-rank excitations of a graph filter. IEEE Trans. Signal Process. **68**, 436–451 (2019)
46. Waradpande, V., Kudenko, D., Khosla, M.: Deep reinforcement learning with graph-based state representations. arXiv:2004.13965 (2020)
47. Yang, K., Dong, X., Toni, L.: Laplacian-regularized graph bandits: algorithms and theoretical analysis. In: Proceedings of International Conference on Artificial Intelligence and Statistics (AISTATS) (2020)
48. Yang, K., Toni, L.: Graph-based recommendation system. In: 2018 IEEE Global Conference on Signal and Information Processing (GlobalSIP) (2018)
49. Yang, L., Wang, M.: Reinforcement learning in feature space: matrix bandit, kernels, and regret bound. In: III, H.D., Singh, A. (eds.) Proceedings of International Conference on Machine Learning (ICML), pp. 10746–10756 (2020)
50. Yuan, K., Ying, B., Zhao, X., Sayed, A.H.: Exact Diffusion for Distributed Optimization and Learning – Part I: Algorithm Development. ArXiv abs/1702.05122 (2017)
51. Zhang, H., Feng, T., Yang, G.H., Liang, H.: Distributed cooperative optimal control for multiagent systems on directed graphs: an inverse optimal approach. IEEE Trans. Cybern. **45**(7), 1315–1326 (2015)

Quantifying Node-Based Core Resilience

Jakir Hossain[1]([✉]), Sucheta Soundarajan[2], and Ahmet Erdem Sarıyüce[1]

[1] University at Buffalo, Buffalo, NY 14260, USA
{mh267,erdem}@buffalo.edu
[2] Syracuse University, Syracuse, NY 13244, USA
susounda@syr.edu

Abstract. Core decomposition is an efficient building block for various graph analysis tasks such as dense subgraph discovery and identifying influential nodes. One crucial weakness of the core decomposition is its sensitivity to changes in the graph: inserting or removing a few edges can drastically change the core structure of a graph. Hence, it is essential to characterize, quantify, and, if possible, improve the resilience of the core structure of a given graph in global and local levels. Previous works mostly considered the core resilience of the entire graph or important subgraphs in it. In this work, we study node-based core resilience measures upon edge removals and insertions. We first show that a previously proposed measure, Core Strength, does not correctly capture the core resilience of a node upon edge removals. Next, we introduce the concept of dependency graph to capture the impact of neighbor nodes (for edge removal) and probable future neighbor nodes (for edge insertion) on the core number of a given node. Accordingly, we define Removal Strength and Insertion Strength measures to capture the resilience of an individual node upon removing and inserting an edge, respectively. As naive computation of those measures is costly, we provide efficient heuristics built on key observations about the core structure. We consider two key applications, finding critical edges and identifying influential spreaders, to demonstrate the usefulness of our new measures on various real-world networks and against several baselines. We also show that our heuristic algorithms are more efficient than the naive approaches.

1 Introduction

The k-cores are proposed as the seedbeds in which cohesive subsets of nodes can be found [36]. A k-core is defined as the maximal connected subgraph in which every vertex has at least k neighbors in the subgraph. Each node is assigned a core number which denotes the maximum k for which the node is a part of k-core. Thanks to its linear time complexity, k-cores are used as a standard tool in various applications at downstream graph analytics. Examples include the analysis of internet topology [11], predicting protein interactions [2], identifying influential spreaders [20], and community detection [3,6,16,21].

Despite its widespread use, k-cores are known to have a weak resilience against a few changes in the graph [1,22]. Inserting or removing a few edges

D. Koutra et al. (Eds.): ECML PKDD 2023, LNAI 14171, pp. 259–276, 2023.
https://doi.org/10.1007/978-3-031-43418-1_16

can drastically change the core structure of a graph. In applications where noise is common or the studied graph has uncertain parts, core decomposition is not reliable. For example, networks are constructed as a result of indirect measurements in various applications, such as the Internet router/AS level graphs by traceroutes [15], biological networks by experimental correlations [35], and social media based networks by limited samples via the APIs [5]. It is essential to characterize, quantify, and, if possible, improve the resilience of the core structure of a given graph in such applications at global and local levels.

In previous works, the resilience of k-core is studied under node or edge removal to improve users' involvement in social networks [29,42,45], bolster connections to protect a social network from unraveling [9] and determining the edges that should be monitored for attacks on technological networks [22]. Those studies only consider the core structure of the entire graph or a few important subgraphs (e.g., maximum k-cores). **There is no holistic study to quantify the node-based core resilience for any given node in the graph upon edge removals and edge insertions.** Considering the query-driven scenarios in uncertain or noisy networks where the properties of the nodes are important, such as identifying influential nodes in spreading processes [26] or information diffusion [27] and finding critical nodes/edges [31], it is crucial to measure the resilience of core numbers against edge removals as well as insertions.

In this work, we study node-based core resilience measures upon edge removals and insertions. We first demonstrate that a previously proposed node-based measure, Core Strength [22], is inaccurate at capturing the changes in the core number upon edge removals. Next, we propose the concept of dependency graph which captures the impact of neighbor nodes (for removal case) and probable future neighbor nodes (for insertion case) on the core number of a given node. In the dependency graph for removal, one-way dependency relationships between neighboring nodes help to identify the resilience of core numbers. Likewise, in the insertion case, we discover the one-way dependency relationships to quantify the likelihood of a change in the core number. Using the dependency graphs, we define a pair of Removal Strength and Insertion Strength measures for each node. Calculating those node strengths for big graphs in a naive way is computationally intensive. For edge removal, we use the equal edges [46] and k-corona [17] properties to design RSC algorithm. For insertion, we design ISC algorithm based on the number of connections a node has with the same or higher core number. As node-level aspects of a graph are important in many real-world applications, we consider two applications to demonstrate the benefit of our new measures: finding the most critical edges to remove/insert such that the number of nodes that changes their initial core numbers is maximized [14,45,46] and identifying influential spreaders [13,28,40]. For both applications we compare our node-based measures against several state-of-the-art baselines.

Our contributions can be summarized as follows:

- We point out that the Core Strength definition (by [22]) is incorrect and provide counterexamples as well as empirical results to show its unreliability.

- To quantify the node resilience upon edge removal and edge insertion, we use the concept of dependency graphs. Accordingly, we introduce a pair of Removal Strength and Insertion Strength measures.
- We design RSC and ISC algorithms to compute the new node resilience measures for removal and insertion.
- We consider two motivating applications to examine the effectiveness of those metrics: finding critical edges and identifying influential spreaders.
- We evaluate our measures and algorithms on real-world networks. We demonstrate the efficiency and effectiveness of our techniques against several baselines on the two applications mentioned above.

2   Background

In this work, we consider $G = (V, E)$ as an undirected and unweighted graph, where V and E represent the set of nodes and edges in G, respectively. We use $\bar{E}$ to denote the complement of E, i.e., $\bar{E} = \{(u, v) | u \in V, v \in V, (u, v) \notin E\}$. We use $N(u, G)$ to represent the set of neighbors of u in G and $\Gamma(u, G)$ to denote the distance-2 neighbors of u. Let $S \subseteq G$ be a subgraph of G. We use $deg(u, S)$ to denote the degree of u in S. In some cases we consider a directed graph G' in which $deg^-(u, G')$ and $deg^+(u, G')$ denotes the in-degree and out-degree of u in G', respectively. In our notations, we omit G when it is obvious.

The k-core, denoted by $C_k(G)$, is the maximal connected subgraph $S \subseteq G$ where every vertex has at least k connections in S, i.e., $deg(u, S) \geq k \; \forall u \in G$. The core number of a vertex is the largest k value for which a k-core contains the vertex. Here, $K(u, G)$ denotes the core number of u in G, and $K(G)$ is the core vector, which is the core numbers of all vertices in G. The maximum k-core(s) of a graph are the (non-empty) k-cores with largest value of k. The k-shell of a graph is the set of nodes with core number k [11] and a subcore is a connected subgraph of nodes with core number k [32]. The k-cores (for all k) are computed by recursively removing vertices with degree less than k and their adjacent edges, while assigning core numbers during the process, which takes $O(|E|)$ time [8].

We define the subset of neighbors of a node u based on the relative core numbers: $\Delta_<(u, G)$ denotes the neighbors with smaller core numbers, i.e., $\{v : v \in N(u, G) \land K(v, G) < K(u, G)\}$ and $\Delta_=(u, G)$ is the neighbors with equal core numbers. Similarly, $\Delta_>(u, G)$ and $\Delta_\geq(u, G)$ are defined.

3   Related Work

Network resilience is the capability of a network to maintain or restore its function under faults. Characterizing the resilience of a network is important for critical systems such as power grids and transportation systems [24]. Characterization of the resilience is made with respect to various graph characteristics, such as components and paths [34]. One interesting direction in this context is the resilience of the core structure. Core decomposition is one of the most widely used graph algorithms thanks to its linear complexity [36]. However, it is quite sensitive to changes in the graph and there are a few studies to characterize and improve its robustness [1,10,14,22,44]. Here we summarize the literature on core resilience and explore its significance in two motivating applications: finding critical edges and identifying influential spreaders.

Table 1. Comparison of previous works on core resilience and our work.

	[1]	[22]	[10]	[14]	[44]	Our work
Graph structure	Max cores	Entire graph	Entire graph	Entire graph	k-shells	Core number
Edge insertion	Yes	No	No	No	Yes	Yes
Edge removal	Yes	Yes	No	No	Yes	Yes

Core Resilience. Adiga and Vullikanti found that the stability of maximum k-cores under noise and sampling perturbations does not degrade in a monotonic way [1]. Laishram et al. defined the core resilience of a graph as the correlation between the core number rankings of the top r% nodes before and after p% edges or nodes are removed at random [22]. As computing this is costly, they proposed Core Strength and Core Influence measures as proxy to quantify the resilience of a node's core number upon node or edge deletions. Burleson-Lesser et al. modeled network robustness by using the histogram of core numbers [10] and found that ecological and financial networks with U-shaped histograms are resilient to node deletion attacks. Dey et al. defined a graph's stability based on changes in each node's core number upon node removals and studied identifying critical nodes to delete to maximize the number of nodes falling from their initial cores [14]. More recently, Zhou et al. studied attack strategies to change the core numbers of the nodes by rewiring edges [44]. Unlike those studies, we focus on node-based core resilience and consider both removal and insertion. For a given node, we quantify the resilience of its core number upon edge insertion and removals. Table 1 compares our work and previous studies on core resilience.

Finding Critical Edges. A related line of work has proposed problems to minimize and maximize the size of a k-core by inserting/removing nodes/edges. For the removal, the motivation is often to find critical nodes/edges that should be kept in the graph to avoid unraveling in social networks or be watched against targeted attacks in infrastructure networks [29,42,43,46]. In the context of core resilience, such nodes/edges are the weak structures with low resilience against removal and are suitable for targeted attacks. Regarding the insertion, the objective is to find new edges that can increase the user engagement [38,45] or incentivize existing nodes to stay engaged so that other nodes are kept engaged as well [9,23,41]. In the scope of core resilience, such nodes/edges are the critical graph structures that are most vulnerable to increases in core numbers or core sizes. All those works consider a specific k-core and study targeted attacks to change the core structure with a minimal number of edge/node changes. In this work, we focus on the core numbers and use our new node-based core resilience measures to select a limited number of edges so as to maximize the number of nodes whose core numbers change (see Sect. 5.2).

Identifying Influential Spreaders. Another application that core numbers are heavily used is identifying influential spreaders [20]. Influential spreaders are the nodes that determine how information spreads over the network or how a virus is propagated [4,18]. SIR (Susceptible-Infected-Recovered) model is a classical tool to measure the influence of a given set of nodes [37]. In the SIR model, a set of initially infected nodes are chosen which will spread the disease at each time step, t. The fraction of infected nodes, denoted by $S(t)$, is used to measure the spread after t iterations. Kitsak et al. demonstrated that the most efficient spreaders are located in the highest k-shells [20]. Wang et al. discovered that greedily choosing multiple spreaders may result in some of them being too close to each other and hence their influence overlaps [39]. They proposed the IKS algorithm to select nodes from different k-shells based on the highest node information entropy, which outperforms the other centrality or core-number based measures. Considering the success of core-based measures, we use node-based core resilience as a proxy to identify influential spreaders (see Sect. 5.3).

4 Node-Based Core Resilience

Earlier studies mostly defined core resilience measures for the entire graph. One exception is the core strength (CS) definition by Laishram et al. [22], which aims to measure the resilience of a node's core number upon edge removals and is defined as $CS(u, G) = |\Delta_{\geq}(u, G)| - K(u, G) + 1$. They claim that in order to decrease $K(u, G)$, at least $CS(u, G)$ connections from u must be removed. Here we show that this claim is not true by a simple counterexample and give empirical evidence to show how frequently it fails in practice.

Consider the toy graph in Fig. 1a. $CS(v_3)$ is 3, which means that at least three edges of v_3 should be removed to decrease its core number, according to Laishram et al. [22]. However, if we remove only (v_3, v_2) and (v_3, v_4), $K(v_3)$ decreases to 1. Note that removing two edges does not always decrease $K(v_3)$, e.g.,. deleting (v_3, v_1) and (v_3, v_2) does not affect $K(v_3)$. Depending on the edges being removed, other nodes may have their core numbers changed too, and this cascading effect may result in decreasing the core number of the vertex of interest. Hence, not only the count but also the position of the removed edges matters in quantifying the node-based core resilience.

One question is how likely to see such structures, where removing less than $CS(u)$ edges decreases $K(u)$, in real-world networks. We perform a simple experiment to check this. We consider the nodes in the maximum k-cores with a CS of at least two. For each node, we remove one of its edges and observe its core number changes. We repeat this for each edge of a node. Removing even a single edge is sufficient around 10% of the time to decrease the core number (as shown in [19]). Hence, the CS definition also fails frequently in practice.

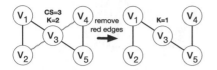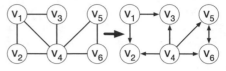

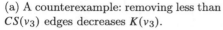

(a) A counterexample: removing less than $CS(v_3)$ edges decreases $K(v_3)$.

(b) A toy graph (left) and its removal dependency graph (right)

Fig. 1. Illustrative examples

As the CS definition is inaccurate in capturing the core resilience of a node upon edge removals, we define a new measure, Removal Strength, to compute the likelihood of a node's core number change (Sect. 4.1). Moreover, we propose a new measure, Insertion Strength, to assess the stability of a node's core number after an edge insertion (Sect. 4.2).

4.1 Resilience Against Edge Removal

We capture a node's core resilience against edge removals by analyzing its dependency on neighbor nodes. We focus on single edge removal, with a conjecture that multiple edge removals can be approximated by considering multiple single edge removals.

We define that the node u is dependent on node v, denoted as a relationship $v \rightarrow u$, if $K(u)$ decrements after removing the edge (u, v). For a given graph $G = (V, E)$, we define the *removal dependency graph*, denoted by $G^{rd} = (V, E^{rd})$, as a directed graph such that an edge $(u, v) \in E^{rd}$ if $(u, v) \in E$ and $K(v, G \setminus (u, v)) < K(v, G)$. We give an example in Fig. 1b. For the toy graph on the left, the corresponding removal dependency graph (G^{rd}) is given on the right. In the G^{rd}, v_2 has two in-neighbors (v_1 and v_4) which means it is dependent on v_1 and v_4. For an edge in G, if neither node is dependent on the other, then no edge will appear in the G^{rd}, such as (v_1, v_4). If each node is dependent on another, then there are two edges in both directions, as for (v_5, v_6).

In-degree and out-degree of a node in the removal dependency graph give important insights about its core resilience. A node with a large in-degree is dependent on many of its neighbors, hence removing a nearby edge could reduce its core number, implying a lower core resilience. We define *In-Degree Removal Strength* of a node u, $RS_{ID}(u)$, to quantify the resilience of u to retain its core number upon edge removal(s): $RS_{ID}(u) = \frac{1}{deg^-(u,G^{rd})}$. The higher a node's out-degree in the dependency graph, the more strength it has to change the other nodes' core numbers. We define *Out-Degree Removal Strength* of a node u, $RS_{OD}(u)$, to quantify the strength of u to change the core number of other nodes: $RS_{OD}(u) = deg^+(u, G^{rd})$.

4.1.1 Removal Strength Computation

A naive way to compute the removal dependency graph is to run incremental core decomposition algorithm for every single edge removal [32,33], which will be costly. Here we propose efficient heuristics by using key observations about the core structure.

We define node $u \in G$ as **vulnerable** if $K(u, G) = |\Delta_{\geq}(u, G)|$. For a vulnerable node u, the set of edges (u, v) where $v \in \Delta_{\geq}(u, G)$ is called the **sensitive edges of** u (also called as equal edges in [46]).

Lemma 1. *If a sensitive edge (u, v) of a vulnerable node u is removed, then $K(u, G)$ will decrease.*

Proof. Proofs of Lemmas 1–7 are available in the extended version [19].

Sensitive edges of a vulnerable node provide a way to group certain edges whose removal yields the same core vector, as first shown in [46].

Lemma 2. *For a vulnerable node u, removing any sensitive edge yields the same core vector, i.e., $K(G \setminus \{(u, v_1)\}) = K(G \setminus \{(u, v_2)\})$ where both edges are sensitive.*

According to [17], k-**corona** is a maximal connected subgraph of vulnerable vertices with the same core number, k. Formally, $S \subseteq G$ is a k-corona if $\forall u \in S$, $K(u, G) = k$ and u is a vulnerable vertex. We define k-**corona adjacent edge set**, $KAES(S)$, as the union of the sensitive edges of the vulnerable nodes in a k-corona S, i.e., $\bigcup_{u \in S} \{(u, v) | v \in \Delta_{\geq}(u, G)\}$.

Lemma 3. *When an edge (u, v) is removed from the graph, there will be a change in the core numbers if and only if the removed edge (u, v) is part of a $KAES$.*

Lemma 4. *For a k-corona S, removing any edge in $KAES(S)$ yields the same core vector, i.e., $K(G \setminus \{(u, v)\}) = K(G \setminus \{(x, y)\})$ for $(u, v), (x, y) \in KAES(S)$.*

We define the subset of nodes whose core numbers change after removing a single edge as **Core Changed Nodes (CCN)**. According to Lemma 4, for a k-corona S, if we choose any edge $(u, v) \in KAES(S)$ to delete, then we will get the same core vector. Hence we denote the set of nodes whose core numbers change after removing any edge in a $KAES(S)$ as $CCN_{KAES(S)}$.

Instead of examining every single edge in a graph, we can utilize $CCN_{KAES(S)}$ to efficiently detect the changes in the core numbers of nodes. Assume w.l.o.g. that $K(u) \leq K(v)$. If u is a vulnerable node, then, by Lemma 1, deleting an edge (u, v) will decrement the core number of u. If u is not a vulnerable node, we need to look at the properties of both u and v. If v is also not a vulnerable node, then the edge $(u, v) \notin KAES$, and there will be no changes in $K(u)$ or $K(v)$ (by Lemma 3). However, if the node v is vulnerable, we need to consider the following two cases to determine the changes in $K(v)$:

Case 1: $K(u) = K(v)$. Here, (u, v) is a sensitive edge, and deleting (u, v) will decrement $K(v)$ (Lemma 1). In this case, $K(u)$ will also decrement if it becomes affected by the changes in $K(v)$. This information is actually captured by the CCN set. If two nodes are in a same CCN, a change in the core number of one node affects the core number of the other node. Hence, if u and v are in the same $CCN_{KAES(S)}$ for any k-corona S, then their core numbers depend on each other.

Case 2: $K(u) < K(v)$. In this case, $K(v)$ will not change, as shown by [32]. Regarding $K(u)$, as u is not a vulnerable node, it has at least $K(u)+1$ neighbors in its k-core. Since v is not in the k-core of u, there will still be at least $K(u)$ neighbors in u's k-core in $G \setminus \{(u,v)\}$, and thus $K(u)$ will not change either.

4.1.2   Removal Strength Algorithm

Building on the definitions and observations above, we propose RSC algorithm (Algorithm 1) to compute RS_{ID} and RS_{OD} for each node in a given graph. At the beginning, we find the k-core(s) of a graph using the classical peeling based algorithm proposed by Batagelj et al. [7] (line 4). Then using the BFS traversal, we compute the set of k-coronas ($\mathcal{S}$) in every k-core subgraph (line 6). Since removing an edge $(u,v) \notin KAES$ does not affect the core number of any node (by Lemma 3), we only consider the edges $(u,v) \in KAES$ in each k-core. For each k-corona S, we find the $KAES$ (line 8). Thanks to Lemma 4, we remove only one edge in $KAES(S)$ and compute $CCN_{KAES(S)}$ for a $KAES(S)$ (line 9) by using the incremental core decomposition algorithm from [33]. Next, we

---

Algorithm 1: RSC: Removal Strength Computation $(G(V, E))$

---

1 **Input:** $G\ (V, E)$: graph
2 **Output:** RS_{ID}, RS_{OD}: in and out-degree removal strength, respectively
3 $G^{rd}\ (V, E')\leftarrow$ empty graph   // removal dependency graph
4 Compute all the k-cores of G, $C_k(G)$, and put in $\mathcal{C}$
5 **foreach** k-core $C_k(G) \in \mathcal{C}$ **do**
6 | Compute all k-coronas in $C_k(G)$ and put in $\mathcal{S}$
7 | **foreach** k-corona $S \in \mathcal{S}$ **do**
8 | | Find $KAES(S)$
9 | | Delete any single edge $e \in KAES(S)$, compute
   | | $CCN_{KAES(S)}$ // by [33]
10 **foreach** $u \in V$ **do**
11 | **if** $K(u) = |\Delta_{\geq}(u, G)|$ **then**
12 | | **foreach** $v \in N_u$ **do**
13 | | | **if** $K(u) \leq K(v)$ **then**
14 | | | | E'.push((v, u))   // $K(u)$ will decrement, by Lemma 1
15 | **else**
16 | | **foreach** v in N_u **do**
17 | | | **if** $K(v) = K(u)$ & $K(v) = |\Delta_{\geq}(v, G)|$ &
18 | | | u and v are in a same $CCN_{KAES(S)}$ **then**
19 | | | | E'.push((v, u))   // $K(u)$ will decrement, by Case 1
20 **foreach** u in V **do**
21 | $RS_{ID}(u) \leftarrow \frac{1}{deg^-(u, G^{rd})}$, $RS_{OD}(u) \leftarrow deg^+(u, G^{rd})$
22 Return RS_{ID}, RS_{OD}

---

use Lemma 1 and the two observations (Case 1 and 2) to quickly determine whether the core numbers will change after each edge removal (lines 10–19). At the end, we calculate and return the in-degree and out-degree removal strengths of all the nodes by using G^{rd} (lines 20–22).

Time and Space Complexity. Line 4, as well as lines 10–19 takes $O(|E|)$ time. In the worst case, lines 5–9 takes $O(|V| \cdot |E|)$ time—if each node is a k-corona, one edge is removed per node, hence $|V|$ edge removals in total (line 9) and each edge removal takes $O(|E|)$ time per [33]. Overall time complexity is $O(|V| \cdot |E|)$, but this is a loose bound as the number of k-coronas is significantly less than $|V|$ in real-world networks (even for large networks we observe the number of k-coronas to be small, requiring us to remove fewer edges, as shown in Table 2 column 4 (% Gain)). In addition to graph $(O(|E|))$, we store $|\Delta_{\geq}(u, G)|$ values $(O(|V|))$, component ids to bookkeep $CCN_{KAES(S)}$ for each node $(O(|V|))$, and RS_{ID}, RS_{OD} values $(O(|V|))$. Overall space complexity is $O(|E|)$.

4.2   Resilience Against Edge Insertion

We now characterize the resilience of a node's core number against edge insertions. We again focus on the impact of a single edge change, consider the changes in a node's core number based on new links it forms with other nodes, and model the resilience accordingly. Regarding the set of edge insertions, it is impractical and unrealistic to think about all possible new links between any pair of unconnected nodes, namely $\bar{E}$. It is impractical because real-world networks are sparse, i.e., $|E| << \binom{|V|}{2}$, which implies $|\bar{E}| >> |E|$. It is unrealistic as it is unexpected that a link will form between two nodes if they have no common neighbors, i.e., if they are not distance-2 neighbors [25,30]. Even the number of non-neighbor node pairs with at least one common neighbor is too large to be considered, reaching up to $100 \cdot |E|$ for some real-world networks. Furthermore, those node pairs are not located homogeneously in the graph; some nodes (mostly low-degree) have very few (or no) distance-2 neighbors, hence it is not clear how to define insertion core resilience for those (see [19] for statistics).

To address these issues, we consider a fixed number (b) of edge insertions for each node and construct the *insertion candidate graph*, G^{ic}, accordingly. Here, we fix $b = 5$ as it is close to the average degrees of the networks used in experiments and no significant advantage is observed for larger b values. For any node $u \in G$, and its distance-2 neighbors $\Gamma(u)$, we consider the below cases to select the edges and add to G^{ic}:

- If $|\Gamma(u)| > b$, choose b random edges (u, v) such that $v \in \Gamma(u)$.
- Else, choose all (u, v) edges such that $v \in \Gamma(u)$ and choose $b - |\Gamma(u)|$ random (u, w) edge(s) such that $w \in V$ (and $w \notin \Gamma(u)$).

Note that b ensures a lower bound on the degree of a node in G^{ic}, there can be nodes with larger degree due to random edges coming from the other nodes.

We define the dependency relationships between nodes by using the insertion candidate graph, G^{ic}. For each edge $(u, v) \in G^{ic}$, we check how the core numbers of u and v change when (u, v) is inserted to G. u is said to be dependent on node v, denoted as a relationship $v \rightarrow u$, if $K(u)$ increases after inserting the edge (u, v). For a given graph $G = (V, E)$ and $G^{ic} = (V, E^{ic})$, we define *insertion dependency graph*, $G^{id} = (V, E^{id})$, as a directed graph such that an edge $(u, v) \in E^{id}$ if $(u, v) \in E^{ic}$ and $K(v, G \cup (u, v)) > K(v, G)$. Here, G^{id} is always a subgraph of G^{ic}. We give an example in Fig. 2. For the toy graph on the left, corresponding insertion candidate graph is given in the middle (for $b = 2$). All the nodes except v_2 has at least two distance-2 neighbors. To ensure v_2 has two edges, we randomly select a node, v_5, and put an edge between them. Straight edges in the candidate graph are the edges due to the distance-2 neighborhood (the if condition above) and the dashed edge is the random edge (from the else condition). The corresponding insertion dependency graph is shown on the right. For example, inserting (v_3, v_5) edge would increase $K(v_5)$ and does not impact $K(v_3)$, hence $(v_3 \rightarrow v_5)$ is put.

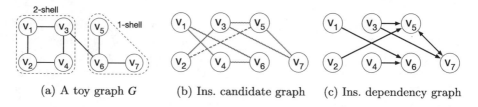

(a) A toy graph G (b) Ins. candidate graph   (c) Ins. dependency graph

Fig. 2. Examples for insertion candidate ($b = 2$) **and dependency graphs.**

A node with a large in-degree is dependent on many of its distance-2 (or random) neighbors, implying a lower core resilience. We define *In-Degree Insertion Strength* of a node u, IS_{ID}, to measure the node's ability to preserve its core number after edge insertion: $IS_{ID}(u) = \frac{1}{deg^-(u, G^{id})}$. A node with a large-out degree implies the ability to increase the core numbers of other nodes. We define *Out-Degree Insertion Strength* of a node u, IS_{OD}, to measure the strength of a node to impact the nodes around it: $IS_{OD}(u) = deg^+(u, G^{id})$.

4.2.1 Insertion Strength Computation

A naive computation of the insertion dependency graph is to run incremental core decomposition algorithm for every single edge insertion [32,33], which is costly. Here we consider four lemmas that help to determine the core number changes without running the incremental algorithm.

Lemma 5. *For a node u such that $K(u, G) = |\Delta_>(u, G)|$, adding a new edge (u, v) s.t. $K(v, G) > K(u, G)$ will increment $K(u)$, i.e., $K(u, G \cup (u, v)) = K(u, G) + 1$.*

Lemma 6. *For two non-neighbor nodes u and v, $(u, v) \notin E$, such that $K(u, G) = K(v, G) = k$, if $|\Delta_>(u, G)| = K(u, G)$ and $|\Delta_>(v, G)| = K(v, G)$, then adding a new edge (u, v) will increment $K(u)$ and $K(v)$.*

Lemma 7. *Consider a node $u \in G$ such that $|\Delta_>(u, G)| = K(u, G) - 1$. Say u has a neighbor w for which $K(u, G) = K(w, G)$ and $|\Delta_>(w, G)| = K(w, G)$. Adding a new edge (u, v) such that $K(v, G) > K(u, G)$ will increment $K(u)$ and $K(w)$.*

4.2.2   Insertion Strength Algorithm

We use the above lemmas (Lemma 5 to Lemma 7) to design ISC (Insertion Strength Computation) algorithm which creates the insertion dependency graph by determining the changes in the core numbers (pseudocode is in [19]). We start by computing the k-cores by [8]. We consider the edges of G^{ic}, which is given, to build the dependency graph of insertion. To construct the G^{id}, we check whether each edge $e \in G^{ic}$ can be handled by the lemmas given in Sect. 4.2.1. If the conditions in any of the lemmas are satisfied, we can readily determine the dependency graph and tell if inserting the new edge (u, v) will change the $K(u)$ and/or $K(v)$. If the edge does not fit to any of the lemmas, we use the incremental core decomposition algorithm [33] to determine the new core numbers. For each of the cases, if there is any increase in $K(u)$ and/or $K(v)$, we update the G^{id} by inserting directed edges based on the core number changes. At the end, we calculate and return the insertion strength measures of each node $u \in G$ by using the G^{id}.

Time and Space Complexity. In the worst case, incremental core decomposition algorithm [33], which takes $O(|E|)$, is run for each edge in G^{ic}. There is $O(b \cdot |V|)$ edges in G^{ic} where b is a constant. In total, the time complexity is $O(|V| \cdot |E|)$. However, this is a loose bound as we show runtime results in Sect. 5. In addition to graph ($O(|E|)$), we store $|\Delta_>(u, G)|$ values ($O(|V|)$) and IS_{ID}, IS_{OD} values ($O(|V|)$). Overall space complexity is $O(|E|)$.

Table 2. Statistics for the networks (first two columns) and runtime results for edge removal and edge insertion (in seconds). %Gain denotes the savings how much less edges are processed by our algorithm than the naive approach for edge removal. $\frac{|E^{ic}|}{|E|}$ denotes the ratio of the number of edges in the insertion candidate graph to the actual graph. Sp. is the speedup of our algorithms against the naive approaches.

Graph	$|V|$	$|E|$	Removal				Insertion			
			% Gain	Naive (s)	RSC (s)	Sp.	$\frac{|E^{ic}|}{|E|}$	Naive (s)	ISC (s)	Sp.
as19971108	3015	5156	50.2 %	4.88	2.93	1.67×	2.79	1.10	0.75	1.46×
as19990309	4759	8896	54.4 %	12.38	6.35	1.95×	2.58	1.70	1.31	1.30×
bio-dmela	7393	25569	79.4 %	56.96	12.85	4.43×	1.40	38.26	26.60	1.44×
ca-CondMat	21363	91286	89.0 %	575.82	67.19	8.57×	1.11	475.15	377.32	1.26×
ca-Erdos992	5094	7515	39.1 %	10.93	7.47	1.46×	3.11	7.48	5.23	1.43×
ca-GrQc	4158	13422	84.4 %	17.82	3.47	5.14×	1.39	32.41	26.66	1.22×
inf-openflights	2939	15677	86.8 %	15.67	2.49	6.29×	0.90	2.64	2.28	1.16×
inf-power	4941	6594	63.8 %	9.36	3.96	2.36×	2.76	504.87	486.43	1.04×
jazz	198	2742	97.8 %	0.43	0.06	7.17×	0.35	1.00	0.94	1.06×
p2p-Gnutella08	6301	20777	80.3 %	40.83	8.99	4.54×	1.45	951.50	918.05	1.04×
p2p-Gnutella09	8114	26013	78.8 %	63.81	14.51	4.40×	1.49	769.12	713.63	1.08×
soc-hamsterster	2426	16630	93.6 %	13.03	1.27	10.26×	0.72	4.82	4.22	1.14×
soc-wiki-Vote	889	2914	81.2 %	0.88	0.29	3.03×	1.46	1.45	1.09	1.33×
tech-routers-rf	2113	6632	77.8 %	4.26	1.30	3.28×	1.50	2.46	1.98	1.25×
tech-WHOIS	7476	56943	89.9 %	128.82	14.51	8.88×	0.65	6.59	5.60	1.18×
USAir97	332	2461	91.2 %	0.28	0.08	3.50×	0.65	0.12	0.09	1.46×
web-spam	4767	37375	91.5 %	52.48	5.28	9.94×	0.63	7.05	5.17	1.36×

5   Experimental Evaluation

We conduct experiments on real-world networks of various types and sizes to evaluate the efficiency and effectiveness of our node-strength measures. Table 2 (first three columns) shows the statistics of the networks, obtained from SNAP[1] and Network Repository[2]. All experiments are performed on a Linux operating system (v. 3.10.0-1127) running on a machine with Intel(R) Xeon(R) Gold 6130 CPU processor at 2.10 GHz with 192 GB memory. We implemented our algorithms in Python 3.6.8. **Our implementation is publicly available[3].**

Since we consider random edge selections to construct G^{ic} and calculate IS_{ID} and IS_{OD}, we repeat insertion experiments 10 times to account for randomness and report the average strength measure for each node. Note that the standard deviation in those computations is quite low, e.g., in `inf-openflights` graph, the standard deviation is less than .18 for most nodes where more than half of the nodes have zero (or close to zero) standard deviation (details are in [19]).

---

[1] http://snap.stanford.edu/.
[2] http://networkrepository.com/.
[3] https://github.com/erdemUB/ECMLPKDD23.

5.1 Runtime Results

We first compare the runtime performances of our RSC and ISC algorithms against the naive strategy which simply runs incremental core decomposition algorithms for each edge removal and edge insertion. One important note is that the three approaches (Subcore, Purecore, and Traversal) proposed in [32] give different behaviors in our removal and insertion experiments. Although the Traversal algorithm is shown to be the best in [32] for both single edge removal and insertion, we observe that the Subcore algorithm can be made faster for edge insertion in our experiments. The key is to precompute all the subcores in each k-core and reuse when handling edge insertions. We use this pre-calculation technique and Subcore algorithm in our edge insertion experiments, whereas the Traversal algorithm is used in our edge removal experiments.

Table 2 gives the results. For the edge removal, we are able to remove 78.2% less edges, on average, when compared to the naive approach (fourth column in Table 2). This translates to 5.11× faster runtime on average. For edge insertion, our algorithm well utilizes the lemmas in Sect. 4.2.1 and gives 1.25× faster computation when compared to the naive approach.

5.2 Finding Critical Edges

Here, we compare our node resilience measures to several baselines for finding critical edges in edge removal and insertion scenarios. We use four baselines: Random, Core Number, Degree, Core Strength. Each method identifies a limited number (c) of critical edges to maximize the impact on the core numbers of affected nodes. For Random, we repeat experiments 50 times and take the average. For Core Number, Degree, and Core Strength; the score of each edge is determined by the sum of its end points' values and c edges with the highest score are considered. We assess each method by the percentage of nodes affected, F, (decreased or increased from the initial core number) by the removal or insertion of the budget number of edges. For all experiments, we vary the budget (c) from 50 to 1000 and evaluate our results. For better visualization, we show the results from budget 600 to 1000 in Fig. 3(c) and Fig. 3(d).

5.2.1 Edge Removal Experiments.

We use RS_{ID} and RS_{OD} to select c critical edges to remove from the graph. For our measures, the score of each edge is set as the sum of its endpoints' RS_{ID} or RS_{OD} values. For RS_{ID}, we choose c edges with the lowest scores as a node with lower RS_{ID} is more likely to change its core number on edge removal, whereas, for RS_{OD}, we select c edges with the highest score as a node with larger RS_{OD} affect other nodes' core numbers more. We also pay attention to not selecting no more than one edge from any $KAES(S)$, as removing any edges in $KAES(S)$ produces the same core vector for a k-corona S by Lemma 4. For Random, we choose c random edges from the graph. Figure 3 (top row) shows the results for four graphs (results for other graphs are in [19]). Both RS_{ID} and RS_{OD} outperform the baselines. RS_{ID} is slightly better than RS_{OD} in some graphs and significantly better in a few.

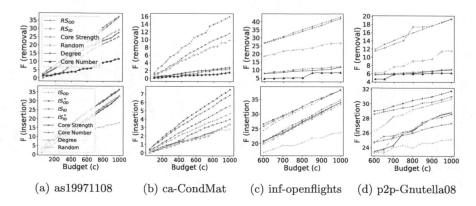

(a) as19971108   (b) ca-CondMat   (c) inf-openflights   (d) p2p-Gnutella08

Fig. 3. Finding critical edges by our methods and baselines for edge removal (top row) and edge insertion (bottom row).

5.2.2   Edge Insertion Experiments

We use IS_{OD} and IS_{ID} to select c critical edges to insert to the graph. We first consider all the non-neighbor node pairs who share at least two common neighbors, called as candidate set, and then select a subset of size c edges of the candidate set by using the baselines or our methods. When inserting an edge (u, v), if core number of both u and v increased by a previous insertion, we skip this edge. For our measures, we define the score of each candidate edge (u, v) as $\max(IS_{ID}(u), IS_{ID}(v))$ (likewise for IS_{OD}), then select the c edges with lowest scores to insert. Here, we consider maximum endpoint strength as the edge score, unlike the edge removal case where we considered sum, to keep the scores more regularized because the space of edge insertions is larger and can yield very large edge scores if the sum is applied. We choose the edges with the lowest score as they are the least resilient for incrementing core numbers. For Random, we choose c random edges from the candidate set. Figure 3 (bottom row) gives the results for four networks (rest are in [19]). Overall, IS_{ID} and IS_{OD} consistently outperform the baselines.

We also define a simple variant of our measures to handle the clique-like structures in which core numbers are difficult to increase. We consider the propagation effect of neighbor nodes by summing up the strength of a node with its neighbors' strengths. We define Neighbor Sum variants as $IS^*_{ID}(u) = IS_{ID}(u) + \sum_{v \in N(u)} IS_{ID}(v)$ (likewise for IS^*_{OD}). As above we define the score of each candidate edge the maximum strength of its endpoints and then select the c edges with the lowest scores to insert. As shown in Fig. 3 (bottom row), IS^*_{ID} and IS^*_{OD} significantly outperform all the other methods in ca-CondMat, which is a co-authorship network formed by cliques of authors on a paper.

5.3   Identifying Influential Spreaders

In this section, we consider the problem of identifying influential spreaders in the SIR model. We use our node resilience measures as well as three baselines to choose 20% nodes in a given graph as the initially infected node set. For our measures ($RS_{ID}, RS_{OD}, IS_{ID}, IS_{OD}$), we choose the node with largest strength from the highest k-shell, then do the same for the next highest shell (($k-1$)-shell), and so on until the 1-shell. Then we repeat this process until 20% of the nodes are chosen. Ties are broken randomly. As the highest strength nodes are more resilient upon graph changes, they are more important for influence maximization than others. Regarding the baselines, we choose the methods that rely on core numbers—the k-shell strategy [20], the IKS method [39], and the Core Strength measure (the nodes with the largest values)—to select the 20% initially infected node set. To ensure a smooth transmission in the SIR model, we fix S→I probability $\mu = 0.01$ and set the value of I→R probability β to be a little bit bigger than $\beta_{min} = \langle k \rangle / \langle k^2 \rangle$ [12], where $\langle k \rangle$ and $\langle k^2 \rangle$ are the first and the second moment of the degree distribution, as done in [39] (exact β values are in [19]). For each method, we run the model 50 times and take the average. We consider the percentage of affected nodes at time t, denoted as $S(t)$, to evaluate the spreading effect of the initially infected node set.

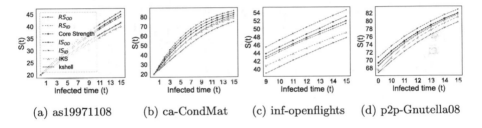

(a) as19971108   (b) ca-CondMat   (c) inf-openflights   (d) p2p-Gnutella08

Fig. 4. Identifying influential spreaders by our measures and baselines.

Figure 4 shows $S(t)$ as a function of $t \in [0, 15]$ for four networks (results for other graphs are in [19]). As t increases, $S(t)$ rises and eventually reaches a steady value. Overall, our node strength measures outperform the k-shell and IKS strategies. Core Strength measure shows superior performance than some of our measures but RS_{OD} consistently outperforms all the methods. The reason for this behavior is that the nodes with large RS_{ID} do not always have large core numbers whereas the nodes with large RS_{OD} are consistently in highest k-cores.

6   Conclusions and Future Work

In this paper, we studied the problem of node-based core resilience upon edge removals and edge insertions. We first showed that the Core Strength [22] does not correctly capture the core resilience of a node upon edge removals. Then we introduced the concept of dependency graph to capture the impact of neighbor nodes (for removal) and probable future neighbor nodes (for insertion) on the core number of a given node. We defined node strengths in dependency graphs based on in- and out-degrees and introduced efficient heuristics to compute those. Experiments show that our heuristics are faster than the naive approaches and our strength measures outperform the existing baselines on two key applications, finding critical edges and identifying influential spreaders. For future work, we plan to speed up the computation of insertion strength measures and also consider more realistic scenarios to construct the G^{ic4}.

Acknowledgments. Hossain and Sarıyüce were supported by NSF Award #1910063 and used resources of the Center for Computational Research at the University at Buffalo. Soundarajan was supported by NSF Award #1908048.

Ethical Statement. Our contribution is algorithmic in nature, building on previously proposed concepts. We work on public datasets. We do not foresee any ethical implications of our work.

References

1. Adiga, A., Vullikanti, A.K.S.: How robust is the core of a network? In: Blockeel, H., Kersting, K., Nijssen, S., Železný, F. (eds.) ECML PKDD 2013. LNCS (LNAI), vol. 8188, pp. 541–556. Springer, Heidelberg (2013). https://doi.org/10.1007/978-3-642-40988-2_35
2. Altaf-Ul-Amine, M., et al.: Prediction of protein functions based on k-cores of protein-protein interaction networks and amino acid sequences. Genome Inf. **14**, 498–499 (2003)
3. Andersen, R., Chellapilla, K.: Finding dense subgraphs with size bounds. In: Avrachenkov, K., Donato, D., Litvak, N. (eds.) WAW 2009. LNCS, vol. 5427, pp. 25–37. Springer, Heidelberg (2009). https://doi.org/10.1007/978-3-540-95995-3_3
4. Anderson, R.M., May, R.M.: Infectious Diseases of Humans: Dynamics and Control. Oxford University Press, Oxford (1992)
5. Bakshy, E., Hofman, J.M., Mason, W.A., Watts, D.J.: Everyone's an influencer: quantifying influence on twitter. In: Proceedings of the Fourth ACM International Conference on Web Search and Data Mining, pp. 65–74 (2011)
6. Balasundaram, B., Butenko, S., Hicks, I.V.: Clique relaxations in social network analysis: the maximum k-plex problem. Oper. Res. **59**(1), 133–142 (2011)
7. Batagelj, V., Zaversnik, M.: An O(m) algorithm for cores decomposition of networks. corr. arXiv preprint cs.DS/0310049 37 (2003)
8. Batagelj, V., Zaversnik, M.: Fast algorithms for determining (generalized) core groups in social networks. Adv. Data Anal. Classif. **5**(2), 129–145 (2011)
9. Bhawalkar, K., Kleinberg, J., Lewi, K., Roughgarden, T., Sharma, A.: Preventing unraveling in social networks: the anchored k-core problem. SIAM J. Disc. Math. **29**(3), 1452–1475 (2015)
10. Burleson-Lesser, K., Morone, F., Tomassone, M.S., Makse, H.A.: K-core robustness in ecological and financial networks. Sci. Rep. **10**(1), 1–14 (2020)
11. Carmi, S., Havlin, S., Kirkpatrick, S., Shavitt, Y., Shir, E.: A model of internet topology using k-shell decomposition. Proc. Natl. Acad. Sci. **104**(27), 11150–11154 (2007)

---

[4] https://ubir.buffalo.edu/xmlui/handle/10477/79221.

12. Castellano, C., Pastor-Satorras, R.: Thresholds for epidemic spreading in networks. Phys. Rev. Lett. **105**(21), 218701 (2010)
13. Chen, D., Lü, L., Shang, M.S., Zhang, Y.C., Zhou, T.: Identifying influential nodes in complex networks. Physica A: Stat. Mech. Appl. **391**(4), 1777–1787 (2012)
14. Dey, P., Maity, S.K., Medya, S., Silva, A.: Network robustness via global k-cores. In: Proceedings of the 20th International Conference on Autonomous Agents and MultiAgent Systems, pp. 438–446 (2021)
15. Faloutsos, M., Faloutsos, P., Faloutsos, C.: On power-law relationships of the internet topology. ACM SIGCOMM Comput. Commun. Rev. **29**(4), 251–262 (1999)
16. Giatsidis, C., Thilikos, D.M., Vazirgiannis, M.: D-cores: measuring collaboration of directed graphs based on degeneracy. Knowl. Inf. Syst. **35**(2), 311–343 (2013)
17. Goltsev, A.V., Dorogovtsev, S.N., Mendes, J.F.F.: k-core (bootstrap) percolation on complex networks: critical phenomena and nonlocal effects. Phys. Rev. E **73**(5), 056101 (2006)
18. Guille, A., Hacid, H., Favre, C., Zighed, D.A.: Information diffusion in online social networks: a survey. ACM Sigmod Rec. **42**(2), 17–28 (2013)
19. Hossain, J., Soundarajan, S., Sarıyüce, A.E.: Quantifying node-based core resilience. arXiv preprint arXiv:2306.12038 (2023)
20. Kitsak, M., et al.: Identification of influential spreaders in complex networks. Nat. Phys. **6**(11), 888–893 (2010)
21. Kortsarz, G., Peleg, D.: Generating sparse 2-spanners. J. Algor. **17**(2), 222–236 (1994)
22. Laishram, R., Sariyüce, A.E., Eliassi-Rad, T., Pinar, A., Soundarajan, S.: Measuring and improving the core resilience of networks. In: Proceedings of the 2018 World Wide Web Conference, pp. 609–618 (2018)
23. Laishram, R., Sariyuce, A.E., Eliassi-Rad, T., Pinar, A., Soundarajan, S.: Residual core maximization: an efficient algorithm for maximizing the size of the k-core. In: Proceedings of the 2020 SIAM International Conference on Data Mining, pp. 325–333. SIAM (2020)
24. Lewis, T.G.: The many faces of resilience. Commun. ACM **66**(1), 56–61 (2022)
25. Liben-Nowell, D., Kleinberg, J.: The link prediction problem for social networks. In: Proceedings of the Twelfth International Conference on Information and Knowledge Management, pp. 556–559 (2003)
26. Lin, J.H., Guo, Q., Dong, W.Z., Tang, L.Y., Liu, J.G.: Identifying the node spreading influence with largest k-core values. Phys. Lett. A **378**(45), 3279–3284 (2014)
27. Liu, C., Zhang, Z.K.: Information spreading on dynamic social networks. Commun. Nonlinear Sci. Numer. Simul. **19**(4), 896–904 (2014)
28. Medo, M., Zhang, Y.C., Zhou, T.: Adaptive model for recommendation of news. EPL (Europhys. Lett.) **88**(3), 38005 (2009)
29. Medya, S., Ma, T., Silva, A., Singh, A.: A game theoretic approach for core resilience. In: International Joint Conferences on Artificial Intelligence Organization (2020)
30. Newman, M.E.: Clustering and preferential attachment in growing networks. Phys. Rev. E **64**(2), 025102 (2001)
31. Purevsuren, D., Cui, G.: Efficient heuristic algorithm for identifying critical nodes in planar networks. Comput. Oper. Res. **106**, 143–153 (2019)
32. Sarıyüce, A.E., Gedik, B., Jacques-Silva, G., Wu, K.L., Çatalyürek, Ü.V.: Streaming algorithms for k-core decomposition. Proc. VLDB Endow. **6**(6), 433–444 (2013)
33. Sarıyüce, A.E., Gedik, B., Jacques-Silva, G., Wu, K.L., Çatalyürek, Ü.V.: Incremental k-core decomposition: algorithms and evaluation. VLDB J. **25**(3), 425–447 (2016)

34. Schaeffer, S.E., Valdés, V., Figols, J., Bachmann, I., Morales, F., Bustos-Jiménez, J.: Characterization of robustness and resilience in graphs: a mini-review. J. Complex Netw. **9**(2), cnab018 (2021)
35. Schwab, D.J., Bruinsma, R.F., Feldman, J.L., Levine, A.J.: Rhythmogenic neuronal networks, emergent leaders, and k-cores. Phys. Rev. E **82**(5), 051911 (2010)
36. Seidman, S.B.: Network structure and minimum degree. Social Netw. **5**(3), 269–287 (1983)
37. Sharkey, K.J.: Deterministic epidemic models on contact networks: correlations and unbiological terms. Theor. Popul. Biol. **79**(4), 115–129 (2011)
38. Sun, X., Huang, X., Jin, D.: Fast algorithms for core maximization on large graphs. Proc. VLDB Endow. **15**(7), 1350–1362 (2022)
39. Wang, M., Li, W., Guo, Y., Peng, X., Li, Y.: Identifying influential spreaders in complex networks based on improved k-shell method. Physica A: Stat. Mech. Appl. **554**, 124229 (2020)
40. Zareie, A., Sheikhahmadi, A.: A hierarchical approach for influential node ranking in complex social networks. Expert Syst. Appl. **93**, 200–211 (2018)
41. Zhang, F., Zhang, W., Zhang, Y., Qin, L., Lin, X.: OLAK: an efficient algorithm to prevent unraveling in social networks. Proc. VLDB Endow. **10**(6), 649–660 (2017)
42. Zhang, F., Zhang, Y., Qin, L., Zhang, W., Lin, X.: Finding critical users for social network engagement: the collapsed k-core problem. In: Thirty-First AAAI Conference on Artificial Intelligence (2017)
43. Zhao, K., Zhang, Z., Rong, Y., Yu, J.X., Huang, J.: Finding critical users in social communities via graph convolutions. IEEE Trans. Knowl. Data Eng. **35**(1), 456–468 (2023)
44. Zhou, B., Lv, Y., Mao, Y., Wang, J., Yu, S., Xuan, Q.: The robustness of graph k-shell structure under adversarial attacks. IEEE Trans. Circ. Syst. II: Express Briefs **69**(3), 1797–1801 (2021)
45. Zhou, Z., Zhang, F., Lin, X., Zhang, W., Chen, C.: K-core maximization: an edge addition approach. In: IJCAI, pp. 4867–4873 (2019)
46. Zhu, W., Chen, C., Wang, X., Lin, X.: K-core minimization: an edge manipulation approach. In: Proceedings of the 27th ACM International Conference on Information and Knowledge Management, pp. 1667–1670 (2018)

Construction and Training
of Multi-Associative Graph Networks

Adrian Horzyk[1]([✉])[ID], Daniel Bulanda[1][ID], and Janusz A. Starzyk[2,3][ID]

[1] AGH University of Krakow, Mickiewicza Av. 30, 30059 Krakow, Poland
horzyk@agh.edu.pl, daniel@bulanda.net
[2] University of Information Technology and Management in Rzeszow,
35225 Rzeszow, Poland
[3] Ohio University, Athens, OH 45701, USA

Abstract. Modern methods and networks of supervised learning use a vast amount of computational resources when adapting to large datasets. They are unable to incorporate new training examples into trained models quickly and to represent internal knowledge for quick adaptation to other computational tasks without retraining. The human brain is capable of representing and retrieving vast amounts of information and can create associations between its various pieces based on frequent relationships and patterns. The backpropagation algorithm is not the best and only way to train neural networks, especially since its use is limited to feed-forward architectures. Brain structures can be modeled using graph architectures that are not feed-forward but recursive with many feedback connections. This paper introduces Multi-Associative Graph Networks that enable the representation of associated training data and objects transformed from relational databases. These graphs store the data along with the most useful relationships to facilitate computational intelligence processes. We describe the associative transformation algorithm allowing for the transformation of any relational database into this graph network, reproducing stored relationships and enriching them with newly detected ones. We also introduce the tuning algorithm that learns to associate different priorities with different neurons representing objects to improve the relational dependencies and classification results. Finally, we draw conclusions from the comparisons to other state-of-the-art models.

Keywords: Associative graph neural networks · Associative transformation of relational databases · Relationship representation and enrichment · Multi-association · Prioritization · Associative inferences

1 Introduction

Supervised learning is currently the most widely used learning strategy working with many different types and structures of artificial neural networks. This type

Supported by AGH grant IDUB 1570, and Adrian Horzyk was partially supported by the Ministry of Education and Science (Agreement Nr 2022/WK/1).

© The Author(s), under exclusive license to Springer Nature Switzerland AG 2023
D. Koutra et al. (Eds.): ECML PKDD 2023, LNAI 14171, pp. 277–292, 2023.
https://doi.org/10.1007/978-3-031-43418-1_17

of learning is very useful in solving many practical tasks where we can collect training data and define targets as labels (for classification problems) or numerical values (for regression problems). On the other hand, supervised learning also has many limitations. First, it requires expert knowledge to label input data or define the target values used during the training process. Training data preparation can be costly and prone to human errors. Second, the initial choice of input values and targets limits the possible applications of trained models to tasks that use similar input features and outputs. Even transfer learning can be used with the same inputs and requires a costly training process to adapt the network. It is not possible to swap inputs with targets without preparing and training new models from scratch.

Human intelligence is based on acquired knowledge and a plastic nervous system. It allows us to create associations between seemingly unrelated pieces of information, which is essential for problem-solving, decision-making, and learning. Knowledge refers to the understanding and awareness of facts and skills acquired through experience or learning. Knowledge develops thanks to the ever-expanding associations between represented objects. Associations represent various relationships with different strengths resulting from the frequency of their occurrences or their reinforcement. So, the well-adapting machine learning knowledge-based system should develop and store associations between various pieces of information and not just focus on some of the feed-forward mathematical transformations that underpin many of today's neural networks.

Today, formal ontologies allow knowledge to be represented in a structured and formal way, e.g., [9,13,19–21], and [3]. We can also use associative graphs, such as knowledge graphs, which allow the representation of relationships between different pieces of information and facilitate the processes of inference, recommendations, and automatic search for significant relationships mentioned in [10], and [3].

This paper describes a relationship-oriented approach to knowledge representation and its use in the introduced Multi-Associative Graph Networks (MAGN) inspired and constructed on the basis of Associative Graph Data Structure (AGDS) [10], Aggregative Sorting Associative graphs (ASA-graphs) [12], and Deep Associative Semantic Neural Graphs (DASNG) [11]. This network facilitates the search for often-used relationships and decreases the computational complexity of various operations. It can be created for any relational database (RDB) using the associative transformation of an RDB or RDBs to a MAGN. Aggregated representations of duplicated features define different objects that share these features. Objects and features can define other objects represented by neurons whose connections represent one-to-one, one-to-many, or many-to-many relationships [16], so no join operations are necessary, saving time and computing power. The introduced reversible associative transformation of RDBs not only does not cause the loss of any data or relationships but automatically enriches the set of relationships represented in MAGNs, which facilitates searching, reasoning, and inference.

While RDBs relate only entities from different tables, the MAGNs aggregate the same and connect similar values of each attribute separately. Hence, the graph enriches the representation of similarities of all entities based on similar values that define them. This graph associates all objects representing entities of the transformed databases not only by means of defined primary and foreign keys but also by means of similarities and normalized distances between represented features, counting their occurrences (duplicates). It allows us to recall other objects according to their similarities and other relationships represented by weighted connections. Due to the proximity of related objects in the graph, we can accelerate processes of inference, recommendations, and classification and limit the number of search processes to closely connected neurons. With aggregated representations of duplicates and connections of neurons representing similar values, we can quickly establish various similarities like similar objects or frequent patterns without looping through many data stored in database tables. These graphs can also remember new relationships found in the form of new graph neurons and connections, facilitating similar processes in the future and updating knowledge representation. The obtained knowledge models representing relationships are necessary for developing advanced cognitive and artificial intelligence systems.

2   Essence of Data Relationship Representation

In computer science, we focus on data, data structures, data search, data retrieval, data sorting, databases, database management systems, data warehouses, data mining, etc., but what we are really interested in is finding valuable data relationships. Whenever we use similarities or dependencies between values or objects, search for larger or smaller values, look for next or previous objects in space or time, compute weighted sums, averages, products, mean values, standard deviations, etc., we aim to find data relationships and their strengths. The ability to find beneficial relationships is a product of human intelligence and knowledge, so we should model and represent them in artificial intelligence models. For example, similarity is one of the most valuable relationships that is often used by various computational intelligence algorithms to determine clusters or classes. We often use the proximity of various objects in space or their chronological order. Therefore, we need to develop efficient structures to store not only data but also detected or defined relationships.

Knowledge about ranges, extreme values, neighbors, duplicates, densities, averages, means, medians, standard deviations, sums, counts, frequent patterns, similarities, etc., facilitates efficient data representation. Therefore, we used ASA-graphs [12], which are self-balancing and self-organizing structures that represent all attribute values in B-trees combined with bidirectional sorted lists of all elements (Fig. 1). ASA-graphs developed the concept of B-trees [4], B+trees [14], clfB-trees [15], AVL-trees [1], and RB-trees [7], automatically aggregating and count all duplicated values representing them by the same nodes and connecting them in order. ASA-graphs use very efficient algorithms for searching, inserting, and removing data, outperforming many commonly used self-balancing trees and other commonly used data structures. Hence, all feature values are accessible in the logarithmic time of the number of unique feature values. The same computational time applies to the insert, remove, or update operations. Thus, the ASA-graphs can efficiently organize all non-key database attributes.

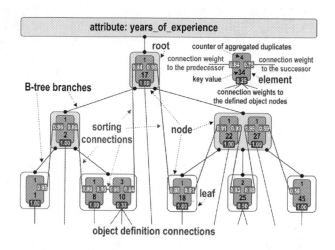

Fig. 1. ASA-graph structure [12] combining a sorted list with a self-balancing search B-tree spanned over all elements, consisting of nodes, B-tree branches, elements storing key values, counters of aggregated duplicates of these key values, and weights of connections that link other elements or object nodes.

RDBs represent some data relationships using primary and foreign keys, but the number and types of represented relationships are very limited. This limitation is due to the fact that RDBs are optimized for storing and retrieving data in a structured and efficient way, not for representing complex relationships. Therefore, RDBs do not efficiently represent complex relationships like hierarchies, causality, or similarity, which are important for knowledge models and AI systems.

To overcome RDB limitations, several approaches have been proposed, such as graph databases and knowledge graphs (KGs), which represent relationships and use ontologies that provide a formal way to represent relationships between different concepts [2,21]. KGs for a more comprehensive and rich representation of knowledge that is essential for natural language understanding, question-answering, and recommendation systems. KGs can be constructed from a variety of sources, such as structured data from databases, unstructured data from text documents, and semi-structured data from social media. KGs integrate different types of information and create a more comprehensive and accurate representation of knowledge. Knowledge graphs also facilitate the inference-making process and retrieval of information. Knowledge-based AI systems utilize knowledge graphs to perform tasks such as question-answering, language understanding, and more.

In this paper, the knowledge graph approach is developed by using the associative transformation of RDBs to a Multi-Associative Graph Network. This transformation automatically enriches the number of directly represented relationships between features and objects that become automatically associated. The created associations have different strengths, allowing for broader and deeper inference-making and classification.

3   Multi-Associative Graph Network

Definition 1. *Multi-Associative Graph Network (MAGN) (Fig. 2) is a graph that consists of neurons representing objects (like database entities), ASA-graphs representing aggregated, counted, and associated features as neurons, and edges representing relationships between features and objects, together with their strengths defined by the normalized distances between features or the number of occurrences of features and objects.*

The duplicated feature values are aggregated, counted, and represented by the same ASA-graph nodes that will be used as neurons. The same feature categories of different tables are consolidated by the same ASA-graph. Duplicates of objects are aggregated, counted, and represented by the same neurons. All relationships defined in the database by primary and foreign keys are transformed into connections between MAGN neurons.

Definition 2. *Two neurons in the MAGN are **associated** if there is at least one path of edges between these neurons with a non-zero product of connection weights on this path.*

There are usually many paths between neurons in the MAGN, so the neurons are usually associated, but these associations can have different strengths.

Definition 3. *Association strength between two neurons in the MAGN is a sum of products of connection weights on independent shortest paths between these two neurons, where independent means that these paths do not share neurons.*

MAGNs can be built for RDBs sharing the same categories of features or for a single RDB. First, entities of the tables that do not contain foreign keys are transformed. Subsequently, in the loop, entities of the tables containing the foreign keys related to the primary keys of the already transformed tables are transformed until all tables are transformed. In each step of the loop, all feature values of the transformed table are transformed into new ASA-graph elements if such values were not previously represented; otherwise, the counters of existing elements are incremented. Elements of ASA-graphs are connected to MAGN neurons representing primary keys of the transformed table. If the transformed

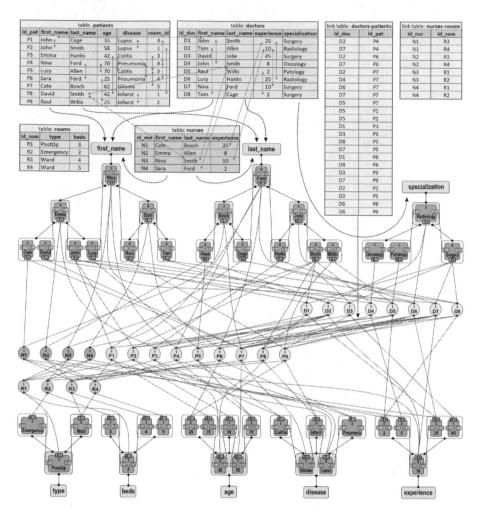

Fig. 2. MAGN constructed for a sample Small Hospital RDB describing patients, doctors, nurses, rooms, and their relationships, using associative transformation, enriching represented relationships. Red arrows present some vertical relationships that are automatically detected during the associative transformation of this RDB. (Color figure online)

table contains some foreign keys, the created MAGN neurons are connected to the existing neurons representing these keys in the MAGN. The transformation process is described by Principle 1 illustrated in Fig. 3 and is called the **associative transformation** of databases to MAGNs because the same features and objects are aggregated and connected due to their values and relationships. Moreover, various undefined relationships in databases are automatically detected, creating new associations between features and objects represented by neurons and their connections in MAGNs, enriching the number of represented relationships and expanding the represented knowledge.

Principle 1. *Transform only these RDB tables that do not contain foreign keys related to the tables that were not yet been transformed into the MAGN.*

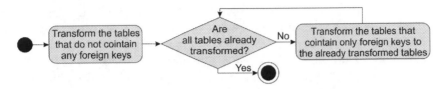

Fig. 3. The associative transformation algorithm of any RDBs used to create a MAGN.

First, it transforms only database tables with no foreign keys. As a result, the MAGN already contains the representation of some tables with which entities of the next tables can be associated until all tables are transformed. This principle does not strictly define the order in which tables are transformed but allows for different orders, which always end up with the same MAGN structure. One possible order of transforming the tables shown in Fig. 2 is: nurses, doctors, rooms, patients, doctor-patients, and nurses-rooms. At the top of this figure, there are tables defining entities of four different objects, defined by several categories, such as *first_name*, *last_name*, *experience*, *specialization*, *age*, *disease*, etc. Some of these categories (e.g., *first_name*, *last_name*, *experience*) are present in several tables, so they are consolidated and associated by the same ASA-graphs to enable broader and automatic inferences.

3.1 Representation of Horizontal and Vertical Relationships

RDB table (T_m) entities are only linked horizontally between tables by primary and foreign keys, while entities from the same tables are not vertically related. This major disadvantage costs search time, especially with Big Data. The MAGNs represent both horizontal and vertical relationships, so related objects are always quickly accessible, regardless of their number.

3.2 Consolidation of Attributes and Aggregation of Duplicates

Different RDB tables often use the same categories like first and last names (of employers, employees, suppliers, contributors, patients, doctors, customers), addresses, phones, e-mails, etc. Associative transformation aggregates all features of the same categories of all tables of all RDBs and represents them by the same ASA-graph (Figs. 1 and 2). This is time and memory efficient and allows for self-associations between objects defined by aggregated features. We can find and use associations between objects because they share the same or similar features represented by connected neurons. They can be used for clustering and classification.

Assuming we have N_C categories represented by N_A attributes in all RDB tables where $N_C \leq N_A$. During the associative transformation process, the attribute values of each transformed table are represented by an existing ASA-graph when that attribute's category is already represented in a MAGN (created during the transformation of another table) or otherwise by a new ASA-graph. After the transformation is finished, we achieve N_C ASA-graphs representing all categories and all attributes of all database tables of all integrated databases. In the example shown in Fig. 2, the same category attributes of different tables define separate ASA-graphs, and all these graphs are integrated with MAGN.

ASA-graphs not only efficiently organize features of the same categories but also weigh connections between adjacent numerical features to express their similarities in view of the range of values of the represented categories. Their connection weights are used in MAGNs. In each ASA-graph representing the numerical values of the C_n category, we can quickly establish the minimum and maximum values ($v_{min}^{C_n}$ and $v_{max}^{C_n}$) and the range of all values ($R^{C_n} = v_{max}^{C_n} - v_{min}^{C_n}$). On this basis, we can define the similarity $s_{i,i+1}^{C_n}$ of any two subsequent numerical values (features) $v_i^{C_n}$ and $v_{i+1}^{C_n}$ (where $v_i^{C_n} < v_{i+1}^{C_n}$) represented by the connected neurons ($V_i^{C_n}$ and $V_{i+1}^{C_n}$) in the ASA graph as:

$$s_{i,i+1}^{C_n} = 1 - \frac{(v_{i+1}^{C_n} - v_i^{C_n})}{R^{C_n}} \tag{1}$$

The similarity is always less than one ($s_{i,i+1}^{C_n} < 1$) because the connected neurons representing neighbor values always differ due to the aggregated representation of the duplicates. The similarity can be equal to zero only if the two extreme values of the attribute (min and max) are connected. Similarities of values are useful for finding similar objects or patterns. The defined similarities (1) between numerical values of the two connected neighbor neurons $V_i^{C_n}$ and $V_{i+1}^{C_n}$ can be used as the weight $w_{i,i+1}^{C_n} = s_{i,i+1}^{C_n}$ of their connection edge.

Non-numeric (symbolic) features are also represented by ASA-graphs in lexicographical order, using this structure, but the connections between adjacent neurons usually have zero weights. Sometimes it is possible to set weights to non-zero values and calculate similarities between symbolic values using various string-based similarity measures [18], e.g., embedding spaces [6], which can also be implemented here. In general, the similarity between any categorical or ordinal values can be measured and represented in ASA-graphs if the distance function $f(v_{i+1}^{C_n}, v_i^{C_n})$ is defined.

3.3   Associating Features and Objects

Features define objects (entities of database tables), so each neuron representing a feature $V_i^{C_n}$ can be used one or more times to define neurons representing objects (entities, patterns) $O_j^{T_m}$ from various tables T_m. Such objects can be related, and the relationships are represented by weighted connections (Fig. 2). The connections are bidirectional, but the weight depends on the direction of movement between the connected neurons. We define the connection weight from the value neuron $(V_i^{C_n})$ to the object neuron $(O_j^{T_m})$ as:

$$w_{V_i^{C_n}, O_j^{T_m}} = \frac{1}{d(V_i^{C_n})} \qquad (2)$$

and in the opposite direction as:

$$w_{O_j^{T_m}, V_i^{C_n}} = 1 \qquad (3)$$

where function d returns the number of duplicates of value $v_i^{C_n}$ represented by the node $V_i^{C_n}$. Hence, if the value node $V_i^{C_n}$ represents only one value $v_i^{C_n}$, this weight is equal to one and expresses that the object $O_j^{T_m}$ is unambiguously defined by that value. When there are some duplicates, no object can be unambiguously defined by this value, so the weight is correspondingly less than one according to (2). In the opposite direction, each defining feature should always be clearly indicated by the object, so the weights of these connections should not be distinguished (3).

Similarly, objects (entities) can define other objects (entities), and the relations between them can be one-to-one, one-to-many, or many-to-many, so depending on the number of objects defined by other objects, we also define the weights of such connections due to the direction of movement between objects and the number of the represented relations as follows:

$$w_{O_k^{T_n}, O_j^{T_m}} = \frac{1}{d(O_k^{T_n})} \qquad (4)$$

where the function d returns how many objects $O_j^{T_m}$ from the table T_m are defined by the object $O_k^{T_n}$.

Corollary 1. *In the MAGN, differently, than in RDBs, objects from different tables related in a many-to-many way are directly connected, so we do not lose time searching for foreign keys and joining related entities of different tables.*

MAGN neurons can be connected not only to the neurons they define but also to neurons representing related objects expressing their sequence or position in space. We can conclude that object B frequently comes after object A, and this frequency is measured and stored in the connection weight between the neurons representing these objects. Similarly, we can use the (frequent or non-frequent) proximity of other objects to the defined object(s). The preservation of such frequencies in the connection weights between related objects creates associations of the calculated strength between them. It allows for quick inference because we do not need to search again for such relationships that are already represented by the connections and their weights. Such weights are only updated locally when new data is inserted, removed, or changed in the MAGN. Weights can express not only the direct succession or proximity but can also vary with distance in sequence or space. Such relations are already used in many different neural networks [5], where the succession and proximity of the represented objects affect the weights of the connected neurons and allow them to process data differently.

3.4 Associative Prioritization Algorithm

MAGNs can solve common machine-learning tasks. Supervised learning is the most common type of machine learning, such as classification and regression. We have developed a prioritization algorithm that improves their efficiency and the representation of relational dependencies [8].

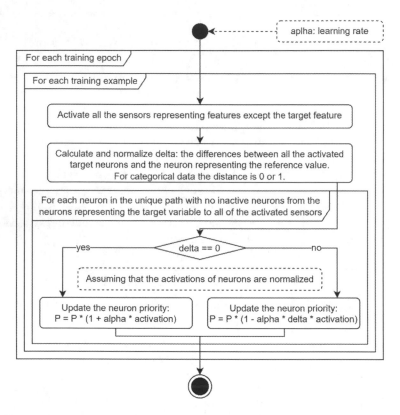

Fig. 4. The Training Phase of the Associative Prioritization Algorithm.

The associative prioritization algorithm is founded on the assumption that neurons are not equally important for the prediction of the target variable. Every MAGN neuron has a property called priority, which is a floating point number greater than or equal to zero, initially equal to one. The sum of the stimuli reaching a neuron is multiplied by its priority before it stimulates the other neurons via connections, so this acts as a simple activation function.

Neuron priorities are trained during the training phase. Only two hyperparameters control the learning process: training epoch number and learning rate α. The learning algorithm recursively searches all paths from the neurons representing the target variable to all inputs that were activated by the training example, avoiding any neurons that are no longer active. Then, the prediction error δ is propagated through each path to penalize neurons that reinforce wrong predictions and favor those that lead to correct predictions in proportion to their activation and learning rate. If $\delta = 0$, then the new priority is given by $P = P \times (1 + \alpha \times z)$, where z is the normalized activation of the neuron in the path, otherwise $P = P \times (1 - \alpha \times \delta \times z)$. In subsequent epochs, the process is repeated. Optionally, an early stop condition can be used to speed up the training phase without significantly affecting performance. Figure 4 is a flowchart that demonstrates the training phase of the associative prioritization algorithm.

Associative Prioritization is a powerful mechanism that enables better discrimination between patterns present in the training data for any arbitrarily selected target variable. This algorithm improved MAGN's overall performance in classification and regression tasks using a variety of popular datasets, as presented in the next section.

3.5   MAGN Implementation and Source Code

The MAGN source code is available at https://github.com/danbulnet/witchnet. The source code can be downloaded and compiled on multiple platforms. There are no specific minimal hardware requirements; however, since this is an in-memory model, the amount of RAM should scale with the amount of data being modeled. The code was tested on popular 64-bit operating systems, such as Windows 11, MacOS 13, and Linux Endevaour OS 2023. Benchmark source code is available at https://github.com/danbulnet/WitchnetBenchmarks.jl

4   Results of Experiments and Comparisons

We divided our experiments into two phases. The first part presents experiments with a machine learning regression task, comparing the results obtained by MAGNs with popular machine learning models. In the second part, we have selected 73 datasets from the Penn Machine Learning Benchmarks (PMLB) collection [17] curated for classification tasks to compare the MAGN performance with other popular machine learning models.

4.1   Regression Benchmark

We have implemented the MAGN to predict flat prices based on 23 numerical and categorical features like address (country, city, district), geographical coordinates, transport accessibility, usable area, floor, number of rooms, places for cars, facilities, and services, technical condition, year of building, and building type. Next, we compared it to the results obtained from popular machine learning models. This dataset contains information about the completed sale transactions of 25156 apartments in the years 2015–2020. The mean flat price is 335432 with a standard deviation equal to 201227. The cheapest flat costs 70500, and the most expensive one is 3115000.

We divided the dataset into 19999 training samples and 5157 test samples using the following models for comparisons:

– Random Forest regressor from the scikit-learn library and BetaML.jl library,
– XGBoost regressor from the XGBoost.jl library,
– SVM regressor from the scikit-learn library,
– AdaBoost regressor from the scikit-learn library,
– KNN regressor from the scikit-learn library.

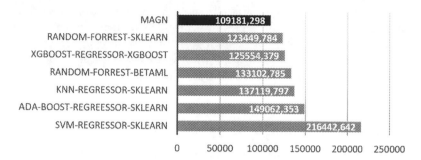

Fig. 5. Comparison of root mean square errors for a regression problem using MAGN and other machine learning algorithms.

MAGN outperformed all of the tested models for the selected metrics: root mean squared error (RMSE) (Fig. 5) and mean absolute error (MAE). For RMSE, MAGN is 12% better than the second-best model - Random Forest, and 7% better in view of MAE.

4.2   Classification Benchmark

We selected 73 benchmark datasets from the PMLB collection [17] dedicated to the classification task, including binary/multi-class classification problems defined by categorical, ordinal, and continuous features. We selected datasets with less than or equal to a thousand records.

The following machine-learning models were selected for all comparisons:

– DecisionTreeClassifier from the DecisionTree.jl package
– RandomForestClassifier from the DecisionTree.jl package
– EvoTreeClassifier from the EvoTrees.jl package
– XGBoostClassifier from the XGBoost.jl package
– KNNClassifier from the NearestNeighborModels.jl package
– LinearClassifier from the MLJLinearModels.jl package
– LGBMClassifier from the LightGBM.jl package
– NeuralNetworkClassifier from the MLJFlux.jl package

We used the default set of hyperparameters for each of the models listed above. The neural network model had 2 hidden fully-connected layers, with 64 and 32 neurons in the consecutive layers. All of the models and benchmarks were implemented in Julia v. 1.9.1. The MAGN was implemented in Rust v. 1.70.0.

Fig. 6. Penn ML Classification Benchmark mean accuracy for 73 datasets with less than 1000 records.

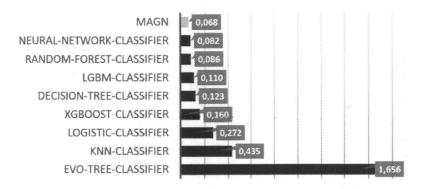

Fig. 7. Penn ML Classification Benchmark mean execution time of the inference phase in seconds for 73 datasets with less than 1000 records.

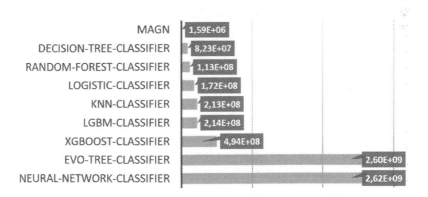

Fig. 8. Penn ML Classification Benchmark mean allocated memory during the entire benchmark (including the training and inference phase) in bytes for 73 datasets with less than 1000 records.

For all of the experiments, we have used a dedicated server with $2 \times$ CPU AMD EPYC 7773X, 256 GB RAM, and GPU NVidia RTX A6000.

Figures 6, 7, and 8 demonstrate that the proposed MAGN achieved very competitive average scores in this benchmark and can be used as a substitute for most modern machine learning models. Note that only allocated memory was measured during the benchmark, so it should be interpreted with caution as it includes all allocations required in the training and inference phase.

5   Conclusions

Understanding and modeling human knowledge is a complex and active research area focused on replicating the capabilities of the human brain in artificial systems. In this paper, we introduced MAGNs, a promising approach that enables the representation of relationships between different pieces of information, enabling inference, recommendation, regression, and classification processes. Unlike traditional feed-forward networks trained using a backpropagation algorithm, MAGNs are constructed and adapted using associative approaches based on frequency, similarities, and other detected data relationships. The relationships are detected during the introduced associative transformation process and represented within the MAGN structure. Sparse connections are used to represent real data relationships so they do not introduce bias as many full-connected structures do. Moreover, MAGNs eliminate the need for predefined input and output data and training goals before the construction phase, so they can be used for multiple applications by easily switching attributes between inputs and outputs. Furthermore, the introduced prioritization algorithm can be used to further improve the final results.

The Multi-Associative Graph Networks aggregate, count, and store all feature values in order, representing duplicates by the same neurons, and all neural object representations (database entities or training examples) are associated due to their existing same or similar values. The described associative transformation of RDBs to a MAGN is lossless and enriches the data with an effective representation of relations while maintaining time and memory efficiency. MAGNs applied to classification and regression tasks show that networks using relationships can achieve reasonable results when compared to other state-of-the-art models and training methods. It is easily scalable and efficient, making it suitable for many computational intelligence applications. The ability to represent and detect many different relationships allows MAGNs to be used as an adaptable model of knowledge representation and use.

Ethical Issues. Our proposed algorithms do not raise any ethical concerns, and the experiments shown used publicly available benchmark datasets.

References

1. Adelson-Velskii, G.M., Landis, E.M.: An algorithm for organization of information. In: Doklady Akademii Nauk, vol. 146, pp. 263–266. Russian Academy of Sciences (1962)
2. Baars, B.J., Gage, N.M.: Cognition, Brain, and Consciousness: Introduction to Cognitive Neuroscience. Academic Press, Cambridge (2010)
3. Starzyk, J.A., Horzyk, A.: Episodic memory in minicolumn associative knowledge graphs. IEEE Trans. Neural Netw. Learn. Syst. **30**(11), 3505–3516 (2019)
4. Bayer, R.: Symmetric binary b-trees: data structure and maintenance algorithms. Acta Informatica **1**(4), 290–306 (1972)
5. Botvinick, M.M., Plaut, D.C.: Short-term memory for serial order: a recurrent neural network model. Psychol. Rev. **113**(2), 201 (2006)
6. Cai, H., Zheng, V.W., Chang, K.C.C.: A comprehensive survey of graph embedding: problems, techniques, and applications. IEEE Trans. Knowl. Data Eng. **30**(9), 1616–1637 (2018)
7. Chen, L., Schott, R.: Optimal operations on red-black trees. Int. J. Found. Comput. Sci. **7**(03), 227–239 (1996)
8. Fu, T.J., Li, P.H., Ma, W.Y.: Graphrel: modeling text as relational graphs for joint entity and relation extraction. In: Proceedings of the 57th Annual Meeting of the Association for Computational Linguistics, pp. 1409–1418 (2019)
9. Guo, Q.E.A.: A survey on knowledge graph-based recommender systems. IEEE Trans. Knowl. Data Eng. **34**(8), 3549–3568 (2022)
10. Horzyk, A.: Associative graph data structures with an efficient access via avb+ trees. In: 2018 11th International Conference on Human System Interaction (HSI), pp. 169–175. IEEE (2018)
11. Horzyk, A.: Associative representation and processing of databases using DASNG and AVB+trees for efficient data access. In: Fred, A., et al. (eds.) IC3K 2017. CCIS, vol. 976, pp. 242–267. Springer, Cham (2019). https://doi.org/10.1007/978-3-030-15640-4_13
12. Horzyk, A., Bulanda, D., Starzyk, J.A.: Asa-graphs for efficient data representation and processing. Int. J. Appl. Math. Comput. Sci. **30**(4), 717–731 (2020)
13. Horzyk, A., Starzyk, J.A., Graham, J.: Integration of semantic and episodic memories. IEEE Trans. Neural Netw. Learn. Syst. **28**(12), 3084–3095 (2017)
14. Jensen, C.S., Lin, D., Ooi, B.C.: Query and update efficient b+-tree based indexing of moving objects. In: Proceedings of the Thirtieth International Conference on Very Large Data Bases, vol. 30, pp. 768–779 (2004)
15. Kim, W.H., Seo, J., Kim, J., Nam, B.: clfb-tree: cacheline friendly persistent b-tree for nvram. ACM Trans. Storage (TOS) **14**(1), 1–17 (2018)
16. Mishra, P., Eich, M.H.: Join processing in relational databases. ACM Comput. Surv. (CSUR) **24**(1), 63–113 (1992)
17. Romano, J.D., et al.: Pmlb v1.0: an open-source dataset collection for benchmarking machine learning methods. arXiv preprint arXiv:2012.00058 (2020)
18. Vijaymeena, M., Kavitha, K.: A survey on similarity measures in text mining. Mach. Learn. Appl. Int. J. **3**(2), 19–28 (2016)

19. Wang, Q., Mao, Z., Wang, B., Guo, L.: Knowledge graph embedding: a survey of approaches and applications. IEEE Trans. Knowl. Data Eng. **29**(12), 2724–2743 (2017)
20. Wang, Z., Zhang, J., Feng, J., Chen, Z.: Knowledge graph embedding by translating on hyperplanes. In: Proceedings of the AAAI Conference on Artificial Intelligence, vol. 28 (2014)
21. Ye, Z., Kumar, Y.J., Sing, G.O., Song, F., Wang, J.: A comprehensive survey of graph neural networks for knowledge graphs. IEEE Access **10**, 75729–75741 (2022)

Skeletal Cores and Graph Resilience

Danylo Honcharov[1]([✉]), Ahmet Erdem Sarıyüce[2], Ricky Laishram[1],
and Sucheta Soundarajan[1]

[1] Syracuse University, Syracuse, NY 13244, USA
{dhonchar,rlaishra,susounda}@syr.edu
[2] University at Buffalo, Buffalo, NY 14260, USA
erdem@buffalo.edu

Abstract. In network analysis, one of the most important structures is the k-core: the maximal set of nodes such that each node in the k-core has at least k neighbors within the core. Recently, the notion of the *skeletal k-core*– a minimal subgraph that preserves the core structure of the graph– has attracted attention. However, the literature to date has contained only a biased greedy heuristic for sampling skeletal cores, which resulted in a skewed analysis of the network. In this work, we introduce a novel MCMC algorithm for sampling skeletal cores uniformly at random, as well as a novel algorithm for estimating the size of the space of skeletal k-cores, which, as we show, is important for understanding the core resilience of the network. With these algorithms, we demonstrate the relationship between *resilience* of the network and the core structure of the graph and suggest fast heuristics for evaluating graph structure from a skeletal cores perspective. We show that the normalized number of skeletal cores in the graph correlates with the resilience of k-core towards edge deletion attacks.

Keywords: networks · robustness · k-cores

1 Introduction

Within the machine learning and network science literature, the study of dense subgraphs has received a great deal of attention. Examples of such structures include cliques [18], k-clubs [21] and k-trusses [7]. Of particular interest is the k-core, which plays a role in applications such as community detection [19,22], influence maximization [11], visualization [3,12], anomaly detection [26] and understanding network topology [3,27]. A network's k-core is defined as the maximal subgraph of the network such that every node in the subgraph has at least k neighbours also in the subgraph [24]. The core number of a node is the highest value of k for which that node belongs to a k-core.

k-cores have a history of being studied in the context of network resilience [17, 20]. To understand the structural properties of k-cores and their effect on resilience, the concept of the *skeletal core* was proposed [16]. The skeletal core of a graph is defined as a minimal subgraph that preserves the core number of each node. Skeletal cores can be seen as a "backbone" of the k-core structure of

D. Koutra et al. (Eds.): ECML PKDD 2023, LNAI 14171, pp. 293–308, 2023.
https://doi.org/10.1007/978-3-031-43418-1_18

the graph, and so play an important role in the structure of the network. While useful for applications such as speeding up community detection, they are crucial in the context of analyzing the network's *resilience* or *robustness* [16]. To this end, understanding the space of skeletal cores can provide valuable insight into the graph structure: understanding when a network's core structure will change, requires understanding when it remains the same.

However, because skeletal cores are a new concept, there are a number of important open problems surrounding them. For instance, the literature contains only a single greedy heuristic for identifying a single skeletal core, and it is not known how to sample skeletal cores of a network uniformly at random, which fundamentally limits the understanding of how skeletal cores are distributed and how they affect the core structure. Relatedly, it is also not known how to estimate the number of skeletal cores to which an edge belongs, making it difficult to gauge the importance of an edge with respect to the overall core structure of the network. Without solving these problems, one cannot properly understand the effect of a network's skeletal core structure on the resilience of the network.

In our work, we first introduce a novel MCMC (Markov Chain Monte Carlo) algorithm for sampling skeletal k-cores uniformly at random and a corresponding algorithm for estimating the number of skeletal cores in the graph. We then use these algorithms to study the relationship between the space of skeletal cores and the robustness of complex networks. We suggest practical heuristics for the estimation of the probability of a given edge being part of a skeletal core and experimentally validate these heuristics with respect to the ground truth.

Our main contributions are as follows:

1. We provide a novel MCMC algorithm for sampling skeletal cores of the graph uniformly at random.
2. We suggest heuristics that can be used to estimate the likelihood of an edge being part of a skeletal core and evaluate them experimentally.
3. We provide a novel algorithm for the estimation of the size of the skeletal core space and experimentally demonstrate the relationship between the number of skeletal cores in the graph and the core resilience of the network.
4. We demonstrate how the proposed algorithms can be used to identify moments of fundamental change of the k-core structure during a process of edge deletion.

2   Related Work

First introduced by Seidman in 1983 [24], the k-core of a graph $G = (V, E)$ is defined as the maximal connected subgraph such that any node in the subgraph has a degree at least k. k-cores are an important part of network analysis, and have been used for many tasks, including community detection [19], speedups of the graph algorithms [22], influence maximization [11], anomaly detection [26], prediction of protein functions [2], and others. k-cores have also been used to gain deeper insight into a graph structure, including through visualization [12].

A skeletal core of a graph G is defined as a minimal subgraph H of G such that all nodes in H have the same core number as in G [16]. The literature contains a greedy algorithm (discussed in more detail in Sect. 4.2) for generating a single skeletal k-core for the given graph and suggests several applications for skeletal cores [16]. However, the greedy algorithm for finding skeletal cores does not sample uniformly at random from the whole space of skeletal cores, and so may lead to bias in analysis. Moreover, because graphs may have many skeletal cores, simply generating one such skeletal core may not provide sufficient insight into the graph structure. The estimation of the *expected* properties of skeletal cores (e.g. expected size of skeletal core or expected overlap between skeletal cores) is a more useful tool for graph analysis, but it requires the ability to sample cores uniformly at random.

Skeletal cores are particularly important to the robustness of networks. While network robustness can be defined in many ways [8,10], of relevance to this work is the resilience of a graph's k-core structure against changes in the graph structure. k-core numbers are used as a way to quantify connectedness and importance of the nodes in the network, and core structure can be used to study the local density of the graphs. As such, it is important to estimate how these properties may be affected if the graph is changed: for example, how do random communications failures in a communications network affect overall connectivity?

The core resilience measure was suggested to measure the propensity of nodes to change core number when edges from the graph are dropped [17], and the impact of noise and sampling process on the k-core of a graph has been studied [1]. Understanding when changes in the graph structure happen during some processes (e.g. edge removal/addition) has been a long-standing research topic in network science. Examples include research on changes in random networks [9], including the emergence of k-cores in the random graphs [23] and dynamics of the k-core during edge removal in the random graphs [13].

3 Background

Here, we introduce concepts necessary for the presentation of our work.

3.1 k-Cores

The k-core is defined as a maximal subgraph for which any node in the subgraph is connected to at least k neighbours in subgraph. A node's core number is the maximum value k such that the node belongs to a k-core. The core numbers of a graph can be obtained using a 'peeling' k-core decomposition technique, which runs in $O(|E|)$ time [4].

3.2 Core Strength

Core strength was introduced in [17]. The core strength of a node u provides an upper bound on the number of edges to same or higher-shell neighbors that can be removed from the node without it decreasing its core number. The proposed MCMC algorithm (Sect. 4.1) uses core strength to identify transitions; and the greedy estimator algorithm from Sect. 4.2 uses it for estimating the number of skeletal cores.

Formally the core strength of u is defined as $CS(u) = |N_{\geq}(u)| - K(u) + 1$, where $N_{\geq}$ is the set of neighbours of u with a core number greater than or equal to that of u (i.e., those that support u's core number) and $K(u)$ denotes the core number of u.[1]

3.3   Core Valid Subgraph and Skeletal k-Core

A Core Valid Subgraph CVS of a graph $G = (V, E)$ is defined as a spanning subgraph of G such that all nodes in G have the same k-core number in CVS as they do in G [16]. In other words, CVS preserves the core structure of G.

A skeletal k-core is defined as a minimal CVS: i.e., one for which removal of any edge would lead to at least one node decreasing its core number [16]. Of interest in the context of our work is the greedy algorithm for finding a single skeletal core [16]. This algorithm serves to identify the starting state for the MCMC algorithm in Sect. 4.2, and can be summarized as follows:

1. Identify a set of edges of G such that any edge in the set can be removed without k-core numbers decreasing. Denote this set as R.
2. Select one of the edges $e \in R$ and remove it from the G.
3. Recompute R and repeat 1-3, until $R = \emptyset$.
4. Return G as a skeletal core.

3.4   Core Resilience

Core resilience was proposed in [17] to measure the robustness of a network's k-core structure against random edge removal. It provides a way to compare the estimated ability of the core structure of different networks to withstand changes (for example, due to failure of the communication channels between nodes or because of network evolution). Consider two graphs: $G = (V, E)$ and $G' = (V, E')$, where G' is a subgraph of G formed by randomly deleting $p\%$ of the edges from G. Denote the top $r\%$ of the nodes with the highest k-core numbers in G as V_r. The resilience $R_r^{(p)}$ of G can then be defined as: $R_r^{(p)} = \tau_b(\{((K(u, G), (K(u, G')), u \in V_r\})$, where $K(u, G)$ denotes the core number of node u in graph G, and τ_b denotes the expected Kendall-Tau rank correlation [14] between the two rankings (other rank correlations may be used). $R_r^{(p_1, p_2)}$ is defined as the mean core resilience as the percentage of dropped edges changes from p_1 to p_2 [17]: $R_r^{(p_1, p_2)} = \frac{\int_{p_1}^{p_2} R_r^{(x)}(G) dx}{p_2 - p_1}$. We use core resilience in our

---

[1] Note that this sometimes overestimates the desired value, as loss of an edge (u, v) can trigger reductions in core numbers of other nodes, and thus lower the core number of other neighbors of u; however, computing the exact value is more computationally intensive.

experimental analysis to show the relationship between skeletal cores and the robustness of the graph.

4   Algorithms to Explore the Space of Skeletal Cores

Here, we introduce an MCMC-based algorithm for sampling skeletal cores u.a.r., and then demonstrate how to estimate the number of skeletal cores in a graph.

Exploring the space of skeletal cores in unbiased way is useful for different applications. Let's consider the scenario of the pandemic of a contagious virus which spreads through the network of personal interactions. As was shown by the research of COVID-19 [25], k-cores of high complexity are known to sustain an outbreak even if the network becomes partially disconnected; thus, estimation of *which* edges are most important for the k-core could be useful to minimize the spread of the disease. While skeletal cores of the personal interaction network provide important insight regarding these edges, application of previously suggested greedy algorithm will provide a biased sample of the skeletal cores, leading to the non-optimal decision-making. Similarly, for the opposite problem of maintaining the k-core structure, a skewed sample of skeletal cores is undesirable. The proposed MCMC algorithm does not suffer from this drawback, and is guaranteed to provide unbiased sampling.

The proposed MCMC algorithm uses the notion of *core strength* [17] (described in Sect. 3.2) to identify transitions between different skeletal k-cores.

In our experimental analysis, we show that the core resilience of a graph is strongly correlated with its skeletal core properties.

4.1   Sampling Skeletal Cores Uniformly at Random

In this section, we describe an MCMC algorithm for sampling skeletal k-cores uniformly at random. At a high level, the proposed method is described as following: First, begin from any skeletal core T_0 (for example, one obtained by the greedy algorithm in [16]). This skeletal core is the initial state of a Markov Chain M. Next, randomly transform T_0 into another skeletal core T_1, or stay at T_0, with probabilities of D/D_{max} and $1 - D/D_{max}$ correspondingly, where D stands for the number of possible transformations from the current state. D_{max} needs to be bigger than any possible number of transitions from one state. This is equivalent to conducting a random walk over M. Repeat the procedure until the process converges to the stationary distribution. If transition probabilities are defined correctly, this stationary distribution will be an uniform distribution over the space of skeletal cores. Once the stationary distribution is reached, return the current skeletal core.

The key idea behind the proposed algorithm is to correctly transition between skeletal cores of the graph. When at a skeletal core T, no edge can be deleted from T without affecting core numbers (because T is skeletal), unless another edge (or edges) is added to compensate. When these replacement edges are added, this may necessitate further removal of edges to ensure that the new subgraph is still skeletal. We consider only allowed transitions that go up to two steps in any direction, and we show in the proof that this is enough to reach any skeletal core, while limiting the number of possible transitions at each step.

More formally, the proposed algorithm consists of the following steps:

1. Begin from some skeletal core T_0 of the original graph $G = (V, E)$. T_0 can be obtained from the original graph by using a greedy algorithm, like that proposed in [16], or in any alternative way.
2. Initialize the set of possible transitions $R_0 = \emptyset$.
3. Denote the current skeletal core as T. To identify possible transitions, iterate over all edges $(u, v) \in T$ and generate all skeletal cores that can be obtained from T by removal of an edge (u, v), followed by the addition of an edge $(u, i) \in G \backslash T$ or an edge $(v, j) \in G \backslash T$ (or both) and corresponding removal of $(i, p) \in T$ and/or $(j, k) \in T$, if needed. Add these transitions to R.
4. Similarly, for all edges $(u, v) \in G \backslash T$, generate all skeletal cores, that can be obtained from T by addition of (u, v), the removal of $(u, i) \in T$ or $(v, j) \in T$ (or both), and corresponding addition of $(i, p) \in G \backslash T$ and/or $(j, k) \in G \backslash T$. Add these transitions to R.
5. Select one of the transitions from R uniformly at random or stay at T with probability $1 - D/D_{max}$, where D_{max} needs to be bigger than any possible number of transitions from one state. D_{max} can be bounded in several ways - for example, it's trivial to show that $D_{max} \leq |E| * d_m^4$, where d_m is the highest degree in the graph.[2]
6. Repeat steps 2–5 until the Markov Chain converges. Convergence can be identified in several ways [6]. One simple example could be running several instances of Markovian chains and comparing their outputs.
7. Return the current skeletal core.

The running time for this algorithm is high. In each iteration, the algorithm iterates over all edges and considers $O(d_m^4)$ possible transitions for every edge in the worst-case scenario. Hence, the running time for one step is $O(|E| * d_m^4)$. The overall running time of the proposed algorithm depends primarily on the mixing time of the Markov chain M. While we do not propose proof that M is rapidly mixing, experiments suggest that the stationary distribution is reached relatively fast in most cases. Nonetheless, the main disadvantage of the algorithm is running time, which makes it prohibitively expensive to run on big graphs.

In the next section, we discuss how properties of the space of skeletal cores can be estimated more quickly.

Theorem 1. *The described MCMC algorithm will sample skeletal cores u.a.r.*

Due to space constraints, the proof of the theorem can be found in the extended version of this paper.[3] In the proof, we show that space of skeletal cores is connected and that transitions between adjacent states are symmetric.

---

[2] Experimentally this bound proved to be very loose, which may reduce the rate of convergence.

[3] Extended version and source code are available at https://github.com/honcharov-danylo/extended_skeletal.

```
def estimator(G = (V, E) : Graph, K : HashTable):
    R = ∅; c = 0; d = 1
    repeat
        CS = getCoreStrength(G)
        R = {(u, v) ∈ E : (CS[u] > 1 ∧ CS[v] > 1)∨
        ∨(CS[u] > 1 ∧ K(u) < K(v))) ∨ (CS[v] > 1 ∧ K(v) < K(u)))}
        d* = |R|; c+ = 1
    until R! = ∅
    return d/c!
def estimate_size(G = (V, E) : Graph, K : HashTable, N : int):
    S = List() ; W = List()
    for i = 0; i < N; i + + do
        | S.add(estimator(G, K))
    end
    return AVG(S)
```
             Algorithm 1: Number of skeletal cores in the graph

4.2 Estimating the Number of Skeletal Cores

Analyzing the properties of the skeletal cores is important for many applications. For instance, the k-core can be seen as a form of the equilibrium in a game-theoretic model [5]; and, correspondingly, the skeletal core can be seen as the minimal edge-induced subgraph that maintains this equilibrium. The question of what this subgraph looks *on average* is crucial for understanding the network as a whole. Another example could be using the average size of skeletal cores to find the "breaking point" of the k-core structure, as shown in Sect. 5.4.

Because the MCMC algorithm is computationally expensive, here we suggest an alternative approach for the estimation of the *expected* properties of skeletal cores. We provide an algorithm that provides the expected number of skeletal k-cores in the graph, and explain how it can be used to estimate properties of skeletal cores (e.g. average size) without relying on the MCMC approach. An outline of the algorithm can be found in Algorithm 1, further referred to as the GE-algorithm. The algorithm takes a graph and k-core numbers of all nodes as input and returns the expected number of skeletal cores in the graph.

The idea behind the algorithm is as follows: first, "unravel" the DAG H, formed by transitions of the greedy heuristic for finding a single skeletal core [16] (discussed in Sect. 3.3) to the tree and count its leaves, adjusting our estimate for overcounting caused by such "unravelling". To improve the estimate, we repeat the process n times and use D_{avg} as the final estimate.

4.3 Proof of the Algorithm Correctness

Theorem 2. *Algorithm 1 returns the expected number of skeletal k-cores in the graph.*

Proof. Denote the original input graph as G. Use a greedy algorithm, (see Sect. 3.3) to obtain a single skeletal core S from G. Next, create a new graph H, where nodes denote graphs that can be obtained during the process above and directed edges denote transitions between these graphs in the greedy algorithm. It can be shown that the greedy algorithm is capable of producing every skeletal core in the graph. H is directed and acyclic, because an edge from $u \in H$ to $v \in H$ requires that v is a subgraph of u in G. Nodes without out-edges are skeletal cores of G (by definition). The root of H is G itself. Next, modify H by "unravelling" the DAG to a tree by making copies of all nodes that have more than one parent. Denote the resulting graph as H_m.

Because H_m is a tree, obtaining the expected number of terminal nodes (leaves) in H_m could be done easily with the algorithm suggested by Knuth [15] for the estimation of the space of the backtracking tree. This algorithm initializes a counter D with 1 at the root of the tree (which denotes the original graph G) and performs a random walk down the tree, multiplying D by the out-degree of every node on the path, until it reaches a leaf. When a leaf is reached, the counter will contain the expected number of the leaves in the graph [15].

However, the skeletal cores (leaves) in H_m may be copied (and counted) several times. As edges removed from G to obtain any skeletal core S_i may have been removed in any order, there are $A_i!$ ways to reach S_i from G in H, where A_i is the number of edges removed from G to obtain S_i. As any of these paths will lead to a unique copy of the skeletal core S_i in H_m, we know that S_i will be counted $A_i!$ times in H_m. Dividing the estimate by $A_i!$ accounts for this.

Theorem 3. *The running time of Algorithm 1 is $O(|E|)$.*

Proof. First, consider the running time of the function *estimator*. To compute core strength, the function requires $O(|E|)$ time in the first iteration. For subsequent iterations, core strength values can be updated in $O(1)$ after every edge deletion (as at most two values of Core Strength will be affected). Identifying a set of edges R takes $O(|E|)$ time the first time, but we can update it quickly if the selected data structure allows us to quickly access and remove edges with one known endpoint. One example of such a data structure could be a hashmap with nodes as keys and edges from R as values. The function *estimate_size* takes $O(k|E|)$ time, where k is the number of samples. Assuming that k is a small fixed constant with $k << |E|$, the overall running time of the algorithm is $O(|E|)$.

4.4   Estimation of Expected Properties of Skeletal Core

We can use a modified version of Algorithm 1 to obtain the expected properties of skeletal cores in the graph. Suppose that we want to get the expected value of property P of the skeletal core (e.g., the number of edges or average degree).

Denote $P(S_i)$ as the value of P for the core S_i and define $C = \sum_{S_i \in S} P(S_i)$. C is the sum of P of all skeletal cores in the space S. Assign 0 as the *cost* of any node in the H which is non-terminal (i.e., not a skeletal core), and assign $P(S_i)$ as the cost of the skeletal core S_i.

In this case, an expected estimate of *total cost* C for one Monte Carlo search will be $P(S_i) * D$ [15], and over multiple experiments it will be $C = \sum_{i=0}^{n} P(S_i) * D_i/n$. The expected value of P will then be $E[P] = C/D_{avg} = P(S_i) * D_i/D_{avg}$.

4.5 Normalized Number of Skeletal Cores

It is useful to introduce a notion of skeletal core density, which allows one to have a sense of the number of skeletal cores that a graph has relative to its size. To this end, we introduce a novel metric of a normalized number of skeletal k-cores. Denoting the expected size of the space of skeletal cores as e_{est} and the expected number of edges in the skeletal core as s_{exp}, we define the *normalized* number of skeletal cores in the graph as $e_n = log(e_{est})/log(\binom{|E|}{s_{exp}})$. The denominator represents the logarithm of the total number of possible subgraphs in G that have s_{exp} edges.

5 Experiments and Analysis

In this section, we demonstrate the relationship between skeletal k-cores and core resilience; and show how skeletal cores can be used to analyze the "breaking point" of the k-core structure.

5.1 Datasets

Networks used in our experiments are listed in Table 1. We compare networks from different domains: AS denotes networks from autonomous systems; P2P stands for peer-to-peer, BIO indicates graphs from bioinformatics; CA denotes co-authorship networks; INF is used for infrastructure-related graphs; CO denotes collaboration networks; SOC indicates social networks; TECH stands for technological networks; WEB is used for internet network; EMAIL indicates email networks; MISC denotes networks that do not fall into the categories above.

5.2 Algorithm Validation

Before using the proposed algorithms to perform network analysis, we demonstrate that they are effective at the desired objectives.

First, we show that the MCMC sampling algorithm reaches its stationary distribution quickly. Any MCMC algorithm needs several steps before convergence. While we do not provide theoretical proof that Markovian chain defined by the suggested algorithm is rapidly mixing, experiments demonstrate fast convergence of the algorithm. To show the speed of convergence of the algorithm experimentally, we perform a sampling of skeletal cores for a different number of steps, setting the number of steps to be equal to the fixed fractions of the number of edges in the original graph.

Intuitively, after convergence, the distribution of the properties of skeletal cores is stable. In Fig. 1, the distribution of sizes of skeletal cores is plotted for a different number of steps of the algorithm. Due to the lack of space, we show

Table 1. Datasets. $|V|$ denotes number of nodes, $|E|$ denotes number of edges, k_{max} denotes highest k-core. † denotes SNAP as a source of the network, ‡ stands for NetworkRepository, § stands for KONECT, §§ stands for Netzschleuder.

Type	Network	$|V|$	$|E|$	k_{max}	Type	Network	$|V|$	$|E|$	k_{max}
AS	auto_as19990111†	549	1249	11	CO	arena_jazz‡	198	2742	29
	auto_as19980318†	3455	6168	10	SOC	wiki‡	889	2914	9
	auto_as19971108†	3015	5156	9		hamsterer†	2426	16630	24
	oregon010331†	10670	22002	17		musae_facebook†	22470	170823	56
P2P	gnutella08†	6301	20777	10		musae_git†	37700	289003	34
BIO	dmela‡	7393	25569	11	TECH	tech_routers‡	2113	6632	15
	protein‡	1870	2203	5		whois‡	7476	56943	88
CA	erdos‡	5094	7515	7		tech_pgp‡	10680	24316	31
	netscience§	1464	2744	19	WEB	webspam†	4767	37375	35
	ca-HepPh‡	12008	118521	238	EMAIL	email_enron†	36692	183831	43
	ca_grq†	4158	13422	43		email_EuAll†	265214	364481	37
INF	openflights‡	2939	15677	28	MISC	moreno_innovation§	245	927	6
	inf-power‡	4941	6594	5		norwegian(net1m)§§	1421	3855	11
						moreno_oz‡	217	2345	14

plots only for 3 networks. For higher number of steps, the distributions of skeletal k-core sizes look very similar, which suggests convergence.[4]

As was seen in Sect. 4.4, we can compute the expected values of properties of skeletal cores. To test this algorithm, we compare these estimated properties to the average properties of skeletal cores sampled uniformly at random using MCMC algorithm. Due to space limitations, we perform only an estimation of the expected number of edges in the skeletal cores for selected graphs.

Results can be seen in Table 2. We compute E_{avg} as a simple average over sizes of skeletal cores, sampled with the greedy algorithm from [16], E_{exp} is the expected value over skeletal cores (method from Sect. 4.4), and E_u is obtained by sampling skeletal cores uniformly at random with the MCMC algorithm. Our goal is to show that E_{exp} is closer to E_u than E_{avg} is to E_u. Indeed, for most graphs, the suggested expected estimate is much closer to E_u, the ground truth obtained from the MCMC algorithm (and for the two networks where it is not closer, the difference is very small).

5.3 Skeletal Core Analysis

Here, we experimentally validate the theoretical results of the GE-algorithm to estimate the number of skeletal cores, as presented in Sect. 4.2. For every graph, we sample 50 skeletal cores and compute the normalized number of skeletal cores as shown in Sect. 4.5. Results are plotted against core resilience $R_{50}^{(0,50)}$ in Fig. 2. (Core resilience is computed as described in Sect. 3.4.)

---

[4] Such convergence diagnostics for MCMC methods don't *guarantee* convergence, and should be seen as a type of statistical analysis [6].

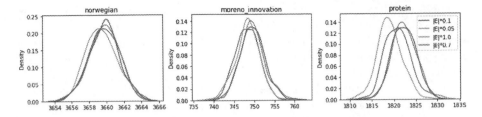

Fig. 1. Distribution of size of skeletal cores, sampled with a different number of steps of MCMC (number of steps are set up as fixed fractions of the number of edges in the graph). Colors denote the number of transitions made by the algorithm until a sample was taken. (Color figure online)

Table 2. Expected number of edges in skeletal cores. E_{avg} is simple average over skeletal cores, sampled with a greedy algorithm, E_{exp} is the expected value over skeletal cores (method from Sect. 4.4), E_u is obtained by MCMC algorithm.

Network	E_{avg}	E_{exp}	E_u
auto_as19971108	4717.13	**4724.53**	4722.28
auto_as19980318	**5649.84**	5648.00	5655.04
auto_as19990111	**1130.45**	1128.28	1131.47
GrQc	11926.69	**11936.83**	11953.45
netscience	2628.29	**2629.01**	2630.30
norwegian	3657.30	**3657.82**	3660.14
wiki	2464.67	**2466.16**	2470.61
erdos	6864.28	**6870.62**	6877.34
protein	1816.31	**1817.76**	1821.81
inf-power	5286.41	**5288.73**	5314.86

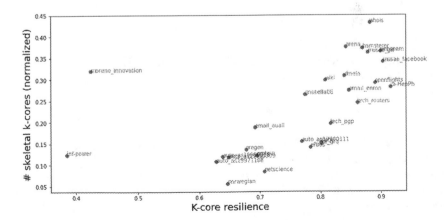

Fig. 2. Normalized number of skeletal cores vs Core Resilience

There is a very strong correlation between the two measures. The greater the density of skeletal cores, the higher core resilience is. This suggests a clear reason why certain networks have high core resilience: the core numbers of nodes are supported in many different ways. The only outlier is the *moreno_innovation* network, discussed below.

Relationships between different skeletal cores of the graph (e.g. overlap) can provide further insight into the network's robustness. One example can be found in Fig. 3. The *moreno_innovation* network has many edges that belong only to a *fraction* of skeletal cores of the network. In other words, there are many edges that can be useful to skeletal cores, but are not always necessary. This property explains the reason for an unusually high number of skeletal cores in this graph, as was seen in Fig. 2, because these edges might support a higher number of skeletal cores comparatively to other networks. This suggests a smaller overlap between different skeletal cores, and so when edges are randomly deleted destruction of many skeletal cores is more likely.

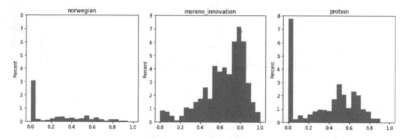

Fig. 3. Fraction of skeletal cores to which each edge belongs. Results were obtained by sampling 200 skeletal cores with MCMC. We ignore edges for which at least one endpoint has a core strength of 1, as they belong to all skeletal cores. *moreno_innovation* has a high normalized number of skeletal cores, but low core resilience; *protein* and *norwegian* networks have a low number of skeletal cores and low core resilience.

Estimating the Probability of an Edge Belonging to a Random Skeletal k-Core. The likelihood that an edge is part of an arbitrary skeletal core can be used for visualizations of skeletal cores or evaluation of the "centralization" of the core structure [16]. As our work is the first that can estimate this likelihood in an unbiased way, we compare against heuristics introduced by [16], which we denote as the *Centralized Skeletal Score (CSS)* heuristics.

In our proposed heuristics, we approximate the probability that an edge connected to a node $u \in V$ will be part of a random skeletal core. Denote the number of edges that can be removed from node u without dropping the k-core number of any node as:

$$\omega(u) = |\{v \in N(u) : K(v) > K(u) \vee (K(u) = K(v) \wedge CS[v] \neq 1)\}|. \quad (1)$$

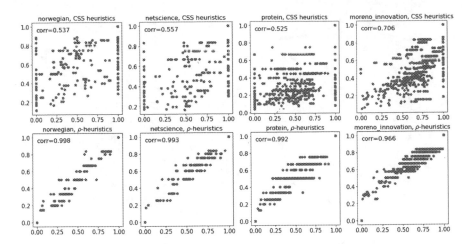

Fig. 4. Comparison of the heuristics. y-axis denotes the heuristics value for the edge, x-axis denotes the proportion of skeletal cores that the edge belongs to (MCMC sample). CSS-heuristics are shown on the top row, ρ-heuristics on the bottom. ρ-heuristics outperform the competition.

Similarly, define the number of edges that cannot be removed from u and must be present in every skeletal core:

$$\gamma(u) = |\{v \in N(u) : K(v) = K(u) \wedge CS[v] = 1\}|. \tag{2}$$

In a skeletal core, u will have at least $K(u)$ neighbours, so we need to select at least $K(u) - \gamma(u)$ nodes from $\omega(u)$ for the skeletal core. Thus, for node u:

$$\rho(u) = \begin{cases} max(\frac{K(u)-\gamma(u)}{\omega(u)}, 0) & \text{if } \omega(u) \neq 0 \\ 1 & \text{if } \omega(u) = 0 \end{cases} \tag{3}$$

For an edge $(u, v) \in E$ we define heuristics as:

$$\rho((u, v)) = \begin{cases} max(\rho(u), \rho(v)) & \text{if } K[u] = K[v] \\ \rho(u) & \text{if } K[u] < K[v] \\ \rho(v) & \text{if } K[u] > K[v] \end{cases} \tag{4}$$

We refer to these heuristics as "ρ-heuristics". In Fig. 4, heuristics from [16] and the proposed ρ-heuristics are plotted against the ground truth, as estimated with the MCMC algorithm. The correlation between ρ-heuristics and ground truth is significantly higher as compared to the earlier CSS heuristics.

5.4   Identifying the "Breaking Point" of the k-Core Structure

The normalized number of skeletal cores from Sect. 5.2 can be interpreted as the "density" of the skeletal cores amongst subgraphs obtained by removal of

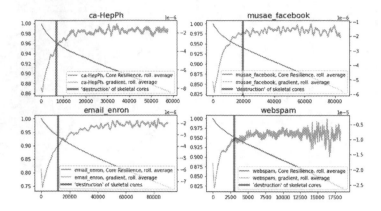

Fig. 5. Skeletal cores and "breaking point" of the network. x-axis denotes number of edges removed, left y-axis denotes the core resilience of the network for a certain percentage of removed edges, and the right y-axis denotes the gradient of Core Resilience. After the destruction of skeletal cores (red line), the gradient of Core Resilience (green line) flattens, indicating a fundamental loss of k-core structure. (Color figure online)

approximately $|E| - s_{exp}$ edges uniformly at random. If we remove edges past this point, the graph will have fewer edges than the expected size of skeletal cores, thus, edges will be unable to support the k-core.

In Fig. 5, we see that the average size of the skeletal core provides a good estimate of when the k-core structure disappears during a random edge removal process. Before the number of deleted edges equals the size of the average skeletal core (red line), core resilience (blue line) drops rapidly; but after that point, it shows a roughly linear decrease (as seen by the gradient, in green, flattening). One explanation is that prior to this point, a single edge deletion can cause a cascade in which many nodes drop their core number. After this point, the core structure is essentially destroyed, and such cascades of are unlikely.

6 Conclusion

In this paper, we introduced an MCMC algorithm for sampling skeletal cores uniformly at random as well as an algorithm for estimating the expected number of skeletal cores and their properties. We demonstrated the relationship between skeletal core structure and the core resilience of the graph, suggested a heuristic to estimate the likelihood of an edge being part of a skeletal core, and showed that skeletal cores can be used to find the "breaking point" of the k-core structure.

Acknowledgements. Honcharov and Soundarajan were supported by NSF Award #1908048. Sarıyüce was supported by NSF Award #1910063.

References

1. Adiga, A., Vullikanti, A.K.S.: How robust is the core of a network? In: Blockeel, H., Kersting, K., Nijssen, S., Železný, F. (eds.) ECML PKDD 2013. LNCS (LNAI), vol. 8188, pp. 541–556. Springer, Heidelberg (2013). https://doi.org/10.1007/978-3-642-40988-2_35
2. Altaf-Ul-Amine, M., et al.: Prediction of protein functions based on k-cores of protein-protein interaction networks and amino acid sequences. Genome Inform. **14**, 498–499 (2003)
3. Alvarez-Hamelin, J.I., Dall'Asta, L., Barrat, A., Vespignani, A.: k-core decomposition: a tool for the visualization of large scale networks. arXiv preprint cs/0504107 (2005)
4. Batagelj, V., Zaversnik, M.: An o(m) algorithm for cores decomposition of networks. arXiv preprint cs/0310049 (2003)
5. Bhawalkar, K., Kleinberg, J., Lewi, K., Roughgarden, T., Sharma, A.: Preventing unraveling in social networks: the anchored k-core problem. SIAM J. Discret. Math. **29**(3), 1452–1475 (2015)
6. Brooks, S.P., Roberts, G.O.: Assessing convergence of Markov chain Monte Carlo algorithms. Stat. Comput. **8**(4), 319–335 (1998)
7. Cohen, J.: Trusses: cohesive subgraphs for social network analysis. National security agency technical report 16.3.1 (2008)
8. Ellens, W., Kooij, R.E.: Graph measures and network robustness. arXiv preprint arXiv:1311.5064 (2013)
9. Erdős, P., Rényi, A., et al.: On the evolution of random graphs. Publ. Math. Inst. Hung. Acad. Sci **5**(1), 17–60 (1960)
10. Freitas, S., et al.: Graph vulnerability and robustness: a survey. IEEE Trans. Knowl. Data Eng. **35**(6), 5915–5934 (2022)
11. Al-garadi, M.A., Varathan, K.D., Ravana, S.D.: Identification of influential spreaders in online social networks using interaction weighted k-core decomposition method. Physica A: Stat. Mech. Appl. **468**, 278–288 (2017)
12. Govindan, P., Wang, C., Xu, C., Duan, H., Soundarajan, S.: The k-peak decomposition: mapping the global structure of graphs. In: Proceedings of the 26th International Conference on World Wide Web, pp. 1441–1450 (2017)
13. Iwata, M., Sasa, S.: Dynamics of k-core percolation in a random graph. J. Phys. A Math. Theor. **42**(7), 075005 (2009)
14. Kendall, M.G.: A new measure of rank correlation. Biometrika **30**(1/2), 81–93 (1938)
15. Knuth, D.E.: Estimating the efficiency of backtrack programs. Math. Comput. **29**(129), 122–136 (1975)
16. Laishram, R., Soundarajan, S.: On finding and analyzing the backbone of the k-core structure of a graph. In: 2022 IEEE International Conference on Data Mining (ICDM), pp. 1017–1022. IEEE (2022)
17. Laishram, R., et al.: Measuring and improving the core resilience of networks. In: Proceedings of the 2018 World Wide Web Conference, pp. 609–618 (2018)
18. Luce, R.D., Perry, A.D.: A method of matrix analysis of group structure. Psychometrika **14**(2), 95–116 (1949)
19. Malvestio, I., Cardillo, A., Masuda, N.: Interplay between k-core and community structure in complex networks. Sci. Rep. **10**(1), 1–12 (2020)
20. Medya, S., Ma, T., Silva, A., Singh, A.: A game theoretic approach for core resilience. In: International Joint Conferences on Artificial Intelligence Organization (2020)

21. Mokken, R.J., et al.: Cliques, clubs and clans. Qual. Quant. **13**(2), 161–173 (1979)
22. Peng, C., Kolda, T.G., Pinar, A.: Accelerating community detection by using k-core subgraphs. arXiv preprint arXiv:1403.2226 (2014)
23. Pittel, B., Spencer, J., Wormald, N.: Sudden emergence of a giantk-core in a random graph. J. Comb. Theory Ser. B **67**(1), 111–151 (1996)
24. Seidman, S.B.: Network structure and minimum degree. Soc. Netw. **5**(3), 269–287 (1983)
25. Serafino, M., et al.: Superspreading k-cores at the center of COVID-19 pandemic persistence. medRxiv (2020)
26. Shin, K., Eliassi-Rad, T., Faloutsos, C.: Corescope: graph mining using k-core analysis–patterns, anomalies and algorithms. In: 2016 IEEE 16th International Conference on Data Mining (ICDM), pp. 469–478. IEEE (2016)
27. Zhang, H., Zhao, H., Cai, W., Liu, J., Zhou, W.: Using the k-core decomposition to analyze the static structure of large-scale software systems. J. Supercomput. **53**, 352–369 (2010)

GDM: Dual Mixup for Graph Classification with Limited Supervision

Abdullah Alchihabi[1]([✉]) and Yuhong Guo[1,2]([✉])

[1] School of Computer Science, Carleton University, Ottawa, Canada
`abdullahalchihabi@cmail.carleton.ca, yuhong.guo@carleton.ca`
[2] Canada CIFAR AI Chair, Amii, Canada

Abstract. Graph Neural Networks (GNNs) require a large number of labeled graph samples to obtain good performance on the graph classification task. The performance of GNNs degrades significantly as the number of labeled graph samples decreases. To reduce the annotation cost, it is therefore important to develop graph augmentation methods that can generate new graph instances to increase the size and diversity of the limited set of available labeled graph samples. In this work, we propose a novel mixup-based graph augmentation method, Graph Dual Mixup (GDM), that leverages both functional and structural information of the graph instances to generate new labeled graph samples. GDM employs a graph structural auto-encoder to learn structural embeddings of the graph samples, and then applies mixup to the structural information of the graphs in the learned structural embedding space and generates new graph structures from the mixup structural embeddings. As for the functional information, GDM applies mixup directly to the input node features of the graph samples to generate functional node feature information for new mixup graph instances. Jointly, the generated input node features and graph structures yield new graph samples which can supplement the set of original labeled graphs. Furthermore, we propose two novel Balanced Graph Sampling methods to enhance the balanced difficulty and diversity for the generated graph samples. Experimental results on the benchmark datasets demonstrate that our proposed method substantially outperforms the state-of-the-art graph augmentation methods when the labeled graphs are scarce.

Keywords: Graph Augmentation · Graph Classification · Limited Supervision

1 Introduction

Graph Neural Networks (GNNs) have successfully tackled a wide range of graph related tasks such as node classification, knowledge graph completion, and graph classification. In particular, the graph classification task has been addressed using various GNN models such as Graph Convolution Networks (GCNs) [11], Graph Attention Networks (GATs) [17], and Graph Isomorphism Networks (GINs) [22]. The effectiveness of such GNN models can be attributed to their natural ability to leverage both the functional information (nodes input features) and structural information (graph adjacency matrix) of graph data using message passing and message aggregation operations.

The success of GNNs in addressing the graph classification task nevertheless has been contingent on the availability of a large set of labeled graph samples, which induces a significant annotation burden in many domains where the labels are scarce and require substantial domain-expertise to generate. To tackle this problem, various graph augmentation methods have been proposed to increase the size and diversity of the training set by generating additional new graph samples. Most common graph augmentation methods, such as DropEdge [14], DropNode [25], and SoftEdge [5], involve perturbing the nodes, edges, or subgraphs of a given graph sample to generate a new graph. However such methods assume that the employed graph-augmentation operations are label invariant, which is difficult to guarantee in many cases. Additionally, these methods use a single graph sample to generate new graph instances, which limits the diversity of the generated graphs. Although mixup-based augmentation methods have demonstrated tremendous success in improving the generalization capacity of deep neural networks on image-based [26] and text-based tasks [16], it remains an open challenge to apply mixup to graph-based tasks given the irregular, discrete and not well-aligned nature of graph data. Few works have proposed methods to adapt mixup to graph data, including G-Mixup [7] and M-Mixup [21]. However, these methods either are computationally expensive and need a relatively large number of graph samples to obtain good performance or generate new graph samples in the manifold space and offer limited improvement in performance.

In this work, we propose a novel mixup-based graph augmentation method named Graph Dual Mixup (GDM) for graph classification, which applies parallel mixup to the functional and structural information of the graph samples to generate new graph instances in the input space. Given the discrete nature of the graph structures, GDM employs a Graph Structural Auto-Encoder (GSAE) to learn a structural embedding of the graph nodes. It then applies mixup to the learned structural node embeddings of existing graphs to generate structural node embeddings for new mixup graph samples, which are subsequently used to produce the graph structures (i.e., adjacency matrices) of the new graph samples using the Graph Structural Decoder. Regarding the functional information, GDM applies mixup directly to the input node features of existing graphs to obtain the input node features of the corresponding mixup graph samples. The new graph instances generated through the parallel mixup over both the input features and graph structures are thereafter used to supplement the original set of labeled graph samples, reduce overfitting, and help GNNs generalize better with scarce graph labels. Furthermore, we propose two Balanced Graph Sampling methods to guide the mixup procedure to achieve balanced difficulty and diversity for the generated graph instances. We conduct comprehensive experiments on six graph classification benchmark datasets. The experimental results demonstrate that our proposed method substantially outperforms state-of-the-art graph augmentation methods in the literature when the number of labeled graphs is limited.

2   Related Works

2.1   Graph Classification

Earlier works have addressed the graph classification task using graph-kernel based methods where the graph samples are decomposed into small subgraphs [8,15,23]. More recently, Graph Neural Networks (GNNs) have been successfully adopted in tackling the graph classification task. Many GNN models such as Graph Convolution Networks (GCNs) [11], Graph Attention Networks (GATs) [17], GraphSAGE [6] and Graph Isomorphism Networks (GINs) [22] have been shown to possess strong capacity to represent the graph data using message passing and message aggregation operations, and facilitate graph classification. Moreover, some works have developed novel graph readout methods to obtain discriminative graph-level representations from the node-level representation learned by various GNN models [1,24].

2.2   Graph Augmentation

Data augmentation methods play a crucial role in regularizing the training of deep models. Common graph augmentation methods are perturbation-based methods that augment graph samples by applying perturbations to graph nodes [9,25], edges [5,14], or subgraphs [13,20]. DropEdge randomly drops a number of edges from the graph structure during training [14]. SoftEdge selects a random subset of edges and assigns random weights to them to generate augmented graphs while preserving the connectivity patterns of the input graphs [5]. DropNode randomly deletes a subset of the nodes in the graph together with their connections to generate augmented graph samples [25]. GraphCrop augments the graphs with sub-structure deletion, which motivates GNNs to learn a robust global-view of the graph samples [20]. Graph Transplant uses subgraph transplantation to augment graphs where node saliency is used to select the transplanted subgraphs [13]. These methods however operate under the strong assumption that the applied graph perturbations are label-invariant insofar the augmented graph shares the same ground-truth label as the original graph. Such an assumption is hard to guarantee in many cases. Meanwhile, although there has been tremendous success of Mixup-based methods in regularizing deep models in domains where the data is regular, well-aligned and continuous such as images [26] and text [16], few works have attempted to adapt mixup to graph data. M-Mixup applies mixup to the graph-level representation in the manifold space learned by GNNs in a similar way to manifold mixup [21]. G-Mixup performs mixup to the graphons of different classes which are learned from the graph samples, and generates augmented graphs by sampling from the mixed graphons [7]. GraphMix is a node-level augmentation method where manifold mixup is applied to a fully-connected network that is trained jointly with a GNN [18]. Further details on graph augmentation methods can be found in [27].

3   Method

3.1   Problem Setup

We consider the following graph classification setting. The input is a set of N labeled graphs: $\mathcal{G} = \{(G_1, \mathbf{y}_1), \cdots, (G_N, \mathbf{y}_N)\}$. Each graph G is made up of a pair (V, E), where V is the set of graph nodes with size $|V| = n$ and E is the set of edges. E is represented by an adjacency matrix A of size $n \times n$. The adjacency matrix can have either binary or weighted values, be symmetric (in the case of undirected graphs) or asymmetric (in the case of directed graphs). Each node in the graph G is associated with a corresponding feature vector of size d. The feature vectors of all the nodes in the graph are represented by an input feature matrix $X \in \mathbb{R}^{n \times d}$. The graphs in the training set $\mathcal{G}$ may potentially have different sizes (different number of nodes), while the feature vectors of the nodes of all graphs have the same size d. The graph label vector $\mathbf{y}$ is a one-hot label indicator vector of size C, where C is the number of classes.

3.2   Graph Classification

GNNs address the graph classification task by utilizing both the graph adjacency matrix and the input node features, which correspond to the structural and functional information of the graphs, respectively. GNN models in the literature are commonly made up of three components: a node representation learning function f_θ, a graph readout function, and a graph classification function g_ϕ. The node representation function f_θ typically consists of multiple (e.g., L) GNN layers, each of which performs message propagation and message aggregation at the node level to learn new node embedding as follows:

$$\mathbf{h}_u^l = \text{AGGREGATE}(\mathbf{h}_u^{l-1}, \mathbf{h}_v^{l-1} | v \in \mathcal{N}(u), \theta^l) \tag{1}$$

where $\mathbf{h}_u^l \in \mathbb{R}^{d_l \times 1}$ is the learned embedding of node u with size d_l at layer l, $\mathcal{N}(u)$ is the set of neighboring nodes of node u, θ^l is the learnable parameters of the l-th GNN layer, and AGGREGATE is the message aggregation function which can be any permutation invariant function (sum, average, max, etc.). The initial node embedding $\mathbf{h}_u^0$ is the input node feature vector $\mathbf{x}_u$. The graph readout function is a permutation-invariant function used to obtain the graph-level embedding from the learned node-level embedding as follows:

$$\mathbf{h}_G = \text{READOUT}(\mathbf{h}_u^L | u \in V) \tag{2}$$

where $\mathbf{h}_u^L \in \mathbb{R}^{d_L \times 1}$ is the embedding of node u obtained from the top layer L of f_θ and $\mathbf{h}_G \in \mathbb{R}^{d_G \times 1}$ is the graph-level embedding. The graph classification function g_ϕ takes the graph-level embedding $\mathbf{h}_G$ as input to produce the predicted class probability vector for the given graph G as follows:

$$\mathbf{p}_G = g(\mathbf{h}_G | \phi). \tag{3}$$

All the components are trained end-to-end by minimizing the following cross-entropy loss over the labeled graphs in the training set:

$$\mathcal{L} = \sum_{G \in \mathcal{G}} \ell(\mathbf{p}_G, \mathbf{y}_G) \qquad (4)$$

where $\ell(\cdot, \cdot)$ is the cross-entropy loss function, $\mathbf{p}_G$ and $\mathbf{y}_G$ are the predicted class probability vector and the ground-truth label indicator vector for graph G, respectively.

3.3 Mixup

Mixup is an interpolation-based augmentation method that has demonstrated significant success in reducing overfitting and improving the generalization of deep neural networks [16,26]. Mixup generates augmented training samples $(\tilde{x}, \tilde{y})$ by applying linear interpolation between a randomly sampled pair of input instances and their corresponding labels as follows:

$$\tilde{x} = \lambda x_i + (1 - \lambda)x_j, \qquad \tilde{y} = \lambda y_i + (1 - \lambda)y_j \qquad (5)$$

where λ is a scalar mixing coefficient sampled from a Beta distribution Beta(α, β) with hyper-parameters α and β. $(\tilde{x}, \tilde{y})$ is the new sample generated by mixing the input labeled samples (x_i, y_i) and (x_j, y_j). Mixup can be readily applied to any classification task where the input data is regular, continuous and well-aligned such as images, text and time-series data. However, mixup cannot be applied directly to graph data given that: (1) graph data is irregular where different graphs may potentially have different sizes (different number of nodes). (2) graphs do not have a natural-ordering of their nodes, therefore aligning a pair of graphs is a non-trivial task. (3) graph structures may be discrete where the edges are binary whereas mixup generates continuous samples. Therefore, it is important to develop new methods that adapt mixup to the discrete, irregular and not well-aligned graph data.

3.4 Graph Dual Mixup

In this section, we introduce our proposed Graph Dual Mixup (GDM) method which generates new graph samples by applying parallel structural (i.e., structure-based) mixup and functional (i.e., feature-based) mixup over each selected pair of existing graph samples. In particular, GDM employs a Graph Structural Auto-Encoder (GSAE) to learn a structural embedding of the graph nodes based on the adjacency matrix. The structural mixup is then applied on the structural node embeddings of the input pair of graphs to produce a new set of node embeddings, which is used to generate the adjacency matrix (i.e., graph structure) of the mixup graph sample using the Graph Structural Decoder of the GSAE. As for the functional information encoded with node features, GDM applies mixup directly to the input node features to obtain the node features of the generated mixup graph sample. In the remainder of this section, we elaborate on the dual mixup procedure of this GDM methodology.

Structural Graph Node Representation Learning. Given the discrete nature of graph structures, mixup cannot be directly applied to the structures of a pair of graphs (represented by their corresponding adjacency matrices) to generate a new graph structure. Therefore, we propose to employ a Graph Structural Auto-Encoder (GSAE) to learn a structural embedding of the graph nodes and support mixup in the learned structural embedding space. This allows us to evade the difficulties associated with applying mixup to the original graph structures. GSAE is made up of a structural encoder $\mathcal{E}_s$ and a structural decoder $\mathcal{D}_s$. The structural encoder $\mathcal{E}_s$ consists of multiple GNN layers that learn the structural node embeddings by propagating and aggregating messages across the graph structure, where the messages reflect solely the structural information of the nodes. The goal is to learn a structural embedding of all the nodes in the graph that would enable us to reconstruct the graph adjacency matrix. Specifically, for a given graph sample $G = (X, A)$, $\mathcal{E}_s$ takes the adjacency matrix $A \in \mathbb{R}^{n \times n}$ and the node degree matrix $D \in \mathbb{R}^{n \times n}$ (represent the initial node structural features) computed from A as input to learn the structural node embeddings as follows:

$$H_s = \mathcal{E}_s(D, A), \qquad \text{where } D[i, i] = \sum_j A[i, j], \tag{6}$$

where the node degree matrix D is an identity matrix whose main diagonal values correspond to the degrees of the associated nodes; $H_s \in \mathbb{R}^{n \times d_s}$ is the learned structural embedding of the nodes in the graph with size d_s. H_s holds solely the structural information of all the nodes in the graph, from which one can reconstruct the connections/edges between the nodes and therefore the original adjacency matrix A using the structural decoder $\mathcal{D}_s$ of the GSAE. In particular, we adopt a simple inner product similarity based decoder as the structural decoder $\mathcal{D}_s$, which takes the learned structural node embeddings as input to reconstruct the graph adjacency matrix A as follows:

$$\hat{A} = \mathcal{D}_s(H_s) = \sigma(H_s H_s^T) \tag{7}$$

where σ is the sigmoid activation function and $\hat{A} \in \mathbb{R}^{n \times n}$ is the decoded/reconstructed adjacency matrix. The GSAE is trained end-to-end to minimize the following graph structure reconstruction loss:

$$\mathcal{L}_{\text{re}}^s = -\sum_{G \in \mathcal{G}} \left[\sum_{(i,j) \in E_G} \log(\hat{A}_G[i, j]) + \sum_{(i,j) \in S_G^{\text{neg}}} \log(1 - \hat{A}_G[i, j]) \right] \tag{8}$$

where E_G is the set of edges for graph G and S_G^{neg} is the set of randomly sampled negative edges of graph G (i.e. edges that do not exist in the original graph). It is important to note that GSAE does not access/use the input node features (functional graph information) as it replaces the input node features with the corresponding node degrees calculated from the adjacency matrix. GSAE also does not make use of the graph class labels as it is learned in a completely self-supervised/unsupervised fashion.

Graph Generation via Dual Mixup. After training the GSAE, our proposed Graph Dual Mixup is ready to apply Structural Mixup and Functional Mixup to the structural and functional information of the graphs respectively to generate new graph samples. To achieve that, for a given pair of graphs and their corresponding label vectors $(G_i, \mathbf{y}_i)$ and $(G_j, \mathbf{y}_j)$, where the two graphs are made up of input node feature matrices and graph adjacency matrices such as $G_i = (X_i, A_i)$ and $G_j = (X_j, A_j)$, GDM randomly aligns the nodes of the graph pair. When G_i and G_j have different sizes $(n_i \neq n_j)$, we pad the input node feature matrix and adjacency matrix of the smaller graph with zeros to match the size of the larger graph. Then we apply functional mixup directly to the input node features and the label vectors of the graph pair to generate the node features of the new graph sample $\tilde{G}$ and its corresponding label vector $\tilde{\mathbf{y}}$ as follows:

$$\tilde{X} = \lambda X_i + (1 - \lambda) X_j, \qquad \tilde{\mathbf{y}} = \lambda \mathbf{y}_i + (1 - \lambda)\mathbf{y}_j \qquad (9)$$

To obtain the structural information of the generated new graph sample $\tilde{G}$, GDM applies structural mixup in the structural embedding space learned by the GSAE as follows:

$$\tilde{H}_s = \lambda \mathcal{E}_s(D_i, A_i) + (1 - \lambda)\mathcal{E}_s(D_j, A_j) \qquad (10)$$

where D_i and D_j are the degree matrices of G_i and G_j, respectively; $\tilde{H}_s \in \mathbb{R}^{\max(n_i, n_j) \times d_s}$ is the structural node embedding matrix of the generated graph $\tilde{G}$. The graph structural decoder is then used to reconstruct the adjacency matrix of graph $\tilde{G}$ from the mixed structural node embeddings:

$$\tilde{A} = \mathcal{D}_s(\tilde{H}_s) = \sigma(\tilde{H}_s \tilde{H}_s^T) \qquad (11)$$

The obtained matrix $\tilde{A} \in \mathbb{R}^{\max(n_i, n_j) \times \max(n_i, n_j)}$ is a weighted adjacency matrix with edge weights between 0 and 1. In order to filter out the noise in the edge weights and sparsify the structure of generated graph sample, we prune the adjacency matrix by dropping off the weak edges with weights smaller than a pre-defined threshold ϵ as follows:

$$\tilde{A}[i,j] = \begin{cases} \tilde{A}[i,j], & \text{if } \tilde{A}[i,j] \geq \epsilon \\ 0, & \text{otherwise.} \end{cases} \qquad (12)$$

Moreover, in order for the structure of the generated graph sample $\tilde{G}$ to match the structural properties of the original graph samples, we post-process $\tilde{A}$ accordingly. In the case that the original graph samples have weighted edges, no post-processing is required. As for the case of the original graph samples being unweighted/binary graphs, we binarize $\tilde{A}$ by replacing all its non-zero values with value 1 as follows:

$$\tilde{A}[i,j] = \begin{cases} 1, & \text{if } \tilde{A}[i,j] > 0 \\ 0, & \text{otherwise} \end{cases} \qquad (13)$$

In this manner, we obtain a new generated graph $\tilde{G}$ with its mixup node features $\tilde{X}$, adjacency matrix $\tilde{A}$ and label vector $\tilde{\mathbf{y}}$.

3.5   Balanced Graph Sampling

Given the limited number of available labeled graph instances, randomly sampling pairs of graphs to generate new graph instances might be inadequate for improving model generalization and reducing overfitting as random sampling does not take the difficulty or diversity of the generated graph instances into consideration. Therefore, we propose two novel Balanced Graph Sampling methods to enhance the diversity and balanced difficulty of the generated graph samples. The proposed methods can separately: (1) generate low difficulty graphs by applying GDM to randomly sampled pairs of low difficulty graphs; (2) generate medium difficulty graphs by applying GDM to mix randomly sampled low difficulty graphs with high difficulty graphs; and (3) generate high difficulty graphs by applying GDM to randomly sampled pairs of high difficulty graphs. The advantage of balanced graph sampling over random sampling is that it guarantees that the generated graph samples have 3 subsets with *equal sizes*: a low difficulty subset, a medium difficulty subset, and a high difficulty subset.

To achieve that, we need to assess/estimate the difficulty level of the original graph instances. This is accomplished by pre-training a GNN model on the original set of labeled graph instances to minimize the classification loss shown in Eq. (1)—Eq. (4). Then the pre-trained GNN model is used to evaluate the difficulty level of each graph G based on its predicted class probability vector $\mathbf{p}_G$. The first balanced graph sampling method is an Accuracy-based method (Acc), which determines the level of difficulty for graph G based on the accuracy/correctness of its predicted class label:

$$\text{Diff}_{\text{Acc}}(G) = \begin{cases} \text{low,} & \text{if argmax } \mathbf{p}_G = \text{argmax } \mathbf{y}_G \\ \text{high,} & \text{otherwise} \end{cases} \qquad (14)$$

The second balanced graph sampling method is an Uncertainty-based method (Unc), which uses the uncertainty/entropy of the model prediction on a sample graph G to determine its level of difficulty. In particular, we sort the graphs from the training set $\mathcal{G}$ based on the entropy of their corresponding predicted class probability vectors, then consider the graphs with the lowest half of entropy scores to be low difficulty ones while the other half of the graphs are taken as high difficulty ones:

$$\text{Diff}_{\text{Unc}}(G) = \begin{cases} \text{low,} & \text{if Ent}(\mathbf{p}_G) \leq \text{Med}(\{\text{Ent}(\mathbf{p}_1), \cdots, \text{Ent}(\mathbf{p}_N)\}) \\ \text{high,} & \text{otherwise} \end{cases} \qquad (15)$$

where Ent(.) is the entropy function and Med(.) is the median function. Therefore, GDM can be applied with Accuracy-based Balanced Graph Sampling (GDM Acc) or Uncertainty-based Balanced Graph Sampling (GDM Unc) to generate a new set of diverse graph samples $\mathcal{G}_{\text{GDM}}$ with balanced difficulty.

Algorithm 1. Augmentation and Training Procedure of Graph Dual Mixup

---

Input: Graph set $\mathcal{G}$; hyper-parameters α, β ϵ, λ_{GDM}
Output: Learned model parameters θ, ϕ
Pre-train a GNN Model on $\mathcal{G}$ to determine the graph difficulty levels
Train GSAE on $\mathcal{G}$ using Eq. (6), (7), (8).
$\mathcal{G}_{\text{low}}$ = Generate low difficulty samples with GDM
$\mathcal{G}_{\text{med}}$ = Generate medium difficulty samples with GDM
$\mathcal{G}_{\text{high}}$ = Generate high difficulty samples with GDM
$\mathcal{G}_{\text{GDM}} = \mathcal{G}_{\text{low}} \cup \mathcal{G}_{\text{med}} \cup \mathcal{G}_{\text{high}}$
Train the final GNN Model on $\mathcal{G}$ and $\mathcal{G}_{\text{GDM}}$ using Eq. (1), (2), (3), and (16).

3.6 Augmented Training Procedure

The combination of Balanced Graph Sampling and Graph Dual Mixup generates a diverse set of new graph instances, which can supplement the limited number of original labeled graph samples. Finally, we train the GNN model using the original graph set $\mathcal{G}$ and the generated graph set $\mathcal{G}_{\text{GDM}}$ by minimizing the following loss function:

$$\mathcal{L}_{\text{total}} = \sum_{G \in \mathcal{G}} \ell_{CE}(\mathbf{p}_G, \mathbf{y}_G) + \lambda_{\text{GDM}} \sum_{G \in \mathcal{G}_{\text{GDM}}} \ell_{CE}(\mathbf{p}_G, \tilde{\mathbf{y}}_G) \quad (16)$$

where λ_{GDM} is a trade-off hyper-parameter controlling the contribution of the generated graph set G_{GDM}. An overview of the graph augmentation process and the GNN augmented training procedure is presented in Algorithm 1.

4 Experiments

4.1 Experimental Setup

Datasets & Baselines. We evaluate our proposed method on 6 graph classification benchmark datasets from the TUDatasets [12], including 3 chemical datasets and 3 social datasets. The chemical datasets are D&D [3], Proteins [2] and NCI1 [19], while the social datasets are IMDB-Binary, IMDB-Multi and Reddit-5K [23]. We employ the same 10-fold train/validation/test split provided by [4]. We apply our proposed Graph Dual Mixup on the Graph Convolution Network (GCN) baseline [11] and compare our proposed method against 5 other graph augmentation methods from the literature: DropNode [25], DropEdge [14], M-Mixup [21], SoftEdge [5] and G-Mixup [7].

Implementation Details. The node representation function f_θ of the GNN model is made up of 4 message passing layers, followed by Global Mean Pooling as the Readout function. The graph classification function g_ϕ is made up of 2 fully connected layers followed by a softmax function. Each message passing layer and fully connected layer is followed by a Rectified Linear Unit (ReLU) activation function. The structural encoder $\mathcal{E}_s$ is made up of 2 GCN message

Table 1. Mean classification accuracy (standard deviation is within brackets) on 6 graph classification benchmark datasets with 10 labeled graphs per class.

Dataset	Proteins	NCI1	D&D	IMDB-B	IMDB-M	Reddit
GCN	$59.3_{(6.8)}$	$51.0_{(1.6)}$	$59.5_{(2.7)}$	$54.5_{(3.9)}$	$36.9_{(3.7)}$	$25.1_{(5.1)}$
DropNode	$61.0_{(8.5)}$	$52.9_{(3.4)}$	$62.1_{(2.9)}$	$59.0_{(5.7)}$	$36.9_{(4.6)}$	$30.8_{(8.4)}$
DropEdge	$59.4_{(5.8)}$	$53.1_{(3.7)}$	$62.6_{(4.5)}$	$57.6_{(5.5)}$	$37.2_{(4.1)}$	$26.7_{(8.4)}$
SoftEdge	$58.9_{(7.2)}$	$52.0_{(3.2)}$	$59.5_{(2.4)}$	$55.3_{(6.6)}$	$36.2_{(3.0)}$	$25.0_{(4.9)}$
M-Mixup	$59.0_{(7.2)}$	$51.9_{(3.3)}$	$59.1_{(5.3)}$	$57.1_{(6.4)}$	$37.4_{(5.3)}$	$23.0_{(2.8)}$
G-Mixup	$60.8_{(2.1)}$	$51.8_{(3.2)}$	$58.7_{(4.2)}$	$55.1_{(8.5)}$	$36.9_{(4.3)}$	$24.1_{(7.3)}$
GDM Acc	$\mathbf{66.0}_{(5.3)}$	$\mathbf{57.5}_{(2.6)}$	$62.1_{(3.7)}$	$\mathbf{61.3}_{(6.7)}$	$\mathbf{40.9}_{(5.4)}$	$\mathbf{36.3}_{(8.0)}$
GDM Unc	$65.1_{(6.1)}$	$56.8_{(3.9)}$	$\mathbf{64.0}_{(4.2)}$	$61.0_{(7.0)}$	$39.8_{(5.5)}$	$34.9_{(9.1)}$

passing layers. The GNN model is pre-trained on the original graph set for 100 epochs and subsequently trained on the original graph set and augmented graph set for 800 epochs, both using the Adam optimizer with learning rate of 1e-2. The Graph Structural Auto-Encoder is trained for 200 epochs using the Adam optimizer with learning rate of 1e-2. The loss trade-off hyperparameter λ_{GDM} and the weak edge pruning threshold ϵ take values 1 and 0.1, respectively. The mixing scalar coefficient λ is sampled from distribution Beta(α, β) with hyperparameters $\alpha = \beta = 1.0$. We use a dropout rate of 0.25 for SoftEdge, DropNode and DropEdge. For G-Mixup, we use the same hyper-parameters reported in [7].

4.2 Comparison Results

We investigate the performance of our proposed GDM with limited numbers of labeled graphs. We aim to use a small number of labeled graphs per class, e.g., {2, 3, 5, 10, 25, 50}, as the training set. To achieve that, we randomly sampled graphs from the training set of each fold in the 10-fold split provided [4] to match the desired label rates. For each label rate, we repeat our experiments 3 times on all the 10-folds and average the test accuracy over all folds and all runs. We evaluate GDM in combination with the proposed two Balanced Graph Sampling methods to obtain: (1) "GDM Acc", where GDM is applied with the Accuracy-based Balanced Graph Sampling; and (2) "GDM Unc", where GDM is applied with Uncertainty-based Balanced Graph Sampling. We report the obtained test accuracy results with 10 labeled graphs per class in Table 1, while the test accuracy results for all label rates are presented in Fig. 1.

The results in Table 1 clearly demonstrate that both variants of our proposed GDM greatly outperform the underlying GCN baseline and the other 5 graph augmentation methods across all 6 datasets. GDM improves the performance of the underlying GCN baseline by 6.7%, 7.5%, 6.8% and 11.2% on the Proteins, NCI1, IMDB-Binary and Reddit-5K datasets, respectively. The performance gain over the other graph augmentation methods is also notable, exceeding 5%, 4.4% and 6.3% on Proteins, NCI1 and Reddit-5K, respectively. Moreover,

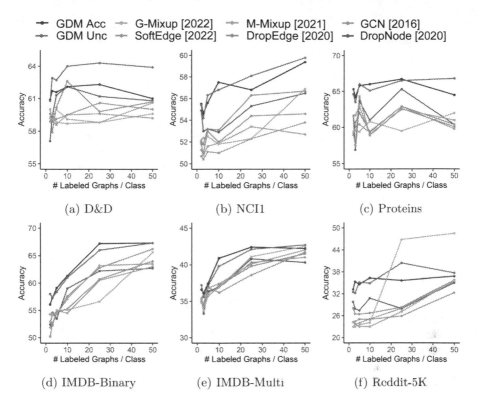

Fig. 1. Mean classification accuracy on 6 graph classification benchmark datasets with few labeled graphs per class (2, 3, 5, 10, 25, 50).

Fig. 1 clearly shows that our proposed GDM consistently outperforms the GCN baseline and the 5 comparison graph augmentation methods on 5 datasets across almost all label rates. Only in the case of the Reddit-5K dataset with label rates of larger than 25 labeled graphs per class, G-Mixup outperforms our proposed method. Nevertheless, GDM consistently improves the performance of the underlying GCN baseline across all the label rates on all the datasets, achieving performance gains over 6%, 5%, 5% and 11% on Proteins, NCI1, IMDB-Binary and Reddit-5K, respectively, in the case of 2 labeled graphs per class. Furthermore, GDM yields remarkable performance gains over the other graph augmentation methods, exceeding 4% on Proteins, Reddit-5K and IMDB-Binary in the case of 2 labeled graphs per class. This highlights the superior performance of the proposed GDM over the existing state-of-the-art graph augmentation methods for graph classification with limited supervision.

4.3 Ablation Study

Impact of Balanced Graph Sampling. We conduct an ablation study to investigate the impact of our balanced graph sampling methods on the pro-

Table 2. Ablation study results on the impact of Balanced Graph Sampling in terms of mean classification accuracy (standard deviation is within brackets) with a few labeled graphs per class (2, 3, 5, 10).

	D & D				IMDB-Multi			
	2	3	5	10	2	3	5	10
GDM Rand	$59.6_{(5.3)}$	$61.2_{(3.9)}$	$61.5_{(3.5)}$	$63.0_{(4.5)}$	$35.4_{(3.8)}$	$35.5_{(4.0)}$	$36.4_{(5.5)}$	$39.7_{(5.3)}$
GDM Acc	$\mathbf{61.0}_{(2.6)}$	$\mathbf{61.7}_{(3.3)}$	$\mathbf{61.6}_{(3.5)}$	$62.1_{(3.7)}$	$\mathbf{36.6}_{(4.9)}$	$\mathbf{36.1}_{(3.8)}$	$37.4_{(4.5)}$	$\mathbf{40.9}_{(5.4)}$
w/o Low Diff	$59.2_{(1.4)}$	$57.7_{(5.7)}$	$59.2_{(2.1)}$	$58.2_{(4.0)}$	$35.0_{(3.6)}$	$34.4_{(2.8)}$	$34.5_{(1.8)}$	$36.5_{(3.1)}$
w/o Med Diff	$60.2_{(3.9)}$	$61.6_{(4.1)}$	$59.9_{(2.1)}$	$59.6_{(3.1)}$	$34.9_{(3.4)}$	$35.4_{(4.7)}$	$38.3_{(4.0)}$	$39.9_{(5.8)}$
w/o High Diff	$60.1_{(3.2)}$	$60.6_{(4.4)}$	$60.6_{(2.7)}$	$61.3_{(4.1)}$	$33.8_{(3.2)}$	$34.4_{(3.9)}$	$\mathbf{38.4}_{(4.3)}$	$39.0_{(5.5)}$
GDM Unc	$\mathbf{60.8}_{(2.8)}$	$\mathbf{62.9}_{(3.7)}$	$\mathbf{62.7}_{(3.2)}$	$\mathbf{64.0}_{(4.2)}$	$\mathbf{37.2}_{(4.9)}$	$\mathbf{35.6}_{(3.6)}$	$37.1_{(5.4)}$	$\mathbf{39.8}_{(5.5)}$
w/o Low Diff	$59.3_{(1.0)}$	$58.8_{(1.0)}$	$58.9_{(1.0)}$	$59.7_{(1.8)}$	$35.8_{(2.9)}$	$34.7_{(3.7)}$	$34.4_{(2.7)}$	$37.0_{(3.4)}$
w/o Med Diff	$\mathbf{60.8}_{(2.9)}$	$60.4_{(4.3)}$	$\mathbf{62.7}_{(3.3)}$	$62.8_{(4.5)}$	$35.3_{(3.6)}$	$34.8_{(3.4)}$	$36.6_{(4.9)}$	$38.8_{(4.6)}$
w/o High Diff	$60.4_{(2.6)}$	$61.5_{(3.7)}$	$62.0_{(4.2)}$	$63.2_{(3.4)}$	$35.7_{(3.2)}$	$35.0_{(3.1)}$	$\mathbf{37.1}_{(4.0)}$	$39.6_{(3.8)}$

posed GDM method. Specifically, we consider four variants of the balanced graph sampling: (1) w/o Low Diff: we do not generate low difficulty samples. (2) w/o Med Diff: we do not generate medium difficulty samples. (3) w/o High Diff: we do not generate high difficulty samples. (4) GDM Rand: we drop the proposed balanced graph sampling method and use random sampling for mixup. We evaluate the first three variants using both the GDM Acc and GDM Unc methods of balanced graph sampling. The comparison results with different label rates—{2, 3, 5, 10} labeled graphs per class—on the D&D and IMDB-Multi datasets are reported in Table 2.

From Table 2, we can see that all variants have a performance drop from the full balanced graph sampling on both datasets with almost all label rates for both GDM Acc and GDM Unc. The w/o Low Diff variant produces the most notable performance degradation, which can be attributed to the GNN models' needs for low difficulty and confident samples to improve generalization and prevent underfitting when learning with very low label rates. The w/o Med Diff and w/o High Diff variants also suffer performance degradations, indicating the importance of medium difficulty and high difficulty samples for inducing better generalization and reducing overfitting. Additionally, the GDM Rand variant also demonstrates notable performance drops compared to both GDM Acc and GDM Unc with almost all label rates, which highlights the importance of ensuring the diversity and balanced difficulty of the generated graph samples. These results validate the contribution of each component in balanced graph sampling.

Impact of Graph Structural Auto-Encoder. We further conduct an ablation study to investigate the impact of the Graph Structural Auto-Encoder on the proposed GDM. Specifically, we compare our proposed GSAE with a Variational Graph Structural Auto-Encoder (VGSAE). The VGSAE learns the parameters of a Gaussian distribution (mean and variance) to represent the underlying

Table 3. Ablation study results on the impact of Graph Structural Auto-encoder in terms of mean classification accuracy (standard deviation is within brackets).

	Proteins				IMDB-Binary			
	2	3	5	10	2	3	5	10
GCN	$59.4_{(6.7)}$	$60.1_{(1.0)}$	$60.4_{(4.6)}$	$59.3_{(6.8)}$	$52.6_{(2.7)}$	$52.5_{(2.5)}$	$55.0_{(6.4)}$	$54.5_{(3.9)}$
GSAE Acc	$\mathbf{65.3}_{(5.5)}$	$\mathbf{64.2}_{(7.9)}$	$\mathbf{65.8}_{(6.2)}$	$\mathbf{66.0}_{(5.3)}$	$\mathbf{56.1}_{(4.6)}$	$57.3_{(6.8)}$	$\mathbf{59.1}_{(6.2)}$	$\mathbf{61.3}_{(6.7)}$
VGSAE Acc	$64.6_{(4.2)}$	$63.4_{(5.1)}$	$65.6_{(6.0)}$	$65.3_{(7.0)}$	$55.9_{(4.0)}$	$\mathbf{58.7}_{(5.2)}$	$57.8_{(6.5)}$	$59.7_{(7.4)}$
GSAE Unc	$\mathbf{64.6}_{(4.0)}$	$63.5_{(7.2)}$	$\mathbf{66.0}_{(5.3)}$	$\mathbf{65.1}_{(6.1)}$	$\mathbf{58.0}_{(6.0)}$	$57.4_{(7.1)}$	$\mathbf{58.4}_{(6.1)}$	$\mathbf{61.0}_{(7.0)}$
VGSAE Unc	$61.8_{(9.4)}$	$\mathbf{63.7}_{(8.4)}$	$65.2_{(5.2)}$	$63.7_{(5.7)}$	$55.2_{(3.9)}$	$\mathbf{57.7}_{(6.6)}$	$56.9_{(6.5)}$	$59.4_{(5.8)}$

Table 4. Ablation study results on the impact of GNN baselines in terms of mean classification accuracy (standard deviation is within brackets).

	IMDB-Binary				IMDB-Multi			
	2	3	5	10	2	3	5	10
GIN	$57.9_{(8.0)}$	$54.5_{(6.1)}$	$54.3_{(6.1)}$	$56.7_{(9.7)}$	$32.6_{(4.8)}$	$31.6_{(6.0)}$	$32.8_{(4.6)}$	$36.0_{(5.2)}$
GDM Acc	$\mathbf{58.8}_{(6.9)}$	$57.0_{(5.5)}$	$57.8_{(6.3)}$	$\mathbf{59.4}_{(6.3)}$	$35.6_{(4.2)}$	$35.1_{(4.6)}$	$36.9_{(3.9)}$	$38.3_{(3.5)}$
GDM Unc	$58.2_{(5.0)}$	$\mathbf{58.0}_{(6.5)}$	$\mathbf{60.5}_{(6.0)}$	$57.7_{(6.2)}$	$\mathbf{36.6}_{(4.2)}$	$\mathbf{37.2}_{(4.8)}$	$\mathbf{37.1}_{(3.9)}$	$\mathbf{39.5}_{(4.5)}$
GAT	$51.2_{(2.1)}$	$50.6_{(1.2)}$	$55.1_{(5.7)}$	$54.4_{(5.5)}$	$31.8_{(2.0)}$	$34.0_{(1.5)}$	$32.6_{(1.9)}$	$33.6_{(2.4)}$
GDM Acc	$\mathbf{55.7}_{(4.3)}$	$56.2_{(6.2)}$	$55.0_{(6.5)}$	$\mathbf{60.0}_{(7.1)}$	$35.6_{(2.9)}$	$\mathbf{36.4}_{(3.8)}$	$\mathbf{37.2}_{(4.3)}$	$38.5_{(5.0)}$
GDM Unc	$54.5_{(3.1)}$	$\mathbf{58.2}_{(6.7)}$	$\mathbf{56.0}_{(6.9)}$	$59.2_{(5.0)}$	$35.8_{(2.8)}$	$34.4_{(3.6)}$	$36.8_{(5.4)}$	$\mathbf{38.8}_{(4.3)}$

structure of the graph [10]. The comparison results with different label rates on the Proteins and IMDB-Binary datasets are reported in Table 3. From the table, it is clear that GSAE outperforms VGSAE on both datasets across almost all label rates. The performance gain of GSAE decreases as the label rate increases, which highlights that VGSAE requires more training samples to obtain good performance. Therefore GSAE is more suitable for the case of learning with limited supervision as it is able to obtain good generalization performance with few samples due to its simple architecture and smaller number of learnable parameters. Nevertheless, the proposed GDM greatly and consistently outperforms the underlying GCN baseline across all different label rates with both GSAE and VGSAE on both datasets.

Impact of GNN Baseline. We also conduct an ablation study to investigate the performance of our proposed GDM on additional GNN baselines. In particular, we applied GDM on the Graph Attention Network (GAT) [17] and Graph Isomorphism Network (GIN) [22] baselines. The comparison results with multiple label rates, $\{2, 3, 5, 10\}$, on the IMDB-Binary and IMDB-Multi datasets are reported in Table 4. The table clearly shows that GDM significantly improves the performance of both the GAT and GIN baselines across all label rates for both datasets. The performance gains are notable, exceeding 6%, 5% for GAT with label rates 5 and 3 for IMDB-Binary and IMDB-Multi, respectively. Similarly,

Table 5. Ablation study results on the impact of graph readout function in terms of mean classification accuracy (standard deviation is within brackets).

	Proteins				IMDB-Binary			
	2	3	5	10	2	3	5	10
Acc Mean	$\mathbf{65.3}_{(5.5)}$	$\mathbf{64.5}_{(4.8)}$	$\mathbf{65.8}_{(5.2)}$	$\mathbf{66.0}_{(5.3)}$	$\mathbf{56.1}_{(4.6)}$	$\mathbf{57.3}_{(6.8)}$	$\mathbf{59.1}_{(6.2)}$	$\mathbf{61.3}_{(6.7)}$
Acc Add	$64.9_{(5.1)}$	$63.2_{(4.9)}$	$65.3_{(4.8)}$	$63.3_{(4.3)}$	$53.0_{(2.8)}$	$55.2_{(5.3)}$	$56.9_{(6.1)}$	$59.9_{(6.7)}$
Acc Max	$63.8_{(4.7)}$	$64.4_{(4.8)}$	$63.2_{(7.0)}$	$63.5_{(7.4)}$	$53.9_{(4.7)}$	$56.0_{(7.8)}$	$58.6_{(7.0)}$	$60.6_{(6.3)}$
Unc Mean	$\mathbf{64.6}_{(4.0)}$	$\mathbf{63.6}_{(6.0)}$	$\mathbf{65.1}_{(5.3)}$	$66.0_{(5.0)}$	$\mathbf{58.0}_{(6.0)}$	$57.4_{(7.1)}$	$\mathbf{58.4}_{(6.1)}$	$\mathbf{61.0}_{(7.0)}$
Unc Add	$61.7_{(6.5)}$	$\mathbf{63.6}_{(6.1)}$	$63.0_{(7.0)}$	$63.4_{(5.5)}$	$55.6_{(4.9)}$	$54.8_{(3.6)}$	$57.4_{(8.2)}$	$60.5_{(6.7)}$
Unc Max	$63.0_{(1.1)}$	$63.4_{(6.6)}$	$61.9_{(7.0)}$	$\mathbf{66.8}_{(5.9)}$	$54.0_{(4.2)}$	$54.4_{(7.6)}$	$57.9_{(7.1)}$	$60.4_{(7.1)}$

GDM yields notable performance boost over GIN, exceeding 7%, 5% with label rates 3 and 5, respectively, for the IMDB-Binary dataset.

Impact of Graph Readout Method. We conduct an ablation study to investigate the impact of the graph Readout function employed in our GNN model. Specifically, in addition to Global Mean Pooling, we consider the following two variants: (1) Add, where Global Add Pooling is used to obtain the graph-level embedding. (2) Max, where Global Max Pooling is used to obtain the graph-level embedding. The comparison results with different label rates on the Proteins and IMDB-Binary datasets are reported in Table 5. From the table, we can see that the Global Max Pooling and Global Add Pooling variants have performance drops compared to the Global Mean Pooling with almost all label rates for both the Proteins and IMDB-Binary datasets. Global Add Pooling suffers from obtaining un-normalized graph-level embeddings which causes generalization issues given that the graphs in each dataset have different sizes. Global Max Pooling only considers one feature per node corresponding to the feature with max value, causing the obtained graph-level embeddings to omit discriminative information present in the other features of the node-level embeddings.

5   Conclusion

In this paper, we proposed a novel Graph Dual Mixup (GDM) augmentation method for graph classification with limited labeled data. The proposed method employs a Graph Structural Auto-encoder to learn the structural embedding of the nodes, and then applies dual mixup on the structural node embeddings and the original node features of a pair of existing graphs in parallel to generate the structural and functional information of a new graph instance. The generated graph samples can augment the set of original graphs to alleviate overfitting and improve the generalizability of the GNN models. Additionally, we further propose two novel Balanced Graph Sampling methods to support GDM and enhance the balanced difficulty and diversity of the generated graph samples.

We conducted experiments on six graph benchmark datasets, the experimental results demonstrate that the proposed method improves the generalization performance of the underlying GNNs when the labeled graphs are scarce and outperforms the state-of-the-art graph augmentation methods.

References

1. Bianchi, F.M., Grattarola, D., Alippi, C.: Spectral clustering with graph neural networks for graph pooling. In: International Conference on Machine Learning (ICML) (2020)
2. Borgwardt, K.M., Ong, C.S., Schönauer, S., Vishwanathan, S., Smola, A.J., Kriegel, H.P.: Protein function prediction via graph kernels. Bioinformatics **21**(suppl_1), i47–i56 (2005)
3. Dobson, P.D., Doig, A.J.: Distinguishing enzyme structures from non-enzymes without alignments. J. Mol. Biol. **330**(4), 771–783 (2003)
4. Errica, F., Podda, M., Bacciu, D., Micheli, A.: A fair comparison of graph neural networks for graph classification. In: International Conference on Learning Representations (ICLR) (2020)
5. Guo, H., Sun, S.: Softedge: regularizing graph classification with random soft edges. arXiv preprint arXiv:2204.10390 (2022)
6. Hamilton, W., Ying, Z., Leskovec, J.: Inductive representation learning on large graphs. In: Advances in Neural Information Processing Systems (NIPS) (2017)
7. Han, X., Jiang, Z., Liu, N., Hu, X.: G-mixup: graph data augmentation for graph classification. In: International Conference on Machine Learning (ICML) (2022)
8. Haussler, D., et al.: Convolution kernels on discrete structures. Technical report, Citeseer (1999)
9. Huang, W., Zhang, T., Rong, Y., Huang, J.: Adaptive sampling towards fast graph representation learning. In: Advances in Neural Information Processing Systems (NeurIPS) (2018)
10. Kipf, T.N., Welling, M.: Variational graph auto-encoders. arXiv preprint arXiv:1611.07308 (2016)
11. Kipf, T.N., Welling, M.: Semi-supervised classification with graph convolutional networks. In: International Conference on Learning Representations (ICLR) (2017)
12. Morris, C., Kriege, N.M., Bause, F., Kersting, K., Mutzel, P., Neumann, M.: Tudataset: a collection of benchmark datasets for learning with graphs. In: ICML Workshop on Graph Representation Learning and Beyond (2020)
13. Park, J., Shim, H., Yang, E.: Graph transplant: Node saliency-guided graph mixup with local structure preservation. In: AAAI Conference on Artificial Intelligence (2022)
14. Rong, Y., Huang, W., Xu, T., Huang, J.: Dropedge: towards deep graph convolutional networks on node classification. In: International Conference on Learning Representations (ICLR) (2020)
15. Shervashidze, N., Schweitzer, P., Van Leeuwen, E.J., Mehlhorn, K., Borgwardt, K.M.: Weisfeiler-Lehman graph kernels. J. Mach. Learn. Res. **12**(9) (2011)
16. Sun, L., Xia, C., Yin, W., Liang, T., Yu, P.S., He, L.: Mixup-transformer: dynamic data augmentation for NLP tasks. arXiv preprint arXiv:2010.02394 (2020)
17. Veličković, P., Cucurull, G., Casanova, A., Romero, A., Liò, P., Bengio, Y.: Graph attention networks. In: International Conference on Learning Representations (ICLR) (2018)

18. Verma, V., et al.: Graphmix: improved training of GNNs for semi-supervised learning. In: AAAI Conference on Artificial Intelligence (2021)
19. Wale, N., Watson, I.A., Karypis, G.: Comparison of descriptor spaces for chemical compound retrieval and classification. Knowl. Inf. Syst. **14**, 347–375 (2008)
20. Wang, Y., Wang, W., Liang, Y., Cai, Y., Hooi, B.: Graphcrop: subgraph cropping for graph classification. arXiv preprint arXiv:2009.10564 (2020)
21. Wang, Y., Wang, W., Liang, Y., Cai, Y., Hooi, B.: Mixup for node and graph classification. In: International World Wide Web Conference (WWW) (2021)
22. Xu, K., Hu, W., Leskovec, J., Jegelka, S.: How powerful are graph neural networks? In: International Conference on Learning Representations (ICLR) (2019)
23. Yanardag, P., Vishwanathan, S.: Deep graph kernels. In: ACM SIGKDD International Conference on Knowledge Discovery and Data Mining (KDD) (2015)
24. Ying, Z., You, J., Morris, C., Ren, X., Hamilton, W., Leskovec, J.: Hierarchical graph representation learning with differentiable pooling. In: Advances in Neural Information Processing Systems (NeurIPS) (2018)
25. You, Y., Chen, T., Sui, Y., Chen, T., Wang, Z., Shen, Y.: Graph contrastive learning with augmentations. In: Advances in Neural Information Processing Systems (NeurIPS) (2020)
26. Zhang, H., Cisse, M., Dauphin, Y.N., Lopez-Paz, D.: mixup: beyond empirical risk minimization. In: International Conference on Learning Representations (ICLR) (2018)
27. Zhao, T., Liu, G., Günnemann, S., Jiang, M.: Graph data augmentation for graph machine learning: a survey. arXiv preprint arXiv:2202.08871 (2022)

Two-Stage Denoising Diffusion Model for Source Localization in Graph Inverse Problems

Bosong Huang[1], Weihao Yu[2], Ruzhong Xie[1], Jing Xiao[1], and Jin Huang[1(✉)]

[1] South China Normal University, Guangzhou, China
{bosonghuang,rzxie,xiaojing,huangjin}@scnu.edu.cn
[2] Research Institute of China Telecom Corporate Ltd., Guangzhou, China
yuwh3@chinatelecom.cn

Abstract. Source localization is the inverse problem of graph information dissemination (information diffusion) and has broad practical applications. However, the inherent intricacy and uncertainty in information dissemination pose significant challenges, and the ill-posed nature of the source localization problem further exacerbates these challenges. Recently, deep generative models, particularly diffusion models inspired by classical non-equilibrium thermodynamics, have made significant progress. While diffusion models have proven to be powerful in solving inverse problems and producing high-quality reconstructions, applying them directly to the source localization problem is infeasible for two reasons. Firstly, it is impossible to calculate the posterior disseminated results on a large-scale network for iterative denoising sampling, which would incur enormous computational costs. Secondly, in the existing methods designed for this field, the training data itself are ill-posed (many-to-one); thus simply transferring the diffusion model would only lead to local optima. To address these challenges, we propose a two-stage optimization framework, the source localization denoising diffusion model (SL-Diff). In the coarse stage, we devise the source proximity degrees as the supervised signals to generate coarse-grained source predictions. This aims to efficiently initialize the next stage, significantly reducing its convergence time and calibrating the convergence process. Furthermore, the introduction of cascade temporal information in this training method transforms the many-to-one mapping relationship into a one-to-one relationship, perfectly addressing the ill-posed problem. In the fine stage, we design a diffusion model for the graph inverse problem that can quantify the uncertainty in the dissemination process. Thanks to the excellent collaboration of the two stages, the proposed SL-Diff yields excellent prediction results within a reasonable sampling time, as demonstrated in extensive experiments on five datasets.

1 Introduction

The exponential growth of network-structured information has aroused widespread interest in studying its dissemination mode [6, 15, 21, 25]. This involves

Fig. 1. Many-to-one (ill-posed) relationship when the supervised signal is the source indicator.

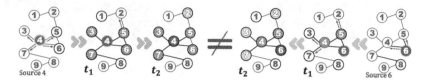

Fig. 2. One-to-one relationship when the supervised signal is the source proximity degree.

modeling the information dissemination (information diffusion[1]) based on the corresponding network structure and dissemination source. While there are few research followers, the inverse problem of information dissemination on graphs and source localization is of great practical significance. For instance, locating the source account for spreading rumors in social networks is crucial for rumor detection [5,24]. Similarly, source localization can aid in virus interception [20], malicious email traceability [23], and other areas [12,30].

However, there are currently several challenges hindering this field: **Chall. 1.** Existing models do not fundamentally address the ill-posed problem because their training data are inherently ill-posed (many-to-one). For instance, in the case of blurred image restoration, the ill-posed problem cannot be solved if the training data consist solely of blurred images. In fact, existing methods unfortunately erase the relative temporal correlation of each node from the cascades when setting the training data, which essentially leads to the ill-posed problem of source localization, as shown in Fig. 1. This abandonment of temporal information also significantly restricts the ability of the model to learn the underlying dissemination pattern. **Chall. 2.** In practical applications, information dissemination in the network will introduce many uncertain factors, that is, the noise irrelevant to the regular dissemination mode. Although some stud-

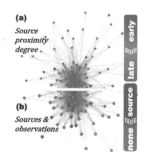

Fig. 3. Two types of supervised signal derived from a cascade.

---

[1] In most studies, this problem is referred to as "graph information diffusion". However, we refer to it as "graph information dissemination" in this paper to disambiguate with the "diffusion model".

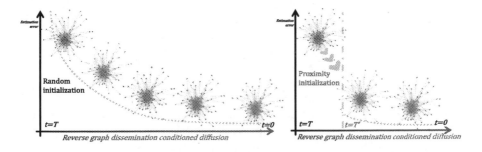

Fig. 4. Random initialization and proximity initialization of sampling.

ies [12,21] have begun to discuss the uncertainty in source localization, how to quantitatively model them and more importantly, eliminate the relevant noise in source localization is unresolved.

The denoising diffusion models [4,7,17] have flourished recently due to their high-quality reconstructions and powerful inverse problem solving abilities. In addition to leveraging its power and further addressing Chall. 2, we have taken the first step in generalizing this powerful model to the source localization problem. However, the existing family of diffusion models poses the following challenges for direct migration. **Chall. 3.** As the inverse problem solver, existing diffusion models need to calculate the conditional posterior probability at each diffusion step for Maximum A Posteriori (MAP) approximation. However, in the case of source localization, the calculation of posterior probability involves simulating information dissemination across the entire network structure at each diffusion step, making it extremely computationally expensive. Therefore, it is almost impossible to directly apply existing diffusion models to source localization. **Chall. 4.** Existing diffusion models [7,16,17,27] that were designed for image or molecule data struggle to model dissemination patterns. For example, the number of nodes in the molecular graph is much smaller than that in the information dissemination network, and does not have the temporal information.

To address the complex challenges outlined above and effectively harness the benefits of current technological developments, we propose a two-stage optimization framework named Source Localization Denoising Diffusion model (SL-Diff). In general, SL-Diff leverages an efficient initialization that is supervised with temporal cascade information and an exquisitely redesigned denoising network structure to achieve a series of outstanding performances. Specifically, for Chall. 1, we ingeniously retain the timing of the cascade (defined as the source proximity degree, shown in Fig. 3(a) and elaborated in Sect. 3.2) during the model training phase while remaining consistent with baselines that only take the disseminated observation (Fig. 3(b)) as the input for prediction during testing. This means that the model in the coarse stage aims to learn the source proximity relationship (i.e., a kind of one-to one mapping correlation, as shown in Fig. 2) through training, which directly addresses the core of Chall. 1. On the other hand, due to the contraction property of stochastic differential equations (SDEs), the error reduction of the diffusion model is exponential. Based on this characteristic, we propose a two-stage optimization framework. In the coarse stage, we use the one-shot method to generate coarse source proximity degrees quickly and efficiently, reducing the predicted source localization error. In the fine stage, the diffusion model simulates information dissemination across the entire network, accurately locating the source. Concretely, we optimize the verbose sampling process (Fig. 4 (left)) into an efficient two-stage process (Fig. 4 (right)) and further balance the two-stage diffusion step ratio to achieve an optimum between efficiency and accuracy through parameter experiments. This approach effectively solves Chall. 3. Since the coarse stage provides excellent initialization of the coarse source proximity relationships, it prominently alleviates the local optimum problem caused by class imbalance in the source localization problem. In addition, we propose a new uncertainty graph information dissemination model that quantizes the dissemination noise and a score function approximating network that adapts to the underlying dissemination mode on the graph to jointly address Chall. 2 and Chall. 4. In summary, our contributions are as follows:

- We propose a training framework that employs source proximity degree supervision, which fundamentally addresses the ill-posed problem of source localization.
- Our contribution lies in proposing, for the first time, a two-stage denoising diffusion model for the source localization problem. The targeted design of the two stages effectively addresses the challenge of migrating the diffusion model to this field.
- We design a new model that approximates graph information dissemination and a score function approximating network to enhance the performance of the diffusion model for source localization.
- Experiments on five real-world datasets demonstrate that our proposed SL-Diff model outperforms state-of-the-art models.

2   Related Work

Graph Information Dissemination and Source Localization. Graph information dissemination modeling aims to predict the nodes to be affected given the source nodes, which is one of the foremost technologies in social network analysis, disease infection prediction, etc. Traditional methods [1,9,10,28] manually model the respective dissemination pattern for different application fields while suffering from poor generalizability and high computational complexity. With the blooming of deep learning, [21,22,26] incorporated recurrent neural networks to capture the dynamic relationship of dissemination cascades. Graph neural networks have further been introduced to aggregate the node neighboring information and model the dissemination pattern to facilitate prediction.

Source localization aims to infer source nodes given an observed set of nodes, which has essential applications in rumor tracing and infection source discovery. Generally speaking, source localization is used to study the traceability method based on the dissemination model. Early studies [5,30,31] were based on specific dissemination models such as Susceptible-Infected (SI) and Susceptible-Infected-Recovered (SIR). [24] argues that a fixed propagation model to be preset is not necessary. Furthermore, [23] focuses on detecting the source in the early propagation stage to reduce the loss caused by propagation. [20] develops a framework for the inverse of graph dissemination models to detect the source. From another perspective, [12] introduces VAE [11] to probabilistically model the uncertainty in source localization.

Diffusion Models. The diffusion model we discuss in this paper is the score-based generative model [17], which applies the stochastic differential equation (SDE) to learn the gradient of the target distribution. The currently popular DDPM [7] is a particular case of it. As the diffusion model separates the noise from the data step by step at a fine-grained level, its powerful generative capabilities have achieved state-of-the-art results in many fields, e.g., image generation [4,7,16,17], graph generation [8,27], and time series generation [14].

3   Preliminaries

3.1   Conditional Score-Based Diffusion Models

Diffusion models aim to approximate the prior distributions by learning the noise of the data reversely. [17] combines SMLD [16] and DDPM [7] into a generalized theoretical framework, known as the Score-Based Diffusion Model. They generally map data to a noise distribution (the prior) with a stochastic differential equation (SDE), and reverse this SDE for generative modeling.

Forward SDE. Given the i.i.d. original dataset samples $\mathbf{x}(0) \sim p_{\mathbf{x}}$, which are further indexed as $\mathbf{x}(t)_{t=0}^{T}$ by the diffusion step $t \in [0, T]$ to indicate the noise degree, the diffusion process can be modeled as the solution to an Itô SDE:

$$d\mathbf{x} = -\frac{\beta(t)}{2}\mathbf{x}dt + \sqrt{\beta(t)}d\mathbf{w} \tag{1}$$

where $\beta(t) \in \mathbb{R}$ is the noise schedule that we uniformly adopt the one in [7] in this paper, $\mathbf{w}$ is the Brownian motion.

Reverse SDE. [2] clarifies that the reverse of a diffusion process is also a diffusion process, which can be modeled as the reverse SDE:

$$dx = \left[-\frac{\beta(t)}{2}\mathbf{x} - \beta(t)\nabla_{\mathbf{x}_t} \log p_t(\mathbf{x}_t) \right] dt + \sqrt{\beta(t)}d\bar{\mathbf{w}}, \tag{2}$$

where dt is the negative diffusion step from T to 0 and $\bar{\mathbf{w}}$ is the corresponding Brownian motion of the reverse process. Since the direct estimation of $\nabla_{\mathbf{x}_t} \log p_t(\mathbf{x}_t)$ is too computationally intensive and badly generalizatial, we train a score-based model to approximate it:

$$\theta^* = \arg\min_{\theta} \mathbb{E}_{t\sim U(\varepsilon,1),\mathbf{x}(t)\sim p(\mathbf{x}(t)|\mathbf{x}(0)),\mathbf{x}(0)\sim p_{\text{data}}} [\xi]$$

$$\xi = \|\mathbf{s}_\theta(\mathbf{x}(t),t) - \nabla_{\mathbf{x}_t} \log p(\mathbf{x}(t) \mid \mathbf{x}(0))\|_2^2 \tag{3}$$

Here $\varepsilon \simeq 0$ is the small positive constant. After acquiring the trained score function approximation network, the initial noise can be denoised to enable sampling based on specific posterior conditions, leading to the generation of expected data.

3.2   Graph Information Dissemination

The graph information dissemination problem involves a graph $G = (V, E)$ with edge set E and node set V. An information dissemination cascade D_i at length $K+1$ on the graph is defined as $D_i = \{(v_{i_k}, k) \mid v_{i_k} \in V, k = 0, 1 \ldots, K-1, K\}$, where k is non-decreasing and the first K_s nodes are defined as source nodes. The source indicator $\mathbf{i} \in \{0,1\}^{|V|}$ is defined as 0 for being the source and 1 for not, while the source proximity degree $\mathbf{x} \in [0,1]^{|V|}$ is defined as $x_k = \frac{k}{K}$. The set of affected nodes' observations is denoted as $\mathbf{y} \in \{0,1\}^{|V|}$, where 0 indicates being affected and 1 indicates not being affected. The goal of the graph information dissemination problem is to predict the affected nodes given the source indicator and graph structure.

Thanks to the outstanding performance of GNN on graph data, the state-of-the-art graph information dissemination methods [6,15,18,21] construct various realistic-meaning attribute variables through GNN at the first stage, and then perform variable dissemination to derive the final affected node sets. Specifically: (1) In the variable construction, we define a neural network $\mathbf{v} = g_{\mathbf{w_1}}(\mathbf{x})$ to construct miscellaneous variables of nodes (such as sender variable or receiver variable). (2) In variable dissemination, we define a dissemination neural network $f_{\mathbf{w_2}}(\mathbf{v})$ to propagate information to neighbour nodes according to the topology of the graph, where w_1 and w_2 are learnable parameters. Thus, the general paradigm of graph information dissemination can be defined as:

$$\mathbf{y} = f_{\mathbf{w_2}}(g_{\mathbf{w_1}}(\mathbf{x})) \tag{4}$$

3.3   Problem Formulation for Source Localization

In order to eliminate ambiguity, the graph mentioned in Subsect. 3.2 is referred to as the whole graph $\mathcal{G}^w = (V^w, E^w)$. Source localization is the corresponding inverse problem of graph information dissemination, which is formally defined as: given the whole graph information $\mathcal{G}^w = (V^w, E^w)$ and affected nodes $\mathbf{y} \in \{0,1\}^{|V|}$, reconstruct the source nodes $\hat{\mathbf{i}} \in \{0,1\}^{|V|}$. For the convenience of mentioning later, we define the cascade graph as $\mathcal{G}_i^c = (V_i^c \in D_i, E^c)$ where $E^c = \{(u,v) \in E^w \mid u \in D_i \text{ or } v \in D_i\}$.

4   SL-Diff Method

4.1   Two-Stage Optimization Framework

To mitigate the computational burden of simulating information dissemination on the whole graph at each diffusion step (chall. 3), and to leverage the cascade temporal information for addressing the ill-posed problem (chall. 3), we propose a two-stage optimization framework, as depicted in Fig. 5. Specifically, in the coarse stage, the supervising sig-

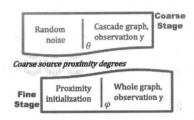

Fig. 5. Two-stage optimization framework

nals for the model are the source proximity degrees (Fig. 3(a)) that fully retain the cascade temporal information. In other words, the final outputs of this stage are the relatively coarse-grained node infection sequence predictions, which are used to initialize the precise source localization for the next stage efficiently. In the second stage, i.e., the fine stage, the supervising signals of model training are source indicators (Fig. 3(b)), which aim to accurately output the predicted source under the given disseminated observation conditions.

4.2   Coarse Proximity Generation

In this section, we propose a coarse proximity generation model (depicted in Fig. 6) at the first stage, which serves to effectively initialize the subsequent

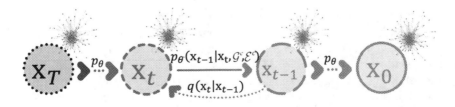

Fig. 6. The forward diffusion and reverse process of the coarse stage.

stage. The "coarse" is used in two senses. Firstly, the source proximity degree derived from the cascade data does not strictly reflect the infection relationships between nodes, as the nodes in a cascade may be infected by their common ancestors rather than by their directly adjacent forward nodes. Secondly, as no dissemination model is incorporated at this stage, it is not feasible to accurately predict the dissemination source in reverse. Nonetheless, the generated coarse source proximity degrees are well-suited for the initialization of the downstream diffusion model. Although the coarse source proximity generation occurs only within the cascade graph, it is incomplete without considering the structure of the entire graph. This is due to the significant impact that the relative position of each node in the graph has on information dissemination. To address this, we utilize Position-aware Graph Neural Networks (P-GNN) [29] to perform node position representation learning on the whole graph of each dataset. Through this process, we obtain the positional embeddings $\mathcal{E}^w = \{\mathbf{e}_i \mid \mathbf{e}_i = \text{P-GNN}(v_i), v_i \in V^w\}$ that reflect the relative position of each node with respect to other nodes on the whole graph. We use this positional representation in the specific cascade $\mathcal{E}^c = \{\mathbf{e}_i \mid \mathbf{e}_i = \text{P-GNN}(v_i), v_i \in V^c\}$ as a conditional input to the score function approximation network, enhancing its ability to fit the underlying features of the cascades.

Let the original source proximity degrees derived from a cascade be denoted as $\mathbf{x}_0$. The reverse SDE here follows the Eq. 2, while the score function conditioned on the the cascade graph structure and the positional embeddings is changed to $\mathbf{s}_\theta(\mathbf{x}_t, t \mid \mathcal{G}^c, \mathcal{E}^c)$. We adopt the same variance schedule as DDPM [7] to discretize the formula, then the estimated reverse Markov chain is defined as follows:

$$\mathbf{x}_{t-1} = \frac{1}{\sqrt{1 - \beta_t}} (\mathbf{x}_t + \beta_t \mathbf{s}_{\theta^*}(\mathbf{x}_t, t \mid \mathcal{G}^c, \mathcal{E}^c)) + \sqrt{\beta_t}\mathbf{z}_t, \quad t = T, T-1, \cdots, 1 \quad (5)$$

in which we use the following re-weighted variant of the evidence lower bound (ELBO) to train the model to obtain the estimated score function:

$$\theta^* = \arg\min_{\theta} \sum_{t=1}^{N} (1 - \alpha_t) \, \mathbb{E}_{p_{\text{data}}(\mathbf{x})} \mathbb{E}_{p_{\alpha_t}(\mathbf{x}_t \mid \mathbf{x})} \left[\|\mathbf{s}_\theta(\mathbf{x}_t, t \mid \mathcal{G}^c, \mathcal{E}^c) - \nabla_{\mathbf{x}_t} \log p_{\alpha_t}(\mathbf{x}_t \mid \mathbf{x})\|_2^2 \right]$$
$$(6)$$

where $\alpha := \prod_{j=1}^{i}(1 - \beta_j)$.

To efficiently approximate the score functions, we propose a new network structure that properly introduces conditional position embeddings while preserving nodes' adjacent characteristics at different orders. Our approach utilizes a multi-head graph attention (GMT) [3] as the basic operation of graph convolution, allowing us to aggregate information across L-layer graphs. Furthermore, we leverage skip connections between each layer to improve the flow of information. Finally, we concatenate the output of each layer and perform multi-layer nonlinear transformations to obtain an estimated score function. The proposed

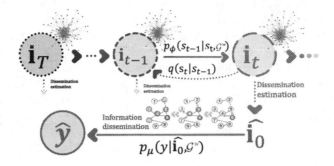

Fig. 7. The forward diffusion and reverse process of the fine stage.

conditional score function approximating network is defined as follows:

$$\mathbf{H}^{l+1} = \mathrm{GMT}(\mathbf{H}^l, \mathcal{G}^c) + \mathbf{H}^l$$
$$\mathbf{s}_\theta(\mathbf{x}_t, t \mid \mathcal{G}^c, \mathcal{E}^c) = \mathrm{MLP}\left(\mathbf{catenate}[\mathcal{E}^c, \mathbf{H}^0, \dots, \mathbf{H}^{L-1}, \mathbf{H}^L, \mathcal{T}(t)]\right) \tag{7}$$

where $\mathbf{H}^0 = \mathbf{x}_t + \mathcal{E}^c$. We use the positional encodings [19] to encode the diffusion step, and the formula is defined as: $\mathcal{T}(t) = \left[\dots, \cos\left(t/r^{\frac{-2d}{D}}\right),\right.$ $\left.\sin\left(t/r^{\frac{-2d}{D}}\right), \dots\right]^{\mathrm{T}}$, where $d = 1, \dots, D/2$ is the dimension of the embedding, and r is a large constant (set to 10^5). After obtaining the trained network $\mathbf{s}_\theta$, we sample according to the Algorithm 1 and get the predicted coarse source proximity degrees.

4.3   Graph Dissemination Conditioned Model

In the second stage, we apply the estimated source proximity degree to initialize the graph dissemination conditioned diffusion model (depicted in Fig. 7). Significantly different from the conditional diffusion in the first stage, the diffusion model here is an inverse problem solver, which aims to recover the source indicator $\mathbf{i}$ from the disseminated observation $\mathbf{y}$. The connection between them is the forward information dissemination process of $\mathbf{i} \rightarrow \mathbf{y}$.

If the assumption is the same as in [17], that is, $p_t(\mathbf{y} \mid \mathbf{i}_t)$ is tractable, then the reverse SDE of the inverse problem is defined as:

$$d\mathbf{i} = \left[-\frac{\beta(t)}{2}\mathbf{i} - \beta(t)\left(\nabla_{\mathbf{i}_t} \log p_t(\mathbf{i}_t) + \nabla_{x_t} \log p_t(\mathbf{y} \mid \mathbf{i}_t, \mathcal{G}^w)\right)\right]dt + \sqrt{\beta(t)}d\bar{\mathbf{w}}, \tag{8}$$

However, in our case, $p_t(\mathbf{y} \mid \mathbf{i}_t)$ is intractable, as the dissemination model cannot support the source with noise as input. To bridge this gap, we introduce the approximation method [4] for $p(\hat{\mathbf{i}}_0 \mid \mathbf{i}_t)$:

$$\hat{\mathbf{i}}_0 \simeq \frac{1}{\sqrt{\bar{\alpha}(t)}}\left(\mathbf{i}_t + (1 - \bar{\alpha}(t))\mathbf{s}_\phi(\mathbf{i}_t, t \mid \mathcal{G}^w)\right) \tag{9}$$

where $\alpha_i \triangleq 1 - \beta_i, \bar{\alpha}_i \triangleq \prod_{j=1}^{i} \alpha_i$ following [7]. Now the problem lies in determining an appropriate dissemination model to calculate the posterior probability of $\mathbf{y}$ from estimated $\mathbf{i}$. In real-world applications, various random factors can impact the information dissemination process, which are not accounted for in the basic dissemination function (Eq. 4). Our proposed model addresses this challenge by qualifying the uncertain trough Gaussian noise $\tilde{\sigma}(t)$ with adaptive variance (parameterized by MLP and taking diffusion step as input). Additionally, our model can eliminate interference from noise to source localization through the powerful iterative denoising process of the diffusion model. Thus, the formula is defined as follows:

$$\mathbf{y} = f\left(g(\mathbf{i})\right) + \tilde{\sigma}(t)\boldsymbol{\epsilon}, \qquad \boldsymbol{\epsilon} \sim \mathcal{N}(\mathbf{0}, \mathbf{I}) \tag{10}$$

From the above formula, we can calculate the partial derivative $\nabla_{\mathbf{i}_0} \log p\left(\mathbf{y} \mid \mathbf{i}_0\right)$. And bring the conclusion in Eq. 8 into it to get an approximate for the derivative of $p\left(\mathbf{y} \mid \mathbf{i}_t\right)$ with respect to $\hat{\mathbf{i}}_t$.

$$\nabla_{\hat{\mathbf{i}}_t} \log p\left(\mathbf{y} \mid \mathbf{i}_t\right) \simeq -\frac{1}{\tilde{\sigma}(t)^2} \nabla_{\mathbf{i}_t} \left\| \mathbf{y} - \hat{\mathbf{y}}\left(\hat{\mathbf{i}}_0\left(\mathbf{i}_t\right)\right) \right\|_2^2 \tag{11}$$

Hence, we can discretize Eq. 8 similarly to formula 5 and deduce the expression for $p(\mathbf{i}_{t-1}) \mid \mathbf{i}_t)$. This allows us to perform iterative denoising of $\mathbf{i}$ given the posterior $\mathbf{y}$, ultimately leading to an accurate estimation of $\mathbf{i}$. For a more thorough explanation of this procedure, please refer to Algorithm 2.

Algorithm 1: Sampling of the coarse stage

Require: ground truth source proximity degree $\mathbf{x}$, number of diffusion steps T_1, variance schedule β_t, the cascade graph $\mathcal{G}_c$
1: $\mathbf{x}_{T_1} \sim \mathcal{N}(\mathbf{0}, \mathbf{I})$
2: **for** $t = T_1 - 1$ to $t = 0$ **do**
3:     $\hat{\mathbf{s}} \leftarrow \mathbf{s}_\phi\left(\mathbf{x}_t, t \mid \mathcal{G}^w, \mathcal{E}^w\right)$
4:     $\mathbf{x}'_{t-1} \leftarrow (2 - \sqrt{1 - \beta_t}\mathbf{x}_t) + \beta_t\left(\hat{\mathbf{s}}\right)$
5:     $\mathbf{z} \sim \mathcal{N}(\mathbf{0}, \mathbf{I})$
6:     $\mathbf{x}_t \leftarrow \mathbf{x}'_{t-1} + \sqrt{\beta_t}\mathbf{z}$
7: **end for**
8: **return** the estimated $\mathbf{x}_0$

Algorithm 2: Sampling of the fine stage

Require: disseminated observation $\mathbf{y}$, coarse source proximity degree $\hat{\mathbf{x}}$, number of diffusion steps T_2, variance schedule β_t, the whole graph $\mathcal{G}_W$
1: $\mathbf{i}_{T_2} \leftarrow \hat{\mathbf{x}}$
2: **for** $t = T_2 - 1$ to $t = 0$ **do**
3:     $\hat{\mathbf{s}} \leftarrow \mathbf{s}_\phi\left(\mathbf{i}_t, t \mid \mathcal{G}^w\right)$
4:     $\mathbf{i}'_{t-1} \leftarrow (2 - \sqrt{1 - \beta_t}\mathbf{i}_t) + \beta_t\left(\hat{\mathbf{s}} - \frac{1}{\tilde{\sigma}(t)^2} \nabla_{\mathbf{i}_t} \left\| \mathbf{y} - \hat{\mathbf{y}}\left(\hat{\mathbf{i}}_0\left(\mathbf{i}_t\right)\right) \right\|_2^2\right)$
5:     $\mathbf{z} \sim \mathcal{N}(\mathbf{0}, \mathbf{I})$
6:     $\mathbf{i}_t \leftarrow \mathbf{i}'_{t-1} + \sqrt{\beta_t}\mathbf{z}$
7: **end for**
8: **return** the estimated $\mathbf{i}_0$

Table 1. Model performance across five datasets.

Datasets	Methods	Netsleuth	OJC	LPSI	GCNSI	IVGD	SL-VAE	SL-Diff
Digg	RE	0.0142	0.0781	0.2352	0.0135	0.2310	0.5420	**0.7813**
	PR	0.0023	0.0554	0.0072	0.2369	0.1397	0.4216	**0.5839**
	F1	0.0040	0.0648	0.0140	0.0255	0.1741	0.4743	**0.6683**
	ACC	0.7714	0.9035	0.9531	0.8064	0.9327	0.9742	**0.9824**
Memetracker	RE	0.0647	0.0256	0.3047	0.2953	0.5954	0.5010	**0.6902**
	PR	0.0247	0.0360	0.1145	0.0172	0.1556	0.4592	**0.4721**
	F1	0.0358	0.0299	0.1665	0.0325	0.2467	0.4792	**0.5607**
	ACC	0.5688	0.6675	0.9174	0.8428	0.8947	0.9420	**0.9562**
Android	RE	0.3172	0.1401	0.3407	0.7434	0.7253	0.6261	**0.8260**
	PR	0.0422	0.0610	0.2323	0.3024	0.4105	0.5284	**0.5945**
	F1	0.0745	0.0850	0.2762	0.4299	0.5243	0.5731	**0.6914**
	ACC	0.6215	0.8337	0.9404	0.8211	0.9530	0.9245	**0.9937**
Christianity	RE	0.2491	0.3478	0.5309	0.7294	0.6433	0.8011	**0.8352**
	PR	0.1184	0.2823	0.6249	0.2300	**0.5202**	0.4894	0.5120
	F1	0.1605	0.3116	0.5741	0.3497	0.5752	0.6076	**0.6348**
	ACC	0.7140	0.9304	0.9122	0.9673	0.9781	0.9529	**0.9818**
Twitter	RE	0.0184	0.0154	0.2091	0.3770	0.6219	0.3273	**0.9037**
	PR	0.0021	0.0238	0.1295	0.3719	0.4427	0.4210	**0.7839**
	F1	0.0038	0.0187	0.1599	0.3744	0.5172	0.3683	**0.8395**
	ACC	0.6348	0.8358	0.9149	0.9231	0.9381	0.9027	**0.9630**

5 Experiments

5.1 Settings

Data. To better demonstrate the practical value of the proposed model, we conducted sufficient experiments on five datasets of various scales: Digg, Memetracker, Android, Christianity, Twitter. Each dataset includes real information cascade data, and the specific dataset details are shown in the Appendix[2]. In order to unify the training standard with the previous method, we define the nodes at the first 5% of the infection time in a cascade as dissemination sources, and all the nodes in the cascade as disseminated observations. We set the ratio of training, validation, and testing to 2:2:6.

Baselines and Metrics. We adopt the following two types of baselines to make a more comprehensive comparison (please refer to the Appendix for details). (1) Methods of presupposing dissemination mode: NetSleuth [13], OJC [30]. (2) Methods compatible with multiple modes of dissemination: LPSI [24], GCNSI [5], IVGD [20], SL-VAE [12].

---

[2] https://github.com/marooncabbage/SL-Diff.

Table 2. Ablation study (— represents GPU memory overflow).

Datasets	Digg		Memetracker		Android		Christianity		Twitter	
	F1	ACC	F1	ACC	F1	ACC	F1	ACC	F1	ACC
SL-Diff(1)	0.4224	0.8510	0.4001	0.7410	0.5188	0.7309	0.4511	0.7792	0.6530	0.8630
SL-Diff(2)	—	—	—	—	—	—	0.6024	0.9530	—	—
SL-Diff(3)	0.6202	0.9627	0.4346	0.9023	0.6427	0.9705	0.6210	0.9722	0.7401	0.9328
SL-Diff(4)	0.5985	0.9329	0.5792	0.9527	0.6132	0.9595	0.6285	0.9717	0.7620	0.9441
SL-Diff	0.6683	0.9824	0.5607	0.9565	0.6914	0.9937	0.6348	0.9818	0.8395	0.9630

Four evaluation matrices are used in the experiments to expose model performance more objectively and comprehensively. First, we use the most commonly used accuracy (ACC), the proportion of correctly classified samples to the total sample. However, since the source localization is essentially an unbalanced classification problem, we added a more appropriate metric, F1-Score (F1)[3] to reconcile the average of precision (PR) and recall (RE). We also attached the results of PR and RE for reference.

Implementation Details. For our SL-Diff model, the details of its implementation are as follows. For the diffusion steps of the coarse stage and the fine stage, we set them to $T_1 = 800$ and $T_2 = 80$, respectively. For the specific dissemination model $f_{\mathbf{w_2}}(g_{\mathbf{w_1}}(\mathbf{i}))$ we chose DeepIS [25]. For the score function approximating network (Eq. 7), four layers of MLP are applied. For other benchmarks, we follow the original structural design. Specifically, for the dissemination model that SL-VAE combines, we adopt DeepIS, while the IC function is used for IVGD.

The models are trained on a single NVIDIA GeForce RTX 3090 GPU. We use a grid search to find the most appropriate combination of parameters for each model. Specifically, the search range for the number of GCN stacks is from 2 to 8. The learning rate is tuned within $\{5 \times 10^{-2}, 10^{-2}, 5 \times 10^{-3}, 10^{-3}\}$. The range of Riemannian SGD weight decay is $\{10^{-2}, 10^{-3}, 10^{-4}, 10^{-5}\}$.

5.2   Overall Performance

We have conducted in-depth comparisons of SL-Diff with state-of-the-art baselines on five real datasets, and the results are presented in Table 1. Generally, models with preset dissemination modes perform relatively poorly, as real information dissemination modes are complex and full of uncertainties. SL-Diff, on the other hand, achieves significantly optimal results in most cases. Among them, the improvement on the Twitter and Android datasets is particularly significant which can be attributed to its ability to denoise the dissemination noise. And this noise is more prominent on datasets with a large cascade length and a large number of nodes. Correspondingly, on the Christianity dataset with a small number of nodes, the performance of SL-Diff is limited. In summary, SL-Diff is more capable of handling large-scale datasets.

---

[3] $F1 = \frac{2PR*RE}{PR+RE}$.

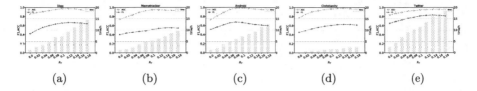

(a)   (b)   (c)   (d)   (e)

Fig. 8. Analysis on the ratio of the diffusion step of the fine stage to the coarse stage.

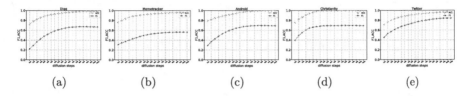

(a)   (b)   (c)   (d)   (e)

Fig. 9. Convergence analysis.

5.3 Ablation Study

To verify the effectiveness of each component of our proposed model, we conduct the following ablation experiments. Compared with the complete model, SL-Diff(1) only retains the coarse stage and is initialized randomly. SL-Diff(2) only retains the fine stage and we take the top 5% of nodes with the largest source proximity degree generated as the source of prediction. SL-Diff(3) is the model with the cascade positional representations removed, and SL-Diff(4) removes the simulated dissemination noise term in Eq. 10. The diffusion step of the above four models is all set to 800. From the results in Table 2, we can conclude that only the coarse stage model can make rough predictions to a certain extent, and it is difficult to make accurate predictions. The model with only the fine stage is not necessarily more accurate than the two-stage model, and the computational overhead is huge, which is not feasible. From the results of SL-Diff(3), we can see that cascade positional representations generally have a more important influence on larger-scale graphs, which may be due to the fact that the relative position of cascades in large-scale graphs will be more complicated, and their influence on propagation will be larger. From the results of SL-Diff(4), we can find that simulated dissemination noise improves the model with a longer cascade length more significantly, which may be because a cascade with a longer propagation chain will introduce relatively more noise.

5.4 Parameter Analysis

In this section, we explore the interdependence of the two stages in greater detail. Specifically, we set the ratio of the diffusion step of the fine stage to the coarse stage as $R_T = \frac{T_2}{T_1}$ and keep the total diffusion step at 800. By adjusting the value of R_T, we gain a deeper understanding of how the two stages mutually reinforce each other, and determine the optimal ratio. As shown in Fig. 8, we observe that the model's performance initially improves significantly with an increasing proportion of the fine stage, but then gradually declines, while the sampling time steadily increases. This suggests that we can identify the most suitable ratio of the two stages at a relatively low time cost across different datasets. The performance degradation resulting from too high R_T may be due to insufficient denoising in the coarse stage. Additionally, we analyze the impact of the diffusion step on the model's performance under the configuration with the optimal R_T. Figure 9 reveals that the convergence of the sampling process is comparatively faster for datasets with smaller scales.

Efficient Analysis. We compared the training time of various models (sampling time is also included since SL-Diff and SL-VAE are generative models). As shown in Fig. 10, the generative model exhibits a shorter overall running time for the source localization task. Among all the models evaluated, SL-Diff effectively controls the computational cost at a lower level, emphasizing the significance of the coarse stage for initialization.

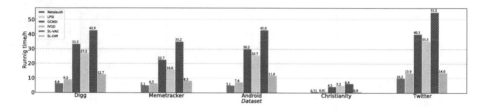

Fig. 10. Model efficiency comparison.

6   Conclusion

In this paper, we propose a new two-stage training paradigm to solve the ill-posed problem in graph source localization from the root. SL-Diff also overcomes the difficulties of introducing the powerful diffusion model into this problem, and achieves optimal results on various real-world datasets. The modeling of dissemination noise further improves the approximation performance of SL-Diff. Overall, by leveraging the diffusion model, we have gained deeper insights into the mechanism of the source localization problem, thereby elevating research in this field to a new level.

Acknowledgments. This work was supported by the National Natural Science Foundation of China under Grants 62177015, and the Natural Science Foundation of Guangdong Province, China under Grants 2022A1515010148.

References

1. Ahmed, M., Spagna, S., Huici, F., Niccolini, S.: A peek into the future: predicting the evolution of popularity in user generated content. In: Proceedings of the Sixth ACM International Conference on Web Search and Data Mining, pp. 607–616 (2013)
2. Anderson, B.D.: Reverse-time diffusion equation models. Stochastic Process. Appl. **12**(3), 313–326 (1982)
3. Baek, J., Kang, M., Hwang, S.J.: Accurate learning of graph representations with graph multiset pooling. arXiv preprint arXiv:2102.11533 (2021)
4. Chung, H., Kim, J., Mccann, M.T., Klasky, M.L., Ye, J.C.: Diffusion posterior sampling for general noisy inverse problems. arXiv preprint arXiv:2209.14687 (2022)
5. Dong, M., Zheng, B., Quoc Viet Hung, N., Su, H., Li, G.: Multiple rumor source detection with graph convolutional networks. In: Proceedings of the 28th ACM International Conference on Information and Knowledge Management, pp. 569–578 (2019)
6. Feng, S., et al.: H-diffu: hyperbolic representations for information diffusion prediction. IEEE Trans. Knowl. Data Eng. **35**, 8784–8798 (2022)
7. Ho, J., Jain, A., Abbeel, P.: Denoising diffusion probabilistic models. Adv. Neural Inf. Process. Syst. **33**, 6840–6851 (2020)
8. Jo, J., Lee, S., Hwang, S.J.: Score-based generative modeling of graphs via the system of stochastic differential equations. arXiv preprint arXiv:2202.02514 (2022)
9. Keeling, M.J., Eames, K.T.: Networks and epidemic models. J. Roy. Soc. Interface **2**(4), 295–307 (2005)
10. Kempe, D., Kleinberg, J., Tardos, E.: Maximizing the spread of influence through a social network. In: Proceedings of the Ninth ACM SIGKDD International Conference on Knowledge Discovery and Data Mining, pp. 137–146 (2003)
11. Kingma, D.P., Welling, M.: Auto-encoding variational bayes. In: International Conference on Learning Representations (2013)
12. Ling, C., Jiang, J., Wang, J., Liang, Z.: Source localization of graph diffusion via variational autoencoders for graph inverse problems. In: Proceedings of the 28th ACM SIGKDD Conference on Knowledge Discovery and Data Mining, pp. 1010–1020 (2022)
13. Prakash, B.A., Vreeken, J., Faloutsos, C.: Spotting culprits in epidemics: how many and which ones? In: 2012 IEEE 12th International Conference on Data Mining, pp. 11–20. IEEE (2012)
14. Rasul, K., Seward, C., Schuster, I., Vollgraf, R.: Autoregressive denoising diffusion models for multivariate probabilistic time series forecasting. In: International Conference on Machine Learning, pp. 8857–8868. PMLR (2021)
15. Sankar, A., Zhang, X., Krishnan, A., Han, J.: Inf-vae: a variational autoencoder framework to integrate homophily and influence in diffusion prediction. In: Proceedings of the 13th International Conference on Web Search and Data Mining, pp. 510–518 (2020)
16. Song, Y., Garg, S., Shi, J., Ermon, S.: Sliced score matching: a scalable approach to density and score estimation. In: Uncertainty in Artificial Intelligence, pp. 574–584. PMLR (2020)
17. Song, Y., Sohl-Dickstein, J., Kingma, D.P., Kumar, A., Ermon, S., Poole, B.: Score-based generative modeling through stochastic differential equations. In: International Conference on Learning Representations (2021)

18. Sun, L., Rao, Y., Zhang, X., Lan, Y., Yu, S.: Ms-hgat: memory-enhanced sequential hypergraph attention network for information diffusion prediction (2022)
19. Vaswani, A., et al.: Attention is all you need. Adv. Neural Inf. Process. Syst. **30**, 1–11 (2017)
20. Wang, J., Jiang, J., Zhao, L.: An invertible graph diffusion neural network for source localization. In: Proceedings of the ACM Web Conference 2022, pp. 1058–1069 (2022)
21. Wang, R., et al.: Dydiff-vae: a dynamic variational framework for information diffusion prediction. In: Proceedings of the 44th International ACM SIGIR Conference on Research and Development in Information Retrieval, pp. 163–172 (2021)
22. Wang, Y., Shen, H., Liu, S., Gao, J., Cheng, X.: Cascade dynamics modeling with attention-based recurrent neural network. In: IJCAI, vol. 17, pp. 2985–2991 (2017)
23. Wang, Z., Hou, D., Gao, C., Huang, J., Xuan, Q.: A rapid source localization method in the early stage of large-scale network propagation. In: Proceedings of the ACM Web Conference 2022, pp. 1372–1380 (2022)
24. Wang, Z., Wang, C., Pei, J., Ye, X.: Multiple source detection without knowing the underlying propagation model. In: Proceedings of the AAAI Conference on Artificial Intelligence, vol. 31 (2017)
25. Xia, W., Li, Y., Wu, J., Li, S.: Deepis: susceptibility estimation on social networks. In: Proceedings of the 14th ACM International Conference on Web Search and Data Mining, pp. 761–769 (2021)
26. Xie, J., et al.: A multimodal variational encoder-decoder framework for micro-video popularity prediction. In: Proceedings of the Web Conference 2020, pp. 2542–2548 (2020)
27. Xu, M., Yu, L., Song, Y., Shi, C., Ermon, S., Tang, J.: Geodiff: a geometric diffusion model for molecular conformation generation. In: International Conference on Learning Representations (2021)
28. Yang, D., et al.: Study on the characteristics of coal and gas outburst hazard under the influence of high formation temperature in deep mines. Energy **268**, 126645 (2023)
29. You, J., Ying, R., Leskovec, J.: Position-aware graph neural networks. In: International Conference on Machine Learning, pp. 7134–7143. PMLR (2019)
30. Zhu, K., Chen, Z., Ying, L.: Catch'em all: locating multiple diffusion sources in networks with partial observations. In: Thirty-First AAAI Conference on Artificial Intelligence (2017)
31. Zhu, K., Ying, L.: Information source detection in the sir model: a sample-path-based approach. IEEE/ACM Trans. Netw. **24**(1), 408–421 (2014)

Interpretability

Sparse Neural Additive Model: Interpretable Deep Learning with Feature Selection via Group Sparsity

Shiyun Xu[1], Zhiqi Bu[1($\boxtimes$)], Pratik Chaudhari[2], and Ian J. Barnett[3]

[1] Department of Applied Mathematics and Computational Science,
University of Pennsylvania, Philadelphia, PA, USA
{shiyunxu,zbu}@sas.upenn.edu

[2] Department of Electrical and Systems Engineering, University of Pennsylvania,
Philadelphia, PA, USA

[3] Department of Biostatistics, Epidemiology, and Informatics,
University of Pennsylvania, Philadelphia, PA, USA

Abstract. Interpretable machine learning has demonstrated impressive performance while preserving explainability. In particular, neural additive models (NAM) offer the interpretability to the black-box deep learning and achieve state-of-the-art accuracy among the large family of generalized additive models. In order to empower NAM with feature selection and improve the generalization, we propose the sparse neural additive models (SNAM) that employ the group sparsity regularization (e.g. Group LASSO), where each feature is learned by a sub-network whose trainable parameters are clustered as a group. We study the theoretical properties for SNAM with novel techniques to tackle the non-parametric truth, thus extending from classical sparse linear models such as the LASSO, which only works on the parametric truth. Specifically, we show that SNAM with subgradient and proximal gradient descents provably converges to zero training loss as $t \to \infty$, and that the estimation error of SNAM vanishes asymptotically as $n \to \infty$. We also prove that SNAM, similar to LASSO, can have exact support recovery, i.e. perfect feature selection, with appropriate regularization. Moreover, we show that the SNAM can generalize well and preserve the 'identifiability', recovering each feature's effect. We validate our theories via extensive experiments and further testify to the good accuracy and efficiency of SNAM (Appendix can be found at https://arxiv.org/abs/2202.12482.).

Keywords: Interpretability · Additive Models · Group LASSO · Feature Selection

1 Introduction

Deep learning has shown dominating performance on learning complex tasks, especially in high-stake domains such as finance, healthcare and criminal justice.

D. Koutra et al. (Eds.): ECML PKDD 2023, LNAI 14171, pp. 343–359, 2023.
https://doi.org/10.1007/978-3-031-43418-1_21

However, most neural networks are not naturally as interpretable as decision trees or linear models. Even to answer fundamental questions like "what is the exact effect on the output if we perturb the input?", neural networks have to rely on complicated and ad-hoc methods to explain the model behavior, with additional training steps and loose theoretical guarantee. As a result, the black-box nature of neural networks makes it difficult and risky for human to trust deep learning models nor to understand them.

There is a long line of work studying the interpretable machine learning. At high level, existing methods can be categorized into two classes: (1) model-agnostic methods, and (2) innately interpretable models. On one hand, model-agnostic methods aim to explain the predictions of models that are innately black-box, via the feature importance and local approximation, which include Shapley values [22,33,35] and LIME [32] as the representatives. On the other hand, directly interpretable models such as the decision-tree-based models and the generalized linear models (GLM, [25]) , are widely applied with demonstrated performance.

To give more details, GLM is a powerful family of models that relates a linear model with its response variable by a link function g.

$$g(\mathbb{E}(\mathbf{y})) = \beta + \sum_{j=1}^{p} \beta_j \mathbf{X}_j \qquad (1)$$

where $\mathbf{y} \in \mathbb{R}^n$ is the response and $\mathbf{X}_j$ is the j-th feature of the input matrix. However, such parametric form with β_j limits the capacity of GLM when the unknown truth function takes a general and non-parametric form. This limitation is overcome by the development of generalized additive models (GAM) [18]:

$$g(\mathbb{E}(\mathbf{y})) = \beta + \sum_{j=1}^{p} f_j(\mathbf{X}_j) \equiv \beta + f(\mathbf{X}). \qquad (2)$$

Here f_j is the unknown truth function to be learned, i.e. the 'effect'.

Recently, the neural additive model (NAM) [1] introduces a new member into the GAM family, which applies sub-networks to learn f_j effectively, making accurate predictions while preserving the explainable power. Similar to regular neural networks, NAM learns a non-parametric model (2) via its trainable parameters, instead of the functional approximation used by the traditional GAM. This parametric formulation allows NAM to be trained efficiently by off-the-shelf optimizers such as Adam. In addition, NAM can leverage arbitrary network architecture to approximate f_j, hence fully exploiting the expressivity of deep learning.

Yet, theoretical results about NAM on some important questions are missing: Does the convergence of NAM behave nicely? Does NAM guarantee to learn the true additive model consistently, as sample size increases? How to modify NAM such as to select features and whether the feature selection is accurate? Can we expect each sub-network in NAM to recover each f_j?

In this paper, we answer these questions in the affirmative. We study the sparse NAM with specific group sparsity regularization, especially the Group

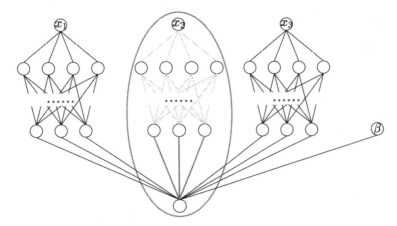

Fig. 1. Architecture of NAM, with each sub-network (blue circle) being a group for Group LASSO regularization in SNAM. Note that in multi-class, multi-label, and multi-task problems, the last layer can have multiple neurons. (Color figure online)

LASSO [16,23], which reduces to NAM when the penalty is zero. Our contributions are as follows:

1. We propose an innately interpretable model – sparse neural additive model (SNAM) – to empower NAM with feature selection. In particular, SNAM can employ the Group LASSO penalty in a unique way to regularize each subnetwork's parameters as one group. Note that we can easily extend to other group sparsity within SNAM, such as the Group SLOPE.
2. We employ efficient optimizers, such as the subgradient and proximal methods (see appendix), to train SNAM with provable convergence.
3. We establish an interesting connection between the LASSO and the SNAM with Group LASSO regularization, showing that the LASSO is indeed a subcase of SNAM. Building on top of this, we rigorously derive the slow rate and the support recovery of SNAM. We show that SNAM approximates the true model, selects important features in a sample-efficient manner, and identifies individual functions f_j asymptotically.
4. We empirically validate our results and advocate the effectiveness of SNAM via synthetic and real datasets . For example, SNAM can be 3× faster than SPAM [31] (see Table 2) and save half of parameters in NAM, while preserving comparable performance (see Table 5).

For theoretical analysis, we focus on the additive model

$$\mathbf{y} = \sum_{j=1}^{p} f_j\left(\mathbf{X}_j\right) + \epsilon \tag{3}$$

where i.i.d. samples $\mathbf{X}_j \sim \mathcal{X}_j$ for $j \in [p]$ where $\mathcal{X}_j$ is some distribution and the noise $\epsilon \sim SG(\sigma^2)$ where SG means sub-Gaussian with variance σ^2. For algorithms and experiments, we generalize from (3) to GAM in (2).

2 Additive Models in a Nutshell

Linear regression is one of the most classic model, on which various extensions are based. One extension is the LASSO [37], a linear model that adds ℓ_1 penalty to the linear model. This penalty not only empowers ordinary linear regression with feature selection but also regularizes the model against overfitting. Another extension is the GLM, which adds a link function to relate the linear model with its response to work on more general problems (e.g. logistic regression for classification). Note that GLM can combine with the ℓ_1 penalty to give sparse logistic regression.

While GLMs are all additive and thus directly interpretable, GAMs further improve the capacity of models by introducing the non-linearity, for instance, in NAM [1] and Explainable Boosting Machines (EBM) [21,27]. In this work, we focus on NAM, a state-of-the-art GAM that incorporates neural networks and uses four types of regularization: dropout, weight decay (ℓ_2 penalty), output penalty, and feature dropout. Unfortunately, all these types of regularization do not enable feature selection for NAM.

Traditionally, one can only allow feature selection on GLMs (with ℓ_1 regularization) or a few special GAMs, e.g. sparse additive model (SPAM by [31], restated in the appendix). As introduced in this paper, SNAM is a new member of GAM with feature selection. In addition, SNAM is the only GAM that is parametric (i.e. containing parameters that are trainable by gradient methods) besides GLMs: traditionally additive models are learned via the 'backfitting algorithm'[1] [8], while neural networks are learned via gradient methods.

$$\boxed{\text{LASSO} \subseteq \text{GLM} \subseteq \text{NAM} \subseteq \text{SNAM} \subseteq \text{GAM}}$$

One drawback of the backfitting algorithm is that the computation time will increase linearly with the number of features. This is due to the asynchronous or sequential estimation for each feature and a lack of theoretical understanding from the convergence viewpoint. The other drawback is the heavy memory complexity when executing the 'smoothing' function (usually some smooth kernel splines) on large sample size. In fact, SNAM can out-speed SPAM by 3 times in Table 2 on synthetic datasets, and SPAM runs out of memory on all real datasets considered here. We give a brief summary of additive models in Table 1[2].

3 SNAM: Model and Optimization

3.1 Model and Linearization Regimes

To analyze SNAM under the regularization, for the j-th sub-network, we write the trainable parameters of as $\boldsymbol{\Theta}_j$ (visualized in Fig. 1 by the blue circle) and

---

[1] The backfitting algorithm can be recovered from SPAM algorithm (see appendix) when $\lambda = 0$.

[2] In 'Non-param truth' column of Table 1, Yes/No means whether a model works without assuming that the truth is parametric.

Table 1. Summary of additive (interpretable) models.

Models	Non-linear model	Non-param truth	Parametric model	Feature selection
LASSO	No	No	Yes	Yes
GLM	No	No	Yes	Yes
EBM	Yes	Yes	No	No
NAM	Yes	Yes	Yes	No
SPAM	Yes	Yes	No	Yes
SNAM	Yes	Yes	Yes	Yes

the output as h_j. Then we write the SNAM output as

$$h(\mathbf{X}, \boldsymbol{\Theta}) = \sum_j h_j(\mathbf{X}_j, \boldsymbol{\Theta}_j) + \beta$$

With these notations in place, we can learn the model via the following SNAM optimization problem with some group sparsity regularization and an arbitrary loss $\mathcal{L}$:

$$\min_{\boldsymbol{\Theta}, \beta} \mathcal{L}\left(\mathbf{y}, \sum_j h_j(\mathbf{X}_j, \boldsymbol{\Theta}_j) + \beta\right) + \text{GroupSparsity}(\{\boldsymbol{\Theta}_j\}). \tag{4}$$

Notably, the group structure defined on sub-networks is the key to feature selection in SNAM: it explicitly penalizes $\boldsymbol{\Theta}_j$ so that the entries in $\boldsymbol{\Theta}_j$ are either all non-zero or all zero. The latter case happens when λ is large, resulting in the j-th feature to be not selected as $h_j = 0$.

In fact, if each sub-network has only a single parameter β_j and no hidden layers at all, then the Group LASSO penalty is equivalent to the LASSO penalty: $\|\beta_j\|_2 = |\beta_j|$. Therefore, we view LASSO as the simplest version of SNAM with Group LASSO regularization. This connection leads to the theoretical findings in this work, since we will analyze the linearization of SNAM.

A long line of research that linearizes the neural networks can be categorized into two main regimes: the neural tangent kernel (NTK) and the random feature (RF). The NTK regime linearizes the network under the 'lazy training' constraint, where $\boldsymbol{\Theta}(t) \approx \boldsymbol{\Theta}(0)$ during entire training process, by applying a first-order Taylor expansion at $\boldsymbol{\Theta}(0)$. This lazy training phenomenon is usually guaranteed using the extremely (even infinitely) wide neural networks, and without any regularization[3] [2,4,11,14,19,42,45]. Such limitation renders the NTK analysis invalid for SNAM.

The other branch of work uses the RF regime [17,24,30,43] to linearize the neural network by fixing the weights in all hidden layers after initialization, and only training the output layer's weights. Mathematically, we decompose $\boldsymbol{\Theta}_j = [\mathbf{w}_j, \boldsymbol{\theta}_j]$. We denote $\mathbf{w}_j$ as the weights of all hidden layers (green in Fig. 1)

---

[3] Unfortunately, $\boldsymbol{\Theta}(t)$ will be pushed away from its initialization $\boldsymbol{\Theta}(0)$ towards zero even under weak regularization, breaking the lazy training assumption [13,15].

and $\boldsymbol{\theta}_j \in \mathbb{R}^m$ as the weights in the output layer (red in Fig. 1). Then we can rewrite the output of SNAM as

$$h(\mathbf{X}, \mathbf{w}, \boldsymbol{\theta}) = \sum_j h_j(\mathbf{X}_j, \mathbf{w}_j, \boldsymbol{\theta}_j) + \beta = \sum_j g_j(\mathbf{X}_j, \mathbf{w}_j)\boldsymbol{\theta}_j + \beta \qquad (5)$$

in which $\boldsymbol{\theta} := [\boldsymbol{\theta}_1, \cdots, \boldsymbol{\theta}_p]$, $\mathbf{w} := [\mathbf{w}_1, \cdots, \mathbf{w}_p]$, and the feature map $g_j : \mathbb{R} \to \mathbb{R}^m$ is the forward propagation of the j-th sub-network until the output layer.

In this RF regime, SNAM is linear in trainable parameters $\boldsymbol{\theta}$ (though non-linear in input $\mathbf{X}$) and is indeed a kernel regression, a topic with rich theoretical understanding.

3.2   Group Sparsity and Optimization Problems

It is well-known that group sparsity allows all parameters in the same group to be simultaneously non-zero or zero. One popular choice is the Group LASSO, with which the SNAM problem becomes

$$\min_{\boldsymbol{\Theta},\beta} \mathcal{L}\left(\mathbf{y}, \sum_j h_j(\mathbf{X}_j, \boldsymbol{\Theta}_j) + \beta\right) + \lambda \sum_j \|\boldsymbol{\Theta}_j\|_2. \qquad (6)$$

For another example, we may consider the Group SLOPE:

$$\min_{\boldsymbol{\Theta},\beta} \mathcal{L}\left(\mathbf{y}, \sum_j h_j(\mathbf{X}_j, \boldsymbol{\Theta}_j) + \beta\right) + \sum_j \lambda_j \|\boldsymbol{\Theta}\|_{2,(j)}, \qquad (7)$$

where the penalty is a decreasing vector $(\lambda_1, \cdots, \lambda_p)$ and $\|\boldsymbol{\Theta}\|_{2(j)}$ denotes the j-th largest element in $\{\|\boldsymbol{\Theta}_1\|_2, \cdots, \|\boldsymbol{\Theta}_p\|_2\}$. We demonstrate other choices of group sparsity in the appendix. In what follows, we focus on SNAM with the Group LASSO.

3.3   Random Feature SNAM

We study the RF neural network as a sub-class of SNAM, with two desirable benefits: (i) we do not restrict to weak (infinitesimal) regularization as in [41]; (ii) we do not need neural networks to be wide. For the ease of presentation, we omit the output layer bias β:

$$h^{\mathrm{RF}}(\mathbf{X}, \boldsymbol{\theta}) = \sum_{j=1}^{p} h_j^{\mathrm{RF}}(\mathbf{X}_j, \boldsymbol{\theta}_j) = \sum_{j=1}^{p} \mathbf{G}_j \boldsymbol{\theta}_j$$

where the random features $\mathbf{G}_j := g_j(\mathbf{X}_j, \mathbf{w}(0)) \in \mathbb{R}^{n \times m}$. Therefore, the corresponding optimization for the RF network is

$$\hat{\boldsymbol{\theta}}^{\mathrm{RF}} := \mathrm{argmin}_{\boldsymbol{\theta}} \mathcal{L}(\mathbf{y}, \mathbf{G}\boldsymbol{\theta}) + \lambda \sum_j \|\boldsymbol{\theta}_j\|_2 \qquad (8)$$

where $\mathbf{G} := [\mathbf{G}_1, \cdots, \mathbf{G}_p]$ is the concatenation of $\mathbf{G}_j$.

3.4   Convergence of SNAM and RF

Algorithmically speaking, the general SNAM (4) can be efficiently optimized by existing optimizers, e.g. the subgradient methods [5,7,34,36] and the proximal gradient descent (ProxGD) [20,26,29] (see appendix for details). In fact, we can show that the subgradient descent and ProxGD both provably find the minimizer of SNAM (4) and its RF variant (8).

Denoting Θ to denote all trainable parameters in SNAM and Θ_j as those in the j-th sub-network, we claim both subgradient descent and ProxGD have the same gradient flow [29, Section 4.2]:

$$\frac{d\Theta}{dt} = -\frac{\partial(\mathcal{L}(\mathbf{y}, h(\mathbf{X}, \Theta)) + \lambda \sum_j \|\Theta_j\|_2)}{\partial\Theta}$$

Let multiply $\frac{\partial\Theta}{\partial t}^\top$ on the left and integrate over time,

$$\int_0^\infty \left\|\frac{d\Theta}{dt}\right\|_2^2 dt = \int_\infty^0 \frac{d(\mathcal{L}(t) + \lambda \sum_j \|\Theta_j(t)\|_2)}{dt} dt \leq \mathcal{L}(0) + \lambda \sum_j \|\Theta_j(0)\|_2.$$

Since the integral is increasing in time but upper bounded, we obtain that $\frac{d\Theta}{dt} \to 0$ and thus $\frac{d\mathcal{L}}{dt} \to 0$, i.e. $\mathcal{L}$ converges to the minimum. The convergence result implies the trainability of SNAMs (and NAMs as a by-product when $\lambda = 0$) in practice.

Henceforth, we focus on the RF SNAM minimizer $\hat{\boldsymbol{\theta}}^{\mathrm{RF}}$ in (3) and drop the super-script 'RF' for clearer presentation.

4   Non-Asymptotic Analysis of SNAM

In this section, we show that SNAM can approximate the truth model well on training set and achieve exact support recovery with finite number of samples.

We study the primal problem

$$\hat{\boldsymbol{\theta}} := \operatorname{argmin}_\theta \frac{1}{2}\|\mathbf{y} - \sum_j \mathbf{G}_j \boldsymbol{\theta}_j\|_2^2 + \lambda \sum_j \|\boldsymbol{\theta}_j\|_2 \qquad (9)$$

and equivalently the dual problem

$$\hat{\boldsymbol{\theta}} := \operatorname{argmin}_{\boldsymbol{\theta}: \sum_j \|\boldsymbol{\theta}_j\|_2 \leq \mu} \frac{1}{2}\|\mathbf{y} - \sum_j \mathbf{G}_j \boldsymbol{\theta}_j\|_2^2 \qquad (10)$$

We point out that although the analysis of SNAM is similar to that of LASSO at high level, our analysis is technically more involved and requires novel tools, due to the fact that the true model (3) is non-parametric (unlike the LASSO whose true model is parametric).

4.1   Slow Rate with Group LASSO Penalty

Similar to the analysis of slow rate for the LASSO [40], our analysis needs SNAM to overfit the training data under the low-dimensional **G** regime.

Assumption 1 (Overfitting of SNAM). *Denoting the truth* $\mathbf{f}_j := f_j(\mathbf{X}_j)$, *we assume there exists* μ *such that*

$$\frac{1}{n}\|\mathbf{y} - \sum_j \mathbf{G}_j \hat{\boldsymbol{\theta}}_j\|_2^2 \le \frac{1}{n}\|\mathbf{y} - \sum_j \mathbf{f}_j\|_2^2 = \frac{1}{n}\|\boldsymbol{\epsilon}\|_2^2.$$

To guarantee a unique solution of SNAM, we further assume that the SNAM feature map **G** has full rank.

Assumption 2 (Full rank of feature map). $\mathbf{G} \in \mathbb{R}^{n \times M}$ *has full column rank* M *and thus* $\mathbf{G}^\top \mathbf{G} \in \mathbb{R}^{M \times M}$ *is invertible.*

Here M is the sum of numbers of neurons at the last hidden layer of each sub-network[4]. Our first result is the slow rate of the SNAM convergence $h(\mathbf{X}, \hat{\boldsymbol{\theta}}) \to f(\mathbf{X})$ as $n \to \infty$. We highlight the definition of estimation error $\|f(\mathbf{X}) - h(\mathbf{X}, \hat{\boldsymbol{\theta}})\|^2/n$, which is different from the prediction error $\|\mathbf{y} - h(\mathbf{X}, \hat{\boldsymbol{\theta}})\|^2/n$.

Theorem 1. *Under Assumption 1 and Assumption 2, supposing* $|f_j|$ *is upper bounded by constant* c_j *and noise* $\epsilon \sim SG(\sigma^2)$, *then with probability at least* $1 - \delta_1 - \delta_2$, *we have for* $\hat{\theta}$ *in* (10),

$$\frac{1}{n}\|\sum_j (\mathbf{f}_j - \mathbf{G}_j \hat{\boldsymbol{\theta}}_j)\|_2^2 \le \frac{2\sigma}{\sqrt{n}}\left(\sum_j \frac{c_j}{\sqrt{\delta_2}} + \mu \max_j \sqrt{\mathbb{E}g_j(\mathcal{X}_j, \mathbf{w}_j(0))^2}\sqrt{2\log(m_j/\delta_1)}\right)$$

where m_j *is the width of output layer in the* j-*th sub-network and* μ *is the penalty coefficient.*

We refer the interested readers to our appendix for the proof. In fact, we may further relax our assumption on the noise distribution in the true model (3), at the cost of a strictly worse bound for any δ_1.

Corollary 1. *Under Assumption 1 and Assumption 2, supposing* $|f_j|$ *is upper bounded by constant* c_j *and noise has* mean(ϵ) = 0, Var(ϵ) = σ^2, *then with probability at least* $1 - \delta_1 - \delta_2$, *we have for* $\hat{\theta}$ *in* (10),

$$\frac{1}{n}\|\sum_j (\mathbf{f}_j - \mathbf{G}_j \hat{\boldsymbol{\theta}}_j)\|_2^2 \le \frac{2\sigma}{\sqrt{n}}\left(\sum_j \frac{c_j}{\sqrt{\delta_2}} + \mu \max_j \sqrt{\mathbb{E}g_j(\mathcal{X}_j, \mathbf{w}_j(0))^2}\sqrt{m_j/\delta_1}\right)$$

The proof only needs slight modification by leveraging the Kolmogorov inequality instead of the maximal sub-Gaussian inequality in Theorem 1. In both Theorem 1 and Corollary 1, the MSE $\frac{1}{n}\|\sum_j(\mathbf{f}_j - \mathbf{G}_j\hat{\boldsymbol{\theta}}_j)\|_2^2$ converges to zero with rate $1/\sqrt{n}$ as $n \to \infty$. We note that the convergence rate of SNAM has the same order as that of LASSO, but SNAM requires two probability quantities δ_1, δ_2 due to the non-parametric true model (3), whereas the LASSO only needs δ_1.

---

[4] When all sub-networks have the same architecture, we write $M = mp$ where the last hidden layer width m. More generally, suppose the j-th sub-network has last hidde layer width m_j, then $M = \sum_j m_j$.

4.2   Exact Support Recovery

There has been a long line of research on the support recovery, particularly on the parametric models such as the LASSO [12,38,40], where the support is defined on the parameters, e.g. $supp(\hat{\boldsymbol{\beta}}) = \{j : \hat{\beta}_j \neq 0\}, supp(\boldsymbol{\beta}) = \{j : \beta_j \neq 0\}$, and the regularization is also defined on the parameters via $\lambda\|\hat{\boldsymbol{\beta}}\|_1$. For non-parametric models like SPAM, the support is instead defined on the functions

$$S = supp(f) = \{j : f_j \neq 0\},$$

and the regularization is on the output function $\{h_j\}$. In contrast, our SNAM sets the sparse regularization on the parameters $\{\boldsymbol{\theta}_j\}$, similar to LASSO. This explicit regularization allows us to borrow from the rich results of traditional support recovery for the LASSO and extend them to SNAM.

First, we assume that an insignificant feature $(j \notin S)$ is small when regressing on the true features.

Assumption 3 (Mutual incoherence). *For some $\gamma > 0$, we have*

$$\left\| \left(\mathbf{G}_S^\top \mathbf{G}_S\right)^{-1} \mathbf{G}_S^\top \mathbf{G}_j \right\|_2 \leq 1 - \gamma, \text{ for } j \notin S \tag{11}$$

where $\mathbf{G}_S$ is the concatenation of $\mathbf{G}_j$ for all $j \in S$.

Next, we assume the regularization is not too large to omit significant features.

Assumption 4 (Maximum regularization). *The Group LASSO penalty coefficient λ in (9) is small enough so that the following solution is dense*

$$\tilde{\boldsymbol{\theta}}_S := \operatorname{argmin}_{\boldsymbol{\theta}_S} \frac{1}{2}\|\mathbf{y} - \sum_{j \in S} \mathbf{G}_j \boldsymbol{\theta}_j\|_2^2 + \lambda \sum_{j \in S} \|\boldsymbol{\theta}_j\|_2 \tag{12}$$

We define the support of any prediction function $h(\cdot; \hat{\boldsymbol{\theta}})$ in two equivalent ways: one on the function and the other on the parameters,

$$supp(h) \equiv \{j : h_j \neq 0\} = \{j : \|\hat{\boldsymbol{\theta}}_j\|_2 \neq 0\}.$$

We prove in the appendix that, with proper Group LASSO regularization, the SNAM recovers the true $supp(f)$ exactly.

Theorem 2. *Under Assumption 2, Assumption 3 and Assumption 4, then*

$$\lambda > \max_{j \notin S} \|\mathbf{G}_j^\top\|_\infty \|\mathbf{y}\|_\infty / \gamma$$

guarantees that the SNAM solution $\hat{\boldsymbol{\theta}}$ in (9) has the exact support recovery, i.e. $supp(h) = supp(f)$.

5   Asymptotic Analysis of SNAM

In this section, we study the asymptotic consistency of SNAM and hence indicate its good generalization behavior. Our results build on top of the asymptotic zero loss between the ground truth and the prediction on training data, given by the slow rate in Theorem 1. The proofs can be found in the appendix.

5.1 Consistency

We show in Theorem 3 that the SNAM h_n, when trained on n samples, converges to the unknown true model f in a probability measure. In other words, large amount of data promises that SNAM as a whole function can learn the truth.

Theorem 3. *Under the assumptions in Theorem 1, we have the convergence in probability measure:*

$$\lim_{n \to \infty} \rho(\{x \in \mathcal{X} : |f(x) - h_n(x)| \geq \varepsilon\}) = 0$$

for arbitrarily small $\epsilon > 0$. Here ρ is the probability measure of $\mathcal{X}$, the joint distribution of data $\mathbf{X}$. In words, the prediction h_n converges to the truth f.

5.2 Effect Identifiability

Another more difficult challenge in the generalized additive models is the identifiability of individual effects, in the sense that we want to have $h_j \to f_j$ for all $j \in [p]$. Notice that since the identifiability is a stronger property than the consistency, we need to assume more about the feature distribution $\mathcal{X}_j$. We show that SNAM is capable of identifying the effects in Theorem 4.

Theorem 4 (Effect Identifiability). *Assuming $h_n \to f$ in probability measure of $\mathcal{X}$ as $n \to \infty$, if $\mathcal{X}_j$ is independent of $\mathcal{X}_{-j}$, then $\lim_{n \to \infty} h_{n,j}(x)$ converges to $f_j(x)$ in probability up to a constant.*

6 Experiments

In this section, we conduct multiple experiments on both synthetic and real datasets. we emphasize that here SNAM is not RF SNAM, i.e. we train all parameters in sub-networks. All experiments are conducted with one Tesla P100 GPU. We use MSE loss for regression, cross-entropy (CE) loss for classification, and wall-clock time for all tasks. Furthermore, we compare SNAM to other possibly sparse interpretable methods: NAM, ℓ_1 linear support vector machine (SVM), LASSO and SPAM [31]. Experiment details such as data pre-processing, model architecture and hyperparamters are listed in the appendix[5].

6.1 Synthetic Datasets

To validate our statistical analysis on SNAM, i.e. the feature selection (or support recovery), the estimation consistency and the effect identifiability, we experiment on synthetic datasets. We emphasize that it is necessary to work with synthetic data instead of real-world ones, since we need access to the truth f_j.

---

[5] Code is available at https://github.com/ShiyunXu/SNAM.git.

Data Generation. We generate a data matrix $\mathbf{X} \in \mathbb{R}^{3000 \times 24}$ and denote the j-th column of $\mathbf{X}$ as $\mathbf{X}_j$. $\mathbf{y}$ is generated by the following additive model, for regression and binary classification, respectively:

$$\mathbb{P}(\mathbf{y} = 1) = \text{sigmoid}(f_1(\mathbf{X}_1) + \cdots + f_{24}(\mathbf{X}_{24})).$$

where all f_j are zero functions except

$$f_1(x) = 2x^2 \tanh x, \quad f_2(x) = \sin x \cos x + x^2$$
$$f_3(x) = 20/(1 + e^{-5\sin x}), \quad f_4(x) = 20\sin^3 2x - 6\cos x + x^2$$

Performance Measures. Denote the output of each sub-network as $\hat{f}_j$. To illustrate the performance on the support recovery, we use precision and recall to compare $\hat{f}_j$ and truth f_j. In particular, we use ℓ_2 norm of a sub-network's weights to indicate whether $\hat{f}_j = 0$.

We now introduce the identification error (iden. error),

$$\min_{c_j \in \mathbb{R}} \|\hat{f}_j(\mathbf{X}_j) - f_j(\mathbf{X}_j) - c_j\|_2^2/n = \|\hat{f}_j(\mathbf{X}_j) - f_j(\mathbf{X}_j) - \hat{c}_j\|_2^2/n$$

in which $\hat{c}_j := \frac{1}{n}\sum_{i=1}^{n}(\hat{f}_j(\mathbf{X}_{ij}) - f_j(\mathbf{X}_{ij}))$. Notice that Corollary 4 claims the convergence up to a constant $\hat{c}_j$.

Table 2. Performance of sparse interpretable methods on synthetic regression.

	ℓ_1 SVM	LASSO	SPAM	SNAM
MSE loss	140.7	139.7	25.75	**10.61**
Precision	0.17	**1.00**	0.17	**1.00**
Recall	**1.00**	**1.00**	**1.00**	**1.00**
Iden. error	5.90	6.09	3.07	**0.69**
Time (sec)	0.005	0.007	152.1	48.52
#. Feature	24	4	4	4
#. Param	24	4	–	127201

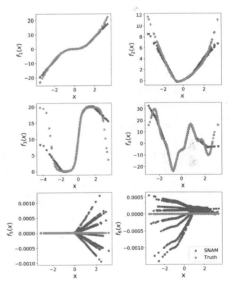

Fig. 2. Individual effect learned by SNAM on synthetic regression. Blue dots are prediction $\hat{f}_j(\mathbf{X}_j)$ and orange dots are truth $f_j(\mathbf{X}_j)$, with $j = 1, \cdots, 6$. (Color figure online)

Table 3. Performance of sparse interpretable methods on synthetic classification.

	ℓ_1 SVM	LASSO	SPAM	SNAM
CE loss	0.27	0.26	–	**0.15**
Test accuracy	73.2	74.2	–	**94.1**
Precision	0.57	0.67	–	**1.00**
Recall	**1.00**	**1.00**	–	**1.00**
Time (sec)	0.005	0.019	–	10.10
#. Feature	13	6	–	4
#. Param	13	6	–	128402

Results. In Table 2, for regression task, SNAM domintes existing sparse interpretable methods in all measures. Especially, SNAM (which includes LASSO as a sub-case) is the only method that achieves exact support recovery, obtaining perfect precision and recall scores. When facing complicated target functions, SNAM, as a non-linear model, significantly outperforms linear models like linear SVM and LASSO, in terms of test loss and identification error. In contrast to SPAM, another non-linear model that achieves low loss, SNAM outperforms in both loss and efficiency, with a 3 times speed-up.

We further visualize the effects learned by SNAM in Fig. 2, demonstrating the strong approximation offered by the neural networks, and leave those learned by other interpretable methods in the appendix.

Similarly in Table 3, for classification task, SNAM again significantly outperforms existing sparse interpretable methods: roughly 20% higher accuracy and 33% higher precision. Here LASSO means ℓ_1 regularized logistic regression and SPAM cannot perform the classification in original text [31].

6.2   California Housing Regression

California Housing [28] is a dataset for studying the effect of community characteristics on housing prices in California districts from 1990 U.S. census. The task is to predict the median housing price based on 20640 examples and 8 features.

In [1], a well-trained NAM deems the median income, latitude and longitude as the most significant features for an accurate prediction. Reassuringly, our SNAM concurs with the their conclusion

Table 4. Performance of interpretable methods on California Housing dataset.

	ℓ_1 SVM	LASSO	NAM	SNAM
MSE loss	0.654	0.712	**0.451**	0.567
MAE loss	0.594	0.654	**0.479**	0.526
R^2 score	0.501	0.457	**0.696**	0.645
Time (sec)	1.37	0.01	343	340
#. Feature	6	2	8	7
#. Param	6	2	42401	37101

by selecting the same features (see appendix). Although the conclusion is the same, we highlight a key difference between the approaches: while the authors in [1] base their conclusion on the ad-hoc visual examination of the shape function $\hat{f}_j$, our approach is based on a hypothesis testing: $\theta_j = 0$ v.s. $\theta_j \neq 0$ where θ_j is all parameters in a sub-network. We recognize a small decrease in the loss as the cost of feature selection, when compared to NAM, but SNAM can save 12.5% in the number of parameters (or memory). Additionally, SNAM still outperforms other sparse interpretable methods. In fact, although SNAM takes longer to achieve its optimal performance in Table 4, it only takes about 14 s to outperform the optimal LASSO and SVM.

6.3   COMPAS Classification

COMPAS is a widely used commercial tool to predict the recidivism risk based on defendants' features and it is known for its racial bias against the black defendants. It has 6172 examples and 13 features[6]. The ProPublica released the recidivism dataset [3], that includes the characteristics of defendants in Broward County, Florida, and the predictions on reoffending by the COMPAS algorithm.

In Table 5, we notice that all interpretable methods perform similarly, and SNAM has the highest AUC score between label and prediction, even though it only contains 54% of NAM's parameters. A closer look at Fig. 3 describes the relations between features and the variation of effect, which is gap between the minimum recidivism risk and the maximum one among all individual samples for a particular feature, i.e. $\max_i \hat{f}_j(X_{ij}) - \min_i \hat{f}_j(X_{ij})$. If the variation of an effect is large, then

Table 5. Performance of interpretable methods on COMPAS dataset.

	ℓ_1 SVM	LASSO	NAM	SNAM
CE loss	**0.486**	**0.484**	0.503	0.504
Test accuracy	75.3	75.4	75.3	**75.6**
AUC score	**0.744**	**0.743**	0.714	**0.745**
Time (sec)	0.106	0.175	27.5	27.4
#. Feature	13	12	13	5
#. Param	13	12	69552	26750

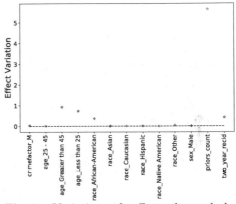

Fig. 3. Variation of effects learned by SNAM on COMPAS dataset.

SNAM indicates the feature is significant. Indeed, the top 5 features selected by SNAM are prior counts, ages, two year recidivism and whether the defendant is African American. The last feature clearly demonstrates SNAM's explanability of the COMPAS algorithm's racial bias. In short, the features selected by SNAM are consistent with NAM's selection based on shape functions (see more figures in appendix).

6.4   Super-Conductivity Regression

We further experiment on the super-conductivity dataset from UCI repository, aiming to predict the critical temperature of super-conductors based on physical quantities (e.g. atomic radius, mass, density...) and chemical formulae. We highlight that the Super-conductivity is a high-dimensional dataset with 21263 samples and 131 features[7], whereas all datasets in [1] have at most 30 features.

---

[6] The data preprocessing follows https://github.com/propublica/compas-analysis.

[7] The original dataset has 168 features. We remove the column `material` and all columns with variance less than 5%.

Table 6. Performance of interpretable methods on super-conductivity dataset.

	ℓ_1 SVM	LASSO	NAM	SNAM
MSE loss	410.0	311.7	**274.1**	**280.3**
MAE loss	15.47	13.43	**11.56**	**12.09**
R^2 score loss	0.654	0.731	**0.787**	**0.775**
Time (sec)	5.00	1.87	682	688
#. Feature	100	50	131	72
#. Param	100	50	6289	3457

We note that SNAM obtains similar performance as NAM and LASSO. In addition, the sparsity in SNAM saves 45% number of parameters. In fact, given that NAM gives the best performance, a practitioner can always choose small penalty in SNAM in order to trade model efficiency for better performance (Table 6).

7 Discussion

In this work, we propose the sparse neural additive model (SNAM) which applies a specific Group LASSO regularization explicitly to NAM. On one hand, SNAM is an interpretable deep learning model where the effect of each feature on the output can be extracted. On the other hand, the Group LASSO regularization empowers the network to select informative features, in the same way that LASSO empowers the linear model. We develop theoretical analysis of the optimization, the slow rate, the support recovery, the consistency of prediction, and the effect identifiability. Additionally, our experiments demonstrate the advantage of SNAM in memory and training efficiency, especially over non-regularized NAM and existing regularized interpretable methods. However, the superiority in performance usually comes at the price of longer training time than simpler methods like LASSO.

For future directions, one may further extend SNAM's theory to the fast convergence rate [39] in sample size, or to the jointly trained SNAM in terms of time. We believe the theoretical analysis and empirical evaluation can be explored for a whole family of interesting SNAMs. For example, while SNAM with Group LASSO penalty contains LASSO as sub-case, we can view SNAM with Group SLOPE [9] penalty as extension of SLOPE [6]. Other possible extensions of elastic net [47], adaptive LASSO [46], K-level SLOPE [10, 44] are also possible with SNAM (see appendix for examples).

Acknowledgements. SX is supported through partnership with GSK. PC was supported by grants from the National Science Foundation (IIS-2145164, CCF-2212519) and the Office of Naval Research (N00014-22-1-2255). IB is supported by the National Institute of Mental Health (R01MH116884).

Ethical Statement. High-stake applications like healthcare, criminal records empowered by deep learning raise people's concern about algorithms' liability, fairness, and interpretability. Our method can help build a fair, trustworthy and explainable community by seeking the reason behind machine learning predictions. Sometimes, the system may predict upon discrimination without realizing it (such as the COMPAS algorithm). Examining into each feature's contribution to the outcome provides a possibility of avoid learning with bias. Our method is useful especially in high dimensional datasets, such as some medical tabular records. Hence, our paper has an important impact on ethical machine learning. Yet, we emphasize that interpretable machine learning does not automatically guarantee its trustworthiness: it can still make mistakes and bias towards certain group, even though it can explain why it does so.

References

1. Agarwal, R., Frosst, N., Zhang, X., Caruana, R., Hinton, G.E.: Neural additive models: interpretable machine learning with neural nets. arXiv preprint arXiv:2004.13912 (2020)
2. Allen-Zhu, Z., Li, Y., Song, Z.: A convergence theory for deep learning via over-parameterization. In: International Conference on Machine Learning, pp. 242–252. PMLR (2019)
3. Angwin, J., Larson, J., Mattu, S., Kirchner, L.: Machine bias. Propublica (2016)
4. Arora, S., Du, S.S., Hu, W., Li, Z., Salakhutdinov, R., Wang, R.: On exact computation with an infinitely wide neural net. arXiv preprint arXiv:1904.11955 (2019)
5. Beck, A., Teboulle, M.: A fast iterative shrinkage-thresholding algorithm for linear inverse problems. SIAM J. Imaging Sci. **2**(1), 183–202 (2009)
6. Bogdan, M., Van Den Berg, E., Sabatti, C., Su, W., Candès, E.J.: Slope-adaptive variable selection via convex optimization. Ann. Appl. Stat. **9**(3), 1103 (2015)
7. Boyd, S., Xiao, L., Mutapcic, A.: Subgradient methods. Lecture notes of EE392o, Stanford University, Autumn Quarter 2004, 2004–2005 (2003)
8. Breiman, L., Friedman, J.H.: Estimating optimal transformations for multiple regression and correlation. J. Am. Stat. Assoc. **80**(391), 580–598 (1985)
9. Brzyski, D., Gossmann, A., Su, W., Bogdan, M.: Group slope-adaptive selection of groups of predictors. J. Am. Stat. Assoc. **114**(525), 419–433 (2019)
10. Bu, Z., Klusowski, J., Rush, C., Su, W.J.: Characterizing the slope trade-off: a variational perspective and the donoho-tanner limit. arXiv preprint arXiv:2105.13302 (2021)
11. Bu, Z., Xu, S., Chen, K.: A dynamical view on optimization algorithms of overparameterized neural networks. In: International Conference on Artificial Intelligence and Statistics, pp. 3187–3195. PMLR (2021)
12. Bühlmann, P., Van De Geer, S.: Statistics for High-Dimensional Data: Methods, Theory and Applications. Springer, Heidelberg (2011). https://doi.org/10.1007/978-3-642-20192-9
13. Chen, Z., Cao, Y., Gu, Q., Zhang, T.: A generalized neural tangent kernel analysis for two-layer neural networks. In: Larochelle, H., Ranzato, M., Hadsell, R., Balcan, M.F., Lin, H. (eds.) Advances in Neural Information Processing Systems, vol. 33, pp. 13363–13373. Curran Associates, Inc. (2020). www.proceedings.neurips.cc/paper/2020/file/9afe487de556e59e6db6c862adfe25a4-Paper.pdf
14. Du, S.S., Zhai, X., Poczos, B., Singh, A.: Gradient descent provably optimizes over-parameterized neural networks. arXiv preprint arXiv:1810.02054 (2018)

15. Fang, C., Dong, H., Zhang, T.: Mathematical models of overparameterized neural networks. Proc. IEEE **109**(5), 683–703 (2021)
16. Hastie, T., Tibshirani, R., Friedman, J.: The Elements of Statistical Learning. SSS, Springer, New York (2009). https://doi.org/10.1007/978-0-387-84858-7
17. Ghorbani, B., Mei, S., Misiakiewicz, T., Montanari, A.: Linearized two-layers neural networks in high dimension. Ann. Stat. **49**(2), 1029–1054 (2021)
18. Hastie, T.J., Tibshirani, R.J.: Generalized Additive Models. Routledge, Abingdon (2017)
19. Jacot, A., Gabriel, F., Hongler, C.: Neural tangent kernel: convergence and generalization in neural networks. arXiv preprint arXiv:1806.07572 (2018)
20. Li, H., Lin, Z.: Accelerated proximal gradient methods for nonconvex programming. Adv. Neural Inf. Process. Syst. **28**, 379–387 (2015)
21. Lou, Y., Caruana, R., Gehrke, J.: Intelligible models for classification and regression. In: Proceedings of the 18th ACM SIGKDD International Conference on Knowledge Discovery and Data Mining, pp. 150–158 (2012)
22. Lundberg, S.M., Lee, S.I.: A unified approach to interpreting model predictions. In: Proceedings of the 31st International Conference on Neural Information Processing Systems, pp. 4768–4777 (2017)
23. Meier, L., Van De Geer, S., Bühlmann, P.: The group lasso for logistic regression. J. Roy. Stat. Soc. Ser. B (Stat. Methodol.) **70**(1), 53–71 (2008)
24. Neal, R.M.: Priors for infinite networks. In: Bayesian Learning for Neural Networks, pp. 29–53. Springer, Heidelberg (1996). https://doi.org/10.1007/978-1-4612-0745-0_2
25. Nelder, J.A., Wedderburn, R.W.: Generalized linear models. J. Roy. Stat. Soc. Ser. A (General) **135**(3), 370–384 (1972)
26. Nitanda, A.: Stochastic proximal gradient descent with acceleration techniques. Adv. Neural Inf. Process. Syst. **27**, 1574–1582 (2014)
27. Nori, H., Jenkins, S., Koch, P., Caruana, R.: Interpretml: a unified framework for machine learning interpretability. arXiv preprint arXiv:1909.09223 (2019)
28. Pace, R.K., Barry, R.: Sparse spatial autoregressions. Stat. Probab. Lett. **33**(3), 291–297 (1997)
29. Parikh, N., Boyd, S.: Proximal algorithms. Found. Trends Optim. **1**(3), 127–239 (2014)
30. Rahimi, A., Recht, B., et al.: Random features for large-scale kernel machines. In: NIPS, vol. 3, p. 5. Citeseer (2007)
31. Ravikumar, P., Lafferty, J., Liu, H., Wasserman, L.: Sparse additive models. J. Roy. Stat. Soc. Ser. B (Stat. Methodol.) **71**(5), 1009–1030 (2009)
32. Ribeiro, M.T., Singh, S., Guestrin, C.: "why should i trust you?" explaining the predictions of any classifier. In: Proceedings of the 22nd ACM SIGKDD International Conference on Knowledge Discovery and Data Mining, pp. 1135–1144 (2016)
33. Shapley, L.S.: 17. A Value for n-person Games. Princeton University Press, Princeton (2016)
34. Shor, N.Z.: Minimization Methods for Non-Differentiable Functions, vol. 3. Springer, Heidelberg (2012). https://doi.org/10.1007/978-3-642-82118-9
35. Strumbelj, E., Kononenko, I.: Explaining prediction models and individual predictions with feature contributions. Knowl. Inf. Syst. **41**(3), 647–665 (2014)
36. Su, W., Boyd, S., Candes, E.: A differential equation for modeling Nesterov's accelerated gradient method: theory and insights. Adv. Neural Inf. Process. Syst. **27**, 2510–2518 (2014)
37. Tibshirani, R.: Regression shrinkage and selection via the lasso. J. Roy. Stat. Soc. Ser. B (Methodol.) **58**(1), 267–288 (1996)

38. Tibshirani, R., Wasserman, L.: Sparsity, the lasso, and friends. Lecture notes from "Statistical Machine Learning," Carnegie Mellon University, Spring (2017)

39. Van De Geer, S.A., Bühlmann, P.: On the conditions used to prove oracle results for the lasso. Electron. J. Stat. **3**, 1360–1392 (2009)

40. Wainwright, M.J.: Sharp thresholds for high-dimensional and noisy sparsity recovery using ℓ_1 -constrained quadratic programming (lasso). IEEE Trans. Inf. Theory **55**(5), 2183–2202 (2009)

41. Wei, C., Lee, J., Liu, Q., Ma, T.: Regularization matters: generalization and optimization of neural nets vs their induced kernel (2019)

42. Xiao, L., Pennington, J., Schoenholz, S.: Disentangling trainability and generalization in deep neural networks. In: International Conference on Machine Learning, pp. 10462–10472. PMLR (2020)

43. Yehudai, G., Shamir, O.: On the power and limitations of random features for understanding neural networks. Adv. Neural Inf. Process. Syst. **32**, 6598–6608 (2019)

44. Zhang, Y., Bu, Z.: Efficient designs of slope penalty sequences in finite dimension. In: International Conference on Artificial Intelligence and Statistics, pp. 3277–3285. PMLR (2021)

45. Zou, D., Cao, Y., Zhou, D., Gu, Q.: Gradient descent optimizes over-parameterized deep relu networks. Mach. Learn. **109**(3), 467–492 (2020)

46. Zou, H.: The adaptive lasso and its oracle properties. J. Am. Stat. Assoc. **101**(476), 1418–1429 (2006)

47. Zou, H., Hastie, T.: Regularization and variable selection via the elastic net. J. Roy. Stat. Soc. Ser. B (Stat. Methodol.) **67**(2), 301–320 (2005)

Learning Locally Interpretable Rule Ensemble

Kentaro Kanamori[✉]

Artificial Intelligence Laboratory, Fujitsu Limited, Tokyo, Japan
k.kanamori@fujitsu.com

Abstract. This paper proposes a new framework for learning a rule
ensemble model that is both accurate and interpretable. A rule ensemble is
an interpretable model based on the linear combination of weighted rules.
In practice, we often face the trade-off between the accuracy and interpretability of rule ensembles. That is, a rule ensemble needs to include a
sufficiently large number of weighted rules to maintain its accuracy, which
harms its interpretability for human users. To avoid this trade-off and learn
an interpretable rule ensemble without degrading accuracy, we introduce a
new concept of interpretability, named local interpretability, which is evaluated by the total number of rules necessary to express individual predictions made by the model, rather than to express the model itself. Then, we
propose a regularizer that promotes local interpretability and develop an
efficient algorithm for learning a rule ensemble with the proposed regularizer by coordinate descent with local search. Experimental results demonstrated that our method learns rule ensembles that can explain individual
predictions with fewer rules than the existing methods, including RuleFit,
while maintaining comparable accuracy.

Keywords: Interpretability · Explainability · Rule ensemble

1   Introduction

In the applications of machine learning models to high-stake decision-making
such as loan approvals, *interpretability* has been recognized as an important element [27,36,37]. One of the well-known interpretable models is a *rule model*,
including decision trees [16], rule lists [2], and rule sets [23]. Because rule models
are expressed using logical rules that are easy to understand, they can explain
how they make predictions in an interpretable manner by themselves. Such explanation helps human users ensure transparency for their critical decision-making,
as well as discover new knowledge from data [12]. In this study, we focus on a
rule ensemble [15,42], which is a rule model based on the linear combination of
weighted rules. For a given input, a rule ensemble makes a prediction depending
on the sum of the weights corresponding to the rules that the input satisfies.

One of the main obstacles to learning rule ensembles is the trade-off between
accuracy and interpretability. While the interpretability of rule models has several definitions depending on their forms and applications [9,24], a common
criterion for evaluating the interpretability of a model is the total number of

© The Author(s), under exclusive license to Springer Nature Switzerland AG 2023
D. Koutra et al. (Eds.): ECML PKDD 2023, LNAI 14171, pp. 360–377, 2023.
https://doi.org/10.1007/978-3-031-43418-1_22

rules required to express the model [12,22]. Due to the cognitive limitations of human users, a model should consist of as few rules as possible, even if the model belongs to the class of inherently interpretable models [23,36]. In practice, however, a rule ensemble requires a sufficiently large number of weighted rules to maintain generalization performance [30]. Therefore, we often need to compromise interpretability to maintain accuracy when learning rule ensembles.

In general, a major approach to addressing the accuracy-interpretability trade-off is to make each individual prediction, rather than a model itself, interpretable. For example, if we need to validate an undesired prediction result (e.g., high risk of default) made by a model, it is often sufficient to explain a reason why the model outputs the prediction in an interpretable way, even if the model consists of too many rules to interpret [6]. To extract an explanation for each individual prediction from a learned model, several model-agnostic methods, such as LIME and SHAP, have been proposed [26,32]. However, because most of these methods construct explanations by locally approximating a model, recent studies have pointed out the risk that their explanations are inconsistent with the actual behavior of the model [17,36,45]. To avoid this risk and provide faithful explanations, we need to explain each individual prediction with the rules that the model actually uses to make the prediction, without approximation.

In this paper, we propose *locally interpretable rule ensemble (LIRE)*, a new framework for learning accurate and interpretable rule ensembles. While a number of weighted rules are required to maintain the accuracy of a rule ensemble model, not all of them are required to make each individual prediction by the model. More precisely, only the weighted rules that a given input satisfies are required to express its prediction, and the other rules are not by the definition of rule ensembles. This fact suggests a chance to learn a rule ensemble with a sufficient number of weighted rules to maintain accuracy but that can express individual predictions using a few weighted rules [36]. Motivated by this fact, we aim to learn a rule ensemble that can explain individual predictions with as few weighted rules as possible, which we refer to as *local interpretability*. To this end, we introduce a regularizer that promotes local interpretability, and propose an efficient algorithm for learning a rule ensemble with the proposed regularizer.

Our Contributions. Our contributions are summarized as follows:

- We introduce a new concept for evaluating the interpretability of rule ensembles. Our concept, named local interpretability, is evaluated by the total number of weighted rules that are necessary to express each individual prediction locally, rather than to express the entire model globally.
- We propose a regularizer that promotes the local interpretability of a rule ensemble, and formulate a task of learning a locally interpretable rule ensemble (LIRE) classifier. Then, we propose an efficient algorithm for learning a LIRE classifier by coordinate descent with local search.
- We conducted experiments on real datasets to evaluate the efficacy of LIRE. We confirmed that our method can learn rule ensembles that are more locally interpretable than the existing methods such as RuleFit [15], while maintaining accuracy and entire interpretability comparable to them.

Table 1. Examples of an input vector x and rule ensemble classifiers on the Adult dataset. The classifiers predict an input as "Income < \$50K" if the sum of the weights of the satisfied rules is greater than their intercept. In (b) and (c), rules that the input x satisfies are highlighted in boldface.

(a) Input vector x with the label "Income < \$50K"

Feature	Value
Age	39
fnlwgt	120985
Education-Num	9
Capital-Gain	0
Capital-Loss	0
House-per-week	40
Workclass	Private
Education	HS-grad
Marital-Status	Divorced
Occupation	Other-service
Relationship	Own-child
Race	White
Sex	Male
Country	United-States

(b) RuleFit [15] (intercept: 0.0, test accuracy: 83.0%)

Rule	Weight
Education-Num ≤ 12 & Capital-Gain ≤ 5119	**1.006**
Marital-Status ≠ Married-civ-spouse & Education ≠ Prof-school	**0.644**
Capital-Loss ≤ 1820 & Marital-Status ≠ Married-civ-spouse	**0.411**
Marital-Status ≠ Married-civ-spouse & Hours-per-week ≤ 44	**0.312**
Age > 31 & Sex = Male	**−0.191**
Marital-Status ≠ Married-civ-spouse & Education ≠ Masters	**0.050**
Marital-Status = Married-civ-spouse & Education ≠ HS-grad	−0.027
Hours-per-week > 43 & Marital-Status ≠ Never-married	−0.014

(c) LIRE (ours, intercept: −1.637, test accuracy: 84.2%)

Rule	Weight
Capital-Gain > 5119	−1.536
Relationship = Own-child & Hours-per-week ≤ 49	**1.255**
Capital-Loss > 1820 & Capital-Loss ≤ 1978	−1.245
Marital-Status = Married-civ-spouse	−1.192
Hours-per-week ≤ 43 & Occupation = Other-service	**0.906**
Education-Num > 12	−0.801
Relationship ≠ Own-child & Capital-Gain > 5095	−0.661

Table 1 presents a demonstration of our framework on the Adult dataset [21]. While Table 1a shows an example of an input vector x, Tables 1b and 1c present examples of rule ensemble classifiers leaned by RuleFit [15] and our LIRE. In Tables 1b and 1c, we denote the weighted rules that the input x satisfies in boldface, and the average total number of them was **3.8** for RuleFit and **1.1** for LIRE, respectively. Table 1 demonstrates that our LIRE (i) could make an accurate prediction for x with fewer weighted rules than RuleFit, and (ii) achieved the test accuracy comparable to RuleFit. These results suggest that our method can learn a locally interpretable rule ensemble without degrading accuracy.

Notation. For a positive integer $n \in \mathbb{N}$, we write $[n] := \{1, \ldots, n\}$. For a proposition ψ, $\mathbb{I}[\psi]$ denotes the indicator of ψ; that is, $\mathbb{I}[\psi] = 1$ if ψ is true, and $\mathbb{I}[\psi] = 0$ if ψ is false. Throughout this paper, we consider a *binary classification problem* as a prediction task. Note that our framework introduced later can also be applied to regression problems. We denote input and output domains $\mathcal{X} \subseteq \mathbb{R}^D$ and $\mathcal{Y} = \{-1, +1\}$, respectively. Let a tuple (x, y) of an input vector $x \in \mathcal{X}$ and output label $y \in \mathcal{Y}$ be an *example*, and the set $S = \{(x_n, y_n)\}_{n=1}^N$ be a *sample* with N examples. We call a function $h \colon \mathcal{X} \to \mathcal{Y}$ a *classifier*. Let $l \colon \mathcal{Y} \times \mathbb{R} \to \mathbb{R}_{\geq 0}$ be a loss function, such as the logistic loss, hinge loss, or exponential loss [28].

2   Rule Ensemble

A *rule ensemble* is a model consisting of a set of rules and their corresponding weights [15]. Each rule is expressed as a form of a conjunction of features (e.g., "Age > 31 & Sex = Male" as shown in Table 1), and has a corresponding weight value. Given an input $x \in \mathcal{X}$, a rule ensemble makes a prediction depending on the linear combination of the weighted rules that the input satisfies. For binary classification, a rule ensemble classifier $h_\alpha \colon \mathcal{X} \to \mathcal{Y}$ is defined as

$$h_\alpha(x) := \operatorname{sgn}\left(\sum_{m=1}^M \alpha_m \cdot r_m(x)\right),$$

where $r_m \colon \mathcal{X} \to \{0, 1\}$ is a rule, $\alpha_m \in \mathbb{R}$ is a weight corresponding to r_m, and $M \in \mathbb{N}$ is the total number of rules. We denote the *decision function* $f_\alpha \colon \mathcal{X} \to \mathbb{R}$ of h_α by $f_\alpha(x) := \sum_{m=1}^M \alpha_m \cdot r_m(x)$, i.e., $h_\alpha(x) = \operatorname{sgn}(f_\alpha(x))$.

To learn a rule ensemble h_α from a given sample S, we first need to obtain a set of rules $R = \{r_1, \ldots, r_M\}$ from S. However, it is computationally difficult to enumerate all the candidate rules on $\mathcal{X} \subseteq \mathbb{R}^D$ because their size grows exponentially with D [19, 29, 42]. To avoid enumerating all of them, we need to efficiently generate a subset of candidate rules that can improve the accuracy of h_α.

Another challenge is to learn a sparse weight vector $\alpha = (\alpha_1, \ldots, \alpha_M) \in \mathbb{R}^M$. By definition, a rule r_m with $\alpha_m = 0$ does not contribute to the predictions of a rule ensemble h_α. While reducing the total number of the rules r_m with nonzero weights is essential to ensure the interpretability of h_α, it often harms the generalization performance of h_α [30]. Therefore, we need to find a weight vector α that is as sparse as possible while maintaining the accuracy of h_α.

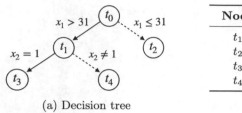

Node	Rule
t_1	$r_1(\boldsymbol{x}) = \mathbb{I}[x_1 > 31]$
t_2	$r_2(\boldsymbol{x}) = \mathbb{I}[x_1 \le 31]$
t_3	$r_3(\boldsymbol{x}) = \mathbb{I}[x_1 > 31] \cdot \mathbb{I}[x_2 = 1]$
t_4	$r_4(\boldsymbol{x}) = \mathbb{I}[x_1 > 31] \cdot \mathbb{I}[x_2 \ne 1]$

(a) Decision tree   (b) Decomposed rules

Fig. 1. Examples of a decision tree and its decomposed rules $R = \{r_1, r_2, r_3, r_4\}$.

2.1   RuleFit

A popular practical framework for learning rule ensembles is *RuleFit* proposed by Friedman and Popescu [15]. RuleFit consists of two steps; it first extracts a set of candidate rules R from a learned ensemble of decision trees, and then optimizes a sparse weight vector $\boldsymbol{\alpha}$ through the ℓ_1-regularization.

Rule Extraction. Given a sample S, RuleFit first learns a tree ensemble model, such as random forests [5] and gradient boosting decision trees [20], on S. It then decomposes each decision tree of the ensemble into a set of rules and collects the decomposed rules over the entire ensemble as R. Because there exist several fast algorithms for learning tree ensemble models, we can efficiently obtain a set of rules R that can improve the accuracy of a rule ensemble $h_{\boldsymbol{\alpha}}$ on S.

Figure 1 shows an example of a decision tree and its decomposed rules. By collecting the branching conditions on the path between the root and each node of the decision tree in Fig. 1a, we can obtain the set of rules shown in Fig. 1b. For example, we can obtain the rule r_3 from the node t_3 by combining the conditions $x_1 > 31$ and $x_2 = 1$ on the path between the root t_0 and t_3.

Weight Optimization. For a set of extracted rules $R = \{r_1, \ldots, r_M\}$, we optimize a weight vector $\boldsymbol{\alpha} \in \mathbb{R}^M$ on the sample S. Because the size of the extracted rules M grows in proportion to the total number of leaves in the tree ensemble, we need to keep $\boldsymbol{\alpha}$ as sparse as possible to avoid overfitting and ensure interpretability. To learn a sparse weight vector $\boldsymbol{\alpha}$, RuleFit uses the ℓ_1-regularization (i.e., the Lasso penalty [39]). Specifically, RuleFit solves the following learning problem.

Problem 1 (RuleFit). For a given sample $S = \{(\boldsymbol{x}_n, y_n)\}_{n=1}^N$, set of M rules $R = \{r_1, \ldots, r_M\}$, and trade-off parameter $\gamma \ge 0$, find an optimal solution $\boldsymbol{\alpha}^* \in \mathbb{R}^M$ to the following problem:

$$\boldsymbol{\alpha}^* = \arg\min_{\boldsymbol{\alpha} \in \mathbb{R}^M} L(\boldsymbol{\alpha} \mid S) + \gamma \cdot \Omega_1(\boldsymbol{\alpha}),$$

where $L(\boldsymbol{\alpha} \mid S) := \frac{1}{N} \sum_{n=1}^N l(y_n, f_{\boldsymbol{\alpha}}(\boldsymbol{x}_n))$ is the empirical risk on S, and $\Omega_1(\boldsymbol{\alpha}) := \|\boldsymbol{\alpha}\|_1$ is the ℓ_1-regularization term that promotes the sparsity of $\boldsymbol{\alpha}$.

Note that we can efficiently solve Problem 1 using the existing algorithms for learning generalized additive models with the ℓ_1-regularization when the loss function l is convex [14]. A common choice of the loss function l for a binary classification task is the logistic loss $l(y, f_\alpha(\boldsymbol{x})) = \log(1 + e^{-y \cdot f_\alpha(\boldsymbol{x})})$ [40,42].

3   Problem Formulation

This section presents our proposed framework, named *Locally Interpretable Rule Ensemble (LIRE)*. We introduce *local interpretability*, a new concept of interpretability for rule ensembles that is evaluated by the total number of rules required to express individual predictions, rather than the model itself. Then, we propose a regularizer that promotes local interpretability, and formulate the task of learning a rule ensemble with our local interpretability regularizer.

3.1   Local Interpretability of Rule Ensemble

In general, the interpretability of a rule ensemble h_α is evaluated by the total number of rules with non-zero weights [15,42]. Let $\mathrm{supp}(\boldsymbol{\alpha}) := \{m \in [M] \mid \alpha_m \neq 0\}$ be the set of rules with non-zero weights, which we call the *support* of h_α. By definition, a rule ensemble classifier h_α can be expressed using only weighted rules in the support, i.e., $h_\alpha(x) = \mathrm{sgn}(\sum_{m \in \mathrm{supp}(\boldsymbol{\alpha})} \alpha_m \cdot r_m(x))$. To ensure interpretability, the existing methods reduce the support size $|\mathrm{supp}(\boldsymbol{\alpha})|$ by the ℓ_1-regularization [39]. In practice, however, since there is a trade-off between the support size of a rule ensemble and its generalization performance, we often need to compromise interpretability to maintain accuracy [30].

On the other hand, not all of the rules with non-zero weights are used for making the individual prediction $h_\alpha(\boldsymbol{x})$ of each input $\boldsymbol{x} \in \mathcal{X}$. This is because a rule r_m with $\alpha_m \neq 0$ but $r_m(\boldsymbol{x}) = 0$ does not contribute to the prediction result $h_\alpha(\boldsymbol{x})$ by the definition of rule ensembles. It suggests that we only need the rules r_m with $\alpha_m \neq 0$ and $r_m(\boldsymbol{x}) = 1$ to express the individual prediction $h_\alpha(\boldsymbol{x})$ for a given input $\boldsymbol{x}$. In some practical situations (e.g., loan approvals and medical diagnoses), even if a model itself is too complex to interpret, it is often sufficient to explain its individual predictions in an interpretable manner [6,36,44].

Motivated by the above facts, we introduce a new concept of interpretability for a rule ensemble model from the perspective of its individual predictions rather than the model itself. We focus on learning a rule ensemble that can express individual predictions using a few rules with non-zero weights, which we call *local interpretability*. To evaluate the local interpretability of a rule ensemble h_α, we define the *local support* of h_α for an input $\boldsymbol{x}$ by

$$\mathrm{lsupp}(\boldsymbol{\alpha} \mid \boldsymbol{x}) := \{m \in [M] \mid \alpha_m \neq 0 \wedge r_m(\boldsymbol{x}) = 1\}.$$

By definition, the prediction $h_\alpha(\boldsymbol{x})$ for $\boldsymbol{x}$ can be expressed using only weighted rules in the local support, i.e., $h_\alpha(x) = \mathrm{sgn}(\sum_{m \in \mathrm{lsupp}(\alpha|x)} \alpha_m)$. To ensure local interpretability, we aim to reduce the local support size $|\mathrm{lsupp}(\boldsymbol{\alpha} \mid \boldsymbol{x})|$ for each $\boldsymbol{x}$ in a given sample S as much as possible.

To promote the local interpretability of a rule ensemble h_α, we propose a *local interpretability regularizer*. By definition, $|\mathrm{lsupp}(\boldsymbol{\alpha} \mid \boldsymbol{x})| \leq |\mathrm{supp}(\boldsymbol{\alpha})|$ holds for any $\boldsymbol{x} \in \mathcal{X}$, which implies that reducing the support size $|\operatorname{supp}(\boldsymbol{\alpha})|$ leads to a decrease in the upper bound on the local support size $|\operatorname{lsupp}(\boldsymbol{\alpha} \mid \boldsymbol{x})|$. However, we need to avoid achieving local interpretability by reducing the support size since it may harm the accuracy of $h_{\boldsymbol{\alpha}}$. To control the local support size separately from the support size, we define our local interpretability regularizer Ω_{L} as

$$\Omega_{\mathrm{L}}(\boldsymbol{\alpha} \mid S) := \frac{1}{N} \sum\nolimits_{n=1}^{N} \frac{|\operatorname{lsupp}(\boldsymbol{\alpha} \mid \boldsymbol{x}_n)|}{|\operatorname{supp}(\boldsymbol{\alpha})|}.$$

That is, we evaluate the ratio of the local support size $|\operatorname{lsupp}(\boldsymbol{\alpha} \mid \boldsymbol{x})|$ to the support size $|\operatorname{supp}(\boldsymbol{\alpha})|$ for each input $\boldsymbol{x}$ in a sample S and average them over S. Minimizing our regularizer Ω_{L} allows us to reduce the average local support size $|\operatorname{lsupp}(\boldsymbol{\alpha} \mid \boldsymbol{x})|$ without directly constraining the support size $|\operatorname{supp}(\boldsymbol{\alpha})|$.

3.2   Locally Interpretable Rule Ensemble

We now formulate our problem of learning a *locally interpretable rule ensemble (LIRE)* classifier. As with RuleFit [15], we assume that we have a set of rules R by extracting them from a tree ensemble leaned on a given sample S in advance. Then, we learn a weight vector $\boldsymbol{\alpha}$ that minimizes the empirical risk $L(\boldsymbol{\alpha} \mid S) = \frac{1}{N} \sum_{n=1}^{N} l(y_n, f_{\boldsymbol{\alpha}}(\boldsymbol{x}_n))$ on S with the regularizers on its interpretability.

Problem 2 (LIRE).   For a given sample $S = \{(\boldsymbol{x}_n, y_n)\}_{n=1}^{N}$, set of M rules $R = \{r_1, \dots, r_M\}$, and hyper-parameters $\gamma, \lambda \geq 0$, find an optimal solution $\boldsymbol{\alpha}^* \in \mathbb{R}^M$ to the following problem:

$$\boldsymbol{\alpha}^* = \arg\min_{\boldsymbol{\alpha} \in \mathbb{R}^M} G_{\gamma,\lambda}(\boldsymbol{\alpha} \mid S) := L(\boldsymbol{\alpha} \mid S) + \gamma \cdot \Omega_{\mathrm{G}}(\boldsymbol{\alpha}) + \lambda \cdot \Omega_{\mathrm{L}}(\boldsymbol{\alpha} \mid S),$$

where $\Omega_{\mathrm{G}}(\boldsymbol{\alpha}) := |\operatorname{supp}(\boldsymbol{\alpha})|$ is the global interpretability regularizer, and $\Omega_{\mathrm{L}}(\boldsymbol{\alpha} \mid S) = \frac{1}{N} \sum_{n=1}^{N} \frac{|\operatorname{lsupp}(\boldsymbol{\alpha} \mid \boldsymbol{x}_n)|}{|\operatorname{supp}(\boldsymbol{\alpha})|}$ is the local interpretability regularizer.

By solving Problem 2, we are expected to obtain an accurate rule ensemble $h_{\boldsymbol{\alpha}^*}$ whose local support size $|\operatorname{lsupp}(\boldsymbol{\alpha} \mid \boldsymbol{x})|$ is small on average. We can control the strength of the global and local interpretability regularizers by tuning the parameters γ and λ. Note that our global interpretability regularizer $\Omega_{\mathrm{G}}(\boldsymbol{\alpha})$ is equivalent to the ℓ_0-regularization term $\|\boldsymbol{\alpha}\|_0$, and the ℓ_1-regularization term $\|\boldsymbol{\alpha}\|_1$ used in RuleFit can be regarded as a convex relaxation of $\|\boldsymbol{\alpha}\|_0$ [39]. We employ $\Omega_{\mathrm{G}}(\boldsymbol{\alpha})$ to penalize the support size of $\boldsymbol{\alpha}$ more directly than the ℓ_1-regularization without degrading the generalization performance of $h_{\boldsymbol{\alpha}}$ [8, 25].

4   Optimization

In this section, we propose a learning algorithm for a LIRE classifier. Because our local interpretability regularizer Ω_{L} is neither differentiable nor convex due to its combinatorial nature, efficiently finding an exact optimal solution to Problem 2 is computationally challenging, even if the loss function l and the global interpretability regularizer Ω_{G} are differentiable and convex. To avoid this difficulty, we propose to extend the existing fast algorithms for learning ℓ_0-regularized generalized additive classifiers [8, 25] to our learning problem.

Algorithm 1. Coordinate descent algorithm with local search for learning LIRE.

Require: a sample S, a set of rules $R = \{r_1, \ldots, r_M\}$ extracted from a tree ensemble
   learned on S in advance, trade off parameters $\gamma, \lambda \geq 0$, an initial weight vector
   $\boldsymbol{\alpha}^{(0)} \in \mathbb{R}^M$, and a maximum number of iterations $I \in \mathbb{N}$ (e.g., $I = 5000$).

Ensure: a weight vector $\boldsymbol{\alpha}^{(i)}$.

 1: **for** $i = 1, 2, \ldots, I$ **do**
 2:     $\boldsymbol{\alpha}^{(i)} \leftarrow \boldsymbol{\alpha}^{(i-1)}$;
 3:     **for** $m \in \mathrm{supp}(\boldsymbol{\alpha}^{(i)})$ **do**
 4:         $\alpha_m^{(i)} \leftarrow \arg\min_{\alpha_m \in \mathbb{R}} G_{\gamma,\lambda}(\boldsymbol{\alpha}_{-m}^{(i)} + \alpha_m \cdot \boldsymbol{e}_m \mid S)$; $\triangleright \boldsymbol{\alpha}_{-m}^{(i)} := \boldsymbol{\alpha}^{(i)} - \alpha_m^{(i)} \cdot \boldsymbol{e}_m$
 5:         **if** $\alpha_m^{(i)} = 0$ **then**
 6:             **break**; $\triangleright$ Delete m
 7:         **end if**
 8:         **for** $m' \in [M] \setminus \mathrm{supp}(\boldsymbol{\alpha}^{(i)})$ **do**
 9:             $\alpha_{m'}^* \leftarrow \arg\min_{\alpha_{m'} \in \mathbb{R}} G_{\gamma,\lambda}(\boldsymbol{\alpha}_{-m}^{(i)} + \alpha_{m'} \cdot \boldsymbol{e}_{m'} \mid S)$;
10:             **if** $G_{\gamma,\lambda}(\boldsymbol{\alpha}_{-m}^{(i)} + \alpha_{m'}^* \cdot \boldsymbol{e}_{m'} \mid S) < G_{\gamma,\lambda}(\boldsymbol{\alpha}^{(i)} \mid S)$ **then**
11:                 $\boldsymbol{\alpha}^{(i)} \leftarrow \boldsymbol{\alpha}^{(i)} - \alpha_m^{(i)} \cdot \boldsymbol{e}_m + \alpha_{m'}^* \cdot \boldsymbol{e}_{m'}$; $\triangleright$ Delete m and insert m'
12:                 **break**;
13:             **end if**
14:         **end for**
15:         **if** $\alpha_m^{(i)} = 0$ **then**
16:             **break**;
17:         **end if**
18:     **end for**
19:     **if** $\boldsymbol{\alpha}^{(i)} = \boldsymbol{\alpha}^{(i-1)}$ **then**
20:         **break**;
21:     **else**
22:         **while** not convergence **do** $\triangleright$ Minimize $G_{\gamma,\lambda}$ with $\gamma = \lambda = 0$
23:             **for** $m \in \mathrm{supp}(\boldsymbol{\alpha}^{(i)})$ **do**
24:                 $\alpha_m^{(i)} \leftarrow \arg\min_{\alpha_m \in \mathbb{R}} L(\boldsymbol{\alpha}_{-m}^{(i)} + \alpha_m \cdot \boldsymbol{e}_m \mid S)$;
25:             **end for**
26:         **end while**
27:     **end if**
28: **end for**

4.1   Learning Algorithm

Algorithm 1 presents an algorithm for solving Problem 2. Our algorithm is based
on a coordinate descent algorithm with local search proposed by Liu et al. [8,25].
Given an initial weight vector $\boldsymbol{\alpha}^{(0)}$, which can be efficiently obtained in practice
by solving Problem 1, we iteratively update it until the update converges or the
number of iterations reaches a given maximum number $I \in \mathbb{N}$. Each iteration
$i \in [I]$ consists of the following steps to update the current weight vector $\boldsymbol{\alpha}^{(i)}$:

Step 1. For each rule $m \in \mathrm{supp}(\boldsymbol{\alpha}^{(i)})$ in the current support, we update its
   weight $\alpha_m^{(i)}$ so that our learning objective function $G_{\gamma,\lambda}$ is minimized with
   respect to the coordinate α_m (line 4). If the weight $\alpha_m^{(i)}$ is updated to 0, then
   we delete m from the support and go to Step 3.

Step 2. For each rule $m \in \text{supp}(\boldsymbol{\alpha}^{(i)})$, we attempt to replace m with another rule $m' \in [M] \setminus \text{supp}(\boldsymbol{\alpha}^{(i)})$ outside the support (line 9). For efficiency, when we find a rule m' that improves the objective value, we immediately delete m by setting its weight to 0 and add m' to the support with a weight $\alpha^*_{m'}$.

Step 3. If the support of $\boldsymbol{\alpha}^{(i)}$ is changed from that of $\boldsymbol{\alpha}^{(i-1)}$, we optimize the weight of each rule in $\text{supp}(\boldsymbol{\alpha}^{(i)})$ so that the empirical risk L is minimized (line 24), and go to the next iteration $i + 1$.

4.2   Analytical Solution to Coordinate Update

In lines 4, 9, and 24 of Algorithm 1, we need to update the weight of each rule m so that our learning objective $G_{\gamma,\lambda}$ is minimized with respect to the coordinate α_m. We show that we can obtain an analytical solution to this coordinate update problem if we employ the exponential loss $l(y, f_{\boldsymbol{\alpha}}(\boldsymbol{x})) = e^{-y \cdot f_{\boldsymbol{\alpha}}(\boldsymbol{x})}$ as the loss function l in $G_{\gamma,\lambda}$. As with the previous study on the ℓ_0-regularized classifier [25], our idea is based on the technique of AdaBoost [13], which iteratively updates the weight of each base learner with an analytical solution that minimizes the exponential loss [28]. In Theorem 1, we extend the technique of AdaBoost to obtain an analytical solution to our coordinate update problem with $G_{\gamma,\lambda}$.

Theorem 1. *For a weight vector $\boldsymbol{\alpha} \in \mathbb{R}^M$ and a rule $m \in [M]$ with $\alpha_m = 0$, we consider the coordinate update problem that is formulated as follows:*

$$\alpha^*_m = \arg \min_{\alpha'_m \in \mathbb{R}} G_{\gamma,\lambda}(\boldsymbol{\alpha} + \alpha'_m \cdot \boldsymbol{e}_m \mid S),$$

where $\boldsymbol{e}_m = (e_{m,1}, \ldots, e_{m,M}) \in \{0,1\}^M$ is a vector with $e_{m,m} = 1$ and $e_{m,m'} = 0$ for all $m' \in [M] \setminus \{m\}$. If the loss function l in the objective function $G_{\gamma,\lambda}$ is the exponential loss $l(y, f_{\boldsymbol{\alpha}}(\boldsymbol{x})) = e^{-y \cdot f_{\boldsymbol{\alpha}}(\boldsymbol{x})}$, then we have

$$\alpha^*_m = \begin{cases} 0 & \text{if } \varepsilon^-_m \in [\frac{1}{2} - B_m, \frac{1}{2} + B_m], \\ \frac{1}{2} \ln \frac{1 - \varepsilon^-_m}{\varepsilon^-_m} & \text{otherwise,} \end{cases}$$

where $\varepsilon^-_m = \frac{\frac{1}{N} \sum_{n \in [N]: y_n \cdot r_m(\boldsymbol{x}_n) = -1} l(y_n, f_{\boldsymbol{\alpha}}(\boldsymbol{x}_n))}{\varepsilon_m}$, $\varepsilon_m = \frac{1}{N} \sum_{n \in [N]: r_m(\boldsymbol{x}_n) = 1} l(y_n, f_{\boldsymbol{\alpha}}(\boldsymbol{x}_n))$, $B_m = \frac{\sqrt{C_m \cdot (2 \cdot \varepsilon_m - C_m)}}{2 \cdot \varepsilon_m}$, $C_m = \gamma + \lambda \cdot \frac{p_m - \Omega_{\text{L}}(\boldsymbol{\alpha} \mid S)}{1 + |\text{supp}(\boldsymbol{\alpha})|}$, and $p_m = \frac{1}{N} \sum_{n=1}^N r_m(\boldsymbol{x}_n)$.

Theorem 1 implies that a rule m outside the current support does not improve the objective value if $\varepsilon^-_m \in [\frac{1}{2} - B_m, \frac{1}{2} + B_m]$; otherwise, we can update its weight as $\alpha^*_m = \frac{1}{2} \ln \frac{1 - \varepsilon^-_m}{\varepsilon^-_m}$. By Theorem 1, we can solve the coordinate update problem in Algorithm 1 analytically. Our proof of Theorem 1 is shown in Appendix [18].

In our experiments, we employed the exponential loss as l for learning LIRE classifiers. In addition to the existence of an analytical solution, another advantage of the exponential loss is that we can efficiently compute the objective value of the updated weight vector $\boldsymbol{\alpha} + \alpha^*_m \cdot \boldsymbol{e}_m$ by simple mathematical operations. This is mainly because we can update the empirical risk L in our learning objective $G_{\gamma,\lambda}$ by multiplying each loss term $l(y_n, f_{\boldsymbol{\alpha}}(\boldsymbol{x}_n))$ by $e^{-y_n \cdot \alpha^*_m \cdot r_m(\boldsymbol{x}_n)}$ if l is the exponential loss [28]. Note that the exponential loss is known to perform well similar to the other popular loss functions, such as the logistic loss [25].

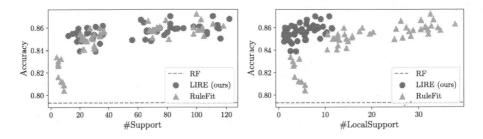

Fig. 2. Experimental results on the accuracy-interpretability trade-off analysis.

5 Experiments

To investigate the performance of our LIRE, we conducted numerical experiments on real datasets. All the code was implemented in Python 3.7 with scikit-learn 1.0.2 and is available at https://github.com/kelicht/lire. All the experiments were conducted on Ubuntu 20.04 with Intel Xeon E-2274G 4.0 GHz CPU and 32 GB memory.

Our experimental evaluation answers the following questions: (1) How is the trade-off between the accuracy and interpretability of LIRE compared to RuleFit? (2) How does our local interpretability regularizer affect the accuracy and interpretability of rule ensembles? (3) How is the performance of LIRE compared to the baselines on the benchmark datasets? Owing to page limitations, the complete settings and results (e.g., dataset details, hyper-parameter tuning, other accuracy criteria, and statistical tests) are shown in Appendix [18].

5.1 Accuracy-Interpretability Trade-Off

First, we examine the trade-off between the accuracy and interpretability of our LIRE compared to RuleFit. We used the Adult dataset ($N = 32561, D = 108$) [21] and conducted 10-fold cross-validation (CV). In each fold, we trained a random forest (RF) with 100 decision trees and obtained $M = 1220.3$ rules on average as R. For interpretability, each decision tree is trained with a maximum depth of 3; that is, the length of each rule is less than or equal to 3. Then, we trained rule ensembles by RuleFit and our LIRE and measured their test accuracy, support size (#Support), and average local support size on the test set (#LocalSupport). To obtain models with different support sizes, we trained multiple models by varying the hyper-parameter γ. For LIRE, we set $\lambda = 1.0$.

Figure 2 shows the results, where the left (resp. right) figure presents the scatter plot between the test accuracy and support size (resp. local support size). From Fig. 2, we can see that LIRE (1) attained a similar trade-off between accuracy and support size to RuleFit, and (2) achieved lower local support size than RuleFit without degrading accuracy. These results suggest that our LIRE could obtain more locally interpretable rule ensembles than RuleFit while maintaining similar accuracy and support size. Thus, we have confirmed that our method can realize local interpretability without compromising accuracy.

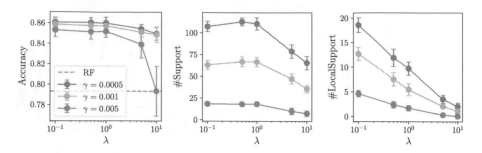

Fig. 3. Experimental results on the sensitivity of the trade-off parameter λ.

5.2   Effect of Local Interpretability Regularizer

Next, we analyze the effect of our local interpretability regularizer Ω_L on rule ensembles by varying the hyper-parameter λ. As in the previous experiment, we used the Adult dataset and conducted 10-fold CV. We trained rule ensembles by varying λ, and measured their average accuracy, support size, and local support size. To control the support size, we set γ to three different values.

Figure 3 shows the average accuracy, support size, and local support size for each λ. For $\gamma \in \{0.0005, 0.001\}$, we could reduce the local support size without significantly degrading accuracy by increasing λ, which indicates that we could obtain accurate and locally interpretable rule ensembles. Furthermore, we can see that the support size also decreased for large λ while maintaining accuracy. In contrast, for $\gamma = 0.005$, the average accuracy decreased when $\lambda > 1.0$. This result suggests that our local interpretability regularizer Ω_L may harm accuracy when γ is large, i.e., the support size is small. Thus, to maintain accuracy with Ω_L, we need to keep the support size larger to some extent by setting γ to be smaller. These observations give us insight into the choice of λ and γ in practice.

5.3   Performance Comparison

Finally, we evaluate the performance of our LIRE on benchmark datasets in comparison with the existing methods. We used five datasets: three datasets are Adult, Bank, and Heart from the UCI repository [21], and two datasets are FICO [11] and COMPAS [3]. In addition to RuleFit, we compared LIRE with the generalized linear rule models (GLRM) [42], another existing method for learning rule ensembles by column generation. We also employed three complex models as baselines: RF [5], LightGBM [20], and KernelSVM. In each fold, we tuned the hyper-parameters of each method through hold-out validation.

Figure 4 shows the test accuracy of each method in 10-fold CV. From Fig. 4, we can see that LIRE achieved comparable accuracy to the other rule ensembles, as well as complex models, regardless of the datasets. Figure 5 shows the results on the support size, local support size, and support ratio, which is defined as the ratio of #LocalSupport to #Support for each rule ensemble. We can see that LIRE stably achieved lower local support sizes and support ratios than

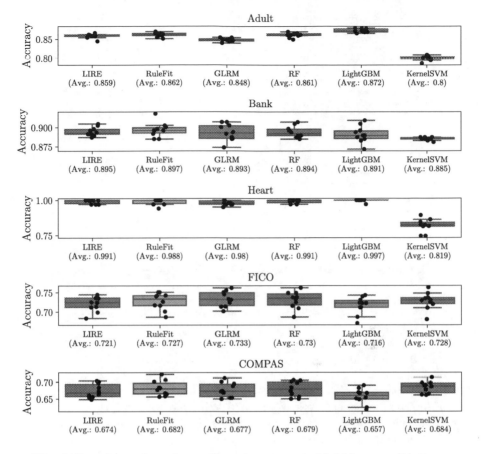

Fig. 4. Experimental results on the test accuracy in 10-fold cross-validation.

RuleFit and GLRM. Furthermore, LIRE also achieved lower support sizes than RuleFit while maintaining similar accuracy, which may be caused by the effect of our global interpretability regularizer Ω_G, i.e., ℓ_0-regularization. These results indicate that our LIRE achieved local interpretability while maintaining not only accuracy but also support size comparable to the baselines. Therefore, we have confirmed that we can learn more locally interpretable rule ensembles than the baselines without degrading accuracy in the benchmark datasets.

Regarding the computational time shown in Appendix [18], LIRE was slower than the baselines because its objective $G_{\gamma,\lambda}$ includes regularizers that have combinatorial nature. For example, the average computation time of LIRE, RuleFit, and GLRM on the Adult was **148.5**, **9.658**, and **75.93** seconds, respectively. However, Figs. 4 and 5 indicate that LIRE achieved higher local interpretability than the baselines without degrading accuracy within a few minutes, even for the dataset with $N > 30000$ and the size of candidate rules with $M > 1000$.

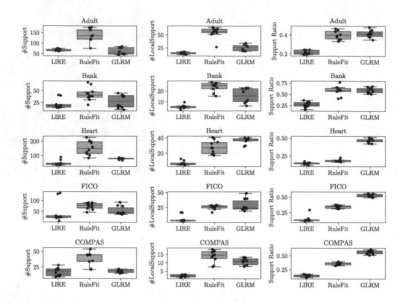

Fig. 5. Experimental results on the support size in 10-fold cross-validation.

6 Related Work

Globally Interpretable Models. This paper mainly relates to the communities of interpretable machine learning [37]. With the emerging trend of leveraging machine learning models in various high-stakes decision-making tasks, interpretable models, such as sparse linear models [8,25,40] and rule models [2,7, 16,23,43], have attracted increasing attention in recent years. Rule ensembles, also known as generalized linear rule models, are one of the popular rule models based on the linear combination of weighted rules [4,10,15,19,29,30,42].

In general, rule ensembles have a trade-off between their accuracy and interpretability. To achieve good generalization, rule ensembles often need to include a sufficiently large number of weighted rules [30]. However, increasing the total number of weighted rules degrades the interpretability of a model because it makes the entire model hard for human users to understand [9,12,24,36]. To address this trade-off, most of the existing methods focus on achieving accuracy with as few weighted rules as possible through ℓ_1-regularization [10,15,19,29,42].

Our contribution is to propose another approach for addressing the accuracy-interpretability trade-off of rule ensembles. We introduced a new concept of interpretability for a rule ensemble model, named local interpretability, focusing on its individual predictions rather than the model itself. Our concept has a similar spirit to the falling rule lists [41] and locally sparse neural networks [44] that can explain individual predictions in an interpretable manner, and is helpful in some practical situations where we need to explain undesired predictions for individual users, such as loan approvals and medical diagnoses [6,36,46]. We also empirically confirmed that we could learn more locally interpretable models than the existing methods while achieving comparable accuracy. Note that our framework can be combined with the existing practical techniques of rule ensembles, such as stabilization [4] and compression [30] of weighted rules.

Local Explanation Methods. Our approach is inspired by the recent methods that extract local explanations of the individual predictions made by a learned model. These methods provide local explanations in a post-hoc manner by locally approximating the decision boundary of a model by the linear models [26,32] or rule sets [33,38]. To improve the quality of local explanations, some papers have proposed to regularize a model during its training so that we can obtain better local explanations in terms of their local approximation fidelity [31] or consistency with domain knowledge [34,35]. Our proposed method also regularizes a rule ensemble for the quality of local explanations, i.e., the total number of weighted rules used for making each individual prediction, during its training.

While several post-hoc local explanation methods have been proposed, recent studies pointed out the issue of their faithfulness to an underlying model [17,45]. Most of the existing methods have a risk that their explanations are inconsistent with the actual behavior of the model because they generate explanations by local approximation [1,36]. In contrast to them, the local explanations provided by our method are faithful to the model since they consist of the weighted rules included in the model actually and they are provided without approximation.

7   Conclusion

In this paper, we proposed a new framework for learning rule ensembles, named locally interpretable rule ensemble (LIRE), that simultaneously achieves accuracy and interpretability. We introduced a new criterion of interpretability, named local interpretability, as the total number of rules that are necessary to explain individual predictions made by the model rather than to explain the model itself. Then, we proposed a regularizer that promotes the local interpretability of a rule ensemble, and developed an efficient learning algorithm with the regularizer by coordinate descent with local search. By experiments, we confirmed that our method learns more locally interpretable rule ensembles than the existing methods, such as RuleFit, while attaining comparable accuracy.

Limitations and Future Work. There are several future directions to improve our LIRE. First, a theoretical analysis of the convergence property of Algorithm 1 is essential to developing a more efficient one [8]. We also need to analyze the sensitivity of the heyper-parameters λ and γ in more detail to decide their default values. Second, it is important to conduct user studies to evaluate our local interpretability in real applications [9,22]. Finally, extending our local interpretability to other rule models, such as decision trees, is interesting for future work [46].

Ethical Statement

Existing Assets

All datasets used in Sect. 5 are publicly available and do not contain any identifiable information or offensive content. As they are accompanied by appropriate citations in the main body, see the corresponding references for more details. Scikit-learn 1.0.2[1] is publicly available under the BSD-3-Clause license. All the scripts and datasets used in our experiments are available in our GitHub repository at https://github.com/kelicht/lire.

Potential Impacts

Positive Impacts. Our proposed method, named locally interpretable rule ensemble (LIRE), is a new framework for learning rule ensemble models. Our LIRE can explain its individual predictions with a few weighted logical rules, i.e., in a transparent manner for human users. Therefore, our LIRE helps decision-makers to validate the prediction results made by machine learning models and ensure the transparency of their decision results in critical tasks, such as loan approvals, medical diagnoses, and judicial decisions [36,37].

Negative Impacts. Because our method provides explanations of its individual predictions in a transparent manner, one might use the output to extract sensitive information from the training dataset. Note, however, that such unintended use can occur not only with our method but also with other interpretable models. One possible way to mitigate this risk is to check whether the features in a dataset used to construct the weighted rules might reveal sensitive information before training the model on the dataset and deploying it publicly.

Limitations

In the real applications of our LIRE, there might exist three limitations. First, as mentioned in our experiments, the computational time of LIRE was certainly longer than those of the baselines. To overcome this limitation, we need to analyze the convergence property of our learning algorithm and develop a more efficient one. Second, since LIRE has two hyper-parameters, λ and γ, users need to determine these values depending on the dataset by themselves, which may incur additional computational costs. Finally, the effectiveness of our local interpretability in real situations has not yet been verified. We plan to conduct user studies to evaluate the usefulness of our concept for human users and analyze how much local support size is acceptable for humans [9,22].

Acknowledgement. We wish to thank Koji Maruhashi, Takuya Takagi, Ken Kobayashi, and Yuichi Ike for making a number of valuable suggestions. We also thank the anonymous reviewers for their insightful comments.

---

[1] https://scikit-learn.org/stable/.

References

1. Alvarez-Melis, D., Jaakkola, T.S.: On the robustness of interpretability methods. In: Proceedings of the 2018 ICML Workshop on Human Interpretability in Machine Learning, pp. 66–71 (2018)
2. Angelino, E., Larus-Stone, N., Alabi, D., Seltzer, M., Rudin, C.: Learning certifiably optimal rule lists. In: Proceedings of the 23rd ACM SIGKDD International Conference on Knowledge Discovery and Data Mining, pp. 35–44 (2017)
3. Angwin, J., Larson, J., Mattu, S., Kirchner, L.: Machine Bias - ProPublica (2016). www.propublica.org/article/machine-bias-risk-assessments-in-criminal-sentencing. Accessed 20 June 2023
4. Bénard, C., Biau, G., da Veiga, S., Scornet, E.: Interpretable random forests via rule extraction. In: Proceedings of the 24th International Conference on Artificial Intelligence and Statistics, pp. 937–945 (2021)
5. Breiman, L.: Random forests. Mach. Learn. **45**(1), 5–32 (2001)
6. Caruana, R., Lou, Y., Gehrke, J., Koch, P., Sturm, M., Elhadad, N.: Intelligible models for healthcare: predicting pneumonia risk and hospital 30-day readmission. In: Proceedings of the 21th ACM SIGKDD International Conference on Knowledge Discovery and Data Mining, pp. 1721–1730 (2015)
7. Dash, S., Günlük, O., Wei, D.: Boolean decision rules via column generation. In: Proceedings of the 32nd International Conference on Neural Information Processing Systems, pp. 4660–4670 (2018)
8. Dedieu, A., Hazimeh, H., Mazumder, R.: Learning sparse classifiers: continuous and mixed integer optimization perspectives. J. Mach. Learn. Res. **22**(135), 1–47 (2021)
9. Doshi-Velez, F., Kim, B.: Towards a rigorous science of interpretable machine learning. arXiv, arXiv:1702.08608 (2017)
10. Eckstein, J., Goldberg, N., Kagawa, A.: Rule-enhanced penalized regression by column generation using rectangular maximum agreement. In: Proceedings of the 34th International Conference on Machine Learning, pp. 1059–1067 (2017)
11. FICO, Google, Imperial College London, MIT, University of Oxford, UC Irvine, UC Berkeley: Explainable Machine Learning Challenge (2018). www.community.fico.com/s/explainable-machine-learning-challenge. Accessed 20 June 2023
12. Freitas, A.A.: Comprehensible classification models: a position paper. ACM SIGKDD Explor. Newsl. **15**(1), 1–10 (2014)
13. Freund, Y., Schapire, R.E.: A decision-theoretic generalization of on-line learning and an application to boosting. J. Comput. Syst. Sci. **55**(1), 119–139 (1997)
14. Friedman, J., Popescu, B.E.: Gradient directed regularization for linear regression and classification. Statistics Department, Stanford University, Technical report (2003)
15. Friedman, J.H., Popescu, B.E.: Predictive learning via rule ensembles. Ann. Appl. Stat. **2**(3), 916–954 (2008)
16. Hu, X., Rudin, C., Seltzer, M.: Optimal sparse decision trees. In: Proceedings of the 33rd International Conference on Neural Information Processing Systems, pp. 7265–7273 (2019)
17. Jacovi, A., Goldberg, Y.: Towards faithfully interpretable NLP systems: how should we define and evaluate faithfulness? In: Proceedings of the 58th Annual Meeting of the Association for Computational Linguistics, pp. 4198–4205 (2020)
18. Kanamori, K.: Learning locally interpretable rule ensemble. arXiv arXiv:2306.11481 (2023)

19. Kato, H., Hanada, H., Takeuchi, I.: Safe rulefit: learning optimal sparse rule model by meta safe screening. IEEE Trans. Pattern Anal. Mach. Intell. **45**(2), 2330–2343 (2023)

20. Ke, G., et al.: LightGBM: a highly efficient gradient boosting decision tree. In: Proceedings of the 31st International Conference on Neural Information Processing Systems, pp. 3149–3157 (2017)

21. Kelly, M., Longjohn, R., Nottingham, K.: The UCI machine learning repository (2023). www.archive.ics.uci.edu/. Accessed 20 June 2023

22. Lage, I., et al.: Human evaluation of models built for interpretability. In: Proceedings of the 7th AAAI Conference on Human Computation and Crowdsourcing, pp. 59–67 (2019)

23. Lakkaraju, H., Bach, S.H., Leskovec, J.: Interpretable decision sets: a joint framework for description and prediction. In: Proceedings of the 22nd ACM SIGKDD International Conference on Knowledge Discovery and Data Mining, pp. 1675–1684 (2016)

24. Lipton, Z.C.: The mythos of model interpretability: in machine learning, the concept of interpretability is both important and slippery. Queue **16**(3), 31–57 (2018)

25. Liu, J., Zhong, C., Seltzer, M., Rudin, C.: Fast sparse classification for generalized linear and additive models. In: Proceedings of the 25th International Conference on Artificial Intelligence and Statistics, pp. 9304–9333 (2022)

26. Lundberg, S.M., Lee, S.I.: A unified approach to interpreting model predictions. In: Proceedings of the 31st International Conference on Neural Information Processing Systems, pp. 4765–4774 (2017)

27. Miller, T.: Explanation in artificial intelligence: insights from the social sciences. Artif. Intell. **267**, 1–38 (2019)

28. Mohri, M., Rostamizadeh, A., Talwalkar, A.: Foundations of Machine Learning. The MIT Press, Cambridge (2012)

29. Nakagawa, K., Suzumura, S., Karasuyama, M., Tsuda, K., Takeuchi, I.: Safe pattern pruning: an efficient approach for predictive pattern mining. In: Proceedings of the 22nd ACM SIGKDD International Conference on Knowledge Discovery and Data Mining, pp. 1785–1794 (2016)

30. Nalenz, M., Augustin, T.: Compressed rule ensemble learning. In: Proceedings of the 25th International Conference on Artificial Intelligence and Statistics, pp. 9998–10014 (2022)

31. Plumb, G., Al-Shedivat, M., Cabrera, A.A., Perer, A., Xing, E., Talwalkar, A.: Regularizing black-box models for improved interpretability. In: Proceedings of the 34th International Conference on Neural Information Processing Systems, pp. 10526–10536 (2020)

32. Ribeiro, M.T., Singh, S., Guestrin, C.: "Why Should I Trust You?": explaining the predictions of any classifier. In: Proceedings of the 22nd ACM SIGKDD International Conference on Knowledge Discovery and Data Mining, pp. 1135–1144 (2016)

33. Ribeiro, M.T., Singh, S., Guestrin, C.: Anchors: high-precision model-agnostic explanations. In: Proceedings of the 32nd AAAI Conference on Artificial Intelligence, pp. 1527–1535 (2018)

34. Rieger, L., Singh, C., Murdoch, W., Yu, B.: Interpretations are useful: penalizing explanations to align neural networks with prior knowledge. In: Proceedings of the 37th International Conference on Machine Learning, pp. 8116–8126 (2020)

35. Ross, A.S., Hughes, M.C., Doshi-Velez, F.: Right for the right reasons: training differentiable models by constraining their explanations. In: Proceedings of the 26th International Joint Conference on Artificial Intelligence, pp. 2662–2670 (2017)

36. Rudin, C.: Stop explaining black box machine learning models for high stakes decisions and use interpretable models instead. Nat. Mach. Intell. **1**, 206–215 (2019)
37. Rudin, C., Chen, C., Chen, Z., Huang, H., Semenova, L., Zhong, C.: Interpretable machine learning: fundamental principles and 10 grand challenges. Stat. Surv. **16**, 1–85 (2022)
38. Rudin, C., Shaposhnik, Y.: Globally-consistent rule-based summary-explanations for machine learning models: application to credit-risk evaluation. J. Mach. Learn. Res. **24**(16), 1–44 (2023)
39. Tibshirani, R.: Regression shrinkage and selection via the lasso. J. Roy. Stat. Soc. Ser. B (Stat. Methodol.) **58**, 267–288 (1994)
40. Ustun, B., Rudin, C.: Learning optimized risk scores. J. Mach. Learn. Res. **20**(150), 1–75 (2019)
41. Wang, F., Rudin, C.: Falling rule lists. In: Proceedings of the 18th International Conference on Artificial Intelligence and Statistics, pp. 1013–1022 (2015)
42. Wei, D., Dash, S., Gao, T., Gunluk, O.: Generalized linear rule models. In: Proceedings of the 36th International Conference on Machine Learning, pp. 6687–6696 (2019)
43. Yang, H., Rudin, C., Seltzer, M.: Scalable bayesian rule lists. In: Proceedings of the 34th International Conference on Machine Learning, pp. 3921–3930 (2017)
44. Yang, J., Lindenbaum, O., Kluger, Y.: Locally sparse neural networks for tabular biomedical data. In: Proceedings of the 39th International Conference on Machine Learning, pp. 25123–25153 (2022)
45. Yoon, J., Arik, S.O., Pfister, T.: LIMIS: locally interpretable modeling using instance-wise subsampling. Transactions on Machine Learning Research (2022). www.openreview.net/forum?id=S8eABAy8P3
46. Zhang, G., Gionis, A.: Regularized impurity reduction: accurate decision trees with complexity guarantees. Data Min. Knowl. Disc. **37**(1), 434–475 (2023)

XAI with Machine Teaching When Humans Are (Not) Informed About the Irrelevant Features

Brigt Arve Toppe Håvardstun[1]([✉]), Cèsar Ferri[2], Jose Hernández-Orallo[2], Pekka Parviainen[1], and Jan Arne Telle[1]

[1] Department of Informatics, University of Bergen, Bergen, Norway
{brigt.havardstun,pekka.parviainen,jan.arne.telle}@uib.no
[2] VRAIN, Universitat Politècnica de València, Valencia, Spain
cferri@dsic.upv.es, jorallo@upv.es

Abstract. Exemplar-based explainable artificial intelligence (XAI) aims at creating human understanding about the behaviour of an AI system, usually a machine learning model, through examples. The advantage of this approach is that the human creates their own explanation in their own internal language. However, what examples should be chosen? Existing frameworks fall short in capturing all the elements that contribute to this process. In this paper, we propose a comprehensive XAI framework based on machine teaching. The traditional trade-off between the fidelity and the complexity of the explanation is transformed here into a trade-off between the complexity of the examples and the fidelity the human achieves about the behaviour of the ML system to be explained. We analyse a concept class of Boolean functions that is learned by a convolutional neural network classifier over a dataset of images of possibly rotated and resized letters. We assume the human learner has a strong prior (Karnaugh maps over Boolean functions). Our explanation procedure then behaves like a machine teaching session optimising the trade-off between examples and fidelity. We include an experimental evaluation and several human studies where we analyse the capacity of teaching humans these Boolean function by means of the explanatory examples generated by our framework. We explore the effect of telling the essential features to the human and the priors, and see that the identification is more successful than by randomly sampling the examples.

1 Introduction

In the field of eXplainable AI (XAI), there are multiple ways to explain humans how an AI system works, one of them being example-based XAI [16,21,24],

A preliminary version of this work was presented as a poster at AAIP@IJCLR2022. Supported by the Norwegian Research Council, project Machine Teaching for XAI.

Supplementary Information The online version contains supplementary material available at https://doi.org/10.1007/978-3-031-43418-1_23.

D. Koutra et al. (Eds.): ECML PKDD 2023, LNAI 14171, pp. 378–393, 2023.
https://doi.org/10.1007/978-3-031-43418-1_23

where the XAI system aims to find examples showing how the machine learning system acts in different situations. Machine teaching is the research area of actively selecting an optimal (e.g., minimal) set of examples so that a learner can identify a given concept or model [27]. The goal is for the teacher to find the smallest training set—known as the *teaching* or *witness* set—such that, a learning algorithm, when given the teaching set as an input, produces a target concept. In this work, we propose a framework based on machine teaching techniques where the XAI system (the teacher) provides explanatory examples to humans (the learners). The target concept is (a part of) the black-box AI system that needs explanation. The machine teaching algorithm must find a small set of labelled examples that will allow the human to build their own model of the AI system and thereby arrive at an explanation of the target concept [17,19]. We demonstrate the validity of our proposal by including some results of an experimental evaluation where we evaluate the results of teaching a black-box model to humans. Specifically, the black box to explain is an artificial neural network learned from images generated by Boolean expressions. We choose Boolean functions because the notions of prototype, centroid, anchors or boundary examples are more elusive in discrete concept classes like this, but we also use neural networks that might use some other features. We analyse the effect of giving humans information about how the examples were chosen and indications about the relevant features. The results show that our framework can generate explanatory examples useful to teach humans Boolean functions, better than sampling examples at random.

The paper is structured as follows. In Sect. 2 we review part of the literature related to XAI and machine teaching. Section 3 describes the framework we developed to generate explanatory witness sets. We instantiate that method for explaining neural network classifiers of images representing Boolean concepts in Sect. 4. Section 5 describes the experiments and human studies, and discusses the results. Finally, Sect. 6 closes the paper with conclusions and future work.

2   Machine Teaching for XAI

Explainable AI (XAI) is an active research field aiming at explaining the decisions of AI systems [16]. Machine learning is a key component of many AI systems, and therefore XAI usually focuses on explaining machine learning models [7,22].

Explainable AI must usually face several trade-offs, such as the tension between fidelity (level of coincidence between the predicted or understood behaviour of the system and the actual behaviour of the model) and comprehensibility (how much effort it takes for the human to understand) [5]. In general, making useful explanations among these tensions requires a great deal of abstraction, additionally modelling machine behaviour [20] in a way that is comprehensible to humans.

XAI approaches are divided into two families. In the first one, the goal is to extract an abstract representation of the AI system to serve as an explanation to a human. An example of this approach is extracting comprehensible rules from models [3]. In the second family, the goal is to use examples such that humans can infer their explanation themselves, known as exemplar-based explanations. An example of this approach is using anchors or partial examples [21].

Machine teaching [26] is a research field that is sometimes considered as an inverse problem to machine learning. In machine teaching the examples are chosen wisely by a teacher to teach a concept to the learner. Figure 1 shows a situation where the teacher has the concept of reversing a list. The teacher could try to explain the concept, but the languages employed by the learner and teacher might not be the same. In this situation, as happens with humans frequently, a few examples may be more effective. In the image, the teacher sends a couple of input-output pairs to the learner, thinking that this would be useful for the learner to build and identify the concept.

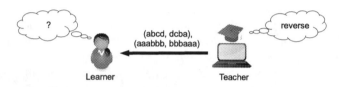

Fig. 1. Machine teaching example. The teacher tries to teach the concept of the *reverse* of a string. The teacher selects two examples carefully and shows them to the learner: the input string *abcd* being mapped into *dcba*, and the input string *aaabbb* being mapped into *bbbaaa*. The learner must infer the concept from only these two examples.

Mainly, machine teaching has been used to comprehend and depict how humans teach. An example is the analysis conducted by [12], which examines the teaching of 1D concepts (intervals) to machines, comparing a machine teaching environment with a curriculum learning environment. In both instances, the question is whether humans provide examples at the boundaries to assist the learner in replicating these boundaries or if they provide examples in clear areas so that the user can interpolate, as outlined by [1].

Our focus lies in machine teaching for the purpose of explaining concepts to humans [8]. In certain models, the teacher can interact with the learner by posing questions (e.g., [15]). On the other hand, some methods have attempted to expand the machine teaching framework by using examples to achieve explainable AI. A few proposals stray from the traditional machine teaching approach and instead utilize well-selected demonstrations in inverse reinforcement learning [9], or in the Cooperative Inverse Reinforcement Learning (CIRL) framework [6].

Yang et al. [25] evaluated the effectiveness of example-based explanations for AI using Bayesian Teaching, with a focus on high sensitivity and high specificity, and we will compare our findings to theirs. Another approach to teaching for XAI is the decomposition of the learner's hypothesis into an attention function and a decision function, as proposed by Chen et al. [2]. Ouyang [18] presents an algorithm for the Bayesian inference of regular expressions using examples. The teaching paradigm proposed is also linked to how humans communicate and how the speaker chooses the appropriate word based on their listener.

3   A MT Framework to Generate Explanatory Teaching Sets

In machine teaching, the teacher T is viewed as a function from concepts to sets of labelled examples, with $T(\theta) = S$ denoting the labelled examples S the teacher employs to teach concept θ. Likewise, the learner L is viewed as a function from sets of labelled examples to concepts, and we require that the concept guessed by the learner is compatible with the given examples S, denoted $L(S) \models S$. Correct teaching is achieved if $L(T(\theta)) = \theta$, i.e. the guessed concept is indeed the one the teacher had in mind. To achieve an efficient teaching protocol we employ simplicity β on concepts and δ on example sets (Occam's razor), as in [23]. β is shared by learner and teacher, and δ is used to prioritise simple witness set. When applying this to XAI the concept θ_{AI} can be the entire AI model to be explained or some particular substructure. To build our XAI system we employ i) an machine learning algorithm L_M modelling the human learner L_H with its simplicity prior β on guessed concepts, ii) a simplicity prior δ on example sets, and iii) a loss function λ giving a penalty for deviations of the guess θ_M from the intended θ_{AI}.

We propose a parameterised framework to generate explanatory examples from a black-box model θ_{AI}. In the framework, we explore the trade-off between fidelity (squared error of the guessed model compared to the black-box model) and teaching complexity (measured as the complexity of the set of labelled examples used as a teaching set) [14,24]. The framework is defined as:

$$T(\theta_{AI}) = \underset{S:\theta_{AI} \models S}{\operatorname{argmin}} \{\delta(S) + \mu \cdot \lambda(\theta_{AI}, \theta_M) : L_M(S) = \theta_M\} \tag{1}$$

$$L_M(S) = \underset{\theta_M:\theta_M \models S}{\operatorname{argmin}} \{\beta(\theta_M)\}$$

In these equations T is a teacher, aiming to teach a concept θ_{AI} to a human learner L_H, by finding a teaching set S such that $L_H(S) = \theta_{AI}$. To achieve automation and increase iteration speed a model L_M of L_H is used, and the teacher will therefore aim for $T(\theta_{AI}) = S$ **s.t.** $L_M(S) = \theta_{AI}$. The fidelity function becomes $1 - \lambda$ and it measures how closely the guessed concept θ_M matches the concept θ_{AI}, while the factor μ allows us to balance the influence of complexity (δ) and fidelity ($1 - \lambda$). In this work, we present an implementation[1] of Eq. 1 tested on a machine learning model trained on images generated by basic Boolean functions.

4   Obtaining Explanatory Examples from a Neural Network

In this section we discuss how the framework presented in the previous section is applied to a black-box model represented by a neural network learned from images generated by basic Boolean functions.

---

[1] https://github.com/BrigtHaavardstun/ExplainableAI.

4.1   The Black-Box Model θ_{AI}

For the experimental setting, we implemented our own θ_{AI}, with the task of learning a Boolean function on four variables, $\phi(A, B, C, D)$. Determining the subjective difficulty of learning Boolean functions has been addressed in the literature, see e.g. [4]. The input to θ_{AI} will be a bitmap containing a subset of letters from the alphabet $\Sigma = \{A, B, C, D\}$, with the letters present being the variables set to True. The bitmaps thus represent an example, with letters being rotated and scaled and placed randomly. This gives us the possibility of extensive training data for our AI. The output space of θ_{AI} is $\{0, 1\}$. For instance, with the concept $\phi = (A \wedge B) \vee (C \wedge D)$, we label an example 1 if ϕ evaluates to True, and 0 if ϕ evaluates to False.

We chose a Convolutional Neural Network (CNN) [13], as a common technique for images, while at the same time not interpretable by themselves, making them a good choice for generating our θ_{AI}. We implemented a CNN with 8 layers in Python using Keras and TensorFlow.

4.2   The Model of the Human L_M

For simplicity, our model L_M of the human learner will not be given bitmaps as examples. Instead, it takes as input the letters present in each image. We thus hypothesise that the human will pay attention to the letters present in the image and disregard other information such as rotation, size and position.

The hypothesis class of L_M will consist of all Boolean functions over the 4-letter alphabet. Then, given a teaching set like $S = \{(AC, 0), (AD, 0), (BD, 0), (AB, 1), (BC, 1), (CD, 1)\}$, we must decide how L_M will act. We assume a human constructs something like a partial truth table, in this case with 3 rows out of $2^4 = 16$ rows total filled with True, 3 rows filled with False, and 10 rows filled with Don't-Cares (x). Applying Occam's razor, we need to define the function β, to choose the Boolean function that is most simple and adheres to these constraints. A commonly accepted answer is the use of Karnaugh maps [11].

We use disjunctive normal form (DNF) which mimics human reasoning. To verify a positive instance you need only to confirm one clause, whereas to confirm a negative instance you always need to check all clauses. The resource-heavy task of confirming a negative compared to a positive is somewhat similar to how humans are poor at negations [10]. For each teaching set the Karnaugh map technique can find many possible DNFs, and in the spirit of K-map minimization we use the following scheme to pick the simplest. The DNFs are sorted in order by fewest clauses, and to break ties we compare clauses starting from the simplest one, using the criteria 1) fewest variables, 2) fewest negations, 3) lexicographic order. This defines β and gives us a unique Boolean formula in DNF form for each teaching set.

4.3   The Fidelity Function $1 - \lambda$

When we want to compare θ_{AI} and θ_M, we need to view the former as an approximation to some Boolean function, but also being affected by the location, rotation, etc., of the letter. Consequently, for each subset of letters (logical example), we estimate the percentage of images containing exactly these letters that θ_{AI} evaluates to True on new images, based on the full training set. We get values like the top row in Table 1. We observe that θ_{AI} predicts some letter groups the same and is more undecided on other letter combinations.

Table 1. Top row shows the percentage of bitmaps on letters for that column for which θ_{AI} evaluates to True. Bottom row shows the truth table of $\theta_M = (A \wedge B) \vee (C \wedge \neg A)$, and $\lambda(\theta_{AI}, \theta_M) = \frac{0.2222}{16} \approx 0.0139$ is the MSE of the difference of all 16 columns, giving fidelity 0.9861.

Symbol	∅	A	B	C	D	AB	AC	AD	BC	BD	CD	ABC	ABD	ACD	BCD	ABCD
θ_{AI} predicts	0.00	0.00	0.00	0.95	0.00	0.99	0.02	0.00	0.63	0.02	0.91	1.00	1.00	0.04	0.74	1.00
θ_M evaluates	0	0	0	1	0	1	0	0	1	0	1	1	1	0	1	1

To evaluate how well the θ_M, returned by the learner as the Boolean formula minimizing β, matches θ_{AI}, we use its truth table as in the bottom row of Table 1. We then compare the two rows (for θ_{AI} and θ_M) using Mean Square Error (MSE) to get λ and fidelity $1 - \lambda$.

We have experimented with various definitions for the complexity function, to punish large and complicated teaching sets S. The chosen δ is a simple squared sum of the number of variables present in each example, plus 0.1 for the empty set (corresponding to setting no variable to True). We thus keep low the total number of variables in all examples while simultaneously putting a high cost on a single large example. Note that the δ values are typically much higher than the λ values, so in our first set of experiments we set the multiplicative factor $\mu = 800$ when computing the aggregated score $\delta(S) + \mu \cdot \lambda(\theta_{AI}, \theta_M)$.

4.4 The Teacher T

The goal of the teacher is to find a teaching set explaining θ_{AI}, by iterating over potential teaching sets. For each teaching set S, we compute $L_M(S) = \theta_M$ as described earlier, and the aggregate score $\delta(S) + \mu \cdot \lambda(\theta_{AI}, \theta_M)$. During the iteration we retain the best aggregate score. For these experiments the iteration is an exhaustive search.

5   Experimental Evaluation

Given the previous setting we performed a set of experiments using different concepts and parameters to analyse the effect of several elements in the machine teaching process on explaining the behaviour of various AI models. In particular, we played with AI models trained on different sized training sets, which approximate the original Boolean function to different levels of accuracy. Depending on how well the AI is approximated by a Boolean function the trade-off parameter μ between fidelity $(1 - \lambda)$ and teaching complexity (δ) has different effects.

5.1   Generation of Teaching Sets

5.1.1   Fixed μ for Varying Models. We trained nine different Θ_{AI} models with differently sized data sets. In this first experiment, all models are trained with the ground truth $\phi = (A \wedge B) \vee C$ and the alphabet $\Sigma = \{A, B, C\}$. The data set sizes used in the experiment are: $\{10, 50, 100, 500, 1000, 2000, 5000, 10000, 50000\}$. Accordingly, we denote the different models: $\{AI_{10}, AI_{50}, AI_{100}, AI_{500}, AI_{1000}, AI_{2000}, AI_{5000}, AI_{10000}, AI_{50000}\}$.

In Table 2 we show several results. In the first row we see the expected result that the accuracy of the models wrt the original concept ϕ increases as more training examples were given to the neural network. In the next rows we show the Boolean expression that best approximates the model, with its associated highest possible fidelity $(1 - \lambda)$ over all Boolean functions. We see that the language of Boolean functions obtains a perfect match for the case of AI_{10} (because the underlying concept is very simple, always predicting True, which is a Boolean function) and almost perfect for AI_{10000} and AI_{50000} (because the number of training examples leads to a concept that is very close to ϕ). Note that also in other cases the most accurate Boolean function is ϕ (from AI_{2000} and up).

Table 2. Several Θ_{AI} models AI_t trained for size t of training examples for $\phi = AB + C = (A \wedge B) \vee C$. We first show accuracy with respect to ϕ. The next two rows show the closest Boolean expression ($AB + C$ from AI_{2000} and on) and its fidelity value $1 - \lambda$. Then we do teaching with $\mu = 800$, and show the Boolean concept taught by the system, the teaching set and its complexity, the fidelity and aggregate score.

AIs	AI_{10}	AI_{50}	AI_{100}	AI_{500}	AI_{1000}	AI_{2000}	AI_{5000}	AI_{10000}	AI_{50000}
Accuracy $AB+C$	62.50	72.85	78.38	81.01	88.47	91.42	94.74	98.72	99.36
Boolean with highest $1-\lambda$	Always True	A+B+C	A+B+C	AB+	AB+	AB+C	AB+C	AB+C	AB+C
				AC+BC	AC+BC				
Highest $1-\lambda$	1	0.927	0.9578	0.9226	0.9843	0.9752	0.9936	0.9994	0.9999
Model taught θ_M	Always True	A+B+C	A+B+C	A+C	AB+	AB+C	AB+C	AB+C	AB+C
					AC+BC				
Teaching Set S	$\{(\emptyset,1)\}$	$\{(\emptyset,0),$	$\{(\emptyset,0),$	$\{(\emptyset,0),$	$\{(A,0),$	$\{(A,0),$	$\{(A,0),$	$\{(A,0),$	$\{(A,0),$
		(A,1),	(A,1),	(A,1),	(AB,1),	(AB,1),	(AB,1),	(AB,1),	(AB,1),
		(B,1),	(B,1),	(C,1)$\}$	(AC,1),	(B,0),	(B,0),	(B,0),	(B,0),
		(C,1)$\}$	(C,1)$\}$		(B,0),	(C,1)$\}$	(C,1)$\}$	(C,1)$\}$	(C,1)$\}$
					(BC,1),				
					(C,0)$\}$				
$\delta(S)$	0.1	3.1	3.1	2.1	15	7	7	7	7
$1 - \lambda(AI_x, \theta_M)$	1	0.927	0.9578	0.9179	0.9843	0.9752	0.9936	0.9994	0.9999
$\delta + 800\lambda$	0.1	61.52	36.71	67.82	27.63	26.84	12.17	7.49	7.09

Now let us look at the next few rows showing results for the teaching framework when run with the chosen parameter $\mu = 800$. First we show the Boolean concept θ_M that is actually taught by the system and note that it is almost always equal to the Boolean concept with highest fidelity $(1 - \lambda)$ value in the 2nd row. The only exception is AI_{500} where the trade-off between δ and λ favours the Boolean concept $A \vee C$ instead of $(A \wedge B) \vee (A \wedge C) \vee (B \wedge C)$ because the teaching set for the former is much simpler ($\delta = 2.1$) than the teaching set for the latter ($\delta = 15$ as can be seen under AI_{1000}). The next rows show the teaching set employed, its δ value, the fidelity value and the aggregate score.

There are three clear cases in the table (AI_{10}, AI_{10000} and AI_{50000}) where a simple teaching set allows the teacher to convey a concept to the learner that very closely captures the model. But there are other cases, such as AI_{1000} and AI_{2000}, where the situation is less clear. For AI_{1000} the fidelity is not bad ($1 - \lambda = 1 - 0.0157 = 0.9843$) but the complexity of teaching becomes high ($\delta = 15$) so even if a sufficiently accurate concept can be taught this is at the cost of a higher effort from the learner. For AI_{2000} we see that this cost is reduced but the fidelity is worse ($1 - \lambda = 1 - 0.0248 = 0.9752$).

5.1.2 Varying μ for a Single Model.
In a second experiment we trained a Θ_{AI} model on a data set of size 350 for $\phi = (A \wedge B) \vee (C \wedge D) = AB + CD$ on 4 variables/letters. The accuracy was 78.25% and the closest Boolean function, with a fidelity value $1 - \lambda$ of $1 - 0.06 = 0.94$, turned out to be $ABC + ABD + ACD + BCD$, which can be interpreted as "True if and only if at least 3 letters present". To investigate the trade-off between fidelity and complexity, teaching was done with varying values of μ, see left column in Table 3. We see that as μ increases more emphasis is put on fidelity at expense of complexity. Note that at $\mu = 3200$ the fidelity is as good as possible (i.e. highest possible $1 - \lambda$) since the teaching set at $\mu = 3200$ is optimal for that optimal θ_M so increasing μ will have no effect. Of course, this comes at the expense of a high complexity. An option worth exploring is to take the characteristics of the human user into account when deciding on the fidelity vs complexity trade-off, e.g., having a high value of μ for an expert and a low value for a non-expert.

Table 3. Results for a single AI model where the closest Boolean function turned out to be $ABC + ABD + ACD + BCD$. Teaching was done with varying values of μ, see left column. As μ increases more emphasis is put on lower fidelity $1 - \lambda = 1 - \lambda(\theta_{AI}, \theta_M)$ at expense of higher teaching complexity δ.

Range μ	Model taught θ_M	$1 - \lambda$	δ	Teaching set
16	A	0.812	1.1	$\{(\emptyset, 0), (A,1)\}$
160–960	AC+BD	0.9119	12	$\{(A,0),(B,0),(C,0),(D,0),(AC,1),(BD,1)\}$
1120–1840	AC+BCD+AD	0.9282	30	$\{(A,0),(AC,1),(AD,1),(BC,0),(BD,0),(CD,0)\}$
1920–2400	AC+ABD+BCD	0.9344	42	$\{(AC,1),(AB,0),(AD,0),(BC,0),(BD,0),(CD,0),$ $(ABD,1),(BCD,1)\}$
3200–∞	ABC+ABD+ ACD+BCD	0.94	60	$\{(AB,0),(AC,0),(AD,0),(BC,0),(BD,0),(CD,0),$ $(ABC,1),(ABD,1),(ACD,1),(BCD,1)\}$

This second experiment also shows that it is not difficult to determine when the language used for the explanation leads to low fidelity and/or complex explanations. Actually, in this case, since the function captured by the AI model does not have a clean Boolean concept, we can detect that teaching will either lead to low fidelity or complex explanation (or both). In sum, the use of the complexity of the teaching set in the trade-off is not only the right choice when doing example-based XAI but it also leads to the same insights as when the complexity of the concept is taken into account.

5.2   Different Hypothesis Spaces

This section will examine the effects of different hypothesis spaces (representation languages) between the AI model, the ground truth, the model of the learner L_M and the actual human learner L_H. In our exemplar-based explanation system, we added letter rotations, letter resizing and letter location as cognitive noise and extra features, so that we have more confounders, and motivated by these spurious variations the neural network will have error with respect to the ground truth. This makes things more realistic, with the neural network creating patterns that are not fully captured by L_M. A neural network trained on images can in principle model functions over all possible images creating an enormous hypothesis space H_{pix}. On the other hand, the ground truth labelling function is on a small set of features, i.e. the presence or absence of k letters, giving the small hypothesis space H_{p^k}, with $p = \{0, 1\}$ indicating the two possibilities of present or absent. When the actual human learner L_H is given a set of labelled images from the example space H_{pix}, they will create a rule based on the features of the images they consider relevant.

Our exemplar-based explanation system has a focus on the simplicity of examples, and so far this has been with respect to the δ function. But simplicity also comes into play when generating images with certain letters present. The simplest images contain letters that all have the same size, with no rotation and with uniform placement, and these can be used as the simplified examples most compatible with the smaller example space H_{p^k}. The research question we want to address with the following experiment is whether using such simplified examples helps align the hypothesis spaces.

The experiment will compare the options for aligning the hypothesis spaces, by three groups that are given the teaching sets in different formats

– Group I: Use original images.
– Group II: Use simplified images, without irrelevant features.
– Group III: Use original images, but alert learners to essential features

We created a 2AFC (two-alternative forced choice) survey. Participants were shown a teaching set of carefully selected images and the (binary) classification of these images into Box 1 or Box 2 (True/False). They were then shown a test set of unclassified images and tasked to classify each image into one either Box 1 or Box 2. In Fig. 2, we display how these tasks were presented to the participants.

The teaching sets were selected according to the system presented in the earlier sections. The test sets were randomly selected with the restriction that exactly one image should contain the same letter combination as one in the teaching set.

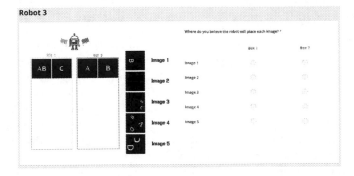

Fig. 2. Participants in group II were presented with this screen when tested on the formula ϕ_3 (C or both A and B). Note the teaching set for Box 1 (True) and Box 2 (False) have images without the noise (rotation, resizing and relocation) found in the five images of the Test Set. For Groups I and III also the teaching set had noise. For group III the following text was displayed prominently: "NB: Size, placement and rotation do not matter. Focus on present/absent letters."

In total, we trained six AI models (called 'robots' in the survey) to be tested. All of them were trained to a high degree of accuracy. Each robot was trained on a different Boolean expression ϕ.

We asked each participant to classify five test instances for each Boolean expression ϕ. The participant's answer to the ith test is denoted $p(\phi, i)$. The correct answer to each test is given by $\phi(i)$. To calculate a participant's score for a single Boolean expression, we use the following formula: $p(\phi) = \frac{1}{6} \sum_{i=1}^{6} [p(\phi, i) = \phi(i)]$ where: $p(\phi, i) = \phi(i)$ is 1 if the participant's answer is correct and 0 otherwise. We then calculate the score of the jth participant across all Boolean expressions as follows: $p_j = \frac{1}{6} \sum_{i=1}^{6} p(\phi_i)$. Here, $p(\phi_i)$ represents the participant's score for the ith Boolean expression.

In total, we had 42 voluntary participants, who were master students, doctoral students or faculty in informatics, none of whom received compensation. The participants were presented with the survey and freely choose to participate. The participants were randomly assigned to the groups, with 12 participants in group I, 17 in group II, and 13 in group III.

The average scores for Groups I, II, and III were 0.564, 0.664, and 0.732, respectively. Furthermore, we observed that group III had the highest average score on 5 out 6 test instances. Though the results are not conclusive due to the small sample size[2], we decided to move on with option III, as we know that the teacher should do something to align the hypothesis spaces of L_M and L_H to achieve efficient learning. Next, we look at the quality of the teaching sets, by comparing our teacher to a teacher randomly selecting teaching sets of similar complexity, with both presenting the teaching sets as group III.

---

[2] We conducted t-tests for all pairs of groups to test whether means differ statistically significantly and got p-values 0.0297, 0.0013, and 0.0747 for pairs (I, II), (I, III) and (II, III), respectively.

5.3   Compare to Teaching Sets Chosen Randomly

In this section, we discuss a second survey where we compare the teaching sets given by our exemplar-based explanation system (the smart teacher) to a system where the teaching sets are chosen randomly but correctly labelled and without repetitions (the random teacher).

To make the comparison of the random teacher and smart teacher fair, both will present their teaching sets as in group III. For a given Boolean formula, we first find the teaching set S_S used by the smart teacher, and then we ensure that the random teaching set S_R has a complexity (δ^*-value[3]) close to S_S (i.e. within some $\pm\epsilon$ additive difference) by choosing S_R as follows, while making sure that no letter combination is repeated in S_R:

1. while $\delta(S_R) < \delta(S_S) - \epsilon \rightarrow$ add a random new image to S_R
2. if $\delta(S_S) - \epsilon \leq \delta(S_R) \leq \delta(S_S) + \epsilon \rightarrow$ use S_R
3. if $\delta(S_S) + \epsilon < \delta(S_R)$ then set $S_R = \emptyset$ and restart from 1.

To avoid bias from the previous survey, we changed most Boolean expressions for the new survey. They were (again) chosen with a variation in terms of expected difficulty, see Table 4. The formulas used can be found in Table 4.

Table 4. Boolean expressions used in the second survey.

Nr	Prior L_H	Short description	Boolean expression
ϕ_1	High	Less Than Two Letters	$(\neg A \wedge \neg B \wedge \neg D) \vee (\neg B \wedge \neg C \wedge \neg D) \vee$ $(\neg A \wedge \neg C \wedge \neg D) \vee (\neg A \wedge \neg B \wedge \neg C)$
ϕ_2	Medium	A or both B and D	$(B \wedge D) \vee A$
ϕ_3	Medium	B or D	$B \vee D$
ϕ_4	High	Exactly One Letter	$(A \wedge \neg B \wedge \neg C \wedge \neg D) \vee (\neg A \wedge B \wedge \neg C \wedge \neg D) \vee$ $(\neg A \wedge \neg B \wedge C \wedge \neg D) \vee (\neg A \wedge \neg B \wedge \neg C \wedge D)$
ϕ_5	Medium	No D	$\neg D$

Both groups G_S given smart teaching sets and G_R given random teaching sets will be shown the same test sets, and we now discuss how to generate the testing sets. When generating testing sets, we want them to be fair with regards to both teaching sets S_S and S_R so that none of them get an unfair advantage. Define $l(S)$ to be the set of letter combinations in the teaching set S, and define X to be the set of all images. We generate test sets for S_S and S_R by choosing images from X as follows, while ensuring that each letter combination appears at most once:

1. As long as there are new letter combinations in $l(X)/(l(S_R) \cup l(S_S))$, choose such an image at random.
2. Otherwise, fill the test set with images from the set of letter combinations in $l(S_R) \cap l(S_S)$, chosen randomly

---

[3] We use $\delta^* = $ *Number of present letters.*

We select a test set of size five by the above protocol, for each Boolean expression, see Table 6. We will thus be able to make a fair comparison between the random and smart teaching sets.

Table 5. Teaching sets used for G_S on left and G_R on right (B1=Box 1, B2=Box 2).

Nr	Teaching set group G_S	$\delta^*(G_S)$	Teaching set group G_R
ϕ_1	B1:{ A , B , C , D } B2:{ AB , AC , AD , BC , BD , CD }	16	B1:{ ∅ , A , B , C } B2:{ AC , ACD , AD , BCD , CD }
ϕ_2	B1:{ A , BD } B2:{ B , D }	5	B1:{ A , AC } B2:{ B }
ϕ_3	B1:{ B , D } B2:{ ∅ }	2.1	B1:{ D } B2:{ C }
ϕ_4	B1:{ A , B , C , D } B2:{ ∅ , AB , AC , AD , BC , BD , CD }	16.1	B1:{ A , B , C } B2:{ AB , ABC , ABD , AD , BCD }
ϕ_5	B1:{ ∅ } B2:{ D }	1.1	B1:{ ∅ } B2:{ BD }

Table 6. Test sets used for both G_S and G_R.

Nr	Test set
ϕ_1	{ ABC , ABCD , ABD , C , AD }
ϕ_2	{ ABD , ACD , C , ∅ , AD }
ϕ_3	{ ABC , BD , ABCD , AB , ACD }
ϕ_4	{ ACD , ABCD , B , AD , C }
ϕ_5	{ AC , CD , A , ABC , BC }

5.4   Overall Results

We will now discuss the results of the second survey. In total, we had 56 participants, none of them overlapping with the previous test. The participants were students in a university-level informatics course. The participants were randomly assigned into two groups, with 22 participants in group G_S and 34 in group G_R.

We start by looking at each group's average score for each ϕ_i. The results are shown in Fig. 3. Our initial observation is that the group G_S has average accuracy over all 5 Boolean expressions of 0.809 versus 0.699 for the group G_R, suggesting that the smart teaching sets have an advantage. This difference is statistically significant ($p = 0.00016$ from t-test). There are two cases where G_R exhibits slightly higher average accuracy than G_S, namely for ϕ_1 and ϕ_4. Notice these concepts are the ones we classified to have high prior for L_H in Table 4 and if we look at Table 5 we see these are also the concepts where our automatic system generates teaching sets with large size (δ-value). When the system is

Task	Group G_S	Group G_R	$G_S + G_R$
ϕ_1	0.882	0.924	0.908
ϕ_2	0.954	0.759	0.836
ϕ_3	0.827	0.547	0.657
ϕ_4	0.873	0.888	0.882
ϕ_5	0.509	0.376	0.428
Total	0.809	0.699	0.742

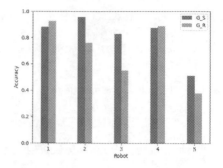

Fig. 3. The table shows average accuracy in Groups G_S, G_R and $G_S + G_R$, for each ϕ_i and Total. The bar plot shows average accuracy in G_S, G_R for each ϕ_i.

aligned[4], as with ϕ_2 and ϕ_3, our system achieves substantially higher accuracy than the random teacher (Fig. 4).

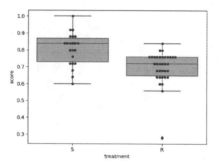

Fig. 4. Boxplot showing results of the two survey groups, to the left teaching sets with the exemplar-based explanation system, and to the right the random teaching sets. There is a clear difference between the groups.

Table 7 gives information on the most common answers for each robot. The most common answer vector of group G_S is the correct one for 4 of the 5 ϕ_is, while for G_R it is the correct one for 3 of the 5.

5.4.1 Detailed Discussion of ϕ_4 (Exactly One Letter in Box 1). Note in Table 7 that for ϕ_4 a full 85 % of the participants in G_R had all answers correct, whereas this drops to 64 % for group G_S. We believe this is because the smart teaching set happens to be compatible with the (wrong) concept 'Odd Number of Letters'. Thus when shown the test set containing 'ACD' almost a third (7/22) of those thought with smart teaching set made a wrong choice,

---

[4] We say that the system is aligned when the prior of L_M is similar to the prior of L_H.

Table 7. The most common answer for both groups. We show how correct the answer is, with 1.0 being all 5 tests correct, and we also show how common it is.

Concept	Most common answer G_S	Score [0..1]	Fraction of participants G_S	Most common answer G_R	Score [0..1]	Fraction of participants G_R
ϕ_1	[2,2,2,1,2]	1.0	59%	[2,2,2,1,2]	1.0	76%
ϕ_2	[1,1,2,2,1]	1.0	82%	[1,1,2,2,1]	1.0	44%
ϕ_3	[1,1,1,1,1]	1.0	68%	[2,1,1,2,1]	0.6	29%
ϕ_4	[2,2,1,2,1]	1.0	64%	[2,2,1,2,1]	1.0	85%
ϕ_5	[2,2,2,2,2]	0.2	41%	[2,2,2,2,2]	0.2	53%

while less than a tenth (3/34) of those taught with the random teaching set selected the wrong box. The teaching sets are in Table 5. This is why we believe the random teaching set is slightly better (accuracy 0.888 vs 0.873, see Fig. 3) for formula ϕ_4 where the procedure built on Karnaugh map used in our system generates a very large smart teaching set.

We also asked participants for how they themselves would explain what they thought each robot was doing. This information is useful to elucidate why the smart teaching set does worse than the random teaching set on ϕ_4.

In the group G_S (the smart teaching set), 10 of the 22 subjects did not write any explanation while 12 subjects had an explanation. 7 people answered wrong for test 'ACD' and 3 of these had no explanation, whereas the other 4 confirm our suspicion that they are focusing on odd/even numbers of letters.

In the group G_R (the random teaching set) 27 subjects had an explanation. 3 people answered wrong for test 'ACD' and 2 of these had no explanation, whereas the 3rd had an explanation that actually should have led the subject to classify 'ACD' correctly.

6   Conclusions

The results of the paper are indeed promising and have the potential to advance the field of explainable AI. Our proposed framework based on machine teaching can effectively teach complex functions to humans using explanatory examples, with a clear advantage over choosing the examples randomly. These findings demonstrate that machine teaching is a valid approach for exemplar-based explainable AI, but also that the expectations on the features and the priors of the humans is critical to get effective explanations from as few examples as possible. As future work, we propose the study of L_M models better aligned with humans. Also, we are considering the use of teaching examples generated by recent language models.

References

1. Basu, S., Christensen, J.: Teaching classification boundaries to humans. In: Twenty-Seventh AAAI Conference on Artificial Intelligence (2013)
2. Chen, Y., Mac Aodha, O., Su, S., Perona, P., Yue, Y.: Near-optimal machine teaching via explanatory teaching sets. In: International Conference on Artificial Intelligence and Statistics, pp. 1970–1978 (2018)
3. Domingos, P.: Knowledge discovery via multiple models. Intell. Data Anal. **2**(1–4), 187–202 (1998)
4. Feldman, J.: Minimization of Boolean complexity in human concept learning. Nature **407**(4), 630–633 (2000)
5. Guidotti, R., Monreale, A., Ruggieri, S., Turini, F., Giannotti, F., Pedreschi, D.: A survey of methods for explaining black box models. ACM Comput. Surv. **51**(5), 93 (2018)
6. Hadfield-Menell, D., Russell, S.J., Abbeel, P., Dragan, A.: Cooperative inverse reinforcement learning. In: NIPS, pp. 3909–3917 (2016)
7. Hernández-Orallo, J.: Gazing into clever hans machines. Nat. Mach. Intell. **1**(4), 172 (2019)
8. Hernández-Orallo, J., Ferri, C.: Teaching and explanations: aligning priors between machines and humans. In: Human-Like Machine Intelligence, pp. 171–198 (2021)
9. Ho, M.K., Littman, M., MacGlashan, J., Cushman, F., Austerweil, J.L.: Showing versus doing: teaching by demonstration. In: NIPS, pp. 3027–3035. Curran (2016). www.papers.nips.cc/paper/6413-showing-versus-doing-teaching-by-demonstration.pdf
10. Hoosain, R.: The processing of negation. J. Verbal Learn. Verbal Behav. **12**(6), 618–626 (1973). https://doi.org/10.1016/S0022-5371(73)80041-6, www.sciencedirect.com/science/article/pii/S0022537173800416
11. Karnaugh, M.: The map method for synthesis of combinational logic circuits. Trans. Am. Inst. Electr. Engineers Part I: Commun. Electron. **72**(5), 593–599 (1953). https://doi.org/10.1109/TCE.1953.6371932
12. Khan, F., Mutlu, B., Zhu, J.: How do humans teach: on curriculum learning and teaching dimension. In: NIPS, pp. 1449–1457 (2011)
13. Lecun, Y., Bottou, L., Bengio, Y., Haffner, P.: Gradient-based learning applied to document recognition. Proc. IEEE **86**(11), 2278–2324 (1998). https://doi.org/10.1109/5.726791
14. Lipton, P.: Contrastive explanation. Roy. Inst. Phil. Suppl. **27**, 247–266 (1990)
15. Liu, W., Dai, B., Li, X., Liu, Z., Rehg, J.M., Song, L.: Towards black-box iterative machine teaching. arXiv preprint arXiv:1710.07742 (2017)
16. Molnar, C.: Interpretable machine learning. https://lulu.com/ (2020)
17. Ortega, A., Fierrez, J., Morales, A., Wang, Z., Ribeiro, T.: Symbolic AI for XAI: evaluating LFIT inductive programming for fair and explainable automatic recruitment. In: Proceedings of the IEEE/CVF Winter Conference on Applications of Computer Vision, pp. 78–87 (2021)
18. Ouyang, L.: Bayesian inference of regular expressions from human-generated example strings. arXiv:1805.08427 (2018)
19. Pisano, G., Ciatto, G., Calegari, R., Omicini, A.: Neuro-symbolic computation for xai: towards a unified model. In: WOA, vol. 1613, p. 101 (2020)
20. Rahwan, I., et al.: Machine behaviour. Nature **568**(7753), 477 (2019)
21. Ribeiro, M.T., Singh, S., Guestrin, C.: Anchors: High-precision model-agnostic explanations. In: Proceedings of the AAAI Conference on Artificial Intelligence, vol. 32 (2018)

22. Samek, W., Müller, K.-R.: Towards explainable artificial intelligence. In: Samek, W., Montavon, G., Vedaldi, A., Hansen, L.K., Müller, K.-R. (eds.) Explainable AI: Interpreting, Explaining and Visualizing Deep Learning. LNCS (LNAI), vol. 11700, pp. 5–22. Springer, Cham (2019). https://doi.org/10.1007/978-3-030-28954-6_1

23. Telle, J.A., Hernández-Orallo, J., Ferri, C.: The teaching size: computable teachers and learners for universal languages. Mach. Learn. **108**, 1653–1675 (2019). https://doi.org/10.1007/s10994-019-05821-2

24. van der Waa, J., Nieuwburg, E., Cremers, A., Neerincx, M.: Evaluating XAI: a comparison of rule-based and example-based explanations. Artif. Intell. **291**, 103404 (2021)

25. Yang, S.C.H., Vong, W.K., Sojitra, R.B., Folke, T., Shafto, P.: Mitigating belief projection in explainable artificial intelligence via Bayesian teaching. Sci. Rep. **11**(1), 9863 (2021). https://doi.org/10.1038/s41598-021-89267-4. www.nature.com/articles/s41598-021-89267-4

26. Zhu, X.: Machine teaching: an inverse problem to machine learning and an approach toward optimal education. In: AAAI, pp. 4083–4087 (2015)

27. Zhu, X., Singla, A., Zilles, S., Rafferty, A.N.: An overview of machine teaching (2018). arxiv.org/abs/1801.05927

Generating Robust Counterfactual Explanations

Victor Guyomard[1,2]([✉]), Françoise Fessant[1], Thomas Guyet[3], Tassadit Bouadi[2], and Alexandre Termier[2]

[1] Orange Innovation, Lannion, France
victor.guyomard@orange.com
[2] Univ Rennes, Inria, CNRS, IRISA, Rennes, France
[3] Inria, AIstroSight, Paris, France

Abstract. Counterfactual explanations have become a mainstay of the XAI field. This particularly intuitive statement allows the user to understand what small but necessary changes would have to be made to a given situation in order to change a model prediction. The quality of a counterfactual depends on several criteria: realism, actionability, validity, robustness, etc. In this paper, we are interested in the notion of robustness of a counterfactual. More precisely, we focus on robustness to counterfactual input changes. This form of robustness is particularly challenging as it involves a trade-off between the robustness of the counterfactual and the proximity with the example to explain. We propose a new framework, CROCO, that generates robust counterfactuals while managing effectively this trade-off, and guarantees the user a minimal robustness. An empirical evaluation on tabular datasets confirms the relevance and effectiveness of our approach.

Keywords: Counterfactual explanation · Robustness · Algorithmic recourse

1 Introduction

The ever-increasing use of machine learning models in critical decision-making contexts, such as health care, hiring processes or credit allocation, makes it essential to provide explanations for the individual decisions made by these models. To this end, Wachter et al. proposed counterfactual explanation [22]. A counterfactual is defined as the smallest modification of feature values that changes the prediction of a model to a given output. The counterfactual can provide actions (or recourse) for individuals to attain more desirable outcomes. This is particularly important in areas where decisions made by algorithms can have significant impacts on people's lives such as finance, health care or criminal

Supplementary Information The online version contains supplementary material available at https://doi.org/10.1007/978-3-031-43418-1_24.

justice. Many methods have been proposed to generate counterfactuals, focusing on some specific properties such as realism [7,14,20], actionability [16,19] or sparsity [3,11,22]. According to Artelt et al. [1], many counterfactual generation methods are vulnerable to small changes, where even a minor change in the value of a counterfactual feature can cause the counterfactual to have a different outcome. Such a situation may arise for example in practical implementation of the counterfactual, due to various factors such as unexpected noise, or adversarial manipulation. As an illustration, a counterfactual may suggest to an individual to raise its salary by 200\$ to obtain a credit, but in practice, the salary is increased by 199\$ or 201\$, potentially resulting in a negative decision (a rejected credit) regarding the decision model. This line of discussions falls into the topic of robustness [4,9,15,21]. To address robustness in the context of counterfactual explanation, Pawelcyk et al. [15] introduce the notion of recourse invalidation rate which represents the probability of obtaining a counterfactual with a different predicted class, when small changes (sampled from a noise distribution) are applied to it. They presented an estimator of the recourse invalidation rate in the context of Gaussian distributions, and also a framework (PROBE) that guarantees the recourse invalidation rate to be no greater than a target specified by the user. A limitation of their approach is that the satisfaction of the user condition is dependent of the estimator quality, which means that in practice, the recourse invalidation rate can be greater than the target fixed by the user. Moreover, PROBE leads in practice to a poor trade-off management between proximity and robustness i.e. the counterfactual is robust but far from the example to explain. In this paper, we introduce a framework called CROCO (Cost-efficient RObust COunterfactuals), which is based on a new minimization problem inspired by PROBE [15]. Our framework introduces the novel concept of soft recourse invalidation rate, as well as an estimator of it. It enables us to derive an upper-bound for the recourse invalidation rate with almost certain probability. This ensures that the user obtains a solution with a recourse invalidation rate lower than the predetermined target. An experimental evaluation on different tabular datasets confirms these theoretical results, and shows that our method better optimizes the two criteria of robustness and proximity.

2   Related Work

Since Wachter et al. seminal paper [22], a variety of counterfactual explanation technics have been proposed. These methods seek to enhance the quality of counterfactuals by incorporating additional properties, such as constraining the counterfactual to support the data distribution in order to produce realistic examples, freezing immutable features (such as race or gender), producing multiple counterfactuals at once, or even adding causality constraints. We refer the readers to Guidotti et al. [6] for a detailed review about counterfactual explanation properties and methods. The property of robustness has been studied recently in the context of counterfactual explanations, where the validity of a counterfactual is determined by its ability to maintain the same predicted class in the presence of changes. Mishra et al. [10] distinguish various types of robustness:

Robustness to model change refers to the evolution of the validity of the counterfactual explanation when machine learning models are re-trained or when training parameters settings are slightly modified. Rawal et al. [17] have demonstrated that state-of-the-art counterfactual generation methods have the tendency to produce solutions that are not robust to model retraining. To address this problem, Ferrario and Loi [5] proposed to use counterfactual data augmentation every time machine learning models are retrained. Upadhyay et al. [18] for their part developed an adversarial training objective that produces counterfactuals that are robust regarding changes in the training data. More specifically, they evaluated the robustness on different types of training data shift which are data correction shift, temporal shift, and geospatial shift. However, the counterfactuals that are generated suffer from a much higher cost of change regarding state-of-the art counterfactual generation methods [15]. In the context of slightly changed training settings, Black et al. [2] achieved robust counterfactual explanations with a regularization method based upon a K-Lipschitz constant.

Robustness to input perturbations refers to how counterfactuals explanations are sensitive to slight input changes. According to Dominguez-Olmedo et al. [4], a counterfactual is said robust if small changes in the example to explain result in valid counterfactuals. They proposed an optimization problem that applies to linear models and neural networks to generate robust counterfactuals in this context. For Artelt et al. [1] robustness means that two examples that are close, must result in two similar counterfactuals. To address this issue they propose to solve an optimization problem that includes a density constraint [1]. They empirically show that having a counterfactual that lies in a dense area has the effect of improving the robustness. Laugel et al. [8] pointed out that such a type of robustness issue cannot solely be attributed to the explainer, but also arises from the decision boundary of the classifier, thus increasing the problem complexity.

Robustness to counterfactual input changes refers to the ability of a counterfactual explanation to remain valid when small feature changes are applied (two similar counterfactuals should have the same predicted class). In this context, Pawelcyk et al. [15] presented PROBE a framework to produce robust counterfactuals that is based on an optimization problem. This framework aims to find a trade-off between two criteria that are the recourse invalidation rate and the proximity, i.e. the distance between the counterfactual and the example to explain. From their side, Maragno et al. [9] introduced an adversarial robust approach that generates counterfactuals that remain valid in an uncertainty set, meaning that for a given example to explain, all the solutions in the set are valid counterfactuals. This approach works for non-differentiable model unlike PROBE. However there is no trade-off between the recourse invalidation rate and the proximity as all the counterfactuals in the uncertainty set are valid. In such a scenario, the robustness constraint cannot be relaxed, then allowing the generation of counterfactuals that are far from the example to explain. Our approach, CROCO, is part of this category of methods. It is inspired by the PROBE framework, and improves its limitations. Indeed, the major criticism that we can make to PROBE is that the guarantees in terms of robustness that it offers to the user are completely dependent on the quality of their estimator (i.e. the guarantee is based on a recourse invalidation rate approximation rather than the true recourse invalidation rate). Our method introduces a new optimization problem that is proved to induce an almost-sure upper bound on the true recourse invalidation rate. This leads to a significant improvement in the trade-off between the robustness of the counterfactual and the proximity with the example to explain.

3   Problem Statement

In this section, we define some notations related to the generation of counterfactuals, and we formalize the robustness of counterfactual generation by introducing the notion of *recourse invalidation rate*.

3.1   Generation of Counterfactuals

We consider the generation of counterfactuals for a binary classifier. Let $\mathcal{X} \subseteq \mathbb{R}^n$ represents the n-dimensional feature space. A binary classifier is a function $h : \mathcal{X} \to \mathcal{Y}$ where $\mathcal{Y} = \{0, 1\}$. We assume that the classification is obtained from a probabilistic prediction i.e. a function $f : \mathcal{X} \to [0, 1]$ that returns $\hat{p}$ which is the predicted probability for the class 1. Then, the predicted class is the most likely class according to $\hat{p}$. For a given example x, $h(x) = g \circ f(x)$ where $g : [0, 1] \to \mathcal{Y}$ is a function that returns the predicted class from the probability vector. We take $g(u) = \mathbb{1}_{>t}(u)$, where t is the decision threshold. $\mathbb{1}_{>t}(u)$ equals 1 if $u > t$ and 0 otherwise.

In this article, we do post-hoc counterfactual generation, meaning that f (and thus h) are given. And for a given example to explain $x \in \mathcal{X}$, whose decision is $h(x)$, we want to generate a counterfactual $\breve{x} \in \mathcal{X}$. A counterfactual is a new example close to the example to explain x, and with a different prediction, i.e. $h(\breve{x}) \neq h(x)$. If it is true that $h(\breve{x}) \neq h(x)$, then $\breve{x}$ is said to be *valid*. A counterfactual $\breve{x}$ is also seen as a change to apply to x: $\breve{x} = x + \delta$ where $\delta \in \mathbb{R}^n$. Thus, a counterfactual is associated to a small change δ that modifies the decision returned by h. Generating a counterfactual is basically solving the following optimisation problem:

$$\min_{\delta} \ell\left(f\left(x + \delta\right), 1 - h(x)\right) + \lambda \left\|\delta\right\|_1 \tag{1}$$

where $\ell : [0, 1]^2 \mapsto \mathbb{R}^+$ quantifies the distance between the predicted probability, $f(\breve{x})$, and $1 - h(x)$ that is the opposite of the predicted class for example x. For instance, Wachter et al. suggested ℓ as the L_2 distance, so as to produce counterfactuals that are close to the desired decision [22]. The other term in the optimization problem, constraints the change δ applied to the example x to be small.

In what follows, we will focus specifically on the generation of counterfactuals in the case of instances that have received a negative decision (which corresponds to instances predicted as class 0). This choice has no limitation and is motivated by the fact that the majority of robustness methods are defined in a recourse context [15,17,18] where the goal is to provide explanations only for negatively predicted instances. We will also assume that the classifier f is differentiable.

3.2 Recourse Invalidation Rate

In order to quantify the robustness of the counterfactual to an input perturbation, the notion of recourse invalidation rate has been introduced by Pawelczyk et al. [15].

Definition 1 (Recourse invalidation rate). *The recourse invalidation rate for a counterfactual $\breve{x}$, of an example x predicted as class 0 can be expressed as:*

$$\Gamma\left(\breve{x}; p_\varepsilon\right) = \mathbb{E}_{\varepsilon \sim p_\epsilon}\left[1 - h\left(\breve{x} + \varepsilon\right)\right]$$

where $\varepsilon \in \mathbb{R}^n$ is a random variable that follows a probability distribution p_ε. Since $h\left(\breve{x} + \varepsilon\right) \in \{0, 1\}$, it ensues $\Gamma(\breve{x}; p_\varepsilon) \in [0, 1]$.

Assuming p_ε is centered, then p_ε defines a region around a counterfactual $\breve{x}$ for *similar* counterfactuals $\breve{x} + \varepsilon$. Intuitively, $\Gamma(\breve{x}; p_\varepsilon)$ gives the rate of *similar* counterfactuals that are not valid, *i.e.* that belong to class 0. Thus, the lower $\Gamma(\breve{x}; p_\varepsilon)$, the more robust is the counterfactual. If $\Gamma\left(\breve{x}; p_\varepsilon\right) = 0$, the counterfactual is considered perfectly robust, given that all the perturbed counterfactuals result in positive outcomes (i.e., there are all predicted as class 1). However, if $\Gamma\left(\breve{x}; p_\varepsilon\right) = 1$, the counterfactual is not at all considered robust, since no noisy counterfactuals lead to positive outcomes (i.e., there are all predicted as class 0).

Figure 1 illustrates the intuition of the recourse invalidation rate. $\Gamma(\breve{x}; p_\varepsilon)$ can be seen as the surface of the neighborhood that overlaps the region, split by the decision frontier, on the side of the example. This neighborhood represents the perturbations on the counterfactuals that we would like to accept without changing its validity. The Figure also shows that finding a robust counterfactual requires to make a trade-off between the robustness and the magnitude of the change.

3.3 The PROBE Framework for Generating Robust Counterfactuals

Pawelczyk et al. [15] have developed a framework named PROBE that generates robust counterfactuals regarding the recourse invalidation rate. It adapts the minimization problem of Eq. 1 by adding a new term that enforces the recourse invalidation rate to be under a target value Γ_t. This target value is chosen by the

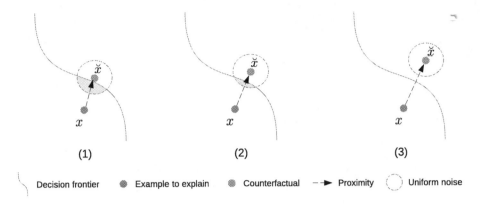

Fig. 1. Illustration of the recourse invalidation rate with a uniform distribution p_ε (dashed-red circle). The recourse invalidation rate is figured out by the area of the region in red. In **(1)** the counterfactual has a low robustness and is at a low distance from the example. In **(2)** the counterfactual has a medium robustness and is at a medium distance, and in **(3)** the counterfactual has a perfect robustness but is far from the example (large distance). (Color figure online)

user. More formally, generating a counterfactual relies on solving the following minimization problem:

$$\min_\delta \ \max\left[\Gamma\left(x+\delta;p_\varepsilon\right)-\Gamma_t,\ 0\right]+\ell\left(f\left(x+\delta\right),\ 1-h(x)\right)+\lambda\left\|\delta\right\|_1 \qquad (2)$$

There are some difficulties with the additional constraint on recourse invalidation rate. Indeed, the true value of Γ can not be evaluated in practice. Then, PROBE proposes a Monte-Carlo estimator of Γ. This means that it is estimated by computing the mean of a sample of perturbations in p_ε:

$$\tilde{\Gamma}\left(\breve{x};K,p_\varepsilon\right)=\frac{1}{K}\sum_{k=1}^{K}\left(1-h\left(\breve{x}+\varepsilon_k\right)\right) \qquad (3)$$

However, $\tilde{\Gamma}$ is non-differentiable, because $h(x)=g\circ f(x)$ and $g(u)=\mathbb{1}_{>t}$. Then, it can not be part of a loss of an optimization problem. To overcome this limitation, the authors proposed a first-order approximation of the true recourse invalidation rate Γ in the context of a Gaussian distribution noise $p_\varepsilon=\mathcal{N}(\mathbf{0},\sigma\mathbf{I})$, named $\tilde{\Gamma}_{\text{PROBE}}$.

Then, the optimization algorithm solves the problem in Eq. 2, replacing Γ by $\tilde{\Gamma}_{\text{PROBE}}$ and stops when the approximation of recourse invalidation rate is under the target value, i.e. when $\tilde{\Gamma}_{\text{PROBE}}(x;\breve{p}_\varepsilon)\leq\Gamma_t$.

Thus, for a given counterfactual $\breve{x}$ returned by PROBE, the user is guaranteed that $\tilde{\Gamma}_{\text{PROBE}}(\breve{x};p_\varepsilon)\leq\Gamma_t$. However, this means that the guarantee depends on the quality of the estimator. Indeed, it is possible to generate a counterfactual where $\tilde{\Gamma}_{\text{PROBE}}(\breve{x};p_\varepsilon)\leq\Gamma_t\leq\Gamma(\breve{x};p_\varepsilon)$ which would then violate the user-selected guarantee. The intuition behind this situation is depicted in Fig. 2.

Fig. 2. Illustration of the potential problem with PROBE. The red region illustrates the true recourse invalidation rate (see Fig. 1) while the green region illustrates the approximated recourse invalidation rate through the approximation of the red region. In this case, the approximation under-estimates the red region and misleadingly encourages finding a $\breve{x}$ that would break the robustness constraint. (Color figure online)

To sum up, PROBE has two limitations: 1) It offers users a guarantee based on the recourse invalidation rate approximation rather than the true recourse invalidation rate; 2) the approximation applies only for Gaussian distribution of counterfactual perturbation. This makes the approach not applicable to dataset with categorical attributes.

Our contribution overcomes the first limitation by introducing a new estimator that is proved to induce an almost-sure upper bound on the true recourse invalidation rate. Furthermore, our approach is independent to the noise distribution, thus enabling the use of various noise distributions.

4   Our Contribution

In this section, we present our method, named CROCO standing for *Cost-efficient RObust COunterfactuals*. It improves the generation of robust counterfactuals according to the recourse invalidation rate.

This method, inspired from PROBE, introduces a new robustness term to the optimization problem presented in Eq. 1. This term is based on an upper-bound of the recourse invalidation rate.

4.1   An Upper Bound of the Recourse Invalidation Rate

As it is not feasible to derive a closed-form expression of Γ without making any assumption about the noise distribution, and given that $\tilde{\Gamma}$ is not differentiable, our idea is to compute an upper-bound of Γ.

Let $\breve{x}$ be a counterfactual for an example $x \in \mathcal{X}$, then we define the soft recourse invalidation rate, $\Theta(\breve{x})$ by:

$$\Theta(\breve{x}; p_\varepsilon) = \mathbb{E}_{\varepsilon \sim p_\varepsilon} \left[1 - f\left(\breve{x} + \varepsilon\right) \right].$$

The Proposition 1 states that the soft recourse invalidation rate, Θ, induces an upper-bound of the recourse invalidation rate, Γ.

Proposition 1. [1] *Let $t \in [0, 1]$ be a decision threshold and $\breve{x}$ be a counterfactual for an example $x \in \mathcal{X}$, an upper bound of the true recourse invalidation rate is given by:*

$$\Gamma(\breve{x}; p_\varepsilon) \leq \frac{\Theta(\breve{x}; p_\varepsilon)}{(1-t)} \tag{4}$$

Similarly to Γ, Θ can not be evaluated directly. However, we can use the following Monte-Carlo estimator, where K is the number of random samples:

$$\tilde{\Theta}(\breve{x}; K, p_\varepsilon) = \frac{1}{K} \sum_{k=1}^{K} (1 - f(\breve{x} + \varepsilon_k)) \tag{5}$$

This quantity can be seen as the mean predicted probability for class 0, computed on perturbed samples that are randomly drawn from the p_ϵ distribution. The proposed estimator is close to the recourse invalidation rate estimation outlined in Eq. 3, but it differs in that it is differentiable as a composition of differentiable functions, thus can be included in an objective function.

Moreover, the Proposition 2 shows that our estimator, $\tilde{\Theta}$, defines an almost-sure upper bound of the true recourse invalidation rate. This means that $\frac{m+\tilde{\Theta}}{1-t}$ has a high probability to be an upper-bound of Γ.

Proposition 2. *Let $t \in [0, 1]$ be a decision threshold, p_ε a noise distribution, $\breve{x}$ be a counterfactual for an example $x \in \mathcal{X}$, then an almost-sure upper-bound of the recourse invalidation rate is given by:*

$$\mathbb{P}\left(\Gamma(\breve{x}; p_\varepsilon) \leq \frac{m + \tilde{\Theta}(\breve{x}; K, p_\varepsilon)}{1-t}\right) \geq 1 - \exp\left(-2m^2 K\right) \tag{6}$$

where $m > 0$ and K is the number of random samples.

With a high number of random samples and a given value of m, the exponential term of Proposition 2 can be arbitrarily small. Then for a given value of our estimator $\tilde{\Theta}(\breve{x}; K, p_\varepsilon)$, we have almost surely that the true recourse invalidation rate will be in the worst case equals to $\frac{m + \tilde{\Theta}(\breve{x}; K, p_\varepsilon)}{1 - t}$. It ensues that if we enforce $\frac{m + \tilde{\Theta}(\breve{x}; K, p_\varepsilon)}{1 - t}$ to be lower than a given threshold $\bar{\Gamma}_t$, then we are almost-sure that the true recourse invalidation rate is lower than $\bar{\Gamma}_t$, *i.e.* that the counterfactual is more robust than the given threshold.

Note that $m \in \mathbb{R}_{>0}$ is a parameter that defines the tightness of the upper-bound. The lower m, the better the upper-bound. In return, low m requires a higher K (*i.e.* more computational resource) to keep the confidence in the bound. Section A.2 in supplementary material provides a table to choose the values of m and K with respect to the desired level of confidence.

---

[1] All proofs are provided in Section A.1 of supplementary material.

Algorithm 1. CROCO optimization for counterfactual generation

Input: x s.t. $f(x) < t$, f, $\lambda > 0$, α, $\bar{\Gamma}_t > 0$, K, p_ε
Output: $x + \delta$
$\delta \leftarrow 0$;
Compute $\tilde{\Theta}(x + \delta; K, p_\varepsilon)$
while $f(x + \delta) < t$ **and** $\frac{m + \tilde{\Theta}(x + \delta; K, p_\varepsilon)}{1 - t} > \bar{\Gamma}_t$ **do**
$\quad \delta \leftarrow \delta - \alpha \cdot \nabla_\delta \mathcal{L}_{\text{CROCO}}(x + \delta; \Theta_t, p_\varepsilon, \lambda)$ ▷ From Eq. 8
$\quad$ Update $\tilde{\Theta}(x + \delta; K, p_\varepsilon)$
end while
Return: $x + \delta$

For instance, with $K = 500$ and $m = 0.1$, and $t = 0.5$, the inequation of the Proposition 2 gives:

$$\mathbb{P}\left(\Gamma(\check{x}) \le 0.2 + 2\tilde{\Theta}(\check{x})\right) \ge 0.999 \tag{7}$$

4.2 Generate Robust Counterfactuals

We propose a minimization problem for the generation of robust counterfactuals according to the recourse invalidation rate.

Given a neighborhood distribution p_ε, a number of samples K, a tightness value $m > 0$ and a target upper-bound $\bar{\Gamma}_t$, a counterfactual $\check{x} = x + \delta$ is found by minimizing the following objective function:

$$\min_\delta \underbrace{\left(\frac{\tilde{\Theta}(x + \delta; K, p_\varepsilon) + m}{1 - t} - \bar{\Gamma}_t\right)^2}_{\text{Robustness}} + \underbrace{\ell(f(x + \delta), 1 - h(x))}_{\text{Validity}} + \underbrace{\lambda \|\delta\|_1}_{\text{Proximity}} \tag{8}$$

The last two terms implement the classical trade-off for counterfactual generation. Indeed, the second term pushes the counterfactual class toward a class that differs from the example class (if $h(x) = 0$ then we want $h(\check{x}) = 1$), while the last term minimizes the distance between the counterfactual and the example to explain.

The first term encourages our new estimator to be close to a target value $\bar{\Gamma}_t$, i.e. the target upper-bound of the recourse invalidation rate. This pushes to choose a counterfactual that has an upper bound close to the objective.

Algorithm 1 describes the optimization process for CROCO. Gradient steps are performed until the counterfactual predicted class is flipped ($f(x + \delta) \ge t$), and the value of the upper-bound $\frac{m + \tilde{\Theta}(x + \delta; K, p_\varepsilon)}{1 - t}$ is below the target value $\bar{\Gamma}_t$.

CROCO has several benefits, it allows the user to generate counterfactuals with almost surely a minimal robustness, and this agnostically to the noise distribution. Moreover, our optimization problem relies on an almost-sure upper bound of the true recourse invalidation rate instead of relying on an approximation as Pawelcyk et al. did with PROBE [15]. Our intuition is that this will in practice improve the trade-off between proximity and robustness.

5   Experiments and Results

We have divided our experiments into two sections. After experimentally confirming that our approach preserves the validity of the counterfactuals, the purpose of the first section is to demonstrate empirically that CROCO provides an effective management of the trade-off between proximity and robustness in comparison to PROBE. In the second section, we demonstrate experimentally that the counterfactuals returned by CROCO exhibits a lower degree of invalidation with respect to the user-defined target than PROBE do.

First of all, we describe the datasets that we used for evaluation, along with the metrics we employed as well as the predictive model details.

5.1   Experimental Setting

For a fair comparison, we used the CARLA library [13], which was also used for evaluating PROBE. It contains three binary classification datasets: *Adult*, *Give Me Some Credit* (GSC), and *COMPAS*. These datasets contain both numerical and categorical features. Both numerical and categorical variables are used to train the classifier, but the counterfactuals are generated by modifying only the numerical variables. The proportion of categorical variables for each dataset are respectively 3/7, 1/12 and 25/40. Additional details about these datasets are available in the section A.4 of the supplementary material. For every dataset, the classification model, f, is the fully connected neural network implemented in the CARLA library[2]. It is composed of 50 hidden layers and ReLU activation functions.

We used for evaluation the following metrics:

Validity A counterfactual $\breve{x}$ of an example x is valid if the classification model predicts different classes for x and $\breve{x}$ [11,12]. Formally:

$$\text{Validity} = \begin{cases} 0, & \text{if } f(\breve{x}) = f(x) \\ 1, & \text{if } f(\breve{x}) \neq f(x) \end{cases}$$

The validity measure lies in $[0, 1]$. The higher it is, the better.

Distance The distance is the L_1 distance between an example, x and its counterfactual, $\breve{x}$ [11,22].

$$\text{Distance} = \|\breve{x} - x\|_1 = \|\delta\|_1$$

A low value indicates fewer changes of features to apply to the original example to obtain the counterfactual. As the distance decreases, the proximity increases. In the context of counterfactual generation, we assume that the lower the distance, the more actionable the counterfactual, the better.

---

[2] Function carla.models.catalog.MLModelCatalog of the CARLA library.

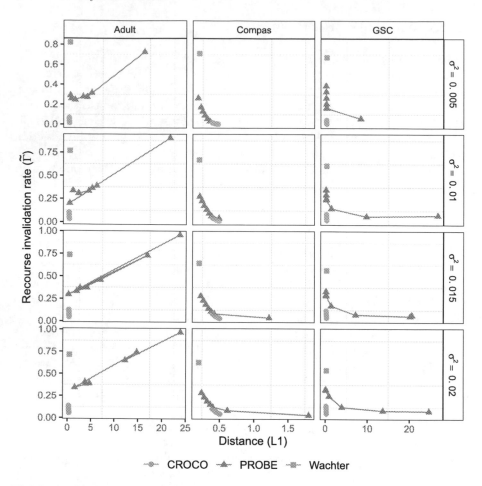

Fig. 3. Trade-off between recourse invalidation rate and distance with Gaussian distribution noises. Each column corresponds to a dataset and each line to a value of $\sigma^2 \in \{0.005, 0.01, 0.015, 0.02\}$. In each subplot the value of σ^2 is fixed. Each point of a curve corresponds to a mean recourse invalidation rate and a mean distance for a given target, we have $target \in \{0.05, 0.10, 0.15, 0.2, 0.25, 0.3, 0.35\}$. The points are connected by target order.

Recourse invalidation rate We used $\tilde{\Gamma}$ (see Eq. 3) to evaluate recourse invalidation rate, i.e. the robustness of the counterfactual. This value indicates the risk to have an invalid counterfactual in case the counterfactual is slightly changing wrt to the automatically recommended counterfactual. The lower, the better.

The recourse invalidation rate makes the assumption of a neighborhood represented by a distribution, p_ϵ. CROCO makes no hypothesis on this distribution but PROBE requires a Gaussian distribution. For the sake of fairness, we use a centered Gaussian distribution with a parameterized variance σ for the two methods.

For each dataset, we run PROBE with $\sigma^2 \in \{0.005, 0.01, 0.015, 0.02\}$ and $\Gamma_t \in \{0.05, 0.10, 0.15, 0.2, 0.25, 0.3, 0.35\}$. Regarding the setting of CROCO, we choose $K = 500$, $m - 0.1$, $t - 0.5$. λ is found through an iterative procedure that is described in section A.5.2 of supplementary material. For each dataset, we run CROCO with the same parameters as PROBE: $\sigma^2 \in \{0.005, 0.01, 0.015, 0.02\}$ and $\bar{\Gamma}_t \in \{0.05, 0.10, 0.15, 0.2, 0.25, 0.3, 0.35\}$.

We also include the approach of Wachter et al. [22] (referred to as *Wachter*) in our experiment. This counterfactual generation method establishes a baseline for recourse invalidation rate.

In our experiments, we generated 500 counterfactuals for each dataset and each parameterized method. We collected their recourse invalidation rate, distance and validity, that are discussed in the following.

5.2 Comparisons Between PROBE and CROCO

In this section, the quality of the counterfactuals generated using CROCO, PROBE and *Watcher* is compared.

First of all, *Watcher* and CROCO achieves a perfect validity for all datasets. PROBE achieved a perfect validity on all datasets, except for two counterfactual sets, that corresponds to the COMPAS dataset where $\sigma^2 = 0.005$ and $\Gamma_t = 0.3$ and also the GSC dataset where $\sigma^2 = 0.02$ and $\Gamma_t = 0.05$. As a consequence, in the following, we focus the analysis on the trade-off between the distance and the recourse invalidation rate. The section A.3.1 of the supplementary material contains details regarding the validity obtained for each dataset, and counterfactual sets that are generated.

Figure 3 compares *Watcher*, PROBE and CROCO regarding the distance and recourse invalidation rate on the three different datasets. Each point of a given curve corresponds to the mean recourse invalidation rate and the mean distance that is obtained from CROCO or PROBE by fixing a target value. Note that *Watcher* has only one point as it has no recourse invalidation rate target parameter. The standard-deviation values are provided in section A.3.2 of supplementary material. Note that for a given curve, the points are linked by order of increasing target value.

For the GSC dataset, CROCO achieves both smaller distances (higher proximities) and lower recourse invalidation rates compared to PROBE, regardless of the value of σ^2. The same conclusion can be drawn for the COMPAS dataset, except for $\sigma^2 = 0.005$ where CROCO achieves smaller recourse invalidation rates but at the cost of higher distances.

Regarding the Adult dataset, we observe that PROBE is unstable, as it can produce solutions with higher recourse invalidation rate than the target fixed by the user (where $\tilde{\Gamma} \geq \Gamma_t$). On the other hand, CROCO is stable and achieves both smaller distances (higher proximities) and lower recourse invalidation rates. We also noticed that on all the datasets, distance values increase when σ^2 increased, thus confirming the presence of a trade-off between the two quantities.

When solutions are closely clustered together in terms of mean distances, both PROBE and CROCO exhibit similar standard deviation values. However,

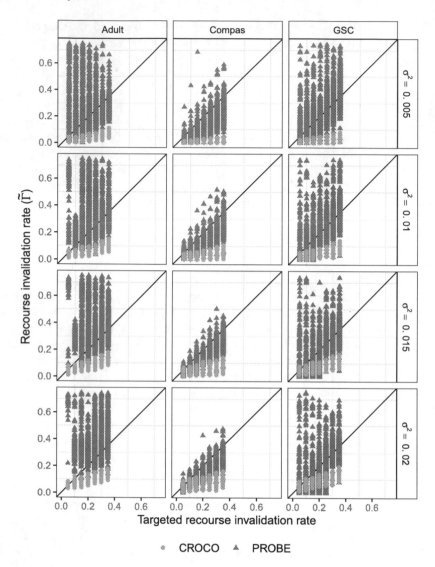

Fig. 4. Comparison between targeted recourse invalidation rate and recourse invalidation rate. Each column corresponds to a dataset and each line to a value of $\sigma^2 \in \{0.005, 0.01, 0.015, 0.02\}$. In each subplot, the value of σ^2 is fixed. Each point corresponds to a counterfactual, on the x-axis is presented the target recourse invalidation rate for the counterfactual, and on the y-axis the recourse invalidation rate that is computed.

when solutions are more widely dispersed, PROBE tends to have higher standard deviation values compared to CROCO (see section A.3.2 of supplementary material).

We observed that for all datasets and values of σ^2, PROBE and CROCO outperform *Wachter* in terms of recourse invalidation rates. The only exception is the Adult dataset when $\Gamma_t = 0.35$, where PROBE produces higher recourse invalidation rates due to instability issues.

5.3   Target Invalidation Study

For each counterfactual that is obtained from PROBE or CROCO, we computed the recourse invalidation rate and compared it with the targeted recourse invalidation rate.[3] The results are provided in Fig. 4. The graphics figure out the diagonal representing the exact match between the targeted and the recourse invalidation rate. All points that are above this diagonal correspond to counterfactuals that do not achieve the robustness requested by the user. We notice that with PROBE, the recourse invalidation rates frequently exceed the target fixed by the user. It illustrates that the approximation of Γ made by PROBE is too loose. In contrast, for CROCO, the recourse invalidation rates are typically lower, indicating that the user-specified target is less invalidated.

We computed the upper bound value derived in Proposition 2 for each counterfactual obtained from CROCO.

Figure 5 of section A.3.3 of the material illustrates the evolution of the upper bound value ($\frac{m+\tilde{\Theta}}{1-t}$) with regard to the recourse invalidation rate for different values of σ^2. Our analysis show that the theoretical bound is not violated. This means that even in cases where CROCO failed to find a solution that matches the user target (i.e., where $\frac{m+\tilde{\Theta}}{1-t} > \bar{\Gamma}_t$), we can still provide the user a guarantee on the true recourse invalidation rate. This guarantee is based on the value of $\tilde{\Theta}$ that is obtained at the end of the optimization.

6   Conclusion

In this paper, we introduce CROCO, a novel framework for generating counterfactuals that are robust to input changes. A robust method guarantees that the slightly perturbed counterfactual is still valid. Our approach leverages a new estimator that provides a theoretical guarantee on the true recourse invalidation rate of the generated counterfactuals. Through experiments comparing CROCO to the state-of-the-art PROBE method, we demonstrate that our approach achieves a better trade-off between recourse invalidation rate and proximity, while also leading to less invalidation regarding the user-specified target. While these initial results are promising, it is necessary to evaluate CROCO on a larger number of datasets to confirm the robustness of the performance obtained. Moving forward, we plan to extend the capabilities of CROCO by adapting it to handle categorical variables. Since our approach is independent to the noise distribution, it seems reasonably possible to generate robust counterfactuals for data with both numerical and categorical variables. CROCO is implemented in the CARLA framework and will be soon available for practical usage.

---

[3] Watcher is not figured out as it does not set a target for recourse invalidation rate.

References

1. Artelt, A., et al.: Evaluating robustness of counterfactual explanations. In: Proceedings of the Symposium Series on Computational Intelligence (SSCI), pp. 01–09. IEEE (2021)
2. Black, E., Wang, Z., Fredrikson, M.: Consistent counterfactuals for deep models. In: Proceedings of the International Conference on Learning Representations (ICLR). OpenReview.net (2022)
3. Brughmans, D., Leyman, P., Martens, D.: Nice: an algorithm for nearest instance counterfactual explanations. arXiv v2 (2021). arxiv.org/abs/2104.07411
4. Dominguez-Olmedo, R., Karimi, A.H., Schölkopf, B.: On the adversarial robustness of causal algorithmic recourse. In: Proceedings of the 39th International Conference on Machine Learning (ICML), vol. 162, pp. 5324–5342 (2022)
5. Ferrario, A., Loi, M.: The robustness of counterfactual explanations over time. Access **10**, 82736–82750 (2022)
6. Guidotti, R.: Counterfactual explanations and how to find them: literature review and benchmarking. Data Min. Knowl. Disc., 1–55 (2022)
7. Guyomard, V., Fessant, F., Guyet, T.: VCNet: a self-explaining model for realistic counterfactual generation. In: Proceedings of the European Conference on Machine Learning and Principles and Practice of Knowledge Discovery in Databases (ECML/PKDD), pp. 437–453 (2022)
8. Laugel, T., Lesot, M.J., Marsala, C., Detyniecki, M.: Issues with post-hoc counterfactual explanations: a discussion. arXiv (2019). arxiv.org/abs/1906.04774
9. Maragno, D., Kurtz, J., Röber, T.E., Goedhart, R., Birbil, S.I., Hertog, D.D.: Finding regions of counterfactual explanations via robust optimization (2023). arxiv.org/abs/2301.11113
10. Mishra, S., Dutta, S., Long, J., Magazzeni, D.: A survey on the robustness of feature importance and counterfactual explanations. arXiv (v2) (2023). arxiv.org/abs/2111.00358
11. Mothilal, R.K., Sharma, A., Tan, C.: Explaining machine learning classifiers through diverse counterfactual explanations. In: Proceedings of the conference on Fairness, Accountability, and Transparency (FAccT), pp. 607–617 (2020)
12. de Oliveira, R.M.B., Martens, D.: A framework and benchmarking study for counterfactual generating methods on tabular data. Appl. Sci. **11**(16), 7274 (2021)
13. Pawelczyk, M., Bielawski, S., van den Heuvel, J., Richter, T., Kasneci, G.: CARLA: a python library to benchmark algorithmic recourse and counterfactual explanation algorithms. In: Conference on Neural Information Processing Systems (NeurIPS) - Track on Datasets and Benchmarks, p. 17 (2021)
14. Pawelczyk, M., Broelemann, K., Kasneci, G.: Learning model-agnostic counterfactual explanations for tabular data. In: Proceedings of The Web Conference (WWW 2020), pp. 3126–3132 (2020)
15. Pawelczyk, M., Datta, T., van-den Heuvel, J., Kasneci, G., Lakkaraju, H.: Probabilistically robust recourse: navigating the trade-offs between costs and robustness in algorithmic recourse. In: Proceedings of the International Conference on Learning Representations (ICLR). OpenReview.net (2023)
16. Poyiadzi, R., Sokol, K., Santos-Rodriguez, R., De Bie, T., Flach, P.: Face: feasible and actionable counterfactual explanations. In: Proceedings of the AAAI/ACM Conference on AI, Ethics, and Society, pp. 344–350 (2020)
17. Rawal, K., Kamar, E., Lakkaraju, H.: Algorithmic recourse in the wild: understanding the impact of data and model shifts. arXiv v3 (2020). arxiv.org/abs/2012.11788

18. Upadhyay, S., Joshi, S., Lakkaraju, H.: Towards robust and reliable algorithmic recourse. Adv. Neural Inf. Process. Syst. **34**, 16926–16937 (2021)
19. Ustun, B., Spangher, A., Liu, Y.: Actionable recourse in linear classification. In: Proceedings of the Conference on Fairness, Accountability, and Transparency (FAccT), pp. 10–19 (2019)
20. Van Looveren, A., Klaise, J.: Interpretable counterfactual explanations guided by prototypes. In: Proceedings of the European Conference on Machine Learning and Knowledge Discovery in Databases (ECML/PKDD), pp. 650–665 (2021)
21. Virgolin, M., Fracaros, S.: On the robustness of sparse counterfactual explanations to adverse perturbations. Artif. Intell. **316**, 103840 (2023)
22. Wachter, S., Mittelstadt, B.D., Russell, C.: Counterfactual explanations without opening the black box: automated decisions and the GDPR. Harvard J. Law Technol. **31**(2), 841–887 (2018)

Neural Models for Factual Inconsistency Classification with Explanations

Tathagata Raha[1], Mukund Choudhary[1], Abhinav Menon[1], Harshit Gupta[1], K. V. Aditya Srivatsa[1], Manish Gupta[1,2(✉)], and Vasudeva Varma[1]

[1] IIIT-Hyderabad, Hyderabad, India
{tathagata.raha,mukund.choudhary,abhinav.m,
harshit.g,k.v.aditya}@research.iiit.ac.in, vv@iiit.ac.in
[2] Microsoft, Hyderabad, India
gmanish@microsoft.com

Abstract. Factual consistency is one of the most important requirements when editing high quality documents. It is extremely important for automatic text generation systems like summarization, question answering, dialog modeling, and language modeling. Still, automated factual inconsistency detection is rather under-studied. Existing work has focused on (a) finding fake news keeping a knowledge base in context, or (b) detecting broad contradiction (as part of natural language inference literature). However, there has been no work on detecting and explaining types of factual inconsistencies in text, without any knowledge base in context. In this paper, we leverage existing work in linguistics to formally define five types of factual inconsistencies. Based on this categorization, we contribute a novel dataset, FICLE (Factual Inconsistency CLassification with Explanation), with ~8K samples where each sample consists of two sentences (claim and context) annotated with type and span of inconsistency. When the inconsistency relates to an entity type, it is labeled as well at two levels (coarse and fine-grained). Further, we leverage this dataset to train a pipeline of four neural models to predict inconsistency type with explanations, given a (claim, context) sentence pair. Explanations include inconsistent claim fact triple, inconsistent context span, inconsistent claim component, coarse and fine-grained inconsistent entity types. The proposed system first predicts inconsistent spans from claim and context; and then uses them to predict inconsistency types and inconsistent entity types (when inconsistency is due to entities). We experiment with multiple Transformer-based natural language classification as well as generative models, and find that DeBERTa performs the best. Our proposed methods provide a weighted F1 of ~87% for inconsistency type classification across the five classes. We make the code and dataset publicly available (https://github.com/blitzprecision/FICLE).

Keywords: deep learning · factual inconsistency classification · explainability · factual inconsistency explanations

D. Koutra et al. (Eds.): ECML PKDD 2023, LNAI 14171, pp. 410–427, 2023.
https://doi.org/10.1007/978-3-031-43418-1_25

1   Introduction

Although Transformer-based natural language generation models have been shown to be state-of-the-art for several applications like summarization, dialogue generation, question answering, table-to-text, and machine translation, they suffer from several drawbacks of which hallucinatory and inconsistent generation is the most critical [14]. Factual inconsistencies in generated text can lead to confusion and a lack of clarity, make the text appear unreliable and untrustworthy, and can create a sense of mistrust among readers. It can lead to inaccurate conclusions and interpretations, and diminishes the overall quality of the text. One approach to tackle this problem is to train robust neural language generation models which produce text with high fidelity and less hallucinations [14]. Another approach is to have human annotators post-check the generated text for inconsistencies. Checking all generated output manually is not scalable. Hence, automated factual inconsistency detection and explanations become crucial.

Claim	The invention of Lying is *only a book.*	
Context	The invention of Lying is *a 2009 American fantasy romantic comedy film* written and directed by Ricky Gervais and Matthew Robinson.	

Inconsistent Claim Fact Triple	Source	The invention of Lying
	Relation	is
	Target	*only a book*
Inconsistent Context Span		*a 2009 American fantasy romantic comedy film*
Inconsistent Claim Component		Target Head
Inconsistency Type		Taxonomic sisters (book vs film)
Coarse Inconsistent Entity-Type		entertainment
Fine-grained Inconsistent Entity-Type		entertainment_movie

Fig. 1. Factual Inconsistency Classification with Explanation (FICLE) Example: Inputs are claim and context. Outputs include inconsistency type and explanation (inconsistent claim fact triple, inconsistent context span, inconsistent claim component, coarse and fine-grained inconsistent entity types).

Accordingly, there have been several studies in the past which focus on detection of false or fake content. Fake content detection studies [8,31,35] typically verify facts in claims with respect to an existing knowledge base. However, keeping the knowledge base up-to-date (freshness and completeness) is difficult. Accordingly, there have been other studies in the natural language inference (or textual entailment) community [4,26,37] where the broad goal is to predict entailment, contradiction or neither. More than a decade back, De Marneffe et al. [9] proposed the problem of fine-grained contradiction detection, but (1) they proposed a tiny dataset with 131 examples, (2) they did not propose any learning method, and (3) they did not attempt explanations like localization of inconsistency spans in claim and context.

Hence, in this paper, we propose the novel problem of factual inconsistency classification with explanations (FICLE). Given a (claim, context) sentence pair, our goal is to predict inconsistency type and explanation (inconsistent claim fact triple, inconsistent context span, inconsistent claim component, coarse and fine-grained inconsistent entity types). Figure 1 shows an example of the FICLE task. Two recent studies are close to our work: e-SNLI [6] and TaxiNLI [15]. Unlike detailed structured explanation (including inconsistency localization spans in

Table 1. Comparison of FICLE with other datasets. #Samples indicates number of contradictory/inconsistent samples (and not the size of full dataset).

Dataset	#Samples	Explanations	#Classes	Inconsistency localized?
Contradiction [9]	131	No	10	No
FEVER [32]	43107	No	1	No
e-SNLI [6]	189702	Yes	1	Yes
TaxiNLI [15]	3014	No	15	No
LIAR-PLUS [1]	5669	Yes	3	No
FICLE (Ours)	8055	Yes	5	Yes

both claim and context) from our proposed system, e-SNLI [6] contains only an unstructured short sentence as an explanation. Unlike five types of inconsistencies detected along with explanations by our proposed system, TaxiNLI [15] provides a two-level categorization for the NLI task. Thus, TaxiNLI focuses on NLI and not on inconsistencies specifically. Table 1 shows a comparison of our dataset with other closely related datasets.

In this work, based on linguistic theories, we carefully devise a taxonomic categorization with five inconsistency types: simple, gradable, set-based, negation, taxonomic relations. First, we obtain English (claim, context) sentence pairs from the FEVER dataset [32] which have been labeled as contradiction. We get them manually labeled with inconsistency types and other explanations (as shown in Fig. 1 by four annotators. Overall, the dataset contains 8055 samples labeled with five inconsistency types, 20 coarse inconsistent entity types and 60 fine-grained inconsistent entity types, whenever applicable.

We leverage the contributed dataset to train a pipeline of four neural models to predict inconsistency type with explanations: M_1, M_2, M_3 and M_4. Given a (claim, context) sentence pair, M_1 predicts the inconsistent subject-relation-target fact triple $\langle S, R, T \rangle$ in the claim and also the inconsistent span in the context. M_2 uses M_1's outputs to predict the inconsistency type and the inconsistent component (subject, relation or target) from the claim. M_3 uses the inconsistent context-span and inconsistent claim component to predict a coarse inconsistent entity type. M_4 leverages both M_3's inputs and outputs to predict fine-grained inconsistent entity type. Overall, the intuition behind this pipeline design is to first predict inconsistent spans from claim and context; and then use them to predict inconsistency types and inconsistent entity types (when inconsistency is due to entities). Figure 3 shows the overall system architecture for FICLE.

We investigate effectiveness of multiple standard Transformer [34]-based natural language understanding (NLU) as well as natural language generation (NLG) models as architectures for models M_1, M_2, M_3 and M_4. Specifically, we experiment with models like BERT [10], RoBERTa [19] and DeBERTa [12] which are popular for NLU tasks. We also experiment with T5 [27] and BART [18] which are popular in the NLG community. DeBERTa seemed to outperform other models for most of the sub-tasks. Our results show that while inconsistency type classification is relatively easy, accurately detecting context span is still challenging.

Overall, in this work, we make the following main contributions (1) We propose a novel problem of factual inconsistency detection with explanations given a (claim, context) sentence pair. (2) We contribute a novel dataset, FICLE, manually annotated with inconsistency type and five other forms of explanations. We make the dataset publicly available[1]. (3) We experiment with standard Transformer-based NLU and NLG models and propose a baseline pipeline for the FICLE task. (4) Our proposed pipeline provides a weighted F1 of ~87% for inconsistency type classification; weighted F1 of ~86% and ~76% for coarse (20-class) and fine-grained (60-class) inconsistent entity-type prediction respectively; and an IoU of ~94% and ~65% for claim and context span detection respectively.

2   Related Work

Factual Inconsistency in Natural Language Generations: Popular natural language generation models have been found to generate hallucinatory and inconsistent text [14]. Krysinski et al. [16] and Cao et al. [7] found that around 30% of the summaries generated by state-of-the-art abstractive models were factually inconsistent. There are other summarization studies also which report factual inconsistency of generated summaries [22,23,25,36,39,41]. Similarly, several studies have pointed out semantic inaccuracy as a major problem with current natural language generation models for free-form text generation [5], data-to-text [11], question-answering [20], dialogue modeling [13,24], machine translation [40], and news generation [38]. Several statistical (like PARENT) and model-based metrics have been proposed to quantify the level of hallucination. Multiple data-related methods and modeling and inference methods have been proposed for mitigating hallucination [14], but their effectiveness is still limited. Hence, automated factual inconsistency detection is critical.

Natural Language Inference: Natural language inference (NLI) is the task of determining whether a hypothesis is true (entailment), false (contradiction), or undetermined (neutral) given a premise. NLI is a fundamental problem in natural language understanding and has many applications such as question answering, information extraction, and text summarization. Approaches used for NLI include earlier symbolic and statistical approaches to more recent deep learning approaches [3]. There are several datasets and benchmarks for evaluating NLI models, such as the Stanford Natural Language Inference (SNLI) Corpus [4], the Multi-Genre Natural Language Inference (MultiNLI) Corpus [37] and Adversarial NLI [26]. FEVER [32] is another dataset on a related problem of fact verification.

Recently there has been work on providing explanations along with the classification label for NLI. e-SNLI [6] provides a one-sentence explanation aiming to answer the question: "Why is a pair of sentences in a relation of entailment, neutrality, or contradiction?" Annotators were also asked to highlight the words that

---

[1] https://github.com/blitzprecision/FICLE.

they considered essential for the label. NILE [17] is a two stage model built on e-SNLI which first generates candidate explanations and then processes explanations to infer the task label. Thorne et al. [33] evaluate LIME [28] and Anchor explanations [29] to predict token annotations that explain the entailment relation in e-SNLI. LIAR-PLUS [1] contains political statements labeled as pants-fire, false, mostly-false, half-true, mostly-true, and true. The context and explanation is combined into a "extracted justification" paragraph in this dataset. Atanasova et al. [2] experiment with LIAR-PLUS dataset and find that jointly generating justification and predicting the class label together leads to best results.

There has also been work on detailed categorization beyond just the two classes: contradiction and entailment. Contradiction [9] is a tiny dataset with only 131 examples that provides a taxonomy of 10 contradiction types. Recently, TaxiNLI [15] dataset has been proposed with 15 classes for detailed categorization with the entailment and not the contradiction category. Continuing this line of work, in this paper, we contribute a new dataset, FICLE, which associates every (claim, context) sentence pair with (1) an inconsistency type (out of five) and (2) detailed explanations (inconsistent span in claim and context, inconsistent claim component, coarse and fine-grained inconsistent entity types).

3   Inconsistency Type Classification

Factual inconsistencies in text can occur because of a number of different sentence constructions, some overt and others that are complex to discover even manually. We design a taxonomy of five inconsistency types following non-synonymous lexical relations classified by Saeed [30, p. 66–70]. The book mentions the following kinds of antonyms: simple, gradable, reverses, converses and taxonomic sisters. To this taxonomy, we added two extra categories, negation and set-based, to capture the FICLE's complexity. Also, we expanded the definition of taxonomic sisters to more relations, and hence rename it to taxonomic relations. Further, since we did not find many examples of reverses and converses in our dataset, we merged them with the simple inconsistency category. Overall, our FICLE dataset contains these five different inconsistency types.

- Simple: A simple contradiction is a direct contradiction, where the negative of one implies the positive of the other in a pair like *pass vs. fail*. This also includes actions/processes that can be reversed or have a reverse direction, like *come vs. go* and *fill vs. empty*. Pairs with alternate viewpoints like *employer vs. employee* and *above vs. below* are also included in this category.
- Gradable: Gradable contradictions include adjectival and relative contradictions, where the positive of one, does not imply the negative of other in a pair like *hot vs. cold, least vs. most*, or periods of time etc.
- Taxonomic relations: We include three kinds of relations in this type: (a) Pairs at the same taxonomic level in the language like *red vs. blue* which are placed parallel to each other under the English color adjectives hierarchy. (b) When a pair has a more general word (*hypernym*) and another more specific word

which includes the meaning of the first word in the pair (*hyponym*) like *giraffe* (hypo) vs. *animal* (hyper). (c) Pairs with a part-whole relation like *nose vs. face* and *button vs shirt*.

- Negation: This includes inconsistencies arising out of presence of explicit negation morphemes (e.g. *not, except*) or a finite verb negating an action (e.g. *fail to do X, incapable of X-ing*) etc.
- Set-based: This includes inconsistent examples where an object contrasts with a list that it is not a part of (e.g. *cat* vs. *bee, ant, wasp*).

4   The FICLE Dataset

4.1   Dataset Curation and Pre-processing

Our FICLE dataset is derived from the FEVER dataset [32] using the following processing steps. FEVER (Fact Extraction and VERification) consists of 185,445 claims generated by altering sentences extracted from Wikipedia and subsequently verified without knowledge of the sentence they were derived from. Every sample in the FEVER dataset contains the claim sentence, evidence (or context) sentence from a Wikipedia URL, a type label ('supports', 'refutes' or 'not enough info'). Out of these, we leverage only the samples with 'refutes' label to build our dataset.

We propose a linguistically enriched dataset to help detect inconsistencies and explain them. To this end, the broad requirements are to locate where an inconsistency is present between a claim and a context, and to have a classification scheme for better explainability.

4.2   Annotation Details

To support detailed inconsistency explanations, we perform comprehensive annotations for each sample in the FICLE dataset. The annotations were done in two iterations. The first iteration focused on "syntactic oriented" annotations while the second iteration focused on "semantic oriented" annotations. The annotations were performed using the Label Studio annotation tool[2] by a group of four

Table 2. Inconsistent Claim Fact Triple, Context Span and Claim Component examples for the context sentence "Prime Minister Narendra Modi enthusiastically hoisted the Indian flag." Subject, relation and target in the claim are shown in bold, italics and underline respectively.

Inconsistent Claim	Inconsistent Context Span	Inconsistent Claim Component
Prime Minister Swami Vivekananda *enthusiastically hoisted* the Indian flag.	Narendra Modi	Subject-Head
President Narendra Modi *enthusiastically hoisted* the Indian flag.	Prime Minister	Subject-Modifier
Prime Minister Narendra Modi *enthusiastically lowered* the Indian flag.	hoisted	Relation-Head
Prime Minister Narendra Modi *halfheartedly hoisted* the Indian flag.	enthusiastically	Relation-Modifier
Prime Minister Narendra Modi *enthusiastically hoisted* the Indian culture.	flag	Target-Head
Prime Minister Narendra Modi *enthusiastically hoisted* the American flag.	Indian	Target-Modifier

---

[2] https://labelstud.io/.

Table 3. Inconsistency Type and Coarse/Fine-grained Inconsistent Entity Type examples. Inconsistent spans are marked in bold in both claim as well as context.

Claim	Context	Incon-sistency Type	Coarse Inconsistent Entity Type	Fine-grained Inconsistent Entity Type
Kong: Skull Island **is not a** reboot.	The film **is a** reboot of the King Kong franchise and serves as the second film in Legendary's MonsterVerse.	Negation	enter-tainment	brand
The Royal Tenenbaums only stars **Emma Stone**.	The film stars **Danny Glover, Gene Hackman, Anjelica Huston, Bill Murray, Gwyneth Paltrow, Ben Stiller, Luke Wilson, and Owen Wilson**.	Set Based	name	musician
Lindsay Lohan began her career as **an adult fashion model**.	Lohan began her career as a **child fashion model** when she was three, and was later featured on the soap opera Another World for a year when she was 10.	Simple	time	age
Karl Malone played the **shooting guard position**.	He is considered one of the best **power forwards** in NBA history.	Taxonomic Relation	profession	sport
The Divergent Series: Insurgent is based on the **third** book in the Divergent trilogy.	The Divergent Series: Insurgent is a 2015 American science fiction action film directed by Robert Schwentke, based on Insurgent, the **second** book in the Divergent trilogy by Veronica Roth.	Gradable	quantity	ordinal

annotators (two of which are also authors). The annotators are well versed in English and are Computer Science Bachelors students with a specialization in computational linguistics, in the age group of 20–22 years. Detailed annotation guidelines are in annotationGuidelines.pdf here (see footnote 1).

Syntactic Oriented Annotations: In this annotation stage, the judges labeled the following syntactic fields per sample. Table 2 shows examples of each of these fields. (1) Inconsistent Claim Fact Triple: A claim can contain multiple facts. The annotators identified the fact that is inconsistent with the context. Further, the annotators labeled the span of source (S), relation (R) and target (T) within the claim fact. Sometimes, e.g., in case of an intransitive verb, the target was empty. Further, for each of the S, R and T, the annotators also labeled head and modifier separately. The head indicates the main noun (for S and T) or the verb phrase (for R) while the modifier is phrase that serves to modify the meaning of the noun or the verb. (2) Inconsistent Context Span: A span marked in the context sentence which is inconsistent with the claim. (3) Inconsistent Claim Component: This can take six possible values depending on the part of the claim fact triple that is inconsistent with the context: Subject-Head, Subject-Modifier, Relation-Head, Relation-Modifier, Target-Head, Target-Modifier.

Semantic Oriented Annotations: In this annotation stage, the annotators labeled the following semantic fields per sample. Table 3 shows examples of each of these fields. (1) Inconsistency Type: Each sample is annotated with one of the five inconsistency types as discussed in Sect. 3. (2) Coarse Inconsistent Entity Type: When the inconsistency is because of an entity, the annotator also labeled one of the 20 coarse types for the entity causing the inconsistency. The types are action, animal, entertainment, gender, geography, identity, material, name, nationality, organization, others, politics, profession, quantity, reality, relationship, sentiment, sport, technology and time. (3) Fine-grained Inconsistent Entity Type: Further, when the inconsistency is because of an entity, the annotator also labeled one of the 60 fine-grained types for the entity causing the inconsistency.

For inconsistency entity type detection, the annotations were performed in two iterations. In the first iteration, the annotators were allowed to annotate the categories (both at coarse and fine-grained level) freely without any limited category set. This was performed on 500 samples. The annotators then discussed and de-duplicated the category names. Some rare categories were merged with frequent ones. This led to a list of 20 coarse and 60 fine-grained entity types (including "others"). In the second iteration, annotators were asked to choose one of these categories. We measured inter-annotator agreement on 500 samples. For source, relation, target and inconsistent context spans, the intersection over union (IoU) was found to be 0.91, 0.83, 0.85 and 0.76 respectively. Further, the Kappa score was found to be 0.78, 0.71 and 0.67 for the inconsistency type, coarse inconsistent entity type and fine-grained inconsistent entity type respectively.

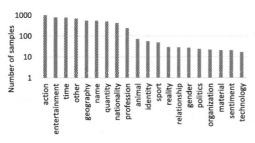

Fig. 2. Distribution of coarse inconsistent entity types in FICLE.

Table 4. Minimum, average, and maximum size (words) of various fields averaged across samples in FICLE dataset.

		Min	Avg	Max
	Claim	3	8.04	31
	Context	5	30.73	138
Incon. Claim	Source	1	2.29	9
	Relation	1	2.17	18
	Target	0	3.39	21
	Incon. Context-Span	1	5.11	94

4.3   FICLE Dataset Statistics

The FICLE dataset consists of 8055 samples in English with five inconsistency types. The distribution across the five types is as follows: Taxonomic Relations (4842), Negation (1630), Set Based (642), Gradable (526) and Simple

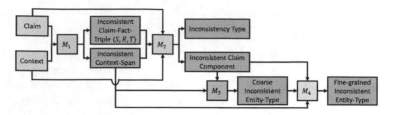

Fig. 3. FICLE: System Architecture

(415). There are six possible inconsistent claim components with distribution as follows: Target-Head (3960), Target-Modifier (1529), Relation-Head (951), Relation-Modifier (1534), Source-Head (45), Source-Modifier (36). The dataset contains 20 coarse inconsistent entity types as shown in Fig. 2. Further, these are sub-divided into 60 fine-grained entity types. Table 4 shows average sizes of various fields averaged across samples in the dataset. The dataset was divided into train, valid and test splits in the ratio of 80:10:10.

5   Neural Methods for Factual Inconsistency Classification with Explanations

We leverage the FICLE dataset to train models for factual inconsistency classification with explanations. Specifically, given the claim and context sentence, our system does predictions in the following stages: (A) Predict Inconsistent Claim Fact Triple (S,R,T) and Inconsistent Context Span, (B) Predict Inconsistency Type and Inconsistent Claim Component, (C) Predict Coarse and Fine-grained Inconsistent Entity Type. Overall, the system architecture consists of a pipeline of four neural models to predict inconsistency type with explanations: M_1, M_2, M_3 and M_4, and is illustrated in Fig. 3. We discuss details of the three stages and the pipeline in this section.

Model Architectures. We experiment with five pretrained models of which two are natural language generation (NLG) models. Specifically, we finetune Transformer [34] encoder based models like BERT [10], RoBERTa [19] and DeBERTa [12]. We also use two NLG models: BART [18] and T5 [27] which are popular in the NLG community.

BERT (Bidirectional Encoder Representations from Transformers) [10] essentially is a transformer encoder with 12 layers, 12 attention heads and 768 dimensions. We used the pre-trained model which has been trained on Books Corpus and Wikipedia using the MLM (masked language model) and the next sentence prediction (NSP) loss functions. RoBERTa [19] is a robustly optimized method for pretraining natural language processing (NLP) systems that improves on BERT. RoBERTa was trained with 160GB of text, trained for larger number of iterations up to 500K with batch sizes of 8K and a larger byte-pair encoding (BPE) vocabulary of 50K subword units, without NSP loss. DeBERTa [12] is trained using a special attention mechanism where content and position embeddings are disentangled. It also has an enhanced mask decoder which leverages absolute word positions effectively. BART [18] is a denoising autoencoder for pre-training sequence-to-sequence models. BART is trained by (1) corrupting text with an arbitrary noising function, and (2) learning a model to reconstruct the original text. T5 [27] is also a Transformer encoder-decoder model pretrained on Colossal Clean Crawled Corpus, and models all NLP tasks in generative form.

When encoding input or output for these models, we prepend various semantic units using special tokens like ⟨claim⟩, ⟨context⟩, ⟨source⟩, ⟨relation⟩, ⟨target⟩, ⟨contextSpan⟩, ⟨claimComponent⟩, ⟨type⟩, ⟨coarseEntityType⟩ and ⟨fineEntityType⟩. NLG models (BART and T5) generate the inconsistency type and all explanations, and are trained using cross entropy loss. For NLU models (BERT, RoBERTa, DeBERTa), we prepend input with a [CLS] token and use its semantic representation from the last layer with a dense layer to predict inconsistency type, inconsistent claim component, and entity types with categorical cross entropy loss. With NLU models, source, relation, target, and context span are predicted using start and end token classifiers (using cross entropy loss) as usually done in the question answering literature [10].

Stage A: Predict Inconsistent Spans
In this stage, we first train models to predict source, relation and target by passing the claim sentence as input to the models. Further, to predict inconsistent context span, we experiment with four different methods as follows. (1) Structure-ignorant: The input is claim and context sentence. The aim is to directly predict inconsistent context span ignoring the "source, relation, target" structure of the claim. (2) Two-step: First step takes claim and context sentences as input, and predicts source, relation and target (SRT). Second step augments source, relation and target to the input along with claim and context, and predicts the inconsistent context span. (3) Multi-task: The input is claim and context sentence. The goal is to jointly predict source, relation, target and inconsistent context span. (4) Oracle-structure: The input is claim and context sentence, and ground truth (source, relation and target). These are all used together to predict inconsistent context span.

Stage B: Predict Inconsistency Type and Claim Component
This stage assumes that (1) SRT from claim and (2) inconsistent context span have already been predicted. Thus, in this stage, the input is claim, context, predicted SRT and predicted inconsistent context span. Using these inputs, to predict inconsistency type and inconsistent claim component, we experiment with three different methods as follows. (1) Individual: Predict inconsistency type and inconsistent claim component separately. (2) Two-step: First step predicts inconsistent claim component. Second step augments the predicted inconsistent claim component to the input, and predicts inconsistency type. (3) Multi-task: Jointly predict inconsistency type and inconsistent claim component in a multi-task learning setup.

Stage C: Predict Inconsistent Entity Types

To find inconsistent entity types, we build several models each of which take two main inputs: inconsistent context span and the span from the claim corresponding to the inconsistent claim component. We experiment with the following different models. (1) Individual: Predict coarse and fine-grained inconsistent entity type separately. (2) Two-step: First step predicts coarse inconsistent entity type. Second step augments the predicted coarse inconsistent entity type to the input, and predicts fine-grained type.

Further, we also attempt to leverage semantics from entity class names. Hence, we use the NLU models (BERT, RoBERTa, DeBERTa) to obtain embeddings for entity class names, and train NLU models to predict the class name which is most similar to semantic representation (of the [CLS] token) of the input. We use cosine embedding loss to train these models. Specifically, using class (i.e., entity type) embeddings, we train the following models. Note that we cannot train NLG models using class embeddings; thus we perform this experiment using NLU models only. (1) Individual Embedding: Predict coarse and fine-grained inconsistent entity type separately using entity type embeddings. (2) Two-step Embedding: First step predicts coarse inconsistent entity type using class embeddings. Second step augments the predicted coarse inconsistent entity type to the input, and predicts fine-grained type using class embeddings. (3) Two-step Mix: First step predicts coarse inconsistent entity type using class embeddings. Second step augments the predicted coarse inconsistent entity type to the input, and predicts fine-grained type using typical multi-class classification without class embeddings.

After experimenting with various model choices for the three stages described in this section, we find that the configuration described in Fig. 3 provides best results. We also attempted other designs like (1) predicting all outputs (inconsistency type and all explanations) jointly as a 6-task setting using just claim and context as input, (2) identifying claim component only as S, R or T rather than heads versus modifiers. However, these alternate designs did not lead to better results.

6   Experiments and Results

For prediction of spans like source, relation, target, and inconsistent context span, we use exact match (EM) and intersection over union (IoU) metrics. EM is a number from 0 to 1 that specifies the amount of overlap between the predicted and ground truth span in terms of tokens. If the characters of the model's prediction exactly match the characters of ground truth span, EM = 1, otherwise EM = 0. Similarly, IoU measures intersection over union in terms of tokens. For classification tasks like inconsistency type prediction as well as coarse and fine-grained inconsistent entity type prediction, we use metrics like accuracy and weighted F1.

Since factual inconsistency classification is a novel task, there are no existing baseline methods to compare with.

Table 5. Source, Relation and Target Prediction from Claim Sentence

Model	Exact Match			IoU		
	Source	Relation	Target	Source	Relation	Target
BERT	0.919	0.840	**0.877**	0.934	0.876	**0.895**
RoBERTa	0.921	**0.865**	0.871	0.936	0.883	0.885
DeBERTa	0.918	0.857	0.864	0.932	0.874	0.893
BART	0.981	0.786	0.741	0.986	0.873	0.842
T5	**0.983**	0.816	0.765	**0.988**	**0.945**	0.894

Table 6. Inconsistent Context Span Prediction

Model	Exact Match			IoU		
	Structure-ignorant	Two-step	Oracle-structure	Structure-ignorant	Two-step	Oracle-structure
BERT	0.483	0.499	0.519	0.561	0.541	0.589
RoBERTa	0.542	0.534	0.545	0.589	0.584	0.632
DeBERTa	0.538	0.540	**0.569**	0.591	0.587	**0.637**
BART	0.427	0.292	0.361	0.533	0.404	0.486
T5	0.396	0.301	0.352	0.517	0.416	0.499

Table 7. Joint Prediction of Source, Relation and Target Prediction from Claim Sentence and Inconsistent Context Span using Multi-Task Setting

Model	Exact Match				IoU			
	Source	Relation	Target	Context Span	Source	Relation	Target	Context Span
BERT	0.769	0.665	0.752	0.524	0.801	0.708	0.804	0.566
RoBERTa	0.759	0.686	0.780	0.572	0.828	0.745	0.836	0.617
DeBERTa	0.788	0.704	0.819	**0.604**	0.843	0.768	0.844	**0.650**
BART	0.973	**0.816**	**0.836**	0.501	0.979	**0.874**	**0.895**	0.549
T5	**0.981**	0.764	0.717	0.570	**0.988**	0.870	0.842	0.602

Source, Relation, Target and Inconsistent Context Span Prediction: Table 5 shows results for source, relation and target prediction from claim sentences. The table shows that T5 works best except for prediction of relation and target using the exact match metric. Further, Table 6 shows that surprisingly structure ignorant method is slightly better than the two-step method. Oracle method with DeBERTa expectedly is the best. NLG models (BART and T5) perform much worse compared to NLU models for context span prediction. Lastly, we show results of jointly predicting source, relation, target and inconsistent context span in Table 7. The table shows while T5 and BART are better at predicting source, relation and target, DeBERTa is a clear winner in predicting the inconsistent context span.

Table 8. Inconsistency Type Prediction

Model	Accuracy			Weighted F1		
	Individual	Two-step	Multi-task	Individual	Two-step	Multi-task
BERT	0.84	0.84	0.84	0.86	0.86	0.86
RoBERTa	0.85	0.85	0.86	0.86	0.86	**0.87**
DeBERTa	0.86	0.85	**0.87**	0.86	**0.87**	**0.87**
BART	0.57	0.60	0.73	0.59	0.64	0.74
T5	0.53	0.61	0.74	0.58	0.66	0.74

Table 9. Inconsistent Claim Component Prediction (6-class classification)

Model	Accuracy		Weighted F1	
	Individual	Multi-task	Individual	Multi-task
BERT	0.83	0.88	0.83	0.88
RoBERTa	0.85	**0.89**	0.85	**0.89**
DeBERTa	0.88	**0.89**	**0.89**	**0.89**
BART	0.80	0.75	0.81	0.76
T5	0.81	0.75	0.81	0.75

Table 10. Coarse Inconsistent Entity Type Prediction. Note that embedding based methods don't work with NLG models.

Model	Accuracy		Weighted F1	
	Individual	Individual Embedding	Individual	Individual Embedding
BERT	0.82	0.84	0.78	0.84
RoBERTa	0.83	0.86	0.80	0.85
DeBERTa	**0.85**	**0.87**	**0.81**	**0.86**
BART	0.73	-	0.71	-
T5	0.74	-	0.73	-

Inconsistency Type and Inconsistent Claim Component Prediction: Tables 8 and 9 show the results for the inconsistency type and inconsistent claim component prediction. Note that the two problems are 5-class and 6-class classification respectively. We observe that joint multi-task model outperforms the other two methods. Also, DeBERTa is the best model across all settings. For this best model, the F1 scores for the inconsistency types are as follows: Taxonomic Relations (0.92), Negation (0.86), Set Based (0.65), Gradable (0.78) and Simple (0.81).

Table 11. Accuracy/Weighted F1 for Fine-grained Inconsistent Entity Type Prediction. Note that embedding based methods do not work with NLG models.

Model	Individual	Two-step	Individual Embedding	Two-step Embedding	Two-step Mix
BERT	0.65/0.59	0.74/0.71	0.64/0.62	0.72/0.70	0.75/0.71
RoBERTa	0.69/0.65	0.75/0.73	0.72/0.68	**0.76/0.73**	0.76/0.75
DeBERTa	**0.70/0.67**	**0.77/0.74**	**0.73/0.70**	**0.76/0.73**	**0.78/0.76**
BART	0.50/0.44	0.64/0.59	-	-	-
T5	0.56/0.48	0.67/0.62	-	-	-

Table 12. Confusion matrix for inconsistency type prediction. We observe a high correlation between actual and predicted values, indicating our model is effective.

		Predicted				
		Taxonomic Relations	Negation	Set Based	Gradable	Simple
Actual	Taxonomic Relations	**456**	16	4	17	9
	Negation	11	**123**	3	0	4
	Set Based	17	4	**22**	1	1
	Gradable	16	1	2	**51**	0
	Simple	6	2	2	2	**36**

Inconsistent Entity Type Prediction: Tables 10 and 11 show accuracy and weighted F1 for coarse and fine-grained inconsistent entity type prediction respectively. We make the following observations from these tables: (1) DeBERTa outperforms all other models for both the predictions. (2) For coarse inconsistent entity type prediction, the embedding based approach works better than the typical classification approach. This is because there are rich semantics in the entity class names that are effectively leveraged by the embedding based approach. (3) For fine-grained inconsistent entity type prediction, two-step method is better than individual method both with and without embeddings. (4) The two-step mix method where we use embeddings based method to predict coarse inconsistent entity type and then usual 60-class classification for fine-grained types performs the best.

Qualitative Analysis To further understand where our model goes wrong, we show the confusion matrix for inconsistency type prediction for our best model in Table 12. We observe that the model labels many set-based examples as 'taxonomic relations' leading to poor F1 for the set-based class. In general most of the confusion is between 'taxonomic relations' and other classes.

Amongst the coarse entity types, we found the F1 to be highest for time, action, quantity, nationality and geography entity types, and lowest for animal, relationship, gender, sentiment and technology entity types.

Further, for inconsistency spans in the context, we observe that the average length of accurate predictions (3.16) is much smaller than inaccurate predictions

(8.54), comparing the lengths of ground truth spans. Further, for inaccurate predictions, we observe that as the length of the inconsistency span increases, the coverage of ground truth tokens by the predicted tokens, decreases on an average. Further, we categorized inaccurate span predictions into 4 buckets (additive, reordered, changed and subtractive). Additive implies more terms compared to ground truth, reordered means same terms but reordered, changed means some new terms were generated by the model, and subtractive means misses out on terms compared to ground truth. We found that ∼91 were of subtractive type, indicating that our inconsistency span predictor model is too terse and can be improved by reducing sampling probability for end of sequence token.

Hyper-parameters for Reproducibility: The experiments were run on a machine with four GEFORCE RTX 2080 Ti GPUs. We used a batch size of 16 and the AdamW optimizer [21] and trained for 5 epochs for all models. We used the following models: bert-base-uncased, roberta-base, microsoft/deberta-base, facebook/bart-base, and t5-small. Learning rate was set to 1e-4 for BART and T5, and to 1e-5 for other models. More details are available in the code[1].

7   Conclusion and Future Work

In this paper, we investigated the problem of detecting and explaining types of factual inconsistencies in text. We contributed a new dataset, FICLE, with ∼8K samples with detailed inconsistency labels for (claim, context) pairs. We experimented with multiple natural language understanding and generation models towards the problem. We found that a pipeline of four models which predict inconsistency spans in claim and context followed by inconsistency type prediction and finally inconsistent entity type prediction works the best. Also, we observed that DeBERTa led to the best results. In the future, we plan to extend this work to multi-lingual scenarios. We also plan to extend this work to perform inconsistency detection and localization across multiple sentences given a paragraph.

Ethical Statement. In this work, we derived a dataset from FEVER dataset[3]. Data annotations in FEVER incorporate material from Wikipedia, which is licensed pursuant to the Wikipedia Copyright Policy. These annotations are made available under the license terms described on the applicable Wikipedia article pages, or, where Wikipedia license terms are unavailable, under the Creative Commons Attribution-ShareAlike License (version 3.0), available at this link: http://creativecommons.org/licenses/by-sa/3.0/. Thus, we made use of the dataset in accordance with its appropriate usage terms.

The FICLE dataset does not contain any personally identifiable information. Details of the manual annotations are explained in Sect. 4 as well as in annotationGuidelines.pdf at https://github.com/blitzprecision/FICLE.

---

[3] https://fever.ai/dataset/fever.html.

References

1. Alhindi, T., Petridis, S., Muresan, S.: Where is your evidence: improving fact-checking by justification modeling. In: Proceedings of the First Workshop on Fact Extraction and Verification (FEVER), pp. 85–90 (2018)
2. Atanasova, P., Simonsen, J.G., Lioma, C., Augenstein, I.: Generating fact checking explanations. In: Proceedings of the 58th Annual Meeting of the Association for Computational Linguistics, pp. 7352–7364 (2020)
3. Bowman, S.R., Angeli, G., Potts, C., Manning, C.D.: A large annotated corpus for learning natural language inference. In: Conference on Empirical Methods in Natural Language Processing, EMNLP 2015, pp. 632–642. Association for Computational Linguistics (ACL) (2015)
4. Bowman, S.R., Angeli, G., Potts, C., Manning, C.D.: A large, annotated corpus for learning natural language inference (2015). Preprint at arXiv:1508.05326. Accessed 21 Jun 2021
5. Brown, T., et al.: Language models are few-shot learners. Adv. Neural. Inf. Process. Syst. **33**, 1877–1901 (2020)
6. Camburu, O.M., Rocktäschel, T., Lukasiewicz, T., Blunsom, P.: e-SNLI: natural language inference with natural language explanations. Adv. Neural. Inf. Process. Syst. **31**, 9539–9549 (2018)
7. Cao, Z., Wei, F., Li, W., Li, S.: Faithful to the original: fact aware neural abstractive summarization. In: Proceedings of the AAAI Conference on Artificial Intelligence, vol. 32 (2018)
8. Ciampaglia, G.L., Shiralkar, P., Rocha, L.M., Bollen, J., Menczer, F., Flammini, A.: Computational fact checking from knowledge networks. PLoS ONE **10**(6), e0128193 (2015)
9. De Marneffe, M.C., Rafferty, A.N., Manning, C.D.: Finding contradictions in text. In: Proceedings of ACL-08: HLT, pp. 1039–1047 (2008)
10. Devlin, J., Chang, M., Lee, K., Toutanova, K.: BERT: pre-training of deep bidirectional transformers for language understanding. arXiv preprint arXiv:1810.04805 (2018)
11. Dušek, O., Kasner, Z.: Evaluating semantic accuracy of data-to-text generation with natural language inference. In: Proceedings of the 13th International Conference on Natural Language Generation, pp. 131–137 (2020)
12. He, P., Liu, X., Gao, J., Chen, W.: DEBERTa: decoding-enhanced BERT with disentangled attention. arXiv preprint arXiv:2006.03654 (2020)
13. Honovich, O., Choshen, L., Aharoni, R., Neeman, E., Szpektor, I., Abend, O.: q^2: evaluating factual consistency in knowledge-grounded dialogues via question generation and question answering. arXiv preprint arXiv:2104.08202 (2021)
14. Ji, Z., et al.: Survey of hallucination in natural language generation. ACM Computing Surveys p, To appear (2022)
15. Joshi, P., Aditya, S., Sathe, A., Choudhury, M.: TaxiNLI: taking a ride up the NLU hill. In: Proceedings of the 24th Conference on Computational Natural Language Learning, pp. 41–55 (2020)
16. Kryściński, W., Keskar, N.S., McCann, B., Xiong, C., Socher, R.: Neural text summarization: a critical evaluation. In: Proceedings of the 2019 Conference on Empirical Methods in Natural Language Processing and the 9th International Joint Conference on Natural Language Processing (EMNLP-IJCNLP), pp. 540–551 (2019)

17. Kumar, S., Talukdar, P.: NILE: natural language inference with faithful natural language explanations. In: Proceedings of the 58th Annual Meeting of the Association for Computational Linguistics, pp. 8730–8742 (2020)

18. Lewis, M., et al.: BART: denoising sequence-to-sequence pre-training for natural language generation, translation, and comprehension. In: Proceedings of the 58th Annual Meeting of the Association for Computational Linguistics, pp. 7871–7880 (2020)

19. Liu, Y., et al.: RoBERTa: a robustly optimized BERT pretraining approach. arXiv preprint arXiv:1907.11692 (2019)

20. Longpre, S., Perisetla, K., Chen, A., Ramesh, N., DuBois, C., Singh, S.: Entity-based knowledge conflicts in question answering. In: Proceedings of the 2021 Conference on Empirical Methods in Natural Language Processing, pp. 7052–7063 (2021)

21. Loshchilov, I., Hutter, F.: Decoupled weight decay regularization. arXiv preprint arXiv:1711.05101 (2017)

22. Mao, Y., Ren, X., Ji, H., Han, J.: Constrained abstractive summarization: preserving factual consistency with constrained generation. arXiv preprint arXiv:2010.12723 (2020)

23. Maynez, J., Narayan, S., Bohnet, B., McDonald, R.: On faithfulness and factuality in abstractive summarization. In: Proceedings of the 58th Annual Meeting of the Association for Computational Linguistics, pp. 1906–1919 (2020)

24. Mesgar, M., Simpson, E., Gurevych, I.: Improving factual consistency between a response and persona facts. In: Proceedings of the 16th Conference of the European Chapter of the Association for Computational Linguistics: Main Volume, pp. 549–562 (2021)

25. Nan, F., et al.: Entity-level factual consistency of abstractive text summarization. In: Proceedings of the 16th Conference of the European Chapter of the Association for Computational Linguistics: Main Volume, pp. 2727–2733 (2021)

26. Nie, Y., Williams, A., Dinan, E., Bansal, M., Weston, J., Kiela, D.: Adversarial NLI: a new benchmark for natural language understanding. In: Proceedings of the 58th Annual Meeting of the Association for Computational Linguistics, pp. 4885–4901 (2020)

27. Raffel, C., et al.: Exploring the limits of transfer learning with a unified text-to-text transformer. J. Mach. Learn. Res. **21**(1), 5485–5551 (2020)

28. Ribeiro, M.T., Singh, S., Guestrin, C.: Why should i trust you? explaining the predictions of any classifier. In: Proceedings of the 22nd ACM SIGKDD International Conference on Knowledge Discovery and Data Mining, pp. 1135–1144 (2016)

29. Ribeiro, M.T., Singh, S., Guestrin, C.: Anchors: high-precision model-agnostic explanations. In: Proceedings of the AAAI Conference on Artificial Intelligence, vol. 32 (2018)

30. Saeed, J.: Semantics. Wiley, Introducing Linguistics (2011)

31. Shi, B., Weninger, T.: Discriminative predicate path mining for fact checking in knowledge graphs. Knowl.-Based Syst. **104**, 123–133 (2016)

32. Thorne, J., Vlachos, A., Christodoulopoulos, C., Mittal, A.: Fever: a large-scale dataset for fact extraction and verification. In: Proceedings of the 2018 Conference of the North American Chapter of the Association for Computational Linguistics: Human Language Technologies, Volume 1 (Long Papers), pp. 809–819 (2018)

33. Thorne, J., Vlachos, A., Christodoulopoulos, C., Mittal, A.: Generating token-level explanations for natural language inference. In: Proceedings of the 2019 Conference of the North American Chapter of the Association for Computational Linguistics:

Human Language Technologies, Volume 1 (Long and Short Papers), pp. 963–969 (2019)

34. Vaswani, A., et al.: Attention is all you need. In: NIPS, pp. 5998–6008 (2017)
35. Vedula, N., Parthasarathy, S.: FACE-KEG: fact checking explained using knowledge graphs. In: Proceedings of the 14th ACM International Conference on Web Search and Data Mining, pp. 526–534 (2021)
36. Wang, A., Cho, K., Lewis, M.: Asking and answering questions to evaluate the factual consistency of summaries. In: Proceedings of the 58th Annual Meeting of the Association for Computational Linguistics, pp. 5008–5020 (2020)
37. Williams, A., Nangia, N., Bowman, S.: A broad-coverage challenge corpus for sentence understanding through inference. In: Proceedings of the 2018 Conference of the North American Chapter of the Association for Computational Linguistics: Human Language Technologies, Volume 1 (Long Papers), pp. 1112–1122. Association for Computational Linguistics, New Orleans, Louisiana (2018). https://doi.org/10.18653/v1/N18-1101, www.aclanthology.org/N18-1101
38. Zellers, R., et al.: Defending against neural fake news. In: Advances in Neural Information Processing Systems, vol. 32 (2019)
39. Zhang, S., Niu, J., Wei, C.: Fine-grained factual consistency assessment for abstractive summarization models. In: Proceedings of the 2021 Conference on Empirical Methods in Natural Language Processing, pp. 107–116 (2021)
40. Zhou, C., Neubig, G., Gu, J., Diab, M., Guzmán, F., Zettlemoyer, L., Ghazvininejad, M.: Detecting hallucinated content in conditional neural sequence generation. In: Findings of the Association for Computational Linguistics: ACL-IJCNLP 2021, pp. 1393–1404 (2021)
41. Zhu, C., et al.: Enhancing factual consistency of abstractive summarization. In: Proceedings of the 2021 Conference of the North American Chapter of the Association for Computational Linguistics: Human Language Technologies, pp. 718–733 (2021)

iSAGE: An Incremental Version of SAGE for Online Explanation on Data Streams

Maximilian Muschalik[1(✉)] [ID], Fabian Fumagalli[2] [ID], Barbara Hammer[2] [ID], and Eyke Hüllermeier[1] [ID]

[1] LMU Munich, MCML Munich, Geschwister-Scholl-Platz 1, Munich, Germany
maximilian.muschalik@ifi.lmu.de
[2] Bielefeld University, CITEC, Inspiration 1, Bielefeld, Germany

Abstract. Existing methods for explainable artificial intelligence (XAI), including popular feature importance measures such as SAGE, are mostly restricted to the batch learning scenario. However, machine learning is often applied in dynamic environments, where data arrives continuously and learning must be done in an online manner. Therefore, we propose iSAGE, a time- and memory-efficient incrementalization of SAGE, which is able to react to changes in the model as well as to drift in the data-generating process. We further provide efficient feature removal methods that break (interventional) and retain (observational) feature dependencies. Moreover, we formally analyze our explanation method to show that iSAGE adheres to similar theoretical properties as SAGE. Finally, we evaluate our approach in a thorough experimental analysis based on well-established data sets and data streams with concept drift.

1 Introduction

If machine learning is used for high-stake decision-making, e.g., in healthcare [47] or energy consumption analysis [21], models learned on data should be transparent and explainable. However, as the best performing models are often opaque in nature, this is typically not the case. The field of explainable artificial intelligence (XAI) addresses this problem by developing methods to uncover the inner working of black box models and to make the input-output relationships represented by such models more understandable [2]. Notably, this includes *global feature importance* (global FI) methods, which quantify the influence of individual input features on the model predictions, and seek to rank the features in terms of their importance.

So far, XAI has mainly focused on static learning scenarios, where a single model is learned from data in a batch mode. However, in modern machine learning applications such as online credit risk scoring for financial services [12], intrusion detection in networks [3], or sensor network analysis [4,15], data is not static but coming in the form of a continuously evolving stream of data.

M. Muschalik and F. Fumagalli—Equal contribution.

D. Koutra et al. (Eds.): ECML PKDD 2023, LNAI 14171, pp. 428–445, 2023.
https://doi.org/10.1007/978-3-031-43418-1_26

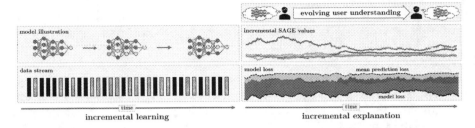

Fig. 1. An incremental model is fitted on a data stream. Incrementally explaining this model with iSAGE efficiently distributes the FI scores according to the model's loss evolving the user understanding of the model over time.

In applications of that kind, online algorithms are needed for learning in an incremental mode, processing data in a sequential manner one by one. Incremental learning should not only be time- and memory-efficient, but must also account for possible changes in the underlying data distribution, which is referred to as *concept drift*. Such drift may occur in different forms and for different reasons, e.g., as a change of energy consumption patterns or hospital admission criteria due to pandemic-induced lockdowns [16].

In dynamic scenarios, where models are constantly evolving and reacting to their changing environment, static explanations do no longer suffice. To effectively monitor dynamic models, explanations need to be updated in real time, keeping pace with the evolving models. As illustrated in Fig. 1, in this work, we compute global FI in an incremental manner, thereby also addressing the challenge of drifting data distributions, where batch methods are likely to yield wrong explanations (cf. Figure 7 in Appendix C).

Providing an incremental global FI method comes with various challenges, not only conceptually and algorithmically, but also computationally, especially because the computation of many FI measures is already prohibitive in the batch setting.

Contribution. We take a first step towards efficient explanations for changing models on data streams and contribute:

- *iSAGE*; a model-agnostic global FI algorithm that provides time- and memory- efficient incremental estimates of SAGE values and is able to react to changes in the model and concept drift.
- *interventional and observational iSAGE*; two conceptual approaches to define SAGE values that extend on the existing discussion of appropriate feature removal techniques with an efficient incremental algorithm.
- *open source implementation*; a well-tested and general implementation of our algorithms that integrates into the *River* [38] Python framework.[1]

---

[1] iSAGE is implemented in iXAI at https://github.com/mmschlk/iXAI.

Related Work. Global FI is an active part of XAI research, and various methods have been proposed [13]. Model-specific methods were developed based on the magnitude of weights for linear models and neural networks (NNs) [23,28], as well as split heuristics for tree-based models [25]. Another common approach to global FI is to aggregate local explanations, such as model-agnostic LIME [42] and SHAP [36] or NN specific methods [6,44–46,51]. Permutation Feature Importance (PFI) [7] is a well-established model-agnostic, global FI method with various extensions [8,33,37]. SAGE is based on the Shapley value [43], similar to SHAP [36] and LossSHAP [35] and overcomes computational limitations of aggregating local SHAP explanations. Retricting a model to compute FI is done either by retaining (*observational*) or breaking (*interventional*) feature dependencies, where it was shown that both methods generate different explanations and the choice should depend on the application [1,11,19].

Traditionally, XAI focuses on the batch learning scenario. However, recently more methods that natively support incremental, dynamic learning environments are proposed. For instance, online feature selection methods compute FI periodically [5,50]. Haug et al. [26] propose a concept drift detection algorithm based on clusterings and changes in SHAP's base value. A model-specific approach for tree-based models is measuring the mean decrease in impurity (MDI) [9,22]. In the notion of explaining change [39], iPFI [20] is a related model-agnostic approach that computes the traditional PFI [7] in an incremental manner. To efficiently restrict the model [14], we rely on geometric sampling [20] (interventional) and a combination of the conditional subgroup approach [37] and the TreeSHAP [35] methodology (observational).

Existing online FI methods are either model-specific or interpretation of the resulting feature importance scores is unintuitive, emphasizing the need for incremental variants of Shapley-based explanations, such as SAGE.

2   Shapley Additive Global Importance (SAGE)

Many feature importance techniques have been proposed in recent years [14], where each method allows to assess an importance ranking of the features. However, interpreting the exact scores and quantifying the difference between the importance of features remains unintuitive in many cases. Shapley-based explanations have attracted a lot of attention due to their unique mathematical properties, in particular the efficiency condition that ensures that the sum of these values over all features equals a specified model property, referred to as *model behavior* [14]. SHapley Additive Global Importance (SAGE) [13] is a well-known Shapley-based explanation technique that quantifies global FI as the contribution of individual features to the model's loss. SAGE is further a *model-agnostic* method that only relies on model evaluations and does not make any assumption about the inherent structure. In the following, we distinguish between the SAGE values ϕ, a statistical concept to define Shapley-based global FI, and the SAGE estimator $\hat{\phi}^{\text{SAGE}}$, an efficient approximator of the SAGE values. For a model $f : \mathcal{X} \to \mathcal{Y}$, the SAGE values $\phi(i)$ for every feature $i \in D$ are constructed, such that the sum is equal to the expected improvement in loss over using the mean prediction $\bar{y} := \mathbb{E}_X[f(X)]$, i.e.

$$\nu(D) := \underbrace{\mathbb{E}_Y\left[\ell(\bar{y}, Y)\right]}_{\text{no feature information}} - \underbrace{\mathbb{E}_{(X,Y)}\left[\ell(f(X), Y)\right]}_{\text{with feature information}} = \sum_{i \in D} \phi(i),$$

where ℓ is a suitable loss (e.g., cross-entropy for classification, absolute error for regression, or kendall tau for rankings) and (X, Y) refers to the joint distribution of the data-generating random variables X and Y. The quantity $\nu(D)$ is viewed as the improvement in loss, if *all features* D are known to the model. It is then also natural to define $\nu(\emptyset) = 0$, i.e. the improvement in loss is expected to be zero, if *no features* are known to the model. To quantify the importance of single features, the expected improvement in loss, if only a subset $S \subset D$ of features is known, is introduced. To restrict this loss, the model is restricted to a subset of features $S \subset D$, by randomizing the features in $D \setminus S$. In the following, we write $f(x) = f(x^{(S)}, x^{(\bar{S})})$ to distinguish the features of x in S, $x^{(S)}$, and the features of x in $\bar{S} := D \setminus S$, $x^{(\bar{S})}$. To randomize the features in $\bar{S}$, we introduce the notation $f(x, S)$ with a set $S \subset D$ and the *observational* approach [13,36]

$$f^{\text{obs}}(x, S) := \mathbb{E}\left[f(x^{(S)}, X^{(\bar{S})}) \mid X^{(S)} = x^{(S)}\right]$$

and the *interventional* approach [11,30]

$$f^{\text{int}}(x, S) := \mathbb{E}\left[f(x^{(S)}, X^{(\bar{S})})\right].$$

The essential difference between the two approaches is that f^{int} breaks the dependence between the features in S and $\bar{S}$. The observational and interventional approach are also referred to as *on-manifold* and *off-manifold* explanation [19], or *conditional* and *marginal* expectation [30], respectively. While f^{int} is easy to approximate using the marginal distribution of the observed data points, approaches using f^{obs} rely on further assumptions on the conditional distribution [1,36]. SAGE values are introduced using the observational approach but the SAGE algorithm relies on the interventional approach for approximation, i.e. assuming feature independence [13]. It was shown that both approaches yield significantly different explanations, if features are correlated [11,19,30]. We thus propose an algorithm for each approach and leave the choice of explanation to the practitioner, as it was concluded that this choice depends on the application scenario [11]. We define the restricted improvement in loss as

$$\nu(S) := \mathbb{E}_Y[\ell(\bar{y}, Y)] - \mathbb{E}_{(X,Y)}\left[\ell(f(X, S), Y)\right] \text{ for } f \in \{f^{\text{int}}, f^{\text{obs}}\}.$$

Then, $\nu : \mathcal{P}(D) \to \mathbb{R}$ defines a function over the powerset $\mathcal{P}(D)$. The SAGE values [13] are then defined as the Shapley value [43] of ν, i.e. the *fair* attribution of $\nu(D)$ to individual features given its axiomatic propoerties.

Definition 1 (SAGE values [13]). *The SAGE values are defined as*

$$\phi(i) := \sum_{S \subset D \setminus \{i\}} \frac{1}{d} \binom{d-1}{|S|}^{-1} [\nu(S \cup \{i\}) - \nu(S)].$$

We refer to the interventional *and* observational *SAGE values, if* f^{int} *and* f^{obs} *are used for* f *in* ν, *respectively.*

Due to the exponential complexity of the Shapley value, the SAGE estimator uses a Monte-Carlo approximation [10] based on the representation

$$\phi(i) = \frac{1}{d!} \sum_{\pi \in \mathfrak{S}_D} \nu(u_i^+(\pi)) - \nu(u_i^-(\pi)) = \mathbb{E}_{\pi \sim \text{unif}(\mathfrak{S}_D)}[\nu(u_i^+(\pi)) - \nu(u_i^-(\pi))],$$

where $\mathfrak{S}_D$ is the set of permutations over D and $u_i^+(\pi)$ and $u_i^-(\pi)$ refer to the set of indices preceding feature i in π, in- and exclusively i. Plugging in the definition of ν and using Monte-Carlo estimation, the SAGE estimator is constructed.

Definition 2 (SAGE Estimator [13]**).** *Given data points* $(x_n, y_n)_{n=1,\ldots,N}$ *and permutations* $(\pi)_{n=1,\ldots,N} \sim unif(\mathfrak{S}_D)$ *the SAGE estimator is defined as*

$$\hat{\phi}^{SAGE}(i) := \frac{1}{N} \sum_{n=1}^{N} \ell(\hat{f}(x_n, u_i^-(\pi_n)), y_n) - \ell(\hat{f}(x_n, u_i^+(\pi_n)), y_n),$$

with $\hat{f}(x, \emptyset) := \frac{1}{N} \sum_{n=1}^{N} f(x_n)$ *and* $\hat{f}(x, S) := \frac{1}{M} \sum_{m=1}^{M} f(x^{(S)}, \tilde{x}_m^{(\bar{S})})$ *for* $\emptyset \neq S \subset D$ *with* $\tilde{x}_m$ *sampled uniformly from* $x_1, \ldots, x_N$.

The mean prediction $\hat{f}(x, \emptyset)$ thereby differs to ensure that the SAGE values sum to the improvement in loss. For each permutation π_n and observation (x_n, y_n), the SAGE estimator can be efficiently computed by iterating through the permutation and evaluating ν on the preceding elements [10,13]. The permutation sampling approach ensures that the efficiency condition of the Shapley value is maintained and thus the SAGE estimates sum approximately to $\nu(D)$. In contrast to other global FI measures, where interpretation of the scores are unintuitive, SAGE yields a meaningful axiomatic interpretation.

3   Incremental Global Feature Importance

In the following, we consider a data stream, where at time t the observations $(x_0, y_0), \ldots, (x_t, y_t)$ have been observed. On this data stream, a model f_t is incrementally learned over time by updating $f_t \rightarrow f_{t+1}$ using the observation (x_t, y_t). [4,34] Our goal is to estimate the (time-dependent) SAGE values ϕ_t alongside the incremental learning process using minimal resources. In particular, in an online learning scenario, where the model is constantly adapting, huge changes in global FI scores can occur, as has been observed by Haug et al. [26] and Fumagalli et al. [20]. To guarantee the reliability of the learned models, it is crucial to understand these global FI scores over time. The main challenge in estimating the SAGE values in an online learning scenario is that the model f_t and the data-generating random variables (X_t, Y_t) change over time and access to observations to compute $\hat{f}_t$ is limited.

While the SAGE estimator provides efficient estimates of static SAGE values for a given dataset, it does not react properly to changes in the model or concept drift. In Appendix C, we show an example (Fig. 7) which illustrates that the SAGE estimator yields wrong importance scores if the underlying distribution or model is not static. Furthermore, computing the SAGE estimator repeatedly in an incremental setting on a data stream quickly becomes infeasible. As a remedy, we propose incremental SAGE (iSAGE), an incremental estimator, which reacts to changing distributions and is able to explain dynamic, time-dependant models. To compare iSAGE in an incremental learning setting, we first propose Sliding Window SAGE (SW-SAGE), a time-sensitive baseline estimator that repeatedly computes the SAGE estimator on a sliding window.

Sliding Window SAGE (SW-SAGE). A naive approach of approximating SAGE values in an incremental manner is by repeated calculations within a sliding window (SW), which we denote as *SW-SAGE*. Applying SW-SAGE, necessitates storing all historical observations (x_t, y_t) for the last w (window length) observations, and recomputing the SAGE estimator from scratch based on the most up-to-date model f_t. The main computational effort of SW-SAGE stems from evaluating the model f_t and, thus, scales linearly with w. The size w of the window has a profound effect on the resulting SAGE estimates. Choosing a large value for w, may increase the quality of the estimated SAGE values, but can also lead to wrong importance scores, as the window may contain outdated observations. Vice versa, a window size too small leads to a high variance.

3.1   Incremental SAGE (iSAGE)

The high computational effort and the inability to reuse past results, because of the dynamic nature of f_t, strictly limits SW-SAGE in many scenarios, further discussed in Sect. 4.1. As a result, we now propose a time- and memory-efficient variant of SW-SAGE, which we refer to as *incremental SAGE* (iSAGE). The iSAGE algorithm computes the (time-dependent) SAGE values ϕ_t at time t and is able to react to changes in the model and concept drift, while updating its estimates efficiently in an incremental fashion with minimal computational effort. At each time step, we observe a sample (x_t, y_t) from the data stream, and our goal is to update the estimate using the current model f_t. We sample $\pi_t \sim \text{unif}(\mathfrak{S}_D)$ to compute the marginal contribution for $i \in D$ as

$$\Delta_t(i) := \ell(\hat{f}_t(x_t, u_i^-(\pi_t)), y_t) - \ell(\hat{f}_t(x_t, u_i^+(\pi_t)), y_t),$$

where $\hat{f}_t(x, S)$ is a time-sensitive approximation of the restricted model, further discussed in Sect. 3.2. These computations are then averaged over time, which yields the iSAGE estimator, outlined in Algorithm 1.

Definition 3 (iSAGE). *The iSAGE estimator is recursively defined as*

$$iSAGE: \hat{\phi}_t(i) = (1 - \alpha) \cdot \hat{\phi}_{t-1}(i) + \alpha \cdot \Delta_t(i),$$

where $\alpha > 0$ and computation starts at $0 < t_0 < t$ with $\hat{\phi}_{t_0-1}(i) := 0$.

Algorithm 1. Incremental SAGE (iSAGE)

Require: stream $\{x_t, y_t\}_{t=1}^{\infty}$, feature indices $D = \{1, \ldots, d\}$, model f_t, loss function ℓ, and inner samples m

1: Initialize $\hat{\phi}^1 \leftarrow 0, \hat{\phi}^2 \leftarrow 0, \ldots, \hat{\phi}^d \leftarrow 0$, and smoothed mean prediction $y_\emptyset \leftarrow 0$
2: **for all** $(x_t, y_t) \in$ stream **do**
3:     Sample π, a permutation of D
4:     $S \leftarrow \emptyset$
5:     $y_\emptyset \leftarrow (1 - \alpha) \cdot y_\emptyset + \alpha \cdot f(x_t)$ {Udpate mean prediction}
6:     lossPrev $\leftarrow \ell(y_\emptyset, y_t)$ {Compute mean prediction loss}
7:     **for** $j = 1$ to d **do** {Iterate over π}
8:         $S \leftarrow S \cup \{\pi[j]\}$
9:         $y \leftarrow 0$
10:         **for** $k = 1$ to m **do** {Marginalize prediction with S}
11:             Sample $x_k^{(\bar{S})} \sim \mathbb{Q}_t^{(x,S)}$ {interventional (Appendix, Algorithm 2) or observational (Appendix, Algorithm 3)}
12:             $y \leftarrow y + f_t(x_t^{(S)}, x_k^{(\bar{S})})$
13:         **end for**
14:         $\bar{y} \leftarrow \frac{y}{m}$
15:         loss $\leftarrow \ell(\bar{y}, y_t)$
16:         $\Delta \leftarrow$ lossPrev $-$ loss
17:         $\hat{\phi}^{\pi[j]} \leftarrow (1 - \alpha) \cdot \phi^{\pi[j]} + \alpha \cdot \Delta$
18:         lossPrev $\leftarrow$ loss
19:     **end for**
20: **end for**
21: **return** $\phi^1, \phi^2, \ldots, \phi^d$

The iSAGE estimator, thus, approximates ϕ_t by exponentially smoothing previous SAGE estimates, as $\mathbb{E}[\Delta_t(i)] = \phi_t(i)$. In the static batch setting, the SAGE estimator computes the restricted model $f_t(x, S)$ by sampling uniformly from observations in the dataset. However, when f_t is incrementally updated in the data stream setting, access to previous observations is limited as observations are discarded after the incremental update of the model. Furthermore, the distribution of previous observations might change over time, so recently observed samples should be preferred. We thus present two sampling strategies to implement the observational and interventional approach incrementally.

3.2   Incremental Feature Removal Strategies

As mentioned in Sect. 2, SAGE is defined using the observational approach, which is then approximated by the interventional approach, i.e. sampling from the marginal distribution and assuming feature independence. Clearly, this constitutes a strong assumption that is rarely satisfied in practice. Instead, we sample from the marginal distribution to compute *interventional* iSAGE and propose a novel approach to compute *observational* iSAGE, by approximating the conditional distribution. This aligns with [11], where it is claimed that the choices of feature removal is dependent on the application scenario. For both approaches we now provide a time- and memory-efficient incremental sampling approach by maintaining time-dependent reservoirs to estimate $f(x, S)$.

Definition 4 (Estimator for $f(x, S)$). *At time t, we define for $\emptyset \neq S \subset D$*

$$\hat{f}_t(x, S) := \frac{1}{M} \sum_{m=1}^{M} f_t(x^{(S)}, \tilde{x}_m^{(\bar{S})}) \text{ with } x_1, \ldots, x_M \sim \mathbb{Q}_t^{(x,S)},$$

where $\bar{S} := D \setminus S$ and $\mathbb{Q}_t^{(x,S)}$ is a sampling distribution over features in $\bar{S}$. Further, $\hat{f}_t(x, \emptyset) := (1 - \alpha) f_{t-1}(x, \emptyset) + \alpha f_t(x_t)$ and $\hat{f}_{t_0-1}(x, \emptyset) := 0$.

The interventional approach breaks the feature dependency and thus $\mathbb{Q}_t^{(x,S)}$ does not depend on the location x, whereas for the observational $\mathbb{Q}_t^{(x,S)}$ does depend on both, the location x as well as the subset S. We now describe incremental sampling algorithms to sample from $\mathbb{Q}^{(x,S)}$ for either approach.

Interventional iSAGE. The interventional approach in the incremental learning setting is defined as $f_t^{\text{int}}(x, S) := \mathbb{E}\left[f_t(x^{(S)}, X_t^{(\bar{S})})\right]$. The batch SAGE algorithm samples uniformly from all observations from the given dataset. In an incremental learning scenario, this approach has significant drawbacks. First, access to previous observations is limited, as storing observations may be infeasible for the whole data stream. Second, the distribution of X_t may change over time, and it is, thus, beneficial to favor *recent* observations over older data points. The geometric sampling strategy, proposed by Fumagalli et al. [20], accounts for both of these challenges. Geometric sampling maintains *one* reservoir of length L, that is updated at each time step with an incoming data point by uniformly replacing a data point from the reservoir. Then, at each time step, observations $\tilde{x}_m$ are uniformly chosen from the reservoir. The geometric sampling strategy (fully initialized at time step $L := t_0$) thus chooses a previous observation from time r at time s with probability $L^{-1}(1 - L^{-1})^{s-r-1}$ for $r \geq L$, which clearly favors more recent observations.

The complete procedure is given in the appendix (Algorithm 2). At any time t, geometric reservoir sampling requires a storage space of $\mathcal{O}(L)$ data points. It has been shown that the geometric sampling procedure is favorable in scenarios with concept drift compared to memory-efficient uniform sampling approaches, such as general reservoir sampling [20].

Observational iSAGE. The interventional approach can generate unrealistic observations when features are highly correlated, resulting in out-of-distribution evaluations of the model. When understanding causal relationships, it might be inappropriate to evaluate the model outside the data manifold [11], and we thus propose an alternative approach that can incorporate feature dependence in the incremental sampling process. The observational approach in the incremental setting is defined as $f_t^{\text{obs}}(x, S) := \mathbb{E}\left[f_t(x^{(S)}, X_t^{(\bar{S})}) \mid X_t^{(S)} = x^{(S)}\right]$. While observing data points x_t, we train for every feature $i \in D$ an incremental decision tree that aims at predicting $x_t^{(i)}$ given the remaining feature values $x_t^{(D \setminus \{i\})}$.

We then traverse the incremental decision tree using the input x_t and maintain a reservoir of length L at each leaf node, using the geometric sampling strategy described above, i.e. uniformly replacing an observation in the leaf's reservoir. This yields a reservoir of length L at every leaf node of the incremental decision tree, where both, the decision tree as well as the reservoir change over time. We propose to use a Hoeffding Adaptive Tree (HAT), a popular incremental decision tree [29], to adaptively maintain the structure. The approach can be viewed as an incremental variant of the *conditional subgroup* approach [37].

Given a subset $S \subset D$ and an observation x_t, we obtain the values of $\tilde{x}_m^{(\bar{S})}$ separately for each feature $j \in \bar{S}$. Using x_t, we traverse the HAT and at every decision node that splits on a feature in $\bar{S}$, we randomly split according to the split ratio of previous observed inputs, a statistic that is inherently available for a HAT. From the reservoir at the resulting leaf node, we then uniformly sample values for $\tilde{x}_m^{(j)}$ and repeat this process for every feature $j \in \bar{S}$ until we obtain all values for $\tilde{x}_m^{(\bar{S})}$. This methodology parallels the TreeSHAP approach of traversing decision trees for absent features, referred to as path dependent TreeSHAP [35]. Notably, our approach allows to extend the conditional subgroup approach to an arbitrary feature subset $S \subset D$ while maintaining only *one* decision tree *per feature* and further extends the approach to an incremental setting. The observational approach via HAT has a space complexity of $\mathcal{O}(d \cdot T^R \cdot L)$ where R refers to the HATs' maximum tree depth, T is the maximum number of tree splits, and L is the size of the reservoir at each leaf node.

3.3   Approximation Guarantees for Static Environments

We presented iSAGE as a time- and memory-efficient algorithm to estimate SAGE values over time incrementally. In contrast to the SAGE estimator, iSAGE reacts to changes in the model as well as concept drift, which we demonstrate empirically in Sect. 4. Analyzing iSAGE theoretically in an incremental learning scenario would require strong assumptions on the data-generating random variables (X_t, Y_t) and the approximation quality of the learned model f_t, as the iid assumption in general is not fulfilled. Instead, we now show theoretically that iSAGE has similar properties as the SAGE estimator in a static learning environment. In the following, we assume that $f \equiv f_t$ is a constant model and $(X, Y) \equiv (X_t, Y_t)$ a stationary data generating process. We further assume that $\mathbb{Q}_t^{(x,S)}$ is the true marginal (interventional) or conditional (observational) distribution and that samples are drawn iid, similar to Covert et al. [13].

Theorem 1. *For iSAGE $\hat{\phi}_t(i) \rightarrow \phi_t(i)$ for $M \rightarrow \infty$ and $t \rightarrow \infty$.*

Theorem 1 shows that iSAGE converges to the SAGE values. Further, the variance is controlled by α.

Theorem 2. *The variance of iSAGE is controlled by α, i.e. $\mathbb{V}[\hat{\phi}_t(i)] = \mathcal{O}(\alpha)$.*

Lastly, we show that iSAGE does not differ much from the SAGE estimator.

Theorem 3. *Given the SAGE estimator $\hat{\phi}_t^{SAGE}(i)$ computed at time t over all previously observed data points, it holds for iSAGE with $M \to \infty$, $\alpha = \frac{1}{t}$ and every $\epsilon > (1-\alpha)^{t-t_0+1}$ that $\mathbb{P}\left(|\hat{\phi}_t(i) - \hat{\phi}_t^{SAGE}(i)| > \epsilon\right) = \mathcal{O}(\frac{1}{t})$.*

While iSAGE admits similar properties as the SAGE estimator in a static environment, we showcase in our experiments that iSAGE is able to efficiently react to model changes and concept drift in an incremental learning setting.

4 Experiments

We now utilize iSAGE in multiple experimental settings. In Sect. 4.1, we show how iSAGE can be efficiently applied in dynamic environments with concept drift. In Sect. 4.2, we construct a synthetic ground-truth scneario for a data stream with concept drift and show that iSAGE is able to efficiently recover the SAGE values. In Sect. 4.3, we illustrate the difference of interventional and observational iSAGE, which yield profoundly different explanations. In Sect. 4.4, we show that iSAGE leads to the same results as the SAGE estimator in a static environment validating our theoretical results. As our iSAGE explanation technique is inherently model-agnostic, we train and evaluate our method on different incremental and batch models.[2]

4.1 iSAGE in Dynamic Environments with Concept Drift

In this experiment, we demonstrate the explanatory capabilities of iSAGE in a dynamic learning scenario with concept drift. We illustrate how iSAGE uncovers hidden changes in black box incremental models applied in real-world incremental learning scenarios where models are updated with every new observation. We compare iSAGE with incremental permutation feature importance (iPFI) [20], which is up to our knowledge, the only model-agnostic explanation method that can be applied in an incremental learning setting. For additional experiments and a comparison with the mean decrease in impurity (MDI) for tree-based models [22], we refer to the supplement material (cf., D.3). Figure 2 explains the incremental learning procedure for an ARF classifier on the *elec2* data stream. Both methods detect similar feature importance rankings with varying absolute values. In contrast to iPFI, iSAGE explanations sum to the time-dependent difference in model loss over the loss using the mean prediction, due to the efficiency axiom of the Shapley value, which naturally increases interpretability of the method. Both methods accurately detect the model changes caused by concept drift in *elec2* [24]. The concept drift, which stems from the *vicprice* feature not having any values in the first $\approx 20k$ observations, would be obfuscated by solely plotting the model performance without any online explanations.

---

[2] All model implementations are based on *scikit-learn* [41], *River* [38], and *torch* [40]. The data sets and streams are retrieved from *OpenML* [17] and *River*. All supplement materials and the appendix can be found at https://github.com/mmschlk/iSAGE-An-Incremental-Version-of-SAGE-for-Online-Explanation-on-Data-Streams.

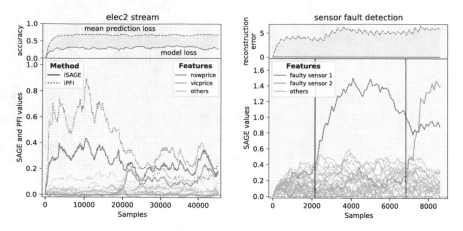

Fig. 2. iSAGE and iPFI of an ARF on *elec2* (left) and iSAGE for an incrementally fitted autoencoder for *fault detection* based on the reconstruction loss (right).

As an illustrative example, we conduct an experiment to show how online SAGE values can detect sensor faults in online sensor networks, which constitutes a challenging predictive maintenance problem [15,48]. Similar to Hinder et al. [27], we simulate sensor network data of water pressures including sensor faults (vertical lines in Fig. 2 denote the time points) via the L-Town [49] simulation tool [32] and explain online learning models. We incrementally fit[3] and explain a NN autoencoder on the sensor readings. Figure 2 shows how the autoencoder's reconstruction error is distributed onto the individual senor values by iSAGE. Notably, the faulty sensor can easily be identified through inspection of the iSAGE values after the sensor faulted.

4.2 Approximation Quality with Synthetic Ground-Truths

We compare iSAGE to the inefficient baseline SW-SAGE, as well as synthetic ground-truth (GT) values estimated using the SAGE estimator. Conducting GT experiments in an incremental learning setting where models change with every new observation is computationally prohibitive. Moreover, it is not defined what constitutes a GT online explanation for real-world data streams with hidden drifts. We construct a data stream that consists of multiple sub-streams, each with different classification functions, i.e. inducing sudden concept drift when sub-streams are switched. Within each substream, we maintain a *static* pre-trained model with a pre-computed (constant) GT explanation. We observe how differently parameterized SW-SAGE and iSAGE estimators approximate the pre-computed GT values, see Fig. 3, and measure the approximation quality in terms of MSE and MAE. We repeat the complete experimental setup 20

---

[3] We update the autoencoder with each new data point using a single gradient update (batch size of 1). For more details on the setup, please see Appendix D.3.

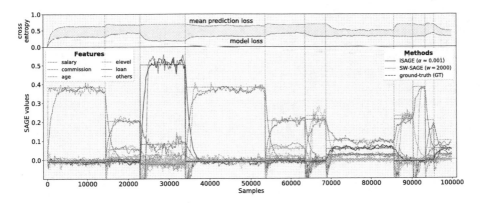

Fig. 3. iSAGE (solid), SW-SAGE (dotted) and GT (dashed) values for an example GT stream. SW-SAGE is computed with a stride of 100 $(0.05 \cdot w)$ resulting in an overhead 20 times higher than iSAGE.

times for each frequency scenario and summarize the resulting approximation errors (MSE) in Table 1 and Fig. 3. Independently of the substantially increased computational overhead (up to 20 times), SW-SAGE's approximation quality is substantially worse compared to iSAGE. In some scenarios, SW-SAGE reaches the GT values faster than iSAGE. Yet, in the important phases of change, SW-SAGE' estimates are substantially worse than iSAGE's (see Fig. 10 for a detailed view). This is a result from SW-SAGE attributing equal weight to outdated observations after a concept drift and the current model f_t classifying the samples differently than before. Yet, iSAGE smoothly transitions between the concepts.

4.3   Interventional and Observational iSAGE

In the presence of dependent variables, the choice of an interventional or observational approach has a profound effect on the SAGE values. In this experiment, we compare both approaches using the efficient incremental algorithms presented in Sect. 3.2. An ARF model is trained and explained on the synthetic *agrawal* data stream. The synthetic classification function is defined in Appendix D.3. In

Table 1. Approximation quality of iSAGE (inc_c) and SW-SAGE (SW_c) on synthetic GT data streams for 20 iterations (c denotes the factor of additional model evaluations compared to iSAGE). The complete results are given in Table 2.

scenario		high		middle		low	
size (w)		500	1 000	500	1 000	500	1 000
$\mathbf{MSE}(\sigma)$	inc_1	**.034** (.021)	**.038** (.022)	**.027** (.023)	**.027** (.026)	**.015** (.012)	**.013** (.009)
	SW_{20}	.283 (.262)	.420 (.360)	.191 (.271)	.320 (.487)	.049 (.043)	.078 (.081)
	SW_1	.248 (.198)	.462 (.413)	.183 (.200)	.399 (.792)	.061 (.067)	.080 (.079)

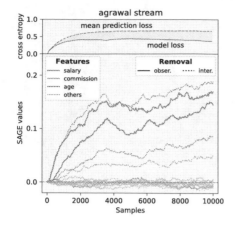

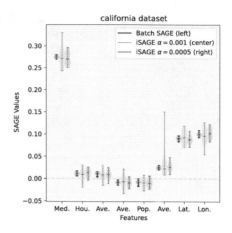

Fig. 4. Interventional and observational iSAGE for an ARF on an *agrawal* stream showcasing profoundly different scores.

Fig. 5. SAGE values (median in red) per feature of the *california* dataset for SAGE and interventional iSAGE. (Color figure online)

this stream the $X_{\text{commission}}$ feature ($X_{\text{com.}}$) directly depends on X_{salary}. Whenever the *salary* of an applicant exceeds 75k, no *commission* is given ($X_{\text{com.}} = 0$), and otherwise the commission is uniformly distributed ($X_{\text{com.}} \sim U(10k, 75k)$). Figure 4 showcases how interventional and observational iSAGE differ.

No significant importance is distributed to the $X_{\text{com.}}$ feature, if observational iSAGE is used, as the information present in $X_{\text{com.}}$ can be fully recovered by the observational approach based on X_{salary}. The importance is distributed onto the remaining two important features X_{salary} and X_{age}. However, when interventional iSAGE is used, the importance is also distributed to $X_{\text{com.}}$, as the model is evaluated outside the data manifold. The unrealistic feature values uncover that the incremental model has picked up on the transient relationship between the target values and the feature $X_{\text{com.}}$.

4.4   iSAGE and SAGE in Static Environments

We consider a static learning scenario, in which we compare interventional iSAGE with Covert et al. [13]'s original SAGE approach for well-established benchmark batch datasets. The models are pre-trained and then explained. We apply Gradient Boosting Trees [18], LightGBM models [31], and NNs. The original SAGE explanations are directly computed from the batch datasets. iSAGE experiences the datasets as a randomly shuffled data stream where the model is not updated incrementally. We run this explanation procedure 20 times and illustrate the SAGE values on the *california* example dataset in Fig. 5 (more datasets in Section D.3). Figure 5 shows that iSAGE approximates SAGE in the static setting on average with a higher variance. The higher variance is a direct result of the iSAGE having no access to future data points and the exponential smoothing mechanism controlled by α. iSAGE, thus, focuses more on recent samples, which is essential for non-stationary environments like incremental learning under concept drift.

5 Conclusion and Future Work

We propose and analyze iSAGE, a novel and model-agnostic explanation procedure to compute global FI in dynamic environments based on time-dependent SAGE values. In contrast to the batch SAGE algorithm [13], iSAGE is able to efficiently react to concept drift and changes in the model while scaling linearly with the number of features in terms of runtime complexity. We further extend SAGE with the observational and interventional SAGE values as distinctive objectives and present efficient incremental iSAGE variants, that are able to estimate these values over time and react to changes in the model and concept drift. In particular, we present an incremental approximation for the observational approach that combines the conditional subgroup approach [37] and the TreeSHAP methodology [35], which could also be used in a static learning environment to further improve the SAGE algorithm. We empirically confirm profound differences in both explanations depending on the choice of approach, which yields supporting arguments in the interventional and observational debate [11,19,30] that the choice should depend on the application scenario [11]. In a static environment, we prove that iSAGE has similar properties as SAGE and that both do not differ significantly. We further illustrate the efficacy of incremental explanations in multiple experiments on benchmark data sets and streams and conduct a ground-truth comparison.

Still, approximating Shapley values remains a computationally challenging problem. Moreover, this approach does not address the problem of incrementally decomposing the interactions between features, which requires further investigation. Finally, the interaction between human users and incrementally created explanations derived from methods like iSAGE need to be vigorously evaluated to identify further research opportunities.

Acknowledgements. We gratefully acknowledge funding by the Deutsche Forschungsgemeinschaft (DFG, German Research Foundation): TRR 318/1 2021 - 438445824. The authors would like to thank Rohit Jagtani for supporting the implementation and engaging discussions, as well as Gunnar König for valuable discussions.

Ethical Statement. We propose iSAGE as a novel XAI method that *enables* explanations for any incrementally trained and dynamic black-box model. This is a novel research direction, which could lead to various use cases. Models, that could not be evaluated before, because of computational restrictions can be investigated with iSAGE. This enables high-performing models to be applied in various critical application domains such as healthcare [47], energy consumption analysis [21], credit risk scoring [12]. These application domains could greatly benefit from XAI methods such as iSAGE, since they can help in uncovering inherent biases or problems with fairness. This could help with more targeted regulation and scrutinization of opaque, yet high-performing, technologies than without explanations. On the other hand, improved interpretability may also lead to an increased acceptance and exploitation of potentially harmful applications using black box models.

References

1. Aas, K., Jullum, M., Løland, A.: Explaining individual predictions when features are dependent: more accurate approximations to Shapley values. Artif. Intell. **298**, 103502 (2021). https://doi.org/10.1016/j.artint.2021.103502
2. Adadi, A., Berrada, M.: Peeking inside the black-box: a survey on explainable artificial intelligence (XAI). IEEE Access **6**, 52138–52160 (2018). https://doi.org/10.1109/ACCESS.2018.2870052
3. Atli, B.G., Jung, A.: Online feature ranking for intrusion detection systems. CoRR abs/1803.00530 (2018)
4. Bahri, M., Bifet, A., Gama, J., Gomes, H.M., Maniu, S.: Data stream analysis: foundations, major tasks and tools. Wiley Interdisc. Rev.: Data Min. Knowl. Discov. **11**(3), e1405 (2021). https://doi.org/10.1002/widm.1405
5. Barddal, J.P., Enembreck, F., Gomes, H.M., Bifet, A., Pfahringer, B.: Boosting decision stumps for dynamic feature selection on data streams. Inf. Syst. **83**, 13–29 (2019). https://doi.org/10.1016/j.is.2019.02.003
6. Binder, A., Montavon, G., Lapuschkin, S., Müller, K.-R., Samek, W.: Layer-wise relevance propagation for neural networks with local renormalization layers. In: Villa, A.E.P., Masulli, P., Pons Rivero, A.J. (eds.) ICANN 2016. LNCS, vol. 9887, pp. 63–71. Springer, Cham (2016). https://doi.org/10.1007/978-3-319-44781-0_8
7. Breiman, L.: Random forests. Mach. Learn. **45**(1), 5–32 (2001). https://doi.org/10.1023/A:1010933404324
8. Casalicchio, G., Molnar, C., Bischl, B.: Visualizing the feature importance for black box models. In: Berlingerio, M., Bonchi, F., Gärtner, T., Hurley, N., Ifrim, G. (eds.) ECML PKDD 2018. LNCS (LNAI), vol. 11051, pp. 655–670. Springer, Cham (2019). https://doi.org/10.1007/978-3-030-10925-7_40
9. Cassidy, A.P., Deviney, F.A.: Calculating feature importance in data streams with concept drift using online random forest. In: 2014 IEEE International Conference on Big Data (Big Data 2014), pp. 23–28 (2014). https://doi.org/10.1109/BigData.2014.7004352
10. Castro, J., Gómez, D., Tejada, J.: Polynomial calculation of the Shapley value based on sampling. Comput. Oper. Res. **36**(5), 1726–1730 (2009). https://doi.org/10.1016/j.cor.2008.04.004
11. Chen, H., Janizek, J.D., Lundberg, S.M., Lee, S.: True to the model or true to the data? CoRR abs/2006.16234 (2020)
12. Clements, J.M., Xu, D., Yousefi, N., Efimov, D.: Sequential deep learning for credit risk monitoring with tabular financial data. CoRR abs/2012.15330 (2020)
13. Covert, I., Lundberg, S.M., Lee, S.: Understanding global feature contributions with additive importance measures. In: Advances in Neural Information Processing Systems 33: (NeurIPS 2020), pp. 17212–17223 (2020)
14. Covert, I., Lundberg, S.M., Lee, S.I.: Explaining by removing: a unified framework for model explanation. J. Mach. Learn. Res. **22**(209), 1–90 (2021)

15. Davari, N., Veloso, B., Ribeiro, R.P., Pereira, P.M., Gama, J.: Predictive maintenance based on anomaly detection using deep learning for air production unit in the railway industry. In: 8th IEEE International Conference on Data Science and Advanced Analytics (DSAA 2021), pp. 1–10. IEEE (2021). https://doi.org/10.1109/DSAA53316.2021.9564181
16. Duckworth, C., et al.: Using explainable machine learning to characterise data drift and detect emergent health risks for emergency department admissions during COVID-19. Sci. Rep. **11**(1), 23017 (2021). https://doi.org/10.1038/s41598-021-02481-y
17. Feurer, M., et al.: OpenML-Python: an extensible Python API for OpenML. J. Mach. Learn. Res. **22**, 100:1-100:5 (2021)
18. Friedman, J.H.: Greedy function approximation: a gradient boosting machine. Ann. Stat. **29**(5), 1189–1232 (2001). https://doi.org/10.1214/aos/1013203451
19. Frye, C., Mijolla, D.d., Begley, T., Cowton, L., Stanley, M., Feige, I.: Shapley explainability on the data manifold. In: International Conference on Learning Representations (2021)
20. Fumagalli, F., Muschalik, M., Hüllermeier, E., Hammer, B.: Incremental Permutation Feature Importance (iPFI): Towards Online Explanations on Data Streams. CoRR abs/2209.01939 (2022)
21. García-Martín, E., Rodrigues, C.F., Riley, G., Grahn, H.: Estimation of energy consumption in machine learning. J. Parallel Distrib. Comput. **134**, 75–88 (2019). https://doi.org/10.1016/j.jpdc.2019.07.007
22. Gomes, H.M., Mello, R.F.D., Pfahringer, B., Bifet, A.: Feature scoring using tree-based ensembles for evolving data streams. In: 2019 IEEE International Conference on Big Data (Big Data 2019), pp. 761–769 (2019)
23. Guyon, I., Weston, J., Barnhill, S., Vapnik, V.: Gene selection for cancer classification using support vector machines. Mach. Learn. **46**(1–3), 389–422 (2002). https://doi.org/10.1023/A:1012487302797
24. Harries, M.: SPLICE-2 Comparative Evaluation: Electricity Pricing. The University of South Wales, Tech. rep. (1999)
25. Hastie, T., Tibshirani, R., Friedman, J.: The Elements of Statistical Learning. SSS, Springer, New York (2009). https://doi.org/10.1007/978-0-387-84858-7
26. Haug, J., Braun, A., Zürn, S., Kasneci, G.: Change detection for local explainability in evolving data streams. In: Proceedings of the 31st ACM International Conference on Information & Knowledge Management (CIKIM 2022), pp. 706–716. ACM (2022). https://doi.org/10.1145/3511808.3557257
27. Hinder, F., Vaquet, V., Brinkrolf, J., Hammer, B.: Model based explanations of concept drift. CoRR abs/2303.09331 (2023)
28. Horel, E., Mison, V., Xiong, T., Giesecke, K., Mangu, L.: Sensitivity based neural networks explanations. CoRR abs/1812.01029 (2018)
29. Hulten, G., Spencer, L., Domingos, P.: Mining time-changing data streams. In: Proceedings of the seventh ACM SIGKDD International Conference on Knowledge Discovery and Data Mining (KDD 2001), pp. 97–106. ACM Press (2001). https://doi.org/10.1145/502512.502529
30. Janzing, D., Minorics, L., Blöbaum, P.: Feature relevance quantification in explainable AI: a causal problem. In: The 23rd International Conference on Artificial Intelligence and Statistics (AISTATS 2020). Proceedings of Machine Learning Research, vol. 108, pp. 2907–2916. PMLR (2020)
31. Ke, G., et al.: LightGBM: a highly efficient gradient boosting decision tree. In: Advances in Neural Information Processing Systems, vol. 30 (NeurIPS 2017) (2017)

32. Klise, K.A., Bynum, M., Moriarty, D., Murray, R.: A software framework for assessing the resilience of drinking water systems to disasters with an example earthquake case study. Environ. Model. Softw. **95**, 420–431 (2017). https://doi.org/10.1016/j.envsoft.2017.06.022

33. König, G., Molnar, C., Bischl, B., Grosse-Wentrup, M.: Relative feature importance. In: Proceedings of International Conference on Pattern Recognition (ICPR 2021), pp. 9318–9325 (2021)

34. Losing, V., Hammer, B., Wersing, H.: Incremental on-line learning: a review and comparison of state of the art algorithms. Neurocomputing **275**, 1261–1274 (2018). https://doi.org/10.1016/j.neucom.2017.06.084

35. Lundberg, S.M., et al.: From local explanations to global understanding with explainable AI for trees. Nat. Mach. Intell. **2**(1), 56–67 (2020). https://doi.org/10.1038/s42256-019-0138-9

36. Lundberg, S.M., Lee, S.I.: A unified approach to interpreting model predictions. In: Advances in Neural Information Processing Systems, vol. 30 (NeurIPS 2017), pp. 4768–4777 (2017)

37. Molnar, C., König, G., Bischl, B., Casalicchio, G.: Model-agnostic feature importance and effects with dependent features - a conditional subgroup approach. CoRR abs/2006.04628 (2020)

38. Montiel, J., et al.: River: machine learning for streaming data in Python. J. Mach. Learn. Res. **22**, 110:1–110:8 (2021)

39. Muschalik, M., Fumagalli, F., Hammer, B., Hüllermeier, E.: Agnostic explanation of model change based on feature importance. KI - Künstliche Intelligenz (2022). https://doi.org/10.1007/s13218-022-00766-6

40. Paszke, A., et al.: Automatic differentiation in PyTorch. In: Advances in Neural Information Processing Systems, vol. 30 (NeurIPS 2017 Workshop) (2017)

41. Pedregosa, F., et al.: Scikit-learn: machine learning in Python. J. Mach. Learn. Res. **12**, 2825–2830 (2011)

42. Ribeiro, M.T., Singh, S., Guestrin, C.: Why should i trust you?: explaining the predictions of any classifier. In: Proceedings of International Conference on Knowledge Discovery and Data Mining (KDD 2016), pp. 1135–1144 (2016)

43. Shapley, L.S.: A value for n-person games. In: Contributions to the Theory of Games (AM-28), Volume II, pp. 307–318. Princeton University Press (1953). https://doi.org/10.1515/9781400881970-018

44. Shrikumar, A., Greenside, P., Kundaje, A.: Learning important features through propagating activation differences. In: Proceedings of the 34th International Conference on Machine Learning (ICML 2017). Proceedings of Machine Learning Research, vol. 70, pp. 3145–3153. PMLR (2017)

45. Springenberg, J.T., Dosovitskiy, A., Brox, T., Riedmiller, M.A.: Striving for simplicity: the all convolutional net. In: 3rd International Conference on Learning Representations (ICLR 2015) (2015)

46. Sundararajan, M., Taly, A., Yan, Q.: Axiomatic attribution for deep networks. In: Proceedings of the 34th International Conference on Machine Learning (ICML 2017). Proceedings of Machine Learning Research, vol. 70, pp. 3319–3328. PMLR (2017)

47. Ta, V.D., Liu, C.M., Nkabinde, G.W.: Big data stream computing in healthcare real-time analytics. In: Procedddings of International Conference on Cloud Computing and Big Data Analysis (ICCCBDA 2016), pp. 37–42 (2016). https://doi.org/10.1109/ICCCBDA.2016.7529531

48. Vaquet, V., Artelt, A., Brinkrolf, J., Hammer, B.: Taking care of our drinking water: dealing with sensor faults in water distribution networks. In: Artificial Neural Networks and Machine Learning - ICANN 2022, pp. 682–693. Springer Nature Switzerland, Cham (2022). https://doi.org/10.1007/978-3-031-15931-2_56
49. Vrachimis, S., et al.: Battle of the leakage detection and isolation methods. J. Water Resour. Plann. Manage. **148**, 04022068 (2022). https://doi.org/10.1061/(ASCE)WR.1943-5452.0001601
50. Yuan, L., Pfahringer, B., Barddal, J.P.: Iterative subset selection for feature drifting data streams. In: Proceedings of the 33rd Annual ACM Symposium on Applied Computing, pp. 510–517 (2018)
51. Zeiler, Matthew D.., Fergus, Rob: Visualizing and understanding convolutional networks. In: Fleet, David, Pajdla, Tomas, Schiele, Bernt, Tuytelaars, Tinne (eds.) ECCV 2014. LNCS, vol. 8689, pp. 818–833. Springer, Cham (2014). https://doi.org/10.1007/978-3-319-10590-1_53

Interpretation Attacks and Defenses on Predictive Models Using Electronic Health Records

Fereshteh Razmi[1], Jian Lou[2], Yuan Hong[3], and Li Xiong[1(✉)]

[1] Emory University, Atlanta, GA 30322, USA
{frazmim,lxiong}@emory.edu
[2] Zhejiang University, Hangzhou, Zhejiang 310027, China
jian.lou@zju.edu.cn
[3] University of Connecticut, Storrs, CT 06269, USA
yuan.hong@uconn.edu

Abstract. The emergence of complex deep neural networks made it crucial to employ interpretation methods for gaining insight into the rationale behind model predictions. However, recent studies have revealed attacks on these interpretations, which aim to deceive users and subvert the trustworthiness of the models. It is especially critical in medical systems, where interpretations are essential in explaining outcomes. This paper presents the first interpretation attack on predictive models using sequential electronic health records (EHRs). Prior attempts in image interpretation mainly utilized gradient-based methods, yet our research shows that our attack can attain significant success on EHR interpretations that do not rely on model gradients. We introduce metrics compatible with EHR data to evaluate the attack's success. Moreover, our findings demonstrate that detection methods that have successfully identified conventional adversarial examples are ineffective against our attack. We then propose a defense method utilizing auto-encoders to denoise the data and improve the interpretations' robustness. Our results indicate that this de-noising method outperforms the widely used defense method, SmoothGrad, which is based on adding noise to the data.

Keywords: Interpretation Models · Electornic Health Records (EHR) · Adversarial Attack · Robustness · Autoencoder

1 Introduction

Machine learning algorithms, particularly deep neural networks, are widely used in various real-world tasks. However, their inner workings are often seen as a black box. Thus, interpretation methods are essential for explaining an algorithm's output, allowing users to understand how and why an algorithm arrived

This work was funded by National Science Foundation (NSF) IIS-2302968, CNS-2124104, CNS-2302689 and CNS-2308730, National Institute of Health (NIH) R01ES033241, R01LM013712, and NSFC (62206207).

D. Koutra et al. (Eds.): ECML PKDD 2023, LNAI 14171, pp. 446–461, 2023.
https://doi.org/10.1007/978-3-031-43418-1_27

at a particular decision. Especially in sensitive applications such as medicine, interpretations improve the system's reliability and enable the discovery of new biomarkers and important features for future decision-making processes. For instance, Quellec et al. [15] use heatmaps to identify local patterns and demonstrate which pixels in retinal fundus photographs are involved in the early signs of retinal disease.

Adversarial examples [23] have been extensively studied in recent years as a potential vulnerability of deep neural networks. Traditionally, they aim to add a small perturbation to the input at inference time, causing the model to classify it differently. With the increasing use of interpretation methods, a new type of attack has emerged. These attacks focus on generating misleading interpretations that deviate significantly from the true classifier interpretations, leading to inaccurate conclusions about the importance of certain features or rendering the interpretations unreliable [8].

Sequential electronic health records (EHR) are crucial data sources in the medical field, containing discrete data of patients' vital values and lab values collected over time and across hospital visits. Due to the importance of these data and their use in many classification based predictive models, recent efforts have been made to enhance the interpretability of models trained on EHR data. Despite the prevalence of interpretation attacks in image classification, to the best of our knowledge, no interpretation attacks have been studied targeting EHR-based models.

Conducting interpretation attacks on EHR data presents significant challenges due to the unique characteristics of the data. Firstly, for building interpretable models using EHR data, models are designed to produce predictions and interpretations simultaneously. In contrast, image interpretations are mostly gradient-based and created via post-hoc approaches. Thus, manipulating the EHR interpretations can easily alter the patient phenotype, consequently affecting the predicted class.

Secondly, the structure of EHR data is vastly different from images. As a result, the widely used L_∞ norm based attacks in image domain are less meaningful in the EHR domain since L_∞ does not capture the distance between the sequential data well (e.g., the temporal trends). Also, unlike images, EHR data consist of multiple attributes, such as heart rate or temperature, whose values are sequential and time-dependent. Therefore, moving across time and attributes significantly influences the interpretations. Consequently, the criteria used for assessing the image interpretation's robustness on previous works cannot be directly applied in the EHR domain.

This work proposes an interpretation attack on EHR data, utilizing specific metrics suitable for this data type. We evaluate our attack against a powerful existing detection technique designed for conventional adversarial examples on EHR data and demonstrate that the attack is not detectable. Furthermore, we aim to make the EHR interpretations robust against the proposed attack. We show that using an auto-encoder to de-noise the input is significantly more effective than using noisy input, as in the state-of-the-art method SmoothGrad.

The source code of our implementation is publicly available on GitHub[1]. We summarize our contributions as follows:

- We propose an interpretation attack on EHR data. This attack is created on top of an interpretable model, so the interpretations are closely tied to the model's predictions. It differs from previous attacks in the image domain, which rely on gradient-based and post-hoc interpretation methods.
- We propose three metrics to assess the EHR interpretation attack. In the previous works, top-K salient explanations between the clean and adversarial images were used for evaluation. However, it is not suitable for EHR data. Two of our evaluation metrics are alternatives to the top-K criteria, and the third metric is based on the Wasserstein distance which better captures the similarity between temporal data.
- We conduct experiments showing that the state-of-the-art detector RADAR, which was designed to detect conventional EHR adversarial examples, are not successful in detecting the proposed attack. We then explore the factors that contribute to this attack evasion.
- Finally, we present a method to enhance the interpretations' robustness and reduce the attack strength. We employ an auto-encoder to boost the robustness of our interpretations through a de-noising process. We show that out approach outperforms SmoothGrad, which is commonly used in gradient-based methods by averaging noisy data.

2   Related Work and Preliminaries

2.1   Attacks on Image Model's Gradients

Post-hoc interpretability are a set of interpretation methods that seek to explain the predictions of models without relying on their underlying mechanisms [11]. Gradient-based approaches are commonly used in image classification to extract these explanations [17,19,20]. They result in a saliency map that explains the output of the model (usually a convolutional neural network (CNN)) by visualizing the areas of the input image that contribute the most to the network's output. However, saliency maps are less common in Recurrent Neural Networks (RNN) since RNNs are typically used for sequential data such as time-series.

Recent research has shown that these methods are vulnerable to interpretation attacks, where small perturbations are deliberately crafted and added to input images to distort the explanations [8]. These attacks primarily focus on images as they rely on gradient-based techniques and face significant challenges in other domains. Several techniques have been proposed to address this issue, including adding randomness to the input called SmoothGrad [21,26], modification of the model architecture [6], or altering the training process using regularization or integrated gradients [3,7]. These approaches are highly dependent on the architecture of image models and their gradients. Interpretation attacks

---

[1] https://github.com/Emory-AIMS/EHR-Interpretation-Attack.

in other domains including EHR have been relatively overlooked due to the difficulty in attacking against complex saliency maps and the lack of a definitive interpretation benchmark.

2.2   Medical Attention-Based Models

Recent research in the medical field has focused on using the attention mechanism to improve the interpretability and accuracy of predictions made using EHR data [4,5]. The attention mechanism is an approach used in machine learning models that assigns a weight to each input feature, indicating its relative importance to the model's final decision. They generally use BERT models [10,16,18] or multi-layer RNNs [9,12,13,25] as the baseline to obtain the attentions. BERT models are mostly focused on binary medical codes and their pre-trained models are often not publicly available due to the sensitive nature of the medical data used for their training. In this work, we use RETAIN [5] as a well-known EHR attention-based RNN model. RETAIN can give interpretation on both visit (temporal point) and attribute levels, and in contrast to other works, it does not need access to extra meta data [9]. We then propose interpretation attacks considering the structure of EHR data and also the intrinsic nature of their non-post-hoc interpretable models.

3   Our Approach

In this section, we first describe the problem setting, then present our approach to the interpretation attack on EHR models and elaborate the rationale behind each objective loss term. We then improve the attack by incorporating dynamic weighing to penalize the attack optimization process and reduce the detectability by modifying the penalty term. We propose new metrics as the current evaluation metrics are unsuitable for EHR data. Finally, we explore methods for defending against the attack and demonstrate that de-noising is more effective than the state-of-the-art method for improving the robustness of interpretations.

3.1   Problem Setting

EHR dataset is a set of clinical trajectories for patients where each trajectory is a sequence of hospital or clinic visits, each visit corresponding to a set of attributes/measurements [1]. For a given dataset with longitudinal EHR data from N patients, we represent the clinical trajectory of patient n as $X^{(n)}$. This trajectory is characterized by a sequence of t_n hospital visits and can be expressed as:

$$X^{(n)} = [X_1, X_2, ..., X_{t_n}], \tag{1}$$

where $X_i \in R^d$ denotes the variables from d vital sign measurements and lab events of the i-th visit made by patient n. Each $x_{i,j}$ shows j-th attribute in the i-th visit. We will exclude the superscript (n) in the subsequent sections to simplify the presentation.

Given a neural network model $f : R^{(t,d)} \rightarrow R^c$ where c is the number of possible classes, we denote the interpretation that is associated with the parameters of function f as $\Phi_f : R^{(t,d)} \rightarrow R^{(t,d)}$ in which every attribute in a specific visit gets a score that shows its importance on the predicted outcome. Given a test input X, the class and explanations of this input is determined by $c^* = \arg\max_c f(X)$ and $\omega = \Phi_f(X)$, respectively. In RETAIN [5], the impact of each input $x_{i,k}$ on the final classification result is calculated using the two-level attention weights:

$$\omega_{i,k} = \alpha_i W(\beta \odot W_{emb}[:,k]) \; x_{i,k}, \tag{2}$$

where α_i is the attention weight assigned to the i-th visit, β_i is an attention weight vector for all attributes and measurements $x_{i,k}$ of the i-th visit, W is the output weight matrix, W_{emb} is the weight matrix at the embedding layer, and the symbol $\odot$ represents element-wise multiplication. $\omega_{i,k}$ is the corresponding contribution to the input $x_{i,k}$. Therefore, we can obtain the contribution matrix ω using all $\omega_{i,k}$.

3.2 Interpretation Attack Formulation

Given a patient record X, the goal is to find a new perturbed record $\widetilde{X}$ that is similar to the original record X both in input space and class predictions but with distorted interpretations. The attack can either be targeted, where we try to make the interpretations of $\widetilde{X}$ closer to a new explanation $\omega^\dagger$, or untargeted, where we attempt to change the interpretations to be far from those of X. Here we aim for a targeted one and formulate the interpretation adversarial attack by

$$\min_{\widetilde{X}} \alpha\|\Phi_f(\widetilde{X}) - \omega^\dagger\| + \gamma\|\widetilde{X} - X\|_1 + \beta(\max\{Logit(\widetilde{X})_i : i \neq c^*\} - Logit(\widetilde{X})_{c^*})^+ \tag{3}$$

where $(r)^+$ represents $max(r,0)$, c^* is the predicted class of X, $Logit$ is the outcome of the neural network before the Softmax layer and $\widetilde{X}$ is the adversarial example resulting in misleading interpretations. α, β and γ are the coefficients to balance the impact of the loss function terms. We will discuss each term one by one:

1. Interpretation Loss: The first term ensures that the interpretations of $\widetilde{X}$ resemble the targeted interpretation $\omega^\dagger$. This attack can be reformulated as an untargeted attack by replacing the current term with $-\|\Phi_f(\widetilde{X}) - \Phi_f(X)\|$. In the case of the targeted attack, $\omega^\dagger$ can come from another set of interpretations with different but still realistic phenotypes, such as the interpretations of a randomly-selected patient, or patients' average interpretations of a different class than the X's class c^*. Since this leads to a more realistic scenario we proceed with targeted attacks.

2. Perturbation Loss: The second term aims to keep the adversarial perturbations small. We optimize the perturbations using L_1 norm rather than widely used L_2-norm or L_∞-norm for images. L_1 norm for adversarial attacks on EHR

Algorithm 1: Interpretation Attack on EHR

Function: MINIMIZE-ATTACK-LOSS(.) : returns X and the corresponding
 Y by minimizing Eq. 3

Input: initial clean sample (X_{clean}, Y_{clean}), initial coefficients $(\alpha_{init}, \beta_{init})$ in
 Eq. 3, number of iterations T, the maximum possible β value $\beta_{treshold}$
 and the number of extra steps for penalizing $steps_{extra}$

Initialize: $\alpha, \beta = \alpha_{init}, \beta_{init}$; $X_0, Y_0 = X_{clean}, Y_{clean}$

1 **for** $t \in \{1, ..., T\}$ **do**
2   X_t, Y_t = MINIMIZE-ATTACK-LOSS(X_{t-1}, α, β)
3   **if** $Y_t \neq Y_{clean}$ **then**   // Dynamically penalize the optimization
4   **while** $Y_t \neq Y_{clean}$ **do**
5            $\alpha, \beta = \alpha/2, \beta \times 2$
6   X_t, Y_t = MINIMIZE-ATTACK-LOSS(X_t, α, β)
7   **if** $\beta > \beta_{threshold}$ **then return** Attack-failure
8   **end**
9   **for** $s_e \in \{1, ..., steps_{extra}\}$ **do**
10   X_t, Y_t = MINIMIZE-ATTACK-LOSS(X_t, α, β)
11   **end**
12        $\alpha, \beta = \alpha_{init}, \beta_{init}$
13   **end**
14 **end**
15 Return X_i from $\{X_1, ..., X_T\}$ with $Y_i = Y_{clean}$ and its interpretations have the
 least distance to the target interpretations (i.e. $\min \|\Phi_f(X_i) - \omega^\dagger\|$)

---

data are more meaningful for several reasons. First, EHR data are sparse, where
many of the values are either zero or imputed and hence do not carry much
information. Second, unlike images, different medical attributes carry different
influences and weights on the output. Consequently, L_1 norm is suitable to meet
both sparsity and heterogeneity of the EHR data [1,22].

3. Classification Loss: The third term aims to keep the class prediction
unchanged. Our interpretation method is non-post-hoc, so the predictions are
highly tied to the interpretations. Thus we need a more powerful function to
keep the class of $\widetilde{X}$ unchanged. We employ the logits based function for this
purpose since it can be well optimized for manipulating the class predictions,
especially for non-linear objective $f(\widetilde{x}) = c^*$ [2]. We will show in Sect. 3.4 that
it can be improved so that the output space $Logit(\widetilde{X})$ resembles $Logit(X)$ and
hence helps the adversarial example remain undetectable.

3.3 Optimization with Dynamic Penalty

Equation 2 denotes how the parameters of the model, including weights and
attributions, are directly involved in the explanations of the input. We observed
that in some cases, the objective to change in interpretations might lead to a
different class label. Given that the interpretation attack is conducted using a
gradient descent algorithm, we use dynamic penalty for the interpretation and
classification loss terms for preventing the prediction change.

Concretely, it involves adjusting the coefficient in Eq. 3 to prioritize the objective of keeping the prediction label unchanged, i.e., incur a higher penalty whenever encountering a label change in any iteration. We can achieve this by decreasing α and increasing β by a factor (e.g., the factor is set to 2 in our implementation) until the original class label is attained. We can then continue using these coefficients for a few more steps to move away from the classification boundaries. If this penalization process continues without successfully restoring the original class, the algorithm is considered to have failed. Algorithm 1 outlines the different components of the attack.

3.4 Minimizing Detectability

To carry out a stealthy attack, two aspects must be considered. The first is to keep the perturbations in the input space minimum, while the second is to maintain the integrity of the output space which includes the final class predictions and their associated logits. The reason is that many state-of-the-art defense methods for adversarial examples check changes both in the input feature space and the output logits space [14,24]. So in order to minimize the detectability, it is necessary to ensure that the logits do not change drastically during the attack. We observed that as we repeatedly apply and remove the penalty according to Algorithm 1, it causes the output space of the adversarial example to oscillate near the classification boundaries. Consequently, while the final label is the same as the original class, the logits do not resemble the original logits, nor does the confidence level of the adversarial prediction. This difference in logits, which we will refer to as output space, can be used to detect the attack.

To address this issue, we propose enhancing (3) by replacing the classification loss with two different alternatives. First we use the Kullback-Leibler divergence to directly compare the distribution of the original sample and adversarial example logits in order to keep them similar. We denote this divergence by $KL \, (\, Logit(X) \, || \, Logit(\widetilde{X}) \,)$ (KL **attack**). Second, similar to the idea of C&W conventional adversarial attacks [2], we use max ($\max\{Logit(\widetilde{X})_i : i \neq c^*\} - Logit(\widetilde{X})_{c^*}, -\kappa$) where κ is a positive adjustable value and maintains a margin between the predicted logit and the second largest logit value to ensure high confidence in the predicted class (**Confident attack** parameterized by κ). Since the classifier is trained based on the clean examples' manifold, it can classify them with high confidence. So by ensuring high confidence predictions for the adversarial examples, we can keep their logits similar to their original counterparts.

3.5 Metrics for Evaluation

For conventional adversarial examples, attack success rate (ASR) is measured as percentage of examples with flipped class labels. However, interpretation attacks aim to alter the multi-dimensional interpretation vector, making it difficult to establish a clear binary metric for measuring the success of the attack. In the

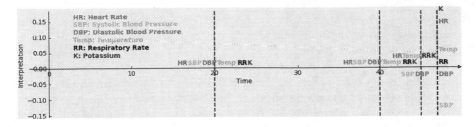

Fig. 1. Interpretations of a patient's EHR data for six attributes *(RR, HR, K, SBP, DBP, Temp)* with heart failure at the final time-stamp. Interpretations of different attributes can be compared with each other in each specific time stamp. Also each attribute separately can be explored for its changes across time. The interpretations for EHR data generally gain more importance as the time of disease onset approaches.

subsequent discussion, we will outline two particular aspects of EHR data that must be taken into account when defining evaluation metrics.

In many application of EHR data, the interpretations may carry either positive or negative connotations, each with its unique significance. For example, when predicting the likelihood of a specific disease, the use of a particular medication may negatively affect the prognosis and decrease the chance of disease onset. For a clinician, the classifier's explanation of such a drug is no less important than the factors that indicate positive interpretations towards the prediction.

Another characteristic of EHR data is the heterogeneity and time sensitivity. Unlike pixels in images, the diverse attributes in EHR data hold distinct meanings, and clinician's interpretation may differ for each attribute. Additionally, the value of interpretations for clinicians is affected by the timing of attribute collection. Clinicians attach more significance to the data points that are closer to the disease onset. Figure 1 displays interpretations of some attributes calculated by RETAIN for predicting heart failure in a patient. Given these factors, we propose three metrics to evaluate the sucess of the interpretation attack, which consider the connotations of the interpretations, the attribute-level heterogeneity, and the visit-level time awareness.

Signed Top-K Intersection Size: According to Ghorbani et al. [8], in many cases, when interpreting a model, the explanations of the most important features are often of interest. In a gradient-based saliency map, the top-K features are determined by their magnitudes. Here we involve the connotation of the interpretations and assess the success of the attack by comparing the proportion of top-K features with consistent signs before and after the attack. So if $A = \{a_1, ..., a_k\}$ and $B = \{b_1, ..., b_k\}$ are the sets of the K largest absolute-value dimensions of $\Phi(\widetilde{X})$ and $\Phi(X)$ respectively, and $C = A \cap B$, then we have

$$topK(C) = |\{c_i \in C : \Phi(\widetilde{X})_{c_i} * \Phi(X)_{c_i} > 0\}|. \tag{4}$$

Asymmetrical Signed Top-K Intersection Size: Since the EHR is sequential and time-sensitive, the importance of different attributes are comparable in each timestamp that they are collected. To reflect that, we suggest a new metric that measures the top-K salient features in corresponding multivariate time series at each time point and then aggregate them.

Also, we assign weight ϕ_i to each time to better attain the perspectives of clinicians who may place greater emphasis on certain times. These weights can be achieved by background knowledge (e.g., higher weight on certain time points before the disease onset) or approximated by how the interpretable model weight different times, e.g., by taking 100 random samples from the clean data and summing up their interpretation values of all attributes at any given time. The resulting values are averaged over all samples to derive the weight that should be assigned to that specific time. For time $t_i \in \{1, \ldots, t\}$, we denote $A_{t_i} = \{a_j^{t_i}\}_{j=1}^k$ and $B_{t_i} = \{b_j^{t_i}\}_{j=1}^k$ as the sets of the K largest absolute-value dimensions of $\Phi(\widetilde{X}_{t_i})$ and $\Phi(X_{t_i})$, respectively, and their intersectino as $C_{t_i} = A_{t_i} \cap B_{t_i}$.

$$topK\_asym = \sum_{i=1}^{t} \phi_i * topK(C_i). \tag{5}$$

Wasserstein Distance: The Wasserstein distance measures the cost of moving a variable mass and is well-suited for comparing changes in time series. Its ability to capture perturbations has made it increasingly popular in the context of adversarial examples. We use the Wasserstein distance to measure the changes of contribution by each attribute as time series - since the modality of data is different across different attributes as discussed before. The resulting distances are then summed to obtain the final Wasserstein distance. Given attribute index $d_j \in [d]$, we denote $X_{[t]}^{d_j}$ as the sequential values of a specific attribute, and $Wass$ as the Wasserstein distance. Then, we calculate the final distance as:

$$Wass\_dist = \sum_{j=1}^{d} W_1(\Phi(\widetilde{X}_{[t]}^j), \Phi(X_{[t]}^j)). \tag{6}$$

where W_1 denotes 1-Wasserstein distance for one dimensional data.

To make Eqs. 4, 5 and 6 consistent with our targeted attack, we calculate these relative metrics:

$$topK^{targeted} = topK(\Phi(\widetilde{X}_i), \omega_i^\dagger)/topK(\Phi(\widetilde{X}_i), \Phi(X_i)); \tag{7}$$

$$topK\_asym^{targeted} = topK\_asym(\Phi(\widetilde{X}_i), \omega_i^\dagger)/topK\_asym(\Phi(\widetilde{X}_i), \Phi(X_i)); \tag{8}$$

$$Wass\_dist^{targeted} = Wass\_dist(\Phi(\widetilde{X}_i), \omega_i^\dagger)/Wass\_dist(\Phi(\widetilde{X}_i), \Phi(X_i)). \tag{9}$$

These three new metrics not only measure how the adversarial interpretations are distant from the original ones, but also reflect how they resemble the target interpretations $\omega^\dagger$. The attacks with larger $topK^{targeted}$ and $topK\_asym^{targeted}$, and with smaller $Wass\_dist^{targeted}$ are more powerful. From now on, when we mention these metrics, we are specifically referring to their targeted version.

3.6 Robustness

To provide robustness, we propose using a sequential auto-encoder to de-noise the input data at inference time and recover the original information. A typical auto-encoder comprises an encoder that compresses the data into a smaller intermediate representation and a decoder that attempts to reconstruct the input data from those embeddings. As the encoder and decoder process the data, the output becomes de-noised. We train the auto-encoder on clean data so it learns the normal manifold. As a result, at inference time, it can remove the noise that caused the input data to become far from this manifold. We then utilize the interpretations of the decoder's output instead of those of the input. Our results show that this approach leads to robust interpretations.

There are two reasons for this. Firstly, the EHR attack perturbations are sparse and have a greater magnitude wherever the features have notable interpretations. Therefore, the de-noiser can restore the original interpretations by reducing the large sparse perturbations on the salient features. Secondly, interpretation attacks differ from traditional adversarial examples in that they aim to modify smoothly distributed, high-dimensional interpretations, especially in EHR data. Once the de-noiser eliminates sudden, sparse perturbations, the interpretations can be regained by relying on the information present in the surrounding neighborhood.

We compare our method with SmoothGrad, a known and strong defense against interpretation attacks [21]. Although the attack in our case is gradient-free, the idea of SmoothGrad is still applicable. It involves adding noise to the data multiple times (usually 10 to 50) and averaging their contributions. However, this method is neither computationally efficient nor effectively provides robustness against EHR attacks as we will show empirically.

4 Experiments

In this section, we will address these questions: 1) What is the effectiveness of the attack in altering the interpretations while maintaining the classification outcomes? 2) Can existing defense methods against adversarial examples detect the interpretation attack? 3) How does the proposed de-noiser approach help with the robustness?

Dataset. The MIMIC-III dataset is a collection of electronic health records from thousands of patients in intensive care units. We use a dataset that was processed by [22] for the binary task of mortality prediction, resulting in 3177 positive samples and 30344 negative samples, each comprising 19 attributes across 48 timestamps including vital signs and lab events. Missing features were filled using the average value across all timestamps, and outliers were removed and imputed according to interquartile range criteria. Finally, each sequence was truncated or padded to 48 h, and each feature was normalized using min-max normalization. We use 80% of the data for training and the rest for testing.

Model Architecture and Parameters. Adversarial examples were generated against RETAIN [5] as our target model, which includes an embedding layer of size 128 and two GRU layers with 128 hidden units. The evaluation results of the test data on the final trained model are $AUROC = 0.92$, $AUPRC = 0.73$, $F1Score = 0.57$ and $Accuracy = 0.86$. We evaluate the detectability of the

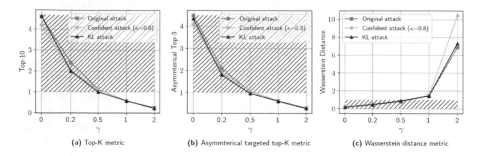

(a) Top-K metric   (b) Asymmterical targeted top-K metric   (c) Wasserstein distance metric

Fig. 2. The comparison of three interpretation attacks, which differ in their penalty term, shown using three metrics. The desirable results are located in the hatched area. A lower perturbation achieved by a smaller γ leads to better attack success, but may also result in a higher detection rate.

interpretation attack using RADAR [24]. It is a robust detection method, specifically developed for traditional EHR adversarial examples where the objective is to change the class. This detector identifies adversarial examples through both changes in input space and also output space relative to the normal manifold, making it well-suited for our purposes. Finally to enhance the data robustness, we de-noised data by the same auto-encoder architecture as that used in RADAR.

4.1 Attack Performance

Comparison of Attacks. We evaluate the attack performance based on three different metrics introduced in Sect. 3.5. We compare the original attack (Eq. 3) with two alternatives, the KL attack and the Confident attack, proposed in Sect. 3.4. In our experiments with the Confident attack, we set $\kappa = 0.8$, as it provides a high level of undetectability. Our comparison is based on different values of the coefficient γ in Eq. 3, which constrains the perturbation size. The higher the value of γ, the more restricted the attack is in terms of its distance from the original sample. Since the parameters α and β are dynamically adjusted by Algorithm 1, we simply select their initial values as 1. Also based on a grid-search we set $T = 1000$ and $steps_{extra} = 10$.

Figure 2 illustrates the results based on the three metrics (Eq. 7, 8, 9) from left to right, respectively. The hatched area in each figure demonstrates the most desirable results. For Fig. 2.a and b, a ratio of over 1 implies that the interpretations are more similar to the targeted interpretations than the original ones, and the larger the ratio, the better. Conversely, in Fig. 2.c, the opposite is true, as this measurement employs a distance metric rather than the intersection of salient features. Although the attacks are very similar, in the next section, we will show the main difference lies in the stealthiness of each of these attacks.

Selection of K. Figure 3 demonstrates that how the selection of K in top-K metrics (7 and 8) impacts our evaluation of the attack's success when $\gamma = 0$. In

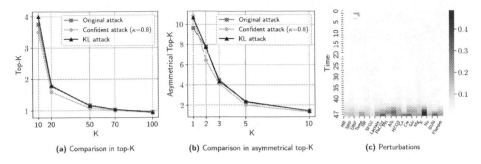

Fig. 3. The comparison of different values of K in two metrics, top-K (a) and asymmetrical top-K (b). The concentration of perturbations on the latest time-stamps (c) confirms that small values of K are sufficient for evaluation.

metric 4 since K is calculated in each time and over a lower dimension than the entire EHR data, we set the value of K to a lower number than in metric 8. As expected, the value of K affects the degree of overlap between interpretations before and after attack. Figure 3.c shows the average perturbations of all the adversarial examples when γ is zero and there is no constraint on the input space. The perturbations are concentrated on the latest time-stamps which hold the most significant interpretations in the model and clinical environments. Therefore, selecting a large K does not yield significant interpretations, particularly since many interpretations that are distant from these timestamps have close to zero. Consequently, considering large K results in overlapping interpretations that do not offer meaningful insights into the attack's success.

4.2 Attack Detectability

Figure 4 illustrates an example before and after the attack and their difference for the confident attack with $\gamma = 0.5$. The attack causes sparse but strong perturbations, which lead the interpretations to shift from the original to the target interpretations. As previously discussed, the low number of perturbations and their sparsity make them undetectable in EHR data. By decreasing γ, the magnitude and density of the perturbations become more flexible. Figure 5 illustrates the interpretations of the original sample and its adversarial counterpart from Fig. 4 as well as the target interpretations across the latest timestamps. Due to space limitations, only three attributes are included in the figure. It reveals that the sparse perturbation attack caused the adversarial interpretations to deviate from their original values and align more closely with the target interpretations.

We evaluated RADAR to demonstrate whether our proposed interpretation attacks can be detected by existing defense methods against conventional adversarial examples. RADAR exhibits a 100% detection rate for conventional adversarial examples on RETAIN. Figure 6 presents the detection percentage of

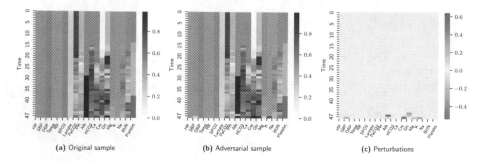

Fig. 4. An input space of a patient's EHRs before (a), and after attack with $\gamma = 5$ (b), and its additive perturbation (c). The perturbation is minimal and sparse.

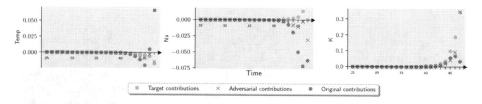

Fig. 5. Comparison of Adversarial, original and target contributions (interpretations) of three attributes of a patient's EHR over time.

different interpretation attacks by RADAR which are significantly lower. As γ increases, the perturbations become smaller, resulting in a decrease in the detection rate in input space. Additionally, considering the detection in output space, when γ is small, the adversarial example has more flexibility during optimization, allowing it to approach the classification decision boundary more closely and activate the penalty process in Algorithm 1 more frequently. In Sect. 3.4, we discussed how KL and confident attacks better maintain similarity between the original and output space in such cases. However, for larger values of γ, the original attack is less likely to trigger the penalty process and remains more stealthy than the KL attack. Generally, the confident attack keeps the output space less detectable and maintains a greater distance from the class boundary.

4.3   Robustness

In this part, we evaluate the effectiveness of the proposed auto-encoder (AE) denoiser based defense method. We report the attack success rate of the attack under the proposed defense method, and compare it with the attack without defense, and the attack with the SmoothGrad defense. We select the confident attack with $\kappa = 0.8$ and $\gamma = 0.5$ as the representative of successful attacks with reasonably high success rate and low detection rate. For SmoothGrad, the best results are reported based on selecting a noise level of 0.1 and calculating the average over 50 samples, which is consistent with the result in paper [21]. Figure 7 displays a comparison of the median and quartile charts of the attack

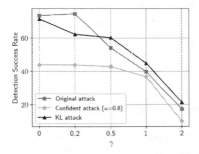

Fig. 6. Detection ratio of interpretation attacks using RADAR.

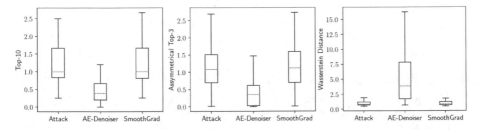

Fig. 7. Robustness of de-noising method vs. SmoothGrad based on three metrics. All figures show the de-noising method outperforms SmoothGrad.

versus the robustness achieved through the de-noising method and SmoothGrad for 100 samples. Smaller values for top-K and asymmetric top-K indicate better robustness, whereas higher values for Wasserstein distance indicate better robustness. As depicted, the de-noising method outperforms SmoothGrad in all metrics.

5   Conclusion

This paper is the first study to develop and adapt interpretation attacks for EHR models. We investigated various aspects of EHR data as well as interpretable models designed specifically for EHR data. We presented interpretation attacks on EHR models optimizing both attack success and detectability and evaluated the attack using customized metrics that address EHR specifications. Our results show that the attack not only can successfully alter the interpretations of the model, but also can evade the detector RADAR, which is capable of detecting 100% of conventional adversarial examples. To counteract the attack, we proposed a de-noiser defense and demonstrated that it improved the robustness and outperformed existing method SmoothGrad. Future research can focus on modifying EHR interpretable models to make them more robust, as well as exploring data preprocessing, data augmentation, and adversarial training to enhance the robustness of EHR models.

References

1. An, S., Xiao, C., Stewart, W.F., Sun, J.: Longitudinal adversarial attack on electronic health records data. In: The World Wide Web Conference, pp. 2558–2564 (2019)
2. Carlini, N., Wagner, D.: Towards evaluating the robustness of neural networks. In: 2017 IEEE Symposium on Security and Privacy (SP), pp. 39–57. IEEE (2017)
3. Chen, J., Wu, X., Rastogi, V., Liang, Y., Jha, S.: Robust attribution regularization. In: Advances in Neural Information Processing Systems, vol. 32 (2019)
4. Chen, P., Dong, W., Wang, J., Lu, X., Kaymak, U., Huang, Z.: Interpretable clinical prediction via attention-based neural network. BMC Med. Inform. Decis. Making **20**(3), 1–9 (2020)
5. Choi, E., Bahadori, M.T., Sun, J., Kulas, J., Schuetz, A., Stewart, W.: Retain: an interpretable predictive model for healthcare using reverse time attention mechanism. In: Advances in Neural Information Processing Systems, vol. 29 (2016)
6. Dombrowski, A.K., Alber, M., Anders, C., Ackermann, M., Müller, K.R., Kessel, P.: Explanations can be manipulated and geometry is to blame. In: Advances in Neural Information Processing Systems, vol. 32 (2019)
7. Dombrowski, A.K., Anders, C.J., Müller, K.R., Kessel, P.: Towards robust explanations for deep neural networks. Pattern Recogn. **121**, 108194 (2022)
8. Ghorbani, A., Abid, A., Zou, J.: Interpretation of neural networks is fragile. In: Proceedings of the AAAI Conference on Artificial Intelligence, vol. 33, pp. 3681–3688 (2019)
9. Kwon, B.C., et al.: RetainVis: visual analytics with interpretable and interactive recurrent neural networks on electronic medical records. IEEE Trans. Vis. Comput. Graph. **25**(1), 299–309 (2018)
10. Li, Y., et al.: BEHRT: transformer for electronic health records. Sci. Rep. **10**(1), 1–12 (2020)
11. Lipton, Z.C.: The mythos of model interpretability: in machine learning, the concept of interpretability is both important and slippery. Queue **16**(3), 31–57 (2018)
12. Luo, J., Ye, M., Xiao, C., Ma, F.: HiTANet: hierarchical time-aware attention networks for risk prediction on electronic health records. In: Proceedings of the 26th ACM SIGKDD International Conference on Knowledge Discovery & Data Mining, pp. 647–656 (2020)
13. Ma, F., Chitta, R., Zhou, J., You, Q., Sun, T., Gao, J.: Dipole: Diagnosis prediction in healthcare via attention-based bidirectional recurrent neural networks. In: Proceedings of the 23rd ACM SIGKDD International Conference on Knowledge Discovery and Data Mining, pp. 1903–1911 (2017)
14. Meng, D., Chen, H.: Magnet: a two-pronged defense against adversarial examples. In: Proceedings of the 2017 ACM SIGSAC Conference on Computer and Communications Security, pp. 135–147 (2017)
15. Quellec, G., Charriere, K., Boudi, Y., Cochener, B., Lamard, M.: Deep image mining for diabetic retinopathy screening. Med. Image Anal. **39**, 178–193 (2017)
16. Rasmy, L., Xiang, Y., Xie, Z., Tao, C., Zhi, D.: Med-BERT: pretrained contextualized embeddings on large-scale structured electronic health records for disease prediction. NPJ Dig. Med. **4**(1), 1–13 (2021)
17. Selvaraju, R.R., Cogswell, M., Das, A., Vedantam, R., Parikh, D., Batra, D.: Gradcam: visual explanations from deep networks via gradient-based localization. In: Proceedings of the IEEE International Conference on Computer Vision, pp. 618–626 (2017)

18. Shang, J., Ma, T., Xiao, C., Sun, J.: Pre-training of graph augmented transformers for medication recommendation. In: Kraus, S. (ed.) Proceedings of the 28th International Joint Conference on Artificial Intelligence, IJCAI 2019, pp. 5953–5959. IJCAI International Joint Conference on Artificial Intelligence, International Joint Conferences on Artificial Intelligence (2019). https://doi.org/10.24963/ijcai.2019/825

19. Shrikumar, A., Greenside, P., Kundaje, A.: Learning important features through propagating activation differences. In: International Conference on Machine Learning, pp. 3145–3153. PMLR (2017)

20. Simonyan, K., Vedaldi, A., Zisserman, A.: Deep inside convolutional networks: visualising image classification models and saliency maps. arXiv preprint arXiv:1312.6034 (2013)

21. Smilkov, D., Thorat, N., Kim, B., Viégas, F., Wattenberg, M.: SmoothGrad: removing noise by adding noise. arXiv preprint arXiv:1706.03825 (2017)

22. Sun, M., Tang, F., Yi, J., Wang, F., Zhou, J.: Identify susceptible locations in medical records via adversarial attacks on deep predictive models. In: Proceedings of the 24th ACM SIGKDD International Conference on Knowledge Discovery & Data Mining, pp. 793–801 (2018)

23. Szegedy, C., et al.: Intriguing properties of neural networks. arXiv preprint arXiv:1312.6199 (2013)

24. Wang, W., Tang, P., Xiong, L., Jiang, X.: RADAR: recurrent autoencoder based detector for adversarial examples on temporal EHR. In: Dong, Y., Mladenić, D., Saunders, C. (eds.) ECML PKDD 2020. LNCS (LNAI), vol. 12460, pp. 105–121. Springer, Cham (2021). https://doi.org/10.1007/978-3-030-67667-4_7

25. Xu, Y., Biswal, S., Deshpande, S.R., Maher, K.O., Sun, J.: RAIM: recurrent attentive and intensive model of multimodal patient monitoring data. In: Proceedings of the 24th ACM SIGKDD International Conference on Knowledge Discovery & Data Mining, pp. 2565–2573 (2018)

26. Yeh, C.K., Hsieh, C.Y., Suggala, A., Inouye, D.I., Ravikumar, P.K.: On the (in) fidelity and sensitivity of explanations. In: Advances in Neural Information Processing Systems, vol. 32 (2019)

An Empirical Evaluation of the Rashomon Effect in Explainable Machine Learning

Sebastian Müller[1,4]([✉]) [iD], Vanessa Toborek[1,4] [iD], Katharina Beckh[3,4] [iD], Matthias Jakobs[2,4] [iD], Christian Bauckhage[1,3,4] [iD], and Pascal Welke[5] [iD]

[1] University of Bonn, Bonn, Germany
semueller@uni-bonn.de
[2] TU Dortmund University, Dortmund, Germany
[3.] Fraunhofer IAIS, Sankt Augustin, Germany
[4] Lamarr Institute, Bonn, Germany
[5] TU Wien, Vienna, Austria

Abstract. The Rashomon Effect describes the following phenomenon: for a given dataset there may exist many models with equally good performance but with different solution strategies. The Rashomon Effect has implications for Explainable Machine Learning, especially for the comparability of explanations. We provide a unified view on three different comparison scenarios and conduct a quantitative evaluation across different datasets, models, attribution methods, and metrics. We find that hyperparameter-tuning plays a role and that metric selection matters. Our results provide empirical support for previously anecdotal evidence and exhibit challenges for both scientists and practitioners.

Keywords: Explainable ML · Interpretable ML · Attribution Methods · Rashomon Effect · Disagreement Problem

1 Introduction

We demonstrate the impact of the Rashomon Effect when analyzing ML models. The Rashomon Effect [8] describes the phenomenon that there may exist many models within a hypothesis class which solve a dataset equally well. The set of these models is referred to as the Rashomon Set [12,37]. From a data-centric perspective this phenomenon is also called Predictive Multiplicity [23], meaning that there exist many strategies to solve a task on a dataset. Other works use Rashomon Sets to analyze and describe data [12,30]. Somewhat surprisingly, the Rashomon Effect has not yet found wider attention in the Explainable Machine Learning (XML) literature. Although a few works have observed the effect it was only anecdotally or without referring to its proper name [14,20,35].

XML has recently become a very active area of research and numerous explanation methods exist [1,9,24]. Many approaches explain black-box models in a post-hoc manner by providing attribution scores [22,27] which assign each input dimension a numerical value that represents this feature's importance with

D. Koutra et al. (Eds.): ECML PKDD 2023, LNAI 14171, pp. 462–478, 2023.
https://doi.org/10.1007/978-3-031-43418-1_28

respect to the model decision. Attribution scores are used to answer questions such as "What feature was the most important in this input sample?" and have been used to uncover spurious correlations in the data [29] and biased behavior of models [21]. However, attribution scores are sometimes ambiguous and their interpretation depends on the application context. It is hard to decide at what magnitude a feature is still important, particularly, if magnitudes of attribution scores can be sorted into an evenly descending order. It follows that the task of comparing different attribution methods is a difficult problem. Several works touch upon the problem of explanation comparison [5,7,19,26,35] from different perspectives.

Our main contribution is an empirical analysis of one novel and two existing perspectives, 1) demonstrating model-specific sensitivity regarding the hyperparameter choice for explanation methods, 2) comparison of different explanations from the same attribution method on differently initialized but otherwise identical model architectures [5,35] and 3) the disagreement between different explanations applied to the same architecture and parameterization [19,26]. We place these three perspectives into a unified framework to investigate how the Rashomon Effect manifests itself in each situation. Our evaluation is conducted on four datasets of entirely different nature, analyzing differences in models explained by five popular attribution methods using both naive and established human-centered similarity measures.[1] Our results highlight the need to fine-tune the hyperparameters of XML methods on a per-model basis. We do find empirical support for the disagreement problem, meaning practitioners cannot expect consistent explanations across methods. Further, the high solution diversity across models hinders the use of XML as an epistemic tool.

Next, Sect. 2 discusses how we connect different parts of the literature for our analysis. Section 3 describes the experimental setup in detail. Sections 4.1, 4.2 and 4.3 present results and discuss the three perspectives we analyze. Section 4.4 summarizes our main findings. Section 5 concludes.

2   Comparing Attribution Scores

Given a classifier and a datum, an attribution method assigns each input dimension a numerical value that represents this feature's importance with respect to the model decision. Hence, an attribution scoring depends on three variables: 1) the model, 2) the input sample, and 3) the attribution method. This distinction enables us to systematically investigate the consequences of the Rashomon Effect on established and novel perspectives in XML in one framework. This framework is the first to bring the different perspectives into a unifying picture which we present in Table 1. Our main mode of comparison is centered around comparing pairs of attribution scores. Hence, we assume that the scores belong to the same sample from the same dataset. We investigate model- or attribution method-dependent effects and do not consider the scenario where the data is the same but both models and methods are different.

---

[1] Our code is available at github.com/lamarr-xai-group/RashomonEffect.

Table 1. We investigate the Rashomon Effect in Explainable Machine Learning for a set of models and a set of attribution methods. Three interesting scenarios arise for a fixed input-sample from a given dataset.

Same Model	Same Sample	Same Attr Method	Scenario	Examples
1	1	1	Numerical Stability	–
0	1	1	Solution Diversity	[12, 17, 35]
1	1	0	Disagreement Problem	[11, 19, 26]

Numerical Stability (111): In Sect. 4.1 we discuss the scenario where the same model and same attribution method are applied to the same sample. This perspective is relevant to non-deterministic explanation methods that can be controlled by hyperparameters. We investigate whether there are model-specific differences regarding optimal parameter choice and find that the hyperparameter choice is significantly dependent on both the investigated model and dataset. This suggests that blindly applying non-optimal hyperparameters can lead to erroneous explanations and thus wrong takeaways in an application scenario. This need for rigorous hyperparameter tuning is mostly overlooked in the literature.

Solution Diversity (011): We can compare how similar or dissimilar two models are w.r.t. their solution strategies by comparing explanations that were computed for each of them using the same attribution method. Comparing any two models not only by one, but by the average difference on explanations over several samples, will only be able to measure a difference, if two models consistently behave differently. This is a coarse, but sufficiently sensitive measure. Using this measure as a basis, we provide a large quantitative view of the Rashomon Effect itself, recently also observed in [35]. In Sect. 4.2, we extend existing results by comparing substantially more models on additional data domains and investigate how diverse the strategies of the models within a Rashomon Set are. We observe very high diversity in most cases and discuss practical implications for machine learning (ML) as an epistemic tool [28, 39].

Disagreement Problem (110): Aiming to find the "right" explanation, prior work compared different attribution methods applied to the same model on the same sample. It was found that explanations of different attribution methods often differ significantly, which is now known as the Disagreement Problem [5, 11, 13, 15, 16, 19, 26]. So far, the Disagreement Problem was only reported on individual or a very small number of models. It has not been sufficiently explored whether the disagreement actually is model-dependent, i.e., whether any pair of attribution methods is consistently less similar than other pairs across models. We investigate this question in Sect. 4.3. We provide quantitative support for anecdotal observations from the literature and add practically relevant insights.

A fundamental question is which metric should be used to compare two attribution scores. One possible approach is to use feature (dis-)agreement, i.e.

the overlap of the top-k "most important" features, which ML practitioners indicated as a key measure for disagreement [19]. Along the same lines, ranking correlation measures are used, such as Kendall's τ [26]. Another option is to base the comparison on typical distance measures, such as cosine similarity [7] or Euclidean distance [11,25]. In previous studies, only one metric or metric type has been considered. In this work, we provide a comparison of both Euclidean and (dis-)agreement based measures.

3   Experimental Framework

Before we report our results we introduce the experimental setup. To emphasize the extent of the Rashomon Effect we will remove randomness from the training process with the exception of model initialization.

3.1   Datasets

For the comparison we chose four publicly available datasets. *AG News* [40], a benchmark dataset for text classification with an average sentence length of 43 words. Three tabular datasets containing only real valued variables: *Dry Bean* [18], a 16-dimensional multi-class dataset with 7 classes of dry beans, *Breast Cancer Wisconsin (Diagnostic)* [36], a classical dataset posing a binary classification problem over 30 features, and *Ionosphere* [31], a binary classification problem over 34 features based on radar signal returns. The amount of data available with each dataset differs greatly. A random subset X_{ref} was held out from each dataset during training and later used for the computation of explanations. X_{ref} contains 300 samples for AG News, 1050 for Dry Bean, 114 for Breast Cancer and 71 for Ionosphere.

3.2   Models: Architecture, Training and Selection

For the tabular datasets we use small, fully connected Feed-Forward Neural Networks with ReLU activation functions. Models for Dry Bean, Breast Cancer and Ionosphere use 3×16, 16 and 8 neurons, respectively. For the AG News dataset we use a Bi-LSTM model with 128 dimensions for each direction and a fully connected output layer. We learn a 128 dimensional word embedding from scratch. We use the softmax function as output activation in all models.

We trained 100 models on each tabular dataset and 20 models on AG News. We fixed all random aspects of the model training except for the initialization of the network parameters. Each model observed exactly the same amount of data in the exact same order. All differences in model behavior will thus only stem from the initialization. To build the final Rashomon Set for each dataset, we choose all models with at most 5% difference in accuracy to the best model. With the exception of the Ionosphere dataset, nearly all models are selected. We present average model accuracy and average pairwise output similarity computed with the Jensen-Shannon-Distance over X_{ref} in Table 2. All models achieve a high accuracy and are nearly indistinguishable by their output distributions.

Table 2. Mean accuracy and mean pairwise Jensen-Shannon-Distance (JSD) of all models over X_{ref}. All models were selected to lie within 5% accuracy of the best model. According to both metrics, all models perform nearly indistinguishably. JSD is bounded to $[0, 1]$.

	AG News	Dry Bean	Breast Cancer	Ionosphere
Mean accuracy on X_{ref}	0.91 ± 0.01	0.89 ± 0.01	0.95 ± 0.01	0.86 ± 0.01
Mean JSD on X_{ref}	0.0315 ± 0.004	0.0207 ± 0.004	0.0019 ± 0.001	0.0103 ± 0.007

3.3   Attribution Methods

We compare five attribution methods. From the family of gradient based methods we use Vanilla Grad (VG) [32], Smooth Grad (SG) [33], and Integrated Gradient (IG) [34]. From the family of perturbation based methods we include KernelSHAP (KS) [22] and LIME (LI) [27] for which we use the implementations provided by Captum[2]. For IG, KS, and LI we use zero-baselines. SG samples with a noise ratio of 10%. Hyperparameters that further impact approximation behavior will be discussed in Sect. 4.1.

3.4   Model Dissimilarity Measures Based on Attribution Scores

We use the following formula to express the scenarios in Table 1:

$$\mathcal{D}(f_a, f_b, X, \phi_1, \phi_2, d) = \frac{1}{|X|} \sum_{x \in X} d(\phi_1(f_a, x), \phi_2(f_b, x)) \tag{1}$$

where f_a, $f_b \in R$ are classifier functions from our Rashomon Set, $X \subseteq X_{\mathrm{ref}} : \{x | x \in X_{\mathrm{ref}} \wedge \arg\max f_a(x) = \arg\max f_b(x)\}$ is a subset of the reference set where both classifiers agree on the label, $\phi_1, \phi_2 \in \Phi = \{\text{VG, SG, IG, KS, LI}\}$ are the aforementioned attribution methods and $d \in D = \{$Feature Disagreement, Sign Disagreement, Euclid, Euclid-abs$\}$ are dissimilarity measures on attribution scores that we introduce now.

Feature Disagreement considers only the k top features (indices of k features of highest magnitude) from each of the two explanations and computes then the fraction of common features between them. *Sign Disagreement* is a more strict version of Feature Disagreement. It applies Feature Disagreement and then subselects only the top features that also have the same sign in both explanations. *Euclid* and *Euclid-abs* are the Euclidean distance and the Euclidean distance over absolute values of two attribution scores. Analogously to [19], for the disagreement measures we set $k = 11$ for AG News, $k = 4$ for Dry Bean, and $k = 8$ for both Breast Cancer and Ionosphere.

---

[2] See project page at github.com/pytorch/captum.

4   Examining the Rashomon Effect

We now present and discuss the experiments on numerical stability (Sect. 4.1), the Rashomon Effect itself (Sect. 4.2) and the Disagreement Problem (Sect. 4.3). Each section provides its own discussion.

4.1   Numerical Stability and the Rashomon Effect (111)

In this section we investigate the setting $\mathcal{D}(f_a, f_a, X = X_{\text{ref}}, \phi_1, \phi_1, \text{Euclid})$ to analyze the numerical stability of all ϕ_* w.r.t. differences of individual f_*.

Attribution methods often require to choose hyperparameters that control approximation behavior. For IG this is the number of steps used to approximate the integral. For SG, KS, and LI one has control over the number of samples evaluated during computation. This allows to adjust the computation time but if the parameter is too small, the resulting explanations may differ between two computations. We investigate this approximation stability across many models: Do explanations converge at the same hyperparameter for all models and if not, how large are the differences between individual models?

On the AG News dataset for SG we evaluate sampling hyperparameters $p \in [25, 50, 75, 100, 150]$, for IG, KS, and LI we evaluate $p \in [25, 50, 100, 150, 300]$. On the tabular datasets we compute the approximation stability for $p \in [25, 50, 75, 100, 125]$ for all methods. We quantify numerical stability in the following way: We compute ten SG, KS, and LI explanations for each sample in X_{ref} for each p. Next, we compute the pairwise Euclidean distances between all ten explanations. To obtain a stability score for one model, the average is taken across all samples in X_{ref}. As a final stability score we report the mean and standard deviation of this score across all models. IG depends deterministically on the number of steps in the integral, hence, we do not compute ten explanations per sample. Instead, we compute the pairwise distance between explanations for the same point obtained by p_i and p_{i+1}. To assess model dependent differences regarding the optimal choice of p, we compute for each model the smallest p_i in the set of parameters, where p_{i+1} did not improve the average stability by a factor of two.

Results for all datasets are presented in Table 3. The rows that start with SG, IG, KS, and LI report numerical stability for each method. The last row (#) reports the accumulated number of models whose explanations are stable at $\leq p$. The aggregated counts correspond to the attribution methods in the order as they appear in the rows: SG, IG, KS, LI. Unsurprisingly, numerical stability improves across all models with increasing p. At the same time, models clearly respond differently to an increase in p. For SG the spread spans four values of p on each dataset and the selected values for p can differ by a factor of up to three. For IG there is no spread on the tabular datasets, but it has the largest spread compared to any other method on AG News. For KS and LI the models mostly split between two consecutive values. Note that KS displays conspicuously large numerical instability for smaller p, even on the smaller tabular datasets. Default parameters for KS and LI are set to 25 and 50 in Captum, which is insufficient

Table 3. Explanation stability for sampling parameter p. We report mean±std across all models and samples for each attribution method. The values for IG describe the difference between using p_{i+1} instead of p_i. The last row (#) accumulates the number of models that converged at $\leq p$ for SG/IG/KS/LI.

	25	50	75	100	150
SG	0.0062 ± 0.0028	0.0044 ± 0.0020	0.0036 ± 0.0016	0.0039 ± 0.0029	0.0027 ± 0.0013
	25	50	100	150	300
IG	0.0734 ± 0.2740	0.0532 ± 0.2201	0.0412 ± 0.1389	0.0329 ± 0.1380	$-$
KS	$6.48e4 \pm 1.3e5$	$3.34e5 \pm 4.94e5$	$6.39e6 \pm 1.15e7$	1.7121 ± 0.1655	0.9515 ± 0.0695
LI	0.0470 ± 0.0117	0.0330 ± 0.0079	0.0220 ± 0.0055	0.0175 ± 0.0045	0.0119 ± 0.0032
#	$-/1/-/-$	$10/2/-/1$	$18/18/-/19$	$19/18/20/19$	$20/20/20/20$

(a) AG News. Total number of models is 20. The set of evaluated parameters is different from other datasets and different for SG from other methods.

	25	50	75	100	125
SG	0.0005 ± 0.0003	0.0004 ± 0.0002	0.0003 ± 0.0002	0.0003 ± 0.0001	0.0003 ± 0.0001
IG	0.0002 ± 0.0001	0.0001 ± 0.0001	0.0001 ± 0.0000	0.0000 ± 0.0000	$-$
KS	0.6087 ± 0.1724	0.2936 ± 0.0576	0.2232 ± 0.0422	0.1872 ± 0.0350	0.1645 ± 0.0306
LI	0.1561 ± 0.0413	0.0956 ± 0.0272	0.0723 ± 0.0219	0.0596 ± 0.0190	0.0515 ± 0.0170
#	$-/-/-/-$	$39/-/73/96$	$62/99/99/99$	$87/99/99/99$	$99/99/99/99$

(b) Beans. Total number of models is 99.

	25	50	75	100	125
SG	0.0253 ± 0.0140	0.0181 ± 0.0099	0.0148 ± 0.0081	0.0128 ± 0.0070	0.0114 ± 0.0063
IG	0.0030 ± 0.0012	0.0013 ± 0.0006	0.0008 ± 0.0004	0.0006 ± 0.0003	$-$
KS	$8.28e4 \pm 1.67e5$	0.4523 ± 0.0735	0.3036 ± 0.0402	0.2462 ± 0.0312	0.2126 ± 0.0265
LI	0.0506 ± 0.0152	0.0345 ± 0.0104	0.0279 ± 0.0085	0.0241 ± 0.0073	0.0215 ± 0.0065
#	$-/-/-/-$	$28/-/-/65$	$58/100/95/86$	$91/100/100/100$	$100/100/100/100$

(c) Breastcancer. Total number of models is 100.

	25	50	75	100	125
SG	0.0298 ± 0.0135	0.0209 ± 0.0095	0.0172 ± 0.0077	0.0148 ± 0.0066	0.0133 ± 0.0060
IG	0.0036 ± 0.0017	0.0017 ± 0.0008	0.0011 ± 0.0005	0.0009 ± 0.0004	$-$
KS	$1.02e5 \pm 2.06e5$	$1.81e3 \pm 3.67e3$	0.1990 ± 0.0279	0.1561 ± 0.0205	0.1325 ± 0.0169
LI	0.0995 ± 0.0239	0.0678 ± 0.0166	0.0547 ± 0.0136	0.0472 ± 0.0119	0.0423 ± 0.0107
#	$-/-/-/-$	$13/-/-/34$	$28/51/42/43$	$47/51/51/50$	$51/51/51/51$

(d) Ionosphere. Total number of models is 51.

for a large number of models. For the remainder of the paper we use explanations computed with the following p for all datasets: SG 100, IG 200, KS and LI 300.

Our results show that, for a rigorous workflow, hyperparameters need to be tuned not only based on the dataset but, in fact, for each model individually. Hence, choosing sensible default parameters is difficult. Providing implementations without default values or with very large values might be an option, though impeding user-friendliness. This learning also impacts any down-stream use of explanations such as benchmarking methods to assess the fidelity of an attribution method [3,4,10,11,17,38] or explanation methods that build atop attributions to extract rules as explanations [2]. In those contexts, numerical stability is a pre-requisite to obtain reliable results.

4.2 Solution Diversity Or: The Rashomon Effect as Seen with Different Dissimilarity Measures (011)

In this section we investigate how the Rashomon Effect manifests under different metrics over different attribution methods. In Table 2 we saw that the output behavior of the models is extremely similar. We are now interested to see how diverse the Rashomon Sets appear if we use the explanation based dissimilarity measure defined above. For each dataset and all dissimilarity measures $d \in D$ we evaluate $\mathcal{D}(f_a, f_b, X, \phi_1, \phi_1, d)$ for all pairs of $f_a, f_b \in R$ with $f_a \neq f_b$. Because all attribution scores are specific to the predicted class, we restrict $X \subseteq X_{\text{ref}}$: $\{x | x \in X_{\text{ref}} \wedge \arg\max f_a(x) = \arg\max f_b(x)\}$.

The distances produced by Feature Disagreement and Sign Disagreement are naturally bounded to the $[0, 1]$ interval. The gradient based attribution scores lie in a bounded range because we compute the gradient through the softmax output. Attribution scores for KS and LI produced distances larger than 1 with the two Euclidean metrics on all datasets. In those cases we normalize the Euclidean distances to the range $[0, 1]$ by dividing by the maximal distance observed. Figure 1 visualizes the pairwise distances of all models as histograms. The x-axis discretizes dissimilarities, the farther to the right the more dissimilar. The y-axis is the number of distances in each bin.

Euclid and Euclid-abs overlap significantly in all cases except for IG and SG on the Ionosphere dataset. The Disagreement measures diverge on AG News and Dry Bean. Naturally, Sign Disagreement produces larger dissimilarity scores than Feature Disagreement.

In most of the cases, the means of the disagreement based measures and the Euclidean based measures lie relatively far apart. The exceptions are IG, KS, and LI on AG News, as well as KS and LI on Dry Bean. This means that one metric always measures significantly more differences than the other, but what metric that is depends both on the dataset and method.

We see that with most attribution methods and metrics the Rashomon Sets produce a large variety of distances across all models. This has strong implications for use cases where ML models, specifically (Deep) Neural Networks, are used as epistemic tools to develop hypotheses about the data generation process as it is becoming frequent practice in several disciplines [28,39]. The variance in our results illustrates that the number of viable solution strategies is extensively large, hence, discovering all possibilities is highly improbable in cases where training a large number of models is infeasible. Methods such as ROAR [17] (despite being developed for a different purpose) could be useful to iteratively narrow down the search space but may still fail to uncover all possible correlations. The Rashomon Effect also has implications in user-centered scenarios. In cases where users interact with model explanations and expect a certain

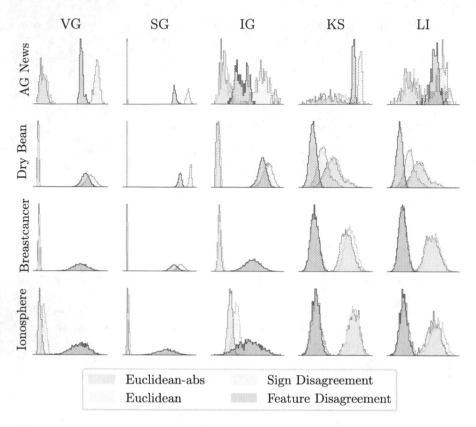

Fig. 1. Histograms over pairwise distances of all models according to Formula 1. Disagreement metrics computed with $k = 11, 4, 8, 8$ for AG News, Beans, Breast Cancer, and Ionosphere, respectively. In the bottom rows both disagreement metrics overlap nearly exactly.

behavioral consistency over time, the deployment of a new model, even if performance itself is very similar, would pose a risk to user trust. Depending on the explanation method, the data domain, and the model, computing explanations can be very costly. Storing explanations for later re-use as a way to mitigate costs only works if the model stays the same.

Table 4. Kendall rank correlation coefficient (τ) between rankings of attribution method pairs. On average we observe a strong or very strong correlation, but the standard deviation indicates that for some models the set of methods that (dis)agree are very different compared to other models.

	AG News	Dry Bean	Breastcancer	Ionosphere
Feature Disagreement	0.67 ± 0.14	0.65 ± 0.26	0.66 ± 0.31	0.63 ± 0.28
Sign Disagreement	0.63 ± 0.10	0.57 ± 0.38	0.64 ± 0.37	0.73 ± 0.24
Euclidean	0.77 ± 0.29	0.69 ± 0.15	0.94 ± 0.12	0.95 ± 0.11
Euclidean-abs	0.79 ± 0.20	0.85 ± 0.15	0.81 ± 0.18	0.84 ± 0.14

In nearly all cases the human-oriented agreement metrics provide a very different picture than the Euclidean distances. Without additional knowledge about the suitability of a metric in a given context, practitioners should not rely on either disagreement or Euclidean measure alone. Use cases like [7], that use explanations to produce training signals for models, could benefit from exploring both kinds of metrics separately or from mixing them in a curriculum.

4.3 The Rashomon Effect and the Disagreement Problem (110)

In this section we investigate the Rashomon Effect on the Disagreement Problem. For all datasets and measures $d \in D$ we compare $\mathcal{D}(f_a, f_a, X, \phi_1, \phi_2, d)$ over all pairs $(\phi_1, \phi_2) \in \Phi \times \Phi$ with $\phi_1 \neq \phi_2$. As before, X is the set of all samples in X_{ref} where the predictions of both models agree.

Existing literature on the Disagreement Problem compares disagreement of method pairs for individual or very few models and only with the disagreement measures [5,11,19,26]. These works report no consistent ranking between method pairs, especially when the data complexity increases.

We now analyze whether we find quantitative support for those observations. Additionally, we extend the analysis of the Disagreement Problem to include results based on the Euclidean distances.

For each individual model we rank the ten possible method pairs from most agreeing to most disagreeing. We calculate Kendall's rank correlation coefficient τ for all model pairs with a sufficiently small p-value (< 0.05). For the remaining τ the mean and standard deviation across all models are reported in Table 4.

Two levels of correlation can be observed: 1) Stronger correlation $\gtrsim 0.8$ for Euclid on AG News, Euclid-abs on Dry Bean as well as both Euclidean based metrics on Breast Cancer and Ionosphere. 2) A moderate correlation ≈ 0.65 for Feature Disagreement on all datasets with a lower standard deviation on AG News. Sign Disagreement also falls in this range on all datasets but Dry Bean, with a notably lower standard deviation on AG News compared to other datasets. The lowest correlation (0.57) is produced by Sign Disagreement on Dry Bean, showing the largest standard deviation (0.38) at the same time. The large standard deviations suggest that a fair amount of models produces very different rankings, particularly in the case of the disagreement based rankings.

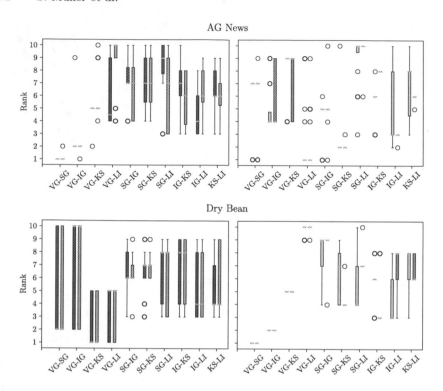

Fig. 2. Box plots of rankings over which pair of attribution methods disagrees most or least for individual models on AG News (top) and Dry Bean (bottom). Higher rank means larger disagreement. Plots on the left: Feature Disagreement Sign Disagreement, plots on the right: Euclid-abs Euclid; Orange lines in each boxplot indicate the median.

Are lower correlations structural? I.e. is it always specific method pairs that tend to swap ranks? We visualize the rank that each pairing occupies for every model in the box plots in Fig. 2 and Fig. 3. The y-axis shows the rank, higher rank meaning stronger disagreement relative to the other methods. Plots on the left pair both disagreement based rankings (blue/ green) while plots on the right show results for Euclidean based rankings (yellow/ red).

Generally, we can make the following observations about the Euclidean metrics: 1) For most explanation pairs, both Euclidean metrics show little to no variance within each dataset, signifying agreement on the ranking of the respective explainability pair, but no consistent ranking across all datasets. 2) All three tabular datasets agree for VG-SG being on rank one and VG-IG being on rank two, both with no variance.

Looking at the results for the disagreement metrics for each dataset in detail, we can see the following: AG News (Fig. 2) shows very stable rankings for both Disagreement metrics for VG-{SG, IG, KS}. For Dry Bean (Fig. 2) across both disagreement metrics, the median lies 8/20 times exactly on one of the quartiles

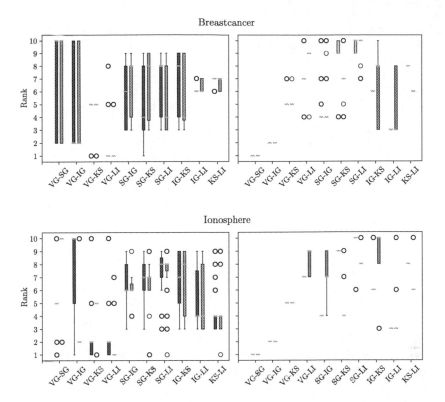

Fig. 3. Box plots of rankings over which pair of attribution methods disagrees most or least for individual models on Breast Cancer (top) and Ionosphere (bottom). Higher rank means larger disagreement. Plots on the left: Feature Disagreement Sign Disagreement, plots on the right: Euclid-abs Euclid; Orange lines in each boxplot indicate the median.

which show no whisker. This means that 50% of the models agree on the respective ranking. This is interesting because at the same time VG-{SG, IG} span nearly the whole ranking, meaning that all rankings in the fourth quartile assign the maximum rank. The pairs SG-{IG, KS} seem to swap places but are otherwise rather consistently placed in the lower middle of the ranking. Breast Cancer (Fig. 3) shows stable rankings for VG-{KS, LI} with both disagreement metrics. More interestingly, for VG-{SG, IG} the medians lie again on "whiskerless"-quartiles and the ranking agrees with the one on Dry Bean (rank 2 for VG-SG and rank 10 for VG-IG). In contrast to Dry Bean, here it is IG-LI and KS-LI that place comparably stable towards the middle of the ranking. On Ionosphere (Fig. 3 bottom) the plot shows smaller boxes compared to the other tasks. Taking outliers into account, multiple pairings span the whole ranking for disagreement based rankings. Ignoring outliers, there are five stable rankings for VG-{IG, SG, KS, LI}, four of which are achieved with Sign Disagreement.

We summarize our observations: We did not see a consistent ranking across all datasets and metrics. Our results for the disagreement based metrics support the observation from the literature that there is no consistent ranking among method pairs. However, we do not observe that results on the more complex AG News appear less correlated than for smaller tabular tasks. Our evaluation of Euclidean based rankings shows them to be notably more stable than their disagreement counterparts.

Interestingly, we cannot identify a single pair of methods that produces high disagreement across all tasks and metrics consistently, but there are pairs of methods for each dataset that consistently take mid-range rankings. Practitioners that seek diverse explanations would be recommended to start their search with comparing VG-KS, SG-{IG, KS}, and KS-LI.

4.4 Summary

In the first scenario in Sect. 4.1 we evaluated how sensitive individual models are to hyperparameter choices for non-deterministic attribution methods. Expectedly, a higher sampling rate always improves the numerical stability of the approximations. However, we found stark differences between the individual models, some requiring larger parameter values by a factor of up to twelve. This has direct implications for scientists and developers using XML methods, as it means that prior knowledge is not necessarily transferable between two models. Choosing default values is de facto impossible. Especially scenarios where parameters have to be chosen as small as possible require rigorous testing.

After verifying the numerical stability of our explanations, in Sect. 4.2 we assessed how the Rashomon Effect manifests itself on different datasets, depending on the different attribution methods and dissimilarity measures. We illustrated the solution diversity under different dissimilarity measures. We found that gradient based attribution methods in conjunction with Euclidean metrics showed smaller distances and low variance on the simpler tabular datasets. Disagreement based dissimilarity measures produced high distances and variances in nearly all cases. The distances are notably higher for Sign Disagreement compared to Feature Disagreement in half of the cases. We saw a large spectrum of distances for perturbation based methods in all cases. Our observation of large magnitudes and high variances in the distances has implications for ML as an epistemic tool. It illustrates how large the space of possible viable solution strategies is, indicating the need to develop informed search strategies in the future [6], especially in complex or resource constrained scenarios. Also, the histograms of Euclidean and disagreement-based measures rarely show overlap, meaning practitioners will have to make context-specific choices on what type of metric to use. In cases where model behavior is explained to users, deploying a model update can lead to irritations as the explanations will likely change drastically between any two models; using the computationally intensive KS or LI seems to give the best chances to maintain somewhat consistent explanations. Conversely to the use-case of ML as an epistemic tool, a possible direction of future work is the inverse search problem of finding a better performing model that functions most similarly.

Investigating the Rashomon Effect on the Disagreement Problem in Sect. 4.3 revealed stark differences between results from the disagreement measures and the Euclidean distances. Neither of the two metric types produced rankings consistent across all datasets. Within tasks, the Euclidean metrics produced very stable rankings while the disagreement measures only occasionally produced a stable rank for a few pairs. Thus, our work provides quantitative support to the observations in [11,19,26] that are based on a small number of models, only. However, contrary to the literature, our results do not look more stable for smaller models on tabular datasets than for the Bi-LSTM model on AG News.

5   Conclusion

We have quantitatively shown how the Rashomon Effect impacts the application and interpretation of XML techniques and argue that it has to be taken into account by the XML community in the future. Along the three variables 1) the model, 2) the datum, and 3) the attribution method, we presented a structured investigation of the Rashomon Effect from three perspectives within XML.

Our quantitative analysis on numerical stability showed models to have individual sensitivity to hyperparameters of explanation methods. We have shown that choosing the most efficient setting requires careful tuning not only to a specific task or architecture, but in fact to every model instance individually, in order to guarantee stable explanations. Assessing the Rashomon Effect itself by measuring the diversity of solution strategies, we found that the solution space appears extensive, especially under the disagreement metrics. This poses challenges to applications of ML as an epistemic tool, as well as use cases where models are offered to consumers that expect consistent behavior. Our study of the Disagreement Problem provides quantitative support for previously anecdotal evidence. No consistent ranking persists across all datasets and the only option for practitioners that seek diverse explanations is trial and error. However, for each dataset individually we were able to identify a pair of methods that consistently take mid-range ranks. Using those rankings to systematically compare methods might yield insight into differences regarding what parts of model behavior each method is sensitive to.

Acknowledgments. This research has been funded by the Federal Ministry of Education and Research of Germany and the state of North-Rhine Westphalia as part of the Lamarr-Institute for Machine Learning and Artificial Intelligence Lamarr22B. Part of PWs work has been funded by the Vienna Science and Technology Fund (WWTF) project ICT22-059.

Ethical Statement. In critical contexts, where persons are directly or indirectly impacted by a model, and where explanations are used to verify that model behavior is compliant with a given standard, proper use of explanation methods is of utmost importance. Hyperparameter choices have to be validated for each model individually. For model testing and validation procedures to be reliable they have to integrate this knowledge. Our work demonstrated that it is unreasonable to expect an explanation computed for one model, to be valid for another model, however similar their performance otherwise may be. Re-using explanations from one model to give as an explanation of behavior for another model is not possible and has to be avoided in critical scenarios.

References

1. Adadi, A., Berrada, M.: Peeking inside the black-box: a survey on explainable artificial intelligence (XAI). IEEE Access **6**, 52138–52160 (2018)
2. Alkhatib, A., Boström, H., Vazirgiannis, M.: Explaining predictions by characteristic rules. In: European Conference on Machine Learning and Principles and Practice of Knowledge Discovery in Databases (ECML/PKDD) (2022)
3. Alvarez-Melis, D., Jaakkola, T.S.: On the robustness of interpretability methods. In: Workshop on Human Interpretability in Machine Learning (WHI@ICML) (2018)
4. Ancona, M., Ceolini, E., Öztireli, C., Gross, M.: Towards better understanding of gradient-based attribution methods for deep neural networks. In: International Conference on Learning Representations, (ICLR) (2018)
5. Atanasova, P., Simonsen, J.G., Lioma, C., Augenstein, I.: A diagnostic study of explainability techniques for text classification. In: Conference on Empirical Methods in Natural Language Processing (EMNLP) (2020)
6. Beckh, K., et al.: Harnessing prior knowledge for explainable machine learning: an overview. In: 2023 IEEE Conference on Secure and Trustworthy Machine Learning (SaTML), pp. 450–463 (2023). https://doi.org/10.1109/SaTML54575.2023.00038
7. Bogun, A., Kostadinov, D., Borth, D.: Saliency diversified deep ensemble for robustness to adversaries. In: AAAI-22 Workshop on Adversarial Machine Learning and Beyond (2021)
8. Breiman, L.: Statistical modeling: the two cultures (with comments and a rejoinder by the author). Stat. Sci. **16**(3), 199–231 (2001)
9. Burkart, N., Huber, M.F.: A survey on the explainability of supervised machine learning. J. Artif. Intell. Res. **70**, 245–317 (2021)
10. DeYoung, J., et al.: ERASER: a benchmark to evaluate rationalized NLP models. In: Annual Meeting of the Association for Computational Linguistics (ACL) (2020)
11. ElShawi, R., Sherif, Y., Al-Mallah, M., Sakr, S.: Interpretability in healthcare: a comparative study of local machine learning interpretability techniques. Comput. Intell. **37**(4), 1633–1650 (2021)
12. Fisher, A., Rudin, C., Dominici, F.: All models are wrong, but many are useful: learning a variable's importance by studying an entire class of prediction models simultaneously. J. Mach. Learn. Res. **20**(177), 1–81 (2019)
13. Flora, M., Potvin, C., McGovern, A., Handler, S.: Comparing explanation methods for traditional machine learning models part 1: an overview of current methods and quantifying their disagreement. arXiv preprint arXiv:2211.08943 (2022)
14. Guidotti, R., Ruggieri, S.: Assessing the stability of interpretable models. arXiv preprint arXiv:1810.09352 (2018)

15. Han, T., Srinivas, S., Lakkaraju, H.: Which explanation should i choose? A function approximation perspective to characterizing post hoc explanations. In: Advances in Neural Information Processing Systems (NeurIPS) (2022)
16. Hancox-Li, L.: Robustness in machine learning explanations: does it matter? In: Conference on Fairness, Accountability, and Transparency (FAT*) (2020)
17. Hooker, S., Erhan, D., Kindermans, P.J., Kim, B.: A benchmark for interpretability methods in deep neural networks. In: Advances in Neural Information Processing Systems (NeurIPS) (2019)
18. Koklu, M., Özkan, I.A.: Multiclass classification of dry beans using computer vision and machine learning techniques. Comput. Electron. Agric. **174**, 105507 (2020)
19. Krishna, S., et al.: The disagreement problem in explainable machine learning: a practitioner's perspective. arXiv preprint arXiv:2202.01602 (2022)
20. Leventi-Peetz, A.M., Weber, K.: Rashomon effect and consistency in explainable artificial intelligence (XAI). In: Future Technologies Conference (FTC) (2022)
21. Liu, F., Avci, B.: Incorporating priors with feature attribution on text classification. In: Annual Meeting of the Association for Computational Linguistics (ACL) (2019)
22. Lundberg, S., Lee, S.I.: A Unified approach to interpreting model predictions. In: Advances in Neural Information Processing Systems (NeurIPS) (2017)
23. Marx, C.T., Calmon, F.P., Ustun, B.: Predictive multiplicity in classification. In: International Conference on Machine Learning (ICML) (2020)
24. Molnar, C.: Interpretable Machine Learning. 2nd edn. (2022)
25. Mücke, S., Pfahler, L.: Check Mate: a sanity check for trustworthy AI. In: Lernen. Wissen. Daten. Analysen. (LWDA) (2022)
26. Neely, M., Schouten, S.F., Bleeker, M.J., Lucic, A.: order in the court: explainable AI methods prone to disagreement. arXiv preprint arXiv:2105.03287 (2021)
27. Ribeiro, M.T., Singh, S., Guestrin, C.: Why should i trust you?: explaining the predictions of any classifier. In: International Conference on Knowledge Discovery and Data Mining (KDD) (2016)
28. Roscher, R., Bohn, B., Duarte, M.F., Garcke, J.: Explainable machine learning for scientific insights and discoveries. IEEE Access **8**, 42200–42216 (2020)
29. Schramowski, P., et al.: Making deep neural networks right for the right scientific reasons by interacting with their explanations. Nat. Mach. Intell. **2**(8), 476–486 (2020)
30. Semenova, L., Rudin, C., Parr, R.: On the existence of simpler machine learning models. In: Conference on Fairness, Accountability, and Transparency (FAccT) (2022)
31. Sigillito, V.G., Wing, S.P., Hutton, L.V., Baker, K.B.: Classification of radar returns from the ionosphere using neural networks. Johns Hopkins APL Tech. Digest **10**(3), 262–266 (1989)
32. Simonyan, K., Vedaldi, A., Zisserman, A.: Deep inside convolutional networks: visualising image classification models and saliency maps. In: International Conference on Learning Representations (ICLR) (2014)
33. Smilkov, D., Thorat, N., Kim, B., Viégas, F., Wattenberg, M.: Smoothgrad: removing noise by adding noise. arXiv preprint arXiv:1706.03825 (2017)
34. Sundararajan, M., Taly, A., Yan, Q.: Axiomatic attribution for deep networks. In: International Conference on Machine Learning (ICML) (2017)
35. Watson, M., Hasan, B.A.S., Al Moubayed, N.: Agree to disagree: when deep learning models with identical architectures produce distinct explanations. In: Winter Conference on Applications of Computer Vision (WACV) (2022)

36. Wolberg, W., Street, N., Mangasarian, O.: Breast Cancer Wisconsin (Diagnostic). UCI Machine Learning Repository (1995)
37. Xin, R., Zhong, C., Chen, Z., Takagi, T., Seltzer, M., Rudin, C.: Exploring the whole rashomon set of sparse decision trees. In: Advances in Neural Information Processing Systems (NeurIPS) (2022)
38. Yeh, C., Hsieh, C., Suggala, A.S., Inouye, D.I., Ravikumar, P.: On the (In)fidelity and sensitivity of explanations. In: Advances in Neural Information Processing Systems (NeurIPS) (2019)
39. Zednik, C., Boelsen, H.: Scientific exploration and explainable artificial intelligence. Minds Mach. **32**(1), 219–239 (2022)
40. Zhang, X., Zhao, J.J., LeCun, Y.: Character-level convolutional networks for text classification. In: Advances in Neural Information Processing Systems (NeurIPS) (2015)

Interpretable Regional Descriptors: Hyperbox-Based Local Explanations

Susanne Dandl[1,2], Giuseppe Casalicchio[1,2], Bernd Bischl[1,2], and Ludwig Bothmann[1,2(✉)]

[1] Department of Statistics, LMU Munich, Ludwigstr. 33, 80539 Munich, Germany
[2] Munich Center for Machine Learning (MCML), Munich, Germany
Ludwig.Bothmann@stat.uni-muenchen.de

Abstract. This work introduces interpretable regional descriptors, or IRDs, for local, model-agnostic interpretations. IRDs are hyperboxes that describe how an observation's feature values can be changed without affecting its prediction. They justify a prediction by providing a set of "even if" arguments (semi-factual explanations), and they indicate which features affect a prediction and whether pointwise biases or implausibilities exist. A concrete use case shows that this is valuable for both machine learning modelers and persons subject to a decision. We formalize the search for IRDs as an optimization problem and introduce a unifying framework for computing IRDs that covers desiderata, initialization techniques, and a post-processing method. We show how existing hyperbox methods can be adapted to fit into this unified framework. A benchmark study compares the methods based on several quality measures and identifies two strategies to improve IRDs.

Keywords: Interpretability · Semi-factual explanations · Hyperboxes

1 Introduction

Supervised machine learning (ML) models are widely used due to their good predictive performance, but they are often difficult to interpret due to their complexity. Post-hoc interpretation methods from the field of interpretable machine learning (IML) can help to draw conclusions about the inner processes of these models: local methods explain individual predictions and global methods explain the expected behavior of the model in general. Doshi-Velez and Kim [3] define model interpretability as "the ability to explain or to present in understandable terms to a human". A topological form that satisfies this notion of interpretability is a hyperbox. In this work, we investigate hyperboxes as local interpretations that describe how the feature values of an observation can be changed without affecting its prediction. We call these boxes interpretable regional descriptors (IRDs). IRDs describe feature spaces by intervals for real-valued features and subsets of possible classes for categorical features (see Table 1).

© The Author(s), under exclusive license to Springer Nature Switzerland AG 2023
D. Koutra et al. (Eds.): ECML PKDD 2023, LNAI 14171, pp. 479–495, 2023.
https://doi.org/10.1007/978-3-031-43418-1_29

Table 1. Credit dataset [4,10] example with 9 *features*, showing the values of a *customer* with a moderate risk prediction. The *IRD* (generated by MaxBox & post-processing (Sect. 4)) shows how all features could be changed simultaneously so that the credit is still of moderate risk. $\bar{B}$ shows how a single feature could be changed (keeping the other features fixed, see Sect. 4.1). For features in the upper half, the IRD covers the full observed value *range* (training data).

Feature	Customer	IRD	$\bar{B}$ (1-dim IRD)	Range
sex	female	{female, male}	{female, male}	{female, male}
saving.accounts	little	{little, moderate rich}	{little, moderate, rich}	{little, moderate, rich}
purpose	car	{car, radio/TV, furniture, others}	{car, radio/TV, furniture, others}	{car, radio/TV, furniture, others}
age	22	[19, 22]	[19, 75]	[19, 75]
job	skilled	{skilled, highly skilled}	{unskilled, skilled, highly skilled}	{unskilled, skilled, highly skilled}
housing	rent	{rent}	{own, free, rent}	{own, free, rent}
checking.account	moderate	{little, moderate}	{little, moderate}	{little, moderate, rich}
credit.amount	4000	[4000, 5389]	[2127, 8424]	[276, 18424]
duration	30	[26, 33]	[6, 44]	[6, 72]

1.1   Motivating Example for the Use of IRDs

A customer applies for a credit of €4000 at a bank to buy a new car. She is 22 years old, skilled, lives in a rented accommodation, has few savings and a moderate balance on her checking account. An ML model predicts whether the credit is of low, moderate or high risk. Due to a moderate risk prediction, the bank rejects the application. The IRD in Table 1 answers the question "to what extent the feature or multiple features can be changed such that the prediction is still in the moderate risk class". From an IRD, multiple insights can be obtained.

First, IRDs offer a set of semi-factual explanations (SFEs) – also called a fortiori arguments – to justify a decision in the form of "even if" statements [23]. Compared to counterfactual explanations [31], SFEs reveal how feature values can be changed *without* affecting the prediction. For these statements to be convincing, domain knowledge is required, e.g., that higher balances in the savings account, and that higher skilled jobs decrease the risk for a bank. Given such knowledge, a multitude of SFEs can be derived from the IRD of Table 1 that (1) justify that a person is in the moderate risk class instead of the low risk class (e.g., "even if you had moderate savings and become highly skilled, your credit is still of moderate risk")[1], and that (2) justify that a person is not in the high risk class ("even if you only have little balance in your checking account,

---

[1] In contrast, a counterfactual would be "if you had rich savings and become highly skilled, your credit would be a *low* risk". Such statements are not covered by IRDs.

your credit would still be of moderate risk"). The latter represents a "safety bound" if some of the features change towards the undesired, higher risk class in the future.

Second, the interval width or cardinality of a feature in an IRD relative to its entire feature space can indicate whether a feature affects a prediction locally (under Theorems 1 and 2). For example, compared to credit amount or duration, savings or purpose seem to have no local effect on the prediction since the regional descriptor encompasses their entire observed feature ranges. These insights also reveal what can be options to change a given prediction.[2]

Third, IRDs are tools for model auditing. If the insights from a box (e.g., an SFE) agree with domain knowledge, users have more trust in the model, while disagreement helps to reveal unintended pointwise biases or implausibilities of a model. For example, an IRD that does not cover male customers *might* indicate that the model classifies individuals differently based on gender.[3] An IRD that covers a credit amount of €300 and high balances in the checking account could indicate an inaccurate model because such customers should pose only a low risk to the bank. Other practical examples of IRDs shows Appendix A.[4]

1.2 Contributions

Our contributions are: 1) We introduce IRDs as a new class of local interpretations to describe regions in the feature space that do not affect the prediction of an observation; 2) We formalize the search for IRDs as an optimization problem and develop desired properties of IRD methods; 3) We introduce a unifying framework for computing IRDs including initialization and post-processing methods; 4) We show how existing hyperbox methods from data mining or IML can be adapted to fit into our unified framework; 5) We present a set of quality measures and compare our derived methods accordingly in a benchmark study; 6) We provide an open-access repository with an R package for the implemented approaches and the code for replicating the benchmark study.[5]

2 Methodology

Let $\hat{f} : \mathcal{X} \to \mathbb{R}$ be the prediction function of an ML model with $\mathcal{X} = \mathcal{X}_1 \times \ldots \times \mathcal{X}_p$ as a p dimensional feature space. For classification models, we consider a predefined class of interest for which $\hat{f}$ returns the predicted score or probability.

2.1 Formalizing the General Task for IRDs

Our goal is to find the largest hyperbox B covering a point of interest $\mathbf{x}' \in \mathcal{X}$ where all data points in B have a sufficiently close prediction to $\hat{f}(\mathbf{x}')$. The

---

[2] However, the concrete strategies can only reveal counterfactual explanations [31].

[3] Note that if all genders are part of the box, it does not mean the model is fair.

[4] https://github.com/slds-lmu/supplementary_2023_ird/blob/main/appendix.

[5] https://github.com/slds-lmu/supplementary_2023_ird.

hyperbox B should have p dimensions $B = B_1 \times \ldots \times B_p$

$$\text{with } B_j = \begin{cases} \{c|c \in \mathcal{X}_j\} & \text{categorical } X_j \\ [l_j, u_j] \subseteq \mathcal{X}_j & \text{numeric } X_j \end{cases},$$

consisting of intervals for numeric features and a subset of possible classes for categorical features. $\mathcal{X}_j$ reflects the value space of the jth feature X_j. In accordance with Lemhadri et al. [22], a prediction is sufficiently close if it falls into a *closeness region*, which is a user-defined prediction interval $Y' = [\hat{f}(\mathbf{x}') - \epsilon_L, \hat{f}(\mathbf{x}') + \epsilon_H]$ with $\epsilon_L, \epsilon_H \in \mathbb{R}_{\geq 0}$.[6] In the bank lending example, the closeness region should cover all model predictions that lead to the moderate risk class, e.g., a predicted probability of 30–60 % of defaulting, i.e., $Y' = [0.3, 0.6]$. To operationalize the above goal, we need three measures [25, 28]:

1. $coverage(B) = \mathbb{P}(\mathbf{x} \in B | \mathbf{x} \in \mathcal{X})$, which measures how much a hyperbox covers the entire feature space. Since, in practice, not all $\mathbf{x} \in \mathcal{X}$ are observable, we use an empirical approximation given data $(\mathbf{x}_i)_{1 \leq i \leq n}$ with $\mathbf{x}_i \in \mathcal{X}$

$$\widehat{coverage}(B) = \frac{1}{n} \sum_{i=1}^{n} \mathbb{I}(\mathbf{x}_i \in B). \tag{1}$$

2. $precision(B) = \mathbb{P}(\hat{f}(\mathbf{x}) \in Y' | \mathbf{x} \in B)$, the fraction of points within a box B whose predictions are inside Y'. Again, we use an empirical approximation

$$\widehat{precision}(B) = \frac{\sum_{i=1}^{n} \mathbb{I}(\mathbf{x}_i \in B \wedge \hat{f}(\mathbf{x}_i) \in Y')}{\sum_{i=1}^{n} \mathbb{I}(\mathbf{x}_i \in B)}. \tag{2}$$

3. an indicator of whether B covers $\mathbf{x}'$

$$locality(B) = \mathbb{I}(\mathbf{x}' \in B). \tag{3}$$

The following operationalizes the search for an IRD [25]:[7]

$$\underset{B \subseteq \mathcal{X}}{arg\,max}(\widehat{coverage}(B))$$
$$\text{s.t. } \widehat{precision}(B) = 1 \text{ and } locality(B) = 1. \tag{4}$$

Definition 1. *A box is maximal if and only if no box could be added under full precision, such that for all numeric X_j, it holds that $(\nexists x_j \in \mathcal{X}_j \wedge x_j < l_j : precision(B \cup [x_j, l_j]) = 1) \wedge (\nexists x_j \in \mathcal{X}_j \wedge x_j > u_j : precision(B \cup [u_j, x_j]) = 1)$, and for all categorical X_j, it holds that $(\nexists x_j \in \mathcal{X}_j \setminus B_j : precision(B \cup x_j) = 1)$.*

---

[6] For classification models, $Y' \subset [0, 1]$ must hold.

[7] For this, we extended the optimization task of Ribeiro et al. [25] to target IRDs by aiming for a precision of 1 and by including the locality constraint.

A box B with maximum coverage satisfies this maximality property. We aim for a maximal B, since B can then detect features that are not locally relevant for a prediction $\hat{f}(\mathbf{x}')$. We prove the following in Appendix B.

Theorem 1. *If B is maximal, $B_j = [min(\mathcal{X}_j), max(\mathcal{X}_j)]$ holds for numeric features X_j and $B_j = \mathcal{X}_j$ for categorical X_j that are not involved in model $\hat{f}$.*

Similarly, we aim for homogeneous boxes B such that $precision(B) = 1$. Then, B can detect features that are locally relevant for $\hat{f}(\mathbf{x}')$. We prove the following in Appendix C.

Theorem 2. *If $precision(B) = 1$, $B_j \subset \mathcal{X}_j$ holds for a feature that is locally relevant for $\hat{f}(\mathbf{x}')$.*

2.2   Desiderata for IRDs

In Sect. 3, we discuss related methods to generate B. The suitability of these methods as IRD methods relies on whether they consider all objectives of Eq. (4) and whether they satisfy the following desired properties for IRDs.

Interpretability. In order for B to be interpretable, we only consider methods that return a *single* p-dimensional hyperbox. The hyperrectangular structure of B allows for a natural interpretation, which is not the case for hyperellipsoids or polytopes formed by halfspaces [22]. According to Eq. (4), B needs to cover $\mathbf{x}'$, which is the case if the following holds: $\forall j \in \{1, ..., p\} : x'_j \in B_j$.

Model-agnosticism. The definition of $\hat{f}$ does not pose any restrictions on the ML model or the feature space. Therefore, methods should be model-agnostic such that they could explain both regression or classification models with various feature types (binary, nominal, ordinal or continuous).

Sparsity Constraints. Eckstein et al. [5] proved that the optimization task for the maximum box problem is $\mathcal{NP}$-hard if the features defining the box are not fixed. This also applies to the search for IRDs, which only additionally requires $\mathbf{x}' \in B$. Since the search space for hyperboxes grows with the number of features, it is infeasible to consider all potential solutions. Furthermore, the fact that IRDs have as many dimensions as the dataset impedes their interpretability – the very goal of IRDs in the first place. To reduce the number of features, methods should be able to adhere to user-defined sparsity constraints such that for some features X_j, $B_j = x'_j$. Section 7 discusses other solutions.

3   Related Work

The optimization task of Eq. (4) can be understood mathematically as finding the preimage of prediction values $\in Y'$ in the neighborhood of $\mathbf{x}'$. Therefore, IRDs can be seen as a subset of a level set for function values $\in Y'$. Level set approximations often consist of points [7], and only a few approaches approximate these via hyperboxes [32, 33] (or other geometric forms). These methods produce multiple boxes instead of one and do not require to contain $\mathbf{x}'$. Hence, they are not interpretable in our sense and, therefore, not useful to produce IRDs.

In data mining, Eckstein et al. [5] proposed a maximum box (MaxBox) approach for datasets with binary outcomes to find the largest homogeneous hyperbox w.r.t. the positive class. Friedman and Fisher [11] derived the patient rule induction method (PRIM) for seeking boxes in the feature space in which the outcome mean is high. Both approaches do not require $\mathbf{x}'$ to be in the box.

Table 2. Overview of approaches that search for hyperboxes in feature spaces.

	Objectives			Desiderata		
	Coverage	Precision	Locality	Interpretable	Agnostic	Sparse
Level set methods						
PBnB [32, 33]	√	√	×	×	√	×
Data mining						
MaxBox [5]	√	√	×	√	×	×
PRIM [11]	×	×	×	√	×	×
Post-hoc IML						
Anchors [25]	√	√	√	√	×	×
MAIRE [28]	√	√	√	√	×	×
LORE [14–16]	×	×	√	√	√	×
Interpretable classifier						
Column generation [1]	√	√	×	×	√	×

As described earlier, IRDs may also be seen as a method to summarize a multitude of SFEs. Most proposed methods for SFEs return only a single point as an explanation [2, 17, 23]. In contrast, LORE by Guidotti et al. [14–16] returns a set of SFEs using surrogate trees. Their approach reveals which feature values are most important for deriving a prediction by following the path to the point of interest. The reliability of such a surrogate tree depends on the assumption that the tree can adequately replicate the underlying model, which may not always be the case [27]. Furthermore, LORE does not directly target Eq. (4) because the level of precision cannot be set [16] and homogeneous boxes are only possible with overfitting/deep-grown trees. This limits its coverage (the box could be larger than the terminal node (Figure S. 5 in the Appendix)) and makes this approach computationally expensive [6, 8]. Therefore, the tree structure is more suitable for deriving SFEs when the underlying model is tree-based [9, 29].

An IML method that utilizes hyperboxes is the Anchors approach [25]. The returned hyperbox indicates how features must be fixed or anchored to prevent a model from changing the classification of a data point. Anchors were originally proposed to aim for hyperboxes that also partly cover observations of other classes; a precision of 0.95 is the default in its implementation [26]. Although the precision can be changed to 1, Anchors are nevertheless not suitable for the generation of IRDs due to their limited search space: Either the box boundary of a feature is set to the full feature range observed in the data, or to the value of $\mathbf{x}$. This bears the risk of "overly specific anchors" with low coverage [25]. For larger coverage, features can be binned beforehand. However, no established discretization technique for Anchors exists so far and the optimization procedure underlying Anchors does not allow adaptions of the bins during optimization.

To overcome the discretization problem, Sharma et al. [28] proposed the model-agnostic interpretable rule extraction (MAIRE) procedure. MAIRE finds more optimal boundaries for continuous features via gradient-based optimization. It still does not allow a more precise choice for categorical features; either the box allows no changes to a feature or it covers all possible values of a feature.

Equation (4) also overlaps with the problem of deriving interpretable (surrogate) models using a combination of rules [12] or hyperboxes [18] that cover the whole feature space (e.g., via column generation [1]). As such, the methods do not focus on locality and are not interpretable in our sense.

Table 2 summarizes whether the addressed methods are suitable for generating IRDs. Overall, none of the methods satisfies all objectives of Eq. (4) and desiderata from Sect. 2.2. Specifically, none of them addresses sparsity constraints, and only a few are model-agnostic. In Sect. 4.4, we modify MaxBox, PRIM, and MAIRE such that they fulfill all of our requirements to transform them into useful IRD methods. All other methods cannot be modified to the required extent due to their underlying, irreplaceable optimization methods that do not directly target Eq. (4) (LORE), target multiple boxes (PBnB) or have a very limited search space. The latter applies in particular to Anchors. However, the method serves as a baseline method for our benchmark study in Sect. 6.

4   Generating IRDs

We now present a unifying framework for generating IRDs, which consists of four steps: restriction, selection, initialization, and optimization. Optionally, a post-processing step can be conducted (Sect. 4.5).

4.1   Restriction of the Search Space

To restrict the initial search space for B, we propose a simple procedure to find the largest local box $\bar{B}$ of $\mathbf{x}'$ such that $B \subseteq \bar{B}$. For a continuous feature X_j, we vary its value x'_j of $\mathbf{x}'$ on an equidistant grid. Upper and lower bounds of $\bar{B}_j$ are set to the minimal changes in x'_j, yielding a prediction outside Y'. This approach is similar to individual conditional expectation (ICE) values [13]. For a categorical feature X_j, $\bar{B}_j$ comprises all classes of $\mathcal{X}_j$ that still lead to a prediction $\in Y'$ after adapting x'_j of $\mathbf{x}'$. If a user sets the sparsity constraint that feature X_j is immutable, $\bar{B}_j = x'_j$ must hold. We prove the following in Appendix D.

486   S. Dandl et al.

Theorem 3. *For any box B that solves the optimization problem of Eq. (4) it holds that $B \subseteq \bar{\underline{B}}$.*

4.2   Selection of the Underlying Dataset

All methods need a dataset $\bar{\mathbf{X}}$ consisting of $\mathbf{x} \in \mathcal{X}$ as an input. This dataset is used for evaluating (competing) boxes w.r.t. the empirical versions of coverage and precision (Eq. (1) and Eq. (2)). For some methods, the dataset also offers a set of potential box boundaries to be evaluated. A suitable dataset is the training data. Since only instances $\in \bar{B}$ are relevant (Theorem 3), we remove all instances $\notin \bar{B}$ from $\bar{\mathbf{X}}$. Consequently, $x_j = x'_j \, \forall \mathbf{x} \in \bar{\mathbf{X}}$ holds for all immutable features X_j. More features and sparsity constraints increase the risk that $\bar{\mathbf{X}}$ is only sparsely populated around $\mathbf{x}'$. Furthermore, training data may not be readily available. Since we aim for IRDs that are faithful to the model and not to the data-generating process (DGP), data can be artificially generated by uniformly sampling from the admissible feature ranges of $\bar{B}$. In Sect. 6, we inspect how double-in-size sampled data[8] within $\bar{B}$ affects the quality of IRDs and IRD methods compared to using training data.

4.3   Initialization of a Box

All methods require an initial box B as an input, which is either set to the largest local box $\bar{B}$ covering all $\bar{\mathbf{X}}$ or the smallest box possible, which only contains $\mathbf{x}'$. We define methods that start with the largest local box as top-down IRD methods, and methods that start with the smallest box possible as bottom-up methods.

4.4   Optimization of Box Boundaries

The last step comprises the optimization of the box boundaries. Top-down methods iteratively shrink the box boundaries of the largest local box to improve the box's precision (upholding that $\mathbf{x}' \in B$), while bottom-up methods iteratively enlarge the box boundaries of the smallest box to improve the box's coverage (upholding the precision at 1). In this section, we describe the MaxBox, MAIRE, and PRIM approaches and our extensions such that the methods optimize Eq. (4) and fulfill the desiderata of Sect. 2.2. Pseudocodes and illustrations of the inner workings of the extended approaches are given in Appendix E. All methods receive as input a dataset $\bar{\mathbf{X}}$ and an initial box B.

MaxBox – Top-down Method. MaxBox was originally proposed for binary classification problems – with a positive and negative class. The method starts with the largest box covering all data. A branch and bound (BnB) algorithm [21] inspects the options to shrink the box to optimize its precision w.r.t. the positive class. The branching rule creates new boxes by bracketing out a sample $\mathbf{x}$ of

---
[8] Double-in-size refers to the size of the training data, not of $\bar{\mathbf{X}}$.

the negative class, such that the box is shrunk to be either below or above the values of $\mathbf{x}$ in at least one feature dimension (categorical features are one-hot encoded). Estimates of the upper bound for the coverage of a box determine which imprecise box is branched next, which sample is used for branching, and which boxes are discarded because their upper bound does not exceed the coverage of the current largest homogeneous box. If no boxes to shrink are left, the largest homogeneous box is returned as an IRD.

Extensions. By labeling observations with predictions $\in Y'$ as positive, the approach becomes model-agnostic. Since the original algorithm does not consider whether corresponding boxes still include $\mathbf{x}'$, we adapted the approach to discard boxes that do not contain $\mathbf{x}'$ to guarantee locality.

PRIM – Top-down Method. The method originally aims for boxes with a high average outcome. The procedure starts with a box that includes all points. In the peeling phase, PRIM iteratively identifies a set of eligible subboxes (defined by the α- and $(1-\alpha)$-quantile for numeric features and each present category for categorical features) and peels off the subbox that results in the highest average outcome after exclusion. This step is repeated until the number of points included in the box drops below a fraction of the total number of points. In the pasting phase, the box is iteratively enlarged by adding the subbox that increases the outcome mean the most. These subboxes consist of at least α observations with the nearest lower or higher values in one dimension (numeric X_j) or with a new category (categorical X_j).

Extensions. We adapted the approach to target Eq. (4): in each peeling iteration, the subbox is excluded such that the resulting box has the highest precision (coverage acts as a tiebreaker), and in each pasting iteration, the largest homogeneous subbox is added. If the precision and coverage are not sufficient to select a best box for peeling or pasting, a subbox is randomly selected from the best ones. Peeling stops as soon as the resulting box is homogeneous, while pasting stops as soon as there exists no homogeneous box to add. Furthermore, only subboxes that do not cover $\mathbf{x}'$ are peeled. According to the authors' recommendation, we use $\alpha = 0.05$ for the benchmark study (Sect. 6).

MAIRE – Bottom-up Method. The method starts with a box covering $\mathbf{x}'$. In each iteration, the box boundaries are adapted via ADAM [19] by optimizing a differentiable approximation of the coverage measure. If the precision falls below a certain threshold or $\mathbf{x}'$ is not part of the box, the method additionally optimizes a differentiable version of Eq. (2) and Eq. (3), respectively. MAIRE stops after a specified number of iterations. In the end, the method returns the largest homogeneous box over the iterations.

Extensions. The method requires 0–1-scaled features. To overcome the one-vs-all issue for categorical features (Sect. 3), we one-hot-encode categorical features. We implemented a convergence criterion for a fair comparison with the other (convergent) approaches: we let MAIRE enlarge the box boundaries until the precision falls below 1, then MAIRE is only allowed to run for another 100 iterations. The implementation for the experiments in Sect. 6 is based on the authors' implementation [28] with the discussed modifications. The hyperparameters were set according to the authors' recommendations. We only set the precision threshold to 1, rather than 0.95.

4.5   Post-processing

All methods described in the previous section determine box boundaries based on a finite number of data points in $\bar{\mathbf{X}}$. The limited access carries the risk that some regions of the feature space are not represented in $\bar{\mathbf{X}}$ and that the boundaries of a generated B are suboptimal: There could be areas in B that have predictions $\notin Y'$, or there could be adjacent areas outside of B that also have predictions $\in Y'$. To improve the box boundaries of a given box B, we developed the following post-processing method using newly sampled data. The procedure consists of peeling and pasting as PRIM.

First, the precision of B is measured based on newly sampled data. If $\exists \mathbf{x} \in B$ with $\hat{f}(\mathbf{x}) \notin Y'$, subboxes with the lowest precision in proportion to their size (according to newly sampled data within this subbox) are iteratively peeled. If all subboxes to peel are homogeneous, peeling stops. In the subsequent pasting step, the largest subboxes that proved to be homogeneous (according to newly sampled data within this subbox) are added. If the best box cannot be determined (because several boxes have the same precision and coverage), a subbox is randomly chosen. The method has three hyperparameters: the number of samples used for evaluation, the relative box size (in relation to the size of $\mathcal{X}_j$) for peeling or pasting boxes for continuous features, and a threshold for the minimum box size. The latter acts as a stopping criterion for pasting. If no homogeneous subbox can be added, the relative box size to add for continuous features is halved as long as the relative box size is not lower than the threshold. The pseudocode of our method displays Appendix F.

Section 6 investigates whether our post-processing method improves IRDs. For the experiments, we set the number of samples to evaluate boxes to 100, the relative box size to 0.1, and the threshold for the minimum box size to 0.05.

5   Quality Measures

We now present a set of quality measures for *generated IRDs* and *IRD methods*. These measures apply to a single instance $\mathbf{x}'$ to be explained, where B is the returned IRD of $\mathbf{x}'$ of an IRD method G. The assessment requires evaluation data $\mathbf{E}$ consisting of $\mathbf{x} \in \mathcal{X}$; for the benchmark study in Sect. 6, we use training data and new data uniformly sampled from $\bar{B}$. Training data helps to assess whether the methods use the training data appropriately during IRD generation (e.g., precision should be 1), while a proliferated number of newly generated data $\in \bar{B}$ leads to a more precise evaluation w.r.t. the model, not the DGP.

Locality. The IRD should cover $\mathbf{x}'$. This property is fulfilled if $locality(B) = \mathbb{I}(\mathbf{x}' \in B)$ equals 1.

Coverage. Given two IRDs with equal precision, we prefer the one with higher coverage (Eq. (1)). To evaluate the coverage, we use samples $\mathbf{x} \in \mathbf{E}$ from the connected convex level set $\mathcal{L}$ covering $\mathbf{x}'$.

Definition 2. *A data point* $\mathbf{x}$ *with* $\hat{f}(\mathbf{x}) \in Y'$ *is part of* $\mathcal{L}$ *of* $\mathbf{x}'$ *iff there exists a path between* $\mathbf{x}$ *and* $\mathbf{x}'$ *for which all intermediate points have a prediction* $\in Y'$.

Paths are identified via the identification algorithm of Kuratomi et al. [20], details are given in Appendix G.

Precision. Given two IRDs with equal coverage, the IRD with higher precision is preferred (Eq. (2)).

Maximality. A box should be maximal (Definition 1) based on $\mathbf{x} \in \mathbf{E}$.

No. of Calls. Lower number of calls to $\hat{f}$ of an IRD method are preferred.[9]

Robustness. If we rerun method G on the same $\mathbf{x}'$ and $\hat{f}$ R times using the same $\underline{\bar{\mathbf{X}}}$, the produced IRDs $B_1, ..., B_R$ should overlap with the originally produced B, such that $robustness(G) = \min_{k \in \{1,...,R\}} \frac{\sum_{\mathbf{x} \in \mathbf{E}} \mathbb{I}(\mathbf{x} \in B \cap B_k)}{\sum_{\mathbf{x} \in \mathbf{E}} \mathbb{I}(\mathbf{x} \in B \cup B_k)}$ has a high value.

6 Performance Evaluation

In a benchmark study, we address the following research questions (RQs):

1. How do MaxBox, MAIRE and PRIM perform against each other w.r.t. the quality measures of Sect. 5 (training data as $\underline{\bar{\mathbf{X}}}$, no post-processing)?
2. What effect do double-in-size sampled data originating from $\bar{B}$ have on the quality compared to using training data?
3. What effect does the post-processing (Sect. 4.5) have on the quality?

As a baseline method, we use the Anchors approach [25] with a precision of 1 and 20-quantile-based bins for numeric features (see Sect. 3 for details).

6.1 Setup

To answer the RQs, we utilize six datasets from the OpenML platform [30], either with a binary, multi-class or continuous target variable. Table 3 summarizes the datasets' dimensions, target and feature types. For each dataset, five data points were randomly sampled to be $\mathbf{x}'$.[10] On each of the datasets, four models were trained: a hyperbox model, a logistic regression/multinomial/linear

---

[9] We prefer this measure over computation time because it is independent of the concrete implementation. We have made our best efforts to implement the methods efficiently, but there is usually room for improvement.

[10] These data points can also be excluded from the data before training a model. However, our experiments showed the results for the RQs are almost the same.

model (depending on the outcome), a neural network with one hidden layer, and a random forest model. The number of trees for the random forest and the neurons on the hidden layer were tuned (details are given in Appendix H). The hyperbox model is derived from a classification and regression tree (CART) model for each $\mathbf{x}'$ individually. For a given $\mathbf{x}'$, the post-processed model predicts 1 if a point falls in the same terminal node as $\mathbf{x}'$ and 0 otherwise.[11]

Table 3. Overview of benchmark datasets.

Name	OpenML ID	Target type	Rows	Continuous	Categorical
diabetes	37	binary	768	8	0
tic_tac_toe	50	binary	958	0	9
cmc	23	three-class	1473	2	7
vehicle	54	four-class	846	18	0
no2	886	regression	500	7	0
plasma_retinol	511	regression	315	10	3

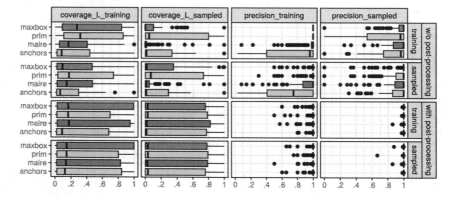

Fig. 1. Comparison of methods w.r.t. coverage and precision. Addendum L means that for the coverage evaluation only training or sampled points within $\mathcal{L}$ are considered. Each point in the boxplot reflects one IRD. Methods were either run or evaluated on training data or uniformly sampled data from $\bar{B}$, and with or without post-processing. Higher values are better.

For classification models, the prediction function returns the probability of the class with the highest probability for $\mathbf{x}$. For binary targets, we set $Y' = [0.5, 1]$. For regression and multi-class targets, Y' is set to $[\hat{f}(\mathbf{x}) - \delta, \hat{f}(\mathbf{x}) + \delta]$

---

[11] The true hyperbox of the CART model might be larger than the terminal node-induced hyperbox (see Figure S. 5 in the Appendix).

with δ as the standard deviation of predictions $\hat{f}$ of the training data. For multi-class, the interval is additionally capped between 0 and 1. For each dataset, model, and $\mathbf{x}'$, we generate IRDs with MaxBox, PRIM, and MAIRE, as well as Anchors – our baseline method. The hyperparameters of the methods were set according to Sect. 4. The methods were either run on training or on uniformly sampled data from $\bar{B}$ (RQ 2), and either without or with post-processing (RQ 3). For the robustness evaluation, we repeated the experiments $R = 5$ times.

The methods and their generated IRDs were evaluated based on the performance measures of Sect. 5 – either evaluated on the training data or 1000 new instances sampled uniformly from $\bar{B}$. We also compared the methods statistically by conducting Wilcoxon rank-sum tests for the hypothesis that the distribution of the coverage and precision values do not differ between two (IRD) methods (RQ 1), for a method using training vs. sampled data (RQ 2), and for a method without vs. with post-processing (RQ 3). The experiments were conducted on a computer with a 2.60 GHz Intel(R) Xeon(R) processor, and 32 CPUs. Overall, generating the boxes took 63 h spread over 20 CPUs. The five repetitions for the robustness evaluation required another 316 h.

Table 4. Comparison of methods w.r.t. maximality and no. of calls to $\hat{f}$ averaged over all datasets, models and $\mathbf{x}'$. Each method was run or evaluated on training data or uniformly sampled data from $\bar{B}$, and without (0) or with (1) post-processing. Higher maximality and lower no. of calls are better.

| | Training data | | | | | | Sampled | | | | | |
| | $\text{Max}_{\text{training}}$ | | $\text{Max}_{\text{sampled}}$ | | No. calls to $\hat{f}$ | | $\text{Max}_{\text{training}}$ | | $\text{Max}_{\text{sampled}}$ | | No. calls to $\hat{f}$ | |
	0	1	0	1	0	1	0	1	0	1	0	1
MaxBox	**0.60**	**0.42**	0.06	**0.41**	184	55769	0.23	**0.45**	0.24	**0.43**	1621	**37627**
PRIM	0.42	0.37	**0.18**	0.39	184	**46070**	0.20	0.42	**0.25**	0.39	1621	42958
MAIRE	0.18	0.41	0.04	**0.41**	184	68126	0.06	0.41	0.11	0.35	1621	92976
Anchors	0.27	**0.42**	0.16	0,40	26402	94448	**0.31**	0.42	0.18	0.36	77818	129276

6.2 Results

Figure 1 compares the coverage and precision values of the methods visually. Table 4 shows the frequency of fulfilling maximality and the number of calls to $\hat{f}$ of the methods. The separate results for each dataset and model, the statistical analysis, and the results of robustness are shown in Appendix I. We omitted the results for the locality measure because all returned IRDs covered $\mathbf{x}'$.

RQ 1 - Comparison of Methods. Without post-processing and training data as $\bar{\mathbf{X}}$ (first row, Fig. 1), MaxBox had the highest precision as evaluated on training and newly sampled data. The IRDs of PRIM had on average the largest coverage, but they also covered sampled data with predictions outside Y'. Due to the randomized choice of a subbox in the case of ties, PRIM is not robust according to our robustness metric. None of the methods outperformed the other methods w.r.t. maximality. By design, MAIRE's optimizer disregards the constraints on the search space ($\bar{B}$), resulting in precisions below 1 on training data. Overall, all methods outperformed the baseline method Anchors according to coverage and precision. While all other methods called $\hat{f}$ $|\bar{\mathbf{X}}|$ times, Anchors evaluates column-wise permutations of the observed data.

RQ 2 - Training vs. Sampled Data. On average, double-in-size sampled data originating from $\bar{B}$ led to slightly higher coverage, precision and maximality rates w.r.t. newly sampled data but not w.r.t. the training data. Due to the increase in the size of $\bar{\mathbf{X}}$, more calls to $\hat{f}$ were necessary.[12]

RQ 3 - Without vs. With Post-processing Post-processing increased the coverage and precision of IRDs for all methods. The difference in the quality of IRDs between the methods and between the underlying data scheme (training data vs. sampled data) diminished. Quality enhancement comes at the cost of efficiency and robustness; on average, post-processing resulted in 57,000 additional calls to $\hat{f}$ and the sampling of new data decreased the robustness. MAIRE required on average the most post-processing iterations, followed by Anchors.

7   Conclusion, Limitations and Outlook

Conclusion. We introduced IRDs that describe regions in the feature space that do not affect the prediction of an instance in the form of hyperboxes. These hyperboxes provide a set of semi-factual explanations to justify a prediction, and indicate which features affect a prediction and whether there might be pointwise biases or implausibilities. We formalized the search for IRDs, and introduced desiderata, a unifying framework and quality measures for IRD methods. We discussed three existing hyperbox methods in detail and adapted them to search for IRDs. The lack of a method "ruling it all" in the benchmark study emphasizes the need for a unifying framework comprising multiple methods. The study also revealed that a larger, uniformly sampled dataset and our post-processing method can further enhance the quality of IRDs (at the cost of efficiency).

Limitations. Our work offers potential for further research, e.g., on the sensitivity of the methods' hyperparameters, on the influence of sampling sizes, on the methods' robustness w.r.t. slight changes in $\mathbf{x}'$ or the underlying data, and if the hyperbox-based explanations adhere to human reasoning (user studies). While we only considered low-dimensional datasets in the benchmark study, for high-dimensional datasets we proposed two strategies to restrict the search space: either by letting users decide which features can be changed and which cannot (Sect. 2.2), or by deriving the largest local box $B \subset \bar{B}$ based on ICE curves (Sect. 4.1). Further research can explore: (1) the use of other IML methods, such as feature importance methods, to select features for which changes are investigated (all other features are set to their admissible value range); (2)

---

[12] The size decuples instead of doubles compared to the training data, because not all training data are $\in \bar{B}$ and, thus, not in $\bar{\mathbf{X}}$.

the consideration of feature correlations or causal relations to generate IRDs, which not only naturally restricts the search space but also makes the IRD faithful to the DGP. While all presented methods are model-agnostic, we leave investigations on image and text data to future research.

Outlook. We believe that our work can also be a starting point for investigations on the application of IRDs in other fields, e.g., for hyperparameter (HP) tuning: if a promising HP set for an ML model was identified by a tuning method, IRDs can reveal its sensitivity and whether there are other equally good but more efficient HP settings. IRDs might also identify high-fidelity regions for interpretable local surrogate models, like LIME [24]. LIME approximates predictions of a black-box model $\hat{f}(\mathbf{x})$ around an observation $\mathbf{x}'$ using a (regularized) linear model $\hat{g}(\mathbf{x})$. Here, it might be useful to understand in which region B the linear model approximates the black-box model (high-fidelity region); $\hat{g}$ only provides valuable insights in the region B around $\mathbf{x}'$ where $\forall \mathbf{x} \in B : \hat{h}(\mathbf{x}) := |\hat{f}(\mathbf{x}) - \hat{g}(\mathbf{x})| \leq \epsilon$ for a user-defined $\epsilon > 0$. With $\hat{h}$ as the prediction model and $Y' = [0, \epsilon]$, IRD methods might identify such high-fidelity regions B in an interpretable manner.

Acknowledgements. This work has been partially supported by the Federal Statistical Office of Germany.

Ethical Statement. For this work, no personal data was collected or processed. Only open source datasets were used for the illustrative example and the benchmark study. Furthermore, our work does not aim at a possible use for policing or military.

References

1. Dash, S., Günlük, O., Wei, D.: Boolean decision rules via column generation. In: Proceedings of the 32nd International Conference on Neural Information Processing Systems, NIPS 2018, pp. 4660–4670. Curran Associates Inc., Red Hook, NY, USA (2018)
2. Dhurandhar, A., et al.: Explanations based on the missing: towards contrastive explanations with pertinent negatives. In: Proceedings of the 32nd International Conference on Neural Information Processing Systems, NIPS 2018, pp. 590–601. Curran Associates Inc., Red Hook, NY, USA (2018)
3. Doshi-Velez, F., Kim, B.: Towards a rigorous science of interpretable machine learning. arXiv 1702.08608 v2, arXiv.org E-Print Archive (2017). 10.48550/arXiv.1702.08608
4. Dua, D., Graff, C.: UCI machine learning repository (2017). www.archive.ics.uci.edu/ml/datasets/statlog+(german+credit+data)
5. Eckstein, J., Hammer, P.L., Liu, Y., Nediak, M., Simeone, B.: The maximum box problem and its application to data analysis. Comput. Optim. Appl. **23**(3), 285–298 (2002). https://doi.org/10.1023/a:1020546910706
6. El Shawi, R., Sherif, Y., Al-Mallah, M., Sakr, S.: Interpretability in healthcare: a comparative study of local machine learning interpretability techniques. Comput. Intell. **37**(4), 1633–1650 (2021). https://doi.org/10.1111/coin.12410

7. Emmerich, M.T.M., Deutz, A.H., Kruisselbrink, J.W.: On quality indicators for black-box level set approximation. In: Tantar, E., et al. (eds.) EVOLVE- A Bridge between Probability, Set Oriented Numerics and Evolutionary Computation, pp. 157–185. Springer, Berlin (2013). https://doi.org/10.1007/978-3-642-32726-1_4

8. Fan, M., Wei, W., Xie, X., Liu, Y., Guan, X., Liu, T.: Can we trust your explanations? Sanity checks for interpreters in android malware analysis. IEEE Tran. Inf. Forensics Secur. **16**, 838–853 (2021). https://doi.org/10.1109/TIFS.2020.3021924

9. Fernandez, G., Aledo, J.A., Gamez, J.A., Puerta, J.M.: Factual and counterfactual explanations in fuzzy classification trees. IEEE Trans. Fuzzy Syst. **30**(12), 5484–5495 (2022). https://doi.org/10.1109/tfuzz.2022.3179582

10. Ferreira, L.: German credit risk (2018). www.kaggle.com/datasets/kabure/german-credit-data-with-risk. Accessed 23 Jan 2023

11. Friedman, J.H., Fisher, N.I.: Bump hunting in high-dimensional data. Stat. Comput. **9**(2), 123–143 (1999). https://doi.org/10.1023/A:1008894516817

12. Fürnkranz, J., Kliegr, T.: A brief overview of rule learning. In: Bassiliades, N., Gottlob, G., Sadri, F., Paschke, A., Roman, D. (eds.) RuleML 2015. LNCS, vol. 9202, pp. 54–69. Springer, Cham (2015). https://doi.org/10.1007/978-3-319-21542-6_4

13. Goldstein, A., Kapelner, A., Bleich, J., Pitkin, E.: Peeking inside the black box: Visualizing statistical learning with plots of individual conditional expectation. J. Comput. Graph. Stat. **24**(1), 44–65 (2015). https://doi.org/10.1080/10618600.2014.907095

14. Guidotti, R., Monreale, A., Giannotti, F., Pedreschi, D., Ruggieri, S., Turini, F.: Factual and counterfactual explanations for black box decision making. IEEE Intell. Syst. **34**(6), 14–23 (2019). https://doi.org/10.1109/MIS.2019.2957223

15. Guidotti, R., Monreale, A., Ruggieri, S., Naretto, F., Turini, F., Pedreschi, D., Giannotti, F.: Stable and actionable explanations of black-box models through factual and counterfactual rules. Data Min. Knowl. Disc. (2022). https://doi.org/10.1007/s10618-022-00878-5

16. Guidotti, R., Monreale, A., Ruggieri, S., Pedreschi, D., Turini, F., Giannotti, F.: Local rule-based explanations of black box decision systems. arXiv 1805.10820, arXiv.org E-Print Archive (2018). 10.48550/arXiv. 1805.10820

17. Kenny, E.M., Keane, M.T.: On generating plausible counterfactual and semi-factual explanations for deep learning. Proc. AAAI Conf. Artif. Intell. **35**(13), 11575–11585 (2021). https://doi.org/10.1609/aaai.v35i13.17377

18. Khuat, T.T., Ruta, D., Gabrys, B.: Hyperbox-based machine learning algorithms: a comprehensive survey. Soft Comput. **25**(2), 1325–1363 (2020). https://doi.org/10.1007/s00500-020-05226-7

19. Kingma, D.P., Ba, J.: Adam: a method for stochastic optimization. arXiv 1412.6980 v9, arXiv.org E-Print Archive (2017). 10.48550/arXiv. 1412.6980

20. Kuratomi, A., Miliou, I., Lee, Z., Lindgren, T., Papapetrou, P.: JUICE: JUstIfied counterfactual explanations. In: Pascal, P., Ienco, D. (eds.) Discovery Science. pp. 493–508. LNCS, Springer, Cham (2022). https://doi.org/10.1007/978-3-031-18840-4_35

21. Land, A.H., Doig, A.G.: An automatic method of solving discrete programming problems. Econometrica **28**(3), 497–520 (1960). https://doi.org/10.2307/1910129

22. Lemhadri, I., Li, H.H., Hastie, T.: RbX: region-based explanations of prediction models. arXiv 2210.08721, arXiv.org E-Print Archive (2022). 10.48550/arXiv.2210.08721

23. Nugent, C., Doyle, D., Cunningham, P.: Gaining insight through case-based explanation. J. Intell. Inf. Syst. **32**(3), 267–295 (2009). https://doi.org/10.1007/s10844-008-0069-0

24. Ribeiro, M.T., Singh, S., Guestrin, C.: Why should I trust you? Explaining the predictions of any classifier. In: Proceedings of the 22nd ACM SIGKDD International Conference on Knowledge Discovery and Data Mining, pp. 1135–1144 (2016)
25. Ribeiro, M.T., Singh, S., Guestrin, C.: Anchors: High-precision model-agnostic explanations. In: Proceedings of the AAAI Conference on Artificial Intelligence, vol. 32, no. 1 (2018). https://doi.org/10.1609/aaai.v32i1.11491
26. Ribeiro, M.T., Singh, S., Guestrin, C.: Anchor. Github repository. www.github.com/marcotcr/anchor (2022), Commit: b1f5e6ca37428613723597e85c38558e8cd21c2e
27. Schwartzenberg, C., van Engers, T.M., Li, Y.: The fidelity of global surrogates in interpretable machine learning. BNAIC/BeneLearn 2020 (2020)
28. Sharma, R., Reddy, N., Kamakshi, V., Krishnan, N.C., Jain, S.: MAIRE - a model-agnostic interpretable rule extraction procedure for explaining classifiers. In: Holzinger, A., Kieseberg, P., Tjoa, A.M., Weippl, E. (eds.) CD-MAKE 2021. LNCS, vol. 12844, pp. 329–349. Springer, Cham (2021). https://doi.org/10.1007/978-3-030-84060-0_21
29. Stepin, I., Alonso, J.M., Catala, A., Pereira-Fariña, M.: Generation and evaluation of factual and counterfactual explanations for decision trees and fuzzy rule-based classifiers. In: 2020 IEEE International Conference on Fuzzy Systems (FUZZ-IEEE), pp. 1–8. IEEE, Glasgow, United Kingdom (2020). https://doi.org/10.1109/FUZZ48607.2020.9177629
30. Vanschoren, J., van Rijn, J.N., Bischl, B., Torgo, L.: OpenML: networked science in machine learning. SIGKDD Explor. Newsl. **15**(2), 49–60 (2014). https://doi.org/10.1145/2641190.2641198
31. Wachter, S., Mittelstadt, B., Russell, C.: Counterfactual explanations without opening the black box: automated decisions and the GDPR. Harvard J. Law Technol. **31**(2), 841–887 (2018)
32. Zabinsky, Z.B., Huang, H.: A partition-based optimization approach for level set approximation: probabilistic branch and bound. In: Smith, A.E. (ed.) Women in Industrial and Systems Engineering. WES, pp. 113–155. Springer, Cham (2020). https://doi.org/10.1007/978-3-030-11866-2_6
33. Zabinsky, Z.B., Wang, W., Prasetio, Y., Ghate, A., Yen, J.W.: Adaptive probabilistic branch and bound for level set approximation. In: Proceedings of the 2011 Winter Simulation Conference (WSC), pp. 4146–4157. IEEE, Phoenix, AZ, USA (2011). https://doi.org/10.1109/WSC.2011.6148103

TIGTEC: Token Importance Guided TExt Counterfactuals

Milan Bhan[1,2](✉), Jean-Noël Vittaut[2], Nicolas Chesneau[1],
and Marie-Jeanne Lesot[2]

[1] Ekimetrics, Paris, France
milan.bhan@ekimetrics.com
[2] Sorbonne Université, CNRS, LIP6, Paris 75005, France

Abstract. Counterfactual examples explain a prediction by highlighting changes in an instance that flip the outcome of a classifier. This paper proposes TIGTEC, an efficient and modular method for generating sparse, plausible and diverse counterfactual explanations for textual data. TIGTEC is a text editing heuristic that targets and modifies words with high contribution using local feature importance. A new attention-based local feature importance is proposed. Counterfactual candidates are generated and assessed with a cost function integrating a semantic distance, while the solution space is efficiently explored in a beam search fashion. The conducted experiments show the relevance of TIGTEC in terms of success rate, sparsity, diversity and plausibility. This method can be used in both model-specific or model-agnostic way, which makes it very convenient for generating counterfactual explanations.

Keywords: XAI · NLP · Counterfactual examples · Local Feature Importance · Attention

1 Introduction

The high level of performance in the field of natural language processing (NLP) achieved by Transformer models [30] comes along with complex architectures. The domain of eXplainable Artificial Intelligence (XAI) aims at understanding and interpreting the predictions made by such complex systems [18]. Among the main categories of XAI methods to explain the prediction of a given instance, local feature importance [3] quantifies the impact of each feature on the considered outcome. Another family of XAI methods consists in explaining with counterfactual examples (see [9] for a recent survey), defined as instances close to the instance of interest but associated with another prediction.

This paper proposes a new method to generate counterfactual explanations in the case of textual data, called Token Importance Guided TExt Counterfactuals (TIGTEC). For example, given a classifier that predicts film synopsis genre and an instance of interest predicted to be a comedy, TIGTEC outputs several slightly modified instances predicted to be horror synopses (see Fig. 1).

The main contributions of TIGTEC are as follows: (*i*) textual counterfactual examples are generated by masking and replacing important words using local

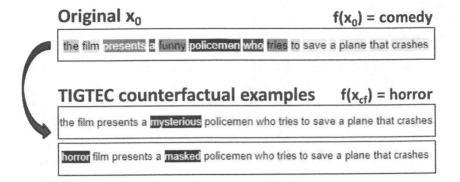

Fig. 1. Example of *sparse, plausible* and *diverse* counterfactual examples generated by TIGTEC for a film genre classifier that discriminates between horror and comedy synopses. Here, the counterfactual generation goes from comedy to horror.

feature importance information, (*ii*) a new model-specific local feature importance method based on attention mechanisms [2] from Transformers is proposed, (*iii*) a new cost function integrating textual semantic distance to preserve the initial content is introduced, (*iv*) the solution space is explored with a new tree search policy based on beam search that leads to diversity in the generated explanations. In this manner, TIGTEC bridges the gap between local feature importance, mask language models, sentence embedding and counterfactual explanations. TIGTEC can be applied to any NLP classifier in a model specific or model-agnostic fashion, depending on the local feature importance method employed.

This paper is organized as follows: we first introduce some basic principles of XAI and the related work in Sect. 2. The architecture of TIGTEC is presented in Sect. 3. Section 4 describes the performed experimental study and compare TIGTEC to a competitor. Finally Sect. 5 concludes this paper by discussing the results and future work.

2   Background and Related Work

We recall here some basic principles of XAI methods and existing counterfactual generation methods in NLP.

2.1   XAI Background

Local Feature Importance. Let $f : \mathcal{X} \to \mathcal{Y}$ be a NLP classifier mapping an input space $\mathcal{X}$ to an output space $\mathcal{Y}$. Let $x_0 = [t_1, ..., t_{|x_0|}] \in \mathcal{X}$ be a sequence of interest with $f(x_0) = y_0$. A local feature importance (or *token importance* in NLP) operator $g : \mathcal{X} \to \mathbb{R}^{|x_0|}$ explains the prediction through a vector $[z_1, ..., z_{|x_0|}]$ where z_i is the contribution of the i−th token. Two common local feature importance methods in NLP are Local Interpretable Model-agnostic Explanations (LIME) [26] and SHapley Additive eXplanations (SHAP) [13]. These methods have the advantage of being model-agnostic since they can be used without any information about the model to explain.

Counterfactual Explanation Counterfactual explanations aim to emphasize what should be different in an input instance to change the outcome of a classifier. Their interest in XAI has been established from a social science perspective [17]. The counterfactual example generation can be formalized as a constrained optimization problem. For a given classifier f and an instance of interest x_0, a counterfactual example x^{cf} must be close to x_0 and is basically defined as:

$$x^{cf} = \underset{z \in \mathcal{X}}{\operatorname{argmin}} \, d(x_0, z) \;\; \text{s.t.} \;\; f(z) \neq f(x_0) \tag{1}$$

with $d : \mathcal{X} \times \mathcal{X} \to \mathbb{R}$ a given distance operator measuring proximity. The counterfactual explanation is then the difference between the generated counterfactual example and the initial data point, $x^{cf} - x_0$.

Many additional desirable properties for counterfactual explanations have been proposed [9,16] to ensure their informative nature that we summarize in three categories. *Sparsity* measures the number of elements changed between the instance of interest and the generated counterfactual example. It is defined as the l_0 norm of $x^{cf} - x$. *Plausibility* encompasses a set of characteristics to ensure that the counterfactual explanation is not out-of-distribution [11] while being feasible [22]. Since several instances of explanation can be more informative than a single one [20,28], *diversity* measures the extent to which the counterfactual examples differ from each other.

2.2 Related Work

This section presents two categories of methods for generating textual counterfactual examples.

Text Editing Heuristics. A first family of methods aims at addressing the problem introduced in Eq. 1 by slightly modifying the input text to be explained with heuristics.

Model specific methods depend structurally on the models they seek to explain. CLOSS [8] focuses on the embedding space of the classifier to explain. After generating counterfactual candidates through optimization in the latent space, the most valuable ones are selected according to an estimation of Shapley values. MiCE [27] iteratively masks parts of the initial text and performs span infilling using a T5 [24] fine-tuned on the corpus of interest. This method targets tokens with high predictive power using model-specific gradient attribution metrics. While the label flipping success rate of CLOSS and MiCE are high and the counterfactual texts are *plausible*, the notions of *semantic distance* and *diversity* are not addressed. We show in Sect. 3 how the TIGTEC approach that we propose tackles these constraints.

Generating counterfactual examples shares similarities with generating *adversarial attacks*, aiming to incorrectly flip the prediction by minimally editing the initial text. Numerous heuristics have been proposed differing in constraints, text transformation methods and search algorithms [19]. Contrary to counterfactual explanations, adversarial attacks seek to fool intentionally a model without explanatory purpose. Therefore, *plausibility* and *sparsity* are not addressed.

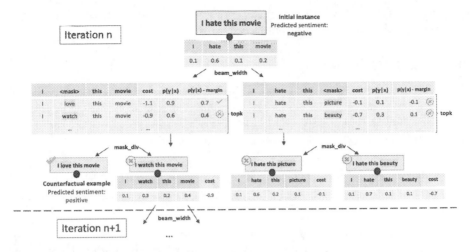

Fig. 2. Illustration of the tree search policy with beam_width = 2, mask_div = 2, strategy = evolutive, margin = 0.2. At each step, the beam_width highest important tokens are masked and replaced. The substitution token is selected considering the cost function depending on the semantic similarity method s and the balancing parameter α. Among the topk candidates, only mask_div one are considered in the tree search. A candidate is accepted if the prediction of the classifier changes and moves margin away from the prediction threshold. Here, "I love this movie" is accepted. Since only one counterfactual candidate was found out of two, the next iteration starts from the nodes with the lowest cost value, here "I watch this movie".

Text Generation with Large Language Models. A second category of methods aims at generating counterfactual examples in NLP with large pre-trained *generative language models*. A first approach [15] applies a Plug and Play language model [6] methodology to generate text under the control of the classifier to explain. It consists in learning latent space perturbations from encoder-decoder models such as BART [12] in order to flip the outcome. Polyjuice [31] proposes to fine-tune a GPT-2 [23] model on a set of predefined tasks. It results in a generative language model capable of performing negation, quantification, insertion of tokens or sentiment flipping based on prompt engineering. Polyjuice needs to be trained in a supervised way on ground truth counterfactual examples in order to be able to generate the expected text. Therefore, the use of Polyjuice to generate counterfactual examples is not generalizable since counterfactual labels do not exist for all classification problems.

3   Proposed Approach: TIGTEC

This section describes the architecture of Token Importance Guided TExt Counterfactuals (TIGTEC) by detailing its four components. The main idea is to iteratively change tokens of the initial text by decreasing order of importance instance to find a compromise between proximity to the initial instance and label flipping. This way, TIGTEC belongs to the *text editing heuristics* category of counterfactual example generators in NLP.

3.1 TIGTEC Overview

TIGTEC is a 4-step iterative method illustrated in Fig. 2. Algorithm 1 describes the generation and evaluation steps, Algorithm 2 summarizes the whole process. The code is available online on a public repository[1]. TIGTEC takes as input a classifier f and a text of interest $x_0 = [t_1, ..., t_{|x_0|}]$.

Targeting. To modify the initial text to explain, tokens with highest impact on prediction are targeted given their local importance. TIGTEC implements two methods of local token importance and a random importance generator as a baseline.

Generating. High importance tokens are masked and replaced, with a fine-tuned or pretrained mask model. Various counterfactual candidates are then generated.

Evaluating. The generated candidates are evaluated by a cost function that balances the probability score of the target class and the semantic distance to the initial instance. Candidates minimizing the cost function are considered valid if they meet acceptability criteria.

Tree Search Policy. The lowest cost candidates are kept in memory and a new iteration begins from the most promising one. The solution space is explored in a beam search fashion until a stopping condition is reached.

As outlined in Fig. 2, the counterfactual search heuristic is a tree search algorithm, in which each node corresponds to a counterfactual candidate, and each edge is a token replacement. Therefore, the root of the tree corresponds to the instance to explain, and the deeper a node is in the tree, the more it is modified.

3.2 Targeting

The first step consists in identifying the most promising tokens to be replaced in the initial instance to modify the outcome of the classifier f. We use token importance metrics to focus on impacting tokens and efficiently guide the search for counterfactual examples. In particular, we integrate the possibility of computing both model-agnostic (e.g. SHAP [13]) and model-specific token importance metrics. We propose a new model-specific token-importance method based on the attention coefficients when the classifier f is a Transformer. Token importance is computed by focusing on the attention of the last encoder layer related to the classification token representing the context of the entire sequence. The efficiency gain of this token importance method is shown in Sect. 4. If the information provided by SHAP is rich, its computation time is high, whereas attention coefficients are available at no cost under a *model-specific* paradigm.

---

[1] https://github.com/milanbhan/tigtec.

Algorithm 1. Mask Language Inference (MLI)

Require: $x = [t_1, ..., t_n]$ an input sequence
Require: $f : \mathcal{X} \rightarrow \mathcal{Y} = \{1,2,...,k\}$ a classifier
Require: i the input token to be masked
Require: $\mathcal{M}$ a BERT-like mask language model
Require: s, α, topk, mask_div
Ensure: $\hat{x} = [\hat{x}_{(1)}, ..., \hat{x}_{(\text{mask\_div})}]$
 1: $t_i \leftarrow [\text{MASK}]$
 2: $x_{\text{mask}} \leftarrow [t_1, ..., [\text{MASK}], ..., t_n]$
 3: $[\hat{t}_1, ..., \hat{t}_{\text{topk}}] = \mathcal{M}(x_{\text{mask}})$ the topk most likely tokens
 4: **for** j in $\{1,...,\text{topk}\}$ **do**
 5:    $\hat{x}_j = x[t_i \leftarrow \hat{t}_j]$
 6:    Compute $\text{cost}(\hat{x}_j)$ see Eq. 4
 7: **end for**
 8: Retrieve in $\hat{x}$ the mask_div sequences with lowest cost
 9: **return** $\hat{x}$

TIGTEC is also defined by its strategy which can take two values. The static strategy consists in fixing the token importance coefficients for the whole search, whereas the evolutive strategy recomputes token importance at each iteration. Since SHAP has a high computational cost, it is not recommended to combine it with the evolutive strategy.

In order to consider several counterfactual candidates at each iteration, several tokens can be targeted in parallel. The beam_width parameter allows to control the number of tokens of highest importance to target at each step to perform a beam search during the space exploration.

3.3   Generating

The second step of TIGTEC generates counterfactual candidates and corresponds to the first part of the mask language inference (MLI) formally described in Algorithm 1, from line 1 to 5. Once high importance tokens have been targeted in the previous step, they are masked and replaced with a BERT-type [7] mask language model denoted $\mathcal{M}$. Mask language models enable to replace tokens considering the context while keeping grammatical correctness and semantic relevance. This step ensures the plausibility of the generated text. Such models take a masked sequence $[t_1, ..., [\text{MASK}], ..., t_n]$ as an input and output a probability score distribution of all the tokens contained in the BERT-type vocabulary. The mask model can be either pretrained or fine-tuned on the text corpus on which the classifier f has been trained.

Since replacing a token with another with low plausibility can lead to out-of-distribution texts, inaccurate prediction and grammatical errors, the number of substitutes proposed by $\mathcal{M}$ is limited to topk. The higher topk, the more we consider tokens with low contextual plausibility.

Algorithm 2. TIGTEC: Token Importance Guided Counterfactual Text Generation

---

Require: $f : \mathcal{X} \to \mathcal{Y}$ a k-class classifier
Require: $x_0 = [t_1, ..., t_n]$ an input sequence of n tokens to be explained
Require: y_{target} : target counterfactual class
Require: p : number of counterfactual examples to generate
Require: g, s, $\mathcal{M}$, α, topk, beam_width, mask_div, strategy, margin, *early_stop*
Ensure: $x^{\text{cf}} = [x_1^{\text{cf}}, ..., x_p^{\text{cf}}]$
1: waiting_list $= [(x_0, \text{cost}(x_0))]$ the priority queue of counterfactual candidates sorted by increasing cost (see Eq. 4)
2: $i \leftarrow 0$ the number of evaluated texts
3: $x^{\text{cf}} \leftarrow []$
4: Compute token importance $[z_1, ..., z_n] = g(x_0)$
5: **while** $len(x^{\text{cf}}) < p$ and $i < early\_stop$ **do**
6:     parent_node $\leftarrow$ waiting_list.pop() the candidate with the lowest cost (see Eq. 4)
7:     $[t_{(1)}, ..., t_{(n)}] \leftarrow$ sort(parent_node) by decreasing importance order with respect to strategy and g
8:     **for** t in $[t_{(1)}, ..., t_{(\text{beam\_width})}]$ **do**
9:         $i \leftarrow i + 1$
10:         $[x_1, ..., x_{\text{mask_div}}] = $ MLI(parent_node , f, t, $\mathcal{M}$, topk, mask_div, s α) (see Algorithm 1)
11:         **for** x in $[x_1, ..., x_{\text{mask\_div}}]$ **do**
12:             **if** $p(y_{\text{target}}|x) \geq \frac{1}{k} + $ margin **then**
13:                 x^{cf}.append(x)
14:             **else**
15:                 waiting_list.push($(x, \text{cost}(x))$) keep in the waiting list rejected candidates with their cost
16:             **end if**
17:         **end for**
18:     **end for**
19: **end while**
20: **return** x^{cf}

3.4 Evaluating

Once the topk candidates are generated, we build a cost function to evaluate them. This evaluation step corresponds to line 6 in Algorithm 1. The cost function has to integrate the need to flip the outcome of the classifier f and the distance to the original instance as formalized in Eq. 1. In order to ensure semantic relevance, we define a distance based on text embedding and cosine similarity measures. Finally, conditions for the acceptability of counterfactual candidates are introduced to ensure the reliability of the explanations.

Distance. The widely used Levenshtein distance and BLEU score [21] do not integrate the notion of semantics. An alternative is to compare sentence embeddings in order to measure the similarity of representations in a latent space. Sentence embeddings have been introduced to numerically represent textual data as real-value vectors, including Sentence Transformers [25]. Such networks have been trained on large corpus of text covering various topics. This encoders are compatible with a model-agnostic approach, as they do not require any prior information about the classifier f.

Another text embedding approach can be used when the classifier f is a BERT-like model and when the prediction is made through the classification token. It consists in using the embedding of the classification token directly from f. This embedding is however strongly related to the task of the classifier f. Therefore, if the model has been trained for sentiment analysis, two texts with the same associated sentiment will be considered similar, regardless of the topics covered.

We derive the textual distance from the normalized scalar product of the two embeddings: $d : \mathcal{X} \times \mathcal{X} \to [0, 1]$ with:

$$d_s(x, x') = \frac{1}{2}(1 - s(x, x')) \tag{2}$$

$$s(x, x') = \frac{\langle e_x, e'_x \rangle}{||e_x|| \cdot ||e'_x||} \tag{3}$$

where e_x is the embedding representation of input sequence x.

Cost. The cost function aims to represent the counterfactual optimization problem introduced in Eq. 1. We propose to integrate the probability score of the target class to define the cost as:

$$\mathsf{cost}(x^{\mathrm{cf}}, x_0) = -\left(p(y_{\mathrm{target}}|x^{\mathrm{cf}}) - \alpha d_s(x^{\mathrm{cf}}, x_0)\right) \tag{4}$$

where y_{target} is the target class and $p(y_{\mathrm{target}}|x^{\mathrm{cf}})$ represents the probability score of belonging to the class y_{target} given x^{cf} from the classifier f. The probability score is the information that guides the heuristic towards the target class. The α coefficient enables for a balanced approach to the need to reach the target class while remaining close to the initial point. The generated topk candidates are evaluated with the cost function defined above.

Acceptability Criteria. A counterfactual candidate x^{cf} is accepted if two conditions are met:

$$f(x^{\mathrm{cf}}) = y_{\mathrm{target}} \tag{5}$$

$$p(y_{\mathrm{target}}|x^{\mathrm{cf}}) \geq \frac{1}{k} + \mathsf{margin} \tag{6}$$

where k is the number of classes of the output space and $\mathsf{margin} \in [0, \frac{k-1}{k}]$ the regularization hyperparameter ensuring the certainty of the prediction of the model f. We assume then that all the counterfactual examples must reach the same target class. The closer margin is to its upper bound, the more polarized the classifier prediction must be in order to satisfy the acceptability criterion, and the stronger the constraint.

3.5 Tree Search Policy

TIGTEC generates a set of diverse counterfactual examples. We address the diversity constraint by considering the mask_div candidates with the lowest cost function among the generated topk from Algorithm 1 and keep them in memory in a priority queue (see line 15 in Algorithm 2). Therefore, we evaluate more possibilities and aim to foster diversity in the counterfactual examples found by TIGTEC. Once these candidates are stored in memory, the iterative exploration step (Algorithm 2 from line 6 to 11) starts again, until a stopping condition is reached. The stopping condition can either be to reach the target number of counterfactual examples or to reach the maximum number of nodes in the tree (see line 5 in Algorithm 2). The higher the maximum number of nodes, the longer TIGTEC can search for counterfactual examples.

The candidate with the lowest cost is then selected from the priority queue (see line 6 in Algorithm 2) in order to apply again the targeting, generation and evaluation sequence. We call predecessor this previous candidate. Since we evaluate several possibilities in parallel through beam search, Algorithm 1 is this time applied to the beam_width tokens with the highest token importance within the predecessor. From this perspective, the exploration approach enables to start from a candidate that seemed less advantageous at a specific stage, but leads to better results by going deeper into the tree. A tree search example is illustrated in Fig. 2.

4 Experimental Analysis

This section presents the conducted experimental study and introduces five metrics to quantitatively assess the counterfactual examples generated by two different versions of TIGTEC and three comparable state-of-the-art competitors.

4.1 Evaluation Criteria

Considering the various objectives to be achieved, we propose a 5-metric evaluation. Given an instance associated with p counterfactual examples, the evaluation metrics are aggregated on average over the generated examples, except for diversity. The same operation is performed on all the instances to be explained, and the average metrics are finally computed.

Success Rate. Since TIGTEC does not guarantee to find counterfactual examples in all cases, the success rate (%S) is calculated.

Sparsity. For some methods we compare to, the lengths of the generated counterfactual examples may differ from the initial instance. Therefore, sparsity (%T) is measured assessed with word-based Levenshtein distance normalized by the length of the sequence.

Proximity. We evaluate *ex-post* the semantic proximity between x_0 and x_{cf} with cosine similarity (s) between Sentence Transformer embedding. This choice is justified by the wish to remain in a general framework that does not depend on the classifier f and the task for which it has been trained. The library used to import the Sentence Transformer is `sentence_transformers` and the model backbone is `paraphrase-MiniLM-L6-v2`.

Plausibility. One approach to evaluate text plausibility is the perplexity score [10]. This score can be computed based on the exponential average loss of a foundation model like GPT-2. We calculate the ratio (Δ**PPL**) between the perplexity of the initial text and its counterfactual examples to compare the quality of the generated text with the original one. The library used to import the pretrained GPT2 is `transformers` and the backbone is `GPT2LMHeadModel`.

Diversity. Based on the distance measure d, we define diversity (**div**) as in [20] where $div_d = det(K)$ with $K_{i,j} = \frac{1}{\lambda + d(x_i^{\text{cf}}, x_j^{\text{cf}})}$ and $\lambda \in \mathbb{R}$ a regularization weight set to 1.

4.2   TIGTEC Agnostic and Specific Variants

Two different versions of TIGTEC are assessed. The first one is model-specific with access to the corpus of interest. Attention coefficients guide the counterfactual example search and a fine-tuned mask language model is used to mask and replace important tokens. We call this version TIGTEC-specific.

The second version is model-agnostic without access to the corpus of interest. SHAP is used to compute token importance and the mask language model is only pre-trained. We call this second version TIGTEC-agnostic. Since SHAP computational cost is high compared to attention, we use the static `strategy` for the *agnostic* version of TIGTEC, whereas the evolutive `strategy` is used for the *specific* one.

4.3   Datasets and Competitors

We apply TIGTEC-agnostic and -specific on two DistilBERT [29] binary classifiers. We limit our analysis to DistilBERT, since it achieves almost the same level of performance as BERT, while being significantly lighter. TIGTEC could, however, be applied to larger models, the methodology remaining the same. The first classifier performs sentiment analysis on the IMDB dataset [14] containing movie reviews. The second classifier is trained on movie genre classification on a dataset of horror and comedy synopses from Kaggle[2]. More information about the datasets and the performance of the classifiers are provided online[3].

The two versions of TIGTEC are compared to Polyjuice [31], MiCE [27] and CLOSS [8]. The objective of each version of TIGTEC is to generate three counterfactual examples associated with an initial instance. We apply Polyjuice by generating three counterfactual examples for each instance to explain. As Polyjuice

---

[2] https://www.kaggle.com/competitions/movie-genre-classification/overview.

[3] See the documentation on the publicly available repository: https://github.com/milanbhan/tigtec.

was trained to flip sentiment on IMDB with negation prompt, Polyjuice's counterfactual examples are generated in the same way. MiCE and CLOSS do not address diversity, they only generate one counterfactual example per initial text. We assess TIGTEC and Polyjuice performance by selecting the instance that is semantically closest to the initial point among the 3 generated to compare them to MiCE and CLOSS. We distinguish the results obtained with one and three counterfactual examples by the notation $TIGTEC_{1d}$ and $TIGTEC_{3d}$ and respectively $Polyjuice_{1d}$ and $Polyjuice_{3d}$.

Each method is evaluated on the same 1000 texts from IMDB. The hyperparameters of TIGTEC are fixed at their optimal level as described in the next section. TIGTEC-specific is also applied on the movie synopsis dataset from Kaggle on 474 texts. Since movie genre classification is a more complex task, we relax the hyperparameters by lowering the margin to 0.05 and alpha to 0.15.

4.4 Hyperparameter Setting

We optimize the nine hyperparameters presented in Sect. 3 with respect to success rate, similarity, diversity and sparsity. The optimization is performed on IMDB with the Optuna [1] library. The solution space is as follows:

- $g \in \{random, attention\}$, the input token importance method.
- $\mathcal{M} \in \{\mathcal{M}_{ft}, \mathcal{M}_{pt}\}$ where $\mathcal{M}_{ft}$ is a mask language model fine-tuned on the corpus in which the classifier f has been trained. $\mathcal{M}_{pt}$ is a pretrained mask language model without fine tuning phase.
- $\alpha \in [0, 1]$ the parameter balancing target probability and distance with the initial point in the cost function
- topk $\in \{10, 11, ..., 100\}$ the number of candidates considered during mask inference
- beam_width $\in \{2, 3, ..., 6\}$ the number of paths explored in parallel at each iteration
- mask_div $\in \{1, 2, 3, ..., 4\}$ the number of candidates kept in memory during a tree search iteration
- strategy $\in \{static, evolutive\}$ where $static$ is the strategy consisting in computing token importance only at the beginning of the counterfactual search. The $evolutive$ strategy consists in computing token importance at each iteration.
- margin $\in \{0.05, 0.3\}$ the probability score spread defining the acceptability threshold of a counterfactual candidate
- $s \in \{sentence\_transformer, CLS\_embedding\}$ the method used to compute the semantic distance.

We perform the optimization over 100 iterations, with the objective to generate 3 counterfactual examples on 20 initial texts. An ablation study thoroughly analyzes the sensibility to TIGTEC to its hyperparameters. For the other hyperparameters, beam_width = 4, mask_div = 4, topk = 50, margin = 0.15 and $\alpha = 0.3$ and Sentence Transformer embedding are reasonable. The maximum number of nodes is set to 1000, which can lead to long searches for counterfactual examples before TIGTEC stops.

Table 1. TIGTEC evaluation on 2 datasets and comparison with competitors on IMDB.

Dataset	Method	Success rate↑%S	Similarity↑%s	Sparsity ↓%T	Plausibility ↓ Δ PPL	Diversity ↑ div
IMDB	Polyjuice$_{1d}$	60.8	55.6	72.2	**1.09**	–
	Polyjuice$_{3d}$	29.6	53.5	74.4	2.16	0.088
	MiCE	**99.6**	81.1	18.0	1.35	–
	CLOSS	97.3	95.4	**2.3**	1.47	–
	TIGTEC-specific$_{1d}$	98.2	**96.8**	4.2	1.25	–
	TIGTEC-specific$_{3d}$	98.2	**95.8**	4.4	1.34	0.019
	TIGTEC-agnostic$_{1d}$	92.7	96.1	4.5	1.24	–
	TIGTEC-agnostic$_{3d}$	92.7	94.6	4.7	1.34	0.075
Movie genre	TIGTEC-specific$_{1d}$	88.4	91.7	8.8	1.42	–
	TIGTEC-specific$_{3d}$	88.4	89.8	9.0	1.38	0.120

4.5   Results

Global Results. Overall, TIGTEC-specific gives very good results on IMDB, succeeding in more than 98% of the time in generating counterfactual examples (Table 1). The counterfactual examples are sparse, plausible and highly similar to their original instance. TIGTEC-agnostic succeeds less than the specific version, with a success rate at circa 93%. Similarity, sparsity and plausibility are at the same level as the specific version, while the counterfactual examples are more diverse. The significant gap in success rates between the agnostic and the specific versions of TIGTEC can be explained by the cumulative effect of the evolutive strategy and the fine-tuned mask model compared to the static strategy and the pretrained mask model. We detail these effects separately in the following ablation study. While the movie genre classification task is more complex (see online[4] for classifier accuracy), TIGTEC manages to generate plausible counterfactual examples close to the initial instance, with more diversity compared to the sentiment analysis task.

Comparative Results. TIGTEC-specific succeeds more often than CLOSS and Polyjuice, while remaining on average closer to the initial instance and being more plausible. The success rate of Polyjuice is low, and the counterfactual examples differ from the original instances in terms of proximity and sparsity. This result is due to the absence of label switching constraint and the independence of the text generation process to the classifier.

MiCE succeeds more often to flip labels than any other counterfactual generator. While the text generated by MiCE is plausible, the counterfactual examples differ strongly from the original instances in terms of semantic proximity and sparsity. TIGTEC-specific succeeds in the same proportion as MiCE and produces much more sparse, similar and plausible counterfactual examples. The low similarity of the counterfactual examples generated by MiCE can be explained by the underlying T5 model used to generate text. Such encoder-decoder models

---

[4] https://github.com/milanbhan/tigtec.

Table 2. Ablation study of token importance, exploration strategy and mask model. With p as the p-value of the one-tailed t-test, *$p < 10\%$, **$p < 5\%$, ***$p < 1\%$. Ref stands for the reference modality.

Hyperparameter		Success rate% mean ± std	Similarity% mean ± std	Sparsity% mean ± std
Token importance	random (ref.)	92.0 ± 14.0	91.4 ± 3.5	9.4 ± 3.0
	attention	**96.2*** ± 7.0	**95.0***** ± 1.7	**4.2***** ± 1.1
	SHAP	**95.6*** ± 7.2	**95.0***** ± 1.5	**4.4***** ± 1.4
Exploration strategy	static (ref.)	93.6 ± 11.4	94.2 ± 2.9	5.9 ± 2.9
	evolutive	95.4 ± 8.5	93.7 ± 2.9	5.8 ± 3.1
Mask model	pretrained (ref.)	94.6 ± 10.5	93.3 ± 3.5	6.0 ± 3.5
	fine-tuned	94.8 ± 9.2	**94.4**** ± 2.1	5.6 ± 2.6

perform mask span infilling by generating text whose meaning and length can sharply change from the masked text.

TIGTEC-agnostic generates more similar, sparse and plausible counterfactual texts than MiCE and Polyjuice. However, if the success rate of TIGTEC-agnostic is high, it is lower than MiCE and CLOSS. Whether in its agnostic or specific version, and with or without the diversity constraint, TIGTEC performs well on all evaluation metrics. Finally, TIGTEC appears to be the best trade-off in terms of success rate, proximity, sparsity, plausibility and diversity.

Ablation Study. This analysis comes from the data resulting from the hyperparameter optimization. We assess the sensitivity of TIGTEC to its hyperparameters through success rate, similarity and sparsity. Each comparison is made with a one-tailed t-test to determine whether the mean of a first sample is lower than the mean of a second one. We first evaluate the impact of hyperparameters specific to the targeting and generating steps of TIGTEC in Table 2. We compare the attention-based token importance and SHAP to a random baseline. The evolutive exploration strategy is compared to the static one and the contribution of the fine-tuned mask model is assessed with respect to the pretrained one. Attention-based token importance and SHAP give better results both in terms of success rate, similarity and sparsity with statistical significance. The fine-tuned mask model induces higher similarity with statistical significance. While the evolutive strategy yields higher success rates on average, the results are not statistically significant.

Besides, we focus on the hyperparameters specific to the exploration and tree search step. The results for the beam_width and mask_div hyperparameters are presented in Table 3. Each beam width is compared to the reference case where beam_width= 2. Mask diversity is also analyzed with respect to the reference case where mask_div= 1. The higher beam_width and mask_div, the higher the similarity and sparsity. This results are statistically significant.

Table 3. Ablation study of beam_width and mask_div. With p as the p-value of the one-tailed t-test, $*p < 10\%$, $**p < 5\%$, $***p < 1\%$. Ref stands for the reference modality.

Hyperparameter		Success rate % mean ± std	Similarity % mean ± std	Sparsity % mean ± std
beam_width	2 (ref.)	94.4 ± 11.3	92.9 ± 3.6	6.6 ± 3.4
	3	96.6 ± 7.4	93.8 ± 2.7	5.8 ± 3.3
	4	96.0 ± 7.8	**94.5**** ± 1.9	**4.5*** ± 1.4
	5	90.2 ± 12.5	**95.1**** ± 1.7	**5.6**** ± 2.7
	6	95.7 ± 6.5	**95**** ± 1.6	**5.1**** ± 2.6
mask_div	1 (ref.)	97.0 ± 7.6	93.2 ± 3.1	6.7 ± 3.3
	2	94.7 ± 10.7	**94.3*** ± 2.0	**4.9*** ± 2.0
	3	90.6 ± 12.2	**94.6*** ± 1.9	**5.5**** ± 3.0
	4	93.3 ± 9.0	**94.4*** ± 3.9	**5.3*** ± 3.3

5   Discussion

We have introduced TIGTEC, an efficient textual counterfactual explainer, generating sparse, plausible, content-preserving and diverse counterfactual examples in an *agnostic* or *specific* fashion. Other NLP counterfactual generators strongly depend on the classifier to explain or the text corpus on which it has been trained. As matter of fact, CLOSS [8] generates counterfactual candidates by optimizing in the latent space from the classifier. MiCE [27] uses gradient-based information from the classifier to target important tokens, while modifying the initial instance with a language model fine-tuned on the corpus of interest. Polyjuice [31] needs to learn to generate counterfactual examples in a supervised way, which requires ground-truth counterfactual data. The adaptability of TIGTEC to any type of NLP classifier and the fact that it works in an *agnostic* way make it particularly flexible.

The proposed framework is versatile and can work with any token importance method. Since the high computational cost of SHAP can be limiting for large-scale applications, other methods such as gradient-based attributions can be used. Besides, the token importance sensitivity analysis highlighted that attention drives TIGTEC as well as SHAP in the search process in terms of success rate, similarity and sparsity. This study therefore favors the interpretabiltiy of self-attention as other recent work [4,5]. If the experimental study has been performed on binary classifiers only, TIGTEC can also be extended to multi-class classifiers by specifiny the target class.

Finally, the use of TIGTEC is not limited to BERT-like classifiers. Our proposed framework can be adapted to any type of classifier as long as a token importance method is given as input. For other NLP classifiers such as recurrent neural networks, SHAP or gradient-based methods could be used to target impactful tokens. TIGTEC can also help in explaining machine learning models such as boosted trees with LIME as token importance method.

6   Conclusion and Future Work

This paper presents TIGTEC, a method for generating sparse, plausible and diverse counterfactual explanations. The architecture of TIGTEC is modular and can be adapted to any type of NLP model and to classification tasks of various difficulties. TIGTEC can cover both model-agnostic and model-specific cases, depending on the token importance method used to guide the search for counterfactual examples.

A way of improvement of TIGTEC could be to cover more types of classifiers as mentioned in the previous section. Other gradient-based token importance methods could also be integrated to TIGTEC. Furthermore, diversity is only implicitly addressed through the exploration strategy. We believe that diversity could be improved by transcribing it into the cost function during the evaluation step or sharpening the exploration strategy.

Finally, automatic evaluation of the counterfactual examples quality has its limits. The metrics introduced above provide good indications of the performance of TIGTEC, but they do not ensure human understanding. From this perspective, human-grounded experiments would be more appropriate to assess the relevance of the generated text and its explanatory quality.

Ethics Statement. Since the training data for mask language models, Sentence Transformers and classifiers can be biased, there is a risk of generating harmful counterfactual examples. One using TIGTEC to explain the predictions of one's classifier must be aware of these biases in order to stand back and analyze the produced results. On the other hand, by generating unexpected counterfactual examples, we believe that TIGTEC can be useful in detecting bias in the classifier it seeks to explain. Finally, as any method based on deep learning, this method consumes energy, potentially emitting greenhouse gases. It must be used with caution.

References

1. Akiba, T., Sano, S., Yanase, T., Ohta, T., Koyama, M.: Optuna: a next-generation hyperparameter optimization framework. In: Proceedings of the 25th ACM SIGKDD International Conference on Knowledge Discovery & Data Mining (2019)
2. Bahdanau, D., Cho, K., Bengio, Y.: Neural machine translation by jointly learning to align and translate. arXiv:1409 (2014)
3. Barredo Arrieta, A., et al.: Explainable Artificial Intelligence (XAI): concepts, taxonomies, opportunities and challenges toward responsible AI. Inf. Fusion **58**, 82–115 (2020)
4. Bhan, M., Achache, N., Legrand, V., Blangero, A., Chesneau, N.: Evaluating self-attention interpretability through human-grounded experimental protocol. arXiv (2023)
5. Bibal, A., et al.: Is attention explanation? An introduction to the debate. In: Proceedings of the Association for Computational Linguistics (ACL) (2022)

6. Dathathri, S., et al.: Plug and play language models: a simple approach to controlled text generation. In: 8th International Conference on Learning Representations, ICLR (2020)

7. Devlin, J., Chang, M., Lee, K., Toutanova, K.: BERT: pre-training of deep bidirectional transformers for language understanding. In: Proceedings of the Association for Computational Linguistics (ACL) (2019)

8. Fern, X., Pope, Q.: Text counterfactuals via latent optimization and shapley-guided search. In: Proceedings of Conference on Empirical Methods in Natural Language Processing (EMNLP) (2021)

9. Guidotti, R.: Counterfactual explanations and how to find them: literature review and benchmarking. Data Mining Knowl. Discov. (2022)

10. Jelinek, F., Mercer, R.L., Bahl, L.R., Baker, J.K.: Perplexity-a measure of the difficulty of speech recognition tasks. J. Acoust. Soc. Am. **62**, 63 (1977)

11. Laugel, T., Lesot, M.J., Marsala, C., Renard, X., Detyniecki, M.: The dangers of post-hoc interpretability: unjustified counterfactual explanations. In: International Joint Conference on Artificial Intelligence (IJCAI) (2019)

12. Lewis, M., et al.: BART: denoising sequence-to-sequence pre-training for natural language generation, translation, and comprehension. In: Proceedings of the Association for Computational Linguistics (ACL) (2020)

13. Lundberg, S.M., Lee, S.I.: A unified approach to interpreting model predictions. In: Advances in Neural Information Processing Systems. NeurIPS (2017)

14. Maas, A.L., Daly, R.E., Pham, P.T., Huang, D., Ng, A.Y., Potts, C.: Learning word vectors for sentiment analysis. In: Proceedings of the Association for Computational Linguistics (ACL) (2011)

15. Madaan, N., Bedathur, S., Saha, D.: Plug and Play Counterfactual Text Generation for Model Robustness. arXiv (2022)

16. Mazzine, R., Martens, D.: A framework and benchmarking study for counterfactual generating methods on tabular data. CoRR (2021)

17. Miller, T.: Explanation in artificial intelligence: insights from the social sciences. Artif. Intell. **267**, 1–38 (2019)

18. Molnar, C.: Interpretable Machine Learning, 2nd edn. (2022). https://christophm.github.io/interpretable-ml-book

19. Morris, J.X., Lifland, E., Yoo, J.Y., Grigsby, J., Jin, D., Qi, Y.: Textattack: a framework for adversarial attacks, data augmentation, and adversarial training in NLP. In: Proceedings of Conference on Empirical Methods in Natural Language Processing (EMNLP) (2020)

20. Mothilal, R.K., Sharma, A., Tan, C.: Explaining machine learning classifiers through diverse counterfactual explanations. In: Proceedings of the 2020 Conference on Fairness, Accountability, and Transparency (FAT*) (2020)

21. Papineni, K., Roukos, S., Ward, T., Zhu, W.J.: Bleu: a method for automatic evaluation of machine translation. In: Proceedings of Association for Computational Linguistics (ACL) (2002)

22. Poyiadzi, R., Sokol, K., Santos-Rodriguez, R., De Bie, T., Flach, P.: FACE: feasible and actionable counterfactual explanations. In: Proceedings of the AAAI/ACM Conference on AI, Ethics, and Society (AIES) (2020)

23. Radford, A., Wu, J., Child, R., Luan, D., Amodei, D., Sutskever, I.: Language models are unsupervised multitask learners. OpenAI blog (2019)

24. Raffel, C., et al.: Exploring the limits of transfer learning with a unified text-to-text transformer. J. Mach. Learn. Res. **21**, 5485–5551 (2019)

25. Reimers, N., Gurevych, I.: Sentence-BERT: sentence embeddings using siamese BERT-networks. In: Proceedings of Empirical Methods in Natural Language Processing (EMNLP) (2019)
26. Ribeiro, M.T., Singh, S., Guestrin, C.: "Why should I trust you?" Explaining the predictions of any classifier. In: Proceedings of the 22nd ACM SIGKDD International Conference on Knowledge Discovery and Data Mining (2016)
27. Ross, A., Marasović, A., Peters, M.: Explaining NLP models via minimal contrastive editing (MiCE). In: Findings of the Association for Computational Linguistics (ACL) (2021)
28. Russell, C.: Efficient search for diverse coherent explanations. In: Proceedings of the Conference on Fairness, Accountability, and Transparency, pp. 20–28. FAT* (2019)
29. Sanh, V., Debut, L., Chaumond, J., Wolf, T.: DistilBERT, a distilled version of BERT: smaller, faster, cheaper and lighter (2020)
30. Vaswani, A., et al.: Attention is all you need. In: Advances in Neural Information Processing Systems (NeurIPS) (2017)
31. Wu, T., Ribeiro, M.T., Heer, J., Weld, D.: Polyjuice: Generating counterfactuals for explaining, evaluating, and improving models. In: Proceedings of the Association for Computational Linguistics (ACL) and the Joint Conference on Natural Language Processing (JCNLP) (2021)

Knowledge Graphs

Towards Few-Shot Inductive Link Prediction on Knowledge Graphs: A Relational Anonymous Walk-Guided Neural Process Approach

Zicheng Zhao[1,2], Linhao Luo[3], Shirui Pan[4], Quoc Viet Hung Nguyen[4], and Chen Gong[1,5(⊠)]

[1] School of Computer Science and Engineering, Nanjing University of Science and Technology, Nanjing, China
chen.gong@njust.edu.cn
[2] Jiangsu Key Laboratory of Image and Video Understanding for Social Security, Nanjing, China
[3] Department of Data Science and AI, Monash University, Melbourne, Australia
[4] School of Information and Communication Technology, Griffith University, Nathan, Australia
[5] Key Laboratory of Intelligent Perception and Systems for High-Dimensional Information of Ministry of Education, Nanjing, China

Abstract. Few-shot inductive link prediction on knowledge graphs (KGs) aims to predict missing links for unseen entities with few-shot links observed. Previous methods are limited to transductive scenarios, where entities exist in the knowledge graphs, so they are unable to handle unseen entities. Therefore, recent inductive methods utilize the sub-graphs around unseen entities to obtain the semantics and predict links inductively. However, in the few-shot setting, the sub-graphs are often sparse and cannot provide meaningful inductive patterns. In this paper, we propose a novel relational anonymous walk-guided neural process for few-shot inductive link prediction on knowledge graphs, denoted as RawNP. Specifically, we develop a neural process-based method to model a flexible distribution over link prediction functions. This enables the model to quickly adapt to new entities and estimate the uncertainty when making predictions. To capture general inductive patterns, we present a relational anonymous walk to extract a series of relational motifs from few-shot observations. These motifs reveal the distinctive semantic patterns on KGs that support inductive predictions. Extensive experiments on typical benchmark datasets demonstrate that our model derives new state-of-the-art performance.

Keywords: Knowledge graphs · Few-shot learning · Link prediction · Neural process

---

Z. Zhao and L. Luo—Equal contribution.

D. Koutra et al. (Eds.): ECML PKDD 2023, LNAI 14171, pp. 515–532, 2023.
https://doi.org/10.1007/978-3-031-43418-1_31

1   Introduction

Knowledge graphs (KGs) are structured representations of human knowledge, where each link represents the fact in the format of a triple (*head entity, relation, tail entity*). Recently, KGs have been widely used in various applications, such as web search [21], community detection [20] and recommender systems [45]. However, the incompleteness of KGs [55] largely impairs their applications. Therefore, many methods have been proposed to complete KGs by predicting the missing links and they achieved impressive performances [2,25].

Despite the success, these traditional methods are often transductive, assuming that all entities are seen during training. However, real-world KGs dynamically evolve over time, with numerous unseen entities emerging every day [22,31]. In this case, transductive methods can hardly model the unseen entities, resulting in an unsatisfactory performance for inductive link prediction. Moreover, unseen entities usually have few links upon their arrival [47], thus providing insufficient information to characterize themselves. Therefore, few-shot inductive link prediction on KGs has recently attracted increasing attention [1,7,43]. As shown in Fig. 1(a), given an unseen node u and its support set $\mathcal{C}_u$ with three observed links (r_1, r_2, r_3), few-shot inductive link prediction aims to predict possible links r_q with other entities e_q in the query set $\mathcal{D}_u$.

Inspired by graph neural networks (GNNs) [40], recent studies utilize a sub-graph around the unseen entity to predict links inductively [24,35,57]. The major motivation behind these methods is that they try to capture the semantic patterns from the graph topology that are agnostic to the target entity. The semantic patterns on KGs are usually reflected as relational paths [44,52], and each of them is a sequence of relations connecting the entities, as shown in Fig. 1(b). Given the observations, an ideal pattern for inductive reasoning should be distinctive and can be matched during the inference. However, in the few-shot setting, the sub-graphs are often sparse, making semantic features captured by relational paths *not general enough and meaningful for inductive link prediction* (**Limitation 1**). For example, as shown in Fig. 1(b), the three relational paths

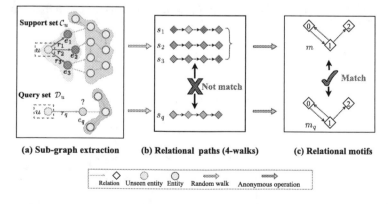

Fig. 1. An illustration of few-shot inductive link prediction on knowledge graphs.

(i.e., $s_1 \sim s_3$) extracted from the support set are distinct, where different colors denote different relations. They cannot provide any inductive and distinctive patterns that can be matched by the relational path extracted from the query set. Therefore, the patterns represented by relational paths cannot be used for supporting the inductive link prediction.

Recently, several meta-learning-based methods have been proposed to tackle the problem of few-shot learning. Meta-learning-based methods quickly adapt to a new entity by updating the model parameters with a few examples [3, 57]. However, due to the limitation of data, the meta-learning-based methods often suffer from overfitting [8] and out-of-distribution problems [13]. Meanwhile, they *fail to quantify the uncertainty in the predictions* (**Limitation 2**), which is essential for generating reliable predictions under few-shot scenarios [49, 56].

To address the aforementioned limitations, we propose a **r**elational **a**nonymous **w**alk-guided **n**eural **p**rocess approach (RawNP) for few-shot inductive link prediction on knowledge graphs. Specifically, we develop a framework based on neural process (NP) [11] to address the challenges mentioned above in few-shot learning. Unlike previous few-shot methods (e.g., meta-learning), NP is based on the stochastic process that models the distribution over the functions conditioned on limited data. Given a few links, we can readily obtain a prediction function from the distribution that is specialized for the unseen entity. By modeling the distribution, RawNP can also estimate the uncertainty of its prediction and generate more reliable results (**addressing Limitation 2**). To capture the representative patterns, we propose a novel relational anonymous walk to extract a series of relational motifs (**addressing Limitation 1**). As shown in Fig. 1(c), the three relational paths (i.e., $s_1 \sim s_3$) in Fig. 1(b) can be represented by one relational motif m, which can be used to guide the inductive predictions by matching with the motif m_q in the query set. The main contributions of our work are summarized as follows:

- We propose a novel neural process approach for few-shot inductive link prediction on knowledge graphs. To the best of our knowledge, this is the first work of developing a neural process framework to solve this problem.
- We propose a novel relational anonymous walk to extract a series of relational motifs. The patterns revealed from these motifs are more general and distinctive than the previous methods for inductive link prediction.
- We conduct extensive experiments on typical public datasets. Experimental results show that RawNP outperforms existing baseline methods, which proves the superiority of our method.

2 Related Work

Link Prediction on Knowledge Graphs. Link prediction on knowledge graphs is an important task to complete the missing facts. Previous methods mainly focus on the transductive setting, where all entities are seen during training [2, 39, 53]. Inspired by the inductive ability of GNNs [41], several methods adopt the graph structure to predict links inductively [5, 19]. For example, GraIL

[35] extracts the enclosing sub-graph of a given triple to capture the topological structure. CoMPILE [24] generates inductive representations by modeling the relations in sub-graphs. To better consider the semantics in knowledge graphs, SNRI [52] adopts relational paths within a sub-graph to provide inductive features. However, the features captured by these methods are not general enough to provide inductive bias for unseen entities, especially in the few-shot setting. Meanwhile, there are several works [14,48] that apply anonymous random walk on temporal graphs to extract temporal network motifs, thus keeping their methods fully inductive. However, they focus on node anonymization and cannot handle complex relations in knowledge graphs.

Several meta-learning-based methods have been proposed for few-shot link prediction. MetaR [6] adapts to unseen relations by a relation-meta learner and updates the parameter by using the meta-learning framework. Meta-iKG [57] utilizes local sub-graphs to transfer sub-graph-specific information and rapidly learn transferable patterns via meta-learning. However, the meta-learning-based methods are sensitive to the quality of given few-shot data and unable to estimate the uncertainty of the model. GEN [1] meta-learns the unseen node embedding for inductive inference and proposes a stochastic embedding layer to model the uncertainty in the link prediction, which achieves state-of-the-art performance among all baseline models.

Neural Process. Neural process (NP) [11], a new family of methods, opens up a new door to dealing with limited data in machine learning [42]. Based on the stochastic process, NP enables to model the distribution over functions given limited observations and provides an uncertainty measure to the predictions. An increasing number of researches focus on improving the expressiveness of the vanilla NP model. For instance, Attentive Neural Process (ANP) [15] leverages the self-attention mechanism to better capture the dependencies and model the distribution. Sequential Neural Process (SNP) [32] introduces a recurrent neural network (RNN) to capture temporal correlation for better generalization. NP has already been applied in many tasks to address the challenge of data limitation, such as recommender systems [18], node classification [4], and link prediction [17, 22]. This also demonstrates the great potential of NP in other machine learning areas. Recently, NP-FKGC [23] applies normalizing flow-based NP to predict the missing facts for few-shot relations. To the best of our knowledge, this is the first work to apply the neural process to the few-shot inductive link prediction on knowledge graphs.

3   Preliminary and Problem Definition

3.1   Neural Process

NP [11] marries the benefits of the stochastic process and neural networks to model the distribution over functions $f : X \rightarrow Y$ with limited data, where X and Y are feature space and label space, respectively. Specifically, the function f is assumed to be parameterized by a high-dimensional random vector z, whose distribution $P(z|\mathcal{C})$ is conditioned on the *context data* $\mathcal{C} = \{(x_\mathcal{C}, y_\mathcal{C})\}$ with x

and y denoting feature and label of a data point accordingly. The $P(z|\mathcal{C})$ is empirically defined as a Gaussian distribution, which is modeled by an *encoder* using the context data. By sampling a z from the distribution, NP can easily obtain the function for a new prediction task. The prediction likelihood over the *target data* $\mathcal{D} = \{(x_{\mathcal{D}}, y_{\mathcal{D}})\}$ is calculated as

$$P(y_{\mathcal{D}}|x_{\mathcal{D}}, \mathcal{C}) = \int_z P(y_{\mathcal{D}}|x_{\mathcal{D}}, z) P(z|\mathcal{C}) dz, \tag{1}$$

where $P(y_{\mathcal{D}}|x_{\mathcal{D}}, z)$ is modeled by a *decoder* network. Since the actual distribution of z is intractable, the training of NP can be achieved by amortized variational inference [16]. The objective expressed by Eq. (1) can be optimized by maximizing the evidence lower **bound** (ELBO), which is formulated as

$$\log P(y_{\mathcal{D}}|x_{\mathcal{D}}, \mathcal{C}) \geq \mathbb{E}_{Q_\psi}(z|\mathcal{C}, \mathcal{D}) \left[\log P_\phi(y_{\mathcal{D}}|x_{\mathcal{D}}, z)\right] - KL\left(Q_\psi(z|\mathcal{C}, \mathcal{D}) \| P_\theta(z|\mathcal{C})\right), \tag{2}$$

where θ and ϕ denote the parameters of encoder and decoder, respectively, and $Q_\psi(z|\mathcal{C}, \mathcal{D})$ denotes the variational posterior of the latent variable z, approximated by another neural network with parameters ψ.

3.2 Problem Definition

A KG can be represented by a set of triples $\mathcal{G} = \{(h, r, t) \subseteq \mathcal{E} \times \mathcal{R} \times \mathcal{E}\}$, where $\mathcal{E}$ and $\mathcal{R}$ denote the set of existing entities and relations in KG respectively, $h, t \in \mathcal{E}$ denote the head and tail entities and $r \in \mathcal{R}$ denotes the specific relations between the entities. The few-shot inductive link prediction on KGs can be formulated as follows:

Definition 1. *Few-shot inductive link prediction on knowledge graphs.* *Given a knowledge graph $\mathcal{G}$ and an unseen entity set $\widetilde{\mathcal{E}}$, where $\mathcal{E} \cap \widetilde{\mathcal{E}} = \emptyset$, we assume that each unseen entity $u \in \widetilde{\mathcal{E}}$ is associated with a K-shot support set $\{(u, r_i, e_i)\}_{i=1}^{K}$, where $e_i \in \mathcal{E} \cup \widetilde{\mathcal{E}}$. For an unseen entity u, our task is to obtain a function f_u that predicts the other entity e_q for each query $q = (u, r_q, ?)$ in the query set $\{(u, r_q, ?)\}$, where $e_q \subset \mathcal{E} \cup \widetilde{\mathcal{E}}$ and r_q is the given query relation.*

In our paper, we propose a neural process-based framework for this task. For each unseen entity u, we treat its support set as the context data $\mathcal{C}_u = \{(u, r_i, e_i)\}_{i=1}^{K}$ and the query set as the target data $\mathcal{D}_u = \{(u, r_q, ?)\}$.

4 Approach

In this section, we present our proposed model RawNP, which consists of three major components: (1) a relational anonymous walk (RAW) to generate a series of relational motifs for each entity and excavate distinctive semantic patterns; (2) a RAW-guided neural process encoder to model the joint distribution over link prediction functions on knowledge graphs and simultaneously estimate the uncertainty for predictions; (3) an inductive neural process link predictor to infer the inductive links given an unseen entity and its associated relation. The overall framework of our proposed model is illustrated in Fig. 2.

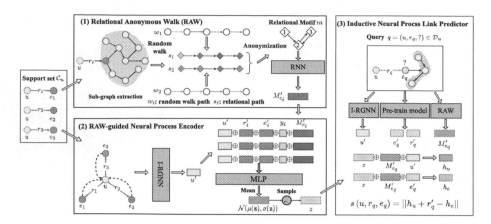

Fig. 2. The framework of our proposed model RawNP for few-shot inductive link prediction on knowledge graphs.

4.1 Relational Anonymous Walk

The relational anonymous walk (RAW) is designed to capture the distinctive semantic patterns on KGs, which better reveal the inductive identity and facilitate the link prediction. Previous methods capture the semantic patterns in the sub-graphs around entities by using relational path [44,52], which is a sequence of relations connecting the entities. Specifically, given a raw path in the knowledge graphs: $w = e_0 \xrightarrow{r_1} e_1 \xrightarrow{r_2} \dots \xrightarrow{r_l} e_l$, the corresponding relational paths s is the sequence of relations in the given path, i.e., $s = \{r_1, r_2, \dots, r_l\}$. However, the relational path is not general enough, as the combinations of relations explode in KGs, making the patterns captured by relational paths not distinguishable. To address this issue, we propose a relational anonymous walk to extract the distinctive semantic patterns in the form of relational motifs. The process of RAW is shown in Algorithm 1.

For each entity e in the triple (u, r, e) of the K-shot support set, we first perform random walk [29] to sample a few l-step paths $\{w_i = e \xrightarrow{r_1} e_1 \xrightarrow{r_2} \dots \xrightarrow{r_l} e_l\}_{i=1}^{L}$ starting from e, where L denotes the number of walks. Then, we could obtain the corresponding relational paths $\{s_i = \{r_1, r_2, \dots, r_l\}\}_{i=1}^{L}$, where relations could be repeated in s_i. Later, we apply an anonymization operation $A(\cdot)$ to each s_i by replacing the actual relations with their first positions in s_i. This can be formulated as

$$m_i = A(s_i) = \{I(r_1), I(r_2), \dots, I(r_l)\}, \tag{3}$$

$$I(r_j) = \min \ pos(r_j, s_i), \tag{4}$$

where $pos(r_j, s_i) \in [1, l]$ denotes the positions of r_j in s_i. The anonymization operation $A(\cdot)$ removes the relation identities and maps the relational paths into a general semantic pattern defined as a *relational motif* m_i. For example, as shown in the bottom of Fig. 2, the two distinct relational paths s_1 and s_2 can be

---

Algorithm 1: Relational anonymous walk (RAW)

Input: Knowledge graph $\mathcal{G}$; unseen entity u; support triple $(u, r, e) \in \mathcal{C}_u$; walks number L; walks length l

Output: Relational motifs set $\mathcal{M}_e$

1   Initialize $\mathcal{M}_e \leftarrow \emptyset$;

2   **for** $i=1$ to L **do**

3   Sample a l-step path w_i starting from e using random walk;

4   Obtain the corresponding relational path s_i;

5   Apply anonymization operation $A(s_i)$ to extract the motif m_i;

6   Add m_i to $\mathcal{M}_e$;

7   **end**

---

anonymized to the same relational motif structure m. In this way, by checking the set of relational motifs $\mathcal{M}_e$, we can find the distinctive features for inductive link predictions.

To obtain the representation of patterns, we first encode each motif $m_i \in \mathcal{M}_e$ by using a recurrent neural network (RNN) and aggregate them with a mean pooling, which is formulated as

$$m'_i = \text{RNN}(\{f_{enc}(I(r_j))|I(r_j) \in m_i\}), \tag{5}$$

$$M'_e = \frac{1}{|\mathcal{M}_e|} \sum_{m_i \in \mathcal{M}_e} m'_i, \tag{6}$$

where f_{enc} is a multi-layer perceptron (MLP) mapping function.

4.2 RAW-Guided Neural Process Encoder

RAW-guided neural process encoder attempts to model the joint distribution over the link prediction functions based on the context data (support set). It first learns a low-dimension vector c_i for each triple in the context data. Then, it aggregates them into a global representation $\mathbf{z}$, which defines the distribution as $\mathcal{N}(\mu(\mathbf{z}), \sigma(\mathbf{z}))$. By sampling a z from the distribution, we can adaptively obtain the prediction function f_u.

For each triple (u, r_i, e_i) in the support set, we first adopt RAW to obtain the pattern representation M'_{e_i} to inject the inductive ability into f_u. Since the relational motifs ignore the identity information, we also obtain the representations of entity e'_i and relation r'_i from a pre-trained model, e.g., TransE [2]. For the unseen node u, we adopt an inductive relational graph neural network (I-RGNN) to generate the representation by aggregating all the triples in its support set, which is formulated as

$$u' = ReLU(\frac{1}{|\mathcal{C}_u|} \sum_{(u, r_i, e_i) \in \mathcal{C}_u} W_{r_i} r'_i + W e'_i), \tag{7}$$

where W_{r_i} denotes a relation-specific weight matrix and W is a weight matrix. Through aggregating from associated triples in the support set, I-RGNN enables the inductive generation of embeddings for unseen entities.

By incorporating the representations of u', r_i', e_i', and M_{e_i}', c_i is generated as follows:

$$c_i = \mathrm{MLP}\left(u' \,\|r_i'\|e_i'\| \, y_i\|M_{e_i}'\right), y_i = \begin{cases} 1, (u, r_i, e_i) \in \mathcal{C}_u \\ 0, (u, r_i, e_i) \in \mathcal{C}_u^- \end{cases}, \tag{8}$$

where we sample a set of negative samples $\mathcal{C}_u^-$ by replacing the e_i in $\mathcal{C}_u$ with the other entities randomly, and y_i is an indicator vector. $\|$ represents concatenation operations.

Then, we aggregate all the latent representations $c_i \in \mathcal{C}_u \cup \mathcal{C}_u^-$ to obtain a global representation $\mathbf{z}$ and define the joint distribution over the link prediction functions. The aggregator function must satisfy the condition of *permutation-invariant* [11,38]. Therefore, we select the mean pooling function, which can be formulated as

$$\mathbf{z} = \frac{1}{|\mathcal{C}_u \cup \mathcal{C}_u^-|} \sum_{c_i \in \mathcal{C}_u \cup \mathcal{C}_u^-} c_i. \tag{9}$$

The distribution $P(\mathbf{z}|\mathcal{C}_u)$ is empirically considered as a Gaussian distribution $\mathcal{N}(\mu(\mathbf{z}), \sigma(\mathbf{z}))$ parameterized by $\mathbf{z}$ [10,15], in which the mean $\mu(\mathbf{z})$ and variance $\sigma(\mathbf{z})$ are modeled by two neural networks:

$$h_z = ReLU(\mathrm{MLP}(\mathbf{z})), \tag{10}$$

$$\mu(\mathbf{z}) = \mathrm{MLP}(h_z), \tag{11}$$

$$\sigma(\mathbf{z}) = 0.1 + 0.9 * Sigmoid(\mathrm{MLP}(h_z)). \tag{12}$$

Noticeably, $\mathcal{N}(\mu(\mathbf{z}), \sigma(\mathbf{z}))$ not only defines the distribution over functions, but also estimates the uncertainty of the model. When the support set is limited, the encoder could generate a distribution with a larger variance, which indicates that the model is more uncertain to its predictions. We detailly analyze the uncertainty captured by RawNP in Sect. 5.7.

4.3   Inductive Neural Process Link Predictor

The inductive neural process link predictor serves the decoder to realize the f_u modeled by $\mathcal{N}(\mu(\mathbf{z}), \sigma(\mathbf{z}))$. Given a query $q = (u, r_q, ?)$, f_u tries to predict the possible entity e_q. The details are as follows:

In the predictor, we obtain the representations of entities and relations (i.e., u', r_q', e_q') with the same process in Sect. 4.2 and combine them with a sampled z by following the paradigm of neural process, which is calculated as

$$\text{Sample } z \sim \mathcal{N}(\mu(\mathbf{z}), \sigma(\mathbf{z})), \tag{13}$$

where each sample of z is regarded as a realization of the function from corresponding stochastic process.

Then, we use two independent MLPs to map z into the space of entities and project u' and e'_q into the hyper-planes defined by z via using an element-wise addition, which can be formulated as

$$u'_z = u' + \text{MLP}^z_u(z), e'_z = e'_q + \text{MLP}^z_e(z). \tag{14}$$

For inductive prediction, we also obtain the relational motif representation M'_{e_q} produced by the relational anonymous walk introduced in Sect. 4.1. Similarly, we inject this representation by another two MLPs, which are formulated as

$$h_u = u'_z + \text{MLP}^M_u(M'_{e_q}), h_e = e'_z + \text{MLP}^M_e(M'_{e_q}). \tag{15}$$

Finally, we use a score function to measure the plausibility of triples, which is formulated as

$$s(u, r_q, e_q) = ||h_u + r'_q - h_e||. \tag{16}$$

4.4   Optimization and Inference

Optimization. Given an unseen entity u and its support set $\mathcal{C}_u$, our objective is to infer the distribution $P(z|\mathcal{C}_u)$ from the context data that minimizes the prediction loss on the target data $\log P(e_q|u, r_q, \mathcal{C}_u)$. The optimization can be achieved by maximizing the evidence lower bound (ELBO), as derived:

$$\log P(e_q|u, r_q, \mathcal{C}_u) = \int_z Q(z) \log \frac{P(e_q, z|u, r_q, \mathcal{C}_u)}{P(z|\mathcal{C}_u)}, \tag{17}$$

$$= \int_z Q(z) \log \frac{P(e_q, z|u, r_q, \mathcal{C}_u)}{Q(z)} + KL(Q(z)\|P(z|\mathcal{C}_u)), \tag{18}$$

$$\geq \int_z Q(z) \log \frac{P(e_q, z|u, r_q, \mathcal{C}_u)}{Q(z)}, \tag{19}$$

$$= \mathbb{E}_{Q(z)} \log \frac{P(e_q, z|u, r_q, \mathcal{C}_u)}{Q(z)}, \tag{20}$$

$$= \mathbb{E}_{Q(z)} \left[\log P(e_q|u, r_q, z) + \log \frac{P(z|\mathcal{C}_u)}{Q(z)} \right], \tag{21}$$

$$= \mathbb{E}_{Q(z)} [\log P(e_q|u, r_q, z)] - KL(Q(z)\|P(z|\mathcal{C}_u)), \tag{22}$$

where $Q(z)$ represents the true posterior distribution of z, which is intractable. To address this problem, we approximate it with $Q(z|\mathcal{C}_u, \mathcal{D}_u)$ calculated by the encoder during training. The detailed derivation of Eq. (22) can be found in the *Appendix*.

We introduce the *reparamterization trick* for sampling z to support gradient propagation, and then we estimate the expectation $\mathbb{E}_{Q(z)} [\log P(e_q|u, r_q, z)]$ via the Monte-Carlo sampling as follows:

$$\mathbb{E}_{Q(z)} [\log P(e_q|u, r_q, z)] \simeq \frac{1}{T} \sum_{t=1}^{T} \log P\left(e_q|u, r_q, z^{(t)}\right), \tag{23}$$

$$z^{(t)} = \mu(\mathbf{z}) + \sigma(\mathbf{z})\epsilon^{(t)}, \text{ with } \epsilon^{(t)} \sim \mathcal{N}(0, 1). \tag{24}$$

The likelihood term $\log P\left(e_q|u, r_q, z\right)$ is calculated by a widely-used margin ranking loss as follows:

$$\log P\left(e_q|u, r_q, z\right) = -\sum_{q,q^-} max\left(0, \gamma + s\left(q^-\right) - s\left(q\right)\right), \tag{25}$$

where γ denotes a margin hyper-parameter, and $q = (u, r_q, e_q)$ denotes the ground truth triples, and q^- denotes the negative triples by randomly corrupting e_q. By maximizing the likelihood, we aim to rank the scores of positive triples higher than all other negative triples.

Inference. In the inference stage, given an unseen entity u, we generate latent distribution $P\left(z|\mathcal{C}_u\right)$ by using its support set $\mathcal{C}_u$. Then, we feed the sampled z together with the embeddings of unseen entity u and its query relation r_q to the decoder and predict the possible entity e_q for the target set $\mathcal{D}_u$. The algorithms of the training and testing process can be found in the *Appendix*.

5 Experiment

5.1 Datasets and Evaluation

We conduct our experiments on two benchmark datasets: FB15k-237 [36] and NELL-995 [50]. To support the inductive setting, we randomly filter a few entities out of KGs as unseen entities. For FB15k-237 dataset, we first select 5000 entities whose related triples are between 10 to 100 and split them into 2,500/1,000/1,500 for training/validation/test. For NELL-995 dataset, we choose 3000 entities whose associated triples are between 7 to 100 and split them into 1,500/600/900 for training/validation/test. The splits are following the same settings in GEN [1] and the statistics of two datasets can be found in *Appendix*.

In the evaluation stage, for a query triple $(u, r_q, ?)$, we construct the candidate set by using all the possible entities in the KG. We obtain the rank of the correct triples and report the results using the mean reciprocal rank (MRR) and the Top-N hit ratio (Hits@N). The N is set to 1, 3, and 10 to directly compare with the existing methods.

5.2 Baseline Models

We select a series of following baseline models for comparison, which can be divided into three categories: (1) **Traditional KGC methods**, including TransE [2], DistMult [53], ComplEx [37], RotatE [34]; (2) **GNN-based methods**, including R-GCN [30], MEAN [12], LAN [46]; (3) **Few-shot inductive methods**, including GMatching [51], MetaR [6], FSRL [54], GEN [1]. Specifically, there are two versions of the GEN model: I-GEN, which does not consider relations between unsees entities, and T-GEN which remedies the defect. More details can be found in the *Appendix*. To avoid the re-implementation bias, we directly use the existing SOTA results reported by GEN [1] in experiments.

5.3 Implementation Details

We implement our model with PyTorch [28] and PyG [9] package and conduct experiments on a single RTX 3090 GPU. The dimensions of entity and relation embedding are set to 100. The length of random walk l in the relational motifs extractor is set to 10, and the walk number L is set to 5. We set the learning rate as 10^{-3}, margin γ as 1, dropout rate as 0.3, and negative sample size as 32 and 64 in FB15k-237 and NELL-995, respectively. We use Adam as the optimizer. We use the pre-trained model (e.g., TransE [2]) to initialize the embeddings of entity and relation, which is fine-tuned during training. We set the embedding of unseen entities as the zero vector. Finally, the best model used for testing is selected according to the metric of MRR on the evaluation set. More detailed experiment settings can be found in the *Appendix*. Code and appendix are available at https://github.com/leapxcheng/RawNP.

5.4 Results and Analysis

We present the results of 1-shot and 3-shot link prediction on FB15k-237 and NELL-995 in Table 1, where the best results are highlighted in bold. From the results, we can see that our RawNP achieves the best performance against all baseline models, demonstrating the superiority and effectiveness of our model.

Traditional KGC methods get the worst results. Because they cannot well represent the emerging unseen entity and barely works under the inductive setting. GNN-based methods achieve better performance as they consider the local structure of the knowledge graph. Specifically, LAN uses the attention mechanism to capture the semantics inherent in the knowledge graph, which achieves the best performance among GNN-based methods. However, with the limitation of the data (e.g., 1-shot), their performance drops quickly. Few-shot methods focus on making predictions with limited data and they reach the second-best results. They often adopt the framework of meta-learning to update the embeddings of new entities with their support triples. However, when the support set is inaccurate and shares different distributions with the query set, the performance of few-shot methods will be affected. Therefore, T-GEN introduces a stochastic embedding layer to account for the uncertainty, which improves the reliability of its predictions. In our method, we not only adopt the framework of the neural process to quantify the uncertainty but also extract the relational motifs to inject the inductive ability into our model, which outperforms all baseline models. Compared with the 3-shot results, the improvement on the 1-shot is relatively small. The possible reason is that the model is less certain about its predictions given a single observation, which impairs the predictions. Detail studies about uncertainty captured by RawNP can be found in Sect. 5.7.

In real-world settings, unseen entities emerge simultaneously. Therefore, we also consider the prediction of links between two unseen entities, i.e., Unseen-to-unseen link prediction. We illustrate the performance of our model RawNP in Table 2, where it achieves comparable results to existing state-of-the-art methods. This demonstrates that RawNP is capable of inferring hidden relationships

Table 1. The results of 1-shot and 3-shot link prediction on FB15k-237 and NELL-995. The best results are highlighted in bold.

Model	FB15k-237								NELL-995							
	MRR		Hit@1		Hit@3		Hit@10		MRR		Hit@1		Hit@3		Hit@10	
	1-S	3-S	1-S	3-S	1-S	3-S	1-S	3-S	1-S	3-S	1-S	3-S	1-S	3-S	1-S	3-S
TransE	.071	.120	.023	.057	.086	.137	.159	.238	.071	.118	.037	.061	.079	.132	.129	.223
DistMult	.059	.094	.034	.053	.064	.101	.103	.172	.075	.134	.045	.083	.083	.143	.131	.233
ComplEx	.062	.104	.037	.058	.067	.114	.110	.188	.069	.124	.045	.077	.071	.134	.117	.213
RotatE	.063	.115	.039	.069	.071	.131	.105	.200	.054	.112	.028	.060	.064	.131	.104	.209
R-GCN	.099	.140	.056	.082	.104	.154	.181	.255	.112	.199	.074	.141	.119	.219	.184	.307
MEAN	.105	.114	.052	.058	.109	.119	.207	.217	.158	.180	.107	.124	.173	.189	.263	.296
LAN	.112	.112	.057	.055	.118	.119	.214	.218	.159	.172	.111	.116	.172	.181	.255	.286
GMatching	.224	.238	.157	.168	.249	.263	.352	.372	.120	.139	.074	.092	.136	.151	.215	.235
MetaR	.294	.316	.223	.235	.318	.341	.441	.492	.177	.213	.104	.145	.217	.247	.315	.352
FSRL	.255	.259	.187	.186	.279	.281	.391	.404	.130	.161	.075	.106	.145	.181	.253	.275
I-GEN	.348	.367	.270	.281	.382	.407	.504	.537	.278	.285	.206	.214	.313	.322	.416	.426
T-GEN	.367	.382	.282	.289	.410	.430	.530	.565	.282	.291	.209	.217	**.320**	.333	**.421**	.433
RawNP	**.371**	**.409**	**.289**	**.323**	**.411**	**.453**	**.532**	**.575**	**.283**	**.314**	**.210**	**.243**	.316	**.352**	.419	**.452**

Table 2. The seen-to-unseen and unseen-to-unseen results of 1-shot and 3-shot link prediction on FB15k-237. Bold numbers denote the best results.

Model	Seen-to-unseen				Unseen-to-unseen			
	MRR		Hit@10		MRR		Hit@10	
	1-S	3-S	1-S	3-S	1-S	3-S	1-S	3-S
I-GEN	.371	.391	.537	.571	.000	.000	.000	.000
T-GEN	.379	.396	**.550**	.588	.185	.175	.220	.201
RawNP	**.383**	**.422**	.549	**.601**	**.204**	**.198**	**.221**	**.220**

among unseen entities and confirms its inductive ability. The I-GEN model ignores the relations between unseen entities, resulting in poor performance.

5.5 Ablation Study

To evaluate the effectiveness of relational anonymous walks (RAW) and neural process (NP), we perform an ablation study by removing each component. The experiment is conducted on the FB15k-237 dataset with a 3-shot support set, and the results are shown in Fig. 3. From the results, we can see that all components (i.e., RAW and NP) are helpful for improving the performance. By removing the RAW, the model ignores the inductive semantic patterns bought by relational motifs, which impairs the ability of inductive reasoning. Without the NP, the model just obtains a deterministic function for the unseen entity, instead of modeling the function distribution. Therefore, the model could suffer from the overfitting problem and fail to generalize to more situations.

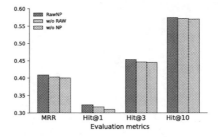

Fig. 3. Ablation study on the FB15k-237 dataset.

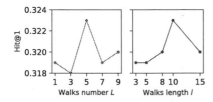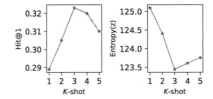

Fig. 4. Parameter studies on walks number L and walks length l.

Fig. 5. Uncertainty analysis under different K-shot support set.

5.6 Parameters Analysis

We study the impact of walks number L and walks length l in relational anonymous walks. The results are illustrated in Fig. 4. From the results, we can see that the performance of RawNP improves as the walks number L increases. The possible reason is that by increasing the walks number, the model could capture more diverse relational motifs, and generate more representative patterns easily. Nevertheless, too many walks could also extract many general patterns that are not dedicated to the unseen entity. The performance of RawNP first increases and then decreases as the walks length l reaches 10. When l is small, the path is too short to represent meaningful patterns (e.g., 1-2-3-4). However, an over large path length could contain redundant motifs that are also not helpful.

5.7 Uncertainty Analysis

The major advantage of RawNP is able to estimate the uncertainty in its predictions. By using the neural process, we can obtain distribution of the prediction function given the support set. The uncertainty of the model can be evaluated by the entropy of z [26]. The higher the entropy, the more uncertain the model is. We illustrate the Hit@1 under different K-shot support sets and calculate the corresponding $Entropy(z)$ by using [33], which are illustrated in Fig. 5.

From the results, we can see that with K increasing, the performance of RawNP first improves. This indicates that RawNP could adaptively incorporate new observations to enhance the distribution. Then entropy of z also supports the claim. With more data in the support set, the $Entropy(z)$ decreases, meaning the model is more certain about its predictions. The performance of the model

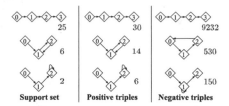

Fig. 6. The Top-3 relational motifs and corresponding occurrence numbers extracted for entity 4192 in FB15k-237.

slightly decreases when $K \geq 4$, which could be caused by the noise in the support set. The $Entropy(z)$ follows the same trend as the model performance. When the model is more uncertain (i.e., larger entropy), the performance is also worse, which indicates that RawNP enables estimating the uncertainty accurately.

5.8 Case Study of Relational Motif

In this section, we conduct a case study to illustrate the relational motifs captured by RawNP. We first select an unseen entity from FB15k-237, and we illustrate the Top-3 distinctive motifs extracted from its support set, positive triples and negative triples, respectively in Fig. 6. From the results, we can see that the relational motifs capture some general semantic patterns (e.g., 1-2-3-4), which widely exist in all sets. However, we also easily find that the motifs from the positive triples are more similar to the motifs from the support set, whereas the motifs from the negative samples cannot match the motifs from the support set. This indicates that RawNP could capture the distinguishable relational motifs of the unseen entity for few-shot inductive link prediction. More detailed cases of motif extraction can be found in the *Appendix*.

6   Conclusion

In this paper, we propose a novel relational anonymous walk-guided neural process approach for few-shot inductive link prediction on knowledge graphs, named RawNP. We first propose a neural process-based approach, which models the distribution over functions conditioned on few-shot observations. Then, we propose a novel relational anonymous walk to extract relational motifs to capture general semantic patterns. The comparison against other baseline models demonstrates the superiority of our method. We plan to unify large language models (LLMs) and knowledge graphs to improve the link prediction performance [27].

Acknowledgement. This research is supported by NSF of China (No: 61973162), NSF of Jiangsu Province (No: BZ2021013), NSF for Distinguished Young Scholar of Jiangsu Province (No: BK20220080), the Fundamental Research Funds for the Central Universities (Nos: 30920032202, 30921013114), CAAI-Huawei MindSpore Open Fund, and "111" Program (No: B13022).

Ethical Statement. In this research, we conducted experiments on publicly available datasets and implemented our approaches using commonly accepted techniques, giving utmost consideration to fairness and avoiding potential biases. We acknowledge the significance of transparency and have furnished comprehensive elucidations regarding our methodology and decision-making process. To conclude, our research adheres to ethical guidelines and poses no potential risks.

References

1. Baek, J., Lee, D.B., Hwang, S.J.: Learning to extrapolate knowledge: transductive few-shot out-of-graph link prediction. Adv. Neural. Inf. Process. Syst. **33**, 546–560 (2020)
2. Bordes, A., Usunier, N., Garcia-Duran, A., Weston, J., Yakhnenko, O.: Translating embeddings for modeling multi-relational data. In: Advances in Neural Information Processing Systems, vol. 26 (2013)
3. Brazdil, P., van Rijn, J.N., Gouk, H., Mohr, F.: Advances in metalearning: ECML/PKDD workshop on meta-knowledge transfer. In: ECML-PKDD Workshop on Meta-Knowledge Transfer, pp. 1–7. PMLR (2022)
4. Cangea, C., Day, B., Jamasb, A.R., Lio, P.: Message passing neural processes. In: ICLR 2022 Workshop on Geometrical and Topological Representation Learning (2022)
5. Chen, J., He, H., Wu, F., Wang, J.: Topology-aware correlations between relations for inductive link prediction in knowledge graphs. In: Proceedings of the AAAI Conference on Artificial Intelligence, pp. 6271–6278 (2021)
6. Chen, M., Zhang, W., Zhang, W., Chen, Q., Chen, H.: Meta relational learning for few-shot link prediction in knowledge graphs. arXiv preprint arXiv:1909.01515 (2019)
7. Chen, M., Zhang, W., Zhu, Y., Zhou, H., Yuan, Z., Xu, C., Chen, H.: Meta-knowledge transfer for inductive knowledge graph embedding. In: Proceedings of the 45th International ACM SIGIR Conference on Research and Development in Information Retrieval, pp. 927–937 (2022)
8. Dong, M., Yuan, F., Yao, L., Xu, X., Zhu, L.: MAMO: memory-augmented meta-optimization for cold-start recommendation. In: Proceedings of the 26th ACM SIGKDD Conference on Knowledge Discovery & Data Mining, pp. 688–697 (2020)
9. Fey, M., Lenssen, J.E.: Fast graph representation learning with pytorch geometric. arXiv preprint arXiv:1903.02428 (2019)
10. Garnelo, M., et al.: Conditional neural processes. In: International Conference on Machine Learning, pp. 1704–1713. PMLR (2018)
11. Garnelo, M., et al.: Neural processes. arXiv preprint arXiv:1807.01622 (2018)
12. Hamaguchi, T., Oiwa, H., Shimbo, M., Matsumoto, Y.: Knowledge transfer for out-of-knowledge-base entities: a graph neural network approach. arXiv preprint arXiv:1706.05674 (2017)
13. Huang, Q., Ren, H., Leskovec, J.: Few-shot relational reasoning via connection subgraph pretraining. In: Advances in Neural Information Processing Systems (2022)
14. Jin, M., Li, Y.F., Pan, S.: Neural temporal walks: motif-aware representation learning on continuous-time dynamic graphs. In: Advances in Neural Information Processing Systems (2022)
15. Kim, H., et al.: Attentive neural processes. arXiv preprint arXiv:1901.05761 (2019)

16. Kingma, D.P., Welling, M.: Auto-encoding variational Bayes. arXiv preprint arXiv:1312.6114 (2013)
17. Liang, H., Gao, J.: How neural processes improve graph link prediction. In: ICASSP 2022–2022 IEEE International Conference on Acoustics, Speech and Signal Processing (ICASSP), pp. 3543–3547. IEEE (2022)
18. Lin, X., Wu, J., Zhou, C., Pan, S., Cao, Y., Wang, B.: Task-adaptive neural process for user cold-start recommendation. In: Proceedings of the Web Conference 2021, pp. 1306–1316 (2021)
19. Liu, S., Grau, B., Horrocks, I., Kostylev, E.: Indigo: GNN-based inductive knowledge graph completion using pair-wise encoding. In: Advances in Neural Information Processing Systems, pp. 2034–2045 (2021)
20. Luo, L., Fang, Y., Cao, X., Zhang, X., Zhang, W.: Detecting communities from heterogeneous graphs: a context path-based graph neural network model. In: Proceedings of the 30th ACM International Conference on Information & Knowledge Management, pp. 1170–1180 (2021)
21. Luo, L., Fang, Y., Lu, M., Cao, X., Zhang, X., Zhang, W.: GSim: a graph neural network based relevance measure for heterogeneous graphs. In: IEEE Trans. Knowl. Data Eng. (2023)
22. Luo, L., Haffari, G., Pan, S.: Graph sequential neural ode process for link prediction on dynamic and sparse graphs. In: Proceedings of the Sixteenth ACM International Conference on Web Search and Data Mining, pp. 778–786 (2023)
23. Luo, L., Li, Y.F., Haffari, G., Pan, S.: Normalizing flow-based neural process for few-shot knowledge graph completion (2023)
24. Mai, S., Zheng, S., Yang, Y., Hu, H.: Communicative message passing for inductive relation reasoning. In: Proceedings of the AAAI Conference on Artificial Intelligence, pp. 4294–4302 (2021)
25. Menon, A.K., Elkan, C.: Link prediction via matrix factorization. In: Gunopulos, D., Hofmann, T., Malerba, D., Vazirgiannis, M. (eds.) ECML PKDD 2011. LNCS (LNAI), vol. 6912, pp. 437–452. Springer, Heidelberg (2011). https://doi.org/10.1007/978-3-642-23783-6_28
26. Naderiparizi, S., Chiu, K., Bloem-Reddy, B., Wood, F.: Uncertainty in neural processes. arXiv preprint arXiv:2010.03753 (2020)
27. Pan, S., Luo, L., Wang, Y., Chen, C., Wang, J., Wu, X.: Unifying large language models and knowledge graphs: a roadmap. arXiv preprint arXiv:2306.08302 (2023)
28. Paszke, A., et al.: PyTorch: an imperative style, high-performance deep learning library. In: Advances in Neural Information Processing Systems, vol. 32 (2019)
29. Perozzi, B., Al-Rfou, R., Skiena, S.: DeepWalk: online learning of social representations. In: Proceedings of the 20th ACM SIGKDD Conference on Knowledge Discovery & Data Mining, pp. 701–710 (2014)
30. Schlichtkrull, M., Kipf, T.N., Bloem, P., van den Berg, R., Titov, I., Welling, M.: Modeling relational data with graph convolutional networks. In: Gangemi, A., et al. (eds.) ESWC 2018. LNCS, vol. 10843, pp. 593–607. Springer, Cham (2018). https://doi.org/10.1007/978-3-319-93417-4_38
31. Shi, B., Weninger, T.: Open-world knowledge graph completion. In: Proceedings of the AAAI Conference on Artificial Intelligence (2018)
32. Singh, G., Yoon, J., Son, Y., Ahn, S.: Sequential neural processes. In: Advances in Neural Information Processing Systems, vol. 32 (2019)
33. Singh, S., Póczos, B.: Analysis of k-nearest neighbor distances with application to entropy estimation. arXiv preprint arXiv:1603.08578 (2016)
34. Sun, Z., Deng, Z.H., Nie, J.Y., Tang, J.: Rotate: knowledge graph embedding by relational rotation in complex space. arXiv preprint arXiv:1902.10197 (2019)

35. Teru, K., Denis, E., Hamilton, W.: Inductive relation prediction by subgraph reasoning. In: International Conference on Machine Learning, pp. 9448–9457. PMLR (2020)
36. Toutanova, K., Chen, D., Pantel, P., Poon, H., Choudhury, P., Gamon, M.: Representing text for joint embedding of text and knowledge bases. In: Proceedings of the 2015 Conference on Empirical Methods in Natural Language Processing, pp. 1499–1509 (2015)
37. Trouillon, T., Welbl, J., Riedel, S., Gaussier, É., Bouchard, G.: Complex embeddings for simple link prediction. In: International Conference on Machine Learning, pp. 2071–2080. PMLR (2016)
38. Van Kampen, N.G.: Stochastic differential equations. Phys. Rep. **24**(3), 171–228 (1976)
39. Wan, G., Pan, S., Gong, C., Zhou, C., Haffari, G.: Reasoning like human: hierarchical reinforcement learning for knowledge graph reasoning. In: Proceedings of the Thirty-First International Joint Conference on Artificial Intelligence, pp. 1926–1932 (2021)
40. Wan, S., Pan, S., Yang, J., Gong, C.: Contrastive and generative graph convolutional networks for graph-based semi-supervised learning. In: Proceedings of the AAAI Conference on Artificial Intelligence, pp. 10049–10057 (2021)
41. Wan, S., et al.: Multi-level graph learning network for hyperspectral image classification. Pattern Recogn. **129**, 108705 (2022)
42. Wan, S., Zhan, Y., Liu, L., Yu, B., Pan, S., Gong, C.: Contrastive graph poisson networks: semi-supervised learning with extremely limited labels. Adv. Neural. Inf. Process. Syst. **34**, 6316–6327 (2021)
43. Wang, C., Zhou, X., Pan, S., Dong, L., Song, Z., Sha, Y.: Exploring relational semantics for inductive knowledge graph completion. In: Proceedings of the AAAI Conference on Artificial Intelligence, pp. 4184–4192 (2022)
44. Wang, H., Ren, H., Leskovec, J.: Relational message passing for knowledge graph completion. In: Proceedings of the 27th ACM SIGKDD Conference on Knowledge Discovery & Data Mining, pp. 1697–1707 (2021)
45. Wang, H., Zhang, F., Zhao, M., Li, W., Xie, X., Guo, M.: Multi-task feature learning for knowledge graph enhanced recommendation. In: Proceedings of the Web Conference 2019, pp. 2000–2010 (2019)
46. Wang, P., Han, J., Li, C., Pan, R.: Logic attention based neighborhood aggregation for inductive knowledge graph embedding. In: Proceedings of the AAAI Conference on Artificial Intelligence, pp. 7152–7159 (2019)
47. Wang, R., et al.: Learning to sample and aggregate: few-shot reasoning over temporal knowledge graphs. In: Advances in Neural Information Processing Systems (2022)
48. Wang, Y., Chang, Y.Y., Liu, Y., Leskovec, J., Li, P.: Inductive representation learning in temporal networks via causal anonymous walks. arXiv preprint arXiv:2101.05974 (2021)
49. Xiao, S., et al.: HMNet: hybrid matching network for few-shot link prediction. In: Jensen, C.S., et al. (eds.) Hmnet: Hybrid matching network for few-shot link prediction. LNCS, vol. 12681, pp. 307–322. Springer, Cham (2021). https://doi.org/10.1007/978-3-030-73194-6_21
50. Xiong, W., Hoang, T., Wang, W.Y.: DeepPath: a reinforcement learning method for knowledge graph reasoning. arXiv preprint arXiv:1707.06690 (2017)
51. Xiong, W., Yu, M., Chang, S., Guo, X., Wang, W.Y.: One-shot relational learning for knowledge graphs. arXiv preprint arXiv:1808.09040 (2018)

52. Xu, X., Zhang, P., He, Y., Chao, C., Yan, C.: Subgraph neighboring relations infomax for inductive link prediction on knowledge graphs. In: Proceedings of the Thirty-First International Joint Conference on Artificial Intelligence (2022)

53. Yang, B., Yih, W.t., He, X., Gao, J., Deng, L.: Embedding entities and relations for learning and inference in knowledge bases. arXiv preprint arXiv:1412.6575 (2014)

54. Zhang, C., Yao, H., Huang, C., Jiang, M., Li, Z., Chawla, N.V.: Few-shot knowledge graph completion. In: Proceedings of the AAAI Conference on Artificial Intelligence, pp. 3041–3048 (2020)

55. Zhang, X., Liang, X., Zheng, X., Wu, B., Guo, Y.: MULTIFORM: few-shot knowledge graph completion via multi-modal contexts. In: Machine Learning and Knowledge Discovery in Databases: European Conference, ECML-PKDD 2022, Grenoble, France, September 19–23, 2022, Proceedings, Part II, pp. 172–187. Springer (2023). https://doi.org/10.1007/978-3-031-26390-3_11

56. Zhang, Z., Lan, C., Zeng, W., Chen, Z., Chang, S.F.: Uncertainty-aware few-shot image classification. In: Proceedings of the Thirtieth International Joint Conference on Artificial Intelligence (2020)

57. Zheng, S., Mai, S., Sun, Y., Hu, H., Yang, Y.: Subgraph-aware few-shot inductive link prediction via meta-learning. IEEE Trans. Knowl. Data Eng. (2022)

Comparing Apples and Oranges? On the Evaluation of Methods for Temporal Knowledge Graph Forecasting

Julia Gastinger[1,2]($\boxtimes$) (ID), Timo Sztyler[1] (ID), Lokesh Sharma[1] (ID), Anett Schuelke[1], and Heiner Stuckenschmidt[2] (ID)

[1] NEC Laboratories Europe, Heidelberg, Germany
{julia.gastinger,timo.sztyler,lokesh.sharma}@neclab.eu
[2] Chair of Artificial Intelligence, University of Mannheim, Mannheim, Germany
heiner.stuckenschmidt@uni-mannheim.de

Abstract. Due to its ability to incorporate and leverage time information in relational data, Temporal Knowledge Graph (TKG) learning has become an increasingly studied research field. To predict the future based on TKG, researchers have presented innovative methods for Temporal Knowledge Graph Forecasting. However, the experimental procedures employed in this research area exhibit inconsistencies that significantly impact empirical results, leading to distorted comparisons among models. This paper focuses on the evaluation of TKG Forecasting models: We examine the evaluation settings commonly used in this research area and highlight the issues that arise. To make different approaches to TKG Forecasting more comparable, we propose a unified evaluation protocol and apply it to re-evaluate state-of-the-art models on the most commonly used datasets. Ultimately, we demonstrate the significant difference in results caused by different evaluation settings. We believe this work provides a solid foundation for future evaluations of TKG Forecasting models, thereby contributing to advancing this growing research area.

Keywords: Temporal Knowledge Graphs · Temporal Graphs · Temporal Knowledge Graph Forecasting

1 Introduction

Temporal Knowledge Graphs (TKG) are Knowledge Graphs (KG) where facts occur, recur or evolve over time [28]. TKG can accommodate time-evolving multi-relational data by extending facts with a timestamp to indicate that a triple is valid at this timestamp [7]. The research field of TKG Forecasting, or TKG Extrapolation, aims at predicting facts at future timesteps, based on the KG history [26]. Recently, various methods have been proposed to advance the field [7,8,12,16–18,26,30].

© The Author(s), under exclusive license to Springer Nature Switzerland AG 2023
D. Koutra et al. (Eds.): ECML PKDD 2023, LNAI 14171, pp. 533–549, 2023.
https://doi.org/10.1007/978-3-031-43418-1_32

Unfortunately, and despite the progress made so far in TKG Forecasting, various reported experimental settings show discrepancies: first, the existing models are evaluated on scores computed with different filter settings; second, models for single-step prediction that predict one step to the future are lumped together with models for multi-step prediction that predict multiple steps to the future; third, multiple versions of the same datasets exist. Last but not least, some models do use the information from the validation set for testing, whereas others do not. These four issues can strongly influence the empirical results and significantly decrease comparability across works. As an example, the best results in single-step setting are in average 6% better than the best results in multi-step setting. Consequently, it is very difficult to understand existing methods' strengths or weaknesses or to identify the currently best-performing method.

In this paper, we address the aforementioned issues in the evaluation of TKG Forecasting models. We first provide an overview of existing models for TKG Forecasting (Sect. 2). We then describe common evaluation settings and compare those settings utilized in state-of-the-art approaches to highlight the inconsistencies (Sect. 3). In this context, we explain the problems we discovered for each setting. As it is essential to evaluate models in a consistent way, we propose a unified evaluation protocol using reasonable and sound evaluation settings (Sect. 4). We re-evaluate state-of-the-art models on this protocol and show results for eight state-of-the-art models on five commonly used datasets (Sect. 5). In addition, we provide insights into the influence of different setups on the result scores. We hope to set a new standard for rigorous evaluations of new models in this growing research field. Our contributions are:

1. A comprehensive discussion of evaluation settings and accompanying problems for TKG Forecasting.
2. The design of a unified evaluation protocol for TKG Forecasting from reasonable evaluation settings.
3. An extensive re-evaluation of state-of-the-art models on a consistent evaluation protocol, showing results and insights on the influence of different evaluation settings on these results.

Our work does not question the methods for TKG Forecasting developed by individual researchers. Instead, it aims at giving a fresh view on the state of the field as a whole and provides a solid basis for working on remaining problems.

2   Terminology and Related Work

2.1   Terminology

A TKG is formalized as a sequence of timestamped Knowledge Graphs, $G = (G_1, G_2, ..., G_t, ...)$. A timestamped KG $G_t = \{\mathcal{V}, \mathcal{R}, \mathcal{E}_t\}$, or KG snapshot, describes the TKG at timestep t, with the set of entities $\mathcal{V}$, the set of relations $\mathcal{R}$, and the set of facts $\mathcal{E}_t$ at discrete timestamp t. Facts $\mathcal{E}_t$ are quadruples (s, r, o, t), with $s, o, \in \mathcal{V}$, and $r \in \mathcal{R}$, for example (Kamala Harris, visit, France,

2021-11-10). Entity prediction for TKG Forecasting is the task of predicting the missing object entity $(s, r, ?, t + k)$ and subject entity $(?, r, o, t + k)$ for a query, with $k \in \mathbb{N}^+$. [18]

2.2   Related Work on Temporal Knowledge Graph Forecasting

In recent years (2017–2022), researchers have proposed various methods for TKG Forecasting:

Graph Neural Networks (GNNs): A large group of models leverages a GNN [22,24] in combination with a sequential approach to integrate the structural and sequential information. RE-Net [12] applies an autoregressive architecture. It learns the temporal dependency from a sequence of graphs and the local structural dependency from the neighborhood. The occurrence of a fact is modeled as a probability distribution conditioned on the temporal sequence of past snapshots. RE-Net can predict full graphs. RE-GCN [18] also models the sequence of the Knowledge Graph snapshots recurrently. For this, it combines a convolutional graph Neural Network with a sequential Neural Network model. Further, RE-GCN introduces a static graph constraint to take into account additional information like entity types. TANGO [8] bases on neural ordinary differential equations to model the temporal sequences combined with a GNN to capture the structural information. In addition, the authors introduce a stochastic jump method to incorporate stochastic events, i.e., triples appearing or disappearing over time. xERTE [7] bases on so-called temporal relational attention mechanisms. To answer a query, it extracts query-relevant subgraphs. Further, it computes and propagates attention scores to identify the relevant evidence in the subgraphs, using a modified time-aware version of a message passing. CEN [16] integrates a Convolutional Neural Network which can handle evolutional patterns of different lengths via a learning strategy that learns these evolutional patterns from short to long. The model can learn in an online setting, meaning that it is updated with historical facts during testing.

Reinforcement Learning: CluSTeR [17] introduces a two-step process: First, a Reinforcement Learning agent, working with randomized beam strategy, searches and induces clue paths related to a given query. Second, an adapted GNN and sequence method models temporal information among the clues to find answers to a query. TimeTraveler [26] leverages a Reinforcement Learning model based on temporal paths. Starting from the query's subject node, the agent traverses outgoing edges across graph snapshots. For this, TimeTraveler samples actions according to transition probabilities, which are based on dynamic embeddings of the query, the path history, and the candidate actions. TimeTraveler uses a time-shaped reward based on Dirichlet distribution [13]. The model is able to predict in the inductive setting.

Rule-based Approaches: TLogic [20], a symbolic framework, learns so-called temporal logic rules via temporal random walks, traversing edges through the graph backward in time. TLogic applies the rules to events that happened prior to the query. For scoring the answer candidates, it takes into account the rules' confidence as well as time differences.

Other: CyGNet [30] predicts future facts purely based on the appearance of historical facts. For this, to answer a query, it first computes each entity's embedding vector. Further, using these embeddings, it computes entity probabilities by combining predictions from a so-called "copy mode" that computes probabilities for historical events based on the repetition of facts in history and a "generation mode" that computes probabilities for every entity.

In our work, we analyze the evaluation discrepancies of the introduced models and evaluate the models on a joint evaluation protocol.

In addition to the described methods, there are also approaches focusing on a slightly different problem setting. We exclude these from our evaluation, but list them below for completeness: Know-Evolve [28] and the Graph Hawkes Neural Network (GHNN) [9] utilize temporal point processes to estimate conditional probabilities of future facts in a continuous time setting. Unlike the other methods discussed in this section, Know-Evolve and GHNN allow scenarios where no facts occur at the same timestamp [18]. Due to their distinct problem setting, where continuous time is considered, these works are not included in our evaluation.

2.3   Related Work on the Evaluation of Graph-Based Machine Learning Models

When conducting empirical evaluations of Machine Learning algorithms, various issues can arise [19]. Such problems have been reported and partially addressed in various subfields, but in the following, we limit the discussion to works in the field of Graph Machine Learning. [25] describe the shortcomings of evaluation strategies for Graph Neural Network models for node classification. [5] focus on graph classification, providing standard practices that should be avoided for a fair comparison. Further, [23] and [27] describe shortcomings in the evaluation of KG link prediction. [10] focus on the evaluation of models for TKG completion (not Forecasting). Our work is the first to study evaluation problems for TKG Forecasting.

3   Description of Evaluation Settings and Evaluation Problems

In this chapter, we subsequently focus on evaluation settings for TKG Forecasting. In each subsection, we first describe a setting, and second, describe problems that we have encountered in that setting. In addition, Table 1, provides an overview, showing the settings each model uses by default. We refer to the respective parts of the table in each subsection. Further, the table contains links to the published code for each model, if available.

3.1   Filter Settings for Link Prediction Metrics

Researchers in TKG Forecasting evaluate the models on metrics known from static link prediction, namely Mean Reciprocal Rank (MRR) and Hits@k, with $k = 1, 3, 10$. There are three settings which have been introduced subsequently, *raw*, *static filter*, and *time-aware filter*:

Raw: As introduced by [2], for each test triple $(s_{test}, r_{test}, o_{test})$, remove the object $(s_{test}, r_{test}, ?)$, and compute the score that the model assigns for each entity $v \in \mathcal{V}$ to be the object in that triple, where the set of all possible triples (s_{test}, r_{test}, v) is termed corrupted triples. Sort the scores in descending order, and note the rank of the correct entity o_{test}. Repeat this by removing the subject $(?, r_{test}, o_{test})$. The MRR is the mean of the reciprocal of these ranks across all queries from the test set, and Hits@k is the proportion of correct entities ranked in the top k.

Static Filter: To avoid counting higher ranks from other valid predictions as errors and thus having flaws in the metrics, [1] propose to remove all triples (except the triple of interest) that appear in the train, valid, and test set from the list of corrupted triples.

Time-Aware Filter: [9] note that the static filter setting is inappropriate for temporal link prediction because it filters out all triples that have ever appeared from the list of corrupted triples, ignoring the time validity of facts. As a consequence, it does not consider predictions of such triples as erroneous. For example, if there is a test query (Barack Obama, visit, India, 2015-01-25) and if the train set contains (Barack Obama, visit, Germany, 2013-01-18), the triple (Barack Obama, visit, Germany) is filtered out for the test query according to the static filter setting, even though it is not true for 2015-01-25 [7]. For this reason, numerous works [7, 8, 16, 17, 20, 26] apply the *time-aware filter* setting which only filters out quadruples with the same timestamp as the test query. In the above example, (Barack Obama, visit, Germany, t) would only be filtered out for the given test query, if it had the timestamp $t = 2015$-01-25, and otherwise stay in the list of corrupted triples.

Problem 1: Different Filter Settings. The works introduced in Sect. 2 do present result scores with MRR and Hits@k using the above-described filter settings. However, not all works report results on all filter settings, which is a problem, as it decreases comparability across works. Further, as mentioned above, the raw, and especially the static filter setting are not appropriate for TKG Forecasting. The first part of Table 1 illustrates the filter settings that each model reports.

3.2   Single-Step and Multi-step Prediction

Methods for Forecasting operate within two distinct prediction settings, single-step and multi-step prediction. Single-step (or one-step) prediction means that the model always forecasts the next timestep [4]. The ground truth facts are then fed before predicting the subsequent timestep. Multi-step prediction means that the model forecasts more than one future time step [4]. More specifically, the model predicts all timesteps from the test set, without seeing any ground truth information in between. As described by [4], multi-step prediction is more challenging, as the model can only leverage information from its own forecasts, and uncertainty accumulates with an increasing number of forecasted timesteps.

Problem 2: Comparison of Multi-step and Single-Step Setting. The models described in Sect. 2 run in different settings. Some can do single-step prediction only, some can do multi-step prediction only, and some do both (see Table 1, second part). Still, single-step models are compared to multi-step models without drawing attention to the different setups. For example, TLogic [20] and TANGO [8] (single-step) are compared to RE-Net [12] (multi-step), xERTE [7] is compared to CyGNet [30], and CEN [16] is compared to CyGNet [30] and RE-Net [12]. The second part of Table 1 shows each model's prediction setting.

3.3   Datasets

Researchers in the domain of TKG Forecasting use the following datasets: Three instances of ICEWS [3]: ICEWS05-15 [6], ICEWS14 [6], and ICEWS18 [11], where the numbers mark the respective years; further, YAGO [21] and WIKI [14], preprocessed according to [11], as well as GDELT [15]. Table 2 shows dataset statistics for dataset version (a), as reported by [18].

Problem 3: Multiple Versions of the Same Dataset. The models described in Sect. 2 report results on different versions of the same dataset. For instance, three versions exist for ICEWS14. This hinders the comparability of results across works, causing confusion and potential errors. The third part of Table 1 shows an overview of different versions of each dataset, describing each version (marked with (a), (b), (c)) by the number of training triples. One version of the ICEWS14 dataset (see Table 1, version (c)) is especially problematic, as it does not contain a validation set. Instead, the test set is used for both validation and testing. Thus, with this setting, the test set is leaked during training.

3.4   Train, Validation, and Test Set

Researchers in TKG Forecasting split each dataset D into a training D_{train}, validation D_{valid}, and test set D_{test}. The model's training is conducted on D_{train}, not using information contained in D_{valid} or D_{test}. D_{valid} can be used for monitoring the training process, and selecting the best model (parameters) across epochs. There are different options to use the validation set during testing:

(a) The model can leverage all information from D_{train}, but not from D_{valid}, to predict D_{test}. This is consistent with the setting in link prediction for static knowledge graphs.

(b) The model can leverage all information from D_{train} and from D_{valid}, to predict D_{test}. This means, if a model has to answer the query $(s, r, ?, n)$ during testing, all quadruples from D_{train} and D_{valid} can be used. This is consistent with the setting used in time-series Forecasting.

Problem 4: Usage of Validation set for Testing. For multi-step setting, during testing, some models (CygNet, TLogic) do not use the information from the validation set (option (a)), whereas others (RE-GCN, RE-Net) do use it (option (b)), see the fourth part of Table 1. Not using the information from the validation set leads to a significantly harder task, as the model needs to forecast more steps in the future: Instead of starting to predict the next unknown timestep $t+1$ for the first test set sample, the model needs to already predict the timestep $t + num_{valid} + 1$, with num_{valid} being the number of timesteps in the validation set, as an information gap between training and testing.

3.5 Problem Summary

When putting all four problems together, a dramatic picture emerges: results have been compared using different filter settings, prediction settings, dataset versions, and dataset splits. Table 1 illustrates the scattered landscape of evaluation settings, where no two models have ever been evaluated on identical settings. Without a uniform and standardized evaluation protocol, we will never be able to gauge true progress in the field. Still, in existing work, the methods are compared to each other, leading to confusion and inconsistencies.

4 A Unified Evaluation Protocol

To tackle the problems introduced in Sect. 3, it is essential to evaluate TKG models in a consistent way. For this reason, we introduce a unified evaluation protocol with clear and reproducible choices.[1]

Filter Settings: We report results on the time-aware filter setting. As explained in Sect. 3.1, this setting avoids counting higher ranks from other valid predictions as errors while taking into account time validity of facts.

Single-Step and Multi-step: While both settings are valid, the comparison of results for different settings is not fair (see Sect. 3.2). The setting to be used depends on the use case and on the methods' capabilities. If the method can predict in single- and multi-step, we re-evaluate it on both settings.

Datasets Versions: The same dataset versions should be used across works to ensure comparability. We suggest using version (a) for each dataset (see Table 1). We selected the dataset versions used by the authors of RE-GCN [18], mainly because these are (among) the most commonly used versions across all works. Table 2 shows dataset statistics.

---

[1] The supplementary material also contains a checklist for benchmark experiments in this field.

Table 1. Methods and their experimental settings: Filter settings (Sect. 3.1), settings for single- and multi-step prediction (Sect. 3.2), dataset versions ((a), (b), (c)) used in papers (Sect. 3.3), and validation set usage (Sect. 3.4). We report dataset versions by the number of quadruples in the training set. An entry ✓ means that the model reported results on the respective setting, and an entry - that it does not. An entry *args* means, that the method provides the option to set this in the args of the code, but does not report the results in the paper. An entry *?* means that we cannot answer this question, as the code is not publicly available.

Name	RE-GCN	RE-Net	xERTE	CyGNet	TLogic	TANGO	Time Traveler	CEN	CluSTeR
Filter settings:									
raw	✓	✓	-	-	-	✓	-	-	✓
static	-	✓	-	✓	-	✓	-	-	-
time-aware	-	-	✓	-	✓	✓	✓	✓	✓
Prediction settings:									
single-step	args	partly[a]	✓	-	✓	✓	✓	✓[b]	?
multi-step	✓	✓	-	✓	args	-	-	-	?
Datasets:									
ICEWS14									
(a): 74845	✓	-	-	-	-	-	-	✓	✓
(b): 63685	-	-	✓	-	✓	-	✓	-	-
(c): 323895 w/o valid[c]	-	✓	-	✓	-	✓	-	-	-
ICEWS18									
(a): 373018	y	✓	✓	✓	✓	✓	✓	✓	✓
ICEWS05-15									
(a): 368868	✓	-	-	-	✓	-	-	-	✓
(b): 322958	-	-	✓	-	-	-	✓	-	-
(c): 369104	-	-	-	-	-	✓	-	-	-
GDELT									
(a): 1734399	✓	✓	✓	-	-	-	-	✓	-
YAGO									
(a): 161540	✓	✓	-	✓	-	✓	✓	-	-
(b): 51205	-	-	✓	-	-	-	-	-	-
WIKI									
(a): 539286	✓	✓	-	✓	-	✓	✓	✓	-
Validation Set for Testing:									
Use Valid	✓	✓	✓	-	-	✓	✓	✓	?
Reference	[18]	[12]	[7]	[30]	[20]	[8]	[26]	[16]	[17]
Code Published	✓[d]	✓[e]	✓[f]	✓[g]	✓[h]	✓[i]	✓[j]	✓[k]	-

a RE-NET published results for the datasets ICEWS18 and GDELT ([12], Table 2, RE-Net w. GT). The published code does not provide the option to set this in the arguments.
b In addition to providing results for single-step setting, CEN has a so-called "online-setting". This means, that the model is re-fit after each test timestep before predicting the next timestep.
c This specific version of ICEWS14 comes without validation set. Instead, the test set is used for validation.
d https://github.com/Lee-zix/RE-GCN
e https://github.com/INK-USC/RE-Net
f https://github.com/TemporalKGTeam/xERTE
g https://github.com/CunchaoZ/CyGNet
h https://github.com/liu-yushan/TLogic
i https://github.com/TemporalKGTeam/TANGO
j https://github.com/JHL-HUST/TITer/
k https://github.com/Lee-zix/CEN

Train, Validation, and Test Set Usage: We use the train, validation, and test sets as described in Sect. 3.4, option (b), where the information from the validation set can be used for testing, to avoid time gaps between training and testing. In addition, we make sure that the test set is never used for model selection and the datasets are split based on ordered timestamps, whereas one timestamp should not belong to two different sets.

Table 2. Dataset Statistics for dataset version (a), as reported by [18].

Dataset	#Nodes	#Rels	#Train	#Valid	#Test	Time Interval
ICEWS14	6869	230	74845	8514	7371	24 h
ICEWS18	23033	256	373018	45995	49545	24 h
ICEWS0515	10094	251	368868	46302	46159	24 h
GDELT	7691	240	1734399	238765	305241	15 min
YAGO	10623	10	161540	19523	20026	1 year
WIKI	12554	24	539286	67538	63110	1 year

5   Experiments

In the following, we show the results for eight models and five datasets[2]. The supplementary material[3] contains additional information on specific experimental settings. Please find the source code with scripts for experiments and evaluation at https://github.com/nec-research/TKG-Forecasting-Evaluation.

We run the experiments on a system with one Nvidia TITAN RTX (24 GB) GPU, 512 GB Memory, and an Intel Xeon Silver 4208 CPU with 16 cores (32 threads).

To eliminate the four problems described in Sect. 3, we follow the evaluation protocol from Sect. 4: We report results on time-aware filter settings for single-step and multi-step settings, use the dataset versions (a), and report the results with the validation set usage option (b). We show aggregated results (mean MRR and Hits@k across all test samples) for the eight models for the datasets GDELT, YAGO, WIKI, ICEWS14, and ICEWS18 in Table 3. The upper part for each dataset contains results in multi-step setting, and the lower part in single-step setting, where models with results for single-step prediction should not be benchmarked against methods with results of multi-step prediction. We mark the best result for each dataset for each setting in **bold**. In addition, for the method CEN, we show results in online setting, where the model is updated continually during testing. For completeness and comparability to related work, the supplementary material reports results on raw and static filter settings. In addition, the supplementary material contains tables with information on the

---

[2] Because of memory and runtime issues for multiple models due to its large amount of timestamps, and its similarity to the other ICEWS datasets, we excluded the dataset ICEWS05-15. By running the script available in our GitHub repository, interested readers can include this dataset.

[3] Please find the supplementary material at https://github.com/nec-research/TKG-Forecasting-Evaluation/blob/main/paper_supplementary_material.pdf.

Table 3. Experimental results for multi-step prediction, single-step prediction, and single-step prediction in online setting (with model updates) with datasets GDELT, YAGO, WIKI (top), and ICEWS14, ICEWS18 (bottom). Results for single-step prediction should not be compared to results for multi-step prediction. We report mean reciprocal rank (MRR), and Hits@k (H@k), with $k = 1, 3, 10$ in time-aware filter setting. The best results for each setting are marked in bold.

multi-step setting (time filter)

	GDELT				YAGO				WIKI			
	MRR	H@1	H@3	H@10	MRR	H@1	H@3	H@10	MRR	H@1	H@3	H@10
RE-GCN	19.64	12.47	20.85	33.62	**75.40**	**71.75**	**77.67**	81.70	62.72	59.48	64.89	67.87
RE-Net	**19.71**	**12.48**	**20.90**	**33.93**	58.21	53.44	61.31	66.26	49.47	47.21	50.70	53.04
CyGNet	19.08	11.88	20.29	33.07	69.02	61.38	74.29	**83.42**	58.26	52.51	62.41	67.56
TLogic	17.68	11.26	18.90	30.29	66.93	63.14	70.63	71.58	**63.99**	**61.31**	**66.36**	**68.22**

single-step setting (time filter)

	GDELT				YAGO				WIKI			
	MRR	H@1	H@3	H@10	MRR	H@1	H@3	H@10	MRR	H@1	H@3	H@10
RE-GCN	19.75	12.51	21.02	33.88	82.20	78.72	84.24	88.48	78.65	74.75	81.71	84.68
xERTE	18.89	12.73	21.09	31.96	87.31	84.20	90.28	**91.22**	74.52	70.30	78.58	80.13
TLogic	19.77	12.23	21.67	**35.62**	76.49	74.02	78.91	79.17	**82.29**	**78.62**	**86.04**	**87.01**
TANGO	19.22	12.19	20.42	32.81	62.39	59.04	64.69	67.75	50.08	48.30	51.41	52.76
Timetraveler	**20.23**	**14.14**	**22.18**	31.17	**87.72**	**84.55**	**90.87**	91.20	78.65	75.15	82.03	83.05
CEN	20.43	12.98	21.81	35.04	82.72	78.81	85.24	89.35	79.29	75.51	82.37	84.91

online setting (single-step with model update) (time filter)

	GDELT				YAGO				WIKI			
	MRR	H@1	H@3	H@10	MRR	H@1	H@3	H@10	MRR	H@1	H@3	H@10
CEN	21.73	13.80	23.51	37.30	83.96	80.08	86.73	90.24	79.82	75.88	83.14	85.47

multi-step setting (time filter)

	ICEWS14				ICEWS18			
	MRR	H@1	H@3	H@10	MRR	H@1	H@3	H@10
RE-GCN	**37.82**	**27.86**	**42.14**	**57.50**	**29.03**	**19.52**	**32.66**	**47.50**
RE-Net	37.00	27.80	40.80	54.92	27.86	18.47	31.43	46.19
CyGNet	36.12	26.66	40.28	54.54	26.01	16.69	29.59	44.43
TLogic	35.48	26.54	39.59	53.11	24.01	15.59	27.23	41.20

single-step setting (time filter)

	ICEWS14				ICEWS18			
	MRR	H@1	H@3	H@10	MRR	H@1	H@3	H@10
RE-GCN	42.11	31.36	47.33	**62.66**	**32.58**	**22.37**	36.78	**52.56**
xERTE	40.91	33.03	45.48	57.07	29.23	20.92	33.50	46.26
TLogic	**42.53**	**33.20**	**47.61**	60.29	29.59	20.42	33.60	48.05
TANGO	36.77	27.29	40.84	55.09	28.35	19.10	31.88	46.27
Timetraveler	40.83	31.90	45.43	57.59	29.13	21.29	32.54	43.92
CEN	41.80	31.85	46.59	60.87	31.50	21.69	35.40	50.69

online setting (single-step with model update) (time filter)

	ICEWS14				ICEWS18			
	MRR	H@1	H@3	H@10	MRR	H@1	H@3	H@10
CEN	43.17	33.20	48.03	62.43	31.78	21.82	35.79	51.27

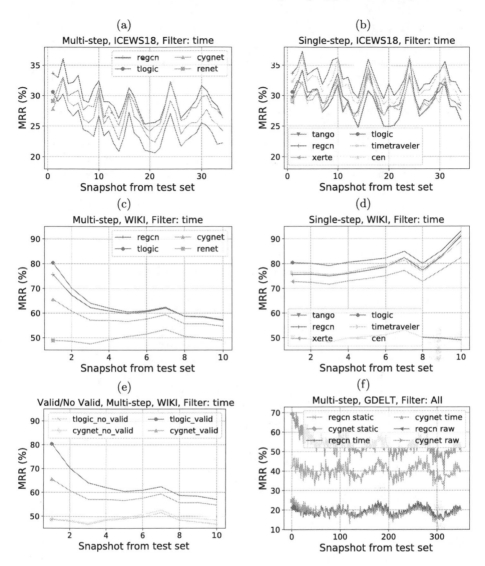

Fig. 1. MRR (in %) over snapshots from test set (one snapshot is one timestamp) per method. (a)-(d): Datasets ICEWS18 (a),(b) and WIKI (c),(d) for multi-step prediction (left) and single-step prediction (right); (e): Using vs. not using the validation set during testing for dataset WIKI; (f) Different filter settings for dataset GDELT.

reproducibility of the results that have been reported by the original works [7,8,12,16,18,20,26,30]. Figure 1 shows the MRR for three selected datasets (ICEWS18, WIKI, and GDELT) over test timestamps (snapshots) for different evaluation settings. In the following, we will discuss important insights.

Single-Step and Multi-step Setting: Table 3 shows the difference in scores for single- vs. multi-step setting: Overall, scores for single-step setting are higher than for multi-step setting. This is especially visible for the two models (TLogic and RE-GCN) that run in both settings, but also true for the other results. Figure 1(a)–(d) shows the MRR (in %) over snapshots in multi-step setting (left) and single-step setting (right).[4] The figure illustrates a contrasting trend between multi-step prediction and single-step prediction with respect to MRR. Specifically, the MRR for multi-step prediction exhibits a decreasing pattern as the timestamps increase, whereas single-step prediction does not display a similar decreasing trend. This is especially visible for the WIKI dataset in a single-step setting, which displays an increasing tendency for the MRR with increasing timestamps for the four best-performing methods. The results reflect the statement from Sect. 3.2, that multi-step prediction is more challenging, and uncertainty accumulates with increasing number of forecasted timesteps, as the models can only leverage information from their own forecasts. Thus, benchmarking models for multi-step prediction against single-step prediction is only fair for the first timestamp.

Validation Set Usage: In Fig. 1(e), we show the MRR (in %) over snapshots in multi-step setting for TLogic and CyGNet[5], when using the validation set for testing (Sect. 3.4, option (b)) vs. not using the validation set for testing (option (a)) for the dataset WIKI.[6] The figure displays a difference in MRR between the two settings for each model, especially in the first two snapshots with a difference in MRR of > 30 for TLogic. This difference is caused by the information gap between the last training timestamp and the first testing timestamp. For the case of WIKI, the number of timestamps in the validation set is $num_{valid} = 11$. The difference decreases with increasing timestamps, because, due to the multi-step setting, there is also a rising information gap when feeding the validation set. Thus, using the information from the validation set for testing and avoiding the information gap is crucial for fair comparison among models.

Filter Settings: Fig. 1(f) shows the MRR (in %) over snapshots in multi-step setting, exemplary for CyGNet and RE-GCN for the dataset GDELT, computed with raw, static, and time-aware filter setting, as described in Sect. 3.1[7]. It reveals a large difference in MRR for static filter setting, vs. raw setting or time-aware filter setting, especially for CyGNet. This is also visible for aggregated results: Where CyGNet does not have the highest MRR scores on any dataset for time-aware filter settings (see Table 3), it has the highest MRR scores on all five datasets in static filter setting (see supplementary material). The static filter setting filters out all triples that have ever appeared from the corrupted triples,

---

[4] The supplementary material shows results for ICEWS14, YAGO, and GDELT.

[5] The two models that run per default in multi-step setting, validation set option (a) from Sect. 3.4.

[6] The supplementary material shows results for YAGO, GDELT, ICEWS14, and ICEWS18.

[7] The supplementary material shows results for YAGO, WIKI, ICEWS14, and ICEWS18.

ignoring the time validity, and does not count a prediction of these triples as error. Thus, for a given query, if a model predicts entities that have appeared in this triple at an earlier timestep, this will not be considered erroneous, even if the predicted fact is not true in the timestep of question. The model will potentially be assigned a higher static filter score than if it would predict previously unseen facts. Thus, the static filter setting favors models that predict repeated facts.

To summarize, we can see that no model shows the best results across all datasets. This evidence remarks the importance of fairly comparing models on different benchmarks. We stressed the clear differences in result scores for single-step and multi-step prediction. In addition, we pointed out that the usage of the validation set during testing does lead to substantially higher test scores. Further, we showed the significant influence of the filter setting used for score computation.

Comparing Results of Original Papers and This Work: It is not straight-forward to compare the results from this study with the results reported in the original papers, when it comes to assessing the state-of-the-art method due to several reasons. Firstly, there exist variations in the evaluation settings and inconsistencies in the evaluations across different methods, as elaborated in Sect. 3. Secondly, the original papers lack complete comparisons between all methods, due to varying factors such as earlier or parallel publication times or results reported only on subsets of datasets.

To illustrate the impact of our proposed evaluation protocol on the ranking of compared methods, we show an example for CyGNet. The original paper reports higher MRRs for CyGNet compared to RE-Net on the datasets ICEWS14, ICEWS18, and GDELT, while lower MRRs on the datasets YAGO and WIKI. However, when employing our evaluation protocol, CyGNet achieves higher MRRs than RE-Net on YAGO and WIKI, but lower MRRs on all other datasets. A plausible explanation for this disparity is the utilization of different filter settings which, as highlighted in the preceding paragraph, notably influences the obtained scores.

6   Conclusion

Summary: In this work, we examined the evaluation of TKG Forecasting models. We uncovered and described inconsistencies that strongly influence the experimental results and thus lead to distorted comparisons among models. To address these problems, we formed a unified evaluation protocol from reasonable evaluation settings and re-evaluated state-of-the-art methods. We illustrated the importance of a consistent evaluation by showing the effect of different evaluation settings on the results. Our work aims at establishing a unified evaluation protocol, stimulating discussions on the evaluation, and raising the community's awareness of experimental issues, with the goal of advancing the research field of TKG Forecasting.

Limitation of this Study: Due to computational infeasibility, we could not conduct multiple repeats for each experiment run[8]. Even with one repetition per run, we experienced significant computation times for many models, e.g., multiple days to weeks for the dataset GDELT; thus, multiple repetitions per model and dataset were not possible. Adding multiple repetitions to the evaluation would have further improved the robustness of our results, which are nonetheless obtained under a unified and reproducible protocol.

Future Work: In future work, we aim to extend the proposed evaluation protocol to: First, evaluate the full predicted graph for methods that can predict full graphs (e.g., RE-Net), instead of exclusively focusing on link prediction. This could be based on graph similarity or computing a percentage of correctly predicted triples. Second, evaluate the change of the predicted graph snapshots over time to analyze if the predictions evolve and if they are able to capture time information. This could be done by comparing the predictions at different time steps. Third, include more fine-grained evaluation to answer what properties the models learned and what they did not. This could, for example, be done using the framework KGxBoard [29], which breaks down the performance measure over individual data subsets.

Acknowledgements. We warmly thank Federico Errica for his time and very valuable feedback.

Ethical Statement. While TKG Forecasting has the potential to enable predictions for complex and dynamic systems, we argue that inconsistencies in experimental procedures and evaluation settings can lead to distorted comparisons among models, and ultimately, misinterpretation of results. Therefore, with our work, we want to highlight the importance of transparency and reproducibility in scientific research, as well as the importance of rigorous and reliable scientific practice. In this context we have identified inconsistencies in evaluation settings and provided a unified evaluation protocol. We ensure transparency by providing a URL to a GitHub repository containing our evaluation code. Within this repository, we use forked submodules to explicitly link to the original assets. Additionally, we report the training details, such as hyperparameters, in the supplementary material of our work.

While we have not focused on increasing the interpretability of individual models, we acknowledge the importance of explainability and interpretability in the field. Therefore, we note that among the compared models, xERTE [7] and TLogic [20] address some aspects of explainability and interpretability.

We did not evaluate the predictions of existing models on bias and fairness as it was out of scope for this work. However, we recognize that it is essential to increase fairness in the comparison of TKG Forecasting models. Therefore, we highlight inconsistencies and provide a unified evaluation protocol to improve comparability and fairness for existing models.

In terms of data collection and use, we used publicly available research datasets for our evaluation. We did not use the data for profiling individuals, and it does not contain offensive content. However, it is important to note that even publicly available

---

[8] One experiment run: A one time training of a model with a given setting on a specific dataset.

data can be subject to privacy regulations, and we have taken measures to ensure that our data usage complies with applicable laws and regulations.

As this study focuses purely on evaluation of existing models, it does not induce direct risk. However, we recognize that TKG Forecasting models can have real-world consequences, especially when applied in domains such as finance and healthcare. Therefore, as the results in Sect. 5 show, we want to stress again that predictions can be unreliable and incomplete, and that these limitations have to be acknowledged when using them for decision making.

References

1. Bordes, A., Usunier, N., García-Durán, A., Weston, J., Yakhnenko, O.: Translating embeddings for modeling multi-relational data. In: Burges, C.J.C., Bottou, L., Ghahramani, Z., Weinberger, K.Q. (eds.) Advances in Neural Information Processing Systems 26: 27th Annual Conference on Neural Information Processing Systems 2013. Proceedings of a Meeting Held 5–8 December 2013, Lake Tahoe, Nevada, United States, pp. 2787–2795 (2013)
2. Bordes, A., Weston, J., Collobert, R., Bengio, Y.: Learning structured embeddings of knowledge bases. In: Burgard, W., Roth, D. (eds.) Proceedings of the Twenty-Fifth AAAI Conference on Artificial Intelligence, AAAI 2011, San Francisco, California, USA, August 7–11, 2011. AAAI Press (2011)
3. Boschee, E., Lautenschlager, J., O'Brien, S., Shellman, S., Starz, J., Ward, M.: ICEWS Coded Event Data (2015)
4. Brownlee, J.: Deep learning for time series forecasting: predict the future with MLPs, CNNs and LSTMs in Python. Machine Learning Mastery (2018)
5. Errica, F., Podda, M., Bacciu, D., Micheli, A.: A fair comparison of graph neural networks for graph classification. In: 8th International Conference on Learning Representations, ICLR 2020, Addis Ababa, Ethiopia, April 26–30, 2020 (2020)
6. García-Durán, A., Dumančić, S., Niepert, M.: Learning sequence encoders for temporal knowledge graph completion. In: Proceedings of the 2018 Conference on Empirical Methods in Natural Language Processing, Brussels, Belgium, October-November pp. 4816–4821. Association for Computational Linguistics (2018)
7. Han, Z., Chen, P., Ma, Y., Tresp, V.: Explainable subgraph reasoning for forecasting on temporal knowledge graphs. In: 9th International Conference on Learning Representations, ICLR 2021, Virtual Event, Austria, 3–7 May 2021 (2021)
8. Han, Z., Ding, Z., Ma, Y., Gu, Y., Tresp, V.: Learning neural ordinary equations for forecasting future links on temporal knowledge graphs. In: Moens, M., Huang, X., Specia, L., Yih, S.W. (eds.) Proceedings of the 2021 Conference on Empirical Methods in Natural Language Processing, EMNLP 2021, Virtual Event/Punta Cana, Dominican Republic, 7–11 November 2021, pp. 8352–8364. Association for Computational Linguistics (2021)
9. Han, Z., Ma, Y., Wang, Y., Günnemann, S., Tresp, V.: Graph Hawkes neural network for forecasting on temporal knowledge graphs. In: Das, D., Hajishirzi, H., McCallum, A., Singh, S. (eds.) Conference on Automated Knowledge Base Construction, AKBC 2020, Virtual, 22–24 June 2020 (2020)
10. Han, Z., Zhang, G., Ma, Y., Tresp, V.: Time-dependent entity embedding is not all you need: a re-evaluation of temporal knowledge graph completion models under a unified framework. In: Moens, M., Huang, X., Specia, L., Yih, S.W. (eds.) Proceedings of the 2021 Conference on Empirical Methods in Natural Language Processing,

EMNLP 2021, Virtual Event/Punta Cana, Dominican Republic, 7–11 November 2021, pp. 8104–8118. Association for Computational Linguistics (2021)

11. Jin, W., Qu, M., Jin, X., Ren, X.: Recurrent event network: autoregressive structure inference over temporal knowledge graphs. arXiv preprint arXiv:1904.05530 (2019). preprint version

12. Jin, W., Qu, M., Jin, X., Ren, X.: Recurrent event network: autoregressive structure inference over temporal knowledge graphs. In: Webber, B., Cohn, T., He, Y., Liu, Y. (eds.) Proceedings of the 2020 Conference on Empirical Methods in Natural Language Processing, EMNLP 2020, Online, 16–20 November 2020, pp. 6669–6683. Association for Computational Linguistics (2020)

13. Kotz, S., Balakrishnan, N., Johnson, N.L.: Continuous Multivariate Distributions. Models and Applications, vol. 1. Wiley, New York (2000)

14. Leblay, J., Chekol, M.W.: Deriving validity time in knowledge graph. In: Champin, P., Gandon, F., Lalmas, M., Ipeirotis, P.G. (eds.) Companion of the The Web Conference 2018 on The Web Conference 2018, WWW 2018, Lyon, France, 23–27 April 2018, pp. 1771–1776. ACM (2018)

15. Leetaru, K., Schrodt, P.A.: Gdelt: global data on events, location, and tone, 1979–2012. In: ISA Annual Convention, pp. 1–49. Citeseer (2013)

16. Li, Z., et al.: Complex evolutional pattern learning for temporal knowledge graph reasoning. In: Proceedings of the 60th Annual Meeting of the Association for Computational Linguistics (Volume 2: Short Papers), Dublin, Ireland, May 2022, pp. 290–296. Association for Computational Linguistics (2022)

17. Li, Z., et al.: Search from history and reason for future: two-stage reasoning on temporal knowledge graphs. In: Zong, C., Xia, F., Li, W., Navigli, R. (eds.) Proceedings of the 59th Annual Meeting of the Association for Computational Linguistics and the 11th International Joint Conference on Natural Language Processing, ACL/IJCNLP 2021, (Volume 1: Long Papers), Virtual Event, 1–6 August 2021, pp. 4732–4743. Association for Computational Linguistics (2021)

18. Li, Z., et al.: Temporal knowledge graph reasoning based on evolutional representation learning. In: Diaz, F., Shah, C., Suel, T., Castells, P., Jones, R., Sakai, T. (eds.) SIGIR 2021: The 44th International ACM SIGIR Conference on Research and Development in Information Retrieval, Virtual Event, Canada, 11–15 July 2021, pp. 408–417. ACM (2021)

19. Liao, T., Taori, R., Raji, I.D., Schmidt, L.: Are we learning yet? A meta review of evaluation failures across machine learning. In: Thirty-fifth Conference on Neural Information Processing Systems Datasets and Benchmarks Track (Round 2) (2021)

20. Liu, Y., Ma, Y., Hildebrandt, M., Joblin, M., Tresp, V.: Tlogic: temporal logical rules for explainable link forecasting on temporal knowledge graphs. In: Thirty-Sixth AAAI Conference on Artificial Intelligence, AAAI 2022, Thirty-Fourth Conference on Innovative Applications of Artificial Intelligence, IAAI 2022, The Twelveth Symposium on Educational Advances in Artificial Intelligence, EAAI 2022 Virtual Event, 22 February–1 March 2022, pp. 4120–4127. AAAI Press (2022)

21. Mahdisoltani, F., Biega, J.A., Suchanek, F.M.: Yago3: a knowledge base from multilingual Wikipedia's. In: CIDR (2015)

22. Micheli, A.: Neural network for graphs: a contextual constructive approach. IEEE Trans. Neural Networks 20(3), 498–511 (2009)

23. Rossi, A., Barbosa, D., Firmani, D., Matinata, A., Merialdo, P.: Knowledge graph embedding for link prediction: a comparative analysis. ACM Trans. Knowl. Discov. Data 15(2), 14:1-14:49 (2021)

24. Scarselli, F., Gori, M., Tsoi, A.C., Hagenbuchner, M., Monfardini, G.: The graph neural network model. IEEE Trans. Neural Networks 20(1), 61–80 (2009)

25. Shchur, O., Mumme, M., Bojchevski, A., Günnemann, S.: Pitfalls of graph neural network evaluation. In: Relational Representation Learning Workshop (R2L 2018), NeurIPS, Montréal, Canada (2018)

26. Sun, H., Zhong, J., Ma, Y., Han, Z., He, K.: Timetraveler: reinforcement learning for temporal knowledge graph forecasting. In: Moens, M., Huang, X., Specia, L., Yih, S.W. (eds.) Proceedings of the 2021 Conference on Empirical Methods in Natural Language Processing, EMNLP 2021, Virtual Event/Punta Cana, Dominican Republic, 7–11 November 2021, pp. 8306–8319. Association for Computational Linguistics (2021)

27. Sun, Z., Vashishth, S., Sanyal, S., Talukdar, P.P., Yang, Y.: A re-evaluation of knowledge graph completion methods. In: Jurafsky, D., Chai, J., Schluter, N., Tetreault, J.R. (eds.) Proceedings of the 58th Annual Meeting of the Association for Computational Linguistics, ACL 2020, Online, 5–10 July 2020, pp. 5516–5522. Association for Computational Linguistics (2020)

28. Trivedi, R., Dai, H., Wang, Y., Song, L.: Know-evolve: deep temporal reasoning for dynamic knowledge graphs. In: Precup, D., Teh, Y.W. (eds.) Proceedings of the 34th International Conference on Machine Learning, ICML 2017. Proceedings of Machine Learning Research, Sydney, NSW, Australia, 6–11 August 2017, vol. 70, pp. 3462–3471. PMLR (2017)

29. Widjaja, H., et al.: KGxBoard: explainable and interactive leaderboard for evaluation of knowledge graph completion models. In: Proceedings of the 2022 Conference on Empirical Methods in Natural Language Processing: System Demonstrations, Abu Dhabi, UAE, December 2022, pp. 338–350. Association for Computational Linguistics (2022)

30. Zhu, C., Chen, M., Fan, C., Cheng, G., Zhang, Y.: Learning from history: modeling temporal knowledge graphs with sequential copy-generation networks. In: Thirty-Fifth AAAI Conference on Artificial Intelligence, AAAI 2021, Thirty-Third Conference on Innovative Applications of Artificial Intelligence, IAAI 2021, The Eleventh Symposium on Educational Advances in Artificial Intelligence, EAAI 2021, Virtual Event, 2–9 February 2021, pp. 4732–4740. AAAI Press (2021)

Improving Few-Shot Inductive Learning on Temporal Knowledge Graphs Using Confidence-Augmented Reinforcement Learning

Zifeng Ding[1,2], Jingpei Wu[1], Zongyue Li[1,3], Yunpu Ma[1,2], and Volker Tresp[1(✉)]

[1] LMU Munich, Geschwister-Scholl-Platz 1, 80539 Munich, Germany
zifeng.ding@campus.lmu.de, Volker.Tresp@lmu.de
[2] Siemens AG, Otto-Hahn-Ring 6, 81739 Munich, Germany
[3] Munich Center for Machine Learning (MCML), Munich, Germany

Abstract. Temporal knowledge graph completion (TKGC) aims to predict the missing links among the entities in a temporal knowledge graph (TKG). Most previous TKGC methods only consider predicting the missing links among the entities seen in the training set, while they are unable to achieve great performance in link prediction concerning newly-emerged unseen entities. Recently, a new task, i.e., TKG few-shot out-of-graph (OOG) link prediction, is proposed, where TKGC models are required to achieve great link prediction performance concerning newly-emerged entities that only have few-shot observed examples. In this work, we propose a TKGC method FITCARL that combines few-shot learning with reinforcement learning to solve this task. In FITCARL, an agent traverses through the whole TKG to search for the prediction answer. A policy network is designed to guide the search process based on the traversed path. To better address the data scarcity problem in the few-shot setting, we introduce a module that computes the confidence of each candidate action and integrate it into the policy for action selection. We also exploit the entity concept information with a novel concept regularizer to boost model performance. Experimental results show that FITCARL achieves stat-of-the-art performance on TKG few-shot OOG link prediction. Code and supplementary appendices are provided (https://github. com/ZifengDing/FITCARL/tree/main).

Keywords: Temporal knowledge graph · Few-shot learning

1 Introduction

Knowledge graphs (KGs) store knowledge by representing facts in the form of triples, i.e., (s, r, o), where s and o are the subject and object entities, and r denotes the relation between them. To further specify the time validity of the facts, temporal knowledge graphs (TKGs) are introduced by using a quadruple

---

Z. Ding and J. Wu—Equal contribution.

© The Author(s), under exclusive license to Springer Nature Switzerland AG 2023
D. Koutra et al. (Eds.): ECML PKDD 2023, LNAI 14171, pp. 550–566, 2023.
https://doi.org/10.1007/978-3-031-43418-1_33

(s, r, o, t) to represent each fact, where t is the valid time of this fact. In this way, TKGs are able to capture the ever-evolving knowledge over time. It has already been extensively explored to use KGs and TKGs to assist downstream tasks, e.g., question answering [12,27,45] and natural language generation [2,20].

Since TKGs are known to be incomplete [19], a large number of researches focus on proposing methods to automatically complete TKGs, i.e., temporal knowledge graph completion (TKGC). In traditional TKGC, models are given a training set consisting of a TKG containing a finite set of entities during training, and they are required to predict the missing links among the entities seen in the training set. Most previous TKGC methods, e.g., [11,17,19,31], achieve great success on traditional TKGC, however, they still have drawbacks. (1) Due to the ever-evolving nature of world knowledge, new unseen entities always emerge in a TKG and traditional TKGC methods fail to handle them. (2) Besides, in real-world scenarios, newly-emerged entities are usually coupled with only a few associated edges [13]. Traditional TKGC methods require a large number of entity-related data examples to learn expressive entity representations, making them hard to optimally represent newly-emerged entities. To this end, recently, Ding et al. [13] propose the TKG few-shot out-of-graph (OOG) link prediction (LP) task based on traditional TKGC, aiming to draw attention to studying how to achieve better LP results regarding newly-emerged TKG entities.

In this work, we propose a TKGC method to improve few-shot inductive learning over newly-emerged entities on TKGs using confidence-augmented reinforcement learning (FITCARL). FITCARL is developed to solve TKG few-shot OOG LP [13]. It is a meta-learning based method trained with episodic training [36]. For each unseen entity, FITCARL first employs a time-aware Transformer [35] to adaptively learn its expressive representation. Then it starts from the unseen entity and sequentially takes actions by transferring to other entities according to the observed edges associated with the current entity, following a policy parameterized by a learnable policy network. FITCARL traverses the TKG for a fixed number of steps and stops at the entity that is expected to be the LP answer. To better address the data scarcity problem in the few-shot setting, we introduce a confidence learner that computes the confidence of each candidate action and integrate it into the policy for action selection. Following [13], we also take advantage of the concept information presented in the temporal knowledge bases (TKBs) and design a novel concept regularizer. We summarize our contributions as follows: (1) This is the first work using reinforcement learning-based method to reason over newly-emerged few-shot entities in TKGs and solve the TKG few-shot OOG LP task. (2) We propose a time-aware Transformer using a time-aware positional encoding method to better utilize few-shot information in learning representations of new-emerged entities. (3) We design a novel confidence learner to alleviate the negative impact of the data scarcity problem brought by the few-shot setting. (4) We propose a parameter-free concept regularizer to utilize the concept information provided by the TKBs and it demonstrates strong effectiveness. (5) FITCARL achieves state-of-the-art performance on all datasets of TKG few-shot OOG LP and provides explainability.

2   Related Work

2.1   Knowledge Graph and Temporal Knowledge Graph Completion

Knowledge graph completion (KGC) methods can be summarized into two types. The first type of methods focuses on designing KG score functions that directly compute the plausibility scores of KG triples [1,4,5,22,25,32,43]. Other KGC methods are neural-based models [28,34]. Neural-based models are built by coupling KG score functions with neural structures, e.g., graph neural network (GNN). It is shown that neural structures make great contributions to enhancing the performance of KGC methods. TKGC methods are developed by incorporating temporal reasoning techniques. A line of works aims to design time-aware KG score functions that are able to process time information [7,19,23,26,42,44]. Another line of works employs neural structures to encode temporal information, where some of them use recurrent neural structures, e.g., Transformer [35], to model the temporal dependencies in TKGs [39], and others design time-aware GNNs to achieve temporal reasoning by computing time-aware entity representations through aggregation [11,17]. Reinforcement learning (RL) has already been used to reason TKGs, e.g., [21,30]. TITer [30] and CluSTeR [21] achieve temporal path modeling with RL. However, they are traditional TKG reasoning models and are not designed to deal with few-shot unseen entities[1].

2.2   Inductive Learning on KGs and TKGs

In recent years, inductive learning on KGs and TKGs has gained increasing interest. A series of works [8,10,24,29,40] focuses on learning strong inductive representations of few-shot unseen relations using meta-learning-based approaches. These methods achieve great effectiveness, however, they are unable to deal with newly-emerged entities. Some works try to deal with unseen entities by inductively transferring knowledge from seen to unseen entities with an auxiliary set provided during inference [15,16,37]. Their performance highly depends on the size of the auxiliary set. [13] shows that with a tiny auxiliary set, these methods cannot achieve ideal performance. Besides, these methods are developed for static KGs, thus without temporal reasoning ability. On top of them, Baek et al. [3] propose a more realistic task, i.e., KG few-shot OOG LP, aiming to draw attention to better studying few-shot OOG entities. They propose a model GEN that contains two GNNs and train it with a meta-learning framework to adapt to the few-shot setting. Same as [15,16,37], GEN does not have a temporal reasoning module, and therefore, it cannot reason TKGs. Ding et al. [13] propose the TKG few-shot OOG LP task that generalizes [3] to the context of TKGs. They develop a meta-learning-based model FILT that achieves temporal reasoning with a time difference-based graph encoder and mines concept-aware

---

[1] TITer can model unseen entities, but it is not designed for few-shot setting and requires a substantial number of associated facts. Besides, both TITer and CluSTeR are TKG forecasting methods, where models are asked to predict future links given the past TKG information (different from TKGC, see Appendix B for discussion).

information from the entity concepts specified in TKBs. Recently, another work [38] proposes a task called few-shot TKG reasoning, aiming to ask TKG models to predict future facts for newly-emerged few-shot entities. In few-shot TKG reasoning, for each newly-emerged entity, TKG models are asked to predict the unobserved associated links happening after the observed few-shot examples. Such restriction is not imposed in TKG few-shot OOG LP, meaning that TKG models should predict the unobserved links happening at any time along the time axis. In our work, we only consider the task setting of TKG few-shot OOG LP and do not consider the setting of [38].

3 Task Formulation and Preliminaries

3.1 TKG Few-Shot Out-of-Graph Link Prediction

Definition 1 (TKG Few-Shot OOG LP). Assume we have a background TKG $\mathcal{G}_{\text{back}} = \{(s,r,o,t)|s,o \in \mathcal{E}_{\text{back}}, r \in \mathcal{R}, t \in \mathcal{T}\} \subseteq \mathcal{E}_{\text{back}} \times \mathcal{R} \times \mathcal{E}_{\text{back}} \times \mathcal{T}$, where $\mathcal{E}_{\text{back}}$, $\mathcal{R}$, $\mathcal{T}$ denote a finite set of seen entities, relations and timestamps, respectively. An unseen entity e' is an entity $e' \in \mathcal{E}'$ and $\mathcal{E}' \cap \mathcal{E}_{\text{back}} = \emptyset$. For each $e' \in \mathcal{E}'$, given K observed e' associated TKG facts $(e',r,\tilde{e},t)$ (or $(\tilde{e},r,e',t)$), where $\tilde{e} \in (\mathcal{E}_{\text{back}} \cup \mathcal{E}')$, $r \in \mathcal{R}$, $t \in \mathcal{T}$, TKG few-shot OOG LP asks models to predict the missing entities of LP queries $(e',r_q,?,t_q)$ (or $(?,r_q,e',t_q)$) derived from unobserved TKG facts containing e' ($r_q \in \mathcal{R}$, $t_q \in \mathcal{T}$). K is a small number denoting shot size, e.g., 1 or 3.

Ding et al. [13] formulate TKG few-shot OOG LP into a meta-learning problem and use episodic training [36] to train the model. For a TKG $\mathcal{G} \subseteq \mathcal{E} \times \mathcal{R} \times \mathcal{E} \times \mathcal{T}$, they split its entities into background (seen) entities $\mathcal{E}_{\text{back}}$ and unseen entities $\mathcal{E}'$, where $\mathcal{E}' \cap \mathcal{E}_{\text{back}} = \emptyset$ and $\mathcal{E} = (\mathcal{E}_{\text{back}} \cup \mathcal{E}')$. A background TKG $\mathcal{G}_{\text{back}} \subseteq \mathcal{E}_{\text{back}} \times \mathcal{R} \times \mathcal{E}_{\text{back}} \times \mathcal{T}$ is constructed by including all the TKG facts that do not contain unseen entities. Then, unseen entities $\mathcal{E}'$ are further split into three non-overlapped groups $\mathcal{E}'_{\text{meta-train}}$, $\mathcal{E}'_{\text{meta-valid}}$ and $\mathcal{E}'_{\text{meta-test}}$. The union of all the facts associated to each group's entities forms the corresponding meta-learning set, e.g., the meta-training set $\mathbb{T}_{\text{meta-train}}$ is formulated as $\{(e',r,\tilde{e},t)|\tilde{e} \in \mathcal{E}, r \in \mathcal{R}, e' \in \mathcal{E}'_{\text{meta-train}}, t \in \mathcal{T}\} \cup \{(\tilde{e},r,e',t)|\tilde{e} \in \mathcal{E}, r \in \mathcal{R}, e' \in \mathcal{E}'_{\text{meta-train}}, t \in \mathcal{T}\}$. Ding et al. ensure that there exists no link between every two of the meta-learning sets. During meta-training, models are trained over a number of episodes, where a training task T is sampled in each episode. For each task T, N unseen entities $\mathcal{E}_T$ are sampled from $\mathcal{E}'_{\text{meta-train}}$. For each $e' \in \mathcal{E}_T$, K associated facts are sampled to form a support set $Sup_{e'} = \{(e',r_i,\tilde{e}_i,t_i)$ or $(\tilde{e}_i,r_i,e',t_i)|\tilde{e}_i \in (\mathcal{E}_{\text{back}} \cup \mathcal{E}'), r_i \in \mathcal{R}, t_i \in \mathcal{T}\}_{i=1}^{K}$, and the rest of its associated facts are taken as its query set $Que_{e'} = \{(e',r_i,\tilde{e}_i,t_i)$ or $(\tilde{e}_i,r_i,e',t_i)|\tilde{e}_i \in (\mathcal{E}_{\text{back}} \cup \mathcal{E}'), r_i \in \mathcal{R}, t_i \in \mathcal{T}\}_{i=K+1}^{M_{e'}}$, where $M_{e'}$ denotes the number of e''s associated facts. Models are asked to simultaneously perform LP over $Que_{e'}$ for each $e' \in \mathcal{E}_T$, given their $Sup_{e'}$ and $\mathcal{G}_{\text{back}}$. After meta-training, models are validated with a meta-validation set $\mathbb{T}_{\text{meta-valid}}$ and tested with a meta-test set $\mathbb{T}_{\text{meta-test}}$. In our work, we also train FITCARL in the same way as [13] with episodic training on the same meta-learning problem.

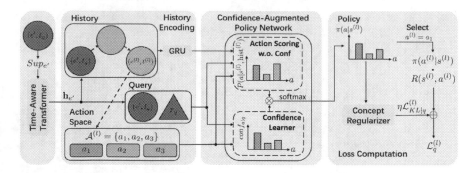

Fig. 1. Overview of FITCARL. To do prediction over the LP query $q = (e', r_q, ?, t_q)$, FITCARL first learns $\mathbf{h}_{e'}$ from a time-aware Transformer. It is then used in history encoding (with GRU) and policy network. To search for the answer, FITCARL starts from node (e', t_q). It goes to $(e^{(l)}, t^{(l)})$, state $s^{(l)}$, at step l. It computes a policy using a confidence-augmented policy network. Assume FITCARL selects action a_1 in current action space $\mathcal{A}^{(l)}$ as the current action $a^{(l)}$. We compute a loss $\mathcal{L}_q^{(l)}$ at step l, considering a_1's probability in policy and reward $R(s^{(l)}, a^{(l)})$, as well as an extra regularization loss $\eta \mathcal{L}_{KL|q}^{(l)}$ computed by a concept regularizer. Please refer to Sect. 4.1, 4.2 and 4.3 for details.

3.2 Concepts for Temporal Knowledge Graph Entities

[13] extracts the concepts of TKG entities by exploring the associated TKBs. Entity concepts describe the characteristics of entities. For example, in the Integrated Crisis Early Warning System (ICEWS) database [6], the entity *Air Force (Canada)* is described with the following concepts: *Air Force, Military* and *Government*. Ding et al. propose three ICEWS-based datasets for TKG few-shot OOG LP and manage to couple every entity with its unique concepts. We use $\mathcal{C}$ to denote all the concepts existing in a TKG and $\mathcal{C}_e$ to denote e's concepts.

4 The Proposed FITCARL Model

Given the support set $Sup_{e'} = \{(e', r_i, \tilde{e}_i, t_i) \text{ or } (\tilde{e}_i, r_i, e', t_i)\}_{i=1}^K$ of $e' \in \mathcal{E}'$, assume we want to predict the missing entity from the LP query $q = (e', r_q, ?, t_q)$ derived from a query quadruple[2] $(e', r_q, \tilde{e}_q, t_q) \in Que_{e'}$. To achieve this, FITCARL first learns a representation $\mathbf{h}_{e'} \in \mathbb{R}^d$ (d is dimension size) for e' (Sect. 4.1). Then it employs an RL agent that starts from the node (e', t_q) and sequentially takes actions by traversing to other nodes (in the form of (*entity, timestamp*)) following a policy (Sect. 4.2 and 4.3). After L traverse steps, the agent is expected to stop at a target node containing $\tilde{e}_q$. Figure 1 shows an overview of FITCARL during training, showing how it computes loss $\mathcal{L}_q^{(l)}$ at step l.

---

[2] For each query quadruple in the form of $(\tilde{e}_q, r_q, e', t_q)$, we derive its LP query as $(e', r_q^{-1}, ?, t_q)$. r_q^{-1} is r_q's inverse relation. The agent always starts from (e', t_q).

4.1 Learning Unseen Entities with Time-Aware Transformer

We follow FILT [13] and use the entity and relation representations pre-trained with ComplEx [32] for model initialization. Note that pre-training only considers all the background TKG facts, i.e., $\mathcal{G}_{\text{back}}$.

To learn $\mathbf{h}_{e'}$, we start from learning K separate meta-representations. Given $Sup_{e'}$, we transform every support quadruple whose form is $(e', r_i, \tilde{e}_i, t_i)$ to $(\tilde{e}_i, r_i^{-1}, e', t_i)$, where r_i^{-1} denotes the inverse relation[3] of r_i. Then we create a temporal neighborhood $\mathcal{N}_{e'} = \{(\tilde{e}_i, r_i, t_i) | (\tilde{e}_i, r_i, e', t_i) \in Sup_{e'}$ or $(e', r_i^{-1}, \tilde{e}_i, t_i) \in Sup_{e'}\}$ for e' based on $Sup_{e'}$, where $|\mathcal{N}_{e'}| = K$. We compute a meta-representation $\mathbf{h}_{e'}^i$ from each temporal neighbor $(\tilde{e}_i, r_i, t_i)$ as $\mathbf{h}_{e'}^i = f(\mathbf{h}_{\tilde{e}_i} \| \mathbf{h}_{r_i})$, where $\mathbf{h}_{r_i} \in \mathbb{R}^d$ is the representation of the relation r_i and $\|$ is the concatenation operation.

We collect $\{\mathbf{h}_{e'}^i\}_{i=1}^K$ and use a time-aware Transformer to compute a contextualized representation $\mathbf{h}_{e'}$. We treat each temporal neighbor $(\tilde{e}_i, r_i, t_i) \in \mathcal{N}_{e'}$ as a token and the corresponding meta-representation $\mathbf{h}_{e'}^i$ as its token representation. We concatenate the classification ([CLS]) token with the temporal neighbors in $\mathcal{N}_{e'}$ as a sequence and input it into a Transformer, where the sequence length is $K + 1$. The order of temporal neighbors is decided by the sampling order of support quadruples.

To better utilize temporal information from temporal neighbors, we propose a time-aware positional encoding method. For any two tokens u, v in the input sequence, we compute the time difference $t_u - t_v$ between their associated timestamps, and then map it into a time-difference representation $\mathbf{h}_{t_u - t_v} \in \mathbb{R}^d$,

$$\mathbf{h}_{t_u - t_v} = \sqrt{\frac{1}{d}}[cos(\omega_1(t_u - t_v) + \phi_1), ..., cos(\omega_d(t_u - t_v) + \phi_d)]. \quad (1)$$

ω_1 to ω_d and ϕ_1 to ϕ_d are trainable parameters. The timestamp for each temporal neighbor is t_i and we set the timestamp of the [CLS] token to the query timestamp t_q since we would like to use the learned $\mathbf{h}_{e'}$ to predict the LP query happening at t_q. The attention $\text{att}_{u,v}$ of any token v to token u in an attention layer of our time-aware Transformer is written as

$$\text{att}_{u,v} = \frac{\exp(\alpha_{u,v})}{\sum_{k=1}^{K+1} \exp(\alpha_{u,k})}, $$
$$\alpha_{u,v} = \frac{1}{\sqrt{d}}(\mathbf{W}_{TrQ}\mathbf{h}_u)^\top(\mathbf{W}_{TrK}\mathbf{h}_v) + \mathbf{w}_{Pos}^\top \mathbf{h}_{t_u - t_v}. \quad (2)$$

$\mathbf{h}_u, \mathbf{h}_v \in \mathbb{R}^d$ are the input representations of token u, v into this attention layer. $\mathbf{W}_{TrQ}, \mathbf{W}_{TrK} \in \mathbb{R}^{d \times d}$ are the weight matrices following original definition in [35]. $\mathbf{w}_{Pos} \in \mathbb{R}^d$ is a parameter that maps $\mathbf{h}_{t_u - t_v}$ to a scalar representing time-aware relative position from token v to u. We use several attention layers and also employ multi-head attention to increase model expressiveness. The output representation of the [CLS] token from the last attention layer is taken as $\mathbf{h}_{e'}$. Figure 2 illustrates how the time-aware Transformer learns $\mathbf{h}_{e'}$ in the 3-shot case.

---

[3] Both original and inverse relations are trained in pre-training.

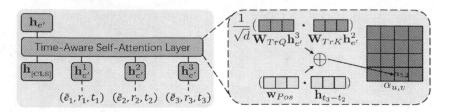

Fig. 2. Time-aware Transformer with one attention layer for learning unseen entity representation in the 3-shot case.

4.2 Reinforcement Learning Framework

We formulate the RL process as a Markov Decision Process, and we introduce its elements as follows. **(1) States:** Let $\mathcal{S}$ be a state space. A state is denoted as $s^{(l)} = (e^{(l)}, t^{(l)}, e', r_q, t_q) \in \mathcal{S}$. $(e^{(l)}, t^{(l)})$ is the node that is visited by the agent at step l and e', r_q, t_q are taken from the LP query $(e', r_q, ?, t_q)$. The agent starts from (e', t_q), and thus $s^{(0)} = (e', t_q, e', r_q, t_q)$. **(2) Actions:** Let $\mathcal{A}$ denote an action space and $\mathcal{A}^{(l)} \subset \mathcal{A}$ denotes the action space at step l. $\mathcal{A}^{(l)}$ is sampled from all the possible outgoing edges starting from $(e^{(l)}, t^{(l)})$, i.e., $\{a = (r, e, t) | (e^{(l)}, r, e, t) \in (\mathcal{G}_{\text{back}} \cup \bigcup_{e'' \in \mathcal{E}_T} Sup_{e''}), r \in \mathcal{R}, e \in (\mathcal{E}_{\text{back}} \cup \mathcal{E}_T), t \in \mathcal{T}\}$. We do sampling because if $e^{(l)} \in \mathcal{E}_{\text{back}}$, there probably exist lots of outgoing edges in $\mathcal{G}_{\text{back}}$. If we include all of them into $\mathcal{A}^{(l)}$, they will lead to an excessive consumption of memory and cause out-of-memory problem on hardware devices. We sample $\mathcal{A}^{(l)}$ in a time-adaptive manner. For each outgoing edge (r, e, t), we compute a score $\mathbf{w}_{\Delta t}^{\top} \mathbf{h}_{t_q - t}$, where $\mathbf{w}_{\Delta t} \in \mathbb{R}^d$ is a time modeling weight and $\mathbf{h}_{t_q - t}$ is the representation denoting the time difference $t_q - t$. $\mathbf{h}_{t_q - t}$ is computed as in Eq. 1 with shared parameters. We rank the scores of outgoing edges in descending order and take a fixed number of top-ranked edges as $\mathcal{A}^{(l)}$. We also include one self-loop action in each $\mathcal{A}^{(l)}$ that makes the agent stay at the current node. **(3) Transition:** A transition function δ is used to transfer from one state to another, i.e., $\delta(s^{(l)}, a^{(l)}) = s^{(l+1)} = (e^{(l+1)}, t^{(l+1)}, e', r_q, t_q)$, according to the selected action $a^{(l)}$. **(4) Rewards:** We give the agent a reward at each step of state transition and consider a cumulative reward for the whole searching process. The reward of doing a candidate action $a \in \mathcal{A}^{(l)}$ at step l is given as $R(s^{(l)}, a) = \text{Sigmoid}\left(\theta - \left\|\mathbf{h}_{\tilde{e}_q} - \mathbf{h}_{e_a}\right\|_2\right)$. θ is a hyperparameter adjusting the range of reward. $\mathbf{h}_{e_a}$ denotes the representation of entity e_a selected in the action $a = (r_a, e_a, t_a)$. $\|\cdot\|_2$ is the L2 norm. The closer e_a is to $\tilde{e}_q$, the greater reward the agent gets if it does action a.

4.3 Confidence-Augmented Policy Network

We design a confidence-augmented policy network that calculates the probability distribution over all the candidate actions $\mathcal{A}^{(l)}$ at the search step l, according to the current state $s^{(l)}$, the search history $\text{hist}^{(l)} = ((e', t_q), r^{(1)}, (e^{(1)}, t^{(1)}), ..., r^{(l)}, (e^{(l)}, t^{(l)}))$, and the confidence $\text{conf}_{a|q}$ of each $a \in \mathcal{A}^{(l)}$. During the search, we represent each visited node with a time-aware representation related to the LP query q. For example, for the node $(e^{(l)}, t^{(l)})$ visited at step l, we compute its representation as $\mathbf{h}_{(e^{(l)}, t^{(l)})} = \mathbf{h}_{e^{(l)}} \| \mathbf{h}_{t_q - t^{(l)}}$. $\mathbf{h}_{t_q - t^{(l)}}$ is computed as same in Eq. 1 and parameters are shared.

Encoding Search History. The search history $\text{hist}^{(l)}$ is encoded as

$$
\begin{aligned}
\mathbf{h}_{\text{hist}^{(l)}} &= \text{GRU}\left(\left(\mathbf{h}_{r^{(l)}} \| \mathbf{h}_{(e^{(l)}, t^{(l)})}\right), \mathbf{h}_{\text{hist}^{(l-1)}}\right), \\
\mathbf{h}_{\text{hist}^{(0)}} &= \text{GRU}\left(\left(\mathbf{h}_{r_{\text{dummy}}} \| \mathbf{h}_{(e', t_q)}\right), \mathbf{0}\right).
\end{aligned}
\tag{3}
$$

GRU is a gated recurrent unit [9]. $\mathbf{h}_{\text{hist}^{(0)}} \in \mathbb{R}^{3d}$ is the initial hidden state of GRU and $\mathbf{h}_{r_{\text{dummy}}} \in \mathbb{R}^{d}$ is the representation of a dummy relation for GRU initialization. $\mathbf{h}_{(e', t_q)}$ is the time-aware representation of the starting node (e', t_q).

Confidence-Aware Action Scoring. We design a score function for computing the probability of selecting each candidate action $a \in \mathcal{A}^{(l)}$. Assume $a = (r_a, e_a, t_a)$, where $(e^{(l)}, r_a, e_a, t_a) \in (\mathcal{G}_{\text{back}} \cup \bigcup_{e'' \in \mathcal{E}_T} Sup_{e''})$. We first compute an attentional feature $\mathbf{h}_{\text{hist}^{(l)}, q|a}$ that extracts the information highly-related to action a from the visited search history $\text{hist}^{(l)}$ and the LP query q.

$$
\begin{aligned}
\mathbf{h}_{\text{hist}^{(l)}, q|a} &= \text{att}_{\text{hist}^{(l)}, a} \cdot \bar{\mathbf{h}}_{\text{hist}^{(l)}} + \text{att}_{q,a} \cdot \bar{\mathbf{h}}_q, \\
\bar{\mathbf{h}}_{\text{hist}^{(l)}} &= \mathbf{W}_1^\top \mathbf{h}_{\text{hist}^{(l)}}, \quad \bar{\mathbf{h}}_q = \mathbf{W}_2^\top \left(\mathbf{h}_{r_q} \| \mathbf{h}_{(e', t_q)}\right).
\end{aligned}
\tag{4}
$$

$\mathbf{W}_1, \mathbf{W}_2 \in \mathbb{R}^{2d \times 3d}$ are two weight matrices. $\mathbf{h}_{r_q}$ is the representation of the query relation r_q. $\text{att}_{\text{hist}^{(l)}, a}$ and $\text{att}_{q,a}$ are two attentional weights that are defined as

$$
\text{att}_{\text{hist}^{(l)}, a} = \frac{\exp(\phi_{\text{hist}^{(l)}, a})}{\exp(\phi_{\text{hist}^{(l)}, a}) + \exp(\phi_{q,a})}, \text{att}_{q,a} = \frac{\exp(\phi_{q,a})}{\exp(\phi_{\text{hist}^{(l)}, a}) + \exp(\phi_{q,a})},
\tag{5}
$$

where

$$
\begin{aligned}
\phi_{\text{hist}^{(l)}, a} &= \bar{\mathbf{h}}_a^\top \bar{\mathbf{h}}_{\text{hist}^{(l)}} + \mathbf{w}_{\Delta t}^\top \mathbf{h}_{t_a - t^{(l)}}, \quad \phi_{q,a} = \bar{\mathbf{h}}_a^\top \bar{\mathbf{h}}_q + \mathbf{w}_{\Delta t}^\top \mathbf{h}_{t_a - t_q}, \\
\bar{\mathbf{h}}_a &= \mathbf{W}_3^\top \left(\mathbf{h}_{r_a} \| \mathbf{h}_{(e_a, t_a)}\right).
\end{aligned}
\tag{6}
$$

$\mathbf{W}_3 \in \mathbb{R}^{2d \times 3d}$ is a weight matrix. $\mathbf{h}_{r_a}$ is the representation of r_a. $\mathbf{h}_{(e_a, t_a)}$ is the time-aware representation of node (e_a, t_a) from action a. $\mathbf{w}_{\Delta t}$ maps time differences to a scalar indicating how temporally important is the action a to the history and the query q. We take $t^{(l)}$ as search history's timestamp because it is the timestamp of the node where the search stops. Before considering confidence, we compute a probability for each candidate action $a \in \mathcal{A}^{(l)}$ at step l

$$
P(a|s^{(l)}, \text{hist}^{(l)}) = \frac{\exp(\bar{\mathbf{h}}_a^\top \mathbf{W}_4 \mathbf{h}_{\text{hist}^{(l)}, q|a})}{\sum_{a' \in \mathcal{A}^{(l)}} \exp(\bar{\mathbf{h}}_{a'}^\top \mathbf{W}_4 \mathbf{h}_{\text{hist}^{(l)}, q|a'})},
\tag{7}
$$

where $\mathbf{W}_4 \in \mathbb{R}^{2d \times 2d}$ is a weight matrix. The probability of each action a is decided by its associated node (e_a, t_a) and the attentional feature $\mathbf{h}_{\text{hist}^{(l)}, q|a}$ that adaptively selects the information highly-related to a.

In TKG few-shot OOG LP, only a small number of K edges associated to each unseen entity are observed. This leads to an incomprehensive action space $\mathcal{A}^{(0)}$ at the start of search because our agent starts travelling from node (e', t_q) and $|\mathcal{A}^{(0)}| = K$ is extremely tiny. Besides, since there exist plenty of unseen entities in $\mathcal{E}_T$, it is highly probable that the agent travels to the nodes with other unseen entities during the search, causing it sequentially experience multiple tiny action spaces. As the number of the experienced incomprehensive action spaces increases, more noise will be introduced in history encoding. From Eqs. 4 to 7, we show that we heavily rely on the search history for computing candidate action probabilities. To address this problem, we design a confidence learner that learns the confidence $\text{conf}_{a|q}$ of each $a \in \mathcal{A}^{(l)}$, independent of the search history. The form of confidence learner is inspired by a KG score function TuckER [4].

$$
\text{conf}_{a|q} = \frac{\exp(\psi_{a|q})}{\sum_{a' \in \mathcal{A}^{(l)}} \exp(\psi_{a'|q})}, \text{ where } \psi_{a|q} = \mathcal{W} \times_1 \mathbf{h}_{(e',t_q)} \times_2 \mathbf{h}_{r_q} \times_3 \mathbf{h}_{(e_a,t_a)}.
\tag{8}
$$

$\mathcal{W} \in \mathbb{R}^{2d \times d \times 2d}$ is a learnable core tensor introduced in [4]. As defined in tucker decomposition [33], $\times_1, \times_2, \times_3$ are three operators indicating the tensor product in three different modes (see [4,33] for detailed explanations). Equation 8 can be interpreted as another action scoring process that is irrelevant to the search history. If $\psi_{a|q}$ is high, then it implies that choosing action a is sensible and e_a is likely to resemble the ground truth missing entity $\tilde{e}_q$. Accordingly, the candidate action a will be assigned a great confidence. In this way, we alleviate the negative influence of cascaded noise introduced by multiple tiny action spaces in the search history. The policy $\pi(a|s^{(l)})$ at step l is defined as

$$
\pi(a|s^{(l)}) = \frac{\exp(P(a|s^{(l)}, \text{hist}^{(l)}) \cdot \text{conf}_{a|q})}{\sum_{a' \in \mathcal{A}^{(l)}} \exp(P(a'|s^{(l)}, \text{hist}^{(l)}) \cdot \text{conf}_{a'|q})}
\tag{9}
$$

4.4   Concept Regularizer

In the background TKG $\mathcal{G}_{\text{back}}$, the object entities of each relation conform to a unique distribution. For each relation $r \in \mathcal{R}$, we track all the TKG facts containing r in $\mathcal{G}_{\text{back}}$, and pick out all their object entities $\mathcal{E}_r$ ($\mathcal{E}_r \in \mathcal{E}_{\text{back}}$) together with their concepts $\{\mathcal{C}_e | e \in \mathcal{E}_r\}$. We sum up the number of appearances n_c of each concept c and compute a probability $P(c|r)$ denoting how probable it is to see c when we perform object prediction[4] over the LP queries concerning r. For example, for r, $\mathcal{E}_r = \{e_1, e_2\}$ and $\mathcal{C}_{e_1} = \{c_1, c_2\}$, $\mathcal{C}_{e_2} = \{c_2\}$. The probability $P(c_1|r) = n_{c_1} / \sum_{c \in \mathcal{C}} n_c = 1/3$, $P(c_2|r) = n_{c_2} / \sum_{c \in \mathcal{C}} n_c = 2/3$. Assume we have an LP query $q = (e', r_q, ?, t_q)$, and at search step l, we have an action probability from policy $\pi(a|s^{(l)})$ for each candidate action $a \in \mathcal{A}^{(l)}$. We collect the concepts $\mathcal{C}_{e_a}$ of e_a in each action a and compute a concept-aware action probability

$$
P(a|\mathcal{C}_{e_a}, q) = \frac{\exp(\sum_{c \in \mathcal{C}_{e_a}} P(c|r_q))}{\sum_{a' \in \mathcal{A}^{(l)}} \exp(\sum_{c' \in \mathcal{C}_{e_{a'}}} P(c'|r_q))}
\tag{10}
$$

---

[4] All LP queries are transformed into object prediction in TKG few-shot OOG LP.

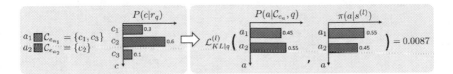

Fig. 3. Concept regularizer. $P(a_1|\mathcal{C}_{e_{a_1}}, q) = \exp(0.3+0.1)/(\exp(0.3+0.1)+\exp(0.6)) = 0.45$. $P(a_2|\mathcal{C}_{e_{a_2}}, q) = \exp(0.6)/(\exp(0.3+0.1)+\exp(0.6)) = 0.55$.

We then compute the Kullback-Leibler (KL) divergence between $P(a|\mathcal{C}_{e_a}, q)$ and $\pi(a|s^{(l)})$ and minimize it during parameter optimization.

$$\mathcal{L}_{\text{KL}|q}^{(l)} = \sum_{a \in \mathcal{A}^{(l)}} \pi(a|s^{(l)}) \log\left(\frac{\pi(a|s^{(l)})}{P(a|\mathcal{C}_{e_a}, q)}\right). \tag{11}$$

Note that $r_q \in \mathcal{R}$ is observable in $\mathcal{G}_{\text{back}}$. $\mathcal{G}_{\text{back}}$ is huge and contains a substantial number of facts of r_q. As stated in FILT [13], although we have only K associated edges for each unseen entity e', its concepts $\mathcal{C}_{e'}$ is known. Our concept regularizer enables a parameter-free approach to match the concept-aware action probability $P(a|\mathcal{C}_{e_a}, q)$ with the action probability taken from the policy $\pi(a|s^{(l)})$. It can be taken as guiding the policy to conform to the distribution of r_q's objects' concepts observed in $\mathcal{G}_{\text{back}}$. We illustrate our concept regularizer in Fig. 3.

4.5 Parameter Learning

Following [13], we train FITCARL with episodic training. In each episode, a training task T is sampled, where we sample a $Sup_{e'}$ for every unseen entity $e' \in \mathcal{E}'_{\text{meta-train}}$ ($\mathcal{E}_T = \mathcal{E}'_{\text{meta-train}}$) and calculate loss over $Que_{e'}$. For each LP query q, we aim to maximize the cumulative reward along L steps of search. We write our loss function (we minimize our loss) for each training task T as follows.

$$\mathcal{L}_T = \frac{1}{\sum_{e'}|Que_{e'}|} \sum_{e'} \sum_{q \in Que_{e'}} \sum_{l=0}^{L-1} \gamma^l \mathcal{L}_q^{(l)}, \quad \mathcal{L}_q^{(l)} = \eta \mathcal{L}_{\text{KL}|q}^{(l)} - \log(\pi(a^{(l)}|s^{(l)}))R(s^{(l)}, a^{(l)}).$$
$$\tag{12}$$

$a^{(l)}$ is the selected action at search step l. γ^l is the lth order of a discount factor $\gamma \in [0, 1)$. η is a hyperparameter deciding the magnitude of concept regularization. We use Algorithm 1 in Appendix E to further illustrate our meta-training process.

5 Experiments

We compare FITCARL with baselines on TKG few-shot OOG LP (Sect. 5.2). In Sect. 5.3, we first do several ablation studies to study the effectiveness of different model components. We then plot the performance over time to show FITCARL's robustness and present a case study to show FITCARL's explainability and the importance of learning confidence. We provide implementation details in Appendix A.

5.1   Experimental Setting

We do experiments on three datasets proposed in [13], i.e., ICEWS14-OOG, ICEWS18-OOG and ICEWS0515-OOG. They contain the timestamped political facts in 2014, 2018 and from 2005 to 2015, respectively. All of them are constructed by taking the facts from the ICEWS [6] TKB. Dataset statistics are shown in Table 1. We employ two evaluation metrics, i.e., mean reciprocal rank (MRR) and Hits@1/3/10. We provide detailed definitions of both metrics in Appendix D. We use the filtered setting proposed in [5] for fairer evaluation. For baselines, we consider the following methods. (1) Two traditional KGC methods, i.e., ComplEx [32] and BiQUE [14]. (2) Three traditional TKGC methods, i.e., TNTComplEx [18], TeLM [41], and TeRo [42]. (3) Three inductive KGC methods, i.e., MEAN [15], LAN [37], and GEN [3]. Among them, only GEN is trained with a meta-learning framework. (4) Two inductive TKG reasoning methods, including an inductive TKG forecasting method TITer [30], and a meta-learning-based inductive TKGC method FILT [13] (FILT is the only previous work developed to solve TKG few-shot OOG LP). We take the experimental results of all baselines (except TITer) from [13]. Following [13], we train TITer over all the TKG facts in $\mathcal{G}_{\text{back}}$ and $\mathbb{T}_{\text{meta-train}}$. We constrain TITer to only observe support quadruples of each test entity in $\mathcal{E}'_{\text{meta-test}}$ for inductive learning during inference. All methods are tested over exactly the same test examples.

Table 1. Dataset statistics.

Dataset	$\mid\mathcal{E}\mid$	$\mid\mathcal{R}\mid$	$\mid\mathcal{T}\mid$	$\mid\mathcal{E}'_{\text{meta-train}}\mid$	$\mid\mathcal{E}'_{\text{meta-valid}}\mid$	$\mid\mathcal{E}'_{\text{meta-test}}\mid$	$\mid\mathcal{G}_{\text{back}}\mid$	$\mid\mathbb{T}_{\text{meta-train}}\mid$	$\mid\mathbb{T}_{\text{meta-valid}}\mid$	$\mid\mathbb{T}_{\text{meta-test}}\mid$
ICEWS14-OOG	7128	230	365	385	48	49	83448	5772	718	705
ICEWS18-OOG	23033	256	304	1268	160	158	444269	19291	2425	2373
ICEWS0515-OOG	10488	251	4017	647	80	82	448695	10115	1217	1228

5.2   Main Results

Table 2 shows the experimental results of TKG 1-shot/3-shot OOG LP. We observe that traditional KGC and TKGC methods are beaten by inductive learning methods. It is because traditional methods cannot handle unseen entities. Besides, we also find that meta-learning-based methods, i.e., GEN, FILT and FITCARL, show better performance than other inductive learning methods. This is because meta-learning is more suitable for dealing with few-shot learning problems. FITCARL shows superior performance over all metrics on all datasets. It outperforms the previous stat-of-the-art FILT with a huge margin. We attribute it to several reasons. (1) Unlike FILT that uses KG score function over all the entities for prediction, FITCARL is an RL-based method that directly searches the predicted answer through their multi-hop temporal neighborhood, making it better capture highly-related graph information through time. (2) FITCARL takes advantage of its confidence learner. It helps to alleviate the negative impact from the few-shot setting. (3) Concept regularizer serves as a strong tool for exploiting concept-aware information in TKBs and adaptively guides FITCARL to learn a policy that conforms to the concept distribution shown in $\mathcal{G}_{back}$.

Table 2. Experimental results of TKG 1-shot and 3-shot OOG LP. Evaluation metrics are MRR and Hits@1/3/10 (H@1/3/10). Best results are marked bold.

Datasets	ICEWS14-OOG								ICEWS18-OOG								ICEWS0515-OOG							
	MRR		H@1		H@3		H@10		MRR		H@1		H@3		H@10		MRR		H@1		H@3		H@10	
Model	1-S	3-S	1-S	3-S	1-S	3-S	1-S	3-S	1-S	3-S	1-S	3-S	1-S	3-S	1-S	3-S	1-S	3-S	1-S	3-S	1-S	3-S	1-S	3-S
ComplEx	.048	.046	.018	.014	.045	.046	.099	.089	.039	.044	.031	.026	.048	.042	.085	.093	.077	.076	.045	.048	.074	.071	.129	.120
BiQUE	.039	.035	.015	.014	.041	.030	.073	.066	.029	.032	.022	.021	.033	.037	.064	.073	.075	.083	.044	.049	.072	.077	.130	.144
TNTComplEx	.043	.044	.015	.016	.033	.042	.102	.096	.046	.048	.023	.026	.043	.044	.087	.082	.034	.037	.014	.012	.031	.036	.060	.071
TeLM	.032	.035	.012	.009	.021	.023	.063	.077	.049	.019	.029	.001	.045	.013	.084	.054	.080	.072	.041	.034	.077	.072	.138	.151
TeRo	.009	.010	.002	.005	.002	.015	.020		.007	.006	.003	.001	.006	.003	.013	.006	.012	.023	.000	.010	.008	.017	.024	.040
MEAN	.035	.144	.013	.054	.032	.145	.082	.339	.016	.101	.003	.014	.012	.114	.043	.283	.019	.148	.003	.039	.017	.175	.052	.384
LAN	.168	.199	.050	.061	.199	.255	.421	.500	.077	.127	.018	.025	.067	.165	.199	.344	.171	.182	.081	.068	.180	.191	.367	.467
GEN	.231	.234	.162	.155	.250	.284	.378	.389	.171	.216	.112	.137	.189	.252	.289	.351	.268	.322	.185	.231	.308	.362	.413	.507
TITer	.144	.200	.105	.148	.163	.226	.228	.314	.064	.115	.038	.076	.075	.131	.011	.186	.115	.228	.080	.168	.130	.262	.173	.331
FILT	.278	.321	.208	.240	.305	.357	.410	.475	.191	.266	.129	.187	.209	.298	.316	.417	.273	.370	.201	.299	.303	.391	.405	.516
FITCARL	**.418**	**.481**	**.284**	**.329**	**.522**	**.646**	**.681**	**.696**	**.297**	**.370**	**.156**	**.193**	**.386**	**.559**	**.584**	**.627**	**.345**	**.513**	**.202**	**.386**	**.482**	**.618**	**.732**	**.700**

5.3 Further Analysis

Ablation Study. We conduct several ablation studies to study the effectiveness of different model components. **(A) Action Space Sampling Variants:** To prevent oversized action space $\mathcal{A}^{(l)}$, we use a time-adaptive sampling method (see Sect. 4.2). We show its effectiveness by switching it to random sample (ablation A1) and time-proximity sample (ablation A2). In time-proximity sample, we take a fixed number of outgoing edges temporally closest to the current node at $t^{(l)}$ as $\mathcal{A}^{(l)}$. We keep $|\mathcal{A}^{(l)}|$ unchanged. **(B) Removing Confidence Learner:** In ablation B, we remove the confidence learner. **(C) Removing Concept Regularizer:** In ablation C, we remove concept regularizer. **(D) Time-Aware Transformer Variants:** We remove the time-aware positional encoding method by deleting the second term of Eq. 2. **(E) Removing Temporal Reasoning Modules:** In ablation E, we study the importance of temporal reasoning. We first combine ablation A1 and D, and then delete every term related to time difference representations computed with Eq. 1. We create a model variant without using any temporal information (see Appendix C for detailed setting). We present the experimental results of ablation studies in Table 3. From ablation A1 and A2, we observe that time-adaptive sample is effective. We also see a great performance drop in ablation B and C, indicating the strong importance of our confidence learner and concept regularizer. We only do ablation D for 3-shot model because in 1-shot case our model does not need to distinguish the importance of multiple support quadruples. We find that our time-aware positional encoding makes great contribution. Finally, we observe that ablation E shows poor performance (worse than A1 and D in most cases), implying that incorporating temporal information is essential for FITCARL to solve TKG few-shot OOG LP.

Table 3. Ablation study results. Best results are marked bold.

Datasets	ICEWS14-OOG								ICEWS18-OOG								ICEWS0515-OOG							
	MRR		H@1		H@3		H@10		MRR		H@1		H@3		H@10		MRR		H@1		H@3		H@10	
Model	1-S	3-S	1-S	3-S	1-S	3-S	1-S	3-S	1-S	3-S	1-S	3-S	1-S	3-S	1-S	3-S	1-S	3-S	1-S	3-S	1-S	3-S	1-S	3-S
A1	.404	.418	.283	.287	.477	.494	.647	.667	.218	.260	.153	.167	.220	.296	.404	.471	.190	.401	.108	.289	.196	.467	.429	.624
A2	.264	.407	.241	.277	.287	.513	.288	.639	.242	.265	.126	.168	.337	.291	.444	.499	.261	.414	.200	.267	.298	.545	.387	.640
B	.373	.379	.255	.284	.454	.425	.655	.564	.156	.258	.106	.191	.162	.271	.273	.398	.285	.411	.198	.336	.328	.442	.447	.567
C	.379	.410	.265	.236	.489	.570	.667	.691	.275	.339	.153	.190	.346	.437	.531	.556	.223	.411	.130	.243	.318	.544	.397	.670
D	–	.438	–	.262	–	.626	–	.676	–	.257	–	.160	–	.280	–	.500	–	.438	–	.262	–	.610	–	.672
E	.270	.346	.042	.178	.480	.466	.644	.662	.155	.201	.012	.117	.197	.214	.543	.429	.176	.378	.047	.239	.194	.501	.506	.584
FITCARL	**.418**	**.481**	**.284**	**.329**	**.522**	**.646**	**.681**	**.696**	**.297**	**.370**	**.156**	**.193**	**.386**	**.559**	**.584**	**.627**	**.345**	**.513**	**.202**	**.386**	**.482**	**.618**	**.732**	**.700**

Performance Over Time. To demonstrate the robustness of FITCARL, we plot its MRR performance over prediction time (query time t_q). We compare FITCARL with two meta-learning-based strong baselines GEN and FILT. From Figs. 4a to 4f, we find that our model can constantly outperform baselines. This indicates that FITCARL improves LP performance for examples existing at almost all timestamps, proving its robustness. GEN is not designed for TKG reasoning, and thus it cannot show optimal performance. Although FILT is designed for TKG few-shot OOG LP, we show that our RL-based model is much stronger.

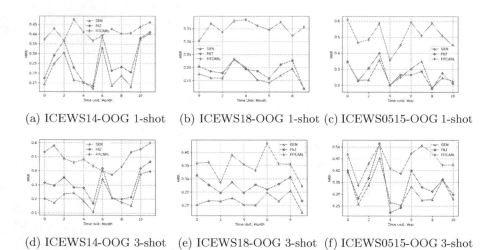

(a) ICEWS14-OOG 1-shot   (b) ICEWS18-OOG 1-shot (c) ICEWS0515-OOG 1-shot

(d) ICEWS14-OOG 3-shot   (e) ICEWS18-OOG 3-shot (f) ICEWS0515-OOG 3-shot

Fig. 4. Performance comparison among FITCARL, FILT and GEN over different query time t_q. Horizontal axis of each subfigure denotes how temporally faraway from the first timestamp. We aggregate the performance of each month to one point in ICEWS14-OOG and ICEWS18-OOG. A point for ICEWS0515-OOG denotes the aggregated performance in each year.

Case Study. We do a case study to show how FITCARL provides explainability and how the confidence learner helps in reasoning. We ask 3-shot FITCARL and its variant without the confidence learner (both trained on ICEWS14-OOG) to predict the missing entity of the LP query (*Future Movement, Express intent to cooperate on intelligence, ?*, 2014-11-12), where *Future Movement* is a newly-emerged entity that is unseen during training and the answer to this LP query is *Miguel Ángel Rodríguez*. We visualize a specific reasoning path of each model and present them in Fig. 5. The relation *Express intent to cooperate on intelligence* indicates a positive relationship between subject and object entities. FITCARL performs a search with length $L = 3$, where it finds an entity *Military Personnel (Nigeria)* that is in a negative relationship with both *Future Movement* and *Miguel Ángel Rodríguez*. FITCARL provides explanation by finding a reasoning path representing the proverb: The enemy of the enemy is my friend. For FITCARL without confidence learner, we find that it can also provide similar explanation by finding another entity that is also an enemy of *Military Personnel (Nigeria)*. However, it fails to find the ground truth answer because it neglects the confidence of each action. The confidence learner assigns high probability to the ground truth entity, leading to a correct prediction.

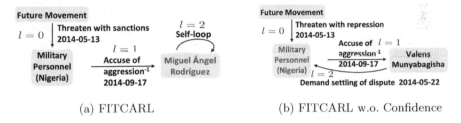

(a) FITCARL   (b) FITCARL w.o. Confidence

Fig. 5. Case study reasoning path visualization. The entity marked in red are the answer predicted by the model. w.o. means without. (Color figure online)

6   Conclusion

We present an RL-based TKGC method FITCARL to solve TKG few-shot OOG LP, where models are asked to predict the links concerning newly-emerged entities that have only a few observed associated facts. FITCARL is a meta-learning-based model trained with episodic training. It learns representations of newly-emerged entities by using a time-aware Transformer. To further alleviate the negative impact of the few-shot setting, a confidence learner is proposed to be coupled with the policy network for making better decisions. A parameter-free concept regularizer is also developed to better exploit concept-aware information in TKBs. Experimental results show that FITCARL achieves a new state-of-the-art and provides explainability.

References

1. Abboud, R., Ceylan, İ.İ., Lukasiewicz, T., Salvatori, T.: Boxe: a box embedding model for knowledge base completion. In: NeurIPS (2020)
2. Ammanabrolu, P., Hausknecht, M.J.: Graph constrained reinforcement learning for natural language action spaces. In: ICLR. OpenReview.net (2020)
3. Baek, J., Lee, D.B., Hwang, S.J.: Learning to extrapolate knowledge: transductive few-shot out-of-graph link prediction. In: NeurIPS (2020)
4. Balazevic, I., Allen, C., Hospedales, T.M.: Tucker: tensor factorization for knowledge graph completion. In: EMNLP/IJCNLP (1), pp. 5184–5193. Association for Computational Linguistics (2019)
5. Bordes, A., Usunier, N., García-Durán, A., Weston, J., Yakhnenko, O.: Translating embeddings for modeling multi-relational data. In: NIPS, pp. 2787–2795 (2013)
6. Boschee, E., Lautenschlager, J., O'Brien, S., Shellman, S., Starz, J., Ward, M.: ICEWS Coded Event Data (2015)
7. Chen, K., Wang, Y., Li, Y., Li, A.: Rotateqvs: representing temporal information as rotations in quaternion vector space for temporal knowledge graph completion. In: ACL (1), pp. 5843–5857. Association for Computational Linguistics (2022)
8. Chen, M., Zhang, W., Zhang, W., Chen, Q., Chen, H.: Meta relational learning for few-shot link prediction in knowledge graphs. In: EMNLP/IJCNLP (1), pp. 4216–4225. Association for Computational Linguistics (2019)
9. Cho, K., et al.: Learning phrase representations using RNN encoder-decoder for statistical machine translation. In: EMNLP, pp. 1724–1734. ACL (2014)
10. Ding, Z., He, B., Ma, Y., Han, Z., Tresp, V.: Learning meta representations of one-shot relations for temporal knowledge graph link prediction. CoRR abs/2205.10621 (2022)
11. Ding, Z., Ma, Y., He, B., Han, Z., Tresp, V.: A simple but powerful graph encoder for temporal knowledge graph completion. In: NeurIPS 2022 Temporal Graph Learning Workshop (2022)
12. Ding, Z., et al.: Forecasting question answering over temporal knowledge graphs. CoRR abs/2208.06501 (2022)
13. Ding, Z., Wu, J., He, B., Ma, Y., Han, Z., Tresp, V.: Few-shot inductive learning on temporal knowledge graphs using concept-aware information. In: 4th Conference on Automated Knowledge Base Construction (2022)
14. Guo, J., Kok, S.: Bique: biquaternionic embeddings of knowledge graphs. In: EMNLP (1), pp. 8338–8351. Association for Computational Linguistics (2021)
15. Hamaguchi, T., Oiwa, H., Shimbo, M., Matsumoto, Y.: Knowledge transfer for out-of-knowledge-base entities: a graph neural network approach. In: IJCAI, pp. 1802–1808. ijcai.org (2017)
16. He, Y., Wang, Z., Zhang, P., Tu, Z., Ren, Z.: VN network: embedding newly emerging entities with virtual neighbors. In: CIKM, pp. 505–514. ACM (2020)
17. Jung, J., Jung, J., Kang, U.: Learning to walk across time for interpretable temporal knowledge graph completion. In: KDD, pp. 786–795. ACM (2021)
18. Lacroix, T., Obozinski, G., Usunier, N.: Tensor decompositions for temporal knowledge base completion. In: ICLR. OpenReview.net (2020)
19. Leblay, J., Chekol, M.W.: Deriving validity time in knowledge graph. In: WWW (Companion Volume), pp. 1771–1776. ACM (2018)
20. Li, J., Tang, T., Zhao, W.X., Wei, Z., Yuan, N.J., Wen, J.: Few-shot knowledge graph-to-text generation with pretrained language models. In: ACL/IJCNLP (Findings). Findings of ACL, vol. ACL/IJCNLP 2021, pp. 1558–1568. Association for Computational Linguistics (2021)

21. Li, Z., et al.: Search from history and reason for future: two-stage reasoning on temporal knowledge graphs. In: ACL/IJCNLP (1), pp. 4732–4743. Association for Computational Linguistics (2021)
22. Lin, Y., Liu, Z., Sun, M., Liu, Y., Zhu, X.: Learning entity and relation embeddings for knowledge graph completion. In: AAAI, pp. 2181–2187. AAAI Press (2015)
23. Messner, J., Abboud, R., Ceylan, İ.İ.: Temporal knowledge graph completion using box embeddings. In: AAAI, pp. 7779–7787. AAAI Press (2022)
24. Mirtaheri, M., Rostami, M., Ren, X., Morstatter, F., Galstyan, A.: One-shot learning for temporal knowledge graphs. In: 3rd Conference on Automated Knowledge Base Construction (2021)
25. Nickel, M., Tresp, V., Kriegel, H.: A three-way model for collective learning on multi-relational data. In: ICML, pp. 809–816. Omnipress (2011)
26. Sadeghian, A., Armandpour, M., Colas, A., Wang, D.Z.: Chronor: rotation based temporal knowledge graph embedding. In: AAAI, pp. 6471–6479. AAAI Press (2021)
27. Saxena, A., Tripathi, A., Talukdar, P.P.: Improving multi-hop question answering over knowledge graphs using knowledge base embeddings. In: ACL, pp. 4498–4507. Association for Computational Linguistics (2020)
28. Schlichtkrull, M., Kipf, T.N., Bloem, P., van den Berg, R., Titov, I., Welling, M.: Modeling relational data with graph convolutional networks. In: Gangemi, A., et al. (eds.) ESWC 2018. LNCS, vol. 10843, pp. 593–607. Springer, Cham (2018). https://doi.org/10.1007/978-3-319-93417-4_38
29. Sheng, J., et al.: Adaptive attentional network for few-shot knowledge graph completion. In: EMNLP (1), pp. 1681–1691. Association for Computational Linguistics (2020)
30. Sun, H., Zhong, J., Ma, Y., Han, Z., He, K.: Timetraveler: reinforcement learning for temporal knowledge graph forecasting. In: EMNLP (1), pp. 8306–8319. Association for Computational Linguistics (2021)
31. Tresp, V., Esteban, C., Yang, Y., Baier, S., Krompaß, D.: Learning with memory embeddings. arXiv preprint arXiv:1511.07972 (2015)
32. Trouillon, T., Welbl, J., Riedel, S., Gaussier, É., Bouchard, G.: Complex embeddings for simple link prediction. In: ICML, JMLR Workshop and Conference Proceedings, vol. 48, pp. 2071–2080. JMLR.org (2016)
33. Tucker, L.R.: The extension of factor analysis to three-dimensional matrices. In: Gulliksen, H., Frederiksen, N. (eds.) Contributions to Mathematical Psychology, pp. 110–127. Holt, Rinehart and Winston, New York (1964)
34. Vashishth, S., Sanyal, S., Nitin, V., Talukdar, P.P.: Composition-based multi-relational graph convolutional networks. In: ICLR. OpenReview.net (2020)
35. Vaswani, A., et al.: Attention is all you need. In: NIPS, pp. 5998–6008 (2017)
36. Vinyals, O., Blundell, C., Lillicrap, T., Kavukcuoglu, K., Wierstra, D.: Matching networks for one shot learning. In: NIPS, pp. 3630–3638 (2016)
37. Wang, P., Han, J., Li, C., Pan, R.: Logic attention based neighborhood aggregation for inductive knowledge graph embedding. In: AAAI, pp. 7152–7159. AAAI Press (2019)
38. Wang, R., et al.: Learning to sample and aggregate: few-shot reasoning over temporal knowledge graphs. In: NeurIPS (2022)
39. Wu, J., Cao, M., Cheung, J.C.K., Hamilton, W.L.: Temp: temporal message passing for temporal knowledge graph completion. In: EMNLP (1), pp. 5730–5746. Association for Computational Linguistics (2020)

40. Xiong, W., Yu, M., Chang, S., Guo, X., Wang, W.Y.: One-shot relational learning for knowledge graphs. In: EMNLP, pp. 1980–1990. Association for Computational Linguistics (2018)
41. Xu, C., Chen, Y., Nayyeri, M., Lehmann, J.: Temporal knowledge graph completion using a linear temporal regularizer and multivector embeddings. In: NAACL-HLT, pp. 2569–2578. Association for Computational Linguistics (2021)
42. Xu, C., Nayyeri, M., Alkhoury, F., Yazdi, H.S., Lehmann, J.: Tero: a time-aware knowledge graph embedding via temporal rotation. In: COLING, pp. 1583–1593. International Committee on Computational Linguistics (2020)
43. Yang, B., Yih, W., He, X., Gao, J., Deng, L.: Embedding entities and relations for learning and inference in knowledge bases. In: ICLR (Poster) (2015)
44. Zhang, F., Zhang, Z., Ao, X., Zhuang, F., Xu, Y., He, Q.: Along the time: timeline-traced embedding for temporal knowledge graph completion. In: CIKM, pp. 2529–2538. ACM (2022)
45. Zhang, Y., Dai, H., Kozareva, Z., Smola, A.J., Song, L.: Variational reasoning for question answering with knowledge graph. In: AAAI, pp. 6069–6076. AAAI Press (2018)

Clifford Embeddings – A Generalized Approach for Embedding in Normed Algebras

Caglar Demir$^{(\boxtimes)}$ (ID) and Axel-Cyrille Ngonga Ngomo (ID)

Data Science Research Group, Paderborn University, Paderborn, Germany
{caglar.demir,axel.ngonga}@upb.de

Abstract. A growing number of knowledge graph embedding models exploit the characteristics of division algebras (e.g., $\mathbb{R}$, $\mathbb{C}$, $\mathbb{H}$, and $\mathbb{O}$) to learn embeddings. Yet, recent empirical results suggest that the suitability of algebras is contingent upon the knowledge graph being embedded. In this work, we tackle the challenge of selecting the algebra within which a given knowledge graph should be embedded by exploiting the fact that Clifford algebras $Cl_{p,q}$ generalize over $\mathbb{R}$, $\mathbb{C}$, $\mathbb{H}$, and $\mathbb{O}$. Our embedding approach, KECI, is the first knowledge graph embedding model that can parameterize the algebra within which it operates. With KECI, the selection of an underlying algebra becomes a part of the learning process. Specifically, KECI starts the training process by learning real-valued embeddings for entities and relations in $\mathbb{R}^m = Cl_{0,0}^m$. At each mini-batch update, KECI can steer the training process from $Cl_{p,q}^m$ to $Cl_{p+1,q}^m$ or $Cl_{p,q+1}^m$ by processing the training loss. In this way, KECI can decide the algebra within which it operates in a data-driven fashion. Consequently, KECI is a generalization of previous approaches such as DistMult, ComplEx, QuatE, and OMult. Our evaluation suggests that KECI outperforms state-of-the-art embedding approaches on seven benchmark datasets. We provide an open-source implementation of KECI, including pre-trained models, training and evaluation scripts (https://github.com/dice-group/dice-embeddings).

Keywords: Knowledge Graphs · Embeddings · Theory Unification

1 Introduction

A plethora of knowledge graph embedding (KGE) models have been developed over the last decade [7,33,34]. Most KGE models map entities $e \in \mathcal{E}$ and relations $r \in \mathcal{R}$ found in a knowledge graph (KG) $\mathcal{G} \subseteq \mathcal{E} \times \mathcal{R} \times \mathcal{E}$ to $\mathbb{V}$, where $\mathbb{V}$ is a d-dimensional vector space and $d \in \mathbb{N}\backslash\{0\}$ [17]. This family of models is currently one of the most popular means to make KGs amenable to vectorial machine learning [33] and has been used in applications including drug discovery, community detection, recommendation, question answering [3,14,15,34]. While early models (e.g., RESCAL [24], DistMult [37]) express embeddings in $\mathbb{R}^d$ and perform well once tuned fittingly [28], later results suggest that embedding

D. Koutra et al. (Eds.): ECML PKDD 2023, LNAI 14171, pp. 567–582, 2023.
https://doi.org/10.1007/978-3-031-43418-1_34

using the more complex division algebras $\mathbb{C}$ and $\mathbb{H}$ can achieve a superior link prediction performance (measured in terms of hits at n, short h@n) [8,28,40,42]. This is at least partially due to the characteristics of (hyper)complex algebras (e.g., $\mathbb{C}$, $\mathbb{H}$) being used to account for logical properties such as the symmetry, asymmetry, and compositionality [30] of relations r found in the input data. While recent works have continued improving the performance of KGE models by including ever more complex neural architectures atop division algebras (see, e.g., ConvE [12], ConEx [9]), a fundamental assumption remains shared: $\mathbb{V}$ is fixed for each approach. This assumption has the advantages of being conducive to rapid implementation, execution and interpretation. However, its main disadvantage is well illustrated by experimental results from recent works [28]: The most adequate algebra for embedding a KG is contingent upon the data to embed. This finding is corroborated by our experimental results (see Fig. 1).

The link between algebras and KGEs can be directly entailed from formal treatments on embeddings. Consider ComplEx [32] embeddings for example. When a KG does not contain triples with an anti-symmetric relation (e.g., the bornIn or hasChild relations), embedding into $\mathbb{C}$ instead of $\mathbb{R}$ is of no advantage. On the contrary, the space and time requirements of an approach based on $\mathbb{C}$ are double that of an approach based on $\mathbb{R}$ (see Sect. 4). Similar insights can be derived for the division algebras $\mathbb{H}$ and $\mathbb{O}$ (see, e.g., QuatE [42] and ConvO [8]). Our goal therefore is to find a hypothesis space, i.e., a suitable algebra underlying $\mathbb{V}$ that is rich enough to embed the input knowledge graph, yet simple enough to ensure reliable generalization over unseen data. We implement this goal by presenting KECI. Our approach exploits the fact that Clifford Algebras $Cl_{p,q}$ (see Sect. 2.1 for an overview) generalize over common division algebras and aims to find a suitable algebra for a particular dataset in a data-driven fashion. We conceived of two ways to find a suitable algebra: (1) Consider p and q as two new hyperparameters to find a suitable $Cl_{p,q}$ or (2) scale the imaginary dimensions of $Cl_{p,q}$ according to the training loss. While finding a suitable $Cl_{p,q}$ via (1) is computationally expensive as it requires multiple training phases, (2) is conceptually simpler. KECI is hence based on (2), and uses the cross-entropy training loss to decide whether it should increase the number of imaginary dimensions of the division algebra within which it operates. This process can be equated with starting the learning process in a small hypothesis space (e.g., $\mathbb{R} = Cl_{0,0}$) and steering the learning process towards a larger hypothesis space as required. Our experiments on seven benchmark datasets (WN18RR, FB15K-237, YAGO3-10, NELL-995-h25, NELL-995-h50, NELL-995-h75, UMLS, and KINSHIP) suggest that KECI outperforms DistMult, ComplEx, QMult and OMult across all datasets and benchmark metrics (MRR, Hit@1,Hit@3, and Hit@10).

2   Preliminaries and Notation

2.1   Clifford Algebras

A Clifford algebra $Cl_{p,q}(\mathbb{R})$ is an associative algebra (i.e., additions and multiplications are associative) generated by the $p + q$ orthonormal basis elements $e_1, \ldots, e_{p+q}$ for which the following relations hold:

$$e_i^2 = +1 \qquad \text{for} \ \ 1 \le i \le p \ , \tag{1}$$

$$e_j^2 = -1 \qquad \text{for} \ \ p < j \le p + q \ , \tag{2}$$

$$e_i e_j = -e_j e_i \ \ \text{for} \ \ i \ne j \ . \tag{3}$$

The lowest-dimensional Clifford algebra $Cl_{0,0}(\mathbb{R})$ is a zero-dimensional algebra with vector space $\mathbb{V}$ that is spanned by the basis element $\{1\}$. Hence, $Cl_{0,0}(\mathbb{R})$ is algebra-isomorphic to $\mathbb{R}$. Analogously, $Cl_{0,1}(\mathbb{R})$ is equivalent to $\mathbb{C}$, and $Cl_{0,2}(\mathbb{R})$ is equivalent to $\mathbb{H}$ [5,16]. In fact, the spaces used by a large portion of the state-of-the-art KGE models are (sub-) algebras of some $Cl_{p,q}(\mathbb{R})$ (see Sect. 3 and Table 1).

2.2 Knowledge Graphs

A KG represents structured collections of assertions describing the world [17]. Formally, a KG is often defined as a set of triples $\mathcal{G} := \{(h, r, t) \in \mathcal{E} \times \mathcal{R} \times \mathcal{E}\}$, where $\mathcal{E}$ and $\mathcal{R}$ stand for a set of entities and a set of relations, respectively [1,2,12]. Each triple $(h, r, t) \in \mathcal{G}$ represents an assertion based on two entities $h, t \in \mathcal{E}$ and a relation $r \in \mathcal{R}$. A relation r is *symmetric* iff $(h, r, t) \Longleftrightarrow (t, r, h)$ holds. Analogously, r is *anti-symmetric* iff $(h, r, t) \in \mathcal{G} \Rightarrow (t, r, h) \notin \mathcal{G}$ for all $h \ne t$. Most publicly available KGs contain missing and erroneous assertions [17]. These triples can be inferred from an existing set of triples by means of designing logical rules or learning continuous vector representations via knowledge graph embedding models [22].

2.3 Knowledge Graph Embeddings

Most KGE models learn continuous vector representations tailored towards link prediction [6,17]. They are often defined as parameterized scoring functions $\phi_\Theta : \mathcal{E} \times \mathcal{R} \times \mathcal{E} \mapsto \mathbb{R}$, where Θ denotes parameters and often comprise entity embeddings $\mathbf{E} \in \mathbb{V}^{|\mathcal{E}| \times d_e}$, relation embeddings $\mathbf{R} \in \mathbb{V}^{|\mathcal{R}| \times d_r}$, and additional parameters (e.g., affine transformations, batch normalizations, convolutions) [1,8]. Since $d_e = d_r$ holds for many models including models reported in Table 1, we will use d to signify the number of real parameters used for the embedding of an entity or relation Given $(h, r, t) \in \mathcal{E} \times \mathcal{R} \times \mathcal{E}$, the prediction $\hat{y} := \phi_\Theta(h, r, t)$ signals the likelihood of (h, r, t) being true [12,33,41]. Since $\mathcal{G}$ contains only assertions that are assumed to be true, assertions assumed to be false are often generated by applying the negative sampling, 1vsAll or Kvsall training strategies [28]. Throughout this paper, we will denote embeddings with bold fonts, i.e., the embedding of h will be denoted $\mathbf{h}$. Moreover, we use $\circ$ and $\cdot$ to denote an element-wise vector multiplication and an inner product in $\mathbb{V}$, respectively.

3 Related Work

In the last decade, a plethora of KGE models have been successfully applied to tackle various tasks, including link prediction, class expression learning, drug discovery among many others [3,11,12,25,28,33,38,39]. Most KGE models are designed to operate in a pre-determined vector space $\mathbb{V}$ based on a normed division algebra to learn embeddings for entities and relations tailored towards predicting missing links. Most of these models can be unified under *a feature composition operator* followed by *an approximation operator* in a respective division algebra. Given a triple (h, r, t), most KGE models $\phi_\Theta : \mathcal{E} \times \mathcal{R} \times \mathcal{E} \mapsto \mathbb{R}$ computes a triple score via linear operations (e.g., element-wise multiplications or additions) on $\mathbf{h}$, $\mathbf{r}$, and $\mathbf{t}$ [4,8,32,37,40,42].

3.1   Inner Product vs Distance

A large portion of the existing KGE approaches can be regarded as instances of one of two paradigms. RESCAL [24], DistMult [37], ComplEx [32], ComplEx-N3 [19], QuatE, OctonionE [42], QMult, and OMult [8] can be unified under the inner product paradigm, where an inner product is used as an approximation operator in a preselected vector space $\mathbb{V}$. TransE [4], TransH [35], TransR [20], CTransR [20], TransD [18], TransO [40], and RotatE [29] can be regarded as belonging to the distance paradigm, where a distance (e.g., the Euclidean distance) is used as an approximation operator in a selected vector space $\mathbb{V}$. Given a triple (h, r, t), all aforementioned models apply element-wise multiplication or addition to obtain a composite representation of the head entity embedding $\mathbf{h}$ and the relation embedding $\mathbf{r}$ in $\mathbb{V}$. A scalar real-valued prediction $\hat{y} := \phi_\Theta(h, r, t)$ is obtained via an inner product or a distance between a resulting composite representation and the tail entity embedding $\mathbf{t}$.

Table 1. State-of-the-art embedding approaches and algebras used for embeddings

Models	Vector Space	$\subseteq Cl_{p,q}(\mathbb{R})$
TransE, DistMult, RESCAL	$\mathbb{R}$	$Cl_{0,0}$
ComplEx, RotatE, ConEx	$\mathbb{C}$	$Cl_{0,1}$
QuatE, QMult, DensE	$\mathbb{H}$	$Cl_{0,2}$
OMult, OctonionE	$\mathbb{O}$	$Cl_{1,3}$

To obtain a more expressive composite representation of $\mathbf{h}$ and $\mathbf{r}$, various KGE models (e.g., HolE [23], ConvE [12], HypER [1], ConvKB [21], ConEx [9], ConvQ [8], ConvO [8] and AcrE [27]) apply 1D or 2D convolutions followed by an non-linear affine transformation as a feature composition operator. These convolution-based models aim to learn a complex composite representation of h and r that is ideally approximately equal to $\mathbf{t}$, while maintaining a parameter efficiency.

3.2   Selecting $\mathbb{V}$

The vector space $\mathbb{V}$ can encode useful prior knowledge that enable KGE models to infer missing triples. For instance, given a triple (h, r, t), DistMult computes a triple score via $(\mathbf{h} \circ \mathbf{r}) \cdot \mathbf{t}$, where $\mathbf{h}, \mathbf{r}, \mathbf{t} \in \mathbb{R}^d$, $\circ$ denotes the element-wise vector multiplication, and $\cdot$ stands for the inner product in $\mathbb{V} = \mathbb{R}$. This formulation leads DistMult to enjoy the linear time and space complexity of multiplication and inner product in $\mathbb{R}$. However, although DistMult can accurately infer missing triples with symmetric relations, missing triples with anti-symmetric relations cannot be accurately inferred. To alleviate this shortcoming and retain parameter and computational efficiency, ComplEx extends DistMult into $\mathbb{C}$, where $\circ$ denotes the element-wise complex vector multiplication and $\cdot$ is a Hermitian inner product. Since this inner product in $\mathbb{C}$ is symmetric in $\mathrm{Re}(\cdot)$ and anti-symmetric in $\mathrm{Im}(\cdot)$, triples with anti-symmetric relations can be accurately predicted [31].

Overall, recent empirical results suggest that the suitability of an algebra is contingent upon the input KG that is to be embedded. For instance, ComplEx outperforms DistMult by absolute 0.5% and 2.2% MRR scores on FB15K-237 and WN18RR, respectively, provided that the models are well tuned and $d = 256$ [28]. On the other hand, a recent work shows that DistMult outperforms ComplEx by 2.1% absolute MRR on FB15K-237, while ComplEx outperforms DistMult by 2.4% and 0.5% absolute MRR on WN18RR and YAGO3-10, respectively. Note that in this experiment, DistMult operates on $\mathbb{R}^{100}$ and ComplEx on $\mathbb{C}^{50}$ [9].[1] Similarly, another recent work suggests that in a low-dimensional setting with $d = 32$, DistMult outperforms ComplEx by 3.5% and 3.2% absolute MRR on FB15K-238 and NELL-995-h100, respectively, while ComplEx outperforms DistMult by 3.6% absolute MRR score on WN18RR [13]. Another recent clinical study pertaining to drug discovery with $d = 200$ shows that the recall@200 performance of ComplEx is 5.7% higher than the performance of DistMult [25]. Many other recent works–including [9, 13, 25, 28]–indicate similar dependencies of the suitability of an algebra on the input KG. On the application side, studies such as Bonner et al. [3] show that determining the selection criteria of a particular KGE model over another real datasets is a viable question. They highlight the importance of understanding the properties of such models w.r.t. the input dataset to improve drug discovery efforts.

We argue that the selection of the algebra underlying the vector space $\mathbb{V}$ within which a KGE model learns embeddings for a given KGE can be a part of the learning problem. In Sect. 4, we introduce the first KGE model that does not only learn embeddings for entities and relations but also a suitable algebra for $\mathbb{V}$ by means of a dimension scaling technique.

4 Methodology

4.1 Clifford Embeddings

Given a triple $(h, r, t) \in \mathcal{G}$, let $\mathbf{h}, \mathbf{r}, \mathbf{t} \in Cl_{p,q}(\mathbb{R}^m)$ denote three multi-vectors representing embeddings of the head entity h, the relation r and the tail entity t, respectively. We defined the multivector $\mathbf{h}$ as

---

[1] Note that the two models have the same complexity w.r.t. the number of real numbers necessary to represent the final embeddings as every element of $\mathbb{C}$ is encoded via two real numbers.

$$\mathbf{h} = h_0 + \sum_{i=1}^{p} h_i e_i + \sum_{j=p+1}^{p+q} h_j e_j, \tag{4}$$

where $h_{(.)} \in \mathbb{R}^m$ with $m = \lfloor d/(p+q+1) \rfloor$. The vectors $\mathbf{r}$ and $\mathbf{t}$ are defined analogously. Hence, every embedding vector can be represented by at most d real numbers. The Clifford multiplication of $\mathbf{h}$ and $\mathbf{r}$ is given by

$$\mathbf{h} \circ \mathbf{r} = h_0 r_0 \qquad + \sum_{i=1}^{p} h_0 r_i e_i \qquad + \sum_{j=p+1}^{p+q} h_0 r_j e_j \tag{5}$$

$$+ \sum_{i=1}^{p} h_i r_0 e_i \qquad + \sum_{i=1}^{p}\sum_{k=1}^{p} h_i r_k e_i e_k \qquad + \sum_{i=1}^{p}\sum_{j=p+1}^{p+q} h_i r_j e_i e_j \tag{6}$$

$$+ \sum_{j=p+1}^{p+q} h_j r_0 e_j \quad + \sum_{j=p+1}^{p+q}\sum_{i=1}^{p} h_j r_i e_j e_i \quad + \sum_{j=p+1}^{p+q}\sum_{k=p+1}^{p+q} h_j r_k e_j e_k. \tag{7}$$

Grouping the terms using the bases and applying the Clifford algebra bases rules (see Sect. 2.1) simplifies the above expression to

$$\mathbf{h} \circ \mathbf{r} = \sigma_0 + \sigma_p + \sigma_q + \sigma_{p,p} + \sigma_{q,q} + \sigma_{p,q}, \tag{8}$$

where $\sigma_{(.)}$ are defined as

$$\sigma_0 = h_0 r_0 + \sum_{i=1}^{p} h_i r_i - \sum_{j=p+1}^{p+q} h_j r_j, \tag{9}$$

$$\sigma_p = \sum_{i=1}^{p} (h_0 r_i + h_i r_0) e_i, \tag{10}$$

$$\sigma_q = \sum_{j=p+1}^{p+q} (h_0 r_j + h_j r_0) e_j, \tag{11}$$

$$\sigma_{p,p} = \sum_{i=1}^{p-1}\sum_{k=i+1}^{p} (h_i r_k - h_k r_i) e_i e_k, \tag{12}$$

$$\sigma_{q,q} = \sum_{j=1}^{p+q-1}\sum_{k=j+1}^{p+q} (h_j r_k - h_k r_j) e_j e_k, \tag{13}$$

$$\sigma_{p,q} = \sum_{i=1}^{p}\sum_{j=p+1}^{p+q} (h_i r_j - h_j r_i) e_i e_j. \tag{14}$$

4.2   Scoring Function Based on Inner Product

Given a triple (h, r, t) and the respective multi-vector embeddings of $\mathbf{h}, \mathbf{r}, \mathbf{t} \in Cl_{p,q}(\mathbb{R}^m)$, KECI's scoring function is given by

$$\text{KECI}(h, r, t)_{p,q} = (\mathbf{h} \circ \mathbf{r}) \cdot \mathbf{t}, \tag{15}$$

where $\cdot$ denotes the inner product between two multi-vectors in $Cl_{p,q}(\mathbb{R}^m)$. Distributing the components of $\mathbf{t}$ simplifies to

$$\text{KECI}(h, r, t)_{p,q} = h_0 r_0 t_0 + \sum_{i=1}^{p} (h_i r_i t_0) - \sum_{j=p+1}^{p+q} (h_j r_j t_0) \tag{16}$$

$$+ \sum_{i=1}^{p} (h_0 r_i t_i + h_i r_0 t_i) e_i \tag{17}$$

$$+ \sum_{j=p+1}^{p+q} (h_0 r_j t_j + r_0 h_j t_j) e_j \tag{18}$$

$$+ \sigma_{p,p} + \sigma_{q,q} + \sigma_{p,q}. \tag{19}$$

Therefore, KECI can be classified as a knowledge graph embedding model using element-wise multiplication as a feature composition operator and the inner product as an approximation operator. Hence, KECI is akin to DistMult, ComplEx, QMult and OMult depending on p and q. More specifically, selecting $p = q = 0$ leads $\text{KECI}(h, r, t)_{0,0}$ to generalize to DistMult:

$$\text{KECI}(h, r, t)_{p,q} = h_0 \circ r_0 \cdot t_0 = \langle \text{Re}(\mathbf{h}), \text{Re}(\mathbf{r}), \text{Re}(\mathbf{t}) \rangle, \tag{20}$$

where $\mathbf{h}, \mathbf{r}, \mathbf{t} \in Cl_{0,0}(\mathbb{R}^d)$, hence, $h_0, r_0, t_0 \in \mathbb{R}^{m=d}$. Similarly, selecting $p = 0 \land q = 1$ leads to $\text{KECI}(h, r, t)_{0,1}$, which is equivalent to ComplEx.

$$\text{KECI}(h, r, t)_{p,q} = \mathbf{h} \circ \mathbf{r} \cdot \mathbf{t} = \langle \text{Re}(\mathbf{h}), \text{Re}(\mathbf{r}), \text{Re}(\mathbf{t}) \rangle \tag{21}$$

$$+ \langle \text{Re}(\mathbf{h}), \text{Im}(\mathbf{r}), \text{Im}(\mathbf{t}) \rangle \tag{22}$$

$$+ \langle \text{Im}(\mathbf{h}), \text{Re}(\mathbf{r}), \text{Im}(\mathbf{t}) \rangle \tag{23}$$

$$- \langle \text{Im}(\mathbf{h}), \text{Im}(\mathbf{r}), \text{Re}(\mathbf{t}) \rangle, \tag{24}$$

where $\mathbf{h}, \mathbf{r}, \mathbf{t} \in \mathbb{C}^{\frac{d}{2}}$. This clearly shows that the triple score computed by KECI does not only depend on learned embeddings of h, r, t but also parameterization of an algebra.

4.3   Learning to Scale Dimensions in $Cl_{p,q}(\mathbb{R})$

Remember that we argue that the selection of the vector space within which a KGE operates should be a part of the learning problem. Hence, instead of fixing p and q for KECI, we argue that KECI should be endowed with the capability of selecting a particular subspace of $Cl_{p,q}$ to operate in.

We propose to learn coefficients $\alpha_1, \ldots \alpha_{p+q}$ for the orthonormal bases $e_1, \ldots e_{p+q}$ of $Cl_{p,q}(\mathbb{R})$, where $\alpha_i \in \mathbb{R}$. Entity embeddings and relation embeddings are now of the forms

$$\mathbf{h}_\alpha = h_0 + \sum_{i=1}^{p} h_i \alpha_i e_i + \sum_{j=p+1}^{p+q} h_j \alpha_j e_j, \text{ and} \tag{25}$$

$$\mathbf{r}_\alpha = r_0 + \sum_{i=1}^{p} r_i \alpha_i e_i + \sum_{j=p+1}^{p+q} r_j \alpha_j e_j, \tag{26}$$

where $\alpha_i, \alpha_j \in \mathbb{R}$ are trainable coefficients for each base vectors. Initializing $\alpha_1, \ldots, \alpha_{p+q} = 0$ leads KECI to start the training process as DistMult in $\mathbb{R}^m$, where $m = \lfloor d/(p+q+1) \rfloor$. Hence, for a given (h, r, t), a triple score is computed as

$$\mathbf{h}_\alpha \circ \mathbf{h}_\alpha \cdot \mathbf{t}_\alpha = h_0 \circ r_0 \cdot t_0, \tag{27}$$

where the valued represented along e_1, e_{p+q} are scaled down to 0. During training, $\alpha_1, \ldots, \alpha_{p+q}$ can be updated iteratively on the basis of the training loss. More specifically, let $\mathcal{L}$ denote the cross-entropy loss function that is defined as

$$\mathcal{L}(y, \hat{y}) = -y\log(\hat{y}) - (1 - y)\log(1 - \hat{y}), \tag{28}$$

where y denotes a binary label of a given triple (h, r, t) and $\hat{y} = \sigma(\phi_\Theta(h, r, t))$ denotes a prediction obtained via the logistic sigmoid function $(\sigma(x) = \frac{1}{1+e^{-x}})$. Moreover, let $\frac{d\mathcal{L}}{d\alpha_i}$ denote the derivative of $\mathcal{L}$ w.r.t. α_i on a single data point (h, r, t). Therefore, a coefficient α_i is updated on the bases of h_i and r_i, $\frac{d\mathcal{L}}{dh_i\alpha_i}h_i + \frac{d\mathcal{L}}{dr_i\alpha_i}r_i$. In the mini-batch training setting, α_i is updated with a batch of respective terms. Consequently, updating α_i in the negative direction of the gradients assists to decrease the loss further. Hence, KECI can learn to select a particular subspace of $Cl_{p,q}$ that is more favorable to decrease the training loss.

5   Experiments

5.1   Datasets

We used the benchmark datasets UMLS, KINSHIP, NELL-995 h25, NELL-995 h50, NELL-995 h100, FB15K-237, and YAGO3-10 for the link prediction problem. An overview of the datasets is provided in Table 2. UMLS describes relationships between medical entities and their relationships, e.g., immunologic_factor, disrupts, and cell. KINSHIP describes the 25 different kinship relations of the Alyawarra tribe and UMLS describes 135 medical entities via 46 relations describing [30]. FB15K-237 and YAGO3-10 are subsets of Freebase and YAGO [12]. They contain information about a general domain, e.g., Stephen_Hawking, and Copley_Medal. The Never-Ending Language Learning datasets NELL-995 h25, NELL-995 h50, and NELL-995 h100 are designed to evaluate multi-hop reasoning capabilities [36].

Table 2. An overview of datasets in terms of number of entities, number of relations, and node degrees in the train split along with the number of triples in each split of the dataset.

Dataset	$|\mathcal{E}|$	$|\mathcal{R}|$	$|\mathcal{G}^{\text{Train}}|$	$|\mathcal{G}^{\text{Validation}}|$	$|\mathcal{G}^{\text{Test}}|$
UMLS	135	46	5,216	652	661
KINSHIP	104	25	8,544	1,068	1,074
NELL-995 h100	22,411	43	50,314	3,763	3,746
NELL-995 h50	34,667	86	72,767	5,440	5,393
NELL-995 h25	70,145	172	122,618	9,194	9,187
FB15K-237	14,541	237	272,115	17,535	20,466
YAGO3-10	123,182	37	1,079,040	5,000	5,000

5.2 Experimental Setup and Optimization

Throughout our experiments, we use the cross-entropy loss function to train each knowledge graph embedding model. We evaluated the link prediction performance of models with benchmark metrics (filtered MRR, Hits@1,Hits@3, and Hits@10). We did not used any regularization technique (e.g., dropout technique or L2 regularization) as we report the training and validation performance of each model on each dataset. Throughout our experiments, each entity and relation is represented with 32-dimensional real valued vector across datasets and models as in [6,13]. Hence, DistMult, ComplEx, QMult, and OMult learn embeddings in $\mathbb{R}^{32}, \mathbb{C}^{16}, \mathbb{H}^{8}$, and $\mathbb{O}^{4}$, respectively. Consequently, all models have the same number of parameters. We report the training, validation and test results to prove a finer-grained overview of performance across datasets and models. We use the Adam optimizer with 0.1 learning rate and train each model for 256 epochs with the batch size of 1024. The implementation of KECI can be found in the dice-embedding framework [10]. Therein, we also provided the pre-trained models[2].

6 Results

6.1 Exhaustive Search

The goal of our first series of experiments was to verify that the performance of KECI is contingent upon different values for p and q. Hence, we did not perform any dimension scaling and tried all combinations of $p \le 4$ and $q \le 4$. Note that we only kept one copy of (p, q) pairs for each equivalent class of $Cl_{p,q}$. For example, $Cl_{1,1}$ is isomorphic to $Cl_{0,2}$.

Figure 1 shows the MRR trajectories of KECI with different (p, q) pairs on the UMLS and KINSHIP benchmark datasets. At the end of each training epoch, the MRR performances on the training and validation splits was registered and

---

[2] https://github.com/dice-group/dice-embeddings#pre-trained-models.

is reported. These results corroborate our hypothesis: The link prediction performance substantially vary depending on the selection of algebras. For instance, KECI performs well with $Cl_{0,1}$ and $Cl_{4,3}$ on both datasets, whereas KECI performs poorly with $Cl_{0,0}$ and $Cl_{3,0}$. Figure 1 also shows that $Cl_{0,0}$, $Cl_{0,1}$, $Cl_{3,4}$ greatly suffer from overfitting, whereas this is not observed for $Cl_{4,3}$.

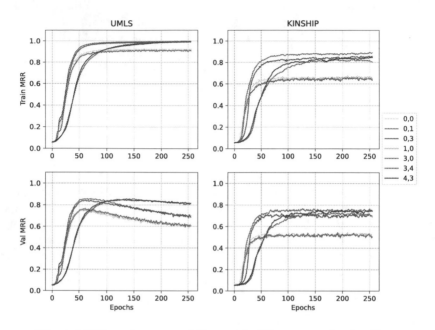

Fig. 1. MRR performance of KECI with different p and q for $Cl_{p,q}$.

Depending on the selection of $Cl_{p,q}$, KECI can greatly benefit from the early stopping technique on UMLS, e.g., terminating the training after observing consecutive decreases in the validation performance [26]. For instance, although KECI with $Cl_{0,1}$ reaches its peak generalization performance around 50–75 epochs, training longer decreases its generalization performance. Yet, a possible overfitting is not observed for any configuration on KINSHIP.

6.2   Comparison with Other Approaches

Tables 3, 4, 5 report the link prediction results on WN18RR, FB15K-237, YAGO3-10, NELL-995-h25, NELL-995-h50, and NELL-995-h75, respectively. We report the link prediction performance of models on the training, validation, and test splits of the respective dataset to allow for a fine-grained performance analysis, e.g., by allowing for overfitting/underfitting to be detected. KECI is trained with the dimension scaling technique (elucidated in Sect. 4.3). Overall, our results corroborates our hypothesis: the suitability of algebras is contingent upon the dataset that is to be embedded. For instance, although DistMult reaches the second best performance on FB15K-237, YAGO3-10, and WN18RR, DistMult performs poorly on NELL-995-h25, UMLS, and KINSHIP. Similarly, although QMult outperforms DistMult, ComplEx, and OMult on FB15K-237, QMult performs poorly on NELL-995-h25, NELL-995-h50, and KINSHIP. Note that all models have the same number of parameters, i.e., DistMult, ComplEx, QMult, OMult, and KECI operate in $\mathbb{R}^d, \mathbb{C}^{d/2}, \mathbb{H}^{d/4} \mathbb{O}^{d/4}$, and $Cl_{p,q}(\mathbb{R}^m)$. Note that each baseline model applies an element-wise vector multiplication followed by an inner product in a respectively fixed algebra, whereas KECI begins the search in $\mathbb{R} = Cl_{0,0}$ and updates the coefficients of the $p + q$ base vectors based on the training loss further as elucidated in Sect. 4.3.

Table 3. Link prediction results on FB15K-237, YAGO3-10 and WN18RR. All models have the same number of parameters. Each entity and relation is represented with 32-dimensional real valued vector. Each sequence of three rows for a model report the model performance on the training, validation and test datasets. Bold and underlined results indicate the best results and second best results.

Models	FB15K-237				YAGO3-10				WN18RR			
	MRR	@1	@3	@10	MRR	@1	@3	@10	MRR	@1	@3	@10
DistMult	0.365	0.259	0.412	0.573	0.644	0.564	0.691	0.794	0.932	0.885	0.978	0.993
	0.212	0.140	0.236	0.355	0.252	0.182	0.275	0.385	0.353	0.342	0.357	0.372
	<u>0.213</u>	<u>0.141</u>	<u>0.235</u>	<u>0.351</u>	<u>0.247</u>	<u>0.174</u>	<u>0.278</u>	<u>0.382</u>	<u>0.351</u>	<u>0.340</u>	<u>0.353</u>	<u>0.371</u>
ComplEx	0.336	0.237	0.379	0.534	0.623	0.543	0.669	0.773	0.906	0.879	0.927	0.948
	0.196	0.128	0.214	0.332	0.227	0.158	0.249	0.364	0.308	0.277	0.326	0.359
	0.197	0.129	0.218	0.333	0.230	0.156	0.257	0.373	0.313	0.282	0.331	0.364
QMult	0.338	0.238	0.381	0.537	0.471	0.382	0.516	0.642	0.996	0.996	0.996	0.997
	0.210	0.143	0.229	0.343	0.176	0.113	0.195	0.300	0.313	0.278	0.337	0.366
	0.207	0.139	0.226	0.341	0.179	0.112	0.202	0.309	0.308	0.274	0.332	0.361
OMult	0.323	0.226	0.362	0.517	0.429	0.334	0.479	0.610	0.977	0.971	0.982	0.988
	0.195	0.131	0.210	0.327	0.160	0.099	0.177	0.282	0.298	0.269	0.314	0.353
	0.192	0.127	0.206	0.325	0.163	0.100	0.181	0.288	0.295	0.263	0.314	0.353
KECI	0.496	0.390	0.551	0.699	0.664	0.579	0.718	0.821	0.967	0.952	0.982	0.989
	0.268	0.191	0.291	0.421	0.260	0.180	0.293	0.414	0.357	0.343	0.365	0.379
	0.262	**0.185**	**0.286**	**0.419**	**0.265**	**0.187**	**0.295**	**0.414**	**0.354**	**0.341**	**0.359**	**0.377**

Table 3 show that KECI finds a suitable subspace of $Cl_{p,q}$ that leads to better training, validation and test performances across datasets. KECI outperforms all models in all metrics on FB15K-237 and YAGO3-10. Although KECI starts the training process as DistMult, KECI finds a subspace of $Cl_{p,q}$ that fits the training data better. For instance, KECI outperforms DistMult by 13.1% absolute difference in MRR on the training split of FB15K-237. Surprisingly, although KECI and QMult reach similar performances on the training split of WN18RR, KECI generalizes better than QMult on WN18RR. This may indicate that learning coefficients for each imaginary dimension of $Cl_{p,q}$ acts as a regularizer. We also observe that as the size of the underlying algebras grows, the performance of a respective model decreases on FB15K-237 and YAGO3-10, e.g., DistMult and ComplEx outperform QMult and OMult in all metrics on FB15K-237 and

YAGO3-10. Hence, as the size of the algebra grows, increasing the embedding size d may be beneficial depending on the input dataset Similarly observation is also reported in [13]. Table 3 also show that all models greatly suffer from overfitting on all datasets, particularly, on WN18RR. This highlights the importance of applying regularization.

Tables 4 and 5 show that KECI generalizes better than all baselines on NELL, UMLS, and KINSHIP benchmark datasets. KECI outperforms all baselines models on NELL-005-h25 in all metrics, while baselines reach better training performance on the other NELL datasets.

Table 4. Link prediction results on NELL-995-h25, NELL-995-h50, and NELL-995-h75. All models have the same number of parameters. Each entity and relation is represented with 32-dimensional real valued vector. Each three rows for a model report performance on the training, validation and test datasets. Bold and underlined results indicate the best results and second best results.

Models	NELL-995-h25				NELL-995-h50				NELL-995-h75			
	MRR	@1	@3	@10	MRR	@1	@3	@10	MRR	@1	@3	@10
DistMult	0.683	0.614	0.725	0.808	0.890	0.840	0.930	0.972	0.929	0.893	0.958	0.984
	0.144	0.101	0.157	0.227	0.170	0.117	0.191	0.275	0.166	0.115	0.180	0.272
	0.140	0.097	0.155	0.224	0.178	0.124	0.197	0.282	0.164	0.112	0.179	0.266
ComplEx	0.854	0.804	0.890	0.939	0.968	0.951	0.982	0.992	0.820	0.750	0.877	0.936
	0.165	0.113	0.182	0.265	0.142	0.090	0.157	0.246	0.138	0.093	0.153	0.223
	0.163	0.112	0.180	0.266	0.150	0.098	0.165	0.252	0.135	0.094	0.146	0.217
QMult	0.518	0.450	0.555	0.641	0.667	0.580	0.729	0.823	0.943	0.914	0.972	0.987
	0.113	0.079	0.123	0.179	0.118	0.075	0.134	0.198	0.145	0.094	0.158	0.249
	0.113	0.076	0.125	0.181	0.125	0.081	0.140	0.208	0.152	0.103	0.165	0.246
OMult	0.513	0.446	0.548	0.638	0.710	0.630	0.761	0.859	0.663	0.565	0.736	0.832
	0.109	0.072	0.119	0.181	0.155	0.102	0.170	0.262	0.109	0.071	0.118	0.179
	0.110	0.075	0.121	0.178	0.161	0.107	0.179	0.266	0.110	0.073	0.120	0.177
KECI	0.882	0.831	0.926	0.963	0.587	0.493	0.648	0.758	0.760	0.674	0.823	0.909
	0.207	0.152	0.229	0.314	0.227	0.162	0.256	0.354	0.225	0.158	0.253	0.356
	0.205	**0.152**	**0.224**	**0.310**	**0.227**	**0.161**	**0.254**	**0.355**	**0.216**	**0.152**	**0.242**	**0.341**

Table 5 shows that KECI outperforms all baselines in all metrics. ComplEx and QMult outperform KECI on the training split of UMLS in 4 metrics, whereas KECI outperform them considerably (up to absolute 15% in MRR). Importantly, although DistMult and KECI reaches similar performance in the training split in terms of MRR performance (e.g., 2% absolute difference in MRR), KECI generalizes considerably better than DisMult (e.g., circa 25% absolute difference in MRR). This is an important result as it implies that although KECI starts the search in $\mathbb{R}$ as DistMult does, KECI finds coefficients for base vectors that leads to an improvement in the generalization. We observe that although ComplEx, QMult and OMult reach on-par link prediction performance on the training dataset of UMLS, this observation cannot be made on KINSHIP. OMult performs worse than ComplEx, QMult on the training, validation and test splits of

Table 5. Link prediction results on UMLS and KINSHIP. All models have the same number of parameters. Each entity and relation is represented with 32-dimensional real valued vector. Each three rows per model report performance on the training, validation and test datasets, respectively. Bold and underlined results indicate the best results and second best results.

Models	UMLS				KINSHIP			
	MRR	@1	@3	@10	MRR	@1	@3	@10
DistMult	0.924	0.887	0.950	0.993	0.657	0.525	0.734	0.938
	0.607	0.471	0.679	0.883	0.511	0.349	0.589	0.874
	0.605	0.469	0.673	0.896	0.520	0.357	0.601	0.888
ComplEx	0.996	0.992	1.000	1.000	0.887	0.818	0.952	0.991
	0.686	0.536	0.801	0.941	0.751	0.627	0.851	0.962
	0.702	0.557	0.813	0.942	<u>0.738</u>	0.614	<u>0.834</u>	<u>0.964</u>
QMult	0.994	0.990	0.999	1.000	0.854	0.772	0.926	0.985
	0.716	0.596	0.807	0.938	0.712	0.575	0.815	0.949
	<u>0.722</u>	<u>0.590</u>	0.816	<u>0.952</u>	0.726	0.597	0.823	0.958
OMult	0.988	0.977	0.999	1.000	0.765	0.658	0.846	0.955
	0.716	0.587	0.810	0.942	0.626	0.481	0.726	0.917
	<u>0.722</u>	0.585	<u>0.836</u>	<u>0.952</u>	0.641	0.497	0.738	0.921
Keci	0.940	0.900	0.976	0.993	0.887	0.823	0.943	0.988
	0.854	0.775	0.919	0.973	0.768	0.648	0.867	0.970
	0.850	**0.768**	**0.917**	**0.976**	**0.764**	**0.644**	**0.855**	**0.974**

KINSHIP. This again corroborates our hypothesis that the selection of the algebra within which a knowledge graph embedding model operates has a tangible impact in the link prediction performance.

7 Conclusion

We introduced the first knowledge graph embedding model–Keci–that can parameterize the algebra within which embeddings for entities and relation are learned. With Keci, the selection of an underlying algebra can be performed in a data-driven fashion. Our extensive experiments on seven benchmark datasets suggest that this ability leads Keci to outperform state-of-the-art models in all metrics. Importantly, our results also show that Learning to scale embedding dimensions makes Keci more robust against overfitting.

Acknowledgements. This work has been supported by the HORIZON Europe research and innovation programme (GA No 101070305), by the Ministry of Culture and Science of North Rhine-Westphalia (GA No NW21-059D), by the German Research Foundation (GA No TRR 318/1 2021 - 438445824) and by the H2020 Marie Skłodowska-Curie programme (GA No 860801).

References

1. Balažević, I., Allen, C., Hospedales, T.M.: Hypernetwork knowledge graph embeddings. In: Tetko, I.V., Kůrková, V., Karpov, P., Theis, F. (eds.) ICANN 2019. LNCS, vol. 11731, pp. 553–565. Springer, Cham (2019). https://doi.org/10.1007/978-3-030-30493-5_52
2. Balažević, I., Allen, C., Hospedales, T.M.: TuckER: tensor factorization for knowledge graph completion. arXiv preprint arXiv:1901.09590 (2019)
3. Bonner, S., et al.: Understanding the performance of knowledge graph embeddings in drug discovery. Artif. Intell. Life Sci. **2**, 100036 (2022)
4. Bordes, A., Usunier, N., Garcia-Duran, A., Weston, J., Yakhnenko, O.: Translating embeddings for modeling multi-relational data. In: Advances in Neural Information Processing Systems, vol. 26 (2013)
5. Brandstetter, J., Berg, R.v.d., Welling, M., Gupta, J.K.: Clifford neural layers for PDE modeling. arXiv preprint arXiv:2209.04934 (2022)
6. Chami, I., Wolf, A., Juan, D.C., Sala, F., Ravi, S., Ré, C.: Low-dimensional hyperbolic knowledge graph embeddings. arXiv preprint arXiv:2005.00545 (2020)
7. Dai, Y., Wang, S., Xiong, N.N., Guo, W.: A survey on knowledge graph embedding: approaches, applications and benchmarks. Electronics **9**(5), 750 (2020)
8. Demir, C., Moussallem, D., Heindorf, S., Ngomo, A.C.N.: Convolutional hypercomplex embeddings for link prediction. In: Asian Conference on Machine Learning, pp. 656–671. PMLR (2021)
9. Demir, C., Ngomo, A.-C.N.: Convolutional complex knowledge graph embeddings. In: Verborgh, R., et al. (eds.) ESWC 2021. LNCS, vol. 12731, pp. 409–424. Springer, Cham (2021). https://doi.org/10.1007/978-3-030-77385-4_24
10. Demir, C., Ngomo, A.C.N.: Hardware-agnostic computation for large-scale knowledge graph embeddings. Softw. Impacts **13**, 100377 (2022)
11. Demir, C., Ngomo, A.C.N.: Learning permutation-invariant embeddings for description logic concepts. arXiv preprint arXiv:2303.01844 (2023)
12. Dettmers, T., Minervini, P., Stenetorp, P., Riedel, S.: Convolutional 2D knowledge graph embeddings. In: Proceedings of the AAAI Conference on Artificial Intelligence, vol. 32 (2018)
13. Gregucci, C., Nayyeri, M., Hernández, D., Staab, S.: Link prediction with attention applied on multiple knowledge graph embedding models. arXiv preprint arXiv:2302.06229 (2023)
14. Hamilton, W., Bajaj, P., Zitnik, M., Jurafsky, D., Leskovec, J.: Embedding logical queries on knowledge graphs. In: Advances in Neural Information Processing Systems, vol. 31 (2018)
15. Hamilton, W., Ying, Z., Leskovec, J.: Inductive representation learning on large graphs. In: Advances in Neural Information Processing Systems, vol. 30 (2017)
16. Hitzer, E.: Extending Lasenby's embedding of octonions in space-time algebra c l (1, 3) cl\left (1, 3\right), to all three-and four dimensional Clifford geometric algebras c l (p, q), n= p+ q= 3, 4 cl\left (p, q\right), n= p+ q= 3, 4. Mathematical Methods in the Applied Sciences (2022)
17. Hogan, A., et al.: Knowledge graphs. ACM Comput. Surv. (CSUR) **54**(4), 1–37 (2021)
18. Ji, G., He, S., Xu, L., Liu, K., Zhao, J.: Knowledge graph embedding via dynamic mapping matrix. In: Proceedings of the 53rd Annual Meeting of the Association for Computational Linguistics and the 7th International Joint Conference on Natural Language Processing (volume 1: Long papers), pp. 687–696 (2015)

19. Lacroix, T., Usunier, N., Obozinski, G.: Canonical tensor decomposition for knowledge base completion. In: International Conference on Machine Learning, pp. 2863–2872. PMLR (2018)

20. Lin, Y., Liu, Z., Sun, M., Liu, Y., Zhu, X.: Learning entity and relation embeddings for knowledge graph completion. In: Proceedings of the AAAI Conference on Artificial Intelligence, vol. 29 (2015)

21. Nguyen, D.Q., Nguyen, T.D., Nguyen, D.Q., Phung, D.: A novel embedding model for knowledge base completion based on convolutional neural network. In: Proceedings of the 2018 Conference of the North American Chapter of the Association for Computational Linguistics: Human Language Technologies, Volume 2 (Short Papers), pp. 327–333. Association for Computational Linguistics, New Orleans, Louisiana (2018). https://doi.org/10.18653/v1/N18-2053, https://aclanthology.org/N18-2053

22. Nickel, M., Murphy, K., Tresp, V., Gabrilovich, E.: A review of relational machine learning for knowledge graphs. Proc. IEEE **104**(1), 11–33 (2015)

23. Nickel, M., Rosasco, L., Poggio, T.: Holographic embeddings of knowledge graphs. In: Proceedings of the AAAI Conference on Artificial Intelligence, vol. 30 (2016)

24. Nickel, M., et al.: A three-way model for collective learning on multi-relational data. In: ICML, vol. 11, pp. 3104482–3104584 (2011)

25. Paliwal, S., de Giorgio, A., Neil, D., Michel, J.B., Lacoste, A.: Preclinical validation of therapeutic targets predicted by tensor factorization on heterogeneous graphs. Sci. Rep. **10**(1), 1–19 (2020)

26. Prechelt, L.: Early Stopping-but When? Neural Networks: Tricks of the Trade: Second Edition, pp. 53–67 (2012)

27. Ren, F., Li, J., Zhang, H., Liu, S., Li, B., Ming, R., Bai, Y.: Knowledge graph embedding with atrous convolution and residual learning. arXiv preprint arXiv:2010.12121 (2020)

28. Ruffinelli, D., Broscheit, S., Gemulla, R.: You CAN teach an old dog new tricks! on training knowledge graph embeddings. In: 8th International Conference on Learning Representations, ICLR 2020, Addis Ababa, Ethiopia, April 26–30, 2020. OpenReview.net (2020). https://openreview.net/forum?id=BkxSmlBFvr

29. Sun, Z., Deng, Z.H., Nie, J.Y., Tang, J.: RotatE: knowledge graph embedding by relational rotation in complex space. arXiv preprint arXiv:1902.10197 (2019)

30. Trouillon, T., Dance, C.R., Gaussier, E., Welbl, J., Riedel, S., Bouchard, G.: Knowledge graph completion via complex tensor factorization. J. Mach. Learn. Res. **18**(1), 4735–4772 (2017)

31. Trouillon, T., Dance, C.R., Welbl, J., Riedel, S., Gaussier, É., Bouchard, G.: Knowledge graph completion via complex tensor factorization. arXiv preprint arXiv:1702.06879 (2017)

32. Trouillon, T., Welbl, J., Riedel, S., Gaussier, É., Bouchard, G.: Complex embeddings for simple link prediction. In: International Conference on Machine Learning, pp. 2071–2080. PMLR (2016)

33. Wang, M., Qiu, L., Wang, X.: A survey on knowledge graph embeddings for link prediction. Symmetry **13**(3), 485 (2021)

34. Wang, Q., Mao, Z., Wang, B., Guo, L.: Knowledge graph embedding: a survey of approaches and applications. IEEE Trans. Knowl. Data Eng. **29**(12), 2724–2743 (2017)

35. Wang, Z., Zhang, J., Feng, J., Chen, Z.: Knowledge graph embedding by translating on hyperplanes. In: Proceedings of the AAAI Conference on Artificial Intelligence, vol. 28 (2014)

36. Xiong, W., Hoang, T., Wang, W.Y.: DeepPath: a reinforcement learning method for knowledge graph reasoning. arXiv preprint arXiv:1707.06690 (2017)
37. Yang, B., Yih, W.t., He, X., Gao, J., Deng, L.: Embedding entities and relations for learning and inference in knowledge bases. arXiv preprint arXiv:1412.6575 (2014)
38. Ye, Z., Kumar, Y.J., Sing, G.O., Song, F., Wang, J.: A comprehensive survey of graph neural networks for knowledge graphs. IEEE Access **10**, 75729–75741 (2022)
39. Yi, H.C., You, Z.H., Huang, D.S., Kwoh, C.K.: Graph representation learning in bioinformatics: trends, methods and applications. Briefings in Bioinformatics **23**(1), bbab340 (2022)
40. Yu, M., et al.: Translation-based embeddings with octonion for knowledge graph completion. Appl. Sci. **12**(8), 3935 (2022)
41. Zamini, M., Reza, H., Rabiei, M.: A review of knowledge graph completion. Information **13**(8), 396 (2022)
42. Zhang, S., Tay, Y., Yao, L., Liu, Q.: Quaternion knowledge graph embeddings. In: Advances in Neural Information Processing Systems, vol. 32 (2019)

Exploring Word-Sememe Graph-Centric Chinese Antonym Detection

Zhaobo Zhang[1,2,3,4], Pingpeng Yuan[1,2,3,4], and Hai Jin[1,2,3,4(✉)]

[1] National Engineering Research Center for Big Data Technology and System, Wuhan, China
[2] Service Computing Technology and System Laboratory, Wuhan, China
[3] Cluster and Grid Computing Laboratory, Wuhan, China
[4] Huazhong University of Science and Technology, Wuhan, China
{zhang_zb,ppyuan,hjin}@hust.edu.cn

Abstract. Antonym detection is a vital task in NLP systems. Pattern-based methods, typical solutions for this, recognize semantic relationships between words using given patterns but have limited performance. Distributed word embeddings often struggle to distinguish antonyms from synonyms because their representations rely on local co-occurrences in similar contexts. Combining the ambiguity of Chinese and the contradictory nature of antonyms, antonym detection faces unique challenges. In this paper, we propose a word-sememe graph to integrate relationships between sememes and Chinese words, organized as a 4-partite graph. We design a heuristic *sememe relevance computation* as a supplementary measure and develop a *relation inference* scheme using related sememes as taxonomic information to leverage the relational transitivity. The 4-partite graph can be extended based on this scheme. We introduce the *Relation Discriminated Learning based on Sememe Attention (RDLSA)* model, employing three attention strategies on sememes to learn flexible entity representations. Antonym relations are detected using a *Link Prediction* approach with these embeddings. Our method demonstrates superior performance in *Triple Classification* and Chinese *Antonym Detection* compared to the baselines. Experimental results show reduced ambiguity and improved antonym detection using linguistic sememes. A quantitative ablation analysis further confirms our scheme's effectiveness in capturing antonyms.

Keywords: Chinese antonym detection · Link prediction · Knowledge graph representation · Word-sememe graph

1 Introduction

Relation Classification focuses on separating word pairs into synonyms, antonyms, and hypernyms. Among them, *Antonym Detection* is one of the most challenging subtasks and is also a key problem in linguistics which has great significance for knowledge discovery and application to many NLP tasks, such as *Sentiment Analysis* [9], *Text Entailment* [5], and *Machine Translation* [28].

© The Author(s), under exclusive license to Springer Nature Switzerland AG 2023
D. Koutra et al. (Eds.): ECML PKDD 2023, LNAI 14171, pp. 583–600, 2023.
https://doi.org/10.1007/978-3-031-43418-1_35

Generally, appearances of words in synonyms and antonyms follow some patterns (e.g., "X or Y" and "X and Y"). Thus, one straightforward way is to extract word pairs according to the given patterns. For example, Lin [15] identified synonyms and antonyms among distributionally large corpus of plain text based on some fixed patterns in English. Nguyen [21] proposed AntSynNET, which encodes simple paths in parse trees using LSTM [11] to train a classifier for antonym detection. However, pattern-based methods are prone to low recall [26] and rely heavily on external resources.

Since words with similar distributions tend to be relevant in meaning, distribution-based methods are becoming popular recently. They can find out target synonyms and antonyms in large corpora and rarely rely on external lexicon resources [1]. Nevertheless, distributed word embeddings based on contextual co-occurrence cannot distinguish between relatedness and similarity because antonyms usually have similar context. Thus, the mining of negative correlations, i.e., antonymous relations, requires a combination of additional knowledge.

Compared with English, Chinese language has more ambiguity due to its multi-layer structure, rich semantic elements, and evolving consensus senses, which exacerbates ambiguity [4,18]. Previous works on Chinese *Relation Classification* focused on semantic opposites using Chinese-specific patterns, such as Chinese four-character patterns antonym compounds [34], universal quantification [43], and *sizige* [37]. Several works aimed to improve the performance of *Antonym Detection* using more features [45], external linguistic knowledge bases [14], or more complex model [29]. However, pattern-based Chinese antonym extraction is limited by outdated and formal corpora [14,37], and methods based on Chinese word embeddings also suffer from confusion between relatedness and similarity for detecting antonyms.

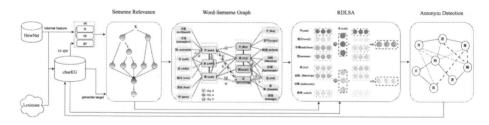

Fig. 1. Illustration of overall architecture

To address these problems on Chinese *Antonym Detection*, we introduce sememe to make implicit features explicit and propose a word-sememe layered knowledge graph. It can be modeled as a 4-partite graph which integrates sememes, words, their relations such as synonym and antonym (Fig. 1). We extract synonym and antonym triples from linguistic corpora and the Internet resources to instantiate the graph. The relations in word-sememe graph often carry properties that can improve integrity, such as reflexivity, symmetry, and transitivity. We then design a framework with some schemes for utilizing relational properties, as shown in Fig. 1. The contributions of our approach are summarized as follows:

Relation Inference. Synonymous and antonymous relations have transitivity and reflexivity properties. So, we develop a *relation inference scheme* with *sememe relevance computation*. The heuristic *sememe relevance computation* method aims to evaluate relevance between sememes based on the synonyms and antonyms of word-sememe graph. This method can help refine the graph and emphasize the direct connections between sememes. Guided by sememe relevance, *relation inference* that combines above-mentioned relational properties and supervision from *sememe relevance* can derive more potential and reliable relations by eliminating transitivity paths [8] with ambiguities.

Relation Discriminated Learning. To model symmetry and discriminate synonyms and antonyms, we also employ a knowledge graph embedding model to encode entities for semantic computation and discovering new antonyms with a distributed-based scheme. Specifically, we utilize three sememe-based attention strategies for building sememe space to obtain semantic separation and disambiguation for entities. By mapping entities vector to the sememe vector space dynamically, we can discriminate similar or opposing features.

Extensive Experiments. We evaluate our approach on *Triple Classification* and Chinese *Antonym Detection*, and results show our model can effectively distinguish between synonyms and antonyms. As we know, it is the first attempt to detect antonyms using the dynamic embedding with sememes motivated by *Link Prediction* on attributed graph [40]. Experimental results and ablation analysis show that our model can achieve significant performance and exactly capture the underlying antonymous relations[1]

2   Word-Sememe Graph-Centric Antonym Detection

Each word is composed of one or more sememes which are the finest semantic unit in Chinese [42]. Synonyms and antonyms share some sememes, making it crucial to identify these shared aspects for *Antonym Detection*. Furthermore, synonymous and antonymous relations are symmetric, reflexive, and transitive, complicating their discrimination and utilization.

In the following, we introduce a word-sememe graph which describes relationships between words and sememes. By this way, it makes the implicit meanings of words explicit and helps addressing the serious 1-N and N-N issues. Based on word-sememe graph, we design a *relation inference scheme* that leverages transitivity. Then, an embedding learning model based on the graph employs the attention strategies to address the problems incurred when detecting antonyms.

2.1   Word-Sememe Graph

Sememes are capable of conveying specific aspects of words. Antonyms and synonyms can be represented as two instances composed of sememe sets in a particular context. Mathematically, antonyms (synonyms) are opposite (same or

---

[1] Code and data: **https://github.com/CGCL-codes/RDLSA**.

similar) in some salient dimensions (sememes), while highly correlated in other dimensions. Discriminating their relationships requires calculating the semantic distance of word vectors, but the implicit dimensions make this inefficient and error-prone. However, the word-sememe graph can clarify these dimensions for antonym and synonym detection.

The graph in Fig. 1 describes relationships between words and sememes, with sets W and S representing words and sememes. Triples are denoted as $(w, composed\_of, s)$, $(w_1, syn/ant, w_2)$. Figure 1 shows the 4-partite graph, with potential relationships between sememes and entities are gathered by the semantic flows represented by arrows (line 1-8). Salient dimensions are linguistically clear, providing a foundation for word-sememe graph-centric antonym detection.

We build the initial graph by extracting sememes from openHowNet [24][2]. New relations can be inferred in Sect. 2.3 with *sememe relevance* (Sect. 2.2) using the synonyms and antonyms in word-sememe graph. Finally, we can obtain more relationships via distribution representations learned from Sect. 2.4.

2.2 Heuristic Sememe Relevance Computation

Sememe relevance refers to a sememe pair's contribution to the establishment of synonyms or antonyms. We primarily examine three features to evaluate this contribution, encompassing the morphological and semantic properties of sememe pairs and their informational popularity.

First, we consider the similarity of sememe strings, characterized by the *Jaro-Winkler Distance*[3] l_s. Second, we assess the angle c_s between sememes vectors, also referred to as cosine similarity. These two features are intrinsically connected as local variables. The third feature is evaluated globally, specifically the variant TF-IDF values of sememe pairs. We employ this feature to represent its prevalence in the knowledge graph to prevent the widespread sememe from obscuring the discovery of triples. The variant TF-IDF value g_s is computed as follow:

$$g(s_i, s_j) = \frac{2 * t(s_i) * t(s_j)}{t(s_i) + t(s_j)}$$

$$where\ t(s) = tf(s) * idf(s) = \frac{freq(s)}{|S_c|} * log\frac{|E|}{|Es_s| + 1} \tag{1}$$

here $freq(s)$ is the frequency of sememe s in sememes of entity c (constant equal to 1), and S_c represents the set of sememes of entity c. E is the set of all entities, and E_s represents the set of entities containing the sememe s.

Taking into account both local and global factors, we define the notion of sememe relevance d_s, i.e., the similarity of sememes from different synonyms and antonyms. For two sememe s_1, s_2, their similarity is calculated as follow:

$$d_s = \alpha l_s + \beta |c_s| + \sigma g_s$$
$$= \alpha\ JW\ (s_1, s_2) + \beta |Cosine\ (\mathbf{v}_{s_1}, \mathbf{v}_{s_2})| + \sigma g(s_i, s_j) \tag{2}$$

---

[2] https://github.com/thunlp/OpenHowNet
[3] https://en.wikipedia.org/wiki/Jaro-Winkler_distance

here α, β, and σ are the parameters that adjust the weights of the three features. We can ensure that the score accurately reflects the degree of relevance between sememes, regardless of whether they are synonyms or antonyms.

We cross-combine the sememes corresponding to existing synonyms and antonyms as positive examples for training. Then, we extract negative examples from combinations of sememes of two Chinese entities in charKG (the dataset built in Sect. 3.1), in descending order of the distance. These sememe pairs s_i & s_j and their features l_s, c_s, g_s are input into XGBoost Regressor, with the sememe relevance as the optimization goal, achieving reliable learning for α, β, and σ.

Algorithm 1: *Relation Inference*

Input　：Two Triples (A, rel_1, B), (A, rel_2, C);
Output　：(B, rel, C) establishment or $False$;
1　$S_{c_1}, S_{c_2} \leftarrow \varnothing; max_1, max_2 \leftarrow 0; S_{max_1}, S_{max_2} \leftarrow \varnothing$;
2　**foreach** s_0 *in A.sememes* **do**
3　　**foreach** s_1 *in B.sememes* **do**
4　　　**if** $d_s(s_0, s_1) > \theta_1$ **then**
5　　　　add s_0, s_1 into S_{c_1} ;
6　　　**else if** $d_s(s_0, s_1) > max_1$ **then**
7　　　　$max_1 \leftarrow d_s(s_0, s_1)$ and $S_{max_1} \leftarrow (s_0, s_1)$;
8　　**foreach** s_2 *in C.sememes* **do**
9　　　**if** $d_s(s_0, s_2) > \theta_2$ **then**
10　　　　add s_0, s_2 into S_{c_2} ;
11　　　**else if** $d_s(s_0, s_2) > max_2$ **then**
12　　　　$max_2 \leftarrow d_s(s_0, s_2)$ and $S_{max_2} \leftarrow (s_0, s_2)$;
13　**if** $S_{c_i} == \varnothing$ **then**
14　　$S_{c_i} \leftarrow S_{max_i}$
15　**if** $S_{c_1} \cap S_{c_2} == \varnothing$ **then**
16　　**return** False
17　**else**
18　　**return** Generated rel by rel_1 and rel_2;

2.3   Proximal Pattern-Based Relation Inference

Synonymous and antonymous relations have transitivity or reflexive transitivity properties. Two synonymous pairs sharing common entity, can infer new synonymous relation using transitivity (Eq. 3), while antonym pairs sharing common entity can generate synonymous relation according to reflexive transitivity. (akin to "two negatives make a positive", Eq. 4). Furthermore, synonym and antonym triples with common entity can create new antonymous relations (Eq. 5):

$$(\underline{A}, syn, \underline{B}) \wedge (\underline{B}, syn, \underline{C}) \rightarrow (\underline{A}, syn, \underline{C}) \tag{3}$$

$$(\underline{A}, ant, \underline{B}) \wedge (\underline{B}, ant, \underline{C}) \rightarrow (\underline{A}, syn, \underline{C}) \tag{4}$$

$$(\underline{A}, syn, \underline{B}) \wedge (\underline{B}, ant, \underline{C}) \rightarrow (\underline{A}, ant, \underline{C}) \tag{5}$$

here $\underline{A}, \underline{B}, \underline{C}$ are entities, *syn* and *ant* refer to synonymy and antonymy, respectively. However, these inferences face challenges due to polysemy, as the synonym and antonym triples may focus on different semantic aspects.

To tackle this, we develop a *relation inference scheme* on word-sememe graph. Specifically, this method applies the transitivity and reflexivity of synonyms and antonyms to provide inference direction, and uses the correlation of sememe to exclude interference items to achieve a proximal pattern-based (i.e., considering transitivity) *relation inference scheme* as shown in Algorithm 1. Note that, we implement this approach using only one-hop extensions to attenuate the noise caused by multiple-hops error superposition. Based on these, inferences in Eqs. 3, 4, and 5 are established under relevant and reliable sememes.

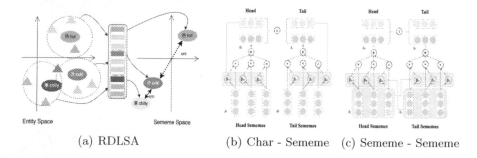

(a) RDLSA   (b) Char - Sememe   (c) Sememe - Sememe

Fig. 2. Illustration of *RDLSA* and attention schemes

2.4 Knowledge Representation Learning via Attention on Sememe

The above relation inference can discover simple relations. Discovering more complex relations relies on distributed representation method on word-sememe graph. Since synonymous and antonymous relations have symmetry and transitive properties etc., it limits the performance improvement of existing embedding methods (e.g. TransE, TransX, and RotatE) on *Antonym Detection*.

TransE struggles with 1-N, N-N problems due to its representation of head entities and semantic symmetry. As Eq. 6 shows, the head entity tends to force different tail entities have similar representations for the same relation.

$$\left. \begin{array}{c} \mathbf{h} + \mathbf{r} - \mathbf{t_1} = \epsilon_1 \\ \mathbf{h} + \mathbf{r} - \mathbf{t_2} = \epsilon_2 \end{array} \right\} \Rightarrow \mathbf{t_2} - \mathbf{t_1} = \epsilon_1 - \epsilon_2 \tag{6}$$

Because of semantic symmetry in *syn* and *ant* relations, the head and tail can be interchanged. Trans$X$ tends to learn zero vectors for the relation representations as Eq. 7 shows:

$$\left. \begin{array}{c} g_{r,1}(\mathbf{h}) + \mathbf{r} - g_{r,2}(\mathbf{t}) = \epsilon_1 \\ g_{r,2}(\mathbf{t}) + \mathbf{r} - g_{r,1}(\mathbf{h}) = \epsilon_2 \end{array} \right\} \Rightarrow 2\mathbf{r} = \epsilon_1 + \epsilon_2 \tag{7}$$

here $g_{r,i}()$ represents a matrix multiplication concerning relation r. RotatE [31] models synonyms as $0°$ rotations and antonyms as $180°$ when learning relations in complex vector space for symmetry. RotatE tends to cluster an entity's synonyms around itself and maximally away from antonyms. It inevitably overlooks the 1-N and N-N problems within these two clusters, as indicated by Eq. 8:

$$\left.\begin{array}{l} \mathbf{h} \circ \mathbf{r} - \mathbf{t_1} = \epsilon_1 \\ \mathbf{h} \circ \mathbf{r} - \mathbf{t_2} = \epsilon_2 \end{array}\right\} \Rightarrow \mathbf{t_2} - \mathbf{t_1} = \epsilon_1 - \epsilon_2 \tag{8}$$

To address these issues, we propose *Relation Discriminated Learning based on Sememe Attention (RDLSA)*, inspired by SE [30], TransD [12], and TKRL [36]. To better represent antonyms, we follow two assumptions from [38]: (a) Antonyms tend to be related in multiple dimensions due to co-occurrence-based learning, but differ in some salient dimensions; (b) In the entire distributional semantic space, the salient dimensions of different antonyms will significantly differ due to their specific polar oppositeness [28,43].

Here, we modify the role of r in the scoring function based on the intensity and symmetry of the relation. We treat r as a deciding factor for scoring functions, where *syn* corresponds to $-$ and *ant* corresponds to $+$ in Eq. 9. This distinction aligns with linguistic rules.

$$f_{syn}(h, t) = \|\mathbf{s_h} \circ \mathbf{h} \pm \mathbf{s_t} \circ \mathbf{t}\| \tag{9}$$

To comply with the mathematical assumptions, we introduce a sememe mutual attention mechanism, enabling dynamic entity mapping and emphasizing salient dimensional differences in entity representations. We design two attention strategies: (1) internal *Char-Sememe (CS)* attention, determining a sememe's weight by calculating its attention with the corresponding entity; (2) external *Sememe-Sememe (SS)* attention, obtaining the maximum attention of a sememe with all the sememes of another entity.

For *CS*, a sememe s_i gets its attention score from the entity as:

$$\beta_{ei} = \frac{\exp(\mathbf{e} \cdot \mathbf{s_i})}{\sum_{s_j \in S_e} \exp(\mathbf{e} \cdot \mathbf{s_j})} \tag{10}$$

here $\mathbf{e} \in \mathbf{h}, \mathbf{t}$ are entities in a triple and S_e indicates the set of sememes of entity e. β_{ei} represents the attention score of i-th sememe in S_e. Bold face $\mathbf{e}$ is the vectors of entity e and $\mathbf{s_j}$ indicates the vector of j-th sememe $\in S_e$.

For *SS*, the attention score of the sememe s_i of the entity e can be calculated with the sememes of another entity $\hat{e}$:

$$\beta_{ei} = \max_{s_j}\left(\frac{d_s(s_i, s_j) \exp(\mathbf{s_i} \cdot \mathbf{s_j})}{\sum_{s_j \in S_{\hat{e}}} \exp(\mathbf{s_i} \cdot \mathbf{s_j})}\right) \tag{11}$$

here $S_{\hat{e}}$ indicates the set of sememes of entity $\hat{e}$. d_s is defined in Sect. 2.2.

Then all the weighted sememes are stacked into a mapping vector (Eq. 12), and the corresponding entities are dynamically mapped to the new sememe space through Hadmard (or element-wise) product for the scoring function, Eq. 9.

$$\mathbf{s_h} = \sum_{i \in |S_h|} \beta_{h_i} \mathbf{s_i}, \quad \mathbf{s_t} = \sum_{j \in |S_t|} \beta_{t_j} \mathbf{s_j} \tag{12}$$

Additionally, we provide a simplified strategy of averaging sememe vectors (*Avg*, in Fig. 1) as projection vectors to verify the feasibility of the sememe attentions. Specifically, we modify Eq. 12 by set β_{h_i} and β_{t_j} to $\frac{1}{|S_h|}$ and $\frac{1}{|S_t|}$.

2.5   Training

The training of feature weight parameters for sememe relevance resembles the method used in [44]. We insert the inferred triples to the training dataset after deduplication, enhancing the integration of transitivity. Initially, we assign pre-trained embeddings to each entity. We similarly initialize sememes to ensure the semantic association of entities to sememes [42]. These embeddings are then adopted in the trained model in Fig. 2 for fine-tuning.

We denote the overall synonym-antonym knowledge graph as G, with triples represented as (h, r, t). Following the optimization scheme in TransE [3], we combine our scoring function to generate an overall optimization objective:

$$\mathcal{L} = \sum_{(h,r,t)\in G_g} \sum_{(h',r',t')\in G_c} [\gamma + f_r(\mathbf{h}, \mathbf{t}) - f_r(\mathbf{h'}, \mathbf{t'})]_+ \tag{13}$$

Gg represents golden triples of antonyms and synonyms in the knowledge graph, while Gc represents corrupted negative triples. For a golden triple $(h, r, t) \in G_g$, we randomly replace the head (tail) to obtain the corresponding negative triple (h', r, t'). Our goal is to minimize the loss as much as possible to extract synonymous and antonymous information comprehensively, while there are far more synonyms than antonyms. To address this data imbalance, we use a hyper-parameter δ to control the sampling ratio of synonyms and antonyms.

3   Experiments

We evaluate our framework on *Triple Classification* and *Antonym Detection*. Furthermore, we conduct an ablation analysis to demonstrate the significant interpretability and efficiency of our models.

3.1   Datasets Construction

We collect basic synonym and antonym triples from various linguistic corpora and Internet resources such as Github[4], Baidu Encyclopedia[5], and Wiktionary[6]. Then, we annotate sememes [6] (Sect. 2.1) for entities in *Character Synonyms-Antonyms Knowledge Graph* (namely, *charKG*, a subinstance of the word-sememe graph for characters, can circumvent the low reliability and out-of-vocabulary issues associated with antonym words in the lexicon). However, since Chinese characters have a limited number and multiple meanings, we extend the original 19178 triples by exploiting the transitivity and trans-transitivity with *relation inference* (Sect. 2.3), resulting in 8808 new triples. We review and integrate the qualified triples into *charKG*.

---

[4] https://github.com/chatopera/Synonyms
[5] https://dict.baidu.com/
[6] https://zh.m.wiktionary.org/wiki/

In addition to the dataset, charKG, we choose Zdic[7] as a complementary test dataset source in closed-world scenarios (named HanDian). We eliminate the triples repeated with the training set and get 132 test antonym triples.

3.2 Experimental Settings

Baseline Models. We choose models from *Knowledge Graph Representation* (KRL) and models migrated from other frameworks as baselines. For KRL models, we select TransE [3], TransR [16], TransD [12], RESCAL [23], DistMult [39], and ComplEx [32] as baselines. We also train embeddings using the RotatE [31] model. These models' training and testing are based on OpenKE [10]. Also, we train advanced HopfE [2] alone. Additionally, we fine-tune RoBERTa, a Chinese pre-trained language model [17], on *Triple Classification*. For pattern-based models, we use an Internet dictionary approach based on Baidu's dictionary for semantic relation classification [14]. We search for antonyms online and compare them to the given character set.

Hyper-parameters and Training Setting. We unify all representations in a 300-dimensional space, use a margin parameter γ of 0.2 in Eq. 13, and initialize character and sememe vectors with existing embeddings [25]. We optimize embeddings using Adaptive Moment Estimation (Adam) with a learning rate of 10^{-5}. For baselines, we adopt their best-performing configurations. We set δ as 3:1 after maximizing prediction accuracy in the validation set.

Table 1. Experimental results of *Antonym Detection* and *Triple Classification*

	charKG						HanDian					
	hit@1	hit@3	hit@10	MRR	MR	TC (%)	hit@1	hit@3	hit@10	MRR	MR	TC (%)
Word2vec	-	-	-	0.0006	4191	18.50	-	-	-	0.0003	4317	9.09
TransE	-	0.0833	0.1574	0.0568	668	62.03	-	0.1705	0.2689	0.1090	298	79.55
TransH	-	0.0556	0.0741	0.0250	1558	61.11	-	0.0341	0.0758	0.0280	1247	62.12
TransR	-	0.0556	0.0926	0.0384	1629	61.11	-	0.4545	0.6098	0.2434	526	78.79
TransD	-	0.0463	0.1296	0.0404	1898	57.41	-	0.1401	0.3409	0.1085	686	74.62
RESCAL	0.0278	0.0463	0.0556	0.0395	1859	55.56	0.0341	0.0530	0.0682	0.0494	1419	63.64
DistMult	0.0555	0.1111	0.2407	0.1129	1079	68.52	**0.5606**	**0.6515**	**0.6931**	0.6149	369	81.81
ComplEx	0.0463	0.0741	0.1296	0.0745	1243	62.04	0.5379	0.6174	0.6364	0.5809	471	80.30
RotatE	0.0463	0.1667	0.2963	0.1279	613	70.37	0.5341	0.6364	0.6515	**0.5883**	296	79.55
HopfE	**0.2045**	**0.2992**	**0.3864**	**0.2698**	518	-	0.5189	0.6174	0.6553	0.5743	312	-
RoBERTa	-	-	-	0.064	656	70.4	0.0227	0.0455	0.0909	0.0514	356	85.6
Internet-Dict	-	-	-	-	-	59.26	-	-	-	-	-	80.30
RDLSA (Avg)	0.1019	0.1481	0.2593	0.1458	389	90.74	0.2424	0.3409	0.4242	0.3071	243	94.72
RDLSA (CS)	0.0926	0.1296	0.2222	0.1388	388	90.74	0.2462	0.3333	0.4205	0.3105	235	95.62
RDLSA (SS)	0.0926	0.1574	0.25	0.1458	**364**	**91.32**	0.2652	0.3674	0.4583	0.3345	**189**	**96.34**

---

[7] https://www.zdic.net/

3.3   Triple Classification

Evaluation Datasets and Protocol. We divide the triples into train, valid, and test datasets in an 8:1:1 ratio. For triple (h, ant, t), we create a corrupted negative triple (h', ant, t') by randomly replacing the head or tail. We represent entities using learned character embeddings and compute scores for both triples. If the golden triple scores below the corrupted triple, we classify it as positive; otherwise, negative.

Experimental Results. From 'TC (%)' results in Table 1, *RDLSA* outperforms all baselines on both datasets. Trans$X$ models struggle to distinguish synonym and antonym relations due to symmetry and 1-N, N-N problems. TransH, TransR, and TransD even perform worse than TransE on both datasets. Mapping entities to the relation vector space does not improve classification performance.

RESCAL, DistMult, ComplEx, RotatE perform better than Trans$X$ except RESCAL. RotatE shows significant performances on charKG, while DistMult obtains the best score among baselines for 3 metrics on HanDian. However, their accuracy is still lower than *RDLSA* due to lack of discrimination for relations.

Character embeddings from word2vec struggle to compute salient oppositions between antonyms, as they can not distinguish semantic relatedness, similarity, and opposites [27]. RoBERTa, after fine-tuning, can effectively identify many relations of triples, particularly for HanDian in the closed-world setting. Internet-Dict performs well on HanDian but not on charKG from the open world, reflecting its closed-world nature. In summary, *RDLSA* outperforms these methods, showing its ability to exploit potential antonymous relations overlooked by co-occurrence or structure-based embeddings and linguistic dictionaries.

3.4   Antonym Detection

Evaluation Datasets and Protocol. We use the same test dataset as in *Triple Classification*, which focuses on detecting opposites. Given an antonym triple (h, ant, t), we compute scores for head (tail) representations and all characters, then sort them. The ranks indicate performance, and we calculate MR, MRR, and Hit@1, Hit@3, and Hit@10 metrics.

Experimental Results. Table 1 summarizes *Antonym Detection* results for baselines and *RDLSA*, with the best results shown in bold. In charKG, *RDLSA* outperforms most baselines on most metrics, demonstrating its excellent ability to capture antonym semantics and perform well on weaker salient opposition dataset (chatKG). This advantage is amplified in the closed-world HanDian, which contains stronger salient oppositions. Overall, our model effectively highlights salient oppositions.

Trans$X$'s MRs indicate that structure-based models have limited success in capturing oppositional salience. The MRs of Trans$X$, mostly miss the hit@1, are insufficient for *Antonym Detection*. The semantic models are consistent with the

Triple Classification results in charKG, and DistMult shows significant improvement in HanDian. ComplEx also improves in HanDian compared to charKG, but the increase is smaller than other semantic models (e.g., DistMult). In particular, RotatE and HopfE keep competitive performance in two datasets and highest hit@10 on charKG for RotatE, and HopfE obtains surprising results on charKG's hit@X and MMR metrics. However, they fit some noise so that they underperform on MR. RoBERTa is good at classification, but it is hard to measure the degree of antonymy which reflected by the weak hit@X performance.

Both experiments show that the semantic models are mostly better at handling potential semantics than the structure-based models. We argue that the semantic model is resistant to symmetry since factorization or bilinear function focus more on head and tail entities [32] instead of relation.

3.5 Ablation Analysis

Accuracy for Different Part-Of-Speech. We examine the difference in accuracy between triples of different POS (*Part-Of-Speech*) in *Triple Classification*. We first compute the POS distribution for the whole test dataset and then show the POS accuracy in Fig. 3.

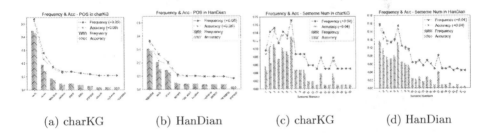

(a) charKG   (b) HanDian   (c) charKG   (d) HanDian

Fig. 3. Frequency & Acc - POS, Frequency & Acc - Sememe Num

To ensure readability, the 'Accuracy' displayed for each POS in Fig. 3 is calculated by multiplying the accuracy by the corresponding frequency. To minimize the impact of noise, we take the data of top 10 POS to visualize. The results indicate that verbs, nouns, and adjectives are the most frequent. In charKG, the highest percentage of verbs has 89.8% accuracy; followed by nouns with 85% accuracy. Adjectives, while less frequent, exhibit a remarkable accuracy of 100%. In HanDian, adjectives have the highest frequency with 94.7% accuracy, while verbs and nouns have 95.7% and 89.2% accuracy respectively. The analysis results of various POSs suggest that adjectives possess a clearer oppositional semantic representation, leading to improved performance on datasets with a higher proportion of adjectives. This conclusion aligns with the observed performance of models on the two datasets.

Accuracy for Different Sememe Number. We count the frequencies of characters corresponding to different numbers of sememe and their accuracies, and display the overall distribution in Fig. 3(c) and (d).

Generally, an inverse relationship between the number of sememes and accuracy can be observed. In charKG, characters with 1 to 7 sememes comprise 77.55% of the knowledge graph. Within this range, characters with fewer sememes tend to perform worse, a trend consistent with HanDian. The average accuracy for characters with fewer sememes is 88.89% in CharKG (93.59% for HanDian), while characters with more sememes have an average accuracy of 94.29% in CharKG (96.70% for HanDian). This demonstrates that a larger number of sememes enables the model to learn more discriminative embeddings.

Role of the Inferred Triples. The pattern-based scheme extends the knowledge graph, charKG, by providing discovered triples. These triples are added to the training dataset to enhance the data after removing duplicates in test datasets. We compare the performance of the dataset before and after enhancement to demonstrate the effectiveness of the pattern-based scheme in supporting the distribution-based scheme.

As shown in the Fig. 4(a), our models all benefit from the extended triples on *Triple Classification*. On the *Antonym Detection* task, our models suffer some weakening in Handian, while making improvements in charKG. Overall, the benefits of *relation inference* are substantial.

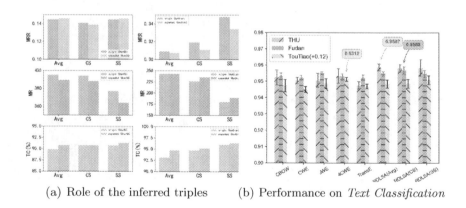

(a) Role of the inferred triples   (b) Performance on *Text Classification*

Fig. 4. Results of *Antonym Detection* and *Text Classification*

3.6   Applications

Improving Performance in Downstream Task. *Text Classification* is a typical downstream task used to test the effect of a well-trained embedding.

Here we use the Fudan[8], THUCNews[9], TouTiao[10] datasets and verify whether our embedding can achieve competitive performances on downstream tasks. An entry in these datasets consists of a sentence and the category it belongs to. Based on these datasets, we implement a CNN-based text classifier and use a 3:1:1 ratio to divide the original dataset into training, testing, and validation datasets. We select some models that can be trained for character representation (CBOW [20], CWE [4], JWE [41], 4CWE [13]), as well as TransE [3], to compare as our baseline model.

We conduct five rounds of experiments and calculate the mean and standard deviation to illustrate the results. In Fig. 4(b), our model performs well on the three datasets. On THU, $RDLSA$(Avg) outperforms the best baseline, 4CWE, by 0.57%. On Fudan, $RDLSA$(CS) achieves a 0.19% advantage over JWE. On TouTiao, $RDLSA$(SS) obtains a competitive result that is only slightly inferior to 4CWE by 0.05% and beats the other baselines.

Enhancing Sentiment Lexicon Based on CharKG. Building on *relation inference*, we find two levels of opposition: character and sememe. Using charKG, we simply infer the relation between sememes by their internal characters based on Sect. 2.2 and combine Algorithm 1 to verify the semantic relation of existing word pairs in HowNet [6] according to their sememes. Sememe-based word antonym derivation is linguistically applicable in various scenarios. For example, enhancing sentiment lexicons can improve sentiment classification performance.

We develop enhanced sentiment lexicons on BosonNLP and HowNet Sentiment Lexicons[11]. In BosonNLP, positive words score positively and the more positive the word the higher the score, and the opposite is true for negative words. HowNet Sentiment Lexicons divides sentiment words into two types (i.e., 1 for positive words and -1 for negative words) and provides 6 lexicons of differently weighted adverbs.

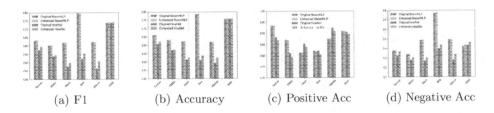

| (a) F1 | (b) Accuracy | (c) Positive Acc | (d) Negative Acc |

Fig. 5. Performance of the original and enhanced dictionaries on different datasets

[8] http://www.nlpir.org/wordpress/download/tc-corpus-answer.rar
[9] http://thuctc.thunlp.org/
[10] https://github.com/aceimnorstuvwxz/TouTiao-text-classfication-dataset
[11] https://www.heywhale.com/

We evaluate the enhancement of the two sentiment lexicons on 5 datasets[12]. Specifically, we insert new content into sentiment lexicons taking the same score for synonyms and negative values for antonyms, and then we test the feasibility on the datasets using two lexicons before and after the enhancement. It is clear that the classification of negative sentiment texts is greatly enhanced (Fig. 5(d)), while the accuracy of positive texts maintains a similar level (Fig. 5(c)). In summary, sentiment classification based on the sentiment lexicon benefits from the new lexicon content (Fig. 5(a) and (b)), i.e., the product of our *Antonym Detection* extends the sentiment lexicon effectively and improves the ability to identify negative texts.

4   Related Works

4.1   Synonym-Antonym Discrimination

Pattern-Based Approach. Lin [15] utilized fixed patterns (e.g., "X and Y") to identify semantically incompatible word pairs in English. Similarly, Wang [34] searched the CCL corpus for Chinese four-character phrases (e.g., a+X+b+!X). Zhang [43] extracted antonym pairs of nouns, adjectives, and verbs in Chinese universal quantification word classes, while Wu [37] identified antonym pairs in Chinese *sizige* using 379 four-character patterns.

Distribution-Based Approach. Nguyen [22] trained word embeddings to decouple synonyms and antonyms by adjusting weights of salient and irrelevant features. Dou [7] used the SkipGram model to train antonym-sensitive embeddings. Li [14] integrated Chinese word embedding and linguistic knowledge into a classification system. Xie [38] employed a mixture-of-experts framework with a divide-and-conquer strategy to learns specialties of different dimensions.

4.2   Knowledge Graph Representation

We introduce three categories of KG representation related to this paper.

Structure-Based Models. TransE [3] projects entities and relations into vector space using $h+r = t$. TransH [35] maps relations to relation-specific hyperplanes based on TransE. TransR [16] models entities and relations in separate spaces, and TransD [12] uses a dynamic mapping matrix to achieve improvements.

Semantic Models. RESCAL [23] treats relations as matrices and learns relations through tensor factorization. DistMult [39] captures compositional semantics via matrix multiplication. ComplEx [32] uses complex numbers to handle symmetries and antisymmetries. HopfE [2] aims to achieve interpretability of inferred relations in the four-dimensional space.

Other Models. TransC [19] differentiates between concepts and instances and utilizes spheres vectors for representation. Wang [33] proposed a novel regularizer to encourage entities with similar semantics to have similar embeddings.

---

[12] https://drive.google.com/drive/folders/1qpLb-52DDEiYDmvpnlYgVfKbRlf428Mq?usp=sharing

5   Conclusion and Future Works

In this paper, we pay attention to the synonymy and antonymy in Chinese and modify *Link Prediction* to *Antonym Detection*. More specifically, we construct a Chinese word-sememe graph with only synonym and antonym relations, and build a framework including *relation inference* and *knowledge representation learning* model based on its transitivity, reflexivity, and symmetry. Afterwards, the experimental results on *Triple Classification* and *Antonym Detection* show that our approach has better representation ability with simplicity, and the ablation analysis also excavates the inherent advantages.

In the future, we will explore more linguistic knowledge and Chinese characteristics to improve the discriminative ability. We want to further extend the approach to unlimited Chinese words based on limited characters and realize complete word-level *Antonym Detection*.

Acknowledgment. The research is supported by The National Natural Science Foundation of China under Grant Nos. 61932004 and 62072205.

Ethical   Issues. Following   the   guidelines   from   *General   ethical issues in Machine Learning* (https://www.w3.org/TR/webmachinelearning-ethics/#general-ethical-issues-in-machine-learning), we will briefly describe our ethical considerations.

Our work mainly focuses on semantic mining in the Chinese domain, without **Bias, Fairness, Security, Privacy, Environmental Impact**, and **Discrimination** against a group or collective. Our method combines external professional linguistic knowledge and has good Transparency and Interpretability.

Our data is sourced from publicly available resources on the internet and all references are cited in the paper, such as Github and other data that follows open-source licenses. Our data does not involve any personal privacy or inference of personal information. Our work is dedicated to researching the potential semantic relationships between words in Chinese and does not have any police or military applications.

References

1. Ali, M.A., Sun, Y., Zhou, X., Wang, W., Zhao, X.: Antonym-synonym classification based on new sub-space embeddings. In: Proceedings of the Thirty-Third AAAI Conference on Artificial Intelligence, AAAI 2019, The Thirty-First Innovative Applications of Artificial Intelligence Conference, IAAI 2019, The Ninth AAAI Symposium on Educational Advances in Artificial Intelligence, EAAI 2019, pp. 6204–6211 (2019)
2. Bastos, A., Singh, K., Nadgeri, A., Shekarpour, S., Mulang, I.O., Hoffart, J.: Hopfe: knowledge graph representation learning using inverse hopf fibrations. In: Proceedings of the 30th ACM International Conference on Information and Knowledge Management, Virtual Event, CIKM 2021, Queensland, Australia, 1–5 November, pp. 89–99. ACM (2021)

3. Bordes, A., Usunier, N., García-Durán, A., Weston, J., Yakhnenko, O.: Translating embeddings for modeling multi-relational data. In: Proceedings of the 27th Annual Conference on Neural Information Processing Systems 2013, NIPS 2013, pp. 2787–2795 (2013)

4. Chen, X., Xu, L., Liu, Z., Sun, M., Luan, H.: Joint learning of character and word embeddings. In: Proceedings of the Twenty-Fourth International Joint Conference on Artificial Intelligence, IJCAI 2015, pp. 1236–1242. AAAI Press (2015)

5. Chen, Z., Feng, Y., Zhao, D.: Entailment graph learning with textual entailment and soft transitivity. In: Proceedings of the 60th Annual Meeting of the Association for Computational Linguistics, ACL 2022, pp. 5899–5910 (2022)

6. Dong, Z., Dong, Q.: Hownet-a hybrid language and knowledge resource. In: Proceedings of the 2003 International Conference on Natural Language Processing and Knowledge Engineering, pp. 820–824 (2003)

7. Dou, Z., Wei, W., Wan, X.: Improving word embeddings for antonym detection using thesauri and sentiwordnet. In: Proceedings of Natural Language Processing and Chinese Computing - 7th CCF International Conference, NLPCC 2018, vol. 11109, pp. 67–79 (2018)

8. Etcheverry, M., Wonsever, D.: Unraveling antonym's word vectors through a siamese-like network. In: Proceedings of the 57th Conference of the Association for Computational Linguistics, ACL 2019, pp. 3297–3307 (2019)

9. Gao, D., Wei, F., Li, W., Liu, X., Zhou, M.: Cross-lingual sentiment lexicon learning with bilingual word graph label propagation. Comput. Linguist. $41(1)$, 21–40 (2015)

10. Han, X., et al.: Openke: an open toolkit for knowledge embedding. In: Proceedings of the 2018 Conference on Empirical Methods in Natural Language Processing, EMNLP 2018, pp. 139–144 (2018)

11. Hochreiter, S., Schmidhuber, J.: Long short-term memory. Neural Comput. $9(8)$, 1735–1780 (1997)

12. Ji, G., He, S., Xu, L., Liu, K., Zhao, J.: Knowledge graph embedding via dynamic mapping matrix. In: Proceedings of the 53rd Annual Meeting of the Association for Computational Linguistics and the 7th International Joint Conference on Natural Language Processing of the Asian Federation of Natural Language Processing, ACL 2015, pp. 687–696 (2015)

13. Jin, H., Zhang, Z., Yuan, P.: Improving Chinese word representation using four corners features. IEEE Trans. Big Data $8(4)$, 982–993 (2022)

14. Li, C., Ma, T.: Classification of Chinese word semantic relations. In: Huang, X., Jiang, J., Zhao, D., Feng, Y., Hong, Yu. (eds.) NLPCC 2017. LNCS (LNAI), vol. 10619, pp. 465–473. Springer, Cham (2018). https://doi.org/10.1007/978-3-319-73618-1_39

15. Lin, D., Zhao, S., Qin, L., Zhou, M.: Identifying synonyms among distributionally similar words. In: Proceedings of the Eighteenth International Joint Conference on Artificial Intelligence, IJCAI 2003, pp. 1492–1493 (2003)

16. Lin, Y., Liu, Z., Sun, M., Liu, Y., Zhu, X.: Learning entity and relation embeddings for knowledge graph completion. In: Proceedings of the Twenty-Ninth AAAI Conference on Artificial Intelligence, AAAI 2015, pp. 2181–2187 (2015)

17. Liu, Y., et al.: Roberta: a robustly optimized BERT pretraining approach. CoRR abs/1907.11692 (2019)

18. Lu, W., Zhang, Z., Yuan, P., Jin, H., Hua, Q.: Learning Chinese word embeddings by discovering inherent semantic relevance in sub-characters. In: Proceedings of the 31st ACM International Conference on Information & Knowledge Management, CIKM, pp. 1369–1378. ACM (2022)

19. Lv, X., Hou, L., Li, J., Liu, Z.: Differentiating concepts and instances for knowledge graph embedding. In: Proceedings of the 2018 Conference on Empirical Methods in Natural Language Processing, EMNLP 2018, pp. 1971–1979 (2018)
20. Mikolov, T., Sutskever, I., Chen, K., Corrado, G.S., Dean, J.: Distributed rep resentations of words and phrases and their compositionality. In: Proceedings of Advances in Neural Information Processing Systems 26: 27th Annual Conference on Neural Information Processing Systems 2013, pp. 3111–3119 (2013)
21. Nguyen, K.A., Walde, S.S.I., Vu, N.T.: Distinguishing antonyms and synonyms in a pattern-based neural network. In: Proceedings of the 15th Conference of the European Chapter of the Association for Computational Linguistics, EACL 2017, pp. 76–85 (2017)
22. Nguyen, K.A., Walde, S.S.I., Vu, N.T.: Integrating distributional lexical contrast into word embeddings for antonym-synonym distinction. In: Proceedings of the 54th Annual Meeting of the Association for Computational Linguistics, ACL 2016 (2016)
23. Nickel, M., Tresp, V., Kriegel, H.: A three-way model for collective learning on multi-relational data. In: Proceedings of the 28th International Conference on Machine Learning, ICML 2011, pp. 809–816 (2011)
24. Qi, F., Yang, C., Liu, Z., Dong, Q., Sun, M., Dong, Z.: Openhownet: an open sememe-based lexical knowledge base. CoRR abs/1901.09957 (2019)
25. Qiu, Y., Li, H., Li, S., Jiang, Y., Hu, R., Yang, L.: Revisiting correlations between intrinsic and extrinsic evaluations of word embeddings. In: Proceedings of Chinese Computational Linguistics and Natural Language Processing Based on Naturally Annotated Big Data - 17th China National Conference, CCL 2018, and 6th International Symposium, NLP-NABD 2018, vol. 11221, pp. 209–221 (2018)
26. Roth, M., Walde, S.S.I.: Combining word patterns and discourse markers for paradigmatic relation classification. In: Proceedings of the 52nd Annual Meeting of the Association for Computational Linguistics, ACL 2014, pp. 524–530 (2014)
27. Samenko, I., Tikhonov, A., Yamshchikov, I.P.: Synonyms and antonyms: Embedded conflict. CoRR abs/2004.12835 (2020)
28. Scheible, S., Walde, S.S.I., Springorum, S.: Uncovering distributional differences between synonyms and antonyms in a word space model. In: Proceedings of the 6th International Joint Conference on Natural Language Processing, IJCNLP 2013, pp. 489–497 (2013)
29. Shijia, E., Jia, S., Xiang, Y.: Study on the Chinese word semantic relation classification with word embedding. In: Huang, X., Jiang, J., Zhao, D., Feng, Y., Hong, Yu. (eds.) NLPCC 2017. LNCS (LNAI), vol. 10619, pp. 849–855. Springer, Cham (2018). https://doi.org/10.1007/978-3-319-73618-1_74
30. Socher, R., Huval, B., Manning, C.D., Ng, A.Y.: Semantic compositionality through recursive matrix-vector spaces. In: Proceedings of the 2012 Joint Conference on Empirical Methods in Natural Language Processing and Computational Natural Language Learning, EMNLP-CoNLL 2012, pp. 1201–1211. ACL (2012)
31. Sun, Z., Deng, Z., Nie, J., Tang, J.: Rotate: knowledge graph embedding by relational rotation in complex space. In: Proceedings of the 7th International Conference on Learning Representations, ICLR 2019, New Orleans, LA, USA, 6–9 May, 2019. OpenReview.net (2019)
32. Trouillon, T., Welbl, J., Riedel, S., Gaussier, É., Bouchard, G.: Complex embeddings for simple link prediction. In: Proceedings of the 33rd International Conference on Machine Learning, ICML 2016, vol. 48, pp. 2071–2080 (2016)

33. Wang, J., Zhang, Z., Shi, Z., Cai, J., Ji, S., Wu, F.: Duality-induced regularizer for semantic matching knowledge graph embeddings. IEEE Trans. Pattern Anal. Mach. Intell. **45**(2), 1652–1667 (2023)
34. Wang, X., Wu, Z., Li, Y., Huang, Q., Hui, J.: Corpus-based analysis of the co-occurrence of Chinese antonym pairs. In: Proceedings of Advanced Data Mining and Applications - 6th International Conference, ADMA 2010, vol. 6441, pp. 500–507 (2010)
35. Wang, Z., Zhang, J., Feng, J., Chen, Z.: Knowledge graph embedding by translating on hyperplanes. In: Proceedings of the Twenty-Eighth AAAI Conference on Artificial Intelligence, AAAI 2014, pp. 1112–1119 (2014)
36. Wu, J., Xie, R., Liu, Z., Sun, M.: Knowledge representation via joint learning of sequential text and knowledge graphs. CoRR abs/1609.07075 (2016)
37. Wu, S.: Iconicity and viewpoint: antonym order in Chinese four-character patterns. Lang. Sci. **59**, 117–134 (2017)
38. Xie, Z., Zeng, N.: A mixture-of-experts model for antonym-synonym discrimination. In: Proceedings of the 59th Annual Meeting of the Association for Computational Linguistics and the 11th International Joint Conference on Natural Language Processing, ACL/IJCNLP 2021, pp. 558–564 (2021)
39. Yang, B., Yih, W., He, X., Gao, J., Deng, L.: Embedding entities and relations for learning and inference in knowledge bases. In: Proceedings of the 3rd International Conference on Learning Representations, ICLR 2015 (2015)
40. Yang, S., et al.: Inductive link prediction with interactive structure learning on attributed graph. In: Proceedings of Machine Learning and Knowledge Discovery in Databases. Research Track - European Conference, ECML PKDD 2021, vol. 12976, pp. 383–398. Springer (2021)
41. Yu, J., Jian, X., Xin, H., Song, Y.: Joint embeddings of Chinese words, characters, and fine-grained subcharacter components. In: Proceedings of the 2017 Conference on Empirical Methods in Natural Language Processing, EMNLP 2017, pp. 286–291 (2017)
42. Zeng, X., Yang, C., Tu, C., Liu, Z., Sun, M.: Chinese LIWC lexicon expansion via hierarchical classification of word embeddings with sememe attention. In: Proceedings of the Thirty-Second AAAI Conference on Artificial Intelligence, (AAAI-18), the 30th innovative Applications of Artificial Intelligence (IAAI-18), and the 8th AAAI Symposium on Educational Advances in Artificial Intelligence (EAAI-18), pp. 5650–5657 (2018)
43. Zhang, J.: Internal semantic structure and conceptual hierarchy of antonymous compounds in modern chinese. In: Proceedings of Chinese Lexical Semantics - 14th Workshop, CLSW 2013, vol. 8229, pp. 181–190 (2013)
44. Zhang, Z., Zhong, Z., Yuan, P., Jin, H.: Improving entity linking in Chinese domain by sense embedding based on graph clustering. J. Comput. Sci. Technol. **38**(1), 196 (2023)
45. Zhou, Y., Lan, M., Wu, Y.: Effective semantic relationship classification of context-free chinese words with simple surface and embedding features. In: Proceedings of Natural Language Processing and Chinese Computing - 6th CCF International Conference, NLPCC 2017. Lecture Notes in Computer Science, vol. 10619, pp. 456–464. Springer (2017)

Distinct Geometrical Representations for Temporal and Relational Structures in Knowledge Graphs

Bowen Song[1,5], Chengjin Xu[2], Kossi Amouzouvi[3,5,6], Maocai Wang[1(✉)],
Jens Lehmann[3,4,5], and Sahar Vahdati[5]

[1] School of Computer Science, China University of Geosciences (Wuhan), Wuhan, China
{songbowen,mcwang}@cug.edu.cn
[2] International Digital Economy Academy, Shenzhen, China
[3] Faculty of Computer Science, TU Dresden, Dresden, Germany
[4] Amazon (work done outside of Amazon), Seattle, USA
[5] Institute for Applied Informatics (InfAI), Dresden, Germany
[6] Department of Mathematics, KNUST, Kumasi, Ghana

Abstract. Geometric aspects of knowledge graph embedding models directly impact their capability to preserve knowledge from the original graph to the vector space. For example, the capability to preserve structural patterns such as hierarchies, loops, and paths present as relational structures in a knowledge graph depends on the underlying geometry. In these years, temporal information has gained lots of attention from researchers. While non-Euclidean geometry, e.g. Hyperbolic Geometry, has been shown to work well in static knowledge graph embedding models for such relational structures, this does not hold for temporal information in knowledge graphs. This is due to the different characteristics of temporal information: time can be seen mostly as a linear construct and using a geometry that is not suitable for this can adversely affect performance. To address this research gap, we provide a novel temporal knowledge graph embedding model that combines different geometries: the non-temporal part of the knowledge is mapped to a hyperbolic space and the temporal part is mapped to a Euclidean space. Our extensive evaluations on several benchmark datasets show a significant performance improvement in comparison to state-of-the-art models.

1 Introduction

Knowledge Graphs (KGs) are a core technology for several AI tasks such as recommendation and prediction services as well as question-answering systems [4]. KGs usually consist of facts represented in the form of triples (subject, relation, object), where subject and object denote the entities and the relation connects those entities. Despite the large quantities of triples in KGs such as Wikidata [29], DBpedia [19], NELL [8], YAGO [25], they remain incomplete. One of the leading approaches to dealing with the incompleteness problem of KGs is the use of Knowledge Graph Embedding (KGE) models. KGE models predict links between existing entities in a KG by providing latent representation of the entities and relations in a low-dimensional space [1,5].

© The Author(s), under exclusive license to Springer Nature Switzerland AG 2023
D. Koutra et al. (Eds.): ECML PKDD 2023, LNAI 14171, pp. 601–616, 2023.
https://doi.org/10.1007/978-3-031-43418-1_36

While many KGE models are designed in Euclidean space, recent works show that non-Euclidean geometry improves model performance for the preservation of several complex relational structures [1]. For example, hyperbolic geometry is shown to be a suitable space for mapping hierarchical structures [3]. Other works provide a combined version of geometries such as GIE [7] that showed promising results in static KGs. Recently, several Temporal Knowledge Graph Embedding (TKGE) models have also considered non-Euclidean geometry or mixed spaces [14,21]. Temporal KGs (TKGs) add time information to triples, which means that some connections between entities have two properties, i.e., relation and time. Facts in TKGs are quadruples in the form of (subject, relation, object, timestamp). Timestamps (τ) can be represented in various forms, e.g., time points, start/end time, or time intervals. While relations are dynamic in forming different structures, time information in knowledge graphs follows a static, linear nature. When previous works used non-Euclidean geometries for knowledge graph embeddings, this choice of geometry also affected time information.

Our main research hypothesis is that this negatively affects the performance of the model. In Fig. 1, we showcase this problem using subgraphs taken from the GDELT dataset [18], which we re-labeled with movie information and year granularity to simplify understanding. As can be seen, the time information is linear while the relations are forming hierarchical structures. In order to preserve the relational patterns of the symbolic space (i.e. the knowledge graph) in the embedding space, geometries with special features such as hyperbolic space are used [14,21]. The hyperbolic space has negative curvature and the distance between two points on its surface grows exponentially with radius increase, while the discrete chain structure of time requires a zero curvature with a polynomial growth of surface with radius increase. For example, changing all timestamps in a subgraph by 10 years should not change the relative distance of entities in this subgraph. For Euclidean geometry this is the case, but not for hyperbolic geometry.

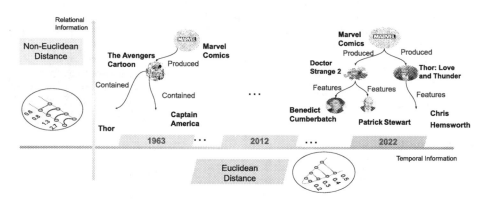

Fig. 1. Movie information is illustrated with different structures of the temporal (Euclidean for linear) and relational part (Non-Euclidean for hierarchical).

In order to address this issue in temporal KGs, we propose a model that captures both the relational and temporal parts appropriately. We provide different views of the underlying temporal knowledge graph: one is the relational part that includes the subject and object entities and their relations, and the other part is the temporal knowledge that includes the subject and object entities and timestamps. Our approach for TKG embedding dubbed TRE (temporal and relational embeddings) that treats these two parts with different geometries. To the best of our knowledge, the proposed approach is the first one using distinct geometries (Euclidean and hyperbolic) simultaneously for Temporal KGs. When providing different views, we first split the quadruples into relational and temporal parts, and then embed the relational parts of the underlying TKG into a hyperbolic space to keep the hierarchies and other complex structures, and embed temporal parts into the Euclidean space that follows the nature of time. One possible issue after splitting a quadruple into relational and temporal parts is that the model can possibly overwrite the relational parts that are same and would normally only be distinguishable with differences in temporal part. We avoid this issue by defining time-related hyperplanes that implicitly keep the temporal information in the relational part. In this way, the embeddings in different time-related hyperplanes that belong to one entity are different. Thereby, our model can even distinguish the same relational parts originally having different temporal parts. Attention based-transformations have been proved to be effective for logical patterns such as symmetry, asymmetry or mixed-behaviour relations (i.e. neither symmetric nor anti-symmetric) in static KGs [9]. In TKGs, timestamps also form relational patterns. We adapt an attention-based rotation and reflection from static KGE models to the temporal KGE model. In this way, our model has a good grasp of facts based on relations and timestamps and the experiments demonstrate that TRE significantly outperforms the other models in low dimensions.

2   Related Work

Geometries in Non-temporal Knowledge Graph Embedding Models. Most of proposed KGE models have geometric and algebraic limitations. Until very recently, many of the KGE models were proposed either in linear or complex spaces. Several state-of-the-art KGE models such as TransE [6] and RotatE [26] represent entities as points in a low-dimensional flat space, and relations are translations and rotations to map subject embeddings to their corresponding object embeddings, respectively. The scores are calculated as geodesic distance between the embeddings of the mapped subject and object entities. There are other KGE models that embed entities as vectors and relations as matrices. For example, RESCAL [23] and ComplEx [27] calculate the scores by a bilinear product of these embeddings. Other track of work is neural-based models such as ConvE [11], ConvKB [22]. All of these models have been designed in Euclidean space, however they used complex or hyper complex algebraic bases where transformations such as Homothety have been made possible. Recently, chain of works focuses on providing non-Euclidean spaces such as MURP [3], AttH [9] and GIE [7], which have shown the outstanding performance on using hyperbolic or spherical geometries. These models are proven to perform best for complex structural patterns such as hierarchical and loop structures but only on static KGs. Although KGEs have widely gained major attention in using non-Euclidean spaces, they have limitations for time-sensitive facts.

Geometries in Temporal Knowledge Graph Embedding Models. TKGE models use embeddings to represent temporal information along entities and relations. Many TKGE models are built based on the existing KGE models. TTransE [17], the temporal version of TransE, treats timestamps as extra translations. HyTE [10], an extension of TransH [30] to TKGs, represents the timestamps by learnable temporal hyperplanes. Both of these temporal KGEs are in Euclidean space. Based on ComplEx model, two models namely TComplEx and TNTComplEx [16] are designed to factorize TKG as a tensor. TeRo [31] defines the temporal evolution of entity embedding as a rotation from the initial time to the current time in the complex vector space. ChronoR [24] treats timestamps and relations as rotation and scale to do the prediction. BoxTE [20] is a box embedding model for TKGC, and is adapted based on the BoxE model from static KGE model to a temporal KGE. Despite the use of different algebraic aspects, all of these models are designed in Euclidean space. Recently, temporal KGE models are also considered non-Euclidean space such as DyERNIE [14] that learns evolving entity representations on a product of Riemannian manifolds with heterogeneous curvatures. HERCULES [21] is a TKGE model in a hyperbolic space, as an extension of ATTH by defining a curvature as a product of both relations and time. While, the overall performance of these models have increased, their evaluation methodology follows static KGE models where time is not taken into account when filtering entities. Therefore, the comparison is not fair to other models that use time-wise filtering. In the case of TKGEs, doing link prediction without timestamps can potentially lead to a fake high ranking of the facts. This is due to the confusion of the model in considering many wrong predictions as correct prediction. Therefore, currently a non-Euclidean temporal KGE model that is designed with a distinct geometrical representation for time and relational structures, also being correctly evaluated is missing. This gap is bridged in this work by contributions on proposing the use of different but more suitable geometries for each parts of time and relational knowledge.

3   Preliminaries

3.1   Temporal Knowledge Graph Completion

TKGs are multi-relational and directed graphs containing temporal information. We define $\mathcal{E}, \mathcal{R}, \mathcal{T}$ as the sets of entities, relations and timestamps, respectively. Each fact in a TKG can be defined as a quadruple $q = (s, r, o, \tau)$, where $s \in \mathcal{E}$ is referred to the subject entity, $o \in \mathcal{E}$ is referred to the object entity, $r \in R$ is a relation between s and o, and $\tau \in \mathcal{T}$ is a timestamp. Temporal Knowledge Graph Embedding (TKGE) models aim at completing TKGs by learning d-dimensional vector representations of entities ($\mathcal{E}$), relations ($\mathcal{R}$), and timestamps ($\mathcal{T}$) denoted by $(\mathbf{s}, \mathbf{r}, \mathbf{o}, \tau)$ per quadruple (s, r, o, τ). The original facts in the TKG without timestamps are assigned with unique timestamp embedding. A TKGE score function computes the plausibility of a quadruple by mapping (s, r, o, sτ) to a real value.

3.2   Hyperbolic Geometry

Hyperbolic geometry is a non-Euclidean geometry with negative sectional curvature. In our work, we use a d-dimensional Poincaré ball from hyperbolic geometry, to model the relational parts of TKGs, i.e. (s, r, o). We denote the non-negative curvature as $-c\,(c > 0)$, and define the Poincaré ball as $\mathrm{B}^{d,c} = \{x \in \mathbb{R}^d : \|x\|^2 < \frac{1}{c}\}$, where $\|\cdot\|$ is the L^2 norm. We therefore denote by T_x^c, the tangent space associated to $x \in B^{d,c}$. By definition, this space contains the tangent vector of all hyperbolic lines in $B^{d,c}$ leaving from x. The tangent space follows a Euclidean geometry.

We can map a tangent vector of T_x^c onto $B^{d,c}$ via the exponential map. Conversely, we can also map vectors of $B^{d,c}$ onto T_x^c via the logarithmic map. Considering the tangent space T_0^c, these two functions are defined as follows:

$$\exp_0^c(x) = \tanh(\sqrt{c}\|x\|)\frac{x}{\sqrt{c}\|x\|}, \tag{1}$$

$$\log_0^c(y) = \operatorname{arctanh}(\sqrt{c}\|y\|)\frac{y}{\sqrt{c}\|y\|}. \tag{2}$$

Due to the non-zero curvature, addition in hyperbolic geometry is replaced with Möbius addition [28], which is a closed operation in the Poincaré ball. It is expressed as follows:

$$x \oplus_c y = \frac{(1 - 2cx^T y - c\|y\|^2)x + (1 + c\|x\|^2)y}{1 - 2cx^T y + c^2\|x\|^2\|y\|^2}. \tag{3}$$

Finally, the hyperbolic distance function between two vectors x and y is defined as:

$$d_c^H(x, y) = \frac{2}{\sqrt{c}}\operatorname{arctanh}(\sqrt{c}\|-x \oplus_c y\|). \tag{4}$$

3.3 Hyperbolic Transformations

We let $R(\Theta)$ and $F(\Phi)$ represent rotations and reflections in the hyperbolic space respectively, which are modeled using the Givens transformation matrices [2]. In 2d space, it is parameterized by a 2×2 matrix:

$$R(\theta) = \begin{bmatrix} \cos(\theta) & -\sin(\theta) \\ \sin(\theta) & \cos(\theta) \end{bmatrix}. \tag{5}$$

These matrices are block diagonalized,

$$R(\Theta) = \operatorname{diag}(R(\theta_1),...,R(\theta_d)), \tag{6}$$

to achieve rotation in high dimension. In Eq. (6), Θ denotes the set $\{\theta_i : i = 1, \ldots, d\}$. Since the blocks are 2×2 matrices $R(\theta_i)$, only rotation in even high dimension can be achieved by this formalism. Equation (6) represents a rotation in $2d$ dimensional Euclidean space. On the other hand, reflection in 2d dimensional Euclidean space, can be represented by the block diagonal matrix

$$F(\Phi) = \operatorname{diag}(F(\phi_1),...,F(\phi_d)) \tag{7}$$

where

$$F(\phi_i) = \begin{bmatrix} \cos(\phi_i) & \sin(\phi_i) \\ \sin(\phi_i) & -\cos(\phi_i) \end{bmatrix} \tag{8}$$

and Φ is the set of reflection angles, ϕ_i, in the 2D plane.

The limitation of Euclidean geometry in preserving hierarchical structures in KG, has created the need to consider rotation and reflection in non-Euclidean space. One way to extend this formalism to hyperbolic spaces, H, is through the use of the exponential and the logarithm maps defined in Eqs. (1) and (2). Let us consider the point $\mathbf{x}^H \in H$. Its tangent vector $\mathbf{x} \in T_0^c$, is obtained by applying the logarithm map as

$$\mathbf{x} = \log_0^c \mathbf{x}^H. \tag{9}$$

By applying the exponential map to the linear transformation $M\mathbf{x}$, we obtain the hyperbolic point

$$\mathbf{y}^H = \exp_0^c (M\mathbf{x}) \tag{10}$$

which is the hyperbolic rotation ($M = R(\Theta)$) or reflection ($M = F(\Phi)$) of $\mathbf{x}^H$.

4   Methodology

The proposed model is designed such that it (1) projects embeddings to time-related hyperplanes, (2) uses rotation and reflection to transform entities, (3) uses time-dependent and relation-specific curvature to make the hyperbolic manifolds time and relation dependent, (4) learns embeddings of relational parts in hyperbolic space, suitable for hierarchical structure. (5) learns embeddings of temporal parts in the Euclidean space, which is suitable for chain structure. The following sections are detailed description.

4.1   Time-Related Hyperplane

For all the facts that are in the form of quadruple (s, r, o, τ), in a TKG, we project the relational parts that has same temporal part τ, onto their associated time-specific hyperplane $\mathcal{H}_\tau$. In this way, we implicitly encode the relational part (s, r, o) with the temporal information denoted by (s_τ, r_τ, o_τ). Thus, the model uses time-related hyperplanes to bring temporal information into the relational parts. Embeddings of the facts with the same relational part but different times, are portrayed on their corresponding time-related hyperplanes. Moreover, the

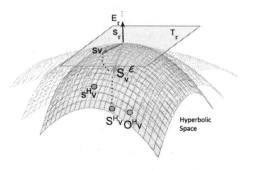

Fig. 2. Time-related Hyperplane and Hyperbolic Space of TRE for a corresponding vector of a subject entity and its temporal part. TRE uses attention mechanism with rotation and reflection to locate the subject vector closer to a possible object vector.

hyperplanes, characterized by their normal unit vector, w_τ, are the direct sum of two Euclidean subspaces: T_τ and E_τ, where the former serves as a tangent space at point 0 of a Poincaré ball and the latter serves as a medium for explicitly propagating time information from subject entities to object entities of temporal facts. We denote entity embeddings by e and their projection onto $\mathcal{H}_\tau$ by $\mathbf{e}_{\mathcal{H}_\tau} = \mathbf{e}_\tau + \mathbf{e}_\nu$ where $\mathbf{e}_\tau \in E_\tau$ and $\mathbf{e}_\nu \in T_\tau$. In other words,

$$\mathbf{e}_{\mathcal{H}_\tau} = \mathbf{e}_\nu + \mathbf{e}_\tau = \mathbf{e} - (w_\tau^T \mathbf{e})w_\tau. \tag{11}$$

We replace e by s or o when we want to refer to the embeddings of the subject or object entities, respectively. As shown in Fig. 2, we illustrate how this mechanism works for the corresponding vector of a subject entity.

4.2   Transformation for Temporal and Relational Parts

Temporal facts with the same timestamp, τ, form a time-related Knowledge Graph, $\mathcal{G}_\tau = \{(s_\tau, r_\tau, o_\tau) : (s, r, o, \tau) \in TKG\}$. Therefore, for each timestamp, τ, we have its corresponding knowledge graph, $\mathcal{G}_\tau$ and its associated hyperplane $\mathcal{H}_\tau$. The relations r_τ exhibit many relational patterns, mainly symmetry or antisymmetry, transitivity, composition, inversion, and so on. In order to preserve these relational patterns, we decided to represent relations by rotation and reflection; these two transformations are widely used in KGE models [26]. While rotation can preserve all the aforementioned relational properties, reflection through a plane, an involutive transformation, fails to adequately preserve antisymmetric relations. However, it is more flexible in preserving symmetric relations.

Given Eq. (11), we define rotation of the subject embeddings on the hyperplanes as

$$\mathbf{S}_{rot} = \begin{bmatrix} R(\Theta_\nu) & 0 \\ 0 & R(\Theta_\tau) \end{bmatrix} \mathbf{s}_{\mathcal{H}_\tau} \tag{12}$$

which could substantially be reduced to

$$\mathbf{S}_{rot} = R(\Theta_\nu)\mathbf{s}_\nu + R(\Theta_\tau)\mathbf{s}_\tau, \tag{13}$$

and reflection as

$$\mathbf{S}_{ref} = F(\Phi_\nu)\mathbf{s}_\nu + F(\Phi_\tau)\mathbf{s}_\tau. \tag{14}$$

Furthermore, in order to better combine the advantages of rotation and reflection, we use the attention mechanism to allow the model to better adapt to symmetric, asymmetric, and composition features. The attention mechanism uses relation and timestamp specific attention vectors and coefficients. The two attention coefficients, α_{rot} and α_{ref}, associated to relation and timestamp, are positive real scalers whose values quantified how much relation and timestamp adhere to rotation or reflection embeddings or to a mixture of both. This adhesion is guided by the relational patterns present in the TKG. The attention vector and coefficients are related by the equation below:

$$(\alpha_{rot}, \alpha_{ref}) = \text{softmax}\left(\alpha^T \mathbf{S}_{rot}, \alpha^T \mathbf{S}_{ref}\right) \tag{15}$$

The model learns the new embeddings in the hyperplanes as:

$$\mathbf{S}_\nu^E + \mathbf{S}_\tau^E = \mathbf{S}^E = \alpha_{rot}\mathbf{S}_{rot} + \alpha_{ref}\mathbf{S}_{ref}. \tag{16}$$

We note that $\mathbf{S}^E$ is separated into two parts, $\mathbf{S}_\nu^E$ and $\mathbf{S}_\tau^E$, which are the projections of $\alpha_{rot}\mathbf{S}_{rot} + \alpha_{ref}\mathbf{S}_{ref}$ from $\mathcal{H}_\tau$ to T_τ and E_τ respectively. Since, the object entity embeddings do not undergo any linear transformation, we conclude $\mathbf{o}_\nu^E = \mathbf{o}_\nu$ and $\mathbf{o}_\tau^E = \mathbf{o}_\tau$ from Eq. (11).

4.3   Geometric Score

Hyperbolic geometric embeddings are designed to capture complex structures such as hierarchies. In order to do so, we set the curvature of the hyperbolic space to a trainable parameter. It is defined in the parametric form

$$c_{\nu,\tau} = softplus(c_\nu \times c_\tau) \tag{17}$$

where c_ν and c_τ refer to relation and timestamp specific curvatures. Through curvatures, the embeddings of the explicit non-temporal parts of the object, $\mathbf{o}_\nu^E$, and transformed subject, $\mathbf{S}_\nu^E$, entities are projected from the hyperplane to the hyperbolic space while keeping the implicit influence of the associated time. This is performed by:

$$\mathbf{S}_\nu^H = \exp_0^{c_{\nu,\tau}}(\mathbf{S}_\nu^E), \quad \mathbf{o}_\nu^H = \exp_0^{c_{\nu,\tau}}(\mathbf{o}_\nu^E). \tag{18}$$

For the transformed subject entities, the projection is followed by a möbius addition, i.e. a hyperbolic translation defined by

$$\mathbf{X}_\nu^H = \exp_0^{c_{\nu,\tau}}(\mathbf{S}_\nu^H \oplus_c \mathbf{r}^H) \tag{19}$$

where $\mathbf{r}^H$ is the hyperbolic embedding of relations. The score function for the hyperbolic geometric interaction is defined as:

$$\begin{aligned} h(s_\tau, r_\tau, o_\tau) &= -d_{\mathbf{c}_{\nu,\tau}}^H(\mathbf{X}_\nu^H, \mathbf{o}_\nu^H) \\ &= -\frac{2}{\sqrt{c_{\nu,\tau}}}\operatorname{arctanh}(\sqrt{c_{\nu,\tau}}\,\|-\mathbf{X}_\nu^H \oplus_c \mathbf{o}_\nu^H\|). \end{aligned} \tag{20}$$

In order to allow the propagation of time information from subject to object entities, we used Euclidean geometry and translation. The score of Euclidean geometric interaction is then defined as

$$g(s, o, \tau) = -d^E(\mathbf{X}_\tau^E, \mathbf{o}_\tau^E) = -\|\mathbf{X}_\tau^E - \mathbf{o}_\tau^E\| \tag{21}$$

where $\mathbf{X}_\tau^E = \mathbf{S}_\tau^E + \tau^E$, and τ represents the timestamp embeddings in E_τ.

4.4   The TRE Model

Different geometries for temporal and relational embeddings (TRE) is the proposed model that treats time flow in a flat space and relational structures in a hyperbolic space. TRE defines two entity embeddings as $\mathbf{e}_\nu^H$ in hyperbolic space, and $\mathbf{e}_\tau^E$ in Euclidean space. Both have two particular latent embeddings $\mathbf{e}_\nu$ and $\mathbf{e}_\tau$, defined on a hyperplane associated to the timestamp of the quadruple in which the subject and object entities co-appear. TRE performs hyperbolic rotation and/or reflection (Eqs. 6, 7, 9, 15, 16, 18) followed by hyperbolic translation (Eq. 19) of subject entity $\mathbf{s}_\nu^H$, and Euclidean rotation and/or reflection (Eqs. 6, 7) followed by translation of $\mathbf{s}_\tau^E$ to transform the subject entity to $\mathbf{X}_\nu^H$ and $\mathbf{X}_\tau^E$ respectively. The model interaction with the object entity is resumed to its embeddings $\mathbf{o}_\nu^H$ and $\mathbf{o}_\tau^E$. The score of quadruples is assessed by the total score function

$$f(s, r, o, \tau) = h(s_\tau, r_\tau, o_\tau) + g(s, o, \tau) + b_s + b_o$$
$$= -d^H_{c_{\nu,\tau}}(\mathbf{X}^H_\nu, \mathbf{o}^H_\nu) - d^E(\mathbf{X}^E_\tau, \mathbf{o}^E_\tau) + b_s + b_o \tag{22}$$

where b_s and b_o are biases related to subject and object entities. For each quadruple (s, r, o, τ), k negative samples are generated by a random corruption of subject or object entities. We use binary cross-entropy as the loss function, which is defined as

$$L = -\frac{1}{N}\sum_{i=1}^{N}\left(log(p_i) + \sum_{j=1}^{k}(log(1 - p_{i,j}))\right). \tag{23}$$

In Eq. (23), N is the total number of training samples, and p_i and $p_{i,j}$ are the probabilities of positive and negative quadruples, where $p = \sigma\left(f\left(s, r, o, \tau\right)\right)$ and $\sigma\left(\cdot\right)$ is the sigmoid function.

5   Experiments

5.1   Experimental Setup

Datasets. In order to provide a fair and comprehensive comparison, three different types of benchmark datasets (ICEWS14 [12], Yago15k [12], and GDELT [18]) that have been used by previous state-of-the-art TKGEs are considered in our work. Statistics on these datasets are provided in Table 1. ICEWS14 provides geopolitical information occurred regularly in 2014. Because of geopolitical events, the relations between entities are sparse and less temporally related. Yago15k is a modification of FB15K [6] with timestamps for some of the facts shown with "occursSince" and "occursUntil". The facts without timestamps are shown as triples and the ones with timestamps are represented in the form of quintuples (subject, relation, object, type of timestamp, timestamp). The third dataset GDELT is a subset of Global Database of Events, Language, and Tone that contains the facts about human behaviors. Thus, facts in this dataset have rich temporal patterns. And it contains facts with timestamps from April 1, 2015 to March 31, 2016. GDELT have only 500 entities and 20 relations, which makes it a dense dataset.

In order to analyse the ability of our model in ablation experiments about representing relational parts and temporal parts, in the three last columns of Table 1, we report the number of relations whose Krackhardt hierarchical score [15] is higher than 60%; and among these relations, we counted and report the number of relations whose maximum path (Max) and average path (Avg) are greater than 2.

Table 1. Statistics and Hierarchical information for ICEWS14, Yago15k and GDELT.

	$|\mathcal{E}|$	$|\mathcal{R}|$	$|\mathcal{T}|$	N_{train}	N_{valid}	N_{test}	$Khs > 60\%$	$Max > 2$	$Avg > 2$
ICEWS14	7128	230	365	72826	8963	8941	217	70	23
YAGO15k	15403	34	198	110441	13815	13800	47	5	4
GDELT	500	20	366	2735685	341961	341961	7	7	7

Evaluation Metrics. For each quadruple (s, r, o, τ) in the test set, two queries of form $(s, r, ?, \tau)$ and $(o, r^{-1}, ?, \tau)$ are created. For each query, the model replaces all possible entities with ? and scores the generated quadruples. The results are then evaluated by Mean Reciprocal Rank (MRR), and H@n where $n \in \{1, 3, 10\}$. MRR is measured by $\sum_{j=1}^{n_t} \frac{1}{r_j}$, where r_j is the rank of the j-th test quadruple and n_t is the number of triples in the test set. It represents the overall performance of a model. H@n is the probability of the number of test quadruples ranked less than n.

Time-Wise Entity Filtering. The time-wise entity filtering [13] is used to remove all the candidate entities which yield correct quadruples. However, several works have evaluated their methods by using only entity filtering that is suitable for non-temporal KGs [14,21]. In this way, time information, that leads to negative but plausible facts, is ignored. Consequently, the removal of such false negative candidates leads to higher rankings. This is avoided in TRE with the time-wise entity filtering method. In our experiments, our model and baseline models are evaluated by time-wise entity filtering.

Baseline Models. TRE is compared to well-performing KGE and TKGE models, namely TERO [31], TNTComplEx [16], ATTH [9], HERCULES [21] and BoxTE [20]. ATTH is a KGE model in hyperbolic space. In the area of TKGE, there are two models built in hyperbolic space, namely DyERNIE [14] and HERCULES. DyERNIE is built on a variable hyperbolic manifold, and HERCULES is the extension of ATTH in TKGs. In our experiments, we only compare TRE to HERCULES as the original results of DyERNIE are achieved by non-temporal KGE filtering and is not reproducible In addition, DyERNIE is outperformed by HERCULES.

Hyperparameter Setting. Evaluations are done in multiple dimensions of entities including 30, 50, and 100. Adam optimizer is used with learning rate of 0.001, 0.005, and the cross-entropy loss is minimized by using negative samples which are uniformly generated from valid entities.

5.2   Analysis and Results

Performance Analysis. As shown in Table 2, TRE outperforms the considered KGE and TKGE models in all the metrics for all three datasets in dimension 30. This is the same for other dimensions, except for H@10 of ICEWS14 in dimensions 50 and 100, and H@1 of Yago15k in dimension 100. As can be seen in Table 1, among the number of relations with high hierarchical scores in Yago15k, there are only 10.6% of the relations that have more than 2 paths and only 8.5% of the relations whose average numbers of paths are more than 2. This means the Yago15k dataset is not rich in hierarchical structures. We observe that although 94.3% of the relations in the ICEWS14 dataset have high hierarchical scores, only 32.3% of the candidate relations have a maximum path greater than 2. Therefore, this dataset has less hierarchical structure. In contrary, GDELT is rich in hierarchical structure since all the 35% of its candidate relations have a maximum and an average path equal to 7. It is noteworthy that ICEWS14 is a sparse TKG and largely temporally uncorrelated across distinct entities. Therefore, TRE shows 5.9% better performance on this dataset compared to other TKGE models that treat the time and relation on the same geometry.

As mentioned before, the Yago15k dataset has either triples without timestamp and quintuples with extra time indicator property. Because of this special pattern, most of

Table 2. Results of performance analyses of baselines and TRE in dimensions 30, 50, and 100 (all the results for these dimensions are produced in this work. The highest values per metric are shown in bold and not achievable results are dashed.)

Datasets		ICEWS14				Yago15k				GDELT			
dim	Model	MRR	H@1	H@3	H@10	MRR	H@1	H@3	H@10	MRR	H@1	H@3	H@10
30	ATTH	0.402	0.281	0.455	0.648	0.252	0.174	0.261	0.444	0.189	0.114	0.201	0.33
	HERCULES	0.419	0.301	0.475	0.652	0.261	0.188	0.265	0.448	0.190	0.116	0.202	0.331
	TERO	0.309	0.185	0.361	0.564	-	-	-	-	0.161	0.0904	0.17	0.3
	TNTComplEx	0.475	0.368	0.534	0.682	0.290	0.224	0.290	0.460	0.208	0.131	0.222	0.359
	BoxTE	0.471	0.350	0.535	0.707	0.221	0.140	0.233	0.407	0.211	0.133	0.225	0.360
	TRE (our)	**0.503**	**0.394**	**0.567**	**0.708**	**0.322**	**0.246**	**0.333**	**0.498**	**0.220**	**0.141**	**0.235**	**0.372**
50	ATTH	0.423	0.301	0.483	0.666	0.304	0.232	0.309	0.487	0.198	0.12	0.211	0.347
	HERCULES	0.436	0.316	0.494	0.671	0.310	0.240	0.316	0.490	0.199	0.121	0.211	0.348
	TERO	0.379	0.254	0.44	0.635	-	-	-	-	0.179	0.103	0.189	0.326
	TNTComplEx	0.504	0.402	0.560	0.700	0.320	0.256	0.321	0.487	0.224	0.144	0.239	0.377
	BoxTE	0.512	0.401	0.578	**0.723**	0.275	0.194	0.287	0.465	0.223	0.143	0.239	0.375
	TRE (our)	**0.544**	**0.445**	**0.604**	0.720	**0.335**	**0.257**	**0.346**	**0.521**	**0.235**	**0.153**	**0.252**	**0.393**
100	ATTH	0.450	0.329	0.511	0.691	0.292	0.215	0.304	0.485	0.206	0.126	0.220	0.361
	HERCULES	0.452	0.332	0.511	0.691	0.284	0.205	0.296	0.476	0.206	0.125	0.219	0.361
	TERO	0.454	0.34	0.522	0.670	-	-	-	-	0.202	0.123	0.215	0.353
	TNTComplEx	0.533	0.435	0.589	0.718	0.338	**0.270**	0.341	0.508	0.242	0.160	0.258	0.400
	BoxTE	0.558	0.457	0.621	**0.743**	0.292	0.215	0.299	0.482	0.241	0.159	0.259	0.400
	TRE (our)	**0.579**	**0.493**	**0.629**	0.733	**0.339**	0.257	**0.354**	**0.531**	**0.255**	**0.171**	**0.274**	**0.416**

the embeddings are affected by non-temporal facts during training. Therefore, these baseline models do not perform well except TNTComplEx as it is specifically designed for this situation. But on this dataset, TRE outperforms TNTComplEx by 11% in 30 dimension in MRR. As the dimension increases, the gap between two models decreases. For the GDELT dataset, TRE outperforms the others in all the metrics, and improves previous performances by a margin of 4.3%. Among these models, ATTH and HER-CULES are hyperbolic models, our model is significantly better. And compared with the box embedding model and tensor models, the overall performance of our model is also much better. Overall the results show that learning relation-related structures in hyperbolic spaces and time-related information in Euclidean spaces is effective.

Impact of Geometric Space. In Table 3, we conducted an experiment by providing three variants of TRE: a) *TRE-original* where two different geometries of Euclidean and hyperbolic are used, b) *TRE-Euclidean* where Euclidean geometry is used for both time and relational parts, c) *TRE-hyperbolic* where hyperbolic space is used for both temporal and relational structures. *TRE-original* shows a higher performance than the other two versions in major cases. *TRE-hyperbolic* performs better on ICEWS14 only in H@10 and for dimensions 30 and 50. This can be due to its sparsity and uncorre-lated time for distinct entities. If we only compare *TRE-hyperbolic* and *TRE-Euclidean*, in Yago15k, we observe that by dimension increase (100), the embeddings of times-tamps are more expressive and distinguishable by *TRE-Euclidean*. While *TRE-original* outperforms the other two versions in all metrics in GDELT dataset, the performance

Table 3. Impact of different geometries is evaluated by three versions of TRE: *TRE-hyperbolic* represents facts on the hyperbolic space for both temporal and relational parts; *TRE-Euclidean* model uses Euclidean for both, and *TRE-original* is the TRE with different geometries.

Datasets		ICEWS14				Yago15k				GDELT			
dim	Model	MRR	H@1	H@3	H@10	MRR	H@1	H@3	H@10	MRR	H@1	H@3	H@10
30	TRE-hyperbolic	0.481	0.361	0.548	**0.713**	0.308	0.226	0.321	**0.502**	0.219	0.140	0.234	0.371
	TRE-Euclidean	0.471	0.350	0.537	0.706	0.294	0.212	0.305	0.489	0.219	0.140	0.234	0.371
	TRE-original	**0.503**	**0.394**	**0.567**	0.708	**0.322**	**0.246**	**0.333**	0.498	**0.220**	**0.141**	**0.235**	**0.372**
50	TRE-hyperbolic	0.511	0.395	0.579	**0.734**	0.331	0.251	0.345	0.519	0.233	0.152	0.250	0.390
	TRE-Euclidean	0.505	0.386	0.572	**0.734**	0.329	0.248	0.342	0.520	0.233	0.151	0.250	0.390
	TRE-original	**0.544**	**0.445**	**0.604**	0.720	**0.335**	**0.257**	**0.346**	**0.521**	**0.235**	**0.153**	**0.252**	**0.393**
100	TRE-hyperbolic	0.575	0.478	**0.635**	0.750	0.335	0.252	0.350	0.528	0.250	0.167	0.269	0.411
	TRE-Euclidean	0.570	0.471	0.630	**0.751**	0.337	0.254	0.353	0.530	0.250	0.167	0.269	0.410
	TRE-original	**0.579**	**0.493**	0.629	0.733	**0.339**	**0.257**	**0.354**	**0.531**	**0.255**	**0.171**	**0.274**	**0.416**

of *TRE-Euclidean* and *TRE-hyperbolic* are similar. As shown in the last three columns of Table 1, this dataset is rich in hierarchical relations. The results show that the hyperbolic space is more suitable to represent relational structures. However, we also observe competitive results in Euclidean space, which is originally not suitable for hierarchical structures but for temporal ones.

Impact of Geometric Operations. In Table 4, we conduct an ablation experiment on several geometric operations of TRE and show results of these versions. In *TRE-Rel*, rotations and reflections are only related to relational structures, and *TRE-Time* is only related to timestamps. *TRE-Rot* only does rotation, and *TRE-Ref* only does reflection. *TRE-NoPlane* does not use time-related hyperplane. These results are in correlation with dataset characteristics shows in Table 1. In the case of Yago15K, the results are higher by *TRE-Rel* which is explained with the low number of timestamps, and presence of time-related information in the entire dataset. In the case of ICEWS14, model setting on *TRE-Time* and *TRE-Ref* show higher performance which is due to the special structure of timestamps. And for GDELT, the results show the richness both in relational and temporal structure.

Impact of Dimensions. With dimension increase, we can see from Fig. 3 that on Yago15k and ICEWS14 datasets, the results of TNTComplEx and BoxTE have larger improvement that TRE. As mentioned above, this is also caused by the characteristics of these datasets. In other words, such models are not capable of capturing characteristics in low dimensions. In GDELT dataset, we can see that the performance improvement of our model is much more than BoxTE and TNTComplEx which is due to its ability in learning temporal information. We conclude that for real world TKGs with rich temporal knowledge and dense graph structures, TRE can show higher performance difference with regard to different dimensions.

Geometry for Time Preservation. To further demonstrate our hypothesis that timestamps can be better represented in the Euclidean space, we show the distribution of

Table 4. Different settings of experiments with planes and transformations. TRE-Time has a focus on temporal part only with both rotation and reflection, TRE-Rel has a focus on relational part also both with rotation and reflection. TRE-Rot is a setting where only a rotation transformation is used for both temporal and relational parts, and TRE-Ref is focused with only reflection on both temporal and relational parts. We additionally show a setting of TRE-NoPlane where time-related hyperplane is removed, also show the results of TRE-original.

Datasets	ICEWS14				Yago15k				GDELT			
Model	MRR	H@1	H@3	H@10	MRR	H@1	H@3	H@10	MRR	H@1	H@3	H@10
TRE-Time	**0.539**	**0.426**	**0.608**	0.748	0.333	0.25	0.35	0.525	0.243	0.159	**0.262**	**0.409**
TRE-Rel	0.530	0.409	0.602	**0.759**	**0.343**	**0.264**	**0.353**	**0.539**	0.244	0.161	0.262	0.406
TRE-Rot	0.526	0.404	0.604	0.76	**0.345**	**0.267**	**0.357**	**0.534**	0.247	0.163	0.265	0.409
TRE-Ref	**0.571**	**0.463**	**0.641**	**0.764**	0.343	0.265	0.353	0.53	**0.252**	**0.167**	**0.271**	**0.416**
TRE-NoPlane	0.552	0.438	0.624	0.764	0.336	0.257	0.345	0.53	0.247	0.163	0.267	0.410
TRE-original	**0.579**	**0.493**	0.629	0.733	0.339	0.257	0.354	0.531	**0.255**	**0.171**	**0.274**	**0.416**

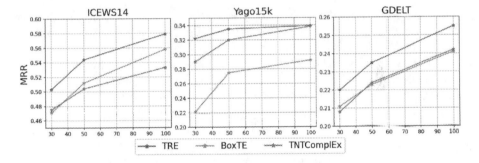

Fig. 3. Impact of dimension on performance increase by comparing on the MRR results of TNT-ComplEx, BoxTE and TRE on dimensions 30, 50, and 100.

time embeddings in Fig. 4. Due to the rich structure both in temporal and relation parts, we selected GDELT for this experiment. For reduction of dimension from 100 to 2, t-SNE is used where timestamps of facts are grouped into 12 months, which are marked with different colors. Because the hyperbolic space in our model is not fixed, and the points in tangent space at 0 point can also reflect the distribution, all time embeddings are analysed in Euclidean space. Figure (a) is time embeddings of TRE-hyperbolic in the tangent space, and figure (b) is time embeddings of TRE-Euclidean in the Euclidean space. We can clearly see that the distribution in (b) is strictly in chronological order, while the distribution of some groups in (a) are scattered. Besides, we can also find that points of TRE-Euclidean have been well classified, while some groups of TRE-hyperbolic are very scattered and messy. So we can conclude that temporal information can be well represented in Euclidean space.

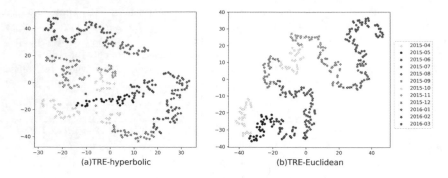

Fig. 4. Distribution of time embeddings on GDELT.

6 Conclusion

In this paper, we proposed a novel TKGE model for temporal knowledge graphs that uses different geometric spaces for the temporal and relation parts. Specifically, the relational part of the TKG is represented in hyperbolic space and the temporal part in euclidean space. Through several studies, we show suitability of hyperbolic space for relational part and Euclidean geometry for capturing the natural chain structure of temporal information. We could positively answer our research hypothesis by showing that the resulting model outperforms most competing models across three different benchmark datasets and multiple dimension sizes. We provided statistics on the extent to which the underlying knowledge graphs have hierarchical structures and their effect in analysis. We also visually illustrated the resultant time embeddings that follows the natural structure of time from symbolic space.

Acknowledgement. We acknowledge the support of the China Scholarship Council for the first author, and contribution of the following EU projects: CALLISTO(101004152), E-Vita (101016453), ScaDS.AI (IS18026A-F). We thank the Natural Science Foundation of China (42271391 and 62006214), Joint Funds of Equipment Pre-Research and Ministry of Education of China Grant No. 8091B022148, the 14th Five-year Pre-research Project of Civil Aerospace in China, and Hubei excellent young and middle-aged science and technology innovation team plan project under Grant No. T2021031. The authors are grateful to the Center for Information Services and High Performance Computing [Zentrum für Informationsdienste und Hochleistungsrechnen (ZIH)] at TU Dresden for providing its facilities for high throughput calculations, and Leipzig universities.

References

1. Ali, M., et al.: Bringing light into the dark: a large-scale evaluation of knowledge graph embedding models under a unified framework. IEEE Trans. Pattern Anal. Mach. Intell. (2021)
2. Anderson, E.: Discontinuous plane rotations and the symmetric eigenvalue problem (2000)
3. Balažević, I., Allen, C., Hospedales, T.: Multi-relational poincaré graph embeddings. In: Advances in Neural Information Processing Systems (2019)

4. Bellomarini, L., Sallinger, E., Vahdati, S.: Chapter 2 Knowledge graphs: the layered perspective. In: Janev, V., Graux, D., Jabeen, H., Sallinger, E. (eds.) Knowledge Graphs and Big Data Processing. LNCS, vol. 12072, pp. 20–34. Springer, Cham (2020). https://doi.org/10.1007/978-3-030-53199-7_2

5. Bellomarini, L., Sallinger, E., Vahdati, S.: Chapter 6 Reasoning in knowledge graphs: an embeddings spotlight. In: Janev, V., Graux, D., Jabeen, H., Sallinger, E. (eds.) Knowledge Graphs and Big Data Processing. LNCS, vol. 12072, pp. 87–101. Springer, Cham (2020). https://doi.org/10.1007/978-3-030-53199-7_6

6. Bordes, A., Usunier, N., Garcia-Duran, A., Weston, J., Yakhnenko, O.: Translating embeddings for modeling multi-relational data. Advances in neural information processing systems 26 (2013)

7. Cao, Z., Xu, Q., Yang, Z., Cao, X., Huang, Q.: Geometry interaction knowledge graph embeddings. In: AAAI Conference on Artificial Intelligence (2022)

8. Carlson, A., Betteridge, J., Kisiel, B., Settles, B., Hruschka, E.R., Mitchell, T.M.: Toward an architecture for never-ending language learning. In: Twenty-Fourth AAAI Conference on Artificial Intelligence (2010)

9. Chami, I., Wolf, A., Juan, D.C., Sala, F., Ravi, S., Ré, C.: Low-dimensional hyperbolic knowledge graph embeddings. arXiv preprint arXiv:2005.00545 (2020)

10. Dasgupta, S.S., Ray, S.N., Talukdar, P.: Hyte: hyperplane-based temporally aware knowledge graph embedding. In: Proceedings of the 2018 Conference on Empirical Methods in Natural Language Processing, pp. 2001–2011 (2018)

11. Dettmers, T., Minervini, P., Stenetorp, P., Riedel, S.: Convolutional 2d knowledge graph embeddings. In: Proceedings of the AAAI Conference on Artificial Intelligence, vol. 32 (2018)

12. García-Durán, A., Dumančić, S., Niepert, M.: Learning sequence encoders for temporal knowledge graph completion. arXiv preprint arXiv:1809.03202 (2018)

13. Goel, R., Kazemi, S.M., Brubaker, M., Poupart, P.: Diachronic embedding for temporal knowledge graph completion. In: Proceedings of the AAAI Conference on Artificial Intelligence, vol. 34, pp. 3988–3995 (2020)

14. Han, Z., Ma, Y., Chen, P., Tresp, V.: Dyernie: dynamic evolution of riemannian manifold embeddings for temporal knowledge graph completion. arXiv preprint arXiv:2011.03984 (2020)

15. Krackhardt, D.: Graph theoretical dimensions of informal organizations. In: Computational Organization Theory, pp. 107–130. Psychology Press (2014)

16. Lacroix, T., Obozinski, G., Usunier, N.: Tensor decompositions for temporal knowledge base completion. arXiv preprint arXiv:2004.04926 (2020)

17. Leblay, J., Chekol, M.W.: Deriving validity time in knowledge graph. In: Companion Proceedings of the The Web Conference 2018, pp. 1771–1776 (2018)

18. Leetaru, K., Schrodt, P.A.: Gdelt: global data on events, location, and tone, 1979–2012. In: ISA Annual Convention, vol. 2, pp. 1–49. Citeseer (2013)

19. Lehmann, J., et al.: Dbpedia-a large-scale, multilingual knowledge base extracted from Wikipedia. Semantic web **6**(2), 167–195 (2015)

20. Messner, J., Abboud, R., Ceylan, I.I.: Temporal knowledge graph completion using box embeddings. In: Proceedings of the AAAI Conference on Artificial Intelligence, vol. 36, pp. 7779–7787 (2022)

21. Montella, S., Rojas-Barahona, L., Heinecke, J.: Hyperbolic temporal knowledge graph embeddings with relational and time curvatures. arXiv preprint arXiv:2106.04311 (2021)

22. Nguyen, D.Q., Nguyen, T.D., Nguyen, D.Q., Phung, D.: A novel embedding model for knowledge base completion based on convolutional neural network. In: Proceedings of the 16th Annual Conference of the North American Chapter of the Association for Computational Linguistics: Human Language Technologies (NAACL-HLT), pp. 327–333 (2018)

23. Nickel, M., Tresp, V., Kriegel, H.P.: A three-way model for collective learning on multi-relational data. In: ICML (2011)
24. Sadeghian, A., Armandpour, M., Colas, A., Wang, D.Z.: Chronor: rotation based temporal knowledge graph embedding. In: Proceedings of the AAAI Conference on Artificial Intelligence, vol. 35, pp. 6471–6479 (2021)
25. Suchanek, F.M., Kasneci, G., Weikum, G.: Yago: a core of semantic knowledge. In: Proceedings of the 16th International Conference on World Wide Web, pp. 697–706 (2007)
26. Sun, Z., Deng, Z.H., Nie, J.Y., Tang, J.: Rotate: knowledge graph embedding by relational rotation in complex space. arXiv preprint arXiv:1902.10197 (2019)
27. Trouillon, T., Welbl, J., Riedel, S., Gaussier, É., Bouchard, G.: Complex embeddings for simple link prediction. In: International Conference on Machine Learning, pp. 2071–2080. PMLR (2016)
28. Ungar, A.: Hyperbolic trigonometry and its application in the poincaré ball model of hyperbolic geometry. Comput. Math. Appl. **41**(1), 135–147 (2001). https://doi.org/10.1016/S0898-1221(01)85012-4
29. Vrandečić, D., Krötzsch, M.: Wikidata: a free collaborative knowledgebase. Commun. ACM **57**(10), 78–85 (2014)
30. Wang, Z., Zhang, J., Feng, J., Chen, Z.: Knowledge graph embedding by translating on hyperplanes. In: Proceedings of the AAAI Conference on Artificial Intelligence, vol. 28 (2014)
31. Xu, C., Nayyeri, M., Alkhoury, F., Yazdi, H.S., Lehmann, J.: Tero: a time-aware knowledge graph embedding via temporal rotation. arXiv preprint arXiv:2010.01029 (2020)

LitCQD: Multi-hop Reasoning in Incomplete Knowledge Graphs with Numeric Literals

Caglar Demir[ID], Michel Wiebesiek, Renzhong Lu,
Axel-Cyrille Ngonga Ngomo[ID], and Stefan Heindorf[✉][ID]

Paderborn University, Paderborn, Germany
{caglar.demir,axel.ngonga,heindorf}@upb.de, michel.wiebesiek@mailbox.org,
renzhong@mail.upb.de

Abstract. Most real-world knowledge graphs, including Wikidata, DBpedia, and Yago are incomplete. Answering queries on such incomplete graphs is an important, but challenging problem. Recently, a number of approaches, including complex query decomposition (CQD), have been proposed to answer complex, multi-hop queries with conjunctions and disjunctions on such graphs. However, these approaches only consider graphs consisting of entities and relations, neglecting literal values. In this paper, we propose LitCQD—an approach to answer complex, multi-hop queries where both the query and the knowledge graph can contain numeric literal values: LitCQD can answer queries having numerical answers or having entity answers satisfying numerical constraints. For example, it allows to query (1) persons living in New York having a certain age, and (2) the average age of persons living in New York. We evaluate LitCQD on query types with and without literal values. To evaluate LitCQD, we generate complex, multi-hop queries and their expected answers on a version of the FB15k-237 dataset that was extended by literal values.

1 Introduction

Knowledge Graphs (KGs) such as Wikidata [30], DBpedia [3], and YAGO [25] have been of increasing interest in both academia and industry, e.g., for major question answering systems [1,9,27] and for intelligent assistants such as Amazon Alexa, Siri, and Google Now. Natural language questions on such KGs are typically answered by translating them into subsets of First-Order Logic (FOL) involving conjunctions ($\land$), disjunctions ($\lor$), and existential quantification ($\exists$) of multi-hop path expressions in the KGs. However, this approach to modeling queries has an important intrinsic flaw: Almost all real-world KGs are incomplete [8,10,20]. Traditional symbolic models, which rely on sub-graph matching, are unable to infer missing information on such incomplete KGs [12]. Hence, they often return empty answer sets to queries that can be answered by predicting missing information. Hence, several approaches (e.g., GQE [12], Query2Box [22], and CQD [2]) have recently been proposed that can query incomplete KGs by performing neural reasoning over Knowledge Graph Embeddings (KGEs). However, all the aforementioned models operate solely on KGs consisting of *entities and relations* and none of them supports KGs with *literal values* such as the age of a person, the height of a building, or the population of a city. Taking literal values into account, however, has been shown to improve predictive performance in many tasks [13,18].

In this paper, we remedy this drawback and propose LitCQD, a neural reasoning approach that can answer queries involving *numerical literal values* over incomplete KGs. LitCQD extends CQD by combining a KGE model (e.g., ComplEx-N3 [19]) that predicts missing entities/relations with a literal KGE model (e.g., TransEA [31]) able to predict missing numerical literal values. Therewith, LitCQD can mitigate missing entities/relations as well as missing numerical values to answer various types of queries. Moreover, we *increase the expressiveness of queries* that can be answered on KGs with literal values by allowing queries (1) to contain filter restrictions involving literals and (2) to ask for predictions of numeric values (see Example 1).

Example 1. The query "*Who ($P_?$) is married to somebody (P) younger than 25?*" with a filter restriction "younger than 25" can be rewritten as $P_?.\exists P, C :$ hasAge$(P, C) \wedge$ lt$(C, 25) \wedge$ married$(P, P_?)$.

To answer this query, we predict the age of all persons P in the knowledge graph and check whether the condition "less than 25" is fulfilled. Then, all persons $P_?$ married to persons P are returned.

To evaluate filter expressions such as "less than 25" on incomplete knowledge graphs, we introduce continuous attribute filter functions (Sect. 4.1, Eqs. 8–10) and improve them by introducing attribute existence checks (Eqs. 11–12). We predict attribute values for a subset of entities that are obtained via beam search with an attribute predictor (Sect. 4.2).

In our experiments (Sect. 5), we use a similar setup to Arakelyan et al. [12] García-Durán and Niepert [11], Hamilton et al. [2] and use the FB15k-237 dataset augmented with literals [11]. However, as previous work did not contain queries with literal values, we generate such queries and their expected answers. Our experiments suggest that LitCQD can effectively answer various types of queries involving literal values, which was not possible before (Tables 3, 4). Moreover, our results show that including literal values during the training process improves the query answering performance even on standard queries in our benchmark (Table 2). Our contributions can be summarized as follows:

- *Filter restrictions with literals:* We propose an approach that can answer multi-hop queries where numeric literals are used to filter valid answers (e.g., "return entities whose age is less than 25").
- *Prediction of literal values:* We propose an approach that can *predict the numeric values* of literals (e.g., "return mean age of married people').
- *Benchmark construction:* We generate multi-hop queries *with numeric literals* and their expected answers.
- *Embeddings with literals:* We show that using knowledge graph embeddings that support literal values even yields better results for traditional queries without literal values.

2   Background and Preliminaries

In this section, we introduce knowledge graphs without literals and queries on them, before introducing our approach with literals in Sect. 4.

2.1   Knowledge Graph Without Literals

A knowledge graph (KG) without literals is defined as $\mathcal{G} = \{(h, r, t)\} \subseteq \mathcal{E} \times \mathcal{R} \times \mathcal{E}$, where $h, t \in \mathcal{E}$ denote entities and $r \in \mathcal{R}$ denotes a relation [12,22]. $\mathcal{G}$ can be regarded as a FOL knowledge base, where a relation $r \in \mathcal{R}$ corresponds to a binary function $\hat{r} : \mathcal{E} \times \mathcal{E} \to \{1, 0\}$ and a triple (h, r, t) corresponds to an atomic formula $\alpha = \hat{r}(h, t)$ [2]. When it is clear from the context that $\hat{r}$ denotes a binary function, we may simply write r as in the following definitions.

2.2   Multihop Queries Without Literals

Conjunctive Queries. A conjunctive graph query [2,12,22,23] $q \in \mathcal{Q}(\mathcal{G})$ over $\mathcal{G}$ is defined as

$$q = E_? \,.\, \exists E_1, \ldots, E_m : \alpha_1 \wedge \alpha_2 \wedge \ldots \wedge \alpha_n, \tag{1}$$

where

- $\alpha_i = r(e, E)$, with $E \in \{E_?, E_1, \ldots, E_m\}$, $r \in \mathcal{R}$, $e \in \mathcal{E}$ or
- $\alpha_i = r(E, E')$, with $E, E' \in \{E_?, E_1, \ldots, E_m\}$, $E \neq E'$, $r \in \mathcal{R}$.

In the query, the target variable $E_?$ and the existentially quantified variables $E_1, \ldots, E_m$ are bound to subsets of *entities* $\mathcal{E}$. The entities bound to $E_?$ represent the answer nodes of the query. The conjunction $\alpha_1 \wedge \alpha_2 \wedge \ldots \wedge \alpha_n$ consists of n atoms defined over relations $r \in \mathcal{R}$, anchor entities $e \in \mathcal{E}$ and variables $E, E' \in \{E_?, E_1, \ldots, E_m\}$.

Example 2. The question "*Which ($D_?$) drugs are to interact with (P) proteins associated with the diseases e_1 and e_2?*" can be represented as the query

$$q = D_? . \exists P : assoc(e_1, P) \wedge assoc(e_2, P) \wedge interacts(P, D_?), \tag{2}$$

where $D_?, P$ are bound to subsets of entities $\mathcal{E}$, $e_1, e_2 \in \mathcal{E}$ are anchor entities, and *interacts, assoc* $\in \mathcal{R}$ are relations.

The dependency graph of a query $q \in Q(\mathcal{G})$ is defined over its query edges α_1, $\alpha_2, \ldots, \alpha_n$ with nodes being either anchor entities or variables [12]. Following Hamilton et al. [12] and Arakelyan et al. [2], we focus on queries whose dependency graph forms a Directed Acyclic Graph (DAG) with anchor entities being source nodes and the target variable being the unique sink node (such queries are called *valid* queries in previous work [2,12]). Figure 1 (left) represents the dependency graph of the query in Eq. (2). Note that for simplicity, we use the term of an entity in a KG interchangeably with a node in a dependency graph.

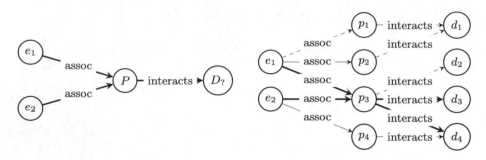

Fig. 1. Example query without literals (see Eq. (2)). Dependency graph of query (left) and symbolic query answering on an incomplete graph (right). Solid bold lines represent paths leading to answer entities. Dashed lines represent missing triples.

The dependency graph of a query encodes the *computation graph* to obtain the answer set $[\![q]\!]$ via *projection* $\mathcal{P}$ and *intersection* $\mathcal{I}$ operators [22]. Starting from a set of anchor nodes (e.g., e_1, e_2), $[\![q]\!]$ is derived by iteratively applying $\mathcal{P}$ and/or $\mathcal{I}$ until the unique sink target node (e.g., $D_?$) is reached. Given a set of entities $S \subseteq \mathcal{E}$ and a relation $r \in \mathcal{R}$, the projection operator is defined as $\mathcal{P}(S, r) := \cup_{e \in S} \{x \in \mathcal{E} : \hat{r}(e, x) = 1\}$ where the binary function $\hat{r} : \mathcal{E} \times \mathcal{E} \to \{1, 0\}$ indicates whether the triple (e, r, x) exists in $\mathcal{G}$. Given a set of entity sets $\{S_1, S_2, \ldots, S_n\}, S_i \subseteq \mathcal{E}$, the intersection operator $\mathcal{I}$ is defined as $\mathcal{I}(\{S_1, S_2, \ldots, S_n\}) := \cap_{i=1}^{n} S_i$. Therefore, the conjunctive query defined in Eq. (2) can be answered via the computation

$$\mathcal{P}\Big(\mathcal{I}(\{\mathcal{P}(\{e_1\}, assoc), \mathcal{P}(\{e_2\}, assoc)\}), interacts\Big). \qquad (3)$$

In the example of Fig. 2 (right), a traditional, symbolic approach yields the answer set $[\![q]\!] = \{d_3, d_4\}$ although the complete answer set taking missing triples into account would be $[\![q]\!] = \{d_2, d_3, d_4\}$. The result is obtained as follows: Starting at the anchor entities e_1 and e_2, the entity p_3 is the only entity for which both $assoc(e_1, p_3)$ and $assoc(e_2, p_3)$ hold. Moving on from p_3, a traditional, symbolic approach can only reach the entities d_3, d_4 via the "interacts" relation, but not the entity d_2 because the edge $(p_3, interacts, d_2)$ is missing. Note that d_1 is not part of the answer set because both p_1 and p_2 are only associated with e_1.

Existential Positive First-order (EPFO) Queries. An EPFO query q in its Disjunctive Normal Form (DNF) is a disjunction of conjunctive queries [2,22]:

$$q = E_? . \exists E_1, \ldots, E_m : (\alpha_1^1 \wedge \cdots \wedge \alpha_{n_1}^1) \vee \cdots \vee (\alpha_{n_1}^d \wedge \cdots \wedge \alpha_{n_d}^d), \qquad (4)$$

where α_i^j are defined as above. Its dependency graph is a DAG having three types of directed edges: *projection*, *intersection*, and *union*; the union $\mathcal{U}$ of entity sets $S_1, S_2, \ldots, S_n \subseteq \mathcal{E}$ is $\mathcal{U}(\{S_1, S_2, \ldots, S_n\}) := \cup_{i=1}^{n} S_i$.

3   Related Work

In this section, we overview the state of the art with regards to knowledge graph embeddings and neural query answering on incomplete knowledge graphs.

3.1   Knowledge Graph Embeddings and Literals

In the last decade, a plethora of knowledge graph embedding (KGE) models have been successfully applied to tackle various tasks, including link prediction, relation prediction, community detection, fact checking, and class expression learning [15–17,20,24,29]. KGE research has mainly focused on learning embeddings for entities and relations tailored towards predicting missing entities/links, i.e., tackling single-hop queries [4,6–8,20,26,29,32,33]. Despite their effectiveness in tackling single-hop queries, KGE models cannot be directly applied to answer multi-hop queries because multi-hop query answering is a strict generalization [21]. Most KGE models do not incorporate literals (e.g., age of a person, height of a person, or date of birth), but there has been a growing interest in designing such models. For instance, Wu and Wang [31] propose TransEA by extending the translation loss used in TransE [5] by adding the attribute loss as a weighted regularization term. García-Durán and Niepert [11] propose KBLRN that is based on relation features, numerical literals, and a KGE model. Kristiadi et al. [18] propose LiteralE, which applies a non-linear parameterized function to merge entity embeddings with numerical literals. Thereby, LiteralE is computationally less demanding than KBLRN as it does not require any rule generation for relation features and is more expressive than TransEA as TransEA integrates the impact of literals linearly.

3.2   Neural Query Answering on Incomplete Knowledge Graphs

In recent years, significant progress has been made on querying incomplete KGs. Hamilton et al. [12] laid the foundations for multi-hop reasoning with graph query embeddings (GQE). Given a conjunctive query (e.g., Eq. (2)), they learn continuous vector representations for queries, entities, and relations and answer queries by performing projection $\mathcal{P}$ and intersection $\mathcal{I}$ operations in the embedding vector space. Ren et al. [22] show that GQE cannot answer EPFO queries (see Eq. (4)) since GQE does not model the union operator $\mathcal{U}$. Hence, they propose Query2Box that represents an EPFO query with a set of box embeddings, where one box embedding is constructed per conjunctive subquery. A query is answered by returning the entities whose minimal distance to one of the box embeddings is smallest.

All the aforementioned models learn query embeddings and answer queries via nearest neighbor search in the embedding space. However, learning embeddings for complex, multi-hop queries involving conjunctions and disjunctions can be computationally demanding. Towards this end, Arakelyan et al. [2] propose complex query decomposition (CQD). They answer EPFO queries by decomposing them into single-hop subqueries and aggregate the scores of a pre-trained single-hop link predictor (e.g., ComplEx-N3). Scores are aggregated using a t-norm and t-conorm—continuous generalizations of the logical conjunction and disjunction [2,14]. Their experiments suggest that CQD outperforms GQE and Query2Box; it generalizes well to complex query structures while requiring orders of magnitude less training data. Zhu et al. [34] highlight that CQD is the only interpretable model among the aforementioned models as it produces intermediate results. In this work, we extend CQD to answer multi-hop queries involving literals.

4   LitCQD: Multi-hop Reasoning with Literals

A knowledge graph with numeric literals (i.e., with scalar values), can be defined as $\mathcal{G}_A = \{(h, r, t)\} \subset (\mathcal{E} \times \mathcal{R} \times \mathcal{E}) \cup (\mathcal{E} \times \mathcal{A} \times \mathbb{R})$, where $\mathcal{R} \cap \mathcal{A} = \emptyset$ and $\mathcal{A}$ and $\mathbb{R}$ denote numeric attributes and real numbers, respectively [18]. The binary function $\hat{a} : \mathcal{E} \times \mathbb{R} \mapsto \{1, 0\}$ indicates whether an entity has attribute $a \in \mathcal{A}$ and we might just write a instead of $\hat{a}$ when this is clear from context. We categorize EPFO queries $q \in \mathcal{Q}(\mathcal{G}_A)$ involving literals depending on the type of their answer sets $[\![q]\!]$: In Sect. 4.1, we define queries with entities as answer set $[\![q]\!] \subseteq \mathcal{E}$; in Sect. 4.2, we define queries with a literal value as answer $[\![q]\!] \in \mathbb{R}$.

4.1   Multihop Queries with Literals and Entity Answers

An EPFO query q on a KG with numeric literals ($\mathcal{G}_A$) can be defined as

$$q = E_? . \exists E_1, \ldots, E_m : (\alpha_1^1 \wedge \cdots \wedge \alpha_{n_1}^1) \vee \cdots \vee (\alpha_1^d \wedge \cdots \wedge \alpha_{n_d}^d), \qquad (5)$$

where

- $\alpha_i^j = r(e, E)$, with $E \in \{E_?, E_1, \ldots, E_m\}$, $r \in \mathcal{R}$, $e \in \mathcal{E}$ or
- $\alpha_i^j = r(E, E')$, with $E, E' \in \{E_?, E_1, \ldots, E_m\}$, $E \neq E'$, $r \in \mathcal{R}$ or
- $\alpha_i^j = a(E, C) \wedge af(C, c)$, with $E \in \{E_?, E_1, \ldots, E_m\}$, $C \in \{C_1, \ldots, C_l\}$, $a \in \mathcal{A}$, $af \in \{\mathrm{lt}, \mathrm{gt}, \mathrm{eq}\}$, $c \in \mathbb{R}$.

In the query, the target variable $E_?$ and the variables $E_1, \ldots, E_m$ are bound to subsets of *entities* $\mathcal{E}$ and the variables $C_1, \ldots, C_l$ are bound to numeric values from $\mathbb{R}$. The binary function $r : \mathcal{E} \times \mathcal{E} \mapsto \{1, 0\}$ denotes whether a relation exists between the two entities, $a : \mathcal{E} \times \mathbb{R} \mapsto \{1, 0\}$ whether an attribution relation exists, and $af : \mathbb{R} \times \mathbb{R} \mapsto \{1, 0\}$ is one of the attribute filter conditions lt (*less-than*), gt (*greater-than*), or eq (*equal-to*). For example, $lt(20, 25)$ returns 1 because $20 \leq 25$. To approximately answer queries defined with Eq. (5) and assuming an incomplete knowledge graph, we propose the following optimization problem:

$$\underset{E_?, E_1, \ldots, E_m}{\arg\max} \; \left(\alpha_1^1 \top \ldots \top \alpha_{n_1}^1 \right) \perp \ldots \perp \left(\alpha_1^d \top \ldots \top \alpha_{n_d}^d \right) \qquad (6)$$

where

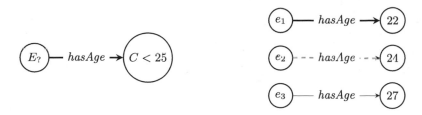

Fig. 2. Example query with literals and entity answer (see Eq. (7)). On the left, the query's dependency graph is shown and on the right, symbolic query answering on an incomplete graph with literal values. Bold lines represent paths leading to answer entities, dashed lines represent missing triples, solid existing triples.

- $\alpha_i^j = \phi_r(e, E)$, with $E \in \{E_?, E_1, \ldots, E_m\}$, $r \in \mathcal{R}$, $e \in \mathcal{E}$ or
- $\alpha_i^j = \phi_r(E, E')$, with $E, E' \in \{E_?, E_1, \ldots, E_m\}$, $E \neq E'$, $r \in \mathcal{R}$ or
- $\alpha_i^j = \phi_{af,a}(\phi_a(E), c)$, with $E \in \{E_?, E_1, \ldots, E_m\}$, $a \in \mathcal{A}$, $af \in \{lt, gt, eq\}$, $c \in \mathbb{R}$,

and $\phi_r : \mathcal{E} \times \mathcal{E} \mapsto [0, 1]$ is a link predictor that predicts a *likelihood* of a link between two entities via a relation r. $\phi_a : \mathcal{E} \mapsto \mathbb{R}$ is an attribute predictor that predicts a *value* of an attribute a given an entity. An attribute filter predictor $\phi_{af,a} : \mathbb{R} \times \mathbb{R} \mapsto [0, 1]$ predicts a *likelihood* that the filter condition is met given the predicted attribute value $\hat{c} := \phi_a(\cdot)$ and the constant value $c \in \mathbb{R}$ specified in the query. All three predictors are derived from a KGE model as described below. A t-norm $\top : [0, 1] \times [0, 1] \mapsto [0, 1]$ is considered as a continuous generalization of the logical conjunction [2,14]. Given a t-norm $\top$, the complementary t-conorm can be defined as $\bot(a, b) = 1 - \top(1 - a, 1 - b)$ [2]. Numerically, the *Gödel t-norm* $\top_{\min}(x, y) = \min\{x, y\}$, the *product t-norm* $\top_{\text{prod}}(x, y) = x \cdot y$, or the *Łukasiewicz t-norm* $\top_{\text{Luk}}(x, y) = \max\{0, x + y - 1\}$ can be used to aggregate predicted likelihoods to obtain a query score [2]. With this formulation, various questions involving numerical values can be asked on incomplete $\mathcal{G}_A$. For example, the question "*Which entities are younger than 25?*" can be represented as

$$q = E_? . \exists C : hasAge(E_?, C) \wedge lt(C, 25). \tag{7}$$

The dependency graph of this query is visualized in Fig. 2 (left). Let $S_?$ be the entities bound to variable $E_?$. Then the projection of $S_?$ with *hasAge* is performed by an attribute prediction model $\phi_{hasAge}(S_?) \in \mathbb{R}^{|E|}$ that predicts the value of the attribute a for each entity in $e \in E$. The answer set is obtained by filtering entities via ϕ_{lt}. A subgraph of $\mathcal{G}_A$ satisfying this query is visualized in Fig. 2 (right). While a symbolic approach only yields the answer set $[\![q]\!] = \{e_1\}$, our approach involving link predictors can identify the full answer set $[\![q]\!] = \{e_1, e_2\}$.

We solve the optimization problem in Eq. (6) approximately with a variant of beam search by greedily searching for sets of entities $S_?, S_1, \ldots S_m$ substituting the variables $E_?, E_1, \ldots, E_m$ in a fashion akin to CQD [2]. In the example in Eq. (7), given the *hasAge* attribute, attribute values $\hat{c} = \phi_{hasAge}(e) \in \mathbb{R}$ are predicted for all entities $e \in \mathcal{E}$. Next, likelihoods of fulfilling the filter condition "less than

25" can be inferred via $\phi_{\mathrm{lt}}(\hat{c}, 25)$. Finally, all entities are sorted by their query scores in descending order and the top k entities are considered to be answers of q. It is important to note that LitCQD like CQD not only computes the final answer but also intermediate steps leading to this answer. In this sense, LitCQD can be considered an interpretable model.

Joint Training of Link and Attribute Predictors. Following Arakelyan et al. [2], we use ComplEx-N3 [19] as entity predictor $\phi_r(\cdot, \cdot)$. As attribute predictor $\phi_a(\cdot)$, we employ TransEA [31]. We jointly train the KGE models underlying both models. The link predictor ComplEx-N3 has previously been found to work well for multi-hop query answering [2] and to perform better than DistMult [2,32]. In a pilot study, we also experimented with the attribute predictor MTKGNN [28]. Overall, it achieved similar performance to TransEA, but we decided to move forward with TransEA, because it slightly outperformed MTKGNN in terms of MRR and required less parameters. KBLRN [11] and LiteralE [18] only compute knowledge graph embeddings based on literal information, but they do not predict the value of attributes which is required in our framework.

Attribute Filter Function without Existence Check. The attribute filter function returns a score indicating the likelihood that the filter condition is met. First, we define a preliminary version $\phi'_{af,a}$ of the function, which does not check whether the attribute relation a actually exist for an entity. The function is defined case by case. For the *equal-to* condition, i.e., for $af = \mathrm{eq}$, we define it as

$$\phi'_{\mathrm{eq},a}(\hat{c}, c) := \frac{1}{\exp(|\hat{c} - c|/\sigma_a)}, \tag{8}$$

where $\hat{c} = \phi_a(e), e \in \mathcal{E}, c \in \mathbb{R}$ is a numeric literal (e.g., 25 in Fig. 2), left) and σ_a denotes the standard deviation of $\mathcal{C}_a$ where $\mathcal{C}_a := \{c \in \mathbb{R} | \hat{a}(e, c) = 1, e \in \mathcal{E}\}$ are all literal values found on $\mathcal{G}_{\mathcal{A}}$ given an attribute a. With $\phi'_{\mathrm{eq},a}(\hat{c}, c)$, we map the difference between the predicted attribute value $\hat{c}$ and the constant value $\hat{c}$ specified in the query into the unit interval $[0, 1]$. As the difference $| \hat{c} - c |$ approaches 0, $\phi_{\mathrm{eq},a}(\hat{c}, c)$ approaches 1. The division by the standard deviation σ_a normalizes the difference $| \hat{c} - c |$. For the attribute filter function with *less-than* ($af = \mathrm{lt}$), we define

$$\phi'_{\mathrm{lt}}(\hat{c}, c) := \frac{1}{1 + \exp((\hat{c} - c)/\sigma_a)}. \tag{9}$$

As $\hat{c} - c \to -\infty$, $\phi_{\mathrm{lt}}(\hat{c}, c) \to 1$. Following Eq. (9), the attribute filter function with *greater-than* is defined as

$$\phi'_{\mathrm{gt}}(\hat{c}, c) := 1 - \phi_{\mathrm{lt}}(\hat{c}, c). \tag{10}$$

We also experimented with a version where the standard deviation σ_a was not computed per attribute but for all literal values independent of a, i.e., σ was computed for $\bigcup_{a \in \mathcal{A}} \mathcal{C}_a$. We picked the latter variant as default for our LitCQD approach as it outperformed the former variant in our experiments.

Attribute Filter Function with Existence Check. The preliminary attribute filter function $\phi'_{af,a}$ assumes that the attribute relation a exists for each entity in the knowledge base which is clearly not the case. Hence, we employ a model $\phi_{\text{exists},a}(e)$ that scores the likelihood that the attribute relation a exists for entity e. Then the final attribute filter function $\phi_{af,a}$ is obtained by combining the attribute existence predictor $\phi_{\text{exist},a}(e)$ with the preliminary filter predictor $\phi'_{af,a}$:

$$\phi_{af,a}(\hat{c}, c) := \phi_{\text{exists},a}(e) \cdot \phi'_{af,a}(\hat{c}, c) \tag{11}$$

Technically, the attribute existence predictor is realized by adding a dummy entity e_{exists} to the knowledge base along with dummy edges $r_a(e, e_{\text{exists}})$ if entity e has an attribute relation a. Then, the existence of an attribute is predicted with the link predictor as

$$\phi_{\text{exists},a}(e) := \phi_{r_a}(e, e_{\text{exists}}) \tag{12}$$

Note that the dummy entity and the dummy relations are only added to the train set but not the validation or test set.

4.2   Multihop Queries with Literals and Literal Answers

Here, we define an EPFO query q on an incomplete $\mathcal{G}_\mathcal{A}$, whose answer $[\![q]\!] \in \mathbb{R}$ is a real number (instead of a subset of entities) as follows

$$q = \psi(C_?) \, . \, \exists E_?, E_1, \ldots, E_m : (\alpha_1^1 \wedge \cdots \wedge \alpha_{n_1}^1) \vee \cdots \vee (\alpha_1^d \wedge \cdots \wedge \alpha_{n_d}^d), \tag{13}$$

where $\psi : 2^\mathbb{R} \mapsto \mathbb{R}$ is a permutation-invariant aggregation function and

- $\alpha_i^j = r(e, E)$, with $E \in \{E_?, E_1, \ldots, E_m\}$, $r \in \mathcal{R}$, $e \in \mathcal{E}$ or
- $\alpha_i^j = r(E, E')$, with $E, E' \in \{E_?, E_1, \ldots, E_m\}$, $E \neq E'$, $r \in \mathcal{R}$ or
- $\alpha_i^j = a(E, C) \wedge af(C, c)$, with $E \in \{E_?, E_1, \ldots, E_m\}$, $C \in \{C_?, C_1, \ldots, C_l\}$ $a \in \mathcal{A}$, $af \in \{\text{lt}, \text{gt}, \text{eq}\}$, $c \in \mathbb{R}$.

Variable bindings $S_?, S_1, \ldots, S_m$ for $E_?, E_1, \ldots, E_m$ are obtained via the same optimization problem as in Sect. 4.1. Then the set of values $C_?$ can be computed by applying the attribute value predictor ϕ_a on the entities in $S_?$.

With this formulation, various questions can be asked on incomplete $\mathcal{G}_\mathcal{A}$. For instance, the question "*What is the average age of Turing Award (TA) winners?*" can be answered by computing the mean of a set of numeric literals $C_?$:

$$\text{mean}(C_?) . \exists E_? : \text{winner}(E_?, \text{turingAward}) \wedge \text{hasAge}(E_?, C_?) \tag{14}$$

Similarly, the question "*What is the minimum age of Turing Award (TA) winners?*" can be answered by computing the minimum of a set of numeric literals $C_?$:

$$\text{min}(C_?) . \exists E_? : \text{winner}(E_?, \text{turingAward}) \wedge \text{hasAge}(E_?, C_?) \tag{15}$$

Figure 3 visualizes a subgraph of $\mathcal{G}_\mathcal{A}$ to answer q defined in Eq. (14). Having found the binding $S_? = \{e_1, e_2\}$ for $E_?$, to each $e \in S_?$, we apply the attribute predictor $\phi_{\text{winner}}(e, \text{turingAward})$ and average the results, yielding the answer $[\![q]\!] = \frac{22+24}{2} = 23$—in contrast to $[\![q]\!] = 22$ by a symbolic approach that neglects missing information.

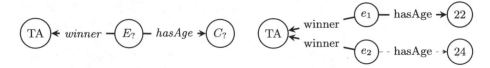

Fig. 3. Example of a query predicting attribute values (see Eq. (14)). On the left, the dependency graph of the query is shown, on the right a subgraph to answer q. Dashed lines represent missing information. Bold lines represent paths leading to the symbolic answer $[\![q]\!] = 22$.

5   Experimental Results

After a brief description of the experimental setup, we evaluate the performance of LitCQD on the query types shown in Table 1. Finally, we show the answers of LitCQD for an example query. Our code is publicly available.[1]

5.1   Experimental Setup

Dataset and Query Generation. We use the FB15k-237 dataset augmented with attributes as done by García-Durán and Niepert [11]. The dataset contains 12,390 entities, 237 entity relations, 115 attribute relations, and 29,229 triples. Queries and their expected answers are generated as by Hamilton et al. [12]. The newly introduced attribute filter conditions (af) are handled as follows: When checking for *equality* $(af(C,c) = eq(C,c))$, we consider all entities whose attribute value lies within one standard deviation from c as correct where the standard deviation is computed per attribute relation a; when checking the *less-than* or *greater-than* criterion, the criterion is checked exactly, i.e., all entities with attribute value "$\leq c$" or "$\geq c$" are considered correct. In a preprocessing step, we normalize all values of an attribute to the unit interval via min-max scaling. Table 1 gives an overview of the newly introduced query types along with previous query types.

Hyperparameters. Per query type, we tried 16 different configurations on the validation set and chose the best before applying the model to the test set. As our framework is derived from the CQD framework, it allows two different optimization algorithms: Continuous optimization (Co), Combinatorial optimization (Beam); two t-norms: Gödel (min), product (prod); and 7 different beam sizes $k \in \{2^2, 2^3, \ldots, 2^8\}$ for the combinatorial optimization algorithm. Each optimization algorithm is computed for both of the t-norms resulting in 2 configurations using the continuous optimization algorithm and 14 using the combinatorial optimization algorithm as every beam size is evaluated for both t-norms.

5.2   Multihop Queries Without Literals

In a first experiment (Table 2), we compare the performance of our approach LitCQD to CQD [2] and Query2Box [22] on multihop entity queries without

---

Table 1. Overview of different query types. Entity queries without literals were proposed by Ren et al. [22]. Entity queries with literals and queries with literal answers are newly proposed in this paper.

	Multihop queries without literals
1p	$E_? \cdot r(e, E_?)$
2p	$E_? \cdot \exists E_1 : r_1(e, E_1) \wedge r_2(E_1, E_?)$
3p	$E_? \cdot \exists E_1 E_2.r_1(e, E_1) \wedge r_2(E_1, E_2) \wedge r_3(E_2, E_?)$
2i	$E_? \cdot r_1(e_1, E_?) \wedge r_2(e_2, E_?)$
3i	$E_? \cdot r_1(e_1, E_?) \wedge r_2(e_2, E_?) \wedge r_3(e_3, E_?)$
ip	$E_? \cdot \exists E_1.r_1(e_1, E_1) \wedge r_2(e_2, E_1) \wedge r_3(E_1, E_?)$
pi	$E_? \cdot \exists E_1.r_1(e_1, E_1) \wedge r_2(E_1, E_?) \wedge r_3(e_2, E_?)$
2u	$E_? \cdot r_1(e_1, E_?) \vee r_2(e_2, E_?)$
up	$E_? \cdot \exists E_1.[r_1(e_1, E_1) \vee r_2(e_2, E_1)] \wedge r_3(E_1, E_?)$

	Multihop queries with literals and entity answers
ai	$E_? \cdot \exists C_1.a(E_?, C_1) \wedge af(C_1, c)$
2ai	$E_? \cdot \exists C_1 C_2.a_1(E_?, C_1) \wedge af_1(C_1, c_1) \wedge a_2(E_?, C_2) \wedge af_2(C_2, c_2)$
pai	$E_? \cdot \exists C_1.r(e, E_?) \wedge a(E_?, C_1) \wedge af(C_1, c_1)$
aip	$E_? \cdot \exists E_1 C_1.a(E_1, C_1) \wedge af(C_1, c_1) \wedge r(E_1, E_?)$
au	$E_? \cdot \exists C_1 C_2.a_1(E_?, C_1) \wedge af_1(C_1, c_1) \vee a_2(E_?, C_2) \wedge af_2(C_2, c_2)$

	Multihop queries with literals and literal answers
1ap	$mean(C_?) \cdot a(e, C_?)$
2ap	$mean(C_?) \cdot \exists E_1.r(e, E_1) \wedge a(E_1, C_?)$
3ap	$mean(C_?).\exists E_1 E_2.r_1(e, E_1) \wedge r_2(E_1, E_2) \wedge a(E_2, C_?)$

literals, which can be answered by all three models—in contrast to more expressive queries that can only be answered by LitCQD. While CQD does not utilize literal information and employs the vanilla ComplEx-N3 [19] model, LitCQD employs a model combining ComplEx-N3 [19] with TransEA [31]. Table 2 shows that LitCQD clearly outperforms CQD and Query2Box in terms of the mean reciprocal rank (MRR), and Hits@k for $k \in \{1, 3, 10\}$.

5.3 Multihop Queries with Literals and Entity Answers

Table 3 shows the evaluation results for the new query types with filter restrictions introduced in Sect. 4.1 (second block in Table 1). For the simple ai query, each filtering expression (*less-than, equals, greater-than*) is evaluated separately; the other query types contain all three filtering expressions. Except for aip queries, all query types with literals can be answered with a performance of at least 0.256 which is comparable to query types without literals (cf. Table 2).

Table 2. Query answering results for multihop queries without literals. Results were computed for test queries over the FB15k-237 dataset and evaluated in terms of mean reciprocal rank (MRR) and Hits@k for $k \in \{1, 3, 10\}$.

Method	Average	1p	2p	3p	2i	3i	ip	pi	2u	up
MRR										
Query2Box	0.213	0.403	0.198	0.134	0.238	0.332	0.107	0.158	0.195	0.153
CQD	0.295	0.454	0.275	0.197	0.339	0.457	0.188	0.267	0.261	0.214
LitCQD (ours)	**0.301**	**0.457**	**0.285**	**0.202**	**0.350**	**0.466**	**0.193**	**0.274**	**0.266**	**0.215**
HITS@1										
Query2Box	0.124	0.293	0.120	0.071	0.124	0.202	0.056	0.083	0.094	0.079
CQD	0.211	0.354	0.198	0.137	0.235	0.354	**0.130**	0.186	0.165	**0.137**
LitCQD (ours)	**0.215**	**0.355**	**0.206**	**0.141**	**0.245**	**0.365**	0.129	**0.193**	**0.168**	0.135
HITS@3										
Query2Box	0.240	0.453	0.214	0.142	0.277	0.399	0.111	0.176	0.226	0.161
CQD	0.322	0.498	0.297	0.208	0.380	0.508	0.195	0.290	0.287	0.230
LitCQD (ours)	**0.330**	**0.506**	**0.309**	**0.214**	**0.395**	**0.517**	**0.204**	**0.296**	**0.295**	**0.235**
HITS@10										
Query2Box	0.390	0.623	0.356	0.259	0.472	0.580	0.203	0.303	0.405	0.303
CQD	0.463	0.656	0.422	0.312	0.551	0.656	0.305	0.425	0.465	0.370
LitCQD (ours)	**0.472**	**0.660**	**0.439**	**0.323**	**0.561**	**0.663**	**0.315**	**0.434**	**0.475**	**0.379**

Moreover, we experimented with different variants of our model and performed an ablation study. As described in Sect. 4.1, Eq. (11), the attribute filter predictor $\phi_{af,a}$ is a product of $\phi_{exists,a}(e)$ and $\phi'_{af,a}(\hat{c}, c)$. We performed three experiments, where we replaced each/both of the two scoring functions by the constant value 1. Table 3 shows that both components are crucial and the performance drops drastically if one of them is removed.

Moreover, the Eq. (8) and Eq. (9) normalize the difference $\hat{c} - c$ by dividing by the standard deviation. Per default (first line), LitCQD employs the universal standard deviation across all attributes of the knowledge base, i.e., the standard deviation σ of $\bigcup_{a \in \mathcal{A}} C_a$. As an alternative, we computed attribute-specific standard deviations σ_a per C_a. Table 3 (last line) shows that using an attribute-specific standard deviation instead of a universal standard deviation leads to a lower performance on five query types, to the same performance on one query type, and to a higher performance on only one query type.

5.4   Multihop Queries with Literals and Literal Answers

Table 4 evaluates the performance of queries asking for literal answers. The predicted numeric values are compared to the actual numeric values in terms of mean absolute error (MAE) and mean squared error (MSE). Interestingly, we notice that the mean absolute error for the 2ap queries is lower than for 1ap queries. This can be explained by the fact that for 1ap queries a single prediction of an attribute value is made whereas 2ap queries average multiple predictions (the number of the beam width). For 3ap queries, the mean absolute error increases again because the relation path becomes longer and errors accumulate.

Table 3. Query answering results for multihop queries with literals and entity answers. Our best-performing model LitCQD is compared to variations thereof. Results were computed for test queries over the FB15k-237 dataset and evaluated in terms of Hits@10.

Method	ai-lt	ai-eq	ai-gt	2ai	aip	pai	au
LitCQD	**0.405**	**0.361**	0.317	**0.336**	**0.182**	0.463	**0.256**
- w/o attribute filter predictor	0.280	0.005	0.237	0.148	0.124	0.421	0.054
- w/o attribute existence predictor	0.206	0.137	0.128	0.104	0.167	**0.470**	0.120
- w/o both	0.015	0.001	0.003	0.001	0.051	0.412	0.003
- with attribute-specific stdev	**0.405**	0.232	**0.329**	0.216	0.174	0.320	0.212

Table 4. Query answering results for multihop queries with literals and literal answers. Results were compute for test queries over the FB15k-237 dataset and evaluated in terms of mean absolute error (MAE) and mean squared error (MSE).

Method	1ap		2ap		3ap	
	MAE	MSE	MAE	MSE	MAE	MSE
LitCQD	0.050	0.011	0.034	0.005	0.041	0.007
Mean Predictor	0.341	0.143	0.346	0.141	0.362	0.152

As a simple baseline, we also report the results of the model that always predicts the mean value $\frac{1}{|\mathcal{C}_a|} \sum_{c \in \mathcal{C}_a} c$ of the attribute a in the whole knowledge graph (mean predictor in the table).

5.5   Example Query and Answers

As an illustration of the model's query-answering ability, consider the query "What are musicians from the USA born before 1972?" and its logical representation

$$E_? \, . \, \exists C_1 . /\text{music/artist/origin}(\text{USA}, E_?) \land$$
$$/\text{people/person/date\_of\_birth}(E_?, C_1) \land lt(C_1, 1972). \tag{16}$$

Table 5 lists the top 10 returned answers. Although the model confuses the band *Funkadelic* as musicians with a date of birth, the model is able to produce a reasonable ranking of entities. Out of these 10 entities, the entity *Robert E. Lee* receives the highest score of 0.95 for the attribute portion of the query. The model is confident that the entity has the attribute `/people/person/date_of_birth` and that its value is less than 1972. The entities *Dio*, *Rob Thomas*, and *Donna Summer* only receive a score of 0.39 for the attribute portion of the query because their predicted values are closer to the threshold of 1972. The model is more certain that the connection /music/artist/origin, *USA* exists for *John Denver* compared to *Robert E. Lee*. While Linus Pauling is a chemist rather than a musician and the dataset does not contain the connection /music/artist/origin, *USA*, the learned embeddings implicitly encode that *Linus Pauling* has another connection to the entity *USA* via the /people/person/nationality relation.

Table 5. Ranking of LitCQD's top 10 answers to the query in Eq. (16) including their expected and predicted attribute value for `date_of_birth`. The star (*) indicates attribute values unseen during training and the double star (**) refers to attribute values not part of the dataset at all. The dash (–) indicates that an entity does not have a date of birth.

Rank	Answer	Expected Attr.	Predicted Attr.
1	Linus Pauling	1901.17	1900.06
2	John Denver	1944.00	1941.52
3	Funkadelic	–	1925.21
4	Friedrich Hayek	1899.42	1900.04
5	Robert E. Lee	1807.08	1794.49
6	Dio	1942**	1935.59
7	Marvin March	1930.42	1922.07
8	Rob Thomas	1972*	1943.72
9	Ezra Pound	1885.83	1882.00
10	Donna Summer	1949.00	1948.55

6   Conclusion

In this paper, we propose LitCQD, a novel approach to answer multihop queries on incomplete knowledge graphs with numeric literals. Our approach allows answering queries that could not be answered before, e.g., queries involving literal filter restrictions and queries predicting the value of numeric literals. Moreover, our experiments suggest that even the performance of answering multihop queries that could be answered before improves as the underlying knowledge graph embedding models now take literal information into account. This is an important finding as most real-world knowledge graphs contain millions of entities with numerical attributes. In future work, we plan to further increase the expressiveness of our queries, e.g., by supporting string literals, Boolean literals, and datetime literals.

Acknowledgements. This work has received funding from the European Union's Horizon 2020 research and innovation programme under the Marie Skłodowska-Curie grant agreement No 860801, the Horizon Europe research and innovation programme under the Marie Skłodowska-Curie grant agreement No 101073307, and the Horizon Europe research and innovation programme under grant agreement No 101070305. This work has also been supported by the Ministry of Culture and Science of North Rhine-Westphalia (MKW NRW) within the project SAIL under the grant No NW21-059D and by the Deutsche Forschungsgemeinschaft (DFG, German Research Foundation): TRR 318/1 2021 - 438445824.

References

1. Adolphs, P., Theobald, M., Schäfer, U., Uszkoreit, H., Weikum, G.: YAGO-QA: answering questions by structured knowledge queries. In: ICSC, pp. 158–161. IEEE Computer Society (2011)
2. Arakelyan, E., Daza, D., Minervini, P., Cochez, M.: Complex query answering with neural link predictors. In: ICLR, OpenReview.net (2021)
3. Auer, S., Bizer, C., Kobilarov, G., Lehmann, J., Cyganiak, R., Ives, Z.: DBpedia: a nucleus for a web of open data. In: Aberer, K., Choi, K.-S., Noy, N., Allemang, D., Lee, K.-I., Nixon, L., Golbeck, J., Mika, P., Maynard, D., Mizoguchi, R., Schreiber, G., Cudré-Mauroux, P. (eds.) ASWC/ISWC -2007. LNCS, vol. 4825, pp. 722–735. Springer, Heidelberg (2007). https://doi.org/10.1007/978-3-540-76298-0_52
4. Balazevic, I., Allen, C., Hospedales, T.M.: TuckER: tensor factorization for knowledge graph completion. In: EMNLP/IJCNLP (1), pp. 5184–5193. Association for Computational Linguistics (2019)
5. Bordes, A., Usunier, N., García-Durán, A., Weston, J., Yakhnenko, O.: Translating embeddings for modeling multi-relational data. In: NIPS, pp. 2787–2795 (2013)
6. Demir, C., Moussallem, D., Heindorf, S., Ngonga Ngomo, A.: Convolutional hypercomplex embeddings for link prediction. In: ACML, Proceedings of Machine Learning Research, vol. 157, pp. 656–671. PMLR (2021)
7. Demir, C., Ngomo, A.-C.N.: Convolutional complex knowledge graph embeddings. In: Verborgh, R., Hose, K., Paulheim, H., Champin, P.-A., Maleshkova, M., Corcho, O., Ristoski, P., Alam, M. (eds.) ESWC 2021. LNCS, vol. 12731, pp. 409–424. Springer, Cham (2021). https://doi.org/10.1007/978-3-030-77385-4_24
8. Dettmers, T., Minervini, P., Stenetorp, P., Riedel, S.: Convolutional 2d knowledge graph embeddings. In: AAAI, pp. 1811–1818. AAAI Press (2018)
9. Diefenbach, D., Tanon, T.P., Singh, K.D., Maret, P.: Question answering benchmarks for Wikidata. In: ISWC (Posters, Demos & Industry Tracks), CEUR Workshop Proceedings, vol. 1963, CEUR-WS.org (2017)
10. Färber, M., Bartscherer, F., Menne, C., Rettinger, A.: Linked data quality of DBpedia, Freebase, OpenCyc, Wikidata, and YAGO. Semantic Web **9**(1), 77–129 (2018)
11. García-Durán, A., Niepert, M.: KBLRN: end-to-end learning of knowledge base representations with latent, relational, and numerical features. In: UAI, pp. 372–381. AUAI Press (2018)
12. Hamilton, W., Bajaj, P., Zitnik, M., Jurafsky, D., Leskovec, J.: Embedding logical queries on knowledge graphs. Advances in neural information processing systems **31** (2018)
13. Heindorf, S., et al.: EvoLearner: learning description logics with evolutionary algorithms. In: WWW, pp. 818–828. ACM (2022)

14. Klement, E., Mesiar, R., Pap, E.: Triangular norms. position paper I: basic analytical and algebraic properties. Fuzzy Sets Syst. **143**(1), 5–26 (2004)
15. Kouagou, N.J., Heindorf, S., Demir, C., Ngonga Ngomo, A.: Learning concept lengths accelerates concept learning in ALC. In: ESWC. LNCS, vol. 13261, pp. 236–252. Springer, Cham (2022). https://doi.org/10.1007/978-3-031-06981-9_14
16. Kouagou, N.J., Heindorf, S., Demir, C., Ngonga Ngomo, A.: Neural class expression synthesis. In: Pesquita, C., et al. (eds.) ESWC. LNCS, vol. 13870, pp. 209–226. Springer, Cham (2023). https://doi.org/10.1007/978-3-031-33455-9_13
17. Kouagou, N.J., Heindorf, S., Demir, C., Ngonga Ngomo, A.: Neural class expression synthesis in ALCHIQ(D). In: ECML, Lecture Notes in Computer Science. Springer (2023)
18. Kristiadi, A., Khan, M.A., Lukovnikov, D., Lehmann, J., Fischer, A.: Incorporating literals into knowledge graph embeddings. In: Ghidini, C., Hartig, O., Maleshkova, M., Svátek, V., Cruz, I., Hogan, A., Song, J., Lefrançois, M., Gandon, F. (eds.) ISWC 2019. LNCS, vol. 11778, pp. 347–363. Springer, Cham (2019). https://doi.org/10.1007/978-3-030-30793-6_20
19. Lacroix, T., Usunier, N., Obozinski, G.: Canonical tensor decomposition for knowledge base completion. In: ICML, Proceedings of Machine Learning Research, vol. 80, pp. 2869–2878. PMLR (2018)
20. Nickel, M., Murphy, K., Tresp, V., Gabrilovich, E.: A review of relational machine learning for knowledge graphs. Proc. IEEE **104**(1), 11–33 (2016)
21. Ren, H., Dai, H., Dai, B., Chen, X., Zhou, D., Leskovec, J., Schuurmans, D.: SMORE: knowledge graph completion and multi-hop reasoning in massive knowledge graphs. In: KDD, pp. 1472–1482. ACM (2022)
22. Ren, H., Hu, W., Leskovec, J.: Query2box: reasoning over knowledge graphs in vector space using box embeddings. In: ICLR, OpenReview.net (2020)
23. Ren, H., Leskovec, J.: Beta embeddings for multi-hop logical reasoning in knowledge graphs. In: NeurIPS (2020)
24. da Silva, A.A.M., Röder, M., Ngomo, A.-C.N.: Using compositional embeddings for fact checking. In: Hotho, A., Blomqvist, E., Dietze, S., Fokoue, A., Ding, Y., Barnaghi, P., Haller, A., Dragoni, M., Alani, H. (eds.) ISWC 2021. LNCS, vol. 12922, pp. 270–286. Springer, Cham (2021). https://doi.org/10.1007/978-3-030-88361-4_16
25. Suchanek, F.M., Kasneci, G., Weikum, G.: Yago: a core of semantic knowledge. In: WWW, pp. 697–706. ACM (2007)
26. Sun, Z., Deng, Z., Nie, J., Tang, J.: RotatE: knowledge graph embedding by relational rotation in complex space. In: ICLR (Poster), OpenReview.net (2019)
27. Tahri, A., Tibermacine, O.: DBPedia based factoid question answering system. Int. J. Web Semantic Technol. **4**(3), 23 (2013)
28. Tay, Y., Tuan, L.A., Phan, M.C., Hui, S.C.: Multi-task neural network for non-discrete attribute prediction in knowledge graphs. In: CIKM, pp. 1029–1038. ACM (2017)
29. Trouillon, T., Welbl, J., Riedel, S., Gaussier, É., Bouchard, G.: Complex embeddings for simple link prediction. In: ICML, JMLR Workshop and Conference Proceedings, vol. 48, pp. 2071–2080. JMLR.org (2016)
30. Vrandecic, D., Krötzsch, M.: Wikidata: a free collaborative knowledgebase. Commun. ACM **57**(10), 78–85 (2014)
31. Wu, Y., Wang, Z.: Knowledge graph embedding with numeric attributes of entities. In: Rep4NLP@ACL, pp. 132–136. Association for Computational Linguistics (2018)

32. Yang, B., Yih, W., He, X., Gao, J., Deng, L.: Embedding entities and relations for learning and inference in knowledge bases. In: ICLR (Poster) (2015)
33. Zhang, S., Tay, Y., Yao, L., Liu, Q.: Quaternion knowledge graph embeddings. In: NeurIPS, pp. 2731–2741 (2019)
34. Zhu, Z., Galkin, M., Zhang, Z., Tang, J.: Neural-symbolic models for logical queries on knowledge graphs. In: ICML, Proceedings of Machine Learning Research, vol. 162, pp. 27454–27478. PMLR (2022)

Large-Scale Learning

Cross Model Parallelism for Faster Bidirectional Training of Large Convolutional Neural Networks

An Xu[1]([✉])[ID] and Yang Bai[2]

[1] ByteDance Inc., Seattle, USA
`an.xu@bytedance.com`
[2] Tencent Inc., Beijing, China
`mavisbai@tencent.com`

Abstract. Large convolutional neural networks (CNNs) have been successful in data mining tasks, but it is hard to train these large-scale models. Model parallelism (MP) places a large CNN to several workers (GPUs) to fit in the memory, but its computation efficiency is low as only one worker is activated at a time and the other workers are idle during training. Pipeline model parallelism (PMP) improves model parallelism by pipelining mini-batches, checkpointing some intermediate activations, and using delayed backward error gradients. But all these techniques have certain limitations, add to the computation cost, and may deteriorate the model performance. To address these important issues and improve the efficiency of model parallelism, we propose a novel cross model parallelism (CMP) method without requiring additional computation overheads and jeopardizing the performance. In cross model parallelism, we reversely place two models to workers and bidirectionally train them at the same time to improve the training throughput. A novel averaging method to synchronize the two models is also proposed in cross model parallelism. Theoretical analysis shows that cross model parallelism converges as fast as model parallelism regarding training epochs. Extensive deep learning experimental results show that our proposed cross model parallelism can achieve a speedup of up to $\times 1.5$ compared with model parallelism regarding training time.

Keywords: Model Parallelism · Convolutional Neural Network

1 Introduction

Deep convolutional neural networks (CNNs) have been very successful in solving various data mining tasks in recent years. As the CNN goes deeper and larger, the performance usually gets better [11, 12, 26, 31]. The backpropagation (BP) [22, 29] algorithm is the most popular method to compute the gradient when training CNNs and consists of the forward pass and the backward pass. However, BP requires the worker (GPU) to store all the intermediate activations in the forward pass in order to calculate the gradient in the backward pass for optimizing the model parameters. A deep CNN model has many layers which lead to many

© The Author(s), under exclusive license to Springer Nature Switzerland AG 2023
D. Koutra et al. (Eds.): ECML PKDD 2023, LNAI 14171, pp. 637–653, 2023.
https://doi.org/10.1007/978-3-031-43418-1_38

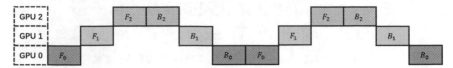

(a) Model Parallelism (MP). Only one model is trained.

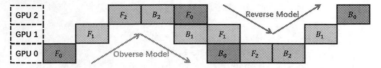

(b) Cross Model Parallelism (CMP). Two models (the obverse and reverse models) are reversely placed to GPUs and trained alternatively and bidirectionally. The blue and red arrows represent the data flow directions and they constitute a "cross".

Fig. 1. The training data flow of model parallelism and our proposed cross model parallelism in the forward and backward pass of backpropagation. The CNN model is placed onto $K = 3$ GPUs. F_i and B_i denote the forward and backward pass of the i-th partition of the model respectively. Different partitions are denoted with different colors. Two consecutive training iterations are displayed. The horizontal axis denotes time. Best viewed in color.

intermediate activations to store, making it too large to fit into one worker's memory during training.

To address the memory issue using a single worker, checkpoint and recomputation [4] have been proposed to train large CNNs with sublinear memory costs regarding the number of layers. During the forward pass of the training, the worker only stores (checkpoints) several layers' activations. While in the backward pass between two consecutive checkpoint layers, the worker recomputes the forward using the stored activation of the lower checkpoint layer and backward with the error gradient from the upper checkpoint layer. Therefore, the peak memory consumption mainly consists of the intermediate activations between the two consecutive checkpoint layers instead of the whole CNN model. But the re-computation introduces non-negligible computation overheads. Other memory-efficient methods include model compression [9] and activation quantization [42], but they usually lead to the loss of performance depending on the compression ratio.

When training large CNN models with multiple workers, data parallelism (DP) [3, 7, 8, 13, 24, 25, 33, 35, 36, 38, 39] and model parallelism (MP) [20, 23] have been the most popular methods and implemented in many existing libraries [1, 28]. In DP with K workers, each worker computes the gradient of a mini-batch of size b and communicates with the other workers to average the gradient. The equivalent mini-batch size is Kb. Nevertheless, as the number of workers K increases, the equivalent mini-batch size grows, hampering the optimization and leading to sharp local optima with worse performance [18]. Besides, in some other tasks such as graph convolutional neural networks [19], each training iteration requires all the data and we cannot sample a mini-batch. MP, on the other hand, divides the CNN model into K partitions and places them to K workers without requirements on the mini-batch size. But MP is inefficient due to the forward and backward computation dependencies [17] of the BP algorithm (Fig. 1a).

In this paper, we focus on **improving the computation efficiency of MP**. Pipeline model parallelism (PMP) [14,15,27,37] pipelines the computation of the workers to decrease the idle time by feeding more batches of data input. Each worker checkpoints the mini-batch but re-computes with a previous checkpointed mini-batch, which leads to staleness and potentially jeopardizes the model performance.

To address the aforementioned important issues and improve the computation efficiency of MP, we propose a novel cross model parallelism (CMP) method (Fig. 1b). In CMP we carefully coordinate the training of two model copies at the same time to achieve **better efficiency with negligible peak memory overheads** in contrast with MP which trains one model. In the first place, we introduce two important and novel concepts in our proposed method below.

- **Reverse placement**: we have two model copies of the same architecture and initialization named as "obverse model" and "reverse model". The first part of the obverse model is placed onto the first worker, while that in the reverse model is placed onto the last worker. The last part of the obverse model is placed onto the last worker, and that of the reverse model is placed onto the first worker. It follows a similar pattern for other parts.
- **Bidirectional training**: the backpropagation algorithm for the two models is conducted in opposite direction due to reverse placement. Therefore we name the training of the two models as bidirectional training.

To the best of our knowledge, CMP is the first synchronous model parallel algorithm more efficient than MP without checkpoint and re-computation overheads. The contributions are summarized as follows.

- We propose a novel cross model parallelism (CMP) training method without requiring a large mini-batch size, computation overheads due to checkpoint and re-computation, and performance deterioration due to staleness as in existing works.
- We propose a novel out-of-step periodic model averaging technique to synchronize the two bidirectionally trained models in CMP.
- Theoretical results show that out-of-step periodic averaging achieves the same convergence rate as SGD. Extensive deep learning experimental results show that CMP can achieve a speedup of up to ×1.5 compared with MP in terms of wall clock time.

2   Background and Related Works

Let $\mathbf{x} \in \mathbb{R}^d$ be the model parameters and $f(\mathbf{x})$ be the objective function. The optimization is to $\min_{\mathbf{x} \in \mathbb{R}^d} f(\mathbf{x})$. Let the data distribution be $\mathcal{D}$ and the sampling random variable be ξ. The SGD optimizer randomly selects a sample with the sampler ξ from the data distribution $\mathcal{D}$ to calculate the stochastic gradient $\nabla F(\mathbf{x}; \xi)$ for model update

$$\mathbf{x} \leftarrow \mathbf{x} - \eta \nabla F(\mathbf{x}; \xi), \tag{1}$$

where η is the learning rate. The stochastic gradient $\nabla F(\mathbf{x}; \xi)$ is usually assumed to be an unbiased estimation of the full gradient $\nabla f(\mathbf{x})$, i.e.,

$$\mathbb{E}_\xi \nabla F(\mathbf{x}; \xi) = \nabla f(\mathbf{x}). \tag{2}$$

Backpropagation. BP is to efficiently compute the stochastic gradient of deep CNNs needed by optimization. Suppose the CNN is split into K partitions and the k-th partition is placed to worker $k \in [K]$. Let $\mathbf{h}^{(k+1)} = F^{(k)}(\mathbf{h}^{(k)}, \mathbf{x}^{(k)})$ be the output activation of worker k with the data sample, where $\mathbf{x}^{(k)}$ and $F^{(k)}(\cdot)$ are the parameters and forward function of the partition on worker k respectively. MP with multiple workers using BP computes the stochastic gradient via Eq. (3).

$$\begin{cases} \nabla_{\mathbf{h}^{(k)}} F(\mathbf{x}; \xi) = \frac{\partial F^{(k)}(\mathbf{h}^{(k)}, \mathbf{x}^{(k)})}{\partial \mathbf{h}^{(k)}} \nabla_{\mathbf{h}^{(k+1)}} F(\mathbf{x}; \xi), \\ \nabla_{\mathbf{x}^{(k)}} F(\mathbf{x}; \xi) = \frac{\partial F^{(k)}(\mathbf{h}^{(k)}, \mathbf{x}^{(k)})}{\partial \mathbf{x}^{(k)}} \nabla_{\mathbf{h}^{(k+1)}} F(\mathbf{x}; \xi), \end{cases} \tag{3}$$

where $\nabla F(\mathbf{x}; \xi) = (\nabla_{\mathbf{x}^{(0)}} F(\mathbf{x}; \xi), \cdots, \nabla_{\mathbf{x}^{(K-1)}} F(\mathbf{x}; \xi))$. The forward in Eq. (3) of the k-th partition to compute activation $\mathbf{h}^{(k+1)}$ requires the activation $\mathbf{h}^{(k)}$ from the $(k-1)$-th partition. The backward pass in Eq. (3) of the k-th partition to compute the gradient $\nabla_{\mathbf{x}^{(k)}} F(\mathbf{x}; \xi)$ requires the error gradient $\nabla_{\mathbf{h}^{(k+1)}} F(\mathbf{x}; \xi)$ from the $(k+1)$-th partition. Such computation dependencies make MP with multiple workers using BP inefficient (Fig. 1a).

Staleness, Checkpoint and Re-computation. PMP pipelines the computation of mini-batches to achieve better efficiency. [37] pipelines the forward of $\mathbf{h}_t^{(k)}$ and $\mathbf{h}_{t-1}^{(k+1)}$, where t denotes the iteration. It is the same with the backward pass. However, the error gradient that worker k receives from worker $k+1$ is at a stale iteration $t' \le t$ as waiting the error gradient at iteration t is inefficient. Worker k has to checkpoint $\mathbf{h}_t^{(k)}$ and re-compute $F^{(k)}(\mathbf{h}_{t'}^{(k)} \mathbf{x}^{(k)})$ in the backward pass. In contrast to [14,15,37] only pipelines the backward pass without pipelining the forward pass. [27] stores the forward intermediate activation without checkpoint and re-computation, leading to large memory overheads. The staleness potentially deteriorates the model performance in all PMP methods.

Model Modification. Other works to address the computation dependencies in MP need careful design. Decoupled Neural Interfaces [17] designed auxiliary networks to predict the error gradient to avoid waiting. Greedy layer-wise learning [2] works in a similar way, where an auxiliary local classifier is introduced to each partition of the CNN model. Therefore, a partition updates its parameters using the error gradient from its local classifier instead of waiting for other partitions. However, these methods have to re-engineer the model architecture, bringing about new challenges and difficulties.

3   New Cross Model Parallelism (CMP)

In this section, we propose the novel cross model parallelism (CMP) to improve the efficiency of MP without re-computation overheads and deterioration of model performance.

3.1   Obverse and Reverse Models

Motivation. In MP, the inefficiency exists in the forward pass because when the first worker 0 is conducting the forward, the last worker $K-1$ has to wait for the forward results and becomes idle. It is the same in the backward pass. When the last worker $K-1$ is conducting backward, the first worker 0 has to wait for the error gradient and becomes idle. However, if we can make this one-directional training bidirectional, the inefficiency issues can be alleviated without the last worker waiting for the first worker or the first waiting for the last.

Based on this motivation, we propose CMP where two models are initialized from the same initialization and we split them into K partitions in the same way to train on K workers (one partition per worker). Of the two models, we place the k-th partition of the *obverse model* to worker $k \in [K]$. In contrast to the obverse model, the partitions of the *reverse model* are reversely placed to the workers, *i.e.*, the k-th partition is placed to worker $K-1-k$. We denote the obverse model parameters as $\mathbf{x}^o$ and the reverse model parameters as $\mathbf{x}^r$. As the obverse model $\mathbf{x}^o$ and reverse model $\mathbf{x}^r$ are placed in opposite direction regarding the workers, their forward and backward passes are also conducted in opposite direction. Therefore, we name the training of the obverse and reverse models as *bidirectional training*. The bidirectional training independently samples data from the distribution $\mathcal{D}$ for both models as the input.

Alternative Forward and Backward. Simply training two the same models will lead to the contention of computation and memory resources and slow down the overall progress. In CMP, however, the obverse and reverse models are placed in the opposite direction regarding workers. Therefore, the obverse model $\mathbf{x}^o$ starts the forward from worker 0 while the reverse model $\mathbf{x}^r$ starts the forward from worker $K-1$ to avoid any conflict and contention. It is similar for the backward. More specifically, we denote the forward and backward pass of the obverse and reverse models with blue and red arrows respectively in Fig. 1b. The bidirectional training of the obverse and reverse models is conducted in an alternative way. We start the forward of the first partition F_0 on the last worker $K-1$ for the reverse model $\mathbf{x}^r$ right after the backward of the last partition B_{K-1} on the last worker $K-1$ for the obverse model $\mathbf{x}^r$ finishes. It is vice versa when we start the forward for the obverse model $\mathbf{x}^o$. Note that F_k and B_k take place on worker k for the obverse model $\mathbf{x}^o$, but worker $K-1-k$ for the reverse model $\mathbf{x}^r$. In contrast to MP, the next batch of training can start before the backward is finished in the previous batch of training. If we assume the model is evenly split to K partitions in terms of the computation cost and the forward and backward consume the same amount of computation time, we have the ideal speedup of CMP over MP as:

Algorithm 1. Out-of-step period averaging for the obverse and reverse models in cross model parallelism.

1: **Input:** period $p \geq 1$, number of iterations T, number of workers K, and learning rate $\{\eta_t\}_{t=0}^{T-1}$.
2: **Initialize:** the initial obverse and reverse models $\mathbf{x}_0^o = \mathbf{x}_0^r = \mathbf{x}_0$.
3: **for** $t = 0, 1, \cdots, T - 1$ **do**
4:     $\mathbf{x}_{t+1}^o = \mathbf{x}_t^o - \eta_t \nabla F(\mathbf{x}_t^o; \xi_t^o)$
5:     $\mathbf{x}_{t+1}^r = \mathbf{x}_t^r - \eta_t \nabla F(\mathbf{x}_t^r; \xi_t^r)$
6:     **if** $\mod (t + 1, p) = 0$ **then**
7:         $\mathbf{x}_{t+1}^o \leftarrow \frac{1}{2}(\mathbf{x}_{t+1}^o + \mathbf{x}_t^r)$
8:         $\mathbf{x}_{t+1}^r \leftarrow \mathbf{x}_{t+1}^o + \frac{1}{2}(\mathbf{x}_{t+1}^r - \mathbf{x}_t^r)$
9:     **end if**
10: **end for**

$$\text{speedup} = \frac{2K}{K + 1}, \tag{4}$$

which approaches $\times 2$ as K increases. This is a simplification because the backward is usually more expensive than forward but it is hard to decide their ratio. As there is no need to split the batch input, CMP does not require a large mini-batch size.

Negligible Memory Overheads. The reverse model $\mathbf{x}^r$ starts the forward on worker k after the obverse model $\mathbf{x}^o$ has finished the backward on worker k. The intermediate activations computed during the forward pass of the obverse model will be *released* from memory before the reverse model starts the forward on worker k. It is vice versa when the obverse model $\mathbf{x}^o$ starts the forward pass. Therefore, CMP introduces no memory overheads of the intermediate activations. Some other memory overheads such as storing two sets of model parameters are negligible in contrast to the intermediate activations.

No Checkpoint and Re-computation. We can further improve the efficiency of CMP by starting the forward of the reverse model $\mathbf{x}^r$ in advance rather than waiting for the backward of the obverse model $\mathbf{x}^o$ to finish on worker k. Nevertheless, the intermediate activations will not be released from memory before the backward pass. It will lead to memory overheads to store two sets of intermediate activations for the obverse and reverse models on worker k. Checkpoint and re-computation can be leveraged to avoid storing additional intermediate activations as in PMP, but it will conflict with our goal to avoid extra computational cost resulting from re-computation. In summary, our proposed CMP improves the efficiency of MP with no compromise of memory and computation overheads.

3.2   Out-of-Step Periodic Averaging

As we are training two models $\mathbf{x}^o$ and $\mathbf{x}^r$ at the same time with mini-batch data sampled from the same data distribution $\mathcal{D}$, they need to be synchronized during the training. Usually, the gradients of the obverse and reverse models need to be averaged before updating $\mathbf{x}^o$ and $\mathbf{x}^r$. But it is practically unfavorable because 1) that the same partition of the obverse and reverse models is not placed on the same worker and averaging gradient introduces communication overheads, and 2) that the obverse model $\mathbf{x}^o$ and the reverse model $\mathbf{x}^r$ are trained alternatively and waiting for the other model's gradient is inefficient.

To address the first important issue, we introduce periodic averaging to CMP from Local SGD [32] in data parallelism (DP). Instead of averaging the gradient of the obverse and reverse models, periodic averaging averages $\mathbf{x}^o$ and $\mathbf{x}^r$ every p updates of $\mathbf{x}^o$ and $\mathbf{x}^r$ to reduce the communication frequency. As the obverse and reverse models are placed to GPUs on a single machine in practice and the GPU to GPU communication is fast via NVLink [5] connection, a small p is enough to make the communication overheads negligible.

To address the second critical issue without loss of efficiency, we propose a novel out-of-step periodic averaging algorithm as shown in Algorithm 1. In CMP, the obverse and reverse models are trained in an alternative manner. When the obverse model $\mathbf{x}^o$ is updated p times, the reverse model is only updated $p-1$ times. Therefore, in line 7 of Algorithm 1 when $\mod(t+1,p) = 0$ (the communication iteration), we synchronize the obverse model to $\frac{1}{2}(\mathbf{x}_{t+1}^o + \mathbf{x}_t^r)$ other than $\frac{1}{2}(\mathbf{x}_{t+1}^o + \mathbf{x}_{t+1}^r)$ because $\mathbf{x}_{t+1}^r$ is still unavailable. The reverse model $\mathbf{x}^r$, however, will be synchronized to the average of the obverse and reverse models in the communication iteration. Note that it equals $\mathbf{x}_{t+1}^o + \frac{1}{2}(\mathbf{x}_{t+1}^r - \mathbf{x}_t^r)$ in line 8 as $\mathbf{x}^o$ has been modified in line 7 of Algorithm 1. After synchronization in the communication iteration, there will be a *synchronization error* $\mathbf{x}_{t+1}^o - \mathbf{x}_{t+1}^r = \frac{\eta_t}{2}\nabla F(\mathbf{x}_t^r; \xi_t^r)$ in out-of-step periodic averaging rather than 0 when using periodic averaging. Intuitively, the synchronization error $\frac{\eta_t}{2}\nabla F(\mathbf{x}_t^r; \xi_t^r)$ will become small as the training converges ($\nabla F(\mathbf{x}_t^r; \xi_t^r) \to \mathbf{0}$) and the learning rate decreases. Consequently, out-of-step periodic averaging will not deteriorate the model performance.

4   Theoretical Analysis

In this section, we provide a rigorous theoretical analysis of CMP with out-of-step periodic averaging to show its same convergence rate as the SGD optimizer. We consider the smooth (Assumption 1) and non-convex optimization problem which is suitable for CNN models. We also make common Assumptions 2 and 3. The average model is denoted as $\bar{\mathbf{x}}_t = \frac{1}{2}(\mathbf{x}_t^o + \mathbf{x}_t^r)$. $\bar{\mathbf{x}}_t$ is an auxiliary variable which will not be computed in real training.

Assumption 1. *(L-Lipschitz) The objective function $f(\cdot)$ is L-smooth, i.e.,*

$$\|\nabla f(\boldsymbol{x}) - \nabla f(\boldsymbol{y})\|_2 \leq L\|\boldsymbol{x} - \boldsymbol{y}\|_2, \forall \boldsymbol{x}, \boldsymbol{y} \in \mathbb{R}^d, \tag{5}$$

Assumption 2. *(Unbiased Gradient and Bounded Variance) Let $\mathcal{D}$ be the data distribution. The stochastic gradient $\nabla F(x; \xi)$ is an unbiased estimation of the full gradient $\nabla f(x)$, i.e.,*

$$\mathbb{E}_\xi \nabla F(x; \xi) = \nabla f(x), \forall x \in \mathbb{R}^d . \tag{6}$$

Its variance is also bounded, i.e.,

$$\mathbb{E}_\xi \|\nabla F(x; \xi) - \nabla f(x)\|_2^2 \le \sigma^2, \forall x \in \mathbb{R}^d . \tag{7}$$

Assumption 3. *(Bounded Full Gradient) The second moment of the full gradient $\nabla f(x)$ is bounded, i.e.,*

$$\|\nabla f(x)\|_2^2 \le G^2, \forall x \in \mathbb{R}^d . \tag{8}$$

Theorem 1. *Under Assumptions 1, 2, and 3, if the learning rate is fixed $\eta_t = \eta$ and $\eta < \min\{\frac{1}{2pL}, \frac{1}{6L}\}$, we have*

$$\frac{1}{T} \sum_{t=0}^{T-1} \mathbb{E}\|\nabla f(\bar{x}_t)\|_2^2 \le \frac{8(f(\bar{x}_0) - f_*)}{\eta T} \tag{9}$$
$$+ (10(2p+1)\eta^2 L^2 + 2\eta L)\sigma^2 + 20\eta^2 L^2 G^2 .$$

In the proof of the convergence rate of out-of-step periodic averaging (Theorem 1), we have to jointly consider two different circumstances $(\mathrm{mod}(t+1,p) \ne 0$ and $\mathrm{mod}(t+1,p) = 0)$ where the update rules of $\bar{x}_t$ are different due to the synchronization error. It differs from the analysis in periodic averaging [40] where the update rule of $\bar{x}_t$ does not change. According to Theorem 1, let $\eta = \mathcal{O}(\frac{1}{\sqrt{T}})$ and $p = \mathcal{O}(\sqrt{T})$, then we will have $\frac{1}{T}\sum_{t=0}^{T-1} \mathbb{E}\|\nabla f(\bar{x}_t)\|_2^2 \le \mathcal{O}(\frac{1}{\sqrt{T}})$ which is at least the same convergence rate as the SGD optimizer. The communication complexity $p = \mathcal{O}(T)$ also matches periodic averaging [40]. Furthermore, we can breakdown the extra terms in Eq. (9) to

$$\underbrace{10\eta^2 L^2(\sigma^2 + 2G^2)}_{\text{out-of-step } \mathcal{O}(\frac{1}{T})} + \underbrace{20p\eta^2 L^2\sigma^2}_{\text{divergence } \mathcal{O}(\frac{1}{\sqrt{T}})} + \underbrace{2\eta L\sigma^2}_{\text{original } \mathcal{O}(\frac{1}{\sqrt{T}})} , \tag{10}$$

where the *out-of-step term* resulting from the synchronization error $\frac{\eta_t}{2}\nabla F(x_t^r; \xi_t^r)$ equals $\mathcal{O}(\frac{1}{T})$. The *divergence term* is caused by the infrequent synchronization every p updates and equals $\mathcal{O}(\frac{1}{\sqrt{T}})$. The obverse model x_t^o and the reverse model x_t^r diverges further (a larger $\|x^o - x^r\|$) with a larger synchronization period p. The *original term* resulting from stochastic sampling as in the SGD optimizer also equals $\mathcal{O}(\frac{1}{\sqrt{T}})$. Therefore, the out-of-step term is trivial in contrast to the other terms and it validates the effectiveness of our proposed out-of-step periodic averaging to address the important issue of synchronizing the alternative and bidirectional training of two models.

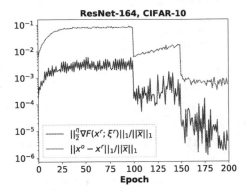

Fig. 2. Verify out-of-step periodic averaging via illustrating a much smaller normalized synchronization (blue) than divergence (green) errors before synchronization in the communication iteration. Best viewed in color.

5 Experimental Results

5.1 Settings

All experiments are implemented using PyTorch [28] and run on a machine equipped with 4 GPUs. The model is split into $K = 4$ partitions and the synchronization period $p = 8$ unless specified otherwise. Each partition is placed on one GPU.

CIFAR. We train the ResNet-164 and ResNet-1001 [11] models on CIFAR-10 [21] image classification task. The model size of ResNet-164 on CIFAR-10 is small and it is fit for fast validation of arguments, while ResNet-1001 is relatively larger on CIFAR-10. We report the mean and standard deviation metrics over 5 runs. The base learning rate is 0.1 and the batch size is 128. The momentum constant is 0.9 and the weight decay is 5×10^{-4}. The model is trained for 200 epochs with a learning rate decay of 0.1 at epoch 100 and 150. Random cropping, random flipping, and standardization are applied as data augmentation techniques.

ImageNet. We train the ResNet-50 model with on ImageNet [30] image classification tasks. The base learning rate is 0.1 and the batch size is 256. The momentum constant is 0.9 and the weight decay is 1×10^{-4}. The model is trained for 90 epochs with a learning rate decay of 0.1 at epoch 30, 60 and 80. Random cropping, random flipping, and standardization are applied as data augmentation techniques. We have also trained other large models including ResNet-152, ResNeXt-101-32x8d [34], Wide ResNet-101-2 [41], and VGG-19 [31].

5.2 Faster Convergence with Out-of-Step Periodic Averaging

Negligible Synchronization Error. We first plot the curves of the training loss and test accuracy of ResNet-164 and ResNet-1001 on CIFAR-10 and ResNet-50 on ImageNet regarding training epochs in Fig. 3. They validate that out-of-step periodic averaging does not jeopardize the final performance of the model.

Table 1. Test Accuracy (%) in Fig. 3. In each row, the first and second sub-rows denote MP and CMP respectively. In the "Epoch" column, the left and right numbers denote the epoch in CIFAR-10 and ImageNet respectively. Mean ± standard deviation are shown for CIFAR-10.

Epoch	CIFAR-10		ImageNet
	ResNet-164	ResNet-1001	ResNet-50
100/30	84.61 ± 0.39	89.06 ± 0.17	55.02
	88.43 ± 0.24	**90.69 ± 0.22**	**59.36**
150/60	93.43 ± 0.14	95.08 ± 0.14	71.00
	94.72 ± 0.11	**96.03 ± 0.07**	**73.44**
200/90	94.89 ± 0.13	95.66 ± 0.09	76.33
	95.28 ± 0.10	**96.19 ± 0.09**	76.38
	94.64†	95.31 ± 0.20†	76.15‡

†From the original paper [12].
‡From https://pytorch.org/docs/stable/torchvision/ models.html

Table 2. Best Top-1 Accuracy (%) of training ResNet-164 on CIFAR-10 using CMP with different period p. Mean ± standard deviation are reported.

Period p	1	2	4
Accuracy	94.80 ± 0.20	95.18 ± 0.09	**95.32 ± 0.05**
Period p	8	16	32
Accuracy	95.28 ± 0.10	95.26 ± 0.11	95.24 ± 0.19

To show the synchronization error $\frac{\eta}{2}\nabla F(\mathbf{x}^r; \xi^r)$ and the divergence error $\mathbf{x}^o - \mathbf{x}^r$ before the communication iteration, we plot their ℓ_1-norm normalized by the ℓ_1-norm of the average model $\overline{\mathbf{x}} = \frac{1}{2}(\mathbf{x}^o + \mathbf{x}^r)$ during training as in Fig. 2. The synchronization and divergence errors affect the out-of-step and divergence terms respectively in Eq. (10). As the training proceeds with decreasing learning rate, the divergence error also decreases and becomes trivial compared with the averaged model $\overline{\mathbf{x}}$. Moreover, the synchronization error is much smaller in contrast to the divergence error, leading to the trivial $\mathcal{O}(\frac{1}{T})$ out-of-step term in contrast to the $\mathcal{O}(\frac{1}{\sqrt{T}})$ divergence term. It empirically validates our analysis.

Faster Convergence. On the contrary of performance deterioration, we empirically find that out-of-step periodic averaging can potentially even improve the convergence speed and final performance. As in the first row of plots in Fig. 3, we can see that our method accelerates the convergence speed both on CIFAR-10 and ImageNet. Although the training loss of MP and CMP becomes very close after the third learning rate decay, their gap is obvious when the learning rate $\eta > 0.0001$. Specifically, out-of-step periodic averaging improves the test accuracy by 3.82%, 1.29%, and 0.39% at epoch 100, 150, and 200 respectively

Table 3. More ImageNet Top-1 Accuracy (%) ($K = 4$)

	ResNet-50	VGG-19	ResNet-152
MP	76.33 ± 0.11	72.39 ± 0.08	78.34 ± 0.14
CMP	76.38 ± 0.13	72.44 ± 0.10	78.36 ± 0.06
PMP [37]	75.80 ± 0.22	71.62± 0.19	77.53 ± 0.15
PMP [27]	75.70 ± 0.27	71.56± 0.25	77.64 ± 0.21

	WideResNet-101-2	ResNext-101-32x8d
MP	78.85 ± 0.12	79.31 ± 0.05
CMP	78.83 ± 0.14	79.34 ± 0.06
PMP [37]	77.76 ± 0.25	78.62 ± 0.22
PMP [27]	77.68 ± 0.19	78.52 ± 0.25

when training ResNet-164 on CIFAR-10. It becomes 1.63%, 0.95%, and 0.53% for ResNet-1001 on CIFAR-10. Consequently, we have a faster and better test accuracy of CMP than MP in CIFAR-10 experiments. The gap also exists for ImageNet but is less obvious at the end of the training, with an improvement of 4.34%, 2.44%, and 0.05% at epoch 30, 60, and 90. We summarize the test accuracy in Table 1. We also compare the results of MP and CMP on more models in ImageNet experiments in Table 3, where PMP leads to considerable performance loss due to asynchronous training. *Why can CMP even improve the model performance?* Periodic averaging [6, 32] also shows an empirical faster convergence, but the theoretical explanation via convergence analysis remains an open problem. [10, 16] empirically showed that the model tends to stay at the edge of the local optima, thus we can reach the center of the local optima via averaging to get better performance. Therefore, CMP can be regarded to have an implicit regularization effect. Empirically, CIFAR-10 benefits more from it than ImageNet, possibly due to the larger randomness in CIFAR-10.

Varying Period p. We summarized the test accuracy of ResNet-164 trained with CMP using different synchronization period p in Table 2. It shows that CMP works well with a wide range of period p without performance deterioration. The performance empirically peaks at $p = 4$, but the performance of other choices is also very close to it. A larger period p means a smaller communication cost and $p = 8$ will suffice to achieve fast training regarding the wall clock time (Fig. 5). Therefore, we simply set $p = 8$ and no other hyper-parameters is introduced in CMP compared with MP.

5.3 Higher Throughput with Cross Model Parallelism

We plot the curves of the training loss and test accuracy regarding training time in Fig. 4. CMP achieves much higher training throughput (faster training speed regarding time) in contrast to MP. The bidirectional training of the obverse and

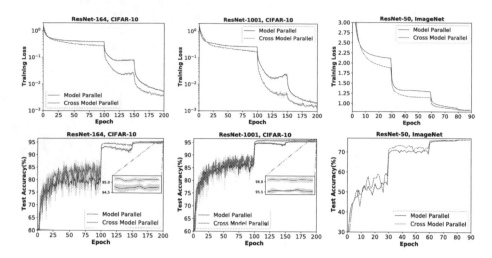

Fig. 3. Training curves regarding epochs. The test accuracy curves at the end of training are not zoomed in for ResNet-50 as they are almost overlapped (Table 1). Best viewed in color.

reverse models are partially overlapped, contributing to a faster training speed by utilizing idle workers more efficiently. Therefore, both the faster convergence of out-of-step periodic averaging and a higher training throughput contribute to the considerably faster training speed of CMP in contrast to MP. We summarize the speedup in Table 4, but it is inferior to the ideal training speedup $\frac{2K}{K+1}$ of CMP from Eq. (4). There are two possible causes. The first is that the workload is not exactly balanced on different workers. We have fine-tuned the partition of the CNN model but a more fine-grained grid search may further improve the speedup. The second is that the forward time and backward time are not empirically equal in Fig. 1. The backward time is usually in the range of $\times 1 \sim \times 2$ the forward time. Therefore, the ideal speedup of CMP is hard to reach in practice.

Scalability. The speedup for various models both on CIFAR-10 and ImageNet is shown in Table 4. CMP is capable of accelerating MP for various large CNNs. For smaller CNNs, we record the speedup of CMP in contrast to MP with $K = 2, 3, 4$. For large CNNs, we record the corresponding metrics with $K = 4$. We achieve the speedup close to ideal with various CNNs and K. In the meantime, the memory overheads are trivial even when we are bidirectionally training two models in CMP. As the activations of the two models are alternatively released in CMP, the memory overheads mainly consist of the additional model parameters and environment setup for training an additional model. The CNNs are usually computationally intensive, so the size of parameters is way less than the activations. Although the absolute memory overhead is 2.4 GiB for training ResNeXt-101-32x8d using CMP, it is only 3.9% compared with the original memory consumption but leads to a 41% improvement of the training speed. Besides, the memory

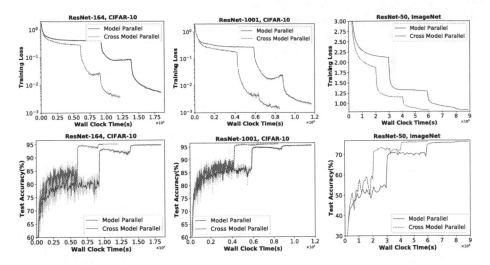

Fig. 4. Training curves regarding wall clock time. Best viewed in color.

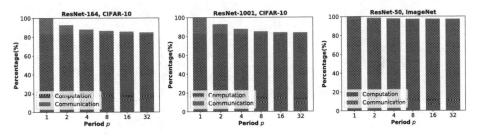

Fig. 5. Running time breakdown using CMP. The computation time and communication time are normalized by the total time of $p = 1$. Best viewed in color.

overheads are way less than naively training two models at the same time, which validates the feasibility of our proposed CMP method.

Running Time Breakdown. We breakdown the running time of CMP on both the CIFAR-10 and ImageNet tasks to show how the synchronization period p helps improve the training speed. As we only have two models for communication, the communication overheads of CMP are not as overwhelming as in data parallelism with many workers. However, the communication still consumes about 16.8% of the total running time when the obverse and reverse models are synchronized every iteration ($p = 1$) in CIFAR-10 experiments. It decreases to 3.2% and 1.9% for ResNet-164 and ResNet-1001 respectively by increasing the synchronization period p to 8. In comparison, the models on ImageNet are much more computationally intensive due to the larger feature size and the communication overheads can be negligible when $p \geq 4$.

Table 4. Speedup and memory (GiB) comparison with K GPUs from small to large models. The first two models are trained on CIFAR-10, while the rest are trained on ImageNet. For larger models, we only show the results with $K = 4$.

Model	MP	CMP		Ideal
	Memory	Memory	Speedup	$\frac{2K}{K+1}$
ResNet-164	4.53	4.59	$\times 1.25$ $(K=2)$	$\times 1.33$
		4.65	$\times 1.35$ $(K=3)$	$\times 1.50$
		4.74	$\times 1.44$ $(K=4)$	$\times 1.60$
ResNet-1001	27.5	27.7	$\times 1.22$ $(K=2)$	$\times 1.33$
		27.7	$\times 1.32$ $(K=3)$	$\times 1.50$
		27.8	$\times 1.40$ $(K=4)$	$\times 1.60$
ResNet-50	21.2	22.1	$\times 1.29$ $(K=2)$	$\times 1.33$
		22.7	$\times 1.41$ $(K=3)$	$\times 1.50$
		23.5	$\times 1.49$ $(K=4)$	$\times 1.60$
VGG-19	20.3	21.8	$\times 1.23$ $(K=2)$	$\times 1.33$
		22.3	$\times 1.33$ $(K=3)$	$\times 1.50$
		23.0	$\times 1.42$ $(K=4)$	$\times 1.60$
Wide ResNet-101-2	42.0	44.4	$\times 1.44$ $(K=4)$	$\times 1.60$
ResNet-152	43.9	45.6	$\times 1.46$ $(K=4)$	$\times 1.60$
ResNeXt-101-32x8d	61.0	63.4	$\times 1.41$ $(K=4)$	$\times 1.60$

6   Conclusion

In this work, we focus on addressing the training difficulty of the large CNNs which are playing a key role in many data mining tasks. We proposed a novel cross model parallelism to improve the efficiency of model parallelism by bidirectionally train two reversely placed models with negligible peak memory overheads. We also introduced a novel out-of-step periodic averaging method to periodically synchronize the two alternatively trained models for lower communication overheads. Both theoretical and experimental results show that the synchronization error is negligible and out-of-step periodic averaging empirically accelerates the convergence. We achieve a speedup of up to $\times 1.5$ compared with model parallelism. In contrast to pipeline model parallelism, cross model parallelism improves the efficiency of model parallelism without these limitations of re-computation overheads and staleness.

Ethical Statement. Our work focuses on improving the model parallelism for distributed training in data-centers. We do not see any potential ethical issues.

References

1. Abadi, M., et al.: Tensorflow: a system for large-scale machine learning. In: 12th {USENIX} Symposium on Operating Systems Design and Implementation ({OSDI} 2016), pp. 265–283 (2016)
2. Belilovsky, E., Eickenberg, M., Oyallon, E.: Greedy layerwise learning can scale to imagenet. In: International Conference on Machine Learning, pp. 583–593. PMLR (2019)
3. Bottou, L.: Large-scale machine learning with stochastic gradient descent. In: Lechevallier, Y., Saporta, G. (eds.) COMPSTAT 2010, pp. 177–186. Springer, Heidelberg (2010). https://doi.org/10.1007/978-3-7908-2604-3_16
4. Chen, T., Xu, B., Zhang, C., Guestrin, C.: Training deep nets with sublinear memory cost. arXiv preprint arXiv:1604.06174 (2016)
5. Foley, D., Danskin, J.: Ultra-performance pascal GPU and NVLink interconnect. IEEE Micro **37**(2), 7–17 (2017)
6. Gao, H., Xu, A., Huang, H.: On the convergence of communication-efficient local SGD for federated learning. In: Proceedings of the AAAI Conference on Artificial Intelligence, vol. 35, pp. 7510–7518 (2021)
7. Gu, B., Xu, A., Huo, Z., Deng, C., Huang, H.: Privacy-preserving asynchronous vertical federated learning algorithms for multiparty collaborative learning. IEEE Trans. Neural Netw. Learn. Syst. **33**(11), 6103–6115 (2021)
8. Guo, P., et al.: Auto-FedRL: federated hyperparameter optimization for multi-institutional medical image segmentation. In: Avidan, S., Brostow, G., Cissé, M., Farinella, G.M., Hassner, T. (eds.) ECCV 2022. LNCS, vol. 13681, pp. 437–455. Springer, Cham (2022). https://doi.org/10.1007/978-3-031-19803-8_26
9. Han, S., Mao, H., Dally, W.J.: Deep compression: compressing deep neural networks with pruning, trained quantization and huffman coding. arXiv preprint arXiv:1510.00149 (2015)
10. He, H., Huang, G., Yuan, Y.: Asymmetric valleys: beyond sharp and flat local minima. In: Advances in Neural Information Processing Systems, pp. 2553–2564 (2019)
11. He, K., Zhang, X., Ren, S., Sun, J.: Deep residual learning for image recognition. In: Proceedings of the IEEE Conference on Computer Vision and Pattern Recognition, pp. 770–778 (2016)
12. He, K., Zhang, X., Ren, S., Sun, J.: Identity mappings in deep residual networks. In: Leibe, B., Matas, J., Sebe, N., Welling, M. (eds.) ECCV 2016. LNCS, vol. 9908, pp. 630–645. Springer, Cham (2016). https://doi.org/10.1007/978-3-319-46493-0_38
13. Huang, Y., et al.: Tangram: bridging immutable and mutable abstractions for distributed data analytics. In: USENIX Annual Technical Conference, pp. 191–206 (2019)
14. Huo, Z., Gu, B., Huang, H.: Training neural networks using features replay. In: Advances in Neural Information Processing Systems, pp. 6659–6668 (2018)
15. Huo, Z., Gu, B., Huang, H., et al.: Decoupled parallel backpropagation with convergence guarantee. In: International Conference on Machine Learning, pp. 2098–2106 (2018)
16. Izmailov, P., Podoprikhin, D., Garipov, T., Vetrov, D., Wilson, A.G.: Averaging weights leads to wider optima and better generalization. arXiv preprint arXiv:1803.05407 (2018)
17. Jaderberg, M., et al.: Decoupled neural interfaces using synthetic gradients. In: International Conference on Machine Learning, pp. 1627–1635. PMLR (2017)

18. Keskar, N.S., Mudigere, D., Nocedal, J., Smelyanskiy, M., Tang, P.T.P.: On large-batch training for deep learning: generalization gap and sharp minima. arXiv preprint arXiv:1609.04836 (2016)
19. Kipf, T.N., Welling, M.: Semi-supervised classification with graph convolutional networks. arXiv preprint arXiv:1609.02907 (2016)
20. Krizhevsky, A.: One weird trick for parallelizing convolutional neural networks. arXiv preprint arXiv:1404.5997 (2014)
21. Krizhevsky, A., Hinton, G., et al.: Learning multiple layers of features from tiny images (2009)
22. LeCun, Y., et al.: Backpropagation applied to handwritten zip code recognition. Neural Comput. **1**(4), 541–551 (1989)
23. Lee, S., Kim, J.K., Zheng, X., Ho, Q., Gibson, G.A., Xing, E.P.: On model parallelization and scheduling strategies for distributed machine learning. In: Advances in Neural Information Processing Systems, pp. 2834–2842 (2014)
24. Li, J., et al.: A general and efficient querying method for learning to hash. In: Proceedings of the 2018 International Conference on Management of Data, pp. 1333–1347 (2018)
25. Li, M., Andersen, D.G., Smola, A.J., Yu, K.: Communication efficient distributed machine learning with the parameter server. In: Advances in Neural Information Processing Systems, pp. 19–27 (2014)
26. Liu, Y., Xu, A., Chen, Z.: Map-based deep imitation learning for obstacle avoidance. In: 2018 IEEE/RSJ International Conference on Intelligent Robots and Systems (IROS), pp. 8644–8649. IEEE (2018)
27. Narayanan, D., et al.: Pipedream: generalized pipeline parallelism for DNN training. In: Proceedings of the 27th ACM Symposium on Operating Systems Principles, pp. 1–15 (2019)
28. Paszke, A., et al.: Pytorch: an imperative style, high-performance deep learning library. In: Wallach, H., Larochelle, H., Beygelzimer, A., d' Alché-Buc, F., Fox, E., Garnett, R. (eds.) Advances in Neural Information Processing Systems, vol. 32, pp. 8024–8035. Curran Associates, Inc. (2019)
29. Rumelhart, D.E., Hinton, G.E., Williams, R.J.: Learning representations by back-propagating errors. Nature **323**(6088), 533–536 (1986)
30. Russakovsky, O., et al.: ImageNet large scale visual recognition challenge. Int. J. Comput. Vision (IJCV) **115**(3), 211–252 (2015). https://doi.org/10.1007/s11263-015-0816-y
31. Simonyan, K., Zisserman, A.: Very deep convolutional networks for large-scale image recognition. arXiv preprint arXiv:1409.1556 (2014)
32. Stich, S.U.: Local SGD converges fast and communicates little. In: International Conference on Learning Representations (2018)
33. Valiant, L.G.: A bridging model for parallel computation. Commun. ACM **33**(8), 103–111 (1990)
34. Xie, S., Girshick, R., Dollár, P., Tu, Z., He, K.: Aggregated residual transformations for deep neural networks. In: Proceedings of the IEEE Conference on Computer Vision and Pattern Recognition, pp. 1492–1500 (2017)
35. Xu, A., Huang, H.: Coordinating momenta for cross-silo federated learning. In: Proceedings of the AAAI Conference on Artificial Intelligence, vol. 36, pp. 8735–8743 (2022)
36. Xu, A., Huang, H.: Detached error feedback for distributed SGD with random sparsification. In: International Conference on Machine Learning, pp. 24550–24575. PMLR (2022)

37. Xu, A., Huo, Z., Huang, H.: On the acceleration of deep learning model parallelism with staleness. In: Proceedings of the IEEE/CVF Conference on Computer Vision and Pattern Recognition, pp. 2088–2097 (2020)
38. Xu, A., Huo, Z., Huang, H.: Step-ahead error feedback for distributed training with compressed gradient. In: Proceedings of the AAAI Conference on Artificial Intelligence, vol. 35, pp. 10478–10486 (2021)
39. Xu, A., et al.: Closing the generalization gap of cross-silo federated medical image segmentation. In: Proceedings of the IEEE/CVF Conference on Computer Vision and Pattern Recognition, pp. 20866–20875 (2022)
40. Yu, H., Jin, R., Yang, S.: On the linear speedup analysis of communication efficient momentum SGD for distributed non-convex optimization. In: International Conference on Machine Learning, pp. 7184–7193 (2019)
41. Zagoruyko, S., Komodakis, N.: Wide residual networks. arXiv preprint arXiv:1605.07146 (2016)
42. Zhou, S., Wu, Y., Ni, Z., Zhou, X., Wen, H., Zou, Y.: Dorefa-net: training low bitwidth convolutional neural networks with low bitwidth gradients. arXiv preprint arXiv:1606.06160 (2016)

Distributed Adaptive Optimization with Divisible Communication

An Xu[1]([✉]) [ID] and Yang Bai[2]

[1] ByteDance Inc., Seattle, USA
an.xu@bytedance.com
[2] Tencent Inc., Beijing, China
mavisbai@tencent.com

Abstract. Synchronous distributed training can scale the training of deep neural networks on large-scale data, thus it has been widely adopted in large-scale applications. Because it often suffers from the communication bottleneck, many methods have been proposed to reduce the communication cost. However, these communication reduction methods often lead to poor performance for the adaptive optimizer, largely due to its non-linearity. To address this challenging issue, we propose a novel method to divide the communication into the foreground and background communication. The foreground communication is more informative but can be of low cost to achieve communication efficiency, while the background communication runs in the background and requires no synchronization time. We use Adam as the base optimizer and achieve ×1024 foreground compression ratio on CIFAR-10, ×128 on *non-iid* CIFAR-10, ×64 on ImageNet image classification tasks, and ×128 on WMT'16 EN-DE machine translation task with comparable performance, which leads to ×7, ×6.4, ×3.5, and ×7 training speedup, respectively. Moreover, we provide rigorous theoretical analysis to prove that our method obtains the same convergence rate as Adam and achieves linear speedup regarding the number of workers.

Keywords: Adaptive Optimization · Communication Efficiency · Distributed Training

1 Introduction

Synchronous distributed learning is widely adopted to accelerate the training of deep neural networks (DNNs) by scaling it to many workers (GPUs). It can be formulated as an optimization problem of

$$\min_x \frac{1}{N} \sum_{i=1}^{N} f_i(x),$$

(1)

Algorithm 1. Vanilla Adam.

1: **Input:** model x, update Δ, lr γ, running average (u, v), coefficient (β_1, β_2), iteration t, and ϵ.

2: **function** ADAM(x, Δ, γ, u, v, β_1, β_2, t, ϵ)

3:     $u' = \beta_1 u + (1 - \beta_1)\Delta$

4:     $v' = \beta_2 v + (1 - \beta_2)\Delta^2$

5:     $x' = x - \gamma \dfrac{u'/(1-\beta_1^{t+1})}{\sqrt{v'/(1-\beta_2^{t+1})}+\epsilon}$

6:     **return** x', u', v'.

7: **end function**

---

where x is the model weight, f_i is the objective function of worker $i \in [N]$. Let the average stochastic gradient

$$\overline{g}_t \stackrel{\Delta}{=} \frac{1}{N} \sum_{i=1}^{N} \nabla F_i(x_t; \xi_t), \tag{2}$$

where $\nabla F_i(x_t; \xi_t)$ is the stochastic gradient and ξ_t is the unbiased data sampling stochastic variable satisfying

$$\mathbb{E}_{\xi_t} \nabla F_i(x_t; \xi_t) = \nabla f_i(x_t). \tag{3}$$

Adam [15,23] is a representative method to solve this optimization problem for DNN related tasks with adaptive learning rate (lr). Specifically, the synchronous distributed Adam updates the model via Algorithm 1:

$$x_{t+1}, u_{t+1}, v_{t+1} = \text{ADAM}(x_t, \overline{g}_t, \gamma, u_t, v_t, \beta_1, \beta_2, t, \epsilon),$$

where t is iteration, γ is the learning rate (lr), u_t is the running average with coefficient β_1, v_t is the second moment running average with coefficient β_2, and ϵ is for numerical stability and controlled adaptivity.

However, averaging the stochastic gradient ($\overline{g}_t$) requires heavy communication [8–10,12,19,21,33,35,37]. It becomes the computational bottleneck for scaling the training task especially for DNNs with large model sizes. There have been many works to improve the efficiency of synchronous distributed (momentum) SGD training, such as compression [2,5,30,31] with error feedback [14,20,32,34,36,40], local SGD with local training and infrequent communication [26,39], or the combination of both [4,8]. We observe that their success is largely due to the linearity of the (momentum) SGD update rule. Nevertheless, there are fewer works perfectly addressing the communication bottleneck of synchronous distributed Adam because its adaptivity (coordinate-wise operator) breaks the linearity, which makes communication-efficient Adam much more challenging.

In this work, we focus on tackling the communication efficiency challenge for synchronous distributed Adam. To address this critical challenge, we propose new concepts called foreground and background communication. The foreground communication is compressed and efficient, while the background communication runs in parallel with the computation so that it does not incur additional synchronization time. In summary, our contributions are as follows.

- We propose a novel communication-efficient distributed Adam variant with foreground and background communication (FB-Adam).
- We introduce a novel running average smoothing technique to stabilize and improve local training.
- We prove that our new method has the same convergence rate as the vanilla distributed Adam without compression.
- Extensive deep learning experiments show that our method achieves ×1024 foreground compression ratio on CIFAR-10, ×64 on *non-iid* CIFAR-10, ×16 on ImageNet image classification tasks, and ×32 on WMT'16 EN-DE machine translation task with comparable performance to Adam, largely improving existing works. We achieve ×7, ×6.4, ×3.5, and ×7 training speedup respectively.

2   Related Works

Local Training. In local SGD [26,39], workers perform local training with (momentum) SGD. The model and momentum statistics are periodically averaged. The same idea is applied to Adam by periodically averaging the model and Adam statistics known as LocalAdam [7]. FedAdam [22], on the other hand, uses SGD for local training and the corresponding local model update to perform server Adam update. However, its convergence analysis does not include the running average u though its algorithm does. Besides, it is only evaluated for federated learning [16] applications.

Compression. Gradient quantization reduces the precision of the gradient to lower bits than the original 32-bit floating-point, e.g., QSGD [2], TernGrad [31], SignSGD [5]. Gradient sparsification [1,3,27] selects partial gradient components for communication, e.g., Top-K.

Communication-Efficient Adam. EfficientAdam [6] directly applies error feedback [14,40] to the compression of Adam model update. But it does not synchronize Adam statistics and its convergence analysis suffers from the model dimensionality d. 1-bit Adam [28] shows that Adam statistics do not change too much during the late training. however, it requires a non-negligible number of warm-up training epochs that limits the overall compression ratio. 1-bit Lamb [18] works on the large-batch training problem by applying a similar idea to the Lamb [38] optimizer.

3   Methodology

3.1   Divisible Communication

The motivation of our FB-Adam is divisible communication, that is, dividing the communication message into the foreground and background communication

Algorithm 2. Distributed Adam with divisible communication (FB-Adam) on worker $n \in [N]$.

1: **Input:** period P, #iterations T, #workers N, server lr γ, local lr η, coefficient (β_1, β_2), and ϵ.

2: **Initialize:** running average $u_0 = u_0^{(n)} = v_0 = v_0^{(n)} = \mathbf{0}$, model $x_0^{(n)} = x_0$, compressor $C(\cdot)$.

3: **for** $t = 0, 1, \cdots, T-1$ **do**

4:    Let $r \triangleq \lfloor \frac{t}{P} \rfloor$

5:    $x_{t+1}^{(n)} = x_t^{(n)} - \frac{\eta}{P} u_r^{(n)} - \eta \nabla F^{(n)}(x_t^{(n)}, \xi_t^{(n)})$

6:    **if** $\mod (t+1, P) = 0$ **then**

7:       **if** $r > 0$ **then**

8:          Wait for the background communication.

9:          $\overline{\Delta}_{r-1} = \widetilde{\Delta}_{r-1} + \overline{e}_r + e_r$

10:          $x_{t+1-P}, u_r, v_r \leftarrow \text{ADAM}(x_{t+1-2P}, \overline{\Delta}_{r-1}, \gamma, u_{r-1}, v_{r-1}, \beta_1, \beta_2, r, \epsilon)$

11:       **end if**

12:       $\Delta_r^{(n)} = \sum_{\tau=t-P+1}^{t} \eta \nabla F^{(n)}(x_\tau^{(n)}, \xi_\tau^{(n)})$

13:       $e_{r+1}^{(n)} = \Delta_r^{(n)} - C(\Delta_r^{(n)})$ and send $C(\Delta_r^{(n)})$ to server.   // Foreground.

14:       Server: // Foreground.

15:          $\widetilde{\Delta}_r = C(\frac{1}{N} \sum_{n=1}^{N} C(\Delta_r^{(n)}))$

16:          $e_{r+1} = \frac{1}{N} \sum_{n=1}^{N} C(\Delta_r^{(n)}) - \widetilde{\Delta}_r$

17:          Broadcast $\widetilde{\Delta}_r$ to workers.

18:          Invoke a new thread in parallel: // Background.

19:             Average $\overline{e}_{r+1} = \frac{1}{N} \sum_{n=0}^{N-1} e_{r+1}^{(n)}$

20:             Broadcast server error e_{r+1} to workers.

21:       $x_{t+1}^{(n)}, u_{r+1}^{(n)}, v_{r+1}^{(n)} = \text{ADAM}(x_{t+1-P}, \widetilde{\Delta}_r + e_{r+1}^{(n)}, \gamma, u_r, v_r, \beta_1, \beta_2, r+1, \epsilon)$

22:    **end if**

23: **end for**

---

message. In foreground communication, workers and the server communicate the most important information of the message, which can be small in terms of the message size. We leave the rest of the message to the background communication that can be conducted in parallel to the training computation. The background message will be stale for one communication round, but its negative effect will be weakened due to less importance. In this way, only the foreground communication requires synchronization, but it will be communication-efficient, while the synchronization time for the background communication will be hidden by the training computation. After background communication, we can restore the vanilla Adam update. The algorithm is summarized in Algorithm 2.

However, the background communication may not be able to be hidden by the computation time of one training iteration. Hence we adopt local training and periodic synchronization to stack the computation of P training iteration together and reduce the communication frequency. Thus, we can ensure that the background communication can be hidden by the local training, resulting in barely any background synchronization time.

In local training, we propose to use SGD with a frozen running average term as shown in Algorithm 2 line 4, and we refer to it as running average smoothing.

Table 1. Compare FB-Adam (ours) with existing methods.

Method	Message Compression	Infrequent Synchronization	Provable Convergence with Adam Statistics	High Communication Reduction Ratio
Efficient Adam	✓	✗	✓	✗
1-bit Adam	✓	✗	✓	✗
LocalAdam	✗	✓	✗	✗
FedAdam	✗	✓	✗	✗
FB-Adam (Ours)	✓	✓	✓	✓

It helps to stabilize local training as the stochastic gradient introduces noise. We do not update this running average term during local training to avoid additional communication for averaging optimization statistics.

Foreground and Background. In particular, the communication message $\Delta_r^{(n)}$ at training round r is the sum of the local training gradient multiplied by the local learning rate. We use a compressor C (e.g., Top-K) to extract the important information of the message for foreground communication. It is efficient both from workers to server and server to workers as shown in Algorithm 2 line 12 and 13. After foreground communication, each worker receives the compressed message $\widetilde{\Delta}_r$. The rest of the message exists as the local error $e_{r+1}^{(n)}$ and server error e_{r+1}. It will be communicated in a background thread in parallel to the next round of local training computation. Finally, we conduct the Adam update at the server side with

$$\widetilde{\Delta}_r + e_{r+1}^{(n)} \tag{4}$$

in Algorithm 2 line 15.

Correction. The updated model based on only the foreground message will deviate from the vanilla Adam method. Therefore, we correct the starting model at training round r by an Adam re-update with the sum of the foreground and background message $\overline{\Delta}_{r-1}$, as shown in Algorithm 2 lines 7 to 9. Note that $\overline{\Delta}_{r-1}$ is the true average message from all workers in training round $r-1$.

Overall, our method FB-Adam features message compression, infrequent communication, and divisible communication techniques. The aforementioned Adam variants suffer from a considerable performance loss when the communication reduction ratio is high, while FB-Adam can restore vanilla Adam's update rule. We compare our method with existing works in Table 1.

4   Convergence Results

Before introducing our main theoretical analysis results, we discuss the following assumptions. These assumptions are mild and have been used in related works frequently. For the combination of Top-K and QSGD compressor, [4] showed that it satisfies Assumption 5.

Assumption 1 *(Lower Bound). Function f has a lower bound f^*.*

Assumption 2 *(Lipschitz Gradient). Function f_n is L-smooth $(L > 0)$ for all $n \in [N]$, i.e., for all $x, y \in \mathbb{R}^d$*

$$\|\nabla f_n(x) - \nabla f_n(y)\| \le L\|x - y\|. \tag{5}$$

Assumption 3 *(Bounded Variance). Function f_n has bounded local variance σ_l, i.e.,*

$$\mathbb{E}\|\nabla F^{(n)}(x, \xi) - \nabla f_n(x)\|^2 \le \sigma_l^2 \tag{6}$$

for all $x \in \mathbb{R}^d$ and $n \in [N]$. Function f has bounded global variance σ_g, i.e., for all $x \in \mathbb{R}^d$,

$$\frac{1}{N} \sum_{n=1}^{N} \|\nabla f_n(x) - \nabla f(x)\|^2 \le \sigma_g^2. \tag{7}$$

Assumption 4 *(Bounded Gradient). Function $F^{(n)}(x, \xi)$ has G-bounded gradient, i.e., for any $n \in [N]$ and $x \in \mathbb{R}^d$, we have*

$$\|\nabla F^{(n)}(x, \xi)\| \le G. \tag{8}$$

Assumption 5 *(Approximate Compressor [14, 32, 40]). For $\delta \in [0, 1]$ and all $x \in \mathbb{R}^d$, the compressor C satisfies*

$$\|C(x) - x\|^2 \le (1 - \delta)\|x\|^2. \tag{9}$$

In the following, we will provide the convergence analysis of our method. The complete proof can be found in the Appendix and here we only show the sketch of our proof.

Theorem 6. *Let Assumptions 1 to 5 hold and*

$$\eta = \frac{1}{160LP\sqrt{R}}, \tag{10}$$

$$\gamma = \frac{\sqrt{PN}G}{L}, \tag{11}$$

$$\epsilon = \frac{G}{(1 - \beta_1)L}. \tag{12}$$

Suppose $z_r \stackrel{\Delta}{=} x_{rP}$ and $T = RP$. Then for large T that satisfies

$$T \ge P^2 N, \tag{13}$$

our algorithm satisfies

$$\frac{1}{R} \sum_{r=0}^{R-1} \mathbb{E}\|\nabla f(z_r)\|^2 \le \frac{640L(f(x_0) - f^*) + \sigma_l^2}{(1 - \beta_1)\sqrt{NT}}$$

$$+ \frac{4PG^2 + PN\sigma_l^2 + ((1 - \delta)P^2 N + P)\sigma_g^2}{(1 - \beta_1)T}. \tag{14}$$

Our convergence bound is free of the model dimensionality d, the first among existing Adam variants with compression to the best of our knowledge, which is significant for deep learning models.

Corollary 1. *According to Theorem 6, our algorithm satisfies*

$$\mathbb{E}\|\nabla f(z_r)\|^2 \leq O(\frac{1}{\sqrt{NT}}) + O(\frac{PN}{T}) + O(\frac{(1-\delta)P^2N}{T}).$$

When T is large enough, the dominating term is $O(\frac{1}{\sqrt{NT}})$. Hence the convergence rate of our algorithm is

$$O(\frac{1}{\sqrt{NT}}), \tag{15}$$

which indicates the linear speedup regarding N.

Corollary 2. *According to Theorem 6, to guarantee the convergence of our algorithm we need*

$$P \leq \frac{T^{1/2}}{N^{1/2}}. \tag{16}$$

When term $O(\frac{1}{\sqrt{NT}})$ is dominating, i.e.,

$$O(\frac{1}{\sqrt{NT}}) \geq O(\frac{P^2N}{T}), \tag{17}$$

P satisfies $P \leq \frac{T^{1/4}}{N^{3/4}}$. Thus, the upper bound of P is

$$O(\frac{T^{1/4}}{N^{3/4}}). \tag{18}$$

Similarly, if the global variance $\sigma_g = 0$ (data-center distributed training) or $\delta = 1$ (no compression), the upper bound of P is

$$O(\frac{T^{1/2}}{N^{3/2}}). \tag{19}$$

5   Experiments

5.1   Experiment Setup

We compare our method FB-Adam with 5 baselines:

(1) vanilla Adam, (2) EfficientAdam (Adam + Error Feedback), (3) Local-Adam, (4) FedAdam, and (5) 1-bit Adam.

The compressor C is the commonly-used Top-K sparsification, so that the foreground compression ratio R_c can be easily adjusted. For our FB-Adam, the overall communication reduction ratio

$$R = R_c P \tag{20}$$

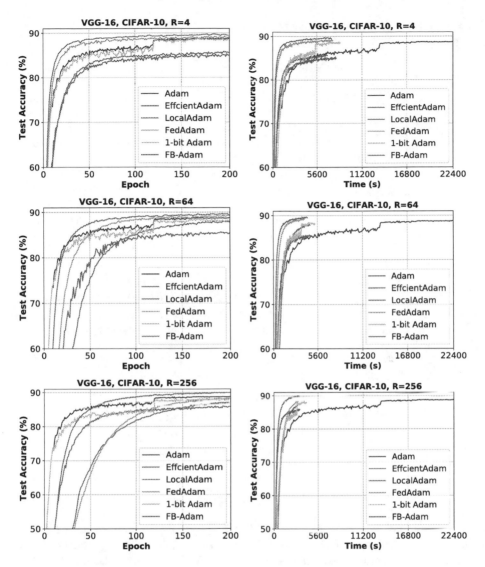

Fig. 1. Test accuracy for training VGG-16 on CIFAR-10.

and $P = 4$ by default, since $P = 4$ is large enough to make sure that there is no background synchronization overheads for all our experiment settings. While $R = R_c$ for EfficientAdam and 1-bit Adam, $R = P$ for FedAdam, and $R = \frac{P}{3}$ for LocalAdam due to its additional communication cost of averaging the running average u and v.

For easy comparison, we report the model performance of 1-bit Adam with the same compressor as the other communication-efficient methods in the tables, though 1-bit Adam require a full-precision pre-training stage (i.e., the warm-up

Table 2. Test accuracy for training VGG-16 on CIFAR-10. × denotes poor convergence.

Ratio(R)	Adam	EfficientAdam	LocalAdam	FedAdam	1-bit Adam	FB-Adam
×1	88.85 ± 0.16	–	–	–	–	–
×4	–	85.64 ± 0.13	86.03 ± 0.11	89.43 ± 0.09	88.45 ± 0.34	**90.01 ± 0.03**
×16	–	85.60 ± 0.45	87.25 ± 0.35	89.62 ± 0.17	88.40 ± 0.18	**89.98 ± 0.14**
×64	–	86.16 ± 0.02	88.15 ± 0.06	89.44 ± 0.19	88.15 ± 0.25	**89.79 ± 0.17**
×256	–	86.20 ± 0.28	87.13 ± 0.52	88.43 ± 0.13	87.88 ± 0.11	**90.09 ± 0.03**
×512	–	86.44 ± 0.15	×	85.58 ± 0.08	87.32 ± 0.28	**89.54 ± 0.03**
×1024	–	84.86 ± 0.13	×	×	86.01 ± 0.19	**89.32 ± 0.18**
×2048	–	×	×	×	×	**88.11 ± 0.09**

Table 3. Test accuracy for training VGG-16 on non-iid CIFAR-10. × denotes poor convergence.

Ratio (R)	EfficientAdam	LocalAdam	FedAdam	1-bit Adam	FB-Adam
×8	×	84.36 ± 0.10	88.87 ± 0.16	88.35 ± 0.31	**89.10 ± 0.20**
×32	×	84.20 ± 0.07	87.96 ± 0.02	88.03 ± 0.22	**89.02 ± 0.06**
×128	×	84.90 ± 0.39	86.94 ± 0.19	87.85 ± 0.26	**88.37 ± 0.13**
×512	×	84.44 ± 0.09	85.26 ± 0.28	86.88 ± 0.39	**87.16 ± 0.10**
×1024	×	×	81.65 ± 0.39	85.32 ± 0.32	**86.90 ± 0.22**
×2048	×	×	×	×	**85.88 ± 0.19**

stage). Therefore 1-bit Adam actually will have a smaller overall compression ratio than other compared methods in Tables 2, 3, 4, and 5. However, when plotting the training curves regarding wall-clock time in the figures, the warm-up stage of 1-bit Adam is communication-heavy and results in *longer wall-clock time* than the other communication-efficient methods with the same compressor, shown in Figs. 1, 2, 3, and 4. The warm-up stage setting follows the original paper [18].

We conduct experiments on CIFAR-10 and ImageNet image classification tasks, and WMT'16 EN-DE machine translation tasks. All experiments run in a cluster of 16 machines where each has 1 NVIDIA P40 GPU and 10 Gb/s networking bandwidth.

5.2 Results on CIFAR-10

For CIFAR-10 [17] image classification task, we train a VGG-16 [25] model. We report the mean and standard deviation metrics over 3 runs. $(\beta_1, \beta_2) = (0.9, 0.999)$ and $\epsilon = 1 \times 10^{-8}$. The batch size is 128 and the weight decay is 5×10^{-4}. The model is trained for 200 epochs. We select the best (server and local) learning rate from

$$\{1 \times 10^{-1}, 5 \times 10^{-2}, 1 \times 10^{-2}, 5 \times 10^{-2}, \cdots\}. \tag{21}$$

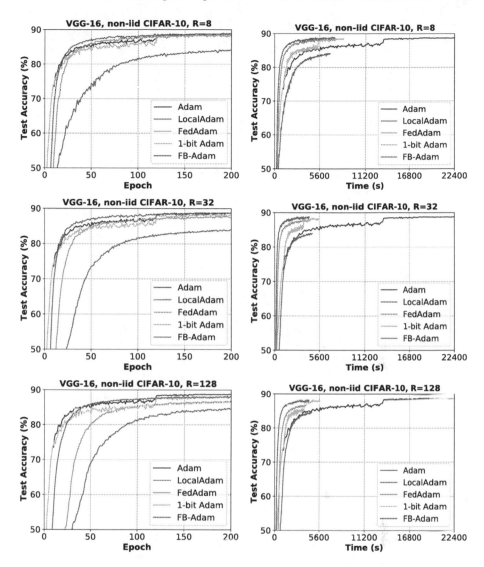

Fig. 2. Test accuracy for training VGG-16 on non-iid CIFAR-10.

Standard data augmentation techniques are applied such as random cropping, random flipping, and standardization. For Adam, there is a learning rate decay of 0.1 at epoch 120 and 160. While for the other methods, we find it better without any learning rate decay.

We plot the training curves regarding both the training epoch and time in Fig. 1 with test accuracy summarized in Table 2. It can be observed from Fig. 1 that 1-bit Adam takes a longer wall-clock training time due to the full-precision warm-up stage, though it converges similarly to vanilla Adam regarding the

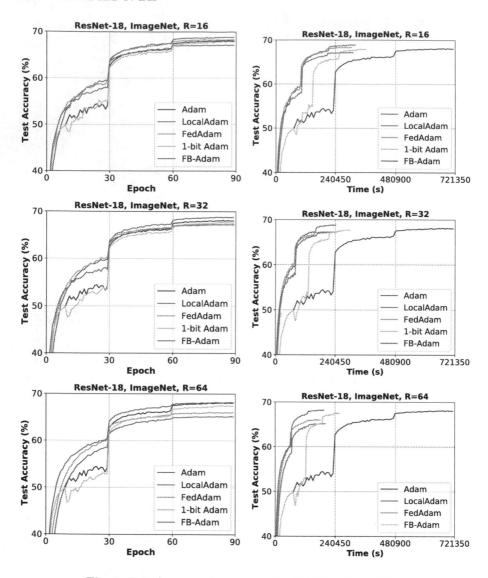

Fig. 3. Test Accuracy for training ResNet-18 on ImageNet

training epochs. In comparison, the proposed FB-Adam converges faster and better regarding the wall-clock time. When the communication reduction ratio $R = 256$, FB-Adam accelerates Adam by $\times 7$ without performance loss. From Table 2, FB-Adam can achieve up to $R = 1024$ with comparable performance to Adam, while the best counterpart only achieves $R = 64$.

We also consider non-IID CIFAR-10. Following the practice in [13], we randomly distribute 80% of the data to workers, but distribute the rest 20% of the data by sorting according to the label. We plot the training curves in Fig. 2

Table 4. Test accuracy for training ResNet-18 on ImageNet. × denotes poor convergence.

Ratio (R)	Adam	EfficientAdam	LocalAdam	FedAdam	1-bit Adam	FB-Adam
×1	68.14	–		–	–	–
×16	–	×	67.21	68.33	67.95	**68.88**
×32	–	×	67.26	67.36	67.88	**68.82**
×64	–	×	65.20	66.06	67.73	**68.22**
×128	–	×	63.15	64.86	67.51	**67.71**

Table 5. Validation loss for training Transformer on WMT'16 EN-DE.

Ratio (R)	Adam	EfficientAdam	LocalAdam	FedAdam	1-bit Adam	FB-Adam
×1	2.0259	–	–	–	–	–
×8	–	2.3693	2.0852	2.0169	2.0268	**2.0090**
×16	–	2.3625	2.0855	2.0259	2.0411	**2.0161**
×32	–	2.3672	2.1180	2.0624	2.0645	**2.0487**
×64	–	–	2.1240	2.1151	2.0859	**2.0674**
×128	–	–	2.1710	2.2339	2.0939	**2.0689**

Table 6. Ablation study of running average smoothing. Test accuracy of FedAdam v.s. FB-Adam without message compression for training VGG-16 on CIFAR-10.

Period P	4	16	64
FedAdam	89.43 ± 0.09	89.62 ± 0.17	89.14 ± 0.19
FB-Adam	$\mathbf{90.01 \pm 0.03}$	$\mathbf{89.98 \pm 0.14}$	$\mathbf{89.54 \pm 0.04}$

with test accuracy summarized in Table 3. EfficientAdam converges poorly when $R = 32$ and 128, therefore we do not include it in these two plots in Fig. 2.

For 1-bit Adam, we observe a similar pattern as in IID CIFAR-10 experiments. When $R = 128$, FB-Adam accelerates Adam by ×6.4 without performance loss. From Table 3, FB-Adam achieves $R = 128$ with comparable performance to Adam, while the best counterpart only achieves $R = 8$.

5.3 Results on ImageNet

For ImageNet [24] image classification task, we train a ResNet-18 [11] model. $(\beta_1, \beta_2) = (0.9, 0.999)$ and $\epsilon = 1 \times 10^{-8}$. The batch size is 256 and the weight decay is 1×10^{-4}. We select the best (server and local) learning rate from

$$\{1 \times 10^{-1}, 5 \times 10^{-2}, 1 \times 10^{-2}, 5 \times 10^{-2}, \cdots\}. \tag{22}$$

The model is trained for 90 epochs with a (server and local) learning rate decay of 0.1 at epoch 30, 60, and 80 for all methods. Random cropping, random flipping,

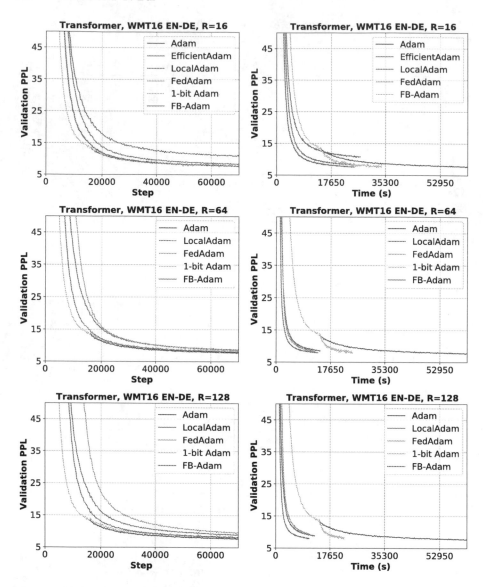

Fig. 4. Validation perplexity (PPL) for training Transformer on WMT'16 EN-DE. Lower is better.

and standardization are applied as data augmentation techniques. We plot the training curves in Fig. 3 with test accuracy summarized in Table 4. EfficientAdam converges poorly for this task and we do not include it.

The proposed FB-Adam converges faster than all other baselines regarding the wall-clock training time. Specifically, FB-Adam accelerates Adam by ×3.5

without performance loss when $R = 64$, while the best counterpart only achieves $R = 16$.

5.4 Results on WMT'16

For WMT'16 EN-DE machine translation task, we train a Transformer [29] model. $(\beta_1, \beta_2) = (0.9, 0.997)$ and $\epsilon = 1 \times 10^{-1}$. The batch size is 4096 and the label smoothing coefficient is 0.1. The dropout ratio is 0.1. The (server) learning rate scheduling follows [29] with 16000 warm-up steps. The local learning rate equals the server learning rate multiplied by a coefficient selected from

$$\{1, 5 \times 10^{-1}, 1 \times 10^{-1}, \cdots\}. \tag{23}$$

We plot the training curves of the validation perplexity (PPL) in Fig. 4 with validation loss summarized in Table 5. 1-bit Adam converges well in this task compared with vanilla Adam regarding the training epochs.

However, when taking the warm-up stage training time into consideration, we find it to be slower than the other communication-efficient counterparts. FB-Adam accelerates Adam by $\times 7$ with comparable performance to Adam when $R = 128$, while the best counterpart only achieves $R = 8$.

5.5 Ablation Study

We conduct an ablation study to show that the performance is improved by running average smoothing during local training in Table 6.

Overall, our proposed method FB-Adam consistently outperforms the counterparts in all tasks. We achieve a high foreground compression ratio due to infrequent synchronization and message compression, with comparable performance to Adam mainly due to the mathematical equivalence using foreground and background communication. Its fast training speed validates the motivation and efficiency of divisible communication.

6 Conclusion

In this work, we proposed a new FB-Adam method with divisible communication (foreground and background) to address the communication efficiency challenge for distributed adaptive optimizers. We also introduced running average smoothing for better local training. Our experimental results on various tasks validated the efficiency of FB-Adam. It achieves $\times 1024$ foreground compression ratio on CIFAR-10, $\times 128$ on *non-iid* CIFAR-10, $\times 64$ on ImageNet, and $\times 128$ on WMT'16 EN-DE machine translation dataset with comparable performance to Adam. Moreover, we showed our method has the same convergence rate as Adam without compression.

Ethical Statement. Our work is to improve the communication efficiency of distributed adaptive optimization. A large part of the work focuses on the theoretical analysis and we do not identify any potential ethical issues.

References

1. Aji, A.F., Heafield, K.: Sparse communication for distributed gradient descent. arXiv preprint arXiv:1704.05021 (2017)
2. Alistarh, D., Grubic, D., Li, J., Tomioka, R., Vojnovic, M.: QSGD: communication-efficient SGD via gradient quantization and encoding. In: Advances in Neural Information Processing Systems, pp. 1709–1720 (2017)
3. Alistarh, D., Hoefler, T., Johansson, M., Konstantinov, N., Khirirat, S., Renggli, C.: The convergence of sparsified gradient methods. In: Advances in Neural Information Processing Systems, pp. 5973–5983 (2018)
4. Basu, D., Data, D., Karakus, C., Diggavi, S.: Qsparse-local-SGD: distributed SGD with quantization, sparsification, and local computations. arXiv preprint arXiv:1906.02367 (2019)
5. Bernstein, J., Wang, Y.X., Azizzadenesheli, K., Anandkumar, A.: signSGD: compressed optimisation for non-convex problems. In: International Conference on Machine Learning, pp. 560–569. PMLR (2018)
6. Chen, C., Shen, L., Huang, H., Liu, W., Luo, Z.Q.: Efficient-adam: communication-efficient distributed adam with complexity analysis (2020)
7. Chen, X., Li, X., Li, P.: Toward communication efficient adaptive gradient method. In: Proceedings of the 2020 ACM-IMS on Foundations of Data Science Conference, pp. 119–128 (2020)
8. Gao, H., Xu, A., Huang, H.: On the convergence of communication-efficient local SGD for federated learning. In: Proceedings of the AAAI Conference on Artificial Intelligence, vol. 35, pp. 7510–7518 (2021)
9. Gu, B., Xu, A., Huo, Z., Deng, C., Huang, H.: Privacy-preserving asynchronous vertical federated learning algorithms for multiparty collaborative learning. IEEE Trans. Neural Netw. Learn. Syst. **33**(11), 6103–6115 (2021)
10. Guo, P., et al.: Auto-FedRL: federated hyperparameter optimization for multi-institutional medical image segmentation. In: Avidan, S., Brostow, G., Cissé, M., Farinella, G.M., Hassner, T. (eds.) ECCV 2022, pp. 437–455. Springer, Cham (2022). https://doi.org/10.1007/978-3-031-19803-8_26
11. He, K., Zhang, X., Ren, S., Sun, J.: Deep residual learning for image recognition. In: Proceedings of the IEEE Conference on Computer Vision and Pattern Recognition, pp. 770–778 (2016)
12. Huang, Y., et al.: Tangram: bridging immutable and mutable abstractions for distributed data analytics. In: USENIX Annual Technical Conference, pp. 191–206 (2019)
13. Karimireddy, S.P., Kale, S., Mohri, M., Reddi, S., Stich, S., Suresh, A.T.: Scaffold: stochastic controlled averaging for federated learning. In: International Conference on Machine Learning, pp. 5132–5143. PMLR (2020)
14. Karimireddy, S.P., Rebjock, Q., Stich, S., Jaggi, M.: Error feedback fixes SignSGD and other gradient compression schemes. In: International Conference on Machine Learning, pp. 3252–3261. PMLR (2019)
15. Kingma, D.P., Ba, J.: Adam: a method for stochastic optimization. arXiv preprint arXiv:1412.6980 (2014)
16. Konečný, J., McMahan, H.B., Yu, F.X., Richtárik, P., Suresh, A.T., Bacon, D.: Federated learning: strategies for improving communication efficiency. arXiv preprint arXiv:1610.05492 (2016)
17. Krizhevsky, A., Hinton, G., et al.: Learning multiple layers of features from tiny images (2009)

18. Li, C., Awan, A.A., Tang, H., Rajbhandari, S., He, Y.: 1-bit lamb: communication efficient large-scale large-batch training with lamb's convergence speed. arXiv preprint arXiv:2104.06069 (2021)
19. Li, J., et al.: A general and efficient querying method for learning to hash. In: Proceedings of the 2018 International Conference on Management of Data, pp. 1333–1347 (2018)
20. Lin, Y., Han, S., Mao, H., Wang, Y., Dally, W.J.: Deep gradient compression: reducing the communication bandwidth for distributed training. arXiv preprint arXiv:1712.01887 (2017)
21. Liu, Y., Xu, A., Chen, Z.: Map-based deep imitation learning for obstacle avoidance. In: 2018 IEEE/RSJ International Conference on Intelligent Robots and Systems (IROS), pp. 8644–8649. IEEE (2018)
22. Reddi, S., et al.: Adaptive federated optimization. arXiv preprint arXiv:2003.00295 (2020)
23. Reddi, S.J., Kale, S., Kumar, S.: On the convergence of adam and beyond. arXiv preprint arXiv:1904.09237 (2019)
24. Russakovsky, O., et al.: ImageNet large scale visual recognition challenge. Int. J. Comput. Vision (IJCV) 115(3), 211–252 (2015). https://doi.org/10.1007/s11263-015-0816-y
25. Simonyan, K., Zisserman, A.: Very deep convolutional networks for large-scale image recognition. arXiv preprint arXiv:1409.1556 (2014)
26. Stich, S.U.: Local SGD converges fast and communicates little. In: International Conference on Learning Representations (2018)
27. Stich, S.U., Cordonnier, J.B., Jaggi, M.: Sparsified SGD with memory. In: Advances in Neural Information Processing Systems, pp. 4447–4458 (2018)
28. Tang, H., et al.: 1-bit adam: communication efficient large-scale training with adam's convergence speed. arXiv preprint arXiv:2102.02888 (2021)
29. Vaswani, A., et al.: Attention is all you need. In: Proceedings of the 31st International Conference on Neural Information Processing Systems, pp. 6000–6010 (2017)
30. Vogels, T., Karimireddy, S.P., Jaggi, M.: Powersgd: practical low-rank gradient compression for distributed optimization. In: Advances in Neural Information Processing Systems, pp. 14259–14268 (2019)
31. Wen, W., et al.: Terngrad: ternary gradients to reduce communication in distributed deep learning. In: Advances in Neural Information Processing Systems, pp. 1509–1519 (2017)
32. Xie, C., Zheng, S., Koyejo, O.O., Gupta, I., Li, M., Lin, H.: CSER: communication-efficient SGD with error reset. In: Advances in Neural Information Processing Systems, vol. 33 (2020)
33. Xu, A., Huang, H.: Coordinating momenta for cross-silo federated learning. In: Proceedings of the AAAI Conference on Artificial Intelligence, vol. 36, pp. 8735–8743 (2022)
34. Xu, A., Huang, H.: Detached error feedback for distributed SGD with random sparsification. In: International Conference on Machine Learning, pp. 24550–24575. PMLR (2022)
35. Xu, A., Huo, Z., Huang, H.: On the acceleration of deep learning model parallelism with staleness. In: Proceedings of the IEEE/CVF Conference on Computer Vision and Pattern Recognition, pp. 2088–2097 (2020)
36. Xu, A., Huo, Z., Huang, H.: Step-ahead error feedback for distributed training with compressed gradient. In: Proceedings of the AAAI Conference on Artificial Intelligence, vol. 35, pp. 10478–10486 (2021)

37. Xu, A., et al.: Closing the generalization gap of cross-silo federated medical image segmentation. In: Proceedings of the IEEE/CVF Conference on Computer Vision and Pattern Recognition, pp. 20866–20875 (2022)
38. You, Y., et al.: Large batch optimization for deep learning: training bert in 76 minutes. arXiv preprint arXiv:1904.00962 (2019)
39. Yu, H., Jin, R., Yang, S.: On the linear speedup analysis of communication efficient momentum SGD for distributed non-convex optimization. In: International Conference on Machine Learning, pp. 7184–7193. PMLR (2019)
40. Zheng, S., Huang, Z., Kwok, J.T.: Communication-efficient distributed blockwise momentum SGD with error-feedback. arXiv preprint arXiv:1905.10936 (2019)

PROPAGATE: A Seed Propagation Framework to Compute Distance-Based Metrics on Very Large Graphs

Giambattista Amati[1], Antonio Cruciani[2(✉)], Daniele Pasquini[3], Paola Vocca[3], and Simone Angelini[1]

[1] Fondazione Ugo Bordoni, Rome, Italy
{gba,sangelini}@fub.it
[2] Gran Sasso Science Institute, L'Aquila, Italy
antonio.cruciani@gssi.it
[3] University of Rome "Tor Vergata", Rome, Italy
{daniele.pasquni,paola.vocca}@uniroma2.it

Abstract. We propose PROPAGATE, a fast approximation framework to estimate distance-based metrics on very large graphs such as: the (effective) diameter or the average distance within a small error. The framework assigns seeds to nodes and propagates them in a BFS-like fashion, computing the neighbors set until we obtain either the whole vertex set (for computing the diameter) or a given percentage of vertices (for the effective diameter). At each iteration, we derive compressed Boolean representations of the neighborhood sets discovered so far. The PROPAGATE framework yields two algorithms: PROPAGATE-P, which propagates all the s seeds in parallel, and PROPAGATE-S which propagates the seeds sequentially. For each node, the compressed representation of the PROPAGATE-P algorithm requires s bits while PROPAGATE-S 1 bit only. Both algorithms compute the average distance, the effective diameter, the diameter, and the connectivity rate (a measure of the sparseness degree of the transitive closure graph) within a small error with high probability: for any $\varepsilon > 0$ and using $s = \Theta\left(\frac{\log n}{\varepsilon^2}\right)$ sample nodes, the error for the average distance is bounded by $\xi = \frac{\varepsilon \Delta}{\alpha}$; the errors for the effective diameter and the diameter are bounded by $\xi = \frac{\varepsilon}{\alpha}$; and the error for the connectivity rate is bounded by ε where Δ is the diameter and α is the connectivity rate. The time complexity of our approaches is $\mathcal{O}(\Delta \cdot m)$ for PROPAGATE-P and $\mathcal{O}\left(\frac{\log n}{\varepsilon^2} \cdot \Delta \cdot m\right)$ for PROPAGATE-S, where m is the number of edges of the graph and Δ is the diameter. The experimental results show that the PROPAGATE framework improves the current state of the art in accuracy, speed, and space. Moreover, we experimentally show that PROPAGATE is also very efficient for solving the All Pair Shortest Path problem in very large graphs.

Keywords: Graph mining · shortest paths · effective diameter · sampling

D. Koutra et al. (Eds.): ECML PKDD 2023, LNAI 14171, pp. 671–688, 2023.
https://doi.org/10.1007/978-3-031-43418-1_40

1   Introduction

The fast computation of distances between pairs of nodes in a graph is a fundamental task in network applications. Distance-based metrics are also used to compute different notions of centrality for nodes or edges that can be used to detect communities in very large graphs, as proposed by Girvan and Newman [26] or Fortunato et al. [25]. The *diameter*, i.e. the maximum distance between all reachable pairs in a graph, is an important parameter for analyzing graphs that, for example, change over the time [30], or real-world graphs as the web and social network graphs, which have small diameters [29] that shrink as they grow [33]. The fastest exact algorithm for computing the diameter of *sparse graphs* is based on solving the All-Pairs Shortest Paths (APSP) problem which, for unweighted graphs, can be computed by executing a Breadth-First Search (BFS) for each vertex, with a time complexity of $\Omega(mn)$, where n is the number of nodes and m the number of edges. For *dense* graphs, the best algorithm is based on matrix multiplication [19], which can be performed in time of $\tilde{\mathcal{O}}(n^\omega)$, where $\omega < 2.38$ [17,40]. However, its well known that computing the diameter of a graph with m edges requires $m^{2-o(1)}$ time under the Strong Exponential Time Hypothesis (SETH), which can be prohibitive for very large graphs [1,20], so *efficient approximation algorithms* for diameter are highly desirable. A trivial 2-approximation algorithm for the exact diameter in undirected graphs can be computed in $\mathcal{O}(m + n)$ time by means of a BFS-visit starting from an arbitrary node. A 3/2-approximation algorithm was first presented by Aingworth *et al.* [2] with a time complexity of $\tilde{\mathcal{O}}(m\sqrt{n} + n^2)$, further improved to $\tilde{\mathcal{O}}(m\sqrt{n})$ [37], and, with the same approximation ratio, to $\tilde{\mathcal{O}}(m^{3/2})$ or $o(n^2)$, depending on the degree of sparsity of the graph [13]. If a graph is weakly connected, experiments with real-world graph data sets show that heuristics may decrease the average running time of the diameter computation [10]. The computation of the exact diameter is however susceptible to outliers. For this reason, it is preferable to use more robust metrics, such as the *effective diameter*, which is defined as the a percentile distance between nodes (e.g. 90th), i.e. the maximum distance that allows to connect that percentage of all reachable pairs [35,38]. For large real graphs, even the exact computation of the effective diameter remains prohibitive since possible approaches are still based either on solving APSP or on computing a transitive closure. Also, some diameter approximation algorithms [10,12] cannot be used to compute the effective diameter, that is because they are based on the computation of the greatest distances from the nodes that do not necessarily pass through all reachable pairs [10] or on merging the diameters independently computed on smaller subgraphs [12]. An alternative approach is to compute the *neighborhood function* to derive distance metrics. A *neighborhood* $N(u, r)$ is the set of all nodes reachable from the node u by a path of length at most r. $N(u, r)$ is also known as the *ball* of center u and radius r. The most efficient algorithms for approximating the effective diameter are based on the estimate of the size of neighborhoods. For example, ANF [36] is based on BFS and the use of Flajolet-Martin (FM) probabilistic counters [24], and HyperANF [7] is based on the same approach as ANF but with the use of HyperLogLog as probabilistic counter [21]. Cohen [16] uses an approach based on a non-probabilistic counter, that uses k hash functions on neighborhoods by keeping only the minimum hash value (MinHash) for each hash function (k-mins sketches). When the hashing values are in the unit interval $[0, 1]$, then it is possible to estimate $|N(u, r)|$ by means of the unbiased cardinality estimator $\frac{1}{\text{MinHash}(N(u,r))}$, with the standard error a function of k. The MHSE framework [4], instead, uses the MinHash approach to derive dense representations (*signatures*) of large and sparse graphs that preserve similarity and thus providing an approximation of the size of the neighborhood of a node using the Jaccard similarity. ANF, HyperANF and MHSE are grounded on the observation that the size of $N(u, r)$ is sufficient to estimate the distance-based metrics.

Our Contributions. We propose a framework to estimate the distance-based metrics on graphs based on a mixed approach: *sampling* and *counting*. The core idea of our approach is to consider a small set of s seed nodes and to count the nodes that can be reached by at least one of these seeds, that is, the size of the neighbourhood set at distance d. We define two implementations of our framework: PROPAGATE-P, and PROPAGATE-S. The time complexity of our approaches is, respectively, $\mathcal{O}(\Delta \cdot m)$, and $\mathcal{O}(s \cdot \Delta \cdot m)$, while the space complexity is $\mathcal{O}(s \cdot n + m)$, and $\mathcal{O}(n + m)$. We provide an estimate on the sample size needed to achieve a good estimate of the distance metrics up to a small error bound. More precisely, we prove that $s = \Theta(\frac{\log n}{\varepsilon^2})$ sample nodes are sufficient to estimate, with probability at least $1 - \frac{2}{n^2}$: (1) the average distance with the error bounded by $\varepsilon \frac{\Delta}{\alpha}$; (2) both the effective diameter and the diameter with the error bounded by $\frac{\varepsilon}{\alpha}$; and, (3) the connectivity rate α with error bounded by ε, where α be the *connectivity rate* of the network (see Sect. 3 for the formal definition). It is important to underline that both the algorithms admit a straightforward and simple implementation in a fully distributed and parallel setting.

In Sect. 2, we give an overview of relevant results on approximation algorithms of distance based metrics. In Sect. 3 we provide some basic preliminaries to understand our work. In Sect. 4, we describe the core idea behind our novel framework, then we introduce the new algorithms PROPAGATE-P and PROPAGATE-S, and provide an unbiased error bound for the computation of the effective diameter, the diameter, the average distance, and the connectivity rate. In Sect. 5, we compare our framework with the state-of-the-art algorithms for approximating the distance-based metrics. Finally, in Sect. 6, we conclude and present future research directions.

2 Related Works

The literature on approximating distance-based metrics being vast, we restrict our attention to approaches that are closest to ours. We, thus, particularly focus on *sampling* and *probabilistic* techniques.

Estimating Diameter by Sampling. There are three main questions to be addressed when sampling from large graphs [32]: how to sample nodes and edges, how to set a good sample size, how to evaluate the goodness of the sample, as well as the goodness of the chosen sampling method. In the case of undirected and connected graphs, the centrality of nodes can be estimated by sampling only $\mathcal{O}(\frac{\log n}{\varepsilon^2})$ nodes and compute all the distances to all other nodes, with an error of $\varepsilon\Delta$, where Δ is the graph diameter [18,22], thus reducing the time complexity to $\mathcal{O}(\frac{\log n}{\varepsilon^2}(n \log n + m))$.

Estimating Diameter by Probabilistic Counters. Palmer et al. proposed the ANF algorithm that exploits the (Flajolet-Martin) FM-counter [24] to derive the distance-based metrics of a graph. The core idea is to count the number of distinct nodes in each neighborhood $N(u, r)$, for all nodes u and radius r. For each set $N(u, r)$, ANF yields a concatenation of l bit-masks (*sketches*), where a bit-mask l has probability $\frac{1}{2^{i+1}}$ of having the i-th bit set to 1. An approximation of the number of distinct elements in a stream is derived by averaging the index of the least significant bit with value 0 in each of the l bitmasks, and is set to $\frac{2^{\text{mean}}}{0.77351}$ [24]. Building upon this approach, Boldi et al. [7] proposed HyperANF that uses the HyperLogLog algorithm [21,23] and improves ANF in terms of speed and scalability, providing a better estimate for the same amount of memory and number of passes. Although HyperLogLog is the best approximate data stream counting algorithm, it is known that it tends to overestimate the real size of small sets [27]. Empirical bias correction has been introduced in [27], where the correction works well in a good range of sizes, however errors persist on small sets where the LinearCounting algorithm [39], provides the best results. Alternatively, the MinHash technique can be used to estimate the size of the neighborhood with respect of All Distance Sketch (ADS) of a node of a weighted graph [15,16]. For each node, an ADS consisting of the first k MinHash is maintained. The estimate of the neighborhood of a node u is given by hashing the nodes in the interval $[0, 1]$ and filtering a node v when its hash value is less than the k-th MinHash of the ADS, and when any other node in ADS is closer to u than to v. This algorithm computes, for each pair (u, v) the *closeness similarity* which generalizes the inverse probability of the MinHash estimate [6] with a Jaccard-like similarity function, that is $\frac{1}{max(\pi_{vx}, \pi_{ux})}$ in the case of $k = 1$, where $\pi_{u,v}$ is the Dijkstra rank of u with respect to the node v according to the position of u by increasing distance from v. If the graph is unweighted, then the BFS visit can be used and Cohen's framework can be considered equivalent in the spirit to HyperANF but with the use of the MinCount probabilistic counter of [6] instead of HyperLogLog probabilistic counter. However, its implementation is very different from the one presented in [6] and does not yield a $O(m)$ space complexity as in [6]. Amati et al. proposed a different probabilistic approach based on the *MinHash* counter [4], and experimentally showed its superiority in comparison to HyperLogLog based counters. Another sketching and sampling based technique to model public-private social network graphs proposes to efficiently preprocess the public graph G and to integrate it with a private user graph node in order to derive graph properties and measures [14].

3   Preliminaries

We proceed by formally introducing the terminology and concepts that we use in what follows. For $k \in \mathbb{N}$, we let $[k] - \{1, \ldots, k\}$. An *undirected graph*[1] is an ordered pair $G = (V, E)$, where V is a set whose elements are called *vertices* or *nodes*, and E is a set of *unordered* pairs of vertices, whose elements are called *edges*, or *links* or *arcs*. In a *directed graph* $G = (V, E)$, E is a set of *ordered* pairs of vertices. Let $d(u, v)$ be the number of edges in the shortest path between u and v. Given a graph $G = (V, E)$, define the *neighborhood at distance at most r* for a node $u \in V$ as $N(u, r) = \{v \in V : d(u, v) \leq r\}$[2]. Additionally, we define the *neighborhood function* at hop r as the size of the set of pairs of nodes within distance r, formally: $|N(r)| = |\{(u, v) \in V \times V : d(u, v) \leq r\}|$. The *diameter* Δ of a graph is the longest shortest path in the graph. In terms of the neighborhood function we have: $\Delta = \min_{r \in [0, n-1]} \{r : \sum_u |N(u, r)| = \sum_u |N(u, r+1)|\}$. Similarly, the *effective diameter* is defined as $\Delta^{\mathrm{eff}} = \min_{r \in [0, n-1]} \{r : \sum_u |N(u, r)| \geq \tau \cdot \sum_u |N(u, \Delta)|\}$ for $\tau \in [0, 1]$. In this work, we consider $\tau = 0.9$, i.e. the 90th percentile distance between the nodes. We can also evaluate the *average distance* of a graph $G = (V, E)$. Let $R(u, v)$ be the reachability function that assumes value 1 if and only if u can reach v and 0 otherwise. Thus we can write: $\mathtt{AvgDist} = \frac{\sum_{u, v \in V} R(u, v) \cdot d(u, v)}{\sum_{u, v} R(u, v)} = \frac{\sum_u \sum_{r \in [\Delta]} (|N(u, r)| - |N(u, r-1)|) \cdot r}{\sum_u |N(u, \Delta)|}$. Observe that the *number of reachable pairs* can be also defined using the neighborhood function as: $\mathtt{Nr.Reachable\ Pairs} = |N(\Delta)|$. Finally, we define the *connectivity rate* α of a graph as the sparseness degree of its transitive closure. $\alpha = \frac{1}{n \cdot (n-1)} \sum_{\substack{u, v \\ u \neq v}} R(u, v) \in [0, 1]$. Notice that the more the graph is connected the higher is α, and vice versa. As extreme values $\alpha = 1$ for a connected undirected graph, while $\alpha = 0$ when all the vertices are isolated.

4   PROPAGATE Framework

Any graph traversal algorithm, efficiently scans the edge list of a graph in a random order. However, if the algorithm needs to be efficient on graphs that do not fit in memory, we can not use standard graph traversal routines. As in [4,7,36], we can find the nodes that are reachable from u within r hops by first retrieving their neighbors reachable in $r - 1$ hops from u. Given u's neighborhood at hop 0, $N(u, 0) = \{u\}$, we can compute $N(u, r)$ incrementally as: $N(u, r) = \bigcup_{(u, v) \in E} N(v, r - 1)$. This technique allows to iterate over the edge set instead of performing a classical graph traversal. Probabilistic counters have been used to efficiently compute in terms of time and space the number of distinct elements in $N(u, r)$. The best known algorithms, namely HyperANF [7], and MHSE [4], use respectively the HyperLogLog [23] and the MinHash counter and drop the required memory down to $2 \cdot s \cdot n \cdot \log_2(\log_2(n/s))$ bits and $2 \cdot s \cdot n \cdot \log_2 n$

---

[1] We use the terms "graph" and "network" interchangeably.

[2] Sometimes, we use the term "ball of radius r centered in u" to denote $N(u, r)$.

(where s is the number of seed nodes from which we are starting the edge scan procedure). Even though their performance are impressive, they turn out to be prohibitive on very large graphs if our memory budget is low. Our novel framework overcomes such problems by using a clever implementation of a boolean array-like data structure allowing to have high-quality approximations of the distance-based metrics on machines with low memory requirements. Given a set of starting nodes $S = \{x_1, x_2, \ldots, x_s\}$, PROPAGATE assigns to each node $u \in V$ a Boolean *signature* array $\mathtt{Sig}(u)$ of length s defined as follows: for all $i \in [s]$ $\mathtt{Sig}_i(u) = \mathbb{1}[u \in S]$, i.e., if the node u is a seed, we set its coordinate to 1. Next, we extend the concept of signature to a *set* of nodes of arbitrary size. Let $K \subseteq V$ be a subset of nodes, then its signature is defined as the *bitwise* OR between the signatures of every node $u \in K$, formally $\mathtt{Sig}_i(K) = \bigvee_{u \in K} \mathtt{Sig}_i(u)$ for every $i \in [s]$. Notice that the ith index of $\mathtt{Sig}(K)$ is equal to 1 if and only if there exists at least one vertex $u \in K$ such that $\mathtt{Sig}_i(u) = 1$. The intuition behind our boolean signature is as follows. Suppose that we have only one seed node x, by definition its signature will be of the form $\mathtt{Sig}(x) = \langle 1 \rangle$ i.e., $\mathtt{Sig}_1(x) = 1$. Subsequently, we expand the *ball* centered in x to its hop-1 neighborhood and for each neighbor $v \in N(x)$ we create a new signature $\mathtt{Sig}_{\mathtt{new}}(v)$ equal to the bitwise OR between $\mathtt{Sig}(x)$ and $\mathtt{Sig}(v)$. After updating all x's neighbors, for each $v \in N(x)$ we count the number of indices in its new signature that assumed value 1 (one), we refer to the number of such indices as *collisions* between the seed's bit and nodes' signatures. The total number of ones will be equal to the size of x's hop-1 neighborhood. Observe that such value can be efficiently computed by summing the number of ones obtained by performing the XOR (exclusive OR) operation between $\mathtt{Sig}(v)$ and $\mathtt{Sig}_{\mathtt{new}}(v)$ for each neighbor v, formally $|N(x)| = \sum_{u \in V} \|\mathtt{Sig}(u) \oplus \mathtt{Sig}_{\mathtt{new}}(u)\|$. If we iterate this process Δ times, we will compute the number of nodes at distance of *exactly* r from x for each $r \in [\Delta]$. By repeating this process Δ times for each node $x \in V$, we will obtain the *exact neighborhood function* $|N(r)|$ for each $r \in [\Delta]$. Recall that, under SETH, computing the exact neighborhood function cannot be done in $\mathcal{O}(n^{3-\varepsilon})$ for $\varepsilon > 0$ [40], thus we run the PROPAGATE framework on a subset of nodes S sampled uniformly at random from V. Given a uniform sample of s nodes from the vertex set V, the PROPAGATE framework can be implemented in two different ways: (1) every node has a signature of s bits, and expands the s balls (one for each seed node) in parallel until there is at least one signature that changed its value; (2) in a sequential fashion, every node spreads its bit until there is a signature that changed its value. We refer to these two implementations as PROPAGATE-P (Sect. 4.1), and PROPAGATE-S (Sect. 4.2). PROPAGATE-S is preferable to PROPAGATE-P when s is very large and $s \cdot n$ bits becomes too big to be kept in the memory of a single machine. For example, when the set of seeds is the entire vertex set V, that is $s = |V|$, then PROPAGATE computes the *exact* neighborhood function. To compute the ground-truth values, PROPAGATE-P needs n^2-bit array that, for big graphs, can be too large to be stored on a single machine. PROPAGATE-S, instead, needs only n bits. Thus, for this task, PROPAGATE-S is preferable to PROPAGATE-P. In Sect. 5.2 we compare the execution times of PROPAGATE-S and the All Pair Shortest Path algorithm to compute the *exact* neighborhood function of big real-world graphs.

4.1   PROPAGATE-P **Algorithm**

Given s sample nodes $\{x_1, \ldots, x_s\} \subseteq V$, PROPAGATE-P (Algorithm 1) works as a synchronous diffusion process. It starts by initializing (line 1–3) the signature s-array for each node $u \in V$, $\texttt{Sig}(u)$ as described in Sect. 4. Subsequently, at each hop r, it computes for each node u the *signature* of the ball $N(u, r) = \{v \in V : d(u, v) \leq r\}$. The variable $\texttt{Count}$ (line 5) keeps track of the number of new collisions at hop r, that is the number of vertices at distance *exactly* r from u. The collisions at hop r are subsequently stored in $\texttt{CountAll}[r]$ and if new collisions have been detected during the current hop, then the diameter lower-bound Δ_{LB} is updated, the approximated neighborhood function at hop r is computed ($R[r]$ contains the number of pairs at distance at most r), the variable $\texttt{AvgDist}$ is increased with the difference between $R[r]$ and $R[r-1]$ times the hop r, and the hop $r+1$ is processed (lines 17–20). Once the stopping criterion is met, i.e. no more collisions have been detected, the algorithm finds the minimum hop r such that the ratio between the reachable pairs at hop r and at the maximum hop is greater than 90% i.e., computes the effective diameter Δ^{eff} (line 21), and normalizes the average distance value by dividing it with the maximum number of reachable pairs (line 22). Algorithm PROPAGATE-P can be implemented using an array of s bits for each vertex, thus we have the following theorem:

Theorem 1. *Algorithm* PROPAGATE-P *(Algorithm 1) computes the: diameter, effective diameter, average distance and number of reachable pairs in* $\mathcal{O}(\Delta \cdot m)$ *time using* $\mathcal{O}(s \cdot n + m)$ *space.*

Algorithm 1: PROPAGATE-P Algorithm

   Data: $G = (V, E) : |V| = n$, s sample of vertices $S \subseteq V$, eff. diameter threshold
     τ.
   Result: Δ^{eff} effective diameter, Δ_{LB} diameter, $R[\Delta_{\text{LB}}]$ number of reach. pairs,
     and `AvgDist` average distance.

 1 $\text{Sig}_i(u) = 0; \quad \forall u \in V, i \in [s]$ `// n × s matrix of the nodes' signature`
 2 **for** *each* $x_i \in S$ **do**
 3   ⌊ $\text{Sig}_i(x_i) = 1$
 4 $\text{CountAll}[0] = s, \text{Count} = 0, \text{AvgDist} = 0, \text{r} = 0, \Delta_{\text{LB}} = 0$
 5 $\text{R} = [0, 0, \ldots, 0]$ `// Neighborhood function`
    `// Process one hop at a time for all the sample vertices` x_i.
 6 **do**
 7      $\text{Count} = 0$ `// Collision counter for hop` r
 8   **foreach** $u \in V$ **do**
 9          $\text{Sig}_{\text{next}}(u) = \text{Sig}(u)$
10   **foreach** $u \rightarrow v$ **do**
11   ⌊ $\text{Sig}_{\text{next}}(u) = \text{Sig}_{\text{next}}(u) \vee \text{Sig}(v)$
12   **foreach** $u \in V$ **do**
13          $\text{Count} = \text{Count} + \|\text{Sig}_{\text{next}}(u) \oplus \text{Sig}(u)\|$
14   ⌊ $\text{Sig}(u) = \text{Sig}_{\text{next}}(u)$ `// Update` u`'s signature`
15      $\text{CountAll}[r] = \text{Count}$ `// Reachable vertices at hop` r
16      $\Delta_{\text{LB}} = \max\{r, \Delta_{\text{LB}}\}$ `// Update diameter lower bound`
17      $\text{R}[r] = R[r-1] + \text{CountAll}[r]$ `// R[−1] treated as 0 when` $r = 0$
18      $\text{AvgDist} = \text{AvgDist} + r \cdot (\text{R}[r] - \text{R}[r-1])$ `// R[−1] treated as 0 when`
        $r = 0$
19      $\text{r} = \text{r} + 1$
20 **while** *Count* > 0
21 $\Delta^{\text{eff}} = \min_k \left\{ k : \frac{R[k]}{R[\Delta_{\text{LB}}]} \geq \tau \right\}$ `// Compute the effective diameter` Δ^{eff}
22 $\text{AvgDist} = \text{AvgDist}/\text{R}[\Delta_{\text{LB}}]$ `// Compute the average distance`
23 $R[\Delta_{LB}] = (n/s) \cdot R[\Delta_{LB}]$ `// Compute the number of reachable pairs`
24 **return** $\Delta^{eff}, \Delta_{LB}, R[\Delta_{LB}], AvgDist$

4.2 PROPAGATE-S **Algorithm**

We derive an even more space efficient algorithm in which we process each sample
vertex at a time using a single bit for each node in the graph, as with a Bernoulli
process. PROPAGATE-S's pseudo code, is presented in the extended version of this
paper [5]. Differently from PROPAGATE-P which maintains a signature s-array
for each vertex $u \in V$, PROPAGATE-S uses a n-array $\text{Sig}(V)$ that represents the
signature of the whole graph $G = (V, E)$. More precisely, given a seed node x_i
$\text{Sig}(V)$, at each hop r, maintains the size of x_i's neighborhood at distance at
most r. Although, PROPAGATE-S has higher running time than PROPAGATE-P,
the independence of the seeds in PROPAGATE-S allows for a very simple implementation of the algorithm in a fully distributed and parallel processing, where

cores or machines can be coupled with hash functions. Additionally, PROPAGATE-S can be implemented using *progressive sampling* heuristics, that establish the sample size "on the fly" (see [5] for PROPAGATE-S's incremental approach). When $s = |V| = n$, all PROPAGATE algorithms can compute the *exact* distance-based metrics of interest. In this case, PROPAGATE-P requires as signature a n bit array for each vertex $u \in V$ thus requiring overall n^2 bits, which for large graphs is impracticable. However, PROPAGATE-S would require only a n-bit array at each iteration and can be used to compute the *exact* values for various graphs faster than the `APSP` algorithm implemented in `WebGraph` [8] (see Sect. 5). For huge graphs, the only feasible algorithm in a standalone setting is the PROPAGATE-S algorithm. The above considerations lead to the following theorem:

Theorem 2. PROPAGATE-S *computes the: diameter, effective diameter, average distance and number of reachable pairs in* $\mathcal{O}(s \cdot \Delta \cdot m)$ *time using* $\mathcal{O}(n+m)$ *space.*

Error Bounds of the Sample Size. We now evaluate the accuracy of the approximations of the PROPAGATE framework. We use Hoeffding's inequality [28] to obtain the sample size s for good approximations of the distance-based metrics of interest.

Theorem 3. *With a sample of* $s = \Theta\left(\frac{\ln n}{\varepsilon^2}\right)$ *nodes, with high probability (at least* $1 - \frac{2}{n^2}$*),* PROPAGATE *framework (*PROPAGATE-P *and* PROPAGATE-S*) compute:*

  i. *the average distance with the absolute error bounded by* $\varepsilon \frac{\Delta}{\alpha}$
 ii. *the effective diameter with the absolute error bounded by* $\frac{\varepsilon}{\tilde{\alpha}}$[3]
iii. *the diameter with the absolute error bounded by* $\frac{\varepsilon}{\tilde{\alpha}}$
 iv. *the connectivity rate* α *with the absolute error bounded by* ε

where α *is the connectivity rate of the graph, and* $\varepsilon > 0$ *a positive constant. Thus,* PROPAGATE-S *requires* $\mathcal{O}(\frac{\ln n}{\varepsilon^2} \cdot \Delta \cdot m)$ *time and* $\mathcal{O}(n+m)$ *space . While,* PROPAGATE-P *requires* $\mathcal{O}\left(n\frac{\log n}{\varepsilon^2} + m\right)$ *space complexity.*

5   Experimental Evaluation

In this section, we summarize the results of our experimental study on approximating the distance-based metrics in real-world networks. We compare our framework with the state-of-the-art algorithms to approximate the distance metrics, i.e., for each algorithm, we compute the *average distance, effective diameter,* and *number of reachable pairs.* Subsequently, we evaluate (using various metrics) how these estimates relates to the *exact* ones computed by the All Pairs Shortest Path algorithm.

---

[3] $\tilde{\alpha}$ is a very close value to α i.e., $\tilde{\alpha} = \alpha \cdot \frac{n-1}{n}$. We actually compute the error bound for the ratio on which the minimum integer is attained, clearly, the smaller the ratio's error the smaller the error bound.

5.1 Experimental Setting

Algorithms. Our study includes several competitor algorithms for approximating the neighborhood function. We provide a short description and a space complexity analysis of the considered algorithms.

HYPERANF: The $\mathcal{O}(\Delta \cdot m)$ algorithm of Boldi et al. [7,8], which uses Hyper-LogLog algorithms [21,23] to approximate the neighborhood function. Hyper-ANF requires for each node $2^b = s$ registers that records the position R with the bit 1 starting the tail ending with all 0s. More precisely, if n is the number of distinct nodes in the graph, HyperANF needs $2 \cdot s \cdot n \cdot \log_2(\log_2(n/s))$ bits for the registers.

MHSE: The $\mathcal{O}(\Delta \cdot m)$ algorithm of Amati et al. [4], which uses the MinHash counter to approximate the neighborhood function. MHSE is based on a BFS visit and it requires an $\mathcal{O}(\log n)$ register for each node to record the signature, hence, it has the same space complexity as ANF (ANF maintains a bitwise $\mathcal{O}(\log n)$ register to count new incoming nodes in the stream, instead). MHSE requires $2 \cdot s \cdot n \cdot \log_2 n$ bits.

rand-BFS: The algorithm by Eppstein and Wang [22], which estimates the distance-based metrics using BFS visits starting from random nodes. Its time complexity is $\mathcal{O}(s \cdot m)$ and needs $\mathcal{O}(n + m)$ space.

APSP: The Java implementation of the All Pair Shortest Path algorithm available in `WebGraph` [8]. The algorithm has been used to compute the exact values of the distance metrics and as a competitor algorithm for the second part of the experimental evaluation.

Networks. We evaluate all of the above competitors on real-world graphs of different nature, whose properties are summarized in Table 1. The networks come from two different domains: social networks and web-crawls. According to Theorem 3, the collection `BlackFriday`[4] should require larger number of samples than other collections, because of a small connectivity rate (see Table 1).

Implementation and Evaluation Details. We released an open source platform for analyzing large graphs. This tool is developed in Java[5] and uses some Web-Graph libraries [8] to load and parse the graph in compressed form. We chose WebGraph both for benchmarking with the compared algorithms and to allow us to: (1) compress very large graphs; (2) iterate the neighbor list of a node with faster random access; and, (3) use its offline methods to process very big graphs that cannot be loaded in memory. We executed the experiments on a server running Ubuntu 16.04.5 LTS equipped with AMD Opteron 6376 CPU (2.3GHz) for overall 32 cores and 64 GB of RAM. All the algorithms are fairly compared, i.e. using the same number of seeds/registers and cores. For the comparison between PROPAGATE, HyperANF, MHSE, and RAND-BFS we use 256

---

[4] The BlackFriday graph is built from Twitter considering retweet and reply activities [3]. This graph is comparable in size to the largest publicly available social network graphs, and is very sparse.

[5] https://github.com/BigDataLaboratory/MHSE/tree/propagate-ecmlpkdd.

Table 1. The data sets used in our evaluation, where n denotes the number of nodes, m the number of edges, Δ the exact diameter, α the exact connectivity rate (type D stands for directed and U for undirected). The first seven graphs have been used in comparison of the four algorithms (PROPAGATE, HyperANF,MHSE, and RAND-BFS) for accuracy and effectiveness, and speed. The last seven have been used to compare the performances of the algorithms on huge graphs. Dashed lines indicate that the exact metrics are not available due to the dimension of the data set.

Graph	n	m	Δ	α	Type	Ref.
BlackFriday	2700815	3811922	70	0.002	D	[3]
Youtube-Links	1138495	4942298	23	0.446	D	[31]
Amazon-2008	7600595	5158388	48	0.854	D	[9]
Web-BerkStan	685230	7600595	715	0.488	D	[34]
Twitch-Gamers	168114	13595114	8	1	U	[31]
Hollywood-2009	1139905	113891327	12	0.88	U	[9]
Orkut-2007	3072441	234370166	61	0.356	U	[9]
it-2004	41291594	1150725436	-	-	D	[9]
gsh-2015-host	68660142	1802747600	-	-	D	[9]
sk-2005	50636154	1949412601	-	-	D	[9]
gsh-2015	988490691	33877399152	-	-	D	[9]
clueweb12	978408098	42574107469	-	-	D	[9]
uk-2014	787801471	47614527250	-	-	D	[9]
eu-2015	1070557254	91792261600	-	-	D	[9]

sample nodes/registers and 32 cores. For the comparison between PROPAGATE-s and APSP we use 32 cores. For the first part of the experiments, we repeat every test 10 times and average over the results for every algorithm (HyperANF, MHSE, RAND-BFS, PROPAGATE-P, and PROPAGATE-S). Whenever we are able to compute the *exact* value $\hat{x}$ and thus the residual $(\hat{x} - \tilde{x})/\hat{x}$ where $\tilde{x}$ its *estimate* we also exhibit a p-value. More precisely, we perform a two-sided unpaired *t-test* [11] with confidence interval of 0.95. Given a set X of estimates of the distance metric y obtained after 10 runs of an algorithm $\mathcal{A}$, the null hypothesis is that its mean $\overline{X}$ is equal to the exact value X. If the displayed p-value is in the range $[0.9, 1.0]$ then we fail to reject the null hypothesis, and conclude that the means are not significantly different. Therefore, we can conclude that algorithm $\mathcal{A}$ provides reliable and statistically significant estimates of y.

5.2   Experimental Results

Accuracy and Effectiveness. In our first experiment, we run on the networks listed in the first group of Table 1 all the discussed approximation algorithms. In Table 4, we show the accuracy and effectiveness of all the competitor algorithms. PROPAGATE-P and PROPAGATE-S are grouped under the name of PROPAGATE, that is because both algorithm produce the same results. We observe that our novel framework leads the scoreboard against its competitors. It provides the best estimations in terms of accuracy and statistical significance. For the average distance, PROPAGATE outperforms all the other algorithms on all the graphs except on Orkut, in which RAND-BFS provides the best estimate. Moreover, it provides the best effective diameter estimates on all the datasets. Finally, for the number of reachable pairs, PROPAGATE provides very accurate estimations on all the networks except on YOUTUBE for which MHSE's estimate has lower residual. Observe that PROPAGATE is the algorithm that provides the higher number of statistically significant estimations and does not perform worse than the competitor algorithms.

Speed. As a second experiment, we compared the average execution times of PROPAGATE-P, PROPAGATE-S, HyperANF, MHSE, and RAND-BFS. In the left side of Table 2, we show the running times (in milliseconds) of the algorithms. We observe that PROPAGATE framework outperform its competitors on almost every data set. Remarkably, PROPAGATE-P, leads the scoreboard with the fastest execution times on four over seven graphs. It is slightly slower than RAND-BFS on balckFriday, Amazon-2008, and Web-BerkStan i.e. the datasets with low connectivity rate and longest diameters for which a classic traversal algorithm should require less time than our framework. We point out that, RAND-BFS does not scale well as the size of the graph increases (as shown in the next experiment). We observe that, on average, PROPAGATE-P is 60% faster than HyperANF and 81% faster than MHSE. Moreover, PROPAGATE-P outperform (in terms of speed) HyperANF, and MHSE on all the graphs. HyperANF's execution time is comparable with the one of PROPAGATE-S while MHSE is the slowest one. More precisely, MHSE is slower than every other algorithm on every network for which it does not require more than 64 GB or RAM i.e., does not generate a memory overflow error.

Table 2. For each network (column 1), we show on the left side of the table the average execution time (in milliseconds) over ten runs for each algorithm. On the right side, we show the execution time (in hours) of PROPAGATE-S, versus WEBGRAPH's APSP algorithm to compute the ground truth distance-based metrics. ✗ indicates that the experiment was interrupted due to a memory overflow error.

Graph	Execution time						
	Milliseconds					Hours	
	Prop-P	Prop-S	HyperANF	MHSE	Rand-BFS	Prop-S	APSP
b.Friday	282.162	2899.075	22495.344	51034.047	**69.21**	**9.513**	33.705
YT-Links	**1761.891**	5040.347	5986.410	6655.706	1771.25	**7.217**	11.118
Amazon	4339.072	12686.703	8451.259	195200.019	**1767.12**	**11.027**	11.914
W.Berk.	1535.781	2477.531	2741.563	5980.219	**645.25**	**33.108**	122.59
Twitch-G.	**1562.219**	2901.497	2288.231	4486.044	1863.10	**0.344**	3.617
Hollywood	**4113.060**	15537.897	11068.953	46409.728	7672.18	**47.77**	158
Orkut	**2875.688**	8121.125	3833.688	✗	12783.13	**840**	960

Estimating Distance Metrics on Huge Graphs. As a third experiment, we run all
the approximation algorithms on the biggest networks available in [9] (see the
second group of data sets in Table 1). We aim to investigate the performances
of all the competitor algorithms on very big graphs that cannot be loaded in
the main memory. In Table 3, we show the running times of the approximation
algorithms. The first column indicates whether the graph can be fully loaded
in memory in its uncompressed form. If this is not possible, we use WebGraph's
offline methods to access the compressed graph from the disk without loading
it in memory. Observe that accessing the compressed graph directly from the
disk, slows down the overall execution of the algorithms. However, it is the only
way to analyze these graphs with our 64 GB memory machines. We observe that
PROPAGATE-S can compute the distance metrics on *every* graph. Considering
the size of the data sets, PROPAGATE-S requires a reasonable amount of time to
approximate the neighborhood function using 256 seeds. PROPAGATE-P can compute the distance metrics for it-2004, gsh-2015-host, and sk-2005. Moreover, it is still possible to run PROPAGATE-P on the remaining graphs by appropriately decreasing the number of sample nodes. Instead, HyperANF can be used
only to compute the approximated neighborhood function only on it-2004, and
sk-2005. Finally, MHSE and RAND-BFS cannot be used on any of these networks. Before comparing the time performances, we point out that the red dash
(–) in Table 3 indicates that the algorithm requires more than 64 GB of memory even with 1 seed/register. Thus, decreasing the number of seeds/registers
is not enough to run these algorithms on these huge networks, we would need
to upgrade the RAM of the machine. From the results in Table 3, we observe
that (on it-2004, and sk-2005) PROPAGATE-P is on average 64% faster than

Table 3. For each network (column 1), we show the loading method (column 2) "Yes"
means that it is possible to load the entire graph in memory, while "No" indicates that
is not possible. In such a case, we use WebGraph's offline methods to iterate trough the
successor lists. For each algorithm, we show the execution time (using 256 seeds/regis-
ters). ✗ indicates that the experiment was interrupted due to a memory overflow error
of the algorithm while initializing the signature/registers array. Here, the red dash
— indicates that the algorithm cannot run even with 1 seed/register.

Graph	In memory	Execution Time				
		Propagate-P	Propagate-S	HyperANF	MHSE	rand-BFS
it-2004	Yes	33.26 min	52.13 min	62.18 min	–	–
gsh-15-h	No	40 min	4.16 h	...	...	...
sk-2005	Yes	44 min	6 h	4 h	...	...
gsh-2015	No	✗	11 h	–	–	–
clueweb12	No	✗	9.56 h	–	–	–
uk-2014	No	✗	39 h	...	...	...
eu-2015	No	✗	7 days	...	...	...

Table 4. The comparison of HyperANF, PROPAGATE, and MHSE using 10 trials and 256 registers and 256 sample nodes respectively. Statistical significance at the 90%, 95% and 99% confidence level are marked with •, * and ** respectively. The algorithms requiring more heap size are marked with ▲ , and ✗indicates that the algorithm needs more than 64 GB of memory.

Graph	Algo.	Neighborhood Function Estimation					
		Av. Dist.	Eff. Diam. 90	Nr. of conn pairs	Residual/$\hat{x}$(p-value)		
					Av. Dist.	Eff. Diam. 90	Nr. of conn pairs
blackFriday	Exact($\hat{x}$)	16.124	22.722	11,300,563,035			
	PROP.	16.143	22.551	11,259,575,354	**−0.001(0.92•)**	**−0.008(0.95•)**	**0.003(0.72)**
	H.ANF$^{(▲)}$	16.214	22.841	11,032,542,659	0.01(0.26)	0.005(0.40)	−0.024(0.34)
	MHSE	16.338	23.029	12,193,068,803	−0.01(0.12)	−0.01(0.23)	−0.07(0.09)
	rnd-BFS	17.381	24.30	8,636,102,833	−0.078(0.60)	−0.069(0.68)	0.24(0.09)
Youtube	Exact($\hat{x}$)	5.104	6.244	577,863,455,179			
	PROP.	5.104	6.291	578,216,139,787	**0(1**)**	**−0.007 (0.44)**	−6e-4 **(0.73)**
	H.ANF	5.131	6.301	602,314,527,291	−0.005 (0.1)	−0.009 (0.11)	−0.042 (0.1)
	MHSE	5.105	6.165	577,569,359,888	0.003(0.25)	0.013(0.08)	**5e-4(0.65)**
	rnd-BFS	5.11	6.217	579,121,217,963	−0.001(0.72)	0.004(0.60)	−0.002(0.01)
Amazon	Exact($\hat{x}$)	12.075	15.544	461,523,315,650			
	PROP.	12.08	15.519	461,523,315,650	**0.00(0.93•)**	−0.002(0.80)	**0.00(1**)**
	H.ANF	12.042	15.47	451,448,606,322	−0.003(0.44)	−0.022(0.31)	−0.022(0.31)
	MHSE	12.1	15.542	462,552,552,254	−0.002(0.54)	**1e-4(0.98*)**	−0.002(0.65)
	rnd-BFS	12.103	15.579	461,522,729,233	−0.002(0.36)	−0.002(0.53)	1.27e-6(0.05)
BerkStan	Exact($\hat{x}$)	13.905	17.777	229,179,533,137			
	PROP.	13.883	17.777	229,015,123,311	**0.02(0.42)**	**0(1**)**	**7e-4(0.65)**
	H.ANF	14.645	17.728	233,108,112,819	0.053(0.40)	−0.003(0.83)	0.017(0.49)
	MHSE	15.29	18.14	239,485,315,387	0.099(**0.61**)	0.02(0.61)	0.045(0.36)
	rnd-BFS	14.341	18.02	228,188,757,612	−0.031(0.44)	−0.02(0.28)	0.004(**0.80**)
Twitch	Exact($\hat{x}$)	2.876	3.127	28,262,316,996			
	PROP.	2.876	3.129	28,262,316,996	**0.0(1**)**	**−0.001 (0.94•)**	**0.00(1.00**)**
	H.ANF	2.891	3.180	28,451,734,342	−0.005 (0.03)	−0.017 (0.06)	−0.007 (0.78)
	MHSE	2.881	3.140	28,262,316,996	−0.002(0.44)	**−0.001(0.62)**	**0.00(1.00**)**
	rnd-BFS	2.868	3.096	28,262,020,235	0.0027(0.33)	0.01(0.29)	1e-5(0.01)
Hollywood	Exact($\hat{x}$)	3.855	4.394	1,143,030,619,175			
	PROP.	3.855	4.397	1,143,485,513,294	**−2e-4(0.92•)**	**−3.9e-4(0.95*)**	**−8e-4(0.90•)**
	H.ANF	3.848	4.374	1,136,104,164,355	0.16(0.49)	−0.46(0.5)	0.61(0.80)
	MHSE	3.857	4.382	1,138,248,927,314	−3.91e-4 (0.86)	0.003 (0.65)	0.0042(0.56)
	rnd-BFS	3.840	4.364	1,143,960,403,951	0.004(0.18)	0.007(0.16)	−0.001(**0.90•**)
Orkut	Exact($\hat{x}$)	6.397	8.906	3,359,893,990,935			
	PROP.	6.402	8.895	3,386,716,107,589	**−7e-4(0.90•)**	**0.001(0.82)**	**−0.008(0.60)**
	H.ANF	6.389	8.917	3,336,311,224,217	0.001(0.53)	**−0.001(0.76)**	0.01(0.45)
	MHSE	✗	✗	✗	✗	✗	✗
	rnd-BFS	6.399	8.929	3,328,105,314,542	−4e-4(**0.91•**)	−0.003(0.61)	0.01(0.32)

HyperANF. Furthermore, PROPAGATE-S is the best algorithm to approximate the neighborhood function on huge data sets. It requires $n \cdot s$ bits, to store the graph *signature*. Indeed, for `eu-2015`, i.e. the biggest graph in Table 1, it needs approximately at most 1 GB to store the graph signature. Thus, using `WebGraph`'s offline methods to scan the graph, PROPAGATE-S could provide the approximated neighborhood function of `eu-2015` using an average *laptop*.

Computing Ground Truth Metrics with PROPAGATE. As a last experiment, we compare PROPAGATE-S with the `WebGraph` implementation of the All Pair Shortest Path (APSP) algorithm to compute the *exact* neighborhood function. Among all the competitor algorithms, HyperANF cannot be used to compute the ground truth values of a graph. That is because its neighborhood function estimator that uses the `HyperLogLog` counter is *asymptotically almost unbiased* [7]. MHSE instead, cannot be employed because of its high space complexity. Observe that RAND-BFS coincides with `WebGraph`'s APSP algorithm. As showed in the proof of Theorem 3 (see [5]) PROPAGATE's distance metrics estimators are all *unbiased*. Thus, our novel framework can be used to compute the ground truth values. Given a n vertices graph $G = (V, E)$, PROPAGATE suffices of the entire vertex set V as set of seeds to compute the exact distance metrics. For this experiment, we use PROPAGATE-S because it needs only n bits to store the graph signature, while PROPAGATE-P would need n^2 bits and with a 64 GB machine can be used only for computing the ground truth metrics of the first three graphs in Table 1. In the right side of Table 2, we show the running times of PROPAGATE-S and APSP. We observe that PROPAGATE-S is faster than `WebGraph`'s APSP implementation on all the data sets. These results suggest that our implementation of PROPAGATE-S is preferable for retrieving exact values of distance-based metrics on very large real-world graphs.

6 Conclusions

We proposed PROPAGATE, a novel framework for estimating distance-based metrics on very large graphs. In Sect. 4, we provided two different implementation of our framework, that, so far, can approximate: average distance, (effective) diameter, and the connectivity rate up to a small error with high probability. Our experimental results are summarized in Sect. 5.1, which depicts the performance of our framework versus the state-of-the-art algorithms. Our approach over-perform in terms of accuracy and running time all its competitors. Moreover, when applied to very large real-world graphs, PROPAGATE-S (and PROPAGATE-P if applicable) clearly outperforms all the other algorithms in terms of scalability. As indicated in Table 3, our framework is the only available option to approximate distance-based metrics when we do not have access to servers with a large amount of memory. In the spirit of reproducibility, we developed an open source framework in Java that allows any user with an *average laptop* to approximate the distance-based metrics considered in this paper on any kind of graph. Some promising future directions are to use PROPAGATE to compute centrality measures on vertices and edges, and to extend our framework to community detection tasks.

Acknowledgements. This work was partially supported by the European Union under the Italian National Recovery and Resilience Plan (NRRP) of NextGenerationEU, partnership on "Telecommunications of the Future" (PE00000001 program "RESTART").

References

1. Abboud, A., Williams, V.V.: Popular conjectures imply strong lower bounds for dynamic problems. In: 55th IEEE Annual Symposium on Foundations of Computer Science, FOCS 2014, Philadelphia, PA, USA, 18–21 October 2014. IEEE Computer Society (2014)
2. Aingworth, D., Chekuri, C., Indyk, P., Motwani, R.: Fast estimation of diameter and shortest paths (without matrix multiplication). SIAM J. Comput. **28**(4), 1167–1181 (1999). https://doi.org/10.1137/S0097539796303421
3. Amati, G., Angelini, S., Capri, F., Gambosi, G., Rossi, G., Vocca, P.: Modelling the temporal evolution of the retweet graph. IADIS Int. J. Comput. Sci. Inf. Syst. **11**(2), 19–30 (2016). ISSN 1646-3692
4. Amati, G., Angelini, S., Gambosi, G., Rossi, G., Vocca, P.: Estimation of distance-based metrics for very large graphs with minhash signatures. In: Proceedings of 2017 IEEE International Conference on Big Data. IEEE (2017)
5. Amati, G., Cruciani, A., Pasquini, D., Vocca, P., Angelini, S.: Propagate: a seed propagation framework to compute distance-based metrics on very large graphs. CoRR (2023). https://doi.org/10.48550/arXiv.2301.06499
6. Bar-Yossef, Z., Jayram, T.S., Kumar, R., Sivakumar, D., Trevisan, L.: Counting distinct elements in a data stream. In: Rolim, J.D.P., Vadhan, S. (eds.) RANDOM 2002. LNCS, vol. 2483, pp. 1–10. Springer, Heidelberg (2002). https://doi.org/10.1007/3-540-45726-7_1
7. Boldi, P., Rosa, M., Vigna, S.: HyperANF: approximating the neighbourhood function of very large graphs on a budget. In: Proceedings of 20th International Conference on World Wide Web, Hyderabad, India, pp. 625–634 (2011)
8. Boldi, P., Vigna, S.: The WebGraph framework I: compression techniques. In: Proceedings of the Thirteenth International World Wide Web Conference (WWW 2004), Manhattan, USA, pp. 595–601. ACM Press (2004)
9. Boldi, P., Vigna, S.: LAW datasets: laboratory for web algorithmics (2022). https://law.di.unimi.it/datasets.php
10. Borassi, M., Crescenzi, P., Habib, M., Kosters, W.A., Marino, A., Takes, F.W.: Fast diameter and radius BFS-based computation in (weakly connected) real-world graphs. Theor. Comput. Sci. **586**, 59–80 (2015)
11. Casella, G., Berger, R.: Statistical Inference. Duxbury Resource Center (2001)
12. Ceccarello, M., Pietracaprina, A., Pucci, G., Upfal, E.: Distributed graph diameter approximation. Algorithms **13**, 216 (2020). https://doi.org/10.3390/a13090216
13. Chechik, S., Larkin, D.H., Roditty, L., Schoenebeck, G., Tarjan, R.E., Williams, V.V.: Better approximation algorithms for the graph diameter. In: Proceedings of the Twenty-fifth Annual ACM-SIAM Symposium on Discrete Algorithms, SODA 2014, pp. 1041–1052. Society for Industrial and Applied Mathematics, Philadelphia (2014). https://dl.acm.org/citation.cfm?id=2634074.2634152
14. Chierichetti, F., Epasto, A., Kumar, R., Lattanzi, S., Mirrokni, V.S.: Efficient algorithms for public-private social networks. In: Proceedings of the 21th ACM SIGKDD International Conference on Knowledge Discovery and Data Mining, Sydney, NSW, Australia, 10–13 August 2015 (2015)
15. Cohen, E.: Size-estimation framework with applications to transitive closure and reachability. J. Comput. Syst. Sci. **55**(3), 441–453 (1997)
16. Cohen, E.: All-distances sketches, revisited: hip estimators for massive graphs analysis. In: Proceedings of 33rd ACM SIGMOD-SIGACT-SIGART Symposium on Principles of Database Systems, Snowbird, Utah, USA, pp. 88–99 (2014)

17. Coppersmith, D., Winograd, S.: Matrix multiplication via arithmetic progressions. J. Symb. Comput. **9**(3), 251–280 (1990)
18. Crescenzi, P., Grossi, R., Lanzi, L., Marino, A.: A comparison of three algorithms for approximating the distance distribution in real-world graphs. In: Marchetti-Spaccamela, A., Segal, M. (eds.) TAPAS 2011. LNCS, vol. 6595, pp. 92–103. Springer, Heidelberg (2011). https://doi.org/10.1007/978-3-642-19754-3_11
19. Cygan, M., Gabow, H.N., Sankowski, P.: Algorithmic applications of baur-strassen's theorem: shortest cycles, diameter, and matchings. J. ACM **62**(4), 28:1–28:30 (2015). https://doi.org/10.1145/2736283. https://doi.acm.org/10.1145/2736283
20. Dalirrooyfard, M., Wein, N.: Tight conditional lower bounds for approximating diameter in directed graphs. In: STOC 2021: 53rd Annual ACM SIGACT Symposium on Theory of Computing, Virtual Event, Italy, 21–25 June 2021. ACM (2021)
21. Durand, M., Flajolet, P.: Loglog counting of large cardinalities (extended abstract). In: Proceedings of 11th Annual European Symposium (ESA), Budapest, pp. 605–617 (2003)
22. Eppstein, D., Wang, J.: Fast approximation of centrality. In: Proceedings of 12th Annual ACM-SIAM Symposium on Discrete Algorithms, Washington, D.C., USA, pp. 228–229 (2001)
23. Flajolet, P., Fusy, É., Gandouet, O., Meunier, F.: Hyperloglog: the analysis of a near-optimal cardinality estimation algorithm. In: Analysis of Algorithms, pp. 137–156. Discrete Mathematics and Theoretical Computer Science (2007)
24. Flajolet, P., Martin, G.N.: Probabilistic counting algorithms for data base applications. J. Comput. Syst. Sci. **31**(2), 182–209 (1985)
25. Fortunato, S., Latora, V., Marchiori, M.: Method to find community structures based on information centrality. Phys. Rev. E **70**(5 Pt 2), 056104 (2004). https://doi.org/10.1103/PhysRevE.70.056104
26. Girvan, M., Newman, M.E.J.: Community structure in social and biological networks. Proc. Natl. Acad. Sci. **99**(12), 7821–7826 (2002)
27. Heule, S., Nunkesser, M., Hall, A.: Hyperloglog in practice: algorithmic engineering of a state of the art cardinality estimation algorithm. In: Proceedings of the 16th International Conference on Extending Database Technology (EDBT), Genoa, pp. 683–692 (2013)
28. Hoeffding, W.: Probability inequalities for sums of bounded random variables. In: Fisher, N.I., Sen, P.K. (eds.) The collected works of Wassily Hoeffding, pp. 409–426. Springer, New York (1994). https://doi.org/10.1007/978-1-4612-0865-5_26
29. Kleinberg, J.: The small-world phenomenon: an algorithmic perspective. In: Proceedings of the Thirty-Second Annual ACM Symposium on Theory of Computing, STOC 2000, pp. 163–170. ACM, New York (2000). https://doi.org/10.1145/335305.335325. https://doi.acm.org/10.1145/335305.335325
30. Kumar, R., Novak, J., Tomkins, A.: Structure and evolution of online social networks. In: Proc. 12th ACM SIGKDD International Conference on Knowledge Discovery and Data Mining, Philadelphia, PA, USA, pp. 611–617 (2006)
31. Kunegis, J.: KONECT - The Koblenz Network Collection. In: Proceedings of International Conference on World Wide Web Companion (2013)
32. Leskovec, J., Faloutsos, C.: Sampling from large graphs. In: Proceedings of 12th International Conference on ACM SIGKDD, Philadelphia, PA, USA, pp. 631–636 (2006)

33. Leskovec, J., Kleinberg, J., Faloutsos, C.: Graphs over time: densification laws, shrinking diameters and possible explanations. In: Proceedings of 11th International Conference on ACM SIGKDD, Chicago, IL, USA, pp. 177–187 (2005)
34. Leskovec, J., Krevl, A.: SNAP Datasets: Stanford large network dataset collection (2014). http://snap.stanford.edu/data
35. Palmer, C., Siganos, G., Faloutsos, M., Faloutsos, C., Gibbons, P.: The connectivity and fault-tolerance of the internet topology. In: Proceedings of Workshop on Network-Related Data Management, vol. 25, S. Barbara, USA (2001)
36. Palmer, C.R., Gibbons, P.B., Faloutsos, C.: ANF: a fast and scalable tool for data mining in massive graphs. In: Proceedings of 8th ACM SIGKDD International Conference on Knowledge Discovery in Data Mining, pp. 81–90. ACM (2002)
37. Roditty, L., Williams, V.V.: Fast approximation algorithms for the diameter and radius of sparse graphs. In: Proceedings of 45th Symposium on Theory of Computing (STOC), Palo Alto, CA, USA, pp. 515–524 (2013)
38. Tauro, L., Palmer, C., Siganos, G., Faloutsos, M.: A simple conceptual model for the Internet topology. In: Global Internet, San Antonio, TX, USA (2001)
39. Whang, K.Y., Vander-Zanden, B.T., Taylor, H.M.: A linear-time probabilistic counting algorithm for database applications. ACM Trans. Database Syst. **15**(2), 208–229 (1990)
40. Williams, V.V.: Multiplying matrices faster than coppersmith-winograd. In: Proceedings of the 44th Symposium on Theory of Computing Conference, STOC 2012, New York, NY, USA, 19–22 May 2012, pp. 887–898 (2012). https://doi.org/10.1145/2213977.2214056. https://doi.acm.org/10.1145/2213977.2214056

Towards Memory-Efficient Training for Extremely Large Output Spaces – Learning with 670k Labels on a Single Commodity GPU

Erik Schultheis[1]([✉])[iD] and Rohit Babbar[1,2][iD]

[1] Aalto University, Espoo, Finland
erik.schultheis@aalto.fi, rb2608@bath.ac.uk
[2] University of Bath, Bath, UK

Abstract. In classification problems with large output spaces (up to millions of labels), the last layer can require an enormous amount of memory. Using sparse connectivity would drastically reduce the memory requirements, but as we show below, applied naïvely it can result in much diminished predictive performance. Fortunately, we found that this can be mitigated by introducing an intermediate layer of intermediate size. We further demonstrate that one can constrain the connectivity of the sparse layer to be of constant fan-in, in the sense that each output neuron will have the exact same number of incoming connections, which allows for more efficient implementations, especially on GPU hardware. The CUDA implementation of our approach is provided at https://github.com/xmc-aalto/ccml23-sparse.

1 Introduction

In this paper, we present findings towards employing sparse connectivity in order to reduce the memory consumption of the classification layer for problems with extremely large output spaces (XMC). Such problems arise in, e.g., tagging of text documents [8], next-word predictions [21], and different kinds of recommendation tasks [1,5,19,24,29]. In order to ensure computational tractability of these tasks, which can have up to several millions of labels, one typically builds a *hierarchical label tree* [14,23,30,32], only exploring branches that are likely to contain relevant labels for the current instance. Even though this is very effective at reducing the computation (from linear to logarithmic in the number of labels), it does not help in addressing the memory consumption, which is still linear in the number of labels times the number of hidden units.

As an illustration consider the AMAZON-3M [18] dataset. If we were to map the inputs to a hidden representation of 1024 units, the fully connected last layer for this dataset would need about 2.9 billion parameters, corresponding to 10.7 GiB[1]. Given that modern deep learning optimizers such as ADAM [16] need to

---

The original version of this chapter was previously published without open access. A correction to this chapter is available at
https://doi.org/10.1007/978-3-031-43418-1_42

[1] Assuming 32-bit floating point numbers.

© The Author(s) 2023, corrected publication 2024
D. Koutra et al. (Eds.): ECML PKDD 2023, LNAI 14171, pp. 689–704, 2023.
https://doi.org/10.1007/978-3-031-43418-1_41

keep track of the value, gradient, and first and second moment, this leads to an overall peak memory consumption of over 40 GiB, making it nigh impossible to train such models on commodity hardware.

Therefore, we want to investigate possibilities for memory efficient *sparse training* of this huge last layer. There are two pre-existing approaches that serve as an indication that this is an idea that could be successful: First, for DiSMEC, a *linear model* applied to tf-idf representations of input text, it is known that the resulting layer can be sparsified *after training* to contain *less than 1%* non-zeros [2]. In a linear model, the different classifiers for each label can be trained *independently*. As a result, only the full weights of the label that is currently trained needs to be kept in memory, and can be pruned as soon as the training for that label has finished. For non-linear models, the MACH [19] algorithm can be interpreted as a special case of training with *static*, random sparsity. It works by hashing the labels into different buckets, and performing training and predictions only on the level of buckets. If enough independent hashes are used, this method allows to solve the original problem in the large output space. However, in practice, the results presented for MACH are not as good as for competing methods.

The contributions of this paper are as follows: We show that naïvely applying a dynamic sparse training algorithm to the last layer of an XMC problem results in strongly reduced predictive performance. Inspired by MACH, we then propose to alleviate this problem by inserting a penultimate layer that is larger than the hidden representation of the inputs, but still much smaller than the size of the label space. Such an increased layer size drastically improves the chances of dynamic sparse training finding a good subnetwork, and enables us to get results only slightly worse than training with a dense last layer. We demonstrate this on several large-scale datasets, for which we train a classification layer on a fixed set of pre-trained features. To ensure memory efficient and quick computations, we propose to restrict the sparsity structure to *constant fan-in*, such that each unit in the output layer receives exactly the same number of inputs. This has several important consequences: (i) it makes it impossible for the training to focus most non-zero weights on a few, prominent head labels, and instead ensures a more even distribution of the representational capacity, (ii) compared to coordinate-format this requires only half the memory to store the indices, and compared to compressed row sparse matrices the data layout is simpler, making it easier to implement the corresponding operations on a GPU, and (iii) it also means that changing the sparsity structure (redistribution of connections) can be implemented as a very cheap operation.

2   Setup and Background

We consider classification problems that map an input instance $x \in \mathcal{X}$ to a subset of a label set with m labels, represented as a binary vector $y \in \{0,1\}^m$. More precisely, we assume that $(x, y) \sim \mathbb{P}$ are jointly distributed according to some probability measure. If almost surely $\|y\|_1 = 1$, it is a multiclass setup, otherwise a multilabel setup. We want to find a classifier $f \colon \mathcal{X} \longrightarrow \{0,1\}^m$ so that predicted labels $\hat{\boldsymbol{y}} = f(x)$ and actual labels are close. Usually, f can be decomposed into two operations: First, the inputs are *embedded* into a fixed-size vector space using a function $\psi \colon \mathcal{X} \longrightarrow \mathbb{R}^e$ (e.g. a linear projection, multilayer perceptron, or transformer-based text model), and then a decoding $\mathbf{W} \in \mathbb{R}^{e \times m}$ is applied to extract scores for each label. The actual prediction is then generated by selecting the k highest scoring labels as positive, $\hat{\boldsymbol{y}} = \mathrm{top}_k(\mathbf{W}^\mathsf{T}\psi(x))$. Consequently, performance is typically measured in terms of *precision-at-k*, defined as the fraction of correct predictions

$$\mathrm{P@}k(\boldsymbol{y}, \hat{\boldsymbol{y}}) = k^{-1} \sum_{j=1}^{m} y_j \hat{y}_j \qquad \text{for } \|\hat{\boldsymbol{y}}\|_1 = k. \tag{1}$$

In order to find the optimal $\mathbf{W}$ that maximizes $\mathrm{P@}k$, one often performs a *One-vs-All (OvA)* reduction [2,3,20]: A binary classification loss ℓ is applied to each label separately. As this involves evaluating the scores $\mathbf{W}^\mathsf{T}\psi(x)$ for each label, many methods select a subset $\mathcal{N} \subset [m]$ of *hard negatives* [7,12,14,15,26], to approximate the sum as

$$\begin{aligned}
l(\boldsymbol{y}, x) = \sum_{j=1}^{m} \ell(y_j, \boldsymbol{w}_j^\mathsf{T}\psi(x)) &= \sum_{j \colon y_j = 1} \ell(1, \boldsymbol{w}_j^\mathsf{T}\psi(x)) + \sum_{j \colon y_j = 0} \ell(0, \boldsymbol{w}_j^\mathsf{T}\psi(x)) \\
&\approx \sum_{j \colon y_j = 1} \ell(1, \boldsymbol{w}_j^\mathsf{T}\psi(x)) + \sum_{j \in \mathcal{N}} \ell(0, \boldsymbol{w}_j^\mathsf{T}\psi(x)).
\end{aligned} \tag{2}$$

This is very effective at reducing the required computations, and could also be beneficial for accuracy because it effectively changes the distribution of labels seen by the classifier [25], but it does not decrease the enormous amount of memory required to store the weight matrix $\mathbf{W}$.

There are several established approaches to handle this problem: The most straightforward method is to place a *bottleneck* layer just before the final classification layer, so that the dimension of the embedding that $\mathbf{W}$ operates on is comparatively low. For example, LightXML [14] project the 3280-dimensional representation used for determining hard negatives down to only 300 units for the extreme-level classification. This approach is limited in its effectiveness, as too small sizes start to severely affect the classification quality. A second strategy is to *prune* the matrix $\mathbf{W}$ after training, turning it into a very sparse matrix. This can reduce the model size to only a tiny fraction of the dense equivalent, without negatively affecting its predictive power, but this does not solve the problem of memory consumption during the training itself. The only exception are linear models, where the weight vectors $\boldsymbol{w}_j$ for different labels can be trained independently, and be sparsified immediately after training, so that the full matrix never has to materialize [2,3]. Additionally, it is possible to exploit the relation between primal and dual of linear problems to achieve sparse training for max margin classifiers with appropriate loss functions [31]. Finally, MACH [19] has shown that it is possible to train an extreme classifier on the level of meta-labels, obviating the need for the large weight matrix $\mathbf{W}$ altogether. However, this corresponds, implicitly, to a multiplication by a sparse, fixed, binary matrix, which therefore limits the expressiveness of the model, and it requires keeping multiple copies of the embedding network ψ.

Thus, existing sparse training methods for XMC either use post-training sparsification, or a fixed sparsity structure. Here, we want to apply the *sparse evolutionary training (*SET*)* algorithm [22] to the classification layer, so that we have sparse training with dynamic sparsity structure. The SET algorithm follows a general prune-redistribute-regrowth cycle, which means that periodically, a subset of existing non-zero weights is selected to be removed (*pruned*), and new structural non-zeros will be inserted (*redistributed*). After that, the training of the sparse layer proceeds just as in any other gradient-based optimization, i.e., the structural non-zeros are updated according to their mini-batch gradient (*regrown*), and the structural zeros are left unchanged, until the next cycle.

This general algorithmic structure can be implemented in various ways, depending on how the pruned weights are selected, and how it is determined where they should be re-distributed. [11] The SET algorithm uses very simple heuristics: The set of least important connections is determined by sorting according to the absolute value of their weight, and removing the fraction α of connections with lowest weight. The same number of new connections is inserted after pruning, by choosing uniformly randomly from the structural zeros.

While there exist more elaborate schemes, they are generally more complex to implement and will require additional memory. For example, [4] chooses its pruning based on weights switching their sign, which means that it needs to store the previous signs of all structural non-zeros. To determine useful locations for inserting the redistributed connections, [9] uses a momentum term, which means that this requires the same amount of memory as the weights for the original dense layer, and thus is infeasible in our setting. This also excludes any strategy that requires, even if only intermittently, a full, dense gradient, such as [10].

A naïve application of SET to the last layer leads to unsatisfactory results, and an implementation using just the available tools in `tensorflow` turns out to be suboptimal in terms of speed and memory consumption. Thus, we present in the next section some modifications to the architecture and training algorithm, as well as insights into an efficient implementation, to alleviate these shortcomings.

3   Method

In principle, implementing a sparse layer in `tensorflow`[2] is straightforward: Replace the dense-dense matrix multiplication with a sparse-dense operation that is supplied by the framework, and the weight matrix with a `SparseTensor`.

There are four problems with this approach: First, it wastes memory due to `tensorflows` requirement that all indices be given as 64-bit integers. Second, completely unstructured sparsity makes efficient implementations challenging, especially on GPUs. Third, the `tensorflow` operations cannot exploit the sparsity in the gradient signal that arises naturally when training with hinge-like

---

[2] `PyTorch` still considers its sparse tensor support to be in beta.

losses. Finally, replacing the dense layer with a highly sparse layer results in underfitting. We will address these problems below.

3.1 Efficient 32-Bit Indexing

In `tensorflow`, sparse tensors are represented in *coordinate* (Coo) format (Fig. 1a), which means that each structural nonzero in a sparse matrix is described by three numbers. Two 64-bit integers define the row and column of the structural nonzero, and a 32-bit floating point number its value. This means that a single sparse weight requires as much memory as five weights in the dense matrix.

Even for extreme-scale classification, however, 32-bit integers would be more than sufficient as column and row indices of **W**. A maximum representable value of around 4 billion is still an order of magnitude larger than even very large scale proprietary problems [19] with 100 s of millions of labels, and three orders of magnitude larger than publicly available benchmark datasets.

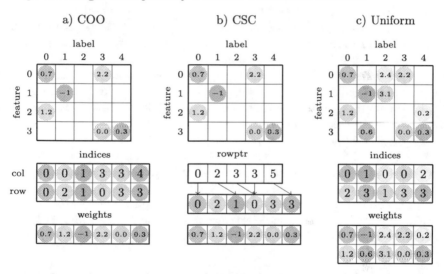

Fig. 1. Schematic depiction of different sparse matrix formats. Note that in Coo format (a), the `indices` array in Algorithm 1 is of shape $2 \times$ nnz. In uniform format (c) it is nnz per column $\times$ labels, and hence only half as big, compared to the Coo format, for the same number of nonzeros.

3.2 Compressed Indexing and Equitable Work Distribution Through Constant Fan-In

Even with 32-bit indices, a sparse weight still consumes three times as much memory as a dense weight, when represented in coordinate format. This could be made much more efficient by switching to *compressed sparse column* (Csc) format, where only row indices are saved directly, and for each column only the offset of its first index is stored (Fig. 1b). While this drastically reduces the amount of memory needed to store the indices, it also increases the complexity of involved computations. For example, in COO format, one can assign each GPU thread to the same amount of structural non-zeros to handle during the matrix multiplication, as getting the corresponding row and column indices is a simple array lookup. In contrast, in CSC format, it is still trivial to assign one column to each thread (i.e., each thread will compute one output), but that can lead to a significant difference in the amount of work each thread has to do, and thus lead to inefficient use of GPU resources. Furthermore, redistribution becomes more involved, as inserting a new structural nonzero in an early column means that all the weights and indices that come after have to be shifted.

This can be simplified if we stipulate that each column should have the exact same amount of structural non-zeros, such that $\forall j : \|\boldsymbol{w}_j\|_0 = s$. Then, a single index array is sufficient, and the starting offset of each column can be calculated simply by multiplying the number of non-zeros per column with the column index, like in regular multidimensional array indexing (Fig. 1c). Distributing a multiplication with a *constant fan-in* sparse matrix across many threads is also easy, as we can simply assign one column (i.e., $\boldsymbol{w}_j$) to each thread, knowing that they correspond to the same amount of work. Finally, connection redistribution is cheaper, because the number of non-zeros stays constant for each column, and thus changes in one column never require moving around the data of other columns. As we will show in Sect. 4.2, the additional constraint on the number of connections per output does not negatively influence the models predictive performance in the overparametrized regime.

Broadly, the implementation works as follows: The sparse weights are represented by two matrices, indices $\in \mathbb{N}^{s \times m}$ and weights $\in \mathbb{R}^{s \times m}$. The input is given as a matrix features $\in \mathbb{R}^{b \times e}$, where b denotes the batch size, and the output is a matrix output $\in \mathbb{R}^{b \times m}$. CUDA threads are generated on a two dimensional grid, with one thread for each output. Thus, threads will be indexed by pairs, each of them consisting of instance $\in [b]$ and label $\in [m]$. Every thread performs the calculations given, schematically, in Algorithm 1.

Algorithm 1. Calculation of the score for a single label label and instance for uniform sparsity (see Fig. 1c) with s non-zeros for each label.

```
value = 0;
for weight_idx in range(s):
    source = indices[weight_idx, label]
    feature = features[instance, source]
    value += feature * weights[weight_idx, label]
output[instance, label] = value
```

3.3 Speeding up Backward Pass Through Implicit Negative Mining

Our experiments with a sparse last layer showed that the largest fraction of time was spent in the backward pass. This is not surprising, as the backward pass requires two sparse matrix multiplications, to calculate the gradient with respect to the inputs, and to calculate the gradient with respect to the weights.

Fortunately, certain margin-based losses can induce high amounts of sparsity in the gradient of XMC problems, which can be exploited to ensure considerable speed-up [27,31]. In the given enormous label space, each instance will have only a tiny subset of labels which are relevant to it, and many for which the decision that they are not relevant is "easy". Thus, if the loss function gives zero penalty for these easy classifications (e.g., if the margin is large enough in hinge-like losses), then the error term to be back-propagated will be highly sparse. For the loss function that is mainly used in this paper, the squared-hinge loss $\ell(y, \hat{y}) = \max(0, 1 - y\hat{y})^2$, the gradient is $\partial\ell/\partial\hat{y} = -2y\max(0, 1 - y\hat{y})$, and thus exactly zero whenever $y\hat{y} \geq 1$.

Therefore, in the backward kernel, it becomes beneficial to explicitly check whether the backpropagated signal $\partial\ell/\partial\hat{y}$, denoted by `backward` $\in \mathbb{R}^{b \times m}$ in the algorithm, is already zero, and if so to skip the corresponding operations. In particular, this means not only that the multiplication with zero can be skipped, but also makes it unnecessary to load the second operand and to store the result. As sparse matrix operations are memory-bound, this can be highly beneficial.

In fact, if we distribute the threads in the same way as the forward pass for the calculation of the gradient with respect to the features (one thread assigned for each `label` and `instance`) then most threads can be skipped entirely.[3] A schematic of the resulting implementation is given in Algorithm 2. Because multiple labels can contribute to the gradient of each input feature, in this case several threads need to update the same part of the gradient array. Therefore, we have to resort to using atomic addition operations here.

For calculating the gradient of the weight values, it is possible to arrange threads so that they can act independently, by using one thread for each gradient entry, i.e., for each `label` $\in [m]$ and `weight_idx` $\in [s]$. In this case, one cannot skip entire threads, but a zero in the backward signal still allows to skip the unpredictable, indirect memory lookup of `feature = features [instance, source]`, as shown in Algorithm 3.

3.4 Mitigating Underfitting by Adding an Intermediate Layer

Finally, we noticed that—even without constant fan-in—replacing the dense layer with a sparse layer results in diminished classification accuracy, which we

---

[3] On a GPU, skipping a single thread might not be helpful, as threads are executed together in groups of 32 as a warp. However, with the very high level of sparsity in the backward signal, it becomes common that all threads within a warp can be skipped.

Algorithm 2. Contribution to the gradient for the input features caused by a given label and instance in the mini-batch.

```
out = backward[instance, label]
if out == 0:
    return

for weight_idx in range(s):
    source = indices[weight_idx, label]
    weight = weights[weight_idx, label]
    atomicAdd(gradient[instance, source], weight * out)
```

Algorithm 3. Calculation of the gradient for a given structural non-zero weight.

```
source = indices[weight_idx, label]
result = 0
for instance in range(batch_size):
    out = backward[instance, label]
    if out == 0: continue

    feature = features[instance, source]
    result += feature * out;
gradient[weight_idx, label] = result
```

attribute to underfitting. Thus, we propose to improve the expressiveness of the model by adding an intermediate layer between the embedding layer and the final classification layer. Because the last layer is sparse, its memory consumption is independent of the size of the preceding layer. Consequently, as long as this new intermediate layer is at least an order of magnitude smaller than the number of labels, this does not impede our goal of reducing memory requirements.

4 Experiments

In this section, we provide the experimental evidence showing that sparse last layers are a viable approach to extreme multilabel classification. We run experiments with several well-known benchmark datasets, measuring duration and peak GPU memory consumption, as well as P@k. After presenting results that justify the architectural choices we made, we provide additional data illustrating the trade-offs between memory consumption and classification accuracy by varying the sparsity and size of the intermediate layer. Then we present investigate the effect of implicit negative mining. The section concludes with a discussion of the results. Additional experiments are given in the supplementary at https://github.com/xmc-aalto/ecml23-sparse.

4.1   Experimental Setup

In this paper we focus on the setting of learning from fixed, low-dimensional representations of the instances. This enables us to do many more experiments than if we had to fine-tune an expensive transformer-based encoder for each run.

We use two different sources for the embeddings: 512-dimensional fast-text based representations as used for SLICE [12], and the final classification embeddings from a trained CASCADEXML [15] model with 768 dimensions. We present results on two datasets, [33], AMAZON-670K [17], and WIKIPEDIA-500K [6].

To update the network's weights, we use the ADAM optimizer [16] with an initial learning rate of 1×10^{-3} that is decayed by $1/2$ whenever validation P@3 stops improving, until reaching 1×10^{-4}. After that, training is stopped once P@3 stops increasing. For sparse layers, we initialize the connections uniformly randomly, potentially subject to the constraint that each label gets the same amount of connections. Every 1000 training steps, each consisting of 32 samples in a minibatch, the 10% lowest-magnitude weights are randomly redistributed. In order to mitigate overfitting, we apply dropout to the input features, dropping 10% for AMAZON-670K and WIKIPEDIA-500K-SLICE features, and 20% for WIKIPEDIA-500K-CASCADE.

The experiments are run on a NVIDIA V100. Even though we want to demonstrate the feasibility of XMC learning on a commodity GPU, in order to be able to make meaningful comparisons, we have to train on the same GPU for all settings, which means that the GPU needs to have enough memory to fit in a dense last layer. To quantify the memory benefits of sparse training, we record the peak memory consumption as reported by `tensorflow` (`tf.config.experimental.get_memory_info("GPU:0")['peak']`). Note, in particular, that all cases with our proposed architecture consume significantly less than 4 GiB of GPU memory, and thus will be feasible, albeit training more slowly, on cheap gaming GPUs.

4.2   Results with Varying Architecture

As a first step, we want to show that the architectural choices described in Sect. 3 are useful. To that end, we compare the training with a dense last layer to the following settings:

- A single, unstructured sparse layer,
- A single, constant fan-in sparse layer,
- An intermediate, dense layer, followed by an unstructured sparse layer,
- An intermediate, dense layer, followed by a constant fan-in sparse layer.

The number of structural non-zeros is chosen such that in the UNSTRUCTURED sparse layers, there are an average of 32 connections per label, and in the CONSTANT-FAN-IN sparse layers there are exactly 32 connections per label. As a baseline with comparable memory consumption, we also trained a BOTTLENECK architecture, that maps the input representation to a low-dimensional space of only 64 dimensions, before projecting into the label space.

Table 1. Comparison of different network architectures. `Con` denotes the (average) number of connections per label, `Int` the intermediate layer's size, `Mem` the peak GPU memory consumption, `Eps` the number of training epochs, and `Time` the duration of a single epoch in seconds. Bold marks the best results in any sparse setting.

Setup			Test			Train			Mem.	Eps.	Time
Sparsity	Con.	Int.	P@1	P@3	P@5	P@1	P@3	P@5	GiB		sec
WIKI500K-SLICE											
DENSE	512	–	58.2	37.9	28.0	97.3	77.5	60.4	6.7	39.4	1 249
UNSTRUCTURED	32	–	45.5	27.3	19.9	58.3	37.7	28.1	4.8	78.0	3 612
CONSTANT-FAN-IN	32	–	37.5	23.2	17.6	42.6	28.0	21.9	0.7	54.8	659
UNSTRUCTURED	32	32k	**59.0**	**38.5**	**28.9**	83.7	61.4	47.7	4.8	40.0	3 977
CONSTANT-FAN-IN	32	32k	58.9	38.4	28.9	**84.2**	**62.2**	**48.4**	1.0	45.8	723
BOTTLENECK	64	64	56.5	36.5	27.5	71.8	50.0	38.5	1.0	41.8	639
WIKI500K-CASCADE											
DENSE	768	–	77.2	58.6	45.1	96.7	79.7	64.2	10.0	25.6	1 744
UNSTRUCTURED	32	–	65.2	43.7	31.4	78.3	54.7	39.8	4.8	100.0	3 870
CONSTANT-FAN-IN	32	–	58.7	42.0	32.2	69.1	51.8	40.4	0.7	59.4	715
UNSTRUCTURED	32	32k	**73.7**	54.7	42.0	92.4	73.5	58.1	4.9	58.0	4 423
CONSTANT-FAN-IN	32	32k	73.6	**54.8**	**42.1**	**93.0**	**74.3**	**58.9**	1.0	67.4	842
BOTTLENECK	64	64	71.9	50.7	37.9	86.4	64.8	49.5	1.0	47.6	678
AMAZON670K-SLICE											
DENSE	512	–	33.8	29.6	26.6	99.2	93.9	88.4	9.0	27.2	472
UNSTRUCTURED	32	–	14.5	11.5	9.5	64.8	49.4	39.0	6.4	73.0	1 357
CONSTANT-FAN-IN	32	–	7.1	6.3	5.6	16.2	13.9	12.4	1.0	24.8	223
UNSTRUCTURED	32	32k	32.7	28.7	25.8	**98.8**	**93.4**	**87.5**	6.4	45.0	1 619
CONSTANT-FAN-IN	32	32k	**32.8**	**28.7**	**25.9**	98.7	93.2	87.3	1.2	38.0	244
BOTTLENECK	64	64	30.7	27.3	24.6	96.4	88.9	80.1	1.1	33.6	219
AMAZON670K-CASCADE											
DENSE	768	–	47.5	42.3	38.3	99.8	94.5	89.0	13.4	28.4	624
UNSTRUCTURED	32	–	30.4	23.8	19.0	88.8	71.4	55.6	6.3	95.0	1 369
CONSTANT-FAN-IN	32	–	37.1	31.6	27.6	92.4	84.0	74.8	1.0	76.2	234
UNSTRUCTURED	32	32k	42.5	37.1	33.0	**99.7**	**94.3**	**88.7**	6.5	36.0	1 512
CONSTANT-FAN-IN	32	32k	**42.6**	**37.1**	**33.1**	99.7	94.3	88.7	1.4	36.4	271
BOTTLENECK	64	64	38.0	33.7	30.4	99.1	93.3	86.4	1.1	31.6	232

We repeated each experiment five times and report the average, expect for the extremely slow settings with unstructured sparsity, which we ran only once.

The results of these experiments are presented in Table 1. Several facts are immediately obvious from the recorded data: First, the naive, tensorflow-based implementation for UNSTRUCTURED sparsity is very slow, to the degree that the sparse matrix multiplication ends up being 2-3× slower than dense multiplication on the large datasets. Second, with the intermediate layer, the classification performance of constant fan-in and unstructured sparsity is almost identical.

Third, without an intermediate layer, there is a significant drop in P@3, both in training and test performance, showing that naïve sparsification leads to severe overfitting. In cases where the unstructured sparse layer fails to perform well even on the training set, the additional constraint does lead to a further drop in performance. The BOTTLENECK baseline outperforms the direct sparse layer, but is significantly weaker than the combination of sparse and intermediate layer.

The measurements further show that for training based on SLICE features, the sparse implementation manages to attain and slightly surpass the classification performance of the equivalent dense layer, whereas for CASCADE features there still remains a noticeable gap between dense and sparse training. As a first possible explanation, one might argue that CASCADE features have been specifically trained so that they work well with a linear extreme classification layer, whereas SLICE are more general features. Therefore, it is not the sparse realizations that perform better, but instead the dense setting that performs disproportionately worse for SLICE features, as it does not have the benefit of the additional intermediate layer that allows non-linear classification boundaries. This argument does not hold up, though, as both features result in comparable model performance on the training set—it is the *generalization gap* that is much increased with SLICE features.

Looking at the memory consumption, we can see that sparsification of the last layer does lead to a noticeable reduction, but only becomes really effective if we use our implementation of constant fan-in sparsity. In this case, the memory consumption reduces to between one third and on tenth of the dense equivalent.

4.3   Results with Varying Network Size

In Table 2, we demonstrate the effect of varying the number of connections per label, and the size of the intermediate layer, for the uniformly sparse setup. Unsurprisingly, increasing the network size results in improved classification performance. For SLICE features, the sparse network can be considerably better than the dense counterpart. For CASCADE features, increasing the size of the sparse layer provides a way of shrinking the gap between sparse and dense performance, while still remaining much more memory efficient than the dense setup. In particular for WIKIPEDIA-500K, the change in memory consumption is only by a few percent, while the improvement in P@k is substantial. Except for AMAZON-670K with CASCADE features, increasing the model size results in reducing the number of training epochs.

The data also shows a clear qualitative difference between AMAZON-670K and WIKIPEDIA-500K: For AMAZON-670K, switching from dense to sparse does not lead to a noticeable decline in the ability of the classifier to fit the training set, whereas for WIKIPEDIA-500K the drop is dramatic, especially in the case of SLICE features. This suggests that for the smaller AMAZON-670K (490 449 instances), even the sparse architectures are overparametrized enough to interpolate the training set, whereas for WIKIPEDIA-500K (1 813 391 instances), this is no longer the case, especially for the smaller sparse models.

700   E. Schultheis and R. Babbar

Table 2. Train and test P@k on AMAZON-670K with varying sparsity and intermediate-layer size, relative to dense performance. Results of a single run.

Setup Sparsity	Con.	Int.	Test P@1	P@3	P@5	Train P@1	P@3	P@5	Mem. GiB	Eps.	Time sec
SLICE FEATURES											
DENSE	512	–	33.8	29.6	26.6	99.2	93.9	88.4	9.0	27.2	472
CONSTANT-FAN-IN	32	16k	−2.0	−1.8	−1.6	−1.0	−1.5	−2.4	1.1	42.0	259
CONSTANT-FAN-IN	32	32k	−1.0	−0.9	−0.7	−0.5	−0.7	−1.0	1.2	38.0	244
CONSTANT-FAN-IN	32	65k	−0.1	**0.1**	**0.3**	−0.2	−0.3	−0.4	1.3	36.0	309
CONSTANT-FAN-IN	32	100k	**0.5**	**0.6**	**0.8**	−0.1	−0.2	−0.2	1.8	35.0	302
CONSTANT-FAN-IN	64	16k	−0.6	−0.4	−0.2	−0.1	−0.1	−0.2	1.9	33.0	301
CONSTANT-FAN-IN	64	32k	**0.2**	**0.3**	**0.5**	−0.1	−0.1	−0.1	2.2	32.0	314
CONSTANT-FAN-IN	64	65k	**0.8**	**0.9**	**1.1**	−0.1	−0.1	−0.1	2.5	30.0	396
CONSTANT-FAN-IN	64	100k	**1.3**	**1.4**	**1.5**	−0.1	−0.2	−0.2	2.6	29.0	411
CASCADE FEATURES											
DENSE	768	–	47.5	42.3	38.3	99.8	94.5	89.0	13.4	28.4	624
CONSTANT-FAN-IN	32	16k	−6.2	−6.3	−6.4	−0.3	−0.5	−1.0	1.2	34.0	270
CONSTANT-FAN-IN	32	32k	−4.9	−5.1	−5.2	−0.1	−0.2	−0.4	1.4	36.4	271
CONSTANT-FAN-IN	32	65k	−3.8	−3.8	−3.9	−0.1	−0.1	−0.2	1.7	39.0	305
CONSTANT-FAN-IN	32	100k	−2.8	−3.0	−3.0	−0.1	−0.2	−0.3	2.4	34.0	334
CONSTANT-FAN-IN	64	16k	−4.2	−4.2	−4.1	−0.0	−0.1	−0.1	2.1	27.0	290
CONSTANT-FAN-IN	64	32k	−3.3	−3.3	−3.2	−0.0	−0.1	−0.1	2.4	31.0	306
CONSTANT-FAN-IN	64	65k	−2.3	−2.4	−2.4	−0.1	−0.1	−0.2	2.5	33.0	391
CONSTANT-FAN-IN	64	100k	−1.9	−1.9	−1.9	−0.1	−0.1	−0.2	2.9	31.0	435
CONSTANT-FAN-IN	72	65k	−2.3	−2.4	−2.3	−0.0	−0.1	−0.	2.7	31.0	440

4.4 Quantifying the Effect of Implicit Negative Mining

Next, we show that the implicit negative mining effect discussed above can have a significant impact on the speed of training. To that end, we use the small model configuration with constant fan-in sparsity with 32 structural non-zeros per output and 16k intermediate units, and train it once using the squared hinge loss (SQH) and once using binary cross-entropy (BCE) loss function. As the BCE loss only goes to zero asymptotically, this means that there will not be many explicit zeros in the signal being back-propagated through the sparse layer, and thus all labels have to be processed.

As shown in Table 3, this has a strong effect on the training time per epoch: The implicit negative mining with SQH reduces the duration by about one third. Additionally, the squared hinge loss results in slightly better P@k, and fewer training epochs.

Table 3. Comparison of training with square hinge loss and binary cross-entropy.

Setup			Test			Train			Mem.	Eps.	Time
dataset	features	loss	P@1	P@3	P@5	P@1	P@3	P@5	GiB		sec
WIKIPEDIA-500K	SLICE	SQH	58.0	37.7	28.4	80.3	58.2	45.1	0.9	59.0	946
WIKIPEDIA-500K	SLICE	BCE	57.1	37.1	28.0	77.0	53.7	41.1	1.0	52.0	1 121
WIKIPEDIA-500K	CASCADE	SQH	73.1	54.2	41.5	90.7	71.4	56.3	0.9	68.0	746
WIKIPEDIA-500K	CASCADE	BCE	71.6	52.4	40.1	89.2	68.6	53.4	1.0	79.0	1 247
AMAZON670K	SLICE	SQH	31.7	27.9	25.0	98.2	92.5	86.0	1.1	42.0	259
AMAZON670K	SLICE	BCE	30.9	27.1	24.4	96.2	89.6	82.0	1.2	54.0	400
AMAZON670K	CASCADE	SQH	41.3	35.9	31.9	99.5	94.0	88.0	1.2	34.0	270
AMAZON670K	CASCADE	BCE	38.4	33.2	29.4	98.2	92.3	85.3	1.3	63.0	423

4.5 Discussion

The results above show that sparsification of the extreme layer is possible without a strong decrease in classification performance, relative to a dense layer. However, it has to be noted that training the dense layer in the common experimental protocol employed here yields worse results than reported state-of-the-art for the same set of features. Thus, even in cases where the sparse architecture outperforms the dense layer, reported results from the literature are still better.

In Table 4, we present the results from SLICE [12] and CASCADE [15], compared against our largest setting with 64 nonzeros per label and 65k intermediate units. Compared to these methods, ours performs up to 4% worse, trading off a little classification accuracy versus a multifold reduction in memory consumption. For example, CASCADE runs for over a day on two NVIDIA A100 GPUs.

Table 4. Comparison of sparse results with state-of-the-art.

Dataset	Method	SLICE			CASCADE		
		P@1	P@3	P@5	P@1	P@3	P@5
WIKIPEDIA-500K	Literature	62.6	41.8	31.6	77.0	58.3	45.1
WIKIPEDIA-500K	Ours	60.5	39.8	29.8	74.5	56.0	43.2
AMAZON-670K	Literature	37.8	33.8	30.7	48.8	43.8	40.1
AMAZON-670K	Ours	34.6	30.5	27.7	45.3	39.8	35.9

5 Conclusion and Outlook

In this paper, we have shown that it is possible to replace an extreme-scale dense classification layer with a memory-efficient sequence of an intermediately-sized layer followed by a constant-fan-in sparsely connected layer, without a strong drop in classification performance, and in some cases even improved P@k.

The experiments performed so far investigate sparse layers in the context of a simple training procedure: Learning with the full label space, from fixed, pre-trained features. To achieve feature-parity with existing approaches, this needs to be extended to allow for end-to-end training, where the featurizer ψ is learned jointly with the classifier. Secondly, even though the implicit negative mining effect allows to reduce the computation for the backward pass to be sub-linear in the overall number of labels, it still requires a full forward pass. In order to get to competitive training times, one thus has to integrate also explicit negative mining into the training pipeline. Finally, the datasets used in this work still do not exceed millions of labels.

We performed some initial experiments using AMAZON-3M [18], which indicate a decrease of memory consumption from 63 GiB to 12 GiB, at the cost of about 5% decrease in precision. While this is still too much memory consumption for cheap gaming GPUs, it is still well within the parameters of common workstation units. A more thorough investigation of this dataset is planned for future work.

We believe that this paper provides a good foundation, from which these goals can be achieved: First, by having the sparse multiplication implemented as a regular tensorflow layer, it can be readily included in a more general model, and automatic differentiation will ensure correct gradient calculations. Second, because we are constraining the sparsity to have constant fan-in, selecting a subset of labels for which scores shall be calculated becomes a trivial matrix slicing operation, similar to the fully-connected case. In follow-up works, we aim to incorporate our approach into existing end-to-end deep extreme classification frameworks while benefiting from explicit negative mining. Furthermore, from a statistical perspective, it is possible that constant-fan-in sparsity also leads to a better coverage of tail-labels, and improvements in the corresponding metrics [13,28], which should be investigated.

Acknowledgements. We acknowledge the support of computational resources provided by the Aalto Science-IT project, and CSC IT Center for Science, Finland. This work is funded in part by the Academy of Finland projects 347707 and 348215.

Ethical Statement. Our work does not provide new datasets or introduce conceptually new learning setups. Instead, we focus on enabling existing methods to run with much reduced hardware requirements. This will make large-scale classification more readily available also to people and organizations that cannot afford to buy latest-grade GPU hardware with enormous RAM, as they can reuse pre-existing and cheaper hardware.

References

1. Agrawal, R., Gupta, A., Prabhu, Y., Varma, M.: Multi-label learning with millions of labels: recommending advertiser bid phrases for web pages. In: Proceedings of the 22nd International Conference on World Wide Web, pp. 13–24 (2013)
2. Babbar, R., Schölkopf, B.: Dismec: distributed sparse machines for extreme multi-label classification. In: Proceedings of the tenth ACM International Conference on Web Search and Data Mining, pp. 721–729 (2017)
3. Babbar, R., Schölkopf, B.: Data scarcity, robustness and extreme multi-label classification. Mach. Learn. **108**(8–9), 1329–1351 (2019)

4. Bellec, G., Kappel, D., Maass, W., Legenstein, R.: Deep rewiring: training very sparse deep networks (2017)
5. Beygelzimer, A., Langford, J., Lifshits, Y., Sorkin, G., Strehl, A.L.: Conditional probability tree estimation analysis and algorithms (2014)
6. Bhatia, K., et al.: The extreme classification repository: multi-label datasets and code (2016). https://manikvarma.org/downloads/XC/XMLRepository.html
7. Chang, W.C., Yu, H.F., Zhong, K., Yang, Y., Dhillon, I.S.: Taming pretrained transformers for extreme multi-label text classification. In: Proceedings of the 26th ACM SIGKDD International Conference on Knowledge Discovery & Data Mining, pp. 3163–3171 (2020)
8. Dekel, O., Shamir, O.: Multiclass-multilabel classification with more classes than examples. In: Proceedings of the Thirteenth International Conference on Artificial Intelligence and Statistics, pp. 137–144. JMLR Workshop and Conference Proceedings (2010)
9. Dettmers, T., Zettlemoyer, L.: Sparse networks from scratch: faster training without losing performance. arXiv preprint arXiv:1907.04840 (2019)
10. Evci, U., Gale, T., Menick, J., Castro, P.S., Elsen, E.: Rigging the lottery: making all tickets winners. In: International Conference on Machine Learning, pp. 2943–2952. PMLR (2020)
11. Hoefler, T., Alistarh, D., Ben-Nun, T., Dryden, N., Peste, A.: Sparsity in deep learning: pruning and growth for efficient inference and training in neural networks. J. Mach. Learn. Res. 22(1), 10882–11005 (2021)
12. Jain, H., Balasubramanian, V., Chunduri, B., Varma, M.: Slice: scalable linear extreme classifiers trained on 100 million labels for related searches. In: WSDM, pp. 528–536 (2019)
13. Jain, H., Prabhu, Y., Varma, M.: Extreme multi-label loss functions for recommendation, tagging, ranking & other missing label applications. In: Proceedings of the 22nd ACM SIGKDD International Conference on Knowledge Discovery and Data Mining, pp. 935–944 (2016)
14. Jiang, T., Wang, D., Sun, L., Yang, H., Zhao, Z., Zhuang, F.: Lightxml: transformer with dynamic negative sampling for high-performance extreme multi-label text classification, vol. 35, no. 9, pp. 7987–7994 (2021)
15. Kharbanda, S., Banerjee, A., Schultheis, E., Babbar, R.: Cascadexml: rethinking transformers for end-to-end multi-resolution training in extreme multi-label classification. In: Advances in Neural Information Processing Systems (2022)
16. Kingma, D.P., Ba, J.: Adam: a method for stochastic optimization. arXiv preprint arXiv:1412.6980 (2014)
17. McAuley, J., Leskovec, J.: Hidden factors and hidden topics: understanding rating dimensions with review text. In: Proceedings of the 7th ACM Conference on Recommender Systems, pp. 165–172 (2013)
18. McAuley, J., Pandey, R., Leskovec, J.: Inferring networks of substitutable and complementary products. In: Proceedings of the 21th ACM SIGKDD International Conference on Knowledge Discovery and Data Mining, pp. 785–794 (2015)
19. Medini, T.K.R., Huang, Q., Wang, Y., Mohan, V., Shrivastava, A.: Extreme classification in log memory using count-min sketch: a case study of amazon search with 50m products, vol. 32 (2019)
20. Menon, A.K., Rawat, A.S., Reddi, S., Kumar, S.: Multilabel reductions: what is my loss optimising? In: Advances in Neural Information Processing Systems, vol. 32 (2019)
21. Mikolov, T., Chen, K., Corrado, G., Dean, J.: Efficient estimation of word representations in vector space. arXiv preprint arXiv:1301.3781 (2013)

22. Mocanu, D.C., Mocanu, E., Stone, P., Nguyen, P.H., Gibescu, M., Liotta, A.: Scalable training of artificial neural networks with adaptive sparse connectivity inspired by network science. Nat. Commun. **9**(1), 2383 (2018)
23. Prabhu, Y., Kag, A., Harsola, S., Agrawal, R., Varma, M.: Parabel: partitioned label trees for extreme classification with application to dynamic search advertising. In: Proceedings of the 2018 World Wide Web Conference, pp. 993–1002 (2018)
24. Prabhu, Y., Varma, M.: Fastxml: a fast, accurate and stable tree-classifier for extreme multi-label learning. In: Proceedings of the 20th ACM SIGKDD International Conference on Knowledge Discovery and Data Mining, pp. 263–272 (2014)
25. Rawat, A.S., et al.: Disentangling sampling and labeling bias for learning in large-output spaces. In: International Conference on Machine Learning, pp. 8890–8901. PMLR (2021)
26. Reddi, S.J., Kale, S., Yu, F., Holtmann-Rice, D., Chen, J., Kumar, S.: Stochastic negative mining for learning with large output spaces. In: The 22nd International Conference on Artificial Intelligence and Statistics, pp. 1940–1949. PMLR (2019)
27. Schultheis, E., Babbar, R.: Speeding-up one-versus-all training for extreme classification via mean-separating initialization. Mach. Learn. **111**, 1–24 (2022)
28. Schultheis, E., Wydmuch, M., Babbar, R., Dembczynski, K.: On missing labels, long-tails and propensities in extreme multi-label classification. In: Proceedings of the 28th ACM SIGKDD Conference on Knowledge Discovery and Data Mining, pp. 1547–1557 (2022)
29. Weston, J., Makadia, A., Yee, H.: Label partitioning for sublinear ranking. In: International Conference on Machine Learning, pp. 181–189. PMLR (2013)
30. Wydmuch, M., Jasinska, K., Kuznetsov, M., Busa-Fekete, R., Dembczynski, K.: A no-regret generalization of hierarchical softmax to extreme multi-label classification. In: Advances in Neural Information Processing Systems, vol. 31 (2018)
31. Yen, I.E.H., Huang, X., Ravikumar, P., Zhong, K., Dhillon, I.: PD-sparse: a primal and dual sparse approach to extreme multiclass and multilabel classification. In: International Conference on Machine Learning, pp. 3069–3077. PMLR (2016)
32. You, R., Zhang, Z., Wang, Z., Dai, S., Mamitsuka, H., Zhu, S.: Attentionxml: label tree-based attention-aware deep model for high-performance extreme multi-label text classification, vol. 32 (2019)
33. Zubiaga, A.: Enhancing navigation on wikipedia with social tags (2012)

Correction to: Towards Memory-Efficient Training for Extremely Large Output Spaces – Learning with 670k Labels on a Single Commodity GPU

Erik Schultheis🆔 and Rohit Babbar🆔

Correction to:
Chapter 41 in: D. Koutra et al. (Eds.): *Machine Learning and Knowledge Discovery in Databases*, **LNAI 14171,**
https://doi.org/10.1007/978-3-031-43418-1_41

The updated version of this chapter can be found at
https://doi.org/10.1007/978-3-031-43418-1_41

© The Author(s) 2024
D. Koutra et al. (Eds.): ECML PKDD 2023, LNAI 14171, p. C1–C2, 2024.
https://doi.org/10.1007/978-3-031-43418-1_42

Author Index

Printed in the United States
by Baker & Taylor Publisher Services